YOUNG EMERSON'S TRANSCENDENTAL VISION

AN EXPOSITION OF HIS WORLD VIEW
WITH AN ANALYSIS
OF THE STRUCTURE, BACKGROUNDS,
AND MEANING OF
NATURE (1836)

By

KENNETH WALTER CAMERON

Trinity College

TRANSCENDENTAL BOOKS—DRAWER 1080—HARTFORD 06101

814.36
+Em35/c

TO MY PARENTS

ALBERT ERNEST CAMERON

ZOE SHOCKLEY BARKER CAMERON

LORD, WITH WHAT CARE HAST THOU BEGIRT US ROUND.
  PARENTS FIRST SEASON US: THEN SCHOOLMASTERS
  DELIVER US TO LAWS; THEY SEND US, BOUND
TO RULES OF REASON, HOLY MESSENGERS,

PULPITS AND SUNDAYES, SORROW DOGGING SINNE,
  AFFLICTIONS SORTED, ANGUISH OF ALL SIZES,
  FINE NETS AND STRATAGEMS TO CATCH US IN,
BIBLES LAID OPEN, MILLIONS OF SURPRISES,

BLESSINGS BEFOREHAND, TYES OF GRATEFULNESSE,
  THE SOUND OF GLORIE RINGING IN OUR EARES;
  WITHOUT, OUR SHAME; WITHIN, OUR CONSCIENCES;
ANGELS AND GRACE, ETERNALL HOPES AND FEARS.

                                    —GEORGE HERBERT.

FOREWORD

The present volume is much more than an abridgment of the two-volume Emerson the Essayist, which has for several years been out of print. Though some chapters have been carried over from that work, many new ones have here been added to provide a critical introduction to what may rightly be called the "key classic" of the American Renaissance. Because I have kept in mind the young scholar's difficulties in establishing a working knowledge of Emerson, Transcendental Vision may effectively open up a "brave new world" to many who have hitherto found American Idealism complex or puzzling.

For the first time, both the beginner and veteran will find herein (1) a useable text of Nature in the midst of sources, interpretations and notes that are integrated and manageable; (2) careful analyses of each chapter of Nature pointing to a synthesis of form and meaning; (3) new sections on significant influences on Emerson up through 1836; and (4) important documents of early Transcendentalism printed without omissions.

Because this volume does not in any way supersede Emerson the Essayist, but rather complements it, the established scholar will not neglect the indexes, bibliographies and encyclopedic resources of the earlier work, which, I hope, may soon be reissued.

Trinity College
Hartford, Connecticut

K. W. C.

January, 1971

3

TABLE OF CONTENTS

THE RISE OF TRANSCENDENTALISM

I) AN ATTEMPT AT A DEFINITION: Transcendentalism was a warm and intuitional religious, aesthetic, philosophical and ethical movement--the American tributary of European Romanticism--a theoretical and practical way of life and a literary expression within the tradition of "Idealism"--a new humanism based upon ancient classical or Neo-Platonic supernaturalism and colored by Oriental mysticism. It maintained the spiritual "infinitude" of the individual person.

II) WORLD BACKGROUND (1775-1849):

A) Political: A period of reform movements----Revolutions----Democratic upheavals----Optimism about man's possibilities and perfectibility----New experiments with constitutions. Transcendentalism reflects contemporary optimism and hope.

B) Economic: The Industrial Revolution and its progressive materialism. Attempts to combat it abroad took the form of experiments in socialism (Fourier and Proudhon)--in collectives which were themselves materialistic. Transcendentalism experimented at Brook Farm and at Fruitlands with collectivism, but its great writers took no real part in it. They were sympathetic however with all efforts at "plain living and high thinking." Thoreau did not favor collectives of any kind, emphasizing rather a simplified living for the individual. Transcendentalism in promoting so vigorously the individual and his private mysticism allowed only a token consideration for society. Stress laid on subjectivism--on personal development.

C) Aesthetic: Romanticism--both a literary movement and a religious movement--was at this time in full blossom throughout the Western hemisphere. Reaction against Neo-Classicism and its restraints in expression. Romanticism was against formalism and conventions in poetry and the fine arts; against austerity and too much emphasis upon mind at the expense of emotions. Favored spontaneity, color, music, intuition; against restraint, balance, cold description and rationality. Form mattered less than inspiration, enthusiasm, emotion, spirituality. Romanticism preferred the Dionysiac to the Apollonian. Transcendentalism shared the Romantic impulse though with somewhat less exaggeration in America because of its associations with New England.

D) Religious: Conventional spirituality was at low ebb everywhere during this period. Aridity of eighteenth-century Deism. Disintegration of Calvinism. Catholicism comparatively weak in the United States. Prevalence of dry and rational utilitarianism and unitarianism. Emphasis upon ethics rather than upon religion. Like so many minor sects (Quakers, Swedenborgians, Brethren, etc.) Transcendentalism reacted against all the prevailing secularism and sought to rediscover the spiritual world----more fully enjoyed in the sweet "long ago." Transcendentalism continued to stress the ethical, basing it upon Kant's Categorical Imperative rather than upon a religion with supernatural sanctions. What religious basis it enjoyed was that of late Neo-Platonism and its derivatives and of the German followers of Kant (Schelling, Fichte, Herder, Goethe, the Schlegels etc.) It deliberately bypassed traditional Christianity. Result: a warm, pantheistic, mystical outlook emphasizing a "god immanent in man and in the world" and at the same time placing the source of everything in an impersonal, transcendent Oversoul. (Valuable insight into the reasons for the rebellion of the Romantic Movement against desiccated Protestant Christianity found in James Baird, Ishmael, Baltimore, 1956.)

E) Philosophic: England and the Continent had long been in the grip of materialistic thought, empiricism and skepticism--stimulated by the inductive philosophy of Bacon and the educational theories (tabula rasa and a posteriori knowledge) of John Locke and his followers. Romanticism proclaimed the Imagination rather than rationality as the principal agency in the creation of poetry; offered an organic concept of nature as opposed to the static or mechanistic views of

the eighteenth century; required symbol and myth for poetic style. (Lovejoy has characterized Romanticism by using the terms (a) organicism, (b) dynamism and (c) diversitarianism. [See Morse Peckham, "Toward a Theory of Romanticism," P M L A, LXVI, 5-23 (March, 1951); also James Benziger, "Organic Union: Leibniz to Coleridge," loc. cit., pp. 24-48.] Transcendentalism attempted to combat materialism and skepticism by emphasizing a philosophy that "transcended" the senses: intuitionalism, a priori thinking, ideas flowing into the mind direct from God, evidence of Divinity in the living heart and conscience. It turned from skepticism to Faith, from cold intellectualism to mysticism, from mere logic to super-logic or intuition, from empiricism to classical idealism.

III) TRANSCENDENTAL OUTLOOK UPON ULTIMATE REALITY: All reality is in a transcendent or spiritual world---the realm of the "Oversoul." The visible (i.e., the phenomenal) world of time and space and matter (including the human body) is less real or, indeed, unreal and without value per se. Only as the Transcendent Spirit shines into man and nature or flows into them or (because of having created them) lingers in them, do they deserve respect. As mere matter, they are dead. Only as God is in them are they alive. The Oversoul is both above man's comprehension  and also within man--an "incarnate Logos" in every human being--though in most people it slumbers and is never awakened, in which case men are bestial. The real SELF in a man is that "higher self" or "true self"---that fragment of the Transcendent (and now Incarnate) Deity-with-him. (Synonymous words are "Conscience," "Intuition," "Influx," "Heart," "Oughtness," "Monitor," etc.) When awake or alive, this inner Godhead is the great guide of life--nay, is LIFE. It has nothing in common with the merely material or utilitarian. It demands spiritual adventuring. Therefore, the right way of viewing the world and ultimates is a spiritual one.

IV) TRANSCENDENTAL VIEW OF MAN: Man is a kind of "mediator" between God and Nature. As we have said, he has within him a fragment of God Himself, often called the "Conscience" or (in Coleridge's system) the "Divine Reason" and that is his true SELF. Self-Reliance, therefore, means leaning on these intuitions from God and actually is synonymous with God-Reliance. (It does not mean "doing as one damn pleases." That sort of antinomianism is the character only of the animal or material man.) When one allows God or the "higher SELF" to become operative-- 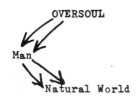 to flow, as it were, through one's life without throwing impediments in His way--when, in other words, one relies on the highest intuitions from the Inner Voice--then the Natural World without us can become a paradise, since (by postulate) the phenomenal world is, at best, a remoter incarnation of Deity and dependent upon man's spiritual condition for its "effects." Whenever man closes his life to God, then the outer world becomes "red in tooth and claw"---unfriendly, to say the least, and filled with war and hate. Man's goal should be to live his life according to the "highest principles" of his intuition, and then cast off his body and personality forever, allowing the God-element in him to return to the Oversoul whence it came. "Onward and upward forever!" [Note: The orthodox Hebrew-Christian world view is neither Transcendental nor Materialistic but a mid-position between them.]

V) TRANSCENDENTAL VIEW OF NATURE: Nature is really a mirage or a dumb and plastic servant of God, not real as the spiritual world is real. Although the natural world is, in a sense, created through man (as we saw in the preceding section), in another sense (though this may sound paradoxical) it is independent of man and serves not only to reflect his interior "spiritual thermometer" reading but also to teach him spiritual truths which God or the Oversoul wishes to impart. (See 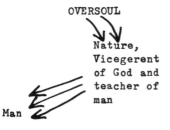 the next section for the way in which this teaching is accomplished-- for the bringing together of the two poles of the battery, as it were, to complete the electric circuit of BEING.) Nature, then, is a kind of mediator between the Oversoul and mankind. It takes the place of TORAH in Jewish thought and of CHRIST in Christian theology. Nature, in this system, therefore, is something infinitely more than the cut-and-dried subject ex-

plored by the departmental scientist of our day. The rich "ministry" of Nature to man is seen both in the Coleridgean and Swedenborgian "systems." Emerson sums them up in his little book, Nature, as (1) practical use or commodity; (2) Beauty; (3) Symbolic Language; (4) Spiritual Discipline; (5) Revelation of the Spirit or Oversoul in Mystical moments. Examples of nature "as language": Joyce Kilmer's tree; Professor "X" is an old fox! Emerson's rhodora. Example of nature as revealing the Spirit: Transparent-eyeball passage in Nature.

[Note: The speculative student will do well to examine the introductory chapters of volume I of Reinhold Niebuhr's The Nature and Destiny of Man for an illuminating discussion of the three ways of looking at God, at Man and at Nature: (1) The uncompromising Transcendental or Rational (Latin: Rationalis) view; (2) the materialistic view; (3) the middle view, which may be denominated the "Hebrew-Christian" or "Orthodox" view. This book can help the beginner make important distinctions. Profitable to the beginner also is the little handbook by John Grier Hibben, The Problems of Philosophy. The "problems" it outlines are expressed in nineteenth-century terms rather than in those of the current day. Hence its value to the student of Emerson's period.]

VI) THE TRANSCENDENTAL THEORY OF KNOWLEDGE. It is concerned, especially, with how Nature is able to teach man and how man is able to receive this teaching. Spiritual growth in this world depends upon the "coincidence of Subject and Object"--that is, the coming together of the "God-within-a-man" and the "God or Spirit pervading or using the outer world. A useful image is that of a battery with positive and negative poles. One sees sparks only when the two poles are brought together. When the God within and the God without meet, Transcendentalists use the term "recognition." (Cf. Emerson's poem, "Rhodora.") So Idea within meets Divine Law without. The electric circuit is completed or, to phrase the thought a little differently, "spirit comes full circle home to itself, the barriers being removed." Since to the Transcendentalist, knowledge is a form of BEING or a condition and not a mere acquirement, at its best it is "mystical union" with God, "being caught up into the Seventh Heaven," a "beholding of the Infinite through transparent phenomena."

The great rule that functions in this "recognition" process is: Quantum sumus, scimus." (Like only can know like.) The Transcendentalists, therefore, tried by every means possible to develop their ethical and/or spiritual condition SO THAT THEY MIGHT BE ABLE TO SEE MORE SPIRITUAL MEANING IN THE OUTER WORLD AND MIGHT MORE FREQUENTLY ENJOY THE BEATIFIC RAPTURE THAN MIGHT BE POSSIBLE OTHERWISE. Self-Reliance, therefore, meant striving to mount into this high, spiritual plane of intuition and occult recognition. (Cf. Wordsworth's "Peter Bell.")

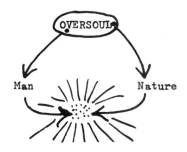

VII) THE TRANSCENDENTAL THEORY OF ART: (See II.E above.) The Oversoul was the author of all genuine art. Man was merely a tool or channel. One ought, therefore, to allow the God-within to absorb as much beauty from the outer world as possible, allowing it to germinate in the highest level--the God-level--of the Mind until it be ready to flow forth with a divine enthusiasm into visible form. Since God was the all-important factor--the source of all aesthetic energy--the Transcendentalists like other Romanticists had contempt for man-made rules of art, man's attempts to restrain the artist by standardized or acceptable "forms," etc. Spontaneity, instantaneity, imagination, new combinations--were more important than neat stylization or patterns. (Hence Coleridge was content with his unfinished Kubla Khan and Christabel--and so are we! Hence Whitman's Leaves of Grass. Hence the interesting mixing of genres during this period, commonly called the "confusion of the arts.")

NATURE'S
MINISTRY
TO MAN

SPIRIT

Nature's highest ministry to man is to confront him with Divinity by unlocking the Divinity within his own breast--to serve as a kind of "burning bush" or channel for the Beatific Vision.

DISCIPLINE

(3) The highest manifestation of Nature as Discipline is in HUMAN FRIENDSHIP, which elevates the mercury in our SPIRIT-UAL THERMOMETER. At its best, it is IMPERSONAL, its values remaining after personal associations end or are forgotten.

(2) The Practical Reason, or MORAL DEPARTMENT of the Soul, as-sists Nature in training the conscience. To the Practical Reason, all objects in Nature are MORAL and shout the Ten Commandments (or, better, Kant's Categorical Imperative). Nature, therefore, trains the Soul not only through indi-vidual objects but also through a TOTAL EFFECT.

(1) Nature trains the Animal Understanding or the Common Sense of Men by making it efficient and discriminating.

LANGUAGE

(3) NATURE AS A WHOLE is a sacramental symbol conveying grace and capable of leading man onward to Mystical Ecstasy or Spiritual Communion with the Ultimate Reality.

(2) Particular natural facts are signs of particular spiritual facts or states of mind. Hence a LAW OF CORRESPONDENCE operates between the Soul (Reason) of Man and certain ob-jects in outer nature. Snake--subtlety. River--flux of things. Light--knowledge. Darkness--ignorance. Lamb--innocence. Fox--cunning.

(1) Most words are signs of natural facts: Right--straight. Wrong--twisted. Spirit--wind. Heart--emotion. Head--thought.

BEAUTY

(3) Abstract Beauty stimulates the "Theoretical Reason" of Man --the realm of contemplation and intuition. There new beauty has its genesis. There man the creator receives inspiration or ideas for producing poems, statues, fiction, painting and the other arts.

(2) Beauty of Moral Actions, which appeals to the "Practical Reason."

(1) Simple Beauty, which the "Understanding" is able to compre-hend.

COMMODITY

Nature's manifold and practical ministry to man's sense: touch, sight, taste, hearing, and smelling.

Cabot, *Memoir*	James Elliot Cabot, *A Memoir of Ralph Waldo Emerson*, (2 vols.) Boston & N.Y., 1887.
Carlyle-Emerson Corr.	*The Correspondence of Thomas Carlyle and Ralph Waldo Emerson, 1834-1872*, (2 vols.) Boston, 1888.
Carlyle, *Sartor Resartus*	[Thomas Carlyle], *Sartor Resartus*, ed. R. W. Emerson, (1st ed.) Boston, 1836.
Coleridge	*Emerson the Essayist*, vol. I, part I, chap. VI.
Coleridge, *Aids* (1829)	S. T. Coleridge, *Aids to Reflection*, ed. James Marsh, (1st American ed.) Burlington, Vt., 1829.
Coleridge, *Aids* (1913)	S. T. Coleridge, *Aids to Reflection*, London (Bohn), 1913.
Coleridge, *Complete Works* (Shedd)	[See "Coleridge, *Works* (Shedd)."]
Coleridge, *Table Talk*	S. T. Coleridge, *Specimens of Table Talk*, (1st ed., 2 vols.) London, 1835.
Coleridge, *Works* (Shedd)	S. T. Coleridge, *The Complete Works*, ed. W. G. T. Shedd, (7 vols.) N.Y., 1853. [Not complete.]
Cousin	*Emerson the Essayist*, vol. I, part I, chap. XIII.
Cousin, *Introduction* (1832)	Victor Cousin, *Introduction to the History of Philosophy*, tr. Henning Gotfried Linberg, Boston, 1832.
Cudworth	*Emerson the Essayist*, vol. I, part I, chap. IV.
Cudworth, *Intellectual System* (1820)	Ralph Cudworth, *The True Intellectual System of the Universe*, ed. Thomas Birch, (new ed., 4 vols.) London, 1820.
Cudworth, *Intellectual System* (1845)	Ralph Cudworth, *The True Intellectual System of the Universe* (with Dr. Mosheim's notes), (3 vols.) London, 1845.
Early Lectures	*Emerson the Essayist*, vol. I, part II.
Emerson's Reading	K. W. Cameron, *Ralph Waldo Emerson's Reading*, Raleigh, N. C., 1941.
E T E	K. W. Cameron, *Emerson the Essayist*, (2 vols.) Raleigh, N. C., 1945.
Ethical Philosophy	R. W. Emerson, "The Present State of Ethical Philosophy" (1821) in *Two Unpublished Essays*, Boston & N. Y., 1896, pp. 43-81.
Gérando, *Histoire* (1804)	Joseph Marie de Gérando, *Histoire Comparée des Systèmes de Philosophie*, (3 vols.) Paris, 1804.
Gérando, *Histoire* (1822)	Joseph Marie de Gérando, *Histoire Comparée des Systèmes de Philosophie*, (2me édition, 4 tomes) Paris, 1822-1823.
Journals	*The Journals of Ralph Waldo Emerson*, ed. E. W. Emerson and W. E. Forbes, (10 vols.) Boston & N. Y., 1909-1914.
Kirby and Spence	*Emerson the Essayist*, vol. I, part I, chap. IX.
Letters	*The Letters of Ralph Waldo Emerson*, ed. Ralph L. Rusk, (6 vols.) N. Y., 1939.

Michael Angelo	[R. W. Emerson], "Michael Angelo," *North American Review*, XLIV (Jan., 1837), pp. 1-16.
Miscellaneous Selections	*Emerson the Essayist*, vol. I, part I, chap. XVI.
Nature	R. W. Emerson, *Nature (1836)*, ed. with introd., index-concordance and bibliographical appendices by K. W. Cameron, N. Y., 1940.
N J M	*New Jerusalem Magazine.*
Notes on the Text of *Nature*	*Emerson the Essayist*, vol. I, part III, chap. III.
Oegger	*Emerson the Essayist*, vol. I, part I, chap. XII.
Orphic Poet	*Emerson the Essayist*, vol. I, part III, last half of chap. I.
Owned	Owned by Emerson and now in his library in Concord.
Plato, *Works* **(Taylor)**	*The Works of Plato*, tr. Floyer Sydenham and Thomas Taylor, (5 vols.) London, 1804.
Plotinus, *Select Works*	*Select Works of Plotinus*, tr. Thomas Taylor, London, 1817.
Plotinus, *Select Works* **(Bohn)**	*Select Works of Plotinus*, tr. Thomas Taylor, London (Bohn's Popular Library), 1929.
RWEMA	Ralph Waldo Emerson Memorial Association.
Sampson Reed	*Emerson the Essayist*, vol. I, part I, chap. XI.
Socrates	R. W. Emerson, "The Character of Socrates" (1820) in *Two Unpublished Essays*, Boston & N.Y., 1896, pp. 3-39.
Sterling-Emerson Corr.	*A Correspondence between John Sterling and R. W. Emerson*, Boston & N.Y., 1897.
Swedenborg	*Emerson the Essayist*, vol. I, part I, chap. X.
Typescript Journals	Typed copies of the complete manuscript journals of R. W. Emerson, now in the Houghton Library of Harvard University and owned by the RWEMA.
Uncollected Lectures	*Uncollected Lectures by Ralph Waldo Emerson* (rptd. from *The Commonwealth*) ed. Clarence Gohdes, N. Y., 1932.
Uncollected Writings	*Uncollected Writings: Essays, Addresses, Poems, Reviews and Letters* by R. W. Emerson, [copyright by Charles C. Bigelow], N. Y., [1912]. For corrections see *M L N*, XXXII (1917), 431-434.
Works	*The Complete Works of Ralph Waldo Emerson*, ed. Edward W. Emerson, (Centenary Edition, 12 vols.) Boston & N. Y., 1903-1904.
Y E S	R. W. Emerson, *Young Emerson Speaks*, ed. Arthur Cushman McGiffert, Jr., Boston, 1938.

THE PRE-PLATONIC PHILOSOPHERS THROUGH THE EYE OF BARON GERANDO

Emerson's first contact with the works of Joseph Marie de Gérando cannot yet be definitely established,[1] but there is evidence that his interest was aroused during the last months of 1829,[2] for he wrote on January 4, 1830:[3] "Degerando Hist. Comparée . . . I am beginning on the best recommendation." The Boston Library Society owned nothing of this author as late as June, 1830, and Harvard had not even a single volume of his works as late as 1834. The Boston Athenæum, however, owned the *Histoire Comparée*——the first edition in three volumes[4]——and this work is probably the first Emerson chose to withdraw from that institution when his membership began there on January 1, 1830.[5] There is evidence that Elizabeth Palmer Peabody had translated for private circulation in manuscript among her friends,[6] probably in 1829, Gérando's *Du Perfectionnement moral, ou de l'éducation de soi-même*, a work of permanent value in developing the moral and spiritual personality, and worthy, indeed, of a modern edition. This she published under the title, *Self-Education*, first in 1830 and again in 1832, when she issued also her translation of Gérando's *Visitor of the Poor*.[7] The Frenchman, therefore, had at least one enthusiastic editor and a coterie of readers in Boston, and it is conceivable that Miss Peabody or one of her circle brought his imposing philosophical work to Emerson's attention.[8] It seems highly probable that after borrowing the first two volumes of the early edition of the *Histoire* from the Athenæum in January and February, 1830, he determined to order for his own library a copy of the second edition

[1] I have a vague recollection of seeing Gérando's name in one of "Cabot's Blotting Books" for the year 1826, but I have not been able to check the *Typescript Journals* a second time.

[2] See *Journals*, II, 279. This reference probably concerns the *Journals* for 1830 rather than 1829. I can find no trace of Gérando's authorship of such a work as the *Dérivation de la Science du Droit*, mentioned in *Journals*, II, 280.

[3] See *Letters*, I, 291.

[4] *Histoire comparée des systèmes de Philosophie*, (3 vols.) Paris, 1804. This edition is interesting from a bibliographical standpoint. The first few signatures were run off on scrap paper containing printed pages of an earlier work, *De la Génération des Connaissances Humaines*, Paris, [1803].

[5] See *Emerson's Reading*, p. 17. Vol. I was taken out on January 1 and returned on February 1; volume II, taken on February 1 and returned March 1.

[6] See the preface to *Self-Education, or the Means and Art of Moral Progress*, tr. from the French, Boston, 1830.

[7] *Visitor of the Poor*, with an introduction by J. Tuckerman, Boston, 1832. See M. Carey's review in the *North American Review* for June, 1833.

[8] Another work by Gérando which circulated in America was the *Discours* [sur l'Industrie]) [Paris, 1802]. See also his article, "De l'Influence de l'esprit de Méditation sur les Lettres," *Mémoires de l'Académie Impériale des Sciences, Littérature et Beaux-Arts*, XV (Turin, 1805). On October 27, 1834, Emerson listed Gérando with Coleridge, Channing, Wordsworth and others, as among those crying out for a systematic moral education. See *Journals*, III, 348. There is a possibility that Miss Peabody was one of Emerson's early pupils. See *Letters*, I, 449. See also the *D. A. B.* Emerson may have been led to Gérando by the recommendation in Victor Cousin, *Cours de Philosophie: Introduction à l'Histoire de la Philosophie*, Paris, 1829.

(1822), which had been augmented and largely rewritten,[9] because the new volumes seem to have arrived before midsummer, when he spoke of Gérando as being on his table.[10] At all events, he wrote on October 27: "I begin the Histoire Comparee . . . ," undoubtedly the revised work, from which, thereafter, he almost consistently quoted.[11] The student who is interested in tracing lustres and ideas in Emerson's writings will do well carefully to examine *both* editions, for although the outlines are the same, the actual contents differ so greatly that the books almost deserve independent titles.

In his introduction to the *Histoire Comparée*——which, except for a few modified footnotes, is the same in both editions——Gérando indicated that the plan of his work, following the recommendation of Lord Bacon, would treat distinctly, severally and in order each of the separate philosophers and their schools, in the hope that from a progressive comparison, not of the peculiar and characteristic details so much as of the fundamental and continuing principles or questions, a core of knowledge about God, the universe and man might emerge in clearer form than might be expected through an eclectic or topical method. His project he believed to be psychologically sound, since one might reasonably suppose that some sects on particular points might be able to see farther and to express themselves more clearly than others. He sought, therefore, to emphasize the harmony running through all patterns of thought——not the discordance——and in so doing to reach the *Prima Philosophia*:[12]

Bacon lui-même justifie cette idée, et nous indique comment elle pourrait être remplie. L'histoire de la philosophie, [xiii] nous dit-il d'abord, occupe le sommet de cette histoire universelle de l'esprit humain; car, soit qu'on considère la philosophie comme une *méthode générale* ou comme la *nomenclature des principes fondamentaux* sur lesquels reposent toutes les sciences et tous les arts, il est certain du moins qu'elle est le centre auquel viennent se réunir tous les rayons de lumière qui dirigent l'esprit humain dans ces diverses applications. De même, les idées qui composent chaque doctrine philosophique en particulier forment un corps et un ensemble par la liaison qu'elles ont dans l'esprit de celui qui les a conçues. Toute doctrine a donc en elle-même ses conditions fondamentales, qui ont déterminé et le dévelop- [xiv] pement de ses détails, et le caractère distinctif de sa physionomie, si l'on peut dire ainsi, et l'influence qu'elle a exercée autour d'elle.

Si donc il y avait en philosophie un petit nombre de questions principales qui, se trouvant à l'origine de toutes les autres, dussent exercer sur celles-ci une influence naturelle, et qui fournissent les dernières données nécessaires à leur solution; si les opinions que les philosophes se seraient formées à l'égard de ce petit nombre de questions primitives avaient dû déterminer par une conséquence secrète ou sensible la suite entière de leurs opinions, en fixant la direction de leurs idées; si ces questions fondamentales, dis-je, pouvaient être reconnues, énumérées, clairement définies, on

---

[9] *Histoire Comparée des Systèmes de Philosophie*, (2ᵐᵉ édition, 4 vols.), Paris, 1822-1823. (Owned).

[10] See *Letters*, I, 306. Margaret Fuller was reading his copy in May, 1837. See *Letters*, II, 78.

[11] Emerson's use of the first edition did not cease. He borrowed the first volume from the Athenæum again on April 6, 1831, returning it on April 15. That he made interesting use of the second edition has been demonstrated by Prof. Carl F. Strauch in his "Gérando: A Source for Emerson," *MLN*, LVIII (1943), 64-67.

[12] See Gérando, *Histoire* (1822), I, xii-xxi. (Page numbers of all quotations here and hereafter will be bracketed within the text.) Emerson has translated and paraphrased this passage in *Journals*, II, 332 (bottom) and 333.

aurait trouvé un moyen simple et assuré de marquer d'une manière gé- [xv] nérale les conditions premières, les caractères essentiels de chaque doctrine; on serait parvenu à saisir les termes qui composent une des lois les plus importantes du monde intellectuel.

Telle est à nos yeux cette véritable *philosophie première* dont parlent Bacon et Descartes, qui renferme en elle l'essence et les élémens constitutifs de toute philosophie, parce que les *principes universels de toutes les sciences* [xxi] ne peuvent résider que dans la nature même de la science, parce qu'avant de décider sur *Dieu, l'univers, l'homme,* ces trois grands objets de toute doctrine philosophique, il faut examiner avant tout en vertu de quel titre l'homme décide sur quelque chose.

Nous avons donc cru reconnaître que les systèmes relatifs aux principes des connaissances humaines ont déterminé constamment et d'une manière presque infaillible les caractères dominans et les destinées principales de chaque doctrine philosophique, parce que ces systèmes renfermaient, si l'on peut dire ainsi, *la législation* de ces doctrines.

In order to review in outline the development of Emerson's thinking up to September, 1836, when he announced "the laws of the First Philosophy,"[13] Part One of the present volume will follow Gérando's method, setting forth in approximately chronological order the principal philosophers that can be shown demonstrably to have had a considerable direct influence on *Nature* and indicating by a progressive comparison some of the "lustres" as well as the core of thought which Emerson appropriated in fashioning his fundamental view of life. Since the first thinkers to command attention will be those who preceded Socrates and Plato, in this chapter we shall turn to Gérando, as did Emerson,[14] for the most useful accounts of the early speculative men of the world.

THALES

"Let us inquire to what end is nature?"[15] Thales attempted to explain the universe by investigating its immediate natural origin, and was the first, according to Cicero, to study nature herself in seeking the laws operating in this time-and-space world. Emerson summarized the chief doctrines of the philosopher-physician in a page of the *Journals*:[16] his teaching that water was the beginning of things; that the essence of the soul is motion; that God is older than the universe, because He was not made; that the universe is the best of all possible universes, because God made it; and that God's omniscience "trieth the very hearts and reins." The original text, which follows this summary, will better serve to introduce the later quotations, to provide a parallel for Emerson's abridgement in the *Journals,* and to reveal at once Gérando's application of his method:[17]

Ce n'est pas que Thalès ait conçu le problème fondamental de la science autrement qu'il avait été posé par les sages de l'Asie et de l'Egypte, du moins si ceux qui nous ont transmis ses opinions ne lui ont pas prêté à cet égard leurs propres idées. Il

---

[13] See *Nature* and also *Journals,* III, 489, 492. See portions of Cabot's *R. O. Pocket Notebook* for June, 1835, in chap. VII.

[14] The second edition was the basis for Emerson's philosophical outlines, found in *Journals,* II, 336-345.

[15] See *Nature,* 6.15.

[16] *Journals,* II, 336.

[17] Gérando, *Histoire* (1822), I, 337-345.

s'agissait toujours d'expliquer [338] l'univers, et de l'expliquer en recherchant quelle pouvait être son origine, ou, comme on disait, ses *principes*. Mais Thalès, renonçant à puiser cette explication dans un ordre de choses surnaturel, dans l'action immédiate de causes invisibles, voulut interroger la nature elle-même, et faire sortir son état présent des seules conditions de son état antérieur; c'est ce qu'atteste expressément Aristote. De là le nom de *physiciens* donné en général aux philosophes de l'école d'Ionie; aussi Thalès est-il appelé, par Tertullien, le prince ou le premier des physiciens; "il fut le premier, dit Cicéron, qui se livra à l'étude de la nature, qui en recherca les lois."

Tel est donc le mérite propre à Thalès, et le caractère qui distingue essentiellement la nouvelle direction à laquelle il s'attacha. Il sépara la physique de la théologie naturelle et de la métaphysique; il sembla, dès l'antiquité, pressentir le célèbre vœu de Newton, et fit ainsi [339] le premier pas pour arriver à cette division des sciences qui s'opéra dans la suite.

La célèbre proposition unanimement attribuée à Thalès, *l'eau est le principe de toutes choses*, doit être entendue comme il l'expliquait lui-même. Il ne prétendait point attacher à l'élément qu'il désignait ainsi, la vertu d'une *cause*, il le considérait seulement comme la *matière* de laquelle s'étaient formés tous les êtres matériels organisés. "Dans l'état liquide, la matière n'a encore aucune forme; c'est en passant à l'état solide qu'elle reçoit les formes diverses sous lesquelles l'organisation nous la présente."

Cet aperçu n'était pas sans quelque motif; c'est, en effet, dans l'état liquide ou fluide que toutes les combinaisons chimiques s'opèrent, et c'est aussi dans le même état que viennent s'unir aux corps organisés les substances qui s'identifient avec eux. Au reste, il ne s'agit point d'apprécier ici le plus ou le moins d'exactitude [340] des notions que Thalès pouvait avoir acquises en physique; nous ne discuterons donc pas avec quelques commentateurs la question de savoir si l'eau, ou le fluide quelconque dont il formait la matière de toutes choses, était composée d'élémens homogènes et hétérogènes. Ce qu'il importe d'observer, c'est que, dans un ordre de recherches qui était entièrement nouveau, Thalès donna aussi, sous trois rapports, un exemple aussi nouveau qu'utile; (1) il ne se borna point, comme ses prédécesseurs, à une affirmation simple et gratuite; il ne se contenta point d'offrir à l'imagination l'aliment dont elle était avide; il voulut s'adresser à la raison; il essaya d'appuyer sur des preuves, bonnes ou mauvaises, mais enfin sur des preuves, l'assertion qu'il avançait; (2) ces preuves, il les chercha dans l'analogie déduite de l'expérience; il généralisa l'observation qu'il avait faite sur la manière dont se nourrissent les corps organisés; (3) enfin, au lieu de considérer les phénomènes naturels comme isolés, détachés les uns des autres, il voulut saisir le nœud qui les unit, il chercha ce nœud dans une loi; le premier, donc, il eut l'idée des lois générales de [341] la nature. Aussi nous dit-on que le système entier des êtres était à ses yeux étroitement enchaîné, et comme il ne concevait pas qu'ils pussent agir les uns sur les autres autrement que par le contact, il fut conduit à les regarder tous comme adhérens, à admettre une absolue contiguité, et il rejeta le vide.

On a reproché à Thalès, et Aristote déjà lui adressait cette critique, on lui a reproché de n'avoir point essayé de découvrir la cause qui préside à la conversion de la matière fluide en un corps concret et dense; mais cette censure est peut-être exagérée; peut-être même faut-il louer la prudence de ce philosophe, lorsque toutes les erreurs accumulées jusqu'à lui provenaient précisément de l'empressement excessif avec lequel on s'était hâté d'imaginer des causes, avant d'avoir bien établi la suite des observations comparées qui seules conduisent à les reconnaître. Il se borna à exposer les faits, tels qu'il les [342] concevait; et s'il les eût conçus en effet tels qu'ils sont dans la nature, il eût mieux préparé les recherches étiologiques, que par des interprétations prématurées.

Ce qu'on nous a transmis des opinions de Thalès sur la psycologie se borne à une seule proposition, sur laquelle Aristote, Plutarque et Stobée sont d'accord. "L'essence de l'âme est le mouvement, un mouvement spontané, quelque chose qui a la faculté de se mouvoir, κινητικον τι, dit Aristote; qui est dans un mouvement continuel, αεικινητον, dit Plutarque; qui se meut par soi-même, αυτοκινητον, dit Stobée. Peut-être, au travers de l'imperfection du langage, peut-on démêler ici un aperçu juste et profond qui ferait consister l'essence de l'âme dans la libre activité. Cependant, il faudrait prendre cette proposition dans son sens littéral, si Thalès dit, comme l'assure Aristote, que "l'aimant a une âme; parce qu'il attire le fer;" et ceci nous expliquerait ce qu'il voulait dire lorsqu'il prétendait que l'univers est plein de dieux, [343] ou plutôt de génies, comme le dit Diogène Laërce; car ces deux expressions sont à peu près équivalentes dans le langage du temps; elles indiqueraient ici des êtres doués d'une mobilité propre, possédant le mouvement par eux-mêmes et capables de l'imprimer. Tertullien, au reste, a cru pouvoir attester que, suivant Thalès, l'âme est immatérielle. Ces diverses idées ne seraient pas aussi incompatibles que plusieurs commentateurs l'ont pensé, et il ne serait pas étonnant que le philosophe de Milet, généralisant l'observation que nous offre le phénomène de la vie, eût conçu le mouvement comme émanant primitivement de l'action des substances spirituelles. . . . [344]

Nous avons vu que Thalès rapportait le principe du mouvement à une cause intellectuelle; le témoignage de quelques anciens semble attester aussi qu'il admettait l'opinion d'une âme du monde. Mais il n'identifiait point, à ce qu'il nous sembler, dans l'idée de *principe*, αρχην, celle d'él[é]ment, et celle de *cause;* il n'attribua donc que la première propriété à son premier principe; du reste, étant plutôt physicien que métaphysicien, s'appliquant à decouvrir les lois matérielles de la nature, et non d'établir un système de théologie naturelle, il n'admit point l'intervention immédiate de la Divinité dans les phénomènes partiels de l'univers; il ne s'occupa point d'établir comment la cause intelligente [345] agit sur la matière, et en cela il paraissait rejeter les Dieux tels que les admettaient les traditions vulgaires, tels que les concevaient les doctrines mystiques; c'est en ce sens qu'il a pu être qualifié d'athée; il a partagé cette accusation avec un grand nombre de sages, avec presque tous ceux qui dans l'antiquité se sont livrés à l'étude des sciences physiques.

Mais au-dessus de ces œuvres matérielles, il paraît qu'il avait conservé l'action de la cause universelle, unie plutôt que confondue avec la matière.

Ainsi s'explique ce que disent Aristote, saint Clément d'Alexandrie, Eusèbe et saint Augustin, que "Thalès n'admettait que des causes matérielles;" ainsi disparaît la contradiction dans laquelle semble tomber Aristote, lorsqu'il annonce cependant que, suivant Thalès, l'univers était plein de Dieux. Ainsi se justifie l'assertion expresse de Cicéron: *Aquam dixit rerum initium; Deum autem, eam mentem quæ ex eâ omnia fingeret;* celle de Diogène Laërce et celle de Plutarque, lorsqu'ils attribuent à Thalès ces trois maximes: *Dieu* [346] *est le plus ancien, car il n'a point été produit; le monde est ce qu'il y a de plus parfait, car il est l'ouvrage de Dieu; aucune action et même aucune pensée n'est cachée à Dieu.*

ANAXIMANDER

Coleridge, who harmonized Plato and Bacon, maintained that the distinction between those thinkers might be expressed simply as follows:[18] "that philosophy being necessarily bipolar, Plato treats principally of the truth, as it manifests itself at the ideal pole, as the science of intellect *(de mundo intelligibili);* while Bacon confines himself . . . to the same truth, as it is manifested at the other or material pole, as the science of nature *(de mundo sensibili).*" Thales had emphasized the physical side; Anaximander sought an absolute or metaphysical basis for the same universe, remarking that "The *infinite* is the principle or source of all that

---

[18] See Coleridge ¶ 143.

exists;"[19]——and it was "such transcendentalism" that showed Emerson "how close is the first and that last step of philosophy"[20]——how perennial the apprehension of the ideal pole! Anaximander, he said, revived in Madame de Staël,[21] and the maxim, "Nothing can come into being *ex nihilo*," was to be echoed in all later philosophy.[22]

Thalès avait essayé de s'appuyer sur une démonstration; Anaximandre[23] voulut rendre cette démonstration plus rigoureuse, il en scruta les fondemens; il se trouva de la sorte conduit à lui donner un principe d'un ordre nouveau, un principe absolu et entièrement métaphysique: *rien ne se fait de rien*. Ainsi vit le jour ce célèbre axiome autour duquel tourna longtemps, comme sur son pivot, la philosophie des écoles grecques. On voit que cet axiome correspondait directement au grand problème qui était jusqu'alors le but essentiel de toutes les investigations, et qui consistait à expliquer *l'origine des choses;* on voit aussi qu'Anaximandre puisa cet axiome dans la généralisation la plus étendue à laquelle puisse donner lieu la chaîne des reproductions naturelles; nous ignorons si, en émettant cette proposition, Anaximandre la conçut comme la simple expression d'un fait, comme le résultat de l'expérience, ou s'il en fit une vérité transcendentale; peut-être n'eut-il pas lui-même une idée bien nette à cet égard, et confondit-il deux points de vue que l'état de la science ne permettait guère de distinguer. [350]

Maintenant, en partant de ce principe fondamental, ce philosophe fut conduit à une conséquence qui étonne par sa hardiesse, il faut même le dire, par sa profondeur, si l'on considère l'époque et les circonstances où elle fut mise au jour. "L'infini, dit-il, est le principe de toutes choses, un infini tout ensemble immuable et immense." En effet, rien de ce qui est inconstant et borné ne lui paraissait pouvoir suffire à la génération universelle et perpétuelle des êtres. Il est digne de remarque que cet aperçu, quelque imparfait qu'il soit, a une analogie assez frappante avec la célèbre démonstration de Clarcke sur l'être nécessaire.

Dans l'idée qu'il se formait de ce principe infini, Anaximandre paraît avoir, comme Thalès, associé et confondu la notion de *cause* et celle *d'élément*, αρχη και στοιχειον απειρον, deux notions que les péripatéticiens et les stoïciens ont ensuite soigneusement distinguées. Il [351] fut le premier, dit le pseudo-Origène, qui attacha à l'expression στοιχειον απειρον, le sens de *cause;* il ne put guère concevoir cette notion dans toute sa netteté et sa rigueur métaphysique. Il voyait en elle, si nous en croyons Cicéron, une source infinie et féconde, *infinitatem naturæ, à quâ omnia gignerentur.*

En saisissant, par une vue aussi remarquable, la distinction du contingent et de l'absolu, en demandant au second le point d'appui qui manque au premier, Anaximandre franchissait la limite de la sphère que Thalès avait assignée à la science; il appelait le métaphysique à servir de base à la physique. Cependant on ne pouvait attendre que les confins de ces deux régions fussent dès lors exactement marqués, et bien moins encore que leurs vrais rapports fussent reconnus. Aussi, Anaximandre ne conçoit-il point l'infini, tel que le donne une légitime abstraction, comme un idéal qui résulte de la suppression de toute limite, et par conséquent comme dégagé de toute divisibilité et de toute composition. Au contraire, son infini est une substance réelle, il remplit l'espace; il a donc une certaine étendue; il tient un milieu entre [352] l'air et l'eau; il a donc une certaine densité; il est matériel, en un mot. C'est ainsi que ce philosophe rentre bientôt dans le domaine des idées de Thalès, dans l'ordre de ses spéculations; c'est ainsi qu'il rallie à la physique et aux choses naturelles la théorie métaphysique à laquelle il avait un instant essayé d'atteindre.

---

[19] See *Nature*, 76.3-17.

[20] *Journals*, II, 337. Cf. *Nature*, 76.3-17.

[21] *Journals*, II, 284.

[22] See *Nature*, 39.19; 45.4; 59.8ff.

[23] The following excerpts come from Gérando, *Histoire* (1822), I, 349-352.

A l'exemple de Thalès, Anaximandre essaya d'établir quelques lois générales de la nature. Telle est celle de l'attraction mutuelle et constante des parties homogènes de la matière les unes vers les autres. Cette attraction donne naissance aux corps, et le mouvement est ainsi, selon lui, éternal comme la reproduction; car les corps, les mondes eux-mêmes, se succèdent par une révolution continuelle, et de la destruction des uns résulte la formation des autres. La chaleur et le froid sont les deux instrumens de ces compositions et de ces décompositions.

ANAXAGORAS[24]

Anaxagoras clarified earlier thinking by separating the Universe from its Cause———that is, by distinguishing mind *(nous)* from matter. Discarding pluralism, he saw an ordered universe———a prevailing unity that pointed to one mind. The phenomenal world, he said, was animated and regulated by one spirit, which revealed itself intimately to man. He, therefore, assisted greatly in the disengagement of the idea of God from the number of things that compose the world, and advanced the concept of the First Cause.[25]

Il survient, maintenant, cet illustre Anaxagoras dont l'antiquité a consacré la mémoire par de si justes et si unanimes hommages; aujourd'hui encore, au travers de tant de siècles, nous le saluons avec un sentiment de joie et de respect. [357] Son nom mériterait sans doute de marquer l'une des époques principales de l'histoire de la philosophie, en considérant l'importance et la grandeur de la doctrine qu'il a établie sur la cause première. Une circonstance remarquable se rattache aussi aux souvenirs de sa vie; il fut le premier philosophe qu'Athènes vit enseigner dans ses murs. Avec Anaxagoras, la philosophie abandonna les colonies grecques en Ionie; la tyrannie des satrapes persans la bannit à jamais de ces belles contrées où elle avait vu le jour; elle fut réduite à fuir avec la liberté qui l'avait protégée à sa naissance.

Nous rangeons cependant Anaxagoras dans l'école d'Ionie, non parce qu'on a supposé qu'il fut le disciple d'Anaximène; car le savant Meiners a montré qu'il est difficile de concilier cette supposition avec les dates; non encore parce qu'il était né à Clazomène, et qu'il vint plus tard s'y réfugier; mais parce que, à l'exemple des Ioniens, il se livra essentiellement à l'étude des sciences physiques; il chercha l'explication des phénomènes dans les analogies fournies par [358] l'expérience; il n'assigna à ces phénomènes, comme causes immédiates, que des agens pris dans la nature. En un mot, c'est en suivant le même ordre de considérations, qu'il se trouva ensuite conduit à des résultats d'un ordre plus relevé.

En prenant pour point de départ cette doctrine des Ioniens, qui avaient banni du champ des phénomènes l'influence immédiate des agens surnaturels, qui avaient affranchi la physique de l'empire du merveilleux, on voit ce qui restait à faire pour replacer la notion sublime de la Divinité dans les vrais rapports qui lui appartiennent avec l'ensemble des lois de l'univers. Déjà on avait assigné ces rapports d'une manière confuse.

La doctrine de la cause première, telle qu'elle a été fondée par Anaxagoras, a eu précisément pour objet d'achever ce grand ouvrage; deux caractères essentiels la distinguent:

(1) Tandis que le système des émanations, [359] que tous les systèmes du panthéisme qui en étaient plus ou moins derivés, que les opinions des premiers Ioniens eux-mêmes avaient associé la matière élémentaire de toutes choses à la cause première

---

[24] See *Journals*, II, 337-339. The following excerpts are taken from *Histoire* (1822), I, 356-369.
[25] See *Nature*, 7.8-9.

de toute production, et conçu ainsi la Divinité comme *l'âme universelle, l'âme du monde,* le monde lui-même comme un tout animé, identique en quelque sorte avec son auteur, Anaxagoras, le premier, détacha, sépara, avec précision et netteté, ces deux notions jusqu'alors confondues. L'univers n'est plus à ses yeux qu'un effet entièrement distinct de la cause qui l'a produit; cette cause n'a rien de commun avec le reste des êtres; elle a sa nature propre exclusivement à elle seule; elle est une, comme elle est éternelle; elle agit sur le monde, comme l'ouvrier sur les matériaux qui lui sont fournis. Aussi l'idée de la cause première, qui, jusqu'alors, s'était essentiellement définie par l'attribut de la *puissance,* fut-elle déterminée par Anaxagoras à recevoir éminemment l'attribut de *l'intelligence.*

(2) Jusqu'alors la vérité la plus auguste, la [360] plus précieuse pour l'humanité, n'avait point été l'objet d'une démonstration explicite et développée; un instinct naturel, un instinct religieux l'enseignait d'une manière confuse chez le plus grand nombre; ceux dont les méditations avaient été plus approfondies, avaient senti que la chaîne des effets devait remonter à une première cause; que cette cause devait opérer en agissant; que l'action supposait un principe doué tout ensemble de la volonté et de la pensée; mais n'avaient point converti cette déduction en un raisonnement méthodique, et surtout n'avaient point fait sortir ce raisonnement de l'harmonie générale des lois de la nature. Ce mérite était réservé à Anaxagoras. Le premier, il comprit clairement, il annonça d'une manière expresse que les phénomènes de l'univers sont étroitement liés entre eux; qu'ils forment un ensemble, un tout; que l'ordre est la grande chaîne qui unit ses parties, la loi suprême qui le gouverne; que ce système universel, dans l'unité qui le constitue, suppose un ordonnateur unique, et par conséquent une intelligence qui le connaît, le dispose et le réalise.

On voit maintenant, et ceci nous paraît ex- [361] trêmement remarquable, on voit que c'est précisément parce que les Ioniens, et Anaxagoras avec eux, avaient banni des phénomènes particuliers l'action immédiate de la Divinité, les causes magiques, l'intervention des génies, qu'une telle démonstration devint possible. En recourant aux agens surnaturels, on avait laissé les phénomènes dans un isolement qui ne permettait pas de saisir la haute sagesse qui préside à leur concert. Il fallut que la physique fût créée, qu'elle prît le rang d'une science, pour que la démonstration cosmologique et téléologique de l'existence de la Divinité et de ses attributs pût obtenir ses bases. L'histoire de l'esprit humain nous montre sans cesse que la superstition a été le plus grand obstacle aux saines idées religieuses.

Aussi, Anaxagoras, alors même qu'il proclamait cette grande révélation de la raison, fut-il accusé d'impiété, persécuté avec acharnement, jeté en prison, et la fuite seule put le soustraire à la vengeance des prêtres et aux fureurs d'une multitude aveuglée. Il avait commis le crime de dire que les astres ne sont point des dieux, et de refuser son culte aux fables de l'astrologie. . . . [362]

La doctrine d'Anaxagoras ne fut point exempte non plus d'erreurs, d'hypothèses gratuites, de contradictions même. Essayons de jeter un coup d'œil rapide sur les opinions qu'on lui attribue, pour mieux apprécier la marche de ses [363] idées da[n]s l'investigation des plus grands problèmes de la science. . . .

Livré par goût à l'étude des sciences physiques, Anaxagoras y avait porté un esprit d'observation qui lui fit soupçonner plusieurs des découvertes modernes, telles que la pesanteur de l'air, par exemple; un aërolithe tombé à Athènes, pendant qu'il habitait cette ville, lui suggéra quelques recherches. Mais il fut rarement heureux lorsqu'il essaya des théories. Suivant les traces de ses prédécesseurs, il voulut en fonder une sur l'origine des choses, et comme eux il prit pour point de départ l'axiome: RIEN NE SE FAIT DE RIEN. Il en tira cette conséquence que tout ce qui est, tout ce qui se produit, résulte de ce qui était, de ce qui a pré- [364] cédé; qu'il y a des élémens primitifs, simples, indivisibles, éternels, immuables; que ces élémens sont divers entre eux; que leurs différentes espèces possèdent déjà les qualités qui appartiennent ensuite à leurs composés. Ainsi se constituèrent ses *homoioméries.* Chacune d'elles est ainsi un germe et comme une esquisse de l'univers. "Toutes sont différentes entre elles; aucune n'est semblable à une autre; leur nombre est infini."

"Tous ces élémens, d'abord mêlés et confondus, formaient le chaos. Ce chaos était immobile et dans un état de mort, environné d'un air ou plutôt d'un éther sans bornes, en sorte qu'il n'existait aucun vide." [365]

"Il fallait donc qu'il existât, en dehors de cette matière universelle, de ce chaos d'élémens, une cause qui vînt leur imprimer le mouvement, leur donner une forme, les coordonner. Cette cause est l'intelligence suprême; car l'intelligence seule peut être un principe d'ordre; et tout ce qu'il y a de bon, de beau, de régulier, émane d'elle seule."

"Cette intelligence doit tout embrasser, tout connaître, le passé, le présent, l'avenir; sa puissance est immense, son activité est spontanée, et elle tire d'elle-même toute son énergie; elle est simple, pure, exempte de tout mélange; elle est, par conséquent, souverainement indépendante, exempte de toute sujétion et de toute influence; en un mot, elle est infinie." ... [367]

"Trois actes principaux manifestent la puissance de la cause première; elle imprime le mouvement; elle assemble les élémens pour en [368] composer des êtres organisés; elle décompose ces êtres pour en former d'autres de leurs débris. L'intelligence suprême conserve, comme elle a produit. Le mouvement a nécessairement commencé. Composition et décomposition, voilà les deux grandes lois de la nature: l'une est le principe de la production, l'autre de la destruction. Ainsi les élémens sont éternels, la forme seule que recoivent leurs combinaisons est l'ouvrage de la sagesse toute-puissante. L'espèce d'élémens qui domine dans un composé en détermine la constitution et les propriétés."

"L'intelligence pénètre tout, régit tout, est présente en toutes choses; *elle les orne en les parcourant,* suivant la belle expression de Platon; mais, elle est bien plus intimement présente aux êtres vivans, sensibles et raison- [369] nables; car elle est le principe de la vie, de la sensibilité et de la connaissance; il n'y a en quelque sorte qu'une seule âme, un seul esprit, répandus dans tous les êtres vivans." ... Anaxagoras distinguait *l'âme,* principe de la vie, de la *raison,* attribut de l'esprit, et il se peut que ce soit seulement le premier de ces deux principes qu'il ait regardé comme étant entièrement commun à l'homme, aux animaux et aux plantes.

THE PYTHAGOREANS[26]

Emerson found the School of Pythagoras exceedingly fertile in ideas, many of which he entered in his *Journals.*[27] Of chief significance are: (1) The strong emphasis on unity[28] as opposed to manifoldness——a concept fundamental in Neo-Platonism. "The true lies in unity; error in the multiple." (2) Polarity, or the system of contrasts obtaining in the time-and-space manifold world, expressed notably in the famous decade of Alcmæon. This principle was coordinate with that of "harmony," which foreshadowed the "Golden Mean" of Aristotle, and, possibly, the doctrine of compensation in Emerson.[29] (3) The Pythagoreans were among the first to hold a majestic view of nature——to give to the world the name of *kosmos* (i.e., beauty, symmetry, order).[30] (4) Virtue, like the Beautiful, was considered the result of a harmony.[31] (5) The principle of inter-

---

[26] See *Histoire* (1822), I, 405-422.   [27] *Journals,* II, 340-341.
[28] Cf. *Nature,* 54.12 through 56.16.
[29] See "Polarity" in the index. Cf. *Nature,* 14.9 for emphasis on temperance.
[30] See *Nature,* 19.5; 29.20-23.
[31] *Nature,* 29.21; 25.3; 27.15. See chapter on Goethe and Moritz, *infra.*

relatedness:[32] Beings are joined by a chain of relations, and all together form a single unified whole. This concept hinted at the "each in all"[33] doctrine of Neo-Platonism as well as at the Aristotelian system of a chain of causes. (6) The centrality of man in the phenomenal world.[34] Rays of relation go out from him not only to the gods but to the lower animals as well. The same intelligence pervades the inferior orders as shines forth in him, but there are distinctions of rank and gradations among creatures.[35] (7) Man's soul is immortal. It is an emanation from the Soul of the World, it fulfills its purpose in the flesh, and it finally returns to its source. (This concept blossomed in Neo-Platonism.)[36] (8) The Reason contemplates the natural world and perceives itself as a universal phenomenon. It acknowledges itself part of a fundamental unity by virtue of the consanguinity existing between the mind or soul of man and nature.[37] "The same can be known only by the same."[38] (9) The two properties attributed to the Divinity are the True and the Good.[39]

De là le principe fondamental de la doctrine pythagoricienne: *les nombres sont les principes des choses*. Encore, l'acception elle-même des termes dont ce célèbre axiome était composé, étant nécessairement fort indéterminée, reçut la valeur la plus étendue, et, dans le vague qui l'entourait, on ne put lui poser aucune limite. L'expression: *principe*, signifia à la fois l'élément intégrant, réel, et la cause active, efficiente, comme chez les premiers Ioniens. L'expression: *nombre* (αριθμος), désigna non-seulement le nombre en général, mais aussi toute espèce de grandeurs et de quantités, toutes les relations qu'ont entre elles les choses commensurables. [406] Deux autres conséquences résultèrent de l'ordre de considérations dans lequel on s'était engagé. Les propriétés des nombres furent transportées sur les objets eux-mêmes; les formules mathématiques furent converties en lois positives de la nature. . . .

[407] Essayons maintenant de tracer rapidement le plan de l'édifice qui fut construit sur ces bases. La *monade*, ou l'unité, occupe le premier rang, compose la première espèce; tout dérive d'elle, puisque tous les nombres se forment par sa répétition; elle est constamment semblable à elle-même; simple, car elle ne résulte d'au- [408] cune combinaison, elle se reproduit encore elle-même, car elle est sa propre puissance mathématique; elle est donc l'élément essentiel comme elle est le principe actif, la cause universelle; elle est éminemment parfaite. De même le point est le principe générateur des corps et des figures; maxime propre à une sous-division particulière de l'école d'Italie. La *dyade*, au contraire, est imparfaite; elle est produite, elle est composée; c'est la matière, le chaos, le principe passif. La *monade* et la *dyade* forment donc les deux genres sous lesquels se range l'universalité des êtres.

Les nombres se partagent en deux espèces: les *pairs* et les *impairs*. Les premiers sont imparfaits, la perfection n'appartient qu'aux seconds; la raison en est que les seconds par leur réunion peuvent former les premiers, et que les pairs ne peuvent jamais donner des pairs en se multipliant; la raison en est encore que les [409] seconds admettent une moyenne proportionnelle que ne donnent point les premiers. La *tryade*, la *tétrade* ont aussi leurs propriétés mystiques; la *tryade* comme formée par les deux premiers nombres, la *tétrade* comme étant le premier carré. La somme

---

[32] See footnote 37.
[33] See the discussion of the "microcosm" in chapter three.
[34] See *Nature*, 13.21; 35.9-12; also 27.16.
[35] Cf. *Nature*, 57.1-12.
[36] See *Nature*, 34.13-17; 73.1-4. See chapters three and five.
[37] See *Nature*, 34.17, 13.21; 43.1; 83.11-21; 29.10-23; also the chapter on Goethe and Moritz.
[38] See *Nature*, 94.5; 44.18; 68.5-7.
[39] Emerson uses the Neo-Platonic triad——Truth, Beauty and Goodness——in *Nature*, 30.20. Cf. 69.2-3.

des quatre premiers nombres constitue la *décade* qui joue par ce motif un rôle éminent dans les symboles des Pythagoriciens. Ils l'appliquent à toutes les branches des connaissances, et contraignent les nomenclatures fondamentales à s'y conformer.

On connaît la célèbre décade attribuée à Alcmæon.

Le fini, περας,	*l'infini,* απειρον,
L'impair, περιττον,	*le pair,* αρτιον,
L'un, εν,	*le multiple,* πληθος,
Le droit, δεξιον,	*le gauche,* αριστερον,
Le mâle, αρρεν,	*le féminin,* θηλυ,
L'objet en repos, ηρεμαν,	*en mouvem.,* κινουμενον,
Le direct, ευθυ,	*le courbe,* καμπυλον,
La lumière, φως,	*les ténèbres,* σκοτος,
Le bon, αγαθον,	*le mauvais,* κακον,
Le carré, τετραγωνον,	*le quadrilatère irrégulier,* ετερομηκες.

[411] On reconnaît, enfin, dans cette décade, le goût que les Pythagoriciens avaient pour les contrastes, et l'usage qu'ils en faisaient. Sextus l'Empirique rapporte qu'ils distinguaient trois grandes espèces de choses; il nomme les deux premières: l'une qui comprend celles qui ont une existence propre et indépendante, comme [412] l'homme, le cheval, la plante, etc., l'autre qui a un caractère exclusif, et qui suppose un contraire, en sorte qu'en affirmant l'un on nie l'autre, comme le mouvement et le repos, la lumière et les ténèbres; il n'indique pas la troisième, mais nous croyons entrevoir que les Pythagoriciens y rangeoient ce qui a un caractère relatif, comme *le plus* et *le moins,* et ce qui admet par conséquent un terme moyen. . . .

[413] Il est, au reste, d'autres genres de mérite qu'on ne peut contester à Pythagore et à ses disciples. Ils avaient aperçu, par exemple, qu'indépendamment de l'unité primitive et simple que entre comme élément dans la formation de tout composé, il y a une autre unité collective qui sert de pivot ou de lien aux idées complexes, et à l'aide de laquelle elles se réunissent en faisceau. Ils avoient remarqué que cette dernière unité est la condition nécessaire pour que les objets prennent rang dans l'ordre de nos connaissances.

Ils avoient appliqué ensuite cette grande vue [414] à la nature: "Les êtres sont liés entre eux par une chaîne de rapports parallèles ou semblables à ceux qui unissent les nombres; tous ces rapports viennent converger à un même centre; le monde forme ainsi un seul tout: la symétrie préside aux systèmes de leur dépendance et de leur connexion." C'est ainsi qu'ils s'élevèrent à cette belle et majestueuse image de l'harmonie de l'univers qui devient le digne et principal but de leurs contemplations. Les premiers ils donnèrent à l'univers cette belle dénomination d'ensemble ordonné (κοσμος), qui exprime si bien la juste admiration que son spectacle nous inspire.

Envisageant la nature sous un tel aspect, ils devoient se trouver naturellement portés à concevoir des notions justes et élevées sur la cause première. Cependant celles qu'on attribue aux premiers Pythagoriciens ne répondent pas entièrement à cette attente. Ils étoient aussi voisins de l'idée d'une intelligence ordonnatrice; mais, ils ne surent point saisir expressément cette [415] conséquence, comme le fit Anaxagoras. Il semble qu'ils croyaient avoir toùt expliqué par les propriétés des nombres, et qu'ayant établi des lois ils ne sentaient pas le besoin des causes; c'est sans doute parce que ces lois avaient un caractère de nécessité, d'immutabilité, parce qu'ils les concevoient comme éternelles. Ils ne parvinrent donc ni à affranchir la notion de la Divinité d'une condition de *lieu* dans l'étendue, puisqu'ils lui assignèrent pour séjour le centre du monde, ni à la dégager des images matérielles, puisqu'ils parurent l'identifier avec le feu, avec la lumière; ils admirent l'antique tradition de l'âme du monde et conçurent l'univers comme un être vivant et animé. Ils adoptèrent ainsi un panthéisme assez grossier, panthéisme que Virgile, Ovide, ont re- [416] vêtu des charmes de la poésie la plus brillante, que saint Justin martyr a défini avec une élégante clarté. Les idées des Pythagoriciens sur ce sujet présentent une analogie remarquable avec le système des émanations, s'ils n'en sont pas simplement un emprunt; elles reçurent ensuite chez les Pythagoriciens récens un caractère éminent de spiritualité et de mysticisme. Pythagore et ses disciples admettaient des hiérarchies de génies, espèce de dieux inférieurs répandus dans les espaces. Ils attachaient une grande importance aux songes, aux prédictions, aux présages, et Pythagore lui-même prétendoit être un augure. Mais, ils rachetaient ce tribut payé aux superstitions vulgaires par de belles notions sur la Providence. "Nous sommes," suivant Philolaus, "les esclaves, la propriété des dieux; les dieux nous gouvernent, veillent sur nous et pourvoient à nos besoins." La vérité et la bonté étaient les deux principaux attributs qu'ils reconnaissaient dans la Divinité.

[417] Les méditations des Pythagoriciens sur la morale produisirent des fruits plus utiles. Ils avaient, à la faveur de leur théorie, aperçu la nature du beau; ils étaient donc bien près d'apercevoir celle du bon; aussi donnèrent-ils les premiers à la vertu cette heureuse définition: *La vertu est une harmonie.* "Ce qui est bien se range sous la loi de *l'unité*, de la détermination, ce qui est mal, sous la catégorie du *multiple;* de l'indéfini. La justice est l'égalité dans le multiple. Dieu est le juge moral de l'homme." Cette dernière maxime liait pour eux l'éthique à la théologie naturelle. On voit, par les règles auxquelles Pythagore soumit ses disciples, qu'il considérait la modération comme le caractère essentiel de la vertu, l'empire sur soi-même comme le moyen de l'obtenir, la paix intérieure comme le fruit qui devait en être la conséquence. Le génie de Pythagore, légis- [418] lateur des cités, auteur d'une association qui devait être le principal ressort de ses institutions, s'était principalement dirigé vers les préceptes pratiques, et les avait fortifiés par la rigueur des exercices qu'il avait imposés à ses disciples, par la retraite, le silence, l'obéissance et la sévérité du régime diététique. Mais, on recueille avec respect, avec admiration, cette belle pensée que Jamblique attribue à Pythagore, et qui devait être comme l'âme de son institut, que *l'amour de la vérité et le zèle du bien sont le présent le plus précieux que Dieu ait pu accorder à l'homme.*

La direction qu'avaient suivie les idées des Pythagoriciens semblait promettre quelques succès dans l'étude des facultés morales et intellectuelles de l'homme; et comme nous avons eu occasion de le remarquer, ces philosophes eurent en effet sur la psychologie certains aperçus qui ne manquent point de sagacité. Mais, l'extrême imperfection qui régnait encore dans l'ordre des idées emprunté à la réflexion, l'amour du merveilleux, l'empressement à généraliser, arrêtèrent les progrès de cette étude, ou l'égarèrent dans sa marche. Suivant les Pythagoriciens: "l'homme a [419] quelque affinité, non-seulement avec les dieux, mais avec les animaux; une même intelligence parcourt l'univers et nous unit à eux. Le langage cependant nous distingue des brutes." Ils distinguaient, toutefois, deux facultés, ou, suivant leur langage, deux parties dans l'âme humaine: l'une, principe des besoins physiques, des passions aveugles; l'autre, des calmes opérations de l'esprit, des résolutions de la sagesse; la seconde raisonnable, la première privée de raison. "Elles ont dans le corps des siéges distincts, comme elles ont une origine différente. L'une d'elles paraît même encore se sous-diviser en deux autres, suivant Platon, en distinguant les affections, des besoins; suivant Jamblique et Plutarque, en distinguant l'intelligence, de la pensée; suivant Diogène Laërce, enfin, en distinguant la raison, de la sensibilité." Dans ces distinctions, quelles qu'elles soient, nous reconnaissons des facultés morales et intellectuelles personnalisées et transformées en substances. Peut-être la première de ces distinctions doit-elle expliquer [420] l'opinion des pythagoriciens sur la similitude de l'homme avec l'animal, en ce sens que le première seulement, la force motrice, source des besoins, seroit commune à l'un et aux autres.

"L'âme est une émanation de la Divinité, une partie de la grande âme du monde, un rayon dérivé du foyer de la lumière. Elle vient du dehors dans le corps humain, comme dans un séjour momentané; elle en sort de nouveau, elle erre dans les régions éthérées, elle revient le visiter, elle passe dans d'autres habitations, car l'âme est immortelle."

"L'âme aspire les représentations des images des choses, comme une sorte d'air. La vérité est dans *l'unité*, l'erreur dans le *multiple;* car, il n'est qu'une route sûre, celle qui est directe; on s'égare en suivant toutes celles qui [421] divergent. Le même ne peut être connu que par le même; ainsi chaque sens a son élément qui lui est propre. L'éther est celui de la vue, l'air celui de l'ouïe, le feu celui de l'odorat, la terre celui du toucher." Suivant Diogène Laërce, les sens étaient, aux yeux des Pythagoriciens, la source de toutes les vues de l'esprit. Suivant Sextus l'Empirique, la raison était pour eux le *critérium* des connaissances, non la raison commune, mais la raison exercée par les disciplines. "Car, comme la raison contemple l'universalité de la nature, elle a avec celle-ci une certaine affinité; et de même que la lumière est aperçue par l'œil, le son par l'ouïe, à l'aide de l'analogie qui existe entre ces objets et ces organes, de même l'universalité de la nature doit être saisie par la raison qui lui est unie par une sorte de consanguinité. Les vrais physiciens doivent donc s'attacher d'abord aux choses universelles, et rechercher en quoi elles consistent. Mais, le principe des choses universelles ne se manifeste point aux sens; [422] car tout ce qui se montre aux sens est composé, et ce qui est composé ne saurait être un principe. L'espèce dépend du genre, et non le genre de l'espèce; le genre est donc connu par lui-même. L'unité n'est que dans le genre." Cependant l'école d'Italie ne négligea point, autant qu'on pourrait le croire, l'étude des sciences naturelles.

XENOPHANES[40]

Xenophanes (1) considered the senses unreliable. Real knowledge, he maintained, was not of things we see, but *a priori*. Only the Reason or spiritual part of man can discover truth, and it does so from within. (2) Thought is the only *real*, continuing, unchangeable substance. The solid-seeming universe is merely phenomenal——a reflection or shadow about which one does well to be skeptical.[41] (3) The Godhead is one and perfect——not manifold or anthropomorphic. It is above man's comprehension, though man can know that God exists. (4) A unity pervades everything. Throughout the multiplicity of the time-and-space world, one can see all signposts pointing to the One.[42] (5) "Like must produce like."[43] There is, therefore, no generation or fundamental alteration or metamorphosis. All that *really* is, is eternal and unchangeable——an aspect of unity. Following the emphasis of Anaximander, Xenophanes set forth a variety of Idealism that pointed to the later rationalism of Descartes and Berkeley.[44] With this subject and its implications Emerson wrestled in Chapter VII of *Nature*.[45]

Xénophane est le premier philosophe qui ait donné pour fondement à la science un raisonnement absolu, entièrement *à priori;* qui se soit placé dans un ordre de pures spéculations antérieur à tous les faits, pour considérer les faits, et qui ait prétendu déterminer ce qui existe par les seules idées que la raison se forme sur ce qui doit être.

---

[40] *Histoire* (1822), I, 453-463.
[41] Emerson in *Journals*, II, 335-336, says: "Idealism seems a preparation for a strictly moral life, and so skepticism seems necessary for a universal holiness."
[42] See *Nature*, 54.15-18.
[43] See footnote 38.
[44] See chapter on Bishop Berkeley, *infra.*
[45] See *Nature*, 78.11-22.

Ainsi que les autres philosophes de l'antiquité, il veut remonter à la génération des choses, aborder le grand problème de l'existence réelle. Mais les autres philosophes s'étaient demandé: *Quelle est la génération des choses?* Xénophane se demande: *Y a-t-il eu en effet une génération quelconque?*

Il s'arrête à cette idée mystérieuse de l'origine, de la naissance, de la transformation des êtres; il veut savoir la raison pour laquelle ce qui n'est pas commencerait à exister; pour laquelle ce qui est viendrait à changer; comment [454] a pu s'opérer la transition de la non existence à l'existence, de tel mode d'existence à tel autre. Il consulte les explications qu'en ont données les philosophes ses prédécesseurs; elles ne peuvent le satisfaire. Il tente donc de pénétrer plus avant encore; il se demande si on peut donner la raison de l'existence, de ses modes, et des transformations qu'ils subissent; si même ces transformations sont possibles.

Rien ne se fait de rien; de ce principe déjà admis confusément par Thalès, Xéno-phane tire une conséquence que Thalès n'avait point imaginée, c'est qu'*une chose ne peut naître d'une autre chose:* "Car, ce qui, dans la première, différerait de la seconde, ce qui serait nouveau, n'aurait aucun principe. L'analogue ne peut produire l'analogue; il ne peut produire que sa propre répétition identique; il peut encore moins produire le dissemblable."

Xénophane appliqua donc aux modifications le même raisonnement que les autres philoso- [455] phes appliquaient aux substances; toute transformation devient à ses yeux une chose contradictoire.

Si l'on considère que l'existence est un fait simple, primitif, un fait qui nous est donné, on comprendra qu'en voulant construire l'existence *à priori*, et par les seules forces de la raison, en cherchant à démontrer le principe même de l'existence, on se proposait un problème insoluble. Xénophane était donc conséquent à lui-même. Mais il transportait dans l'ordre des réalités une vérité qui n'a de valeur que dans l'ordre intellectuel, et l'impossibilité où est l'esprit humain d'expliquer par d'autres faits le fait primitif, devenait pour lui l'impossibilité réelle de toute naissance et de toute génération. Or, rien ne peut être que sous une certaine manière d'être; il était donc conséquent encore lorsqu'il soumettait la manière d'être à la même loi que l'existence elle-même. De là résulta cette conséquence générale, que "tout ce qui est, est éternel, immuable, et doit subsister toujours."

"De même que les choses qui existent ne peuvent changer, elles ne peuvent être di- [455] verses; ainsi, *tout est un:* on ne peut concevoir des êtres dissemblables. L'être est unique." "La pensée, suivant ce philosophe, est la seule substance réelle, persévérante, immuable."

Xénophane, dans ses vues sur la théologie naturelle, dut s'élever au-dessus des superstitions vulgaires, aussi ne craignit-il point de les tourner en ridicule; "Dieu est un, et il ne peut y avoir qu'un Dieu; il est toujours semblable à lui-même; on ne peut le concevoir sous la forme humaine; il est parfait; on ne peut lui appliquer ni le mouvement, ni la limitation; il n'est cependant ni immobile, ni infini." Xénophane, dans ces deux dernières maximes, entendait sans doute que les notions de la limitation et du mouvement, telles que nous les donne la matière, ne peuvent avoir aucun rapport avec les attributs de la divinité. . . .

[457] On considère généralement Xénophane comme ayant admis le panthéisme à l'exemple de tous les philosophes de son temps, et cette supposition nous paraît fondée, quoique Xénophane n'ait rien avancé expressément qui la confirme. Mais son panthéisme, dans aucun cas, ne consistait point à identifier la Divinité avec l'univers physique; il ne pouvait consister qu'à considérer Dieu comme la substance unique, universelle, comme la seule réalité dans le sens qu'il donnait à la réalité, et qui va achever de s'expliquer, c'est-à-dire comme existant hors du domaine du monde sensible.

Rien n'est plus surprenant, au premier abord, que de voir Xénophane, après avoir érigé le système que nous venons de retracer, s'occuper cependant d'une cosmologie physique, distin- [458] guer quatre élémens, spéculer sur les lois de la nature, et s'il en fallait croire un fragment conservé par les anciens, mais dont l'authenticité est douteuse, affirmer que tout provient de la terre, se résoud en elle, que l'homme est composé de terre et d'eau. On reconnaît du moins qu'il a le premier avancé la célèbre hypothèse géologique des Neptuniens; il la déduisit de l'observation que lui présentèrent des poissons de mer pétrifiés qui furent trouvés à Syracuse. Il paraîtrait même qu'il étendit cette hypothèse à tous les autres corps célestes. Comment concilier ces idées avec sa doctrine sur l'immutabilité absolue des êtres?

Il nous semble, cependant, qu'on peut donner une explication propre à concilier ces deux ordres de systèmes admis à la fois par le même philosophe; cette explication acquiert quelque [459] vraisemblance, si l'on se reporte à la maxime déjà citée de Xénophane, que *la pensée est la seule substance*, et si l'on s'arrête à un passage fort important de Simplicius, d'après lequel *l'unité* de Xénophane n'appartenait point à la physique. Il n'est guère possible d'attribuer à Xénophane une contradiction aussi choquante que celle qui résulterait de son système d'immutabilité absolue, et de ses hypothèses sur les transformations de la nature matérielle, s'il les avait appliquées à la fois au même ordre d'idées. Mais la contradiction disparaît, si l'on suppose que Xénophane distinguait le monde physique du monde intellectuel, qu'il les isolait entièrement l'un de l'autre, et en faisait l'objet de deux sciences distinctes. Au second seulement il aurait attribué la réalité proprement dite, la véritable existence; dans le second seulement il consentait à reconnaître des substances, ou plutôt la substance unique et permanente. Au premier, à l'univers matériel, il eût accordé une simple valeur phénoménale; ce n'était point le monde de la raison, mais un monde inférieur, soumis, subordonné [460] à la raison, comme il le disait lui-même. Xénophane n'aurait fait ainsi que pressentir d'une manière confuse, supposer d'une manière implicite, les mêmes maximes que Parmenide après lui exprima d'une manière positive.

Cette solution se confirmerait encore par la distinction que Xénophane établissait entre la science et l'opinion. "La seconde, disait-il, dépend des impressions sensibles, et chacun de nous reçoit par les sens des impressions différentes; aucun n'aperçoit par leur secours les choses telles qu'elles sont par elles-mêmes; il ne faut donc point commencer par ces opinions prises au hasard, ni par les apparences, mais par ce qui est ferme et stable; à la raison seule appartient le privilége de nous le faire découvrir."

Il paraît cependant que Xénophane lui-même trouva quelque difficulté à concilier ses propres systèmes; d'après le témoignage de Timon le syllographe, et d'après un fragment curieux que nous a conservé Sextus l'Empirique, il se plaignait que, dans les derniers temps de sa [461] vie, il ne pouvait se féliciter de rien savoir avec certitude; "quelque part qu'il portât ses regards, tout se résolvait pour lui dans l'unité; il ne lui apparaissait partout qu'une substance semblable a elle-même." Son poëme sur la nature se terminait par les vers que nous traduisons ici, et dont Sextus l'Empirique nous a encore conservé le texte: "Aucun homme ne sait rien de certain sur ce qui concerne les Dieux, ni sur ce que je dis sur le tout universel; aucun ne peut le savoir. Car, si l'un d'entre eux atteignait à la vérité, *il ne pouvait du moins savoir qu'il l'a obtenue;* mais l'opinion étend son voile sur toutes choses." Ailleurs enfin Sextus rapporte, mais seulement comme un récit transmis par d'autres, que Xénophane ne rejetait pas toutes les notions, mais seulement celles qui auraient un caractère scientifique et positif; qu'il conservait celles qui sont simplement vraisemblables. . . . [462] Le scepticisme de Xénophane, quel qu'il fût, ne doit s'entendre que du monde sensible et phénoménal, et non des vérités métaphysiques. C'est ce que nous atteste Aristote; c'est ce que répète expressément Aristoclès, dans le passage rapporté par Eusèbe. C'était l'idéalisme, en un mot, système qui, aux yeux des observateurs superficiels, se con- [463] fond avec le scepticisme, et qui souvent aussi se résout en effet dans ce dernier.

PARMENIDES[46]

Gérando quotes at length from Parmenides' "Poem on Nature" to illustrate its highly colorful idealism and, at the same time, its tendency to "confound the abstract concept of *being* with objective reality"——to identify thought with its object——to confuse the ideal with the real—— a mistake common among philosophers down through the Romantic Movement and explanatory of the pantheistic note in early nineteenth-century poetry. The "Poem on Nature" continues the tradition of early spiritualists: "May custom never allure you to follow the sense, the eye and the ear. It is in warding off such guides, with the help of Reason alone, that you should penetrate to what I reveal. Sensation, if one yields to it, drags one from the way of truth." Parmenides insists that the truth as it was in the beginning, is *now* and *ever shall be*, and that since "like only can produce like," what truly exists or is *real* (in the philosophic sense) cannot become manifold. The emphasis, then, is placed upon a great spiritual unity as the substratum of the universe.

Nous avons, sous le nom de Parménide, un poëme presque complet, et dont l'authenticité, si elle n'est pas absolument certaine, est du moins appuyée sur de fortes probabilités. La doctrine que ce poëme contient est d'ailleurs dans un parfait accord avec celle que le témoignage unanime des anciens attribue à cet Éléatique. Ce poëme porte chez Sextus l'Em- [464] pirique le titre ordinaire aux ouvrages philosophiques de ce siècle: *Sur la nature*. Le prologue est une allégorie dans laquelle le poète philosophe semble peindre les méditations du sage qui se dirige à la recherche de la vérité, et la route par laquelle la sagesse le conduit au but; il se termine ainsi; c'est la grande déesse qui parle: "Je te salue, ô toi que les coursiers de la déesse conduisent à ma demeure; réjouis-toi, ce n'est point un sort malheureux qui t'a conduit sur cette voie inconnue aux mortels; *Thémis* et *Dicée* sont tes guides. Tu discerneras ces choses immuables et éternelles que la vérité enseigne, et tu les distingueras des apparences sensibles et des opinions humaines. Marche constamment dans cette voie, dans tes recherches; que jamais l'habitude ne t'entraîne à suivre tes sens, ton œil et ton oreille. C'est en écartant de tels guides, avec le secours de la raison seule, que tu dois pénétrer ce que je t'annonce. Le sentiment, si on s'abandonne à lui, écarte de la vraie route."

La première partie qui succède à ce prologue est intitulée *De l'Intelligible*, ou *De la* [465] *vérité*, ou *De l'être unique*. C'est une sorte de traité d'ontologie. Ici la déesse révèle "ce que la raison découvre dans ses recherches. La raison enseigne *que ce qui est, est*, que le néant ne peut être conçu. *La parole, la pensée, l'être, ont ainsi la réalité entière*. Les hommes aveuglés par les sens confondent tour à tour, et séparent l'être et le néant. Suis donc la route qui te montre *l'être* des choses. Plusieurs motifs prouvent que ce qui est n'a point commencé et ne peut cesser d'être. Il est tout, il est un; il est immuable, infini; car, dis-moi, d'où serait-il dérivé? à quelle source emprunterait-il pour s'accroître? du néant? c'est ce qu'on ne peut concevoir. Car, personne ne saurait concevoir, ou dire comment quelque chose n'est pas, et quelle puissance aurait pu lui prescrire de sortir de son néant, d'apparaître, précisément à cet instant, non plus tôt ou plus tard? Il faut donc qu'un être soit toujours, ou ne soit jamais; car cette maxime est éternellement vraie, *que quelque chose ne peut par soi-même naître de rien*. [466] Fondé en lui-même, l'être universel repose sur lui-même, il subsiste permanent; les chaînes puissantes de la nécessité l'enveloppent ... *La pensée et l'objet de la pensée ne sont qu'un;* car il ne peut y avoir de pensée sans une réalité qu'elle saisisse; au-delà de ce qui est, il n'y a rien. Ce sont donc des mots vides de sens que ceux qu'emploie le

---

[46] See *Histoire* (1822), I, 463-480. Cf. *Journals*, II, 343-344. For an elucidating discussion of "subject and object" or of "Nature and self"—a passage which Emerson indexed in his copy of the book, see Coleridge, *Biographia Literaria*, chap. XII.

préjugé humain, lorsqu'il parle de naissance et de fin, de changement de lieu, de transformation. La forme du tout est parfaite; elle ressemble à la sphère où le centre est également éloigné de tous les points de la surface. Il n'y a point de néant qui interrompe la continuité du réel; il n'y a donc point de vide; on ne peut enlever au tout aucune partie; car, il est partout semblable à lui-même, et toujours le tout." [47]

La première partie du poëme se termine par ce passage qui sert de transition à la seconde: "Je termine ici cet entretien qui renferme la doctrine de la vérité; maintenant, considère les illusions des opinions humaines; ce qui va maintenant s'offrir à [467] toi, n'est qu'une vaine apparence sensible."

La seconde partie du poëme est intitulée *l'Opinion;* c'est un tableau du monde sensible, de la nature matérielle, une suite d'hypothèses sur ses principes et ses lois. La déesse assigne deux principes opposés à l'univers; l'un des deux cependant mérite veritablement ce titre, c'est le feu éthéré, subtil et doux, semblable à lui-même, séparé de tout le reste; l'autre n'est que la nuit, vain fantôme, substance épaisse et dure." Cette dernière partie, dont il ne reste que des fragmens incomplets, se termine par ce passage remarquable: "L'entendement est à l'homme ce que le membre est à son corps; car ce qui pense en nous est un avec l'ensemble de nos organes; tout est rempli par la pensée."

[468] Ce double système qu'admet à la fois Parménide, l'accord qu'il cherche à établir entre deux ordres de considérations si incompatibles, explique la manière de voir que nous avons prêtée à Xénophane son prédécesseur, et semble confirmer notre hypothèse.

On voit que ces philosophes avaient confondu la notion abstraite de l'être avec sa réalité objective, et cru pouvoir conclure de l'une à l'autre. Nous nous sommes attachés à rapporter les propres expressions de Parménide, parce qu'elles nous offrent de la manière la plus sensible, et, si l'on peut dire ainsi, dans toute son ingénuité, cette grande méprise qui, bien que sous des formes plus subtiles, a égaré pendant le cours des siècles un grand nombre de métaphysiciens, à laquelle Descartes lui-même n'a pas échappé. . . .

[479] One voit que Xénophane, Parménide, Mélissus, Zénon, forment ensemble un groupe que l'histoire de la philosophie ne peut point diviser; ils s'éclairent, se complètent réciproquement. Ils s'accordaient tous à donner l'idée de la substance unique, absolue et réelle, pour base à la philosophie, à montrer que le principe, *rien ne se fait de rien,* ne pouvait être transporté dans le domaine de l'experience sans donner lieu à des contradictions manifestes. Xénophane identifiait la réalité, Dieu, l'univers, dans l'unité de l'être. Les attributs qu'il accordait à son tout universel et réel, étaient [480] preque entièrement négatifs, à l'exception de la toute-puissance et de l'intelligence. Parménide, en admettant cette idée, l'appliquait plus à l'univers qu'à la Divinité, à l'existence qu'à la cause; Mélissus et Zénon en conclurent que la simplicité de la substance unique ne se prête point à remplir l'espace; le premier aperçut cette conséquence, et le second la développa. Ainsi, à mesure que cette notion fondamentale fut mieux déterminée, à mesure qu'on en pressa les déductions avec plus de rigueur, elle se dépouilla graduellement de tout attribut, et, d'abstraction en abstraction, elle s'évanouit presque comme une conception vide de sens et sans valeur.

HERACLITUS[48]

The philosophy of Heraclitus is especially interesting as an introduction to the great schools of thought which followed him. He believed (1) that constant laws govern nature[49] and that although the several phenomena may seem to be discordant, changing, conflicting, there is harmony in the

---

[47] Cf. *Nature,* 56.7-14.
[48] See *Histoire* (1822), I, 482-489. Also *Journals,* II, 344-345.
[49] See *Nature,* 60.15-23.

whole. The continual flux[50] is the result of attraction and repulsion——
of polarity.[51] He was among the first to announce a "unity in diversity."[52]
(2) The force that maintains the perpetual movement is an ethereal fire
——a kind of soul——the later "Soul of the World." (3) There are two
orders of things or two worlds: one is invisible, intellectual and accessible
only to reason; the other, physical and accessible only to sense. (4) His
fundamental principle of human knowledge was that "the same can be
conceived or understood only by the same," or that "what we are, that
only can we see,"[53] a statement which Emerson considered to be a truth
of the first class. (5) Our sensations do not, therefore, adequately characterize objects or give us certain knowledge. The qualities we observe are
in ourselves and vary with individuals and with man's changing moods
or conditions.[54] The testimony of the senses should be rejected and Reason
embraced, though Reason sometimes may profitably make use of the
sensual channels. (6) The human soul insofar as it is endowed with Reason
is an emanation from the universal soul and not separated in any way
from it. But it is united to a flesh body, which it shares with the beasts
of the field. (7) Such a combination results in conflict, and virtue arises
as a result of governing the passions——in self-control. (8) Wisdom lies
in being faithful to the Reason or the True——both in thought, word and
deed. It consists in a discovery of the fundamental law which governs
things——in the destiny or necessity that may be called "regulative
Reason." (9) The judgments which men have in common——the "common sense" of the world—furnishes significant evidence of the diffusion
of the divine Reason. Wisdom, then, is accessible to all not only through
one's own experience, but through the accrued corporate experience of
the race, kept alive by memory. (10) Human laws receive their force or
prove their value from divine law. Heraclitus, therefore, urged conformity
to the laws of nature.

Aussi, c'est à l'investigation des lois de l'univers que paraissent se diriger essentiellement les recherches d'Héraclite. "Tout dans la nature est régi par des lois con-
stantes; les phénomènes eux-mêmes qui paraissent discordans, concourent à l'harmonie
du tout; c'est un accord qui resulte des dissonances." Belle et philosophique pensée, qui
[483] explique en effet tout l'univers, et qui semble avoir inspiré le génie de Platon.
"Ainsi les êtres divers, quelle que soit leur variété, sont unis, coordonnés, dans le même
plan, ne forment qu'un seul ensemble, tendent au même but." Héraclite avait donc évité
l'écueil contre lequel Xénophane avait été porté par ses déductions spéculatives; il
avait compris comment l'unité peut se concilier avec la diversité, il pénétrait le principe
qui renferme la solution du grand problème.

Le Destin, suivant Héraclite, n'est que cette grande harmonie, ou plutôt son principe;
c'est la loi générale imposée à l'univers, la puissance intelligente de laquelle émane cette
loi, l'expression de la raison qui est l'attribut de cette puissance. C'est ainsi qu'il rectifia
la notion du destin, admise dans la théologie vulgaire, lui enleva le caractère d'une
puissance aveugle, et ne fit dériver la nécessité que de la sagesse. Le destin, dans sa
pensée, était, si l'on peut dire aïnsi, la raison régulatrice.

---

[50] See *Nature*, 34.10ff.

[51] See index.

[52] See *Nature*, 29.14-17; 54.12-15.

[53] See *Nature*, 94.5; 68.5-7; 44.18. See also the interesting parallels listed under these
references in the editorial notes, *infra*.

[54] See *Nature*, 59.8 through 60.15.

"Cependant, tous les êtres sont sujets à des variations continuelles; chaque instant ne [484] les retouve plus tels qu'ils étaient à l'instant précédent; c'est un torrent qui roule incessamment ses flots." Comment, du milieu d'une telle mobilité, concevoir des lois générales et fixes? "Au milieu de ces révolutions, répond Héraclite, la nature suit une marche constante; les parcelles élémentaires et indivisibles ($\Psi\eta\gamma\mu\alpha\tau\alpha$) se combinent, se séparent; *l'attraction, la répulsion* opèrent ce double changement, une sorte de condensation et d'évaporation en résultent. Une activité aussi universelle que persévérante met en jeu ces deux grands ressorts. On ne peut donc dire proprement que les choses *sont*, mais seulement, qu'elles *passent*, qu'elles naissent et disparaissent;" quelle est enfin cette force immense, infatigable, qui entretient ce grand mouvement de toutes choses, cette vie, cette reproduction? "C'est le feu; le feu doué d'une énergie expansive, le feu qui pénètre de toutes parts, qui dissout, [485] qui volatilise, qui transforme; non précisément le feu extérieur tel qu'il s'offre à nos sens, mais un feu éthéré aérien, doué d'une mobilité prodigieuse, une exhalaison, une vapeur, une sorte de force ignée, lumineuse, immatérielle, intelligente, *une âme*," en un mot, ainsi que le dit expressément Aristote. "C'est l'âme du monde; cette exhalaison que tous les êtres respirent est la nourriture de tous les êtres; car le mouvement est la vie, et le repos est la mort. Ainsi, la pensée est l'attribut essentiel du principe universel."

Héraclite établit d'une manière plus expresse et plus explicite que les anciens Éléatiques la distinction de deux ordres de choses, de deux mondes: l'un invisible, intellectuel, accessible à la raison seule; l'autre physique, accessible aux sens. [486]

"L'âme humaine, en tant qu'elle est douée de raison, est une émanation de cette âme universelle; mais elle est unie à une autre substance animée, celle qui nous est commune avec les animaux, d'une nature différente, d'une origine matérielle. L'homme respire l'âme universelle; uni sans obstacle à cette intelligence suprême, il est dans l'état de veille; le sommeil est une suspension de cette communication immédiate.

Héraclite introduisit, sur le principe de la connaissance humaine, une maxime spécieuse, qui eut après lui un grand succès, et exerça sur la philosophie une grande influence. *Le même ne peut être conçu que par le même;* "la conception ne peut se fonder que sur la similitude entre l'objet et le sujet." Cette maxime appliquée aux idées qu'Héraclite s'était faites, et de l'univers, et de l'âme humaine, le conduisait naturellement à rejeter le témoignage des sens, à n'accorder d'autorité qu'à [487] la raison: cependant les sens étaient, suivant lui, comme autant de canaux ouverts, par lesquels, pour emprunter ses expressions, nous aspirons la raison divine.

"Nos sensations n'appartiennent point aux objets; elles ne résident qu'en nous-mêmes; car elles varient selon les individus; elles varient dans un même sujet suivant la disposition de ses organes." "Les sens ne peuvent donc nous donner aucune connaissance certaine des objets, puisque leurs instructions n'ont ni uniformité ni constance. L'entendement seul presente dans ses instructions ce caractère absolu; lui seul peut donc connaître la vérité." De son hypothèse qui faisait aspirer par l'âme humaine une exhalaison de la raison divine, Héraclite déduisit encore une seconde conséquence qu'on n'attendait guère d'un philosophe accoutumé à traiter avec beaucoup de dédain les opinions vulgaires, mais qui présente assez d'intérêt par sa nouveauté, par les applications qu'elle pouvait recevoir. Il [488] fonda sur cette hypothèse l'autorité de *sens commun.* "Les jugemens dans lesquels s'accordent tous les hommes sont un témoignage certain de la vérité; cette lumière commune, qui les éclaire tous à la fois, n'est autre chose que la raison divine répandue dans tous les êtres pensans, par une effusion immédiate." De là aussi les prérogatives singulières qu'il accorda à la mémoire. "L'entendement se représente la marche de l'univers telle qu'elle a été conservée par la mémoire; nous parvenons donc à la vérité, lorsque nous empruntons à la mémoire le tableau fidèle dont le dépot lui est confié." "La sagesse est donc accessible à tous les hommes." . . .

[489] Héraclite faisait consister la vertu dans l'empire que l'homme exerce sur lui-

même, en maîtrisant ses passions; comme il faisait consister la sagesse dans la fidélité à ce qui est vrai, dans ses recherches, ses paroles et ses actions. "La fin de l'homme, disait-il, est sa propre satisfaction;" mais la preuve qu'il ne faisait point consister cette satisfaction dans la volupté sensuelle, se montre assez dans le mépris qu'il recommande pour tout ce qui appartient au corps, "dont on ne doit, disait-il, user que comme d'un instrument." Sa morale était encore un corollaire de sa théorie principale, et il en tirait cette belle maxime: "Que les lois humaines reçoivent leur force de cette loi divine qui règle tout à son gré, qui triomphe de toutes choses." C'est pourquoi il recommandait d'agir conformément à la nature, maxime que lui ont empruntée les Stoiciens.

Gérando's *Histoire* (1822) served Emerson well in his attempt to discover the "First Philosophy." Its rich table of contents introduced him immediately to Socrates, Plato, the Gnostics and the Neo-Platonists[55]——to name only a few——and helped him in his book on nature to clarify his thoughts on man:[56]

L'homme étant l'objet le plus immédiat de sa propre étude, l'homme étant l'intermédiaire entre Dieu et la nature, le point de convergence de tous les phénomènes de l'univers, il devint aussi le type sur lequel se réglèrent toutes les conceptions relatives au système des êtres; on généralisa, on reproduisit sous diverses formes [280] l'idée qu'il avait conçue de lui-même, pour en faire le principe d'une solution commune; mais comme les études de la réflexion étaient très-imparfaites, à peine ébauchées, l'emploi de cette donnée fut lui-même très-défectueux, en considérant dans l'homme ce phénomène complexe qui résulte de l'union de l'esprit et de la matière, on conçut le monde extérieur comme un corps organisé; en considérant la prééminence de l'intelligence et l'action de la volonté, on expliqua la nature par les doctrines mystiques.

---

[55] Among the more interesting subjects in the *Histoire* (1822) are: "The Development of Language," I, 230ff.; 284-293. "Ideas of Unity and Emanation in Early Idealism," I, 249-258. "Symbolism and Mythology," I, 303-307. "The Sophists," II, 42-120. "Socrates," II, 121-169. "Plato," II, 206-279. "Oriental and Greek Influences on Idealism," III, 286-331. "Neo-Platonism," III, 332-480.

[56] *Histoire* (1822), I, 279-280.

PLATO AND PLATONISM

Emerson apparently began his study of Plato as an undergraduate in Harvard College,[1] using for the most part the summaries found in the philosophical handbooks current in his day.[2] We lack a record of his library borrowings from the summer of 1818 until 1823,[3] but can chart rather well, with the aid of collateral records,[4] the progress of his early reading in metaphysical works. Translations of Plato were scarce,[5] and since as late as March 17, 1828, Emerson admitted that he was "profoundly ignorant of the original" Greek version,[6] he could have had, during his undergraduate period, only a few volumes in English at his disposal.[7] For his Bowdoin prize essay on "The Character of Socrates," compiled toward the end of his Junior year (1820),[8] Emerson consulted the writings of both Plato[9] and Xenophon,[10] especially *The Works of Plato Abridg'd*,[11] a copy of which, in two volumes, he borrowed from the Boston Library Society[12] and used with profit. In the dissertation on "The Present State of Ethical Philosophy," submitted to the committee on the Bowdoin Prize in July, 1821, he referred briefly to Socrates and his principal biographer as "alone among the sons of Adam, qualified to institute and methodize the science of morality."[13] On June 10, 1822, in discussing the reformation of the legitimate stage, he praised the Platonist's belief in

---

[1] We lack definite information about Emerson's courses, though the outline of the curriculum in 1820 is helpful. See the chapter on his Harvard College days. See also Edgeley W. Todd, "Philosophical Ideas at Harvard College, 1817-1837," *N E Q*, XVI (1943), 63-90.

[2] See a forthcoming article on "Emerson's Handbooks."

[3] See *Emerson's Reading*, 13 and 44.

[4] See *Letters*, I, xxxi-xxxii, liv-lvi, *et passim*.

[5] See Bronson Alcott's lament about the deficiency of New England libraries in philosophical books as late as September 25, 1835: *The Journals of Bronson Alcott*, ed. Odell Shepard, Boston, 1938, pp. 65-66.

[6] See *Letters*, I, 228.

[7] See *A Catalogue of the Library of Harvard University*, (3 vols.) Cambridge, 1830-1831, vol. II, *s.v.* These books will be mentioned below.

[8] The MS., dated at "Cambridge, July 21st 1820," is in the Harvard College library. It was first edited by Edward Everett Hale in *Two Unpublished Essays*, Boston, 1896, pp. 3-39, and reprinted in Hale's *Ralph Waldo Emerson . . . together with two early essays*, Boston, 1899. Anr. edition: Boston, 1904. See the present writer's forthcoming edition of both these essays with other early prose pieces.

[9] *Journals*, I, 84. At Harvard he probably consulted *Socrates his Apology, and Phedo* (1673); *The Republic*, tr. H. Spens, Glasgow, 1763. Thomas Taylor's translation probably reached the library too late for his use in the essay. See *infra*.

[10] Although Harvard College Library did not possess a copy, he indicates in his essay that he used *Xenophon's Memoirs of Socrates*. It was probably the frequently reprinted translation made by Sarah Fielding and included the "Defense of Socrates before his Judges." He certainly withdrew her volume (3rd ed., London, 1788) from the Boston Library Society, keeping it from April 16 through May 21, 1829.

[11] *The Works of Plato Abridg'd, with an account of his life, philosophy, morals, and politicks, together with a translation of his choicest dialogues . . . illustrated with notes* by M. [André] Dacier, (2 vols.) London, 1772. This work passed through many editions: (2 vols.) London, 1701, 1719, 1739, 1749, 1761, 1772, 1839; New York, 1833.

[12] Vols. 1 and 2 were withdrawn Dec. 30, 1819, and returned on Jan. 20, 1820. Vol. 1 was again in his hands between Apr. 15 and May 13, 1820; also between May 27 and June 15. For his later use of this work, see the list of library borrowings in Vol. II of *E T E*.

[13] See *Two Unpublished Essays*, ed. cit., p. 50. See also p. 59. (The entire essay covers pp. 43-81. The MS. at Harvard is dated "July 1821.")

"two warring principles" as a realistic interpretation of human life,[14] and, on July 13, spoke of the moral law as sometimes seeming to sanction "that Platonic dream"——the doctrine of the transmigration of souls.[15] In October of this year he added to his library a sixteenth-century edition of the *Opera*[16] and, in November, exchanged some philosophic opinions with William Withington,[17] but during the next two years Plato remained for the most part unexplored. Emerson, nonetheless, praised him for helping to popularize in all subsequent literature the doctrine of the immortality of the soul,[18] and frequently mentioned his name in letters to Aunt Mary. The long epistle to that "venerable Shade," written in the *Journals* of 1824,[19] is a tribute to the thought of ancient Athens as well as a condemnation of the cacaphony of more recent times. Aunt Mary's imaginary letter *from* Plato, prepared as a rejoinder, might be considered as a challenge to her nephew for his greater exploration of the classics.[20] Certainly, at the end of Emerson's journal for 1825, the *Dialogues* were listed together with Montaigne's *Essays* among the "Books to Read,"[21] and during the following year he seems to have begun the systematic study which he continued throughout his life.[22]

Although the Harvard College Library acquired its set of the Sydenham-Taylor translation of Plato's *Works*[23] by bequest from Thomas Palmer in 1820, Emerson does not seem to have examined it much before November

---

[14] *Journals*, I, 148.

[15] *Ibid.*, I, 164.

[16] *Platonis Atheniensis Philosophi Summi ac Penitus Divini Opera*, Basileæ (Froben), 1561. The volume is autographed and dated. Emerson's books are now preserved in the building of the Concord Antiquarian Society and in his Concord home.

[17] From a photostat of Emerson's letter to William Withington, dated November 21, 1822, I transcribe the following: "My first question regards Plato; For the love of Athens, I pray you tell me, what golden thoughts you have culled from the oracle of so many centuries? Have you found the source of heresies, and the models of all bad creeds? and chiefly, have you found that 'etherial imagination,' which all books ascribe to Plato, and which, of all his excellencies, I am the least willing to take upon trust. I confide in your scholarly character, that you spurn translations, and read the Greek. From my very limited knowledge of the philosopher, I should judge, that of all the ancients, he is most a citizen of the world; that is, soared above his time, and judged of men and things then, as a speculative man does today. One difficulty always meets me there, to wit, how to distinguish Socrates from his disciple. When a man writes a biography of Socrates, he ransacks Plato as if he were another Boswell. But when Plato is the hero of the tale, poor Socrates becomes a theoretic personage, yea, the mere mouth of his disciple. Now these contradictions it is incumbent upon your learning to reconcile, and I shall expect your solutions with impatience. If Plato be the thing I have imagined him to be, namely—A philosophy not too profound for easy comprehension, mixed and softened with a proportion of imagination and poetry—enough to adapt it to an idle eye and a vacant hour,—why, in that case, nothing but his Greek should appal me."

[18] See *Letters*, I, 128 (Jan. 3, 1823). Emerson probably was referring to the *Phaedo*, though he might have meant the *Republic* or the *Phaedrus*.

[19] See *Journals*, I, 380-388.

[20] See *Journals*, I, 331 (1823); 359 (Mar. 21, 1824); *Letters*, I, 160, 169.

[21] *Journals*, II, 68. See also footnote 12 *supra*.

[22] See the references to Alcibiades in March and September, and one to the *Phaedo*, in October: *Journals*, II, 89, 122, 128.

[23] *The Works of Plato: viz, his fifty-five dialogues and twelve epistles*, tr. from the Greek; (nine dialogues by Floyer Sydenham and the others by Thomas Taylor, with commentaries), (5 vols.) London, 1804. The contents are as follows:

2, 1826,[24] when he withdrew volume four——the tome containing the *Apology of Socrates* and the *Phaedo*. (He twice withdrew the same quarto from Harvard during the next three years.) There is evidence, of course, that Taylor's Plato lacked Emerson's complete approval, for on March 17, 1828, in admitting that it was the standard translation, he declared it "faulty" because of its difficult and "very Greek" style.[25]

When Emerson came into possession of Taylor's *The Cratylus, Phaedo, Parmenides and Timaeus of Plato*[26] is not yet established, but there is evidence that he kept borrowing volumes of the *Works* until 1845,[27] the year during which he quite possibly purchased the Charles Lane copy of the Taylor translation, now in Concord.[28] His interest in Plato was especially keen between 1830 and 1836, while he was struggling to work out his basic philosophy. In those six years he began to see "forms or ideas" in whatever he studied,[29] and to consider Plato as the father of the art of exposition as well as the progenitor of all scientists and philosophers who seek a principle of classification for the particulars of life.[30] On December 8, 1834, he expressed the belief that lovers of the "primal philosophy" would welcome a course of lectures on Plato alone or on Plato and Aristotle, with Bacon and Coleridge included.[31] He asserted, moreover, that Plato's "purple light" was the test of all great intellects[32] and that Plato's use of fables must necessarily be adopted by the great thinkers of the world, since fables are admirable conveyors of truth and can be approached

VOLUME I	The Sophista	VOLUME V
General Introduction	The Phaedrus	The Euthyphro
Explanation of Platonic Terms	The Greater Hippias	The Meno
Life of Plato by Olympiodorus	The Banquet (Symposium)	The Theages
The First Alcibiades	Proclus on the Parmenides	The Laches
The Republic	Damascius on the Parmenides	The Lysis
Proclus on the First Alcibiades	Proclus on the Phaedrus	The Charmides
More Notes on the Republic		The Lesser Hippias
	VOLUME IV	The Euthydemus
VOLUME II	The Theaetetus	The Hipparchus
The Laws	The Politicus	The Rivals
The Epinomis, or the Philosopher	The Minos	The Menexenus.
The Timaeus	The Apology of Socrates	The Clitopho
The Critias, or Atlanticus	The Crito	The Io
Proclus on the Timaeus	The Phaedo	The Cratylus
	The Gorgias	The Twelve Epistles
VOLUME III	The Philebus	Proclus on the Cratylus
The Parmenides	The Second Alcibiades	

[24] See *Emerson's Reading*, 46 and 97.

[25] See *Letters*, I, 228. *The Works of Plato Abridg'd* he considered "very much more intelligible than this Taylor," and borrowed vol. 1 from the Boston Library Society Feb. 18 through Mar. 2, 1830, and again on March 15, 1831. Vol. 2 was in his hands between Mar. 15 and Mar. 31, 1831.

[26] Published in London in 1793. It is now in his library at Concord. For an excellent bibliography of the original works and translations of Thomas Taylor, and for a bibliography of works about him, see *Thomas Taylor the Platonist (1758-1835), List of Original Works and Translations*, compiled by Ruth Balch, Chicago (Newberry Library), 1917.

[27] See *Emerson's Reading*, 97.

[28] See *Letters*, I, 228 footnote, and III, 257.

[29] See *Journals*, II, 274 (April 17, 1832).

[30] See *Journals*, III, 284 (April 27, 1834); 294 (May 3, 1834); 468 (April 16, 1835); 529 (Aug. 3, 1835). Cf. *Nature*, 83.9-14.

[31] See *Journals*, III, 386. He also would treat Heraclitus, Hermes Trismegistus, Giordano Bruno, Vyasa, Plotinus and Swedenborg. See also *Journals*, III, 485.

[32] See *Journals*, III, 419 (Dec. 28, 1834) and 529 (Aug. 3, 1835).

from either side of the eternal conflict between the Reason and the Understanding.[33] Yet when his first book was taking form in the spring of 1836, Emerson dared to write that his indebtedness to Plato did not extend beyond "a certain number of sentences."[34] That this assertion is sheer understatement and that the *Dialogues*, taken together, had a profound, even if indirect, influence upon him will appear in what follows. It remains to be determined how many of his "sentences" are like the two which he puts into the mouth of Plato in *Nature:*

> 68.19   "The problem of philosophy," according to Plato, "is, for all that exists conditionally, to find a ground unconditioned and absolute."

> 86.14   . . . we accept the sentence of Plato, that, "poetry comes nearer to vital truth than history."

The first example Emerson copied from *The Friend* (Section II, essay 5)[35] of Coleridge, who had taken it not from Plato at all, but from Kant's *Critique of Pure Reason.*[36] The second may represent a free paraphrase of the line: "Action comes less near to vital truth than description," which Emerson claimed in his journal came from *The Republic* (Book V),[37] meaning, perhaps, Aristotle's *De Poetica* (Section 9), for the passages somewhat correspond.[38]

A brief analysis of Plato's philosophy at this point will help bring out contrasts with Neo-Platonism, which will be considered later. References to *Nature* in footnotes will provide a rough resumé of some of the more striking parallels and give hints of Emerson's indebtedness to the Athenian before the fall of 1836.[39]

---

[33] *Ibid.*, III, 467-468 (Apr. 14, 1835). Cf. *Nature*, 92.21.

[34] See *Journals*, IV, 23 (Mar. 14, 1836).

[35] See this passage in chapter VI below, Coleridge ¶ 131.

[36] See René Wellek, "Emerson and German Philosophy," *N E Q*, XVI (1943), 42.

[37] See *Journals*, II, 439 (Dec. 20, 1831). Emerson quoted the line with a slight variation to Benjamin Peter Hunt in a letter written on Jan. 23, 1835. See *Letters*, I, 431. See also Plato, *Works* (Taylor), I, 312, for a possible original. Cf. also *Journals*, III, 352.

[38] See the translation of Ingram Bywater in *The Basic Works of Aristotle*, ed. Richard McKeon, N.Y., [1941], pp. 1463-1464: "From what we have said it will be seen that the poet's function is to describe, not the thing that has happened, but a kind of thing that might happen, i.e. what is possible as being probable or necessary. The distinction between historian and poet is not in the one writing prose and the other verse—you might put the work of Herodotus into verse, and it would still be a species of history; it consists really in this, that the one describes the thing that has been, and the other a kind of thing that might be. Hence poetry is something more philosophic and of graver import than history, since its statements are of the nature rather of universals, whereas those of history are singulars." Emerson copied the significant line from this into *Journals*, II, 440.

[39] This analysis will serve its intended purpose if it indicates the major distinctions existing between Platonism and Neo-Platonism. It is based chiefly on the excellent study by Raphael Demos, *The Philosophy of Plato*, N.Y. etc. (Charles Scribner's Sons), [1939], and compiled by permission. Like all attempts to systematize Plato's thought, the present outline is admittedly defective. The reader is referred to Demos for a comprehensive presentation, and also to A. E. Taylor, *Plato: The Man and His Work*, N.Y., 1936. See also the *Encyclopædia of Religion and Ethics*, (ed. princ.), X, 54-61.

BASIC CONSIDERATIONS

(A) The Unchanging and Timeless Creative Factors. (The order in which they appear is unimportant.)

(1) GOD——The Best of Causes——The Maker and Father[40]——The Energy of Creation——The Psyche[41]——The Principle of Inherent Sponteneity.

(2) THE PATTERN——The Limit or Limiting Factor——The Principle of Order, System, Harmony——The Factor in Actualizing Ideas——The Sublime Model ——The Forms——God's Ideas.

(3) THE RECEPTACLE——The Locus of Creation——The Unlimited——Pure Potentiality of all Shapes——Not Stuff or Matter——Fusion of all Forms—— Space or Space-Time——Factor of Concreteness and Indefiniteness——Chaos and Disorder——The Matrix of Creation——The Boundless——The Negation of God's Being——"Other" than God and yet not antithetical to him——The Factor of Perishing——The Principle of Birth and Novelty——The Factor of Movement and Change——Its nature is both receptive and resistant.

(4) THE GOOD——The Cause or Source of all Being——It transcends Being——It is beyond Knowledge——The Fit, the Timely, the Just——The Principle of Perfection——God's "Purpose"——The "Why" of the Universe——The Principle of the Best——The Motive for Creation——The Valuational Note in the Universe ——It has no reference to anything beyond itself——Its grounds are (a) Desirableness, (b) Self-sufficiency, (c) Plenitude of Being, and (d) Measure—— The Good is a Cause without being itself caused——It is a universal and fixed norm.

(B) Intermediary Factor:

(5) EROS——Intermediary between the Creator and the Creature——Between the Infinite and the Finite——The Principle of Betweenness——It functions in two directions: (a) The love of God for the world; (b) the aspiration of the mortal for the immortal——The Life Force. (See also under "Soul").

(C) The Derivative, Relative, Imitative Factor:

(6) THE VISIBLE WORLD——The Creature[42]——The Mixture——The result of the union between the Pattern (*i.e.*, the Forms) and the Receptacle——A "becoming" rather than a "state of being"——The Prey of Dissolution.

THE SOUL

(1) IT IS MOTION, ACTIVITY, BECOMING——It is any self-motion or self-activity, vital or rational——It is in all organic things (plants and animals)——The Principle of Life——Inherent Spontaneity that perpetually renews itself from within——Principle of Transition——Coeval with Time——Its Essence is in *doing*, not *cognizing*[43]——If the Soul thinks, it is because to think is to act.

(2) IT IS EROS——Patterned Activity——Principle of Betweenness——A process of realizing the Good——The Drive of Life itself——Pursuit of Perfection and the Preservation of Values——Leads to Creation[44]——Act of Duration——Factor in the Intensification of Life. (See "Eros" above).

(3) IT IS A MIXTURE OF THE INDIVISIBLE AND THE DIVISIBLE——A Complex——More integrated a mixture than the body——Soul is concrescence of all the elements in the Universe——A Microcosm——Togetherness of all Things ——Not a body, though it has a bodily part——The Link between the realm of Forms and the realm of Particulars, yet not of either——Channel God uses to transmit his activity into the Receptacle.

---

[40] *Nature*, 35.4.
[41] *Nature*, 35.1; 77.3.
[42] *Nature*, 80.16ff.
[43] Cf. *Nature*, 75.13.
[44] *Nature*, 43.22.

(4) IT MAY BE CLASSIFIED (as to levels of activity) under (a) star souls, (b) souls of the winged kind, dwelling in the air, (c) water souls, and (d) land souls. As regards function, the Soul may be (a) reason, (b) spirit, (c) desire, (d) mere vital activity.

GOD

GOD is one of the creative factors along with the GOOD and the RECEPTACLE ——The Artificer and Demiurge——The Shepherd and Father——Creative Intelligence ——Purposive Cause——Timeless and Ungenerated——He creates because of his abundance, and not out of need——God transforms the timeless Receptacle by winning it over; thus he brings order out of chaos——God governs by moral appeal and by reason[45]——His government is free——God has a moral nature and intelligence—— Both are self-communicative——God doesn't absorb the world——He is distinct from it ——Communion between them is, therefore, possible——God is both transcendent and immanent——God is to be distinguished from the "created gods," who are merely natural forces——God is above the latter——He is timeless; they are temporal and impure mixtures——Plato rationalizes polytheism into the principle of the "one and the many." [46]

THE FORMS OR IDEAS

Distinction between *appearance* and *reality* is basic in Plato.[47] His doctrine of ideas[48] is postulated to explain the facts of our daily experience, which facts fall into three groupings:

(1) Facts concerning the making of things: Artists and craftsmen create according to patterns or ideas. They draw upon standards within themselves.

(2) Facts concerning human knowledge: The existence of exact, certain, and universal knowledge in this world implies the existence of a world above experience. The qualities of the phenomenal world lack purity. There must be a *real* world which consists of the "Forms"—each of which is pure, definite and precisely what it is.[49]

(3) Facts concerning nature: There is order in nature, yet the order does not seem to come from nature itself. A supernatural realm must have imposed its character upon the realm of the natural.[50]

Forms may be considered either (a) as *essences* of things or (b) as *archetypes*.[51] To seek the forms, it is not necessary to abandon things, but rather to penetrate into their true nature. When we discover the forms in things, we grasp what the things *really are*.[52] Every concrete thing has an *appearance* (i.e., a sensible aspect) and *reality* (its essential nature). The actual world is not a state of being, but a "becoming."[53] It is constantly moving from a state of incompleteness toward completeness. The forms, however, are *never* completely realized.

ART AND BEAUTY

In Plato's thought, art does not have a distinct function.[54] It is tested by "moral purpose." [55] It must not be separated from the ordinary pursuits of daily life and work.[56] There are various degrees of the observation of beauty, beginning with sensuous perception and ending with the apprehension of abstract beauty.[57] The vision of the latter is dormant in man and must, like innate knowledge, be aroused. The awakening process involves various stages: (a) beauty through art, (b) beauty in nature, (c) beauty in bodies, (d) beauty in souls, (e) beauty in institutions, (f) beauty in sciences and philosophy, and (7) ideal beauty. Man begins his education with the beauty of the concrete and rises to the abstract. When he begins to see the "vision" in the thing, his creative impulse is released, to issue forth in the actual creation of new beauty.[58] All

---

[45] *Nature*, 51.12.
[46] *Nature*, 29.16; 54.13ff.
[47] *Nature*, 79.4; 59.11.
[48] *Nature*, 70.10.
[49] *Nature*, 92.21; 74.6ff.
[50] *Nature*, 69.1; 77.23ff.; 84.2.
[51] *Nature*, 84.12.

[52] *Nature*, 92.21ff.
[53] *Nature*, 93.20.
[54] *Nature*, 53.4ff.; 24.3.
[55] *Nature*, 25.3.
[56] *Nature*, 24.13ff.
[57] *Nature*, 20.19ff.
[58] *Nature*, 29.1ff.

nature is an exhibition of the beautiful.[59]

MAN

Man is both earthly and divine.[60] He has a mortal and an immortal part. This duality in his nature makes any discussion of his soul a difficult matter. Tension exists within man.[61] It results from the conflict between his reason (which strives after the Best) and the irrational animal nature, or "pleasure principle." Men are good by constitution; evil-doing is the result of missing the good.[62] When the soul is born into a body, it enters a state of flux, forgetting its real essence——its affection for and knowledge of the Good. Incarnation is definitely a fall,[63] but there are other falls.[64] A soul might descend to a mere animal or bestial level. Why, then, does the soul come into the flesh in the first place? It must be because it possesses a "disease" or a "downward tendency" or an "unruly element." Evil, forgetfulness, ignorance——seem to have their roots in the soul before it enters the body. How does the soul undo the evils of incarnation? It is by the process of "Recollection."[65] The mind, which was put to sleep at birth, must be awakened.[66] *Latent* knowledge must be made *conscious*.[67] The agent or helper in this task is the wise man:[68] He draws one's true nature forth. Society and the individual are reflections of each other. Society is merely a large individual; a man is a miniature society.[69]

MISCELLANEOUS OBSERVATIONS

(1) We see, then, that Plato's system is complex. The universe is reducible to no one factor. Plato was not a mystic in the sense that he saw the universe converging in a simple unity. Ultimate reality, to him, was a society of contrasted beings.

(2) Though absolute knowledge be impossible in this life, Plato advised a continuance of the search for truth, the exercise of the reasoning faculty, and a holding on to "the second best." When the spoken word cannot be enjoyed, he recommended books. When the Reason does not function, one may obey the written laws. Through all doubts, one must have faith in the soundness of the Reason. Books are of value chiefly for those who are old and forgetful. They have no primary value.[70]

(3) We all have an idea of a god or perfect being, and we go about seeking a person who will image it for us. We love others because they are symbols of our god. In loving a person, we teach him to be a better image. Teaching, then, becomes a function of friendship. Love awakens the lover and the beloved, and assists in the process of "recollecting" our ideal.[71]

(4) The life of appetite is one of flux. Appetites manifest nothing of measure or restraint, but are insatiable. The natural man is one whose appetites war against each other. A group of such men cannot form a society, for appetites are selfish and independent. The life of Reason is all-embracing. One who is governed by the appetites separates himself from others. Where ends are private and self-centered, a state of war exists.[72]

(5) Justice, to Plato, is the rule of limitation. In the state, justice requires that everyone perform a special task and ignore others. We might call this specialization by its modern term, "division of labor." Character is strong in proportion as one *selects* from the "number of things" that make up life and excludes the irrelevant. Even the gods had their peculiar functions.[73]

(6) "For all things in nature being linked together in relationship, and the soul having heretofore known all things, nothing hinders but that any man, who has recalled to mind, or, according to the common phrase, who has learnt, one thing only, should of himself recover all his ancient knowledge, and find out again all the rest of

---

[59] *Nature*, 29.22; 30.22ff.; 19.5.
[60] *Nature*, 7.8ff.
[61] *Nature*, 61.22; 89.14; 48.10ff.
[62] *Nature*, 92.6.
[63] *Nature*, 88.1.
[64] *Nature*, 89.17.
[70] See Plato's *Phædrus*, 276d. Cf. *The American Scholar*: "Books are for the scholar's idle times." (*Works*, I, 91).
[71] *Nature*, 58.4ff.

[65] *Nature*, 91.5.
[66] *Nature*, 73.18; 6.11; 40.11; 93.13ff.; 91.5ff.; 45.8.
[67] *Nature*, 88.14.
[68] *Nature*, 89.12ff.
[69] *Nature*, 87.13; 35.10ff.; 84.16ff.
[72] *Nature*, 89.18.
[73] *Nature*, 92.1ff.

things. . . . For inquiry and learning is reminiscence all."[74]

(7) Plato uses the word *idol* for an exact or inexact reflection of a form or idea. Creation is a process of producing idols or appearances. "The divine act of creation is one of self-representation; the creature is an imitation of the creator. The process is self-continuing; the image mirrors itself in another image, and so on. God created the cosmos in his image; the world-soul in its turn created the particular souls and physical objects in its own image; for, as the cosmos is a whole and a plenitude, so are its creatures wholes and plenitudes, though in a lesser degree. The principle of creation as self-reflection determines a descending hierarchy of creatures and images."[75]

(8) "But the concrete world is not wholly unreal;[76] it lies between complete being and complete not-being, partaking of each.[77] It would seem that there is an objective contradiction in nature; the concrete world both is and is not."[78] "Plato's ambivalence with respect to the world of opinion is an ambivalence about the image. At times, perhaps for the most part, Plato is an iconoclast; the creation of images is a fall, and art is doubly a fall. Man is urged to rise to realities, ignoring images. And at other times, Plato seems to regard imitation as the natural overflow of the really real, and the created world as the expression of God to himself."[79]

(9) A man's life has value only if he can perform his proper work.[80] If his health becomes impaired so that he cannot lead a normal life or further the welfare of the State, it is best that he die without benefit of physic.

Emerson seems to have drawn much inspiration from Plato's dialogues during the period preceding the publication of *Nature* in 1836. There is evidence that he liked especially the *Phædo*, the *Protagoras*, the *Phædrus*, the *Timæus*, the *Republic* and the *Apology of Socrates*.[81] The *Parmenides*, moreover, supplied him with a discussion of the "ideas" or "forms."[82] But Thomas Taylor's five volumes, which Emerson began to read regularly after 1826, led him beyond Plato into the spirit of the Neo-Platonic School——largely through the "General Introduction," the remarks prefacing each dialogue, the elaborate appendices and the exhaustive footnotes. One can see in the following excerpt from Taylor's introductory essay all that one associates with the religious philosophy of the later school of Plotinus, and one must look forward to its stronger influence if one is to understand what, to Emerson, during the formative years of his philosophy, proved more attractive than the bare text of Plato's dialogues. In a sense, Plotinus, Proclus, Iamblichus and the other Neo-Platonists served as the basis for all Emerson's study of the Orient.[83]

---

[74] See Plato's *Meno*, 81d, in *Five Dialogues* (Everyman ed.), p. 91. Cf. *Nature*, 56.22; 56.7ff. See under "Man" *supra*.

[75] See Demos, *op. cit.*, p. 198. Cf. *Nature*, 79.14ff.

[76] *Nature*, 61.9.

[77] *Nature*, 79.14; 69.12.

[78] From Demos, *op. cit.*, p. 180. Cf. *Nature*, 78.11ff.

[79] From Demos, *op. cit.*, p. 215. Cf. *Nature*, 78.9ff.

[80] Cf. *Nature*, 18.8; 24.20; 92.1ff.

[81] See "Books" in Emerson's *Works*, VII, 199.

[82] See Plato's *Works* (Taylor), III, 3-200; 533-600.

[83] From Taylor's general summary of what he calls "Platonism" in Plato's *Works* (Taylor), I, lvi-lvii.

And now having with venturous, yet unpresuming wing, ascended to the ineffable principle of things, and standing with every eye closed in the vestibules of the adytum, found that we could announce nothing concerning him [God, or the One], but only indicate our doubts and disappointment, and having thence descended to his occult and most venerable progeny, and passing through the luminous world of ideas, holding fast by the golden chain of deity, terminated our downward flight in the material universe, and its undecaying wholes, let us stop awhile and contemplate the sublimity and magnificence of the scene which this journey presents to our view. Here then we see the vast empire of deity, an empire terminated upwards by a principle so ineffable that all language is subverted about it, and downwards by the vast body of the world. Immediately subsisting after this immense unknown we in the next place behold a mighty all-comprehending one, which, as being next to that which is in every respect incomprehensible, possesses much of the ineffable and unknown. From this principle of principles, in which all things causally subsist absorbed in superessential light and involved in unfathomable depths, we view a beauteous progeny of principles, all largely partaking of the ineffable, all stamped with the occult characters of deity, all possessing an over-flowing fulness of good. From these dazzling summits, these ineffable blossoms, these divine propagations, we next see being, life, intellect, soul, nature and body depending; *monads* suspended from *unities*, deified natures proceeding from deities. Each of these monads too, is the leader of a series which extends from itself to the last of things, and which while it proceeds from, at the same time abides in, and returns to its leader. And all these principles and all their progeny are finally centered and rooted by their summits in the first great all-comprehending one. Thus all beings proceed from, and are comprehended in the first being; all intellects emanate from one first intellect; all souls from one first soul; all natures blossom from one first nature; and all bodies proceed from the vital and luminous body of the world. And lastly, all these great monads are comprehended in the first one, from which both they and all their depending series are unfolded into light. Hence this first one is truly the unity of unities, the monad of monads, the principle of principles, the God of gods, one and all things, and yet one prior to all.

THE OLD MANSE — Parsonage of Rev. William Emerson, it was the first home of Nathaniel Hawthorne and his bride Sophia Peabody. "Mosses from an Old Manse" describes their life here

NEO-PLATONISM———THE SCHOOL OF PLOTINUS

Later, perhaps, a now unknown reading record, personal letter or journal may offer evidence for the specific date on which Emerson acquired his copy of the *Select Works of Plotinus*,[1] the octavo volume which for many years he kept within easy reach of his writing table and which he marked and indexed as a favorite possession. I have found no proof of his acquaintance with it, either in his own or in other libraries,[2] before the publication of *Nature,* and must conclude, therefore, that his chief sources for Neo-Platonic thought before September, 1836, (apart from the elaborate footnotes and appendices of *The Works of Plato,* edited by Thomas Taylor) were Gérando's *Histoire Comparée,*[3] Cudworth's *True Intellectual System,*[4] and a number of philosophical handbooks[5]—all together a convenient and rather respectable collection of ancient lore. The references to Plotinus both in the *Journals*[6] and in the text of *Nature* as well[7] point to no primary sources, but the fact remains, as this and later chapters will make clear, that through one channel or another Emerson absorbed the wisdom of the "New Platonists" before owning or reading Thomas Taylor's translations of them.[8] It becomes necessary, therefore, to give at this point a general outline of the system of Plotinus and his fellows[9] in the hope that its relevance to what precedes and follows may later become apparent.

---

[1] *Select Works of Plotinus . . . and extracts from the Treatise of Synesius on Providence,* tr. (with the substance of Porphyry's life of Plotinus) by Thomas Taylor, London, 1817.

[2] The Boston Library Society owned none of the works of Plotinus as late as 1835. The Boston Athenæum had none until very late and still lacked the *Select Works* in 1857. Harvard College had acquired nothing in English through 1834.

[3] Gérando, *Histoire* (1822), III, 332-480.

[4] See the next chapter for a full discussion of this work.

[5] See a forthcoming article for an account of these. To the list may be added the rich prose works of Coleridge, which quoted from the Neo-Platonists (*e.g., Biographia Literaria,* chap. XII), and the poems of Wordsworth.

[6] See *Journals,* II, 323, 357-385, 364, 377; III, 402, 439. Cf. *Works,* III, 55. The first Journal entry is apparently Emerson's rewriting of two passages in Coleridge's *Works* (Shedd), II, 384, and III, 231: "As, according to the eldest philosophy, life being in its own nature aeriform, is under the necessity of renewing itself by inhaling the connatural, and therefore assimilable, air, so is it with the intelligential soul with respect to truth; for it is itself of the nature of truth." (Plotinus, *Ennead* III.1.8 slightly altered, in "The Friend").

"[I]t is profanation to speak of these mysteries . . . 'to those to whose imagination it has never been presented, how beautiful is the countenance of justice and wisdom; and that neither the morning nor the evening star are so fair. For in order to direct the view aright, it behooves that the beholder should have made himself congenerous and similar to the object beheld. Never could the eye have beheld the sun, had not its own essence been soliform,' (*i.e. pre-configured to light by a similarity of essence with that of light*) 'neither can a soul not beautiful attain to an intuition of beauty.'" (Plotinus, *Ennead* I.6. ss. 4 and 9, in "Biographia Literaria").

[7] See the quotation on the title page, which Emerson took from Cudworth; and *Nature,* 72.20 and 72.23.

[8] See the excellent bibliography: *Thomas Taylor the Platonist (1758-1835), List of original works and translations,* compiled by Ruth Balch, Chicago (Newberry Library), 1917.

[9] The following list of Neo-Platonic writers is taken with slight modification from the end papers of Kenneth Sylvan Guthrie, *The Philosophy of Plotinos,* Phila., [1896]:

THE DIVINITY[10]

The Neo-Platonic system is one of necessary Emanation, Procession, Aspiration and Reversion to source.[11] All existence flows from the Divinity and strives to return to its origin and there remain. This Divinity is a graded Triad——*not* a Trinity. Its three *personæ* or hypostases are: (1) The ONE or First Existent, (2) the DIVINE MIND[12] or the First Thinker, and (3) the ALL-SOUL or Over Soul, which is the First Principle of Life. These three stages are often spoken of collectively as One Transcendent Being——One Divine Realm——The Godhead——The Triad——The Eternal.[13] The Divinity is communicated and approached by any one of the three hypostases. Each overflows, producing the stage beneath, without itself lapsing in any particular. The Divine Mind contemplates its source——the One; the All-Soul contemplates the Divine Mind. The flow of spiritual energy is cyclic. Even in the realms of Nature and Matter, one finds a striving upward, an aspiration, a contemplation of Godhead——or, at least, a power to receive form from the Godhead. All is in a state of flux.[14] One cautionary observation should be made: The order of the hypostases in the Divine Triad is *not* one of space, but of dependence. In the spiritual world, for example, body may be said to be in soul, soul in mind, and mind in the One. Reality is the Triad-in-unity: the One, the Divine Mind and the All-Soul. It is (1) thought, (2) the thing and (3) the relation between them. This is the Doctrine of Correspondence and of Mutual Dependence of subject and object.[15] It operates up and down the whole scale of being, beginning with the Divine Triad. *Like only sees like.*[16] The accompanying diagram must, therefore, be interpreted spiritually rather than spatially.

(1) THE ONE: Various names may be applied to the highest realm of existence: The First, The Good, The Simple, The Absolute, The Transcendent, The Infinite, The Unconditioned, or The Father.[17] It is unknowable, has a super-nature, is the goal of all that exists and transcends even the quality of Being. It (or He) is ineffable. It is *not* the Creator and not rightly called the "First Cause," though all that *is* depends from it. The One stands in contrast to The Many, for unity is more fundamental than manifoldness. The One is, therefore, above even thinking, for thinking implies making distinctions, classifying, or entertaining thoughts. Hence it partakes of the "many"

Philo Judæus (A.D. 1-50), who read Plato into the Bible.
Plutarch (A.D. 1-66), who taught about the soul of matter, and about Providence.
Apollonius of Tyana (A.D. 1-50), who purified Roman religions.
Cornutus (*fl.* A.D. 68), known for his Stoic allegories on the nature of the Gods.
Apuleius (*fl.* A.D. 130), mystic, Platonist and moralist.
Seneca (*fl.* A.D. 141), moralist, dramatist, Stoic.
Numenius (*fl.* A.D. 150), mystic; father of Neo-Platonism.
Alcinous and Albinus, who wrote introductions to Platonism.
Maximus of Tyre (*fl.* A.D. 180), moralist and systematizer of organic nature.
Philostratus (*fl.* A.D. 210), who edited the life of Apollonius.
Amelius (A.D. 200-250), pupil of Numenius and secretary of Plotinus.
Plotinus (A.D. 205-270), who united Plato, Aristotle and the Stoics.
Porphyry (A.D. 233-304), Stoic, moralist and theurgist.
Jamblichus (A.D. 280-330), who applied Platonism to the Mysteries.
Julian *the emperor* (*fl.* A.D. 361), purifier of philosophy and Platonist.
Macrobius (*fl.* A.D. 395), who saved Cicero's *Dream of Scipio*.
Proclus (A.D. 411-485), who studied Plato's *Parmenides*.
Boethius (A.D. 470-523), who in prison wrote *De Consolatione Philosophiæ*.
Miscellaneous writers (*ca.* A.D. 500-533): Damascius, Sallustius, works of Dionysius the Areopagite on the Celestial Angel Hierarchies.

[10] For good analyses of Neo-Platonism consult the following: Kenneth Sylvan Guthrie, *op. cit.*; Thomas Whittaker, *The Neo-Platonists*, (2nd ed.) Cambridge (Eng.), 1928; *The Essence of Plotinus*, compiled by Grace A. Turnbull, N.Y., 1934; Plotinus, *The Ethical Treatises* (First Ennead), tr. Stephen Mackenna, London, 1917, esp. the Appendix; see also the *Encyclopædia of Religion and Ethics* (ed. princ.), IX, 307-319.

[11] *Nature*, 86.1ff.; 34.11; 56.10.
[12] *Nature*, 80.23; 56.17.
[13] *Nature*, 74.19; 87.10.
[14] *Nature*, 34.9-13.
[15] *Nature*, 46.19; 91.20; 43.1; 83.21; 51.9.
[16] *Nature*, 94.5; 68.5-7; 46.19; 44.18.
[17] *Nature*, 35.4.

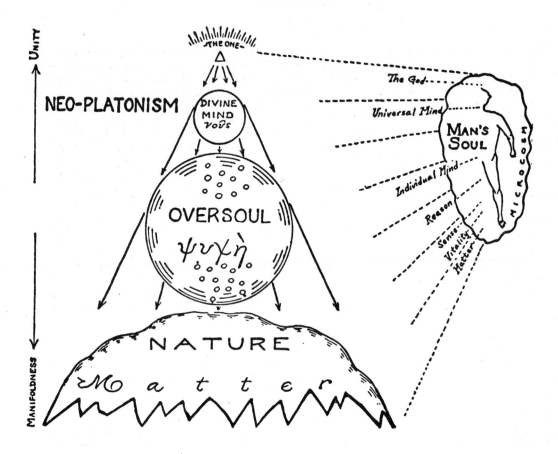

or the "manifold" and belongs to the stage beneath the One. The One is also above even Divine Goodness, for goodness implies the existence of a subject or an object. The One is, therefore, above all categories of Life, Being, Thought and Activity.[18] He is then above the Prime Mover of Aristotle. He is above Beauty. He is unknowable and infinite, and can be defined only negatively, in terms of what He is *not*. No name is really adequate for Him.[19] Since Divine Love is a necessity in each stage of ultimate reality, The One generates worlds and souls, not because of any decay or degeneration in his being, but rather because his divine nature (love) is sufficient for begetting everything.[20] And since his nature is eternal, so are also the natures of his offspring. (Because the One is the source of all things, He may be said to be everywhere; yet, being *other* than all things, He may be said to be *nowhere*. It is the second fact that precludes pantheism from Neo-Platonic philosophy.) God is a spiritual sun which gives light to the Universe and rules all existence.[21] He is the center around which all revolves. Through Him, every part of the Universe is organically related to every other part and to the whole.[22]

(2) THE DIVINE MIND. It may be called Intellectual Principle, Universal Intelligence, Divine Intelligence, Divine Intellect, Supreme Soul, Spiritual Universe, or Nous. As offspring and image of the One, it is the mediator between Creation and the Unknowable. Plurality, complexity or multiplicity begins with this second member of the Triad. The Divine Mind is composed of the Intelligibles, the Ideas, or the Divine Thoughts——all of them Real Beings or Powers——Archetypes or Forms of all that exist in the lower levels.[23] This Divine Mind or Intelligible Universe contains (or *is*) all particular minds or intelligences, which, in the lower levels, are phantasms or

---

[18] *Nature*, 79.10ff.
[19] *Nature*, 77.7-9.
[20] *Nature*, 29.7; 91.15; 79.11.
[21] *Nature*, 76.17; 92.8.

[22] *Nature*, 34.11; 56.10; 74.14-18.
[23] *Nature*, 44.2; 84.12; 87.13; 70.10; 71.4-5.

shadows of the real. The Divine Mind acts in two directions: (a) It contemplates the One; (2) it generates or creates the Over-Soul or All-Soul.[24] Since "eternity" is only the intensity of "intelligible action," the Divine Mind may be said to live in eternity, and not in time. It, therefore, comprehends all things that have existed, that now exist or that shall exist. It, therefore, knows no distinction between potentiality and actuality in thought. The One, we said, was *above* Being; the Divine Mind, on the other hand, is *full* Being. Since Being and Thought are identical, the system of "thoughts" of the Divine Mind is "reality."

(3) THE ALL-SOUL or OVER-SOUL emanates from the Divine Mind and is a reflection. It likewise has two functions or principles: (a) It contemplates the Divine Mind above it; (b) it looks toward Nature and generates the lower and material universe according to the models (or "ideas") of the Divine Mind. The Over-Soul is the eternal cause of the existence of the *cosmos* or sense-grasped universe.[25] It is the Creator and Vital-Principle of all that is lower than the Divinity or Divine Triad. It contains all souls. The sphere of the Over-Soul is "intelligible light." Time begins in the Over-Soul. (Space does not exist in the Godhead.)[26] The soul is, therefore, said to "bring forth time." The Over-Soul is really alive according to Plotinus. Each Idea is an *energeia*, the original type of a definite individual. Plotinus does not, therefore, conceive of the Over-Soul in terms of a great undifferentiated spiritual mass——one that absorbs all individuality of private souls. Individuality pre-exists in the soul-world. All things there are together, yet distinct. Plurality exists prior to embodiment. A word may be said about these individual souls: Before descent into the world of Nature and after reascent to the Over-Soul, each one's thoughts are revealed to other souls in direct vision, though without discourse. Although it would seem better for souls to remain above, yet self-will (*i.e.*, the individual nature of the unincarnate soul) makes it want to venture forth to birth and become separated from the whole. Coming down is one fault; entering into bodies is another. If the soul returns quickly, it usually suffers no hurt.[27] Descent and reascent both seem to be the result of natural law or necessity,[28] yet there is also "free will," for from another viewpoint, incarnation is self-caused. The universal law is not outside, but *within* each soul. We may say, further to express the paradox between necessity and free will, that the soul does not willingly go to a worse state; yet the course that it takes is its own. It must, therefore, suffer retribution for the original error and for any evil that it may do while in its incarnate state——and this retribution is required under the inexorable law of justice.[29] In a very real sense, however, the soul is obliged to descend in order to put forth its powers, which would otherwise remain latent.[30] The soul *must* communicate its gifts as do all the gradations of reality and value. When the soul descends into the body, it creates according to what it has seen in the Spiritual World.[31]

CREATION[32]

(1) NATURE:[33] The Sensible World is a reflection of the Eternal World in the mirror of matter.[34] The realm of "spiritual being" known as Nature (or "Vitality" or "Vegetable Life") is *unconscious* thought.[35] Nature is the active faculty of the Universal Soul.[36] It is simple and purposeless, yet manifold.[37] It may be said to have sensation much as a sleeping body might have it.[38] Its products are the materials that "dreams are made on."[39] It works quietly with the certainty of instinct, without the interruption which thinking entails. It begets, as its offspring, the realm of Matter by the same inner necessity of love, mentioned above as being prevalent throughout all levels of the spiritual universe.[40] This external world has much to teach us about

---

[24] *Nature*, 39.19.
[25] *Nature*, 70.14; 7.9.
[26] Cf. *Nature*, 71.19.
[27] *Nature*, 88.8.
[28] *Nature*, 43.22.
[29] *Nature*, 91.6.
[30] *Nature*, 59.9.
[31] *Nature*, 73.4; 34.18; 79.22; 94.1.
[32] *Nature*, 44.7; 79.4.

[33] See *Nature*, title page.
[34] *Nature*, 80.16; 6.14; 77.12; 41.20; 61.20; 70.14; 76.13.
[35] See next chapter.
[36] *Nature*, 7.20; 80.18-20.
[37] *Nature*, 29.15.
[38] *Nature*, 57.20; 83.4.
[39] *Nature*, 70.12; 78.7; 72.17.
[40] *Nature*, 76.18.

ultimate truth.[41] Plotinus believed it to be beautiful[42]——to be the image of God[43]—— to be a teacher that reminds man of the goodness of God.[44] Man can come to know much about God by contemplating the world as God's image.[45] The stars have souls as men do. Thus a refined astrology enters into Neo-Platonism.[46] The heavens become a kind of celestial writing.[47] Since all levels of the universe are interdependent, subject to the law of coherence or sympathy, we can deduce from the condition of one part of the cosmic system the condition of other parts. (This is the doctrine of "each in all." See under *Microcosm, infra*). We must remember that animals and vegetables have souls like human souls, only infinitely less developed.[48] Just as in the human body all members are in mutual harmony, so in Nature there is a unity or harmony of sounds, low and high.[49] Things act and react on each other, whether by physical or by psychical forces. This phenomenon is described as the "doctrine of action and reaction" or of "sympathy."[50]

(2) MATTER[51] is the ultimate and least significant emanation of the creative power of the All-Soul.[52] It is the point at which the creative process comes to a stop. It is almost non-Being, but not quite. It is the stage of greatest possible manifoldness. Matter is *not material*, and should not, therefore, be confused with the *stuff* to which modern science applies the term. It is intangible and impalpable——a mere abstraction. Matter is evil only in the sense that it is farthest removed from God, proximity to Whom alone is goodness. Considered in itself, Matter is perfect. It is seriously defective only when seen from a higher level of existence. Good and evil are not opposite principles in Neo-Platonism. There is *no* dualism in the system. In one sense, evil does not exist at all. Nor can evils be said to come from God. They are merely degenerations or declinations of qualities already possessed by the person or thing. Unmixed evil certainly does not exist. In still another sense, evil is a lower form of good, and necessary to the completeness of the world. Matter may be summed up as formless stuff without quality——a weak image or shadow of the spiritual——the lowest level of value and the lowest level in the scale of ethical being.

MAN——HIS NATURE, POWERS AND DESTINY

The human soul may be described as the All-Soul or Over-Soul particularized for the space of the mortal life of man.[53] It is the All-Soul incarnated or set in touch with the lower realms. Since particularization is a limitation, incarnation must always be regarded as a "fall." [54] The "human soul divine" has the following three[55] major elements in its composition or psychology. They are indissolubly bound together while the soul is incarnate, and the bond is broken only at death, when the soul discards the body as a man might shed an old coat.[56]

---

[41] *Nature*, 76.14; 54.9.
[42] *Nature*, 29.21.
[43] *Nature*, title page.
[44] *Nature*, 30.14; 77.13; 41.3; 65.8; 52.5; 53.21-22; 53.4; 51.22; 76.4; 63.4.
[45] *Nature*, 80.23.
[46] *Nature*, 10.2-6; 34.21; 9.8; 9.12; 25.20.
[47] *Nature*, 9.8.

[48] *Nature*, 57.2-6.
[49] *Nature*, 29.21.
[50] See Wordsworth's *Ode on Intimations of Immortality* for the phrase, "primal sympathy." Cf. *Nature*, 41.23.
[51] *Nature*, 72.20-23.
[52] *Nature*, 80.17; 77.5-6; 46.11; 81.10; 69.18.

[53] *Nature*, 34.14; 25.12; 80.2; 88.1; 87.13; 76.17.

[54] *Nature*, 81.4; 88.8ff.

[55] Guthrie, *op. cit.*, p. 23, prefers to list seven elements, but the result is the same if one will group the first three and the last three together:

1) *Ho Theos*——The God.
2) *Nous Koinos*——Universal Mind.
3) *Nous Idios*——Individual Mind.
4) *Logos Dianoia*——Reason.
5) *To Aisthetikon Meros*——The psychological mechanism of sensation.
6) *To Phutikon Meros*——Vegetable life.
7) *To Soma*——The form, body, matter.

[56] *Nature*, 73.4.

(1) THE INTELLECTIVE-SOUL:[57] It is the highest level of the soul of man. It is not subject to the vicissitudes of our mortal life, remains untouched by the flesh, and is eternally separated from the body.[58] Its function is true *knowing*, meditation on Real Existence, and intuition from the higher levels of the spiritual universe.[59] It is not perceived by man until by a life of philosophical morality (sanctity or sagehood) he has identified himself with the second level of being (the Divine Mind or God-the-Knowable).[60] To live by this soul is to exist as a god and to experience instantaneous intuitions of true-knowing.[61]

(2) THE REASONING-SOUL:[62] It is the characteristically human element in man's psychology. It constitutes our normal nature. It is the element of individuality in the human soul. It can be separated from the body (*i.e.*, at death), but is not separated during the period of incarnation. Its task is "discursive reasoning," that is, a step-by-step approach to what is, at best, *imperfect* knowledge. The route is that of doubt and logic. This Rational Soul (or faculty of reason) has the power to identify itself with the highest faculties of human psychology[63] or to sink itself into the lower levels. When the Soul sinks into the sensual region, the higher faculties become quiescent or latent, and sometimes may atrophy. (They may always, of course, be revived.)[64]

(3) THE UNREASONING-SOUL is the principle of animal life added to the incarnate soul so that it can function in the realm of Nature or flesh. The Unreasoning-Soul and the fleshly body compose the Animal as distinguished from the Man. (This combination is often called the "couplement.") The faculties of the Unreasoning Soul are: a sense-grasping imagination, a sense-grasping memory, appetites rooted in the flesh, sensation, and the vegetative-nutritive-generative faculties.[65]

SUMMARY: We can say that a man may live on three planes, and that his rank in the scale of existence depends on his choice. (a) He may live an external life——on the level of natural instincts; (b) he may be obedient to his Reasoning-Soul (the Discursive-Reason) and live the life of an intelligent, unspiritual man; or (c) he may in his Intellective-Soul attain to the "life of gods and godlike men." The Soul, being a microcosm, has affinities with every step of the spiritual ladder, reaching from earth to heaven. These stages shade off into each other.

MISCELLANEOUS

MICROCOSM and MACROCOSM ("Each in all"):[66] Plotinus borrowed the philosophy of the word *microcosm* ("little universe") from Aristotle, whose conception was that man is the cosmos in miniature just as the universe *(macrocosm)* is a man enlarged.[67] The relation of all that *is* becomes apparent. If a man follows the ancient precept, "Know thyself," and if he will rely on that higher self,[68] which is the God in him, he will come to understand all Being.[69] In order to know the universe, one has only to look within. One must know oneself before one can understand *man as such*. This doctrine of "each in all" becomes especially meaningful in the study of human beings. Each human faculty, while bound up indissolubly with the other faculties, exists in a universe (or level of existence) all its own. The physical body dwells in the realm of

---

[57] Cf. Coleridge's "Reason" as opposed to the "Understanding."
[58] *Nature*, 74.21; 75.4-10; 34.18; 62.6-8; 68.17.
[59] *Nature*, 79.17; 28.8-9; 86.18; 93.9; 94.14.
[60] *Nature*, 74.11-12; 92.8.
[61] *Nature*, 79.9; 49.20; 71.4-6; 88.1; 71.17; 88.3.
[62] Cf. Coleridge's "Understanding."
[63] See the fourth element in footnote 55.
[64] *Nature*, 28.23.
[65] See Emerson's references to "Understanding" in Index-Concordance of *Nature* as well as Coleridge ¶s. 1-65.
[66] *Nature*, 54.21-23; 29.12; 29.16; 55.1; 55.23; 56.1-22; 30.21; 53.15.
[67] *Nature*, 27.16; 35.10; 85.3ff.; 86.1ff.; 80.8; 51.9; 57.11; 84.16.
[68] That is, the "Intellective-Soul."
[69] *Nature*, 80.6; 6.9.

matter, and a man's diviner elements have rays of relation with all levels of the Divinity.[70]

ALL SOULS were originally equal——parts of the same Divine Mind. That they are alike as to *idea* and *nature* is proved by the fact that they can understand one another.[71] In the Intelligible World they can communicate, being in the same place at the same time. Yet in spite of their common origin, there are many differences between souls in this phenomenal world. These may be accounted for in part by original characteristic variations, by the amount of experience got in former incarnations, by unlike bodies, or by education and discipline.[72] Divine justice operates in all souls, however, and happiness is ultimately the reward of merit or goodness.[73] "The good alone are happy." The difference between men and the gods is only one of development.

FREE WILL: it is only as regards the lowest faculties of a human Soul that a person may be considered rigidly conditioned. In its highest faculties, the Soul is as free as self-existence can make it. A person will, therefore, be free or not free according to whether he will identify himself with the highest or lowest elements in his nature. If the Discursive Reason identifies itself with the Unreasoning-Soul, that man is a slave to his body and in no sense free. Freedom comes when one is serving one's highest good.[74]

THE GODS:[75] They may be either (a) the entire Divinity, (b) the Ideas or Archetypes, (c) exalted Beings——ministers of the Divinity——vaguely supposed to exist above men, (d) the stars and earth in their soul-part, (e) souls of lofty men, or (f) a vague conception of the ancient Greek pantheon. THE DAIMONES——Supernals, Celestials, Divine Spirits, Blessed Spirits—are lofty powers beneath the gods, though often, in practice, confounded with the gods.

THE CONTEMPLATIVE LIFE[76] is of chief interest to Neo-Platonists, for therein does the Soul attain to a knowledge of God, face to face, in a glow of ecstasy. The Soul is the only object worthy of consideration, and things have value only insofar as they promote the higher interests of man. Knowing the Soul means knowing the highest self. Since "Know thyself!" and "Trust thyself!"[77] are the two chief commandments of human life, the contemplative side of one's nature aids one most.[78] Even the morally handicapped may contemplate the soul and grow in grace. The perfect life——that of the wise man——is lived not in community but in detachment. Practical activity is discouraged, but if it cannot be avoided, then the spirit of detachment should be preserved within one's Soul. (Plotinus didn't share Plato's belief in the desirability of reforming the practical life.[79] Worldly business and activity were usually regarded as escape mechanisms.) The best practice issues from theory and returns to it.[80] Since action involves multiplicity of detail, the better soul will attempt to reduce the "many" in his life and approach simplicity or "oneness." [81] Mysticism is the obvious corollary of Neo-Platonic psychology. (See below.)

MORALITY: It is the "half-existence" of Matter that necessitates morality. The Divine perfection is above morals——is unmoral. The realm of pure Matter, on the other hand, is submoral. Morality is for man.[82] Since man is divine in the highest level of his soul, human at the mean level, and brute (or vegetable or matter) in his lowest

---

[70] *Nature*, 35.11.
[71] This paragraph provides part of the philosophic background of Emerson's essay on "Friendship."
[72] See *Nature*, chap. V. Also 46.4; 59.6.
[73] *Nature*, 94.20.
[74] *Nature*, 25.10; 82.4.
[75] *Nature*, 70.13-15; 71.3; 71.11-13.
[76] *Nature*, 29.3; 74.20; 82.11; 92.3.
[77] "Trust thyself!" means essentially "Rely upon the God-in-you!" This doctrine is developed in Emerson's essay, "Self-Reliance." See chapters VI-VIII below.
[78] *Nature*, 75.12-14; 74.20.
[79] *Nature*, 7.2.
[80] *Nature*, 7.2; 82.4.
[81] *Nature*, 74.23.
[82] *Nature*, 53.5; 53.21; 72.4; 51.22; 52.5.

characteristics, he must elevate his being and raise his line of vision constantly, if he intends to grow. How, then, may one account for the troubles of the righteous——troubles like poverty and disease? Plotinus asserts with Stoical fervor that they are unimportant to those who possess the true-good: Virtue.[83] Misfortunes and accidents have, moreover, some disciplinary value. He counsels against worry. The soul may safely trust Divine Justice.[84] One incarnation is not all vouchsafed to us, and one need not despair, therefore, if a single short life seems incomplete or unfair.

REINCARNATION: Since the aim of life is an ethical one and the end of spiritual striving is the vision of God, man's greatest problem is to become worthy. Merit can be increased only in the incarnate state, and incarnation, accordingly, has a moral purpose. Through reincarnation, souls are given more than one chance to improve themselves, to receive compensation for unmerited suffering in earlier states, and to endure retribution for earlier offenses. Plotinus' scheme of reincarnation is "rational." He does not believe, for example, that human Reason can ever be placed in animal bodies. Bad masters in one life, at the worst, become slaves in the next. Rich people who have misused their wealth may return to live in poverty. Murderers may be murdered. When souls no longer need reincarnation, they are placed on stars. The purest turn their faces toward the Divine Mind.

THE PATH OF ENLIGHTENMENT: Neo-Platonism stresses the ethical and practical techniques of self-improvement. Virtues are considered purifications through which the soul disentangles itself from fleshly lusts. Purifications cannot modify the soul, for it is incapable of being harmed, but they do alter its relation to the body by giving it the upper hand.[85] When the soul gains ascendancy, it appears in its original purity——in its likeness to God. The impediments of the soul are anger, cupidity, lust, pain, fear, gluttony, intemperance and avarice. (Compare the "Seven Deadly Sins" [86] of Christendom.) One should strive for temperance, fortitude, modesty, calmness and divinity of mind. A virtue is an energy of the soul——that is, whatever is good for her according to her nature. Neo-Platonism adopts the four Cardinal Virtues of Platonism: Temperance, Courage, Magnanimity and Prudence. *Temperance* means fleeing from physical lusts, gratification of sense, and pleasure in order to achieve utter purity. *Courage* includes overcoming the fear of death——that is, the soul's fear of being outside the body. Courage also means being indifferent to earthly preferment or to anything that cannot be taken away by the soul at death. *Magnanimity* is also characterized by a contempt for earthly advantages. *Prudence* is the virtue of those who turn away from lower interests for the things above. The natural appetites are in themselves good as long as they are not misused. The world of Nature, therefore, is beautiful and useful in reminding souls of God, but one should flee from the natural lusts of the flesh because that side of one's being is fixed and determined—far from free. One's freedom is found only in the world of Soul——in identifying oneself with one's highest nature. When the soul is inside the body, it is handicapped or preordained; outside of the body it is free. The path of enlightenment has seven degrees, beginning with the purification of oneself through the virtues and ending with *becoming God*. Each soul must progress in its own manner and live according to its own nature. There are three kinds of souls: the Musician, the Philosopher, and the Lover.[87]

THE CONSCIENCE OR DAEMON appears to be the psychological attractiveness of the level of one's own soul next above that with which the Reasoning-Soul has identified itself.[88] In other words, Conscience is the God within man summoning him to know his *true self*. The Soul is not a conglomeration of different elements, but a system of organic unities, of which God is the highest phase. To enter into oneself, then, is to enter into God. To rely on self is to rely on God. The process is one of simplification. At long last, we catch the beatific vision. Ours is a "flight from the alone to the alone."

ECSTASY OR MYSTICAL UNION WITH GOD: Man strives *actually* to become divine as, indeed, potentially he is.[89] His duty and his happiness lie in bringing his

---

[83] *Nature*, 12.1; 15.15; 71.10.
[84] *Nature*, 80.5; 94.20; 13.1; 34.16; 6.6.
[85] *Nature*, 80.15; 91.6.
[86] Pride, Wrath, Envy, Lust, Avarice, Gluttony and Sloth.
[87] *Nature*, 68.18; cf. 69.2.
[88] See "Reasoning-Soul" above.
[89] *Nature*, 13.5-8.

entire being into harmony with the Divine within him. Through his Inner-Divine, a
man may in ecstasy break with all that links him to Matter and attain to the "possession" of the Godhead in an act of union, securing thereby an advance taste of the
blessedness surrounding his incarnate life. The pure in heart, therefore, do enter into
ecstatic union with the Deity. They experience an inrushing of Divine Power, and they
are lifted up "to the Seventh Heaven." For those who cannot mount so high, there
always remains "spiritual bliss or happiness." In all such mystical experiences, a
person passively *accepts* what God sends.[90]

AESTHETICS:[91] The One is above Beauty, but the Divine Mind is beautiful because
it is the image of God. The Over-Soul is beautiful because it is the image of the Divine
Mind. The human soul, in like manner, reflects its divine origin, and so does Nature.
Beauty characterizes all existence. It may be sensual or incorporeal, the latter being
higher. Sensual beauty pertains to the eye and ear and is not ultimate; incorporeal
beauty is that of virtue or of the soul, which is the Divine Light. Corporeal beauty is
outside of a man; incorporeal beauty is within him. One must be beautiful himself
before he can behold beauty, since *only like can see like*.[92] Every soul, therefore, strives
after the good and the beautiful,[93] and ultimately for the beauty of the vision of God.
Man takes delight in sensible beauty probably because his soul perceives in it something
akin to his own nature.[94] Beauty may be *in parts* as well as *in the whole*, but perception
seizes the unity and presents that unity to the soul.[95] The beauty of action, virtue and
knowledge, though not perceived through the senses, is understood only by those who
have felt it themselves.[96] The beautiful is definitely in the soul of man. The highest level
of beauty is intellectual, or beauty that is at one with intellect.[97] Love of the beautiful
gives pain as well as pleasure; it reminds one of one's distant spiritual origin as well
as inspires one to recover the lost radiance of the pre-incarnate state.

A few relevant passages from Gérando will conclude this chapter. They
will illustrate one of the channels through which Emerson gained much
information, and the next chapter will deal with another. When, in the
following, Gérando quotes from a Neo-Platonic writer, he is usually
following Victor Cousin's French translation of the original.

UNITY[98]

La doctrine de Platon aspirait tout entière a l'unité systematique; unité dans le but,
unité dans le principe fondamental, unité dans le système des connaissances, comme
dans le système des êtres. Les idées des Mystiques offraient le moyen de réaliser cette
unité, de la porter dans ce double système au plus haut degré qu'il fut possible de
concevoir.

TRUTH, BEAUTY, GOODNESS[99]

"La fin de la nature intellectuelle n'est autre que la fin de la nature morale; car, le
beau, le bon, le vrai sont identiques, comme ils sont tels par leur propre essence. La
pratique de la vertu se confond avec la recherche de la vérité. L'une et l'autre ne tendent
qu'à l'union intime avec l'essence divine. Les erreurs, comme les vices, proviennent de
ce que l'âme humaine, descendue sur cette terre, a oublié sa céleste origine; elle rec-
tifiera les unes, corrigera les autres, en se dirigeant de nouveau vers sa source première;
l'âme, en se livrant à la contemplation, rentre dans sa véritable patrie."

---

[90] *Nature*, 75.12; 75.6.
[91] *Nature*, 30.20-23.
[92] *Nature*, 44.18; 94.5.
[93] *Nature*, 30.17; 19.3.
[95] Gérando, *Histoire* (1822), III, 339.
[94] *Nature*, 30.15.
[95] *Nature*, 30.3; 19.3 through 20.2.
[96] *Nature*, 27.7;   26.7;   26.16;   25.3;
25.21; 69.1.
[97] *Nature*, 28.5; 28.21.
[98] *Ibid.*, III, 381-382. Gérando is quoting from one of Plotinus' *Enneads*. In III, 338,
Gérando says: "La morale de Platon était éminemment désintéressée, repoussait les
séductions de la volupté, faisait rechercher la vertu pour elle-même, comme le type du
beau et du bon." Cf. *Nature*, 30.20; 69.1-4.

APULEIUS ON THE GODDESS——NATURE[100]

Invocation à la Déesse: "Toi que les dieux célestes honorent, que les divinités infernales redoutent; déesse qui imprimes le mouvement à notre globe, qui éclaires le soleil, gouvernes l'univers et foules au pied le Tartare; les astres t'obéissent; tu règles l'ordre des saisons; les élémens te sont asservis; les vents ne soufflent et les nuages ne s'assemblent qu'à ton gré; les semences ne peuvent germer, ni croître sans toi.

Réponse de la Déesse: "Me voici; la nature, mère de toutes choses, souveraine de tous les élémens, l'origine des siècles, la première des divinités, la reine des mânes, la plus ancienne habitante des cieux, l'image uniforme des dieux et des déesses. Les voûtes éclatantes du ciel, les vents salutaires de la mer, et le déplorable silence des enfers reconnaissent mon pouvoir absolu. Je suis la seule divinité révérée dans l'univers, sous plusieurs formes, avec diverses cérémonies et sous différens noms, etc."

IAMBLICHUS ON THE REGIONS OF THE GODS[101]

"Les Dieux qui composent cette région supérieure, contemplent leurs propres *idées* divines; les astres, ou Dieux visibles, ne sont que des simulacres apparens, engendrés des exemplaires divins et intelligibles. Un lien d'unité associe ces deux ordres de choses d'une manière indissoluble; les Dieux visibles sont contenus dans les Dieux intellectuels. Plus nous nous élevons dans l'échelle des êtres, remontant à l'identité des causes premières, par les genres et les essences, plus nous nous dirigeons des parties au tout, et mieux aussi nous découvrons cette unité parfaite et sublime qui renferme en elle et la variété et la multitude. Tel est le caractère de la cause et de l'action divine, que l'unité se répand du sommet aux régions inférieures suivant un ordre divin. La hierarchie des Dieux se termine elle-même à l'unité absolue; là réside ce Dieu suprême, permanent dans la solitude de sa propre unité, qui n'est mêlé à rien d'étranger, qui n'est rien autre que cette unité même.

"Cette connaissance des Dieux est intimement unie à notre propre essence; elle est antérieure à toute faculté d'examen et du jugement, à tout raisonnement; elle a co-existé, dès le commencement, avec la tendance essentielle de notre âme vers le bien. Il en est de même de ces natures supérieures dont la hiérarchie remplit l'intervalle qui sépare les Dieux de l'âme humaine, qui forment entre ceux-ci et celle-là un lien inter-médiaire, chaîne immense qui unit ce qu'il y a de plus élevé avec ce qu'il y a de plus infime, qui constitue la communauté, la connexion, l'ordre et l'harmonie de toutes choses; échelle universelle par laquelle les essences suprêmes descendent aux derniers degrés, par laquelle les êtres inférieurs montent au sommet de la perfection; tels sont ces génies, ces héros, ces âmes pures qui parviennent à la même condition. Compagnons immortels des Dieux, ces esprits nous sont connus ainsi qu'eux par une notion innée."

PROCLUS ON THE DESCENT OF THE SOUL[102]

"L'âme, en descendant dans le corps, se trouva séparée des esprits divins qui la remplissaient d'intelligence, de puissance et de pureté; elle se trouva unie à l'ordre des choses produites, à la nature matérielle, qui l'environnerent d'oubli, d'erreur et d'ignorance; elle se trouva comme enveloppée de vêtemens divers et mélangés qui l'empêchaient de se livrer à la contemplation des choses supérieures. Mais, elle peut remonter à ces régions sublimes, aux essences divines, déposer ces vêtemens importuns, se dépouiller de la composition, s'élever à la vie intellectuelle, aux simples et pures intuitions, contempler les genres des êtres, l'essence intelligible. Elle ressuscite ainsi son existence primitive et suprême, par laquelle elle redevient une, et subordonne à son unité tout ce qui en elle est complexe. Notre entendement se trouve ainsi en contact avec l'entendement divin; il

---

[100] This passage comes from one of his poems translated by Saint-Croix. Apuleius called Nature "la mère commune, l'unité multiforme," in his *Metamorphoses*, Bk. II. See *Histoire* (1822), I, 304. Cf. *Nature*, 73.11-16.
[101] See Gérando, *Histoire* (1822), III, 398-400. Cf. *Nature*, 70.13 through 71.12.
[102] Gérando, *Histoire* (1822), III, 439-440. Cf. *Nature*, 70.13 through 71.12.

atteint ainsi cette unité première qui est le lien de toutes choses, qui est comme la fleur de son essence, et, par cette communication, il exerce en quelque sorte lui-même une fonction divine; nous devenons pour ainsi dire divins quand, fuyant ce qui est multiple en nous, nous nous refugions dans notre propre unité."

GÉRANDO'S SUMMARY OF NEO-PLATONISM[103]

S'il fallait essayer de définir par des caractères généraux le système entier de la philosophie des nouveaux Platoniciens, nous dirons qu'elle constitue: Un système de *Panthéisme*, en ce qu'elle identifie la substance et la cause, et rappelle ainsi tout ce qui existe à une substance unique; Un système de *Spiritualisme*, en ce qu'elle réduit la matière à n'être qu'une simple privation, et n'accorde de réalite qu'à l'intelligence; Un système *d'Idéalisme*, en ce qu'elle identifie l'objet et le sujet, ne reconnaît aucune existence positive aux objets externes, et ne déduit la connaissance que de l'identité absolue; Un système de *Mysticisme*, en ce qu'elle fait dériver toutes les lumières de l'esprit de l'union intime, directe et immédiate avec Dieu, par l'état de l'extase; Enfin, un système de Théurgie, en ce qu'elle suppose le pouvoir de diriger par l'évocation des Génies les opérations de la nature.

THE WAYSIDE — Rebuilt many times, it was the home of the Alcotts, Hawthorne, and Margaret Sidney

---

[103] Gérando, *Histoire* (1822), III, 455-456.

CUDWORTH——"A MAGAZINE OF QUOTATIONS"[1]

Emerson's chief guide to Plotinus and Neo-Platonic thought before 1837 was Ralph Cudworth's *The True Intellectual System of the Universe*,[2] a copy of which (in four volumes) he seems to have acquired for his library sometime in 1834 or early in 1835.[3] This outstanding work of the school of seventeenth-century philosophical divines known as the "Cambridge Platonists"[4] he found to be a veritable encyclopædia of ancient wisdom,[5] divine pages for every torpid hour,[6] and "an armory for a poet to furnish himself withal."[7] In his address before the American Institute of Education in August, 1835, he placed it in a class second only to that of Chaucer, Spenser, Shakespeare and Milton.[8] He confessed that it encouraged his self-reliance by pointing out in the works of old philosophers exact parallels to his own thoughts, and thereby convinced him that truth was as accessible to him in the present as it had been to others in the past.[9] It claimed his attention in later years, even after the separate volumes of Thomas Taylor's Neo-Platonic translations had found their way to his shelves,[10] and it was one of three works which he prescribed for the Dartmouth College Library and for which he forwarded funds out of a remitted honorarium.[11] His failure to copy long passages[12] into his journals, however, is understood when one examines his well-marked copy, observing the carefully prepared indexes and marginal scorings, for the *Intellectual System*, like the *Select Works of Plotinus* or Jeremy Taylor's *Sermons*, was a vade mecum——not an ordinary book——and

---

[1] See *Journals*, VII, pp. 95-96 (September, 1845): "[Cudworth's book] is a magazine of quotations, of extraordinary ethical sentences, the shining summits of ancient philosophy . . . wonderful revelations. . . ." For a good working bibliography on Cudworth and on his philosophy, see *C.B.E.L.*, I, 877.

[2] Ralph Cudworth, *The True Intellectual System of the Universe, wherein all the reason and philosophy of Atheism is confuted*, ed. Thomas Birch, 4 vols., London, 1820.

[3] He may have consulted the appendix to this work as early as 1832, for he refers directly or indirectly to Cudworth's "Discourse concerning the True Notion of the Lord's Supper" [See *Intellectual System* (1820), IV, 215-286] in his famous sermon before the Second Church on September 9 of that year. (See *Works*, XI, p. 4). Earlier references to Cudworth in the *Journals* and in his Bowdoin prize essay [*Ethical Philosophy* (1821)] point to a posthumous work, "A Treatise on Immutable Morality," which appeared for the first time as *A Treatise concerning Eternal and Immutable Morality*, ed. Edward Chandler, London, 1731. This work was in the Harvard College Library, and Emerson apparently borrowed it several times between 1818 and 1823—— a period for which library records are missing. See *Emerson's Reading*, p. 44, footnote.

[4] The chief members of this group were: Nathanael Culverwel (d. 1651?), Benjamin Whichcote (1609-1683), John Smith (1618-1652), and Ralph Cudworth (1617-1688).

[5] See *Journals*, III, 489 (June 10, 1835): "Cudworth is like a cow in June which breathes of nothing but clover and scent-grass. He has fed so entirely on ancient bards and sages that all his diction is redolent of their books. He is a stream of Corinthian brass in which gold and silver and iron are molten together out of ancient temples."

[6] See *Journals*, III, 485-486 (May 29, 1835).

[7] *Ibid.*, IV, 8 (Jan. 24, 1836).

[8] See Cabot, *Memoir*, II, 715.

[9] See "Literary Ethics," read at Dartmouth College, July 24, 1838, in *Works*, I, 160.

[10] See *Letters*, II, 451.

[11] *Ibid.*, II, 144.

[12] The only copied quotation is found in *Journals*, IV, 7 (Jan. 22, 1836). It was taken from the *Intellectual System* (1820), II, 271.

was, therefore, accorded special consideration and treatment. The following excerpts, *with the Greek and Latin parentheses omitted*,[13] will not do justice to such an important influence on Emerson's life and writings, but they will suggest, in a measure, how Cudworth contributed to the thought of *Nature*[14] and why he was chosen to supply the motto[15] for its title page:

NATURE EVER DEPENDENT ON GOD[16]

¶ 1

Wherefore, since neither all things are produced fortuitously, or by the unguided mechanism of matter, nor God himself may reasonably be thought to do all things immediately and miraculously; it may well be concluded, that there is a plastic nature under him, which, as an inferior and subordinate instrument, doth drudgingly execute that part of his providence, which consists in the regular and orderly motion of matter; yet so as that there is also, besides this, a higher Providence to be acknowledged, which, presiding over it, doth often supply the defects of it, and sometimes over-rule it; forasmuch as this plastic nature cannot act electively, nor with discretion. And by this means the wisdom of God will not be shut up nor concluded wholly within his own breast, but will display itself abroad, and print its stamps and signatures every where throughout the world; so that God, as Plato (after Orpheus) speaks, will be not only the beginning and end, but also the middle of all things; they being as much to be ascribed to his causality; as if himself had done them all immediately, without the concurrent instrumentality of any subordinate natural cause. Notwithstanding which, in this way it will appear also to human reason, that all things are disposed and ordered by the Deity, without any solicitous care or distractious providence.

¶ 2

Now, if there be a plastic nature, that governs the motion of matter every where, according to laws, there can be no reason given, why the same might not also extend farther to the regular disposal of that matter, in the formation of plants and animals, and other things, in order to that apt coherent frame and harmony of the whole universe.

ANCIENT OPINION ON NATURE[17]

¶ 3

And as this plastic nature is a thing, which seems to be in itself most reasonable, so hath it also had the suffrage of the best philosophers in all ages. For, first, it is well known, that Aristotle concerns himself in nothing more zealously than this, that mundane things are not effected merely by the necessity and unguided motion of matter, or by fortuitous mechanism; but by such a nature as acts regularly and artificially for ends; yet so as that this nature is not the highest principle neither, or the supreme Numen, but subordinate to a perfect mind or intellect; he affirming, that mind, together with nature, was the cause of this universe;—and that heaven and

---

[13] When Cudworth quotes, he always gives the Greek or Latin original and then follows with his own translation. In order to eliminate this duplication and to simplify the problem of editing and typesetting, I here omit the ancient tongues *without* indicating the omissions by the usual dots. The English equivalent, however, is always given. Cudworth's famous work deserves a modern edition prepared on some such principle, because, as it stands, it is a formidable undertaking for the average printer and provides unnecessary evidence of erudition for the modern reader.

[14] See pages 24-26 of the "Index-Concordance" to my facsimile of *Nature* for a rapid summary of Emerson's beliefs on the subject. Nature is altered and moulded by spirit (69.12; 72.2; 77.13; 79.14; 93.21); it always speaks of spirit (76.14); it is an accident and effect (61.20); its aspect is devout (76.18); it becomes ancillary to man (28.3); it is deaf and dumb (57.1; 57.20); it is as meek as the Savior's ass (50.22); it is an apparition of God (6.14; 77.11); it is not fixed but fluid (93.20); it is not rivaled by art (24.3); it is not shorter lived than Spirit (61.9); it is thoroughly mediate (50.21); it withdraws before God (62.21); it is not explicable by carpentry (78.10). Compare man's "chipping, baking and patching" in 8.2.

[15] See *Intellectual System* (1820), I, 338-339.

[16] See *Intellectual System* (1820), I, 322-323; 324.

[17] *Ibid.*, I, 324-325.

earth, plants and animals, were framed by them both; that is, by mind as the principal and directive cause, but by nature as a subservient or executive instrument; and elsewhere joining in like manner God and nature both together, as when he concludes, That God and nature do nothing in vain.

¶ 4

Neither was Aristotle the first broacher or inventor of this doctrine, Plato before him having plainly asserted the same. For in a passage already cited, he affirms, that nature, together with reason, and according to it, orders all things; thereby making nature, as a distinct thing from the Deity, to be a subordinate cause under the reason and wisdom of it. And elsewhere he resolves, that there are certain causes of a wise and artificial nature, which the Deity uses as subservient to itself;—as also, that there are con-causes, which God makes use of, as subordinately co-operative with himself.

POLARITY IN NATURE——NOT DUALISM[18]

¶ 5

Moreover, before Plato, Empedocles philosophized also in the same manner, when, supporting two worlds, the one archetypal, the other ectypal, he made friendship and discord to be the active principle and immediate operator in this lower world; he not understanding thereby, as Plutarch and some others have conceited, two substantial principles in the world, the one of good, the other of evil; but only a plastic nature, as Aristotle in sundry places intimates; which he called by that name, partly because he apprehended, that the result and upshot of nature in all generations and corruptions amounted to nothing more than mixtures and separations, or concretion and secretion of pre-existent things; and partly because this plastic nature is that, which doth reconcile the contrarieties and enmities of particular things, and bring them into one general harmony in the whole. Which latter is a notion, that Plotinus, describing this very seminary reason or plastic nature of the world (though taking it in something a larger sense than we do in this place), doth ingeniously pursue after this manner: The seminary reason or plastic nature of the universe, opposing the parts to one another, and making them severally indigent, produces by that means war and contention. And, therefore, though it be one, yet, notwithstanding, it consists of different and contrary things. For there being hostility in its parts, it is nevertheless friendly and agreeable in the whole; after the same manner as in a dramatic poem, clashings and contentions are reconciled into one harmony. And, therefore, the seminary and plastic nature of the world may fitly be resembled to the harmony of disagreeing things.——Which Plotinic doctrine may well pass for a commentary upon Empedocles, accordingly as Simplicius briefly represents his sense[:] Empedocles makes two worlds, the one united and intelligible, the other divided and sensible; and in this lower sensible world, he takes notice both of unity and discord.

NATURE NOT MYSTERIOUS——IS RULED BY AN INTELLIGENCE[19]

¶ 6

But because some may pretend, that the plastic nature is all one with an occult quality, we shall here shew, how great a difference there is betwixt these two. For he that asserts an occult quality for the cause of any phenomenon, does indeed assign no cause at all of it, but only declare his own ignorance of the cause: but he that asserts a plastic nature, assigns a determinate and proper cause, nay, the only intelligible cause, of that which is the greatest of all phenomena in the world, namely the orderly, regular, and artificial frame of things in the universe, whereof the mechanic philosophers, however, pretending to solve all phenomena by matter and motion, assign no cause at all. Mind and understanding is the only true cause of orderly regularity; and he that asserts a plastic nature, asserts mental causality in the world; but the fortuitous Mechanists, who, exploding final causes, will not allow mind and understanding to have any influence at all upon the frame of things, can never possibly assign any cause of this grand phenomenon, unless confusion may be said to be the cause of order, and fortune or chance of constant regularity; and, therefore, themselves must resolve it into an occult quality. Nor, indeed, does there appear any great reason, why such men should assert an infinite mind in the world, since they do not allow it to act any where at all, and therefore must needs make it to be in vain.

---

[18] *Ibid.*, I, 325-327.   [19] *Ibid.*, I, 331-332.

THE ART OF NATURE AND OF MAN CONTRASTED[20]

¶ 7

In the next place, we are to observe, that though the plastic nature be a kind of·
art, yet there are some considerable pre-eminences which it hath above human art;
the first whereof is this, that whereas human art cannot act upon the matter otherwise
than from without and at a distance, nor communicate itself to it, but with a great
deal of tumult and hurliburly, noise and clatter, it using hands and axes, saws and
hammers, and after this manner, with much ado, by knockings and thrustings, slowly.
introducing its form or idea (as, for example, of a ship or house) into the materials;
nature, in the mean time, is another kind of art, which, insinuating itself immediately
into things themselves, and there acting more commandingly upon the matter as an
inward principle, does its work easily, cleverly, and silently. Nature is art as it were
incorporated and embodied in matter, which doth not act upon it from without
mechanically, but from within vitally and magically; Here are no hands, nor feet, nor
any instrument, connate or adventitious, there being only need of matter to work upon,
and to be brought into a certain form, and nothing else. For it is manifest that the
operation of nature is different from mechanism, it doing not its work by trusion or
pulsion, by knockings or thrustings, as if it were without that which it wrought upon.—
But as God is inward to every thing, so nature acts immediately upon the matter, as
an inward and living soul, or law in it.

¶ 8

Another pre-eminence of nature above human art is this, that whereas human artists
are often to seek and at a loss, and therefore consult and deliberate, as also upon
second thoughts mend their former work; nature, on the contrary, is never to seek
what to do, nor at a stand; and for that reason also (besides another that will be
suggested afterwards) it doth never consult nor deliberate. Indeed Aristotle intimates,
as if this had been the grand objection of the old Atheistic philosophers against the
plastic nature, that because we do not see natural bodies to consult or deliberate,
therefore there could be nothing of art, counsel, or contrivance in them; but all came
to pass fortuitously.——But he confutes it after this manner: It is absurd for men
to think nothing to be done for ends, if they do not see that which moves to consult,
although art itself doth not consult.——Whence he concludes, that nature may act
artificially, orderly, and methodically, for the sake of ends, though it never consult or
deliberate. Indeed human artists themselves do not consult properly as they are artists,
but whenever they do it, it is for want of art, and because they are to seek, their art
being imperfect and adventitious: but art itself, or perfect art, is never to seek, and
therefore doth never consult or deliberate; and nature is this art, which never hesitates
nor studies, as unresolved what to do, but is always readily prompted; nor does it
ever repent afterwards of what it had formerly done, or go about, as it were, upon
second thoughts, to alter and mend its former course; but it goes on in one constant
unrepenting tenor, from generation to generation, because it is the stamp or impress
of that infallibly omniscient art, of the· Divine understanding, which is the very law
and rule of what is simply the best in every thing.

¶ 9

And thus we have seen the difference between nature and human art; that the
latter is imperfect art, acting upon the matter from without, and at a distance; but
the former is art itself, or perfect art, acting as an inward principle in it. Wherefore,
when art is said to imitate nature, the meaning thereof is, that imperfect human art
imitates that perfect art of nature, which is really no other than the Divine art itself;
as, before Aristotle, Plato had declared in his Sophist, in these words: Those things,
which are said to be done by nature, are indeed done by Divine art.——

NATURE'S ART INFERIOR TO DIVINE ART[21]

¶ 10

Notwithstanding which, we are to take notice in the next place, that as nature is
not the Deity itself, but a thing very remote from it, and far below it, so neither is it
the Divine art, as it is in itself pure and abstract, but concrete and embodied only;
for the Divine art considered in itself, is nothing but knowledge, understanding, or
wisdom in the mind of God. . . . Art is defined by Aristotle to be the reason of the
thing without matter;——and so the Divine art or knowledge in the mind of God is

---

[20] *Ibid.*, I, 333-336.   [21] *Ibid.,* I, 336-338.

unbodied reason; but nature is *ratio mersa et confusa*, reason immersed and plunged into matter, and, as it were, fuddled in it, and confounded with it. Nature is not the Divine art archetypal, but only ectypal; it is a living stamp or signature of the Divine wisdom; which, though it act exactly according to its archetype, yet it doth not at all comprehend nor understand the reason of what itself doth. And the difference between these two may be resembled to that between the reason of the mind and conception, —called *verbum mentis*, and the reason of external speech;—the latter of which, though it bear a certain stamp and impress of the former upon it, yet itself is nothing but articulate sound devoid of all understanding and sense. . . . Thus nature may be called the manuary opificer, that acts subserviently under the architectonical art and wisdom of the Divine understanding, which does do without knowing the reason of what it doth.—

HOW NATURE FALLS SHORT OF HUMAN ART[22]

¶ 11

Wherefore, as we did before observe the pre-eminences of nature above human art, so we must here take notice also of the imperfections and defects of it, in which respect it falls short of human art, which are likewise two; and the first of them is this, that though it act artificially for the sake of ends, yet itself doth neither intend those ends, nor understand the reason of that it doth. Nature is not master of that consummate art and wisdom, according to which it acts, but only a servant to it, and a drudging executioner of the dictates of it. This difference betwixt nature and abstract art or wisdom is expressed by Plotinus in these words: How doth wisdom differ from that which is called nature? verily in this manner, that wisdom is the first thing, but nature the last and lowest; for nature is but an image or imitation of wisdom, the last thing of the soul,[23] which hath the lowest impress of reason shining upon it; as when a thick piece of wax is thoroughly impressed upon by a seal, that impress, which is clean and distinct in the superior superficies of it, will in the lower side be weak and obscure; and such is the stamp and signature of nature, compared with that of wisdom and understanding, nature being a thing, which doth only do, but not know.—— And elsewhere the same writer declares the difference between the spermatic λογοι, or reasons, and knowledges or conceptions of the mind in this manner: Whether are these plastic reasons or forms in the soul knowledges? but how shall it then act according to those knowledges? for the plastic reason or form acts or works in matter, and that which acts naturally is not intellection nor vision, but a certain power of moving matter, which doth not know, but only do, and makes as it were a stamp or figure in water.

¶ 12

And with this doctrine of the ancients, a modern judicious writer,[24] and sagacious inquirer into nature, seems fully to agree, that nature is such a thing as doth not know, but only do; for after he had admired that wisdom and art, by which the bodies of animals are framed, he concludes that one or other of these two things must needs be acknowledged, that either the vegetative or plastic power of the soul, by which it fabricates and organizes its own body, is more excellent and Divine than the rational; or else, That in the works of nature there is neither prudence nor understanding, but only it seems so to our apprehensions, who judge of these Divine things of nature according to our own arts and faculties, and patterns borrowed from ourselves; as if the active principles of nature did produce their effects in the same manner as we do our artificial works.——Wherefore we conclude, agreeably to the sense of the best philosophers, both ancient and modern, that nature is such a thing, as, though it act artificially, and for the sake of ends, yet it doth but ape and mimic the Divine art and wisdom, itself not understanding those ends which it acts for, nor the reason of what it doth in order to them; for which cause also it is not capable of consultation or deliberation, nor can it act electively, or with discretion.

---

[22] *Ibid.*, I, 338-344.

[23] Here and in the lines following Emerson found the motto which he put on the title page of the first edition of *Nature*.

[24] William Harvey, *Exercitationes De Generatione Animalium*, London, 1651, ex. 49, p. 145.

¶ 13

Moreover, that something may act artificially and for ends, without comprehending the reason of what it doth, may be further evinced from those natural instincts that are in animals, which without knowledge direct them to act regularly, in order both to their own good, and the good of the universe. As for example: the bees in mellifi-, cation, and in framing their combs and hexagonial cells, the spiders in spinning their webs, the birds in building their nests, and many other animals in such like actions of their's, which would seem to argue a great sagacity in them, whereas notwithstand- ing, as Aristotle observes, They do these things, neither by art, nor by counsel, nor by any deliberation of their own;——and, therefore, are not masters of that wisdom, according to which they act, but only passive to the instincts and impresses thereof upon them. And indeed to affirm, that brute animals do all these things by a knowledge of their own, and which themselves are masters of, and that without deliberation and consultation, were to make them to be endued with a most perfect intellect, far transcending that of human reason; whereas it is plain enough, that brutes are not above consultation, but below it, and that these instincts of nature in them are nothing but a kind of fate upon them.

¶ 14

There is, in the next place, another imperfection to be observed in the plastic nature, that as it doth not comprehend the reason of its own action, so neither is it clearly and expressly conscious of what it doth; in which respect, it doth not only fall short of human art, but even of that very manner of acting, which is in brutes them- selves, who, though they do not understand the reason of those actions, that their natural instincts lead them to, yet they are generally conceived to be conscious of them, and to do them by fancy; whereas, the plastic nature in the formation of plants and animals seems to have no animal fancy, no express con-sense or consciousness of what it doth. Thus the often commended philosopher [Plotinus]: Nature hath not so much as any fancy in it; as intellection and knowledge is a thing superior to fancy, so fancy is superior to the impress of nature, for nature hath no apprehension nor conscious perception of any thing. In a word, nature is a thing, that hath no such self- perception or self-enjoyment in it, as animals have.

The value of the *Intellectual System* as a textbook of Neo-Platonism can also be illustrated by a few typical excerpts, but these should merely encourage any future editor of Emerson's works to make a careful exami- nation of Ralph Cudworth for many of the lusters which adorn the essays and poems.[25] Since it would require a dissertation adequately to set forth his complete significance in American Transcendentalism, this chapter must, therefore, be considered suggestive rather than exhaustive:

THE NEO-PLATONIC TRIAD OR TETRAD[26]

¶ 15

Wherefore Proclus, and some others of those Platonists, plainly understood this Trinity no otherwise, than as a certain scale or ladder of beings in the universe; or a gradual descent of things from the first or highest, by steps downward, lower and lower, so far as to the souls of all animals. For which cause, Proclus, to make up this scale complete, adds to these three ranks and degrees, below that third of souls, a fourth of natures also; under which there lies nothing but the passive part of the universe, body and matter. So that their whole scale of all that is above body was indeed not a Trinity, but a quarternity, or four ranks and degrees of beings, one below another; the first of henades or unities, the second of noes, minds or intellects, the third of souls, and the last of natures; these being, as it were, so many orbs and spheres, one within and below another. In all which several ranks of being, they supposed one first universal, and unparticipated, as the head of each respective rank, and many particular or participated ones: as one first universal Henade, and many secondary particular henades; one first universal Nous, Mind, or Intellect, and many

---

[25] Cudworth provides an interesting background for the poem, "Rhodora," in *Intellectual System* (1820), III, pp. 282-285. His discussion centers about the postulate, basic in Neo-Platonism, that "eyes *were* made for seeing."

[26] *Intellectual System* (1820), III, 53-55.

secondary and particular noes or minds; one first universal Soul, and many particular souls; and lastly, one universal Nature, and many particular natures. In which scale of beings, they deified, besides the first Το 'εν, and Τ'αγαθον, One, and good——not only the first Mind, and the first Soul, but also those other particular henades and noes universally; and all particular souls above human: leaving out, besides them and inferior souls, that fourth rank of natures, because they conceived, that nothing was to be accounted a god, but what was intellectual and superior to men. Wherein, though they made several degrees of gods, one below another, and called some eternal, and some generated——or made in time; yet did they no where clearly distinguish betwixt the Deity properly so called, and the creature, nor shew how far in this scale the true Deity went, and where the creature began. But as it were melting the Deity by degrees, and bringing it down lower and lower, they made the juncture and commissure betwixt God and the creature so smooth and close, that where they indeed parted was altogether undiscernible; they rather implying them to differ only in degrees, or that they were not absolute but comparative terms, and consisted but in more and less.

THE SCALE OF BEING[27]
¶ 16
There is unquestionably a scale or ladder of nature, and degrees of perfection and entity, one above another, as of life, sense, and cogitation, above dead, senseless, and unthinking matter; of reason and understanding above sense, &c. And if the sun be nothing but a mass of fire, or inanimate subtile matter agitated, then hath the most contemptible animal that can see the sun, and hath consciousness and self-enjoyment, a higher degree of entity and perfection in it, than that whole fiery globe; as also than the materials (stone, timber, brick and mortar), of the most stately structure, or city. Notwithstanding which, the sun in other regards, and as its vastly extended light and heat hath so great an influence upon the good of the whole world, plants and animals, may be said to be a far more noble and useful thing in the universe, than any one particular animal whatsoever. Wherefore there being plainly a scale or ladder of entity, the order of things was unquestionably, in way of descent, from higher perfection downward to lower; it being as impossible for a greater perfection to be produced from a lesser, as for something to be caused by nothing. Neither are the steps or degrees of this ladder (either upward or downward) infinite; but as the foot, bottom, or lowest round thereof, is stupid and senseless matter, devoid of all life and understanding; so is the head, top, and summity of it a perfect omnipotent Being, comprehending itself, and all possibilities of things. A perfect understanding Being is the beginning and head of the scale of entity; from whence things gradually descend downward; lower and lower, till they end in senseless matter. Mind is the oldest of all things,——senior to the elements, and the whole corporeal world. . . .

UNITY AND DEPENDENCE[28]
¶ 17
The chief ground of this Platonic doctrine of an essential dependance, and therefore gradual subordination, in their trinity of Divine hypostases, is from that fundamental principle of their theology, that there is but one Original of all things, and only one Fountain of the Godhead; from whence all other things whatsoever, whether temporal or eternal, created or uncreated, were altogether derived. And therefore this second hypostasis of their trinity, since it must accordingly derive its whole being from the first, as the splendour from the original light——must of necessity have also an essential dependence upon the same; and, consequently, a gradual subordination to it.

EMANATION DESCRIBED BY ANALOGY[29]
¶ 18
Which gradual subordination and essential dependence of the second and third hypostasis upon the first is by these Platonics illustrated several ways. Ficinus resembles it to the circulations of water, when some heavy body falling into it, its superficies is depressed, and from thence every way circularly wrinkled. "Alius (saith he) sic ferme profluit ex alio, sicut in aqua circulus dependet a circulo;" one of these Divine hypostases doth in a manner so depend upon another, as one circulation of water depends upon another.——Where it is observable also, that the wider the

---

[27] *Ibid.*, IV, 131-132.
[28] *Ibid.*, III, 114.
[29] *Ibid.*, III, 102-104.

circulating wave grows, still hath it the more subsidence and detumescence, together with an abatement of celerity, till at last all becomes plain and smooth again. But, by the Pagan Platonists themselves, each following hypostasis is many times said to be a print, stamp or impression, made by the former, like the signature of a seal upon wax. Again, it is often called by them an image, and representation, and imitation; which if considered in *audibles*, then will the second hypostasis be looked upon as the echo of an original voice; and the third as the repeated echo, or echo of that echo: as if both the second and third hypostases were but certain replications of the first original Deity with abatement; which though not accidental or evanid ones, but substantial, yet have a like dependence one upon another, and a gradual subordination. Or if it be considered in *visibles*, then will the second hypostasis be resembled to the image of a face in a glass, and the third to the image of that image reflected in another glass, which depend upon the original face, and have a gradual abatement of the vigour thereof. Or else the second and third may be conceived as two parhelii, or as a second and third sun. For thus does Plotinus call the universal Psyche, or third hypostasis, the image of mind (which is the second) retaining much of the splendour thereof.—— Which similitude of theirs, notwithstanding, they would not have to be squeezed or pressed hard; because they acknowledge, that there is something of dissimilitude in them also, which then would be forced out of them. Their meaning amounts to no more than this, that as an image in a glass is said essentially to belong to something else, and to depend upon it; so each following hypostasis doth essentially depend upon the former or first, and hath a subordination to it. But we meet with no expression in any of these Pagan Platonists so unhandsome and offensive, as that of Philo's, in his second book of allegories, The word is the shadow of God, which he made use of, as an instrument, in the making of the world.

"NATURE NOT A GODDESS"——PROCLUS[30]
¶ 19

Nature is the last of all causes, that fabricate this corporeal and sensible world, and the utmost bound of incorporeal substances. Which, being full of reasons and power, orders and presides over all mundane affairs. It proceeding (according to the Magic Oracles) from that supreme goddess, the Divine wisdom, which is the fountain of all life, as well intellectual, as that which is concrete with matter. Which wisdom this nature always essentially depending upon, passes through all things unhinderably; by means whereof even inanimate things partake of a kind of life, and things corruptible remain eternal in their species, they being contained by its standing forms or ideas, as their causes. And thus does the oracle describe nature, as presiding over the whole corporeal world, and perpetually turning round the heavens.——Here have we a description of one universal, substantial life, soul, or spirit of nature, subordinate to the Deity. . . . Where it may be observed, by the way, that this Proclus, though he were a superstitious Pagan, much addicted to the multiplying of gods (subordinate to one supreme) or bigotic Polytheist, who had a humour of deifying almost every thing, and therefore would have this nature, forsooth, to be called a goddess too; yet does he declare it not to be properly such, but abusively only (viz. because it was no intellectual thing), as he saith the bodies of the sun, moon, and stars, supposed to be animated, were called gods too, they being the statues of Gods. This is the meaning of those words: Nature is a god or goddess, not as having godship properly belonging to it, but as the Divine bodies are called gods, because they are statues of the gods.

INTERPRETING THE PAGAN GODS[31]
¶ 20

Wherefore the truth of this whole business seems to be this, that the ancient Pagans did physiologize in their theology; and whether looking upon the whole world animated, as the supreme God, and consequently the several parts of it as his living members; or else, apprehending it at least to be a mirror, or visible image of the invisible Deity, and consequently all its several parts, and things of nature, but so many several manifestations of the Divine power and providence, they pretended, that all their devotion towards the Deity ought not to be huddled up in one general and confused acknowledgment of a supreme invisible Being, the creator and governor of

---

all; but that all the several manifestations of the Deity in the world, considered singly and apart by themselves, should be made so many distinct objects of their devout veneration. And, therefore, in order hereunto, did they speak of the things in nature, and the parts of the world, as persons,——and consequently as so many gods and goddesses; yet so, as that the intelligent might easily understand the meaning, that these were all really nothing else but so many several names and notions of that one Numen, divine force and power, which runs through the whole world, multiformly displaying itself therein.

For Emerson, however, Cudworth's chief significance was not so much his powerful attack against atheism or the rich gleanings from the ancients, to be found in all his works, but rather his valliant championing of the good life against the debauchery and atheism which followed in the wake of the seventeenth-century materialistic philosophies. In the inductive aspect of Hobbes' thinking, for example, the distinctions between right and wrong had been attributed to rational necessity and convenience rather than to divine revelations available to all men, and the senses alone were believed to provide all knowledge. Starting with the condition of nature (that is, with the condition of early man without social organization) Hobbes had assumed that each human being inevitably and normally waged war against all others in a selfish, competitive or cunning manner and that only as society progressed had men learned slowly to cooperate with others for mutual benefit. He, therefore, denied the existence in man of a mystical or supernatural moral quality (or a universal soul) that enabled all men to know the distinction between an objective good and evil. Nevertheless Hobbes spoke respectfully of the simple religion of the Gospels, but in his inability to demonstrate the existence of a universal morality, common to all men, he recommended that they accept Biblical truths by faith. The result of his ethical thinking in England and France, especially among the common people, who did not understand all the values of his thought or his fruitful inconsistencies, was the espousal of a philosophy of naturalism and atheistic fatalism against which the Cambridge Platonists launched a vigorous campaign. The chief note in the works of the Cambridge school was the belief in a spiritual universe that was present to every man.

In his *Treatise on Immutable Morality*,[32] published posthumously in 1731 by Edward Chandler, Bishop of Durham, Cudworth sought to show that the mind has many conceptions which, though occasioned or stimulated by sensible objects, are not cognizable by the senses but formed by a higher faculty. He believed that the universe had a spiritual constitution and that sense could reveal only appearance, whereas reality consisted in intelligible forms or ideas arising within the soul of man. Emerson's "The Present State of Ethical Philosophy," written shortly after his eighteenth birthday, expresses his early sympathies in rather strong language:[33]

---

[32] Usually found as an appendix to the *True Intellectual System of the Universe*, but not included in the 1820 edition of that work. For the volume which Emerson probably consulted, see footnote 3. All references to the *Treatise* in this chapter are made to volume II, pp. 361-497 of Cudworth's *The True Intellectual System etc.*, (1st American edn.) 2 vols., Andover & N.Y., 1837.

[33] From the MS. of the Bowdoin Prize Dissertation in Harvard College Library, folios 14-15. Cf. also *Ethical Philosophy*, pp. 56-57. Emerson may not have read much or any of Cudworth in college, but may have drawn his facts from encyclopedias or

An important controversy which has been much agitated among modern philosophers whether benevolence or selfishness be the ground of action arose chiefly from the malevolent spirit of Mr Hobbes, whose shrewd speculations discovered to society that all their relations were artificial and grotesque; and that nature which they had ignorantly judged to be so sublime and aspiring, would lead them to the character and circumstances of bears and tigers. This opinion that nature tends to savageness and stupidity is not true. For the impulse to exertion, which urges all our faculties to their highest possible degree, is very powerful, and prompts men to social intercourse where alone they have their widest range. We delight in every exertion of active moral power and exclaim against every retrograde step, and against sloth the antagonist vice as the mother of ignorance. Few men, probably, feel any inclination to perform the experiment of weakening the magnet; all prefer to see its power accumulating. The system of fanatic philosophy, which in the course of time was the result of these speculations of Mr Hobbes, and the accursed fruits of whose prevalence were abundantly reaped in France, sweeps away all the duties which we owe to others; this would elevate the ostrich to a higher rank on the scale of merit and wisdom than the man old and honourable whose parental affection dictates actions of wise and profound calculation. Dr Cudworth attacked the system of Hobbes in his Immutable Morality with ability and success, and modern opinion has concurred in his boldest positions. The fine remark of the eloquent Burke may be extended to moral nature. "Nature is never more truly herself than in her grandest forms; the Apollo of Belvidere is as much in nature as any figure from the pencil of Rembrandt, or any clown in the rustic revels of Teniers."

In his essay, Cudworth attacked Hobbes and Locke, vigorously declaring that "the soul is not a mere rasa tabula, a naked and passive thing, which has no innate furniture or activity of its own, nor any thing at all in it, but what was impressed upon it without; for if it were so, then there could not possibly be any such thing as moral good and evil, just and unjust."[34] The following excerpts will present his principal ideas. As might be expected from what has been said above, he draws heavily upon the Neo-Platonists.[35]

GOD——THE ETERNAL MIND[36]

¶ 21

Now the plain meaning of all this is nothing else, but that there is an eternal wisdom and knowledge in the world, necessarily existing, which was never made, and can never cease to be or be destroyed; or, which is all one, that there is an infinite eternal mind necessarily existing, that actually comprehends himself, the possibility of all things, and the verities clinging to them. In a word, that there is a God, or an omnipotent and omniscient being, necessarily existing, who therefore cannot destroy his own being or nature, that is, his infinite power and wisdom.

¶ 22

Just as when a thousand eyes look upon the sun at once, they all see the same individual object. Or as when a great crowd or throng of people hear one and the same orator speaking to them all, it is one and the same voice that is in the several ears of

---

from such a work as Dugald Stewart's *A General View of the Progress of Metaphysical, Ethical and Political Philosophy . . . In two Dissertations*, (2 vols.) Boston, [1817]-1822. See *Letters*, I, 125. Compare Emerson's opinion at the age of twenty (*Journals*, I, 379-380): "For Morals and Metaphysics, Cudworth and Locke may both be true, and every system of religion yet offered to man wholly false. To glowing hope, moreover, 't is alarming to see the full and regular series of animals from mites and worms up to man; yet he who has the same organization and a little more mind pretends to an insulated and extraordinary destiny to which his fellows of the stall and field are in no part admitted, nay are disdainfully excluded."

[34] *Intellectual System* (1837), II, 490.

[35] *Ibid.*, II, 424: "And thus Plotinus argues, when he endeavors to prove that the immediate τα νοητα, objects of knowledge and intellection, are not things without the mind acting upon it at a distance, but contained and comprehended within the mind itself."

[36] *Ibid.*, II, 475; 479.

all those several auditors; so in like manner, when innumerable created understandings direct themselves to the contemplation of the same universal and immutable truths, they do all of them but as it were listen to one and the same original voice of the eternal wisdom that is never silent; and the several conceptions of those truths in their minds are but like several echos of the same verba mentis of the divine intellect resounding in them.

HUMAN MINDS RELATED TO THE DIVINE MIND[37]

¶ 23

The mind being a kind of notional or representative world, as it were a diaphanous and crystalline sphere, in which the ideas and images of all things existing in the real universe may be reflected or represented. For as the mind of God which is the archetypal intellect, is that whereby he always actually comprehends himself, and his own fecundity, or the extent of his own infinite goodness and power; that is, the possibility of all things; so all created intellects being certain ectypal models, or derivative compendiums of the same; although they have not the actual ideas of all things, much less are the images or sculptures of all the several species of existent things fixed and engraven in a dead manner upon them; yet they have them all virtually and potentially comprehended in that one vis cognitrix, cognoscitive power, of the soul, which is a potential omniformity, whereby it is enabled as occasion serves and outward objects invite, gradually and successively to unfold and display itself in a vital manner, by framing intelligible ideas or conceptions within itself or whatsoever hath any entity or cogitability.

IDEAS NOT GAINED THROUGH SENSE[38]

¶ 24

That there are some ideas of the mind which were not stamped or imprinted upon it from the sensible objects without, and therefore must needs arise from the innate vigour and activity of the mind itself, is evident, in that there are, first, ideas of such things as neither are affections of bodies, nor could be imprinted or conveyed by any local motions, nor can be pictured at all by the fancy in any sensible colours; such are the ideas of wisdom, folly, prudence, imprudence, knowledge, ignorance, verity, falsity, virtue, vice, honesty, dishonesty, justice, injustice, volition, cogitation, nay, of sense itself, which is a species of cogitation, and which is not perceptible by any sense; and many other such like notions as include something of cogitation in them, or refer to cogitative beings only; which ideas must needs spring from the active power and innate fecundity of the mind itself, because the corporeal objects of sense can imprint no such things upon it. Secondly, in that there are many relative notions and ideas, attributed as well to corporeal as incorporeal things that proceed wholly from the activity of the mind comparing one thing with another. Such as are cause, effect, means, end, order, proportion, similitude, dissimilitude, equality, inequality, aptitude, inaptitude, symmetry, asymmetry, whole and part, genus and species, and the like.

UNITY OF NATURE PERCEIVED WITHIN[39]

¶ 25

The same is to be affirmed of that huge and vast automaton, which some will have to be an animal likewise, the visible world or material universe, commonly called κοσμος, cosmos or mundus, the world, from the beauty of it. Whether we mean thereby that one single vortex, to which our planetary earth belongs, or a system of as many vortices, as we see fixed stars in the heavens, their central suns and circumferential planets moving round about them respectively. Now sense looking round about, and making many particular views, sees now one fixed star, and then another; now the moon, then the sun; here a mountain, there a valley; at one time a river, at another a sea, particular vegetables and animals one after another. But it cannot sum up or unite all together, nor rise to any comprehensive idea of the whole at once, as it is one or many mechanical automatons, self-movers, most curiously and artificially framed of innumerable parts; in which there are all manner of logical scheses, relations,

[37] *Ibid.*, II, 426.
[38] *Ibid.*, II, 432.
[39] *Ibid.*, II, 441. Cf. *Nature*, 19.5ff.; 29.10ff.

possible offered to the mind, but all so fitly proportioned with such admirable symmetries and correspondencies in respect of one another and the whole, that they perfectly conspire into one most orderly and harmonious form.

THE BOOK OF NATURE[40]
¶ 26

But now, in the room of this artificial book in volumes, let us substitute the book of nature, the whole visible and material universe, printed all over with the passive characters and impressions of divine wisdom and goodness, but legible only to an intellectual eye; for to the sense both of man and brute, there appears nothing else in it but as in the other, so many inky scrawls, i.e. nothing but figures and colors; but the mind or intellect, which hath an inward and active participation of the same Divine Wisdom that made it; and being printed all over with the same archetypal seal, upon occasion of those sensible delineations represented to it, and taking notice of whatsoever is cognate to it, exerting its own inward activity from thence, will not have only a wonderful scene and large prospect of other thoughts laid open before it, and variety of knowledge, logical, mathematical, metaphysical, moral, displayed; but also clearly read the divine wisdom and goodness, in every page of this great volume, as it were written in large and legible characters.

RICH PERCEPTION DEPENDS MORE ON SOUL THAN SENSE[41]
¶ 27

Now there is yet a pulchritude of another kind; a more interior symmetry and harmony in the relations, proportions, aptitudes and correspondences of things to one another in the great mundane system, or vital machine of the universe, which is all musically and harmonically composed; for which cause the ancients made Pan, that is, nature to play upon an harp; but sense, which only passively perceives particular outward objects, doth here, like the brute, hear nothing but mere noise and sound and clatter, but no music or harmony at all; having no active principle and anticipation within itself to comprehend it by, and correspond or vitally sympathize with it; whereas the mind of a rational and intellectual being will be ravished and enthusiastically transported in the contemplation of it; and, of its own accord, dance to this pipe of Pan, nature's intellectual music and harmony.

BOOKS ARE FOR THE SCHOLAR'S IDLE TIME[42]
¶ 28

[S]cientifical knowledge is best acquired by the soul's abstraction from the outward objects of sense, and retiring into itself, that so it may the better attend to its own inward notions and ideas. And therefore it is many times observed, that over-much reading and hearing of other men's discourses, though learned and elaborate, doth not only distract the mind, but also debilitates the intellectual powers, and makes the mind passive and sluggish, by calling it too much outwards. For which cause that wise philosopher Socrates altogether shunned that dictating and dogmatical way of teaching used by the sophisters of that age, and chose rather an aporetical and obstetricious method; because knowledge was not to be poured into the soul like liquor, but rather to be invited and gently drawn forth from it; nor the mind so much to be filled therewith from without, like a vessel, as to be kindled and awakened.

---

[40] *Intellectual System* (1837), II, 447-448.
[41] *Ibid.*, II, 446. Cf. Wordsworth's "Peter Bell," Part I, stanza 12.
[42] *Intellectual System* (1837), II, 427. Cf. Emerson's "The American Scholar," *Works*, I, 91.

THE IDEALISM OF BISHOP BERKELEY[1]

"Idealism insists that the only world which is known to us is the world which appears in consciousness. Whether there is an external world corresponding, is a matter of surmise, but never of certainty."[2] Bishop George Berkeley (1685-1753), one of the outstanding exponents of this tradition, maintained that nothing exists except as it is perceived by the perceiving self or ego and that *esse est percipi.* He declared that he wished to deny not the validity of man's perceptions but only the existence of abstract matter, and he conveniently summarized his metaphysical opinions in *A Treatise Concerning the Principles of Human Knowledge,* part one of which appeared in 1710.[3] This work Emerson probably discovered for the first time in one of the philosophical courses at Harvard,[4] for it seems early to have been significant in shaping his transcendentalism:[5]

I know but one solution to my nature & relations, which I find in the remembering the joy with which in my boyhood I caught the first hint of the Berkleian philosophy, and which I certainly never lost sight of afterwards. There is a foolish man who goes up & down the country giving lectures on Electricity;—this one secret he has, to draw a spark out of every object, from desk, & lamp, & wooden log, & the farmer's blue frock, & by this he gets his living: for paupers & negroes will pay to see this celestial emanation from their own basket & their own body. Well, I was not an electrician, but an Idealist. I could see that there was a cause behind every stump & clod, & by the help of some fine words could make every old wagon & woodpile & stone wall oscillate a little & threaten to dance; nay, give me fair field,—& the Selectmen of Concord & the Reverend Doctor Poundmedown himself began to look unstable & vaporous. You saw me do my feat—it fell in with your own studies——and you would give me gold & pearls. Now there is this difference between the Electrician,—Mr Quimby——is his name?— (I never saw him)——and the Idealist, namely, that the spark is to that philosopher a toy, but the dance is to the Idealist terror & beauty, life & light. It is & it ought to be; & yet sometimes there will be a sinful empiric who loves exhibition too much. This Insight is so precious to society that where the least glimmer of it appears all men should befriend & protect it for its own sake.

In the succeeding pages will appear, first, some significant paragraphs from the *Principles of Human Knowledge* and, second, one of Emerson's short themes——possibly a college exercise——which is both an excellent summary of Berkeley's idealism and a useful introduction to chapter six of *Nature.*[6] By 1827, Emerson was convinced that the philosophy of the

[1] See *Encyclopædia of Religion and Ethics,* (ed. princ.), II, 524-529; also Harald Höffding, *A History of Modern Philosophy,* (tr. B. E. Meyer, 2 vols.) London, 1935, I, 414-423.

[2] See John Grier Hibben, *The Problems of Philosophy,* N. Y. &c., [1898], p. 109.

[3] Part one was published at Dublin. A revised edition appeared in London in 1734. A copy of the latter was owned by the Boston Library Society and seems to have been borrowed by Emerson for two weeks on Oct. 10, 1829. See vol. II of the present work.

[4] See the Harvard curriculum, set forth later in the present volume. In his *Ethical Philosophy,* written in his senior year, however, Emerson speaks of "the visionary schemes of Mr. Hume and Bishop Berkeley." Mary Moody Emerson expressed an indirect admiration for Berkeley in a letter of May 24, 1822, and probably encouraged R. W. E.'s study in idealism. See *Letters,* I, 116, footnote. There is evidence that she also feared at times that Berkeley was tainted with pantheism. See George Tolman, *Mary Moody Emerson,* ed. Edward W. Forbes, [Cambridge, Mass., 1929], p. 6.

[5] See *Letters,* II, 384-385.

[6] For Berkeley's influence on *Nature,* see 59.8 through page 67; 74.21——75.14; 76.14

Bishop of Cloyne could "never be got the better of."[7]

THERE IS NO PROOF THAT THE EXTERNAL WORLD EXISTS APART FROM THE HUMAN MIND AND INDEPENDENT OF A SPIRITUAL UNIVERSE[8]

¶ 1

Some truths there are so near and obvious to the mind, that a man need only open his eyes to see them. Such I take this important one to be, to wit, that all the choir of heaven and furniture of the earth, in a word all those bodies which compose the mighty frame of the world, have not any subsistence without a mind, that their being is to be perceived or known; that consequently so long as they are not actually perceived by me, or do not exist in my mind or that of any other created spirit, they must either have no existence at all, or else subsist in the mind of some eternal spirit: it being perfectly unintelligible, and involving all the absurdity of abstraction, to attribute to any single part of them an existence independent of a spirit. To be convinced of which, the reader need only reflect and try to separate in his own thoughts the being of a sensible thing from its being perceived.

MATTER IS A SHADOW——SPIRIT IS THE ONLY REAL SUBSTANCE[9]

¶ 2

From what has been said, it follows, there is not any other substance than *spirit*, or that which perceives. But for the fuller proof of this point, let it be considered, the sensible qualities are colour, figure, motion, smell, taste, and such like, that is, the ideas perceived by sense. Now for an idea to exist in an unperceiving thing, is a manifest contradiction; for to have an idea is all one as to perceive: that therefore wherein colour, figure, and the like qualities exist, must perceive them; hence it is clear there can be no unthinking substance or *substratum* of those ideas.

EVEN IF MATTER WERE REAL, OUR SENSES COULD NOT PROVE THAT FACT[10]

¶ 3

But though it were possible that solid, figured, moveable substances may exist without the mind, corresponding to the ideas we have of bodies, yet how is it possible for us to know this? Either we must know it by sense, or by reason. As for our senses, by them we have the knowledge only of our sensations, ideas, or those things that are immediately perceived by sense, call them what you will: but they do not inform us that things exist without the mind, or unperceived, like to those which are perceived. This the materialists[11] themselves acknowledge. It remains therefore that if we have any knowledge at all of external things, it must be by reason, inferring their existence from what is immediately perceived by sense. But what reason can induce us to believe the existence of bodies without the mind from what we perceive, since the very patrons of matter themselves do not pretend there is any necessary connexion betwixt them and our ideas? I say it is granted on all hands (and what happens in dreams,[12]

——78.22; 79.14ff.; 82.8ff. See also 72.13.

[7] See *Journals*, II, 165. Cf. S. T. Coleridge, *Specimens of Table Talk*, (2 vols.), London, 1835, I, 88: "Berkeley can only be confuted, or answered, by one sentence. . . . His premise granted, the deduction is a chain of adamant." See Emerson's playing with Berkeleian ideas in his letter to Charles (Oct. 8, 1827) in *Letters*, I, 214. In his essay, "Plutarch" (1871), he called the ancient moralist a pronounced idealist who, like Bishop Berkeley, did not hesitate to say that matter was itself privation. (*Works*, X, 307). See also *Letters*, I, lvi-lvii. A convenient analysis of Berkeley's philosophy appears in Gérando, *Histoire* (1802), I, 448-456, a volume which Emerson was reading in January, 1830. See also footnote 3, *supra*.

[8] This and the following excerpts are drawn from George Berkeley's "A Treatise Concerning the Principles of Human Knowledge," in his *Works* (3 vols.), London, 1820, vol. I, pp. 1-100. I shall indicate only the section numbers which appear in the body of this essay. See section 6. All titles are supplied by the present editor.

[9] *Ibid.*, section 7.

[10] *Ibid.*, section 18 and the first part of 20. Cf. *Nature*, 59.8——60.15.

[11] Berkeley was referring to the school of Thomas Hobbes. See the *Encyclopædia of Religion and Ethics* (ed. princ.), VIII, 488-492, for a discussion of 17th- and 18th-century materialism.

[12] See the first main subdivision of Emerson's theme at the end of this chapter.

frenzies, and the like, puts it beyond dispute), that it is possible we might be affected with all the ideas we have now, though no bodies existed without resembling them. Hence it is evident the supposition of external bodies is not necessary for the producing our ideas: since it is granted they are produced sometimes, and might possibly be produced always, in the same order we see them in at present, without their concurrence. . . . In short, if there were external bodies, it is impossible we should ever come to know it; and if there were not, we might have the very same reasons to think there were that we have now.

IDEAS ARE CAUSED NOT BY OBJECTS WITHOUT BUT BY THE SPIRIT BEHIND ALL CREATION[13]

¶ 4

We perceive a continual succession of ideas, some are anew excited, others are changed or totally disappear. There is therefore some cause of these ideas whereon they depend, and which produces and changes them. That this cause cannot be any quality or idea, or combination of ideas, is clear from the preceding section.[14] It must therefore be a substance; but it has been shewn that there is no corporeal or material substance: it remains therefore that the cause of ideas is an incorporeal active substance or spirit.

MY IDEAS ARE NOT PRODUCED BY MY OWN, BUT BY A HIGHER WILL[15]

¶ 5

But whatever power I may have over my own thoughts, I find the ideas actually perceived by sense have not a like dependance on my will. When in broad day-light I open my eyes, it is not in my power to choose whether I shall see or no, or to determine what particular objects shall present themselves to my view: and so likewise as to the hearing and other senses, the ideas imprinted on them are not creatures of my will. There is therefore some other will or spirit that produces them.

THE ORDER AND COHERENCE OF NATURE'S LAWS POINT TO DIVINE WISDOM——EXPERIENCE TEACHES US TO VALUE THE NATURAL ORDER[16]

¶ 6

The ideas of sense are more strong, lively, and distinct than those of the imagination; they have likewise a steadiness, order and coherence, and are not excited at random, as those which are the effects of human wills often are, but in a regular train or series, the admirable connexion whereof sufficiently testifies the wisdom and benevolence of its Author. Now the set rules or established methods, wherein the mind we depend on excites in us the ideas of sense, are called the *laws of nature:* and these we learn by experience, which teaches us that such and such ideas are attended with such and such other ideas, in the ordinary course of things.

THE LAWS OF NATURE ARE DEPENDABLE——THEY DISCIPLINE US[17]

¶ 7

This gives us a sort of foresight, which enables us to regulate our actions for the benefit of life. And without this we should be eternally at a loss: we could not know how to act any thing that might procure us the least pleasure, or remove the least pain of sense. That food nourishes, sleep refreshes, and fire warms us; and to sow in the seed-time is the way to reap in the harvest, and, in general, that to obtain such or such ends, such or such means are conducive, all this we know, not by discovering any necessary connexion between our ideas, but only by the observation of the settled laws of nature, without which we should be all in uncertainty and confusion, and a grown man no more know how to manage himself in the affairs of life, than an infant just born.

---

[13] Berkeley, *Human Knowledge,* section 26.
[14] *I.e.,* section 25.
[15] Berkeley, *Human Knowledge,* section 29.
[16] *Ibid.,* section 30.
[17] *Ibid.,* section 31. Cf. *Nature,* 60.16——61.11.

FOR ALL PRACTICAL PURPOSES THE NATURAL ORDER MAY BE TREATED AS REAL[18]

¶ 8

If any man thinks this detracts from the existence or reality of things, he is very far from understanding what hath been premised in the plainest terms I could think of. Take here an abstract of what has been said. There are spiritual substances, minds, or human souls, which will or excite ideas in themselves at pleasure: but these are faint, weak, and unsteady, in respect of others they perceive by sense, which being impressed upon them according to certain rules or laws of nature, speak themselves the effects of a mind more powerful and wise than human spirits. These latter are said to have more *reality* in them than the former: by which is meant that they are more affecting, orderly, and distinct, and that they are not fictions of the mind perceiving them. And in this sense, the sun that I see by day is the real sun, and that which I imagine by night is the idea of the former. In the sense here given of *reality*, it is evident that every vegetable, star, mineral, and in general each part of the mundane system, is as much a *real being* by our principles as by any other. Whether others mean any thing by the term *reality*, different from what I do, I entreat them to look into their own thoughts and see.

ONE MUST TRUST ONE'S SENSES[19]

¶ 9

But say what we can, some one perhaps may be apt to reply, he will still believe his senses, and never suffer any arguments, how plausible soever, to prevail over the certainty of them. Be it so, assert the evidence of sense as high as you please, we are willing to do the same. That what I see, hear, and feel, doth exist, that is to say, is perceived by me, I no more doubt than I do of my own being. But I do not see how the testimony of sense can be alleged, as a proof of the existence of any thing, which is not perceived by sense. We are not for having any man turn *sceptic*, and disbelieve his senses; on the contrary we give them all the stress and assurance imaginable; nor are there any principles more opposite to scepticism, than those we have laid down, as shall be hereafter clearly shewn.

THE TESTIMONY OF DREAMS[20]

¶ 10

It will be objected, that we see things actually without or at a distance from us, and which consequently do not exist in the mind, it being absurd that those things which are seen at the distance of several miles, should be as near to us as our own thoughts. In answer to this, I desire it may be considered, that in a dream we do oft perceive things as existing at a great distance off, and yet for all that, those things are acknowledged to have their existence only in the mind.

THE MIND IS RESPONSIBLE FOR THE FORMS AND QUALITIES BELIEVED TO EXIST IN THE EXTERNAL WORLD[21]

¶ 11

The reason . . . that any particular body seems to be of a finite magnitude, or exhibits only a finite number of parts to sense, is, not because it contains no more, since in itself it contains an infinite number of parts, but because the sense is not acute enough to discern them. In proportion therefore as the sense is rendered more acute, it perceives a greater number of parts in the object; that is, the object appears greater, and its figure varies, those parts in its extremities which were before unperceivable, appearing now to bound it in very different lines and angles from those perceived by an obtuser sense. And at length, after various changes of size and shape, when the sense becomes infinitely acute, the body shall seem infinite. During all which there is no alteration in the body, but only in the sense. Each body therefore considered in itself, is infinitely extended, and consequently void of all shape or figure. From which it follows, that though we should grant the existence of matter to be ever so

---

[18] Berkeley, *Human Knowledge*, section 36. Cf. *Nature*, 60.16——61.11.

[19] *Ibid.*, section 40.

[20] *Ibid.*, section 42.

[21] *Ibid.*, section 47. Cf. *Nature*, pp. 62-67.

certain, yet it is withal as certain the materialists themselves are by their own principles forced to acknowledge, that neither the particular bodies perceived by sense, nor any thing like them, exists without the mind. Matter, I say, and each particle thereof, is according to them infinite and shapeless, and it is the mind that frames all that variety of bodies which compose the visible world, any one whereof does not exist longer than it is perceived.

ATHEISM IS BOUND UP WITH A BELIEF IN THE EXISTENCE OF MATTER[22]

¶ 12

For as we have shewn the doctrine of matter or corporeal substance, to have been the main pillar and support of scepticism, so likewise upon the same foundation have been raised all the impious schemes of Atheism and irreligion. Nay, so great a difficulty hath it been thought, to conceive matter produced out of nothing, that the most celebrated among the ancient philosophers, even of these who maintained the being of a God, have thought matter to be uncreated, and coeternal with him. How great a friend material substance hath been to Atheists in all ages, were needless to relate. All their monstrous systems have so visible and necessary a dependence on it, that when this corner-stone is once removed, the whole fabric cannot choose but fall to the ground; insomuch that it is no longer worth while to bestow a particular consideration on the absurdities of every wretched sect of Atheists.

EMPIRICAL SCIENCE IS APT TO CLOUD THE SIGHT[23]

¶ 13

As in reading other books, a wise man will choose to fix his thoughts on the sense and apply it to use, rather than lay them out in grammatical remarks on the language; so in perusing the volume of nature, it seems beneath the dignity of the mind to affect an exactness in reducing each particular phenomenon to general rules, or shewing how it follows from them. We should propose to ourselves nobler views, such as to recreate and exalt the mind, with a prospect of the beauty, order, extent, and variety, of natural things: hence, by proper inferences, to enlarge our notions of the grandeur, wisdom, and beneficence, of the Creator: and lastly, to make several parts of the creation, so far as in us lies, subservient to the ends they were designed for; God's glory, and the sustentation and comfort of ourselves and fellow-creatures.

THROUGHOUT NATURE, SPIRIT IS PRESENT[24]

¶ 14

But though there be some things which convince us, human agents are concerned in producing them; yet it is evident to every one, that those things which are called the works of nature, that is, the far greater part of the ideas or sensations perceived by us, are not produced by, or dependent on the wills of men. There is therefore some other Spirit that causes them, since it is repugnant that they should subsist by themselves. . . . I say if we consider all these things, and at the same time attend to the meaning and import of the attributes, one, eternal, infinitely wise, good and perfect, we shall clearly perceive that they belong to the aforesaid Spirit, *who works all in all*, and *by whom all things consist*.

NATURE ALWAYS SPEAKS OF SPIRIT AND IS ITSELF ONLY A PERPETUAL EFFECT[25]

¶ 15

But you will say, hath nature no share in the production of natural things, and must they be all ascribed to the immediate and sole operation of God; I answer, if by *nature* is meant only the visible *series* of effects, or sensations imprinted on our minds according to certain fixed and general laws; then it is plain, that nature taken in this sense cannot produce any thing at all. But if by *nature* is meant some being distinct from God, as well as from the laws of nature and things perceived by sense, I must confess that word is to me an empty sound, without any intelligible meaning annexed

---

[22] Berkeley, *Human Knowledge*, section 92.
[23] *Ibid.*, section 109. Cf. *Nature*, 82.8ff.
[24] *Ibid.*, section 146. Cf. *Nature*, 79.14ff.
[25] Berkeley, *Human Knowledge*, section 150. Cf. *Nature*, 76.14——77.15; 61.19——62.22.

to it. Nature in this acceptation is a vain chimera introduced by those heathens, who had not just notions of the omnipresence and infinite perfection of God.

THE SOUL SHOULD AVOID A TOO TRIVIAL STUDY OF NATURE[26]

¶ 16

As for the mixture of pain or uneasiness which is in the world, pursuant to the general laws of nature, and the actions of finite imperfect spirits: this, in the state we are in at present, is indispensably necessary to our well-being. But our prospects are too narrow: we take, for instance, the idea of some one particular pain into our thoughts, and account it *evil;* whereas if we enlarge our view, so as to comprehend the various ends, connexions, and dependences of things, on what occasions and in what proportions we are affected with pain and pleasure, the nature of human freedom, and the design with which we are put into the world; we shall be forced to acknowledge that those particular things, which considered in themselves appear to be *evil,* have the nature of *good,* when considered as linked with the whole system of beings.

IDEAL THEORY[27]

By RALPH WALDO EMERSON

It is an interesting inquiry, to examine our knowledge of material world. Doubts have been started which affect its existence.

In the first place what are the foundations of our belief of its existence. These are the evidence of our senses   The eye informs us of colour & extension of the beauty & proportions of the earth & the planets about us   The ear informs us of sound produced by concussions which the eye beholds   The *smelling* and tasting senses unite with the eye & ear and their evidence is in perfect harmony with the first. The sense of touch the most substantial & infallible of all ascertains the correctness of the sensations produced by the rest. But beside these we have no means of determining the existence of things. Shut up the organs of the senses successively & this will be proved. Take away sight smell hearing tasting touch and you leave a blank which we cannot concieve. If therefore it be proved possible that the senses can be decieved your knowledge is entirely unsettled   you have no further proof that what appears to exist does exist.

     I   The senses may be shut up and your perceptions continue
     II   There is no reason why your senses should not be decieved

     I   Now that the senses may be entirely decieved or rather that they may not operate at all is evident from dreams in which we firmly believe that we see things which in fact we do not see and are delighted or displeased quite as powerfully as when awake by scenes & sounds & faces, which, though apparently present to us, are in fact a thousand miles off. Sometimes in a dream you think for a moment that you are dreaming & then become unconscious that you are not awake. Are you sure that you are not dreaming now,[27a] that your senses are not shut up and that those objects which seem to affect them are not separated by a great gulf from yourself?

     II   What are these senses upon which you depend thus absolutely, and in what manner are they affected? They are only powers of giving the mind information of certain different qualities of external objects. They do not themselves percieve those properties of which they give us knowledge   The organs of the eye do not recieve pleasure from the pictures which they recieve any more than the glass sees through which we look at an object. It is the mind alone which is affected. But what we wish

------

[26] Berkeley, *Human Knowledge,* section 153. Cf. *Nature,* 74.21——75.14.
[27] From *Letters,* VI, 337-338. Professor Rusk dates the "Undated Prose Fragments" (see page 333) as belonging to 1821-1822.
[27a] Cf. *Nature,* 78.6-8.

to say is that the senses cannot ascertain their own truth or their relation to the qualities which so affect them and of which they inform the mind. It is manifest, then that we have no knowledge of the substances which affect the senses in any other manner than as they affect them. Therefore if it be possible to affect them in any other manner than by matter there is no need of the universe to account for our perceptions.

Now it is plainly possible for the Deity to give the air or any subtle fluid whatever the property of affecting certain organs in such & such a manner. Perhaps the mind is at rest in a point of infinite space; for the sake of perspicuity let us suppose encompassed with a subtle fluid which the Deity has established that an impulse upon one organ shall give the idea of touch upon another of sight and these impulses following certain laws will supersede the necessity of any other creation   Perhaps there are a multitude of minds in a corner of space deeming themselves surrounded with bodies and a vast universe which exist alone in their own imaginations. Perhaps space is peopled with these little assemblies of disembodied dreamers. I do not know that it sets aside any system of morals, any one bond of moral obligation any faith or doctrine of a Christian scheme; if the delusion be perfect & consistent it may be delusion still.

In Emerson's first sermon (October 15, 1826) Berkeley's philosophical idealism yielded to a Christian idealism that was strongly permeated with ethical teaching as the following paragraphs will prove:

It has been one of the best uses of the Christian religion to teach, that the world of spirits is more certain and stable than the material universe. Every thoughtful man has felt that there was a more awful reality to thought and feeling, than to the infinite panorama of nature around him. The world he has found indeed consistent and uniform enough throughout the mixed sensations of thirty or forty years, but it seems to him at times, when the intellect is invigorated, to ebb from him, like a sea, and to leave nothing permanent but thought. Nevertheless it is a truth not easily nor early acquired, and the prejudice that assigns greater fixture and certainty to the material world is a source of great practical error.[28]

Is it not outside shews, the pleasures of appetite, or at best of pride; is it not bread and wine and dress and our houses and our furniture, that give the law to the great mass of actions and words? This is the great error which the strong feeling of the reality of things unseen must correct. It is time greater force should be given to the statement of this doctrine; it is time men should be instructed that their inward is more valuable than their outward estate; that thoughts and passions, even those to which no language is ever given, are not fugitive undefined shadows, born in a moment, and in a moment blotted from the soul, but are so many integral parts of the imperishable universe of morals.[29]

On October 27, 1830, he observed that Idealism seemed to be a preparation for moral living.[30] Echoing Coleridge,[31] he wrote on December 29, 1834:[32]

Excite the soul, and it becomes suddenly virtuous. Touch the deep heart, and all these listless, stingy. beef-eating bystanders will see the dignity of a sentiment; will say, This is good, and all I have I will give for that. Excite the soul, and the weather and the town and your condition in the world all disappear; the world itself loses its solidity, nothing remains but the soul and the Divine Presence in which it lives. Youth and age are indifferent in this presence.

---

[28] See *Y E S*, 1-2.
[29] See *Y E S*, 2-3.
[32] *Journals*, III, 425. Cf. *Nature*, 13.2-18; 62.4-22; 79.8ff.
[30] *Journals*, II, 335-336.
[31] See ¶s. 237-238 in next chapter.

Beginning in January, 1835, and continuing until the publication of *Nature* (September, 1836) the Ideal Theory continued to challenge his thinking and to show a decided Neo-Platonic and Coleridgean[33] direction:

There is an elevation of thought from which things venerable become less, because we are in the presence of their Source. When we catch one clear glimpse of the moral harmonies which accomplish themselves throughout the everlasting Now and throughout the omnipresent Here, how impertinent seem the controversies of theologians. God is before us, and they are wrangling about dead gods.[34]

The dreams of an idealist have a poetic integrity and truth. Their extravagance from nature is yet within a higher nature, and terrible hints are thrown to him out of a quite unknown intelligence. I have been startled two or three times by the justice as well as the significance of the intimations of this phantasmagoria. Once or twice the conscious fetters of the Spirit have been unlocked and a freer utterance seemed attained.[35]

Why must always the philosopher mince his words and fatigue us with explanation? He speaks from the Reason, and being, of course, contradicted word for word by the Understanding, he stops like a cog-wheel at every notch to explain. Let him say, *I idealize*, and let that be once for all; or, *I sensualize*, and then the Rationalist may stop his ears. Empedocles said bravely, "I am God; I am immortal; I contemn human affairs"; and all men hated him.[36]

The ideal philosophy is much more akin to virtue than to vice. When the mountains begin to look unreal, the soul is in a high state, yet in an action of justice or charity things look solid again.[37]

Idealism is not so much prejudiced by danger as by inconvenience. In our speculative habits we sometimes expect that the too solid earth will melt. Then we cross the ocean sweltering, seasick, reeling, week after week, with tar, harness-tub, and bilge, and, as an ingenious friend says, it is carrying the joke too far.[38]

We all know how life is made up; . . . [trifles] eat up the hours. How then is any acquisition, how is any great deed or wise and beautiful work possible? Let it enhance the praise of Milton, Shakspear and Laplace. These oppress and spitefully tyrannize over me because I am in Idealist.[39]

The book is always dear which has made us for moments idealists. That which can dissipate this block of earth into shining ether is genius. I have no hatred to the round earth and its gray mountains. I see well enough the sand-hill opposite my window. I see with as much pleasure as another a field of corn or a rich pasture, whilst I dispute their absolute being. Their phenomenal being I no more dispute than I do my own. I do not dispute, but point out the just way of viewing them. Religion makes us idealists. Any strong passion does.[40]

[G]rant us the Ideal theory, and the universe is solved. Otherwise, the moment a man discovers that he has aims which his faculties cannot answer, the world becomes a riddle. Yet Piety restores him to Health.[41]

Is the pretension of the Ideal Theory enormous? Every possible statement of the connexion between the world and you involves pretensions as enormous.[42]

---

[33] See ¶s. 275ff. in next chapter.
[34] *Journals*, III, 433-434 (Jan. 8, 1835). Cf. *Nature*, 74.13-14; 5.2ff.; 75.1ff.
[35] *Journals*, III, 463 (Mar. 31, 1835).
[36] *Journals*, III, 467 (Apr. 16, 1835). Cf. *Nature*, 65.3-10. See next chapter, ¶s. 1-56.
[37] *Journals*, III, 486 (May 30, 1835). Cf. *Nature*, 62.15-19.
[38] *Journals*, III, 495 (June 24, 1835). See *Hamlet*, I.ii.129.
[39] *Journals*, III, 562 (Oct. 22, 1835).
[40] *Journals*, IV, 12 (Feb. 24, 1836). Cf. *Nature*, 60.16—61.21. See next chapter, ¶s. 59ff., 122a, 126, 237-238.
[41] *Journals*, IV, 14 (Feb. 24, 1836).   [42] *Journals*, IV, 67 (June 14, 1836).

In *Nature* (1836), he devoted chapter VI to a thorough discussion of "Idealism," but in the following chapter, "Spirit," confessed that the Ideal Theory, though indispensable, was defective on the side of Nature. He wished, however, to let it stand as a "useful introductory hypothesis, serving to apprize us of the eternal distinction between the soul and the world."[43] The best summary of Emerson's thought and experience in the Ideal philosophy seems to be the following paragraph from "Circles," published in 1841:

> There are degrees in idealism. We learn first to play with it academically, as the magnet was once a toy. Then we see in the heyday of youth and poetry that it may be true . . . in gleams and fragments. Then its countenance waxes stern and grand, and we see that it must be true. It now shows itself ethical and practical. We learn that God is; that he is in me; and that all things are shadows of him. The idealism of Berkeley is only a crude statement of the idealism of Jesus, and that again is a crude statement of the fact that all nature is the rapid efflux of goodness executing and organizing itself.

---

[43] See *Nature*, 79.2-4.

EMERSON'S COLERIDGE IN REVIEW

Nothing would facilitate or stimulate research in English and American authors of the nineteenth century so much as a complete and well-documented edition of Coleridge's prose works in chronological order, equipped with analyses, notes, indexes and concordances. Until such a scholarly apparatus exists, we shall remain, as at present, vague about his real influence on contemporaries and successors, for notwithstanding his clear style and careful definitions, he has never easily divulged his riches. President Marsh in his "Introduction" to the *Aids to Reflection* (1829) was, doubtless, correct in putting the blame largely upon the reader, who all too often expects to read *as he runs* and who comes to Coleridge with little or no knowledge of philosophy or English theology. *The Friend*, the *Aids*, the *Statesman's Manual*, *Biographia Literaria*, and *Church and State* deserve to be better known, and they will reveal "hands and feet" when they are read, reread and studied without haste. Evidence that they are usually ignored altogether can be found in most dictionaries of quotations, which give borrowers credit for sentences and phrases which they have taken from him.

Emerson's philosophy deepened greatly between 1825 and 1836, because Coleridge's volumes were always on his working table. He used them throughout the year as inspiration for Sunday sermons, as stimulation for daily prose paragraphs in his blotting books, and as much-needed encouragement for a faith sorely tried during a most troublous and difficult decade. The ideas of no other author appear so frequently in the pages of the early *Journals*——a fact that should long ago have suggested the need for a detailed study, because, indeed, Coleridge is pre-eminent among the teachers of Emerson. This chapter and the next two, however, are in no sense intended as definitive. They are merely to suggest the broad outlines of the intellectual relationship between the two thinkers, and to indicate possibilities for extended research. On the basis of Emerson's letters, journals and published writings, I have selected and numbered specimen portions of Coleridge's prose works which, with a few exceptions to be indicated, Emerson studied more or less in detail before 1836. The headings and footnotes have been added the more quickly to call attention to content and context, but they are not intended as substitutes for the paragraphs themselves.

THE DISTINCTION BETWEEN THE UNDERSTANDING AND THE REASON

¶ 1

UNDERSTANDING

1) Understanding is discursive.

2) The Understanding in all its judgments refers to some other Faculty as its ultimate authority.

3) Understanding is the Faculty of *Reflection*.

REASON

1) Reason is fixed.

2) The Reason in all its decisions appeals to itself, as the ground and *substance* of their truth. (*Hebrews* vi. v. 13).

3) Reason [is the faculty] of Contemplation. Reason indeed is far nearer to SENSE than to Understanding: for Reason (says our great HOOKER) is a direct Aspect of Truth, an inward Beholding, having a similar relation to the Intelligible or Spiritual, as SENSE has to the Material or Phenomenal.

The Result is, that neither falls under the definition of the other. They differ *in kind*:[1] and had my object been confined to the establishment of this fact, the preceding Columns would have superseded all further disquisition.[2]

REASON IS THE SOURCE OF TRUTHS THAT ARE THEIR OWN EVIDENCE——IT HAS TWO FUNCTIONS——IN REFERENCE TO ABSTRACT TRUTH, IT IS "SPECULATIVE REASON"——IN REFERENCE TO MORAL TRUTH, IT IS "PRACTICAL REASON," AND AS SUCH COMPREHENDS THE WILL, THE CONSCIENCE AND THE MORAL BEING——AS RESPECTS THEIR REASON, ALL MEN ARE EQUAL——FROM THE PRACTICAL POINT OF VIEW, HOWEVER, MEN DO POSSESS REASON IN VARYING DEGREES——COLERIDGE APPEARS THEN TO CONTRADICT HIMSELF BY SAYING THAT REASON IS EITHER WHOLLY PRESENT OR WHOLLY ABSENT——REASON DEMANDS FREEDOM FOR MAN——CONSCIENCE REQUIRES THAT HE OBEY THE REASON——IN ITS HIGHEST SENSE, REASON IS BEING——MEANING OF "WE POSSESS REASON"——IT DOES NOT BELONG TO US, BUT WE ARE ITS ——REASON IS THE "IMMEDIATE" IN EVERY MAN, BUT IT DOES NOT IN EVERY MAN RISE INTO CONSCIOUSNESS——REASON INCLUDES SENSE, UNDERSTANDING AND IMAGINATION WITHIN ITSELF, THOUGH IS NONE OF THEM——EACH INDIVIDUAL MUST FIND IT FOR HIMSELF——IT DWELLS IN US ONLY AS WE DWELL IN IT——REASON IS THE SCIENCE OF THE UNIVERSAL——REASON AND RELIGION ARE APPLICATIONS OF THE SAME POWER——BY REASON WE BECOME POSSESSED OF PRINCIPLES——GOD, SOUL, AND ETERNAL TRUTH ARE REASON——CONSCIOUS SELF-KNOWLEDGE IS REASON——REASON BRINGS UNITY INTO OUR CONCEPTIONS AND SEVERAL KNOWLEDGES——IT ASSUMES "THE ONE" AS GROUND OF ALL EXISTENCE

¶ 2

Reason is the Power of universal and necessary Convictions, the Source and Substance of Truths above Sense, and having their evidence in themselves. Its presence is always marked by the *necessity* of the position affirmed: this necessity being *conditional*, when a truth of Reason is applied to Facts of Experience or to the rules and maxims of the Understanding, but *absolute*, when the subject matter is itself the growth or offspring of the Reason. Hence arises a distinction in the Reason itself, derived from the different mode of applying it, and from the objects to which it is directed: according as we consider one and the same gift, now as the ground of formal principles, and now as the origin of *ideas*. Contemplated distinctively in reference to *formal* (or abstract) truth, it is the *speculative* Reason; but in reference to *actual* (or moral) truth, as the fountain of ideas and the *Light* of the Conscience, we name it the *practical* Reason.[3]

¶ 3

But if not the abstract or speculative Reason, and yet a reason there must be in order to a rational Belief—then it must be the *Practical* Reason of Man, comprehending the Will, the Conscience, the Moral Being with its inseparable Interests and Affections—that Reason, namely, which is the Organ of *Wisdom*, and (as far as Man is concerned) the Source of living and actual Truths.[4]

¶ 4

In respect of their reason all men are equal. The measure of the understanding and of all other faculties of man, is different in different persons: but reason is not susceptible of degree. For since it merely decides whether any given thought or action is or is not in contradiction with the rest, there can be no reason better, or more reason, than another.[5]

---

[1] This important distinction is discussed in most of Coleridge's prose works, and I treat it here separately. The student should remember that Emerson found a somewhat similar collection of excerpts on this theme in the extensive notes and appendices of President Marsh's edition of the *Aids*, Burlington, 1829. Marsh drew from volumes not easily obtainable in America and thus provided the reading public with a rich survey of all Coleridge's principal works in advance of American editions.

[2] *Aids* (1829), 142.

[3] *Aids* (1829), 137. For some "necessary" truths, see *Journals*, II, 357-358. See *Nature*, 74.10.

[4] *Aids* (1829), 115.   [5] *Works* (Shedd), II, 176.

¶ 5

Christianity is especially differenced from all other religions by being grounded on facts which all men alike have the same means of ascertaining with equal facility, and which no man can ascertain for another. Each person must be herein querist and respondent to himself ... Am I at one with God, and is my will concentric with that holy power, which is at once the constitutive will and the supreme reason of the universe?[5a]

¶ 6

[A]ll men have not only Reason equally, but likewise all the materials on which the reason, considered as *Conscience*, is to work. But when we pass out of ourselves, and speak, not exclusively of the *agent as meaning* well or ill, but of the action in its consequences, then of course experience is required, judgment in making use of it, and all those other qualities of the mind which are so differently dispensed to different persons, both by nature and education. And though *the reason itself* is the same in all men, yet the means of exercising it, and the materials (i.e. the facts and Ideas) on which it is exercised, being possessed in very different degrees by different persons, the *practical Result* is, of course, equally different——and the whole ground work of Rousseau's Philosophy ends in a mere Nothingism.[6]

¶ 7

Observe, the understanding may be deranged, weakened, or perverted; but the reason is either lost or not lost, that is, wholly present or wholly absent.[7]

¶ 8

Reason! best and holiest gift of God and bond of union with the giver;——the high title by which the majesty of man claims precedence above all other living creatures; ——mysterious faculty, the mother of conscience, of language, of tears, and of smiles; ——calm and incorruptible legislator of the soul, without whom all its other powers would 'meet in mere oppugnancy;'[8]——sole principle of permanence amid endless change,——in a world of discordant appetites and imagined self-interests the one only common measure.[9]

¶ 9

Thrice blessed faculty of reason! all other gifts, though goodly and of celestial origin, health, strength, talents, all the powers and all the means of enjoyment, seem dispensed by chance or sullen caprice;——thou alone, more than even the sunshine, more than the common air, art given to all men, and to every man alike. To thee, who being one art the same in all, we owe the privilege, that of all we can become one, a living whole,——that we have a country. Who then shall dare prescribe a law of moral action for any rational being, which does not flow immediately from that reason, which is the fountain of all morality? Or how without breach of conscience can we limit or coerce the powers of a free agent, except by coincidence with that law in his own mind, which is at once the cause, the condition, and the measure of his free agency? Man must be free; or to what purpose was he made a spirit of reason, and not a machine of instinct? Man must obey; or wherefore has he a conscience? The powers, which create this difficulty, contain its solution likewise: for their service is perfect freedom. And whatever law or system of law compels any other service, disennobles our nature, leagues itself with the animal against the god-like, kills in us the very principle of joyous well-doing, and fights against humanity.[10]

¶ 10

Reason may or rather must be used in two different yet correlative senses, which are nevertheless in some measure reunited by a third. In its highest sense, and which is the ground and source of the rest, reason is being, the Supreme Being contemplated objectively, and in abstraction from the personality. The Word or Logos is life, and communicates life; is light and communicates light. Now this light contemplated *in abstracto* is reason. Again as constituents of reason we necessarily contemplate unity and distinctity. Now the latter as the polar opposite to the former implies plurality; therefore I use the plural, distinctities, and say, that the distinctities considered apart from the unity are the ideas, and reason is the ground and source of ideas. This is the first and absolute sense.[11]

[5a] *Works* (Shedd), I, 455. Cf. *Nature*, 43.3-4. See ¶ 252 *infra*.
[6] *Aids* (1829), notes, 310-311. Also *Works* (Shedd), II, 148.
[7] *Works* (Shedd), II, 142. Also *Aids* (1829), notes, 306.
[8] *Troilus and Cressida*, I.iii.109.
[9] *Works* (Shedd), II, 176.
[10] *Works* (Shedd), II, 176-177.
[11] *Works* (Shedd), I, 460 fn.

¶ 11

The second sense comes when we speak of ourselves as possessing reason; and this we can no otherwise define than as the capability with which God had endowed man of beholding, or being conscious of, the divine light. But this very capability is itself that light, not as the divine light, but as the life or indwelling of the living Word, which is our light; that is, a life whereby we are capable of the light, and by which the light is present to us, as a being which we may call ours, but which I can not call mine: for it is the life that we individualize, while the light, as its correlative opposite, remains universal.[12]

¶ 12

"While we reflect on our own idea of Reason, we know that our own souls are not it, but only partake of it; and that we have it κατα μεθεξιν and not κατ' ουσιην. Neither can it be called a Faculty, but far rather a Light, which we enjoy, but the Source of which is not in ourselves, nor rightly, by any individual, to be denominated *mine*."[13]

¶ 13

It can not in strict language be called a faculty, much less a personal property, of any human mind. He, with whom it is present, can as little appropriate it, whether totally or by partition, as he can claim ownership in the breathing air or make an inclosure in the cope of heaven.[14]

¶ 14

On the IMMEDIATE, which dwells in every man, and on the original intuition, or absolute affirmation of it, (which is likewise in every man, but does not in every man rise into consciousness), all the *certainty* of our knowledge depends; and this becomes intelligible to no man by the ministry of mere words from without. The medium, by which spirits understand each other, is not the surrounding air; but the *freedom* which they possess in common, as the common ethereal element of their being, the tremulous reciprocations of which propagate themselves even to the inmost of the soul. Where the spirit of man is not *filled* with the consciousness of freedom (were it only from its restlessness, as one struggling in bondage) all spiritual intercourse is interrupted, not only with others, but even with himself. No wonder then, that he remains incomprehensible to himself as well as to others. . . . To remain unintelligible to such a mind, exclaims Schelling on a like occasion, is honor and a good name before God and man.[15]

¶ 15

[The Reason] is an *intuition* or *immediate* Beholding, accompanied by a conviction of the necessity and universality of the truth so beheld not derived from the Senses, which Intuition, when it is *construed* by *pure* Sense, gives birth to the Science of Mathematics, and when applied to Objects supersensuous or spiritual, is the Organ of Theology and Philosophy.[16]

¶ 16

The reason . . . as the integral spirit of the regenerated man, reason substantiated and vital, *one only*, yet *manifold, overseeing all, and going through all* understanding; *the breath of the power of God, and a pure influence from the glory of the Almighty;* which *remaining in itself* regenerateth all other powers, *and in all ages entering into holy souls maketh them friends of God and prophets;* (Wisdom of Solomon, c. vii.) this reason without being either the sense, the understanding, or the imagination, contains all three within itself, even as the mind contains its thoughts, and is present in and through them all; or as the expression pervades the different features of an intelligent countenance. Each individual must bear witness of it to his own mind, even as he describes life and light: and with the silence of light it describes itself, and dwells in us only as far as we dwell in it.[17]

¶ 17

Reason and Religion differ only as a two-fold application of the same power. But if we are obliged to distinguish, we must *ideally* separate. In this sense I affirm, that Reason is the knowledge of the laws of the WHOLE considered as ONE: and as such it is contradistinguished from the Understanding, which concerns itself exclusively with

---

[12] *Works* (Shedd), I, 460 fn.
[13] Quoted from John Smith, one of the Cambridge Platonists. See *Aids* (1829), notes, 323. Cf. *Nature*, 34.17-19.
[14] *Works* (Shedd), I, 461.
[15] *Works* (Shedd), III, 329.
[16] *Aids* (1829), notes, 305.
[17] *Works* (Shedd), I, 461.

the quantities, qualities, and relations of *particulars* in time and space. . . . The REASON, on the other hand, is the science of the *universal*, having the ideas of ONENESS AND ALLNESS as its two elements or primary factors. In the language of the old schools,

$$\text{Unity} + \text{Omn\"eity} = \text{Totality.}$$

The Reason first manifests itself in man by the *tendency* to the comprehension of all as one. We can neither rest in an infinite that is not at the same time a whole, nor in a whole that is not infinite. Hence the natural Man is always in a state either of resistance or of captivity to the understanding and the fancy, which cannot represent totality without limit; and he either loses the ONE in the striving after the INFINITE (i.e. Atheism with or without polytheism) or the INFINITE in the striving after the ONE, (i.e. anthropomorphic monotheism.)[18]

¶ 18

By the pure 'reason,' I mean the power by which we become possessed of principles, ——the eternal verities of Plato and Descartes, and of ideas, not images——as the ideas of a point, a line, a circle, in mathematics; and of justice, holiness, free-will, and the like, in morals. Hence in works of pure science the definitions of necessity precede the reasoning, in other works they more aptly form the conclusion.[19]

¶ 19

Thus, God, the Soul, eternal Truth, &c. are the objects of Reason; but they are themselves *reason*. We name God the Supreme Reason; and Milton says, "Whence the Soul *Reason* receives, and Reason is her Being."[20] Whatever is conscious *Self*-knowledge is Reason; and in this sense it may be safely defined the organ of the Supersensuous.[21]

¶ 20

The Understanding suggests the materials of reasoning: the Reason decides upon them. The first can only say,——This *is*, or *ought* to be so. The last says,——it *must* be so.[22]

¶ 21

It is the office, and as it were, the instinct of Reason to bring a unity into all our conceptions and several knowledges. On this all system depends: and without this we could reflect connectedly neither on nature or our own minds. Now this is possible only on the assumption or hypothesis of a ONE as the ground and cause of the Universe, and which in all succession and through all changes is the subject neither of Time or Change. The ONE must be contemplated as Eternal and Immutable.[23]

REASON, RELIGION AND THE WILL——THE PRINCIPLE OF ALL IN EACH ——PITFALLS OF RELIGION——TEMPTATIONS OF THE WILL——SPIRIT *VS*. A NATURE IN RELATION TO THE WILL——HOW THE WILL BECOMES RE-GENERATE——MEANING OF REDEMPTION——THE WILL HAS POWER OF ORIGINATING AN ACT OR STATE——COLERIDGE OFFERS AN EXAMPLE ——RELATION OF THE FINITE WILL TO THE ABSOLUTE WILL——REASON SUMMARIZED IN RELATION TO FAITH.

¶ 22

There exists in the human being, at least in man fully developed, no mean symbol of Tri-unity, in Reason, Religion, and the Will. For each of the three, though a distinct agency, implies and demands the other two, and loses its own nature at the moment that from distinction it passes into division or separation. The perfect frame of a man is the perfect frame of a state: and in the light of this idea we must read Plato's REPUBLIC. For, if I judge rightly, this celebrated work is to 'The History of the Town of Man-soul,' what Plato was to John Bunyan.[24]

¶ 23

Reason as the science of All as the Whole, must be interpenetrated by a Power, that represents the concentration of All in Each——a Power that acts by a contraction of

---

[18] *Aids* (1829), notes, 371-372.
[19] *Works* (Shedd), II, 164 fn. Also *Aids* (1829), notes, 316.
[20] *Paradise Lost*, V, 486.
[21] *Aids* (1829), notes, 308. Also *Works* (Shedd), II, 145.
[22] *Table Talk*, I, 23. See section VIII of Emerson's "Statement of the First Philosophy" in the next chapter.
[23] *Aids* (1829), 110.   [24] *Aids* (1829), notes, 372-373.

universal truths into individual duties, as the only form in which those truths can attain life and reality. Now this is RELIGION, which is the EXECUTIVE of our nature, and on this account the name of highest dignity, and the symbol of sovereignty.[25]

¶ 24

Yet this again—yet even Religion itself, if ever in its too exclusive devotion to the *specific* and *individual* it neglects to interpose the contemplation of the *universal*, changes its being into Superstition; and becoming more and more earthly and servile, as more and more estranged from the one in all, goes wandering at length with its pack of amulets, bead-rolls, periapts, fetisches, and the like pedlary, on pilgrimages to Loretto, Mecca, or the temple of Juggernaut, arm in arm with sensuality on one side and self-torture on the other, followed by a motley group of friars, pardoners, faquirs, gamesters, flagellants, mountebanks, and harlots.[26]

¶ 25

But neither can reason or religion exist or co-exist as reason and religion, except as far as they are actuated by the WILL, (the platonic θυμος,) which is the sustaining, coercive and ministerial power, the functions of which in the individual correspond to the officers of war and police in the ideal Republic of Plato. In its state of immanence (or indwelling) in reason and religion, the WILL appears indifferently, as wisdom or as love: two names of the same power, the former more intelligential, the latter more spiritual; the former more frequent in the Old, the latter in the New Testament. But in its utmost abstraction and consequent state of reprobation, the Will becomes satanic pride and rebellious self-idolatry in the relations of the spirit to itself, and remorseless despotism relatively to others; the more hopeless as the more obdurate by its subjugation of sensual impulses——by its superiority to toil and pain and pleasure; in short, by the fearful resolve to find in itself alone the one absolute motive of action, under which all other motives from within and from without must be either subordinated or crushed.[27]

¶ 26

[A] *Nature* in a Will implies already a *Corruption* of that Will; that a *Nature* is as inconsistent with *freedom*, as free choice with an incapacity of choosing aught but evil.[28]

¶ 27

I have attempted then to fix the proper meaning of the words Nature and Spirit, the one being the *antithesis* to the other: so that the most general and *negative* definition of Nature is, Whatever is not Spirit; and *vice versâ* of Spirit, That which is not comprehended in Nature: or in the language of our elder Divines, that which transcends Nature. But Nature is the term in which we comprehend all things that are representable in the forms of Time and Space, and subjected to the Relations of Cause and Effect: and the cause of whose existence therefore is to be sought for perpetually in something Antecedent. The word itself expresses this in the strongest manner possible: Natura, that which is *about to be* born, that which is always *becoming*. It follows, therefore, that whatever originates its own acts, or in any sense contains in itself the cause of its own state, must be *spiritual*, and consequently *super-natural:* yet not on that account necessarily *miraculous*. And such must the responsible WILL in us be, if it be at all.[29]

¶ 28

Whenever by self-subjection to this universal Light, the Will of the Individual, the *particular* Will, has become a Will of Reason, the man is regenerate: the Reason is then the *Spirit* of the regenerated man, whereby the Person is capable of a quickening intercommunion with the Divine Spirit. And herein consists the mystery of Redemption, that this has been rendered possible for us.[30]

¶ 29

These are truths which can scarcely be too frequently impressed on the Mind that is in earnest in the wish to *reflect* aright. Nature is a Line in constant and continuous evolution. Its *beginning* is lost in the Super-natural: and *for our understanding*, therefore, it must appear as a continuous line without beginning or end. But where there is

---

[25] *Aids* (1829), notes, 373.
[26] *Aids* (1829), notes, 373.
[29] *Aids* (1829), 155.
[30] *Aids* (1829), 137. Cf. *Nature*, 91.5-19; 94.13—95.12.
[27] *Aids* (1829), notes, 373-374.
[28] *Aids* (1829), notes, 330.

no discontinuity there can be no origination, and *every appearance of origination in Nature is but a shadow of our own casting.* It is a reflection from our own *WILL* or Spirit. Herein, indeed, the Will consists. This is the essential character by which WILL is *opposed* to Nature, as *Spirit,* and raised *above* Nature as *self-determining* Spirit—this, namely, that it is a power of *originating* an act or state.[31]

¶ 30

A young friend or, as he was pleased to describe himself, *a pupil of mine, who is beginning to learn to think,* asked me to explain by an instance what is meant by "*originating* an act or state." My answer was—This morning I awoke with a dull pain, which I knew from experience the getting up would remove; and yet by adding to the drowsiness and by weakening or depressing the *volition* . . . the very pain seemed to *hold me back,* to fix me (as it were) to the bed. After a peevish ineffectual quarrel with this painful disinclination, I said to myself: Let me count twenty, and the moment I come to nineteen I will leap out of bed. So said and so done. Now should you ever find yourself in the same or in a similar state, and should attend to the *Goings-on* within you, you will learn what I mean by *originating* an act. At the same time you will see that it belongs *exclusively* to the Will *(arbitrium);* that there is nothing analogous to it in outward experiences; and that I had, therefore, no way of explaining it but by referring you to an *Act* of your own, and to the peculiar self-consciousness preceding and accompanying it. As we know what Life is by *Being,* so we know what Will is by *Acting.*[32]

¶ 31

[A] *finite* Will does indeed originate an *act,* and may originate a *state* of being; but yet only *in* and *for* the Agent himself. A finite Will *constitutes* a true Beginning; but with regard to the series of motions and changes by which the free act is manifested and made *effectual,* the *finite* Will *gives* a beginning only by co-incidence with that *absolute* WILL, which is at the same time *Infinite* POWER! Such is the language of Religion, and of Philosophy too in the last instance. But I express the same truth in ordinary language when I say, that a finite Will, or the Will of a finite Free-agent, acts outwardly by confluence with the Laws of Nature.[33]

¶ 32

Such as the nature and objects of the reason are, such must be the functions and objects of the conscience. And the former we shall best learn by recapitulating those constituents of the total man which are either contrary to, or disparate from, the reason.

I. Reason, and the proper objects of reason, are wholly alien from sensation. Reason is supersensual, and its antagonist is appetite, and the objects of appetite the lust of the flesh.

II. Reason and its objects do not appertain to the world of the senses, inward or outward; that is, they partake not of sense or fancy. Reason is super-sensuous, and here its antagonist is the lust of the eye.

III. Reason and its objects are not things of reflection, association, discursion, discourse in the old sense of the word as opposed to intuition; "discursive or intuitive," as Milton has it. Reason does not indeed necessarily exclude the finite, either in time or in space, but it includes them *eminenter.* Thus the prime mover of the material universe is affirmed to contain all motion as its cause, but not to be, or to suffer, motion in itself.[34]

¶ 33

Reason is not the faculty of the finite. But here I must premise the following. The faculty of the finite is that which reduces the confused impressions of sense to their essential forms,——quantity, quality, relation, and in these action and reaction, cause and effect, and the like; thus raises the materials furnished by the senses and sensations into objects of reflection, and so makes experience possible. Without it, man's representative powers would be a delirium, a chaos, a scudding cloudage of shapes; and it is therefore most appropriately called the understanding, or substantiative faculty. Our elder metaphysicians, down to Hobbes inclusively, called this likewise discourse,

---

[31] *Aids* (1829), notes, 327. Cf. *Nature,* 80.16—81.16.
[32] *Aids* (1829), notes, 327.   [33] *Aids* (1829), notes, 328.
[34] From "An Essay on Faith," rptd. from *Literary Remains* as an appendix to *Aids* (1913), 345.

discursus, discursio, from its mode of action as not staying at any one object, but running, as it were, to and fro to abstract, generalize, and classify. Now when this faculty is employed in the service of the pure reason, it brings out the necessary and universal truths contained in the infinite into distinct contemplation by the pure act of the sensuous imagination, that is, in the production of the forms of space and time abstracted from all corporeity, and likewise of the inherent forms of the understanding itself abstractedly from the consideration of particulars, as in the case of geometry, numeral mathematics, universal logic, and pure metaphysics. The discursive faculty then becomes what our Shakespeare, with happy precision, calls "discourse of reason." [35]

¶ 34

IV. Reason, as one with the absolute will *(In the beginning was the Logos, and the Logos was with God, and the Logos was God),* and therefore for man the certain representative of the will of God, is above the will of man as an individual will. We have seen in III. that it stands in antagonism to all mere particulars; but here it stands in antagonism to all mere individual interests as so many selves, to the personal will as seeking its objects in the manifestation of itself for itself——*sit pro ratione voluntas;* ——whether this be realized with adjuncts, as in the lust of the flesh, and in the lust of the eye; or without adjuncts, as in the thirst and pride of power, despotism, egoistic ambition. The fourth antagonist, then, of reason, is the lust of the will.[36]

¶ 35

Now, the reason has been shown to be super-individual, generally, and therefore not less so when the form of an individualization subsists in the *alter,* than when it is confined to the *idem;* not less when the emotions have their conscious or believed object in another, than when their subject is the individual personal self. For though these emotions, affections, attachments, and the like, are the prepared ladder by which the lower nature is taken up into, and made to partake of, the highest room,——as we are taught to give a feeling of reality to the higher *per medium commune* with the lower, and thus gradually to see the reality of the higher (namely, the objects of reason), and finally to know that the latter are indeed, and pre-eminently real, as if you love your earthly parents whom you see, by these means you will learn to love your Heavenly Father who is invisible;——yet this holds good only so far as the reason is the president, and its objects the ultimate aim; and cases may arise in which the Christ as Logos, or Redemptive Reason, declares, *He that loves father or mother more than me, is not worthy of me;* nay, he that can permit his emotions to rise to an equality with the universal reason, is in enmity with that reason. Here, then, reason appears as the love of God; and its antagonist is the attachment to individuals wherever it exists in diminution of, or in competition with, the love which is reason.[37]

¶ 36

The will of God is the last ground and final aim of all our duties, and to that the whole man is to be harmonized by subordination, subjugation, or suppression alike in commission and omission. But the will of God, which is one with the supreme intelligence, is revealed to man through the conscience. But the conscience, which consists in an inappellable bearing-witness to the truth and reality of our reason, may legitimately be construed with the term reason, so far as the conscience is prescriptive; while as approving or condemning, it is the consciousness of the subordination or insubordination, the harmony or discord, of the personal will of man to and with the representative of the will of God. This brings me to the last and fullest sense of Faith, that is, the obedience of the individual will to the reason, in the lust of the flesh as opposed to the supersensual; in the lust of the eye as opposed to the supersensuous; in the pride of the understanding as opposed to the infinite; in the φρονημα σαρκος in contrariety to the spiritual truth; in the lust of the personal will as opposed to the absolute and universal; and in the love of the creature, as far as it is opposed to the love which is one with the reason, namely, the love of God .... Faith subsists in the *synthesis* of the Reason and the individual Will. By virtue of the latter, therefore, it must be an energy, and, inasmuch as it relates to the whole moral man, it must be exerted in each and all of his constituents or incidents, faculties and tendencies;—— it must be a total, not a partial—a continuous, not a desultory or occasional—— energy. And by virtue of the former, that is, Reason, Faith must be a Light, a form

---

[35] *Aids* (1913), 345-346.
[36] *Aids* (1913), 346-347.
[37] *Aids* (1913), 347-348. See Emerson on "personal relations" in *Nature,* 92.6-11; 58.3ff. Cf. the impersonal note in Emerson's essay on "Friendship."

of knowing, a beholding of Truth.[38]

THE UNDERSTANDING OF MAN IS THE GENERALIZING AND REFLECTIVE FACULTY——IT FUNCTIONS IN THREE STEPS: (1) ATTENTION; (2) ABSTRACTION; (3) GENERALIZATION——IT CONSTITUTES SENSIBLE EXPERIENCE AND GIVES RISE TO RULES OR MAXIMS——IT HAS TWO ORGANS: (1) THE OUTWARD SENSE; (2) "THE MIND'S EYE" OR REASON

¶ 37

The Understanding then (considered exclusively as an organ of human intelligence), is the Faculty by which we reflect and generalize. Take, for instance, any Object consisting of many parts, a House, or a Group of Houses: and if it be contemplated, as a Whole, *i.e.* (as many constituting a One), it forms what in the technical language of Psychology is called a *total impression*. Among the various component parts of this, we direct our attention especially to such as we recollect to have noticed in other total impressions. Then, by a voluntary Act we withhold our attention from all the rest to reflect exclusively on these: and these we henceforward use as *common characters*, by virtue of which the several Objects are referred to one and the same sort. Thus, the whole Process may be reduced to three acts, all depending on and supposing a previous impression on the Senses: first, the appropriation of our Attention; 2. (and in order of the continuance of the first) Abstraction, or the voluntary withholding of the Attention. and 3. Generalization. And these are the proper Functions of the Understanding: and the power of so doing is what we mean when we say we possess Understanding, or are created with the Faculty of Understanding.[39]

¶ 38

[The Understanding is] a reflective and discursive Faculty, or *mediate* Apprehension, which, taken by itself and uninfluenced by the [Reason], depends on the Senses for the Materials on which it is exercised, and is contained within the Sphere of the Senses. And this Faculty it is, which, in generalizing the Notices of the Senses, constitutes Sensible Experience, and gives rise to Maxims or Rules, which may become more and more *general*, but can never be raised to universal Verities, or beget a consciousness of absolute Certainty; though they may be sufficient to extinguish all doubt.[40]

¶ 39

A Maxim is a conclusion upon observation of matters of fact, and is merely retrospective: an Idea, or, if you like, a Principle, carries knowledge within itself, and is prospective. Polonius is a man of maxims. Whilst he is descanting on matters of past experience, as in that excellent speech to Laertes[41] before he sets out on his travels, he is admirable; but when he comes to advise or project, he is a mere dotard. You see, Hamlet, as the man of ideas, despises him. A man of maxims only is like a Cyclops with one eye, and that eye placed in the back of his head.[42]

¶ 40

[The Understanding] may be defined the conception of the Sensuous, or the faculty by which we generalize and arrange the phænomena of perception: that faculty, the functions of which contain the rules and constitute the possibility of outward Experience. In short, the Understanding supposes something that is understood. This may be merely its own acts or forms, that is, formal Logic; but *real* objects, the materials of *substantial* knowledge, must be furnished, we might safely say *revealed*, to it by Organs of Sense.[43]

¶ 41

Again, the Understanding and Experience may exist without Reason. But Reason cannot exist without Understanding; nor does it or can it manifest itself but in and through the understanding, which in our elder writers is often called *discourse*, or the discursive faculty, as by Hooker, Lord Bacon, and Hobbes: and an understanding enlightened by reason Shakspear gives as the contra-distinguishing character of man, under the name *discourse of reason*. In short, the human understanding possesses two distinct organs, the outward sense, and "the mind's eye" which is reason: wherever we use that phrase (the mind's eye) in its proper sense, and not as a mere synonyme of

---

[38] *Aids* (1913), 348-349.
[39] *Aids* (1829), 143.
[40] *Aids* (1829), notes, 305.
[43] *Aids* (1829), notes, 308. Also *Works* (Shedd), II, 145.
[41] *Hamlet*, I.iii.55-81.
[42] *Table Talk*, I, 69.

the memory or the fancy. In this way we reconcile the promise of Revelation, that the blessed will see God, with the declaration of St. John, God hath no one seen at any time.[44]

¶ 42

To generalize is a faculty and function of the Human Understanding, and from its imperfection and limitation are the use and the necessity of generalizing derived. Generalization is a Substitute for Intuition, for the Power of *intuitive* (that is, immediate) knowledge. As a Substitute, it is a gift of inestimable Value to a finite Intelligence, such as *Man* in his present state is endowed with and capable of exercising; but yet a *Substitute* only, and an imperfect one to boot. To attribute it to God is the grossest Anthropomorphism; a[n]d grosser instances of Anthropomorphism than are to be found in the controversial writings on Original Sin and Vicarious Satisfaction, the Records of Superstition do not supply.[45]

¶ 43

[Some say "Reason" but mean] the understanding considered as using the Reason, so far as by the organ of Reason only we possess the ideas of the Necessary and the Universal; and this is the more common use of the word, when it is applied with *any* attempt at clear and distinct conceptions. In this narrower and derivative sense the best definition of Reason, which I can give, will be found in the third member of the following sentence, in which the understanding is described in its three-fold operation, and from each receives an appropriate name. The Sense, (vis sensitiva vel intuitiva) *perceives*: Vis regulatrix (the understanding, in its own peculiar operation) *conceives*: Vis rationalis (the Reason or rationalized understanding) *comprehends*. The first is impressed through the organs of sense; the second combines these multifarious impressions into individual *Notions*, and by reducing these notions to Rules, according to the analogy of all its former notices, constitutes *Experience;* the third subordinates both these notions and the rules of Experience to ABSOLUTE PRINCIPLES or necessary LAWS.[46]

THE UNDERSTANDING HAS VALIDITY ONLY WITHIN ITS OWN SPHERE ——IT SHOWS UNBELIEF AND MISBELIEF TOWARD ALL BEYOND SENSE EXPERIENCE——FUTILITY OF APPLYING THE METHODS OF THE UNDERSTANDING TO SPIRITUAL REALITIES——ON THE CONTRARY, WHEN A WIDESPREAD DOCTRINE DOES NOT MAKE SENSE TO THE UNDERSTANDING, OR COMES FROM IT IN THE FORM OF CONTRADICTORY CONCEPTIONS, THE PRESUMPTION SHOULD BE IN ITS FAVOR——EULER'S LAW OF ARCHES——THE IMAGINATION IS THE COMPLETING POWER WHICH GIVES THE UNDERSTANDING DEPTH

¶ 44

In close connexion . . . is the Subject of the legitimate exercise of the Understanding and its limitation to Objects of Sense; with the errors both of unbelief and of misbelief, that result from its extension beyond the sphere of possible Experience. Wherever the forms of Reasoning appropriate only to the *natural* world are applied to *spiritual* realities, it may be truly said, that the more strictly logical the Reasoning is in all its *parts*, the more irrational it is as a *whole*.[47]

¶ 45

I am firmly persuaded, that no doctrine was ever widely diffused among various nations through successive ages, and under different religions (such as is the doctrine of original sin, and redemption, those fundamental articles of every known religion professing to be revealed) which is not founded either in the nature of things or in the necessities of our nature. In the language of the schools, it carries with it presumptive evidence, that it is either *objectively or subjectively* true. And the more strange and contradictory such.a doctrine may appear to the understanding, or discursive faculty, the stronger is the presumption in its favour; for whatever satirists may say, the sciolists imagine, the human mind has no predilection for absurdity.[48]

---

[44] *Aids* (1829), notes, 308. Also *Works* (Shedd), II, 145.
[45] *Aids* (1829), notes, 329.
[46] *Aids* (1829), notes, 309.
[47] *Aids* (1829), 156. Hence the emptiness and sophistry of the so-called systems of Natural Theology, Religion of Nature, and Light of Nature——all of which are based on the Understanding alone.   [48] *Aids* (1829), notes, 276.

¶ 46

Plato's works are preparatory exercises for the mind. He leads you to see, that propositions involving in themselves a contradiction in terms, are nevertheless true; and which, therefore, must belong to a higher logic——that of ideas. They are self-contradictory only in the Aristotelian logic, which is the instrument of the understanding.[49]

¶ 47

The celebrated Euler, treating on some point respecting arches, makes this curious remark:——"All experience is in contradiction to this; *sed potius fidendum est analysi;* but this is no reason for doubting the analysis." The words sound paradoxical; but in truth mean no more than this, that the properties of space are not less certainly the properties of space because they can never be entirely transferred to material bodies.[50]

¶ 48

In short, Understanding in its highest form of Experience remains commensurate with the experimental notices of the senses, from which it is generalized. Reason, on the other hand, either predetermines Experience, or avails itself of a past Experience to supersede its necessity in all future time; and affirms truths which no Sense could perceive, nor Experiment verify, nor experience confirm.[51]

¶ 49

Yea, this is the test and character of a truth so affirmed, that in its own proper form it is *inconceivable.* For *to conceive* is a function of the Understanding, which can be exercised only on subjects subordinate thereto. And yet to the forms of the Understanding all truth must be reduced, that is to be fixed as an object of reflection, and to be rendered *expressible.* And here we have a second test and sign of a truth so affirmed, that it can come forth out of the moulds of the Understanding only in the disguise of two contradictory conceptions, each of which is partially true, and the conjunction of both conceptions becomes the representative or *expression* (= the *exponent*) of a truth *beyond* conception and inexpressible. Examples. Before Abraham *was, I am.*——God is a Circle whose centre is every where and circumference no where.[52]——The Soul is all in every part.[53]

¶ 50

Of the *discursive* understanding, which forms for itself general notions and terms of classification for the purpose of comparing and arranging phænomena, the Characteristic is Clearness without Depth. It contemplates the unity of things in their *limits* only, and is consequently a knowledge of superficies without substance. So much so, indeed, that it entangles itself in contradictions in the very effort of comprehending the *idea* of substance. The completing power which unites clearness with depth, the plenitude of the sense with the comprehensibility of the understanding, is the IMAGINATION,[54] impregnated with which the understanding itself becomes intuitive, and a living power.[55]

---

[49] *Table Talk,* I, 105.

[50] *Works* (Shedd), II, 432. Also *Aids* (1829), notes, 274. President Marsh explains that "a fact may be above our understandings, which is not inconsistent with reason, and which reason requires us to believe; it may be inconceivable under those conditions, which limit the powers of conception in the understanding, and yet its truth be discovered intuitively by the reason; it may be irrepresentable under the forms of time and space, i.e. something, of which neither extension, nor place, nor the attributes of time, as before and after, can be predicated, and yet its reality force itself upon our conviction." See *Nature,* 69.22ff.

[51] *Aids* (1829), notes, 304.

[52] This sentence is of unknown origin. Some have traced it to a lost treatise of Empedocles. It is quoted in the *Roman de la Rose* and by St. Bonaventura in his *Itinerarius Mentis ad Deum.* Emerson assigns it to St. Augustine in *Works,* II, 301. See Swedenborg ¶ 54.

[53] *Aids* (1829), notes, 304. The phrase, *all in every part,* appears also in ¶ 260. In *Works* (Shedd), III, 244, a couplet from Cowley's *All Over Love* has been altered to read:

And like a God by spiritual art,
Be all in all, and all in every part.

[54] See *Nature,* 65.10-12.   [55] *Aids* (1829), notes, 375.

ANIMALS POSSESS INSTINCTS AND MAY, TO A DEGREE, PARTAKE OF
UNDERSTANDING, BUT CANNOT HAVE REASON——MAN'S UNDERSTAND-
ING IS WHAT IT IS BECAUSE IT COEXISTS WITH THE REASON——MAN
DIFFERS FROM ANIMALS CHIEFLY BECAUSE OF HIS REASON

¶ 51

Beasts, we have said, partake of Understanding. If any man deny this, there is a
ready way of settling the question. Let him give a careful perusal to Hüber's two small
volumes, on Bees and on Ants (especially the latter), and to Kirby and Spence's
Introduction to Entomology: and one or other of two things must follow. He will either
change his opinion as irreconcilable with the facts: or he must deny the facts, which
yet I cannot suppose, inasmuch as the denial would be tantamount to the no less
extravagant than uncharitable assertion, that Hüber, and the several eminent Naturalists, French and English, Swiss, German, and Italian, by whom Hüber's observations
and experiments have been repeated and confirmed, had all conspired to impose a
series of falsehoods and fairy-tales on the world.[56]

¶ 52

[If] I suppose the Adaptive Power in its highest species or form of Instinctive
Intelligence to co-exist with Reason, *Free* will, and Self-consciousness, it instantly
becomes UNDERSTANDING: in other words, that Understanding differs indeed from the
noblest form of Instinct, but not in itself or in its own essential properties, but in
consequence of its co-existence with far higher Powers of a diverse kind in one and
the same Subject. INSTINCT in a rational, responsible, and self-conscious Animal, is
Understanding.[57]

¶ 53

The understanding of the higher Brutes has only organs of outward sense, and
consequently material objects only; but man's understanding has likewise an organ of
inward sense, and therefore the power of acquainting itself with invisible realities or
spiritual objects. This organ is his Reason.[58]

¶ 54

It should seem easy to give the definite distinction of the Reason from the Understanding, because we constantly imply it when we speak of the difference between
ourselves and the brute creation. No one, except as a figure of speech, ever speaks
of an animal *reason;* but that many animals possess a share of Understanding, perfectly distinguishable from mere Instinct, we all allow. Few persons have a favorite
dog without making instances of its intelligence an occasional topic of conversation.
They call for our admiration of the *individual* animal, and not with exclusive reference
to the Wisdom in Nature, as in the case of the *storgè* or maternal instinct of beasts;
or of the hexangular cells of the bees, and the wonderful coincidence of this form with
the geometrical demonstration of the largest possible number of rooms in a given
space. Likewise, we distinguish various *degrees* of Understanding there, and even
discover, from inductions supplied by the Zoologists, that the Understanding appears
(as a general rule) in an inverse proportion to the Instinct.[59]

¶ 55

The definition and proper character of Man—that, namely, which should contra-
distinguish him from the Animals—is to be taken from his Reason rather than from
his Understanding: in regard that in other creatures there may be something of
Understanding but there is nothing of Reason.[60]

¶ 56

This Reason applied to the *motives* of our conduct, and combined with the sense of
our moral responsibility, is the conditional cause of *Conscience,* which is a spiritual
sense or testifying state of the coincidence or discordance of the FREE WILL with the
REASON. But as the reasoning consists wholly in a man's power of seeing, whether any
two ideas, which happen to be in his mind, are, or are not, in contradiction with each
other, it follows of necessity, not only that all men have reason, but that every man
has it in the same degree. For Reasoning (or Reason, in this its *secondary* sense) does
not consist in the Ideas, or in their clearness, but simply, when they *are* in the mind,

[56] *Aids* (1829), 138-139.
[57] *Aids* (1829), 152.
[58] *Aids* (1829), notes, 308. Also *Works* (Shedd), II, 145.
[59] *Aids* (1829), notes, 307.   [60] *Aids* (1829), 135.

in seeing whether they contradict each other or no.[61]

BIOGRAPHIA LITERARIA[62]

LANGUAGE HAS BECOME MECHANIZED AND ARTIFICIAL——IT NOW SAVES PEOPLE THE TROUBLE OF THINKING——LITERATURE NOW BEING MANUFACTURED OUT OF STEREOTYPE PIECES——WORKS OF GENIUS ARE RARE[63]

¶ 56a

In the days of Chaucer and Gower, our language might . . . be compared to a wilderness of vocal reeds, from which the favorites only of Pan or Apollo could construct even the rude *syrinx;* and from this the constructors alone could elicit strains of music. But now, partly by the labors of successive poets, and in part by the more artificial state of society and social intercourse, language, mechanized as it were into a barrel-organ, supplies at once both instrument and tune. Thus even the deaf may play, so as to delight the many. Sometimes . . . I have attempted to illustrate the present state of our language, in relation to literature, by a press-room of larger and smaller stereotype pieces, which, in the present Anglo-Gallican fashion of unconnected, epigrammatic periods, it requires but an ordinary portion of ingenuity to vary indefinitely, and yet still produce something, which, if not sense, will be so like it as to do as well. Perhaps better: for it spares the reader the trouble of thinking; prevents vacancy, while it indulges indolence; and secures the memory from all danger of an intellectual *plethora.* Hence, of all trades, literature at present demands the least talent or information; and, of all modes of literature, the manufacturing of poems. The difference indeed between these and the works of genius is not less than between an egg and an egg-shell; yet at a distance they both look alike.

SENSIBILITY IS A COMPONENT PART OF GENIUS——IT MAY BE SENSIBILITY EXCITED BY PERSONAL INTERESTS, BUT USUALLY IT IS NOT—— GENIUS LIVES IN THE IDEAL WORLD[64]

¶ 56b

Sensibility indeed, both quick and deep, is not only a characteristic feature, but may be deemed a component part, of genius. But it is not less an essential mark of true genius, that its sensibility is excited by any other cause more powerfully than by its own personal interests; for this plain reason, that the man of genius lives most in the ideal world, in which the present is still constituted by the future or the past; and because his feelings have been habitually associated with thoughts and images, to the number, clearness, and vivacity of which the sensation of self is always in an inverse proportion.

THE MYSTICS AND COLERIDGE——THEY POINTED TO VALUES BEYOND THOSE OF THE UNDERSTANDING[65]

¶ 57

One assertion I will venture to make, as suggested by my own experience, that there exist folios on the human understanding, and the nature of man, which would have a far juster claim to their high rank and celebrity, if in the whole huge volume there could be found as much fulness of heart and intellect, as burst forth in many a simple page of George Fox, Jacob Behmen, and even of Behmen's commentator, the pious and fervid William Law.

¶ 58

For the writings of these Mystics acted in no slight degree to prevent my mind from being imprisoned within the outline of any single dogmatic system. They contributed

---

[61] *Aids* (1829), notes, 310.

[62] With a few paragraphs on related topics from other works. The *Biographia* was first issued in two volumes (London, 1817). Emerson considered it "the best book of criticism in the English language" (see Cabot, *Memoir*, II, 723), and Coleridge himself thought that the second half——containing his criticism of Wordsworth's poetry—— might be worthy of preservation. (See ¶ 284 *infra.*)

[63] *Works* (Shedd), III, 171. Cf. *Nature*, 37.23——39.20.

[64] *Works* (Shedd), III, 175-176. Cf. *Nature*, 75.8-13.

[65] *Works* (Shedd), III, 254; 255.

to keep alive the heart in the head; gave me an indistinct, yet stirring and working presentiment, that all the products of the mere reflective faculty partook of death, and were as the rattling twigs and sprays in winter, into which a sap was yet to be propelled from some root to which I had not penetrated, if they were to afford my soul either food or shelter. If they were too often a moving cloud of smoke to me by day, yet they were always a pillar of fire throughout the night, during my wanderings through the wilderness of doubt, and enabled me to skirt, without crossing, the sandy deserts of utter unbelief. That the system is capable of being converted into an irreligious Pantheism, I well know.

"IMAGINATION" AND "FANCY" DEFINED[66]

¶ 59

The IMAGINATION then I consider either as primary, or secondary. The primary Imagination I hold to be the living power and prime agent of all human perception, and as a repetition in the finite mind of the eternal act of creation in the infinite I AM. The secondary Imagination I consider as an echo of the former, co-existing with the conscious will, yet still as identical with the primary in the *kind* of its agency, and differing only in *degree*, and in the *mode* of its operation. It dissolves, diffuses, dissipates, in order to re-create: or where this process is rendered impossible, yet still at all events it struggles to idealize and to unify. It is essentially *vital*, even as all objects (*as* objects) are essentially fixed and dead.

¶ 60

FANCY, on the contrary, has no other counters to play with but fixities and definites. The fancy is indeed no other than a mode of memory emancipated from the order of time and space; while it is blended with, and modified by that empirical phenomenon of the will, which we express by the word Choice. But equally with the ordinary memory the Fancy must receive all its materials ready made from the law of association.

"IMAGINATION" AND "FANCY" ILLUSTRATED AND COMPARED[67]

¶ 61

You may conceive the difference in kind between the Fancy and the Imagination in this way,——that if the check of the senses and the reason were withdrawn, the first would become delirium, and the last mania. The Fancy brings together images which have no connection natural or moral, but are yoked together by the poet by means of some accidental coincidence; as in the well-known passage in Hudibras:——

> "The sun had long since in the lap
> Of Thetis taken out his nap,
> And like a lobster boyl'd, the morn
> From black to red began to turn."[68]

¶ 62

The Imagination modifies images, and gives unity to variety; it sees all things in one, *il più nell' uno*.[69] There is the epic imagination, the perfection of which is in Milton; and the dramatic, of which Shakspeare is the absolute master. The first gives unity by throwing back into the distance; as after the magnificent approach of the Messiah to battle, the poet, by one touch from himself——

> ——"far off their coming shone!"——[70]

makes the whole one image. And so at the conclusion of the description of the appearance of the entranced angels, in which every sort of image from all the regions of earth and air is introduced to diversify and illustrate,——the reader is brought back to the single image by——

> "He call'd so loud that all the hollow deep
> Of Hell resounded."[71]

The dramatic imagination does not throw back, but brings close; it stamps all nature

---

[66] *Works* (Shedd), III, 363-364. Cf. *Nature*, 65.10-23.
[67] *Table Talk*, II, 330-334.
[68] Samuel Butler, *Hudibras*, Part II, canto 2, lines 29-32.
[69] See ¶ 291a and *Nature*, 30.1-5. See *Journals*, IV, 7.
[70] *Paradise Lost*, VI, 768. [71] *Paradise Lost*, I, 314-315.

with one, and that its own, meaning, as in Lear throughout.[72]

THE IMAGINATION AND THE POET[73]

¶ 63

The poet, described in ideal perfection, brings the whole soul of man into activity, with the subordination of its faculties to each other according to their relative worth and dignity. He diffuses a tone and spirit of unity, that blends, and (as it were) *fuses*, each into each, by that synthetic and magical power, to which I would exclusively appropriate the name of Imagination. This power, first put in action by the will and understanding, and retained under their irremissive, though gentle and unnoticed, control, *laxis effertur habenis*, reveals itself in the balance or reconcilement of opposite or discordant qualities: of sameness, with difference; of the general with the concrete; the idea with the image; the individual with the representative; the sense of novelty and freshness with old and familiar objects;[74] a more than usual state of emotion with more than usual order; judgment ever awake and steady self-possession with enthusiasm and feeling profound or vehement; and while it blends and harmonizes the natural and the artificial, still subordinates art to nature; the manner to the matter; and our admiration of the poet to our sympathy with the poetry. Doubtless, as Sir John Davies observes of the soul——(and his words may with slight alteration[75] be applied, and even more appropriately, to the poetic Imagination)——

> Doubtless this could not be, but that she turns
> Bodies to *spirit* by sublimation strange,
> As fire converts to fire the things it burns,
> As we our food into our nature change.
>
> From their gross matter she abstracts *their* forms,
> And draws a kind of quintessence from things;
> Which to her proper nature she transforms
> To bear them light on her celestial wings.
>
> *Thus* does she, when from *individual states*
> She doth abstract the universal kinds;
> *Which then re-clothed in divers names and fates*
> *Steal access through the senses to our minds.*[76]

THE POET'S VERSATILE IMAGINATION IS TRUSTWORTHY BECAUSE OF THE "ALL IN EACH" OF HUMAN NATURE[77]

¶ 64

By what *rule* that does not leave the reader at the poet's mercy, and the poet at his own, is the latter to distinguish between the language suitable to suppressed, and the language, which is characteristic of indulged, anger? Or between that of rage and that of jealousy? Is it obtained by wandering about in search of angry or jealous people in uncultivated society, in order to copy their words? Or not far rather by the power of imagination proceeding upon the *all in each* of human nature? By meditation, rather than by observation? And by the latter in consequence only of the former?

THE IMAGINATION OF SHAKESPEARE AND MILTON[78]

¶ 65

What then shall we say? even this; that Shakspeare, no mere child of nature; no *automaton* of genius; no passive vehicle of inspiration possessed by the spirit, not possessing it; first studied patiently, meditated deeply, understood minutely, till knowledge, become habitual and intuitive, wedded itself to his habitual feelings, and at length gave birth to that stupendous power, by which he stands alone, with no equal

---

[72] See *Nature*, 65.17-23. Emerson drew from *Lear* his illustrations for the discussion of the imagination in his introductory lecture on English literature (Nov. 5, 1835).
[73] *Works* (Shedd), III, 374. Cf. *Nature*, 64.16——68.10.
[74] See *Nature*, 92.13-18; 11.16-19.
[75] The italics in the following stanza represent Coleridge's alterations.
[76] From Sir John Davies, "Of the Soul of Man."
[77] *Works* (Shedd), III, 428. Cf. *Nature*, 68.5-10.
[78] *Works* (Shedd), III, 381; 379; 378-379. Cf. *Nature*, 65.14ff.

or second in his own class; to that power, which seated him on one of the two glory-smitten summits of the poetic mountain, with Milton as his compeer not rival. While the former darts himself forth, and passes into all the forms of human character and passion, the one Proteus[79] of the fire and the flood; the other attracts all forms and things to himself, into the unity of his own ideal. All things and modes of action shape themselves anew in the being of Milton; while Shakspeare becomes all things, yet forever remaining himself.

¶ 66

As of higher worth, so doubtless still more characteristic of poetic genius does the imagery become, when it moulds and colors itself to the circumstances, passion, or character, present and foremost in the mind. For unrivalled instances of this excellence, the reader's own memory will refer him to the *Lear, Othello*, in short to which not of the *"great, ever-living, dead man's"* dramatic works? *Inopem me copia fecit.*[80] How true it is to nature, he has himself finely expressed in the instance of love in his 98th Sonnet.

¶ 66a

[I]mages, however beautiful, though faithfully copied from nature, and as accurately represented in words, do not of themselves characterize the poet. They become proofs of original genius only as far as they are modified by a predominant passion; or by associated thoughts or images awakened by that passion; or when they have the effect of reducing multitude to unity, or succession to an instant; or lastly, when a human and intellectual life is transferred to them from the poet's own spirit . . . . Shakspeare even in his earliest, as in his latest, works surpasses all other poets. It is by this, that he still gives a dignity and a passion to the objects which he presents. Unaided by any previous excitement, they burst upon us at once in life and in power,

> "Full many a glorious morning have I seen
> *Flatter* the mountain tops with sovereign eye." [Sonnet 23]

ALL KNOWLEDGE RESTS IN COINCIDENCE OF SUBJECT WITH OBJECT——"KNOW THYSELF"——NATURE *VS.* INTELLIGENCE——OBJECTIVE *VS.* SUBJECTIVE——UNCONSCIOUS *VS.* CONSCIOUS[81]

¶ 67

The postulate of philosophy and at the same time the test of philosophic capacity, is no other than the heaven-descended KNOW THYSELF! (*E cœlo descendit*, Γνωθι σεαυτον.) And this at once practically and speculatively. For as philosophy is neither a science of the reason or understanding only, nor merely a science of morals, but the science of BEING altogether, its primary ground can be neither merely speculative nor merely practical, but both in one. All knowledge rests on the coincidence of an object with a subject. . . . For we can *know* that only which is true: and the truth is universally placed in the coincidence of the thought with the thing, of the representation with the object represented.

¶ 68

Now the sum of all that is merely OBJECTIVE, we will henceforth call NATURE, confining the term to its passive and material sense, as comprising all the *phænomena* by which its existence is made known to us. On the other hand the sum of all that is SUBJECTIVE, we may comprehend in the name of the SELF or INTELLIGENCE. Both con-

---

[79] See *Journals*, IV, 72. Emerson calls himself a "Proteus."

[80] "Plenty makes me poor." (Ovid, *Metamorphoses*, III, 466.)

[81] *Works* (Shedd), III, 335, 335, 348, 587 fn. Coleridge recognized the difficulties arising from the theory of coincidence and also understood the two dominant schools of thought: (a) Kant's Critical School and (b) the Influx School of Plotinus. See *Aids* (1829), notes, 396: "Whether Ideas are regulative only, according to Aristotle and Kant; or likewise CONSTITUTIVE, and one with the power and Life of Nature, according to Plato, and Plotinus . . . is the highest *problem* of Philosophy, and not part of its nomenclature." See also *Works* (Shedd), III, 270-271, for Professor Shedd's important note on Coleridge and Schelling, and on the chief problem presented by the theory of identity of subject and object——PANTHEISM. Shedd points out that although both men emphasized the Identity Theory, the mind of neither was content with it. "At any rate, all such teaching of Coleridge as that the *moral* Reason is the highest form of Reason, and that no merely speculative decisions can set aside those of *Conscience*, are in the very vein and spirit of the Critical philosophy, and a protest against a theory which obliterates all the fixed lines and immutable distinctions of Theism."

ceptions are in necessary antithesis. Intelligence is conceived of as exclusively representative, nature as exclusively represented; the one as conscious, the other as without consciousness. Now in all acts of positive knowledge there is required a reciprocal concurrence of both, namely, of the conscious being, and of that which is in itself unconscious. Our problem is to explain this concurrence, its possibility and its necessity.

¶ 69

We begin with the I KNOW MYSELF, in order to end with the absolute I AM. We proceed from the SELF, in order to lose and find all self in GOD.

¶ 70

Poor unlucky Metaphysics! and what are they? A single sentence expresses the object, and thereby the contents of this science. Γνωθι σεαυτον:

Nosce te ipsum,
Tuque Deum, quantum licet, inque Deo omnia noscas.

Know thyself: and so shalt thou know God, as far as is permitted to a creature, and in God all things.——Surely, there is a strange——nay, rather a too natural——aversion in many to know themselves.

COLERIDGE CRITICIZES STANZA EIGHT OF THE *ODE* AS AN EXAMPLE OF WORDSWORTH'S USE OF THOUGHT AND IMAGE TOO GREAT FOR THE SUBJECT——SAYS THE WISDOM ATTRIBUTED TO THE CHILD IS NOT EVEN GOOD PANTHEISM——TEACHERS OF THE *EN KAI PAN* MAKE A DISTINCTION AT LEAST BETWEEN *A PART* AND *THE WHOLE*[82]

¶ 71

[W]ithout examining the propriety of making a "Master *brood* o'er a Slave," or "the *Day*" brood *at all;* we will merely ask, what does all this mean? In what sense is a child of that age a *Philosopher?* In what sense does he *read* "the eternal deep?" In what sense is he declared to be *"forever haunted"* by the Supreme Being? or so inspired as to deserve the splendid titles of a *Mighty Prophet,* a *blessed Seer?* By reflection? by knowledge? by conscious intuition? or by *any* form or modification of consciousness? These would be tidings indeed; but such as would pre-suppose an immediate revelation to the inspired communicator, and require miracles to authenticate his inspiration. Children at this age give us no such information of themselves; and at what time were we dipped in the Lethe, which has produced such utter oblivion of a state so godlike? There are many of us that still possess some remembrances, more or less distinct, respecting themselves at six years old; pity that the worthless straws only should float, while treasures, compared with which all the mines of Golconda and Mexico were but straws, should be absorbed by some unknown gulf into some unknown abyss.

¶ 72

But if this be too wild and exorbitant to be suspected as having been the poet's meaning; if these mysterious gifts, faculties, and operations, are not accompanied with consciousness; who else is conscious of them? or how can it be called the child, if it be no part of the child's conscious being? For aught I know, the thinking Spirit within me may be *substantially* one with the principle of life, and of vital operation. For aught I know, it may be employed as a secondary agent in the marvellous organization and organic movements of my body. But, surely, it would be strange language to say, that *I* construct my *heart!* or that *I* propel the finer influences through my *nerves!* or that *I* compress my brain, and draw the curtains of sleep round my own eyes! Spinoza and Behmen were, on different systems, both Pantheists; and among the ancients there were philosophers, teachers of the EN KAI ΠΑΝ, who not only taught that God was All, but that this All constituted God. Yet not even these would confound the *part, as* a part, with the whole, *as* the whole. Nay, in no system is the distinction between the individual and God, between the Modification and the one only Substance, more sharply drawn, than in that of Spinoza.

¶ 73

In what sense can the magnificent attributes, above quoted, be appropriated to a *child,* which would not make them equally suitable to a *bee,* or a *dog,* or *a field of corn;* or even to a *ship,* or to the wind and waves that propel it? The omnipresent Spirit works equally in them, as in the child; and the child is equally unconscious of it as they.

---

[82] *Works* (Shedd), III, 481-482, 482, 483.

WORDSWORTH DID NOT ACCEPT A LITERAL INTERPRETATION OF THE DOCTRINE OF PRE-EXISTENCE[83]

¶ 74

[T]he ode was intended for such readers only as had been accustomed to watch the flux and reflux of their inmost nature, to venture at times into the twilight realms of consciousness, and to feel a deep interest in modes of inmost being, to which they know that the attributes of time and space are inapplicable and alien, but which yet can not be conveyed, save in symbols of time and space. For such readers the sense is sufficiently plain, and they will be as little disposed to charge Mr. Wordsworth with believing the Platonic pre-existence in the ordinary interpretation of the words, as I am to believe, that Plato himself ever meant or taught it.

THE PURPOSE OF *LYRICAL BALLADS* (1798)[84]

¶ 75

[I]t was agreed, that my endeavors should be directed to persons and characters supernatural, or at least romantic; yet so as to transfer from our inward nature a human interest and a semblance of truth sufficient to procure for these shadows of imagination that willing suspension of disbelief for the moment, which constitutes poetic faith. Mr. Wordsworth, on the other hand, was to propose to himself as his object, to give the charm of novelty[85] to things of every day, and to excite a feeling analogous to the supernatural, by awakening the mind's attention to the lethargy of custom, and directing it to the loveliness and the wonders of the world before us; an inexhaustible treasure, but for which, in consequence of the film of familiarity and selfish solicitude we have eyes, yet see not, ears that hear not, and hearts that neither feel nor understand.

THE FRIEND[86]

QUOTATIONS ON MAN FROM SAMUEL DANIEL AND JOHN DONNE[87]

¶ 75a

Knowing the heart of man is set to be
The centre of this world, about the which
These revolutions of disturbances
Still roll; where all the aspects of misery
Predominate; whose strong effects are such,
As he must bear, being powerless[88] to redress:
And that unless above himself he can
Erect himself, how poor a thing is man![89]

¶ 75b

The recluse hermit ofttimes more doth know
Of the world's inmost wheels, than *worldlings* can.

---

[88] *Works* (Shedd), III, 490. Coleridge reprints stanzas V and IX on pp. 498-499.
[84] *Works* (Shedd), III, 365.
[85] Cf. *Nature*, 92.13-18; 93.3-7; 93.15.
[86] First published serially in 1809-1810 and reissued with supplements in 1812. It appeared greatly augmented and revised in three volumes, London, 1818, the edition which Emerson owned. Coleridge considered vol. III, pages 67-265 (or Essays I-X inc. of "Section the Second") to be especially worthy of preservation (see ¶ 284). Emerson concurred (Cabot, *Memoir*, II, 723-724), finding in the whole work many important suggestions on the Reason and the Understanding; a valuable discussion on method, theory and law; and a warm spiritual philosophy.
[87] *Works* (Shedd), II, 96; 108.
[88] Emerson changed the word to "helpless" in *Journals*, II, 347, and in *Parnassus*, Boston, 1875, p. 517.
[89] Coleridge used this stanza as a motto for Essay XIV in the "General Introduction." The lines came from Daniel's poem, "To the Lady Margaret, Countess of Cumberland," [89-96]. The final couplet was much quoted. See Wordsworth, "The Excursion," IV, 330-331. See Emerson, in "Circles," *Works*, II, 307; in "Civilization" (*Society and Solitude*), *Works*, VII, 30. See also Coleridge ¶s. 178 and 225. Emerson copied the eight lines from Coleridge into his journals, changing the one word mentioned in note 88.

As man is of the world, the heart of man
Is an epitome of God's great book
Of creatures, and men need no farther look.[90]

ABSTRACT TRUTH IS MOST PRACTICAL[91]——ONE SHOULD RESPECT THE LAW OF REASON AGAINST THE MAXIMS OF THE UNDERSTANDING——THE DUTIES TO ONE'S MORAL BEING——SHADOW OF DIVINITY IN HUMAN NATURE——RESPECT THYSELF![92]

¶ 76

An honest man . . . possesses a clearer light than that of history. He knows, that by sacrificing the law of his reason to the maxim of pretended prudence, he purchases the sword with the loss of the arm that is to wield it. The duties which we owe to our own moral being, are the ground and condition of all other duties; and to set our nature at strife with itself for a good purpose, implies the same sort of prudence, as a priest of Diana would have manifested, who should have proposed to dig up the celebrated charcoal foundations of the mighty temple of Ephesus, in order to furnish fuel for the burnt-offerings on its altars. Truth, virtue, and happiness, may be distinguished from each other, but can not be divided. They subsist by a mutual co-inherence, which gives a shadow of divinity even to our human nature.

MORAL TRUTH IS SUPERIOR TO MERE VERBAL TRUTH——IMPORTANCE OF THE INTENTION OF THE SPEAKER——THOUGH DIFFICULT EVER TO CONVEY THE "WHOLE TRUTH,"[93] REASON DEMANDS THAT WE COMMUNICATE A RIGHT NOTION OF IT[94]

¶ 77

By verbal truth, we mean no more than the correspondence of a given fact to given words. In moral truth, we involve likewise the intention of the speaker, that his words shall correspond to his thoughts in the sense in which he expects them to be understood by others; and in this latter import we are always supposed to use the word, whenever we speak of truth absolutely, or as a possible subject of moral merit or demerit. . . . Veracity, therefore, not mere accuracy; to convey truth, not merely to say it, is the point of duty in dispute: and the only difficulty in the mind of an honest man arises from the doubt, whether more than veracity, that is, the truth and nothing but the truth——is not demanded of him by the law of conscience; whether it does not exact simplicity; that is, the truth only, and the whole truth.

¶ 78

The conscience, or effective reason, commands the design of conveying an adequate notion of the thing spoken of, when this is practicable: but at all events a right notion, or none at all. A schoolmaster is under the necessity of teaching a certain rule in simple arithmetic empirically . . . ;——the necessary truth of the rule [he does not give because that requires] a knowledge of the higher mathematics for its demonstration. He, however, conveys a right notion, though he can not convey the adequate one.

WHAT CONSCIENCE REQUIRES IN COMMUNICATING RIGHT, THOUGH INADEQUATE, NOTIONS OF THE TRUTH: (1) RIGHT INTENTION; (2) SELF-RESPECT; (3) INTEGRITY; (4) CERTAINTY THAT THE INADEQUACY OF THE TRUTH WILL NOT OUTWEIGH ITS VALUE, BUT RATHER THAT THE VALUE WILL GREATLY OUTWEIGH THE ELEMENT OF ERROR; (5) ALSO THAT THE ERROR WILL NOT PRECLUDE THE RECIPIENT'S GAINING MORE COMPLETE TRUTH LATER——NATURE'S METHOD——THE CHIEF EVILS IN MAN'S METHOD——MAN'S DROWSY AND HALF-OPENED EYE[95]

¶ 79

[T]he conscience demands: 1. That it should be the wish and design of the mind to convey the truth only; that if in addition to the negative loss implied in its inadequate-

---

[90] Coleridge's modification of Donne's *Eclogue* of Dec. 26, 1613——lines from the first speech of Idios. The alterations appear here in italics. Emerson copied Coleridge's version into *Journals*, II, 347-348, without suspecting the changes. He printed Coleridge's lines as Donne's in *Parnassus*, p. 517. Cf. also *Journals*, III, 298.

[91] Cf. *Nature*, 7.2.   [93] Cf. *Nature*, 56.17.

[92] *Works* (Shedd), II, 45.   [94] *Works* (Shedd), II, 48-49, 49.

[95] *Works* (Shedd), II, 50-51, 51-52, 52, 53, 67.

ness, the notion communicated should lead to any positive error, the cause should lie in the fault or defect of the recipient, not of the communicator, whose paramount duty, whose inalienable right, it is to preserve his own integrity, the integral character of his own moral being. Self-respect; the reverence which he owes to the presence of humanity in the person of his neighbor; the reverential upholding of the faith of man in man; gratitude for the particular act of confidence; the religious awe for the divine purposes in the gift of language; are duties too sacred and important to be sacrificed to the guesses of an individual, concerning the advantages to be gained by the breach of them.

¶ 80

It is further required, that the supposed error shall not be such as will pervert or materially vitiate the imperfect truth, in communicating which we had unwillingly, though not perhaps unwittingly, occasioned it. A barbarian so instructed in the power and intelligence of the infinite Being as to be left wholly ignorant of his moral attributes, would have acquired none but erroneous notions even of the former. . . . This must be the case with all organized truths; the component parts derive their significance from the idea of the whole. Bolingbroke removed love, justice, and choice, from power and intelligence, and yet pretended to have left unimpaired the conviction of a Deity. He might as consistently have paralyzed the optic nerve, and then excused himself by affirming, that he had, however, not touched the eye.

¶ 81

[Another] condition of a right though inadequate notion is, that the error occasioned be greatly outweighed by the importance of the truth communicated. The rustic would have little reason to thank the philosopher, who should give him true conceptions of the folly of believing in ghosts, omens, dreams, &c. at the price of abandoning his faith in divine providence, and in the continued existence of his fellow-creatures after their death. . . . [The French Encyclopedists] taught many truths, historical, political, physiological, and ecclesiastical . . . and the sole price which their scholars paid for these treasures of new information, was to believe Christianity an imposture, the Scriptures a forgery, the worship, if not the belief, of God superstition, hell a fable, heaven a dream, our life without providence, and our death without hope. . . . What can be conceived more natural than the result,——that self-acknowledged beasts should first act, and next suffer themselves to be treated, as beasts. We judge by comparison. To exclude the great is to magnify the little.

¶ 82

One condition yet remains: that the error foreseen shall not be of a kind to prevent or impede the after acquirement of that knowledge which will remove it. Observe, how graciously nature instructs her human children. She can not give us the knowledge derived from sight without occasioning us at first to mistake images of reflection for substances. But the very consequences of the delusion lead inevitably to its detection; and out of the ashes of the error rises a new flower of knowledge. We not only see, but are enabled to discover by what means we see. So, too, we are under the necessity, in given circumstances, of mistaking a square for a round object: but ere the mistake can have any practical consequences, it is not only removed, but in its removal gives us the symbol of a new fact, that of distance.

¶ 83

The evils occasioned by [the promulgation of truth], with few and rare exceptions, have their origin in the attempts to suppress or pervert it . . . or in the extravagances of ignorance and credulity roused from their lethargy, and angry at the medicinal disturbance——awaking, not yet broad awake, and thus blending the monsters of uneasy dreams with the real objects, on which the drowsy eye had alternately half-opened and closed, again half-opened and again closed.

IMPORTANCE OF GUARDING MAN'S LIBERTIES, ESPECIALLY THAT OF FREEDOM OF THE PRESS——BOOKS ARE JUDGED ONLY AFTER PUBLICA-TION——WORDS ARE MORAL ACTS[96]

¶ 84

Nor let any one falsely persuade himself, that those who keep watch and ward for liberty, are meddling with things that do not concern them, instead of minding their own business. For all men should know, that all blessings are stored and protected

---

[96] *Works* (Shedd), II, 74-76.

in this one, as in a common repository. . . . We have reason then . . . to rest satisfied with our laws, which no more prevent a book from coming into the world unlicensed, lest it should prove a libel, than a traveller from passing unquestioned through our turnpike-gates, because it is possible he may be a highwayman. Innocence is presumed in both cases. The publication is a part of the offence, and its necessary condition. Words are moral acts, and words deliberately made public the law considers in the same light as any other cognizable overt act.

THE REASON CONTRIBUTES TO THE DIGNITY OF MAN——REASON IS OBLIGATORY ON ALL MANKIND——WHAT THEN IS OF PERMANENT VALUE TO ONE MUST BE SO TO ALL——A PERSON NOT TRUE TO HIMSELF, THERE-FORE, ROBS HIS NEIGHBOR, AND WHEN HE ROBS HIS NEIGHBOR, HE SINS AGAINST HIMSELF[97]

¶ 85

This again is the mystery and the dignity of our human nature, that we can not give up our reason, without giving up at the same time our individual personality. For that must appear to each man to be his reason which produces in him the highest sense of certainty; and yet it is not reason, except so far as it is of universal validity and obligatory on all mankind. There is a one heart for the whole mighty mass of humanity, and every pulse in each particular vessel strives to beat in concert with it. He who asserts that truth is of no importance except in the signification of sincerity, confounds sense with madness, and the word of God with a dream. If the power of reasoning be the gift of the supreme Reason, that we be sedulous, yea, and militant in the endeavor to reason aright, is his implied command. But what is of permanent and essential interest to one man must needs be so to all, in proportion to the means and opportunities of each. Woe to him by whom these are neglected, and double woe to him by whom they are withholden; for he robs at once himself and his neighbor. That man's soul is not dear to himself, to whom the souls of his brethren are not dear. As far as they can be influenced by him, they are parts and properties of his own soul, their faith his faith, their errors his burthen, their righteousness and bliss his righteousness and his reward——and of their guilt and misery his own will be the echo.

COLERIDGE ON GOVERNMENTS——SYSTEMS OF POLITICAL PHILOSOPHY CAN BE REDUCED TO THREE CLASSES[97a]

¶ 85a

The first denies all truth and distinct meaning to the words, *right* and *duty;* and affirming that the human mind consists of nothing but the manifold modifications of passive sensation, considers men as the highest sort of animals indeed, but at the same time the most wretched; inasmuch as their defenceless nature forces them into society: while such is the multiplicity of wants engendered by the social state, that the wishes of one are sure to be in contradiction to those of some other. The assertors of this system consequently ascribe the origin and continuance of government to fear, or the power of the stronger, aided by the force of custom. This is the system of Hobbes.

¶ 85b

The second system corresponds to the second point of view under which the human being may be considered, namely, as an animal gifted with understanding, or the faculty or suiting measures to circumstances. According to this theory, every institu-tion of national origin needs no other justification than a proof, that under the par-ticular circumstances it is expedient.

¶ 85c

The third and last system . . . denies all rightful origin to government, except as far as it is derivable from principles contained in the reason of man, and judges all the relations of man in society by the laws of moral necessity, according to ideas. I here use the word in its highest and primitive sense, and as nearly synonymous with the modern word *ideal,*——according to archetypal ideas co-essential with the reason, the consciousness of these ideas being indeed the sign and necessary product of the full development of the reason. The following then is the fundamental principle of this theory: Nothing is to be deemed rightful in civil society, or to be tolerated as such, but what is capable of being demonstrated out of the original laws of the pure reason. . . . Whatever is not everywhere necessary, is nowhere right.

---

[97] *Works* (Shedd), II, 94. This is another instance of "All in each, and each in all."
[97a] *Works* (Shedd), II, 154; 163; 165.

MAN MADE IN GOD'S IMAGE——HENCE HAS IMMORTALITY AND SELF-
DETERMINATION —— MAN'S REASON —— REFLECTIVE SELF-CONSCIOUS-
NESS——PRINCIPLES *VS.* MAXIMS——LAW OF CONSCIENCE——DUTY——
THE GREAT IDEAS OF THE SOUL: GOD, FREE WILL AND IMMORTALITY[98]

¶ 86

God created man in his own image. To be the image of his own eternity created he
man! Of eternity and self-existence what other likeness is possible, but immortality
and moral self-determination? In addition to sensation, perception, and practical judgment ... God gave us reason, and with reason he gave us reflective self-consciousness;
gave us principles, distinguished from the maxims and generalizations of outward
experience by their absolute and essential universality and necessity; and above all,
by superadding to reason the mysterious faculty of free-will and consequent personal
amenability, he gave us conscience——that law of conscience, which in the power,
and as the indwelling word, of a holy and omnipotent legislator commands us ... to
attribute reality, and actual existence, to those ideas and to those only, without which
the conscience itself would be baseless and contradictory, to the ideas of soul, of free-
will, of immortality, and of God. To God, as the reality of the conscience and the
source of all obligation; to free-will, as the power of the human being to maintain the
obedience which God through the conscience has commanded, against all the might of
nature; and to the immortality of the soul, as a state in which the weal and woe of
man shall be proportioned to his moral worth. With this faith all nature ... presents
itself to us, now as the aggregated material of duty, and now as a vision of the Most
High revealing to us the mode, and time, and particular instance of applying and
realizing that universal rule, pre-established in the heart of our reason.

QUOTATIONS FROM GIORDANO BRUNO——THE WISE MAN PURSUES A
LOFTY CONTEMPLATION——MAN IS A GREAT MIRACLE——TRIES TO BE-
COME ALL THINGS——GOD IS INFINITE, AND YET EVERYTHING EVERY-
WHERE[99]

¶ 87

"A wise spirit does not fear death, nay, sometimes——as in cases of voluntary
martyrdom——seeks and goes forth to meet it, of its own accord. For there awaits all
actual beings, for duration eternity, for place immensity, for action omniformity. We
pursue, therefore, a species of contemplation not light or futile, but the weightiest
and most worthy of an accomplished man, while we examine and seek for the splendor,
the interfusion, and communication of the Divinity and of nature ... in the august
palace of the Omnipotent, in the illimitable ethereal space, in the infinite power, that
creates all things, and is the abiding being of all things."

¶ 87a

"Let us then cast our eyes upon the omniform image of the attributes of the all-
creating Supreme, nor admit any representation of his excellency but the living
universe, which he has created! Thence was man entitled by Trismegistus, the great
miracle, inasmuch as he has been made capable of entering into union with God, as if
he were himself a divine nature; tries to become all things, even as in God all things
are; and in limitless progression of limited states of being, urges onward to the
ultimate aim, even as God is simultaneously infinite, and everywhere all!"[100]

REASON IN ACTION——EACH TRUTH MAN DISCOVERS IMPLIES OTHERS——
EXAMPLE OF THE CIRCLE[101]

¶ 88

Every man must feel, that though he may not be exerting different faculties, he is
exerting his faculties in a different way, when in one instance he begins with some
one self-evident truth,——that the *radii* of a circle, for instance, are all equal,——and
in consequence of this being true sees at once without any actual experience, that some
other thing must be true likewise, and that, this being true, some third thing must be
equally true, and so on till he comes, we will say, to the properties of the lever, con-

[98] *Works* (Shedd), II, 106-107.
[99] From Bruno's *De Monade* in *Works* (Shedd), II, 109-110. Coleridge requests the
reader to make allowances for Bruno's peculiar bias.
[100] This is "Each in all; all in each."
[101] *Works* (Shedd), II, 147. Cf. *Nature*, 56.3-14.

sidered as the spoke of a circle; which is capable of having all its marvellous powers demonstrated even to a savage who had never seen a lever, and without supposing any other previous knowledge in his mind, but this one, that there is a conceivable figure, all possible lines from the middle to the circumference of which are of the same length.

TRUTHS OF THE REASON ARE SUBLIME AND VALID——BUT THE REASON IN EVERY MAN DOES NOT QUALIFY HIM TO BE A LEGISLATOR FOR MAN-KIND——IT EXISTS FOR HUMILITY, SELF-CONQUEST AND SELF-GOVERN-MENT[102]

¶ 89

[B]y detecting the true source of the influence of these principles, we shall at the same time discover their natural place and object; and that in themselves they are not only truths, but most important and sublime truths; and that their falsehood and their danger consist altogether in their misapplication. Thus the dignity of human nature will be secured, and at the same time a lesson of humility taught to each individual, when we are made to see that the universal necessary laws, and pure ideas of reason, were given us, not for the purpose of flattering our pride, and enabling us to become national legislators; but that, by an energy of continued self-conquest, we might establish a free and yet absolute government in our own spirits.

ROUSSEAU IN THEORY RECOGNIZES HUMAN LIMITATIONS, BUT IN PRAC-TICE HE MAKES EVERY MAN A POTENTIAL LEGISLATOR AND MOUTH-PIECE OF PURE REASON——HE ASSUMES THAT LEGISLATURES CAN ELIMINATE THE SELF-LOVE OF MEN[103]

¶ 90

[Rousseau] states the problem of a perfect constitution of government in the following words . . . "to find a form of society according to which each one uniting himself with the whole shall yet obey himself only and remain as free as before." This right of the individual to retain his whole natural independence, even in the social state, is absolutely inalienable [according to Rousseau]. He can not possibly concede or compromise it: for this very right is one of his most sacred duties. He would sin against himself, and commit high treason against the reason which the Almighty Creator has given him, if he dared abandon its exclusive right to govern his actions. Laws obligatory on the conscience, can only therefore proceed from that reason which remains always one and the same, whether it speaks through this or that person: like the voice of an external ventriloquist, it is indifferent from whose lips it appears to come, if only it be audible.

¶ 91

The individuals indeed [says Rousseau] are subject to errors and passions, and each man has his own defects. But when men are assembled in person or by real representatives, the actions and reactions of individual self-love balance each other; errors are neutralized by opposite errors; and the winds rushing from all quarters at once with equal force, produce for the time a deep calm, during which the general will arising from the general reason displays itself.

COLERIDGE POINTS OUT ROUSSEAU'S FALLACY——REMINDS HIM OF DIS-TINCTION BETWEEN THE WILL OF THE MOB AND THE WILL OF REASON[104]

¶ 92

It is a mere probability, against which other probabilities may be weighed: as the lust of authority, the contagious nature of enthusiasm, and other of the acute or chronic diseases of deliberative assemblies. But which of these results is the more probable, the correction or contagion of evil, must depend on circumstances and grounds of expediency: and thus we already find ourselves beyond the magic circle of the pure reason, and within the sphere of the understanding and the prudence. Of this important fact Rousseau was by no means unaware in his theory, though with gross inconsistency he takes no notice of it in his application of the theory to practice. He admits the possibility . . . that the most numerous popular assemblies, nay even whole

---

[102] *Works* (Shedd), II, 171.
[103] *Works* (Shedd), II, 177-178. Reference is made to *Le Contrat Social*.
[104] *Works* (Shedd), II, 178.

nations, may at times be hurried away by the same passions, and under the dominion of a common error. This will of all is then of no more value, than the humors of any one individual: and must therefore be sacredly distinguished from the pure will which flows from universal reason. . . . [F]or in this distinction, established by Rousseau himself, between the *volonté de tous* and the *volonté générale*,——that is, between the collective will, and a casual overbalance of wills——the falsehood or nothingness of the whole system becomes manifest.

ROUSSEAU'S OVER-SIMPLIFICATION DEMONSTRATED——LIMITATIONS OF SELF-RELIANCE——THE REASON IN MAN IS INVIOLABLE ONLY IN PERSONAL MORALITY——PROBLEMS OF SOCIETY AND PROPERTY REQUIRE THE ACTIVITY OF THE UNDERSTANDING OR COMMON SENSE——PURE REASON IS, THEREFORE, INAPPLICABLE AND INEFFECTIVE——GEOMETRY AS AN ILLUSTRATION——COMPLEXITY OF HUMAN GOVERNMENT SPRINGS FROM MAN'S OWN COMPLEXITY[105]

¶ 93

Apply [Rousseau's] principles to any case, in which the sacred and inviolable laws of morality are immediately interested, all becomes just and pertinent. No power on earth can oblige me to act against my conscience. No magistrate, no monarch, no legislature, can without tyranny compel me to do any thing which the acknowledged laws of God have forbidden me to do. So act that thou mayest be able, without involving any contradiction, to will that the maxim of thy conduct should be the law of all intelligent beings——is the one universal and sufficient principle and guide of morality. And why? Because the object of morality is not the outward act, but the internal maxim of our actions. And so far it is infallible. But with what show of reason can we pretend, from a principle by which we are to determine the purity of our motives, to deduce the form and matter of a rightful government, the main office of which is to regulate the outward actions of particular bodies of men, according to their particular circumstances? Can we hope better of constitutions framed by ourselves, than of that which was given by Almighty Wisdom itself?[106]

¶ 94

That reason should be our guide and governor is an undeniable truth, and all our notion of right and wrong is built thereon: for reason is one of the two fountain-heads in which the whole moral nature of man originated and subsists. From reason alone can we derive the principles which our understandings are to apply, the ideal to which by means of our understandings we should endeavor to approximate. This, however, gives no proof that reason alone ought to govern and direct human beings, either as individuals or as states. It ought not to do this, because it can not. The laws of reason are unable to satisfy the first conditions of human society . . . unaided by the positive and conventional laws in the formation of which the understanding must be our guide, and which become just because they happen to be expedient. The chief object for which men first formed themselves into a state was not the protection of their lives, but of their property. . . . Now it is impossible to deduce the right of property from pure reason.

¶ 95

Geometry holds forth an ideal which can never be fully realized in nature, even because it is nature; because bodies are more than extension, and to pure extension of space only the mathematical theorems wholly correspond. In the same manner the moral laws of the intellectual world, as far as they are deducible from pure intellect, are never perfectly applicable to our mixed and sensitive nature, because man is something besides reason; because his reason never acts by itself, but must clothe itself in the substance of individual understanding and specific inclination, in order to become a reality and an object of consciousness and experience. . . . [For] universal principles, as far as they are principles and universal, necessarily suppose uniform and perfect subjects, which are to be found in the ideas of pure geometry and, I trust, in the realities of heaven, but never, never, in creatures of flesh and blood.

---

[105] *Works* (Shedd), II, 180, 184-185, 186-187.
[106] Coleridge means the "Ten Commandments," Torah, "Sermon on the Mount," etc.

LAW OF POLARITY DEFINED——SYNTHESIS AND ANTITHESIS——IDENTITY AND OPPOSITION[107]

¶ 96

There is, in strictness, no proper opposition but between the two polar forces of one and the same power. Every power in nature and in spirit must evolve an opposite as the sole means and condition of its manifestation: and all opposition is a tendency to re-union. This is the universal law of polarity or essential dualism, first promulgated by Heraclitus, 2000 years afterwards re-published, and made the foundation both of logic, of physics, and of metaphysics by Giordano Bruno. The principle may be thus expressed. The identity of *thesis* and *antithesis* is the substance of all being; their opposition the condition of all existence or being manifested; and every thing or *phenomenon* is the exponent of a *synthesis* as long as the opposite energies are retained in that *synthesis*. Thus water is neither oxygen nor hydrogen, not yet is it a commixture of both; but the *synthesis* or indifference of the two: and as long as the *copula* endures, by which it becomes water, or rather which alone is water, it is not less a simple body than either of the imaginary elements, improperly called its ingredients or components.

LUTHER WAS AIDED BY THE SPIRIT OF THE TIMES——BELIEVED WHAT ALL THE BEST BELIEVED——FAITHFULLY FOLLOWED HIS OWN IDEAL[108]

¶ 97

[My] readers must think of Luther not as he really was, but as he might have been, if he had been born in the age and under the circumstances of the Swiss philosopher [Rousseau]. For this purpose I must strip him of many advantages which he derived from his own times, and must contemplate him in his natural weaknesses as well as in his original strength. Each referred all things to his own ideal.[109] The ideal was indeed widely different in the one and in the other: and this was not the least of Luther's many advantages, or, to use a favorite phrase of his own, not one of his least favors of preventing grace. Happily for him he had derived his standard from a common measure already received by the good and wise;[110] I mean the inspired writings, the study of which Erasmus had previously restored among the learned. To know that we are in sympathy with others, moderates our feelings as well as strengthens our convictions: and for the mind, which opposes itself to the faith of the multitude, it is more especially desirable, that there should exist an object out of itself, on which it may fix its attention, and thus balance its own energies.

LUTHER WAS A WARRIOR WHOSE FAITH REMOVED MOUNTAINS——A POET WHO ACTED RATHER THAN WROTE POEMS[111]

¶ 98

If this Christian Hercules, this heroic cleanser of the Augean stable of apostasy, had been born and educated in the present or the preceding generation, he would, doubtless, have holden himself for a man of genius and original power. But with this faith alone, he would scarcely have removed the mountains which he did remove. The darkness and superstition of the age, which required such a reformer, had moulded his mind for the reception of impressions concerning himself, better suited to inspire the strength and enthusiasm necessary for the task of reformation, impressions more in sympathy with the spirits whom he was to influence.[112] He deemed himself gifted with supernatural influxes, an especial servant of heaven, a chosen warrior, fighting as the general of a small but faithful troop, against an army of evil beings, headed by the prince of the air. These were no metaphorical beings in his apprehension. He was a poet indeed, as great a poet as ever lived in any age or country; but his poetic images were so vivid, that they mastered the poet's own mind! He was possessed with them, as with substances distinct from himself: Luther did not write, he acted poems.[113]

---

[107] *Works* (Shedd), II, 91. See ¶s. 138-139, 155.
[108] *Works* (Shedd), II, 125.
[109] This phrase appears frequently in Emerson. Cf. *Nature*, 58.14.
[110] Cf. Cabot, *Memoir*, II, 713.
[111] *Works* (Shedd), II, 131.
[112] Emerson describes Luther's achievements as of the "material sublime" rather than the "moral." See *Journals*, III, 367, and ¶s. 296-297.
[113] Quoted in *Journals*, III, 367 (Nov. 19, 1834).

PURPOSE OF *THE FRIEND* IS TO POINT MEN TO ABSOLUTE PRINCIPLES[114]

¶ 99

To refer men's opinions to their absolute principles,[115] and thence their feelings to the appropriate objects, and in their due degrees; and finally, to apply the principles thus ascertained, to the formation of steadfast convictions concerning the most important question of politics, morality, and religion——these are to be the objects and the contents of his work.

¶ 99a

But what are my metaphysics?——Merely the referring of the mind to its own consciousness for truths indispensable to its own happiness! To what purpose do I, or am I about to, employ them? To perplex our clearest notions and living moral instincts? To deaden the feelings of will and free power, to extinguish the light of love and of conscience, to make myself and others worthless, soulless, God-less? No! to expose the folly and the legerdemain of those who have thus abused the blessed machine of language; to support all old and venerable truths; and by them to support, to kindle, to project the spirit; to make the reason spread light over our feelings, to make our feelings, with their vital warmth, actualize our reason.

TRUTH IS MADE ONE'S OWN ONLY BY AN ACT OF THE WILL——SPECULATIVE TRUTHS ARE DISCOVERED BY FIRST MAKING A POSTULATE—— THE MORAL BEING IS THE SOURCE OF THE INTELLECTUAL——SELF-KNOWLEDGE IS BEGINNING OF WISDOM[116]

¶ 100

How can a truth, new to us, be made our own without examination and self-questioning——any new truth, I mean, that relates to the properties of the mind, and its various faculties and affections? But whatever demands effort, requires time. Ignorance seldom vaults into knowledge, but passes into it through an intermediate state of obscurity, even as night into day through twilight. All speculative truths begin with a postulate, even the truths of geometry.[117] They all suppose an act of the will; for in the moral being lies the source of the intellectual.[118] The first step to knowledge, or rather the previous condition of all insight into truth, is to dare commune with our very and permanent self. It is Warburton's remark, not the Friend's, that of all literary exercitations, whether designed for the use or entertainment of the world, there are none of so much importance, or so immediately our concern, as those which let us into the knowledge of our own nature. Others may exercise the understanding or amuse the imagination; but these only can improve the heart and form the human mind to wisdom.

NATURE DECREES SELF-RELIANCE[119]

¶ 101

Nature has irrevocably decreed, that our prime dependence in all stages of life after infancy and childhood have been passed through (nor do I know that this latter ought to be excepted) must be upon our own minds; and that the way to knowledge shall be long, difficult, winding, and oftentimes returning upon itself.

FAITH AND WORKS——PALEY EMPHASIZES THE LATTER BY ASSERTING "GENERAL CONSEQUENCES"[120] TO BE CHIEF AND BEST CRITERION OF THE RIGHT AND WRONG OF ACTIONS——COLERIDGE'S REFUTATION—— MAKES FAITH (OR INTENTION) AND GOOD WORKS INSEPARABLE—— "THE ROOT BEARS *THEE*"——MEANING OF "GOOD EXAMPLE"[121]

¶ 102

First: [Paley's theory of "General Consequences"] depends on, and must vary with, the notions of the individual, who, in order to determine the nature of an action, is to

---

[114] *Works* (Shedd), II, 27; 103.
[115] See *Nature*, 28.8-11; 71.13-20; 80.4-8.
[116] *Works* (Shedd), II, 108. See "will is deeper than mind" in ¶ 282.
[117] See *Nature*, 68.20 through 69.21, esp. 69.20.
[118] See *Journals*, III, 530.
[119] *Works* (Shedd), II, 374.
[120] See William Paley, *Moral and Political Philosophy*, Bk. II, chaps. i-viii.
[121] *Works* (Shedd), II, 286-287; 287-288; 288-289; 291.

make the calculation of its general consequences. Here, as in all other calculation, the result depends on that faculty of the soul in the degrees of which men most vary from each other, and which is itself most affected by accidental advantages or disadvantages of education, natural talent, and acquired knowledge——the faculty, I mean, of foresight and systematic comprehension. But surely morality, which is of equal importance to all men, ought to be grounded, if possible, in that part of our nature which in all men may and ought to be the same,——in the conscience and the common sense.

¶ 103

Secondly: this criterion confounds morality with law; and when the author adds, that in all probability the divine Justice will be regulated in the final judgment by a similar rule, he draws away the attention from the will, that is, from the inward motives and impulses which constitute the essence of morality, to the outward act; and thus changes the virtue commanded by the gospel into the mere legality, which was to be enlivened by it. One of the most persuasive, if not one of the strongest, arguments for a future state, rests on the belief, that although by the necessity of things our outward and temporal welfare must be regulated by our outward actions, which alone can be the objects and guides of human law, there must yet needs come a juster and more appropriate sentence hereafter, in which our intentions will be considered, and our happiness and misery made to accord with the grounds of our actions. Our fellow-creatures can only judge what we are by what we do; but in the eye of our Maker what we do is of no worth, except as it flows from what we are. Though the fig-tree should produce no visible fruit, yet if the living sap is in it, and if it has struggled to put forth buds and blossoms which have been prevented from maturing by inevitable contingencies of tempests or untimely frosts, the virtuous sap will be accounted as fruit.

¶ 104

Just and generous actions may proceed from bad motives, and both may, and often do, originate in parts, and, as it were, fragments of our nature. A lascivious man may sacrifice half his estate to rescue his friend from prison, for he is constitutionally sympathetic, and the better part of his nature happened to be uppermost. The same man shall afterwards exert the same disregard of money in an attempt to seduce that friend's wife or daughter. But faith is a total act of the soul: it is the whole state of the mind, or it is not at all; and in this consists its power, as well as its exclusive worth. . . . The Apostle tells those who would substitute obedience for faith (addressing the man as obedience personified), Know that *thou bearest not the root, but the root thee*[122]——a sentence which, methinks, should have rendered all disputes concerning faith and good works impossible among those who profess to take the Scriptures for their guide. . . . As if an action could be either good or bad disjoined from its principle. As if it could be, in the Christian and only proper sense of the word, an action at all, and not rather a mechanic series of lucky or unlucky motions!

¶ 105

God will judge each man before all men: consequently he will judge us relatively to man. But man knows not the heart of man; scarcely does any one know his own. There must therefore be outward and visible signs, by which men may be able to judge of the inward state; and thereby justify the ways of God to their own spirits, in the reward or punishment of themselves and their fellow-men. Now good works are these signs, and as such become necessary. In short there are two parties, God and the human race;——and both are to be satisfied. First, God, who seeth the root and knoweth the heart: therefore there must be faith, or the entire and absolute principle. Then man, who can judge only by the fruits: therefore that faith must bear fruits of righteousness, that principle must manifest itself by actions. But that which God sees, that alone justifies. What man sees, does in this life show that the justifying principle may be the root of the thing seen. . . . Good works may exist without saving principles, and therefore can not contain in themselves the principle of salvation; but saving principles never did, never can, exist without good works.

¶ 106

The duty of setting a good example is no doubt a most important duty; but the example is good or bad, necessary or unnecessary, accordingly as the action may be, which has a chance of being imitated. I once knew a small, but (in outward circumstances at least) respectable congregation, four fifths of whom professed that they

---

[122] Romans 11:18.

went to church entirely for the example's sake; in other words to cheat each other and act a common lie! These rational Christians had not considered that example may increase the good or evil of an action, but can never constitute either. If it was a foolish thing to kneel when they were not inwardly praying, or to sit and listen to a discourse of which they believed little and cared nothing, they were setting a foolish example.

WORDSWORTH'S WORDS ARE THUNDER[123]

¶ 107

But if my readers wish to see the question of the efficacy of principles and popular opinions for evil and for good proved and illustrated with an eloquence worthy of the subject, I can refer them with the hardiest anticipation of their thanks to the late work concerning the relations of Great Britain, Spain, and Portugal,[124] by my honored friend, William Wordsworth, *quem quoties lego, non verba mihi videor audire, sed tonitrua.*[125]

PROGRESS IS NOT ALWAYS OBVIOUS——THROUGH SLEEP AND APPARENT INACTIVITY ENERGY IS BEING STORED UP——SOLITARY MINDS LABOR FOR TRUTH EVEN IN EVIL DAYS[126]

¶ 108

The progress of the species neither is nor can be like that of a Roman road in a right line. It may be more justly compared to that of a river, which, both in its smaller reaches and larger turnings, is frequently forced back towards its fountains by objects which can not otherwise be eluded or overcome; yet with an accompanying impulse that will insure its advancement hereafter, it is either gaining strength every hour, or conquering in secret some difficulty, by a labor that contributes as effectually to further it in its course, as when it moves forward uninterrupted in a line, direct as that of the Roman road with which I began the comparison.

¶ 109

It suffices to content the mind, though there may be an apparent stagnation, or a retrograde movement in the species, that something is doing which is necessary to be done, and the effects of which will in due time appear; that something is unremittingly gaining, either in secret preparation or in open and triumphant progress. But in fact here, as everywhere, we are deceived by creations which the mind is compelled to make for itself; we speak of the species not as an aggregate, but as endued with the form and separate life of an individual. But human kind,——what is it else than myriads of rational beings in various degrees obedient to their reason; some torpid, some aspiring; some in eager chase to the right hand, some to the left; these wasting down their moral nature, and these feeding it for immortality? A whole generation may appear even to sleep, or may be exasperated with rage,——they that compose it, tearing each other to pieces with more than brutal fury. It is enough for complacency and hope, that scattered and solitary minds are always laboring somewhere in the service of truth and virtue; and that by the sleep of the multitude the energy of the multitude may be prepared; and that by the fury of the people the chains of the people may be broken.

———————

WORDS OF A SOLDIER IN PARLIAMENT'S ARMY DURING THE ENGLISH CIVIL WAR: A MAN IS MOST HONORABLE WHO DEFENDS A TRUTH SINGLE HANDED AGAINST THE WORLD——WHO LOVES TRUTH ABOVE HIS OWN LIFE——WHAT A MAN IS *WITHIN*, THAT ONLY CAN HE SEE *WITHOUT*[127]

---

[123] *Works* (Shedd), II, 169.

[124] William Wordsworth, [*Concerning the Relations of Gt. Britain, Spain and Portugal &c.,* London, 1809].

[125] See *Journals*, II, 405, 429-430.

[126] *Works* (Shedd), II, 362-363.

[127] *Works* (Shedd), II, 377-378. Coleridge's condensed version occupies pages 377-381. On the last page he characterizes the soldier as having "a mind so constituted and disciplined as to find in its own wants and instincts an interest in truths for their truth's sake." He continues: "To possess the end in the means, as it is essential to morality in the moral world, and the contra-distinction of goodness from mere prudence, so is it, in

¶ 110

"I judge it ten times more honorable for a single person, in witnessing a truth to oppose the world[128] in its power, wisdom, and authority, this standing in its full strength, and he singly and nakedly, than fighting many battles by force of arms, and gaining them all. I have no life but truth; and if truth be advanced by my suffering, then my life also. If truth live, I live; if justice live, I live; and these can not die, but by any man's suffering for them are enlarged, enthroned. Death can not hurt me.[129] I sport with him, am above his reach. I live an immortal life. What we have within, that only can we see without.[130] I can not see death; and he that hath not this freedom is a slave. He is in the arms of that, the phantom of which be beholdeth and seemeth to himself to flee from."

PARLIAMENTARIANS SEE EVIL IN OTHERS BECAUSE THEIR OWN HEARTS ARE EVIL——THEY PURSUE THINGS OF HOPE IN THE SPIRIT OF FEAR—— THEY LACK INNER INTEGRITY[131]

¶ 111

"Thus, you see that the king hath a will to redeem his present loss. You see it by means of the lust after power in your own hearts.[132] For my part I condemn his unlawful seeking after it. I condemn his falsehood and indirectness therein. But if he should not endeavor the restoring of the kingliness to the realm, and the dignity of its kings, he were false to his trust, false to the majesty of God that he is intrusted with. The desire of recovering his loss is justifiable. Yea, I should condemn him as unbelieving and pusillanimous, if he should not hope for it. But here is his misery and yours too at present, that ye are unbelieving and pusillanimous, and are, both alike, pursuing things of hope in the spirit of fear. Thus you condemn the parliament for acknowledging the king's power so far as to seek to him by a treaty; while by taking such pains against him you manifest your own belief that he hath a great power."

THE SPARK OF GOD CANNOT BE SUPPRESSED BY FORCE——ALL THINGS TEND TO THEIR CENTER——NATURAL ORDER CANNOT BE THWARTED—— VIOLENCE DEFEATS ITSELF[133]

¶ 112

"But as you give testimony to his power, so you take a course to advance it; for there is nothing that hath any spark of God in it, but the more it is suppressed, the more it rises. If you did indeed believe, that the original of power were in the people, you would believe likewise that the concessions extorted from the king would rest with you. And, doubtless, such of them as in righteousness ought to have been given would do so, but that your violent courses disturb the natural order of things, in which they still tend to their centre. These courses, therefore, so far from being the way to secure what we have got, are the way to lose them, and (for a time at least) to set up princes in a higher form than ever. For all things by force compelled from their nature will fly back with the greater earnestness on the removal of that force;[134] and this, in the present case, must soon weary itself out, and hath no less an enemy in its own satiety than in the disappointment of the people."

SUFFERING STIMULATES SYMPATHY——MEN NATURALLY PITY SUFFERERS[135]

¶ 113

"Again, you speak of the king's reputation, and do not consider that the more you crush him, the sweeter the fragrance that comes from him. While he suffers, the spirit of God and glory rests upon him. There is a glory and a freshness sparkling in him by suffering, an excellency that was hidden, and which you have drawn out. And naturally men are ready to pity sufferers. When nothing will gain me, affliction will. I confess

---

the intellectual world, the moral constituent of genius, and that by which true genius is contra-distinguished from mere talent."

[128] See *Journals*, III, 368, for lines which were possibly inspired by this soldier.
[129] Cf. *Nature*, 71.10-17; 27.5-8.
[130] Cf. *Nature*, 94.5 and ¶ 259.
[131] *Works* (Shedd), II, 378.
[132] "Like only can know like." Cf. *Nature*, 44.18-19; 94.5.
[133] *Works* (Shedd), II, 378-379.
[134] Cf. *Nature*, 41.23: "Action is equal to reaction."
[135] *Works* (Shedd), II, 379.

his sufferings make me a royalist, who never cared for him. He that doth and can suffer shall have my heart; you had it while you suffered. But now your severe punishment of him for his abuses in government, and your own usurpations, will not only win the hearts of the people to the oppressed suffering king, but provoke them to rage against you, as having robbed them of the interest which they had in his royalty."

SELF-INTEREST INCOMPATIBLE WITH HIGH PURPOSE——THE CHRISTIAN CANNOT SERVE WITH A DIVIDED HEART[136]

¶ 114

"To assume the office and the name of champions for the common interest, and of Christ's soldiers, and yet to act for self-safety is so poor and mean a thing that it must needs produce most vile and absurd actions, the scorn of the old pagans, but for Christians who in all things are to love their neighbor as themselves, and God above both, it is of all affections the unworthiest. Let me be a fool and boast, if so I may show you, while it is yet time, a little of that rest and security which I and those of the same spirit enjoy, and which you have turned your backs upon; self, like a banished thing, wandering in strange ways."

LAW OF COMPENSATION OPERATES[137]——LIKE ONLY CAN KNOW LIKE—— RECONCILIATION ENGENDERS RECONCILIATION——ENMITY BEGETS EN- MITY——MAIN TASK IS TO ENLARGE ONE'S OWN SOUL——RESULTANT PEACE AND SECURITY[138]

¶ 115

"First, then, I fear no party, or interest, for I love all, I am reconciled to all, and therein I find all reconciled to me. I have enmity to none but the son of perdition. It is enmity begets insecurity: and while men live in the flesh, and in enmity to any party, or interest, in a private, divided, and self good, there will be, there can not but be, perpetual wars; except that one particular should quite ruin all other parts and live alone, which the universal must not, will not, suffer. For to admit a part to devour and absorb the others, were to destroy the whole, which is God's presence therein; and such a mind in any part doth not only fight with another part, but against the whole. Every faction of men, therefore, striving to make themselves absolute, and to owe their safety to their strength, and not to their sympathy, do directly war against God who is love, peace, and a general good, gives being to all and cherishes all, and, there- fore, can have neither peace nor security. But we being enlarged into the largeness of God, and comprehending all things in our bosoms by the divine spirit, are at rest with all, and delight in all; for we know nothing but what is, in its essence, in our own hearts.[139] Kings, nobles, are much beloved of us, because they are in us, of us, one with us, we as Christians being kings and lords by the anointing of God."[140]

AMOUR DE MOI-MEME——SELF-LOVE WELL CALCULATED——UTILITY—— SELF-LOVE AS A SYSTEM OF MORALITY——SELF-INTEREST COMPARED WITH SENSE OF DUTY——EVEN IF RESULTS WERE THE SAME, THERE WOULD BE A GREAT DIFFERENCE BETWEEN THE AGENTS——CHRISTIAN PRINCIPLE OF LOVE OF GOD——THE SPIRIT OF HONOR[141]

¶ 116

Amour *de moi-même, mais bien calculé*——was the motto and maxim of a French philosopher. Our fancy inspirited by the more imaginative powers of hope and fear enables us to present to ourselves the future as the present, and thence to accept a scheme of self-love for a system of morality. And doubtless, an enlightened self- interest would recommend the same course of outward conduct, as the sense of duty would do; even though the motives in the former case had respect to this life exclu- sively. But to show the desirableness of an object, or the contrary, is one thing; to excite the desire to constitute the aversion, is another: the one being to the other as a common guide-post to the "chariot instinct with spirit," which at once directs and

---

[136] *Works* (Shedd), II, 380.
[137] Cf. *Journals*, II, 357-358 (Feb. 23, 1831).
[138] Cf. *Nature*, 80.15.
[139] This is the "Quantum sumus, scimus."
[140] *Works* (Shedd), II, 380-381.
[141] *Works* (Shedd), II, 388-389.

conveys; or employing a more familiar image, we may compare the rule of self-interest to a watch with an excellent hour-plate, hand, and regulator, but without its spring and wheel-work.

¶ 117

But let it be granted, that in certain individuals from a happy evenness of nature, formed into a habit by the strength of education, the influence of example, and by favorable circumstances in general, the actions diverging from self-love as their centre should be precisely the same as those produced from the Christian principle, which requires of us that we should place our self and our neighbor at an equal distance, and love both alike as modes in which we realize and exhibit the love of God above all;——wherein would the difference be then? I answer boldly,——even in that, for which all actions have their whole worth and their main value,——in the agents themselves. So much indeed is this of the very substance of genuine morality, that wherever the latter has given way in the general opinion to a scheme of ethics founded on utility, its place is soon challenged by the spirit of honor.

GENERAL AND LONG-CONTINUED ASSENT IS A QUALIFICATION FOR ACCEPTANCE OF TRUTHS WHICH MAN CAN KNOW ONLY IMPERFECTLY——FAITH IN IMMORTALITY IS AN EXAMPLE[142]

¶ 118

But lest in uttering truth I should convey falsehood and fall myself into the error which it is my object to expose, it will be requisite to distinguish an apprehension of the whole of a truth, even where that apprehension is dim and indistinct, from a partial perception of the same rashly assumed as a perception of the whole. The first is rendered inevitable in many things for many, in some points for all, men from the progressiveness no less than from the imperfection of humanity, which itself dictates and enforces the precept, Believe that thou mayest understand. The most knowing must at times be content with the *facit* of a sum too complex or subtle for us to follow nature through the antecedent process. Hence in subjects not under the cognizance of the senses wise men have always attached a high value to general and long-continued assent, as a presumption of truth. After all the subtle reasonings and fair analogies which logic and induction could supply to a mighty intellect, it is yet on this ground that the Socrates of Plato mainly rests his faith in the immortality of the soul, and the moral government of the universe. It had been holden by all nations in all ages, but with deepest conviction by the best and wisest men, as a belief connatural with goodness and akin to prophecy.

HUMAN MIND HAS NO PREDILECTION FOR ABSURDITY——BELIEFS OR DOCTRINES WIDELY DIFFUSED AMONG VARIOUS NATIONS OVER LONG PERIODS ARE FOUNDED IN THE NATURE OF THINGS OR IN HUMAN NATURE——SUCH DOCTRINES ARE VALID THOUGH IRRECONCILABLE TO THE UNDERSTANDING——THEY MAY NOT BE COMPLETE TRUTH, BUT TRUTH WILL BE PRESENT[143]

¶ 119

I am indeed firmly persuaded, that no doctrine was ever widely diffused among various nations through successive ages, and under different religions (such, for instance, as the tenets of original sin and redemption, those fundamental articles of every known religion professing to have been revealed), which is not founded either in the nature of things, or in the necessities of human nature. Nay, the more strange and irreconcilable such a doctrine may appear to the understanding, the judgments of which are grounded on general rules abstracted from the world of the senses, the stronger is the presumption in its favor. For whatever satirists may say, or sciolists imagine, the human mind has no predilection for absurdity. I would even extend the principle (proportionately I mean) to sundry tenets, that from their strangeness or dangerous tendency appear only to be generally reprobated.

¶ 120

I am far from asserting that such a doctrine (. . . [*e.g.,*] that of a latent mystical sense in the words of Scripture and the works of nature, according to Origen and

---

[142] *Works* (Shedd), II, 391. Cf. the rule of Catholic truth as formulated in the *Commonitorium* of St. Vincent of Lerins: "Id quod ubique, quod semper, quod ab omnibus creditum est." (This is the test of time, universality and general acceptance.)
[143] *Works* (Shedd), II, 392-393; 393.

Emanuel Swedenborg) shall be always the best possible, or not a distorted and dangerous, as well as partial, representation of the truth on which it is founded. For the same body casts strangely different shadows in different positions and different degrees of light. But I dare, and do, affirm that it always does shadow out some important truth, and from it derives its main influence over the faith of its adherents, obscure as their perception of this truth may be, and though they may themselves attribute their belief to the supernatural gifts of the founder, or the miracles by which his preaching had been accredited.

CAN MIRACLES ALONE WORK TRUE CONVICTION?——SOME SPIRITUAL TRUTHS DERIVE THEIR EVIDENCE ONLY FROM WITHIN MAN'S SOUL—— THESE A MAN'S RISING FROM THE DEAD COULD NOT STRENGTHEN—— OLD TESTAMENT PUNISHED MIRACLES ATTESTING FALSE DOCTRINE—— THE ONE ESSENTIAL MIRACLE IS THE CREATING OF A NEW HEART AND CONSCIENCE——THE INFALLIBLE CRITERION OF MIRACLES FROM GOD, THEREFORE, IS THAT THEY ACCOMPANY MORAL TRUTH[144]

¶ 121

But we have the highest possible authority, that of Scripture itself, to justify us in putting the question,——whether miracles can, of themselves, work a true conviction in the mind. There are spiritual truths which must derive their evidence from within, which whoever rejects, *neither will he believe though a man were to rise from the dead*[145] to confirm them. And under the Mosaic law a miracle in attestation of a false doctrine subjected the miracle-worker to death; and whether the miracle was really or only seemingly supernatural, makes no difference in the present argument, its power of convincing, whatever that power may be, whether great or small, depending on the fulness of the belief in its miraculous nature. *Est quibus esse videtur.* Or rather, that I may express the same position in a form less likely to offend, is not a true efficient conviction of a moral truth, is not *the creating of a new heart*,[146] which collects the energies of a man's whole being in the focus of the conscience, the one essential miracle, the same and of the same evidence to the ignorant and the learned, which no superior skill can counterfeit, human or demoniacal?

¶ 122

Is it not emphatically that leading of the Father, without which no man can come to Christ? Is it not that implication of doctrine in the miracle and of miracle in the doctrine, which is the bridge of communication between the senses and the soul;—— that predisposing warmth which renders the understanding susceptible of the specific impression from the historic, and from all other outward, seals of testimony? Is not this the one infallible criterion of miracles, by which a man can know whether they be of God? The abhorrence in which the most savage or barbarous tribes hold witchcraft, in which however their belief is so intense as even to control the springs of life,——is not this abhorrence of witchcraft under so full a conviction of its reality a proof, how little of divine, how little fitting to our nature, a miracle is, when insulated from spiritual truths, and disconnected from religion as its end?

GENIUS——TALENT——[COMMON] SENSE——CLEVERNESS[147]

¶ 122a

The first I use in the sense of most general acceptance, as the faculty which adds to the existing stock of power and knowledge by new views, new combinations; by discoveries not accidental but anticipated, or resulting from anticipation. In short, I define Genius, as originality in intellectual construction; the moral accompaniment, and actuating principle of which consists, perhaps, in the carrying on of the freshness and feelings of childhood into the powers of manhood.[148]

¶ 123

By Talent, on the other hand, I mean the comparative facility of acquiring, arranging, and applying the stock furnished by others, and already existing in books or other conservatories of intellect.[149]

---

[144] *Works* (Shedd), II, 393-394.
[145] Luke 16:31.
[146] Psalm 51:10.
[147] *Works* (Shedd), II, 384-385.
[148] Cf. *Nature*, 11.18-19; 92.13-18. See ¶s. 173-174.
[149] *Table Talk*, I, 144: "Talent, lying in the understanding, is often inherited; genius, being the action of reason and imagination, rarely or never."

¶ 124

By Sense I understand that just balance of the faculties which is to the judgment what health is to the body. The mind seems to act at once and altogether by a synthetic rather than an analytic process: even as the outward senses, from which the metaphor is taken, perceive immediately, each as it were by a peculiar tact or intuition, without any consciousness of the mechanism by which the perception is realized. . . . The general accompaniment of sense is a disposition to avoid extremes, whether in theory or in practice, with a desire to remain in sympathy with the general mind of the age or country, and a feeling of the necessity and utility of compromise. If genius be the initiative, and talent the administrative, sense is the conservative, branch in the intellectual republic.

¶ 125

By Cleverness (which I dare not with Dr. Johnson call a low word, while there is a sense to be expressed which it alone expresses) I mean a comparative readiness in the invention and use of means, for the realizing of objects and ideas——often of such ideas, which the man of genius only could have originated, and which the clever man perhaps neither fully comprehends nor adequately appreciates, even at the moment that he is prompting or executing the machinery of their accomplishment. In short, cleverness is a sort of genius for instrumentality. It is the brain in the hand. In literature, cleverness is more frequently accompanied by wit, genius and sense by humor.

GENIUS *VS.* TALENT[150]

¶ 126

But to find no contradiction in the union of old and new, to contemplate the Ancient of days with feelings as fresh, as if they then sprang forth at his own *fiat*——this characterizes the minds that feel the riddle of the world, and may help to unravel it! To carry on the feelings of childhood into the powers of manhood,[151] to combine the child's sense of wonder and novelty with the appearances which every day for perhaps forty years has rendered familiar,

> With sun and moon and stars throughout the year,
> And man and woman————[152]

this is the character and privilege of genius, and one of the marks which distinguish genius from talent. And so to represent familiar objects as to awaken the minds of others to a like freshness of sensation concerning them——that constant accompaniment of mental, no less than of bodily, health——to the same modest questioning of a self-discovered and intelligent ignorance . . . this is the prime merit of genius, and its most unequivocal mode of manifestation.

COLERIDGE ON THE METHOD FOR ARRIVING AT THE TRUTH——A TRUE METHOD REQUIRES A SOMEWHAT PROGRESSIVE[153]——A CONTINUOUS TRANSITION PRECEDED BY A PRECONCEPTION[154]

¶ 127

For method implies a progressive transition, and it is the meaning of the word in the original language. The Greek μεθοδος is literally a way or path of transit. Thus we extol the Elements of Euclid, or Socrates' discourse with the slave in the Menon of Plato, as methodical, a term which no one who holds himself bound to think or speak correctly, would apply to the alphabetical order or arrangement of a common dictionary. But as without continuous transition there can be no method, so without a preconception there can be no transition with continuity.[155] The term, method, can not

---

[150] *Works* (Shedd), II, 104.   [151] See *Nature*, 11.18 and 92.13ff.
[152] Milton's Sonnet XXII, "To Mr. Cyriack Skinner."
[153] Emerson reflects the following passage in *Nature*, 76.3-9.
[154] *Works* (Shedd), II, 416-417. Cf. *Nature*, 6.15, for application of this method.
[155] Emerson has much to say about the unifying Idea (*Nature*, 68.19 through 70.3), the guess which is better than facts (*Nature*, 83.2), or the dream which can interpret the dry categories of the scientist (*Nature*, 83.4). Coleridge develops this point in sub-

therefore, otherwise than by abuse, be applied to a mere dead arrangement, containing in itself no principle of progression.

TWO KINDS OF RELATION IN WHICH OBJECTS OF THE MIND MAY BE CONTEMPLATED——LAW AND THEORY
¶ 128

It has been observed ... that the relations of objects are prime materials of method, and that the contemplation of relations is the indispensable condition of thinking methodically. It becomes necessary therefore to add, that there are two kinds of relation, in which objects of mind may be contemplated. The first is that of law, which, in its absolute perfection, is conceivable only of the Supreme Being, whose creative idea not only appoints to each thing its position, but in that position, and in consequence of that position, gives it its qualities, yea, gives it its very existence, as that particular thing. Yet in whatever science the relation of the parts to each other and to the whole is predetermined by a truth originating in the mind, and not abstracted or generalized from observation of the parts, there we affirm the presence of a law,[156] if we are speaking of the physical sciences, as of astronomy for instance; or the presence of fundamental ideas, if our discourse be upon those sciences, the truths of which, as truths absolute, not merely have an independent origin in the mind, but continue to exist in and for the mind alone.[157]

¶ 129

The second relation is that of theory, in which the existing forms and qualities of objects, discovered by observation or experiment, suggest a given arrangement of many under one point of view; and this not merely or principally in order to facilitate the remembrance, recollection, or communication of the same; but for the purposes of understanding, and in most instances of controlling them. In other words, all theory supposes the general idea of cause and effect. The scientific arts of medicine, chemistry, and physiology in general, are examples of a method hitherto founded on this second sort of relation.[158]

LAW IN ITS PERFECT FORM IS CONSIDERED AS AN ATTRIBUTE OF THE SUPREME BEING[159]
¶ 130

I have thus assigned the first place in the science of method to law; and first of the first, to law, as the absolute kind which, comprehending in itself the substance of every possible degree, precludes from its conception all degree, not by generalization, but by its own plenitude. As such, therefore, and as the sufficient cause of the reality correspondent thereto, I contemplate it as exclusively an attribute of the Supreme Being, inseparable from the idea of God; adding, however, that from the contemplation of law in this its only perfect form, must be derived all true insight into all other grounds and principles necessary to method. ... Alienated from this intuition or steadfast faith, ingenious men may produce schemes conducive to the peculiar purposes of particular sciences, but no scientific system.

STATEMENT OF THE GRAND PROBLEM OF PHILOSOPHY ACCORDING TO KANT[160]——SINCE THE MIND BEARS INDEPENDENT WITNESS TO THE SAME LAWS THAT GOVERN THE MATERIAL WORLD,[161] WE SEEK THE HIGHEST LAW OR THE ABSOLUTE GROUND OF BOTH[162]
¶ 131

The grand problem, the solution of which forms, according to Plato,[163] the final object and distinctive character of philosophy, is this: for all that exists conditionally (that is, the existence of which is inconceivable except under the condition of its dependency on some other as its antecedent) to find a ground that is unconditional and absolute, and thereby to reduce the aggregate of human knowledge to a system. For the relation common to all being known, the appropriate orbit of each becomes discoverable, together with its peculiar relations to its concentrics in the common

---

sequent paragraphs.
[156] See *Nature*, 68.21-23.
[157] *Works* (Shedd), II, 418.
[158] *Works* (Shedd), II, 422-423.
[159] *Works* (Shedd), II, 418.
[160] See Chapter II.
[161] See *Nature*, 83.6 through 87.2.
[162] *Works* (Shedd), II, 420-421.
[163] Cf. *Nature*, 68.18-23.

sphere of subordination. Thus the centrality of the sun having been established, and the law of the distances of the planets from the sun having been determined, we possess the means of calculating the distance of each from the other. . . . And now the remarkable fact forces itself on our attention, namely, that the material world is found to obey the same laws as had been deduced independently from the reason; and that the masses act by a force, which can not be conceived to result from the component parts, known or imaginable.

HOW PLATO WOULD EXPLAIN THE COINCIDENCE BETWEEN REASON AND EXPERIENCE, OR BETWEEN THE IDEAS OF PURE INTELLECT AND THE LAWS OF MATTER——RELIGION IS THE ULTIMATE AIM OF PHILOSOPHY[164]

¶ 132

Plato has proved incontrovertibly that in both [the atomic doctrine of Democritus and the pure rationalism of Zeno the Eleatic] alike the basis is too narrow to support the superstructure; that the grounds of both are false or disputable; and that, if these were conceded, yet neither the one nor the other scheme is adequate to the solution of the problem,——namely, what is the ground of the coincidence between reason and experience; or between the laws of matter and the ideas of the pure intellect. The only answer which Plato deemed the question capable of receiving, compels the reason to pass out of itself and seek the ground of this agreement in a supersensual essence, which being at once the ideal of the reason and the cause of the material world, is the pre-establisher of the harmony in and between both. Religion therefore is the ultimate aim of philosophy, in consequence of which philosophy itself becomes the supplement of the sciences, both as the convergence of all to the common end, namely wisdom; and as supplying the copula, which, modified in each in the comprehension of its parts in one whole, is in its principles common to all, as integral parts of one system. And this is method, itself a distinct science, the immediate offspring of philosophy, and the link or mordant by which philosophy becomes scientific, and the sciences philosophical.

BOTANY STILL NEEDS A PHILOSOPHER TO STATE THE UNIFYING PRINCIPLE AND THEREBY ESTABLISH A TRUE METHOD[165]

¶ 133

[W]hat is botany at this present hour? Little more than an enormous nomenclature; a hugh catalogue,[166] well arranged, and yearly and monthly augmented, in various editions, each with its own scheme of technical memory and its own conveniences of reference. A dictionary in which (to carry on the metaphor) an Ainsworth arranges the contents by the initials; a Walker by the endings; a Scapula by the radicals; and a Cominius by the similarity of the uses and purposes. The terms system, method, science, are mere improprieties of courtesy, when applied to a mass enlarging by endless appositions, but without a nerve that oscillates, or a pulse that throbs, in sign of growth or inward sympathy.[167] The innocent amusement, the healthful occupation, the ornamental accomplishment of amateurs (most honorable indeed and deserving of all praise as a preventive substitute for the stall, the kennel, and the subscription-room), it has yet to expect the devotion and energies of the philosopher.

COLERIDGE GIVES EXAMPLE OF A "PRECONCEPTION"——HE EARLY BELIEVED THAT BOTANICAL METHOD SHOULD BE BUILT ON ANTITHESIS RATHER THAN ON ANALOGY——HIS GUESS WAS LATER CORROBORATED[168]

¶ 134

So long back as the first appearance of Dr. Darwin's *Phytologia*,[169] I . . . presumed to hazard the opinion,[170] that the physiological botanists were hunting in a false direction, and sought for analogy where they should have looked for antithesis. . . . Since that time, the same idea has dawned in the minds of philosophers capable of demonstrating its objective truth by induction of facts in an unbroken series of correspondences in nature. From these men, or from minds enkindled by their labors, we may

[164] *Works* (Shedd), II, 422.
[165] *Works* (Shedd), II, 426. Cf. *Nature*, 82.3 through 84.2.
[166] Cf. *Nature*, 69.15; 35.14-19.
[167] See *Nature*, 82.12-20.
[168] *Works* (Shedd), II, 427.
[169] Erasmus Darwin, *Phytologia*, London, 1800. (Also Dublin, 1800).
[170] Cf. *Nature*, 83.2.

hope hereafter to receive it, or rather the yet higher idea[171] to which it refers us, matured into laws of organic nature, and thence to have one other splendid proof, that with the knowledge of law alone dwell power and prophecy,[172] decisive experiment, and, lastly, a scientific method, that dissipating with its earliest rays the gnomes of hypothesis and the mists of theory may, within a single generation, open out on the philosophic seer discoveries that had baffled the gigantic, but blind and guideless, industry of ages.

THE UNIFYING LAW OR PRINCIPLE OF CONNECTION IS SANCTIONED BY THE CORRESPONDENCE BETWEEN MIND AND NATURE[173]

¶ 135

Such, too, is the case with the assumed indecomponible substances of the laboratory. They are the symbols of elementary powers, and the exponents of a law, which, as the root of all these powers, the chemical philosopher, whatever his theory may be, is instinctively laboring to extract. This instinct, again, is itself but the form, in which the idea, the mental correlative of the law, first announces its incipient germination in his own mind: and hence proceeds the striving after unity[174] of principle through all the diversity of forms, with a feeling resembling that which accompanies our endeavors to recollect a forgotten name; when we seem at once to have and not to have it; which the memory feels but can not find. . . . It is the sense of a principle of connection given by the mind, and sanctioned by the correspondency of nature.[175]

PLATO'S WORKS AIM TO EXEMPLIFY THE ART OF METHOD AND NOT TO CONVEY SPECIFIC INFORMATION——PLATO WAS CONCERNED WITH EDU- CATION OF THE INTELLECT BY STIMULATING SELF-DEVELOPMENT[176]

¶ 136

From Shakspeare to Plato, from the philosophic poet to the poetic philosopher, the transition is easy, and the road is crowded with illustrations of our present subject. For of Plato's works, the larger and more valuable portion have all one common end, which comprehends and shines through the particular purpose of each several dialogue; and this is to establish the sources, to evolve the principles, and exemplify the art of method. This is the clue, without which it would be difficult to exculpate the noblest productions of the divine philosopher from the charge of being tortuous and labyrin- thine in their progress, and unsatisfactory in their ostensible results. . . . But with the clear insight that the purpose of the writer is not so much to establish any par- ticular truth, as to remove the obstacles, the continuance of which is preclusive of all truth, the whole scheme assumes a different aspect, and justifies itself in all its dimen- sions. We see, that to open anew a well of springing water, not to cleanse the stagnant tank, or fill, bucket by bucket, the leaden cistern; that the education of the intellect, by awakening the principle and method of self-development, was his proposed object, not any specific information that can be conveyed into it from without;——not to assist in storing the passive mind with the various sorts of knowledge most in request, as if the human soul were a mere repository or banqueting-room, but to place it in such relations of circumstance as should gradually excite the germinal power that craves no knowledge but what it can take up into itself, what it can appropriate, and repro- duce in fruits of its own. To shape, to dye, to paint over, and to mechanize the mind, he resigned, as their proper trade, to the sophists, against whom he waged open and unremitting war.

EXAMPLES OF PRIOR ACTION OF THE MIND IN SCIENCE——EULER'S LAW OF ARCHES——PHYSICS[177]

¶ 137

The celebrated Euler, treating on some point respecting arches, makes this curious remark:——"All experience is in contradiction to this; *sed potius fidendum est analysi;*

---

[171] Cf. *Nature*, 92.20-23.
[172] See *Nature*, 68.21: "a law determines all." Cf. *Nature*, 69.13.
[173] *Works* (Shedd), II, 427-428.
[174] Cf. *Nature*, 29.16; 54.13-17; 56.5; 83.11-14.
[175] The doctrine of correspondences is common throughout Emerson. See *Nature*, 12.5; 33.20; 36.21; 46.19; 91.20 etc.
[176] *Works* (Shedd), II, 429-430.   [177] *Works* (Shedd), II, 432.

but this is no reason for doubting the analysis." [178] The words sound paradoxical; but in truth mean no more than this, that the properties of space are not less certainly the properties of space because they can never be entirely transferred to material bodies. But in physics,[179] that is, in all the sciences which have for their objects the things of nature, and not the *entia rationis*——more philosophically, intellectual acts and the products of those acts, existing exclusively in and for the intellect itself——the definition must follow, and not precede, the reasoning. It is representative not constitutive, and is indeed little more than an abbreviature of the preceding observation, and the deductions therefrom.

EXAMPLE OF A UNIFYING IDEA——THE LAW OF POLARITY, WHICH DESCRIBES THE MANIFESTATION OF ONE POWER IN OPPOSITE FORCES ——ILLUSTRATED IN THE PHENOMENA OF ELECTRICITY[180]

¶ 138

How many centuries, we might have said *millennia*, have passed, since the first accidental discovery of the attraction and repulsion of light bodies by rubbed amber! Compare the interval with the progress made within less than a century, after the discovery of the *phaenomena* that led immediately to a theory of electricity. That here as in many other instances, the theory was supported by insecure hypothesis; that by one theorist two heterogeneous fluids are assumed, the vitreous and the resinous; by another, a *plus* and *minus* of the same fluid; that a third considers it a mere modification of light; while a fourth composes the electrical *aura* of oxygen, hydrogen, and caloric;——this does but place the truth we have been evolving in a stronger and clearer light. For abstract from all these suppositions, or rather imaginations, that which is common to, and involved in, them all; and we shall have neither notional fluid or fluids, nor chemical compounds, nor elementary matter,——but the idea of two ——opposite——forces, tending to rest by *equilibrium*. These are the sole factors of the *calculus*, alike in all the theories. These give the law, and in it the method, both of arranging the *phænomena* and of substantiating appearances into facts of science; with a success proportionate to the clearness or confusedness of the insight into the law.

¶ 139

For this reason, I anticipate the greatest improvements in the method, the nearest approaches to a system of electricity, from these philosophers, who have presented the law most purely, and the correlative idea as an idea;——those, namely, who since the year 1798, in the true spirit of experimental dynamics, rejecting the imagination of any material substrate, simple or compound, contemplate in the *phænomena* of electricity the operation of a law which reigns through all nature, the law of polarity, or the manifestation of one power by opposite forces;——who trace in these appearances, as the most obvious and striking of its innumerable forms, the agency of the positive and negative poles of a power essential to all material construction. . . . The time is, perhaps, nigh at hand, when the same comparison between the results of two unequal periods,——the interval between the knowledge of a fact, and that from the discovery of the law,——will be applicable to the sister science of magnetism.

THE INEFFECTIVE NATURALIST IGNORES THE UNIFYING IDEA[181]

¶ 140

The naturalist, who can not or will not see, that one fact is often worth a thousand, as including them all in itself, and that it first makes all the other facts,——who has not the head to comprehend, the soul to reverence, a central experiment or observation (what the Greeks would perhaps have called a *protophænomenon*),——will never receive an auspicious answer from the oracle of nature.

BACON, FATHER OF THE INDUCTIVE METHOD, ALSO INSISTS UPON REQUIRING A "PRECONCEPTION" OR MENTAL INITIATIVE IN APPROACHING THE FACTS OF SCIENCE[182]

¶ 141

In the first instance, Lord Bacon equally with myself demands what I have ventured to call the intellectual or mental initiative, as the motive and guide of every philosoph-

---

[178] See *Nature*, 69.21ff. See also ¶ 229. Emerson paraphrases Coleridge.
[179] See *Nature*, 69.18ff.
[180] *Works* (Shedd), II, 433-434. Cf. ¶s. 96, 155.
[181] *Works* (Shedd), II, 436. Cf. *Nature*, 69.13ff.; 82.8——84.23; 86.10——87.2; 91.14; 92.1.   [182] *Works* (Shedd), II, 443-444.

ical experiment; some well-grounded purpose, some distinct impression of the probable results, some self-consistent anticipation as the ground of the *prudens quæstio*, the forethoughtful query, which he affirms to be the prior half of the knowledge sought, *dimidium scientiæ*. With him, therefore, as with me, an idea is an experiment proposed, an experiment is an idea realized. . . . If again we ask, what it is which gives birth to the question . . . the answer is,——*lux intellectus, lumen siccum*, the pure and impersonal reason, freed from all the various idols enumerated by our great legislator of science (*idola tribus, specus, fori, theatri*); that is, freed from the limits, the passions, the prejudices, the peculiar habits of the human understanding, natural or acquired; but above all, pure from the arrogance, which leads man to take the forms and mechanism of his own mere reflective faculty, as the measure of nature and of Deity. In this indeed we find the great object both of Plato's and of Lord Bacon's labors. They both saw that there could be no hope of any fruitful and secure method, while forms, merely subjective, were presumed as the true and proper moulds of objective truth.

BACON THUS STRESSES THE UNIVERSAL REASON[183] OR SPIRIT OR INTELLECTUAL INTUITION AS THE CONDITION OF ALL SCIENCE——AT BEST THE UNDERSTANDING HAS SERIOUS LIMITATIONS[184]

¶ 142

To adopt the bold but happy phrase of a late ingenious French writer, it is the *homme particulier*, as contrasted with *l'homme général*,[185] against which, Heraclitus and Plato, among the ancients, and among the moderns, Bacon and Stewart (rightly understood), warn and preadmonish the sincere inquirer. Most truly, and in strict consonance with his two great predecessors, does our immortal Verulam teach, that the human understanding, even independently of the causes that always, previously to its purification by philosophy, render it more or less turbid or uneven . . . is itself only a *phænomenon* of the inner sense, and requires the same corrections as the appearances transmitted by the outward senses. But that there is potentially, i[f] not actually, in every rational being, a somewhat, call it what you will, the pure reason, the spirit, *lumen siccum* . . . intellectual intuition, or the like,——and that in this are to be found the indispensable conditions of all science, and scientific research, whether meditative, contemplative, or experimental,——is often expressed, and everywhere supposed, by Lord Bacon.

PLATO AND BACON COMPARED AND RECONCILED——TRUTH SEEN FROM OPPOSITE POINTS——*IDEA* AND *LAW* DEFINED[186]

¶ 143

Thus the difference, or rather distinction, between Plato and Lord Bacon is simply this: that philosophy being necessarily bipolar, Plato treats principally of the truth, as it manifests itself at the ideal pole, as the science of intellect (*de mundo intelligibili*); while Bacon confines himself, for the most part, to the same truth, as it is manifested at the other or material pole, as the science of nature (*de mundo sensibili*). It is as necessary, therefore, that Plato should direct his inquiries chiefly to those objective truths that exist in and for the intellect alone, the images and representatives of which we construct for ourselves by figure, number, and word; as that Lord Bacon should attach his main concern to the truths which have their signatures in nature, and which (as he himself plainly and often asserts) may indeed be revealed to us through and with, but never by the senses, or the faculty of sense.

¶ 144

Hence too, it will not surprise us, that Plato so often calls ideas living laws, in which the mind has its whole true being and permanence; or that Bacon, *vice versa*, names the laws of nature ideas;[187] and represents what I have in a former part of this disquisition called facts of science and central *phænomena*, as signatures, impressions, and symbols of ideas. A distinguishable power self-affirmed, and seen in its unity with the Eternal Essence, is, according to Plato, an idea: and the discipline, by which the human mind is purified from its idols (ειδωλα), and raised to the contemplation of ideas, and thence to the secure and ever-progressive, though never-ending, investigation of truth and reality by scientific method, comprehends what the same philosopher so highly extols under the title of dialectic.

---

[183] See ¶s. 1-21 *supra*.
[184] *Works* (Shedd), II, 444-445.
[187] Cf. *Nature*, 68.15——69.1. See ¶ 231.

[185] See *Nature*, 87.13.
[186] *Works* (Shedd), II, 445; 446.

¶ 145

According to Lord Bacon, as describing the same truth seen from the opposite point, and applied to natural philosophy, an idea would be defined as——*intuitio sive inventio, quæ in perceptione sensus non est (ut quæ puræ et sicci luminis intellectioni est propria) idearum divinæ mentis, prout in creaturis per signaturas suas sese pate-faciant.* "That (saith the judicious Hooker) which doth assign unto each thing the kind, that which doth moderate the [f]orce and power, that which doth appoint the form and measure, of working, the same we term a law." [188]

THE IDEA IS REQUISITE FOR THE RIGHT DEVELOPMENT OF SCIENCE, SOCIETY AND EDUCATION——ON IT DEPENDS TRUE CULTURE OR CULTIVATION——MAN MUST FIND IT WITHIN BEFORE TRUTH CAN BE REFLECTED ON THE MIND FROM WITHOUT[189]

¶ 146

[W]ithout this guiding light [of the regulating Idea or Law—the "master-light"[190]] neither can the sciences attain to their full evolution, as the organs of one vital and harmonious body, nor that most weighty and concerning of all sciences, the science of education, be understood in its first elements, much less display its powers, as the *nisus formativus* of social man, as the appointed protoplast of true humanity. Never can society comprehend fully, and in its whole practical extent, the permanent distinction, and the occasional contrast, between cultivation and civilization; never can it attain to a due insight into the momentous fact . . . that a nation can never be a too cultivated, but may easily become an over-civilized race: never, I repeat, can this sanative and preventive knowledge take up its abode among us, while we oppose ourselves voluntarily to that grand prerogative of our nature, a hungering and thirsting after truth, as the appropriate end of our intelligential, and its point of union with our moral nature; but therefore after truth, that must be found within us before it can be intelligibly reflected back on the mind from without.[191]

NECESSITY FOR CONSIDERING *FINAL CAUSES* IN STUDYING MAN OR NATURE——ONE MUST *EAST* ONESELF BEFORE HANDLING PARTICULARS[192]

¶ 147

Hence proceeds the introduction of final causes in the works of nature equally as in those of man. Hence their assumption, as constitutive and explanatory, by the mass of mankind; and the employment of the presumption, as an auxiliary and regulative principle, by the enlightened naturalist, whose office it is to seek, discover, and investigate the efficient causes. Without denying, that to resolve the efficient into the final may be the ultimate aim of philosophy, he, of good right, resists the substitution of the latter for the former, as premature, presumptuous, and preclusive of all science; well aware, that those sciences have been most progressive, in which this confusion has been either precluded by the nature of the science itself, as in pure mathematics, or avoided by the good sense of its cultivator. Yet even he admits a teleological ground in physics[193] and physiology; that is, the presumption of a something analogous to the [causality] of the human will, by which, without assigning to nature, as nature, a conscious purpose, he may yet distinguish her agency from a blind and lifeless mechanism. Even he admits its use, and, in many instances, its necessity, as a regulative principle; as a ground of anticipation, for the guidance of his judgment and for the direction of his observation and experiment;——briefly in all that preparatory process, which the French language so happily expresses by *s'orienter*, to find out the east for one's self.

---

[188] Cf. *Nature*, 68.23ff.
[189] *Works* (Shedd), II, 446-448.
[190] This term appears in *Works* (Shedd), II, 448.
[191] Another instance of "like only can know like."
[192] *Works* (Shedd), II, 450-451. In *Nature*, Emerson is seeking the final cause which, he says, many plodding scientists miss. He asks (*Nature*, 6.16) "to what end is nature?" and deals with the question throughout. See *Nature*, 15.3-8; 45.4; 59.8-10; 76.12-14. Emerson adopts the verb "east" in *Journals*, III, 239 (misprinted *cast*) ; 476.
[193] Cf. *Nature*, 69.17-18; 49.17-18.

THE METHOD BEING GRANTED, HOW SHOULD MAN BE EDUCATED? IN EDEN THE EMPHASIS WAS PUT UPON HUMANITY, MORAL SENSE, AND CULTIVATION OF THE REASON AND THE WILL[194]

¶ 148

In the childhood of the human race, its education commenced with the cultivation of the moral sense; the object proposed being such as the mind only could apprehend, and the principle of obedience being placed in the will. . . . The aim, the method throughout was, in the first place, to awaken, to cultivate, and to mature the truly human in human nature, in and through itself, or as independently as possible of the notices derived from sense, and of the motives that had reference to the sensations; till the time should arrive when the senses themselves might be allowed to present symbols and attestations of truths, learnt previously from deeper and inner sources. Thus the first period of the education of our race was evidently assigned to the cultivation of humanity itself, or of that in man, which of all known embodied creatures he alone possesses, the pure reason, as designed to regulate the will. And by what method was this done? First, by the excitement of the idea of their Creator as a spirit, of an idea which they were strictly forbidden to realize to themselves under any image; and secondly, by the injunction of obedience to the will of a supersensual Being. . . . Thus were the very first lessons in the divine school assigned to the cultivation of the reason and of the will; or rather of both as united in faith.

BAD EDUCATION DEVELOPS WITH INCREASE OF CIVILIZATION AND DECLINE OF CULTIVATION——THE REASON BECOMES ATROPHIED—— MEN COME TO LIVE ONLY IN REALM OF THE UNDERSTANDING[195]

¶ 149

Those, on the contrary, who wilfully chose a mode opposite to this method, who determined to shape their convictions and deduce their knowledge from without, by exclusive observation of outward and sensible things as the only realities, became, it appears, rapidly civilized. They built cities, invented musical instruments, were artificers in brass and in iron, and refined on the means of sensual gratification, and the conveniencies of courtly intercourse. They became the great masters of the agreeable, which fraternized readily with cruelty and rapacity; these being, indeed, but alternate moods of the same sensual selfishness. Thus, both before and after the flood, the vicious of mankind receded from all true cultivation, as they hurried towards civilization. Finally, as it was not in their power to make themselves wholly beasts, or to remain without a semblance of religion; and yet continuing faithful to their original maxim, and determined to receive nothing as true, but what they derived, or believed themselves to derive from their senses . . . *à posteriori*, they became idolaters of the heavens and the material elements.[196]

TRADE AND LITERATURE ARE THE TWO MAIN DIRECTIONS OF HUMAN ACTIVITY——THEY MEET RESPECTIVELY THE WANTS OF THE BODY AND THE WANTS OF THE MIND——FUNDAMENTAL CHARACTER OF A MAN OR A NATION DEPENDS ON THEIR PROPORTIONS[197]

¶ 150

As there are two wants connatural to man, so are there two main directions of human activity, pervading in modern times the whole civilized world; and constituting and sustaining that nationality which yet it is their tendency, and, or more or less, their effect, to transcend and to moderate,——trade and literature. . . . The natural law of increase and the instincts of family may produce tribes, and, under rare and peculiar circumstances, settlements and neighborhoods; and conquest may form empires. But without trade and literature, mutually commingled, there can be no nation; without commerce and science, no bond of nations. As the one hath for its object the wants of the body, real or artificial, the desires for which are for the greater part, nay, as far as the origination of trade and commerce is concerned, altogether excited from without; so the other has for its origin, as well as for its object, the wants of the mind, the gratification of which is a natural and necessary condition of its growth and sanity. And

---

[194] *Works* (Shedd), II, 452-453.
[195] *Works* (Shedd), II, 453-454.
[196] This passage is one of the sources for Emerson's Orphic Poet and context. Cf. *Nature*, 88.11——89.6; 89.12——90.4.
[197] *Works* (Shedd), II, 458-459.

the man (or the nation, considered according to its predominant character as one man) may be regarded under these circumstances, as acting in two forms of method, inseparably co-existent, yet producing very different effects accordingly as one or the other obtains the primacy.

¶ 151

[U]nder the ascendency of the mental and moral character the commercial relations may thrive to the utmost desirable point, while the reverse is ruinous to both, and sooner or later effectuates the fall or debasement of the country itself——this is the richest truth obtained for mankind by historic research; though unhappily it is the truth, to which a rich and commercial nation listens with most reluctance and receives with least faith.

HOW SHALL WE RESTORE THE WORLD?——BY THE NURTURE OF OUR HUMANITY——BY SEEKING THE COMMON GROUND OF THE WORLD AND MAN——BY LOOKING INTO OUR OWN BEING——THE DIVINE COMMAND IS "KNOW THYSELF"—MAN'S RELATION TO NATURE[198]

¶ 152

In the pursuits of commerce the man is called into action from without, in order to appropriate the outward world, as far as he can bring it within his reach, to the purposes of his senses and sensual nature. His ultimate end is appearance and enjoyment. Where on the other hand the nurture and evolution of humanity is the final aim, there will soon be seen a general tendency toward, an earnest seeking after, some ground common[199] to the world and to man, therein to find the one principle of permanence and identity, the rock of strength and refuge, to which the soul may cling amid the fleeting surge-like objects of the senses. Disturbed as by the obscure quickening of an inward birth; made restless by swarming thoughts, that, like bees when they first miss the queen and mother of the hive, with vain discursion seek each in the other what is the common need of all; man sallies forth into nature——in nature, as in the shadows and reflections of a clear river, to discover the originals of the forms presented to him in his own intellect. Over these shadows, as if they were the substantial powers and presiding spirits of the stream, Narcissus-like, he hangs delighted: till finding nowhere a representative of that free agency which yet is a fact of immediate consciousness sanctioned and made fearfully significant by his prophetic conscience, he learns at last that what he seeks he has left behind, and that he but lengthens the distance as he prolongs the search. Under the tutorage of scientific analysis, haply first given to him by express revelation,

E cœlo descendit, Γνωθι σεαυτον,

he separates the relations that are wholly the creatures of his own abstracting and comparing intellect, and at once discovers and recoils from the discovery, that the reality, the objective truth, of the objects he has been adoring, derives its whole and sole evidence from an obscure sensation, which he is alike unable to resist or to comprehend, which compels him to contemplate as without and independent of himself what yet he could not contemplate at all, were it not a modification of his own being.[200]

WORDSWORTH'S *ODE ON INTIMATIONS OF IMMORTALITY* REVEALS THE PART NATURE PLAYS IN MAN'S EDUCATION[201]

¶ 153

Earth fills her lap with pleasures of her own;
Yearnings she hath in her own natural kind,
And, even with something of a mother's mind,
    And no unworthy aim
    The homely nurse doth all she can
To make her foster-child, her inmate man,
    Forget the glories he hath known,
And that imperial palace whence he came.

---

[198] *Works* (Shedd), II, 459-460. Cf. *Nature*, 91.5-8.
[199] Cf. *Nature*, 68.15-20.
[200] "Like only can know like."
[201] *Works* (Shedd), II, 460-461 (stanzas VI and IX of the *Ode*). Coleridge also reprints stanzas V and IX in *Biographia Literaria* [*Works* (Shedd), III], 498-499.

¶ 154

O joy! that in our embers
Is something that doth live,
That nature yet remembers
What was so fugitive!
The thought of our past years in me doth breed
Perpetual benedictions: not indeed
For that which is most worthy to be blest;
Delight and liberty, the simple creed
Of childhood, whether busy or at rest,
With new-fledged hope still fluttering in his breast:—
Not for these I raise
The song of thanks and praise;
But for those obstinate questionings
Of sense and outward things,
Fallings from us, vanishings;
Blank misgivings of a creature
Moving about in worlds not realized,
High instincts, before which our mortal nature
Did tremble like a guilty thing surprised!
But for those first affections,
Those shadowy recollections,
Which, be they what they may,
Are yet the fountain light of all our day,
Are yet a master light of all our seeing;
Uphold us—cherish——and have power to make
Our noisy years seem moments in the being
Of the eternal silence: truths that wake,
To perish never;
Which neither listlessness, nor mad endeavor,
Nor man nor boy,
Nor all that is at enmity with joy,
Can utterly abolish or destroy!
Hence, in a season of calm weather,
Though inland far we be,
Our souls have sight of that immortal sea
Which brought us hither;
Can in a moment travel thither—
And see the children sport upon the shore,
And hear the mighty waters rolling evermore.

MAN'S SPIRITUAL RESPONSE TO NATURE SUGGESTS THAT BOTH SHARE
SOMETHING SPIRITUAL——MAN MUST LEARN, THEREFORE, TO COMPRE-
HEND NATURE IN HIMSELF——SELF-KNOWLEDGE IS THE METHOD
WHEREBY HE DISCOVERS THE GREAT COMMON CENTER OR THE UNI-
VERSAL LAW WHICH LIES BEHIND ALL THINGS——POLARITY——HE
THEN SEES THE RELATIONS OF THINGS TO THE SPIRITUAL CENTER
AND TO EACH OTHER[202]

¶ 155

Long indeed will man strive to satisfy the inward querist with the phrase, laws of
nature. But though the individual may rest content with the seemly metaphor, the race
can not. If a law of nature be a mere generalization, it is included in the above as an
act of the mind. But if it be other and more, and yet manifestable only in and to an
intelligent spirit, it must in act and substance be itself spiritual: for things utterly
heterogeneous can have no intercommunion.[203] In order therefore to the recognition of
himself in nature man must first learn to comprehend nature in himself, and its laws
in the ground of his own existence.[204] Then only can he reduce *phænomena* to prin-

---

[202] *Works* (Shedd), II, 461-462. This paragraph is basic for understanding *Nature*.
See 25.12-13; 51.9; 73.20; 78.20-22; 84.14-17.
[203] "Like only can know like."
[204] Man's condition is a solution to the questions he would ask: *Nature*, 6.9; 35.10ff.;
36.21; 85.12.

ciples;[205] then only will he have achieved the method, the self-unravelling clue, which alone can securely guide him to the conquest of the former;——when he has discovered in the basis of their union the necessity of their differences, in the principle of their continuance the solution of their changes. It is the idea alone of the common centre, of the universal law, by which all power manifests itself in opposite yet interdependent forces[206] . . . which enlightening inquiry, multiplying experiment, and at once inspiring humility and perseverance will lead him to comprehend gradually and progressively the relation of each to the other, of each to all, and of all to each.

ABSOLUTE EXISTENCE CONSIDERED——MAN'S REALIZATION THAT HE EXISTS IS ATTENDED BY AWE AND WONDER——THE MYSTERIOUS FORCE BEHIND HIS LIFE——INSTANTANEOUS LIGHT——IT RAISES MEN TO VISION AND CREATES FOUNDERS OF LAW AND RELIGION——WHAT NAME SHALL WE GIVE THIS POWER?[207]

¶ 156

Hast thou ever raised thy mind to the consideration of existence, in and by itself, as the mere act of existing? Hast thou ever said to thyself thoughtfully, It is! heedless in that moment, whether it were a man before thee, or a flower, or a grain of sand,—— without reference, in short, to this or that particular mode or form of existence? If thou hast indeed attained to this, thou wilt have felt the presence of a mystery, which must have fixed thy spirit in awe and wonder.[208] The very words,——there is nothing! or, ——There was a time, when there was nothing! are self-contradictory. There is that within us which repels the proposition with as full and instantaneous a light, as if it bore evidence against the fact in the right of its own eternity. Not to be, then, is impossible: to be,[209] incomprehensible. If thou hast mastered this intuition of absolute existence, thou wilt have learnt likewise, that it was this, and no other, which in the earlier ages seized the nobler minds, the elect among men, with a sort of sacred horror. This it was which first caused them to feel within themselves a something ineffably greater than their own individual nature. It was this which, raising them aloft, and projecting them to an ideal distance from themselves, prepared them to become the lights and awakening voices of other men, the founders of law and religion, the educators and foster-gods of mankind. The power, which evolved this idea of being, being in its essence, being limitless, comprehending its own limits in its dilatation, and condensing itself into its own apparent mounds——how shall we name it?

THE TRUE *SELF* OR INDIVIDUALITY OF MAN IS NOT HIS OWN——HE BELONGS TO *IT*——IS NOT THAT DREAD UNIVERSAL ESSENCE GOD?[210]

¶ 157

The idea itself, which like a mighty billow at once overwhelms and bears aloft—— what is it? Whence did it come? In vain would we derive it from the organs of sense. . . . I have asked then for its birth-place in all that constitutes our relative individuality, in all that each man calls exclusively himself. It is an alien of which they know not: and for them the question itself is purposeless, and the very words that convey it are as sounds in an unknown language, or as the vision of heaven and earth expanded by the rising sun, which falls but as warmth on the eyelids of the blind. To no class of *phænomena* or particulars can it be referred, itself being none; therefore, to no faculty by which these alone are apprehended. As little dare we refer it to any form of abstraction or generalization; for it has neither co-ordinate nor *analogon;* it is absolutely one;[211] and that it is, and affirms itself to be, is its only predicate. And yet this power, nevertheless, is;——in supremacy of being it is;——and he for whom it manifests itself in its adequate idea, dare as little arrogate it to himself as his own, can as little appropriate it either totally or by partition, as he can claim ownership in the breathing air,

---

[205] Cf. *Nature*, 68.18-23.
[206] *I.e.*, the law of Polarity. See ¶s. 96, 138, 139.
[207] *Works* (Shedd), II, 463-464. For emphasis on *being* or *to be*, see *Nature*, 49.21; 71.1-20, esp. line 17, and also the first stanza of Alcott's poem in *Psyche*, p. 12+6.
[208] Cf. *Nature*, 95.7-12.
[209] Cf. *Nature*, 49.21.
[210] *Works* (Shedd), II, 464-465.
[211] This paragraph has influenced Emerson's chapter on "Spirit." Cf. *Nature*, 79.8-19.

or make an inclosure in the cope of heaven.[212] He bears witness of it to his own mind, even as he describes life and light: and, with the silence of light,[213] it describes itself and dwells in us only as far as we dwell in it.[214] The truths which it manifests are such as it alone can manifest, and in all truth it manifests itself. By what name then canst thou call a truth so manifested? Is it not revelation?[215] . . . And the manifesting power, the source and the correlative of the idea thus manifested——is it not God?

THE CREATOR ADAPTS MEANS TO ENDS[216]——THE MATERIAL WORLD MUST HAVE BEEN MADE FOR THE SAKE OF MAN[217]

¶ 158

Look round you, and you behold everywhere an adaptation of means to ends. Meditate on the nature of a being whose ideas are creative, and consequently more real, more substantial than the things that, at the height of their creaturely state, are but their dim reflexes; and the intuitive conviction will arise that in such a being there could exist no motive to the creation of a machine for its own sake; that, therefore, the material world must have been made for the sake of man, at once the high-priest and representative of the Creator, as far as he partakes of that reason in which the essences of all things co-exist in all their distinctions yet as one and indivisible. But I speak of man in his idea, and as subsumed in the divine humanity, in whom alone God loved the world.

EACH LEVEL OF CREATION SHARES UNIVERSAL LAWS BUT IS ALSO GOVERNED BY PARTICULAR LAWS WHICH MODIFY OR TEMPER THE UNIVERSAL——MUST NOT MAN ENJOY A SPECIAL DISPENSATION ALSO ——HE WHO IS THE ONLY RATIONAL, ETHICAL AND PROGRESSIVE CREATURE——THE CENTER IN WHICH ALL LINES CONVERGE?[218]

¶ 159

In all inferior things . . . we behold——first, a subjection to universal laws by which each thing belongs to the whole, as interpenetrated by the powers of the whole; and, secondly, the intervention of particular laws by which the universal laws are suspended or tempered for the weal and sustenance of each particular class. Hence and thus we see too that each species, and each individual of every species, becomes a system, a world of its own. If then we behold this economy everywhere in the irrational creation, shall we not hold it probable that by some analogous intervention a similar temperament will have been effected for the rational and moral? Are we not entitled to expect some appropriate agency in behalf of the presiding and alone progressive creature? To presume some especial provision for the permanent interest of the creature destined to move and grow towards that divine humanity which we have learnt to contemplate as the final cause of all creation, and the centre in which all its lines converge?[219]

MAN'S SPECIAL DISPENSATION LIES IN NOT HAVING HIS MENTAL LIFE LIMITED TO THE UNDERSTANDING AND FANCY ALONE——TEMPTATIONS WHICH THE UNDERSTANDING STILL PUTS IN HIS PATH[220]

¶ 160

To discover the mode of intervention requisite for man's development and progression, we must seek then for some general law, by the untempered and uncounteracted action of which man's development and progression would be prevented and endangered. But this we shall find in that law of his understanding and fancy, by which he is impelled to abstract the changes and outward relations of matter and to arrange them

---

[212] Cf. *Nature*, 34.17——35.2.

[213] For "light" imagery, see *Nature*, 43.12; 92.21; 92.8-9; 34.5.

[214] Cf. *Nature*, 79.16-17.

[215] Cf. *Nature*, 5.10.

[216] Cf. *Nature*, 52.5-14.

[217] *Works* (Shedd), II, 466. This thought is basic in Emerson's *Nature*, which attempts to show just how the material or natural world serves man. See especially Herbert's poem on "Man" in *Nature*, 85.3——86.9.

[218] *Works* (Shedd), II, 466-467.

[219] Cf. *Nature*, 27.16; 35.10-14.

[220] *Works* (Shedd), II, 467. The last half of this paragraph contributed ideas to the Orphic Poet passages etc. in *Nature*, 88.11——90.4.

under the form of causes and effects. And this was necessary, as the condition under which alone experience and intellectual growth are possible. But, on the other hand, by the same law he is inevitably tempted to misinterpret a constant precedence into positive causation, and thus to break and scatter the one divine and invisible life of nature into countless idols of the sense; and falling prostrate before lifeless images, the creatures of his own abstraction, is himself sensualized, and becomes a slave to the things of which he was formed to be the conqueror and sovereign. From the fetisch of the imbruted African to the soul-debasing errors of the proud fact-hunting materialist we may trace the various ceremonials of the same idolatry, and shall find selfishness, hate, and servitude as the results.

HUMAN LIFE, THEREFORE, IS PENETRATED BY A MYSTERIOUS SPIRIT WHICH THE UNDERSTANDING CANNOT UNDERSTAND——TO INEXPLICABLE PHENOMENA WE GIVE THE NAME "MIRACLES"——SIGNIFICANCE AND EVALUATION OF MIRACLES[221]

¶ 161

If therefore by the overruling and suspension of the phantom-cause of this superstition; if by separating effects from their natural antecedents; if by presenting the *phænomena* of time (as far as is possible) in the absolute forms of eternity; the nursling of experience should, in the early period of his pupilage, be compelled by a more impressive experience to seek in the invisible life alone for the true cause and invisible *nexus* of the things that are seen, we shall not demand the evidences of ordinary experience for that which, if it ever existed, existed as its antithesis and for its counteraction.

¶ 162

Was it an appropriate mean to a necessary end? Has it been attested by lovers of truth; has it been believed by lovers of wisdom? Do we see throughout all nature the occasional intervention of particular agencies in counter-check of universal laws? (And of what other definition is a miracle susceptible?) These are the questions: and if to these our answers must be affirmative, then we too will acquiesce in the traditions of humanity, and yielding as to a high interest of our own being, will discipline ourselves to the reverential and kindly faith, that the guides and teachers of mankind were the hands of power, no less than the voices of inspiration: and little anxious concerning the particular forms, proofs, and circumstances of each manifestation we will give an historic credence to the historic fact, that men sent by God have come with signs and wonders on the earth.[222]

¶ 163

If it be objected, that in nature, as distinguished from man, this intervention of particular laws is, or with the increase of science will be, resolvable into the universal laws which they had appeared to counterbalance, we will reply: Even so it may be in the case of miracles; but wisdom forbids her children to antedate their knowledge, or to act and feel otherwise or further than they know. But should that time arrive, the sole difference, that could result from such an enlargement of our view, would be this;—— that what we now consider as miracles in opposition to ordinary experience, we should then reverence with a yet higher devotion as harmonious parts of one great complex miracle, when the antithesis between experience and belief would itself be taken up into unity of intuitive reason.

WHAT PHILOSOPHY WILL GAIN BY ACCEPTING COLERIDGE'S OUTLOOK ——REMOVAL OF PRESENT BARRIER BETWEEN PHILOSOPHY AND FAITH ——THE "INWARD EYE" CAN OPEN TO THE VISION OF GOD[223]

¶ 164

And what purpose of philosophy can this acquiescence answer? A gracious purpose, a most valuable end; if it prevent the energies of philosophy from being idly wasted, by removing the contrariety without confounding the distinction between philosophy and faith. The philosopher will remain a man in sympathy with his fellow-men. The head will not be disjoined from the heart, nor will speculative truth be alienated from practical wisdom. And vainly without the union of both shall we expect an opening of the

---

[221] *Works* (Shedd), II, 467-468.
[222] Emerson quoted this entire paragraph at the end of his sermon on "Miracles" (Jan. 23, 1831). See *Y E S*, 126.
[223] *Works* (Shedd), II, 468.

inward eye[224] to the glorious vision of that existence which admits of no question out of itself, acknowledges no predicate but the I AM THAT I AM![225]

INEVITABILITY OF WONDER IN CONTEMPLATING THE INCOMPREHENSIBLE GROUND OF ALL THINGS——MYSTERY OF THAT LIFE-EBULLIENT STREAM[226]

¶ 165

In wonder . . . says Aristotle, does philosophy begin; and in astoundment . . . says Plato, does all true philosophy finish. As every faculty, with every the minutest organ of our nature, owes its whole reality and comprehensibility to an existence incomprehensible and groundless, because the ground of all comprehension; not without the union of all that is essential in all the functions of our spirit, not without an emotion tranquil from its very intensity, shall we worthily contemplate in the magnitude and integrity of the world that life-ebullient stream[227] which breaks through every momentary embankment, again, indeed, and evermore to embank itself, but within no banks to stagnate or be imprisoned.

ALL TRUE REALITY HAS BOTH ITS GROUND AND EVIDENCE IN THE WILL ——WITHOUT THE WILL TO COMPLETE IT, SCIENCE IS MEANINGLESS ——INDIVIDUALITY RESTS IN THE INFINITE——FINITE FORMS APPEAR REAL BUT ARE NOT VIEWED BY THE DIVINE IMAGINATION THROUGH ITS OMNIFORMITY——IN FINITE FORMS WE SEE ONLY THE LIGHT SHINING THROUGH REALITY AND NOT THE REALITY ITSELF[228]

¶ 166

But here it behooves us to bear in mind, that all true reality has both its ground and its evidence in the will, without which as its complement science itself is but an elaborate game of shadows, begins in abstractions and ends in perplexity. For considered merely intellectually, individuality, as individuality, is only conceivable as with and in the universal and infinite, neither before nor after it. No transition is possible from one to the other, as from the architect to the house, or the watch to its maker. The finite form can neither be laid hold of by, nor can it appear to, the mere speculative intellect as any thing of itself real, but merely as an apprehension, a frame-work which the human imagination forms by its own limits, as the foot measures itself on the snow; and the sole truth of which we must again refer to the divine imagination, in virtue of its omniformity. For even as thou art capable of beholding the transparent air as little during the absence as during the presence of light, so canst thou behold the finite things as actually existing neither with nor without the substance. Not without, ——for then the forms cease to be, and are lost in night: not with it,——for it is the light, the substance shining through it,[229] which thou canst alone really see.

THE TWO DIRECTIONS OF MAN'S EDUCATION——(1) INTUITION THROUGH THE REASON WHEN HE IS *AT ONE* WITH THE WHOLE——(2) SCHOOL OF THE UNDERSTANDING, WHICH RECONCILES ANTITHESES OF NATURE TO MIND, SUBJECT TO OBJECT, AND THING TO THOUGHT——BASIS OF COLERIDGE'S ROMANTICISM[230]

¶ 167

The ground-work, therefore, of all pure speculation is the full apprehension of the difference between [1] the contemplation of reason, namely, that intuition of things which arises when we possess ourselves, as one with the whole, which is substantial knowledge, and [2] that which presents itself when[,] transferring reality to the negations of reality, to the ever-varying frame-work of the uniform life, we think of our-

---

[224] See the phrase in Wordsworth's "I Wandered Lonely as a Cloud," and Coleridge's criticism of its misuse in *Biographia Literaria* [*Works* (Shedd), III], 478-479.

[225] See *Nature*, 79.10ff.

[226] *Works* (Shedd), II, 468-469. For comment on this note of wonder, see *Nature*, 77.3-9; 95.11.

[227] See *Nature*, 13.6-7.

[228] *Works* (Shedd), II, 469.

[229] See *Nature*, 13.5; 43.11-12; 62.17; 91.10.

[230] *Works* (Shedd), II, 469-470. Emerson's philosophy rests firmly on this analysis. For an example of the first method, see *Nature*, 13.2-13; of the second, see esp. chapters III and IV. For the higher synthesis, see *Nature*, 43.1-13; 79.8——80.23. See also his poem "Γνωθι Σεαυτον" re-edited in the next chapter.

selves as separated beings, and place nature in antithesis to the mind, as object to subject, thing to thought, death to life. This is abstract knowledge, or the science of the mere understanding. By the former, we know that existence is its own predicate, self-affirmation, the one attribute in which all others are contained, not as parts, but as manifestations. It is an eternal and infinite self-rejoicing, self-loving, with a joy unfathomable, with a love all-comprehensive. It is absolute; and the absolute is neither singly that which affirms, nor that which is affirmed; but the identity and living *copula* of both. . . . [It] is by this abstract knowledge that the understanding distinguishes the affirmed from the affirming. Well if it distinguish without dividing![231] Well if by distinction it add clearness to fulness, and prepare for the intellectual re-union of the all in one in that eternal Reason whose fulness hath no opacity,[232] whose transparency[233] hath no *vacuum*.

THE DIALECTIC INTELLECT OF MAN CAN LEAD HIM TO A KNOWLEDGE OF THE ABSOLUTE, BUT IT CANNOT SOLVE THE PROBLEM OF THE RELATION BETWEEN GOD AND THE WORLD——IDEALISM HAS LIMITATIONS[234]——TO THE PHILOSOPHER, PANTHEISM IS AN EVER-PRESENT THREAT——ONLY THE SPIRIT AND RELIGION OF MAN CAN FILL UP THE CHASM LEFT BY SPECULATION[235]

¶ 168

If we thoughtfully review . . . we shall find the conclusion to be;——that the dialectic intellect by the exertion of its own powers exclusively can lead us to a general affirmation of the supreme reality of an absolute being. But here it stops. It is utterly incapable of communicating insight or conviction concerning the existence or possibility of the world, as different from Deity. It finds itself constrained to identify, more truly to confound, the Creator with the aggregate of his creature, and, cutting the knot which it can not untwist, to deny altogether the reality of all finite existence, and then to shelter itself from its own dissatisfaction, its own importunate queries, in the wretched evasion that of nothings, no solution can be required; till pain haply, and anguish, and remorse, with bitter scoff and moody laughter inquire;——Are we then indeed nothings?[236]——till through every organ of sense nature herself asks;——How and whence did this sterile and pertinacious nothing acquire its plural number? . . . and lastly;——What is that inward mirror, in which these nothings have at least relative existence? The inevitable result of all consequent reasoning, in which the intellect refuses to acknowledge a higher or deeper ground than it can itself supply, and weens to possess within itself the centre of its own system, is——and from Zeno the Eleatic to Spinosa, and from Spinosa to the Schellings, Okens and their adherents, of the present day, ever has been——pantheism under one or other of its modes, the least repulsive of which differs from the rest, not in its consequences, which are one and the same in all, and in all alike are practically atheistic, but only as it may express the striving of the philosopher himself to hide these consequences from his own mind. This, therefore, I repeat, is the final conclusion. All speculative disquisition must begin with postulates, which the conscience alone can at once authorize and substantiate: and from whichever point the reason may start, from the things which are seen to the one invisible, or from the idea of the absolute one to the things that are seen, it will find a chasm, which the moral being only, which the spirit and religion of man alone, can fill up.[237]

IN WRITING THE PRECEDING CHAPTERS COLERIDGE BEGAN WITH AN ANTECEDENT PRINCIPLE——NOW IN CONCLUDING HE HAS COME FULL CIRCLE TO THE STARTING POINT——TO THE PRINCIPLE OF RELIGION AND FAITH, IN WHICH THE WILL FINDS SUPPORT AND WHICH THROWS LIGHT ON THE RIDDLE OF THE WORLD AND OF OURSELVES——SUFFER-

---

[231] See *Nature*, 78.17——79.4.
[232] See *Nature*, 91.9-11. See ¶ 254.
[233] See *Nature*, 13.5; 43.11; 62.17.
[234] Emerson faces this problem at length in his chapter on "Spirit." See *Nature*, 78.1——79.4.
[235] *Works* (Shedd), II, 470-471.
[236] Cf. *Nature*, 78.13.
[237] Emerson here apparently received the hint for his chapter on "Spirit"——for the "somewhat progressive." See *Nature*, 76.3ff.

ING IS INCONSEQUENTIAL TO THE MAN OF FAITH——MEANING OF *LIFE IN THE IDEA*——IMPORTANCE OF MAN'S HEART[238]

¶ 169

Thus I prefaced my inquiry into the science of method with a principle deeper than science, more certain than demonstration. For that the very ground, saith Aristotle, is groundless or self-grounded, is an identical proposition. From the indemonstrable flows the sap that circulates through every branch and spray of the demonstration. To this principle I referred the choice of the final object, the control over time, or, to comprise all in one, the method of the will. From this I started, or rather seemed to start; for it still moved before me, as an invisible guardian and guide, and it is this the re-appearance of which announces the conclusion of the circuit, and welcomes me at the goal. Yea (saith an enlightened physician), there is but one principle, which alone reconciles the man with himself, with others, and with the world; which regulates all relations, tempers all passions, gives power to overcome or support all suffering, and which is not to be shaken by aught earthly, for it belongs not to the earth; namely, the principle of religion, the living and substantial faith *which passeth all understanding*, as the cloud-piercing rock, which overhangs the stronghold of which it had been the quarry and remains the foundation. This elevation of the spirit above the semblances of custom and the senses to a world of spirit, this life in the idea, even in the supreme and godlike, which alone merits the name of life,[239] and without which our organic life is but a state of somnambulism; this it is which affords the sole sure anchorage in the storm, and at the same time the substantiating principle of all true wisdom, the satisfactory solution of all the contradictions of human nature, of the whole riddle of the world. This alone belongs to and speaks intelligibly to all alike, the learned and the ignorant, if but the heart listens.[240] For alike present in all, it may be awakened, but it can not be given.[241] But let it not be supposed, that it is a sort of knowledge: no! it is a form of BEING,[242] or indeed it is the only knowledge that truly *is*, and all other science is real only so far as it is symbolical of this. . . . For it is an immutable truth, that what comes from the heart, that alone goes to the heart; what proceeds from a divine impulse, that the godlike alone can awaken.[243]

AIDS TO REFLECTION[244]

---

[238] *Works* (Shedd), II, 471-472.

[239] See *Nature*, 49.21; 71.1-20; 80.4-8.

[240] See *Nature*, 71.2-6.

[241] Reason is in all men, though it may slumber. See ¶s. 1-56. Cf. *Nature*, 80.6-8; 43.1-13.

[242] See footnote 239, *supra*.

[243] *I.e.*, "Like only can know like."

[244] The *Aids* first appeared in London, 1825, but the first American edition, prepared by James Marsh (Burlington, Vt., 1829), is of chief interest here both because Emerson used it and because its notes and appendices, drawn from Coleridge's other prose works, made it a small encyclopedia. Its contents may be roughly described as follows: (a) "Preliminary Essay" by Marsh (pp. vii-liv), reprinted in vol. II of the present work; (b) the text itself (pp. 1-249); (c) "Notes" by Coleridge and Marsh (pp. 251-342); (d) "Selection from Mr. Coleridge's Literary Correspondence" [Rptd. from *Blackwood's Magazine* for Oct., 1820] (pp. 345-367); (e) "Appendix to the *Statesman's Manual*" (pp. 369-396); (f) "Additional Definitions, extracted from [Coleridge's] other works" (pp. 396-399). Through this one volume alone Emerson and his contemporaries had access to the heart of Coleridge's teaching, and that fact cannot be overemphasized. Marsh's "Preliminary Essay" has an interest all its own. It was itself a trumpet blast against the metaphysics of John Locke as well as a commentary on contemporary thought in the United States. Marsh called attention to a growing dissatisfaction with prevailing opinions on man and man's will, mentioning in particular the "Correspondence with the Editors" in the September, 1829, issue of *The Quarterly Christian Spectator* (Vol. I: New Haven, 1829, pp. 530-547) wherein "Pacificus" commented on the review dealing with "Human Depravity" (pp. 343-383). That review had considered a sermon by Nathaniel W. Taylor, delivered at Yale on Sept. 10, 1828, and a rejoindre by Joseph Harvey, printed at Hartford in the same year. (Subsequent correspondence on the issues appeared on pp. 547-552). Marsh surveyed the shortcomings of Paley and Locke, attempted to answer critics of Coleridge's language, pointed to Victor Cousin as the French counterpart of Coleridge, and appealed to the learned to

JAMES MARSH DEFINES COLERIDGE'S TERMS——*LIFE-GIVING BREATH*——*INWARD PRINCIPLE*——*THE INFORMING WORD*——*QUICKENING SPIRIT*——*LAW OF LIFE*[245]

¶ 170

"It will give the reader at least some clue to the author's meaning and to his sentiments . . . if by the enlivening Breath he understands the life-giving Breath or Spirit, and by the informing word the inward power or principle, which in all organized bodies modifies the living agency, appoints the measure of its working, and determines the specific *form* of its developement in each several kind. This specific principle of organization, which, as an antecedent law preexisting in the seed of every plant and so in the germs of all organized bodies, awaits the *actuating* power of life, predetermining the several shapes or forms, in which it is to be unfolded, and by which alone it is manifestable to the senses, I understand the author to mean *the* WORD; and both the actuating, quickening spirit, and the informing word belong to all organized bodies in common. . . .[246] [It] is consonant with the language of the Old Testament to represent not only the thoughts, the ideas, but the Breath and the Word of the Divine Being as living, formative, creative. Thus too, in reference to the higher powers of spiritual life in Christians, our Saviour says the *words* that I speak unto you, they are *spirit*, and they are *life*, i.e. have in them a living and life-giving energy."

¶ 171

If the reader clearly apprehends the *law of life*, as a living power or agency, antecedent to and independent of the visible and tangible forms, which it constructs, he will have little difficulty in understanding what is said of the transfusion of a higher gift and specially inbreathed, of a soul, having its life in itself, and independent for its subsistence of the inferior powers, with which it co-exists. He will be prepared to apprehend at least the meaning of the doctrine, that distinct specific forms or laws of being are superadded to that life, which is common to all, each having its own developement, and by their living agency constituting our intellectual, moral and spiritual life.

PHILOSOPHY AND RELIGION ARE STRONGEST IN UNION—DIVORCE IS FATAL TO BOTH[247]

¶ 172

"Naturam hominis hanc Deus ipse voluit, ut duarum rerum cupidus et appetens esset ——religionis et sapientiæ. Sed homines ideo falluntur, quod aut religionem suscipiunt omissâ sapientiâ; aut sapientiæ soli student omissâ religione, cum alterum sine altero esse non possit verum."—Lactantius *De Falsâ Sapientiâ*, Lib. III. B. 11.

IMPORTANCE OF REFLECTION IN GIVING NOVELTY TO FAMILIAR OBJECTS——GENIUS SEES THE MIRACULOUS IN THE COMMON——EXTREMES MEET——TO RESTORE A TRUTH TO PRISTINE LUSTRE TRANSLATE IT INTO ACTION[248]

¶ 173

It is the prerogative of Genius to produce novel impressions from familiar objects:[249] and seldom can philosophic genius be more usefully employed than in thus rescuing admitted truths from the neglect caused by the very circumstance of their universal admission. Extremes meet.[250] Truths, of all others the most awful and interesting, are too often considered as *so* true, that they lose all the power of truth, and lie bed-ridden in the dormitory of the soul, side by side with the most despised and exploded errors.

¶ 174

There is one sure way of giving freshness and importance to the most *common-place* maxims——that of *reflecting* on them in direct reference to our own state and conduct, to our own past and future being. To restore a common-place truth to its first *uncom-*

---

promote the virtue of self-knowledge. It would be a great service to American scholarship if the entire edition might be reissued in facsimile and if the editor would prepare a useful index and simplified concordance to complete it.

[245] *Aids* (1829), notes, 252.

[246] See John 1:1. The "living and specific agencies here spoken of are the inherent *forms* of the Peripatetics, the *ideas* of Plato and Ld. Bacon."

[247] *Aids* (1829), vi.

[248] *Aids* (1829), 1.

[249] See *Nature*, 92.13-18; cf. 11.18-19. Also ¶s. 63, 75, 186.

[250] See also *Works* (Shedd), VI, 155; *Table Talk*, I, 35; II, 15.

mon lustre, you need only *translate* it into action.[251] But to do this, you must have *reflected* on its truth.

KNOW THYSELF——STAY AT HOME——TURN TO THE RICH WORLD *WITHIN*——SELF-RELIANCE[252]

¶ 175

"It is the advice of the wise man, 'Dwell at home,' or, with yourself; and though there are very few that do this, yet it is surprising that the greatest part of mankind cannot be prevailed upon, at least to visit themselves sometimes; but, according to the saying of the wise Solomon, *The eyes of the fool are in the ends of the earth.*"—LEIGHTON.

¶ 176

It is a matter of great difficulty, and requires no ordinary skill and address, to fix the attention of men (especially of young men) on the world within them, to induce them to study the processes and superintend the works which they are themselves carrying on in their own minds: in short, to awaken in them both the faculty of thought and the inclination to exercise it. For alas! the largest part of mankind are nowhere greater strangers than at home.

REFLECTION IS THE SPIRITUAL EYE——THOUGHT——BECOMING CONSCIOUS OF THE SPIRITUAL WORLD——REFLECTION *IS* SELF-RELIANCE[253]

¶ 177

"And man became a living soul." [254] He did not merely *possess* it, he *became* it. It was his proper *being*, his truest *self*, *the* man *in* the man. None then, not one of human kind, so poor and destitute, but there is provided for him, even in his present state, *a house not built with hands.*[255] Aye, and spite of the philosophy (falsely so called) which mistakes the causes, the conditions, and the occasions of our becoming *conscious* of certain truths and realities for the truths and realities themselves——a house gloriously furnished. Nothing is wanted but the eye, which is the light of this house, the light which is the eye of this soul. This *seeing* light, this *enlightening* eye, is Reflection. It is more, indeed, than is ordinarily meant by that word; but is what a *Christian* ought to mean by it, and to know too, whence it first came, and still continues to come ——of what light even this light is *but* a reflection. This, too, is THOUGHT; and all thought is but unthinking that does not flow out of this, or tend towards it.

HOW CAN MAN OVERLOOK THE NEED FOR SELF-SUPERINTENDENCE OR SELF-KNOWLEDGE?——AN HOUR WISELY SPENT CAN AWAKEN THE FACULTY OF REFLECTION OR SELF-RELIANCE——TRUTHS OF THE INNER MAN APPEAR AS PARADOXES TO WORLDLINGS——OUTWARD SENSES SEE SURFACES, NOT SUBSTANCE——FEAR OF INNER SELF IS CHIEF IMPEDIMENT TO SELF-KNOWLEDGE——POWER, FREEDOM, MORALITY ARE OFTEN MIXED WITH SIN——DISTINCTION BETWEEN GOOD AND EVIL[256]

¶ 178

Self-superintendence! that any thing should overlook itself! Is not this a paradox, and hard to understand? It is, indeed, difficult, and to the imbruted sensualist a direct contradiction: and yet most truly does the poet exclaim,

> ——Unless *above* himself he can
> Erect himself, how mean a thing is man![257]

¶ 179

An hour of solitude passed in sincere and earnest prayer, or the conflict with, and conquest over, a single passion or "subtle *bosom* sin," will teach us more of thought, will more effectually awaken the *faculty*, and form the *habit*, of reflection, than a year's study in the schools without them.

---

[251] See *Aids* (1829), notes, 357: "To know the *whole* truth, we must likewise ACT: and he alone acts, who *makes*——and this can no man do, estranged from Nature. Learn to know thyself in Nature, that thou mayest understand Nature in thyself."

[252] *Aids* (1829), 1-2; 3. For other examples of the theme "Know Thyself" or "Trust Thyself," see ¶s. 67-70, 100, 152, 155, 181, 188, 189, 216, 246, 260, 264, 275, 302.

[253] *Aids* (1829), 3-4. Cf. *Nature*, 62.5-22; 74.11-13; 95.10-12.

[254] *Genesis*, 2:7.

[255] Hebrews 9:11. See ¶s. 211-212.

[256] *Aids* (1829), 4, 4, 4, 7, 10.

[257] See footnote 89 *supra*.

¶ 180

In a world, whose opinions are drawn from outside shows, many things may be *paradoxical*, (that is, contrary to the common notion) and nevertheless true: nay, *because* they are true. How should it be otherwise, as long as the imagination of the Worldling is wholly occupied by surfaces, while the Christian's thoughts are fixed on the substance, that which *is* and abides, and which, *because* it is the substance, the outward senses cannot recognize. Tertullian had good reason for his assertion, that the simplest Christian (if indeed a Christian) knows more than the most accomplished irreligious philosopher.

¶ 181

In countries enlightened by the gospel, however, the most formidable and (it is to be feared) the most frequent impediment to men's turning the mind inward upon themselves is that they are afraid of what they shall find there. There is an aching hollowness in the bosom, a dark cold speck at the heart, an obscure and boding sense of a somewhat, that must be kept *out of sight* of the conscience; some secret lodger, whom they can neither resolve to eject or retain.

¶ 182

Woe to the man, who will believe neither power, freedom, nor morality; because he no where finds either entire, or unmixed with sin, thraldom and infirmity. In the natural and intellectual realms, we distinguish what we cannot separate; and in the moral world, we must distinguish *in order to* separate. Yea, in the clear distinction of good from evil the process of separation commences.

REFLECTION MAY BE OF THREE KINDS——(1) PRUDENTIAL, (2) MORAL, (3) SPIRITUAL——THESE ARE BASED RESPECTIVELY UPON (1) THE UNDERSTANDING, (2) THE HEART AND CONSCIENCE, (3) THE WILL AND THE REASON[258]

¶ 183

It may be an additional aid to reflection, to distinguish the three kinds severally, according to the faculty to which each corresponds, the faculty or part of our human nature which is more particularly its organ. Thus: the prudential corresponds to the sense and the understanding; the moral to the heart and the conscience; the spiritual to the will and the reason, *i.e.* to the finite will reduced to harmony with, and in subordination to, the reason, as a ray from that true light which is both reason and will, universal reason, and will absolute.

JOHN SMITH ON THE REASON——WE ARE NOT THE REASON AND CANNOT CALL IT OUR OWN[259]

¶ 184

Take one passage among many from the posthumous Tracts (1660) of John Smith, not the least Star in that bright Constellation of Cambridge Men, the cotemporaries of Jeremy Taylor. "While we reflect on our own idea of Reason, we know that our own Souls are not it, but only partake of it; and that we have it κατα μεθεξιν and not κατ' ουσιην. Neither can it be called a Faculty, but far rather a Light, which we enjoy, but the Source of which is not in ourselves, nor rightly, by any individual, to be denominated *mine*."

REASON IS THE LIGHT WHICH LIGHTETH EVERY MAN——BLINDNESS OF THE UNDERSTANDING——ST. JOHN'S *HYMN TO THE LOGOS* QUOTED[260]

¶ 185

But the cause of . . . "false doctrine, blindness of Heart and contempt of the Word," is best declared by the philosophic Apostle: "they did not *like* to retain God in their knowledge," (Rom. i. 28,) and though they could not *extinguish* "the Light that lighteth every *man*," and which "shone in the Darkness;" yet because the Darkness could not *comprehend* the Light, they refused to bear witness of the Light, and worshipped, instead, the shaping Mist, which the Light had drawn upward from *the Ground* (i.e. from the mere Animal nature and instinct), and which that Light alone had made visible (*i.e.* by super-inducing on the animal instinct the principle of Self-consciousness).

---

[258] *Aids* (1829), 15.
[259] *Aids* (1829), notes, 323.

[260] *Aids* (1829), notes, 305-306.

NEED FOR DISTINCTION IN USE OF TERMS——FOR RESCUING WORDS NOW MEANINGLESS BECAUSE FAMILIAR[261]

¶ 186

In the business of moral and religious reflection . . . we have to rescue words, already existing and familiar, from the false or vague meanings imposed on them by carelessness, or by the clipping and debasing misusage of the market. And surely happiness, duty, faith, truth, and final blessedness, are matters of deeper and dearer interest for all men, than circles to the geometrician, or the characters of plants to the botanist, or the affinities and combining principle of the elements of bodies to the chemist, or even than the mechanism (fearful and wonderful though it be!) of the perishable Tabernacle of the Soul can be to the anatomist. Among the *aids to* reflection, place the following maxim prominent: let distinctness in expression advance side by side with distinction in thought.

SERMONS OF TWO CENTURIES COMPARED——THEIR SIGNIFICANCE IN THE HISTORY OF EDUCATION AND LEARNING[262]

¶ 187

It is my full conviction, that in any half dozen Sermons of Dr. Donne, or Jeremy Taylor, there are more thoughts, more facts and images, more excitements to inquiry and intellectual effort, than are presented to the congregations of the present day in as many churches or meetings during twice as many months. Yet both these were most popular preachers of their times, were heard with enthusiasm by crowded and promiscuous Audiences, and the effect produced by their eloquence was held in reverential and affectionate remembrance by many attendants on their ministry, who, like the pious Isaac Walton, were not themselves men of learning or education.

THE BEASTS WITHIN US——SELF-KNOWLEDGE IS A CHRISTIAN DUTY[263]

¶ 188

"What, will you say, have I beasts within me? Yes, you have beasts, and a vast number of them. And, that you may not think I intend to insult you, is anger an inconsiderable beast, when it barks in your heart? What is deceit, when it lies hid in a cunning mind; is it not a fox? Is not the man who is furiously bent upon calumny, a scorpion? Is not the person who is eagerly set on resentment and revenge, a most venomous viper? What do you say of a covetous man; is he not a ravenous wolf? And is not the luxurious man, as the prophet expresses it, a neighing horse? Nay, there is no wild beast but is found within us. And do you consider yourself as lord and prince of the wild beasts, because you command those that are without, though you never think of subduing or setting bounds to those that are within you? What advantage have you by your reason, which enables you to overcome lions, if, after all, you, yourself, are overcome by anger? To what purpose do you rule over the birds, and catch them with gins, if you, yourself, with the inconstancy of a bird, or hurried hither and thither, and sometimes flying high, are ensnared by pride, sometimes brought down and caught by pleasure?" LEIGHTON.

¶ 189

Art thou under the tyranny of sin? a slave to vicious habits? at enmity with God, and a skulking fugitive from thy own conscience? O, how idle the dispute, whether the listening to the dictates of *prudence* from prudential and self-interested motives be virtue or merit, when the *not* listening is guilt, misery, madness, and despair! The best, the most *Christianlike* pity thou canst show, is to take pity on thy own soul. The best and most acceptable service thou canst render, is to do justice and show mercy to *thyself*.

ALL TEACHERS OF MORAL TRUTH CALL MEN'S ATTENTION TO THE LAW OF THEIR OWN HEARTS——IT IS NO MEAN EMPLOYMENT——SALVATION IS FOUND WITHIN——SELF-RELIANCE IS THE PRINCIPLE OF MORAL AND SPIRITUAL GROWTH——IMPORTANCE OF FAITH AND BELIEF[264]

¶ 190

"What the Apostles were in an extraordinary way befitting the first annunciation of a Religion for all Mankind, this all Teachers of Moral Truth, who aim to prepare for

[261] *Aids* (1829), 20. Cf. *Y E S*, 158.   [262] *Aids* (1829), 254-255.
[263] *Aids* (1829), 26-27. Cf. *Nature*, 33.19——34.4.
[264] *Aids* (1829), 37; 39. Emerson set about becoming such a teacher of moral truth.

its reception by calling the attention of men to the Law in their own hearts, may, without presumption, consider themselves to be under ordinary gifts and circumstances: namely, Ambassadors for the Greatest of Kings, and upon no mean employment, the great Treaty of Peace and Reconcilement betwixt him and Mankind." LEIGHTON.

¶ 191

"If . . . they can read the characters of God's image in their own souls, those are the counter-part of the golden characters of His Love, in which their names are written in the book of life. Their believing writes their names under the promises of the revealed book of life (the Scriptures) and thus ascertains them, that the same names are in the secret book of life which God hath by himself from eternity. So that finding the stream of grace in their hearts, though they see not the fountain whence it flows, nor the ocean into which it returns, yet they know that it hath its source in their eternal election, and shall empty itself into the ocean[265] of their eternal salvation." LEIGHTON.

MAN MAKES THE MOTIVE, AND NOT MOTIVE THE MAN——BEHIND A MAN IS THE INTELLIGENT WILL, WHICH IS THE SPIRITUAL ELEMENT IN HIM——INFLUENCE ON HIM OF THE ORGANIZED UNIVERSE——UNITY IN PHYSICAL WORLD SUGGESTS A SPIRITUAL UNITY IN MORAL AND SPIRITUAL BEINGS——THE ALL-PRESENT POWER WITHIN AND WITHOUT MAN MAY BE CALLED *LAW, THE WORD, THE SPIRIT*[266]

¶ 192

We need only reflect on our own experience to be convinced, that the Man makes the *motive*, and not the motive the Man. What is a strong motive to one man, is no motive at all to another. If, then, the man determines the motive, what determines the Man ——to a good and worthy act, we will say, or a virtuous Course of Conduct? The intelligent Will, or the self-determining Power? True, *in part* it is; and therefore the Will is pre-eminently the *spiritual* Constituent in our Being. But will any reflecting man admit, that his own Will is the only and sufficient determinant of all he *is*, and all he does? Is nothing to be attributed to . . . the system to which he belongs, and to the pre-established Fitness of the Objects and Agents, known and unknown, that surround him, as acting *on* the will, though doubtless, *with* it likewise? a process, which the co-instantaneous yet reciprocal action of the Air and the vital Energy of the Lungs in Breathing may help to render intelligible.

¶ 193

Again: in the World we see every where evidences of a Unity, which the component Parts are so far from explaining that they necessarily pre-suppose it as the cause and condition of their existing *as* those parts: or even of their existing at all. This antecedent Unity, or Cause and Principle of each Union, it has since the time of Bacon and Kepler been customary to call a Law. . . . Now will Reason, will Common Sense, endure the assumption, that in the material and visible system it is highly reasonable to believe a Universal Power, as the cause and pre-condition of the harmony of all particular Wholes . . . and yet unreasonable and even superstitious or enthusiastic to entertain a similar belief in relation to the System of intelligent and self-conscious Beings, to the moral and personal World? But if in *this* too, in the great Community of *Persons*, it is rational to infer a One universal Presence, a One present to all and in all, is it not most irrational to suppose that a finite will can exclude it? Whenever, therefore, the man is determined (i.e. impelled and directed) to act in harmony of intercommunion, must not something be attributed to this all-present power as acting *in* the Will? and by what fitter names can we call this than THE LAW, as empowering; THE WORD, as informing; and THE SPIRIT, as actuating?

THE ABOVE APPROACH IS ADMITTEDLY NEGATIVE, BUT IT IS REASONABLE——REAL EVIDENCE FOR THE EXISTENCE OF SPIRITUAL REALITIES MUST BE SPIRITUALLY DISCERNED——THE WILL OF MAN IS THE SUPERNATURAL ELEMENT AND PRINCIPLE OF HIS PERSONALITY[267]

¶ 194

A *positive* Insight belongs to a more advanced stage: for spiritual truths can only spiritually be discerned.[268] This we know from Revelation, and (the existence of

---

[265] Cf. *Y E S*, 245.14.
[266] *Aids* (1829), 41-42; 42-43. See *Nature*, chap. VII.
[267] *Aids* (1829), 43-44.
[268] Variation of "Like only can know like."

spiritual truths being granted) Philosophy is compelled to draw the same conclusion. But though merely negative, it is sufficient to render the union of Religion and Morality *conceivable*; sufficient to satisfy an unprejudiced Inquirer, that the spiritual Doctrines of the Christian Religion are not at war with the reasoning faculty, and that if they do not run on the same Line (or Radius) with the Understanding, yet neither do they cut or cross it. It is sufficient, in short, to prove, that some distinct and consistant meaning may be attached to the assertion of the learned and philosophic Apostle, that "the spirit beareth witness with our spirit"——i.e. with *the Will*, as the Supernatural in Man and the Principle of our Personality——of that, I mean, by which we are responsible Agents; *Persons*, and not merely living *Things*.

COLERIDGE ASSUMES THE EXISTENCE OF THE SPIRITUAL WORLD BE-CAUSE OF A MORAL NATURE BELIEVED COMMON TO ALL MEN——PROOF OF SUCH A WORLD NO ONE CAN GIVE ANOTHER——SPEECH INADE-QUATE——EACH MAN MUST FIND IT WITHIN——SELF-RELIANCE[269]

¶ 195

This then is the distinction of Moral Philosophy——*not that* I begin with one or more *Assumptions*, for this is common to *all* science; but——that I assume a something, the proof of which no man can give to another, yet every man may *find* for himself.[270] If any man assert, that he *can* not find it, I am *bound* to disbelieve him! I cannot do otherwise without unsettling the very foundations of my own moral Nature. For I either find it as an *essential* of the Humanity *common* to Him and Me: or I have not *found* it at all, except as an Hypochondriast finds *Glass* Legs. If, on the other hand, he *will* not find it, he excommunicates himself. He forfeits his *personal* Rights, and becomes a *Thing*, i.e. one who may rightfully be *employed* or *used*, as a means to an end, against his will, and without regard to his interest.

THE PHILOSOPHY OF THE CHRISTIAN IS GROUNDED ON THE *CATE-GORICAL IMPERATIVE*——THE UNIVERSAL *OUGHT*——HE KNOWS THREE FACTS: (1) LAW OF CONSCIENCE; (2) RESPONSIBLE WILL; (3) EXIST-ENCE OF EVIL——HE ACCEPTS WITH WONDER THE MYSTERY SUR-ROUNDING ULTIMATE REALITY[271]

¶ 196

The *Christian* likewise grounds *his* philosophy on assertions; but with the best of all reasons for making them——viz. that he *ought*[272] so to do. He asserts what he can neither prove nor account for, nor himself comprehend; but with the strongest of *inducements*, that of understanding thereby whatever else it most concerns him to understand aright. And yet his Assertions have nothing in them of Theory or Hypothesis; but are in immediate reference to three ultimate *Facts;* namely, the Reality of the LAW OF CONSCIENCE; the existence of a RESPONSIBLE WILL, as the subject of that law; and lastly, the existence of EVIL——of Evil essentially such, not by accident of outward circumstances, not derived from its physical consequences, or from any cause, out of itself. The first is a Fact of Consciousness; the second a Fact of Reason necessarily concluded from the first; and the third a Fact of History interpreted by both. *Omnia exeunt in mysterium*, says a Schoolman: *i.e. There is nothing, the absolute ground of which is not a Mystery*. The contrary were indeed a contradiction in terms: for how can that, which is to explain all things, be susceptible of an explanation? It would be to suppose the same thing first and second at the same time.[273]

¶ 197

In Wonder all Philosophy began: in Wonder it ends: and Admiration fills up the interspace. But the first Wonder is the Offspring of Ignorance: the last is the Parent of Adoration. The First is the birth-throe of our knowledge: the Last is its euthanasy and apotheosis.

BY INTUITION AND SELF-RELIANCE WE KNOW THAT THE INFINITE PENETRATES THE FINITE——THAT ETERNITY ENTERS TIME——THAT WE EXIST ONLY SO FAR AS GOD IS WITH US——THAT WE POSSESS OUR-SELVES ONLY IN POSSESSING HIM[274]

---

[269] *Aids* (1829), 88.
[270] See *Nature*, 56.16-18.
[271] *Aids* (1829), 89-90; 145-146.
[272] Cf. *Y E S*, 95.9.
[273] Cf. *Nature*, 77.3-10.
[274] *Aids* (1829), 55.

¶ 198

[T]here is something in the human mind which makes it know (as soon as it is sufficiently awakened to reflect on its own thoughts and notices), that in all finite Quantity there is an Infinite, in all measures of Time an Eternal; that the latter are the basis, the substance, the true and abiding *reality* of the former; and that as we truly *are*, only as far as God is with us, so neither can we truly *possess* (*i.e.* enjoy) our Being or any other real Good, but by living in the sense of his holy presence.

REASON IS CALLED *SPIRIT* IN JOHN'S GOSPEL[275]——*IDEAS* ARE CALLED *TRUTHS SPIRITUALLY DISCERNED*——SENECA'S TESTIMONY OF THE SPIRIT'S ACTIVITY[276]

¶ 199

And here it will not be impertinent to observe, that what the eldest Greek Philosophy entitled *the Reason* (ΝΟΥΣ) and *ideas*, the Philosophic Apostle names *the Spirit* and *Truths spiritually* discerned: while to those who in the pride of Learning or in the overweening meanness of modern Metaphysics decry the doctrine of the Spirit in Man and its possible communion with the Holy Spirit, as *vulgar* enthusiasm! I submit the following Sentences from a Pagan Philosopher, a Nobleman and a Minister of State—— "Ita dico, Lucili! *sacer intra nos Spiritus sedet*, malorum bonorumque nostrorum observator et custos. Hic prout a nobis tractatus est, ita nos ipse tractat. *Bonus vir sine Deo nemo est.*"——SENECA.

THE SPIRIT OR WILL OF MAN KNOWS ITS OWN STATE BY ACTION—— MAN'S DIVIDED SELF——HIS INCONSISTENCY DESCRIBED——THE REMEDY MUST BEGIN AT THE HEART, WHICH IS RESTLESS AWAY FROM GOD ——CHRISTIANITY BEGINS THERE

¶ 200

Now the Spirit in Man (that is, the Will) knows its own State in and by its Acts alone: even as in geometrical reasoning the Mind knows its constructive *faculty* in the *act* of constructing, and contemplates the act in the *product* (*i.e.* the mental figure or diagram) which is inseparable from the act and co-instantaneous.[277]

¶ 201

God and the World we worship both together,
    Draw not our Laws to Him, but His to ours;
Untrue to both, so prosperous in neither,
    The imperfect Will brings forth but barren Flowers!
Unwise as all distracted Interests be,
Strangers to God, Fools in Humanity:
Too good for great things, and too great for good,
While still, "I dare not" waits upon "I would." [278]

¶ 202

All true remedy must begin at the heart; otherwise it will be but a mountebank cure, a false imagined conquest. The weights and wheels are *there*, and the clock strikes according to their motion. Even he that speaks contrary to what is within him, guilefully contrary to his inward conviction and knowledge, yet speaks conformably to what is within him in the temper and frame of his heart, which is double, *a heart and a heart*, as the Psalmist hath it, Psal. xii.2.——LEIGHTON.[279]

¶ 203

Though the heart once gone from God turns continually further away from him, and moves not towards Him till it be renewed, yet, even in that wandering, it retains that natural relation to God, as its centre, that it hath no true rest elsewhere, nor can by any means find it. It is made for Him, and is therefore still restless till it meet with him.[279a] It is true, the natural man takes much pains to quiet his heart by other things,

---

[275] See *Nature*, chap. VII.
[276] *Aids* (1829), 96.
[277] *Aids* (1829), 56. Cf. *Nature*, 6.11; 47.18. Cf. also 56.19. See ¶ 218.
[278] *Aids* (1829), 59. This is an adaptation of stanza lxvi of Fulke Greville Lord Brooke's "A Treatise of Warres," which is given in its original form on page 471 of *The Poetical Works of S. T. Coleridge*, ed. James Dykes Campbell, London, 1925. Cf. *Nature*, 89.13-18.
[279] *Aids* (1829), 68.
[279a] A possible echo of St. Augustine's famous line: "Thou hast made us, O Lord, for

and digests many vexations with hopes of contentment in the end and accomplishment of some design he hath; but still the heart misgives. Many times he attains not the thing he seeks; but if he do, yet he never attains the satisfaction he seeks and expects in it, but only learns from that to desire something further, and still hunts on after a fancy, drives his own shadow before him, and never overtakes it; and if he did, yet it is but a shadow.[280]

¶ 204

In preventing the rank vapours that steam up from the corrupt *Heart* Christianity restores the *Intellect* likewise to its natural clearness. By relieving the mind from the distractions and importunities of the unruly passions, she improves the *quality* of the Understanding: while at the same time she presents for its contemplations Objects so great and so bright as cannot but enlarge the Organ, by which they are contemplated. The Fears, the Hopes, the Remembrances, the Anticipations, the inward and outward Experience, the Belief and the Faith, of a Christian form of themselves a Philosophy and a sum of Knowledge, which a Life spent in the Grove of Academus, or the "painted Porch," could not have attained or collected.[281]

CHRISTIANITY——HOW COMPREHENDED?——HOW PROVED?[282]

¶ 205

To the first question I should answer: Christianity is not a Theory, or a Speculation; but a *Life*. Not a *Philosophy* of Life, but a Life and a living process. To the second: TRY IT. It has been eighteen hundred Years in existence: and has one Individual left a record, like the following? I tried it; and it did not answer. I made the experiment faithfully according to the directions; and the result has been, a conviction of my own credulity.

EXTREMES IN THE CHRISTIAN FAITH CAN BE AVOIDED BY AN AWARENESS OF THE DIVERSITY BETWEEN THE *UNDERSTANDING* AND THE *REASON*——SIR THOMAS BROWNE AND ULTRA-FIDIANISM—— MINIMIFIDIANISM[283]

¶ 206

Sir Thomas Brown,[284] in his Religio Medici, complains, that there are not impossibilities enough in Religion for his active faith; and adopts by choice and in free preference such interpretations of certain texts and declarations of Holy Writ, as place them in irreconcilable contradiction to the demonstrations of science and experience of mankind, because (says he) I love to lose myself in a mystery, and 'tis my solitary recreation to pose my apprehension with those involved enigmas and riddles of the Trinity and Incarnation——"and because he delights (as thinking" it no vulgar part of faith) to believe a thing not only above but contrary to Reason, and against the evidence of our proper sense. For the worthy knight could answer all the objections of the Devil and Reason (!!)[285] "with the odd resolution he had learnt of Tertullian: Certum est quia impossibile est. It is certainly true because it is quite impos[s]ible!" Now this I call ULTRA-FIDIANISM.

¶ 207

Again, there is a scheme constructed on the principle of retaining the social sympathies, that attend on the name of Believer, at the least possible expenditure of Belief ——a scheme of picking and choosing Scripture texts for the support of doctrines that had been learned beforehand from the higher oracle of Common Sense; which, as applied to the truths of Religion, means the popular part of the philosophy in fashion. . . . And this extreme I call MINIMIFIDIANISM. Now if there be one Preventive of both these extremes more efficacious than another, and preliminary to all the rest, it is the being made fully aware of the diversity of Reason and Understanding.

Thyself, and our hearts are restless till they return to Thee." Quoted in *The Select Works of Archbishop Leighton*, ed. George B. Cheever, Boston, 1832, p. 524.

[280] *Aids* (1829), 79. Cf. *Nature*, 76.16; 89.3-6.
[281] *Aids* (1829), 123.   [283] *Aids* (1829), 135-136.
[282] *Aids* (1829), 131.   [284] *I.e.,* "Browne."
[285] Coleridge's term is "Understanding." See ¶ 43.

UNDERSTANDING IS NOT THE MEASURE OF SPIRITUAL MATTERS—
GREAT TRUTHS CAN BE PERCEIVED ONLY BY A HIGHER AGENCY—
INADEQUACY OF THE *RELIGION OF NATURE*————SIMONIDES————
POMPONATIUS[286]

¶ 208

I would disturb no man's faith in the great articles of the (falsely so called) Religion
of Nature. But before the man rejects, and calls on other men to reject, the revelations
of the Gospel and the Religion of all Christendom, I would have him place himself in
the state and under all the privations of a Simonides, when on the fortieth day of his
meditation the sage and philosophic Poet abandoned the Problem in despair. Ever and
anon he seemed to have hold of the truth; but when he asked himself, what he *meant*
by it, it escaped from him, or resolved itself into meanings, that destroyed each other.
I would have the Sceptic, while yet a Sceptic only, seriously consider whether a Doctrine, of the truth of which a Socrates could obtain no other assurance than what he
derived from his strong *wish* that it should be true; or that which Plato found a
Mystery hard to discover, and when discovered, communicable only to the fewest of
men; can, consonantly with History or Common Sense, be classed among the Articles,
the belief of which is ensured to all men by their mere common sense? Whether, without gross outrage to fact, they can be said to constitute a Religion of nature, or a
Natural Theology antecedent to Revelation or superseding its necessity? Yes! in
prevention (for there is little chance, I fear, of a *cure*) of the pugnacious dogmatism
of *partial* Reflection, I would prescribe to every man, who feels a commencing alienation
from the Catholic Faith, and whose studies and attainments authorise him to argue on
the subject at all, a patient and thoughtful perusal of the arguments and representations which Bayle supposes to have passed through the mind of Simonides. Or I should
be fully satisfied if I could induce these Eschewers of Mystery to give a patient, manly,
and impartial perusal to the single Treatise of Pomponatius, De Fato.

CHRISTIAN FAITH AS *IN-EVIDENCE*————MIRACLES OF CHRIST A PROOF
OF HIS AUTHORITY[287]

¶ 209

"True Christian Faith must have in it something of in-evidence, something that must
be made up by duty and by obedience."[288] But most readily do I admit, and most
fervently do I contend, that the Miracles worked by Christ, both as miracles and as
fulfilments of prophecy, both as signs and as wonders, made plain discovery, and gave
unquestionable proof, of his divine character and authority; that they were to the whole
Jewish nation true and appropriate evidences, that He was indeed come who had
promised and declared to their Forefathers.

MEANING OF PHRASE *STEDFAST BY FAITH* TO THE ORTHODOX
CHRISTIAN[289]

¶ 210

Stedfast by Faith. This is absolutely necessary for resistance to the Evil Principle.
There is no standing out without some firm ground to stand on: and this Faith alone
supplies. By Faith in the Love of Christ the power of God becomes ours. When the Soul
is beleaguered by enemies, Weakness on the Walls, Treachery at the Gates, and Corruption in the Citadel, then by faith she says——Lamb of God, slain from the foundation of the World! thou art my Strength! I look to thee for deliverance! And thus she
overcomes. The pollution (*miasma*) of Sin is precipitated by his Blood, the power of Sin
is conquered by his Spirit. The Apostle says not——stedfast by your own resolutions
and purposes; but *stedfast by faith.* Nor yet stedfast in your Will, but *stedfast in the
faith.* We are not to be looking to, or brooding over ourselves, either for accusation or
for confidence, or by a deep yet too frequent self-delusion) to obtain the latter by
making a *merit* to ourselves of the former. But we are to look to CHRIST and "him
crucified." The Law "that is very nigh to thee, even in thy heart;" the Law that con-
demneth and hath no promise; that stoppeth the guilty PAST in its swift flight, and
maketh it disown its name; the Law will accuse thee enough. Linger not in the Justice-

---

[286] *Aids* (1829), 147-148.
[287] *Aids* (1829), 207-208.
[288] Jeremy Taylor, *Worthy Communicant*, [edition uncertain], p. 160.
[289] *Aids* (1829), 188-189. Cf. Emerson's sermon, "Religious Liberalism and Rigidity."

court, listening to thy indictment! Loiter not in waiting to hear the Sentence! No! Anticipate the verdict! *Appeal to Cæsar!* Haste to the King for a Pardon! ... Fix thy thought on what *Christ* did, what *Christ* suffered, what *Christ* is——as if thou wouldst fill the hollowness of thy Soul with Christ!

IMPORTANCE OF SELF-RELIANCE——FAITH ADMITS US TO OUR SPIRITUAL HOUSE——TO THE *HOUSE NOT MADE WITH HANDS*[290]

¶ 211

Oh take counsel of thy Reason! It will show thee how impossible it is, that even a World should merit the love of Eternal Wisdom and all-sufficing Beatitude, otherwise than as it is contained in that all-perfect Idea, in which the Supreme Mind contemplateth itself and the plenitude of its infinity——the only-begotten before all ages! the beloved Son in whom the Father is indeed well pleased! And as the Mind, so the Body with which it is to be clothed! as the Indweller, so the House in which is to be the Abiding-place!

¶ 212

St. Paul ... asserts the same doctrine when speaking of the "celestial body" provided for "the New Man" in the spiritual Flesh and Blood, (i.e. the informing power and vivific life of the incarnate Word: for the Blood is the Life, and the Flesh the Power) ——when speaking, I say, of this "celestial body," as an "house not made with hands, *eternal in the heavens,*" yet brought down to us, made appropriable by faith, and *ours* ——he adds: "For in this earthly house (i.e. this mortal life, as the inward principle or energy of our Tabernacle, or outward and sensible Body) we groan, earnestly desiring to be *clothed upon with* our house which is from heaven: not that we would be unclothed, but *clothed upon,* that Mortality might be swallowed up of life." 2 Cor. v. 1-4.

DOCTRINE OF A FUTURE LIFE BELONGS TO ALL RELIGIONS AND IS NOT A PECULIARITY OF CHRISTIANITY——JESUS CITED AS EVIDENCE[291]

¶ 213

Yes! fervently do I contend, that to satisfy the Understanding, that there is a Future State, was not the *specific* Object of the Christian Dispensation; and that neither the Belief of a Future State, nor the *Rationality* of this belief, is the *exclusive* Attribute of the Christian Religion. An *essential,* a *fundamental,* Article of *all* Religion it is, and therefore of the Christian; but ... before sentence is passed against me, as heterodox, on this ground, let not my Judges forget, who it was that assured us, that if a man did not believe in a state of retribution after death, previously and on other grounds, "neither would he believe, though a man should be raised from the dead." ... He held such Questioners, who could not find a sufficing proof of this great all-concerning verity in the words, "The God of Abraham, the God of Isaac, and the God of Jacob," unworthy of any other answer! men not to be satisfied by *any* proof!——by any such proofs, at least, as are compatible with the ends and purposes of all religious conviction! by any proofs, that would not destroy the faith they were intended to confirm, and reverse the whole character and quality of its effects and influences!

RICHARD HOOKER ON PRIDE——COMPENSATION——VALUE IN OUR FAULTS——GOOD EMERGES FROM EVIL——STRENGTH COMES FROM WEAKNESS[292]

¶ 214

"I am not afraid to affirm it boldly with St. Augustine, that Men puffed up through a proud Opinion of their own Sanctity and Holiness receive a benefit at the hands of God, and are assisted with his Grace when with his Grace they are *not* assisted, but permitted (and that grievously) to transgress. Whereby, as they were through over-great Liking of themselves supplanted *(tripped up),* so the dislike of that which did supplant them may establish them afterwards the surer. Ask the very Soul of Peter, and it shall undoubtedly itself make you this answer: My eager protestations made in the glory of my spiritual strength, I am ashamed of. But my shame and the Tears, with which my Presumption and my Weakness were bewailed, recur in the songs of my Thanksgiving. My Strength had been my Ruin, my Fall hath proved my Stay."—SERMON ON PRIDE.

---

[290] *Aids* (1829), 189-190; notes, 333. See ¶ 177.
[291] *Aids* (1829), 209-210.   [292] *Aids* (1829), 127.

THE DIVINE SPIRIT IS DEEPER THAN OUR CONSCIOUSNESS——LOCKE ERRED IN TAKING ONLY HALF THE TRUTH[293]

¶ 215

If any reflecting mind be surprised that the aims of the Divine Spirit should be deeper than our Consciousness can reach, it must arise from the not having attended sufficiently to the nature and necessary limits of human Consciousness. For the same impossibility exists as to the first acts and movements of our own will——the farthest back our recollection can follow the traces, never leads us to the first foot-mark——the lowest depth that the light of our Consciousness can visit even with a doubtful Glimmering, is still at an unknown distance from the Ground: and so, indeed, must it be with all Truths, and all modes of Being that can neither be counted, coloured, or delineated. Before and After, when applied to such Subjects, are but allegories, which the Sense or Imagination supply to the Understanding. The Position of the Aristotelians, *Nihil in intellectu quod non prius in sensu*, on which Mr. Locke's Essay is grounded, is irrefragable: Locke erred only in taking half the truth for a whole Truth. Conception is consequent on Perception. What we cannot *imagine*, we cannot, in the proper sense of the word, *conceive*.

DISTINCTION BETWEEN *THOUGHT* AND *ATTENTION*——SELF-KNOWLEDGE REQUIRES THOUGHT[294]

¶ 216

In ATTENTION, we keep the mind *passive:* in THOUGHT, we rouse it into activity. In the former, we submit to an impression——we keep the mind steady in order to *receive* the stamp. In the latter, we seek to *imitate* the artist, while we ourselves make a copy or duplicate of his work. We may learn arithmetic, or the elements of geometry, by continued attention alone; but *self*-knowledge, or an insight into the laws and constitution of the human mind and the *grounds* of religion and true morality, in addition to the effort of attention requires the energy of THOUGHT.[295]

NATURE AND *THE WILL* DIFFERENTIATED——WILL IS THE SPIRITUAL PART OF MAN——THE UNDERSTANDING BEHOLDS CAUSE AND EFFECT IN NATURE——ACTION AND REACTION[296]

¶ 217

Whatever is representable in the forms of Time and Space, is Nature. But whatever is comprehended in Time and Space, is included in the Mechanism of Cause and Effect. And conversely, whatever, by whatever means, has its principle in itself, so far as to *originate* its actions, cannot be contemplated in any of the forms of Space and Time ——it must, therefore, be considered as *Spirit* or *Spiritual* by a mind in that stage of its Developement which is here supposed, and which we have agreed to understand under the name of morality, or the Moral State: for in this stage we are concerned only with the forming of *negative* conceptions, *negative* convictions; and by *spiritual* I do not pretend to determine *what* the Will *is*, but what it is *not*——namely, that it is not Nature.

¶ 218

Whatever is comprized in the Chain and Mechanism of Cause and Effect, of course *necessitated*, and having its necessity in some other thing, antecedent or concurrent——

---

[293] *Aids* (1829), 45; notes, 397: "By knowledge, *a priori*, we do not mean, that we can know any thing previously to experience, which would be a contradiction in terms; but, that having once known it by occasion of experience, (i.e., something acting upon us from without,) we then know, that it must have pre-existed, or the experience itself would have been impossible. By experience only, I know that I have eyes; but then my reason convinces me, that I must have had eyes in order to the experience." See *Nature*, chap. VII. See also Marsh's note in *Aids* (1829), 334: "In his Literary Life, vol. 1. c. 12, the Author has distinguished transcendental and transcendent, according to the scholastic use of them. In philosophical enquiries, that is *transcendental*, which lies beneath, or, as it were *behind* our ordinary consciousness, but of which we become conscious by a voluntary effort of self-inspection. That is *transcendent*, which is out of the reach of all thought and self-consciousness, and cannot, therefore, become an object of knowledge——and a transcendent cause is a cause, the knowledge of which *as it is in itself*, lies beyond the reach of all our cognitive faculties."
[294] *Aids* (1829), 251-252.
[295] Cf. *Nature*, 25.14; 51.7; 62.5; 74.11-12; 79.5.
[296] *Aids* (1829), 45, 273, 87, 326-327. See ¶s. 1ff.; 200. See *Nature*, 71.17-20.

this is said to be *Natural;* and the Aggregate and System of all such things is NATURE. It is, therefore, a contradiction in terms to include in this the Free-will, of which the verbal definition is——that which *originates* an act or state of Being. In this sense therefore, which is the sense of St. Paul, and indeed of the New Testament throughout, *Spiritual* and *Supernatural* are synonymous.

¶ 218a

If there be aught *Spiritual* in Man, the Will must be such. *If* there be a Will, there must be Spirituality in Man. . . . I suppose the Reader . . . convinced, that there is more in man than can be rationally referred to the life of Nature and the Mechanism of Organization; that he has a will not included in this mechanism; and that the Will is in an especial and pre-eminent sense the spiritual part of our Humanity.

¶ 219

The Power which we call nature, may be thus defined: a Power subject to the Law of Continuity *(Lex Continui.——In Naturâ non datur Saltus,)* which law the human Understanding, by a necessity arising out of its own constitution, can conceive only under the form of Cause and Effect. That this *form* (or law) of Cause and Effect is (relatively to the World *without,* or to Things as they subsist independently of our perceptions) only a form or mode of *thinking;* that it is a law inherent in the Understanding itself (just as the symmetry of the miscellaneous objects seen by the kaleidoscope inheres in (*i.e.* results from) the mechanism of the kaleidoscope itself)——this becomes evident as soon as we attempt to apply the pre-conception directly to any operation of Nature. For in this case we are forced to represent the cause as being at the same instant the effect, and vice versâ the effect as being the cause——a relation which we seek to express by the terms Action and Re-action;[297] but for which the term Reciprocal Action or the Law of Reciprocity (*germanicè* Wechselwirkung) would be both more accurate and more expressive.

JEREMY TAYLOR ON ORIGINAL SIN——ADAM TURNED HIS BACK ON THE SUN[298]——SIN LEFT HIM IGNORANT AND A VICTIM OF HIS OWN *NATURE*[299]

¶ 220

"Adam turned his back on the Sun, and dwelt in the Dark and the Shadow. He sinned, and brought evil into his *Supernatural* endowments, and lost the Sacrament and instrument of Immortality, the Tree of Life in the centre of the Garden. He then fell under the evils of a sickly Body, and a passionate and ignorant Soul. His Sin made him sickly, his Sickness made him peevish: his Sin left him ignorant, his Ignorance made him foolish and unreasonable. His sin left him to his *Nature:* and by Nature, whoever was to be born at all was to be born a child, and to do before he could understand, and to be bred under laws to which he was always bound, but which could not always be exacted; and he was to choose when he could not reason, and had passions most strong when he had his understanding most weak; and the more need he had of a curb, the less strength he had to use it! And this being the case of all the world, what was *every* man's evil became *all* men's greater evil; and though alone it was very bad, yet when they came together it was made much worse."

MAN IS A FALLEN CREATURE——HIS WILL IS DISEASED——HIS FREEDOM IS, THEREFORE, IMPAIRED——MEANING OF *ORIGINAL SIN*——ADAM RESPONSIBLE ONLY IN SENSE OF *UNIVERSAL MAN*[300]

¶ 221

Man was and is a *fallen* Creature, not by accidents of bodily constitution, or any other cause, which *human* Wisdom in a course of ages might be supposed capable of removing; but diseased in his *Will,* in that Will which is the true and only strict synonime of the Word, I, or the intelligent Self.

¶ 222

For this is the essential attribute of a Will, and contained in the very *idea,* that whatever determines the Will acquires this power from a previous determination of the

---

[297] See *Nature,* 41.23.
[298] *Nature,* 76.16-17.   [299] *Aids* (1829), 159.
[300] *Aids* (1829), 90; 172; 174; 176. Emerson avoids Coleridge's view of Original Sin, yet emphasizes an *atrophied* Will. Cf. *Nature,* 91-95. In other words, he accepts Coleridge's Neo-Platonism, but rejects his orthodoxy or theology.

Will itself. The Will is ultimately self-determined, or it is no longer a *Will* under the Law of perfect Freedom, but a *Nature* under the mechanism of Cause and Effect. And if by an act, to which it had determined itself, it has subjected itself to the determination of Nature (in the language of St. Paul, to the Law of the Flesh), it receives a nature into itself, and so far it becomes a Nature: and this is a corruption of the Will and a corrupt Nature. It is also a *Fall* of Man, inasmuch as his Will is the condition of his Personality; the ground and condition of the attribute which constitutes him *Man*. And the ground-work of *Personal* Being is a capacity of acknowledging the Moral Law (the Law of the Spirit, the Law of Freedom, the Divine Will) as that which should, of itself, suffice to determine the Will to a free obedience of the Law, the Law working thereon *by its own exceeding lawfulness*. This, and this alone, is *positive* Good: good in itself, and independent of all relations. Whatever resists and, as a positive force, opposes *this* in the Will is therefore evil.

¶ 223

A moral Evil is an Evil that has its origin in a Will. An Evil common to all must have a ground common to all. But the actual existence of moral evil we are bound in conscience to admit; and that there is an evil common to all is a Fact; and this Evil must therefore have a common ground. Now this evil ground cannot originate in the Divine Will: it must therefore be referred to the Will of Man. And this evil Ground we call Original Sin. It is a *Mystery*, that is, a Fact, which we see, but cannot explain; and the doctrine a truth which we apprehend but can neither comprehend nor communicate. And such by the quality of the Subject *(viz.* a responsible *Will)* it must be, if it be truth at all.

¶ 224

The Corruption of my will may very warrantably be spoken of as a *Consequence* of Adam's Existence; as a consequence, a link in the historic Chain of Instances, whereof Adam is the first. But that it is *on account* of Adam; or that this evil principle was, a priori, inserted or infused into my Will by the Will of another——which is indeed a contradiction in terms, my Will in such case being no *Will*——*this* is nowhere asserted in Scripture explicitly or by implication. It belongs to the very essence of the doctrine, that in respect of Original Sin *every* man is the adequate representative of *all* men. What wonder, then, that where no inward ground of preference existed, the choice should be determined by outward relations, and that the first *in time* should be taken as the Diagram? Even in Genesis the word, Adam, is distinguished from a Proper Name by an Article before it. It is *the* Adam, so as to express the *genus*,[301] not the Individual ——or rather, perhaps, I should say, *as well as* the Individual.

ALL THINGS STRIVE TO ASCEND——MAN SHOULD STAY ERECT[302]

¶ 225

And who that hath watched their ways with an understanding heart, could contemplate the filial and loyal Bee; the home-building, wedded, and divorceless Swallow; and above all the manifoldly intelligent Ant tribes . . . and not say to himself, Behold the Shadow of approaching Humanity, the Sun rising from behind, in the kindling Morn of Creation! Thus all lower Natures find their highest Good in semblances and seekings of that which is higher and better. All things strive to ascend, and ascend in their striving. And shall man alone stoop? Shall his pursuits and desires, the *reflections* of his inward life, be like the reflected Image of a Tree on the edge of a Pool, that grows downward, and seeks a mock heaven in the unstable element beneath it, in neighbourhood with the slim water-weeds and oozy bottom-grass that are yet better than itself and more noble, in as far as Substances that appear as Shadows are preferable to Shadows mistaken for Substance! No! it must be a higher good to make you happy. While you labour for any thing below your proper Humanity, you seek a happy Life in the region of Death. Well saith the moral Poet——

Unless above himself he can
Erect himself, how mean a thing is man![303]

---

[301] Cf. *Nature*, 87.13.
[302] *Aids* (1829), 72. Cf. stanza on title-page of 1849 edition of *Nature*.
[303] See note 89.

CHILDLIKE HUMILITY NEEDED FOR DISCOVERING TRUTH, BEAUTY OR GOODNESS——THE BIAS WHICH WE SHARE WITH ALL HUMANITY NEED NOT PROVE A HANDICAP IN THE QUEST——LOVE OF TRUTH FOR ITS OWN SAKE IS POSSIBLE[304]

¶ 226

There is small chance of Truth at the goal where there is not child-like Humility at the Starting-post. . . . And that a love of Truth for its own sake, and merely as Truth, is possible, my Soul bears witness to itself in its inmost recesses. But there are other Interests——those of Goodness, of Beauty,[305] of Utility. It would be a sorry proof of the Humility I am extolling, were I to ask for Angels' wings to overfly my own Human Nature. I exclude none of these. It is enough if the *"lene clinamen,"* the gentle Bias, be given by no interest that concerns myself other than as I am a Man, and included in the great family of Mankind; but which does therefore especially concern me, because being a common Interest of *all* men it must needs concern the very *essentials* of my Being, and because these essentials, as existing in *me*, are especially intrusted to my particular charge.

PRIDE (THE DESIRE TO BE DISTINGUISHED) COMES BETWEEN THE SELF AND TRUTH——SELF-RELIANCE IMPOSSIBLE WHEN ONE YIELDS TO EXTERNAL APPRAISALS[306]

¶ 227

Widely different from this social and truth attracted Bias, different both in its nature and its effects, is the Interest connected with the desire of *distinguishing* yourself from other men, in order to be distinguished by them. Hoc reverâ *est inter* te et veritatem. This Interest does indeed stand between thee and truth. I might add between thee and thy own soul. It is scarcely more at variance with the love of truth than it is unfriendly to the attainment that deserves that name. By your own act you have appointed the Many as your Judges and Appraisers: for the anxiety to be admired is a loveless passion, ever strongest with regard to those by whom we are least known and least cared for, loud on the Hustings, gay in the Ball-room, mute and sullen at the family Fireside.

QUANTUM SUMUS, SCIMUS——WHAT WE ARE, THAT ONLY CAN WE KNOW[307]

¶ 228

Quantum *sumus, scimus*. That which we find within ourselves, which is more than ourselves, and yet the ground of whatever is good and permanent therein, is the substance and life of all other knowledge.

SUBJECTIVE *VS.* OBJECTIVE TRUTH——EULER AND THE PROPERTIES OF ARCHES[308]

¶ 229

The celebrated Euler having demonstrated certain properties of Arches, adds: "All experience is in contradiction to this; but this is no reason for doubting its truth." The words *sound* paradoxical; but mean no more than this——that the mathematical properties of figure and space are not less certainly the properties of Figure and Space because they can never be perfectly realized in wood, stone, or iron. Now this assertion of Euler's might be expressed at once, briefly and simply, by saying, that the properties in question were *subjectively* true, though not objectively——or that the Mathematical Arch possessed a *subjective reality*, though incapable of being realized *objectively*.

MORALITY DISTINGUISHED FROM PRUDENCE[309]

¶ 230

Morality, as distinguished from Prudence[,] implying (it matters not under what name, whether of Honour, or Duty, or Conscience, still, I say, implying), and being grounded in, an awe of the Invisible and a Confidence therein beyond (nay occasionally

---

[304] *Aids* (1829), 124. Cf. *Nature*, 82.18-20.
[305] Cf. *Nature*, 30.20.
[307] *Aids* (1829) notes, 257.
[308] *Aids* (1829), notes, 285. See ¶s. 47, 137.
[306] *Aids* (1829), 124-125.
[309] *Aids* (1829), notes, 277-278.

in apparent contradiction to) the inductions of outward Experience, is essentially religious.

IDEA DEFINED——CORRELATIVE OF *LAW*[310]

¶ 231

What is an IDEA? In answer to this I commence with the *absolutely* Real, as the PROTHESIS; the *subjectively* Real as the THESIS; the *objectively* Real as the ANTITHESIS: and I affirm, that Idea is the INDIFFERENCE of the two——so namely, that if it be conceived as in the Subject, the Idea is an Object, and possesses Objective truth; but if in an Object, it is then a Subject, and is necessarily thought of as exercising the powers of a Subject. Thus an IDEA conceived as subsisting in an Object becomes a LAW; and a Law contemplated *subjectively* (in a mind) is an Idea.

THE STATESMAN'S MANUAL[311]

MIRACLES——SIGNS AND WONDERS WERE ONCE USED TO BREAK DOWN SUPERSTITION AND STARTLE THE UNDERSTANDING——BIBLICAL MIR-ACLES WERE ACCOMPANIED BY TRUTHS AND SUBSERVED THESE TRUTHS ——SUCH MIRACLES WERE REALLY SUPERFLUOUS——SHOULD NEVER BE SOUGHT FOR THEMSELVES ALONE——TRUTH SUFFICIENT IN ITSELF—— WICKED GENERATIONS SEEK AFTER A SIGN[312]

¶ 232

In the infancy of the world signs and wonders were requisite in order to startle and break down that superstition,——idolatrous in itself and the source of all other idolatry,——which tempts the natural man to seek the true cause and origin of public calamities in outward circumstances, persons, and incidents: in agents therefore that were themselves but surges of the same tide, passive conductors of the one invisible influence, under which the total host of billows, in the whole line of successive im-pulse, swell and roll shoreward; there finally, each in its turn, to strike, roar, and be dissipated.

¶ 233

But with each miracle worked there was a truth revealed, which thenceforward was to act as its substitute. And if we think the Bible less applicable to us on account of the miracles, we degrade ourselves into mere slaves of sense and fancy, which are indeed the appointed medium between earth and heaven, but for that very cause stand in a desirable relation to spiritual truth then only, when, as a mere and passive medium, they yield a free passage to its light. It was only to overthrow the usurpation exercised in and through the senses, that the senses were miraculously appealed to; for reason and religion are their own evidence. The natural sun is in this respect a symbol of the spiritual. Ere he is fully arisen, and while his glories are still under veil, he calls up the breeze to chase away the usurping vapors of the night-season, and thus converts the air itself into the minister of its own purification: not surely in proof or elucidation of the light from heaven, but to prevent its interception.

¶ 234

Wherever, therefore, similar circumstances co-exist with the same moral causes, the principles revealed, and the examples recorded, in the inspired writings render miracles superfluous: and if we neglect to apply truths in expectation of wonders, or under pretext of the cessation of the latter, we tempt God, and merit the same reply which our Lord gave to the Pharisees on a like occasion. *A wicked and an adulterous genera-tion seeketh after a sign, and there shall no sign be given to it, but the sign of the prophet Jonas* (Matt. xvi. 4): that is, a threatening call to repentance.

---

[310] *Aids* (1829), notes, 286. See ¶s. 134-145. Cf. *Nature*, 69.1.
[311] The first edition appeared in London, 1816. The work is important for its comments on the *Understanding* and the *Reason*. Marsh reprinted the valuable "Appendix" in *Aids* (1829), and Emerson was, therefore, acquainted with it before he owned a separate copy of the *Manual* (Burlington, 1832).
[312] *Works* (Shedd), I, 425-426.

ORIGIN OF HUMAN EVENTS LIES IN SPIRITUAL WORLD——HISTORY
SHOULD BE READ FOR THE WORKING OF *IDEAS* OR GENERAL *PRIN-
CIPLES*, NOT FOR FACTS——MIRACLES INADEQUATE BECAUSE THEY
LIMIT THE ATTENTION TO FACTS, ESPECIALLY TO FACTS IN PRESENT
TIME[312a]

¶ 234a

The true origin of human events is so little susceptible of that kind of evidence
which can compel our belief; so many are the disturbing forces which in every cycle
of changes modify the motion given by the first projection; and every age has, or
imagines it has, its own circumstances which render past experience no longer applicable to the present case; that there will never be wanting answers, and explanations,
and specious flatteries of hope to persuade a people and its government that the
history of the past is inapplicable to their case. And no wonder, if we read history for
the facts instead of reading it for the sake of the general principles, which are to
the facts as the root and sap of a tree to its leaves: and no wonder, if history so read
should find a dangerous rival in novels, nay, if the latter should be preferred to the
former on the score even of probability.

MACHIAVELLI'S CLASSIFICATION OF TYPES OF MINDS——HIGHEST RE-
VEALS SELF-RELIANCE——IMPORTANCE OF SPECULATIVE PHILOSOPHY——
METAPHYSICAL SYSTEMS COINCIDENT WITH REVOLUTIONS IN WORLD
HISTORY——LACK OF SELF-RELIANCE AT PRESENT TIME[313]

¶ 235

The politic Florentine[314] has observed, that there are brains of three races. The one
understands of itself; the other understands as much as is shown it by others; the
third neither understands of itself, nor what is shown it by others. In our times there
are more perhaps who belong to the third class from vanity and acquired frivolity of
mind, than from natural incapacity. It is no uncommon weakness with those who
are honored with the acquaintance of the great, to attribute national events to particular persons, particular measures, to the errors of one man, to the intrigues of
another, to any possible spark of a particular occasion, rather than to the true proximate cause (and which alone deserves the name of a cause), the predominant state of
public opinion. And still less are they inclined to refer the latter to the ascendancy of
speculative principles, and the scheme or mode of thinking in vogue. I have known
men, who with significant nods and the pitying contempt of smiles have denied all
influence to the corruptions of moral and political philosophy, and with much solemnity
have proceeded to solve the riddle of the French Revolution by Anecdotes! Yet it
would not be difficult, by an unbroken chain of historic facts, to demonstrate that the
most important changes in the commercial relations of the world had their origin in
the closets or lonely walks of uninterested theorists;——that the mighty epochs of
commerce, that have changed the face of empires; nay, the most important of those
discoveries and improvements in the mechanic arts . . . had their origin not in the
cabinets of statesmen, or in the practical insight of men of business, but in the visions
of recluse genius.

¶ 236

To the immense majority of men, even in civilized countries, speculative philosophy
has ever been, and must ever remain, a *terra incognita*. Yet it is not the less true,
that all the epoch-forming revolutions of the Christian world, the revolutions of
religion and with them the civil, social, and domestic habits of the nations concerned,
have coincided with the rise and fall of metaphysical systems. So few are the minds
that really govern the machine of society, and so incomparably more numerous and
more important are the indirect consequences of things, than their foreseen and direct
effects.

BOTH NATIONS AND INDIVIDUALS ARE PRACTICAL WHEN TRANQUIL——
PHILOSOPHY ARISES UNDER PASSION —— SHAKESPEARE PUT GREAT

[312a] *Works* (Shedd), I, 426.
[313] *Works* (Shedd) I, 427; 428.
[314] Niccolo Machiavelli, *Il Principe*, chap. xxii.

MAXIMS IN MOUTHS OF THE PASSIONATE————SIGNIFICANCE FOR
IDEALISM?[315]

¶ 237

It is with nations as with individuals. In tranquil moods and peaceable times we are
quite practical. Facts only and cool common sense are then in fashion. But let the
winds of passion swell, and straightway men begin to generalize; to connect by
remotest analogies; to express the most universal positions of reason in the most
glowing figures of fancy; in short, to feel particular truth and mere facts, as poor,
cold, narrow, and incommensurate with their feelings.

¶ 238

With his wonted fidelity to nature, our own great poet has placed the greater number
of his profoundest maxims and general truths, both political and moral, not in the
mouths of men at ease, but of men under the influence of passion, when the mighty
thoughts overmaster and become the tyrants of the mind that has brought them forth.
In his Lear, Othello, Macbeth, Hamlet, principles of deepest insight and widest interest
fly off like sparks from the glowing iron under the loud forge-hammer.

BIBLE CONSIDERED AS TEXTBOOK FOR LEADERS————MISTAKES IN HIS-
TORY ARE RESULT OF NEGLECTING MAXIMS OF CLEAR REASONING————
FRENCH REVOLUTION CITED————BIBLE IS RICHEST COLLECTION OF IM-
PORTANT TRUTHS FOR STATESMEN————HAS TWO PECULIAR ADVANTAGES
AS A MANUAL————(1) THE HEBREW LAWS FLOWED FROM UNIVERSAL
PRINCIPLES————SPRANG FROM THE REASON ITSELF————(2) SINCE WE LIVE
BY FAITH, BIBLE TRUTHS BEST MEET OUR HUMAN NATURE————ITS PRIN-
CIPLES ARE UNDERSTOOD IN PROPORTION AS BELIEVED————FAITH IS
SELF-TRUST————FAITH IS GROUND AND SOURCE OF ALL EXPERIENCE————
IT IS SIGHT[316]

¶ 239

[T]he fearful blunders of the late dread Revolution, and all the calamitous mistakes
of its opponents . . . every failure with all its gloomy results may be unanswerably
deduced from the neglect of some maxim or other that had been established by clear
reasoning and plain facts in the writings of Thucydides, Tacitus, Machiavel, Bacon, or
Harrington. . . . and yet I dare challenge all the critical benches of infidelity to point
out any one important truth, any one efficient practical direction or warning, which
did not pre-exist (and for the most part in a sounder, more intelligible, and more
comprehensive form) in the Bible.

¶ 240

In addition to this, the Hebrew legislator, and the other inspired poets, prophets,
historians and moralists of the Jewish Church have two peculiar advantages in their
favor. First, their particular rules and prescripts flow directly and visibly from universal principles, as from a fountain: they flow from principles and ideas that are not
so properly said to be confirmed by reasons as to be reason itself. Principles in act
and procession, disjoined from which, and from the emotions that inevitably accompany
the actual intuition of their truth, the widest maxims of prudence are like arms without hearts, muscles without nerves.

¶ 241

Secondly, from the very nature of those principles, as taught in the Bible, they are
understood in exact proportion as they are believed and felt. The regulator is never
separated from the main-spring. For the words of the Apostle are literally and
philosophically true: We (that is the human race) live by faith.[317] Whatever we do
or know that in kind is different from the brute creation, has its origin in a determination of the reason to have faith and trust in itself. This, its first act of faith, is
scarcely less than identical with its own being. Implicite, it is the copula——it contains
the possibility——of every position, to which there exists any correspondence in
reality. It is itself, therefore, the realizing principle, the spiritual substratum of the
whole complex body of truths. This primal act of faith is enunciated in the word, God:
a faith not derived from, but itself the ground and source of, experience, and without

---

[315] Works (Shedd), I, 428. Emerson seems to have had this passage in mind when
speculating on Idealism. See chapter V. Cf. also Nature, 39.5-20; 65.1ff.
[316] Works (Shedd), I, 429-430. Cf. Y E S, 250.28-32.
[317] See II Corinthians 5:7.

which the fleeting chaos of facts would no more form experience, than the dust of the grave can of itself make a living man. The imperative and oracular form of the inspired Scripture is the form of reason itself in all things purely rational and moral.

BIBLE APPEALS TO THE REASON OF MAN——NOT TO HIS UNDERSTANDING——HENCE ITS TRUTHS ARE POSITIVE AND SURE——THEY *MUST* BE——THEY ARE CERTAIN KNOWLEDGE——AS SURE AS GOD LIVETH—— TO BELIEVERS THE PRINCIPLE OF KNOWLEDGE IS THE SPRING AND PRINCIPLE OF ACTION——MAN MAKES THE MOTIVE, NOT MOTIVES THE MAN[318]

¶ 242

If Scripture be the word of Divine Wisdom, we might anticipate that it would in all things be distinguished from other books, as the Supreme Reason, whose knowledge is creative, and antecedent to the things known, as distinguished from the understanding, or creaturely mind of the individual, the acts of which are posterior to the things which it records and arranges. Man alone was created in the image of God: a position groundless and inexplicable, if the reason in man do not differ from the understanding. For this the inferior animals (many at least) possess in degree: and assuredly the divine image or idea is not a thing of degrees.

¶ 243

Hence it follows that what is expressed in the Scriptures is implied in all absolute science. The latter whispers what the former utter as with the voice of a trumpet. *As sure as God liveth*,[319] is the pledge and assurance of every positive truth, that is asserted by the reason. The human understanding musing on many things snatches at truth, but is frustrated and disheartened by the fluctuating nature of its objects; its conclusions therefore are timid and uncertain, and it hath no way of giving permanence to things but by reducing them to abstractions. *Hardly do we guess aright at things that are upon earth, and with labor do we find the things that are before us; but all certain knowledge is in the power of God, and a presence from above.* So only have the ways of men been reformed, and every doctrine that contains a saving truth, and all acts pleasing to God (in other words, all actions consonant with human nature, in its original intention) are through wisdom; that is, the rational spirit of man.

¶ 244

This then is the prerogative of the Bible; this is the privilege of its believing students. With them the principle of knowledge is likewise a spring and principle of action. And as it is the only certain knowledge, so are the actions that flow from it the only ones on which a secure reliance can be placed. The understanding may suggest motives, may avail itself of motives, and make judicious conjectures respecting the probable consequences of actions. But the knowledge taught in the Scriptures produces the motives, involves the consequences; and its highest *formula* is still: *As sure as God liveth*, so will it be unto thee! Strange as this position will appear to such as forget that motives can be causes only in a secondary and improper sense, inasmuch as the man makes the motive, not the motives the man; yet all history bears evidence to its truth.

ENTHUSIASM——NOTHING GREAT ACHIEVED WITHOUT IT——DEFINED AS OBLIVION OF SELF AND ENLARGEMENT OF SOUL——PROVIDES A CONDITION FOR INTUITION AND ATTESTS PRESENCE OF ULTIMATE PRINCIPLES——*PRINCIPLES* COMPARED WITH MERE *NOTIONS*——KNOWLEDGE (WHICH CONSISTS OF IDEAS AND PRINCIPLES) IS POWER[320]

¶ 245

But histories incomparably more authentic than Mr. Hume's (nay, spite of himself even his own history) confirm by irrefragable evidence the aphorism of ancient wisdom, that nothing great was ever achieved without enthusiasm.[321] For what is enthusiasm but the oblivion and swallowing up of self in an object dearer than self, or in an idea more vivid? . . . in the genuine enthusiasm of morals, religion, and patriot-

---

[318] *Works* (Shedd), I, 430-431.
[319] For the dozens of uses of the phrase "as the Lord liveth," see any Bible concordance.
[320] *Works* (Shedd), I, 433. Cf. *Nature*, 13.2-13; 62.1-22; 90.13. Coleridge also has much to say about the dangers of enthusiasm.
[321] See Emerson's "Circles," *Works*, II, 321.

ism, this enlargement and elevation of the soul above its mere self attest the presence, and accompany the intuition, of ultimate principles alone. These alone can interest the undegraded human spirit deeply and enduringly, because these alone belong to its essence, and will remain with it permanently. Notions, the depthless abstractions of fleeting *phænomena,* . . . have effected their utmost when they have added to the distinctness of our knowledge. For this very cause they are of themselves adverse to lofty emotion . . . . But every principle is actualized by an idea; and every idea is living, productive, partaketh of infinity, and (as Bacon has sublimely observed) containeth an endless power of semination. Hence it is, that science, which consists wholly in ideas and principles, is power. *Scientia et potentia* (saith the same philosopher) *in idem coincidunt.*[322]

IN THE PRESENCE OF IDEAS AND PRINCIPLES THE SOUL OF MAN AWAKES WITH JOY——THE FREE AGENCY OF MEN CONTAINS THE IDEA OF FREE WILL———THROUGH SPIRITUAL FREEDOM MAN INTUITIVELY KNOWS HIMSELF[323]

¶ 246

At the annunciation of principles, of ideas, the soul of man awakes and starts up, as an exile in a far distant land at the unexpected sounds of his native language, when after long years of absence and almost of oblivion, he is suddenly addressed in his own mother-tongue. He weeps for joy, and embraces the speaker as his brother. How else can we explain the fact so honorable to Great Britain, that the poorest amongst us will contend with as much enthusiasm as the richest for the rights of property? These rights are the spheres and necessary conditions of free agency. But free agency contains the idea of the free will; and in this he intuitively knows the sublimity, and the infinite hopes, fears, and capabilities of his own nature.

AN IMPOVERISHED PHILOSOPHY LEADS TO AN IMPOVERISHED RELIGION ——PRESENT AGE OF *MECHANIC PHILOSOPHY* IS UNDER THE DOMINION OF THE UNDERSTANDING——IT CONFUSES *SYMBOL* WITH *ALLEGORY*—— THE WORD *SYMBOL* DEFINED——BIBLE USES SYMBOLS——ALL ITS FACTS AND PERSONS HAVE TWO-FOLD SIGNIFICANCE———HISTORY BECOMES PROPHETIC; PROPHECY BECOMES HISTORY[324]

¶ 247

Eheu! paupertina philosophia in paupertinam religionem ducit: A hunger-bitten and idea-less philosophy naturally produces a starveling and comfortless religion. It is among the miseries of the present age that it recognizes no *medium* between literal and metaphorical. Faith is either to be buried in the dead letter, or its name and honors usurped by a counterfeit product of the mechanical understanding, which in the blindness of self-complacency confounds symbols with allegories. Now an allegory is but a translation of abstract notions into a picture-language, which is itself nothing but an abstraction from objects of the senses. . . . On the other hand a symbol . . . is characterized by a translucence of the special in the individual, or of the general in the special, or of the universal in the general; above all by the translucence of the eternal through and in the temporal. It always partakes of the reality which it renders intelligible; and while it enunciates the whole, abides itself as a living part in that unity of which it is the representative.

¶ 248

The histories and political economy of the present and preceding century partake in the general contagion of its mechanic philosophy, and are the product of an unenlivened generalizing understanding. In the Scriptures they are the living educts of the imagination; of that reconciling and mediatory power, which incorporating the reason in images of the sense, and organizing (as it were) the flux of the senses by the permanence and self-circling energies of the reason, gives birth to a system of symbols, harmonious in themselves, and consubstantial with the truths of which they are the conductors. . . . Hence, by a derivative, indeed, but not a divided, influence, and though in a secondary yet in more than a metaphorical sense, the Sacred Book is worthily

---

[322] Quoted from Bacon's *Novum Organum.* Cf. *Nature,* 45.11-12 and "Old Age," *Works,* VII, 321.
[323] *Works* (Shedd), I, 434. Cf. *Nature,* 62.19-22; 89.3-4.
[324] *Works* (Shedd), I, 437-438; 436-437.

entitled *the Word of God*. Hence too, its contents present to us the stream of time continuous as life and a symbol of eternity, inasmuch as the past and the future are virtually contained in the present. According therefore to our relative position on the banks of this stream the Sacred History becomes prophetic, the Sacred Prophecies historical, while the power and substance of both inhere in its laws, its promises, and its comminations.[325] In the Scriptures therefore both facts and persons must of necessity have a twofold significance, a past and a future, a temporary and a perpetual, a particular and a universal application. They must be at once portraits and ideals.

SELF-RELIANCE OF ALL SCRIPTURAL CHARACTERS——THE BIBLE RECONCILES FREE WILL AND NECESSITY———THE ULTIMATE NECESSITY IS KNOWN BY INTUITION, THAT IS, BY THE IMMEDIATE SPIRITUAL CONSCIOUSNESS——THE IDEA OF GOD IS ITS OWN EVIDENCE[326]

¶ 249

In the Bible every agent appears and acts as a self-subsisting individual; each has a life of its own, and yet all are one life. The elements of necessity and free-will are reconciled in the higher power of an omnipresent Providence, that predestinates the whole in the moral freedom of the integral parts. Of this the Bible never suffers us to lose sight. The root is never detached from the ground. It is God everywhere: and all creatures conform to his decrees, the righteous by performance of the law, the disobedient by the sufferance of the penalty.

¶ 250

Suffer me to inform or remind you, that there is a threefold necessity. There is a logical, and there is a mathematical necessity; but the latter is always hypothetical, and both subsist formally only, not in any real object. Only by the intuition and immediate spiritual consciousness of the idea of God, as the One and Absolute, at once the ground and the cause, who alone containeth in himself the ground of his own nature, and therein of all natures, do we arrive at the third, which alone is a real objective, necessity. Here the immediate consciousness decides: the idea is its own evidence, and is insusceptible of all other.[327] It is necessarily groundless and indemonstrable; because it is itself the ground of all possible demonstration. The reason hath faith in itself in its own revelations. . . . *Ipse dixit*. So it is: for it is so.

RELIGIOUS FAITH PRESUPPOSES KNOWLEDGE AND CONVICTION——IN A SPIRITUAL SENSE, TO KNOW GOD IS TO POSSESS HIM——KNOWLEDGE IS *BEING*[328]

¶ 251

If it be said, that we should endeavor not so much to remove ignorance, as to make the ignorant religious: religion herself through her sacred oracles answers for me, that all effective faith pre-supposes knowledge and individual conviction. . . . I do not here mean veracity, which can not but be enforced in every code which appeals to the religious principle of man; but knowledge. . . . Not that knowledge can of itself do all. The light of religion is not that of the moon, light without heat; but neither is its warmth that of the stove, warmth without light. Religion is the sun whose warmth indeed swells, and stirs, and actuates the life of nature, but who at the same time beholds all the growth of life with a master-eye, makes all objects glorious on which he looks, and by that glory visible to others. . . . For to know God is (by a vital and spiritual act in which to know and to possess are one and indivisible)——to know God, I say, is——to acknowledge him as the infinite clearness in the incomprehensible fulness, and fulness incomprehensible with infinite clearness.

UNIQUENESS OF CHRISTIANITY——FOUNDED ON SPIRITUAL FACTS DIRECTLY ACCESSIBLE TO ALL MEN——THE REASON IS IN ALL MEN——SELF-RELIANCE IS, THEREFORE, AN INDISPENSABLE CONDITION OF GROWTH[329]

---

[325] Cf. Hill Shine, *Carlyle's Fusion of Poetry, History, and Religion by 1834*, Chapel Hill, N. C., 1938.
[326] *Works* (Shedd), I, 438-439. Cf. *Nature*, 43.1-13.   [327] Cf. *Nature*, 7.2-4.
[328] *Works* (Shedd), I, 448-449.   [329] *Works* (Shedd), I, 455. Cf. *Nature*, 43.3-4.

¶ 252

Christianity is especially differenced from all other religions by being grounded on facts which all men alike have the same means of ascertaining with equal facility, and which no man can ascertain for another. Each person must be herein querist and respondent to himself; Am I sick, and therefore need a physician?——Am I in spiritual slavery, and therefore need a ransomer?——Have I given a pledge, which must be redeemed, and which I can not redeem by my own resources?——Am I at one with God, and is my will concentric with that holy power, which is at once the constitutive will and the supreme reason of the universe?

BIBLE CONTAINS A SCIENCE OF REALITIES——TEACHES THAT THE INFINITE EXISTS POTENTIALLY IN THE FINITE——THE UNDERSTANDING SEES THIS TRUTH AS AN ASCENT OF CAUSES AND A PROGRESSION OF EFFECTS OR AS ACTION AND REACTION——THE REASON SEES IT AS *ALL IN EACH* OR AS THE MICROCOSM[330]

¶ 253

All other sciences are confined to abstractions, unless when the term science is used in an improper and flattering sense,——Thus we may speak without boast of natural history; but we have not yet attained to a science of nature.[331] The Bible alone contains a science of realities: and therefore each of its elements is at the same time a living germ, in which the present involves the future, and in the finite the infinite exists potentially. That hidden mystery in every the minutest form of existence, which contemplated under the relations of time presents itself to the understanding retrospectively, as an infinite ascent of causes, and prospectively as an interminable progression of effects;——that which contemplated in space is beholden intuitively as a law of action and re-action,[332] continuous and extending beyond all bound;——this same mystery freed from the *phænomena* of time and space,[333] and seen in the depth of real being, reveals itself to the pure reason as the actual immanence or in-being of all in each. Are we struck with admiration at beholding the cope of heaven imaged in a dewdrop?[334] The least of the *animalculæ* to which that drop would be an ocean, contains in itself an infinite problem of which God omnipresent is the only solution.[335] The slave of custom is roused by the rare and the accidental alone;[336] but the axioms of the unthinking are to the philosopher the deepest problems as being the nearest to the mysterious root, and partaking at once of its darkness and its pregnancy.

WE NEED THE *IDEA* (THE GODLIKE WITHIN US) BEFORE WE CAN DISCOVER THE TREASURES IN THE BIBLE——LIGHT IS THE MATERIAL SYMBOL OF THE IDEA——KEPLER AND NEWTON[337]

¶ 254

O what a mine of undiscovered treasures, what a new world of power and truth would the Bible promise to our future meditation, if in some gracious moment one solitary text of all its inspired contents should but dawn upon us in the pure untroubled brightness of an idea, that most glorious birth of the God-like within us, which even as the light, its material symbol,[338] reflects itself from a thousand surfaces, and flies homeward to its Parent Mind enriched with a thousand forms, itself above form and still remaining in its own simplicity and identity! O for a flash of that same light, in which the first position of geometric science that ever loosed itself from the generalizations of a groping and insecure experience, for the first time revealed itself to a human intellect in all its evidence and all its fruitfulness, transparence without *vacuum*, and plenitude without opacity![339] O that a single gleam of our own inward experience would make comprehensible to us the rapturous Eureka, and the grateful hecatomb, of the philosopher of Samos;——or that vision which from the

---

[330] *Works* (Shedd), I, 450. For the microcosm in *Nature*, see 29.16; 30.21; 53.15-17; 54.20——55.2; 55.23; 56.2; 56.7-8; 56.22; 78.19.

[331] See *Nature*, 6.17-20.
[332] *Nature*, 41.23ff.
[333] *Nature*, 71.17-20; 60.8; 50.1-2; 90.20-22.
[334] See *Nature*, 54.21.
[335] Cf. *Nature*, 68.18-20; 43.13.
[336] Cf. *Nature*, 92.13ff.
[337] *Works* (Shedd), I, 450-451. Another application of "Like only can know like."
[338] Cf. *Nature*, 43.12; 92.21; 92.8-9; 34.5.
[339] See similar expression in ¶ 167. Cf. *Nature*, 91.9-11.

contemplation of an arithmetical harmony rose to the eye of Kepler, presenting the planetary world, and all its orbits . . . or which, in the falling of an apple, revealed to the ethereal intuition of our own Newton the constructive principle of the material universe.

CONSCIENCE DEFINED AS A TESTIFYING STATE OR AS THE PEACE OF GOD[340]

¶ 255

The conscience is neither reason, religion, or will, but an experience *sui generis* of the coincidence of the human will with reason and religion. It might, perhaps, be called a spiritual sensation; but that there lurks a contradiction in the terms, and that it is often deceptive to give a common or generic name to that, which being unique, can have no fair analogy. In strictness, therefore, the conscience is neither a sensation nor a sense; but a testifying state, best described in the words of Scripture, as *the peace of God that passeth all understanding.*

THE GREAT BOOK OF NATURE IS A REVELATION OF GOD——IT HAS COR-RESPONDENCES AND SYMBOLS OF THE SPIRITUAL WORLD[341]

¶ 256

If you have accompanied me thus far, thoughtful reader, let it not weary you if I digress for a few moments to another book, likewise a revelation of God——the great book of his servant Nature. That in its obvious sense and literal interpretation it declares the being and attributes of the Almighty Father,[342] none but the fool in heart has ever dared gainsay. But it has been the music of gentle and pious minds in all ages, it is the poetry of all human nature, to read it likewise in a figurative sense, and to find therein correspondences and symbols of the spiritual world.

NATURE IS HAPPY AND UNTROUBLED LIKE A SLEEPING INFANT WITH ITS MOTHER[343]——SUGGESTS TO MAN THAT HE HAS FALLEN[344]—— IN-SPIRES HIM WITH HOPE OF REGAINING THROUGH HIS SPIRIT WHAT HE HAS LOST[345]——GOD'S LOVE AND WISDOM SHINE THROUGH NATURE AND US[346]——NATURE IS UNCONSCIOUS OF WHAT IT REFLECTS[347]——MAN MUST BE MADE CONSCIOUS——PRAYER IS IMPORTANT[348]

¶ 257

I have at this moment before me, in the flowery meadow, on which my eye is now reposing, one of its most soothing chapters, in which there is no lamenting word, no one character of guilt or anguish. For never can I look and meditate on the vegetable creation without a feeling similar to that with which we gaze at a beautiful infant that has fed itself asleep at its mother's bosom, and smiles in its strange dream of obscure yet happy sensations. The same tender and genial pleasure takes possession of me, and this pleasure is checked and drawn inward by the like aching melancholy, by the same whispered remonstrance, and made restless by a similar impulse of aspiration. It seems as if the soul said to herself: From this state hast thou fallen! Such shouldst thou still become, thyself all permeable to a holier power! thyself at once hidden and glorified by its own transparency, as the accidental and dividuous in this quiet and harmonious object is subjected to the life and light of nature; to that life and light of nature, I say, which shines in every plant and flower, even as the transmitted power, love and wisdom of God over all fills, and shines through, nature! But what the plant is by an act not its own and unconsciously——that must thou make thyself to become——must by prayer and by a watchful and unresisting spirit, join at least with the preventive and assisting grace to make thyself, in that light of conscience which inflameth not, and with that knowledge which puffeth not up![349]

---

[340] *Works* (Shedd), I, 459. Also in *Aids* (1829), 374.
[341] *Works* (Shedd), I, 461. Cf. *Nature*, chap. IV on "Language," pp. 32-45, esp. 45.2-4.
[342] Cf. *Nature*, 35.1-4.
[343] Cf. *Nature*, 73.11-16.
[344] Cf. *Nature*, 80.21——81.3, 88.18-23; 89.3-6.
[345] Cf. *Nature*, 80.14-15; 91.5-9.
[346] Cf. *Nature*, 79.10-18.
[347] Cf. *Nature*, 80.16-19.
[348] Cf. *Nature*, 92.3-11.
[349] *Works* (Shedd), I, 461-462. Influence on the "Orphic Poet" and related passages is evident.

THE REASON IN ITS RELATION TO NATURE IS SPIRIT——UNITY OF IMPRESSION FOUND IN NATURE——LIGHT IS THE SYMBOL OF THE HIGHER LIFE OF REASON——NATURE'S BOOK ILLUSTRATES UNITY IN VARIETY[350]

¶ 258

I seem to myself to behold in the quiet objects, on which I am gazing, more than an arbitrary illustration, more than a mere *simile*, the work of my own fancy. I feel an awe, as if there were before my eyes the same power as that of the reason——the same power in a lower dignity, and therefore a symbol established in the truth of things. I feel it alike, whether I contemplate a single tree or flower, or meditate on vegetation throughout the world, as one of the great organs of the life of nature. Lo![351] ——with the rising sun it commences its outward life and enters into open communion with all the elements, at once assimilating them to itself and to each other. At the same moment it strikes its roots and unfolds its leaves, absorbs and respires, steams forth its cooling vapor and finer fragrance, and breathes a repairing spirit, at once the food and tone of the atmosphere, into the atmosphere that feeds it. Lo!——at the touch of light how it returns an air akin to light, and yet with the same pulse effectuates its own secret growth, still contracting to fix what expanding it had refined. Lo!——how upholding the ceaseless plastic motion of the parts in the profoundest rest of the whole it becomes the visible *organismus* of the entire silent or elementary life of nature and, therefore, in incorporating the one extreme becomes the symbol of the other; the natural symbol of that higher life of reason, in which the whole series (known to us in our present state of being) is perfected, in which, therefore, all the subordinate gradations recur, and are reordained *in more abundant honor*. We had seen each in its own cast, and we now recognize them all as co-existing in the unity of a higher form, the crown and completion of the earthly, and the mediator of a new and heavenly series. Thus finally, the vegetable creation, in the simplicity and uniformity of its internal structure symbolizing the unity of nature, while it represents the omniformity of her delegated functions in its external variety and manifoldness, becomes the record and chronicle of her ministerial acts, and enchases the vast unfolded volume of the earth with the hieroglyphics[352] of her history.

NATURE DEFIES OUR CLASSIFICATIONS——CANNOT BE MEASURED BY METHODS OF THE UNDERSTANDING ALONE——LIKE ONLY CAN KNOW LIKE——WHAT WE ARE, THAT ONLY CAN WE KNOW——*QUANTUM SUMUS, SCIMUS*[353]

¶ 259

Man of understanding, canst thou command the stone to lie, canst thou bid the flower bloom, where thou hast placed it in thy classification?——Canst thou persuade the living or the inanimate to stand separate even as thou hast separated them?—— And do not far rather all things spread out before thee in glad confusion and heedless intermixture, even as a lightsome chaos on which the Spirit of God is moving?—— Do not all press and swell under one attraction, and live together in promiscuous harmony, each joyous in its own kind, and in the immediate neighborhood of myriad others that in the system of thy understanding are distant as the poles?——If to mint and to remember names delight thee, still arrange and classify and pore and pull to pieces, and peep into death to look for life, as monkeys put their hands behind a looking-glass! Yet consider in the first sabbath which thou imposest on the busy discursion of thought, that all this is at best little more than a technical memory: that

---

[350] *Works* (Shedd), I, 462-463. Cf. Nature, 34.9——35.1; 52.10-14; 54.12-15; 79.8-18. See also index-concordance to *Nature* under "Spirit." See *Nature*, chap. VII.

[351] Coleridge's note: "The remainder of this paragraph might properly form the conclusion of a disquisition on the spirit, as suggested by meditative observation of natural objects, and of our own thoughts and impulses without reference to any theological dogma, or any religious obligation to receive it as a revealed truth, but traced to the law of the dependence of the particular on the universal, the first being the organ of the second, as the lungs in relation to the atmosphere, the eye to light, crystal to fluid, figure to space, and the like."

[352] Cf. *Nature*, 6.10; 34.22.

[353] *Works* (Shedd), I, 464-465. Also *Aids* (1829), 378-379. This and the following paragraph profoundly influenced Emerson's Γνωθι Σεαυτον. See next chapter, footnote 43. See *Nature*, 94.5.

like can only be known by like: that as truth is the correlative of being, so is the act of being the great organ of truth: that in natural no less than in moral science, *quantum sumus, scimus.*

KNOW THYSELF——WHAT WE FIND WITHIN IS THE LIFE OF ALL OUR KNOWLEDGE——THE MIND OF MAN IS A MYSTERY, PRESENTING A PROBLEM OF WHICH GOD IS THE ONLY SOLUTION——THE LANGUAGE OF NATURAL SYMBOLS——NATURE'S POWER IS *ALL IN EVERY PART*[354]

¶ 260

That which we find in ourselves is *(gradu mutato)* the substance and the life of all our knowledge.[355] Without this latent presence of the 'I am,' all modes of existence in the external world would flit before us as colored shadows, with no greater depth, root, or fixture, than the image of a rock hath in a gliding stream or the rainbow on a fast-sailing rain-storm. The human mind is the compass, in which the laws and actuations of all outward essences are revealed as the dips and declinations. (The application of geometry to the forces and movements of the material world is both proof and instance.) The fact, therefore, that the mind of man in its own primary and constituent forms represents the laws of nature, is a mystery which of itself should suffice to make us religious: for it is a problem of which God is the only solution, God, the one before all, and of all, and through all![356]——True natural philosophy is comprised in the study of the science and language of symbols. The power delegated to nature is all in every part:[357] and by a symbol I mean, not a metaphor or allegory or any other figure of speech or form of fancy, but an actual and essential part of that, the whole of which it represents. Thus our Lord speaks symbolically when he says that *the eye is the light of the body.* The genuine naturalist is dramatic poet in his own line: and such as our myriad-minded Shakspeare is, compared with the Racines and Metastasios, such and by a similar process of self-transformation would the man be, compared with the doctors of the mechanic school, who should construct his physiology on the heaven-descended, Know Thyself.

WE ARE TO DO OUR OWN WORK——ALL THINGS CONTRIBUTE TO AN INCREASE OF MAN'S CONSCIOUSNESS——OUR WILL MUST CONQUER OUR CORNER OF THE UNIVERSE IN COOPERATION WITH THE *REASON*—— NOVELTY AND FRESHNESS WILL THEN CHARACTERIZE OUR VIEW OF THE WORLD[358]

¶ 261

But whatever of good and intellectual our nature worketh in us, it is our appointed task to render gradually our own work. For all things that surround us, and all things that happen unto us, have (each doubtless its own providential purpose, but) all one common final cause: namely, the increase of consciousness in such wise that whatever part of the *terra incognita* of our nature the increased consciousness discovers, our will may conquer and bring into subjection to itself under the sovereignty of reason.

¶ 262

To find no contradiction in the union of old and new, to contemplate the Ancient of days, his words and his works, with a feeling as fresh as if they were now first springing forth at his *fiat*——this characterizes the minds that feel the riddle of the world[359] and may help to unravel it.

GOD'S UNITY AND INFINITY OVERFLOW INTO THE SOUL OF MAN—— RELIGION DOES NOT REQUIRE ABSTRACTION——WHAT MEN RECEIVE INTUITIVELY, THAT THEY TEND TO BECOME——ALL IS IN EACH—— MEANEST OBJECTS REVEAL A MYSTERY OF INFINITE SOLUTION—— BEHOLDING GOD LEADS TO BECOMING——THE EYE IS A SYMBOL——

---

[354] *Works* (Shedd), I, 465 and 472. Also *Aids* (1829), 378-379.
[355] Cf. *Nature*, 6.9.
[356] See Ephesians 4:6.
[357] See ¶ 49 and footnote 53.
[358] *Works* (Shedd), I, 470; 434-435. Also in *Aids* (1829), 384. See "Orphic Poet" and related passages in *Nature* and esp. 45.5-12; 50.13——51.9; 94.1——95.12. See also 80.20-21; 92.12-18.
[359] See *Nature*, 43.21. Cf. *Journals*, IV, 14.

REDEMPTION OF CREATION COMES ABOUT THROUGH A RENEWAL OF FORFEITED POWER——THROUGH ENTERING THE *HIGHER SELF*—— RELIGION IS A TOTAL ACT OF THE SOUL——IT IS LIFE WITHIN LIFE—— IT EVER ORGANIZES THE SOUL ANEW[360]

¶ 263

In religion there is no abstraction. To the unity and infinity of the Divine Nature, of which it is the partaker, it adds the fulness, and to the fulness, the grace and the creative overflowing. That which intuitively it at once beholds and adores, praying always, and rejoicing always——that doth it tend to become. In all things and in each thing——for the Almighty Goodness doth not create generalities or abide in abstractions——in each, the meanest, object[361] it bears witness to a mystery of infinite solution. Thus *beholding as in a glass the glory of the Lord, it is changed into the same image from glory to glory.* (2 Cor. iii. 18.) For as it is born and not made, so must it grow. As it is the image or symbol of its great object, by the organ of this similitude, as by an eye,[362] it seeth that same image throughout the creation; and from the same cause sympathizeth with all creation in its groans to be redeemed. *For we know that the whole creation groaneth and travaileth in earnest expectation* (Rom. viii. 20-23) of a renewal of its forfeited power, the power,[363] namely, of retiring into that image, which is its substantial form and true life, from the vanity of self, which then only is when for itself it hath ceased to be. Even so doth religion finitely express the unity of the infinite Spirit by being a total act of the soul. And even so doth it represent his fulness by its depth, by its substantiality, and by an all-pervading vital warmth which ——relaxing the rigid, consolidating the dissolute, and giving cohesion to that which is about to sink down and fall abroad, as into the dust and crumble of the grave—— is a life within life, evermore organizing the soul anew.

SELF-RELIANCE AND SELF-KNOWLEDGE ARE THE KEYS TO SPIRITUAL GROWTH——LOOK *WITHIN* FOR THE TRUTH——TRUE RELIGION CONVERTS *KNOWING* INTO *BEING*——INTUITIVELY WE LEARN THE DISTINCTION BETWEEN THE *UNDERSTANDING* AND THE *REASON*——THROUGH THE *REASON* WE BECOME SONS OF GOD——REASON IS COMMON TO ALL MEN[364]

¶ 264

Join with me, reader! in the fervent prayer that we may seek within us what we can never find elsewhere, that we may find within us what no words can put there, that one only true religion, which elevateth knowing into being, which is at once the science of being, and the being and the life of all genuine science.

¶ 265

[W]hen educated men shall be ashamed to look abroad for truths that can be only found within; within themselves they will discover, intuitively will they discover, the distinctions between *the light that lighteth every man that cometh into the world;* and the understanding, which forms the *peculium* of each man, as different in extent and value from another man's understanding, as his estate may be from his neighbor's estate. . . . Being rejected, [the Reason——the universal light] leaves the understanding to a world of dreams and darkness: for in it alone is life and the *life is the light of men.*

¶ 266

On the other hand, if the light be received by faith, to such understandings it delegates the privilege (ʼεξουσιαν) to become sons of God, expanding while it elevates, even as the beams of the sun incorporate with the mist, and make its natural darkness and earthly nature the bearer and interpreter of their own glory. . . . The very same truth is found in a fragment of the Ephesian Heraclitus, preserved by Stobæus. . . . it behooves us to derive strength from that which is common to all men (*the light that lighteth every man*). For all human understandings are nourished by the one Divine Word, whose power is commensurate with his will, and is sufficient for all and over-

[360] *Works* (Shedd), I, 471. Cf. the last two chaps. of *Nature*, esp. 79.5-23.
[361] Cf. *Nature*, 45.7-9.
[362] Cf. *Nature*, 13.5-6.
[363] One of God's attributes is power, which overflows into human souls. (In theological language the equivalent term is "grace.") Coleridge and Emerson emphasize power through *Self-* (i.e., *God-*) *Reliance*. See *Nature*, 38.7; 45.12; 50.14; 57.16; 79.8-13; 80.3; 89.7; 89.19; 90.1; 90.21-22.
[364] *Works* (Shedd), I, 472; 475; 475-476.

floweth *(shineth in darkness, and is not contained therein, or comprehended by the darkness).*

ARE IDEAS REGULATIVE OR CONSTITUTIVE?[365]

¶ 267

Whether ideas are regulative only, according to Aristotle and Kant; or likewise constitutive, and one with the power and life of nature, according to Plato, and Plotinus . . . is the highest problem of philosophy, and not part of its nomenclature.

ON THE CONSTITUTION OF CHURCH AND STATE[366]

MEANING OF THE PHRASE *ACCORDING TO THE IDEA*——COLERIDGE INTENDS TO DISCUSS THE CHURCH AND THE STATE AS *IDEAS* OR IN VIEW OF THEIR ULTIMATE AIM————NOT AS THEY ACTUALLY ARE AT ANY PARTICULAR TIME[367]

¶ 268

By an idea I mean (in this instance) that conception of a thing, which is not abstracted from any particular state, form, or mode, in which the thing may happen to exist at this or at that time; nor yet generalized from any number or succession of such forms or modes; but which is given by the knowledge of its ultimate aim.

¶ 269

[A] Constitution is an idea arising out of the idea of a State; and because our whole history from Alfred onwards demonstrates the continued influence of such an idea, or ultimate aim, on the minds of our forefathers, in their characters and functions as public men, alike in what they resisted and in what they claimed; in the institutions and forms of polity which they established, and with regard to those, against which they more or less successfully contended; and because the result has been a progressive, though not always a direct or equable, advance in the gradual realization of the idea; and because it is actually, though even because it is an idea not adequately, represented in a correspondent scheme of means really existing; we speak, and have a right to speak, of the idea itself, as actually existing, that is, as a principle existing in the only way in which a principle can exist,——in the minds and consciences of the persons whose duties it prescribes, and whose rights it determines.

DEFINITION OF *LAW* AND *IDEA*[368]

¶ 270

That which, contemplated objectively (that is, as existing externally to the mind), we call a law; the same contemplated subjectively (that is, as existing in a subject or mind), is an idea. Hence Plato often names ideas laws; and Lord Bacon, the British Plato, describes the laws of the material universe as the ideas in nature. *Quod in natura naturata lex, in natura naturante idea, dicitur.*

LAW OF COMPENSATION AND THE PRINCIPLE OF COMPROMISE[369]

¶ 271

But alike in the works of nature and the institutions of man, there is no more effectual preservative against pedantry and the positiveness of sciolism, than to meditate on the law of compensation and the principle of compromise; and to be fully impressed with the wide extent of the one, the necessity of the other, and the frequent occurrence of both.

---

[365] *Works* (Shedd), I, 484.

[366] First published in 1830. The subtitle reads: "According to the Idea of Each." Emerson valued the work highly (See Cabot, *Memoir*, II, 723-724). He rejoiced in Coleridge's concept of an *idea* being worked out through many generations. He valued especially the appendix for Coleridge's eloquent reply to the author of the *Natural History of Enthusiasm*. The reply was a most succinct statement of Transcendental thought. Isaac Taylor's book had appeared in London in 1829. (Also N. Y., 1831).

[367] *Works* (Shedd), VI, 30; 34-35.

[368] *Works* (Shedd), VI, 31. Cf. ¶s. 145, 231. See *Nature*, 68.23——69.1.

[369] *Works* (Shedd), VI, 36.

MAN'S SPIRIT IS THE INTELLIGENT WILL————IT WORKS WITH THE
REASON FOR ULTIMATE ENDS————NOT SO THE UNDERSTANDING————
MORAL IDEAS DEFINED————THE IDEA OF THE *RESPONSIBLE WILL*[370]

¶ 272

Now the spirit of a man, or the spiritual part of our being, is the intelligent will:
or (to speak less abstractly) it is the capability, with which the Father of Spirits hath
endowed man of being determined to action by the ultimate ends, which the reason
alone can present. The understanding, which derives all its materials from the senses,
can dictate purposes only, that is, such ends as are in their turn means to other ends.
The ultimate ends, by which the will is to be determined, and by which alone the will,
not corrupted, *the spirit made perfect*, would be determined, are called, in relation to
the reason, moral ideas. Such are the ideas[371] of the eternal, the good, the true, the
holy, the idea of God as the absoluteness and reality (or real ground) of all these, or
as the Supreme Spirit in which all these substantially are, and are one: lastly, the
idea of the responsible will itself; of duty,[372] of guilt, or evil in itself without reference
to its outward and separable consequences.

COLERIDGE POINTS OUT THE EVIL IMPLICATIONS OF TAYLOR'S BELIEF THAT GOD DARE NOT REVEAL HIMSELF TO THE WORSHIPER[373]

¶ 273

I find two errors predominate, and both, it appears to me, dangerous errors. First,
that the rational and consequently the only true ideas of the Supreme Being are
incompatible with the spirit of prayer and petitionary pleading taught and exemplified
in the Scriptures. Second, that this being the case, and "supplication with arguments
and importunate requests" being irrational and known by the supplicant to be such,
it is nevertheless a duty to pray in this fashion. In other words, it is asserted that the
Supreme Being requires of his rational creatures, as the condition of their offering
acceptable worship to him, that they should wilfully blind themselves to the light,
which he had himself given them, as the contra-distinguishing character of their
humanity, without which they could not pray to him at all; and that drugging their
sense of the truth into a temporary doze, they should make believe that they know
no better! As if the God of Truth and Father of all lights resembled an oriental or
African despot, whose courtiers, even those whom he had himself enriched and placed
in the highest rank, are commanded to approach him only in beggars' rags and with
a beggarly whine!

¶ 274

The Essayist would bring down his understanding to his religion: I would raise up
my understanding to my reason, and find my religion in the *focus* resulting from their
convergence. We both alike use the same penitential, deprecative and petitionary
prayers; I in the full assurance of their congruity with my reason, he in a factitious
oblivion of their being the contrary.

COLERIDGE'S CONCEPT OF GOD, MAN, AND THE UNIVERSE————*KNOW THYSELF* INTRODUCES ONE TO ANOTHER WORLD, BUT NOT TO COME———— THE SPIRITUAL WORLD PENETRATES EACH MICROCOSM————POLARITY— ————MACROCOSM————THE CREATOR HAS GIVEN US *IDEAS* FOR A PURPOSE ————THERE IS AN APPROACHABLE SPIRITUAL WORLD CORRESPONDENT TO THEM[374]

¶ 275

The world in which I exist is another world indeed, but not to come.[375] It is as
present as (if that be at all) the magnetic planet, of which, according to the astrono-

---

[370] *Works* (Shedd), VI, 103-104.
[371] See *Nature*, 30.20-21; 69.1-4; 70.9-17. See ¶ 275.
[372] See *Nature*, 91.22-23.
[373] *Works* (Shedd), VI, 132-133.   [374] *Works* (Shedd), VI, 135-136.
[375] See also *Works* (Shedd), VI, 99-100: "The true and only contra-position of the
Christian Church is to the World. Her paramount aim and object, indeed, is another
world, not a world to come exclusively, but likewise another world that now *is*, and to
the concerns of which alone the epithet *spiritual* can, without a mischievous abuse of
the word, be applied." Coleridge seems here to be attempting a quite orthodox com-

mer Halley, the visible globe which we inverminate is the case or travelling-trunk;——
a neat little world where light still exists *in statu perfuso*, as on the third day of the
creation, before it was polarized into outward and inward, that is, while light and life
were one and the same, neither existing formally, yet both *eminenter*: and when herb,
flower, and forest rose as a vision, *in proprio lucido*, the ancestor and unseen yesterday
of the sun and moon. Now, whether there really is such an Elysian *mundus mundulus*
encased in the macrocosm, or great world, below the adamantine vault that supports
the mother waters, which support the coating crust of that *mundus immundus* on
which we and others less scantily furnished from nature's storehouse crawl, delve,
and nestle——(or, shall I say the Lyceum, where walk οι τουτου κοσμου φιλοσοφοι)——
Dr. Halley, may, perhaps, by this time have ascertained; and to him and the philosophic
ghosts, his compeers, I leave it.

¶ 276

But that another world is enshrined in the microcosm I not only believe, but at
certain depths of my being, during the more solemn Sabbaths of the spirit, I have
holden commune therewith, in the power of that faith, which is *the substance of the
things hoped for*, the living stem that will itself expand into the flower, which it now
foreshows. How should it not be so, even on grounds of natural reason, and the
analogy of inferior life? Is not nature prophetic up the whole vast pyramid of organic
being? And in which of her numberless predictions has nature been convicted of a lie?
Is not every organ announced by a previous instinct or act? . . . Do not the eyes, ears,
lungs of the unborn babe give notice and furnish proof of a transuterine, visible,
audible, atmospheric world? We have eyes, ears, touch, taste, smell; and have we not
an answering world of shapes, colors, sounds, and sapid and odorous bodies? But likewise——(alas! for the man for whom the one has not the same evidence of fact as the
other)——the Creator has given us spiritual senses, and sense-organs——ideas[376] I
mean——the idea of the good, the idea of the beautiful, ideas of eternity, immortality,
freedom, and of that which contemplated relatively to will is holiness, in relation to
life is bliss. And must not these too infer the existence of a world correspondent to
them.

THE INNER WORLD IS THERE FOR ALL MEN——DIFFERENCES AMONG MEN
TRACEABLE TO DIFFERENCES IN THE WILL——MAN IS OFTEN AN ABSEN-
TEE OWNER OF HIS PROPER HOME——THE DEFECTIVE WILL DESCRIBED[377]

¶ 277

Another and answerable world there is; and if any man discern it not, let him not,
whether sincerely or in contemptuous irony, pretend a defect of faculty as the cause.
The sense, the light, and the conformed objects are all there and for all men.[378] The
difference between man and man in relation thereto results from no difference in their
several gifts and powers of intellect, but in the will. As certainly as the individual is
a man, so certainly should this other world be present to him: yea, it is his proper
home. But he is an absentee and chooses to live abroad.[379] His freedom and whatever
else he possesses which the dog and the ape do not possess, yea, the whole revenue of
his humanity, is derived from this;——but with the Irish land-owner in the theatres,
gaming-houses, and maitresseries of Paris, so with him. He is a voluntary absentee.
I repeat it again and again,——the cause is altogether in the will: and the defect of
intellectual power, and "the having no turn or taste for subjects of this sort," are
effects and consequences of the alienation of the will, that is, of the man himself.
There may be a defect, but there was not a deficiency, of the intellect. . . . Was it
only of the world to come that Luther and his compeers preached? Turn to Luther's
Table Talk, and see if the larger part be not of that other world which now is, and
without the being and working of which the world to come would be either as unintelligible as *Abracadabra*, or a mere reflection and elongation of the world of sense.

---

mentary on the last clause of the Nicene Creed——"I believe in . . . the life of the
world to come." He does not deny a future existence, but indicates that eternal life for
the Christian begins here and now. He is dealing with the problem of time and eternity.
See also Revelation 4:1, 8.

[376] See ¶ 272.

[377] *Works* (Shedd), VI, 137. This passage is echoed in the "Orphic Poet" passages of
Nature.

[378] See *Nature*, 43.3. [379] Cf. *Nature*, 43.4; 88.11——89.6.

THE ART OF CONTEMPLATING THINGS ABSTRACTEDLY——THAT IS, APART FROM PERSONAL AND IMPERMANENT RELATIONS[380]

¶ 278

Learn the art and acquire the habit of contemplating things abstractedly from their relations. . . . and you will gradually (that is, if you choose and sincerely will it) acquire the power and the disposition of contemplating your own imaginations, wants, appetites, passions, and opinions, on the same principles, and distinguish that which alone is and abides from the accidental and impermanent relations arising out of its co-existence with other things or beings.

IN THE SCALE OF ORGANIC NATURE EACH HIGHER STAGE PRESUPPOSES A LOWER AS A CONDITION OF ITS EXISTENCE——STAGES OF (1) GROWTH, (2) IRRITABILITY AND (3) SENSIBILITY[381]

¶ 279

My second rule or maxim requires its *prolegomena*. In the several classes and orders that mark the scale of organic nature, from the plant to the highest order of animals, each higher implies a lower as the condition of its actual existence;——and the same position holds good equally of the vital and organic powers. Thus, without the first power, that of growth, or what Bichat and others name the vegetive life or productivity, the second power, that of totality and locomotion (commonly but most infelicitously called irritability) could not exist, that is, manifest its being. Productivity is the necessary antecedent of irritability, and in like manner irritability of sensibility. But it is no less true that in the idea of each power the lower derives its intelligibility from the higher: and the highest must be presumed to inhere latently or potentially in the lowest, or this latter will be wholly unintelligible, inconceivable;——you can have no conception of it. Thus in sensibility we see a power that in every instant goes out of itself, and in the same instant retracts and falls back on itself.

THE HIGHER QUALITIES IN ORGANIC NATURE INCLUDE THE LOWER——A SELF-CONTAINING POWER PRESUPPOSES A SELF-CAUSING POWER——A PROBLEM WHICH IS ITS OWN SOLUTION——WILL IS DEEPER THAN MIND[382]

¶ 280

For all sensibility is a self-finding; whence the German word for sensation or feeling is *Empfindung*, that is, an inward feeling. Therefore sensibility can not be excluded: and as it does not exist actually, it must be involved potentially. Life does not yet manifest itself in its highest dignity, as a self-finding; but in an evident tendency thereto, or a self-seeking;——and this has two epochs or intensities. Potential sensibility in its first epoch, or lowest intensity, appears as growth: in its second epoch, it shows itself as irritability or vital instinct. In both, however, the sensibility must have pre-existed, or rather pre-inhered, though as latent.

¶ 281

Again: what has been said of the lowest power of life relatively to its highest power ——growth to sensibility, the plant to the animal——applies equally to life itself relatively to mind. Without the latter the former would be unintelligible, and the idea would contradict itself. If there had been no self-retaining power, a self-finding would be a perpetual self-losing.

---

[380] *Works* (Shedd), VI, 138-139. Cf. *Nature*, 50.1-2; 60.8-10; 68.15-17; 92.6-11; cf. 58.10-20 for an application of this abstracting to friendship. See also *Aids* (1829), notes, 358, for Coleridge's method of considering Nature by abstraction: "I seldom look at a fine prospect or mountain landscape, or even at a grand picture, without abstracting the lines with a feeling similar to that with which I should contemplate the graven or painted walls of some temple or palace in Mid Africa——doubtful whether it were mere Arabesque, or undeciphered characters of an unknown tongue, framed when the language of men was nearer to that of nature——a language of symbols and correspondences. . . . 'Should any one interrogate Nature *how* she works if graciously she vouchsafe to answer, she will say, it behooves thee to understand me (*or better and more literally*, to go along with me) in silence, even as I am silent, and work without words;' but you have a Plotinus, and may construe it for yourself.——(Ennead 3.1.8. c.3.)."

[381] *Works* (Shedd), VI, 139. Cf. *Nature*, 49.1-4; 51.14-23; 57.2-6.

[382] *Works* (Shedd), VI, 140-141.

¶ 282

Again: a self-retaining mind——that is, memory (which is the primary sense of mind . . .),——a self-retaining power supposes a self-containing power, a self-conscious being. And this is the definition of mind in its proper and distinctive sense, a subject that is its own object,——or where *A contemplant* is one and the same subject with *A contemplated*. Lastly . . . the self-containing power supposes a self-causing power. . . . Here alone we find a problem which in its very statement contains its own solution[383]——the one self-solving power, beyond which no question is possible. . . . Even in man will is deeper than mind: for mind does not cease to be mind by having an antecedent; but will is either the first . . . or it is not will at all.[384]

AN ORIGINAL LETTER FROM MR. COLERIDGE[385]

¶ 283

28th Feb. 1819, Highgate.

Dear Sir,

First permit me to remove a very natural, indeed almost inevitable mistake, relative to my lectures; not that I *have* them, or that the lectures of one place or season are in any way repeated in another. So far from it, that on any point that I had ever studied (and on no other should I dare discourse——I mean, that I would not lecture on any subject for which I had to *acquire* the main knowledge, even though a month's or three months' previous time were allowed me; on no subject that had not employed my thoughts for a large portion of my life since earliest manhood, free of all outward and particular purpose)——on any point within my habit of thought, I should greatly prefer a subject I had never lectured on, to one which I had repeatedly given; and those who have attended me for any two seasons successively will bear witness that the lecture given at the London Philosophical Society, on the *Romeo and Juliet* for instance, was as different from that given at the Crown and Anchor as if they had been given by two individuals who, without any communication with each other, had only mastered the same *principles* of philosophic criticism. This was most strikingly evidenced in the coincidence between my lectures and those of Schlegel; such, and so close, that it was fortunate for my moral reputation that I had not only from five to seven hundred ear-witnesses that the passages had been given by me at the Royal Institution two years before Schlegel commenced his lectures at Vienna, but that notes had been taken of these by several men and ladies of high rank.

¶ 284

The fact is this: during a course of lectures, I faithfully employ *all* the intervening days in collecting and digesting the materials, whether I have or have not lectured on the same subject before, making no difference. The day of the lecture, till the hour of commencement, I devote to the consideration, what of the mass before me is best fitted to answer the purposes of a lecture——*i.e.* to keep the audience awake and interested during the delivery, and to leave a *sting* behind——*i.e.* a disposition to study the subject anew, under the light of a new principle. Several times, however, partly from apprehension respecting my health and animal spirits, partly from the wish to possess copies that might afterwards be marketable among the publishers, I have previously written the lecture; but before I had proceeded twenty minutes, I have been

---

[383] Cf. *Nature*, 7.1-3.

[384] See *Journals*, III, 530. See ¶ 100: The moral being is the source of the intellectual.

[385] Reprinted from *The Literary Gazette and Journal of the Belles Lettres* (London), Sept. 13, 1834, pp. 628-629. Emerson referred to this document in *Journals*, III, 361 (Nov. 15, 1834), and in his lecture on the "Modern Aspects of Letters" (Jan. 4, 1836). See Cabot, *Memoir*, II, 723-724. The original footnote to the letter as first published read: "Mr. Britton has kindly favoured us with this characteristic letter, which was addressed to him in answer to inquiries respecting Mr. Coleridge's giving a course of lectures at the Russell Institution." The first two paragraphs as here printed are only *one* in the original. I have made the separation for convenience of reference.

obliged to push the MSS. away, and give the subject a new turn. Nay, this was so notorious, that many of my auditors used to threaten me, when they saw any number of written papers on my desk, to steal them away; declaring they never felt so secure of a good lecture as when they perceived that I had not a single scrap of writing before me. I take far, far more pains than would go to the set composition of a lecture, both by varied reading and by meditation; but for the words, illustrations, &c. I know almost as little as any one in my audience (*i.e.* those of any thing like the same education with myself) what they will be five minutes before the lecture begins. Such is *my way*, for such is *my nature*; and in attempting any other, I should only torment myself in order to disappoint my auditors——torment myself during the delivery, I mean; for in all other respects it would be a much shorter and easier task to deliver them from writing. I am anxious to preclude any semblance of *affectation*; and have therefore troubled you with this lengthy preface before I have the hardihood to assure you that you might as well ask me what my dreams were in the year 1814, as what my course of lectures was at the Surrey Institution. *Fuimus Troës.* I regret that I cannot say the same of all my intellectual life. At least, were it in my power, my works should be confined to the second volume of my "Literary Life,"[386] the Essays of the third volume of the "Friend," from page 67 to page 265,[387] with about fifty or sixty pages from the two former volumes, and some half dozen of my poems.

¶ 285

If, therefore, I *should* be able to employ the time required for a course of six or eight lectures at the Russell Institution, that is, comparatively with other employment for the bread and beef of the day——God knows how laboriously, and yet scarcely earned!——I should greatly prefer your committee's making their own choice of the subjects from English, Italian, or German literature; and even of the Fine Arts, as far as the *philosophy* of the same is alone concerned. I have learnt, what I might easily have anticipated, that the *Lear* of Shakspeare is not a good subject for a whole lecture, in *my* style; with that exception, any of the plays of Shakspeare, the *Twelfth Night*, or the *Tempest*, the *Henry IVth's*, *Richard II.* with the character of *Richard III.*, *Romeo and Juliet*, *Antony and Cleopatra*, *Macbeth*, *Hamlet*, *Othello*, &c. &c.; the *Paradise Lost*, with the character of Milton, (which I appear to remember was the favourite lecture of those given at the Surrey Institution); Spencer, Dante, old English ballads and metrical romances; on the uses of poetry in the process of the mind's education, especially on the supernatural; the comparison of English poetry from Chaucer to Milton, with the period from Dryden (inclusive) to the Wartons;——of all these, and of any other congenerous subjects, the committee might take their choice; and it would be much more agreeable to me (who am so utterly unfit to arrange any pecuniary matters, and have in consequence suffered so much in *mind*, to leave all else unnoticed, that I have vowed and promised never to attempt it again, but to leave it to some friend) if the committee would state the sum they are disposed to offer, and I would instantly decide.——Oh! how much more genial would my feelings be, could I but address so respectable an audience with unhired eloquence. Even as it is, and bleak as my vineyard (potatoe-ground would be a metaphor more *germain* to the occasion) lies on the north aspect of Parnassus, yet the accounts I have received, from the best authority, of the character of the audience at the Russell Institution, have *alone* induced me to return an hesitating answer to the inquiry which, at all events, I must have acknowledged as a high compliment to,

dear sir,

yours with unfeigned respect,

S. T. COLERIDGE.

To J. Britton, Esq.

---

[386] *Biographia Literaria, or Biographical Sketches of my Literary Life and Opinions,* (2 vols.), London, 1817. The second volume included his comments on Shakespeare, Wordsworth and the Imagination.

[387] *The Friend* (3 vols.), London, 1818. The pages indicated cover the first ten essays of "Section the Second." Coleridge's failure to include the important "Essay XI"

THEORY OF LIFE————TENDENCY TO INDIVIDUATION EXISTS WITH TENDENCY TO JOIN ———— END OF NATURE IS TO PRODUCE HIGHEST INDIVIDUALITY[388]

¶ 286

By Life I everywhere mean the true Idea of Life, or that most general form under which Life manifests itself to us, which includes all its other forms. This I have stated to be the *tendency to individuation,* and the degrees or intensities of Life to consist in the progressive realization of this tendency. The power which is acknowledged to exist, wherever the realization is found, must subsist wherever the tendency is manifested. The power which comes forth and stirs abroad in the bird, must be latent in the egg. I have shown, moreover, that this tendency to individuate can not be conceived without the opposite tendency to connect, even as the centrifugal power supposes the centripetal, or as the two opposite poles constitute each other, and are the constituent acts of one and the same power in the magnet. We might say that the life of the magnet subsists in their union, but that it lives (acts or manifests itself) in their strife. Again, if the tendency be at once to individuate and to connect, to detach, but so as either to retain or to reproduce attachment, the individuation itself must be a tendency to the ultimate production of the highest and most comprehensive individuality. This must be the one great end of Nature, her ultimate production of the highest and most comprehensive individuality. This must be the one great end of Nature, her ultimate object, or by whatever other word we may designate that something which bears to a final cause the same relation that Nature herself bears to the Supreme Intelligence.

THE MOST GENERAL LAW BEHIND THE TENDENCY TO INDIVIDUATION IS THAT OF POLARITY——IT IS THE LAW OF DUALISM WHICH IS ESSENTIAL TO ALL ACTUAL EXISTENCE[389]

¶ 287

According to the plan I have prescribed for this inquisition, we are now to seek for the highest law, or most general form, under which this tendency acts, and then to pursue the same process with this, as we have already done with the tendency itself, namely, having stated the law in its highest abstraction, to present it in the different forms in which it appears and reappears in higher and higher dignities. I restate the question. The tendency having been ascertained, what is its most general law? I answer——*polarity*, or the essential dualism of Nature, arising out of its productive unity, and still tending to reaffirm it, either as equilibrium, indifference, or identity. In its *productive* power, of which the product is the only measure, consists its incompatibility with mathematical calculus. For the full applicability of an abstract science ceases, the moment reality begins. Life, then, we consider as the copula, or the unity of thesis and antithesis, position and counterposition,——Life itself being the positive of both; as, on the other hand, the two counterpoints are the necessary conditions of the *manifestations* of Life. These, by the same necessity, unite in a synthesis; which again, by the law of dualism, essential to all actual existence, expands, or *produces* itself, from the point into the *line*, in order again to converge, as the initiation of the same productive process in some intenser form of reality. Thus, in the identity of the two counter-powers, Life *sub*sists; in their strife, it *con*sists: and in their reconciliation it at once dies and is born again into a new form, either falling back into the life of the whole, or starting anew in the process of individuation.

MAN IS RELATED TO ALL NATURE, YET HAS A WORLD WITHIN——MAN IS A COMPENDIUM OF NATURE OR A MICROCOSM——THE MOST SELF-RELIANT MAN IS, THEREFORE, THE TRUEST————GENIUS AND ORIGINALITY DE-

---

(which belongs to the preceding group) was probably the result of an oversight. Emerson made note of Coleridge's remark in his own copy of this very edition.

[388] *Works* (Shedd), I, 391. This and the next two paragraphs are taken from "Hints toward the Formation of a More Comprehensive Theory of Life," first published in 1848, and now in *Works* (Shedd), I, 373-416. Emerson could not have known this essay when writing *Nature* (1836), but it is printed here because it serves as a good commentary on the conclusion of Part II. of *The Friend.*

[389] *Works* (Shedd), I, 391-392.

PENDENT UPON THE SUPREME WILL——MAN LIVES AT THE MID-POINT BETWEEN TWO WORLDS[390]

¶ 288

Man possesses the most perfect osseous structure, the least and most insignificant covering. The whole force of organic power has attained an inward and centripetal direction. He has the whole world in counterpoint to him, but he contains an entire world within himself. Now, for the first time at the apex of the living pyramid, it is Man and Nature, but Man himself is a syllepsis, a compendium of Nature——the Microcosm! Naked and helpless cometh man into the world. Such has been the complaint from eldest time; but we complain of our chief privilege, our ornament, and the connate mark of our sovereignty. *Porphyrigeniti sumus!* In Man the centripetal and individualizing tendency of all Nature is itself concentred and individualized——he is a revelation of Nature; Henceforward, he is referred to himself, delivered up to his own charge; and he who stands the most on himself, and stands the firmest, is the truest, because the most individual, Man. In social and political life this acme is interdependence; in moral life it is independence; in intellectual life it is genius. Nor does the form of polarity, which has accompanied the law of individuation up its whole ascent, desert it here. As the height, so the depth. The intensities must be at once opposite and equal. As the liberty, so must be the reverence for law. As the independence, so must be the service and the submission to the Supreme Will! As the ideal genius and the originality, in the same proportion must be the resignation to the real world, the sympathy and the inter-communion with Nature. In the conciliating mid-point, or equator, does the Man live, and only by its equal presence in both its poles can that life be manifested!

CONDITIONS UNDER WHICH NATURE REVEALS HER CLOSE AFFINITY WITH MIND——THE *INWARD EYE*[391]

¶ 289

When the bodily organ, steadying itself on some chance thing, imitates, as it were, the fixture of "the inward eye" on its ideal shapings, then it is that Nature not seldom reveals her close affinity with mind, with that more than man which is one and the same in all men, and from which

"the soul receives
Reason: and reason is her *being!*"[392]

¶ 290

Then it is, that Nature, like an individual spirit or fellow soul, seems to think and hold commune with us. If, in the present contempt of all mental analysis not contained in Locke, Hartley, or Condillac, it were safe to borrow from "scholastic lore" a technical term or two, for which I have not yet found any substitute equally convenient and serviceable, I should say, that at such moments Nature, as another *subject* veiled behind the visible *object* without us, solicits the intelligible object hid, and yet struggling beneath the subject within us, and like a helping Lucina, brings it forth for us into distinct consciousness and common light. Who has not tried to get hold of some half-remembered name, mislaid as it were in the memory, and yet felt to be there? And who has not experienced, how at length it seems *given* to us, as if some other unperceived had been employed in the same search?

THE THREE SILENT REVOLUTIONS IN ENGLAND[393]

¶ 291

There have been three silent revolutions in England:——first, when the professions fell off from the church; secondly, when literature fell off from the professions; and, thirdly, when the press fell off from literature.

DEFINITION OF BEAUTY[394]

¶ 291a

The old definition of beauty in the Roman school of painting was, *il più nell' uno*—— multitude in unity; and there is no doubt that such is the principle of beauty. And as

---

[390] *Works* (Shedd), I, 411-412.
[391] *Aids* (1829), notes, 362-363. Cf. *Nature*, 13.2-18; 43.1-13; 44.20——45.12; 62.5-22.
[392] *Paradise Lost*, V, 486-487.   [393] *Table Talk*, II, 42.
[394] *Table Talk*, II, 18. See also II, 279. See ¶ 62; *Nature*, 30.1-2; and *Journals*, IV, 7.

one of the most characteristic and infallible criteria of the different ranks of men's intellects, observe the instinctive habit which all superior minds have of endeavouring to bring, and of never resting till they have brought, into unity the scattered facts which occur in conversation, or in the statements of men of business.

WILLIAM SHAKESPEARE[395]
¶ 292

[H]e had as unequivocally proved the indwelling in his mind of imagination, or the power by which one image or feeling is made to modify many others, and by a sort of fusion to force many into one;——that which afterwards showed itself in such might and energy in Lear, where the deep anguish of a father spreads the feeling of ingratitude and cruelty over the very elements of heaven;——and which, combining many circumstances into one moment of consciousness, tends to produce that ultimate end of all human thought and human feeling, unity, and thereby the reduction of the spirit to its principle and fountain, who is alone truly one. Various are the workings of this the greatest faculty of the human mind, both passionate and tranquil. . . . Or this power acts by impressing the stamp of humanity, and of human feelings, on inanimate or mere natural objects:——

> Lo! here the gentle lark, weary of rest,
> From his moist cabinet mounts up on high,
> And wakes the morning, from whose silver breast
> The sun ariseth in his majesty,
> Who doth the world so gloriously behold,
> The cedar-tops and hills seem burnish'd gold.

¶ 293

[Shakespeare had] that poetic power . . . of making every thing present to the imagination——both the forms, and the passions which modify those forms, either actually, as in the representations of love, or anger, or other human affections; or imaginatively, by the different manner in which inanimate objects, or objects unimpassioned themselves, are caused to be seen by the mind in moments of strong excitement, and according to the kind of the excitement,——whether of jealousy, or rage, or love, in the only appropriate sense of the word, or of the lower impulses of our nature, or finally of the poetic feeling itself.

¶ 294

The wonderful faculty which Shakspeare above all other men possessed, or rather the power which possessed him in the highest degree, of anticipating everything, evidently is the result——at least partakes——of meditation, or that mental process which consists in the submitting to the operation of thought every object of feeling, or impulse, or passion observed *out* of it. I would be willing to live only as long as Shakspeare were the mirror to Nature.

¶ 295

It was Shakspeare's prerogative to have the universal, which is potentially in each particular, opened out to him, the *homo generalis*, not as an abstraction from observation of a variety of men, but as the substance capable of endless modifications, of which his own personal existence was but one, and to use this one as the eye that beheld the other, and as the tongue that could convey the discovery. There is no greater or more common vice in dramatic writers than to draw out of themselves.

THE SUBLIME——MATERIAL, MORAL, ARITHMETICAL
¶ 296

Schiller has the material Sublime;[396] to produce an effect, he sets you a whole town on fire, and throws infants with their mothers into the flames, or locks up a father in an old tower. But Shakspeare drops a handkerchief, and the same or greater effects follow.[397]

---

[395] The first two paragraphs are found in *Literary Remains* (1836). See *Works* (Shedd), IV, 48-49; 49-50. The third comes from *Letters, Conversations and Recollections*, (2 vols.), London, 1836, I, 196. Cf. *Nature*, 64.16——68.4. For the fourth, see *Works* (Shedd), IV, 257.

[396] "This expression . . . like a hundred others which have slipped into general use, came originally from Mr. Coleridge, and was by him, in the first instance, applied to Schiller's *Robbers*."   [397] *Table Talk*, I, 2.

¶ 297

Sublimity is the pre-eminent characteristic of the *Paradise Lost*. It is not an arithmetical sublime like Klopstock's, whose rule always is to treat what we might think large as contemptibly small. Klopstock mistakes bigness for greatness. There is a greatness arising from images of effort and daring, and also from those of moral endurance; in Milton both are united. The fallen angels are human passions, invested with a dramatic reality.[398]

GOTHIC ARCHITECTURE——CATHEDRAL IS PETRIFIED RELIGION——"I AM NOTHING"[399]

¶ 298

The contemplation of the works of antique art excites a feeling of elevated beauty, and exalted notions of the human self; but the Gothic architecture impresses the beholder with a sense of self-annihilation; he becomes, as it were, a part of the work contemplated. An endless complexity and variety are united into one whole, the plan of which is not distinct from the execution. A Gothic cathedral is the petrifaction of our religion.[400]

¶ 299

When I enter a Greek Church, my eye is charmed, and my mind elated; I feel exalted, and proud that I am a man. But the Gothic art is sublime. On entering a cathedral, I am filled with devotion and with awe; I am lost to the actualities that surround me, and my whole being expands into the infinite; earth and air, nature and art, all swell up into eternity, and the only sensible impression left, is 'that I am nothing!'[401]

DISTINCTION BÈTWEEN *SIMILAR* AND THE *SAME*——PLANTS AND ANI-MALS COMPARED——ANTECEDENT UNITY STRIVES TO BECOME *IDEA*[402]

¶ 300

Now, compare a plant . . . with an animal. In the former, the productive energy exhausts itself, and as it were, sleeps in the product or *organismus*——in its root, stem, foliage, blossoms, seed. . . . But in the animal it is otherwise. Here the antecedent unity ——the productive and self-realizing idea——strives, with partial success, to re-emancipate itself from its product, and seeks once again to become *idea:* vainly indeed: for in order to this, it must be retrogressive, and it hath subjected itself to the fates, the evolvers of the endless thread——to the stern necessity of progression. *Idea* itself it can not become, but it may in long and graduated process, become an image, an ANALOGON, an anti-type of IDEA. And this εἰδωλον may approximate to a perfect likeness. *Quod est simile nequit esse idem.*

COLERIDGE'S FAITH IN GOD WOULD REMAIN STEADFAST EVEN IF SCRIPTURES SHOULD PROVE TO BE FORGERIES——HIS INNER REASON IS PROOF ENOUGH——DISTINCTION BETWEEN FAITH AND BELIEF[403]

¶ 301

"Mr. Coleridge used very frequently to insist upon the distinction between belief and faith. He once told me, with very great earnestness, that if he were that moment con-vinced . . . that the New Testament was a forgery from beginning to end——wide as the desolation in his moral feelings would be, he should not abate one jot of his faith in God's power and mercy through some manifestation of his being towards man, either in time past or future, or in the hidden depths where time and space are not. This was, I believe, no more than a vivid expression of what he always maintained, that no man had attained to a full faith who did not *recognize* in the Scriptures a correspondency to his own nature, or see that his own powers of reason, will, and understanding were preconfigured to the reception of the Christian doctrines and promises."——THE EDITOR.

---

[398] *Works* (Shedd), IV, 303-304.
[399] *Works* (Shedd), IV, 233-234; 235.
[400] See *Nature*, 55.9-10. Emerson characteristically modifies his original.
[401] Cf. Coleridge's reaction to Gothic churches with Emerson's reaction to God's first temple, the woods, in *Nature*, 13.2-15. Note the identical words in 13.6.
[402] *Works* (Shedd), IV, 356-357.   [403] *Table Talk*, II, 77-78.

SELF-KNOWLEDGE[404]

¶ 302

——E cœlo descendit γνωθι σεαυτον.
——Juvenal, xi. 27.

Γνωθι σεαυτον!——and is this the prime
And heaven-sprung adage of the olden time!——
Say, canst thou make thyself?——Learn first that trade;——
Haply thou mayst know what thyself had made.
What hast thou, Man, that thou dar'st call thine own?——
What is there in thee, Man, that can be known?——
Dark fluxion, all unfixable by thought,
A phantom dim of past and future wrought,
Vain sister of the worm,——life, death, soul, clod——
Ignore thyself, and strive to know thy God!

EMERSON'S GRAVE AT CONCORD

---

[404] Appeared in *The Poetical Works of S. T. Coleridge*, (3 vols.), London, 1834. Apparently composed in 1832.

COLERIDGE AND THE "FIRST PHILOSOPHY"[1]

In 1841, Emerson wrote of Landor: "He is a man full of thoughts, but not, like Coleridge, a man of ideas. Only from a mind conversant with the First Philosophy can definitions be expected. Coleridge has contributed many valuable ones to modern literature. Mr. Landor's definitions are only enumerations of particulars; the generic law is not seized."[2] Just when Emerson first became acquainted with the works of Samuel Taylor Coleridge is not certain, though he did read disapprovingly some of his poetry[3] during undergraduate days at Harvard, and may then have glanced through the *Biographia Literaria*.[4] We do not hear again of the English philosopher and critic until 1826, when, according to Cabot, Emerson studied Coleridge's "proposed reconstruction of Christian theology" at the Harvard Divinity School.[5] Though such study is highly probable, the only evidence for the statement seems to be the two letters which Emerson wrote to his Aunt Mary before being approbated to preach on October 10[6] of that year, both of which reflect the thought of English Romanticism. In the first,[7] he spoke of his sense of wonder at life,[8] of a past now irreparable, and of his mind's being aware of a Presence[9] that might vouchsafe a revelation. He rejoiced in all that pointed to his connection with the Mysterious——to a relationship with God which assured him of his immortality.[10] He was grateful for the view of a deity that was no longer stern and distant but able to bring close together the natural order and our moral nature. In the second,[11] he condemned the sudden shift in philosophy from coldness to sentiment and feelings.[12] He agreed with the modernists, however, in believing it wrong constantly to think of ourselves in an historical light, allowing time to come between us and God.[13] It were

---

[1] All ¶ numbers (but *not* letters) cited in the notes of this chapter refer to sections in the foregoing chapter. The reader should look up the references as he reads in order that the demonstration may be progressive and as clear as possible. The present chapter will have meaning only if chapter VI is kept constantly in mind.

[2] First published in the *Dial* for October, 1841. Now in *Works*, XII, 346. For Emerson's concept of the "generic law," see ¶s. 128, 130, 131, 138, 139, 145, 193.

[3] See Cabot, *Memoir*, I, 58.

[4] See Cabot, *Memoir*, I, 241. The charging lists of the Boston Library Society indicate that the *Biographia Literaria* (Philadelphia, 1818) was borrowed on March 25, 1819, and returned two days later.

[5] Cabot, *Memoir*, I, 159. While at the Divinity School he was, doubtless, introduced to the thought of *The Statesman's Manual, or the Bible the Best Guide* (London, 1816); *The Friend* (London, 1818); and the *Aids to Reflection*, which had appeared in 1825. There is evidence that Sampson Reed owned the last by the end of 1826 and was circulating it among his friends. See his letter to Theophilus Parsons, Jr., of Jan. 31, 1827, in *E T E*, II.

[6] *Letters*, I, 170.

[7] Dated Aug. 1, 1826. (*Letters*, I, 169-171).

[8] See ¶s. 126, 156, 165, 196.

[9] See Wordsworth's "Tintern Abbey," lines 93ff. See *Emerson's Reading*, 50, for his borrowing of Wordsworth's poetry from the library of the Divinity School.

[10] Probably an allusion to Wordsworth's "Ode on Intimations of Immortality."

[11] *Letters*, I, 174-175 (Sept. 23, 1826).

[12] See Coleridge's excellent condemnation of misguided sentiment or sensibility in the second section of *Aids to Reflection*. It appears in *Aids* (1829), 31ff.

[13] See ¶ 198.

better to consider "every moment of the existence of the universe as a new creation, and all as a revelation proceeding each moment from the Divinity to the mind of the observer."[14] It followed, for him, that Christianity was the expounder of the Moral Law, which, existing in every breast,[15] needed not to be supported by antiquated institutions. He noted the distinction between relative and absolute truth and spoke of the recoil of the understanding from the speculations of the mystics. In his first sermon (October 15, 1826)[16] he mentioned again that the past is irrevocable and deserves no tears of regret; and that there remain for us all only the present and the future.[17] Extolling God as supreme and omniscient, he cast away "the deceptive subterfuges of language" and proclaimed that man's reason and virtue *are God* and that only man's free will is absolutely his own.[18] Coleridge was later to supply for Emerson a rich psychology within which the will gained even greater significance, but there is no strong trace of the English philosopher at this point. One must, instead, assume from the two letters and from the earliest sermons that Emerson, though standing on the brink, had read little of Coleridge at first hand. He was to begin his serious quest for the *prima philosophia* in the *Biographia Literaria*, which he withdrew from Harvard on November 16.[19] Its influence upon his developing transcendentalism can hardly be exaggerated, for it not only became the basis of his mature criticism and introduced him to Coleridge's principal definitions, but also led him eventually to *The Friend* and to the *Aids to Reflection*.

We lack a well-documented study of Coleridge's reputation and influence in New England before 1830——a study based upon printed and manuscript resources.[20] We know from a letter[21] that Sampson Reed owned and circulated a copy of the *Aids* among eager readers near the end of 1826; and it is possible that his *Observations on the Growth of the Mind* (1826)[22] owed something to the influence of *The Friend*. President James Marsh of the University of Vermont, moreover, must have developed his interest in Coleridge several years before the appearance of his elaborate edition of the *Aids* (Burlington, 1829), but the Vermont school still awaits serious investigation. Library records in the Boston area are disappointing, for as late as 1830 neither Harvard College, the Boston Athenæum, nor the Boston Library Society had acquired *The Friend*, the *Aids* or *The Statesman's Manual*;[23] and the supporters of the library of the Harvard Divinity School——a library which consisted of only a few volumes for many years after its feeble organization in the spring of 1827——lamented its inability to secure the latest theological works.[24] Marsh's edition of the

---

[14] Cabot, *Memoir*, I, 159-160. Cf. ¶ 157. [15] See ¶ 196.
[16] See "Pray Without Ceasing," *Y E S*, 1-12. [17] *Ibid.*, 8.
[18] *Ibid.*, 4. This thought is repeated in a later sermon (June 19, 1831) on p. 236. He contrasts (Nov. 28, 1830) the will of Jesus with the wills of other men, on p. 234.
[19] See *Emerson's Reading*, 46.
[20] *E.g.*, periodical literature, newspaper advertisements, sermons, letters, diaries, reading circles, and school curricula. See also the lists of dissertations read at annual examinations—for example, those of the Harvard Divinity School ("The Theological School"), which appear regularly in the *Christian Examiner*.
[21] See note 5 above.
[22] The first edition is reprinted in *E T E*, II.
[23] I use as evidence the printed catalogues of these institutions, a bibliography of which appears in *Emerson's Reading*, 13-15, and in the preface to the Boston Library Society charging list in vol. II.
[24] For an interesting account of the problems confronting the Harvard Divinity School

Aids, however, with its almost encyclopedic appendices and notes, **reached the booksellers** probably in December, 1829,[25] and awakened all circles to the fact that Coleridge could no longer be ignored and that his was a voice which the materialists had cause to fear. Emerson was reading the *Aids*, probably Marsh's edition, sometime after December the thirteenth.[26] His "Book Memoranda"———all referring to pages in Marsh's volume———must have been interpolated in the journals several weeks thereafter and *not two months before*, as their present position suggests.[27]

<h1 style="text-align:center">1829</h1>

Emerson was called as colleague-pastor of the Second Church of Boston on January 11, and was ordained to the active ministry on March 15.[28] His increased responsibility for sermons drove him to new religious books for suggestions, and Coleridge, who had long been inviting his attention, began slowly to establish a powerful influence over his mind. Among Emerson's books now in Concord is the 1818 edition of *The Friend*, probably the first work by the English critic to enter Emerson's library and the edition about which he was so enthusiastic in his letter to Aunt Mary of December 10-13.[29] It seems that the three volumes had been on his table for several months and there had been casually read along with other books of interest. His letter suggests that he had already reached the valuable third volume and that his aunt, too, had read the set and formed an opinion.[30] If he acquired them before the preceding June, they would help account for the strong Romantic note in his sermon on "Summer" (June 14),[31] in which man's relation to the "book of Nature"[32] is so lyrically set forth:[33] Nature exists for the soul of man;[34] it speaks a language through its constant analogies;[35] and in supplying emblems or hieroglyphics as well for us as for Adam,[36] it is, indeed, a monitor and prophet of the human race.[37] *The Friend*, moreover, would have given him meat for his sermon on "Faith and Works," delivered on September 6, as

---

in Cambridge and the establishment of its small library, see the *Christian Examiner*, II (1825), 395-396; IV (1827), 192-196. In the issue of March-April, 1827, we learn that the small collection of books had "just commenced in Divinity Hall."

[25] The work bears a copyright notice dated October 27, 1829, and an "Advertisement" dated November 16, 1829. A short review appears in the *Journal of Humanity* (Andover, Mass.), Dec. 23, 1829, p. 123. Two Boston periodicals indicate that the book was put on sale in parts of Boston on Jan. 5 and Jan. 8, 1830. See *New-England Galaxy and Boston Mercury*, Boston, Jan. 8, 1830; also *New England Palladium* for Jan. 5, 1830.

[26] The *Aids* appears in the reading list for 1829. See *Journals*, II, 280. Emerson mentions *The Friend*, but not the *Aids*, in writing to his Aunt Mary on Dec. 10 and 13, 1829. See *Journals*, II, 276-279. See also *Letters*, I, 291, for evidence that he had been reading the *Aids* before Jan. 4, 1830.

[27] See *Journals*, II, 268. As they stand they are dated *ca.* Oct. 9, 1829.

[28] *Y E S*, xiv-xv.

[29] See *Journals*, II, 276-279. See Cabot, *Memoir*, I, 161-162, 163. The following volumes appear in Emerson's library in Concord: *The Friend*, (3 vols.) London, 1818; *The Statesman's Manual*, Burlington, Vt., 1832; *Biographia Literaria*, (2 vols. in 1) N.Y., 1834; *Specimens of Table Talk*, (2 vols. in 1), N.Y., 1835; *Letters, Conversations and Recollections*, (2 vols.) London, 1836; *Literary Remains*, (2 vols.) London, 1836; *The Poetical and Dramatic Works of S. T. Coleridge*, (3 vols.) Boston, 1854.

[30] Scholarship would profit by an edition of the letters of Mary Moody Emerson. They would supply facts of great value for an outline of Emerson's philosophical development.

[31] See *Y E S*, 39-45, esp. 43-44.
[32] See ¶s. 256 and 258.
[33] See ¶s. 152-157.
[34] See ¶s. 158-159.
[35] See ¶ 135.
[36] See ¶ 258. See *Nature*, 94.6-7.
[37] See *Nature*, 32-45, esp. 36.15-20.

may be seen in the preceding chapter (¶s. 102-106). Of course, the *Biographia Literaria*,[38] particularly the critical sections on Wordsworth,[39] helped inspire "Summer" as well as the sermon on "Atheism and Ignorance" (October 11).[40] One theme of the latter was that men have a common nature and that when each man understands himself, he is able to understand all other human beings[41]——a thought correlative with the command, "Know Thyself,"[42] and the axiom, "Like only can know like,"[43] repeatedly set forth in Coleridge, especially in *The Friend*. If Emerson did have access to this work in the summer or early fall, that fact would help explain his considered judgment of the English philosopher on December 10-13:[44]

He has a tone a little lower than greatness——but what a living soul, what a universal knowledge! I like to encounter these citizens of the universe, that believe the mind was made to be spectator of all, inquisitor of all, and whose philosophy compares with others much as astronomy[45] with the other sciences, taking post at the centre and, as from a spectacular mount, sending sovereign glances to the circumference of things. . . . [T]here are few or no books of pure literature so self-imprinting, that is so often remembered as Coleridge's.

People wag their heads and say, I can't understand Coleridge. Yet it is only one more instance of what is always interesting, the restless human soul bursting the narrow boundaries of antique speculation and mad to know the secrets of that unknown world, on whose brink it is sure it is standing——yea, can now and then overhear passing words of the talk of the inhabitants.[46] I say a man so learned and a man so bold, has a right to be heard, and I will take off my hat the while and not make an impertinent noise. At least I become acquainted with one new mind I never saw before,——an acquisition in my knowledge of man not unimportant, when it is remembered that so gregarious are even intellectual men that Aristotle thinks for thousands, and Bacon for his ten thousands,[47] and so, in enumerating the apparently manifold philosophies and forms of thought, we should not be able to count more than seven or eight minds.

'T is the privilege of his independence and of his labour to be counted for one school. His theological speculations are, at least, *God viewed from one position;*[48] and no wise man would neglect that one element in concentrating the rays of human thought to a true and comprehensive conclusion. Then I love him that he is no utilitarian,[49] nor

---

[38] It appears in the reading list for 1829. See *Journals*, II, 280. See ¶s. 67-70.
[39] Chapters xiv, xvii—xix, xxii.
[40] See *Y E S*, 243.
[41] For Coleridge's use of this doctrine of the "common nature of man" and the "all in each" see esp. ¶s. 64 and 169 end. See also ¶s. 5, 8, 13, 23, 85, 195, 253, 263, 266, 295. For the "εν και παν" see ¶ 72. Relevant also are the terms *microcosm* and *macrocosm*, q.v. in the index.
[42] For "Know Thyself" or "Γνωθι Σεαυτον" see ¶s. 67-70, 152, 175, 176, 260, 275, 302. See also related ¶s. on self-knowledge: 100, 155, 181, 188, 189, 216, 246, 264.
[43] For "Like only can know life" and its variations ("What we are, that only can we see" and *Quantum sumus, scimus*) see ¶s. 110, 111, 115, 146, 152, 155, 169 end, 194, 228, 259. See *Nature*, 94.5.
[44] See *Journals*, II, 277; 278-279; 279.
[45] Emerson's fondness for the circle in his imagery—especially when discussing *truth*—springs in part from his study of astronomy and in part from his literary sources. See ¶s. 49 and 88. See also the index of the present work and all available index-concordances under: *circle, sphere, circumference, center, point*, etc. See *Y E S*, 171.15, and note 329 *infra*.
[46] This seems to refer to Wordsworth's *Ode* ["Ode on Intimations of Immortality"], lines 164-168.
[47] An illusion to I Samuel 18:7-8; 21:11; 29:5.
[48] Cf. "the absolute Ens seen from one side" in *Nature*, 56.13.
[49] He is probably referring to the dominant philosophy of the period—that of the school of John Locke.

necessarian,[50] nor scoffer, nor *hoc genus omne*,[51] tucked away in the corner of a sentence of Plato.

1 8 3 0

On January 1, apparently resolved to secure as many of the writings of the Englishman as possible, Emerson withdrew his first book from the library of the Boston Athenæum[52]————the *Sibylline Leaves*,[53] which contained almost all Coleridge's poetry written between 1793 and 1817. He wrote William three days later that he was reading *The Friend* with great interest and the *Aids to Reflection* with still greater.[54] That the latter had challenged him to more extensive reading is apparent from the memoranda on certain pages in Marsh's edition which he inscribed in a small corner of the journal, probably sometime in January.[55] An examination of the pages which he cites and the context indicates that he had found his way to the very heart of the *Aids*, had been squarely confronted by the distinction between the Understanding and the Reason, and was quarrying in Marsh's extensive appendices. His notations for further exploration covered the following: the writings of John Smith (1618-1652), one of the Cambridge Platonists;[56] François and Jean Pierre Huber on bees and ants;[57] William Kirby and William Spence, *Introduction to Entomology*;[58] William Derham (1657-1735); Bernardus Nieuwentyt; Pierre Lyonnet (1707-1789);[59] the article, "Simonides," in Pierre Bayle's *Dictionary*;[60] Petrus Pomponatius (1462-1525), *De Fato*;[61] Henry More, *Antidote to Atheism*;[62] and John Donne, *Sermons*.[63] How energetically he followed up these suggestions may be seen in the reading record for the period 1830-1832.[64]

On January 4,[65] he recorded the famous principle, *quantum sumus, scimus*,[66] which Coleridge repeated again and again, and which was to become one of the central Emersonian ideas, a correlative of the doctrine of self-reliance. He asserted, following Coleridge, that the humblest Christian could teach the great scholar many things, that the "inward eye" is

---

[50] An allusion to the Calvinists, whose predestinarian tenets denied freedom of the will.

[51] See the first sentence above. Emerson is apparently praising Coleridge for drawing upon a great variety of sources and handling them all with respect. He may have had in mind Coleridge's effort to reconcile Plato and Bacon. See ¶s. 143-144.

[52] See *Emerson's Reading*, 17, 65.

[53] London, 1817. He returned the volume on Jan. 11.

[54] *Letters*, I, 291 (Jan. 4, 1830).

[55] See *Journals*, II, 268. The passage is misdated in the printed text and belongs certainly to 1830, or even later.

[56] *Aids* (1829), 156; 323. See ¶ 184.

[57] See ¶ 51.

[58] See ¶ 51.

[59] *Aids* (1829), 157.

[60] See ¶ 208. Emerson had quoted Simonides twice before: *Journals*, I, 150; II, 274. I am inclined to believe that the second quotation (the year of which is uncertain) is a paraphrase of Coleridge's passage in the *Aids*. R. L. Rusk, however, gives possible evidence for the conjectural date in *Letters*, I, 287.

[61] See ¶ 208.

[62] *Aids* (1829), 97, 99, 316-320.

[63] *Aids* (1829), 5, 254. See ¶ 187.

[64] See esp. *Emerson's Reading*, augmented by the index to the *Letters*.

[65] *Journals*, II, 282.

[66] See note 43 *supra*. On Mar. 15, 1829, he expressed this thought in a sermon. See *Y E S*, 32.20.

the source of a man's truth, and that all things *exeunt in mysterium*.[67] In his sermon of January 10, "Love to Christ,"[68] he echoed Coleridge's argument for Christianity.[69] On January 24, he developed the theme of reliance on the "inward eye" in his sermon, "Non-Conformity."[70] On February 7, he found inspiration for "Benevolence and Selfishness"[71] in *The Friend*.[72] On February 10, he wrote:[72a] "Coleridge supposes that a miracle can have no effect upon the soul except when the doctrine it accompanies is true; that a miracle is religious gratification only to a religious man. Every thing changes its nature to the good." On February 28, in "The Power of the Soul,"[73] and on April 11, in "The Good Heart,"[74] he again drew upon the favorite source. On April 25, he spoke of "The Childlike Character" and probably stressed Coleridge's ideas about humility, genius and the ability to retain youth's sense of wonder and freshness of impressions even in adulthood.[75] On May 16, in "Religious Liberalism and Rigidity,"[76] he drew his concept of the "rigid" or traditional party from Coleridge's theological opinions——especially from the discussion of sin and faith in the *Aids*[77]——and distinguished between S. T. C. the philosopher and S. T. C. the theologian. Reacting against the incomplete evidence for the Trinity in the *Aids*,[78] he asserted that the doctrine seemed to him only incidentally a part of Christianity and in no sense a deduction from "first principles."[79] On May 30, in "The Authority of Jesus," he mentioned the categorical imperative——the *ought* and the *ought not*——as the basis of Christian moral dominion.[80] On July 18, in "The Virtue of Humility," he touched on another theme in the *Aids*.[81] On August 1, in "Acquiring True Knowledge,"[82] he seems to have developed Coleridge's familiar themes: that one should *know oneself*,[83] that knowing is *being* or *becoming*, and that *knowing* God is equivalent to *possessing* God.[84] "Self-Culture,"[85] delivered on September 5, set forth principles for the education of a soul "having its life in itself."[86] Emerson reiterated that "we want principles,"[87] and observed, following Coleridge, that the Christian

---

[67] *Journals*, II, 282-283. For Coleridge on the simple Christian, see ¶s. 180, 204; on the fundamental mystery underlying existence and the phrase quoted by Emerson, see ¶ 196; on the "inward eye," see ¶s. 41, 164, 289. See also *Biographia Literaria* [*Works* (Shedd), III], 478-479, for Coleridge's criticism of the use of "inward eye" in Wordsworth's "I Wandered Lonely as a Cloud."

[68] *Y E S*, 235.26.

[69] See ¶ 205.

[70] *Y E S*, 266.14.

[71] *Y E S*, 242.9ff.

[72] See ¶s. 85, 116, 117.

[72a] See *Typescript Journals*, "Blotting Book Y," p. 24. See *infra* under Jan. 23, 1831.

[73] *Y E S*, 266.22. See ¶s. 63, 184, 245, 246, 263 *et passim*.

[74] *Y E S*, 266.30. Examine Emerson's references to the *heart* in the Index-Concordances. Cf. ¶s. 164, 169, 183, 191, 202.

[75] *Y E S*, 266.32. Cf. ¶s. 63, 71, 75, 122a, 126, 156, 226.

[76] *Y E S*, 83.29ff.

[77] See ¶ 210.

[78] *Aids* (1829), 116ff.

[79] *Y E S*, 84.17ff.

[80] *Y E S*, 94.33ff. Cf. ¶ 196. See also *Y E S*, 93.25, 95.9, 105.6, 111.26.

[81] *Y E S*, 267.9. See ¶ 226.

[82] *Y E S*, 267.13.

[83] See note 42.

[84] See ¶s. 243, 251, 263, 264.

[85] *Y E S*, 99-104.

[86] See ¶s. 2ff., 170-171. Cf. also the utility of the regulative principle in ¶s. 99, 133, 147.

[87] *Y E S*, 99.15, 99.17, 99.20, 99.23.

religion discovered them not without but *within* ourselves.[88] Man possesses the Divine eye within;[89] he must make his actions yield to the higher Will (*i.e.*, make his will yield to the Reason);[90] he must submit to the law of the mind——to the Divine Mind.[91] The "law of all action" is that love begets love, hate responds to hate, measure is met by measure——a corollary of the *quantum sumus, scimus* (the world mirrors our own thought), which one might call Coleridge's "law of all knowledge."[92] In the same vein, on September 12, came "The Oracle Within."[93] On October 24, in "Reason and Revelation,"[94] he minimized the value of the past and stressed the immediacy of spiritual knowledge through the "know thyself"——through an inner spiritual world——not one of remote antiquity or of the distant future, but present *now*.[95] On October 31, his theme was the same——"The Kingdom of Heaven is Within."[96] On November 10, he spoke of Coleridge's distinction between the *similar* and the *same*.[97] On November 21, in "The Fear of Death,"[98] he echoed the *Aids* on Jesus, immortality, miracles, and the God of Abraham, Isaac and Jacob.[99] As the year drew to a close, the *Aids* and *The Friend* (on December 3) furnished ideas for "Trust Yourself."[100] Religion supposes, he said, that every man's immortal soul can receive divine truth and act on it;[101] Christianity urges self-respect, self-trust or self-reliance as an inevitable deduction;[102] it requires the activity of the mind in *reflection*;[103] our goal is to become passive to universal thought (*i.e.*, to the Reason), which belongs to no human being but is above all.[104] We must follow the inner voice and sedulously avoid imitation of all that contradicts it.[105] Each has within a concept of *universal man* by which he can judge the imperfections of his fellow men.[106] Self-reliance is not to be identified with selfishness, but with dependence upon the soul——the Bethel within.[107] The Bible is locked to us until we first hear God's voice inside ourselves;[108] then correspondences become evident between the printed record and the living soul. Emerson again emphasized the precept, "Know Thyself."[109]

---

[88] *Y E S*, 100.6. See also under "within" in the Index-Concordances. See ¶s. 178-182, 190, 191, 195, 196, 254, 264-266.

[89] *Y E S*, 100.7. Cf. ¶ 289.

[90] *Y E S*, 100.10. Cf. ¶s. 148, 160, 166, 183, 192-194, 196, 221, 261, 272, 277.

[91] *Y E S*, 100.17. Cf. ¶s. 2ff.

[92] *Y E S*, 102.17; 101.30ff. See note 43. See also ¶ 115.

[93] *Y E S*, 267.20; xxvi.4ff.

[94] *Y E S*, 267.28; xxvi-xxvii.

[95] See note 42. See also ¶ 198. Cf. *Nature*, 5.17.

[96] *Y E S*, 267.30. See note 88.

[97] *Journals*, II, 320. See ¶ 300.

[98] *Y E S*, 244.42ff. He repeated the same statement in his sermon, "A Future Life," delivered on Sept. 11, 1831.

[99] See ¶s. 209, 213.   [100] *Y E S*, 105-111.

[101] *Y E S*, 105.4ff. Cf. ¶s. 2ff., 177.

[102] *Y E S*, 105.17, 105.21, 106.13. For *Self-Respect*, see ¶ 79. For *Self-Trust* or *Self-Reliance*, see ¶s. 2ff., 101, 136, 157, 175-178, 180-181, 184, 190-191, 195, 198, 211, 227, 249, 252, 264-266, 288. For Coleridge on the related theme of *Self-Knowledge*, see note 42.

[103] *Y E S*, 108.25ff. For Coleridge on reflection, see esp. ¶s. 173-177, 179, 183, 185. It should be remembered that his great work was *Aids to Reflection*.

[104] *Y E S*, 109.15ff. Cf. ¶s. 2ff.

[105] *Y E S*, 109.30ff. Cf. ¶ 227.

[106] *Y E S*, 110.13ff. Emerson speaks of the universal man again in 181.5-6. For Coleridge's use of the concept, see ¶s. 224, 295.

[107] *Y E S*, 110.20ff. For Coleridge on the voice *within*, see note 88. For the soul as God's house, see ¶s. 211-212.

[108] *Y E S*, 111.5. See ¶ 254. Also "Like only can know like" in note 43.

[109] *Y E S*, 111.9. See note 42.

On December 11, he paraphrased the opinion, common with Coleridge, that corroboration of the truth of Christianity is in one's soul and that the New Testament is not indispensable.[110] On the last day of the year, in "How Old Art Thou?"[111] he employed concepts from St. John's gospel[112] reminiscent of the manner of Coleridge,[113] and sometime before the end of the year, he made a collection of poetic and prose gems on the themes, "search thine own heart," "God is within thee," and *quantum sumus, scimus.*"[114] Two were taken from *The Friend*——excerpts which Coleridge had drawn from Samuel Daniel and (with considerable modification) from John Donne.[115] These two later appeared in the anthology, *Parnassus,*[116] without having been checked in the works of the original authors. Emerson never suspected Coleridge's adaptations.

1 8 3 1

On January 10, Emerson approved the discussion of faith and works in *The Friend*.[117] Two days later, he built a sermon ("Self and Others") around several paragraphs on benevolence and God's judgment——in the same source. Coleridge had chosen as text the saying of a French philosopher: *amour de moi-même, mais bien calculé.* Emerson translated the "proverb," and followed completely the succinct analysis of *The Friend*. He showed the inadequacy of selfishness, declared that the Eternal dwells in each human heart, that for this reason each man is but a copy of ourselves and that all men have common duties through allegiance to God, their common bond. God must, therefore, be the basis of benevolence—— and not self-love. From Him we have received all we possess; we have got nothing by our own efforts. So, in doing good, we but show gratitude to the Divine as he appears *in our neighbor*.[118] In the peroration on the Eternal Eye and the Eternal Voice present in every breast, Emerson was, doubtless, thinking of his frail and declining wife; and a few of the following thoughts assumed poetic form six months later——after her death ——in *Gnothi Seauton*:[119]

My friend . . . have you never suspected a greater inmate in your frail body than a frail animal life? Have you never perceived that while all things change, a soul possesses you[120] which changes not; which amid doubts, doubts not; which amidst dejection, intimates that all will be well;[121] a soul which amid the clamors of temptation, breathes the low thunders of his admonition; a soul which though disregarded and forgotten in the din of affairs still meets you again with its unruffled supremacy on its own occasions when you are alone; a soul before which you are known though you wear a mask to all the world; a soul which never participates in your guilt,[122] but as God in Heaven beholds it all from an infinite superiority; a soul which assures you that integrity and truth and love can never be a loss, nor crime a gain?

[110] *Journals*, II, 325. Cf. ¶ 301.
[111] *Y E S*, 112-119.
[112] Especially from the gospel of John, chaps. 1, 3, 5 and 6.
[113] See ¶s. 10, 34, 41, 157, 170, 185, 199, 258, 265-266, and throughout all the works of Coleridge, the Cambridge Platonists, and other Neo-Platonic writers.
[114] *Journals*, II, 347-351.
[115] See ¶s. 75a, 75b.
[116] Boston, 1875, p. 517.
[117] *Journals*, II, 353-354. See ¶s. 102-105.
[118] *Y E S*, 128.12ff. Cf. ¶s. 85, 116, 117.
[119] *Y E S*, 136.8ff. Cf. ¶ 110.
[120] See ¶s. 11-13.
[121] See ¶ 169 (last half).
[122] See "Γνωθι Σεαυτον" under July 6, *infra*, line 88.

On January 23, in "Miracles," he drew heavily upon the "eloquent" Mr. Coleridge and comparatively little from New England tradition.[123] It is especially significant that he concluded his discourse with a quotation from *The Friend*——the longest borrowed passage in his published sermons.[124] On January 30, in "Independence in Faith," he again stressed the independent connection which the soul must establish with God—— the necessary self-reliance which takes priority over forms of social worship——and spoke of the doctrine of *quantum sumus, scimus* in its practical functioning: As we purify the soul within we are rewarded more frequently with the sight of God, whom only the pure in heart can see.[125] On February 8, Ellen died, and Emerson's sermon twelve days later ("Consolation for the Mourner") stressed Duty——*the soul's everlasting object*——the duty of continuing to face life and to discharge one's appointed trusts.[126] A passage in the *Aids*, which, doubtless, had given him consolation, seems to have suggested his text.[127]

On February 23, he began deliberately to make use of Coleridge's distinction between Reason and the Understanding, compiling in his journals a number of the "necessary truths" which spring only from the former.[128] The paragraph in his blotting book reveals many of Coleridge's favorite themes: that the sublime truths of the Reason are not comprehended by the Understanding,[129] that spiritual truths can only be spiritually discerned,[130] that great truths are their own evidence,[131] that like must know like,[132] and that one truth is related to all others.[133]

It is worth recording that Plotinus said, "Of the Unity of God, nothing can be predicated, neither being, nor essence, nor life, for it is above all these." Grand it is to recognize the truth of this and of every one of that first class of truths which are *necessary*. Thus, "Design proves a designer," "Like must know like," or "the same can only be known by the same," out of which come the propositions in ethics, "*Si vis amari, ama*," and "God without can only be known by God within," and "the scriptures can be explained only by that spirit which dictated them," [134] and a thousand sayings more which have a *quasi* truth instantly to the ear, the real truth of which is this elementary fact in all, "like must know like." It would be well for every mind to collect with care every truth of this kind he may meet, and make a catalogue of "necessary truths." They are scanned and approved by the Reason far above the understanding. They are the last facts by which we approximate metaphysically to God.[135]

---

[123] *Y E S*, 120-126. See ¶s. 87a, 120-122, 161-163, 209, 232-234. See above under Feb. 10, 1830.

[124] See ¶ 162.

[125] See *Y E S*, 237.29; xxv.33ff. This idea is later expressed as the gain or loss of power. See *Journals*, II, 362 bottom. The thought reappears in "Γνωθι Σεαυτον," lines 92-95. See *Nature*, 62.19-22.

[126] *Y E S*, 138-144, esp. 143.23ff. Coleridge stressed the theme in his poetic soliloquy, "Duty Surviving Self-Love: the Only Sure Friend of Declining Life," and also in ¶s. 76, 86, 196, 272. Emerson, doubtless, had Wordsworth's "Ode to Duty" in mind and possibly Milton, who had risked his eyesight for the Commonwealth and had striven to serve his Maker when blind.

[127] *Y E S*, 138.2ff. See ¶s. 211, 212. An echo of the "house not made with hands" appears in his letter to Edward on Sept. 16, 1831 (*Letters*, I, 331).

[128] See ¶s. 2, 15, 115.

[129] See ¶s. 44ff., 89, 178.

[130] See ¶ 194.

[131] See ¶ 2.

[132] See note 43.

[133] See ¶ 88.

[134] This was the remark of George Fox. See *Journals*, II, 497-498; III, 225; *Nature*, 44.18-19.

[135] *Journals*, II, 357-358.

On March 6, he preached on "God in the Soul," a sermon which, I believe, may be considered the prose original of his poem, *Gnothi Seauton*. "It is not our soul that is God but God is *in* our soul." He spoke of the "pure and holy inmate of every human breast, this conscience, this Reason," this "spark of God" in us——this "domestic God." He was apparently rereading the *Aids* and *The Friend*, and finding Coleridge's discussion of the Reason and the Understanding both consoling and encouraging.[136] On March 13, in his journal, he referred to the Reason for evidence of God's immanence and unifying energy——paraphrasing and condensing Coleridge's apologetic in the *Aids*.[137] A week later, in a sermon ("The Holy Spirit"), he quoted Coleridge's tests of universality, permanence and general acceptance for testing the basic truth of current dogmas.[138] The following Sunday (March 27), in "The Common Basis of Truth," he dealt with the same theme.[139]

On April 29,[140] he withdrew from the Boston Athenæum Coleridge's translation of Schiller's *Wallenstein* (London, 1800), a work which he seems greatly to have admired throughout his life.[141] In this volume, which was strongly Coleridgean in flavor, he found consolation in his recent bereavement, a necessary escape from the realities of his environment, many useful lustres, and confirmation for his developing ideas of honor, "God within," and self-reliance. A few of the many gems follow:

THE SPIRIT'S LADDER——CIRCLES[142]
¶ A
                         [B]ut whate'er
Full of mysterious import Nature weaves,
And fashions in the depths——the spirit's ladder,
That from this gross and visible world of dust
Even to the starry world, with thousand rounds,
Builds itself up; on which the unseen powers
Move up and down on heavenly ministeries——
The circles in the circles, that approach
The central sun with ever-narrowing orbit——
These see the glance alone, the unsealed eye,
Of Jupiter's glad children born in lustre.

JUDGMENT IS INSTANTANEOUS[143]
¶ B
Who sows the serpent's teeth, let him not hope
To reap a joyous harvest. Every crime
Has, in the moment of its perpetration,
Its own avenging angel——dark Misgiving,
An ominous Sinking at the inmost heart.

---

[136] *Y E S*, 268.18; xxv.8; xxv.11. See ¶s. 2ff., esp. 12. For Coleridge on the conscience, see ¶s. 2, 3, 6, 8-9, 79, 86, 93, 196, 255. For the source of "spark of God" see ¶ 112.

[137] *Journals*, II, 361. Cf. ¶s. 192-194.

[138] *Y E S*, 230.37ff. Cf. ¶s. 118-120. This test of place, time and general response is ancient in Christianity, and appears in the *Commonitorium* of St. Vincent of Lerins, who flourished in the fifth century: *Id quod ubique, quod semper, quod ab omnibus creditum est* is the rule of Catholic faith.

[139] *Y E S*, 230.40ff.

[140] See *Emerson's Reading*, 18, 103. He returned it on May 11.

[141] See quotations and references in *Journals*, II, 377-378, 423; III, 262, 347, 428; IV, 153. See *Parnassus*, Boston, 1875, *passim*.

[142] Schiller, *Wallenstein* (tr. Coleridge), Part One, I.xi.96ff.

[143] *Ibid.*, Part One, IV.vii.250ff.

SELF-RELIANCE *VS.* SELF-CONTRADICTION[144]

¶ C

For, by the laws of Spirit, in the right
Is every individual character
That acts in strict consistence with itself.
Self-contradiction is the only wrong.

MAN AND THE SOUL OF THE WORLD[145]

¶ D

There exist moments in the life of man,
When he is nearer the great Soul of the world
Than is man's custom, and possesses freely
The power of questioning his destiny.

THE INNER WORLD——THE MICROCOSM[146]

¶ E

Know, that the human being's thoughts and deeds
Are not, like ocean billows, blindly moved.
The inner world, his microcosmus, is
The deep shaft, out of which they spring eternally.

MAN'S WILL AND SELF-RESPECT[147]

¶ F

We all do stamp our value on ourselves.
The price we challenge for ourselves is given us.
There does not live on earth the man so stationed,
That I despise myself compared with him.
Man is made great or little by his own will.

SELF-RELIANCE AND GRIEF[148]

¶ G

Leave her alone with him: for there are sorrows,
Where of necessity the soul must be
Its own support. A strong heart will rely
On its own strength alone. In her own bosom,
Not in her mother's arms, must she collect
The strength to rise superior to this blow.

THE ORACLE WITHIN *VS.* DEAD BOOKS[149]

¶ H

         If to be the chieftain asks
All that is great in nature, let it be
Likewise his privilege to move and act
In all the correspondencies of greatness.
The oracle within him, that which lives,
He must invoke and question——not dead books,
Not ordinances, not mould-rotted papers.

SELF-RELIANCE *VS.* DOUBT[150]

¶ I

In your own bosom are your destiny's stars.
Confidence in yourself, prompt resolution,
This is your Venus! and the sole malignant,
The only one that harmeth you is Doubt.

---

[144] *Ibid.*, Part One, IV.vii.191ff. Emerson quotes this in *Journals*, III, 262.
[145] *Ibid.*, Part One, V.iii.54ff.
[146] *Ibid.*, Part One, V.iii.106ff.
[147] *Ibid.*, Part Two, III.viii.73ff.
[148] *Ibid.*, Part Two, IV.iii.57ff.
[149] *Ibid.*, Part One, I.iv.54ff. Emerson copied lines 46-60 into *Journals*, II, 377.
[150] *Ibid.*, Part One, I.xi.82ff. Emerson inserted these in *Journals*, II, 377.

MYTHOLOGY——FABLE——LOVE——IDEALISM[151]

¶ J

This visible nature, and this common world,
Is all too narrow: yea, a deeper import
Lurks in the legend told my infant years
Than lies upon that truth, we live to learn.
For fable is Love's world, his home, his birth-place:
Delightedly dwells he 'mong fays and talismans,
And spirits; and delightedly believes
Divinities, being himself divine.

HEROISM——SELF-RELIANCE[152]

¶ K

                           At the approach
Of extreme peril, when a hollow image
Is found a hollow image and no more,
Then falls the power into the mighty hands
Of Nature, of the spirit giant-born,
Who listens only to himself, knows nothing
Of stipulations, duties, reverences,
And, like the emancipated force of fire,
Unmastered scorches, ere it reaches them,
Their fine-spun webs.

MISCELLANEOUS[153]

¶ L

All powerful souls have kindred with each other.

¶ M

Not every one doth it beseem to question
The far-off high Arcturus. Most securely
Wilt thou pursue the nearest duty——let
The pilot fix his eye upon the pole-star.

¶ N

A brave man hazards life, but not his conscience.

¶ O

If your heart speak to you,
Follow its impulse. 'Tis the voice of God.

¶ P

                Come, friend! Be noble-minded!
Our own heart, and not other men's opinions,
Forms our true honour.

¶ Q

The dearest thing a man has is himself.

Special mention should be made of the passage beginning, "He is gone——
is dust," in which Wallenstein mourns the death of Max Piccolomini.[154]
The strong affirmation of immortality and the beautiful tribute to the
dead, doubtless, gave Emerson comfort in Ellen's absence, for it sprang to
his lips in 1834 at the time of Edward's decease[155] and seems to have
influenced his prose lament for Charles, in 1836.[156] On May 28,[157] he again

---

[151] *Ibid.*, Part One, II.iv.115ff. Lines 110-138 appear in *Parnassus*, 120.
[152] *Ibid.*, Part One, IV.vii.169ff. They appear in *Journals*, II, 377-378, and in *Parnassus*, 195.
[153] *Ibid.*, Part One, II.xi.61; Part Two, II.vi.137ff.; III.vi.39; III.vii.51-52; III.viii.65ff.; III.ix.17.
[154] *Ibid.*, Part Two, V.i.38-68. See *Parnassus*, 459.
[155] See *Journals*, III, 346-347.
[156] See *Journals*, IV, 39-40.
[157] *Emerson's Reading*, 18, 103. He kept the volume for nearly a month, returning it on June 25.

withdrew *Wallenstein* from the Athenæum and apparently took it with him when he left Boston on Monday, May 30,[158] for a two-week vacation[159] in Vermont. It is significant that after this sojourn he brought back a monody on death and an elegy on Ellen. To that short trip, moreover, he seems to have owed the opportunity for reflection on the deep spiritual themes which he expressed in permanent form three weeks later (July 6) in two other poems, one of them unmistakably Coleridgean.[160] It represented the culmination of many months of thought on the nature of his own soul; it foreshadowed the declaration of independence from organized religion, which came a year later; and it announced the conviction which reappeared in the first and concluding parts of *Nature* (1836).[161] Emerson believed that the Christian revelation had expressly and implicitly declared men to be the children of God and sharers of His divine being.[162] What, then, might the highest and holiest religion require if not that the *individual* should know his *true self*——that is, the godlike that dwelt (potentially, at least) within every breast?[163] Was not the Divine Reason, described by Coleridge as possessed by no man, yet possessing all and dwelling in all——was it not man's true empire and rightful king?[164] Did it not manifest itself as the source of "necessary truths" above the Understanding,[165] as the Moral Law or Voice of Duty, and (less frequently, perhaps) as a warm, ebullient stream of spiritual life? In yielding to it, then, one might expect to find one's conscience——the testifying state of man——enjoying the "peace of God which passeth all understanding."[166] Did it not become man's highest vocation to make his behavior conform to the pure idea of his mind[167]——to make his will ONE with the Divine Will[168]——to keep the Understanding and the senses subordinate to his inner Magistrate? Was not this the only process of regeneration and redemption?[169] If one had to have a symbolism, a mythology or a fable to describe spiritual growth, there was the imagery of St. John or Plotinus ——a thousand times preferable to the crass atonement theories of orthodox or "rigid" Christianity. So, for Emerson, the individual soul——the microcosm——was under command to preserve its dignity; was never to use people or things as crutches; and was to remember that it already possessed potentially the entire spiritual wealth and opportunity of mythical Adam on the first day of creation, or of a Julius Caesar at the height of his power in Rome.[170] The first, last, and eternal admonition for the soul was *know thyself,* and only as individuals obeyed that voice might one hope for improvement in society at large.[171] In the following poem,

---

[158] See *Letters,* I, 323, in which he speaks of leaving "next Monday morn."

[159] See *Journals,* II, 384.

[160] There is also a possible indebtedness to Taylor's translation of the *Works of Plato.* See chap. II, *supra.* Emerson had been reading vols. II and III from Jan. 3 to Mar. 7; and vol. III alone from Mar. 25 to Apr. 29.

[161] *Nature,* "Introduction" and "Prospects," esp. pp. 5-6 and 91-95.

[162] See "Self and Others" (Jan. 12, 1831), *Y E S,* 133.2ff. Cf. ¶ 22.

[163] See ¶s. 11-13.

[164] See "Γνωθι Σεαυτον" below, line 49.   [166] See ¶ 255.

[165] See note 128.   [167] See *Nature,* 94.14ff.

[168] See *Y E S,* 132.31, 135.9, 160.16, 210.19, 259.23; see ¶s. 25, 27-30.

[169] *Y E S,* 119.11; see *Nature,* 91.5ff.

[170] See *Nature,* 94.6ff.

[171] For the emphasis upon the individual rather than on society, see "The Individual and the State" (Apr. 8, 1830); "The Oracle Within" (Sept. 12, 1830), *Y E S,* xxv.12ff.; and "Religion and Society" (Oct. 27, 1833), *Y E S,* 191-202.

therefore, Emerson assumed for background many of his recent sermons and all his favorite reading. Herein lies the heart of his religious philosophy, which the months and years were not greatly to alter, but rather to make more explicit.

GNOTHI SEAUTON[172]

By RALPH WALDO EMERSON

I

If thou[173] canst bear
Strong meat of simple truth,
If thou durst my words compare
. With what thou thinkest in the soul's free youth,[174]
5   Then take this fact unto thy soul,——
God dwells in thee.[175]
It is no metaphor nor parable,[176]
It is unknown to thousands, and to thee;
Yet there is God.

II

10   He is in thy world,
But thy world knows him not.[177]
He is the mighty Heart
From which life's varied pulses part.[178]
Clouded and shrouded there doth sit
15   The Infinite
Embosomed in a man;[179]
And thou art stranger[180] to thy guest,
And know'st not what thou dost invest.
The clouds that veil his life within[181]
20   Are thy thick woven webs of sin,

---

[172] The poem seems to owe much to ¶s. 152-157. (I prefer to use Roman letters for the title rather than the Greek: Γνωθι Σεαυτον). Except for the emendations, which I have made on the basis of the *Typescript Journals*, I reprint the text as given in *Journals*, II, 395-399, inserting strophe and line numbers for convenience of reference. For the theme "know thyself" in Coleridge, see note 42. See also ¶s. 2ff. for the philosophic framework which Emerson had by this time made his own. Read over ¶s. 259-260. Cf. *Y E S*, 111.9, 111.28, 168.3, 183.3, 200.25-28-30-34.

[173] Emerson is addressing himself in soliloquy. It is a deeply moving meditation in spirit not unlike Wordsworth's *Ode*. It seems to reflect his continued grief and his quest for spiritual certainty in the midst of his troubled world. See Coleridge's poem on the same subject in ¶ 302.

[174] A possible reference to childhood as described in the first strophe of Wordsworth's *Ode*. See also "the *simple creed* of childhood" in strophe VIII. See Coleridge's comment in ¶s. 71-74, and Emerson's discussion of Coleridge in his letter to Edward under date of May 31, 1834, *infra*.

[175] See ¶s. 86 and 264-266. Also ¶ 157: "it describes itself and dwells in us only as far as we dwell in it." This thought appears strongly expressed in earlier sermons, esp. in "God in the Soul" (Mar. 6, 1831), still unpublished. See *Y E S*, 110-111, 116, 133-134, 137. See ¶ 191.

[176] See *Y E S*, xxii.16.

[177] An echo of John 1:10. See note 112.

[178] Cf. *Y E S*, 186.27. Emerson may be echoing the last two lines of Wordsworth's sonnet, "Composed upon Westminster Bridge."

[179] See ¶s. 14, 16-17, 25, 31, 157, 198, 253, 263.

[180] See ¶ 14. Cf. *Y E S*, 132.14-15; 162.18. Cf. *Nature*, 81.4.

[181] Line 176 of Wordsworth's *Ode* speaks of the "radiance which was once so bright," and line 197, of the "clouds that gather round the setting sun." The imagery in the first part of Emerson's poem is that of light, darkness, clouds, glory, sun—is predominantly

Which his glory struggling through
Darkens to thine evil hue.[182]

III

Then bear thyself, O man!
Up to the scale and compass of thy guest;

25   Soul of thy soul.[183]
Be great[184] as doth beseem
The ambassador who bears
The royal presence where he goes.[185]

IV

Give up to thy soul——

30   Let it have its way——[186]
It is, I tell thee, God himself,[187]
The selfsame One[188] that rules the Whole,[189]
Tho' he speaks thro' thee with a stifled voice,[190]
And looks through thee, shorn of his beams.[191]

35   But if thou listen to his voice,
If thou obey the royal thought,
It will grow clearer to thine ear,
More glorious to thine eye.
The clouds will burst that veil him now

40   And thou shalt see the Lord.[192]

V

Therefore be great,[193]
Not proud,——too great to be proud.[194]
Let not thine eyes rove,
Peep not in corners; let thine eyes

45   Look straight before thee, as befits
The simplicity of Power.[195]
And in thy closet carry state;
Filled with light, walk therein;
And, as a king[196]

50   Would do no treason to his own empire,

Neo-Platonic like the fifth strophe of Wordsworth's *Ode*, which was based on a work of Proclus (See *M P*, XXVI, 201-213). See chap. III of the present work, and ¶s. 10, 11, 16, 28, 36, 166, 185, 254, 258, 264-266, 203, 220.

[182] See note 43; Swedenborg ¶s. 23ff.; Sampson Reed ¶s. 58-70; *Y E S*, 101.31.

[183] *I.e.*, the Reason. See ¶s. 1-56, 184, 264.   [184] Best commentary is *Y E S*, 133-134.

[185] Prose commentary appears in *Journals*, II, 388 top. Emerson was probably influenced by ¶ 190. For the theme "independence of circumstances," which is implied here, see Index-Concordance to the Sermons, *s.v.*

[186] See ¶s. 28, 34, 36. Also note 42.

[187] Cf. *Y E S*, xxv.7-9 (Mar. 6, 1831). The poem may indicate development.

[188] See chap. III *supra*, and the excerpt from Taylor's *Works of Plato* at the end of chap. II. See also ¶s. 21, 168, 193.

[189] Cf. line 116. The phrase "rules the whole" might be paraphrased as "informs the whole." See ¶s. 170-171, 157, and 87a. This is the εν και παν.

[190] On the "voice of God" or "conscience" see the Index-Concordances.

[191] Similar imagery appears in ¶ 266.

[192] See his sermon, "Independence in Faith" (Jan. 30, 1831), quoted in *Y E S*, xxv.33ff. See *Nature*, 80.15. Also ¶ 86.

[193] For the idea that man was born great but has "shrunk to a drop," see *Nature*, 88.20.

[194] See ¶ 89. This foreshadows his advice in the Orphic Poet passage, *Nature*, 94.6-13.

[195] See "power" in the Index-Concordances. See ¶s. 193, 245 bottom, 263.

[196] See end of ¶ 115. Wordsworth's *Ode* speaks of the "glories he hath known" and of

So do not thou to thine.[197]

VI

This is the reason why thou dost recognize
Things now first revealed,
Because in thee resides
55 The Spirit that lives in all;
And thou canst learn the laws of nature
Because its author is latent in thy breast.[198]

VII

Therefore, O happy youth,
Happy if thou dost know and love this truth,
60 Thou art unto thyself a law,[199]
And since the soul of things is in thee,
Thou needest nothing out of thee.[200]
The law, the gospel,[201] and the Providence,
Heaven, Hell, the Judgment,[202] and the stores
65 Immeasureable of Truth and Good,
All these thou must find
Within[203] thy single mind,
Or never find.[204]

VIII

Thou art the *law*;
70 The *gospel* has no revelation[205]
Of peace or hope until there is response
From the deep chambers of thy mind thereto,——
The rest is straw.
It can reveal no truth unknown before.
75 The *Providence*[206]

---

[197] See ¶s. C, H, I, K, Q *supra*. Man's "empire" is described in *Nature*, 94.11ff.

[198] For the background of this strophe and a discussion of *subject* and *object*, see ¶s. 67-70 and notes 42 and 43.

[199] Probably an echo of Romans 2:14.

[200] For "Self-Reliance" and "Know Thyself" references, see note 42.

[201] See above under date of Dec. 11, 1830. The best commentary on this line, with evidence that Coleridge's distinction between the Reason and the Understanding was in his mind, appears in *Journals*, III, 377. There he indicates that the "Law and Gospel" are Luther's and St. Paul's terms and that they are to be translated into philosophical terminology.

[202] For collateral commentary on Emerson's Doctrine of Compensation and Instantaneous Judgment, see *Y E S*, 100.9, 101.18-26, 102.23, 210.2. See also ¶s. 115, 214, 271. The terms "Heaven," "Hell," "Judgment," "Providence" are used here in a strongly Swedenborgian sense. The first two are dealt with in *A Treatise Concerning Heaven and Its Wonders and also Concerning Hell*. Emerson owned an edition published in London, 1823. There was an American edition of *The Divine Providence* available in 1829. See esp. Swedenborg ¶s. 6-13, 29, 45-46, 50, 56.

[203] See note 88. Also ¶ 115.

[204] See ¶ 7 and *Nature*, 43.4. For "Like only can know like" or *Quantum sumus, scimus*, see note 43.

[205] See *Y E S*, 111.5 and ¶ 254. See note on line 57 *supra*. See his unpub. sermon, "Reason and Revelation," dated Oct. 24, 1830.

[206] Emerson's view is that man creates his own world (*Nature*, 94.13-22) and that nothing can harm a man but himself. See *Y E S*, 209.31. The latter view is proverbial. See Burton Stevenson, *Home Book of Quotations*, 3d ed., N.Y., 1937, p. 544, under "Man His Own Enemy." See also Erasmus, *Adages*: "No one is injured save by himself." Also St. Chrysostom's *Letter to Olympia*: "No one can harm the man who does himself no wrong." See *Journals*, III, 208: "Not easy are [the laws of nature] to be enumerated, but he has some idea of them who considers such propositions as St. Bernard's,—

Thou art thyself that doth dispense
Wealth to thy work, want to thy sloth,
Glory to goodness, to neglect, the moth.
Thou sow'st the wind, the whirlwind reapest,[207]
80   Thou payest the wages
Of thy own work, through all ages.
The almighty energy within
Crowneth virtue, curseth sin.[208]
Virtue sees by its own light;[209]
85   Stumbleth sin in self-made night.

IX

Who approves thee doing right?
God in thee.[210]
Who condemns thee doing wrong?[211]
God in thee.
90   Who punishes thine evil deed?
God in thee.
What is thine evil meed?[212]
Thy worse mind, with error blind
And more prone to evil[213]
95   That is, the greater hiding of the God within:
The loss of peace[214a]
The terrible displeasure of this inmate
And next the consequence
More faintly as more distant wro't[214b]
100   Upon our outward fortunes
Which decay with vice
With Virtue[214c] rise.

X[214d]

The selfsame God
By the same law[215]
105   Makes the souls of angels[216] glad
And the souls of devils sad
See
There is nothing else but God

Nobody can harm me but myself,—or who develops the doctrine in his own experience that nothing can be given or taken without an equivalent."

[207] Hosea 8:7.

[208] Doctrine of Compensation. See note on line 64 *supra*. "Curse" may be an allusion to Genesis 3:17.

[209] An echo of Milton's *Comus*, lines 372-374.

[210] See ¶s. 76, 86, 93, 196, 255.

[211] See *Y E S*, 200.13.

[212] The word appears incorrectly as *need* in *Journals*, II, 398.

[213] See the discussion of the "path of enlightenment" in chap. III. Emerson's view of evil is optimistic. He anticipates the possibility of eliminating it in *Nature*, 94.13ff., esp. in 95.7. Cf. Swedenborg ¶s. 41, 44-47, 56; Sampson Reed ¶s. 55, 59-62; *Nature*, 88.11—90.4.

[214a] Lines 96-102 inclusive are reproduced from the *Typescript Journals* (Blotting Book III). On the loss of peace consequent on evil, see *Y E S*, 141.7. See ¶ B *supra*.

[214b] *I.e.*, "wrought."

[214c] For definition of this term, see the Index-Concordances. For virtue as a source of spiritual power, see *Y E S*, 94.4-6; 87.27; 35.23. Cf. Milton's *Comus*. See ¶ 263 on the renewal of forfeited power.

[214d] This entire stanza follows the *Typescript Journals* (Blotting Book III).

[215] Emerson insists with Coleridge that the moral order of God is the same as that of man. The Moral Law is universal. See *Y E S*, xxiii.32ff. See ¶s. 192-193.

[216] MS. originally read "good men."

> Where eer I look
> 110   All things hasten back to him[217]
> Light is but his shadow dim.[218]
>
> ### XI
>
> Shall I ask wealth or power of God, who gave
> An image of himself to be my soul?
> As well might swilling[219] ocean ask a wave,
> 115   Or the starred firmament a dying coal,——
> For that which is in me lives in the whole.[220]

On the same day (July 6), Emerson showed that he had become acquainted with Coleridge's important chapters on theory, law and method, in *The Friend*——keys to Coleridge's and his own Transcendentalism.[220a] On July 15, Emerson remarked that there was nothing more true than that "spiritual things must be spiritually discerned."[221] Two days later, in "Spiritual Discernment," he again developed his favorite Coleridgean themes, emphasizing the fact that *faith* is spiritual perception——is spiritual sight or insight.[222] (This sermon he preached sixteen times!) On July 21,[223] he illustrated the "moral sublime"[224] by a passage in *Othello* to which Coleridge had called his attention,[225] and applied to all such lofty utterances the words which Coleridge had written in describing Wordsworth's early prose: *Non verba sed tonitrua audio.*[226] On July 24, he preached on "We Are Not Our Own," the theme of which Coleridge had made so much: "Thou bearest not the root, but the root thee."[227] Five days later, in a long passage in his journals, he again explored the *Aids*, declared the distrust of Reason to be suicidal, and indicated clearly that dependence on *it* was what he meant by "self-reliance" or "self-trust." "To think is to receive;" and "to reflect is to receive truth immediately."[228] On the last day of the month, in "The Limits of Self-Reliance,"[229] he seems to have felt obliged to answer those who misunderstood his doctrine. He clearly indicated that the thesis rested on the meaning of the word "self" ——on the "self" not made by man. He declared that the *origin* of man's

---

[217] A modification of Xenophanes' observation that all things were rushing back to unity. See Gérando, *Histoire* (1822), I, 460, and chap. I of the present work. See *Nature*, 54.15-18 and Emerson's poem, "Xenophanes," *Works*, IX, pp. 137, 449. The poem is dated Concord, 1834. Xenophanes appears frequently in the *Journals*: II, 343, 398; III, 310; IV, 21.

[218] See ¶s. 11, 12, 16, 157 end, 166 end, 171 end, 184, 185, 254, 258.

[219] This is the correct reading of the MS.

[220] Compare line 32. For an excellent commentary see ¶ 167.

[220a] See *Journals*, II, 400. Emerson announced that when one discovers a fundamental law, it automatically classifies all pertinent facts, and a person thereafter does not need to collect further instances. He cited Kepler's Law as an example. See ¶s. 127ff. For passages on Kepler, see *The Friend* in *Works* (Shedd), II, 432-433 footnote, and the "Conclusion" of *Aids*. See also under May 3, 1834, *infra*, and esp. ¶ 254 end.

[221] See *Journals*, II, 404. Cf. ¶ 194.

[222] See *Y E S*, 250.28ff. For parallels on "faith" in Coleridge, see ¶s. 36 end, 190-191, 209, 241, 251, 301.

[223] *Journals*, II, 405.

[224] See ¶s. 296-297.

[225] See *The Friend* [*Works* (Shedd), II], 285.

[226] See ¶ 107.

[227] See *Y E S*, 268.43. Cf. ¶s. 11-13, 104, 157, 184, 198. See *Nature*, 34.17-18.

[228] See *Journals*, II, 409-410. Cf. ¶ 177.

[229] See *Y E S*, 268.45; 237.47ff. He may also have profited by Coleridge's criticism of Rousseau in ¶s. 89-95.

higher nature had always to be kept in mind——that man was *not his own*——that we do not bear the root, but the root bears us. To think otherwise was to inflame pride and invite mental and spiritual darkness.

On August 15,[230] he drew upon Coleridge's idealism[231] for the motif of the "transparency" of the phenomenal world——a motif which was to reappear in *Nature*.[232] All things, he believed, revealed their "reason" within themselves.[233] On September 11, in "A Future Life," he revived a theme which he had used a year earlier.[234] On November 18, he commended Wordsworth's "Happy Warrior" by repeating Coleridge's tribute in Latin.[235] On December 3, he characterized wisdom and ignorance respectively as *insight* and *outward sight*——a variation of his "look within" philosophy.[236] In "The Choice of Theisms" (December 4), he recommended the habit of reflection as a means of making the overworked phrase, "faith in God," meaningful,[237] and again suggested that too often men were strangers *to themselves*.[238]

1832

It is clear, indeed, that the larger outlines of Emerson's philosophy were complete in 1831. During the following year, he read widely rather than deeply, and his sermons, on the whole, show little new development beyond a wrestling with himself in the attempt to bring his own life under the full sway of his theories. On January 15, he defined *religion* as self-respect or doing oneself no harm.[239] On May 13, in "Thinking Well of Human Nature," he said Divine Providence had honored the human form and that men should, therefore, respect it in each other. Every individual soul has worth, infinitude and capacity for virtue.[240] On June 10, in "A Living Religion," he followed the implications of *The Statesman's Manual* and included the "Book of Nature" in God's revelation of himself. He frowned upon a faith recorded only in a Bible, and demanded a religion that should flow from all things.[241] Finally, in "The Genuine Man," delivered on October 21, the day on which he severed all connections with the Second Church,[242] he attempted to justify the steps which he had taken by reiterating themes from the *Aids*, which had so long nourished him: There is a man within us greater than that which acts without.[243] This is the Reason,[244] and it can be observed to speak through the man of genuine

---

[230] *Journals*, II, 410.

[231] See ¶s. 167, 254.

[232] See *Nature*, 13.5, 43.11, 62.17, 91.10.

[233] Apparently a modification of Coleridge's "truths that are their own evidence." See ¶s. 2, 233, 250. Cf. the thought of "Rhodora." See *Journals*, II, 411.

[234] See under Nov. 21, 1830.

[235] *Journals*, II, 429-430. See under July 21, *supra*.

[236] *Journals*, II, 434-435.

[237] *Y E S*, 158.18ff. Cf. ¶s. 173-174.

[238] See ¶s. 175-177.

[239] *Y E S*, 269.35.

[240] *Y E S*, xxi.17ff., 221.43ff., 270.20. Cf. ¶s. 158-159, 198, 253, 263. See also *The Friend* [*Works* (Shedd), II], 99: "We are bad ourselves, because we despair of the goodness of others." (Again: *Quantum sumus, scimus*.)

[241] See *Y E S*, xxxv.25ff. Coleridge's treatment of the Bible had profound influence on Emerson, and the following sections cannot be too carefully read: ¶s. 245-246, 250-254, 256-262, 264-266.

[242] *Y E S*, 180-190, xv.9.

[243] *Y E S*, 181.5ff.

[244] *Y E S*, 186.20.

worth. The genuine man ignores the external trappings of society and reverences his true nature——his higher self——God's image and likeness within.[245] The voice of supreme, universal Reason, though common to all men, is not yours or mine, but belongs to the Infinite——is the Infinite in the flesh.[246] The secret of true greatness lies in believing in the sovereignty of this inner voice——God's voice——and in accepting it as one's rightful leader.[247] The more one trusts it, the more trustworthy it becomes. In other words, the humble follower of God's guidance will be able to cast all responsibility for his words, his actions, and their consequences upon God himself, and walk henceforth in peace.[248] Following a distinction set forth in *The Friend*, Emerson made his genuine man go beyond mere literal truth in his utterance and speak *in the spirit of truth*.[249] On December 22 or 25,[250] the young clergyman sailed for Europe, and Coleridge was among those whom he wished most to see on the other side.

1 8 3 3

Frederic Henry Hedge's review of Coleridge's works, together with a synopsis of German metaphysics, appeared in March, and Emerson read it enthusiastically——in the fall, after his return from England.[251] In the meantime, on July 11, while in Paris, he pledged himself (following Coleridge) to "demonstrate that all necessary truth is its own evidence; that no doctrine of God need appeal to a book;" and that, since the stress of Christianity is upon moral truth, "it is a rule *of life*, not a rule of faith."[252] On August 5, he spent an hour with Coleridge at Highgate, and has preserved the record of his visit in *English Traits*.[253] Of chief importance in the interview, from our standpoint, is Emerson's inquiry about the passage from the Independent's pamphlet, set forth in the last part of *The Friend*. He declared the thought to be excellent and expressed the wish to see the entire work, for it dealt with his favorite themes: love of truth for its own sake,[254] self-reliance, greatness of a man who stands against the world, "what we have within that only can we see without," the integrity of man, the "spark of God" within all men, compensation, immediate retribution, perils of self-interest, "like only can know like," peace through enlarging one's soul, and the truth that Christians are kings and lords.[255] Coleridge did not, however, put the work into his hands.[256] On September 1, at Liverpool, Emerson wrote of his indebtedness to the works of Coleridge, Landor, Carlyle and Wordsworth, but indicated that he found the persons themselves deficient. They possessed, he said, no idea of the particular species of moral truth which he called the "first philoso-

---

[245] *Y E S*, 182.22ff.
[246] *Y E S*, 186.18ff.
[247] *Y E S*, 184.4ff.; 186.30ff.
[248] *Y E S*, 188.12ff. This last idea is also strongly Swedenborgian.
[249] See ¶s. 77-80. Cf. *Y E S*, 186.33ff.
[250] *Letters*, I, 360. Cf. *Journals*, III, 3.
[251] This has been reprinted in vol. II. See *Letters*, I, 402.
[252] *Journals*, III, 160. Cf. ¶s. 2, 205, 252, 301.
[253] *Works*, V, 10-14.
[254] See Index-Concordances, *s.v.*
[255] See ¶s. 110-115.
[256] Coleridge said the title was "A Protest of One of the Independents" or something to that effect. I have been unable to find such a book listed among the Thomason Tracts in the B.M. and cannot verify S.T.C's remarks or learn to what extent he "filtered it."

phy."[257] Coleridge's ideas, however, continued to inspire him. On September 8, he wrote that the purpose of life seemed to be self-knowledge and that man is "to live in the real future by living to the real present. The highest revelation is that God is in every man."[258] He arrived in New York on October 7,[259] and four days later wrote from Boston asking William to secure the July issue of *Fraser's Magazine*, which he had inadvertently left on the boat. It contained, he said, an excellent engraving of Coleridge which he did not wish to lose. On October 27, a year and one week after his final sermon as pastor of the Second Church, he returned to his old congregation and preached what to them must have been a familiar message, but in it there was an unusually strong note of optimism and conviction; it was delivered by one who had found himself and who knew that henceforth the inner voice would be all-sufficient for his greatest needs :[260]

There is a solemn interest settling upon the future which may well withdraw our interest from what is already around us, were it far more excellent. The dawn is reddening around us, but the day has not come.[261] The Teacher is teaching but has not finished his word.[262] That word never will be finished. It was before the heavens and shall be after them. But a part of this message is spoken this day and every day. There are truths now being revealed. There is a revolution of religious opinion taking effect around us as it seems to me the greatest of all revolutions which have ever occurred that, namely, which has separated the individual from the whole world and made him demand a faith satisfactory to his own proper nature, whose full extent he now for the first time contemplates. A little while ago men were supposed to be saved or lost as one race; Adam was the federal head[263] and, in books of theology, his sin was a federal sin which cut off the hopes of all his posterity. The atoning blood of Christ, again, was a sacrifice for all, by which the divine vengeance was averted from you and me. But now, men have begun to feel and to inquire for their *several stake* in the joy and the suffering of the whole. What is *my* relation to Almighty God? What is *my* relation to my fellow man? What am I designed for? What are my duties? What is my destiny?——The soul peremptorily asks these questions——the Whence and the Why——and refuses to be put off with insufficient answers. It is because so many false answers have been offered that in many earnest well-intentioned men, reason has been so far shaken from her seat, that they have assorted with the infidel and the atheist so called. The questions are now again presented, because the wonder of the surrounding creation begins to press upon the soul with the force of a personal address. And what is the answer?[264]

Man begins to hear a voice in reply that fills the heavens and the earth, saying, that God is within him,[265] that *there* is the celestial host. I find that this amazing revelation of my immediate relation to God, is a solution to all the doubts[266] that oppressed me. I recognize the distinction of the outer and the inner self——of the double consciousness—as in the familiar example, that I may do things which I do not approve; that is, there are two selfs, one which does or approves that which the other does not and approves not; or within this erring passionate mortal self, sits a supreme calm immortal mind, whose powers I do not know, but it is stronger than I am, it is wiser than I am, it never approved me in any wrong. I seek counsel of it in my doubts; I repair to it

[257] See *Journals*, III, 185-186.
[258] See *Journals*, III, 201. Cf. ¶s. 173ff., 254, 275 *et passim*.
[259] *Letters*, I, 396.
[260] See "Religion and Society," *Y E S*, 199-201.
[261] See the conclusion of Sampson Reed's "Oration on Genius," in vol. II, p. 11.
[262] On the need for a great teacher, see the letter of *Mathetes* in *The Friend* [*Works* (Shedd), II], 347-358.
[263] Coleridge was in no sense fundamentalistic in his treatment of Adam. See ¶s. 221-224.
[264] See *Nature*, 6.4-12.
[265] This paragraph is an echo of the poem "Γνωθι Σεαυτον," discussed above.
[266] See the excerpts from *Wallenstein*, ¶ I *supra*. See *Nature*, 6.4-16.

in my dangers; I pray to it in my undertakings. It is the door of my access to the Father. It seems to me the face which the Creator uncovers to his child.

It is the perception of this depth in human nature——this infinitude[267] belonging to every man that has been born——which has given new value to the habits of reflexion and solitude.[268] This has caused the virtue of independent judgment to be so much praised. This has given its odour to spiritual interpretations. Many old and almost forgotten maxims have been remembered up from where they lay in the dust of centuries and are seen to beam new light. Such are the old pregnant maxims, 'Know Thyself'; Est deus in nobis, agitante calescimus illo;[268a] the Stoical precept, 'The good Man differs from God in nothing but duration,' Bonus Vir nil nisi tempore a deo differt;[269] the inscription on the gate of Athens, 'But know thyself a man and be a God'; 'Revere Thyself.'

And let me add that in this doctrine as deeply felt by him, is the key by which the words that fell from Christ upon the character of God can alone be well and truly explained. Read by the torch of this faith, it seems to me, those discourses shine with heavenly meaning. The Father is in me——I in the Father. Yet the Father is greater than I.[270]

I anticipate auspicious effects from the farther opening of this faith upon the public mind, from the studies and the actings of good men in the course wherein its light will lead them. It will be inspiration to prophets and heroes. It will be day without night. It will be power to the hands and wisdom to the understanding and society to the solitary. In a particular manner will not the increased clearness of the spiritual sight produce a great reform in the tone and character of our public religious teaching? Will it not put an end to all that is technical, allegorical, parabolical in it?

On November 5, in his introductory lecture before the Boston Society of Natural History ("Uses of Natural History"),[271] he remarked how the study of nature helps man to self-knowledge by reason of the identity of subject and object——that is, because of the correspondence between the outward world of nature and the inward world of thought and emotion. Nature unlocks the truth within us and helps us interpret what would otherwise remain unconscious knowledge.[272] Attempting to understand itself and to perceive man's true place in the system of being, the mind asks questions; and all these the external world answers——but in hieroglyphics.[273] All minerals and plants have a relation to man, and if rightly understood, they would explain a corresponding secret in him.

1834

It was probably during 1834 that Emerson purchased for his library the copy of the *Biographia Literaria* which is now in Concord.[274] On January 6, in his Franklin Lecture "On the Relation of Man to the Globe,"[275] he observed that long before the human being appeared on our planet, the lower forms of life had prepared for his coming by trying to produce him in themselves;[276] that not only was there a relation of *usefulness* between

---

[267] See note 240 above.
[268] This paragraph echoes the introductory section of *Aids*. See ¶s. 173-182.
[268a] Found in Victor Cousin, *Introd. to the History of Philosophy*, Boston, 1832, p. 165. The quotation is originally from Ovid's *Fasti*, Bk. VI, lines 5-6.
[269] See also *Y E S*, xxiii-xxiv, for the use of this quotation in another sermon.
[270] John 14:11; 17:21; 14:28.
[271] At the Masonic Temple. See Cabot, *Memoir*, I, 223-224, 227; II, 710-711.
[272] Cf. ¶s. 67-70, 135, 256, 260, 290. See *Nature*, 44.20—45.12.
[273] See ¶ 258. Cf. *Nature*, 6.4-16.
[274] *Biographia Literaria*, (2 vols.) N.Y., 1834. Emerson has marked and indexed his copy.
[275] Cabot, *Memoir*, I, 223-224; II, 711.   [276] See ¶s. 225 and 152.

the world and man, but, significantly, one of *beauty* also.[277] On February 1, he may have referred to Coleridge's distinction between *cultivation* and *civilization*.[278] On May 3, he recorded at length his approval of the important chapters on *theory* and *method* set forth in the last part of *The Friend*[279]——chapters from which, during subsequent months, he was to draw dozens of ideas and lustres, and in which, ultimately, he discovered the method which he followed in writing *Nature* (1836) :[280] Men have not yet seized the "Idea" that explains the universe; they fail to see the harmony of all things. Natural science encourages merely arbitrary classification and omits philosophical method, which alone can discover systems of permanent value. We must look beyond details and find the pure, plastic *Idea,* which will integrate particulars. That Idea will be the true theory of animated nature. It will be the true classification. Plato's dialogues are valuable chiefly because they are concerned primarily with unfolding an idea rather than conveying facts. Once the idea is seized in a science, additional facts find their places automatically——for they have been predicted. When will botany yield to such a principle of classification and go beyond counting stamens? A true method is not an enumeration of particulars or the ordering of successive points. It carries its evidence *in itself*——is brief and complete——is its own apologetic. At present, natural history cannot assume that its theory has been attained. It is merely full of tendency. Four days later (May 7) these thoughts entered into his lecture on "The Naturalist," delivered in Boston.[281] In addition to the points already mentioned were the following : Natural history shows man in the center of the world with rays of relation extending from him to all things.[282] The study of external nature is a discipline that sharpens the powers of discrimination and enables one to distinguish between the *similar* and the *same*.[283] He concluded by emphasizing the necessity for the marriage of mind and nature——for an awareness of the identity of subject and object——in order that nature might fulfill her purpose of instructing man and that man might become fruitful through self-knowledge.[284] On May 31, Emerson wrote enthusiastically to his brother Edward, stressing the usefulness of Coleridge's view of the Understanding and the Reason :[285]

Philosophy affirms that the outward world is only phenomenal & the whole concern of dinners of tailors of gigs of balls whereof men make such account is a quite relative & temporary one—an intricate dream——the exhalation of the present state of the Soul—wherein the Understanding works incessantly as if it were real but the eternal Reason when now & then he is allowed to speak declares it is an accident a smoke nowise related to his permanent attributes. Now that I have used the words, let me ask you do you draw the distinction of Milton Coleridge & the Germans between Reason & Understanding. I think it a philosophy itself. & like all truth very practical.[286] So now lay away the letter & take up the following dissertation on Sunday. Reason is

[277] See ¶s. 158 and 257. See *Y E S*, 43.29——44.6. See chap. III ("Beauty") in *Nature.*
[278] *Journals*, III, 253. Cf. ¶s. 146, 149.
[279] See *Journals*, III, 292-296, and ¶s. 127-147; 253. See also under July 6, 1831.
[280] See *Nature*, 6.14-20; 35.5——36.20; 56.1ff.; 68.21——70.3; 82.8——84.21; 92.23.
[281] See Cabot, *Memoir*, I, 224-227; II, 712.
[282] See ¶s. 87a, 152, 155, 158-159, 288.
[283] See ¶ 300 and under date of Nov. 10, 1830. This discipline in the perception of differences was developed in *Nature*, 47.1-19; 48.14——49.16.
[284] See note 272. Cf. *Nature*, 46.19; 91.20.
[285] See *Letters*, I, 412-413. Cf. ¶s. 1-56.   [286] See *Nature*, 7.1-2; 82.4-5.

the highest faculty of the soul—what we mean often by the soul itself; it never *reasons*, never proves, it simply perceives; it is vision. The Understanding toils all the time, compares, contrives, adds, argues, near sighted but strong-sighted, dwelling in the present the expedient the customary. Beasts have some understanding but no Reason. Reason is potentially perfect in every man—Understanding in very different degrees of strength. The thoughts of youth, & 'first thoughts,' are the revelations of Reason. the love of the beautiful & of Goodness as the highest beauty the belief in the absolute & universal superiority of the Right & the True   But understanding that wrinkled calculator the steward of our house to whom is committed the support of our animal life contradicts evermore these affirmations of Reason & points at Custom & Interest & persuades one man that the declarations of Reason are false & another that they are at least impracticable. Yet by & by after having denied our Master we come back to see at the end of years or of life that he was the Truth. . . . The manifold applications of the distinction to Literature to the Church to Life will show how good a key it is. So hallelujah to the Reason forevermore.

On June 20, he improvised on the same theme and manifested ability to use the distinction in speculation and to express it in his own colorful idiom:[287]

It occurred that the gestures of the Reason are graceful and majestic, those of the Understanding quick and mean. The uplifted eye of Memory, the solemn pace, perfect repose, and simple attitudes of Meditation inspire respect, but the moment the senses call us back, and the Understanding directs us, we run, start, look askance, or turn and look behind us, we skulk, fumble, exceed in manner and voice, and suffer. Live by reason, and you will not make the foul mouths, nor utter the foul breath nor drag disgracefully sleepy days that convince Alexander that he is mortal. When Minerva, they say, saw her distorted face in a brook, she threw away her hautboy.

On August 17, he considered Scott and Coleridge to be professors of the art of poetry, but not true poets.[288] Ten days later he spoke of the *general mind*——of the universal man that speaks with complete indifference as to its mouthpiece.[289] On September 7, *The Friend*[290] supplied him with the theme for his sermon, "The Miracle of our Being,"[291] the thoughts of which point toward *Nature*. He began by drawing upon his earlier lectures ——condemning the kind of knowledge that limits itself to mere categories of facts and that fails to see the wonder *within* as well as without us.[292] He admitted, with Coleridge, that we have animal wants and that "commerce" springs naturally from them; yet the fact that some never recognize the higher wants of spiritual beings——never see that there is something extraordinary in life——this distressed him.[293] Reflection——self-knowledge——these alone can save a man from his brutishness by making him aware of the wonder of his condition. Only when awake to his better self will he adore; only then will he be aware of truth and virtue——the double office of the Reason; only then will he find contentment with his lot in life and escape from the limitations of the finite to breathe immortal breath.[294] Emerson then discussed the infinite number of relations existing among things, each of which is a microcosm.[295] How much more wonderful

---

[287] *Journals*, III, 310-311.   [288] *Journals*, III, 328.
[289] *Journals*, III, 329. See ¶s. 90, 142. Cf. *Nature*, 87.13.
[290] See ¶ 87a.
[291] *Y E S*, 203-212.
[292] *Y E S*, 204-205. Cf. ¶s. 126, 156, 165, 196-197.
[293] *Y E S*, 206. Cf. ¶s. 150-152.
[294] *Y E S*, 207. Cf. ¶s. 167-170. See *Nature*, 80.1-8.
[295] Cf. ¶s. 156, 159, 253, 257, 258. See *Nature*, 54.12—56.14; 60.2ff.

is man, who stands on the summit of organized nature——at its very heart![296] He has a perfect world within his reach——the Divine Reason ——whatever may be his trade or condition.[297] The laws of the spiritual or moral universe he learns by exercising his volition—by acting and then observing the results.[298] Judgment on his behavior is instantaneous—— swifter than lightning.[299] He gives to the external world the hue of his own thought.[300] When he yields his will to the Divine Will and opens himself to the spiritual world within (*i.e.,* to the Divine Reason), eternal laws become known to him. Heaven begins in his very soul. His heart is dilated with God's spirit.[301] For when man yields to the empire of Reason, his Understanding is brought into the service of his soul and ennobled. He comes to regard his troubles, sicknesses or handicaps as mere trifles, for the Spirit transforms everything into benefits.[302] Like St. Augustine, the spiritual man will let others wrangle while he stands apart enchanted or in a state of wonder.[303]

On September 14, Emerson stated Coleridge's view of the will as "the doctrine of infallible guidance if one will abdicate choice." He defined it further as "striving to act unconsciously, to resume the simplicity of childhood," and to act without regard to selfish advantages or personal relations.[304] The following day he translated the parabolic language of Dr. George Washington Blagden into Coleridge's terms. Instead of St. Paul's expressions, "carnal mind" and "spiritual mind," which are ever in conflict, he preferred substituting respectively the *Understanding* and the *Reason*.[305] On October 14, he withdrew Coleridge's *On the Constitution of Church and State* (1830) from the Boston Athenæum and kept it nearly three months![306] In the appendix of this work Coleridge had attempted to refute Isaac Taylor's opinion that God found it expedient to conceal himself from men. Coleridge declared that God was neither remote from man nor separated from him by history, by a Bible or by anything else. Rather, He was *immediately* present and within reach of everyone.[307] On October

---

[296] *Y E S*, 208.16ff.; 209.16ff. See note 282 and ¶ 288. Cf. *Nature*, 35.11-14; 84.15-21.

[297] See *Y E S*, 208.29ff; 209.1ff.; ¶s. 1ff.; *Nature*, 25.6-15; 94.3ff.

[298] *Y E S*, 209.29ff. For Coleridge on *action*, see ¶s. 174, 200, 205, 244, 253. On the discovery of truth through action, see *Nature*, 5.14, 6.11, 25.6-8, 47.18, 56.19, 93.8-10. On the exercise of the will in extending one's power or dominion, see *Nature*, 25.6-15, 38.1-8, 45.9-12, 50.13—51.9, 80.3-15, 89.6—91.4. For some of Emerson's sources in Coleridge for the doctrine of the will, see ¶s. 22ff., 100, 148, 166, 183, 192-194, 196, 200, 217, 218, 221, 261, 272, 277, 282.

[299] *Y E S*, 210.1ff. See note 202.   [300] *Y E S*, 210.5ff. See note 182.

[301] *Y E S*, 210.14ff. See ¶s. 1-56. On yielding one's will to the Divine Will, see *Nature*, 50.14-16; 92.6-11; 93.18-19. On the dilated spirit, see *Nature*, 13.5-13, 43.11-12, 62.15-22, 90.18—91.4, 95.2-7.

[302] *Y E S*, 210.24ff. Cf. *Nature*, 12.23ff., 75.6-14, 95.7, and the Index-Concordance under "Understanding." See ¶ 169.

[303] *Y E S*, 204.34. In a letter to his Aunt Mary, dated Aug. 1, 1826 (*Letters*, I, 170), Emerson paraphrased this quotation of St. Augustine, which he probably had discovered in his reading at the Divinity School: "Others laugh, weep, sell, or proselyte. I admire." Another reference appears in *Journals*, II, 304 (Aug. 28, 1830): "*Alii disputent, ego mirabor,* said Augustine. It shall be my speech to the Calvinist and the Unitarian." See also "Thoughts on Modern Literature," contributed to *The Dial* in Oct., 1840 (*Works*, XII, 327): "Wrangle who pleases, I will wonder." Cf. *Nature*, 74.20ff.

[304] *Journals*, III, 337-338. For Coleridge on the child, see ¶s. 71, 122a, 226. For the sense of novelty and wonder which is possessed by children and by men of genius— those who "feel the riddle of the world," see ¶s. 75, 122a, 126, 174, 218, 262. See *Nature*, 11.16-19; 74.20ff.; 89.8-10; 92.6-15.

[305] *Journals*, III, 340. See Romans 8:6-9.

[306] Until Jan. 5, 1835. See *Emerson's Reading*, 21, 65.   [307] See ¶s. 272-282.

27 and November 1, Emerson cited Euler on arches to illustrate how truth can be known by the Reason of a contemplative man and be denied by one dominated by the Understanding. He noted, moreover, that Coleridge was among those calling for a system of moral education and urged that men stop multiplying facts and begin to search out the underlying meanings of those already available.[308] On November 15, he read with pleasure Coleridge's letter in *The Literary Gazette* (of London) and resolved to follow his example and never speak or write for any occasion on topics which had not previously attracted his interest or deserved his meditation.[309] He also commented on the unhappy divorce of religion and philosophy.[310] Four days later he quoted Coleridge on Luther[311] and added that the German's literary achievements deserved the estimate of "material sublime" rather than "moral."[312] He also composed for his journal three lines of blank verse which, thereafter, he often inscribed in the albums of autograph hunters——lines which echo *Gnothi Seauton* and seem to convey the sentiments of the unknown Independent soldier, whom he greatly admired.[313] He recorded the hope that his degraded generation might yet rise up to new heights of genius, once the sleep of the Reason had ended.[314]

On November 26, he quoted the following from Coleridge's reply to Isaac Taylor: "The world in which I exist is another world indeed, but not to come."[315] On December 2, he again preferred the terms *Understanding* and *Reason* to the preacher's *natural man* and *God*. He also applied Coleridge's chief distinction to stages in the life of man: Adolescence, for example, he defined as a critical period of transition from unconscious to conscious living——a leaving behind of the protective Reason for the dominion of the near-sighted Understanding.[316] He was by this time applying the terms to all departments of life. On December 6, he read, to his Aunt Mary, Coleridge's defense of God's immediacy against Isaac Taylor's *Natural History of Enthusiasm*, and she approving it remarked that man's Reason was sufficiently distinct from the Universal Reason so that he could rightly pray to the latter, yet so joined with it that he could be certain of being heard.[317] Two days later, he recommended that Coleridge be considered as the subject for a course of lectures.[318] On December 9, he indicated that his doctrine of self-reliance was based upon Coleridge's doctrine of the Reason and that he subscribed to all the limitations and provisos which Coleridge had set forth against its perversion.[319] Take, for example, the vulgar man's bad logic——his boast that *his* opinion is as valuable as that of any other man:

---

[308] See *Journals*, III, 348-349, 356. See ¶s. 47, 137, 140, 229.
[309] *Journals*, III, 361. See ¶s. 283-285.
[310] *Journals*, III, 362. See ¶s. 132, 164, 172, 247.
[311] *Journals*, III, 367. See ¶ 98 end.
[312] See ¶s. 296-297.
[313] *Journals*, III, 368. See ¶ 110. See his visit to Coleridge, *supra*, under Aug. 5, 1833.
[314] *Journals*, III, 365. This is the optimistic note found in the last chap. of *Nature*.
[315] See ¶ 275 and footnote. Cf. *Journals*, III, 371.
[316] *Journals*, III, 376-377. See Wordsworth's *Ode*, lines 72ff.
[317] *Journals*, III, 383. See note 307.
[318] *Journals*, III, 386.
[319] *Journals*, III, 389-390. See ¶s. 1-56; 89-95. See above under July 31, 1831.

"Every man's Reason can show him what is right. Therefore every man says what is right, whether he use his Reason or no." I hate this fallacy the more that it is, beside being dire nonsense, a profanation of the dearest truths. Democracy, Freedom, has its root in the sacred truth that every man hath in him the divine Reason, or that, though few men since the creation of the world live according to the dictates of Reason, yet all men are created capable of so doing. That is the equality and the only equality of all men. To this truth we look when we say, Reverence thyself; Be true to thyself. Because every man has within him somewhat really divine, therefore is slavery the unpardonable outrage it is.

[Coleridge's] doctrine affirms that there is imparted to every man the Divine light of reason, sufficient not only to plant corn and grind wheat by, but also to illuminate all his life, his social, political, religious actions. Sufficient according to its faithful use. Sufficient, if faithfully used. The propositions are true to the end of the world, with this inseparable condition; Every man's Reason is sufficient for his guidance, *if used.*

On December 14, Emerson declared that his Reason and Understanding were good company for each other *in the woods.*[320] He apparently was still thinking of his dead wife. On December 20, his Reason was convinced of its own immortality, but "its down-looking brother, the Understanding," was not.[321] On December 22, he praised Coleridge for circulating many new truths[322] and spoke well of Coleridge's philosophy of *waiting*——the procedure whereby powers that cannot be exercised are stored up or "hived" for another occasion.[323] On December 23, he wrote that a single thought was only *one side* of Nature and that when stressed too much it became one of Bacon's Idols of the Cave.[324] On December 29, he listed some of the spiritual laws which the Reason approved but which seemed contradictory to the Understanding or the "common sense."[325]

Thus I should begin with my old saws, that nothing can be given; everything is sold; love compels love; hatred, hatred; action and reaction always are equal;[326] no evil in society but has its check which coexists; the moral, the physical, the social world is a *plenum,* and any flood in one place produces equal ebb in another; nothing is free but the will of man, and that only to procure his own virtue:[327] on every other side but that one he beats the air with his pompous action; that punishment not follows but accompanies crime.[328]

"Every truth," he added, "is a full circle"——a figure which he seems to have drawn from his study of astronomy, from Coleridge and from his general lustre reading.[329] Probably his last reference to the Understanding and Reason during 1834 concerned the irreconcilable philosophies of men. Consistent Epicureanism, he said, belonged to the realm of the Understanding; Stoicism, to that of the Reason. So, respectively, did the con-

---

[320] *Journals,* III, 392; 453. Cf. *Nature,* 12.22ff.
[321] *Journals,* III, 398.
[322] *Journals,* III, 405.
[323] *Journals,* III, 403. See ¶s. 108-109. For another reference to "hiving knowledge" see *Nature,* 48.10-13.
[324] *Journals,* III, 408-409. See ¶s. 141-142. Cf. *Nature,* 56.12-14.
[325] *Journals,* III, 423. Cf. ¶s. 44-56. See a similar list under Feb. 23, 1831.
[326] See ¶s. 219, 112, 253. Coleridge's discussion is more illuminating than Emerson's.
[327] Cf. *Y E S,* 4.14. See ¶s. 28, 30, 36, 86, 110, 222. See note 298.
[328] See note 202.
[329] *Journals,* I, 59-60; III, 422; and note 45 *supra.* The line just quoted may be, in part, an echo of *King Lear,* V.iii.176: "The wheel has come full circle." See *Wallenstein* excerpts above, ¶ A. Circles are prominent in the plates of Jacob Behmen's works, *q.v.* See index-concordances under such terms as: *radius, circuit, cycle, sphere, rings,* etc. A clear example appears in *Nature,* 56.7-14. See also paragraphs I-II of Emerson's "Statement of the First Philosophy" under June 10, 1835.

sistent sinner and the consistent saint.[330]

1835

On January 7, Emerson observed that all the religious enthusiasts owed their genius to the discovery that God must be found *within* and not without. Meditation or reflection, he said, was the key to wisdom; and the prerequisite of reflection was absolute submission of the will——both familiar Coleridgean themes.[331] On January 9, he conceived of prayer as the temporary subjugation of the Understanding to the Reason,[332] and wrote of the need for a theory that might interpret the great myths of the world, which are creations of the imagination and Reason of man. He was particularly interested in the account of Prometheus, whom he regarded as the Jesus of ancient legend.[333] On January 13, he commented on the vigorous contributions made to the English language by the great writers and the lazy acceptance of that same mother tongue by his contemporaries. His generation did not think. As Coleridge expressed the fact, language was made *to think for it.*[334] On January 23, he remarked that Carlyle had become the foremost thinker of the age, now that Coleridge was dead.[335] On February 2, he copied Coleridge's famous line into his blotting book: "Nothing great was ever achieved without enthusiasm."[336] In his lecture, "Michael Angelo," delivered on February 5, he noted that the ancient Greeks called the world *kosmos* or beauty,[337] and that the Italian artists assigned the phrase *il piu nell' uno* (the *many in one* or *multitude in unity*) to the "standard of beauty"——the "beauty of the whole."[338] On February 12, he lectured on "Martin Luther" and seems to have found Coleridge's criticism useful in estimating the reformer's genius.[339] On or about March 4, he lent his copy of the important third volume of *The Friend* to Mrs. Bliss (Elizabeth Davis Bancroft).[340] Writing to Carlyle on March 12, he implied that Coleridge had aroused a group of minds and that Transcendentalism was about to burst into life:[341]

---

[330] *Journals*, III, 426-427.

[331] *Journals*, III, 432.

[332] *Journals*, III, 435. See ¶ 257 end. See *Nature*, 92.1-11.

[333] See *Journals*, III, 435, augmented by *Works*, II, 30-31 (orig. a part of the journal of this date). He had apparently just read Coleridge's "On the Prometheus of Æschylus," *Works* (Shedd), IV, 344-365, first pub. in 1825 and rptd. in *Transac. Royal Soc. of Lit.*, II, 1834. See also *Aids* (1829), 171, 243. See section VII of his "Statement of the First Philosophy," under June 10, 1835.

[334] *Journals*, III, 439. Cf. ¶ 56a, and *Nature*, 37.1—39.20.

[335] *Letters*, I, 432. Coleridge had died six months earlier, on July 25, 1834.

[336] *Journals*, III, 447. Cf. ¶ 245. See *Works*, II, 321.

[337] See *Works*, XII, 216. *Aids* (1913), 217-218: ". . . it was necessary, that God should be *manifested in the flesh*, that the Eternal Word, through whom and by whom the world (κοσμος, the order, beauty, and sustaining law of visible natures) *was* and *is*, should be made flesh, assume our humanity personally etc." See *Journals*, II, 340; III, 477. See *Nature*, 19.5.

[338] See *Works*, XII, 218. Cf. ¶s. 62, 291a; *Nature*, 30.1-5, and *Journals*, IV, 7.

[339] See Cabot, *Memoir*, II, 713, and essays I-II of the First Landing Place in *The Friend* [*Works* (Shedd), II], 121-131. Cf. ¶s. 97-98, and under Nov. 19, 1834, *supra*. See *Journals*, III, 367.

[340] *Letters*, I, 440.

[341] *Carlyle-Emerson Correspondence*, I, 48, 50-51. I believe that the term "Transcendentalism" sprang from the term *Transcendental* and *Transcendentalist*, as used here and in chap. XII of *Biographia Literaria*. See chap. VI of the present work, footnote 293. Cf. *Journals*, III, 272, for the phrase "on the brink."

[Dr. Channing] lay awake all night, he told my friend last week, because he had learned in the evening that some young men proposed to issue a journal, to be called *The Transcendentalist*, as the organ of a spiritual philosophy. . . . [W]e aspire to have a work on the First Philosophy in Boston. I hope, or wish rather. Those that are forward in it debate upon the name. I doubt not in the least its reception if the material that should fill it existed. Through the thickest understanding will the reason throw itself instantly into relation with the truth that is its object, whenever that appears. But how seldom is the pure loadstone produced! Faith and love are apt to be spasmodic in the best minds. Men live on the brink of mysteries and harmonies into which yet they never enter, and with their hand on the door-latch they die outside.

On March 19, he called the Understanding a rebellious and incorrigible liar and declared that a person is not consistently truthful beyond two minutes at a stretch.[342] On April 10, he quoted Coleridge on "poetic genius" and on the ability of the poet to write well about himself.[343] Two days later he indicated that Coleridge was being quoted in Boston pulpits.[344] On April 16, he wrote:[345]

Why must always the philosopher mince his words and fatigue us with explanation? He speaks from the Reason, and being, of course, contradicted word for word by the Understanding, he stops like a cog-wheel at every notch to explain. Let him say, *I idealize*, and let that be once for all; or, *I sensualize*, and then the Rationalist may stop his ears. Empedocles said bravely, "I am God; I am immortal; I contemn human affairs"; and all men hated him.

On May 9, he paraphrased a line from the lecture on the "General Character of the Gothic Mind in the Middle Ages:" "A Gothic Church," said Coleridge, "is a petrified religion."[346] Two days later, he echoed Coleridge on "genius."[347] On May 13, he spoke of the desirability of having a rule that would enable the mind at any moment *to east itself*——to escape from the Understanding and from error into the spiritual vision of the Reason, for "not in his goals but in his transition man is great."[348] On June 4, he wrote:[349]

Heaven is the name we give to the True State, the world of Reason, not of the Understanding; of the Real, not the Apparent. It exists always, whether it is ever to be separated from the Hell or not. It is, as Coleridge said, another world, but not to come.[350] The world I describe is that, where only the laws of mind are known;[351] the only economy of time is saying and doing nothing untrue to self.

On or about June 10, Emerson set down an outline of the "First Philosophy," built firmly upon Coleridge's foundation, but enriched with a strong emphasis on practical virtue, which note, stressed in the works of Sampson Reed, Emerson had made his own.[352] He had praised and sought after virtue since childhood, he had extolled Milton for holding to that ideal, he had preached about it in his sermons, he had missed it in the English thinkers whom he had visited, and now he announced it as the chief glory

[342] *Journals*, III, 455.   [344] *Journals*, III, 466.
[343] *Journals*, III, 463-464. Cf. ¶ 56b.   [345] *Journals*, III, 467.
[346] *Typescript Journals*, "B," Part I, p. 37. See ¶ 298 and *Nature*, 55.9.
[347] See *Journals*, III, 474. Cf. ¶s. 56a, 122a, 126, 288.
[348] *Journals*, III, 476-477. For the origin of the term *east*, see ¶ 147 end. Cf. also Wordsworth's *Ode*, line 72: "The Youth, who daily from the east must travel. . . ."
[349] *Journals*, III, 488. The "heaven" and the "hell" in each man are Swedenborgian concepts. See Swedenborg ¶s. 8-10, 29-30; Sampson Reed ¶s. 58, 60-62, 27, 29-32.
[350] See ¶ 275. See above under dates: Oct. 14, Nov. 26, Dec. 6, 1834.
[351] See ¶s. 9, 18, 76, 145, 231, 270.   [352] See above under date of Sept. 1, 1833.

of his spiritual universe. The bent of his thought, therefore, was to be ethical and religious rather than strictly philosophic, and it is to his lofty moral tone as well as to his literary ability that one must attribute his high rank in the history of American letters. The following statement deserves careful study, for like a *Janus bifaced* it looks back over the preceding six years of earnest reflection, and forward to *Nature* and the great *Essays*.

A STATEMENT OF THE FIRST PHILOSOPHY[353]
By RALPH WALDO EMERSON

I

I endeavor to announce the laws of the First Philosophy. It is the mark of these that their enunciation awakens the feeling of the moral sublime,[354] and great men are they who believe in them. Every one of these propositions resembles a great circle in astronomy.[355] No matter in what direction it be drawn, it contains the whole sphere. So each of these seems to imply all truth. Compare a page of Bacon with Swift, Chesterfield, *Lacon*,[355a] and see the difference of great and less circles. These are gleams of a world in which we do not live: they astonish the understanding.[356]

II

The *first* Philosophy, that of mind,[357] is the science of what *is*,[358] in distinction from what *appears*. It is one mark of its laws that their enunciation awakens the feeling of the moral sublime, and *great men* are they who believe in them. They resemble great circles in astronomy, each of which, in what direction soever it be drawn, contains the whole sphere. So each of these seems to imply all truth. These laws are Ideas of the Reason, and so are obeyed easier than expressed.[359] They astonish the Understanding, and seem to it gleams[360] of a world in which we do not live.

III

Our compound nature differences us from God, but our Reason is not to be distinguished from the divine Essence.[361] We have yet devised no words to designate the attributes of God which can adequately stand for the universality and perfection of our own intuitions.[362] To call the Reason "ours"[363] or "Human" seems an impertinence, so absolute and unconfined it is. The best we can say of God, we mean of mind as it is

[353] The dating of some of the following sections in the printed *Journals* is incorrect. The locations of all the parts are as follows: Pt. I: *Journals*, III, 489-490; Pt. II: *Ibid.*, III, 235; Pt. III: *Ibid.*, III, 235-236 (Much of this section was originally composed, it seems, on Aug. 19, 1832. *Ibid.*, II, 508-509); Pt. IV: *Typescript Journals*, Cabot's R. O. Pocket Notebook, p. 4; Pt. V: *Ibid.*, pp. 5-6; Pt. VI: *Ibid.*, p. 6; Pt. VII: *Ibid.*, p. 7; Pt. VIII: *Journals*, III, 236; IX: *Typescript Journals* (as above), p. 8; Pt. X: *Journals*, III, 236-237; Pt. XI: *Ibid.*, III, 237; Pt. XII: *Ibid.*, III, 237-238—cf. 458; Pt. XIII: *Ibid.*, III, 239; Pt. XIV: *Ibid.*, III, 239-240. The first two sections are really different versions of the same introduction.
[354] See ¶s. 296-297.
[355] See note 329 and *Nature*, 56.7-14.
[355a] Charles Caleb Colton, *Lacon: or Many Things in Few Words*. Many editions. One appeared in 2 vols., Phila., 1824 (from the 8th London edition). See *Journals*, III, 489, 544.
[356] See ¶s. 37-56.
[357] See ¶ 216.
[358] The *real* world is the Ideal world, not the phenomenal. See ¶s. 19, 156-157, 164, 198, 251, 260. Cf. *Nature*, 49.21; 59.3 *et passim*.   [360] See *Nature*, 90.5.
[359] See ¶s. 145, 231, 270. Cf. *Nature*, 68.23.   [361] See ¶ 19.
[362] On the difficulty of determining attributes, see ¶s. 8, 9, 15, 16, 157. On the intuition, see ¶s. 15, 198, 245, 246, 250, 263, 265.   [363] See ¶s. 10-13, and *Nature*, 34.13-19.

known to us. Thus when you say,

"The gods approve
The depth, but not the tumult of the soul
(A fervent, not ungovernable love),"[364]

the sublime in the sentiment is, that to the soul itself depth,[365] not tumult, is desirable. When you say (Socrates said it), "Jupiter prefers integrity to charity," your finest meaning is the "soul prefers," etc. When Jesus saith, "Who giveth one of these little ones a cup of cold water shall not lose his reward," is not the best meaning the love at which the giver has arrived? And so on throughout the New Testament there is not a volition attributed to God considered as the external cause but gains in truth and dignity by being referred to the soul.

IV

Man is conscious of a twofold nature which manifests itself in perpetual self-contradiction.[366] Our English philosophers to denote this duality, distinguish the Reason and the Understanding.[367] Reason is the superior principle. Its attributes are Eternity[368] & Intuition.[369] We belong to it, not it to us.[370] Human individuality[371] is an upstart[372] just now added to this Eternal Beatitude.[372a]

V

Time & Space are below its sphere.[373] It considers things according to more intimate properties. It beholds their essence[374] wherein is seen what they can produce. It is in all men, even in the worst,[375] & constitutes them men.[376] In bad men it is dormant; in the good, efficient. But it is perfect & identical in all, underneath the peculiarities, the vices, & the errors of the individual. A man feels that his fortune, friendships, opinions, yea, all the parts of his individual existence, are merely superficial[377] to the principle of Right. Compared with the self-existence of the laws of Truth & Right whereof he is conscious, his personality is a parasitic deciduous atom. Hence the doctrine of Cosmism,[378] that the Soul which was, shall be, but that our private life which was created, may be dissipated. The authority of Reason cannot be separated from its vision. They are not two acts, but one. The sight commands, & the command sees.[379]

VI

The Understanding is the executive faculty,[380] the hand of the mind.[381] It mediates between the soul & inert matter. It works in time & space, & therefore successively. It divides, compares, reasons, invents.[382] It lives from the Reason, yet disobeys it. It commands the material world, yet often for the pleasure of the sense.[383]

---

[364] Wordsworth's "Laodamia," line 75ff. The reporter makes Emerson attribute this statement to Socrates in *Uncollected Lectures*, N.Y., 1932, 50.

[365] See ¶ 50 and *Y E S*, 201.17.

[366] See ¶s. 45-47, 49.

[367] See ¶s. 1-56.

[368] See *Nature*, 87.10.

[369] See ¶ 42.

[370] See *Nature*, 34.17-19.

[371] See ¶ 35.

[372] See his lecture, "On the Relation of Man to the Globe" (Jan. 6, 1834): "man is no upstart in the creation, but has been prophesied in nature for a thousand thousand ages." Cabot, *Memoir*, I, 223.

[372a] Cf. *Nature*, 57.1-12.

[373] See ¶s. 32, 33, 198, 275-277. Cf. *Nature*, 50.2, 60.8, 71.18, 79.17, 90.21.

[374] Cf. *Nature*, 7.20, 77.3, 77.9.

[375] Cf. ¶s. 6-7. See *Nature*, 80.6-8.

[376] See ¶ 52.

[377] Cf. *Nature*, 13.9ff., 74.20—75.14.

[378] See *Y E S*, 245.13-15.

[379] Cf. ¶s. 86, 196, 241, 255.

[380] See ¶s. 37-56. Cf. *Nature*, 46.11-20, 47.1-17, 48.14—49.7, 89.18ff.

[381] See *Nature*, 47.17.

[382] See *Nature*, 46.14-15.

[383] See *Nature*, 62.5-8.

VII

The Ideas of the Reason assume a new appearance as they descend into the Understanding. Invested with space & time they walk in masquerade.[384] It incarnates the Ideas of Reason. Thus the gods of the ancient Greeks[385] are all Ideas (as Cupid, Apollo, the Muse, &c or Love, Poesy, Wisdom, &c) but make an awkward appearance joined with the appetites of beasts.

VIII

Reason, seeing in objects their remote effects, affirms the effect as the permanent character. The Understanding, listening to Reason, on the one side, which says *It is*, and to the senses on the other side, which say *It is not*, takes middle ground and declares *It will be*.[386] Heaven[387] is the projection of the Ideas of Reason on the plane of the understanding.

IX

The mind reveals that Virtue is happiness; that good spirits associate;[387a] that the only Rank is Character; that Virtue is the key to the secrets of the world.[388] The Understanding accepts the oracle, but, with its short sight not apprehending the truth, declares that in Futurity it is so, & adds all manner of fables of its own.[389]

X

Jesus Christ was a minister of the pure Reason. The beatitudes[389a] of the Sermon on the Mount are all utterances of the mind contemning the phenomenal world.[390] "Blessed are the righteous poor, for theirs is the kingdom of heaven. Blessed are ye when men revile you," etc. The Understanding can make nothing of it. 'T is all non-sense.[391] The Reason affirms its absolute verity.

XI

Various terms are employed to indicate the counteraction of the Reason and the Understanding, with more or less precision, according to the cultivation of the speaker. A clear perception of it is the key to all theology, and a theory of human life. St. Paul marks the distinction by the terms natural man and spiritual man.[392] When Novalis says, "It is the instinct of the understanding to counteract the Reason," he only translates into a scientific formula the sentence of St. Paul "The Carnal mind is enmity against God."[393]

XII

The mind is very wise, could it be roused into action.[394] But the life of most men is aptly signified by the poet's personification, "Death in Life."[395] We walk about in a

[384] See *Nature*, 5.16.

[385] See under Jan. 9, 1835. See Schiller's *Wallenstein* (tr. Coleridge), Part One, II.iv.110-138; also *Parnassus*, p. 120. See *Nature*, 92.22.

[386] See ¶ 20.

[387] See under June 4, 1835, and ¶ 255.

[387a] See *Wallenstein* excerpts above, ¶ L., but see especially Emerson's conversation with the Swedenborgians in *Journals*, II, 455-456. See Swedenborg ¶s. 53-55.

[388] See *Nature*, 25.3, 25.15, 27.5, 44.22, 51.12-23, 53.4-9, 57.22, 74.10-13, 80.10. See also with the Swedenborgians in *Journals*, II, 455-456. See Swedenborg ¶s. 53-55.

[389] See ¶ 247. Cf. *Nature*, 92.18—93.8.

[389a] See Matthew 5:1-12. Cf. Luke 6:20-23.

[390] Cf. *Nature*, 72.5-18.

[391] See under Dec. 29, 1834.

[392] 1 Cor. 2:14-16. See above under Sept. 15 and Dec. 2, 1834.

[393] See under Sept. 15, 1834. See Romans 8:7. Novalis is the pseudonym for Friedrich von Hardenberg.

[394] See under May 13, 1835. See ¶s. 63, 245, 246, 263. See *Nature*, 5.13, 28.13, 47.18, 56.19, 76.11, 87.1, 90.7.

[395] He is referring to Coleridge's "Epitaph," composed Nov. 9, 1833:

sleep.[396] A few moments in the year, or in our lifetime, we truly live; we are at the top of our being; we are pervaded, yea, dissolved by the Mind;[397] but we fall back again presently. Those who are styled Practical Men are not awake,[398] for they do not exercise the Reason; yet their sleep is restless.[399] The most active lives have so much routine as to preclude progress almost equally with the most inactive. We bow low to the noted merchants[400] whose influence is felt, not only in their native cities, but in most parts of the globe; but our respect does them and ourselves great injustice, for their trade is without system, their affairs unfold themselves after no law of the mind, but are bubble built on bubble without end; a work of arithmetic, not of commerce, much less of humanity. They add voyage to voyage,[401] and buy stocks,——that they may buy stocks,——and no ulterior purpose is thought of. When you see their dexterity in particulars, you cannot overestimate the resources of good sense; and when you find how empty they are of all remote aims, you cannot underestimate their philosophy.

XIII

Such is the inaction of men. We have an obscure consciousness of our attributes.[402] We stand on the edge of all that is great, yet are restrained in inactivity and unconscious of our powers, like neuters of the hive, every one of which is capable of transformation into the Queen bee.[402a] We are always on the brink, etc.[402b] Much preparation, little fruit. But suddenly in any place, in the street, in the chamber, will the heavens open and the regions of wisdom be uncovered, as if to show how thin the veil, how null the circumstances. As quickly, a Lethean stream washes through us and bereaves us of ourselves.[403]

XIV

What a benefit if a rule could be given whereby the mind, dreaming amid the gross fogs of matter, could at any moment [E]AST[404] *ITSELF and* FIND THE SUN! But the common life is an endless succession of phantasms; and long after we have deemed ourselves recovered and sound, light breaks in upon us and we find we have yet had no sane hour. Another morn rises on mid-noon.[405]

Stop, Christian passer-by!——Stop, child of God,
And read with gentle breast. Beneath this sod
A poet lies, or that which once seem'd he.——
O, lift one thought in prayer for S.T.C.;
That he who many a year with toil of breath
Found death in life, may here find life in death!
Mercy for praise——to be forgiven for fame
He ask'd, and hoped, through Christ.
    Do thou the same!

See also Shakespeare, *Rape of Lucreece*, line 406, for the same phrase.
    [396] See Wordsworth's *Ode*, line 59: "Our birth is but a sleep and a forgetting."
    [397] See *Nature*, 62.15-22. The word "dissolve" came from Emerson's conversation with the Swedenborgians recorded in *Journals*, II, 455-456.
    [398] See ¶s. 150-152.
    [399] See ¶ 203. Cf. *Nature*, 89.2-6.
    [400] Emerson treats this theme at length in his sermons: "Trifles" and "The Genuine Man." See esp. *Y E S*, 182.4-25. See ¶s. 149-152.
    [401] Possibly an echo of Isaiah 5:8 or 30:8. It suggests the Old Testament prophets.
    [402] See the last chapter of *Nature*, esp. 89.2ff.
    [402a] See also *Journals*, III, 326 (Aug. 14, 1834).
    [402b] For this phrase see under Mar. 12, 1835, and *Journals*, III, 272 (Apr. 12, 1834).
    [403] Cf. *Nature*, 13.5, 43.11, 62.17. See *Journals*, III, 454, for an earlier use of the "Lethean Stream."
    [404] The *Journals* print it as "cast." See above under May 13, 1835, and compare this paragraph with *Journals*, III, 476-477. See ¶ 147.
    [405] See *Paradise Lost*, V, 310-311.

On June 20, Emerson praised Coleridge's language, at the same time admitting with the English critic that we cannot ever put truth into words, but can only *suggest* it.[406] On June 21, having in mind Coleridge's concept of the Imagination, he applied the distinction between the Reason and the Understanding to poetry and prose.[407] On June 24, he quoted from *Table Talk* on the three "silent revolutions" in England.[408] On July 2, he criticized *An Essay Towards the Theory of an Ideal or Intelligible World*[409] by John Norris (1657-1711) because it fought for the Reason with weapons meet for the Understanding.[410] On July 15, he lamented the plagiarism from Schelling, of which Coleridge was being accused by De Quincey in a series of essays on the English Lake Poets.[411] He also expressed faith in the "intuition" of good men——men who lived in the realm of the Reason.[412] On July 24, he spoke of the strong individual peculiarities of Coleridge and other great men of England, noting the apparent lack of a conventional manner among the eminent.[413] On July 27, he praised the *Table Talk*, which had probably been in his hands for some time,[414] and saw in *The Record of a School*[415] a remark that reminded him of Coleridge's "unifying Idea."[416] On July 30, he mourned that each day facts were slipping by him because he did not possess the principle that would give them meaning.[417] On the following day, he spoke of Coleridge's distinction between *talent* and *genius*.[418]

On August 1, he commented on the difference between *fancy* and *imagination*.[419] On August 3, he again discussed the reception of truth by intuition, ecstasy and insight, declaring that men are pensioners upon, or prisoners of, Ideas.[420] Although he realized that the Reason would always prove to be a mystery to the Understanding, yet he did not have an appetite for the deep mysteries and contradictions which delighted Sir Thomas Browne.[421] Again he spoke of the "unifying idea" and the principle of classification.[422] He recorded having written Miss Peabody that he believed

---

[406] See *Journals*, III, 491. Cf. ¶s. 77-83, 195. See *Nature*, 56.17-18.
[407] See *Journals*, III, 492. For Coleridge on Reason, Poetry and the Imagination, see ¶s. 59, 62-66. [409] In 2 vols., London, 1701-1704.
[408] *Journals*, III, 494. Cf. ¶ 291. [410] *Journals*, III, 500.
[411] *Journals*, III, 503-504. De Quincey's essays had begun to appear in Tait's *Edinburgh Magazine* in 1834.
[412] *Journals*, III, 504-505. See ¶s. 15, 42, 198, 245, 246, 250, 263, 265.
[413] *Journals*, III, 508. He turned this observation to the praise of the British in his *English Traits*.
[414] *Letters*, I, 448. Emerson owned the second edition (2 vols. in 1), N.Y., 1835, and quoted from it on Feb. 5, in "Michael Angelo," unless that lecture, as we now have it, represents a later revision of the original. In his copy of *Table Talk*, Emerson has indexed "Plotinus vs. Aristotle," p. 125; "Plotinus," p. 138.
[415] Issued anonymously by Elizabeth Palmer Peabody, the full title for the first edition being: *Record of a School, exemplifying the General Principles of Spiritual Culture*, Boston (James Munroe & Co.), 1835.
[416] *Journals*, III, 511. See above under May 3, 1834.
[417] *Journals*, III, 517. Cf. ¶s. 18, 86, 133, 147, 170, 171.
[418] *Journals*, III, 523-524. Cf. ¶s. 123, 126.
[419] *Journals*, III, 525-526. Cf. ¶s. 59-64. See *Nature*, 65.10-23.
[420] See *Journals*, III, 530, together with *Works*, II, 328-329, which apparently belongs with the journal of 1835. See ¶s. 216, 193; also *Nature*, 13.2-13, which was inspired by ¶ 299. See note 412 and sections IV-V, XIII-XIV of the "Statement of the First Philosophy" under June 10, 1835.
[421] *Journals*, III, 531. See *Letters*, I, 450, and compare ¶ 206.
[422] *Journals*, III, 532. See under May 3, 1834.

the spiritual to contain the intellectual nature——that is, that the moral
nature is prior to the intellectual in God's dispensation.[423] He next applied
Coleridge's distinction between the Reason and the Understanding to wit
and humor.[424] On August 5, he implied that he was leaning too heavily
upon Coleridge and needed greater self-reliance.[425] Three days afterwards
he discussed facts as seen by the Understanding and the Reason. To the
former, they were seen as *isolated*; to the "iron lids" of the eye of Reason,
they were classified at once.[426] On August 13, he paid tribute to Coleridge
as an acute psychologist,[427] and the following day lamented his death and
the fact that the world was unaware that it had lost an important chapter
on the analysis of the Imagination.[428] On October 10, he suggested or
implied Coleridge's judgment on the character of ancient as against
modern sermons,[429] and urged that the criterion of any literature should
be the prevalence in it of the great ideas which spring from the Reason:
God, Justice, Free Will, Necessity, War, and Intellectual Beauty.[430] On
October 25, he recalled Coleridge's distinction between telling the truth
and speaking in the spirit of truth.[430a] On October 28,[431] he reiterated his
opinion that man stands "on the point" between the spiritual world within
and the world of Nature without. He emphasized the correspondences
between the two, echoed Bacon's definition of man as *naturæ minister et
interpres,* and implied the related Baconian theme: *scientia et potentia
verè in idem coincidunt.*[432] On October 30, he praised Coleridge's idealiza-
tion of English institutions——especially of the church and state as *Ideas
yet to be realized.*[433]

In the first of a series of ten lectures on English literature, delivered at
weekly intervals and beginning on November 5, Emerson wrote much
which appeared ten months later in *Nature.*[434] Coleridge's influence is
observable at the following points: (1) The discussion and assumptions

---

[423] *Journals*, III, 530. Cf. ¶ 100 middle.
[424] *Journals*, III, 529.
[425] *Journals*, III, 536.
[426] *Journals*, III, 539. See under May 3, 1834. For the "eye of Reason," "inward eye,"
or "mind's eye," see ¶s. 39, 41, 83, 164, 263, 289.
[427] *Journals*, III, 539-540.
[428] *Journals*, III, 540. Coleridge had died a little more than a year before, on July 25,
1834. Emerson is referring to chap. XIII of the *Biographia Literaria*, in which Coleridge had printed a letter from one who had urged him to withhold his treatment of the
subject because the public would not appreciate its appearing in his literary life.
Coleridge yielded, and the dissertation never appeared. I believe Emerson attempted to
supply the loss in his "Poetry and Imagination," *Works*, VIII, 1-75.
[429] *Journals*, III, 549. Cf. ¶ 187.
[430] *Journals*, III, 551. On the Reason as source of ideas and for lists of the great ideas,
see ¶s. 2, 3, 18, 43, 86, 199, 245, 246, 276 end. Cf. *Nature*, 34.13-19.
[430a] *Journals*, III, 564. Cf. Coleridge ¶s. 77-85.
[431] *Journals*, III, 566. This he repeated almost verbatim in his lecture of Nov. 5, 1835.
See notes 273 and 282 *supra*.
[432] Both are parts of a single sentence in Bacon's *Novum Organum*. See also "Of
Heresies," in his *Religious Meditations*: "Nam et ipsa scientia potestas est." For the
power over Nature which is unlocked in man by seeing objects rightly, *vide Nature*,
40.19, 45.7-12, 50.13—51.9. Emerson says in *Nature* that man's original or elemental
power will return to him and his control over Nature will increase when he becomes
aware of his inner self—the Reason—and when his will yields to that Reason. See
Nature, 89.7, 89.12ff., 95.7-12.
[433] *Journals*, III, 567. Cf. ¶s. 268-270.
[434] See my brief synopsis under this date in Part II of the present work. For Cabot's
summaries, see *Memoir*, II, 716; I, 238-239.

regarding man——his standing as the central figure between the outer and inner worlds, his ability to discover the correspondences between the two realms, and his use of the Reason and Understanding. (2) Emphasis on the unifying Idea, Law or Principle as a tool of science or philosophy in interpreting particulars in Nature and the facts in history. (3) List of the eternal necessary Ideas which God reveals to man through his Reason and in communion with which he becomes a more spiritual being. (4) The distinction between an *idea* and a *notion*.[435] (5) Emphasis on generic or universal man, the each in all, and the common nature of men that assures the poet of being understood.[436] (6) Inveighing against *custom*, which makes things fixed, and the extolling of *thought*, which makes the universe fluid. (7) Treatment of the poet, of the imagination, and of Shakespeare.[437] (8) Thoughts on language and the causes of its degradation.[438] (9) Modification of Machiavelli's grouping of men.[439] On November 12, in "Permanent Traits of English National Genius,"[440] he attempted to define and illustrate with anecdotes the *Ideas* which could give unity and meaning to English life and manners throughout the centuries. He was obviously applying the method outlined in *The Friend* and illustrated in *Church and State*. On November 19, in "The Age of Fable,"[441] he again made some use, it seems, of Coleridge's scattered paragraphs on mythology and of the essay *On the Prometheus of Æschylus*. On December 10 and 17, he delivered two lectures on Shakespeare and drew upon Coleridge's theory of the imagination and his criticism of the English bard.[442] On December 24, in "Lord Bacon," he profited by Coleridge's discussion of method and theory and of Bacon and Plato——in the last third of *The Friend*.[443]

1836

On January 7, in his lecture on "Ethical Writers," he spoke of the moral sense (the eternal Reason) which is alike in all men at all times and which speaks a universal language.[444] On January 14, in "Modern Aspects of Letters,"[445] he paid tribute publicly to Coleridge and referred again to Coleridge's letter in *The Literary Gazette* (of London) :[446]

Coleridge's true merit is not that of a philosopher or of a poet, but a critic. He possessed extreme subtlety of discrimination, surpassing all men in the fineness of his distinctions, and he has taken the widest survey of the moral, intellectual, and social world. His *Biographia Literaria* is the best book of criticism in the English language; nay, I do not know any to which a modern scholar can be so much indebted. His works are of very unequal interest; in his own judgment half the *Biographia* and part of the third volume of the *Friend*, with a few of his poems, were all he would preserve, and if you add the inestimable little book called *Church and State*, I suppose all good judges would concur.

---

[435] See ¶ 245.
[436] See ¶ 64.
[437] See ¶s. 59-66.
[438] See ¶ 56a and 278 footnote.
[439] See ¶ 235.
[440] Cabot, *Memoir*, II, 716-717.
[441] Cabot, *Memoir*, II, 717-718.
[442] See Cabot, *Memoir*, II, 718-720. Cf. ¶s. 59-60, 237-238, 292-295.
[443] See Cabot, *Memoir*, II, 720; *The Friend* [*Works* (Shedd), II], 439-448 *et passim*.
[444] Cabot, *Memoir*, II, 772. Cf. ¶s. 1ff., 195, 239-244, 246, 265-266, 295.
[445] Cabot, *Memoir*, II, 723-724.
[446] See ¶ 284. Also under Nov. 15, 1834.

On January 22, he spoke of the scholar who reveals *the principle which classifies facts*.[447] On February 24, he noted how any strong passion made men idealists.[448] Four days later he applied the adjective *beautiful* only to a life conformed to an Idea.[449] On March 17 and 22, he commented on the "each in all" and on Goethe's belief in it also.[450] On March 21,[451] he returned to the Coleridgean themes: the "*Ideas* of God," the union of head and heart,[452] and the centrality of man:

> Without the ideas of God, Freedom, Virtue, Love, in his *head*, man would be vermin: but put them in his *heart* and he is one with God. All is naught without the Idea which is its nucleus & soul: for this reason no natural fact interests until connected with man.

On March 22, he called the arbitrary classification of facts *immature* science, but classification by means of an Idea, science *perfect*. On March 27, he dwelt at length upon the discovery of laws through ideas.[453] On May 22, he extemporized on the valuable habit of abstraction——or rising above personal relations to behold impersonal ideas.[454] Throughout June and July, the "each in all," the microcosm, and the macrocosm continued uppermost in his thoughts. The ocean was only a huge rain drop, and the drop was a miniature ocean.[455] On June 17, he spoke of looking within himself to find God——the Universal Unity "that IS before the World was." [456] On June 22, he called himself a "Proteus," borrowing the concept from Coleridge's discussion of Shakespeare's genius.[457] Again he improvised with concepts of the Reason and the Understanding:[458]

> The Understanding, the usurping understanding, the lieutenant of Reason, his hired man,——the moment the Master is gone, steps into his place; this usher commands, sets himself to finish what He was doing, but instantly proceeds with his own dwarf architecture, and thoroughly cheats us, until presently for a moment Reason returns, and the slave obeys, and his work shrinks into tatters and cobwebs. . . . The Reason refuses to play at couples with Understanding; to subserve the private ends of the understanding.[459]

On July 20,[460] he acknowledged Frederic Henry Hedge's letter of a month earlier and gave his opinions about a projected "symposium" led by individuals whose Reason functioned along with their Understanding. He recommended Alcott for membership and mentioned that Alcott set Coleridge in the zenith. On September 8, at Harvard College, Emerson, Hedge and others seem to have made definite plans.[461] On September 9

---

[447] *Journals*, IV, 7-8. Cf. ¶ 127ff.
[448] *Journals*, IV, 12. Cf. ¶s. 237-238.
[449] *Journals*, IV, 16. Cf. ¶ 169, 97, 146.
[450] *Journals*, IV, 26, 28. See note 41.
[451] *Typescript Journals*, "B," Part II, p. 204.
[452] See ¶s. 164, 169, 183, 202.
[453] *Journals*, IV, 33.
[454] *Journals*, IV, 53-54. Cf. *Journals*, IV, 12, 62, 68, and ¶ 278.
[455] *Journals*, IV, 60, 70, 71, 76. Cf. note 41. See ¶s. 253, 275. On the Pantheistic interpretation of εν και παν see ¶s. 71ff.
[456] *Journals*, IV, 71. Cf. ¶ 49.
[457] *Journals*, IV, 72. Cf. ¶ 65.
[458] *Journals*, IV, 73-74; 75.
[459] See "Understanding" in the Index-Concordance of *Nature*.
[460] *Letters*, II, 29-30.
[461] See *Journals*, IV, 84-85.

and 10, *Nature* was published.[462] On the nineteenth, the projected meeting of the transcendentalists was held in Boston, and I turn to Hedge's reminiscences for the details:

THE TRANSCENDENTALISTS[463]

By FREDERIC HENRY HEDGE

In September, 1836, on the day of the celebration of the second centennial anniversary of Harvard College, Mr. Emerson, George Ripley, and myself, with one other, chanced to confer together on the state of current opinion in theology and philosophy, which we agreed in thinking very unsatisfactory. Could anything be done in the way of protest and introduction of deeper and broader views? What precisely we wanted it would have been difficult for either of us to state. What we strongly felt was dissatisfaction with the reigning sensuous philosophy, dating from Locke, on which our Unitarian theology was based. The writings of Coleridge, recently edited by Marsh,[464] and some of Carlyle's earlier essays, especially the "Characteristics" and the "Signs of the Times," had created a ferment in the minds of some of the young clergy of that day. There was a promise in the air of a new era of intellectual life.

We four concluded to call a few like-minded seekers together on the following week. Some dozen of us met in Boston, at the house, I believe, of Mr. Ripley. Among them I recall the names of Orestes Brownson (not yet turned Romanist), Cyrus Bartol, Theodore Parker, and Wheeler and Bartlett, tutors in Harvard College.[465] There was some discussion, but no conclusion reached, on the question whether it were best to start a new journal as the organ of our views, or to work through those already existing. The next meeting, in the same month, was held by invitation of Emerson, at his house in Concord. A large number assembled; besides some of those who met in Boston, I remember Mr. Alcott, John S. Dwight, Ephraim Peabody, Dr. Convers Francis, Mrs. Sarah Ripley, Miss Elizabeth Peabody, Margaret Fuller, Caleb Stetson, James Freeman Clarke. These were the earliest of a series of meetings, held from time to time, as occasion prompted, for seven or eight years. Jones Very was one of those who occasionally attended; H. D. Thoreau another.

There was no club, properly speaking; no organization, no presiding officer, no vote ever taken. How the name *Transcendental*, given to these gatherings and the set of persons who took part in them, originated, I cannot say. It certainly was never assumed by the persons so called. I suppose I was the only one who had any first-hand acquaintance with the German transcendental philosophy, at the start. The *Dial* was the product of the movement, and in some sort its organ.

---

[462] See *Nature*, iv-v.
[463] Cabot, *Memoir*, I, 244-246.
[464] Marsh edited the *Aids to Reflection*, Burlington, 1829; *The Friend*, Burlington, 1831; *The Statesman's Manual*, Burlington, 1832.
[465] Emerson (*Journals*, IV, 85-86) gives details of this meeting, which was held at George Ripley's home, and lists the following guests: Frederic Henry Hedge, Convers Francis, A. Bronson Alcott, James Freeman Clarke, Orestes A. Brownson, and George Ripley.

COLERIDGE AS THE KEY TO *NATURE*

In the preceding chapter, I pointed out Emerson's growing esteem for Coleridge's works, the use of ideas which he found in the *Aids* and in *The Friend*, his frequent employment of the distinction between the Reason and the Understanding, and the strong influence of Coleridge upon "Gnothi Seauton" and upon the "Statement of the First Philosophy." In *Nature*, Emerson's most complete presentation of Transcendentalism, the evidence again points to Coleridge as the background or necessary setting for the lustres drawn from Goethe, Swedenborg, Oegger, Reed, Alcott and others. To approach that important work from any other standpoint, in view of the facts already set forth and the parallels that are to follow, seems to be like turning in astronomical speculation from Copernicus back to Ptolemy.

Nature has been widely appreciated, but seldom understood, largely, I think, because the philosophic portions are highly compressed summaries of earlier lectures and notes (still unpublished); because, in taking for granted his "Statement of the First Philosophy," Emerson did not feel obliged to give his readers many definitions of terms; and because the descriptions of Concord and the sparkling colors gleaned from his wide reading have tended to hide the basic structure of the work. In other words, the literary character of the book, since its first publication, has tended to conceal from most readers rather than reveal to them, its ultimate meaning and purpose. We shall see later that the early non-transcendental reviewers, who at different times disapproved of both Coleridge and Emerson because of their seeming lack of clarity, were aware of their common purpose; but today the relationship between American Transcendentalism and English Romanticism appears to be somewhat vague. It will be the purpose of the present chapter, therefore, to recapitulate Coleridge's major doctrines and to allow *Nature*, if it will, to analyze itself.

In the parallel columns, chiefly for reasons of space, I have not attempted to give completely verbatim quotations from either writer——Coleridge has usually required great condensation, and Emerson, some expansion and commentary——but in every instance I have indicated where the original sentences may be consulted promptly. My aim has been to summarize and interpret——not to protract an already long discussion. I have, therefore, regularly omitted irrelevant phrases, employed italics for emphasis, expanded fragments that proved meaningless when isolated, and, as seemed necessary, repeated a few of the shorter elements. Parentheses in the left-hand column refer always to the paragraphic system of Chapter VI. Those on the right-hand side cite page and first line in the facsimile of the first edition of *Nature*. The value chiefly intended in the method employed is that of immediate utility.[1]

---

[1] Coleridge is on the left; Emerson's *Nature*, on the right. When the Coleridge summary alone is given, it will occupy the width of two columns. In four instances, I have allowed one column to overflow into the other. See pp. 204, 207, 213, 215.

CHART OF NATURE'S MINISTRY TO MAN—COLERIDGE'S SYSTEM

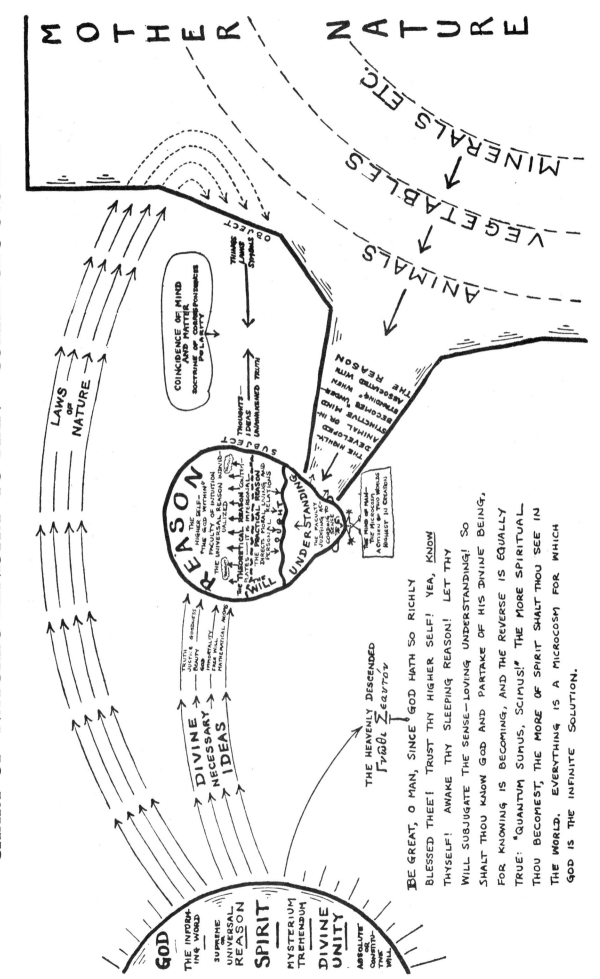

I

REASON——THE HIGHER FACULTY IN MAN'S MIND[2]

A

Reason is the Immediate within every man, and on it all the certainty of our knowledge depends. Our intuition, which is the affirmation of it, does not in every man rise to consciousness, for some men allow it to slumber, preferring to live on the plane of the Understanding. (14). Reason is an intuition, accompanied by a conviction of the necessity of the truth so beheld. It appeals only to itself for the ground of the truth of its decisions. It is an inward beholding. It is related to the "Intelligible" or Spiritual world rather than to the material or phenomenal. It is the source and substance of truths above sense. It is the organ of the supersensuous. Its objects are alien from sensation. It is not the faculty of the finite. It is *conscious self-knowledge*. Reason is the Power by which man becomes possessed of absolute and universal principles—— of "necessary ideas" and of the eternal verities of Plato and Descartes——of ideas in mathematics and morals. Among them are the ideas of the Good, the Beautiful, Eternity, Immortality, Freedom, Holiness, etc. (1, 15, 18——19, 32——33, 86, 250, 276).

B

Reason is the *common factor* in men ——the basis of the doctrine of *each in all*. If a man will trust this higher self, he can understand all mankind and gain insight into nature also. But "like only can know like," and if he neglects his spiritual nature, his external vision will be clouded. "Only what we are within can we see without." (4-5).

C

Reason is the capacity in man for beholding or being conscious of, the Divine Light. This capability is itself light, life, the Indwelling Living Word, and the fountain of truth. It is not strictly ours. We really belong to It. (11-13).

A

Reason is thought. It mars one's faith in the external world. It overcomes the despotism of the senses. (62.4). Reason is a higher agency and sees farther than the animal eye. (62.9). The highest is present to the soul of man. Many truths arise out of the recesses of consciousness. (79.6). Reason or Spirit hath life in itself. (32.2). Men and women reveal best the power and order that lie at the heart of things. They rest on the unfathomed sea of thought and virtue whereto they alone, of all organizations, are the entrances. (57.15). Reason's momentary grasp of the scepter is manifested in an instantaneous in-streaming causing power. (90.19). Intellectual science fastens the attention upon immortal, necessary, uncreated natures, that is, upon ideas. We ascend into their region and know that these are the thoughts of the Supreme Being. (70.10). Man is conscious of a universal soul within or behind his individual life, wherein, as in a firmament, the natures of Justice, Truth, Love, Freedom arise and shine. This universal soul he calls Reason. (34.13).

B

Reason enables man to act upon nature with his entire force. (90.7). Sensible objects conform to the premonitions of Reason and reflect man's conscience. To the moral person all things are moral. (51.10). When the eye of Reason is stimulated to earnest vision, outlines and surfaces become transparent; causes and spirits are seen through them. (62.11). Imagination may be defined as the use Reason makes of the material world. (65.10). What we are, that only can we see. (94.5).

C

Reason is not mine or thine or his, but we are its. We are its property and its men. Our private earth is buried in the blue sky, which is the type of Reason. (34.17).

---

[2] Emerson's discussion of the distinction between the Understanding and the Reason is treated at greater length in the preceding chapter, to which the student is referred.

D

Reason is, therefore, the best and holiest gift of God. It is the sole principle of permanence amid the endless change of the phenomenal world, and it gives man precedence above all other living creatures. (8).

E

Reason is the knowledge of the laws of the whole considered *as one*. It is the science of the Universal. It first manifests itself in man as a tendency to comprehend the ALL AS ONE. Its emphasis is on the fundamental unity of all things. It brings unity into our conceptions and several knowledges. It is the source of all true systems. We assume from it that a ONE is the ground and cause of the universe——is behind all that is. Because of the great unifying Reason, we see that each truth implies or includes every other truth. Like the Reason they all have validity in themselves. (17, 21, 88-89).

F

The contemplation of Reason is the intuition of things which arises when we possess ourselves as one with the whole. This intuition is *substantial* knowledge. By it we know that existence is its own predicate. *We are. We exist.* It is an eternal and infinite self-rejoicing and self-loving——with a joy unfathomable and a love all-comprehensive. (167).

G

In the highest sense, then, Reason is *being*. Reason is the Supreme Being contemplated objectively and in abstraction from the personality. God, the soul and Eternal Truth are the Supreme Reason. (10, 19).

H

Regarded with reference to abstract truth, it is the *Speculative Reason*, and in this sense Reason is *being*. It contemplates reality quite apart from personal relations. This Reason is one with the Absolute Will. It is super-individual. An individual and personal attachment should lead to a higher and impersonal one of ideas and thoughts. (2, 10, 34-35).

D

To the senses and the unrenewed Understanding belongs a sort of instinctive belief in the absolute existence of nature. The presence of Reason mars this faith. (61.22). The soul prefers the human form: "It can speak again. It can yield me thought formed and alive." (57.7).

E

So intimate is this Unity that it lies under the undermost garment of nature and betrays its source in Universal Spirit. For it pervades Thought also. Every universal truth implies or supposes every other truth. *Omne verum vero consonat.* (56.7). Reason perceives the analogy which marries matter and mind. (46.17). The soul seeks beauty, which in its largest and profoundest sense, is one expression for the universe. God is the all-fair. Truth, goodness and beauty are but different faces of the same All. (30.14).

F

No man touches these divine natures without becoming in some degree himself divine. We are transported out of the district of change. We apprehend the absolute. As it were, for the first time *we exist*. We become immortal. (71.5). What noble emotions dilate the mortal as he enters into the counsels of the creation, and feels by knowledge the privilege *to be*. (49.19).

G

This universal Soul man calls the Reason. (34.17).

H

Speculative Reason is philosophy. In the light of thought the world is phenomenal. (74.10). Thought relaxes the despotism of the senses. (62.5). Intellect endlessly inquires: What is Truth? (93.17). A faithful thinker, resolute to detach every object from personal relations, sees it in the light of thought. (92.7). The philosopher and poet postpone the apparent order and relations of the phenomenal world to the empire of thought. (68.17). The intellect searches

I

Regarded with reference to moral truth——as the fountain of ideas regulating man's conduct, action, and personal relations——as the light of the conscience and as the origin of wisdom, it is called the *Practical Reason*. It comprehends the will, the conscience, and the moral being. (2-3).

J

The Reason is called Spirit in John's gospel; and the ideas of Reason are there called "truths spiritually discerned." The Eternal Reason is fullness without opacity; transparency without vacuum. The grandeur of the Reason within man, far from making him proud, should teach him humility. It challenges him to self-conquest and self-government. (89, 167, 199).

out the absolute order of things as they stand in the mind of God, and without the colors of affection. (28.8). Beauty remains for the apprehension and pursuit of the intellect. (28.6,22).

I

Practical Reason, or virtue, subordinates the phenomenal world to the mind. (74.10). The Moral Sentiment is in the soul of man. (53.21).

J

That which intellectually considered we call Reason, considered in relation to nature we call Spirit. (34.22). If the Reason be stimulated to earnest vision, outlines and surfaces become transparent. (62.15). When man lives in the Understanding, external things are no longer seen to be transparent, but opake. (91.9). In the uttermost meaning of the words, thought is devout, and devotion is thought. (91.18). Is not prayer a study of truth? (92.3). Truth is learned by entire humility. (82.19).

II

UNDERSTANDING——THE LOWER FACULTY IN MAN'S MIND

The Understanding is the generalizing faculty. (Generalization is the substitute for Intuition.) The Understanding depends on the senses for materials. It constitutes sensible experience. It gives rise to maxims or rules, but never to universal verities. It can never beget a consciousness of absolute certainty. The Understanding may exist without Reason, as in the highest of the lower animals, but human Understanding differs from mere animal nature or instinct by being associated with the Reason. (There is no Reason in lower animals.) The well-controlled human Understanding looks in two directions: to the Reason or "inward eye" and to the senses. (37-38, 41). The science of Being embraces both the sciences of the Reason and the Understanding. (67).

The worldling, under the dominion of the Understanding and the senses, is wholly occupied with surfaces. The man of Reason fixes his gaze on the *substance* or *reality* beneath the phenomena——on that which *is* and which *abides*. When

Space, time, climate, food and all the properties of matter contribute to educate the Understanding. (46.10). Nature supplies tedious training to form the "hand of the mind." She disciplines it in intellectual truths——in everyday facts. (47.1,17). Right training of the Understanding is important, for the character and fortune of the individual are affected by his ability to distinguish differences, weigh, compare, separate and grade. (48.15). When the Understanding and Reason are both used, man acts upon nature with entire force. (90.7).

The Understanding or animal eye sees outlines and surfaces. Reason sees causes and spirits through them. (69.2). The "practical" English are dominated by the senses and the Understanding. (22.4). The wintry light of the Understanding freezes subjects which it touches——makes them seem hard and permanent. (92.3). To the senses and the unrenewed Understanding belongs a sort of instinctive belief in the absolute existence of nature. (61.22). The man of

we exercise the Understanding, we do not conceive of ourselves as *one with the whole*, but as separated beings. We place nature in antithesis to mind, as object over against subject, as thing against thought, and as death against life. (167, 180). Nature cannot be fathomed or measured by the Understanding. It can best be approached with the spiritual axiom: *Quantum sumus, scimus.* (259).

Nature is a power subject to the Law of Continuity. It has no power of self-origination, for it depends entirely on the spiritual world. Yet the human Understanding (because of its character) can conceive of nature only under the form of cause and effect. This cause and effect, or action and reaction, or law of reciprocity is really, therefore, only a *mode of thinking* inherent in the Understanding. The Understanding has validity only *in its own sphere.* In trying to go beyond that sphere, it manifests unbelief and

Understanding approaches nature with manure, compass, machinery and tools. He does not see that nature is more than utility. Those who live in the Understanding are half-men and exercise only a penny wisdom. (89.12). The behavior of the Understanding is best described as "gymnastics." (48.11). The Understanding, yielding to the despotism of the senses, sees man as a part of the flux of nature. Reason shows us nature aloof and afloat. (62.5). The ruin or blank that we see when we look at nature is in our own eye. The cause is man's disunity within himself. (91.7).

––––––––––

misbelief. It simply cannot comprehend higher truths––––cannot conceive them. Truth comes out of the moulds of the Understanding only in the disguise of two contradictory conceptions. (44, 49, 119, 219).

III

THE WILL OF MAN––––FREE TO OBEY THE REASON

Will is the supernatural or spiritual in man and the principle of his personality. By it he is a responsible agent. (217, 194). Reason, Religion and the Will in man constitute a trinity in unity. (22). Will is the sustaining, coercive and ministerial power––––the police officer. In its relation to the Reason it is wisdom. In its relation to religion, it is love. (25). The responsible will is responsible to the law of conscience. By self-subjection to the Universal Light of Reason, the will of the individual (*i.e.,* the *particular* will) becomes a "will of Reason," and its possessor is considered regenerate. The Reason then becomes the Spirit of the regenerate man, and by its presence a person is capable of a quickening intercommunion with the Divine Spirit. (28, 31). Free Will is the power of the human being to maintain the obedience which God through conscience has commanded against all the might of nature. (86).

A virtuous will has nothing to do with time and space relations, for they belong to matter. The will is free––––is related to Reason and the truths of Reason. (71.4-20). Power in man comes from the universal light of Reason, and hence is superior to his will and to his narrow animal self. (89.9). A virtuous will says (with Jesus): "Thy will be done." (50.16). Beauty is the mark God sets upon a free will. (25.2).

By exercising a will of the Reason, man extends his kingdom over the world and makes the world his double, for nature yields itself passive to an educated will (*i.e.,* to one educated in spiritual wisdom). (7.23, 25.14, 30.12, 50.13, 51.8, 93.19). A corrupt or unenlightened will, however, limits its influence to a man's own body, for nature only recognizes *spiritual* sovereignty. (80.21). The will is exercised in every event. (50.13).

The ultimate ends by which the will is to be determined and by which alone the will, not corrupted, should be determined are called *moral ideas*, and these spring from the

Reason. They are the ideas of the Eternal, the Good, the True, the Holy, and the Idea-of-God-as-the-Ground-of-all or the Idea of the Supreme Spirit in which all these dwell *substantially* and in which they are *one*. (272). The uncorrupt or responsible will is characterized by freedom. It is then not subject to anything under the forms of Time and Space——under the relations of Cause and Effect. It has ability to originate its own acts. A corrupt or fallen will has yielded its independence by admitting into itself a "nature" or an element *not free*. (26-27, 86). Since nature is an extension of the supernatural and has no power of its own to originate anything, every appearance of discontinuity or origination in nature is a shadow of our own casting——a reflection from our own will or spirit, which results from an inner maladjustment. (29).

IV

THE CONSCIENCE——A TESTIFYING STATE

The conscience is neither Reason, Religion or Will, but an *experience sui generis* of the coincidence of the human will with Reason and Religion. It is best described as the peace of God which passeth all understanding. (255). The Will of God, which is the final aim of all our duties, is revealed to man through the conscience. Conscience is hard to define. It is a witness-bearer to the truth or reality of our Reason, and may be construed with the term *Reason*. Conscience is the *effective Reason*. (36, 78).

Nature always wears the colors of the spirit. (14.14). Sensible objects, therefore, conform to the premonitions of Reason and reflect the conscience. All things are moral; and in their boundless changes have an increasing reference to spiritual nature. Every animal function from the sponge up to Hercules shall hint or thunder to man the laws of right and wrong, and echo the Ten Commandments. Nature is always an ally of Religion. (51.10).

Conscience is a spiritual sense or testifying state of the coincidence or discordance of the Free Will with the Reason. (56). The Law of Conscience has the power of a holy and omnipotent legislator. It is the indwelling Word of the Supreme Legislator. It commands us to attribute reality and actual existence only to those ideas without which the conscience itself would be baseless and contradictory to the *ideas of the soul:* free will, immortality, God, etc. God is the reality of the conscience and the source of all obligation. (86).

V

FAITH——A SYNTHESIS OF REASON AND THE WILL

An effective faith presupposes knowledge and individual conviction. By a vital and spiritual act, *to know* and *to possess* are one and indivisible. To know God is to possess Him. Knowledge is *being*. Faith may also be called *self-trust, reliance* on the Reason etc. (36, 241, 251). Faith is a total act of the soul. It is the whole state of the mind, or it is not at all. Faith subsists in the synthesis of the Reason and the individual will. As regards the latter, it is a constant energy permeating the whole man. As regards the former, it is a light ——a form of knowing——an actual beholding of the Truth. (36, 104).

In the woods we return to Reason and faith. Mean egotism vanishes. I am nothing. The currents of the Universal Being circulate through me. (12.22). Whilst we behold the divine natures, we learn the difference between the absolute and the relative. For the first time *we exist*. (71.13). What noble emotions dilate the mortal as he feels by knowledge the privilege *to be*. (49.19).

VI

MAN AND NATURE——MIND AND MATTER——UNIVERSAL SPIRIT BEHIND
BOTH——POLARITY NECESSARY FOR EXISTENCE——THE DIVINE UNITY
MANIFESTS ITSELF IN EITHER POLE AS THE *ALL IN EACH*

A

The remarkable fact is that the material world is found to obey the same laws as have been deduced independently from the Reason. And masses act by a force which cannot be conceived to result from the component parts, known or imaginable. (131). That *ideas* in the mind of man correspond to the *laws* of nature is a mystery which of itself should suffice to make us religious; for it is a problem of which God is the only solution——God, the One *before* all, and *of* all, and *through* all. (260).

B

The objective world of nature and the subjective world of the self or intelligence are related. (68). Polarity functions in man. He has liberty, yet he must reverence Divine Law. He is independent, yet must submit to the Supreme Will. He must yield to the *real* world within, yet show sympathy for and hold commune with, the phenomenal world of nature. In the conciliating mid-point or equator does man live, and only by its equal presence in both poles can his life be manifested. (288). Every power in nature and in Spirit must evolve an opposite as the sole means and condition of its manifestation. *Identity* of thesis and antithesis is the substance of all being; *opposition* is the condition of all existence or of *being* manifested. (96, 138, 287).

C

That hidden mystery in every the minutest form of existence appears (to the Understanding) under the aspect of *time* retrospectively as an infinite ascent of causes, and prospectively as an interminable progression of effects. And under the aspect of *space*, it appears intuitively as a law of action and reaction, continuous and extending beyond all bound. This same mystery, freed from the phenomenal world and seen in the depth of *real* being, reveals itself to the pure Reason as the actual immanence or

A

This miracle——the relation between the mind and matter——is not fancied by some poet, but stands in the will of God. It is the standing problem which has exercised every genius since the world began. (43.1). A Law of nature when in the mind is an Idea. (68.23). Nature is the symbol of Spirit. (32.10). Universal Spirit speaks to man through nature and strives to lead him back to it. (77.14). Nature is pierced with an Informing Soul. (69.12). Behind nature, throughout nature, Spirit is present. That Spirit is *one* and not compound. (79.14).

B

Things have a relation to virtue (Practical Reason) and to thought (Theoretical Reason). (28.7). Friends are coextensive with our inner Idea. Each answers to a certain affection of the soul. (58.6). The whole of nature is a metaphor of the human mind. (41.16). The laws of moral nature (*i.e.*, the Reason) answer to those of matter as face to face in a glass. (41.18). Reason perceives the analogy that marries Matter to Mind. (46.19). Forms of flowers, shells, animals etc. are related to the mind of man. Science must be built upon *ideas*. (83.23). There seems to be a necessity in Spirit to manifest itself in material forms. (43.22).

C

The rule of one art or a law of one organization holds true throughout nature (56.3). Each creature is only a modification of the other. (55.22). The sailor, shepherd, miner and merchant have each an experience precisely parallel and leading to the same conclusions. (53.13). A wise man in doing one thing does all. (56.22). Every universal truth implies or supposes every other truth. (56.7). Truth, Beauty and Goodness are different faces of the same ALL. (30.21). Unity lies under the undermost garment of nature. (56.4). The Reason sees Unity in Variety. Every particular in nature

in-being of *all in each*. Heaven is imaged in a dew-drop. The least animalcule in a drop of water is a microcosm, of which God omnipresent is the only solution. The same Spirit that dwells in man stands behind nature. (253).

D

Man has the whole world in counterpoint to him, but he also contains the whole world within himself. We speak of *man* and *nature*, but man himself is a compendium of nature——a microcosm! In man the centripetal and individualizing tendency of all nature is itself concentred and individualized. He is a revelation of nature. Henceforward he is referred to himself and delivered up to his own charges, and he who relies most on himself and stands the firmest, is the truest because the most *individual*, man. (288).

E

Man is the only rational, ethical and progressive creature——the final cause of all creation, the centre in which all its lines converge. (159). See above.

——a leaf, a drop, a crystal, a moment of time——is related to the whole. Each particle is a microcosm and faithfully renders the likeness of the world. (54.13). A work of art is an abstract or epitome of the world. (29.12).

D

It is a wonderful congruity which subsists between man and the world, of which he is lord, its most subtle inhabitant, its head and heart. Man finds something of himself in every great and small thing——in every law of color and fact of astronomy. This mystery was seen by George Herbert in his little poem on man. (84.13).

E

Man is an analogist, and studies relations in all objects. He is placed in the centre of beings, and a ray of relation passes from every other being to him. And neither can man be understood without these objects, nor these objects without man. (35.9). Words and actions introduce us to the human form. All other organizations in nature appear to be degradations. (57.4).

VII

MAN'S EDUCATION DEPENDS ON THE CONCURRENCE OF MIND AND MATTER——ACTION IS, THEREFORE, INEVITABLE——UNLOCKED KNOWLEDGE IS SPIRITUAL POWER IN THE ETERNAL PRESENT

A

Both the unconscious world and the conscious must concur in all acts of positive knowledge. (68). All knowledge rests in the coincidence of an object with a subject. (67). To know the whole truth we must likewise *act;* and he alone acts, who *makes*. This no man can do estranged from nature. Learn to know thyself in nature, that thou mayest understand nature in thyself. (174fn.). The spirit in man (*i.e.*, the will) knows its own state in and by its acts alone. (200).

other, but they are like the alternate periods of feeding and working in animals. (28.11). "Good thoughts are no better than good dreams, unless they be executed." (47.18).

A

Whilst the abstract question occupies your intellect, Nature brings it in the concrete to be solved by your hands. (93.9). Every man's constitution is a solution in hieroglyphic to the questions he would ask. He *acts* the solution before he apprehends it as truth. (6.10). Nature invites man to action through the powers which are supplied in her floods of life. (5.13). An action is the perfection and publication of thought. (56.19). All right education is concerned with man's true position as regards nature ——his connection with her. (73.18). The intellectual (*i.e.*, the contemplative) and the active powers seem to succeed each other in man, and the exclusive activity of the one generates the exclusive activity of the other. There is something unfriendly in each to the

B

There are times when the eye rests steadily upon nature, much as the "inward eye" concentrates on its Ideas, and nature then reveals her affinity with mind. She then becomes like an individual spirit or fellow soul and seems to think and hold commune with us. At such moments, nature——as another *subject*, veiled behind the visible *object* without us——solicits the intelligible object hid and yet struggling beneath the subject within us, and like a helping Lucina, brings it forth for us into consciousness and common light. (289).

C

There is a spiritual world penetrating the world of nature. The world in which I exist is not the world of nature. It is another world, but *not to come*. It is *present*. It is a world in which light still shines *as on the third day of the creation*, before it was polarized into outward and inward——*i.e.*, while light and life were one and the same. This world to which I refer is enshrined in the microcosm, and I have held commune therewith. The Creator has given us spiritual senses and sense-organs——Ideas, I mean: the idea of the Good, the Beautiful, Eternity, Immortality, Freedom, etc. And must not these infer the existence of a world corresponding to them? (275-277).

B

Every object in nature, rightly seen, unlocks a new faculty of the mind. What was before unconscious truth *within* man becomes, when defined in an object, *conscious truth and power*. (45.9). Under the principle, "Like only can know like," nature is so pervaded with human life that there is something of humanity in all and in every particular. (78.18). The forms of nature are keys to power for man. They can awaken his sleeping thoughts. (40.19). The lesson of power is taught in every event. Man learns that he can reduce nature under his will by accepting her discipline. (50.14). Nature yields herself passive to the educated Will of man (*i.e.*, to the Will of the Reason). (93.19).

C

Religion is a present experience: We are embosomed in nature, whose floods of life stream around us. We need not grope in the dry bones of the past. The sun shines *today!* (5.11). The Spirit does not act upon us from without, that is, in space and time, but spiritually, or *through ourselves*. A man rests upon the bosom of God. (79.16).

VIII

NATURE THEN BECOMES A LANGUAGE OF SYMBOLS AND HIEROGLYPHICS——A BOOK OF CORRESPONDENCES[3]

The great book of God's servant, nature, has an obvious sense and literal interpretation that declares the being and attributes of the Almighty Father. But there is more in nature than that. To the pious minds in all ages it has been music and poetry. They have read the book in a figurative sense and found therein correspondences and symbols of the spiritual world from which it sprang. (256). Spiritual reflection can help us by giving novelty to familiar natural objects, making them reveal the miraculous. Ancient truths will be restored to their pristine lustre. (173-174).

True natural philosophy is comprised in the study of the science and language of symbols. The power delegated to nature is *all in every part*. A symbol is not a figure of speech or an allegory; it is an actual and essential part of that, the whole of which it represents. The genuine naturalist is a dramatic poet in his own line. So is any scientist who forsakes Locke and builds his physiology on the heaven-descended *Know Thyself*. (260).

---

[3] In order to save space, I give no parallels from Emerson at this point, but refer the student to *Nature*, chap. IV, pp. 32-45; also to 92.18——93.8.

A symbol is characterized by a translucence of the special in the individual, or of the general in the special, or of the universal in the general; but above all by the translucence of the eternal through and in the temporal. It always partakes of the reality which it renders intelligible; and while it enunciates the whole, abides itself as a living part in that unity of which it is the representative. (247).

IX

MAN SUMMARIZED——THE GREAT RULE OF HIS BEING IS *KNOW THYSELF* ——THE GROUND OF ALL KNOWLEDGE IS WITHIN——EACH MUST LEARN EVERYTHING FOR HIMSELF[4]

No man can learn for another, yet all men have the same means for ascertaining the facts. Each person must be herein querist and respondent to himself: "Am I at one with God, and is my will concentric with that Constitutive Will and the Supreme Reason of the Universe? (5).

The highest man is a thinking, spiritual being. He aims in his pursuits to find a ground common to the world and to himself, wherein he may find the *one* principle of permanence and identity. He may sally forth into nature and find temporary delight in her forms, but he will be disappointed to find no Free Will like that which prompts him. At last he will conclude that what he is seeking he has *left behind*——in himself! He will be shocked at the realization that the objective world which he once thought was so *permanent* gains whatever character it has from his own mind. Whatever its validity, his inner thought has created it. Deep within himself he will experience "an obscure sensation"——powerful yet incomprehensible——assuring him that the objective world is only a modification of himself, and that he would not be able to comprehend it were it not for the fact that *like only can know or see like*. (152).

Man will then try energetically to satisfy the voice within himself, by accepting the so-called laws of nature outside of him, but he must soon see that these laws are the formulations of his own mind. And since he is an intelligent or spiritual being, he must assume that nature, which he can observe and enjoy, must be *spiritual* also. (If it were not like himself, he could have no communion with it.) He is forced to conclude, then, that before he can recognize himself in nature, he must learn to understand nature *within himself*. The laws of nature must be studied in the depths of his own being. Only then can he interpret the natural world. Only then will he have power over it. Only then will he discover the method for interpreting the facts of the outward scene. Finally, he will come upon the idea of the *common ground* of man and nature——the Universal Idea or Law by which all power manifests itself in opposite, though interdependent, forces. Then will dawn upon his mind the relation of the outer world to the inner, and of the relation of both to the great ALL behind everything. (155).

We are to begin, then, with "I know myself" in order to end with the absolute I AM. We proceed from *self* in order to lose and find all self in *God*. (67). *Self* is the Reason ——the Godlike in man——the spiritual element common to all men. So in knowing the self, one at once comes to know God, the Ground of everything and the nature of all men and of all things. Our human nature thus has a shadow of divinity in it. (69-70, 76). Since the Reason is not our own, such things as pride, self-love and self-will are out of place. A childlike humility is needed for the discovery of spiritual truth. (226-227, 175ff.). Self-knowledge requires more than mere attention to the voice within. It demands the energy of *thought*. (216).

---

[4] I have shown in the preceding chapter how prominent this theme was in Emerson's thinking during the six years before the publication of *Nature*. The phrases, "Know Thyself," "Trust Thyself," "Revere Thyself," etc. do not appear in his little book, but they are all implied in the "Introduction" and in "Prospects." See also *Nature*, 79.5 —80.8.

Quantum sumus, scimus. That which we find within ourselves, which is more than ourselves and yet the ground of whatever is good and permanent therein, is the substance and life of all other knowledge. (228). Join in the fervent prayer that we may seek *within us* what we can never find elsewhere——what no words can put there—— that one, only, true religion which elevates *knowing* into *being*, which is at once the science of being, and the being and the life of all genuine science. (264).

X

MAN'S GREAT PROBLEM——PHILOSOPHY FAILS TO MASTER IT——ONLY RELIGION CAN PROVIDE THE SOLUTION

A

The grand problem, the solution of which forms, according to Plato [he means Kant], the final object and distinctive character of philosophy, is this: for all that exists conditionally (that is, the existence of which is inconceivable except under the condition of its dependency on some other as its antecedent) to find a ground that is unconditional and absolute, and thereby to reduce the aggregate of human knowledge to a system. For the relation common to all being known, the appropriate orbit of each becomes discoverable, together with its peculiar relations to its concentrics in the common sphere of subordination. (131; cf. 68).

B

Philosophy has limitations. The dialectic intellect of the philosopher can lead him to a knowledge of the Absolute, but it cannot solve the problem of the relation between God and the World. Pantheism constantly threatens those who try the philosophical path. Only the Spirit and the Religion of man can fill up the chasm left by metaphysical speculation. (168).

C

Plato has faced this problem of finding what is the ground of the coincidence between Reason and experience, or between the Laws of matter and the Ideas of pure intellect. And his only answer is that the Reason must pass out of itself and seek the ground of this agreement in a supersensual essence, which being at once the Ideal of the Reason and the Cause of the material world, is the pre-establisher of the harmony in and be-

A

"The problem of philosophy," according to Plato, "is for all that exists conditionally to find a ground unconditioned and absolute." Although the poet proposes Beauty as his main end and the philosopher, truth——both postpone the apparent order of things to the empire of thought. They proceed on the faith that a law determines all phenomena, which being known, the phenomena can be predicted. (68.18). That which intellectually considered we call Reason, considered in relation to nature we call Spirit. (35.1). That Spirit is one and not compound. (79.15).

B

Idealism does not satisfy the demands of Spirit. (78.12). Let it stand, however, in the present state of our knowledge, merely as a useful introductory hypothesis. Let us go further and take the invisible steps of *thought* (spiritual contemplation) to make our inquiry. We shall then learn that the highest is present to the soul of man. (79.5). Of that ineffable essence which we call Spirit, he that thinks most will say least. Both language and thought desert us. That essence refuses to be recorded in propositions. (77.3).

C

The problem is solved by the redemption of the soul. The reason why the world lacks unity and lies broken and in heaps is that man is disunited with himself. He must satisfy all the demands of Spirit. Love is as much its demand as perception. Thought is devout, and devotion is thought. (91.5). The relation between mind and matter is not fancied by some poet, but stands in the will of God, and so (knowledge of it being a matter

tween *both. Religion is, therefore, the ultimate aim of philosophy.* It supplies the copula between philosophy and the sciences. Religion can be used in each field to comprehend the parts in one whole. It is *the* principle *common to all men.* It enables philosophy to become scientific and the sciences to become philosophical. (132).

D

When a man raises his mind to consider existence in and by itself——apart from personal relations——he feels the presence of a mystery, and his soul stands in awe and wonder. Intuition of the great Universal Power sweeps like a light through him. He is aware of Something greater than his own individual nature——Something which shakes him from his petty preoccupation with personal interests and makes him aware that he is a mouthpiece of the Spirit, and its tabernacle. The great educators and law-givers of the world have had this experience, have yielded to the inner voice, and have *dilated* with an energy not their own. (156).

of religion) *it is free to be known by all men.* (43.1).

D

When a faithful thinker is resolute to detach every object from personal relations and see it in the light of Thought, then will God go forth anew into the creation. (92.6). Following the invisible steps of Thought, we learn that the highest is present to the soul of man, that the dread universal essence, which is not wisdom, or love, or beauty, or power, but all in one, and each entirely, is that for which all things exist, and that by which they *are.* That spirit does not act upon us from without, that is, in space and time, but spiritually, or through ourselves. (79.5). It is an instantaneous, in-streaming, causing power. (90.21). I become a transparent eye-ball. I am nothing. I see all. The currents of the Universal Being circulate through me. The name of the nearest friend sounds then foreign and accidental. (13.5). What noble emotions *dilate* the mortal as he enters into the counsels of the creation and feels by knowledge the privilege *to be!* (49.19).

XI

ADVANTAGES OFFERED BY THE RELIGIOUS APPROACH

Reason, Religion and the Will in man constitute a trinity in unity. Reason is the science of the *All as the Whole.* Religion is the same power that represents the concentration of the *All in Each.* It converts universal truth into individual duties. (22-23).

Philosophy will gain much by accepting Coleridge's outlook. The barriers between it and Faith will fall. The philosopher will no longer be alienated from sympathy with his fellow men. His head will not be disjoined from his heart. Speculative truth will not be separated from practical wisdom. And with the union of Religion and Philosophy, the Inward Eye (*i.e.*, the Reason) will open upon a glorious vision of the I AM THAT I AM ——that which cannot be described in mere words. (164).

The Principle of Religion——of a living and substantial faith——passeth all understanding. Religion elevates the spirit above the semblances of custom and the senses to the world of Spirit. It is "life in the Idea." It is the only sure anchorage in the storm, and at the same time the substantiating principle of all true wisdom and the satisfactory *solution* of all the contradictions of human nature and of the whole riddle of the world. Religion alone speaks intelligibly to all alike, if only the *heart* listens. For the Reason is present in all and can be awakened, but it cannot be given. Religion is not just a sort of knowledge; it is rather a form of *being,* for it is the only knowledge that truly *is.* (169).

There is something in the human mind which makes it know (as soon as it is sufficiently awakened to reflect on its own thoughts and notices), that in all finite quantity there is an Infinite; in all measures of Time, an Eternal; that the latter are the basis, the substance, the true and abiding *reality* of the former, and that as we truly *are,* only as far as God is with us, so neither can we truly *possess* (*i.e.*, enjoy) our Being or any other real good, but by living in the sense of his holy Presence. (198).

This great Idea which, like a mighty wave, bears us aloft and for the description of which man has no adequate faculty——this great Idea is *Unity Absolute*. It is *Existence*. And man dares not arrogate it to himself. It is *not* his own, but superior to his will. It dwells in him only so far as he dwells in it. The truths which it manifests are such that it alone can manifest. Are they not perpetual Revelation? And is it not *God?* (157).

Being enlarged into the largeness of God and comprehending all things in our bosoms by the Divine Spirit, we are not disturbed by trifles, do not enter into factions, are at rest with all and delight in all. For we know nothing but what is, in its essence, *in our own hearts*. (110, 115). Yea, religion reconciles the man with himself, with others and with the world. It regulates all relations, tempers all passions, gives power to overcome or support suffering, and is not to be shaken by aught earthly, for it belongs not to the earth. (169). A wise spirit does not fear death. He pursues a species of contemplation not light or futile, but the most worthy of an accomplished man. He seeks for the splendor, the interfusion and communication of the Divinity and of nature. (87).

No man touches the divine natures without becoming, in some degree, himself divine. They renew the body. We tread on air. Life is no longer irksome, and we think it will never be so. No man fears age or misfortune or death in their supreme company, for he is transported out of the district of change. (71.4). The soul holds itself off from a too trivial and microscopic study of the universal tablet. It respects the end too much to immerse itself in the means. It accepts from God the phenomenon as it finds it, as the pure and awful form of religion in the world. It is not hot and passionate at the appearance of what it calls its own good or bad fortune, at the union or opposition of other persons. (74.21). When the currents of the Universal Being circulate through one, the name of the nearest friend sounds foreign. To be brothers or acquaintances——master or servant—— is then only a trifle. (13.7).

XII
THE RIGHT METHOD FOR THE DISCOVERY OF TRUTH IN THE RELATED WORLDS OF MIND AND MATTER

A

One must begin with a preconception or a prior action of the mind before one can initiate a true method. It is often necessary to trust the intuition and to make a guess. A true method must have continuous transition or a principle of progression. Mere deduction from particulars or the arrangement of facts in a series is *no method at all*. When one begins with an Idea——the right Idea—— he often discovers in the external world a corresponding Law, which slowly and inevitably explains the known facts, predicts others not yet observed, and interprets all that shall occur. It progressively extends its influence, making for greater and greater unity and simplicity. (127-134).

A

In inquiries respecting the laws of the world, the highest (*i.e.*, the most spiritual) reason is always the truest. That which seems faintly possible, because it is so refined, is often faint and dim because it is deepest seated in the mind among the eternal verities. (82.3). It is essential to a true theory of Nature and of man that it should contain somewhat progressive. Facts that end in the statement (as one finds them in the lifeless classifications of botany) cannot be all that is true of this brave lodging wherein man is harbored. Nature always speaks *of Spirit*. (That is its unifying and explanatory Idea!) (76.3).

B

A guess inspired by intuition often becomes fruitful. Coleridge gives an example of one of his guesses which was later proved true in the scientific field. Once man seizes the Unifying Idea or Law, it becomes its own proof and answer. It extends its jurisdiction over the earth and makes further collection of particulars unimportant. (The Law of Polarity is an example of such an Idea. It functions in physics, botany and throughout the universe.) (134-138).

---

true theory appears, it will be its own evidence. Its test is that it will explain all phenomena. (7.3). We make fables to hide the baldness of the fact and conform it to the higher law of the mind. But when the fact is seen *under the light of an Idea*, the gaudy fable fades and shrivels. We behold the real higher Law. (92.18).

C .

Without the guiding light of a Regulative Idea, the sciences cannot attain their full evolution, cannot recognize their fundamental laws. *Truth must be found within us before it can be intelligibly reflected back on the mind from without.* We must consider final causes in the works of nature as well as in the works of man. The scientist must admit a teleological ground in physics and physiology before he can find the *one law* which prevails throughout *all existence.* Although the strict scientist cannot assign to nature a *conscious* purpose, he must be able to distinguish her agency from a blind and lifeless mechanism. (146-147).

D

Botany still needs a philosopher to state the unifying principle and thereby establish a true method. At present, that science is little more than a huge catalogue of particulars. The ineffective

B

Every surmise and vaticination of the mind is entitled to a certain respect, and we learn to prefer imperfect theories and sentences which contain glimpses of truth to digested systems which have no one valuable suggestion. (86.16). The true scientist will perceive that there are far more excellent qualities in the student than preciseness and infallibility; that a guess is often more fruitful than an indisputable affirmation, and that a dream may let us deeper into the secret of nature than a hundred concerted experiments. It is not so pertinent to man to know all the individuals of the animal kingdom, as it, is to know whence and whereto is this tyrannizing unity. in his constitution. When I behold a rich landscape, it ought to be my purpose to know why all thought of multitude is lost in a tranquil sense of unity. (83.1). All science has one aim, namely, to find a theory of nature. (6.17). Whenever a

C

Empirical science is apt to cloud the sight and, by the very knowledge of functions and processes, to bereave the student of the manly contemplation of the whole. But the best read naturalist with *devout* attention to truth will see that there remains much to learn in his relation to the world and that it is not to be learned by any addition or subtraction or other comparison of known quantities, but is arrived at by *untaught sallies of the spirit.* (82.8). Once the Idea is captured by the mind, a spiritual life is imparted to nature, and the solid-seeming block of matter is pervaded and dissolved by a thought. The feeble human being penetrates vast masses of nature with an informing soul and recognizes himself in their harmony——that is, seizes their *law!* In physics, when this is attained, the memory disburthens itself of its cumbrous particulars and carries centuries of observation in a single formula. (69.7).

D

Science often sees only with half sight. The end is lost in attention to the means. (86.12). I cannot greatly honor minuteness of details so long as there is no hint to explain the relation between things

naturalist ignores the Unifying Idea——
in truth, ignores his Reason, his higher
Self and Religion. Until he emerges from
under the dominion of the Understanding, he will never receive an answer
from the oracle of nature. (133, 140).

and thoughts——no ray upon the *metaphysics* of botany to the mind so that
science can be built upon *ideas*. (83.19).
All the facts of natural history taken by
themselves have no value, but are barren
like a single sex. But marry natural history to human history, and it is full of
life. Whole floras are but dry catalogues
of facts. (35.14).

E

In whatever science the relation of the
parts to each other and to the whole is
predetermined by a truth originating in
the mind, and not abstracted or generalized from observation of the parts,
a law is present. Law, in its perfect
form, is an attribute of the Supreme
Being, inseparable from the Idea of God.
What is *Idea* in the mind becomes *Law*
in Nature. (128 *et passim*).

E

A law determines all phenomena,
which being known, the phenomena can
be predicted. That law, when in the mind,
is an Idea. (62.21).

Bacon, father of the Inductive Method, insists upon a preconception or mental
initiative before one approaches the facts of science. Plato and Bacon are really in
complete agreement. They saw the same truth from opposite viewpoints: Philosophy
being necessarily bipolar, Plato treats principally of the truth as it manifests itself at
the *ideal* pole, as the science of intellect, while Bacon confines himself, for the most part,
to the same truth as it is manifested at the other or material pole, as the science of
nature. (141-143).

All speculative truths, in beginning with a postulate, require an *act of the will*.
Truth is made one's own, therefore, only if the will *acts*. Since the will is the officer
presiding over the moral being, it may be said that the *intellectual* rests upon the *moral*.
The will is deeper than mind; the moral being is deeper than the intellectual. The mind
doesn't cease to be mind by having an antecedent, but the will is either first or it is not
a will at all. (100, 282).

XIII
PROSPECTS——WHAT OF THE FUTURE?——HOW RESTORE THE WORLD?

A

In the childhood of the race (from
Adam through Moses), education began
with training the moral sense——the
will being taught obedience. The aim was
to cultivate the truly human (the Reason) in man's nature and to do so as
independently as possible from the senses
until the time should come when the
outer world would serve to attest the
truths previously learned from the
deeper inner sources. Emphasis was on
the pure Reason and on training the will
——or on both as united in faith. Men
were not allowed to make images to represent their Creator, but were taught to
consider the Creator as Spirit. (148). At

A

Once upon a time man was permeated
and dissolved by spirit. (He lived in his
Reason.) His mind externalized itself in
the world of nature. (88.11). His elemental power was, therefore, not his
own——not deliberately achieved by himself——not consciously sought after nor
given as a reward for his merit. It came
not through the functioning of his Understanding. Rather it sprang from
above him. It was superior to his will, or
transcendental. His *law* became paramount or supreme in nature only by his
submitting his individual will to the demands of the Universal Will——to the
Universal Reason. (Exposition of 89.6-

the Creation, man *became a living soul.* He did not merely *possess* it; he *became it.* It was his proper being, his truest self, the *man* in him. (177).

10).

B

Man is a fallen creature, not by accidents of bodily constitution, but by disease in his will, which is no longer self-determined——no longer free and yielding to the Divine Will, but under the domination of the mechanical universe. (221-222). Man determined to exercise his Understanding alone——to shape his convictions and deduce his knowledge from without (*a posteriori*), emphasizing visible and tangible things. He built cities etc. *Civilization* replaced *cultivation* of the Spirit. He became an idolater of the senses, lived almost completely in the Understanding, and determined to receive nothing as true unless the senses bore witness to it. He thus became almost a beast, but not quite. A semblance of religion continued; the Reason still dwelt in him, though it slept. (149). So the heart once gone from God turned continually further away, yet even in wandering it retained a natural relation to God as its center. It found no true rest elsewhere. Man attempted to quiet his heart by things, but, unsuccessful, drove his own shadow before him. (203). Thus did Adam (generic man) turn his back on the sun and dwell in the dark and shadow. (220, 224). But the other world remains for man, though he discerns it not. It is the Reason that dwells in all. Men do not differ in their several gifts

B

At present, man applies to nature but half his force. He works on the world with his Understanding alone. He lives in the world, but masters it only by a penny-wisdom. And he that works hardest is at best only a half-man. His arms are strong enough, and his digestion is good, but *his mind is imbruted*, and he is a selfish savage. His relation to nature, his power over it, is through the senses ——the realm of the Understanding: witness his attempt to conquer nature by manure, steam engines, harnessing of wind, development of water power, and use of the compass. (89.12). Yet sometimes man starts in his slumber and wonders at himself and his house, and muses strangely at the resemblance betwixt him and it. (89.2). Nature ever admonishes him. She stands like a great shadow, pointing as always to the sun behind him. (76.16).

and powers of intellect, but in their wills. The other world is really their proper home. But man is an absentee and chooses to live abroad. His freedom and his Reason (which characterize him as human and above the beasts) he repudiates. The will is alienated, and the Reason slumbers. (277).

C

As I look at nature I seem to see the same Power as that of the Reason—— the same power, but in a lower dignity ——and, therefore, a symbol of that higher life of Reason in which the whole series of forms is perfected. (258). Nature's book shows no evidence of guilt or anguish. It is like a mother nursing her child, the child smiling in its strange dream of obscure yet happy sensations. In the presence of nature, man's soul seems to say to itself: "From this state hast thou fallen! Such shouldst thou still become, thyself all permeable to a holier power! thyself at once hidden and glorified by its own transparence." But what

C

The world proceeds from the same spirit as the body of man. It is a remoter and inferior incarnation of God, a projection of God in the unconscious. But it differs from the body in one important respect. It is not, like that, now subjected to the degenerated human will. Its serene order is inviolable by us. It is, therefore, to us the present expositor of the divine mind. It is a fixed point whereby we may measure our departure. As we degenerate, the contrast between us and our house is more evident. We find we do not know the use of more than a few plants. We are becoming strangers. Yet the landscape, every glimpse of which has

the plant is by an act not its own and unconsciously, that must thou make thyself to become——must by prayer and by a watchful and unresisting spirit, join with the preventing and assisting grace to make thyself. (257).

grandeur, continues to be a face of God. (80.16).

D

How restore the world? By the nurture and evolution of our proper humanity (*i.e.*, the Reason, which is the true Self). When this aim becomes uppermost in man's pursuits, he will seek the ground common to the world and human beings, therein to find the one principle of permanence and identity——*the Spirit*. (152). At the annunciation of principles, of ideas, the soul of man awakes and starts up, and an exile in a far-distant land leaps up at the unexpected sounds of his native language, when after long years of absence and almost of oblivion he is suddenly addressed in his own mother-tongue. (246). We must have a birth of the godlike *within* us before the symbols *without* become alive with meaning. Once the Idea is grasped, then all nature will become transparence without vacuum; plenitude without opacity. (254).

D

The problem of restoring the world to its original and eternal beauty concerns not the external order, but our inner selves. It is solved *by the redemption of the soul*. (91.5). In the thick darkness there are not wanting gleams of a better light——occasional examples of the action of man upon nature with his entire force——with Reason as well as Understanding. (90.4). When Reason momentarily grasps the sceptre, man experiences a power which is supplied not in the time-and-space world, but comes from above. It is transcendental——an instantaneous, in-streaming, causing power. (90.19).

E

Religion partakes of the unity and infinity of the Divine Nature. It adds fullness and creative overflowing. That which men intuitively behold and adore, praying always and rejoicing always, that do they tend to become. The meanest object bears witness to a mystery of infinite solution. The whole creation groans and travails in earnest expectation of renewal of its forfeited power ——the power of retiring from vanity of self into its true life——that of the Reason or Spirit. Religion expresses the unity of the Infinite Spirit by being a total act of the soul. It is a life within life, evermore organizing the soul anew. (263).

E

Man is disunited with himself. He cannot be a naturalist until he satisfies all the demands of spirit. Love is as much its demand as perception. (91.13). His power over nature is now limited to the Understanding. (89.19). It is ineffective. It is such a resumption of power as if a banished king should buy his territories inch by inch, instead of vaulting at once into his throne. Meanwhile, there are gleams of a better light ——examples of man's action upon nature with his entire force——with both Reason and Understanding. And then he manifests the energy of the instantaneous in-streaming causing power. (90.1).

F

Nothing great is achieved without enthusiasm, which is the swallowing up of self in an object dearer than self, or in an *Idea* more vivid. In the genuine enthusiasm of morals, religion etc., this enlargement and elevation of the soul attest the presence and accompany the in-

F

There are not wanting examples of the action of man upon nature with his entire force. (90.5). These include the miracles of enthusiasm, such as those reported of Swedenborg, Hohenlohe and the Shakers. They are examples of Reason's momentary ascendancy——of the

tuition of ultimate principles alone. Every principle is actualized by an idea, and every idea is living, productive, characterized by infinity, and filled with endless power of semination. Hence wisdom (consisting wholly of ideas and principles) is *power*. (245).

G

But every living human being today ——no matter how poor and destitute he may be, even in his present state——has access to that world of the soul——to the house not made with hands. All he needs is the *eye*, which is the light of this *house*——the light which is the eye of the soul. (177).

H

It is our appointed task to render gradually our own work. All things surrounding us and all experiences that can happen to us have a providential purpose and one final cause——namely, *to increase consciousness*, so that whatever part of the *terra incognita* of our being the increased consciousness discovers, our will may conquer and bring into subjection to itself under the sovereignty of Reason. (261). And we shall find our speculations beginning and ending in *wonder* before the Incomprehensible and Groundless. The life-ebullient stream shall break through every momentary embankment and sweep through us. *Omnia exeunt in mysterium.* (165, 196-197).

ideal force of man. (90.13). Such enthusiasts rebuild the world by conforming their lives to the pure transcendental idea within their own minds. (94.13).

G

When we breathe the infinite we understand that man has access to the entire mind of the Creator——is himself the creator in finite. This view animates me to create my own world through the purification of my soul. (80.4). The highest is present to the soul of man. (79.9). All that Adam had, all that Caesar could, you have and can do. Adam called his house, heaven and earth. Caesar called his, Rome. You, perhaps, call yours a cobbler's trade. Yet your dominion is as great as theirs, though without fine names. (94.6).

H

A man is fed, not that he may be fed, but that he may work. (18.6). Whilst the abstract question occupies one's intellect, nature brings it in the concrete to be solved by one's hands. (93.8). That which was unconscious truth becomes, when interpreted and defined in an object, a part of the domain of knowledge ——a new amount to the magazine of power. (45.9). Man should, therefore, build his own world. As fast as he conforms his life to the pure idea in his mind, that mind will unfold its great proportions. (94.13). More and more with every thought will his kingdom stretch over things until the world becomes, at last, only a *realized will*—— the double of a man. (51.6). In proportion to the energy of his thought and will, he will take up the world into himself. (25.13). The kingdom of man over nature——a dominion such as now is beyond his dream of God——he shall enter without more wonder than the blind man feels who is gradually restored to perfect sight. (95.7).

We are now ready for a rapid survey of *Nature*, beginning with the "Introduction," which seems to have been composed last of all and which, therefore, reflects as well as foreshadows all that follows it. The work opens with a call for the age to be self-reliant (that is, *God-reliant*) because God and Nature are as close to the moderns as they once were to the ancients. "The sun shines today also!" Nature continually invites us to increase our spiritual power by acting in accordance with the divine order of things. That system includes an outer world and an inner world (matter and mind), the one objective and the other subjective, with a transcendent Spirit over, behind and through both.

Man is a citizen of both these worlds and the sole interpreter of them. Rays of relation extend from him to God (who also dwells within his breast), on the one hand, and to every created thing, on the other. Because he is the universe in little (the microcosm), he holds within him the means of answering all questions concerning himself or the cosmos. He is a veritable key to all existence. Convinced that he belonged to such a divine order, Emerson believed it possible to discover an adequate theory of nature. (The scientists thus far had failed to produce one befitting the beauty, grandeur and richness that he and a few contemporaries had seen in the creation.) The method which he intended to use in making the search was one which, he believed, Plato (the greatest philosopher) and Bacon (the greatest scientist) had both approved. (Coleridge had apparently reconciled them!!)

That method was subjective and intuitional. It began with a preconception, a clue from the Reason, a hint from the God within, or a guess from the world of Thought. To the average scientist counting stamens or sorting leaves, this approach might seem rather futile, but Coleridge and Emerson knew that the phenomenal world (*i.e.*, the realm of nature) was less *real* than the world of Ideas or Spirit, and that the most effective approach to an analysis of the material universe was, therefore, through the mind. (Abstract truth is always in the end most practical.) And since matter and mind throughout the universe coincided, the one unlocking the other and both penetrated by the same "Something" or Divine Unity, then the great *Ideas* of the mind of man were paralleled by the great unifying *Laws* organizing the kingdom of nature. And since one's powers of observation *without* depended upon one's spiritual state *within*——since "what we are within, that only can we see without" (*Quantum sumus, scimus*), the best way of finding the Theory or Law of outer nature was to begin with an Idea in one's own mind——an Idea supplied by the Indwelling Reason. In a sense, the Ideas within were not only parallel to the Laws without, but *prior to them*.

How might one recognize a true theory of nature, if it should be discovered? In the first place, it would have the simplicity of a unifying principle. In the second, it would be its own evidence; it would meet the pragmatic test. In the third, it would manifest a "somewhat progressive" ——that is, it would grow and expand in its application, to cover not only the known facts but even those yet undiscovered and, when they should come to light, would find a place for them in the great whole. It would be like the great Law of Polarity, which, Coleridge believed, not only manifested itself in physics by positive and negative poles of the magnet, and in botany and zoology by male and female sexes, but also throughout existence by antithesis of mind and matter. Such a progressive quality one might expect to find in a true theory of nature. It would extend its simple operation in ever-widening circles throughout the length and breadth of the time-and-space world. It would be seen in the lowest levels of life as well as in the highest, modified perhaps and called by different names, but always recognizably the same. It would seem in the lowest levels to be preparing itself for the higher ones by an unceasing development.

Coleridge and Emerson were dissatisfied with the complacency of contemporary science. The botanist seemed happy if he discovered a new species and classified it with thousands of others under a particular genus. Nature was treated as if dead——recorded in dry catalogues of particulars. There was nothing progressive in the method. Each field of science seemed distinct and unrelated to the others. The final mystery, the great ends, the complete natural order, the relation between animal life and human life——these did not concern the narrow insect hunter or the specialist in lichens, with their blotters and bottles of chloroform. Coleridge and Emerson believed that since matter and mind were related, then the apple, the Rhodora, the dog, the ant or the spider not only were *facts*, but were *facts with a meaning* (if one were only awake), and the meaning had a way of becoming *deeper* as man became a *better* human being. (The human quality in man was his Reason.) Coleridge and Emerson were disturbed by the blind spots in the eyes of the so-called learned men, who lived only in the tradition of John Locke——that is, under the dominion of the sense-loving, nearsighted Understanding. A true theory of nature would not concern itself with "facts that end in the statement" or with "uses that are exhausted or may be" (76.5). In other words, plants were something more than the source of animal food. That might be their least value. They were also symbols of simple truths, and if regarded with spiritual energy, they might point to fundamental spiritual laws. The true theory of nature was expected to unify all existence and show that *nothing* in the natural world could be comprehended *in a statement*. Its influence would be perpetually growing. Its wealth for spiritual beings could never be exhausted, and this because it had relations with mind and matter, and with that "Something" behind them both.

Emerson did not lack a good example of the use of the so-called "Plato-Bacon" method. The conclusion to *The Friend* had shown what it could accomplish and how one might begin with a great idea, execute a full circle, and come successfully back to the starting point in the end. Let me summarize rather than quote a significant paragraph from Coleridge: "Thus I prefaced my inquiry into the science of method with a principle deeper than science, more certain than demonstration: *God, the Groundless or the Self-Grounded.* From this I started, or rather seemed to start; for it still moved before me as an invisible guardian and guide, and it is *this* the reappearance of which announces the conclusion of the circuit, and welcomes me at the goal. There is but one principle, and it is the principle of *religion*. It elevates the spirit above the semblances of custom and the senses to a world of spirit——to life in the Idea."[5]

Emerson chose the very same Idea as his postulate or assumption, and attempted to show in *Nature* (1) its progressive quality when applied to every level of the phenomenal world and (2) its remarkable ability for unifying all fields of knowledge and experience. With regard to the first,

---

[5] Read carefully the complete paragraph (¶ 169).

he showed nature in no way exhausted in her first uses. "When a thing has served an end to the uttermost, *it is wholly new for an ulterior service. In God, every end is converted into a new means.*" (52.10). He then put the common fact-hunter to shame by revealing nature first *as our home,* then *as beauty* mounting from material to spiritual levels, then *as a language* in several different degrees, then *as a discipline* in various senses, and finally *as the revealer* of the great Unifying Fact behind all other facts——the cause of all the progressive tendency——THE SPIRIT. Emerson thus gave us an excellent demonstration of Coleridge's progressive method, and the true theory of nature was stated as follows: *It is the organ of the Spirit, designed to yield the activity of man an infinite scope.* (76.9). In other words, it is God's agent in helping the soul of man to grow and develop. Since the Divine Spirit aids man from *within* and from *without* (through nature), who dares set bounds to the possibilities of the spiritual man? (80.3).

As for his second objective——the demonstration of a progressive and tyrannizing unity throughout creation——he began with the separate fields of science and pointed out (what the scientists themselves had already pointed out) that there is a unity in each department of knowledge. For example, the field of comparative anatomy shows the human hand in the flipper of the fossil saurus. (55.5). He next called attention to the unity in objects "wherein there is great superficial unlikeness" (55.7)—— to observations made by his philosophic sources (Goethe, Staël-Holstein, Coleridge and others), showing how this unity transcends special fields: Architecture is frozen *music!* A Gothic church is petrified *religion!* The artist needs the surgeon's knowledge of human *anatomy!* And so on for a page. (55.3ff.) Next he showed a central unity, not in *things* but in *deeds*: "The same central Unity is still more conspicuous in actions." (56.15). "The axioms of *physics* translate the laws of *ethics.*" Thus, the "whole is greater than its part; reaction is equal to action." (41.21). "A rule of one art or a law of one organization *holds throughout nature,*" and the intimate unity "betrays its source in universal Spirit." (56.2). As with things and actions, so with thoughts: "Every universal truth which we express in words implies or supposes *every other truth.*" It is "like a great circle on a sphere, comprising all possible circles." (56.10). Ultimately, "truth and goodness and beauty are but different faces of the same ALL," which is manifested in and by one Spirit. (30.20 and 79.8). The progressive character of his "true theory" is patent. The tyrannizing unity organized not only the little departments of man's knowledge, but swept through all existence.

In "Prospects" he wrote *from the Reason,*[6] making the Orphic Poet present the everlasting and omnipresent truth of his theory in fables and symbols.[7] Language, at best, never communicates the whole truth, and except in moments of great inspiration (92.22), men must rely upon picturesque or symbolical statements to stimulate their dull imagination. (Coleridge, also, had ended his great works with mythological summaries.) The fable was addressed to spirits suffering from torpor and from the

---

[6] See *Journals,* III, 467.
[7] See *Journals,* IV, 287: "We say Paradise was; Adam fell; the Golden Age, and the like. We mean man is not as he ought to be; but our way of painting this is on Time and we say *was.*" Cf. "A Statement of the First Philosophy," sections VIII-IX.

domination of the senses and the Understanding. It proclaimed that in "inquiries respecting the laws of the world and the frame of things, "the highest reason is always the truest."[8] It announced that the Reason in man was the source of his humanity; that it was within the reach of all; that it gave unity to life and explained all experience. It promised, to those who would dwell in that Reason and submit their wills to it, the ability to create a brave new world, or (to use the language of the fable) the power to shape a new Eden or Paradise.

So, like Coleridge, Emerson came full circle to his starting point——to that ineffable, ever-present universal Essence or Supreme Being, who acted upon the soul of man, not from without, "that is, in space and time, but spiritually, or through ourselves." Its revelation was continuous. It depended not on time or upon the expressions of an historic religion, with creeds and institutions which dotted the centuries and which were recorded in dusty books. It did not hark back to "special revelations" in Eden, on Sinai, or at the Reformation. It was the *immediate* in every man, who needed only to have his Reason awakened (79.8ff.) to discover God in greater wonder than ever before in history.

In the early 1820's, Emerson had joyfully discovered Bishop Berkeley's Idealism and esteemed it highly because it gave the lie to the smugness of the school of Locke and introduced him to a mysterious universe. He always thereafter had respect for Berkeley's system. (It is that particular system of Idealism which was uppermost in his mind while he composed chapter VI of *Nature*.) But Coleridge, in the 1830's, brought Emerson still greater joy and still greater hope and encouragement——and not Emerson only, but Sampson Reed, Bronson Alcott and James Marsh, to name only a few. Berkeley had advanced an hypothesis that accounted for nature "by other principles than those of carpentry and chemistry" (78.9), but he had not answered Emerson's deepest spiritual needs or contributed a warm, transcendental assurance of the Spirit. Berkeley's system, in denying the existence of abstract matter, seemed unfortunately to deny "substantive being to men and women." (78.16). If matter did not exist, were the bodies of human beings to be considered phantoms also? And what of the abundant evidence which Coleridge had set forth for the coincidence of mind and matter, of subject and object, of man's recapitulating nature and of nature's seeming reflection of human life?

Man is the point wherein matter and spirit meet and marry. The Idealist says, God paints the world around your soul. The spiritualist saith, Yea, but lo! God is within you. The self of self creates the world through you, and organizations like you. The Universal Central Soul comes to the surface in my body.[9]

Berkeleian Idealism left God out of Emerson (78.13), and his heart, therefore, resisted it. (78.15). It could, henceforth, stand only as a "useful introductory hypothesis," serving to guard one against pantheism by apprizing him of "the eternal distinction between the soul and the world." (79.1).

---

[8] See *Nature*, 82.3. See also *Journals*, IV, 64 (June 7, 1836): "So you have undertaken to solve the problem of the world. God speed you, fair sir, in your modest attempt. Remember this, however, that the greatest reason is always the truest."
[9] See *Journals*, IV, 78 (July 30, 1836).

Coleridge's postulate, with its Unifying Idea, proved superior to Berkeley's; and with its aid Emerson was able to interpret the spiritual writers of all ages and to gather from them his richest lustres. He was able, moreover, to conclude his little work, *Nature*, in the spirit of Coleridge, who had said: "All teachers of moral truth who aim to prepare for its reception call men's attention to the Law of their own hearts."[10] The Orphic Poet's lines reflect the speaker of those words.

I have by no means pointed out Coleridge's complete influence on *Nature*, for it seemed wise to dwell on the major outline. I might have called attention to Emerson's adaptation of Coleridge's Shakespearean criticism and his Theory of the Imagination, as it appears in the section on "Idealism." I might also have given an account of the lustres which Emerson carried over or modified, but most of them are indicated in earlier footnotes.[11] Two of special interest will be mentioned, however, in concluding this chapter——the first because it was a favorite with Coleridge to whose distinction between the Reason and the Understanding and between objective and subjective truth it gave picturesque support; the second, because it supplied Emerson with the description of a man under the influence of lofty sentiments and seems to have been the original of the much-discussed "transparent eyeball" passage (12.17ff.). The student will see in the latter parallel an interesting contrast between the backgrounds of the two men—geographical, educational, symbolical and social——for although their views on philosophical subjects almost coincided, Emerson's solitary worship in the New England pine woods (which were God's *first* temples),[12] stands out distinct from Coleridge's losing himself in a gothic cathedral. Whereas Emerson strongly emphasized the individual, Coleridge was most at home in society. For the one, the woods provided the best atmosphere for contemplation. For the other, that atmosphere was, doubtless, congregational worship in the One, Holy, Catholic and Apostolic Church.[13]

EULER'S LAW OF ARCHES

The celebrated Euler having demonstrated certain properties of Arches, adds: "All experience is in contradiction to this; but this is no reason for doubting its truth." The words *sound* paradoxical; but mean no more than this——that the mathematical properties of figure and space are not less certainly the properties of Figure and Space because they can never be perfectly realized in wood, stone, or iron. (229).

Thus even in physics, the material is ever degraded before the spiritual. The astronomer, the geometer, rely on their irrefragable analysis, and disdain the results of observation. The sublime remark of Euler on his law of arches, "This will be found contrary to all experience, yet is true;" had already transferred nature into the mind, and left matter like an outcast corpse. (69.18).

---

[10] See ¶s. 190-191.
[11] See chapter VI, above.
[12] See *Journals*, III, 570-571.
[13] See *Journals*, IV, 152-153: "I told Miss Peabody last night that Mr. Coleridge's churchmanship is thought to affect the value of his criticism, etc. I do not feel it. It is a harmless freak and sometimes occurs in a wrong place, as when he refuses to translate some alleged blasphemy in Wallenstein. Some men are affected with hemorrhage of the nose; it is of no danger, but unlucky when it befals where it should not, as at a wedding or in the rostrum. But Coleridge's is perfectly separable. I know no such critic. Every

SPIRITUAL EXALTATION——THE MYSTICAL ECSTASY

The contemplation of the works of antique art excites a feeling of elevated beauty, and exalted notions of the human self; but the Gothic architecture impresses the beholder with a sense of self-annihilation; he becomes, as it were, a part of the work contemplated. An endless complexity and variety are united into one whole, the plan of which is not distinct from the execution. A Gothic cathedral is the petrifaction of our religion.[14] (298). [T]he Gothic art is sublime. On entering a cathedral, I am filled with devotion and with awe; I am lost to the actualities that surround me, and my whole being expands into the infinite; earth and air, nature and art, all swell up into eternity, and the only sensible impression left, is '*that I am nothing!*' (299).

In the woods, is perpetual youth. Within these plantations of God, a decorum and sanctity reign, a perennial festival is dressed. In the woods, we return to reason and faith. Standing on the bare ground,——my head bathed by the blithe air, and uplifted into infinite space,——all mean egotism vanishes. I become a transparent eye-ball. *I am nothing.* I see all. The currents of the Universal Being circulate through me; I am part or particle of God. In the wilderness, I find something more dear and connate than in streets or villages. In the tranquil landscape, and especially in the distant line of the horizon, man beholds somewhat as beautiful as his own nature.[15] (12.17).

EMERSON HOUSE — Built in 1828. Owned by Ralph Waldo Emerson from 1835 to 1882

opinion he expresses is a canon of criticism that should be writ in steel, and his italics are italics of the mind."

[14] This line appears slightly modified in *Nature*, 55.9.

[15] Cf. *Journals*, III, 392.

EMERSON AND THE *ENTOMOLOGY* OF KIRBY AND SPENCE[1]

Men have perhaps always conceived of nature in some degree as a book of emblems and symbols, and Emerson certainly found the theory not only in the ancient Trismegisti,[2] and in Coleridge and Swedenborg, but throughout dozens of contemporary works, ranging from books on the formation and history of language, and pious works on nature and the seasons of the year, to volumes dealing strictly with science. Of special interest, in the group last mentioned, is the *Introduction to Entomology* by William Kirby and William Spence——one, though not necessarily the most significant, of many semi-pious scientific works which Boston was reading in the 1820's and the 1830's.[3] I mention it here because Coleridge knew it well and referred to it in the *Aids*[4] in support of his distinction between the Reason and the Understanding, and because it almost certainly came to Emerson's attention through a long review by Sampson Reed, which appeared in many installments, during three years, in the *New Jerusalem Magazine*.[5] It reflects the vulgate doctrine of the period and serves conveniently to prepare the reader for the Swedenborgian attitude toward animals——to be considered in later chapters.

Emerson may or may not have followed the review carefully, though he had access to the magazine in which it appeared. At all events, he seems not to have consulted the *Introduction* itself until after Coleridge had called it to his attention, for it is first listed in the journals[6] (*ca.* January, 1830) among the books suggested by the *Aids*. On July 15, following,[7] he withdrew the first two volumes from the Boston Athenæum, and the third, fifteen days later.[8] On October 19, he again called for volume one and kept it for exactly one month. On May 28, 1831,[9] he secured it for the third time and kept it for three weeks. In 1848, when he was in England, Emerson had the pleasure of making the acquaintance of William Spence, and after returning to America, received several pamphlets from him.[10] For convenience and because of their relevance to later chapters, I have drawn the following excerpts from the review in the *New Jerusalem Magazine*.

---

[1] William Kirby and William Spence, *An Introduction to Entomology.* It was first issued in London, 1815-1816.

[2] See *Carlyle-Emerson Corr.*, I, 32-33.

[3] Perhaps the most famous are the Bridgewater Treatises on the Power, Wisdom and Goodness of God as Manifested in Creation (13 vols., 1833-1837).

[4] For example, see ¶ 51.

[5] See esp. *N J M*, II (1828-1829), 171ff., 203ff., 248ff., 274ff., 302ff., 333ff., 368ff.; III (1829-1830), 16-20, 138-146, 239-245, 277-285; IV (1830-1831), 62.

[6] See *Journals*, II, 268. In chapter VII above I have dated it conjecturally as of January or February, 1830, and given negative evidence in support.

[7] *Emerson's Reading*, 17 and 83. He returned both on July 23.

[8] *Ibid.*, 17 and 83. He returned it on August 20.

[9] *Ibid.*, 17, 18, 83. Oct. 19 to Nov. 19, 1830; May 28 to June 20, 1831.

[10] See *Letters*, IV, 84 (June, 1848).

SEEING GOD IN ALL THINGS——SOLOMON ON NATURAL HISTORY—— JESUS' SYMBOLICAL REFERENCE TO ANIMALS

¶ A

'To see all things in God' has been accounted one of the peculiar privileges **of a** future state; and in this present life, 'to see God in all things,' in the mirror **of the** creation to behold and adore the reflected glory of the Creator, is no mean attainment; and it possesses this important advantage, that thus we sanctify our pursuits, and instead of loving the creatures for themselves, are led by the survey of them, and their instincts, to the love of Him who made and endowed them.[11]

¶ B

Solomon, the wisest of mankind, made natural history a peculiar object of study, and left treatises behind him upon its various branches, in which *creeping things* or insects were not overlooked; and a wiser than Solomon directs our attention to natural productions, when he bids us consider the lilies of the field, teaching us that they are more worthy of our notice than the most glorious works of man; he also not obscurely intimates that insects are symbolical beings, when he speaks of scorpions as synonymous with evil spirits; thus giving into our hands a clue for a more profitable mode of studying them, as furnishing moral and spiritual instruction.[12]

THE BOOK OF NATURE AS A BOOK OF SYMBOLS——ANALOGIES IN SITUATION, STRUCTURE AND USE

¶ C

Whichever way we turn our eyes on the objects of creation, above—below—athwart *analogies* meet us in every direction, and it appears clear, that the book of nature is a book of symbols, in which one thing represents another in endless alternation. And not only does one animal, &c. symbolize another, but even between the parts and organs of one set of animals there is often an *analogy* as to their *situation* and *use*, when there is little or no *affinity* as to their *structure*; or again, the analogy is in their *situation*, without affinity in either structure or use.[13]

SYSTEM OF CORRELATION OR CHAIN OF AFFINITIES——ASCENT IN CREATION TOWARDS MAN, THE CENTER OF ALL——EVIL AND MALIGNANCY IN THE SYSTEM

¶ D

When the Almighty Creator willed to bring into existence this mundane system, he formed it according to a preconcerted plan, with all its parts beautifully linked together and mutually corresponding. All things were ordered in *measure*, and *number*, and *weight*. There was nothing deficient, nothing superfluous; but the whole in the strictest sense 'was very good,' and calculated in the highest degree to answer the purpose of its Great Author. I call it a system of *Correlation*, because there is discernible in it, in the first place, a concatenation of its parts, by which, as to their forms and uses, objects are linked together in groups by a chain of affinities; so that we pass from one to the other by gentle gradations, without having to overleap any *wide* interval. We see also a gradual ascent from low to high, from less to more excellent. And this leads us to another kind of relationship between natural objects, by which, though placed in distinct groups or in a different series, they in some sort represent and symbolize each other. Examples of this relationship by analogy are to be found in every kingdom of nature, and often form an ascending series from the lowest to the highest; for, as we shall see hereafter, these resemblances appear to maintain a certain correspondence with each other as to their relative situations; so that, for instance, in the animal kingdom they ascend step by step, without being linked by affinity or having any real juxtaposition, from the lowest groups, towards man, who stands alone at the head, or in the centre of all.[14]

---

[11] *N J M*, II (1828-1829), 174.
[12] *N J M*, II (1828-1829), 176.
[13] *N J M*, II (1828-1829), 370.
[14] *N J M*, II (1828-1829), 370-371.

¶ E

All the analogies I have here particularized, ascending from the insect, terminate in races of a corresponding character and aspect amongst the *Mammalia*, and thus lead us towards *man* himself, or rather to men in whose minds those bad and malignant qualities prevail, which, when accompanied by power, harass and lay waste mankind; and thus ascending from symbol to symbol, we arrive at an animal who in his own person unites both matter and spirit, and is thus the member both of a visible and invisible world: and we are further instructed by these symbols,—perpetually recurring under different forms,—in the existence of evil and malignant spirits, whose object and delight is the corporeal and spiritual ruin of the noble creature who is placed at the head of the visible works of God.[15]

NATURE WAS DESIGNED TO INSTRUCT MAN——IT IS A BOOK OF EMBLEMS AND SYMBOLS OF SPIRITUAL VERITIES——IT IS A *JANUS BIFRONS*, IN ONE DIRECTION LOOKING TOWARD GOD

¶ F

The Almighty Creator, when he clothed the world that he had made with *plants*, and peopled it with *animals*, besides the manifestation of his own glory, appears to have had *two* most important purposes in view:—the one, to provide a supply for mutual wants . . . and the other, that by them he might *instruct* his creature man in such civil, physical, moral and spiritual truths, as were calculated to fit him for his station in the visible world, and gradually prepare him to become an inhabitant of that invisible one for which he was destined. . . . The last,—or the instruction of man in his primeval state of integrity and purity,—was best secured by placing before him for his scrutiny a book of emblems or symbols, in which one thing, either by its form or qualities, or both, might represent another. If he was informed by his Creator that the works of creation constituted such a book, by the right interpretation of which he might arrive at spiritual verities as well as natural knowledge, curiosity and the desire of information concerning these high and important subjects would stimulate him to the study of the mystic volume placed before him; in the progress of which he would doubtless be assisted by that Divine guidance, which even now is with those who honestly seek the truth. Both divines and philosophers have embraced this opinion, which is built upon the Word of God itself.[16]

¶ G

This last purpose of the Creator was the root of the analogies, connecting different objects with each other that have no real affinity, observable in the works of creation: so that from the bottom to the top of the scale of being, there is many a series of analogous forms, as well as of concatenated ones; and the entire system of nature is *representative*, as well as operative: it is a kind of *Janus bifrons*, which requires to be studied in two aspects looking different ways.[17]

¶ H

[C]reated things are representative or symbolical: and we find, when we view them in this light, that as we ascend from the lowest beings in the scale of creation, we are led from one to another till we reach the summit or centre of the whole, and are thus conducted to the boundaries of this visible and material system; from whence we may conclude that we ought not here to stop, but go on to something invisible and extramundane, as the ultimate object intended to be reflected from this great speculum of creation—the Creator himself, and all those spirits, virtues, and powers that have emanated from him.[18]

---

[15] *N J M*, II (1828-1829), 372.
[16] *N J M*, II (1828-1829), 372-373.
[17] *N J M*, II (1828-1829), 373.
[18] *N J M*, II (1828-1829), 373.

THOUGH THE ASCENT IN NATURE IS CONTINUOUS, EACH FORM MAIN-
TAINS A LIFE CYCLE OR ORBIT——CIRCLE WITHIN CIRCLE——WHEEL
WITHIN WHEEL——MAN IS THE CENTER AND SUMMIT

¶ J

Mr. W. S. MacLeay[19] and (without consultation nearly at the same time) **Professor**
Agardh, Mr. Fries, &c. have given to the learned world an opinion which approximates
more nearly to what we see in nature: viz. That the arrangement of objects is indeed
in a continuous series, but which in its progress forms various convolutions, each of
which may be represented by a *circle*, or a series that returns into itself. According to
this opinion,—which seems the most consistent of any yet advanced, and which reconciles facts which upon no other plan can be reconciled,—the series of beings is involved
in the highest degree, rolling wheel within wheel, *ad infinitum*, and revolving, if I may
so speak, round its centre and summit—*man:* who, though not including in himself all
that distinguishes them, is still the great type in which they terminate, and from which
they degrade on all sides.[20]

---

[19] William Sharp MacLeay (1792-1865). For the basis of his system, see *N J M*, III
(1829-1830), 17: "(1) That all natural groups, whether kingdoms or any subdivision of
them, return into themselves; a distribution which he expresses by circles. (2) That
each of these circles is formed precisely of *five* groups, each of which is resolvable into
five other smaller groups, and so on till you reach the extreme term of such division.
(3) That proximate circles or larger groups are connected by the intervention of lesser
groups, which he denominates *osculant*. (4) That there are relations of analogy between
the corresponding points of contiguous circles. This system he has represented by tables
of circles inscribed with the five primary divisions of each group." Cf. *Nature*, 56.10.

[20] Kirby and Spence suggested a pattern of *seven* instead of five. *N J M*, II, 374.

SWEDENBORG IN BOSTON——EMERSON AND THE NEW CHURCH THROUGH 1836

Emerson became acquainted with the doctrines of Emanuel Swedenborg (1688-1772) chiefly through four agencies: (1) Sampson Reed and his writings (beginning in 1821); (2) articles in the *New Jerusalem Magazine* (after September, 1827); (3) the works of Swedenborg (beginning *ca.* 1828); (4) G. Oegger's *The True Messiah*, which was available in a manuscript translation in 1835. It will be convenient to discuss Reed and Oegger in separate chapters and here to deal succinctly only with the second and third. The divisions are admittedly artificial and by no means mutually exclusive, for the *New Jerusalem Magazine* published many of Reed's influential compositions and long extracts from Swedenborg's works; yet the proposed sectioning will have advantages.

An outline history of the New Church in America, especially in Boston, is now easily obtainable,[1] though the important contribution of Sampson Reed and his little circle to American thought remains still to be adequately evaluated. By way of summary it will be sufficient here to state that the Swedenborgian tradition did not really strike root in Boston until 1816, when members of the Worcester family began enthusiastically to propagate its truths.[2] There were only twelve members in the society when it was organized by Samuel Worcester on August 15, 1818, and they included two Harvard students, Thomas Worcester and Thomas B. Hayward. Sampson Reed did not join until two years later.[3] The society early began a circulating library and soon afterwards (in 1823) became a corporation.[4] In September, 1827, the *New Jerusalem Magazine* came into being as a principal missionary enterprise, with the Rev. Thomas Worcester as editor. The New Church then, as always, placed a strong emphasis on printed literature, and the back pages of the early numbers of the *N J M* list the books and pamphlets offered for sale by Adonis Howard, whose particular "use"[5] in the community, after he had left the drug business in 1827, was to print, import and sell editions of Swedenborg, as well as commentaries, tracts, catechisms and sermons. The New Church was so completely and effectively organized through the dedication of its members that growth was inevitable. It considered itself as the "new Jerusalem, coming down

---

[1] See Marguerite Block, *The New Church in the New World: A Study of Swedenborgianism in America*, N.Y., 1932. Also Sampson Reed, *A Biographical Sketch of Thomas Worcester, D.D.*, (with an address by the Rev. James Reed), Boston, 1880. See also Sampson Reed, "History of the Boston Society up to 1837. An Address," *N J M*, XI, 118ff.

[2] Block, *op. cit.*, 101; Reed, *Thomas Worcester*, 14ff.

[3] Block, *op. cit.*, 102-104. Reed, *Thomas Worcester*, 29 and 75, gives a list of converts among Harvard students: Thomas Worcester and Thomas B. Hayward were two of the founding members of the Boston Society in 1818. John H. Wilkins and Sampson Reed joined in 1820; Nathaniel Hobart, Caleb Reed and Warren Goddard, in 1821; Theophilus Parsons, in 1823; Taylor G. Worcester, in 1830; William Parsons, in 1845; and John Angier, in 1848.

[4] See Sampson Reed's letter to Theophilus Parsons, Jr., under March 6, 1823, in *E T E*, II.

[5] For the Doctrine of Uses, see below ¶s. 18-20. See also Sampson Reed ¶s. 35-37.

from God out of heaven, prepared as a bride adorned for her husband"[6] and pledged itself to redeem a New England that had somehow lost the Christian faith. Its note was optimistic. Its philosophic premises were predominantly Neo-Platonic and, therefore, might be expected to make an appeal to all who found joy in the English Romantic Movement. Emerson, who came to esteem Coleridge for his philosophic teaching rather than for doctrinal beliefs, was prepared to value the Swedenborgians for their general truths rather than for specific religious tenets, and on November 20, 1834, wrote to Carlyle that this sect "must contribute more than all other sects to the new faith which must arise out of all."[7] The New Church welcomed his interest at first, but soon became wary of the Transcendentalists of New England when, as became apparent, they showed little respect for important dogmas and traditional beliefs. With the succeeding years, it was inevitable that the two movements should drift into a mood of hostility. As early as November, 1833, Frederic Henry Hedge had discussed the recent "heresy" in his review entitled "Emanuel Swedenborg,"[8] and had established the attitude which was to prevail in the Transcendental group.[9] Though he had written with charity and depth, praising the Swedenborgians for their progressive character and sanctity of life, he received no thanks from them for questioning the value of Swedenborg's revelation. Interesting for us in that review is Hedge's discussion of the three types of mysticism and his classification of Swedenborg under the second:[10]

The first stage is, when the brooding mind, ascending from forms to principles, and from the visible manifestation to the invisible power, first begins to spiritualize nature, and loses itself in the contemplation of one pervading intelligence, which, itself infinite, possesses every form of finite being, and constitutes the life and essence of all created things;——when, not content with knowing the obvious relations and powers of animate and inanimate beings, or the obvious meaning of revealed truth, it seeks to interpret all things in conformity with its own spiritual views. This is *contemplative* mysticism; it may be compared to the first budding of a noble plant, it is the vine in its blossom, the fresh bloom and early fragrance of a visionary mind. Such was the mysticism of Plato and Pythagoras among the ancients, of St. Austin and others in the early ages of Christianity, of Jacob Boehm, and the Quietists in later times.

The second stage is, when the mind returns again from the universal to the particular, from abstract essences to determinate forms, and, leaving the contemplation of the one, endeavours to deduce the many,——when, having annihilated the creations of sense,—— the crude conceptions of its childhood, it devises a creation of its own, and constructs, on principles more ethereal, new theories of nature and new systems of religion. This is *constructive* mysticism, the plant in production, the vine hung with full clusters of rich, ripe fruit. Of this kind was the mysticism of those eastern sages, whose names have come down to us as founders of certain mystic sects,——of Hermes in Egypt, of Zoroaster in Persia, of Budha in India, &c.

[The third] stage occurs, when mysticism becomes enthusiasm, when the mind, having completed its creative process, solved all its problems, and constructed its theory of temporal and spiritual things, grows dissatisfied with intellectual intuitions, and burns to express itself in outward acts,——when, according to the nature of its doctrine, it

---

[6] Revelation 21:2. Compare 3:12.
[7] *Carlyle-Emerson Corr.*, I, 33.
[8] F. H. Hedge, "Emanuel Swedenborg," *The Christian Examiner*, XV (1833), 193-218. For a good reply to Hedge's review see "Notice of Emanuel Swedenborg in the *Christian Examiner*," *N J M*, VIII (1834-1835), 23-36; 54-57.
[9] See *Letters*, I, 402.
[10] See Hedge, *loc. cit.*, XV, 195, 195, 196.

either disjoins itself from the mother church and riots in ascetic enormities, or inflamed with the fierce zeal of proselytism waxes intolerant of received opinions, and snatching the sword of persecution attempts to force its heresies upon the world. This is *practical mysticism*,——the plant in its manufactured produce, the fruit divorced from the vine, pressed and fermented into a maddening wine. Such is the character of the self-torturing, self-destroying mystics on the banks of the Ganges. Of this character was the mysticism of those Christian madmen of the fourth and fifth centuries, the followers of Simeon Stylites, who, with the hope of drawing nearer to God, devoted themselves to a life of wretchedness and pain.

Following the Neo-Platonic tradition, Swedenborg believed in the Identity Philosophy, in the doctrine of the scale or degrees of existence, in the correspondence between the outward and inward worlds, in the microcosm and macrocosm (*i.e.*, the "all in each" and the "each in all"), in the centrality of man in nature, in the unity running through all things, in the gravitation of like towards like, in an instantaneous compensation or retribution, and in the derivative doctrine that everyone builds his own spiritual house or state or world.[11] From Plato he took his philosophy of the "forms," and his "Greatest Man" reflects Plato's "Universal Man." From the school of Plotinus came the doctrine of the Influx. His uniqueness, for Emerson, lay not in his theory of correspondence but in his wide application of it. He was the first to "put the fact into a detached and scientific statement"[12] ——to pierce thoroughly to the "emblematic or spiritual character of the visible, audible, tangible world." He went beyond the poets in showing "the mysterious bond that allies moral evil to the foul material forms," and he deserved praise for announcing in "epical parables a theory of insanity, of beasts, of unclean and fearful things,"[13] namely, that of "affections clothed." Swedenborg, indeed, gave Emerson sufficient evidence that he was dealing with great and universal ideas——ideas that could unify and explain in spiritual terms the myriad phenomena of this life, and therein lay his chief attraction. He repelled Emerson, however, by his symbolism based upon details found in the Hebrew-Christian scriptures rather than upon objects appropriate for all ethical systems and *all* sacred traditions. He thereby failed, said Emerson, to become "human and universal," and though he went farther than others in his experiment, he still remained a pedant and a theologian.[14]

By 1837, Emerson owned a few of Swedenborg's works,[15] but he continued to find the *New Jerusalem Magazine* the most satisfactory approach to the Swedish mystic. The numbered paragraphs set forth below are, therefore, drawn not only from volumes bearing Swedenborg's name like *Influx*,[16] but also from articles (exclusive of Sampson Reed's) in the New-

[11] Emerson lists most of these points in his "Swedenborg; or the Mystic," *Works*, IV, 106-107; 125.   [12] *Ibid.*, IV, 117.

[13] *Ibid.*, I, 113. Emerson was interested in such speculation, though not in the details, the fable or the mythology of any particular system. See *Nature*, 7.5-7; 92.15——93.1.

[14] See *Works*, IV, 120. Emerson made it clear in *Nature*, 44.14ff., that he did *not* subscribe to all Swedenborg's terminology. He adopted it only when it could stimulate the fancy. He ever felt the need of "more vital expositors."

[15] His holdings of Swedenborg's works before 1837 were few: *On the Intercourse between the Soul and the Body which is supposed to take place either by Physical Influx or by Spiritual Influx*, Boston (Adonis Howard), 1828; *The Apocalypse Revealed*, (3 vols.) Boston, 1836; *The Doctrine of the New Jerusalem Concerning the Lord*, Boston, 1833; and probably *A Treatise Concerning Heaven and its Wonders and also Concerning Hell*, London, 1823.

[16] The early editions of this work include: *A Theosophic Lucubration on the Nature of*

Church missionary journal, which Emerson seems to have read regularly. Any one of the themes represented in the following excerpts might have been illustrated by dozens of parallels.

DOCTRINE OF CORRESPONDENCE DEFINED——ILLUSTRATED IN ANIMALS ——MAN IS BOTH A HEAVEN AND A WORLD[17]

¶ 1

Since, then, without a perception of what correspondence is there can be no clear knowledge of the spiritual world or of its inflow into the natural world, neither of what the spiritual is in its relation to the natural, nor any clear knowledge of the spirit of man, which is called the soul, and its operation into the body, neither of man's state after death, it is necessary to explain what correspondence is and the nature of it.

¶ 2

The whole natural world corresponds to the spiritual world, and not merely the natural world in general, but also every particular of it; and as a consequence every thing in the natural world that springs from the spiritual world is called a correspondent. It must be understood that the natural world springs from and has permanent existence from the spiritual world, precisely like an effect from its effecting cause. All that is spread out under the sun and that receives the heat and light from the sun is what is called the natural world; and all things that derive their subsistence therefrom belong to that world. But the spiritual world is heaven; and all things in the heavens belong to that world.

¶ 3

Since man is both a heaven and a world in smaller form after the image of the greatest, there is in him both a spiritual and a natural world. The interior things that belong to his mind, and that have relation to understanding and will, constitute his spiritual world; while the exterior things that belong to his body, and that have relation to its senses and activities, constitute his natural world. Consequently, every thing in his natural world (that is, in his body and its senses and activities), that has its existence from his spiritual world (that is, from his mind and its understanding and will) is called a correspondent.

¶ 4

But at the present day no one can know the spiritual things in heaven to which the natural things in the world correspond except from heaven, since the knowledge of correspondences is now wholly lost. But the nature of the correspondence of spiritual things with natural I shall be glad to illustrate by some examples. The animals of the earth correspond in general to affection, mild and useful animals to good affections, fierce and useless ones to evil affections. In particular, cattle and their young correspond to the affections of the natural mind, sheep and lambs to the affections of the spiritual mind; while birds correspond, according to their species, to the intellectual things of the natural mind or the spiritual mind. . . . Man is like an animal so far as his natural man is concerned, and is therefore likened to animals in common speech; for example, if he is gentle he is called a sheep or lamb, if fierce a bear or wolf, if cunning a fox or serpent, and so on.[18]

SWEDENBORG'S PREPARATION——HIS CHIEF DOCTRINE EPITOMIZED[19]

¶ 5

[After he] had searched the sciences of his century, and had been honored with the applause of single connoisseurs and whole academies, he began——to see ghosts. His apologist[20] says: "he considered the visible world and the relation of his parts as the

Influx, tr. T. Hartley, London, 1770; *A Theosophic Treatise on the Nature of Influx*, London, 1784; *A Treatise on the Nature of Influx*, tr. Thos. Hartley, Boston, 1794. The last is the edition which Emerson's father probably owned. (See the inventory of the Rev. William Emerson's library in *E T E*, II.)

[17] Swedenborg, *Heaven and its Wonders and Hell*, N.Y., 1939, nos. 88-90; 110. See *Nature*, 12.4-7; 36.21——37.3; 41.15-21; 43.18; 44.8——45.4; 46.19.

[18] See *Nature*, 33.20——34.7.

[19] From "Emanuel Swedenborg," *N J M*, V (1831-1832), 437. Cf. *Journals*, II, 500-501 (July 15, 1832) and *Nature*, 41.19-21.

[20] Counsellor Samuel Sandels. See Nathaniel Hobart, "Life of Swedenborg," *N J M*, II (1828-1829), 40.

dial plate of the invisible one; and after being acquainted with the visible world, he
ventured upon the invisible universe, first with conjectures, and then by degrees reared
his system."

THE SPIRITUAL WORLD DESCRIBED——OUR HEAVEN OR HELL BEGINS IN THIS LIFE——WE MAKE OUR OWN ETERNAL CONDITION[21]

¶ 6

The spiritual world is a world of *causes*, and the natural world is a world of *effects*.
The spiritual world lies within the natural world; and man, who is born to live for ever,
must . . . begin life with his spiritual form or body enveloped in a material form or
body. Then, the world in which he is to live for ever lies about him also in a material
body; and thus this world, which exists for him, is adapted to him both in the temporary
condition in which he begins life, and in the later condition in which he lives for ever.
The man and the world are *here* clothed with a material covering or body, and *hereafter*
both the man and the world are free from it; but they are not hereafter the less real,
nor the less perfectly adapted to each other. On the contrary, they then stand in a
closer relation to each other, are nearer together, and the man perceives the reality,
the variety, the use, the beauty, the laws and the powers of the world, infinitely more
clearly than he could do before.

¶ 7

It may seem that, as every man differs in some respects from others, every one in the
spiritual world must, as a consequence of these laws of representation, have a world of
his own; one in which no others live, and which no others can inhabit or use or enjoy.
But another doctrine concerning the spiritual world answers this objection. We learn
that *there*, all are associated according to and by the influence of internal sympathy.
Like seeks and meets its like.[22] Hence, they who form one society, are they whose
principles and feelings are the same, and in whose thoughts, wishes or endeavors, there
is no discordance, no opposition. Of course there would prevail around them both a
similarity and a difference, representative of their internal likeness and unlikeness.

¶ 8

The main difference between that world and this, remains to be stated. It consists in
the fact, that there *space* and *time* are not, but only appearances of them; in their
stead, are *state*, and changes of state. Accustomed as we are to think of nothing but in
space and time, it is difficult to divest our mind of the influence of these ideas; perhaps
. . . impossible. . . . [T]he first question which the mention of a real spiritual world
suggests is, *Where is it?* The answer is, every where, in the spiritual sense,——but
no where in the natural sense. It lies within us and around us. It is where we are and
wherever any thing is. Still it does not occupy space, because it is only thought and
feeling in form. . . . [H]eaven is not a place, nor is hell. They are states,——conditions
of the will and the understanding. He is in heaven, in whom the love of the Lord and
of the neighbor are not only predominant, but absolute; holding all things within the
man in due subservience to them. He is in hell, in whom the love of self and the love
of the world have the mastery, and exercise entire dominion.[22a]

¶ 9

If we would know with more of detail what heaven and hell are, we have the means
of at least beginning this knowledge, while we live here; for they meet on earth. If
we can imagine every thing good, beautiful, useful, delightful, which we now have any
glimpse of, separated from every thing of an opposite nature, and suppose it exalted
beyond measure and constantly approaching perfection, we may form some idea of
heaven. And the opposite course will lead us into some idea of hell. There is nothing
good on earth which does not come from, and accord with and represent something in
heaven; nor is there any evil thing on earth which does not hold a similar relation to
something in hell.

¶ 10

It is from this that every one after death comes into the society of his own, that is,
of those who are in a like love, and that he recognizes these as relatives and as friends;
and what is wonderful, when he meets them and sees them it is as if he had been

---

[21] Theophilus Parsons, "The Spiritual World," *N J M*, IX (1835-1836), 272-281. See
esp. pp. 277, 278-279, 279-280, 281.
[22] Cf. chap. VII, note 43.   [22a] Cf. *Nature*, 95.9.

acquainted with them from infancy. Spiritual relationship and friendship are the cause of this. And what is more, no one in a society can occupy any house but his own, each one in a society has his own house, and this he finds ready for him as soon as he enters the society. Outside of his house he may be in close association with others, but he cannot stay anywhere except in his own house. And still further, in another's apartment no one can sit any where except in his own place; if he sits elsewhere he loses his self-possession and becomes dumb; and what is wonderful, whenever one enters a room he knows his own place.[23]

EARTHLY LIFE PASSES GRADUALLY INTO THE IMMORTAL——MAN DOES NOT DIE——RESUSCITATION CALLED RESURRECTION[24]

¶ 11

When the body is no longer able to perform the bodily functions in the natural world that correspond to the spirit's thoughts and affections, which the spirit has from the spiritual world, man is said to die. This takes place when the respiration of the lungs and the beatings of the heart cease. But the man does not die; he is merely separated from the bodily part that was of use to him in the world, while the man himself continues to live.

¶ 12

After the separation the spirit of man continues in the body for a short time, but only until the heart's action has wholly ceased, which happens variously in accord with the diseased condition that causes death, with some the motion of the heart continuing for some time, with others not so long. As soon as this motion ceases the man is resuscitated; but this is done by the Lord alone. Resuscitation means the drawing forth of the spirit from the body, and its introduction into the spiritual world; this is commonly called the resurrection.

¶ 13

When he has come into the enjoyment of light the spiritual angels render to the new spirit every service he can possibly desire in that state; and teach him about the things of the other life so far as he can comprehend them. But if he has no wish to be taught the spirit longs to get away from the company of the angels. Nevertheless, the angels do not withdraw from him, but he separates himself from them; for the angels love every one, and desire nothing so much as to render service, to teach, and to lead into heaven; this constitutes their highest delight. When the spirit has thus withdrawn he is received by good spirits, and as long as he continues in their company every thing possible is done for him.

HEAVEN IS A UNITY——IT APPEARS AS A SINGLE MAN WITH MANY PARTS WORKING TOGETHER——HEAVEN IS CALLED THE *GREATEST MAN*[25]

¶ 14

That heaven in its whole complex reflects a single man is an arcanum hitherto unknown in the world, but fully recognized in the heavens. To know this and the specific and particular things relating to it is the chief thing in the intelligence of the angels there, and on it many things depend which without it as a general principle would not enter distinctly and clearly into the ideas of their minds. Knowing that all the heavens with their societies reflect a single man they call heaven the Greatest Man and the Divine Man——Divine because it is the Divine of the Lord that makes heaven.

¶ 15

The angels, it is true, do not see heaven in its whole complex in the human form, for heaven as a whole does not come within the view of any angel; but remote societies, consisting of many thousands of angels, they sometimes see as a one in the human form; and from a society, as from a part, they draw their conclusion as to the general, which is heaven. For in the most perfect forms generals are like the parts, and parts are like the generals, with simply such a difference as there is between like things of

---

[23] This last paragraph is taken from *Angelic Wisdom Concerning the Divine Providence*, N.Y., 1939, no. 338.

[24] *Heaven and its Wonders and Hell*, N.Y., 1939, nos. 445, 447, 450. Cf. *Nature*, 88.1-4. See also an exposition of this theme in Sampson Reed, "We are passing from Time into Eternity," *N J M*, I, 107ff.

[25] *Ibid.*, nos. 59, 62, 70, 64. Cf. Plato's doctrine of Universal Man, which Emerson mentions in *Nature*, 87.13-15.

greater or less magnitude.[26]

¶ 16

It must be understood that although all in a heavenly society when seen together as one appear in the likeness of a man; yet no one society is just such a man as another. Societies differ from one another like the faces of different individuals of the same family . . . that is, they differ as the good in which they are, and which determines their form, differs. The societies of the inmost or highest heaven, and in the centre there, are those that appear in the most perfect and beautiful human form.

¶ 17

So many different things in man act as a one, because there is no least thing in Him that does not do something for the general welfare and perform some use. The general performs a use for its parts, and the parts for the general. . . . [T]hey provide for each other, have regard for each other, and are joined together in such a form that each thing and all things have reference to the general and its good.

THE USES OR FUNCTIONS OF MEN AND ANGELS[27]

¶ 18

The soul of man, upon the immortality of which many have written, is his spirit, for this is in every respect immortal. This is what thinks in the body, for it is spiritual, and what is spiritual receives what is spiritual and lives spiritually, which is to think and to will. Therefore, all rational life that appears in the body belongs to the soul, and nothing of it to the body; for the body, as just said, is material, and the material, which is the property of the body, is added to and apparently almost joined to the spirit, in order that the spirit of man may be able *to live and perform uses in the natural world.*[28]

¶ 19

[T]he universe was created by God for the existence of uses, wherefore it may be called a theatre of uses. And since man is the principal end of creation, it follows that all things were created for his sake, and therefore that all things pertaining to order, both in general and in particular, were brought together and concentrated in him, so that through him God might accomplish primary uses. . . . [U]se is the end which love purposes and accomplishes through the cause; and when use results, then love and wisdom acquire a real existence; in use they make for themselves a habitation and a seat, where they may be at rest as in their home. It is the same with man; the love and wisdom of God abide in him when he performs uses; and for the sake of performing divine uses he was created an image and likeness, or form, of divine order.[29]

¶ 20

Man, when first created, was endued with the love of wisdom, not for his own sake but in order that he might share it with others. Hence it is inscribed on the wisdom of the wise, that no one should be wise or live for himself alone; for then society could not exist. To live for others is to perform uses; uses are the bonds of society, and their number is infinite. There are spiritual uses, pertaining to the love of God and of the neighbour; there are moral and civil uses, pertaining to the love of one's community and fellow-citizens; there are natural uses, pertaining to the love of the world and its necessities; and there are corporeal uses, pertaining to the love of self-preservation for the sake of higher uses. This orderly succession of uses is inscribed on a man's very nature. Those who perform the first or spiritual uses and therefore all the others, are wise. Those who neglect the first, but perform civil and moral uses, and therefore all the lower ones, are not really but only superficially wise.[30]

THE SPIRIT FLOWS BY INFLUX FROM THE SPIRITUAL WORLD INTO THE NATURAL WORLD[31]

¶ 21

It is thence manifest to me that there are two worlds which are distinct from each other; one in which all things are spiritual, which is thence called the spiritual world;

---

[26] An analogue of the "Each in all" and the "All in each."
[27] This doctrine together with Plato's Universal Man may have influenced Emerson's concept of the functions of men in a society. In his Phi Beta Kappa Address he called the scholar "man thinking."
[28] *Heaven and its Wonders and Hell*, N.Y., 1939, no. 432.
[29] *The True Christian Religion*, N.Y. (Everyman ed.), 1936, no. 67. Cf. *Nature*, 18.7.
[30] *Ibid.*, no. 746.
[31] *On the Intercourse between the Soul and the Body* (usually called by its subtitle,

and another in which all things are natural, which is thence called the natural world; and that spirits and angels live in their own world, and men in theirs; and also that every man passes by death from his own world into the other, and lives therein to eternity. A knowledge concerning each of these worlds should be premised, in order that [the doctrine of] influx, which is the subject here treated of, may be unfolded from its beginning; for the spiritual world flows-in into the natural world, and actuates it in all its particular parts as well with men as with beasts, and also constitutes the vegetative principle in trees and herbs.[32]

THE TWO SUNS——ONE THE SOURCE OF THE SPIRITUAL WORLD AND THE OTHER, OF THE NATURAL WORLD——FOLLY OF THOSE BLIND TO THE FORMER[33]

¶ 22

The reason why there is one sun of the spiritual world and another sun of the natural world, is because those worlds are altogether distinct; and a world derives its origin from its sun; for a world in which all things are spiritual cannot originate from a sun from which all the things that proceed are natural, for thus influx would be physical, which, nevertheless, is contrary to order. That the world existed from the sun, and not *vice versa,* is manifest from an effect derived from this cause, viz. that the world in all and singular its parts subsists by means of the sun, and subsistence demonstrates existence, wherefore it is said that subsistence is perpetual existence; from whence it is evident, that if the sun were removed, its world would fall into chaos, and this chaos into nothing.

¶ 23

The man . . . who knows nothing concerning the sun of the spiritual world, easily falls into absurdity *(delirat)* in his idea concerning the creation of the universe, which, when he deeply considers it, he apprehends no otherwise than as proceeding from nature; and as the origin of nature is the sun, he no otherwise apprehends the creation of the universe than as proceeding from its sun as a creator. Moreover no one can apprehend [the doctrine of] spiritual influx, unless he also knows the origin of it; for all influx proceeds from a sun, spiritual influx from its sun, and natural influx from its sun; the internal sight of man, which is that of his mind, receives influx from the spiritual sun, but his external sight, which is that of his body, receives influx from the natural sun; and both are conjoined in operation in like manner as the soul is conjoined with the body.[34] Hence it is evident into what blindness, darkness, and fatuity they may fall, who know nothing concerning the spiritual world and its sun; they may fall into *blindness,* because the mind which depends on the sight of the eye alone, becomes in its reasonings like a bat, which flies by night with a wandering course.

LOVE AND WISDOM——THE ROUTE TAKEN BY DIVINE INFLUX AFTER IT ENTERS MAN——SOUL> MIND> SENSES> ACTIONS[35]

¶ 24

The reason that life from God flows-in into man through the soul, and through this into the mind, that is, into the affections and thoughts of the mind, and from these into the senses, speech, and actions of the body, is because these are [the derivatives] of life in successive order; for the mind is subordinate to the soul, and the body is subordinate to the mind: and the mind has two lives, one of the will and another of the understanding; the life of its will is the good of love, the derivations of which are called affections, and the life of its understanding is the truth of wisdom, the derivations of which are called thoughts; by means of these and the former the mind lives: but the life of the body are the senses, speech, and actions; that these are derived from the soul through the mind, follows from the order in which they stand, and from which they manifest themselves to a wise man without scrutiny. The human soul, forasmuch as it is a superior spiritual substance, receives influx immediately from God; but the human mind, forasmuch as it is an inferior spiritual substance, receives influx from

_____

Influx), Boston, 1828, no. 3, pp. 7-8, hereafter called *Soul and Body.* The brackets are in the original.

[32] See *Nature,* 94.16-17.
[33] *Soul and Body,* no. 4, pp. 8-9; 9-10. Brackets are in the original.
[34] See *Nature,* 76.16-17.
[35] *Soul and Body,* no. 8, pp. 18-19. Brackets are in the original.

God mediately through the spiritual world; and the body, forasmuch as it originates from the substances of nature, which are called material, receives influx from God mediately through the natural world. That the good of love and the truth of wisdom[36] flow-in from God into the soul of man conjointly, that is united into one, but that they are divided by man in their progress, and are conjoined only with those who suffer themselves to be led by God, will be seen in the following articles.

AFFECTIONS CLOTHED——THE SPIRITUAL CLOTHES ITSELF WITH THE NATURAL AS A MAN DONS A GARMENT[37]

¶ 25

It is known that in every operation there is what is active and what is passive, and that from what is active alone nothing exists, and nothing from what is passive alone: the case is similar with what is spiritual and what is natural; what is spiritual, forasmuch as it is a living power, being active, and what is natural, forasmuch as it is a dead power, being passive; hence it follows that whatever has existed in this solar world from the beginning, and afterwards exists every moment, is from what is spiritual through what is natural, and this not only in the subjects of the animal kingdom, but also in the subjects of the vegetable kingdom.[38]

¶ 26

Another fact similar to this is also known, viz. that in every thing which is effected there is what is principal and what is instrumental, and that these two, when any thing is done, appear as one, though they are distinctly two; wherefore it is one of the rules of wisdom that the principal cause and the instrumental cause make together one cause: so also do what is spiritual and what is natural: the reason that these two in producing effects appear as one, is because what is spiritual is within what is natural as the fibre is within the muscle, and as the blood is within the arteries; or as the thought is inwardly in the speech and the affection in the tones of the voice, causing themselves to be apprehended by means of what is natural.

¶ 27

[F]rom these considerations, but yet [obscurely] as [objects appear when seen] through a window, it appears, that what is spiritual clothes itself with what is natural as a man clothes himself with a garment. The organical body with which the soul clothes itself, is here compared to a garment, because a garment invests the body, and the soul also puts off the body, and casts it away as old clothes, (exuviæ) when it emigrates by means of death from the natural world into its own spiritual world;[39] for the body grows old like a garment, but not the soul, because this is a spiritual substance, which has nothing in common with the changes of nature, which advance from their beginnings to their ends, and are periodically terminated.

THE RATIONAL AND MORAL MAN DESCRIBED[40]

¶ 28

From the principle established above, viz. that the soul clothes itself with a body as a man clothes himself with a garment, this follows as a conclusion: for the soul flows-in into the human mind, and through this into the body, and carries life with it, which it continually receives from the Lord, and thus transfers it mediately into the body, where by the closest union it makes the body appear to live; whence, and from a thousand testimonies of experience, it is evident, that what is spiritual united to what is material, as a living power with a dead power, causes man to speak rationally and to act morally: it appears as if the tongue and lips spoke from a certain life in themselves, and that the arms and hands act in a like manner, but it is the thought, which in itself is spiritual, which speaks, and the will, which likewise is spiritual, which acts, both by means of their own organs, which in themselves are material, as being taken from the natural world.

---

[36] Cf. *Nature*, 79.10-12; 80.8-15; 91.15.
[37] *Soul and Body*, no. 11, pp. 25, 25-26, 26. All brackets are in the original except the initial capital letter in ¶ 27.
[38] Cf. *Nature*, 5.8-18.
[39] Quoted in *Journals*, IV, 8 (Jan. 24, 1836). Cf. *Nature*, 44.15.
[40] *Soul and Body*, no. 12, pp. 28-29.

RECEPTION OF THE INFLUX OF LOVE AND WISDOM DEPENDS ON THE STATE OF LOVE AND WISDOM IN A MAN——"AFFECTIONS" DEFINED—— DANGERS OF SELF-LOVE[41]

¶ 29

That man is not life, but an organ recipient of life from God, and that love together with wisdom is life; also, that God is love itself and wisdom itself, and thus life itself;[42] has been demonstrated above: hence it follows, that so far as a man loves wisdom, or so far as wisdom in the bosom of love is with him, so far he is an image of God, that is, a receptacle of life from God; and on the contrary, so far as he is in opposite love, and thence in insanity,[43] so far he does not receive life from God, but from hell, which life is called death. Love itself and wisdom itself are not life, but are the esse of life, but the delights of love and the pleasantnesses of wisdom, which are affections, constitute life, for the Esse of life Exists by means of these: the influx of life from God carries with it those delights and pleasantnesses, like the influx of light and heat at the time of spring[44] into human minds, and also into birds and beasts of every kind, yea into vegetables, which then germinate and become prolific: for the delights of love and the pleasantnesses of wisdom expand men's minds (animi) and adapt them to reception, as joy and gladness expand the face, and adapt it to the influx of the hilarities of the soul.

¶ 30

I will here add an arcanum confirming these things from heaven: all the angels of heaven turn their forehead to the Lord as a sun, and all the angels of hell turn the back of the head to him,[45] and the latter receive the influx into the affections of their will, which in themselves are concupiscences, and make the understanding favour them, but the former receive the influx into the affections of their understanding, and make the will favour them, whence these are in wisdom, but the others are in insanity; for the human understanding dwells in the cerebrum, which is under the forehead, and the will in the cerebellum, which is in the back of the head: who does not know that a man who is insane from falses, favours the cupidities of his own evil, and confirms them by means of reasons drawn from the understanding, and that a wise man sees from truths the quality of the cupidities of his own will and restrains them; a wise man does this because he turns his face to God, that is, he believes in God, and not in himself, but an insane[46] man does the other because he averts his face from God, that is, he believes in himself and not in God; to believe in himself, is to believe that a man loves and is wise from himself and not from God, and this is signified by eating of the tree of the science of good and evil; but to believe in God, is to believe that a man loves and is wise from God and not from himself, and this is signified by eating of the tree of life, Rev. ii. 7.[47]

MEN AND BEASTS COMPARED[48]

¶ 31

They who judge of things only as they appear before the senses of the body, conclude that beasts have will and understanding as well as men, and hence that the only distinction consists in man's being able to speak, and thus to describe the things which he thinks and desires, while beasts can only express them by sounds: yet beasts have not will and understanding, but only a resemblance of each, which the learned call something analogous. The reason that a man is a man, is because his understanding is capable of being elevated above the desires of his will, and thus can know and see them, and also govern them; but a beast is a beast because its desires drive it to do whatever it does; wherefore a man is a man in consequence of this, that his will is under the obedience of his understanding; but a beast is a beast in consequence of this, that its understanding is under the obedience of its will.

¶ 32

[F]rom these considerations this conclusion follows, viz. that the understanding of man, forasmuch as it receives the light influent from heaven, and apprehends and apperceives this as its own, and therefrom thinks analytically with all variety altogether as from itself, is alive, and is thence truly understanding; and that the will of

---

[41] *Soul and Body*, no. 13, pp. 31-32; 32-33.
[42] See *Nature*, 79.8-23.
[43] See *Nature*, 94.19.
[44] Cf. Sampson Reed ¶ 59 and note.
[45] Cf. *Nature*, 76.17.
[46] See *Nature*, 94.13-20.
[47] See Sampson Reed ¶s. 55-62.
[48] *Soul and Body*, no. 15, pp. 39; 39-40; 41. Initial brackets in ¶ 32 are mine. Cf. *Nature*, 7.7; 16.7.

man, forasmuch as it receives the influent love of heaven, and therefrom acts as from itself, is alive, and is thence truly will; but that the contrary is the case with beasts. Wherefore they who think from the lusts of the will, are compared to beasts, and in the spiritual world they likewise at a distance appear as beasts; they also act like beasts, with this only difference, that they are able to act otherwise if they will: but they who restrain the lusts of their will by means of the understanding, appear in the spiritual world as men, and are angels of heaven.

¶ 33

The life of a beast may be compared with a sleep walker, who walks and acts by virtue of the will while the understanding sleeps: and also with a blind man,[49] who walks through the streets with a dog leading him: and also with an idiot, who from custom and the habit thence acquired does his work in a regular manner: it may likewise be compared with a person void of memory, and thence deprived of understanding, who still knows or learns how to clothe himself, to eat dainties, to love the sex, to walk the streets from house to house, and to do such things as sooth the senses and indulge the flesh, by the allurements and pleasures of which he is drawn along, though he does not think, and thence cannot speak.

HOW THE SOUL FORMS THE BODY OF MAN————THE SPIRITUAL BODY DESCRIBED[50]

¶ 34

The soul forms and fashions the body out of the elements of nature, by its living principle, as the seed takes to itself of the elements and makes of them a tree and determines its form and quality exactly according to its own principle of life. And when the body falls from man, the spiritual body, formed by the soul out of spiritual substances according to the same principle, continues to exist; it bears no relation to death; it always exists within the natural body, and is the medium by which the soul forms that body; and its senses and powers lie within the natural senses and powers, and give to them form and being. Thus, after death, the man remains, clothed with a body, possessing perfectly all his senses, and provided with a world, exactly accommodated, like this world, to those senses. He has there affections and thoughts, and these flowing forth, are seen and known by him in external forms, and the complex of these forms constitutes a universe wherein he dwells.

PHYSICAL CONDITION OF THE WORLD IS DEPENDENT ON THE MORAL CHARACTER OF MAN——A MORAL ADVANCE IS NEEDED TO MAKE THE FEROCIOUS AND TERRIBLE DISAPPEAR[51]

¶ 35

When man departed from the state of pristine innocence and simplicity, in which he was originally created, inferior natures felt a corresponding change. Nor do we believe it to be a wild and chimerical idea, a mere fancy of the poet, or whim of speculative philosophy, that when the moral nature of man shall have become renovated, when he shall have returned to the laws of order from which he has wandered; when the chords of human society shall vibrate in harmonious unison, and mutual benevolence shall characterize the intercourse of man with man,——inferior natures, also, yielding to the resistless impulse of an influence from within, will again find their place in the scale of being, and the same universal harmony be restored which reigned on the morning of creation.

¶ 36

[H]ow, in view of the facts recorded in history, sacred or profane, or elicited by daily experience, shall we repudiate, as unphilosophical, the necessary conclusion, that the physical condition of the world is dependent upon the moral character of man. Or who will venture to assert, that when in the progress of moral advancement, the disorders of human society shall cease to exist; when we shall have learned to act from purer and more exalted motives; when sordid selfishness and demoniac ambition shall

---

[49] Cf. *Nature*, 95.11.

[50] "Concerning Nature," *N J M*, III (1829-1830), pp. 267-276. See p. 273. Cf. *Nature*, 80.16-19.

[51] Thomas H. Perry, "The Physical Condition of the World Dependent upon the Moral Character of Man," *N J M*, IX (1835-1836), pp. 58-62. See pp. 59-60, 61, 61-62. The entire article is reproduced in *E T E*, II, 99-101. Cf. *Nature*, 81.2-11; 94.13-22.

no longer be suffered to belittle and pollute humanity; to array mankind in envious and jealous animosity; nor be appealed to and fostered as motives of action;——the time may not yet arrive, when the pernicious, the ferocious, and the terrible, shall disappear in the useful, and inferior natures learn to regard man as a friend and a protector, rather than to fear him and to detest him, as a common enemy, a tyrant, and a scourge.

¶ 37

Though, as the lord of this sublunary creation, he is ever prone to pride himself upon his fancied superiority, he finds, even in the disorder and confusion which his follies and his crimes have introduced, the record of the steps of his deviations. He beholds it in the apparent external distraction which Providence permits to exist as the proper ultimates of human evil, alike in the diseases which prey upon his physical constitution, in the ferocity of the tiger, the venom of the serpent, and in the fatal poison of the deadly night-shade. On what side soever he turns himself, he witnesses every where the consequences of his aberrations, and under circumstances in which, because, perhaps, he does not consider them as exclusively his own, he is comparatively free from the temptation to palliate or excuse them, he beholds faithfully and forcibly depicted, his own passions, feelings and propensities.

APPEARANCE OF DISORGANIZATION IN THE NATURAL WORLD IS THE RESULT OF MAN'S FALLEN CONDITION——GOD IS THE TRULY HUMAN—— THE GRAND MAN[52]

¶ 38

The appearance, of which we have been speaking, is the necessary consequence of the state we are in as degenerate,[53] fallen men, and will subside only in proportion as we have his joy fulfilled in ourselves, by following him in the regeneration. We shall in this way learn that the laws of God make one with his love and wisdom, that they are himself. That he is truly *human*, nay the only MAN, and that we become men only by becoming images of him. That by fulfilling these laws upon earth, as man, he was as really and fully engaged in a divine and glorious work, as when he formed the everlasting hills, and meted out the heavens with a span. The only cause of any appearance to the contrary is to be found in our own states. We are always supposing him to be a God, afar off, and not near at hand.[54]

NOTE, HOWEVER, THAT MAN'S AFFECTIONS CLOTHE THEMSELVES IN THE NATURAL WORLD ONLY IN A *GENERAL* WAY——NATURE ACTS COERCIVELY UPON US[55]

¶ 39

The world *without* man *corresponds* to and is created from the world *within* him. It is his infinite variety of thoughts and feelings and faculties and states which are represented by the infinite variety of the world without man. But, in this world, this representation is only *general*, and not *particular*. Here, the whole world without represents the whole within; and the world without any one man does not represent in an especial manner the world within that individual. It does not vary with his changing states,—— it is fixed, and made steadfast by its material covering, because the man lives here to be changed himself, and disciplined, and acted upon in some sort, forcibly. In the other world, the man lives *freely* what he has made himself here; and there the world without any individual represents exactly and is the living index of the world within him; it changes freely with his changes, because it is no longer necessary that it should act upon him coercively.

AS MAN DEGENERATES HE GRADUALLY BECOMES BLIND TO THE SUN AND MOON OF THE SPIRITUAL WORLD, TURNS HIS BACK ON THEM, AND WORSHIPS THE SUN AND MOON IN NATURE[56]

---

[52] "Ye That Have Followed Me in the Regeneration," *N J M*, III (1829-1830), pp. 40-45. See p. 45.

[53] See *Nature*, 81.2; "As we degenerate . . . ." See also *Nature*, 91.5-9.

[54] Sampson Reed developed this thought in his admirable discussion of time and eternity in "Growth of the Mind," *E T E*, II, 15-17. See also Reed ¶s. 1-3. Emerson reflects Reed in *Letters*, I, 174.

[55] Theophilus Parsons, "The Spiritual World," *N J M*, IX (1835-1836), pp. 272-281. See pp. 277-278. This important qualification is assumed in *Nature*, 80.19—81.11; 94.13-22.   [56] See *Nature*, 76.16-17; 81.2-9; 88.12-23; 89.1-3.

¶ 40

To the angels the sun of the world appears like a dense darkness opposite to the sun of heaven, and the moon like a darkness opposite to the moon of heaven, and this constantly; and for the reason that the world's fieriness corresponds to the love of self, and the light from it corresponds to what is false from that love; and the love of self is the direct opposite of the Divine love; and what is false from that love is the direct opposite of the Divine truth; and the opposite of the Divine love and the Divine truth is to the angels darkness. Therefore, in the Word, to worship the sun and moon of this world and bow down to them, signifies to love self and the falsities that spring from the love of self, and it is said that such will be cut off.[57]

¶ 41

As it is from the Divine love that is in and from Him that the Lord appears in heaven like a sun, so all in the heavens are turned constantly to Him, those in the celestial kingdom to Him as a sun, and those in the spiritual kingdom to Him as a moon. But those that are in hell turn themselves to an opposite darkness and dense darkness, that is, they turn backwards away from the Lord; and this for the reason that all in the hells are in love of self and the world, thus antagonistic to the Lord. . . . In respect to his spirit man turns himself in the same way as a spirit does, backwards from the Lord if he is in love of self and the world, and towards the Lord if he is in love to the Lord and the neighbor. But of this man is ignorant, because he is in the natural world where quarters are determined by the rising and setting of the sun.[58]

¶ 42

As most things in the Word have also a contrary sense, so have "sun" and "moon" and in that sense "sun" signifies the love of self, and "moon," the falsities therefrom. "Sun and moon" have this signification because those who are in natural thought only, and not in spiritual thought, do not think beyond nature; therefore when they see that from these two luminaries, or from their light and heat, all things arise and, as it were, live upon earth, they suppose that these luminaries rule the universe; above this they do not raise their thoughts. This all do who are in the love of self and in the evils and falsities therefrom, for such are merely natural and sensual men, and the merely natural and sensual man does not think beyond nature, for what he does not see and touch he believes to be nothing. With the ancients, all things of the church consisted of the representatives of spiritual things in natural; with them, therefore, "the sun" signified the Lord in relation to Divine good, and "the moon" the Lord in relation to Divine truth, consequently in worship they turned their faces to the rising of the sun; and those among them who were in love of self, and were therefore merely natural and sensual, began to worship as their highest gods the sun and the moon that they saw with their eyes.[59]

¶ 43

As they fell from this high estate, all intelligent understanding of spiritual things, of which that of correspondences formed an essential part, was lost. This was a gradual process. The knowledge that external things were in some way significative continued after all knowledge of the heavenly things which they signified had disappeared. As the heavens of the angels were withdrawn, they were left, as it were, gazing into the heavens of the natural world; and the bodies there seen, especially the sun, responded to their highest conceptions of the Divinity, and became objects of their adoration and worship.[60]

EVEN IN DEGRADATION MAN STILL RETAINS A MEMORY OF THE DIVINE ORDER IN AND BY WHICH HE WAS CREATED[61]

¶ 44

A departure in man from the order and influence of the Lord through heaven, gives existence in him to opposing qualities. His love becoming evil his thoughts cannot be

---

[57] *Heaven and its Wonders and Hell*, N.Y., 1939, no. 122. Swedenborg refers to Deut. 17:3; Jeremiah 8:2; Ezekiel 8:16.

[58] *Ibid.*, no. 123.

[59] *Apocalypse Explained*, (6 vols., N.Y., 1928), II, no. 401g.

[60] Sampson Reed, "Correspondences," *N J M*, n.s. III (May, 1879), 52. (I include it here because it is the sort of commentary with which Emerson was familiar.)

[61] "On the Human Form," *N J M*, VII (1833-1834), 335-342; 374-380. See pp. 340-341. (The article is rptd. in *E T E*, II, 69-75.) Cf. *Nature*, 89.3-10.

true. He still carries with him, however, in his interior form, as well as exterior conformation, while he remains man, an image, of that order, in and by which the heavens and the earth, and angels and men were created. There is still in him a progression, of and from the end aimed at, or his love, in and by its means, real or apparent truth, to an accomplishment in the effect, its form. There is in him an image of humanity within and without, though there be not a likeness of Him from whom it has receded. Did he not possess *that* he could never be restored to *this*. He is, therefore, capable of perceiving the form of good, that by embracing it he may feel its power. He can elevate his understanding to apprehend truth, and by willing obedience to it, may know it more fully in the good it contains.

THE PROCESS OF REDEMPTION OR REGENERATION[62]

¶ 45

This is the way in which we follow him in the regeneration. Not by exerting our own strength, and exercising our own wisdom, and endeavoring by our own reasoning to judge of what is good by searching out what is expedient; but by acknowledging that of our own selves we can do nothing, and by ascribing all the power and the glory to Him who must be in us before we can have life. Thus is the regeneration of man, an image of the glorification of the Lord. The victories which the Lord is continually gaining over the evil and the false, within the wills and understandings of those who are suffering him to regenerate them and to reign over them, are, however, only partial and incomplete.

¶ 46

And though it is not man, but the Lord in man, who fights and overcomes, yet the evil and the false are not entirely overcome and expelled, because man does not entirely submit his own will and understanding to the operation of divine influx. They are therefore only removed from the centre to the circumference, where they remain inefficient and harmless so long as man depends upon the Lord for power over them and salvation from them, but ready to rush in and seize their victim the moment he ascribes the merit to himself, and thus relies upon his own strength to resist their assaults.

IMPROVEMENT WILL BE GRADUAL, FOR THE SPIRIT DOES NOT ACT IN HASTE——A BRIGHT FUTURE LIES AHEAD[63]

¶ 47

We are taught that Divine Providence does not act by violence or sudden change. That improvement, to be solid and permanent, must be gradual; and that if we would go along the pathways which lead to eternal life, we must journey in them step by step and day by day. The growth of faith and charity, of wisdom and of love, in the mind, is like that of the plant whose fruits correspond to the good works which are the evidence and the result of regeneration. . . . Let us not despond, and feel as if that which cannot be to-day nor tomorrow, will never be. The obstacles we encounter are the signs and the effects of interposing evils,——and these cannot be safely removed otherwise than "little by little," as were the nations before the children of Israel, "lest wild beasts come up and possess the land." In a future time and state, which will assuredly come after these evils have been subdued, "the reaper will tread upon the heels of the sower," and good and truth will follow each other in unbroken succession.

INSTINCT IN ANIMALS AND MEN IS A RESULT OF SPIRITUAL INFLUX[64]

¶ 48

Every bird, beast, fish, reptile, and insect has its own natural, sensual, and bodily loves which reside in their brains; by means of the brain, the spiritual world directly influences their bodily senses, and through these determines their actions; this is why their bodily senses are far keener than those of men. This influx from the spiritual world is rightly called instinct, because it exists quite apart from thought. . . . Man

---

[62] *N J M*, III (1829-1830), 44. See *Journals*, III, 337-338 (Sept. 14, 1834): "What is the doctrine of *infallible guidance if one will abdicate choice*, but striving to act unconsciously, to resume the simplicity of childhood?" See *Nature*, 11.18-19; 91.5-7. See Sampson Reed ¶s. 66-70.

[63] Theophilus Parsons, "On the Doctrine of Progressive Order," *N J M*, IX (1835-1836), 192ff. See pp. 192-193. Cf. *Nature*, 95.11-12; 88.1-4.

[64] *The True Christian Religion*, N.Y., [1936], no. 335. Cf. *Nature*, 89.10.

also has no connate ideas, because he has no connate thought; for where there is no thought, there are no ideas, these being interdependent. Consider new-born infants, who can do nothing but suck and breathe. . . . [N]othing is connate in man, except the power of acquiring knowledge, intelligence, and wisdom, and the inclination to love not only these but also the neighbour and God.

HOW THE LORD MANIFESTS HIS INFINITY IN NATURE——GOD IS A CIRCLE[65]

¶ 49

Infinity is also represented in nature. The Lord is the centre of all things; and man is the centre of all created things.[66] Man is thus the definite and universal standard. Things depart from man into immeasurableness, both upwards and downwards, both into largeness and smallness, and this equally. This was always known to a certain extent, and it became better known as science advanced. As the time for the consumating manifestation of truth drew near, new means of science were provided for man, that natural forms of truth might be prepared, into which spiritual truths might descend. Thus the telescope was given that we might look into the glittering sky with something better than vague admiration, with the knowledge that space is sown thick with innumerable worlds. The microscope is also given that we may advance in an opposite direction; that we may see every leaf to be a world to innumerable inhabitants, and know that the least fibres of our flesh are composed of fibrils, which are again only a congeries of smaller but similarly compounded parts. There is no end to our progress on either side. . . . [T]he limit of nature, whether in its smallness or in its greatness, though it be perpetually approached, will never be reached. The oldest philosophy of which we have any distinct record, declares the Divine to be a circle whose centre is everywhere and whose circumference is nowhere.[67]

TRUE RELIGION SHOULD BE CONCERNED WITH PURIFYING THE INNER AFFECTIONS——OUTWARD EXAMPLE IS SECONDARY[67a]

¶ 50

It is frequently urged by parents and teachers that this and that should be done for the sake of example. It is a constant theme with the moralist and the externally religious, that men should set a good example, that they should become models for others to imitate and follow. It is true that the example afforded by an orderly life, provided it be at the same time a religious, spiritual life, is calculated to have a beneficial effect on society. But it is questionable whether an exemplary life, a religious exterior deportment superinduced upon a mind impure and selfish; where, from the nature of the case, the internal man is at war with the external; where pride of character is the life and soul of all the good which is manifested;——it is questionable whether an example which is the offspring of motives like those above intimated, will produce any beneficial effect on others. It is said that example is contagious, but we apprehend that the outward form of man's conduct is less contagious than the sphere of his life——his thoughts, affections, ends, motives. These are contagious. Men of even dissimilar external habits and manners are frequently brought together and become associated in a way, at the time, unaccountable to themselves, when it afterwards becomes manifest to them that they were led to each other by the tendency of similar though unapparent affections and motives. All societies which are permanent and endure in the spiritual world, are formed by propinquity of affections, by a oneness of ends and motives. Do we, then, wish to benefit our fellow-men by setting a good example, let us purify and chasten our affections, correct our thoughts, and see that our ends and motives are regulated by the precepts of the Holy Scriptures. It will not be necessary for us to go out of our way to search for objects on which to confer the benefit of this kind of example. Our use will be provided for us by the Lord, while we shall be but willing instruments in performing it.

---

[65] Theophilus Parsons, "On the Infinite in Nature," *N J M*, IV (1830-1831), 144-146. See pp. 145-146. (The article is rptd. in *E T E*, II, 58-59.) Cf. *Nature*, 80.4; 92.5.

[66] Cf. *Nature*, 27.16; 35.10.

[67] For the disputed source of this line, see chap. VI, note 52. Emerson said the author was St. Augustine.

[67a] Nathaniel Hobart, "Example," *N J M*, III (1829-1830), 8-11. Excerpt is from page 8. Cf. *Journals*, III, 375 (Dec., 1834).

MILTON'S INSIGHT INTO THE STATE OF HEAVEN IS A FRAGMENT OF THE EARLIEST PHILOSOPHY————EARTHLY FORMS ARE IDENTICAL WITH HEAVENLY ONES[67b]

¶ 51

When Milton, in his paradise lost, said

> What surmounts the reach
> Of human sense, I shall delineate so,
> By likening spiritual to corporeal forms,
> As. may express them best; *though what if earth*
> *Be but the shadow of Heaven, and things therein*
> *Each to the other like, more than on earth is thought!*

he did not merely paint a picture, the forms and colors of which were supplied by his imagination. But, in this as in many other cases, he brought his learning into use, and the poet turned to good account the acquirements of the scholar. . . . The passage above cited, is but a poetical form of an apothegm which has come down as one of the few remaining fragments of the very earliest philosophy; namely,——"that there is nothing on earth which is not in the heavens in a heavenly form, and nothing in the heavens which is not on the earth in an earthly form."

TRUE FRIENDSHIP IS SPIRITUAL AND IMPERSONAL[67c]

¶ 52

Many people say, I love such an one because he loves me, and does me good. But yet to love him for that reason only, is not to love him interiorly, unless he that so loves is in good, and in consequence of it, loves the goodness of the other. The one is in charity; but the other is only in friendship, which is not charity. He who out of charity loves his neighbor, connects himself with the good that is in him; and not with his person, except so far and so long as he is in good. Such a man is spiritual, and loves his neighbor spiritually. But he who barely out of friendship loves another, connects himself with his person, and then at the same time with the evil that is in him. This man after death is with difficulty separated from the person who is in evil; whilst he who being in charity, loves spiritually, is easily so separated.—*Doctrine of Faith*, n. 21.

SPIRITUAL INFLUENCE IS RECIPROCAL————DEATH IS NO BARRIER TO FRIENDSHIP[67d]

¶ 53

[W]e learn, that all of us, who are in the natural world, are internally and spiritually associated either with good or evil spirits, who are similar to ourselves: that if we act from good affections, we are internally associated with, and act with, good spirits; and that if we act from evil affections, we are internally associated with evil spirits, and act with them: also, that we can come out of an evil society into a good one, by resisting our evil affections, and cherishing those which are good; and that we go out of a good society into an evil one, when we resist the good, and cherish the evil.

¶ 54

We learn that when a person dies, he comes into manifest association with the spirits that he was before internally and secretly associated with; that for this purpose he is divested of every thing which is not in agreement with his ruling affections. If his internal and ruling affections are good, he is cleansed from all external impurities; but if they are evil, he is divested of all the external appearances of goodness, which would enable him to deceive.

[67b] Theophilus Parsons, "The Spiritual Sense of the Word," *N J M*, IX (1835-1836), 414-420. Excerpt is from pp. 414-415.

[67c] "Extract from Swedenborg," *N J M*, VI (1832-1833), 40. It is quoted from Swedenborg's *Doctrine of Faith*, no. 21. Cf. Emerson's essay on "Friendship" and Notes on the Text of *Nature* under 58.4-15.

[67d] "Funeral Service from the *Book of Worship*," *N J M*, IX (1835-1836), 354-358. The excerpts come from pp. 355-356; 356. See Notes on the Text of *Nature* under 58.4-15. See also Caleb Reed, "Dependence of Men Upon Spirits and Angels," *N J M*, VIII (1834-1835), 243-245.

¶ 55

We learn that if we are internally and spiritually united to any person while here, the union is not severed by death: that, although he is then invisible to us, and we are invisible to him, yet his influence still continues to operate upon us, and that our influence continues to operate upon him: that we are still spiritually near together: that his affection for us still contributes to our happiness, and that our affection for him still contributes to his happiness. We thus learn not to mourn at the death of our friends, as if they had ceased to exist, nor as if they had ceased to be what they were, nor as if we were entirely separated from them: but at the same time, we learn to mourn on account of those habits of thinking and feeling which bind our spirits to the earth, and make us unmindful of the world to which our friends have gone, and to which we are going. We learn to mourn, not because our friends are dead, but because we ourselves have so little of spiritual life.

MAN'S POTENTIAL DIVINE HUMANITY——WITHIN *VS.* WITHOUT——GOD
ABIDES WITHIN——NECESSITY FOR LOOKING WITHIN——*WITHIN* AND
ABOVE ARE SYNONYMS[67e]

¶ 56

But we consider the New Jerusalem dispensation altogether an *internal* dispensation. By this we mean that it is addressed to the internal man, and operates by motives from *within*. It does not oppose any of the arguments or motives in favour of goodness which may be derived from any other dispensation; it rather illustrates and strengthens them: but they do not belong to it, excepting as it includes all other dispensations, and was the *end* of them all. It stands upon higher ground; it occupies a higher region of the mind; it employs higher powers; it requires higher qualities, and inspires and gratifies higher desires and hopes. It is the same thing, whether we say *higher*, or more *internal*. From the centre proceeds the circumference: the cause lies *within* the effect, and is not only prior in point of order, but *higher* in degree and nature. God is all *in* all; he is the *inmost;* and whatever is nearer to him is better than the more remote; therefore, the more *internal*, and the more *exalted*, are the same thing. Now the New Jerusalem dispensation requires, properly speaking, no new conduct, no new form of action, because the christian dispensation, and before this the commandments of the Jewish law, required perfection; obedience to them make one's *external* conduct perfect. But the New Church says, "be ye perfect, even as your Father in heaven is perfect," and says also, be perfect, as your Father in heaven is perfect," because your Father in heaven only is perfect man, and the manhood of all human beings is solely derived from the complete, essential, and only absolute manhood of our Father; because men are men by being images and likenesses of God, and thus by being forms receptive of influx from the Deity; and because that which flows from the Father as perfect man, and is received into men as into forms receptive of him, constitutes all their humanity. Hence, be ye perfect as your Father, has a wide and infinite, but a real and distinct, meaning; be ye the children of your Father; receive into your affections the love, and into your understandings the wisdom, which constitute the divine humanity; be ye *men*. Not that the New Church commands man to become God, but that it shews *how* Divinity can abide with us, and dwell in us; and if the New Church seems to liken man to God profanely or presumptuously, it is because it teaches a world utterly ignorant that there is *truth* in the text, that man is "made in the image and likeness of God;" and the light shineth in darkness. . . . Thus with the New Church there is no looking forward, but within, for the reward.

POETRY DRAWS ITS POWER FROM CORRESPONDENCES——TESTIMONY
OF FRANCIS JEFFREY IN THE *EDINBURGH REVIEW*[67f]

¶ 57

It is well understood by the New Church that poetry derives its power solely from the correspondence of natural things with spiritual. Even the fables of the muses, and

---

[67e] Theophilus Parsons, "Internal and External Evidence," *N J M,* II (1828-1829), 141-145. Excerpt is on pp. 142-143. This seems to have influenced Emerson's "Self and Others" (see esp. *Y E S,* 132-133) and also explains Emerson's phrase "redemption of the soul" in *Nature,* 91.6-7. See also Caleb Reed's "Recompense of Reward," *N J M,* II (1828-1829), 178-181. See chap. VII for a list of Emerson's references to *inner, outer, within* and *without.*

[67f] Caleb Reed, "Essence of Poetry," *N J M,* III (1829-1830), 191-192 (Feb., 1830).

of the flying horse, have the same origin, being a part of the drapery which fell from the ancient church. Whatever may be the boasted power of dry, argumentative reason, such is necessarily the constitution of the human mind, that the illustration of spiritual truth with' corresponding external objects, will carry conviction over the head and above the reach of reason. . . . The following extracts are from a notice of the poems of Mrs. Hemans, in the last number of the Edinburgh Review, said to be from the pen of Mr. Jeffrey, its late editor.

¶ 58

"It has always been our opinion, that the very essence of poetry, apart from the pathos, the wit, or the brilliant description which may be embodied in it, but may exist equally in prose, consists in the fine perception and vivid expression of that subtle and mysterious analogy which exists between the physical and the moral world——which makes outward things and qualities the natural types and emblems of inward gifts and emotions, and leads us to ascribe life and sentiment to every thing that interests us in the aspects of external nature. The feeling of this analogy, obscure and inexplicable as the theory of it may be, is so deep and universal in our nature, that it has stamped itself on the ordinary language of men of every kindred and speech: and that to such an extent, that one half of the epithets by which we familiarly designate moral and physical qualities, are in reality so many metaphors, borrowed reciprocally, upon this analogy, from those opposite forms of existence. The very familiarity, however, of the expression, in these instances, takes away its poetical effect——and indeed, in substance, its metaphorical character. The original sense of the word is entirely forgotten in the derivative one to which it has succeeded; and it requires some etymological recollection to convince us that it was originally nothing else than a typical or analogical illustration. Thus we talk of a penetrating understanding, and a furious blast——a weighty argument, and a gentle stream——without being at all aware that we are speaking in the language of poetry, and transferring qualities from one extremity of the sphere of being to another. In these cases, accordingly, the metaphor, by ceasing to be felt, in reality ceases to exist, and the analogy being no longer intimated, of course can produce no effect. But whenever it is intimated, it does produce an effect; and that effect we think is poetry.

¶ 59

"It has substantially two functions, and operates in two directions. In the *first* place, it strikes vividly out, and flashes at once on our minds, the conception of an inward feeling or emotion, which it might otherwise have been difficult to convey, by the presentment of some bodily form or quality, which is instantly felt to be its true representative, and enables us to fix and comprehend it with a force and clearness not otherwise attainable; and, in the *second* place, it vivifies dead and inanimate matter with the attributes of living and sentient mind, and fills the whole visible universe around us with objects of interest and sympathy, by tinging them with the hues of life, and associating them with our own passions and affections. This magical operation the poet too performs, for the most part, in one of two ways——either by the direct agency of similes and metaphors, more or less condensed or developed, or by the mere graceful presentment of such visible objects on the scene of his passionate dialogues or adventures, as partake of the character of the emotion he wishes to excite, and thus form an appropriate accompaniment or preparation for its direct indulgence or display. The former of those methods has perhaps been most frequently employed, and certainly has most attracted attention. But the latter, though less obtrusive, and perhaps less frequently resorted to of set purpose, is, we are inclined to think, the most natural and efficacious of the two; and is often adopted, we believe, unconsciously by poets of the highest order;——the predominant emotion of their minds overflowing spontaneously on all the objects which present themselves to their fancy, and calling out from them, and coloring with its own hues, those that are naturally emblematic of its character, and in accordance with its general expression. It would be easy to show how habitually this is done by Shakspeare, and Milton especially, and how much many of their finest passages are indebted both for force and richness of effect to this general and diffusive harmony of the external character of their scenes with the passions of

The quoted passages are from Francis Jeffrey's review of Felicia Hemans' poems in the *Edinburgh Review*, no. 99 (Oct., 1829).

their living agents——this harmonizing and appropriate glow with which they kindle the whole surrounding atmosphere, and bring all that strikes the sense into unison with all that touches the heart."

SUMMARY OF THE NEW-CHURCH VIEW OF NATURE, WHICH IS MAN'S LARGE EXTERNAL HOUSE——CORRESPONDENCE BETWEEN THE OUTER AND INNER WORLDS——THE SPIRITUAL MAN *VS.* THE NATURAL[67a]

¶ 60

The "natural man" lives in "nature;" there he finds his proper sphere and his home. He dwells there in heart and in life; its limits are boundless to him, because he cannot fill them; they are perpetually opening before him, for the mysteries of nature, as fast as they are developed, disclose other mysteries in an unending series, and the uses and functions of nature, as he discovers and turns them to account, become means for bringing other uses and functions within his dominion. Thus his horizon recedes as he advances, or rather widens as he ascends; whatever he learns of the substances, laws, powers and qualities of nature, suggests to him something he had not before thought of, to study and learn. He remains always within nature, because he finds there constantly enlarging room for all his activity, new objects of thought perpetually springing up to satisfy all the demands of his intellect, and ample space and means for the display, developement and gratification of all his affections; thus neither in act, nor in thought, nor in affection does he go where nature is not. . . . Thus is he bounded by nature in act, in thought and affection, in the whole of his life and being.

¶ 61

The spiritual is within the natural, as the soul is within the body; and the man who has become spiritual from being natural, does not abandon or lose the thoughts, knowledge and pleasures of the natural man; he does not give up the natural world, nor could he, any better than the natural man, act, think, or live without it. But, he makes a totally different use of it. In the spiritual man, the forms of the natural man, that is, the forms of action, thought, and affection, are filled with a spiritual life. His senses remain the same, and through them he acts upon and with the external world as before, but to totally different ends and on totally different principles. He still may seek the necessaries of life, or a comfortable subsistence, or authority and means of influence, but it is no longer for their own sakes; it is now for the sake of the uses which he is by them enabled to discharge towards his neighbor. . . . And the final cause, the sole end for which the external world exists, is, that it may subserve these spiritual uses.

¶ 62

This correspondence between the things within man and the things without, is the law of their being, because the things without man are formed by means of the things within him. The external world not only *was* but perpetually *is* created, (for *subsistence* is perpetual *creation*,) by efflux from the Divine, which flowing through man, passes into the material elements of nature and impresses upon them the signature of man. This creative efflux passes through man as its medium or instrument, from highest to lowest; and as the natural man is the lowest form of man, is proximate to nature, as it were in contact with nature,——nature gives back the impression, true beyond the possibility of error, and equally true in all its parts and in all the relations between them. Thus nature is indeed in the image and likeness of man, and thus man, in nature, may see and learn what he is, and what manner of things are within him. There may his senses read concerning his spirit, and if he permits the sensual forms which his mind first receives from nature to be filled with the spirit of truth, there may he find a wisdom that will lead him along the path by which it descended from on high.

¶ 63

In man, the affections or feelings awaken, form, and are within the thoughts; flowing through the thoughts, they, by the thoughts as their medium or means, determine, terminate in, and are manifested by the actions; and these altogether constitute the man. Now, efflux from the Divine flowing through these affections and thoughts and receiving from them their form and pressure, passes into material elements, and fashions them according to that form and pressure. Thus material things correspond to, and because they correspond to, exactly represent and become the signs of spiritual things.

[67a] Theophilus Parsons, "Concerning Nature," *N J M*, III (1829-1830), 267-276 (May, 1830). The excerpts are from pp. 268-269; 270-271; 271-272; 272-273. Cf. Orphic Poet IV. See also *Nature*, 76.5—77.2.

This is equally true, and true on the same ground and for the same reason, in regard to the external world of the *natural* body, and in regard to the external world of the *spiritual* body; the one world being material, like the material body, the other world being spiritual, like the spiritual body, for, as in each particular case something spiritual forms and is represented by a corresponding natural something, so is it with all things taken together, and the whole natural world exists in nature, because there exists in spirit, a complete, perfectly analogous and most real spiritual world. The soul forms and fashions the body, out of the elements of nature, by its living principle, as the seed takes to itself of the elements and makes of them a tree and determines its form and quality exactly according to its own principle of life. And when the body falls from man, the spiritual body, formed by the soul out of spiritual substances according to the same principles, continues to exist; it bears no relation to death; it always exists within the natural body, and is the medium by which the soul forms that body; and its senses and powers lie within the natural senses and powers, and give to them form and being.

Emerson had considerable respect for the Swedenborgians even from the time of their incorporation in Boston. Writing in his journal as early as December 10, 1824, he classified them as a quiet sect like the Quakers.[68] Sampson Reed's *Observations on the Growth of the Mind,* published on August 29, 1826, doubtless, aroused him to active interest,[69] for by January, 1827, he paid the New Church a significant tribute. Characterizing the early nineteenth century as an age of "Transcendentalism," a time when metaphysical and ethical speculation *looked within,* he declared the four representative figures of the period to be Madame de Staël, Wordsworth, Sampson Reed and Swedenborg respectively of France, England, America and Germany.[70] When the initial number of the *New Jerusalem Magazine* appeared in September, 1827, Emerson began to look especially for Reed's unsigned articles. It is possible, moreover, that he purchased his first volume of Swedenborg's works during 1828, for his copy of *Intercourse between the Soul and the Body* or *Influx*[71] was published in that year.[72] His father had owned an earlier edition of the same work.[73] At all events, on March 22, 1829, in a sermon ("The Best Part of Life Unseen") one observes Swedenborgian terminology in his remark that Jesus received "a miraculous *influx* of light into the soul which superseded the necessity of painful progress from the elements of knowledge."[74] On October 9, 1829, he rejoiced that the New-Church interpretations of the Bible could be accepted in America, for they were right and eternal, even though the writers of Holy Writ "meant no such things" as the commentators claimed.[75] On November 3, 1830, he saw a great likeness between Swedenborgians, Methodists and Quakers, and declared their supposed differences to be only superficial.[76] A year later, after the death of his wife and while he was thinking seriously about his uncertain future, he highly approved the Swedenborgian Doctrine of Uses:[77]

---

[68] See *Journals,* II, 25.

[69] See *Journals,* II, 116-117 (Sept. 10, 1826). It is conceivable, however, that Reed's "Oration on Genius" (1821) aroused his interest in the Swedenborgians, but I have discovered no evidence.

[70] *Journals,* II, 164.

[71] For the various titles of this work see note 16 above.

[72] See note 15 *supra.*

[73] See item 184 of the catalogue of the Rev. William Emerson's library in *E T E,* II.

[74] See *Y E S,* 234.43-45. Italics are mine.   [75] *Journals,* II, 267-268.

[76] *Journals,* II, 318.   [77] See ¶s. 18-20 *supra.* See Sampson Reed ¶s. 35-37.

Is it not true that every man has before him in his mind room in one direction to which there is no bound, but in every other direction he runs against a wall in a short time? One course of thought, affection, action is for him——that is his *use*, as the new men say.[78]

About this time, to the strong Swedenborgian influence was added that of Coleridge——especially the distinction between the Reason and the Understanding, and in the poem, "Gnothi Seauton,"[79] completed on July 6, 1831, Emerson confessed that he had truly made the transcendentalism of the age his own by turning forever from the outer world of sense to the rich inner world of spiritual reality. Again, on the following Christmas day, he observed that "all our philosophy" hangs on the words "in" and "out" and that this important distinction forms the substance of the writings of both Wordsworth and Swedenborg.[80]

1 8 3 2

On January 27,[81] he wrote of having talked with Thomas Worcester and Sampson Reed on the mutual influence of spirits and of discovering that the New-Church speculation on this point was in no sense distinctive. Rather it was a confirmation of universally accepted truths, for did not the ancient Stoics maintain that a wise man could influence sages everywhere in the world by merely raising his finger? The Swedenborgians were, it seemed, reflecting the best thought of all ages in emphasizing the interaction of the unconscious or spiritual levels of the inner beings of men.[82] This conversation supplied Emerson with a word which, during the months to come, he was to put to good use in his best descriptions of spiritual activity: "God," said Worcester, "not so much sees as *dissolves* us."[83] On February 19, Emerson was still meditating on the ecumenical truth of New-Church doctrine.[84] On April 17, he wrote:[85]

A strange poem is Zoroastrism. It is a system as separate and harmonious and sublime as Swedenborgianism——congruent. One would be glad to behold the truth which they all shadow forth. For it cannot but be truth that they typify and symbolize, as the play of every faculty reveals an use, a cause and a law to the intelligent. One sees in this, and in them all, the element of poetry according to Jeffrey's[86] true theory, the effect produced by making every thing outward only a sign of something inward.

On July 15, he quoted Swedenborg's view of the visible world as the "dial plate of the invisible one."[87] On August 18, he emphasized the genuineness of Fox, Washington and Swedenborg, the last of whom had said: "My writings will be found another self."[88] The examples of those men remained in his mind during the following difficult weeks. On September 9, he delivered his famous sermon on "The Lord's Supper" and two days later

---

[78] See *Journals*, II, 426 (Nov., 1831).
[79] See chap. VII under July 6, 1831.
[82] This thought is strongly implied in the later essays on "Friendship" and "Love." Cf. *Nature*, 58.1-20, esp. line 16; also 89.8-9. See Sampson Reed's "Growth of the Mind," *E T E*, II, 24: "All minds, whatever may be their condition, are not unconnected with God; and consequently not unconnected with each other."
[83] Italics mine. See section XII of his "Statement of the First Philosophy" in chap. VII; see the Orphic Poet's line in *Nature*, 88.12. See "Self-Reliance," *Works*, II, 66.
[84] *Journals*, II, 466.
[85] *Journals*, II, 473-474.
[88] *Journals*, II, 507. Apparently a paraphrase of parts of a long article, published

[80] *Journals*, II, 440. Cf. ¶ 56.
[81] *Journals*, II, 455-456. Cf. ¶s. 53-55.
[86] See ¶s. 57-59.
[87] See ¶ 5. See also *Journals*, II, 500-501.

handed his resignation to the proprietors of the Second Church.[89] Sometime during the early part of October, while recovering from a relapse,[90] he seems to have sought intellectual companionship among his New-Church friends, but came away disappointed at their inability to explain the doctrines which they promulgated: "They are *possessed with* the ideas, but do not *possess* them."[91] His respect for Swedenborg, however, remained undiminished, and in his farewell sermon, "The Genuine Man," delivered on October 21, he publicly praised that "eminent religious teacher of the last generation" whose writings were, indeed, "another self."[92]

1 8 3 3

Emerson resigned his office in the Unitarian Church because he, too, sought to make his words and deeds genuine expressions of his inner convictions. Most of this year he spent abroad, but he carried with him an enthusiasm for the writings of Sampson Reed and the belief that the New Church would contribute more than any other sect to the universal religion of the future.[93] After his return from Europe, writing on October 21, he was no less enthusiastic, even though he qualified his praise with a characteristic reservation: Fox and Swedenborg, he said, "wanted but little, or . . . exceeded but little, of being true prophets."[94] During this period, moreover, he seems to have purchased a copy of *The Doctrine of the New Jerusalem Concerning the Lord*.[95] On November 2, he noted how people under the influence of passion clothe their thoughts in material or natural garments and that this fact was a possible illustration of the manner in which spirits clothe themselves with bodies. He then went on to discuss the doctrine of correspondences and to speak of nature as being a language or a universal book——one that he wished very much to read. He implied that the Swedenborgians might help him in this great task.[96] On December 22,[97] he praised Hedge's review of Swedenborg for the help it gave him.[98]

1 8 3 4

At New Bedford, on March 21, he recorded with evident pleasure a tribute from his Swedenborgian friend, Dr. Artemas Stebbins, who had said that he felt excused from preaching while Emerson was in the vicinity because the people were receiving from him as much New Jerusalem doctrine as they could bear.[99] On May 3, he declared the Swedenborgian

serially, by Nathaniel Hobart, on the "Life of Swedenborg." Cf. *N J M*, II (1828-1829), 36. This article had some influence upon Emerson's lecture, "Swedenborg," in *Representative Men*.   [91] *Journals*, II, 520. Italics are mine.

[89] *Letters*, I, 355-357.   [92] *Y E S*, 186.9. See above under Aug. 18, 1832.
[90] *Letters*, I, 357 note.   [93] See *Carlyle-Emerson Corr.*, I, 17 and 33.
[94] *Journals*, III, 222.   [95] Printed in Boston in 1833.

[96] See *Journals*, III, 227. Cf. *Nature*, 38.18. See ¶s. 1-5, 25-27, 34, 39, 49. Note how this thought is expressed in the Orphic Poet's lines in *Nature*, 93.20-24; 94.1-3; 94.13-15. See also *Nature*, 34.4; 43.21——44.4; 93.5-8.

[97] *Letters*, I, 402.

[98] A quotation from this review appears at the beginning of the present chapter. See *Christian Examiner*, XV, 193-218 (Nov., 1833).

[99] See *Journals*, III, 266. Dr. Artemas Stebbins is described as a genial and lovable old pioneer, who was a medical doctor and a preacher in the "Old Church." He early

doctrine of "affections clothed" to be an important unifying idea.[100] On May 21, he resolved to trust his instincts,[101] that is, the promptings of the Universal Mind or Spirit flowing into him, for he discovered that whenever he "deviated from the instinct," some Goethe, Swedenborg[102] or Carlyle would come along with a profound theory teaching that he ought to have followed it.[103] This doctrine of Self-Reliance (i.e., God-Reliance) he reinforced by the observation that whenever he had refused to listen to the inner voice and had yielded to the opinions of others, he was later obliged with embarrassment to return to his *first* idea. Dugald Stewart had rightly said: "Our first and third thoughts coincide."[104] Emerson distinguished, however, between following the high principles of his teachers and yielding to a superstitious worship of their *tastes*. For this reason he wished no more to imitate Baron Swedenborg than Jesus Christ![105] On November 20, he wrote to Carlyle of the important contribution which the New-Church sect would surely make to the coming universal religion:[106]

Swedenborgianism, if you should be fortunate in your first meetings, has many points of attraction for you; for instance, this article, "The poetry of the Old Church is the reality of the New,"[107] which is to be literally understood, for they esteem, in common with all the Trismegisti, the Natural World as strictly the symbol or exponent of the Spiritual, and part for part; the animals to be the incarnations of certain affections; and scarce a popular expression esteemed figurative, but they affirm to be the simplest statement of fact. Then is their whole theory of social relations——both in and out of the body——most philosophical, and, though at variance with the popular theology, self-evident. It is only when they come to their descriptive theism, if I may say so, and then to their drollest heaven, and to some autocratic not moral decrees of God, that the mythus loses me. In general, too, they receive the fable instead of the moral of their Æsop. They are to me, however, deeply interesting, as a sect which I think must contribute more than all other sects to the new faith which must arise out of all.

On November 23, he wrote that since every institution, thought or person seemed to embody itself externally in clothing, in a house, or in a society, he saw no reason for objecting to the Swedenborgian doctrine that the affections clothe themselves in appropriate habiliments and dwellings.[108] On November 26, he probably had in mind the Doctrine of Uses as well as the New-Church belief in the afterlife[109] when he wrote about the fear of

---

became attracted to Swedenborgian doctrines and began to distribute New-Church literature. In 1824, the New-Church Society was legally organized in Bridgewater, Mass., with Dr. Stebbins as its leader. He was not ordained until 1838. After 1840 he was inactive, but lived until November 26, 1871. He was eighty-four years old when he died. See "Early History of the New Jerusalem Church in Bridgewater, Mass.," *N J M*, XLIV, 471-476 (March, 1872).

[100] *Journals*, III, 293.   [101] See *Nature*, 89.10.
[102] See ¶s. 24, 28-30, 48. Also Sampson Reed ¶s. 27-28, 46-47, 66-70.
[103] *Journals*, III, 299.
[104] See the quotation from Stewart in *Journals*, II, 388 (June, 1831). That Emerson was fond of it is evident in his frequent paraphrases. See *Y E S*, 110.1-5 (Dec. 3, 1830); *Letters*, I, 338 (Dec. 10, 1831); *Letters*, I, 413 (May 31, 1834); and *Journals*, III, 533 (Aug. 5, 1835).
[105] *Journals*, III, 337 (Sept. 13, 1834) and III, 518.
[106] *Carlyle-Emerson Corr.*, I, 32-33. See Sampson Reed ¶s. 38-43. See *Y E S*, 199-201.
[107] See Sampson Reed ¶ 57. Emerson had apparently enclosed "Self-Love Essential Evil"—pages 338-346 of *N J M*, IV, no. xlv, May, 1831.
[108] *Journals*, III, 370. See note 96 above. See ¶s. 25-27, 29-30, 34-37, 39. See also Sampson Reed ¶s. 18-19, 58, etc. as well as the chapter on Oegger.   [109] See ¶s. 6-13.

death:[110] "do your duty, and you are already immortal; the taste . . . of death has already vanished."[111] Sometime during December, recalling Coleridge's denunciation of the hypocrisy of churchgoers,[112] he wrote with respect: "George Fox and Emanuel Swedenborg never advise people to go to church for the sake of example."[113] On December 2, he compared Coleridge's terms, *Understanding* and *Reason* to Swedenborg's *love of self* and *love of the Lord*.[114] On December 22, he seems to have described poetically the parallel suns of Swedenborg:[115]

> The sun is the sole inconsumable fire
> And God is the sole inexhaustible giver.

On December 27, he spoke of the "sane moments"[116] when he experienced "ineffable peace" and the *"influx* of God," which came with humility and love.[117] On December 28, he criticized the prolix sermons and prayers heard in most churches, but excepted the utterances of that "living Methodist," Edward Taylor, whom he called a poet, and those of the Swedenborgians, if, as he assumed, their pulpit had any resemblance whatsoever to their literature.[118] On the following day, however, he wrote with a customary independence:[119] "When I rest in perfect humility, when I burn with pure love, what can Calvin or Swedenborg say to me?"

1 8 3 5

On January 5, he visited for the first time the Swedenborg Chapel in Boston, found the service simple, said he had not been deceived in his expectations, and declared to Sampson Reed that the sermon, except at one point, would not have surprised or alarmed the congregation of any other sect.[120] On January 7, he wrote that the parallel element in biographies of enthusiasts like Luther, Fox, Swedenborg and Madame Guyon[121] was the realization that God must be found *within*. Each saw that instruction from without had no value, that wisdom came only by reflection or meditation, and that the conditions of spiritual growth were innocence[122] and sub-mission. "Swedenborg and the Quakers have much to say of a new name that shall be given in heaven."[123] On January 9, he compared Madame Guyon's inability to talk in the presence of faultfinders with Swedenborg's revelation that in heaven the angels are unable to utter what they do not believe.[124] On January 23, he wrote that natural laws interested him par-

---

[110] See Sampson Reed ¶ 64.

[111] *Journals*, III, 373-374.

[112] See Coleridge ¶ 106.

[113] *Journals*, III, 375. See ¶ 50.

[114] See *Journals*, III, 377. Cf. ¶s. 8, 30, 45-46; Sampson Reed ¶s. 59-62.

[115] *Journals*, III, 408. Cf. ¶s. 22-23, 40-43; Sampson Reed ¶s. 58-59.

[116] See section XIV of his "Statement of the First Philosophy" in chap. VII. Cf. *Nature*, 62.19.

[117] *Journals*, III, 415-416 (italics mine). The opposite of humility is "love of self." See note 114 above. Cf. Sampson Reed ¶s. 46-47.

[118] *Journals*, III, 421.

[119] *Journals*, III, 423.

[120] See *Letters*, I, 430 (Jan. 7, 1835) and *Journals*, III, 430-432 (Jan. 6, 1835).

[121] *I.e.*, Jeanne Marie de la Motte-Guyon (1648-1717), a French mystic who practiced semiquietism.

[122] See the index to Swedenborg's *Heaven and its Wonders and Hell* as well as the indices of his other works for excellent commentary on this word. Cf. *Nature*, 88.2.

[123] See *Journals*, III, 432-433. Cf. Revelation 2:17 and 3:12. See under those verses in Swedenborg's *Apocalypse Revealed* and *Apocalypse Explained*.

[124] See *Journals*, III, 435. The reference is to the *Apocalypse Revealed*, no. 294: "In

ticularly for their correspondences with spiritual laws——for their symbolic and prophetic values.[125] On April 14, he praised Swedenborg's early education, which had provided a sound foundation for his later religious doctrines.[126] On June 4, he suggested a parallel between the New-Church theory of heaven and hell within every man and Coleridge's Reason and Understanding.[127] Writing to Elizabeth Peabody on August 3, he endorsed the general truth which Swedenborg taught but, like her, did not wish to be confined to his associations.[128] He condemned, however, the cheap jests which the ignorant and sensual kept hurling at that mystic.[129] On November 5, in his "Introductory Lecture on English Literature," he discussed the doctrine of correspondences in a long section on language.[130]

1 8 3 6

Sometime in early January, he added to his library *The Apocalypse Revealed*[131] and marked the first two volumes as he read. Several excerpts were copied into his journals on January 22.[132] Two days later he seems to have reread with "sublime emotion" *On the Intercourse Between the Soul and the Body* (or *Influx*) and copied from it a passage which influenced *Nature*.[133] On June 16, when about to compose his Orphic Poet's lines, he wrote significantly that Swedenborg would soon become popular, that he needed only to be considered *as a poet*——"to be read and admired for his verities," and that his dogmatic theology could be easily overlooked.[134] In *Nature*, published in September, he spoke of Swedenborg among other great men who had tried to solve the problem of the relation between mind and matter,[135] cited his miracles as an evidence of man's action on nature with all his force,[136] and drew upon him and his followers for lustres and fable materials with which to decorate the chapters on "Language," "Spirit," and "Prospects."[137] The influence of the Swedenborgians upon the lines of the Orphic Poet will be discussed in a later section (pages 361-399) of the present study.

---

the natural world man has a twofold speech, because he has a twofold thought, an exterior and an interior: for a man can speak from interior thought, and at the same time from exterior thought; and he can speak from exterior thought, and not from the interior, and even against the interior: hence come simulations, flatteries, and hypocrisies. But in the spiritual world man's speech is not twofold, but single. He there speaks as he thinks: otherwise the sound is harsh, and offends the ear. But still he can be silent, and thus not divulge the thoughts of his mind." Swedenborg tells of an experiment made by some of the angels, trying to say what they did not believe: "But they could not. They twisted and folded their lips into many curves, and could not articulate any other words than those that agreed with the ideas of their thought. . . . They twisted their lips into folds even to indignation, and wished to compel their mouth to utter it, and to force it out: but they were not able." The same thoughts occur in "On the Name of the Lord Jesus Christ," *N J M*, VIII (1834-1835), 103.

[125] *Letters*, I, 433.
[126] *Journals*, III, 467.
[127] *Journals*, III, 488.
[132] See *Journals*, IV, 6.
[134] *Journals*, IV, 70-71.
[135] *Nature*, 43.18.
[128] *Letters*, I, 451. See also *Journals*, III, 531.
[129] See *Journals*, III, 529.
[130] See my abstract of this lecture in a later section.
[131] Published in 3 vols., Boston, 1836.
[133] See ¶ 27. Cf. *Nature*, 44.15; 79.19-23.
[136] *Nature*, 90.14. These miracles were discussed in Hedge's "Emanuel Swedenborg," *The Christian Examiner*, XV, 193-218 (Nov., 1833).
[137] See esp. *Nature*, chap. IV *passim;* 79.15-23; 80.16——81.11; 87.17-22; 88.1——89.11; 91.5-19; 93.3-8; 93.15——94.3; 94.13——95.12.

SAMPSON REED——"MY EARLY ORACLE"[1]

Sampson Reed was born in Bridgewater (now West Bridgewater), Mass., on June 10, 1800, one of the sons[2] of the Rev. John Reed, D.D.,[3] by whom he was educated during the first fourteen years of his life. After a boyhood spent for the most part on his father's farm, he was taken to Harvard College in 1814 for the entrance examinations. "[W]e spent the night," he wrote later,[4] "at Morse's tavern. Our room was separated by a board partition from an adjoining one, in which I heard two students reciting to each other the Latin Grammar preparatory to the examination till I fell asleep myself. The next day I recognized the voices which I had heard as those of [Timothy] Osgood and [James] Swan." During his first year at the college he met Thomas Worcester, whose influence upon his life was to be incalculable:[5]

We occupied rooms in the same building, it being a private residence near to that of Dr. Kirkland, then president of the university. Mr. Worcester, for some time previous to his entering college, had been under the instruction of the Rev. Pitt Clark, and resided in his family in Norton. Mr. Clark and my father were intimate friends, and being ministers in neighboring towns sometimes exchanged with each other, and Mr. Worcester had met my father at Mr. Clark's house. This was the occasion of our being first brought together. It happened that neither of us had a congenial chum the first year, and it was arranged that we should occupy a room together in one of the college buildings the second; and this was continued during the rest of our college life. This arrangement was very satisfactory to my father, who had been favorably impressed with his short acquaintance with Mr. Worcester, and who had great respect for his father; both of them having renounced the Calvinistic faith and adopted views similar to his own on religious subjects, especially upon the doctrine of the Lord.

Mr. Worcester was then nineteen years old, and I was five years his junior, and, as I look back, I cannot well see why he should have chosen me for a room-mate, as I could hardly have been a companion for him at that time; but I can see in this, very clearly, the hand of Divine Providence; certainly so far as I was concerned. All my life has been shaped differently from what it might have been under other circumstances, for which I can never be sufficiently thankful to my Heavenly Father. Mr. Worcester is remembered at that time as tall and slender, but possessed of a good degree of physical strength. He, as well as myself, was poor and our expenses were very largely paid by waiting on the tables, which was then the custom in college for those who needed

---

[1] See *Journals*, IV, 74 (June 22, 1836). For biographical details see: (1) Reed's note to Francis Brinley of July 13, 1864, printed as Letter XI in *E T E*, II, and referred to hereafter as *Autobiography*; (2) his *A Biographical Sketch of Thomas Worcester, D.D.*, Boston, 1880, referred to hereafter as *Thomas Worcester*; (3) Marguerite Bloch, *The New Church in the New World*, N.Y., 1932; (4) Warren Goddard, "Sampson Reed," *N J M*, n.s. IV, 285-289 (Sept., 1880); (5) "Sampson Reed," *N J M*, n.s. IV, 301-302 (Sept., 1880); *Dictionary of American Biography*; (7) Jacob Whittemore Reed, *History of the Reed Family*, Boston, 1861. A list of some of Sampson Reed's periodical publications is given within the present chapter.

[2] His brothers both became distinguished Massachusetts citizens. The Hon. John Reed was a member of Congress for sixteen years or more and served for several years as Lieutenant Governor of the Commonwealth. Caleb Reed became active in the New Church and for many years was editor of the *N J M*. The latter is discussed at considerable length in *Thomas Worcester*. See also Goddard, *loc. cit.*, 286.

[3] See *Autobiography*. His father "officiated for half a century as clergyman in that place and was for six years member of Congress in the administration of Washington and the elder Adams."

[4] See *Autobiography*.   [5] *Thomas Worcester*, 14-15.

assistance; and by keeping school during the long winter vacation, which was somewhat extended for that purpose.

During his four years as an undergraduate, Reed stood high as a scholar and often received the highest mark in his class on themes and compositions. Warren Goddard remembered one time "when several of us having received our compositions from the professor, and holding them folded in our hands on our way to our rooms, we saw, in the deep impressions of the professor's pencil, plainly on the outside of his, the word *Optimé.*" Although Reed did not soon become a follower of his roommate's Swedenborgian opinions, he was not uninfluenced by them. Beginning in the junior year, Worcester's "principal employment was in reading the *Heavenly Doctrines* and in communicating a knowledge of them" to his fellow students.[6] His pursuit of a set of Swedenborg's works, deposited in the college library many years earlier by the Rev. William Hill,[7] deserves to be quoted in his own words because of the picture they give of the Harvard Library and of the atmosphere in which Reed lived during his last two years as an undergraduate. Worcester writes:[8]

Upon my return to college, after I had begun to read Swedenborg, I went to the library the second time to see if I could find any of his works. The librarian looked into the catalogue again, and found the alcove and shelves where they ought to have been; but they were not there. Then we began a thorough search. We looked through the whole library, in place and out of place, but could not find them. Then we began to think of other rooms. At that time the library was in the second story of the west end of Harvard Hall. In the east end was a large room, called the "Philosophical Room." And between this room and the library was a small room, which for the want of a proper name was called the "Museum."[9] It was filled with rubbish, old curiosities, cast off, superseded, and obsolete philosophical apparatus, and so forth, all covered with dust. We could see no reason for hunting here, except that we had hunted everywhere else, without finding what we wanted.

There was a long table in the room. Upon it, and under it, were piles of useless articles; and beyond it were shelves against the wall, where various things were stored away. On the under shelf, as far out of sight as possible, I saw some books. I told the librarian, and he went round and worked his way until he got at them, and found that the large books were volumes of the *Arcana Cœlestia.*[10] There were also several other works of Swedenborg, all of them covered with dust. I immediately got an order from President Kirkland, giving me authority to take the books and keep them in my room; and this I did for the rest of my college life. By what means or for what purpose these *Heavenly Doctrines* were cast out of the library of Harvard College must be left to conjecture. Of the 50,000 or 60,000 volumes then belonging to the library, these were the only ones that were treated in this manner. The fact seems to represent the state of the New Church at that time.

After the transfer, Sampson Reed's room must have resembled a small library, and one may assume that it was the setting for many student discussions and conferences.

---

[6] *Thomas Worcester,* 15-16.

[7] Hill came to America from Liverpool in 1794. See Bloch, *op. cit.,* 100-101.

[8] *Thomas Worcester,* 17-18.

[9] Bloch, *op. cit.,* 101-102, reports that the museum contained some stuffed crocodiles among other discarded objects.

[10] These were probably the *Arcana Cœlestia,* (7 vols. in quarto), London, 1749-1754, listed in the *Catalogue of the Library,* Cambridge, 1830, II, 814. By 1830, Harvard had an excellent collection of Swedenborg's writings, including another set of the *Arcana Cœlestia,* (5 vols. in octavo), London, 1792.

In 1818, when Emerson was about to begin his sophomore year, Sampson Reed and Thomas Worcester were graduated from Harvard and entered the Theological School in Cambridge. Reed did so upon the advice of his father, who expected him probably to become "a minister of the Unitarian denomination." He had, however, become "somewhat interested" in the works of Swedenborg while in college, "and now commenced reading them in earnest."[11] In 1819, his classmate, John H. Wilkins, who had developed New-Church tendencies during his senior year,[12] entered the theological school and, doubtless, strengthened Reed's purpose. The three friends were soon giving most of their time to Swedenborgian doctrine and preparing only as much class work as was required to maintain their standing.[13] Meanwhile, Mrs. Thomazine E. Minot (neé Bond), one of the twelve original members of the Boston Society,[14] hoping to further the work of the church among Harvard students, rented a large boarding house in Cambridge and provided a home as well as a religious center for the three theologians and a few others.[15] In 1820, Wilkins and Reed were formally admitted into the Boston New-Church family, accepting all the responsibilities which such membership involved.[16]

1 8 2 1

The year 1821 was one of importance and crisis. The Society asked Thomas Worcester to become its pastor on March 10; Worcester married Alice Clark on May 8; and Mrs. Minot saw that her work in Cambridge was at an end. Moving to a large house in Boston, located in what is now Hayward Place, she planned to accommodate the new pastor, his wife, and other New-Church boarders, thus providing a home and social center for the developing church. Wilkins and Reed went to Boston with her, quitting the Divinity School without completing the course. They had no means, no business experience and no prospects, yet they had hope of becoming teachers in a community rather unsympathetic with New-Church principles.[17] Wilkins began working at once on an elementary textbook in astronomy, which met with immediate success, and soon afterwards entered the bookstore of Cummings, Hilliard and Company.[18] Reed had trained himself chiefly for the ministry, but there were no vacancies in his adopted church, which at this time was much in need of financial support from its laymen.[19] Sometime during the year, therefore, he became a teacher in a small school in Boston "on the neck."[20] On August 21, he delivered an "Oration on Genius"[21] at the Harvard Commencement for the degree of Master of Arts, and Emerson who was then completing work for his bachelor's degree, heard the essay with much pleasure.[22] The following outline will indicate its principal ideas:

---

[11] *Thomas Worcester*, 38.
[12] See *Thomas Worcester*, 36 and 68.
[15] See *Thomas Worcester*, 44; also the college catalogues for Oct., 1819, and Oct., 1820.
[16] *Thomas Worcester*, 75.
[17] *Thomas Worcester*, 43-47.
[18] *Thomas Worcester*, 69.
[13] *Thomas Worcester*, 68.
[14] See Bloch, *op. cit.*, 102-103.
[19] See "Sampson Reed," *N J M*, n.s. IV, 302.
[20] *Autobiography*.
[21] See *E T E*, II, 9-12.
[22] For a contemporary comment on this address and for a statement of its popularity among members of the Emerson household, see *Letters*, III, 74.

INTRODUCTION

At birth every man is given a form of mind peculiar to himself, and it becomes the basis of his character and the force that urges him onward. Growth is merely the expansion of his rudimentary self by the assimilation of what he can use. Nations, like individuals, also have distinctive characters, but behind nations, individuals, and centuries is a force called *love*, which stimulates all minds, lies behind all affections, and may be diverted to good or evil purposes.

I. FALSE GENIUS——THOSE WHOM THE WORLD CALLS GREAT

So-called great men are esteemed only because they meet the artificial standards of their society. In a savage community, for example, greatness depends upon physical strength; in a civilization, upon the arts and sciences; but in Heaven, on something still different——on the awareness that love and wisdom *come from God*. The proud and the lovers of self forget that nothing they possess is their own. Mankind seems unable to see God in everything. Though God is the source of truth, one sees men boasting of their discoveries. True genius is not man-made. It does not spring from ambition. It is not the creation of self-love.

II. TRUE GENIUS IS FROM GOD

True genius is divine——not when a man thinks he is God, but when he acknowledges that all his powers are from God. He then is humble with a humility that exalts. We see the genius of such men as Luther, Shakespeare, Milton and Newton only when Divine Truth has cleared the mental atmosphere of man so that their bright side[23] is seen to be toward us.

III. THE WORKS OF TRUE GENIUS REFLECT THE DIVINE

All the *arts* which result from human invention and which men have taken from nature will perish or return to nature. The only imperishable arts are those which spring spontaneously from divine inspiration and which, therefore, have a spiritual value. Music and poetry may be either worthless or heavenly. The *sciences*, also, will have permanence only insofar as they depend upon the Divine. How can one be a true scientist if one regards not the Author of nature and the giver of the Ten Commandments? One cannot love the natural world without respecting the moral order. When the heart is purified, science like poetry will become a spontaneous growth. Until that time, it will be learned "by the sweat of the brow." *Religion* characterizes true genius, yet today men consider the inspiration of genius to be quite distinct from religion. The reason, in part, is that the church has long been too much concerned with death, but the truly great man must be a good and humble man. Greatness and goodness are not separable.

IV. AFTERTHOUGHTS

Therefore be genuine! Be your true self! Let heaven direct your life, even as it began it. Flee ambition, which is death to the genuine and the cause of blindness to one's duty to one's neighbor. Since self-love is death, get rid of your shroud! When the heart is pure, genius will find its seat within the church, and the arts will spring in full-grown beauty from Him who is the source of all beauty. In place of sterile knowledge there will be wisdom that flows from the heart. Genius of the mind will unite with the genius of nature. Thoughts will fall to earth with power, and nature will become a living language. Adam and Eve had no need for words. The Spirit shone into their hearts and supplied their needs. Our science will be full of life as we come to see God in the natural world, but before we can have a living natural science, we shall need a new science of the mind. John Locke's system is definitely inadequate, and a better day is about to dawn.

Reed soon abandoned the schoolroom, probably because he found opposition to his religious views. He next entered his name with Dr. James Mann in the hope of becoming a physician, but being straitened in his circumstances, he gave up hope of a profession and sought a trade, binding himself as an apprentice for a period of three years to a druggist named

---

[23] Emerson speaks of turning "our best side" to the sun in *Journals*, II, 117-118.

William B. White.[24] When, in 1822, the Society adopted the tithing system, he faithfully contributed one tenth of his modest earnings.[25] Later he wrote:[26]

Perhaps no one thing has had a more important influence on the character and history of this society than the early introduction of this principle of tithing, and the deep sense of religious obligation which it engendered in the minds of the members, to give to the church an affectionate and substantial support, each according to his ability. The question was not, how much they required for their own wants, and how much, if anything, could be conveniently spared for the society; but a tenth part of their income was religiously devoted to the uses of the church, and it was regarded as a duty to keep the private expenditures within the remaining portion.

1 8 2 3

On March 6,[27] Reed wrote to his classmate, Theophilus Parsons, Jr., who had recently joined the Society,[28] an account of his life during the preceding year and a half, mentioning his great uncertainty about the particular "use"[29] which he believed the Lord intended him to perform in the church. Until recently he had felt that his gifts were not being exercised to advantage:

I have been for this year and a half past, between heaven and earth. Seven years were spent in indolent study. The result of the whole was a few pieces of composition which had met with considerable applause; and on which my own mind rested with comfortable satisfaction. Here as far as I knew, was my whole man.——I was then put in a situation where I was obliged to work. The duties to be performed of necessity pressed on me continually——and between these, and the sum total of my old acquirements, there was to my knowledge, no connection. That I was sad, and unfit for any thing worthy to be named, was of course a necessary result. When I met any of my old acquaintance, I retreated into my former enclosure, ashamed of my present occupation; thence I was dragged again, by main strength. It is but lately that I have thought I could discover in my own mind, any thing like an essential incipient use, by which the two things will be united. This is so tender, as itself to require protection, though with this protection, it "may be the greatest among herbs; and become a tree, so that the birds of the air may come and lodge in the branches thereof." [30]

Reed did eventually find his use, chiefly as a writer and apologist for the Swedenborgian way of life. Still later, when both his leisure and income increased, he became well known as an editor of religious publications and beloved for his hospitality to the saints. On May 31, following his first letter, he again wrote Parsons,[31] lamenting the small amount of writing he had done recently. He commented unfavorably on the New-Church publication just begun by the New York Society and implied that the faithful in Boston should not expect to find that organ an adequate outlet for their articles. Of chief interest to the literary historian are his interesting views of poetry, which were developed three years later in the work

---

[24] See *Autobiography*. See also Goddard, *loc. cit.*, 287: "Mr. Reed's love of the church was manifest in the beginning, and continued unwavering to the end. For had he not avowed his belief in the doctrines taught by Swedenborg, his own talents as well as his father's influence with the faculty of Harvard, and all so-called liberal Christians, would at once have secured to him one of the very first positions in that denomination."

[25] See Bloch, *op. cit.*, 106-107; Goddard, *loc. cit.*, 287.

[26] *Thomas Worcester*, 77-78.   [28] *Thomas Worcester*, 75.

[27] See Letter II in *E T E*, II.   [29] See below ¶s. 35-37 and Swedenborg ¶s. 18-20.

[30] The kingdom of Heaven is likened to a mustard seed in Matthew 13:31-32 and in Mark 4:30-32.   [31] See Letter III in *E T E*, II.

for which he is now famous. It is difficult not to think of Walt Whitman and *Leaves of Grass* when one reads the following defense of what is now called "free verse:"

> If you keep the Word before you as essential poetry, I think you must know where to look for every thing else, as instinctively as animals know the point of compass. The different kinds of poetry as they have been classified by writers on the subject, are something, that I know very little about——but I should think that the natural mind had made divisions here, as elsewhere, many of which would disappear before a single view of goodness and truth united. Whether Lyric, Pastoral, Heroic, or what not—— poetry can have but one essence, love, but one form, nature. There may be infinite variety in the time, but they all require articulation and sound. I can see no rhymes in nature, and hardly blank verse, but a happy assemblage of living objects, not in straight lines and at a fixed distance, but springing up in Gods own order, which by its apparent want of design, leaves on the heart an image of its essential innocence and humility.

"The poet," he said later on, "should be free and unshackled as the eagle."[32] In a letter of June 1,[33] the use of the *New Jerusalem Missionary* (of New York) as a possible organ for the Boston Society was still being discussed.

Sometime during 1825, Reed opened his own retail drug store at 44 Hanover Street, opposite Elm, borrowing $900 for capital. His helper was Adonis Howard.[34] He now found more time for writing, and eventually prepared for the *North American Review* an article which the editor recommended to be published as a book. Reed read the manuscript to Warren Goddard one day when the two were alone in the store, and the latter enjoyed what he called "some essential poetry of a very high order."[35]

1 8 2 6

Reed's *Observations on the Growth of the Mind*[36] was published on August 29, by the press of Cummings, Hilliard and Company, where his classmate and brother churchman, John H. Wilkins, was employed. The title page bore the following quotation:

> So build we up the Being that we are;
> Thus deeply drinking-in the Soul of Things
> We shall be wise perforce; and while inspired
> By choice, and conscious that the will is free,
> Unswerving shall we move, as if impell'd
> By strict necessity, along the path
> Of order and of good.
>   WORDSWORTH[37]

The following analysis of the famous little book will emphasize its major divisions and most significant ideas:

---

[32] See ¶ 51 *infra*.
[33] See Letter IV in *E T E*, II.
[34] See *Autobiography* and Goddard, *loc. cit.*, 287. See also the *Boston Directory* for 1825, 1826 and 1827.
[35] Goddard, *loc. cit.*, 287-288.
[36] See the *Boston Daily Advertiser* under that date. The complete text of the first edition appears in *E T E*, II, 12-31.
[37] "The Excursion," IV, 1264-1270. Emerson quoted the last two lines in a sermon preached on Dec. 31, 1830. See *Y E S*, 116.29-30.

INTRODUCTION

Conditions in the world are changing, and men are looking to the future rather than to the past.[38] As man's moral and intellectual character improves we may expect an altered world. Brute force will yield to the powers of the mind. There is no place, however, for easy optimism, because man's fallen state[39] is a fact. It is difficult for him to know his true condition unless he accepts the Creator as the only immutable standard.[40] Then his so-called progress seems empty, and he becomes necessarily humble.[41]

All changes in the external world must originate in the mind,[42] which now seems to be changing under the influence of revelation.[43] In a material sense, there is nothing fixed in the philosophy of mind. Its interaction with the outer world seems capable of infinite possibilities. New classifications and new terminology appear and are succeeded by others. From the view of the immutable First Cause, however, the laws of the mind[44] are fixed and perfect, applicable to existence both in this life and the next, but man has wandered from them. Fortunately, Divine revelation, which always gives a right direction to every power of the mind, is awakening us to the truth, and we may expect new inventions and new discoveries. The appearance of nature will change as we come to behold truth, and the world will again become a paradise.[45] The purpose of this work is to see the mind from the highest viewpoint——that is, in its revealed character: (1) its powers of acquiring and retaining truth; (2) the steps in the mind's development toward usefulness and happiness.

I. POWER OF THE MIND IN ACQUIRING AND RETAINING TRUTH ——THE MEMORY

Truth is retained only by the continuous exertion of the same powers by which it is acquired. Memory is ultimately related to the affections——to the heart——to the condition *within* rather than to facts without. Attention, on which memory principally depends, is easily directed to those things which a man likes. Memory is the effect of learning. It varies in different individuals largely because men differ in their degree of involvement in time-and-space relations. Simple Divine truth has nothing to do with time, and the development of the mind depends upon training the memory in this higher truth. When the soul emphasizes its eternal state, the past and future are swallowed up in the present.[46]

Time is difficult to define, though we know it is a condition of the material world. It is not real as far as our minds are concerned. Eternity, on the other hand, is to the mind what time is to nature. We should, therefore, cultivate the memory for values in the timeless world and accustom it to approach the eternal I AM.[47] But we live in two worlds, and since all truth is practical, it should be put to use. The memory can hold it only when it is *applied*——when identified with external objects.[48] Locke's theory of *tabula rasa* or an empty mind awaiting impressions from without is erroneous. The mind is rather a delicate germ in a husk (the body), assimilating to itself what it can use. Its energies are evoked from within. From this discussion of time and eternity we see that God is *immediately* present and not distant. "My Father worketh hitherto and I work." The child feels at home in its Father's house. It doesn't wonder because it sees God always at hand. Men show amazement because they have lost the perceptions of children. Miracles will cease to be miracles only when man sees all phenomena to be properly classified *in the Lord*.

The memory is an active power, exerting effort. It *possesses* rather than retains truth and is a consciousness of the will and of the character. It becomes alive when man's affections are applied to their proper objects. Since a person's individuality is the result of the habitual thoughts which he entertains, the will is involved in the memory process, and the way to develop the memory is deliberately to develop the affections. The mind must grow from an internal principle rather than from external accretion. The germ is given to it at birth together with a principle of freedom. The mind must not confine

---

[38] Cf. *Nature*, 5.2—6.3.
[39] See *Nature*, 88.1.
[40] Cf. *Nature*, 80.16—81.11.
[41] Cf. *Nature*, 76.18ff.; 82.20; 91.15ff.
[46] Cf. *Nature*, 5.6-17. See also footnote 143 below.
[47] See *Nature*, 79.16-23.
[42] Cf. *Nature*, 91.5-7.
[43] Cf. *Nature*, 5.8-11.
[44] Cf. *Nature*, 88.15-18.
[45] Cf. *Nature*, 94.13—95.12; 81.2-11.
[48] See *Nature*, 40.20ff.

itself, however, to the inner world, for affections must have objects.[49] Body and mind must grow together.

II. GENERAL REQUIREMENTS FOR THE DEVELOPMENT OF THE HUMAN MIND

(A) NATURAL SCIENCES DEVELOP THE MIND——POETRY AND MUSIC INCLUDED

Laws of the animal, vegetable and mineral kingdoms are the basis for all useful knowledge and are important to man everywhere. The natural world is the proving ground for our inner affections and is essential to an enlightened independence of thought and action. The natural world is perfectly adapted to invigorate and strengthen the intellectual and moral man. It has many uses, ranging from the support of vegetable and animal life up to the drawing forth of the latent energies of man's soul. The natural world humbly depends upon its Creator and serves as an example for man.[50]

Providence has endowed the infant mind with the germ of every science. How could one learn sciences if it were otherwise? The mind cannot be healthy and athletic without descending into the natural world.[51] Eloquence warms the heart because it uses natural imagery. Poetry enlivens the imagination by making use of the material world. Science develops our early love of nature into a knowledge of her laws, relations and uses. Our affections are expanded into astronomy, botany etc. The natural sciences are the spontaneous productions of the human mind. To these should be added poetry and music, for the harmony of the natural world suggests both.

Poetry may be defined as all those illustrations of truth by natural imagery which spring from the fact that this world is a mirror of Him who made it. Poetry embraces all that is in exact agreement with the creative spirit of God. The true poet feels this spirit and is governed by it. He rises above the senses, inspires the inward efforts of things and feels the power of creation. The true poetic spirit is the soul of science.[52] Without it, science is a cheerless, heartless study, distrusting the presence and power of Him to whom it owes its existence. The state of poetry has always indicated the state of science and religion. Poetry shall be kindled in its immortal part when men shall see God in everything, and when nature and the sciences are not regarded apart from Him,[53] for there is a language not of words, but of *things*. The savagery in nature which we see about us is the result of man's abuse of power.[54] Let a man's language spring from his true self, and then there will be poetry. Rhyme is unnecessary and is not sanctioned in nature. The poet should be as free and unshackled as an eagle.

Music is not confined to songs of the angels and men or to the singing of birds and the lowing of cattle,[55] but extends to the harmony that pervades all orders of creation. It includes the music of the morning and evening. Orpheus once played to animals, plants and natural objects, which listened with attention. Now the mind of man is mute, and the stones cry out.[56] He had better listen to them. Poetry and music are related. They suffer degradation and are exalted together. Only that music which is in unison with the Divine Mind deserves the name.[57] Modern music is chiefly profane. Its opposite is sacred.

(B) SOCIETY DEVELOPS THE MIND

Religious (*i.e.*, spiritual and moral) institutions as well as civil institutions (including the family) provide the atmosphere which surrounds and protects the mind while it sends out branches and bears fruit. It gathers strength from the warmth of surrounding affections. Society is a spiritual influence. All minds, whatever their condition, are connected with God and with each other.[58] Each person makes his own contribution to the whole. "It is not for time or space to set limits to the effects of the life of a single

---

[49] *Nature*, 43.21—44.13.
[50] This paragraph probably influenced *Nature*, 76.5—77.2.
[51] Cf. *Nature*, 88.15-23.   [54] See *Nature*, 81.2ff.; 94.13—95.7.
[52] See *Nature*, 82.8-12; 86.13-16; 93.1.   [55] Cf. *Nature*, 40.16.
[53] Cf. *Nature*, 92.6-11.   [56] An allusion to Luke 19:40.
[57] *Nature*, 5.8-9. See Reed's letter of March 6, 1823 (partly quoted above), printed in *E T E*, II. See also ¶s. 48-52.   [58] See *Nature*, 79.8-9.

man." [59] So love of family spreads to love of country and to the betterment of society. But man is fallen, and society cannot help him as before his degeneration. It cannot raise him above its own corrupt level. But there is a society coming in the future in which men may hope. The natural world cannot help man as it once did, because he has lost the key[60] to the correspondences between it and the mind. The lower orders of creation, moreover, have suffered a change as a consequence of man's fall,[61] and cannot restore man to that moral order, the want of which has changed them.

(C) THE WORD OF GOD DEVELOPS THE MIND

The Bible, which is a part of revelation, has a tendency to effect the union of the Divine and human in man by conjoining the soul with God. It restores spiritual consciousness, gives hope for immortality and removes the fear of death. The mind in its development must have the spirit of God. Knowledge of the Bible is only gradually achieved, however. It begins when the child learns the alphabet and then slowly opens out its riches. The Bible is not for the learned, who indulge in artificial speculation, but for the practical, and it achieves a practical end when it helps the human mind to become conformed to the spirit of Christianity.

The Bible is not always appreciated, especially by those who say it resembles ordinary books. Dull people said of Jesus: "Is not this the carpenter's son?" [62] and they, therefore, miss the *internal* sense. There is but one law of criticism, and it applies especially to the Bible: A scripture can be interpreted only by a spirit akin to that which gave it forth.[63] When a man becomes himself a *living* poem he can understand poetry. If a man would understand the Bible, he must cleanse his mind and dwell in the moral universe. The Bible differs from other books as our Lord differed from men. When a man's heart opens to Divine influence, the Bible will become the living voice of God. It can be understood only by such illumination.

The inadequacy of the reason to judge the Bible is seen in the fact that men using their reason believe the Biblical miracles to be *extraordinary* rather than as parts of the harmonious laws of Divine operation. The reason does not see the higher unity that gives miracles an ordinary place in the scheme of existence.[64] The resurrection of our Lord must have been a very different miracle to the angels at the tomb than to Mary, because they had experienced death and could see the resurrection from the other side of the grave. Mary could see it only as an insulated fact. Man is unhappy today largely because he has left his place in creation.[65] He doubts his spiritual worth and questions existence in a future state. The Bible can help him.

III. SPECIAL REQUIREMENTS AND CONCLUDING ADVICE

When man reaches the period of mental maturity, he becomes his own master, begins to rely upon himself, finds his peculiar character in full flower, and knows that he is accountable. Having banished his tutors, however, he must watch how he uses his liberty. It is so with groups called nations. They, too, have a distinctive character.[66] They, too, come to self-realization——to a knowledge of the parts they are to play in the regeneration of the world. They must be well-organized divisions of *one* body.

Every individual possesses peculiar powers which should be brought to bear on society through observing appropriate duties. Man's task is to develop the peculiar organization given him at infancy, and the advance in his development should not occasion any surprise.[67] With his fundamental inheritance from God he should seek employment for the mind in which all its energies may be warmed into existence. There is something

---

[59] Cf. *Nature*, 80.1-4.
[60] Cf. *Nature*, 81.3-9.
[61] Cf. *Nature*, 81.6-7; 94.16-22.
[65] Cf. *Nature*, 88.18—89.3. See under August 3, 1835, in the last half of this chapter.
[62] See Matthew 13:55 and Mark 6:3.
[63] Cf. *Nature*, 44.18—45.4.
[64] Cf. *Nature*, 75.4.
[66] Coleridge, in *The Friend* (Section II, Essay I), characterized the individuality of England, France and Germany. Cousin, however, comes nearest expressing the Swedenborgian view of the character of each nation. See his chapter *infra*. The concept was evidently quite common in the period. Cf. *Nature*, 22.2-7.   [67] Cf. *Nature*, 95.10-12.

that everyone can do better than anyone else,[68] and a man cannot be other than what he is. Of course, each man has infinite possibilities for growth in moral goodness, but the original stamina of his mind remain the same.

We ought, then, to cherish this peculium——this patrimony of God——as that which unites us to the whole vine——as the forming power within us.[69] Let us not seek to be great but to *be ourselves*. By finding appropriate objects for our desires and by doing our duty[70] we shall perceive in our hearts that Providence is working with us. Since the end of all education is a life of active usefulness in some particular sphere,[71] we should desire nothing that cuts a man off from his fellow men by giving him a false dignity to guard. We seek rather a character that cannot be hurt by circumstances because it is protected *from above*. The palms of our hands should be the book of our life as we behold our duty and share the blessings of mankind.

The *Growth of the Mind* was reviewed in the October number of *The Christian Examiner* and called "unintelligible and useless."[72] *The United States Review* for November[73] was a little more charitable, but took issue with Reed's definitions of the words *time, miracle, memory, revelation* and *music*.[74] On November 17,[75] Reed's friend, John H. Wilkins, married Mrs. Thomazine E. Minot, who, it seems, was still presiding over her boarding house and dedicating her best efforts to the growth of the New Church.

1827

Reed not only returned to writing, but he also found time for studies and for conversation with his friends. In a letter to Parsons of January 31,[76] he indicated his ownership of Coleridge's *Aids to Reflection* (1825) as well as the neighborhood demand for the volume. He was one of the leading spirits who founded the *New Jerusalem Magazine*, the first number of which made its appearance in September. In that publication the Boston Society at last had an appropriate outlet for literary talent or religious apologetic, and Sampson Reed found his principal *use* as writer and teacher to an ever-widening circle of men like Emerson, who were eager for new truth. Since the *N J M* was only one of many publishing ventures, Adonis Howard left Reed's drug store and found his *use* as publisher and distributor of New-Church books. For his new partner, Reed chose Dr. Abraham T. Lowe, and the firm of Lowe and Reed became in time an exclusively wholesale business.[77] Reed's article on the "Free Agency of Man" appeared in October.[78]

---

[68] See *Journals*, III, 416-417.

[69] Emerson stresses this note of self-reliance throughout the early sermons. See, for instance, *Y E S*, 108.25ff., 182.31ff., 186.13ff., and 237.40ff.

[70] See *Journals*, III, 373-374. Cf. Emerson's sermon, "Religion is Doing One's Duty."

[71] For the Doctrine of Uses, see Swedenborg ¶s. 18-20 and Sampson Reed ¶s. 35-37. See Emerson's sermon, "The Objects of Education" and note 240 below.

[72] See *The Christian Examiner*, III (no. 5, Sept.-Oct., 1826), 418-426. See p. 426: "We intended to controvert some of the opinions taken by this writer; but we soon found, that the very principles assumed by him, were mere assumptions so far as we could discern, leaving us, of course, no common ground on which to stand."

[73] See the *U. S. Review and Literary Gazette*, I (no. 1, Nov., 1826), 109ff. See esp. pp. 110-113.

[74] See ¶s. 1-3, 11-17, 25, 41-43, and *E T E*, II, 23.

[75] From information in the Harvard University Archives. Reed, *Thomas Worcester*, 74, gives the date as Nov. 19, 1826.   [76] See Letter VI in *E T E*, II.

[78] *N J M*, I, no. 2, 49-52. See *E T E*, II, 32-33.   [77] See Goddard, *loc. cit.*, 277.

The *N J M* published "Miracles" [79] in January, 1828, and "On Animals" in September.[80] Reed was now boarding at Ephraim Holland's Coffee House on Howard Street[81] and preparing to open a new store at 111 State Street.[82] By 1830, he had consolidated his resources, had abandoned the shop at 44 Hanover, and had begun to board with Dr. Samuel A. Shurtleff, a physician living at Pemberton Hall, Tremont, and later at 52 Hanover Street.[83] In May, 1831, appeared "Self-Love Essential Evil,"[84] a copy of which Emerson sent to Carlyle.[85] By 1832, Lowe and Reed, Druggists, had moved to 24 Merchants Row, and Reed was boarding at 47 Chambers Street.[86] In September of that year, he published "External Restraint,"[87] and in November, "Sleep."[88] On December 25, the day on which Emerson sailed for Europe,[89] Reed married Catharine Clark, daughter of John Clark of Waltham and sister to the wife of the Rev. Thomas Worcester.[90] Between 1832 and 1835 he and his wife lived at 26 Howard Street.[91] On December 8, 1834, their first child, James, was born. He was later to enter the Swedenborgian ministry and to become assistant to Thomas Worcester in the Boston Society.[92] In 1836, Sampson Reed moved into a house at Louisburg Square, where he remained for the duration of his life, entertaining generously all who loved the Church.[93] A son, Thomas, apparently named for Worcester, was born on February 3, 1837. When the third edition of *Growth of the Mind* came from the press in 1838, it contained several appendices[94] and a preface which deserves mention because it discouraged purchase by the Concord philosophers, who had been circulating the book, and clearly denounced prevalent Transcendentalism:[95]

The present age is characterized by the love of pleasing, as opposed to the love of truth. Fashionable education, as it is often pursued, may almost be defined the cultivation of the art of pleasing. This is but too frequently the end for which so much labor is bestowed, by which a wardrobe of accomplishments is provided, which may be used as occasion requires. When the disposition to please takes the first place, it is obvious that truth must be sought only as it is subservient to this object. "How can ye believe, which receive honor one of another, and seek not the honor that cometh from God only." The love of pleasing is opposed to the love of truth, when a person desires to please others, in order that he may gain an influence over them, for the sake of promoting his own private ends or personal advantage. The love of pleasing is consistent with the love of truth, when a person desires to please, for the sake of promoting the good of others, and the cause of truth itself.

[79] *N J M*, I, no. 5, 148-156.
[80] *N J M*, II, no. 1, 23-29. See *E T E*, II, 34-37.
[81] See the *Boston Directory* for 1828 and 1829.
[82] See the *Boston Directory* for 1829.
[83] See the *Boston Directory* for 1830 and 1831.
[84] *N J M*, IV (1830-1831), 338-346.
[85] See *Carlyle-Emerson Corr.*, I, 32-33, and ¶ 57.
[86] See the *Boston Directory* for 1832.
[87] *N J M*, VI (1832-1833), no. lxi, 30-32. See ¶s. 29-32.
[88] See *N J M*, VI (1832-1833), 88-89. See ¶s. 33-34.
[89] *Journals*, III, 3. Compare, however, *Letters*, I, 360.
[90] See *Autobiography* and *Journals*, II, 455-456.
[91] See the *Boston Directory* for 1833, 1834 and 1835.
[92] See *Autobiography*.
[93] See Goddard, *loc. cit.*, 288; *Boston Directory* for 1836.
[94] The appendices consisted of the following, all but the last, it seems, reprints from the *N J M:* "Miracles," "Conscience," "Home," "Self-Love," "External Restraint," "Hereditary Evil," "Marriage in the Heaven," and "Children's Books."
[95] I have taken the following paragraphs from the fifth edition (Boston, 1865, iv-vii), in which they were reprinted.

The New Church can discern, in almost every moral or religious writer of any acknowledged merit at the present day, some outbreakings of its own power; while its principles are pressing into the natural sciences, like so many gushing streams from an inexhaustible fountain above them. It is painful to see how little willingness there is to acknowledge the source of truth; and how often a man seems to think that it has answered its legitimate purpose, when he has bedecked his own person therewith, so as to command the admiration of the multitude.

The time is approaching when the claims of the New Church on the public attention may not be easily set aside. There is a problem to solve, to which those who reject the claims of this Church, will find it difficult to furnish a solution; and the misrepresentations and ignorance which have often prevailed in regard to it, will, before many years, be seen to be neither consistent with good manners nor good scholarship. The writings of Swedenborg are so pure in their character and influence, that the moral sense of the community will bear testimony that there is no wilful imposture; and they are so perfect in their method and logic, that the rationality of the community will bear testimony that there is no insanity.[96] The voice of these two witnesses cannot be silenced; and the day is approaching, when the assertion that these writings are not of sufficient importance to command the attention of the public, will not be hazarded by any one, who either is a man of intelligence or seeks to be so esteemed.

Still, the natural mind is ever backward to receive *revealed truth*, both from the character of this truth itself, and from the fact of its being revealed—from the character of the truth, because it is opposed to the affections and principles of the natural mind, and calculated to reform and regenerate them—from the fact of its being revealed, because it leaves no place for the pride of discovery. "Whosoever will, let him take the water of life freely." The water of life is really as free as natural water; and this we all know is the common gift of Providence to man and beast. But the condition is, that we should *will to receive it*—that we should acknowledge it to be the water of life, and endeavor to live from it—that we should seek to be purified and regenerated by its influence. And alas! how few are disposed to comply with these conditions, and how much do these find in themselves, which requires to be subdued and put away!

From these causes it is not to be expected that the truths of the spiritual sense of the Sacred Scripture, which the Lord has now revealed through his servant Emanuel Swedenborg, will find a very ready reception. *Transcendentalism*[97] will rather be caressed. This is the product of man's own brain; and when the human mind has been compelled to relax its grasp on sensualism, and the philosophy based on the senses, it may be expected first to take refuge here. *Transcendentalism*, even now, offers indications of an approaching popularity in this country. It may be something gained, when the idolater no longer literally worships the work of his own hands; even though he be in heart an idolater still, and worship the creations of his own imagination. So it may be a step forwards from *sensualism* to *transcendentalism*. It may be a necessary step in the progress of the human mind. But they still lie near each other—almost in contact. There is among insects a class called parasites. Their instinct leads them to deposit their eggs in the bodies of other insects, where, when the young is hatched, it has only to open its mouth and eat up its brother. It would seem to be in a way analogous to this, that Providence often permits one falsity to be removed by another. *Transcendentalism* is the parasite of *sensualism*; and when it shall have done its work, it will be found to be itself a worm, and the offspring of a worm.

Two other children were born to Sampson Reed: Elizabeth, on July 10, 1838, and Joseph Sampson, on December 13, 1841. Reed contributed to the *N J M* throughout his life, becoming one of its editors in 1854. He also had complete management of the *Children's New Church Magazine* from its beginning until his death.[98] In 1844, he became a proprietor of the

---

[96] Cf. Emerson's "Swedenborg" *Works*, IV, 97 and 119.
[97] Sampson Reed's note: "By *Transcendentalism*, I mean such transcendentalism as we now find, without any reference to its origin, or to the original meaning of the word."   [98] *Autobiography*.

Boston Athenæum[99] and withdrew books, which are still listed in the charging records.[100] In 1852 and 1853, he was a member of the Board of Aldermen, and in the latter year he attended the Constitutional Convention. In 1854, he became chairman of the Committee of Finance in the Massachusetts House of Representatives and also editor of the *N J M*. In January, 1861, he retired from the drug business, transferring his interest in the firm of Reed, Cutler & Co. to his son, Thomas.[101] On July 8, 1864, he prepared the autobiographical sketch which I have used throughout this introduction,[102] and, in 1880, published in Boston *A Biographical Sketch of Thomas Worcester, D.D.* He died greatly beloved on July 8 of that year, having served as a member of the Church Committee and as superintendent of the Boston Sabbath School throughout the latter part of his life.[103]

WE ARE WRONG TO PUT DISTANCE AND TIME BETWEEN GOD AND US[104]——GOD IS IMMEDIATELY PRESENT——ETERNITY AND TIME——MIND AND MATTER

¶ 1

Another object of the preceding remarks . . . is that we may be impressed with the immediate presence and agency of God, without which a correct understanding of mind or matter can never be attained; that we may be able to read on every power of the mind, and on every particle of matter the language of our Lord, "My Father worketh hitherto, and I work." We usually put the Divine Being to an immense distance, by supposing that the world was created many years ago, and subjected to certain laws, by which it has since been governed. We find ourselves capable of constructing machines, which move on without our assistance, and imagine that the world was constructed in the same way. We forget that the motions of our machines depend on the uniform operation of what we call the laws of nature; and that there can be nothing beyond, on which these depend, unless it be the agency of that Being from whom they exist. . . . We simply place things in a situation to be acted upon by an all-pervading power——but what all-pervading power is there by which gravitation is itself produced, unless it be the power of God? [105]

¶ 2

[W]e find that our idea of a year is continually changing,[106] as the mind becomes conversant with different objects, and is susceptible of different impressions; and the days of the old man as they draw near their close, seem to gather rapidity from their approach to the other world. We have all experienced the effect of pleasure and pain in accelerating and retarding the passing moments; and since our feelings are constantly changing, we have no reason to doubt, that they constantly produce a similar effect, though it may not be often noticed. The divisions of time then, however real they may seem to be, and however well they may serve the common purposes of conversation, cannot be supposed to convey the same impression to any two minds, nor to any one mind in different periods of its existence. . . . Time then, is nothing real so far as it exists in our own minds.[107]

---

[99] See *Catalogue of the Library of the Boston Athenæum, 1807-1871*, (5 vols.), Boston, 1874-1882, V, pp. 5 and 19.

[100] See *Emerson's Reading*, 137. A record of Reed's early reading at college is also preserved in the Harvard College Library.

[101] See *Autobiography*.

[102] See Letter XI in *E T E*, II.

[103] See Goddard, *loc. cit.*, 285; 289.

[104] Cf. Emerson's letter to his Aunt Mary, Sept. 23, 1826, in Cabot, *Memoir*, I, 159-160, and in *Letters*, I, 174-175. Cf. *Nature*, 5.2ff.

[105] "Growth of the Mind," *E T E*, II, 17. For the theme of God's power being above space and time, see *Nature*, 79.15ff.; 90.20ff. See note 143 below.

[106] See *Nature*, 88.17; 92.15.

[107] "Growth of the Mind," *E T E*, II, 16. See note 143 below.

¶ 3

Eternity is to the mind what time is to nature. We attain a perception of it, by regarding all the operations in the world within us, as they exist in relation to their first cause; for in doing this, they are seen to partake somewhat of the nature of that Being on whom they depend. We make no approaches to a conception of it, by heaping day upon day or year upon year. This is merely an accumulation of time; and we might as well attempt to convey an idea of mental greatness by that of actual space, as to communicate a conception of eternity by years or thousands of years. Mind and matter are not more distinct from each other than their properties; and by an attempt to embrace all time we are actually farther from an approach to eternity than when we confine ourselves to a single instant——[108] because we merely collect the largest possible amount of natural changes, whereas that which is eternal approaches that which is immutable. This resembles the attempt to ascend to heaven by means of the tower of Babel, in which they were removed by their pride from that which they would have approached, precisely in proportion to their apparent progress. It is impossible to conceive of either time or space without matter.[109] The reason is, they are the effect of matter; and as it is by creating matter that they are produced, so it is by thinking of it that they are conceived of. It need not be said how exceedingly improper it is to apply the usual ideas of time and space to the Divine Being; making him subject to that which he creates.[110]

ADAM AND EVE——THE ANCIENT CHURCH——THE GOLDEN AGE

¶ 4

The most ancient church, represented by Adam, enjoyed an uninterrupted intercourse with the spiritual world. Inhabitants at once of the spiritual world and the natural, and conscious of their union with God, their residence on earth was simply the commencement of that course of life, in the progress of which, according to the divine order, at a certain period their internals divested themselves of that which was earthly, and they became as the angels of heaven. In the development of their powers, there was nothing of violence; and death was regarded as a necessary consequence of this development. They were conscious of the presence of a divine power working within them, unloosing the cords which would confine them to a stifled sense of the use for which they were created, and pushing them on to a full and perfect evolution.[111] Instead of shuddering at the thought of annihilation and a new creation, they attained to such a clear perception of the inward endeavours of the soul, that no longer fearing death, they actually co-operated with the Lord in this great event of their spiritual progress. They were not afraid to die;[112] for they were not afraid to be more fully what they were already. Like a child, who has not yet left his father's house,[113] they were strangers to the ills and the fears which have attended the wanderings of their posterity.[114]

¶ 5

Adam and Eve knew no language but their garden. They had nothing to communicate by words; for they had not the power of concealment. The sun of the spiritual world shone bright on their hearts, and their senses were open with delight to natural objects. In the eye were the beauties of paradise; in the ear was the music of birds; in the nose was the fragrance of the freshness of nature; in the taste was the fruit of the garden; in the touch, the seal of their eternal union. What had they to *say*?[115]

A LANGUAGE OF THINGS, NOT OF WORDS——CORRESPONDENCES IN NATURE——GOD THE CREATOR AT WORK[116]

¶ 6

There is a language, not of words but of things.[117] When this language shall have been made apparent, that which is human will have answered its end, and being as it

---

[108] *Nature*, 54.20-22.   [109] See *Nature*, 71.18.
[110] "Growth of the Mind," *E T E*, II, 15. Cf. *Nature*, 74.13-20; 87.10ff.; 79.15ff.; 90.20ff.
[111] See *Nature*, 79.16ff.
[112] Reed told Emerson in conversation that he had not feared death for the past ten years. See *Letters*, I, 315 (Dec. 24? 1830). Cf. *Nature*, 71.10ff.
[113] Cf. *Nature*, 81.3.
[114] "Miracles," *N J M*, I (1827-1828), 148-156. See pp. 148-149. Cf. *Nature*, 94.1ff.
[115] "Oration on Genius," *E T E*, II, 11.
[116] "Growth of the Mind," *E T E*, II, 22.   [117] Cf. *Journals*, III, 492 (June 20, 1835).

were resolved into its original elements, will lose itself in nature. The use of language is the expression of our feelings and desires; the manifestation of the mind. But every thing which is, whether animal or vegetable, is full of the expression of that use for which it is designed, as of its own existence. If we did but understand its language,[118] what could our words add to its meaning? It is because we are unwilling to hear, that we find it necessary to say so much; and we drown the voice of nature, with the discordant jargon of ten thousand dialects. Let a man's language be confined to the expression of that which actually belongs to his own mind;[119] and let him respect the smallest blade which grows and permit it to speak for itself. Then may there be poetry[120] which may not be written perhaps, but which may be felt as a part of our being. Every thing which surrounds us, is full of the utterance of one word, completely expressive of its nature. This word is its name; for God, even now could we but see it, is creating all things, and giving a name to every work of his love, in its perfect adaptation to that for which it is designed.

NATURE——HOW UNDERSTOOD——DECEITFULNESS OF THE WORLD OF APPEARANCES——THE SPIRITUAL EYE——SPIRITUAL TRUTHS SPIRITUALLY DISCERNED

¶ 7

Rightly to understand natural science, is to understand the true uses[121] of natural things. But all things of this world have respect, either directly or indirectly, to the spiritual and immortal part of man; and are created for it and from it. How can those therefore understand natural science, whose minds rest on the ultimate effect, without any knowledge of this relation? Suppose a watch for the first time to be submitted to the inspection of a savage. He is pleased with the motion of the wheels——he gradually learns the connexion of the parts——he may even make some rude imitation. Yet is all this an idle curiosity, and he may cast it away as a useless toy, unless its true use be disclosed to him, in unfolding its relation to the sun. Yet such precisely is the extent of scientific knowledge among those in the world who are usually called learned.[122]

¶ 8

Such is the present state of the human mind formed by hereditary errors, perverted from truth by a false philosophy, that man forms his opinion from appearances of natural things without reflecting that apparent truth is not, at all times, real truth; those opinions denominated truths, are so received, until by some happy discovery or elevation of thoughts above the prejudices of education, they are demonstrated to be false. In our philosophical conjectures, by attempting to account for natural effects by natural causes, we close our eyes to the sublime truth revealed by God, that all things, visible to the natural eye, are forms of invisible spiritual essences.[123] "The natural man, neither can he know them [spiritual things] because they are spiritually discerned;" [124] that is, seen only by the spiritual eye.[125]

NATURE EXISTS FOR THE SOUL OF MAN——ITS COMMODITY IS ONLY A MEANS TO A HIGHER USE——ITS END IS DEVELOPMENT OF THE MORAL BEING——IT REINFORCES THE *TEN COMMANDMENTS*[126]

¶ 9

The natural world was precisely and perfectly adapted to invigorate and strengthen the intellectual and moral man. Its first and highest use[127] was not to support the vegetables which adorn, or the animals which cover its surface; nor yet to give sustenance to the human body——it has a higher and holier object, in the attainment of which these are only means. It was intended to draw forth and mature the latent energies of the soul; to impart to them its own verdure and freshness; to initiate them into its own mysteries; and by its silent and humble dependence on its creator, to leave on them when it is withdrawn by death, the full impression of his likeness.[128]

---

[118] Cf. *Nature*, 41.12-15.
[119] Cf. *Nature*, 37.18ff.
[120] Cf. *Nature*, 37.1ff.
[124] I Corinthians 2:14, and Coleridge ¶ 194.
[125] "Natural Diseases of Spiritual Origin," *N J M*, V (1831-1832), 133-139; 169-175. See p. 139.
[127] *Nature*, 52.10ff.; 76.9—77.2.
[128] "Growth of the Mind," *E T E*, II, 20. Cf. *Nature*, 77.9-15.

[121] Cf. *Nature*, 81.7ff.; 15.3ff.
[122] "On Animals," *E T E*, II, 36.
[123] Cf. *Nature*, 80.23.
[126] See *Nature*, 51.12—52.10; 53.1-23.

¶ 10

If, then, science be from Him who gave the ten commandments, must not a life according to the latter facilitate the acquirement of the former? Can *he* love the works of God who does not love his commandments? It is only necessary that the heart be purified, to have science like poetry its spontaneous growth. Self-love has given rise to many false theories, because a selfish man is disposed to make things differently from what God has made them. Because God is love, nature exists; because God is love, the Bible is poetry. If, then, the love of God creates the scenery of nature, must not he whose mind is most open to this love be most sensible of natural beauties?[129]

MIRACLES——THEY ARE PART OF THE UNIFORM SPIRITUAL ORDER IF RIGHTLY UNDERSTOOD——THEY ARE ALSO EVIDENCE OF MAN'S DE-GENERATION——THEY MEASURE HIS ALIENATION FROM GOD——HOW THE POWER BEHIND BIBLICAL MIRACLES MANIFESTS ITSELF TODAY ——RIGHTLY SEEN GOD'S LAWS ARE UNIFORM AND HARMONIOUS

¶ 11

In process of time, this church degenerated. The love of self and of the world took the place of the love of the Lord and the neighbour; and a knowledge of the means to obtain selfish and worldly ends was substituted for a knowledge of the laws of divine order and of the things of the spiritual world.[130] The communication of the Lord with man, became necessarily miraculous; for the cause and ground of miracles is to be found in the aversion of man to that which is concealed within the miracle. God remained, as he must, unchangeably the same; but man no longer continued to behold him in his works, in the order, the beauty, and the harmony of creation, because he had ceased to love him. As divine things became less and less familiar to the human mind, there was more and more a feeling of something strange[131] and incongruous when they were presented. Mankind were as one who has been stolen in his childhood by a band of robbers, and made familiar to all their scenes of violence: to whom the recollections of his infancy appear like a strange dream,[132] by which he is terrified far more than by crimes.[133]

¶ 12

The miraculous is the measure of our alienation from God;[134] it represents the opposition of revealed truth to human depravity, and its want of coincidence with merely natural reason. There is something of the nature of a miracle in the relation between the word of God and the human mind, precisely to that degree that we have not followed the Lord in the regeneration, and become conformed to his spirit. Miracles are not, strictly speaking, confined to those particular acts recorded in the sacred scriptures, to which the term is usually applied. The whole word is to the natural man a living miracle.[135]

¶ 13

The world appears to be under a decidedly false impression, in regard to the design of miracles, in supposing them intended primarily as evidence of a divine mission. Their effect on the mind, in some states, in this respect, is merely an incidental circumstance. Miracles were not wrought by our Lord with this end; and in proportion as we take delight, that "the blind see, the lame walk, the lepers are cleansed, the deaf hear, the dead are raised, and to the poor the gospel is preached,"——we shall not make this use of them, any more than we shall look for a reward for the performance of our duty, when the act finds no opposition in our hearts. The miracles wrought by our Lord were not a momentary exhibition of power, which then ceased to operate, that the mind should find it necessary to go back to that period in order to realize its existence. The eternal fountain of divine love was opened. The same power which removed blindness, raised the dead, cast out devils, now imparts vision and life, and delivers from evil; and the only true practical belief in those miracles, consists in a perception of this fact.[136]

---

[129] "Oration on Genius," *E T E*, II, 10.
[130] Cf. *Nature*, 89.12ff.
[131] Cf. *Nature*, 81.4 and 89.5.
[132] Cf. *Nature*, 89.3ff.
[133] "Miracles," *N J M*, I (1827-1828), 148-146. See p. 149. Cf. "Growth of the Mind," *E T E*, II, 17-18.
[134] Emerson paraphrases this line in *Journals*, II, 289 (Feb. 10, 1830).
[135] "Miracles," *N J M*, I, 149.   [136] "Miracles," *N J M*, I, 152.

¶ 14

It can never be too deeply impressed on the mind, that a miracle derives its specific character as such, not more from the nature of the act itself, than from the state of those by whom it is witnessed. There are no miracles connected with the revelation of the spiritual sense of the sacred scriptures, because with those who receive it, religion can no longer be regarded as a prodigy or a monster. It no longer retains a secluded, insulated seat in their minds, approached from motives of fear or interest, and secretly held as a tyrant, or viewed with contempt. It becomes their constant daily meat and drink, assimilating all things of the man to itself, and clothing itself with flesh and blood, as with a garment.[137] The very cause of miracles is removed. The spiritual truths of the word are not only not supported by any new miracles, but to those who follow them aright, that which is recorded as miraculous in its letter, ceases to appear such. They create a sense of the presence and agency of God as constant and uniform as the laws of nature, and felt more powerfully in the operation of these laws, than they ever could have been in their apparent interruption.[138]

¶ 15

The laws of Divine Operation are perfectly uniform and harmonious; and a miracle is a particular instance of Divine Power, which for a want of a more interiour and extended knowledge of the ways of God, appearing to stand alone, and to have been the result of an unusual exertion of the Divine Will, creates in the minds of men, what its name implies, a sensation of wonder.[139] That there are miracles in the Bible, proves that there are laws of the Divine Operation and of the Divine Government, which are not embraced within the utmost limits of that classification and arrangement, which is the result of natural reason. . . . [Miracles] are insulated examples of laws as boundless as the universe, and by the manner in which we are affected by them, prove how much we have to learn, and how utterly incompetent we are to judge of the ways of God, from that reason, which is founded on our own limited and fallacious observation. The resurrection of our Lord must have been a very different miracle to the angels at the sepulchre, from what it was to Mary. They saw it from the other side of the grave, with a knowledge of the nature of that death which they had themselves experienced; she saw an insulated fact.[140]

¶ 16

When the child is first told that the sun, moon and stars do not revolve round the earth, he is filled with astonishment; but when the comparative size and uses of these several bodies, with the immense distance they would have to pass, are explained, this astonishment ceases. When we see simply the fact that the dead were restored to life by our Lord, we cannot but marvel; but when we understand what life is, the connexion of things natural with spiritual, and of all with the Lord, our admiration ceases entirely, or is altogether changed as to its quality.[141]

¶ 17

It is agreeable to the laws of moral and intellectual progression, that all phenomena, whether of matter or mind, should become gradually classified; till at length all things, wherever they are found; all events, whether of history or experience, of mind or matter; shall at once conspire to form one stupendous miracle, and cease to be such.[142] They will form a miracle, in that they are seen to depend constantly and equally on the power of the Lord;[143] and they will cease to be a miracle, in that the power which pervades them, is so constant, so uniform and so mild in its operation, that it produces nothing of fear, nothing of surprise.[144] From whatever point we contemplate the scene, we feel that we are still in our Father's house; go where we will, the paternal roof, the broad canopy of heaven is extended over us.[145]

[137] Cf. *Nature*, 38.19; 44.15; 56.5.
[138] "Miracles," *N J M*, I, 153.
[139] Cf. *Nature*, 89.1-6; 95.10-12.
[140] "Growth of the Mind," *E T E*, II, 28. Cf. ¶ 57.
[141] "Miracles," *N J M*, I, 155.
[142] See "Self-Reliance," *Works*, II, 66: "All things are dissolved to their centre by their cause, and in the universal miracle petty and particular miracles disappear."
[143] *Ibid.*, II, 66: "Whenever a mind is simple and receives a divine wisdom, old things pass away. . . . It lives now, and absorbs past and future into the present hour."
[144] Cf. *Nature*, 95.10ff.
[145] "Growth of the Mind," *E T E*, II, 18.

INFLUX PASSES FROM HEAVEN INTO MAN AND THROUGH HIM INTO THE
ANIMAL AND MINERAL KINGDOMS——MAN IS, THEREFORE, RESPON-
SIBLE FOR DISORGANIZATIONS IN THE ANIMAL WORLD[146]

¶ 18a

The divine operation is first into the highest heavens and thence into the lower, becoming as it were veiled and accommodated to the condition of every recipient. The heavens
rest on the church as their basis, without which they could not subsist. But the church
also has its basis in the formation of animals less and less perfect, till we come to the
vegetable and mineral kingdoms. Were there no intervening media between man and
inorganised matter, the passage of the influx would be like that of lightning, rupturing
and destroying the natural mind.

¶ 18b

[I]t appears to us, that as all animals were created for use in relation to man, that
an essential change in his moral character must have required and produced a corresponding change in these, in order that they might answer the end for which they were
created; and that there is no reason to doubt that some species have ceased, and others
have come into existence.

¶ 18c

That the real cause of their creation is the Cause of causes is obvious; but that the
formative cause is with spirits and men is also obvious, if not in itself, from this consideration—that we find among them those which are possessed of instincts and forms
essentially diabolical, which could not be produced by an unperverted operation of the
divine influence, and that man is the only being capable of this perversion by a life in
opposition to the divine order and commandments, and thus of manifesting his own evils
in the animals beneath him.

ANIMALS ARE IMPORTANT TO MAN NOT ONLY AS SYMBOLS BUT AS
RECIPIENTS OF HIS STATES OF MIND AND AS THE NECESSARY PROJEC-
TIONS OF HIS AFFECTIONS——GOD IS THE CAUSE OF ALL THINGS, BUT
MAN IS A MEDIATE CREATOR[147]

¶ 18d

We wish that it may be remembered, that correspondences of natural things with
spiritual, stand in the relation to each other, of effects to their causes—that the wonderful things which we find without us, are not merely representative and symbolical,
according to the empty meaning often attached to these words, but are actually created
from things within us. In this way the instruction afforded, becomes in the highest
possible sense, not theoretical, but practical. We are thus permitted to see ourselves as
we are projected out of, and beyond ourselves. The instruction afforded by animals,
important as it may appear, and exalted as it may be above the present condition of the
world, is indeed only a secondary use. As they are the effects of certain affections which
we possess, so are they the only means by which these affections could be brought forth
into existence and manifestation. We could no more breathe without them, than without the atmosphere. They are produced from the developement of human affections, in a
way corresponding to that in which angels and men are from the Divine Love. The
operation of the spirit of God—the influence of the sun of the spiritual world is indeed
strictly speaking the cause of all things. But what we say, is, that this influence as it is
first exerted on angels and men, is there moulded into particular forms, which are thus
transmitted to, and made manifest in the lower orders of creation, which could not
otherwise exist.[148]

---

[146] "Review of Kirby and Spence," *N J M*, II (1828-1829), 370, 252, 369. See *Nature*,
79.15—80.3; 80.8; 80.16—81.9; 88.13-19; 94.13-22. Reed compares Spence's opinions with
those of the New Church on page 370: "But though Mr. Spence withholds his consent
from the supposition that animals are produced by mediate influx, we are happy to
observe that he simply withholds his consent, without opposition. This is the only
alternative he has left himself, and if he moves at all it must be in this direction. Indeed
we might suppose, from the following extracts, that our authors were not far distant
from what we consider the truth on the subject."
[147] "Review of Kirby and Spence," *N J M*, II (1828-1829), 248.
[148] Cf. *Nature*, 80.8; 88.12-18.

HUMAN AFFECTIONS BECOME THE SOULS OF ANIMALS, BUT ANIMAL BODIES ARE RESPONSIBLE FOR THEIR LIFE CYCLES[149]

¶ 18e

Thus in the spiritual world animals are simply the bodies of which human affections, as they pass forth out of the individual, are the souls. But with animals in the natural world there are superinduced material bodies, by which the animals themselves acquire a kind of free-agency and independent existence. The animal, or form of affection as it exists in the spiritual world, has nothing exterior to itself on which it can act, consequently no proper will of its own; but in this world it has a material body, by which it acquires a fixed existence and becomes in itself a subject of pleasure and pain. It is because the natural world furnishes substances, by which the souls of animals become clothed, and in this way they react of themselves and possess a kind of will and free-agency, that they are not created directly from the spiritual world, but are capable of propagating their own species.

CORRESPONDENCE ILLUSTRATED——INSECTS NEVER SLEEP——HOW THE ANT ILLUSTRATES GOD'S PERPETUAL ACT OF CREATION[150]

¶ 18f

It must, we think, be obvious, on reflection, that insects cannot be said, properly speaking, to sleep. They may appear to rest; so also do plants close their petals and recline their heads, and seem to wait for the rising sun to awake them. . . . The ants have been celebrated for their industry, but we were not, till lately, aware with how much justice. They have been observed at all hours of the night, and never been found idle. We behold, in the uninterrupted operation of the supervoluntary organs, an illustration of the truth of the Lord's words, "My Father worketh hitherto and I work," but we did not expect to find so near an approach to the same thing in any animals.

CREATION IS FROM WITHIN OUTWARDS——SAVAGE ANIMALS ACCOUNTED FOR BY THE EVILS OF MEN——THE DEGRADATION OF MAN ——IGNORANCE OF HIS CONDITION——ANIMALS ADMONISH HIM[151]

¶ 18g

[A]ll creation is from within outwards; from spiritual to natural. The body is produced from the soul. Man having in his own freewill alienated himself from God, evil dispositions are hereditarily transmitted from one generation to another. The divine influx of love and wisdom is forever the same; but it is changed according to the state of the recipients. The existing evils in the human race are thus satisfactorily accounted for, by the nature of free agency. But animals also are forms of certain existing affections, from which they are created; nor have they now, or ever had they power to change those affections. How then can we account for those evil beasts and reptiles, which are forms of affections which have no prototype in the Creator? It is impossible for the Lord to communicate an affection which does not exist in himself; and it is impossible that these animals should have changed their character like man, from good to evil. The spiritual sense of the Sacred Scriptures affords the only possible explanation. From this we learn that bad animals correspond to, and are produced by the affections of evil spirits and men;[152] thus that they are created by the divine influx as it is perverted by the hells——and that good animals correspond to and are produced by the affections of good spirits and men; thus that they are created by the Lord through the heavens. The fact that some animals are symbolical, is we believe universally admitted. The lamb is another name for innocence; the fox for cunning.[153]

¶ 19

But man has abused his power, and has become insensible to the real character of the brute creation, still more so, to that of inanimate nature, because in his selfishness, he is disposed to reduce them to slavery. Therefore he is deaf. We find the animal world,

[149] "Review of Kirby and Spence," *N J M*, III (1829-1830), 20. Cf. *Nature*, 80.16-23.

[150] "Review of Kirby and Spence," *N J M*, III (1829-1830), 284. Cf. *Nature*, 36.13-20: "The instincts of the ant are very unimportant considered as the ant's; but the moment a ray of relation is seen to extend from it to man, and the little drudge is seen to be a monitor, a little body with a mighty heart, then all its habits, even that said to be recently observed, that it never sleeps, become sublime."

[151] "On Animals," *E T E*, II, 34. Cf. ¶s. 58ff.

[152] Cf. *Nature*, 81.2ff.; 94.13-22.　　　　[153] Cf. *Nature*, 34.1-3.

either in a state of savage wildness, or enslaved submission. It is possible that as the character of man is changed, they may attain a midway condition equally removed from both. As the mind of man acknowledges its dependance on the Divine Mind, brutes may add to their instinct submission to human reason; preserving an unbroken chain from our Father in Heaven, to the most inanimate parts of creation . . . and man will become conscious of the use of every thing.[154]

¶ 20

There was a time, when the human mind was in more perfect harmony with the Divine Mind, than the lower orders of creation; and the tale of the harp of Orpheus, to which the brutes, the vegetables and the rocks listened, is not altogether unfounded in reality——but when the selfish and worldly passions usurped the place of love to our God and our neighbour, the mind of man began to be mute in its praise. The original order was reversed. The very stones cry out, and we do well to listen to them.[155]

¶ 21

Since the fall of man, nothing has been more difficult for him than to know his real condition, since every departure from divine order is attended with a loss of the knowledge of what it is. When our first parents left the garden of Eden, they took with them no means by which they might measure the depths of degradation to which they fell; no chart by which they might determine their moral longitude.[156]

USES OF ANIMALS ARE YET SCARCELY KNOWN——WE ARE STRANGERS IN NATURE[157]

¶ 22

The proportion of animals, the use of which is known, is probably exceedingly small in comparison with those whose use is not acknowledged. It might appear very strange to most people, should they be told that, independently of any obvious external advantages derived from animals, man could not exist without them. Yet such is probably the fact. The Lord still suffers the devils to enter into the swine, and unclean beasts, and reptiles. . . . The manner in which the smallpox, one of the most loathsome and dangerous diseases, becomes modified in animals, by which man himself gains protection from danger, is probably a true illustration of their use to us in regard to those diseases which are spiritual.

THE INDIVIDUAL MIND——ITS UNIQUENESS——ITS COMPLETENESS AT BIRTH——ITS EDUCATION——ITS DEVELOPMENT BY ASSIMILATION—— REED'S OPPOSITION TO JOHN LOCKE——THE MEMORY

¶ 23

Every man has a form of mind peculiar to himself. The mind of the infant contains within itself the first rudiments of all that will be hereafter, and needs nothing but expansion; as the leaves and branches and fruit of a tree are said to exist in the seed from which it springs. He is bent in a particular direction.[158]

¶ 24

There prevails a most erroneous sentiment, that the mind is originally vacant, and requires only to be filled up; . . . The mind is originally a most delicate germ, whose husk is the body; planted in this world, that the light and heat of heaven may fall upon it with a gentle radiance, and call forth its energies. The process of learning is not by synthesis, or analysis. It is the most perfect illustration of both. As subjects are presented to the operation of the mind, they are decomposed and reorganized in a manner peculiar to itself, and not easily explained.[159]

¶ 25

[T]he true way to store the memory is to develop the affections.[160] The mind must grow, not from external accretion, but from an internal principle. Much may be done by

---

[154] "Growth of the Mind," *E T E*, II, 22. Cf. *Nature*, 94.13-22; 81.7ff.

[155] "Growth of the Mind," *E T E*, II, 23.

[156] "Growth of the Mind," *E T E*, II, 13. Cf. *Nature*, 88.11——89.11.

[157] "On Animals," *E T E*, II, 37. Cf. *Nature*, 81.7ff.

[158] "Oration on Genius," *E T E*, II, 9. See also "Growth of the Mind," *E T E*, II, 20: "It was the design of Providence that the infant mind should possess the germ of every science. If it were not so, they could hardly be learned."

[159] "Growth of the Mind," *E T E*, II, 17. Reed here condemns Locke's theory of the *tabula rasa*.

[160] Emerson quotes this line in his section on "Memory" in the *Natural History of the*

others in aid of its development; but in all that is done, it should not be forgotten, that even from its earliest infancy, it possesses a character and a principle of freedom, which *should* be respected, and *cannot* be destroyed. Its peculiar propensities may be discerned, and proper nutriment and culture supplied——but the infant plant, not less than the aged tree, must be permitted, with its own organs and absorption, to separate that which is peculiarly adapted to itself; otherwise it will be cast off as a foreign substance, or produce nothing but rottenness and deformity. . . . The best affections we possess will find their home in the objects around us, and, as it were, enter into and animate the whole rational, animal and vegetable world. . . . The mind will see itself in what it loves and is able to accomplish. Its own works will be its mirror; and when it is present in the natural world, feeling the same spirit which gives life to every object by which it is surrounded, in its very union with nature it will catch a glimpse of itself.[161]

¶ 26

[A] man cannot be other than what he is. . . . It becomes us then to seek and to cherish this *peculium* of our own minds, as the patrimony which is left us by our Father in heaven——as that by which the branch is united to the vine——as the forming power within us, which gives to our persons that by which they are distinguished from others ——and by a life entirely governed by the commandments of God, to leave on the duties we are called to perform, the full impress of our real characters. Let a man's ambition to be great, disappear in a willingness to be what he is.[162]

INFANCY ILLUSTRATES THE IDEAL OF SPIRITUAL CONSCIOUSNESS—— THE LORD PERPETUALLY ENDEAVORS TO GIVE US THE CHILD'S CHARACTER[163]

¶ 27

The infant is nearly passive, and his motions are mostly involuntary. He does not will or think, according to the usual understanding of volition and thought; but possesses that kind of consciousness which we should have, if we ascended, within ourselves, above those principles which appear to be at all the work of our own hands. Thus to ascend into the elements and beginning of our own creation, where the Lord *stretcheth forth the heavens;* and thence, by our cooperation, to permit the lower principles of the mind to be formed after the same pattern, is *to be born again, to become as little children,* to ascend to where the good and the true are perpetually born within us from the Lord . . . save that the innocence of infancy, as it now descends, becomes clothed with the wisdom and strength of manhood. The infant is associated with the celestial angels, of whom our Lord said, that they *do always behold the face of my Father, who is in the heavens;* and the term of infancy is of considerable duration, in order that the highest principles of the mind may acquire strength to overcome the resistance to divine order, which hereditary evil will perpetually offer beneath; or if, in later periods, he be borne away by his own will, he may yet not be entirely insensible to the presence of the Lord within him, by which his evils may still possibly be curbed and subdued. . . . Each succeeding period of life presents an image of what is seen in infancy. It is the perpetual[164] endeavour of the Lord, as the interior principles are formed, thence to descend into those which are beneath, that all may be made in his image and likeness; and this is effected so far as it can be done consistently with the freedom of the individual.

¶ 28

There is formed in the mind of the child, from his most familiar observations, however imperfect they may be, as it were a little nucleus, which serves as the basis of his future progress. This usually comprises a large proportion of those natural appearances, which the philosopher in later periods of life, finds it most difficult to explain. The child grows up in his Father's house, and collects and arranges the most familiar operations and events. Into this collection, he afterwards receives whatever history or

---

Intellect. See *Works,* XII, 104.

[161] "Growth of the Mind," *E T E,* II, 19.

[162] "Growth of the Mind," *E T E,* II, 30-31. Cf. lines 41-42 of Γνωθι Σεαυτον.

[163] "Free Agency of Man," *E T E,* II, 33. Cf. ¶s. 66-70 below, esp. ¶ 69. Cf. "Oration on Genius," *E T E,* II, 9: "The hand of the Almighty is visible to all in the stroke of death; but few see his face in the smiles of the new-born babe." See *Journals,* III, 337-338 (Sept. 14, 1834): "What is the doctrine of *infallible guidance if one will abdicate choice,* but striving to act unconsciously, to resume the simplicity of childhood?"   [164] Cf. *Nature,* 88.6-10, esp. line 7.

science may communicate, and still feels at home; a feeling with which wonder[165] is never associated.[166]

TENDENCIES TO EVIL IN THE NATURAL MAN————IMPORTANCE OF EXTERNAL RESTRAINTS[167]

¶ 29

Few realize, to what the natural man is continually inclined, and what crimes would be perpetrated, were it not for external restraints. We are told by Swedenborg that the natural man is of himself continually inclined to the lowest hell, and that he is withdrawn and withheld solely by the Divine influence. Swedenborg also informs us, that man is of himself more savage than the wild beasts. This appears to be strong language. Yet it is not only true, but capable of demonstration; for in evil spirits and men is the very fountain of the life by which these beasts are impelled to action.

¶ 30

The natural man grows up under restraints imposed by the order of society and the civil law, of the extent of which he is himself ignorant. He is not aware that the life externally correct, is not internally good also, till he begins to shun evils, not because they are disreputable or dangerous, but because they are sins. The true quality of his own life is then revealed to him, as he is able to see it. He is generally impressed with the belief that he is worse than any one else; for he dares not impute to others such tendencies as he finds in himself. Such a persuasion, however, is not true, nor does it possess all the humility which it appears to have. It is not unattended with the latent belief, that as his evil is his own, so he still has of himself, (perhaps to a very small degree,) something good. But true humility perceives that one man is of himself neither better nor worse than his neighbor; for all are of themselves essentially evil. There is none good but one, God; nor can any thing good exist for a moment, independent of its source.

¶ 31

If the man who leads a moral life, but is as yet insensible of his own evil tendencies, would know what he is internally, let him reflect how he would appear to those around him, if every affection and thought of which he is conscious, were made visible to those in whose company he is. In the present state of society, the power of concealment is common to all, and is by all insensibly practised. But if any one in his natural state should from any cause lose the power of suppressing the spontaneous suggestions of his heart, he would at once be excluded from all society, though this society may differ from him in no other respect, than that of possessing the power which he has lost.

¶ 32

Herein exists a remarkable difference between the spiritual world and the natural. In the former, things without represent the true quality of things within, being created directly from them, and bearing their image. The affections and thoughts pass forth and become actually visible in the things which correspond to them. But in the natural world the spontaneous thoughts are for the most part not permitted to pass forth till they have been scrutinized and are thought to answer. It is to a considerable extent the case, that the opposite is instantly and almost imperceptibly substituted for the true thought. This is an important part of what constitutes the politeness of artificial society.

SLEEP————ITS RELATION TO REGENERATION AND DEPENDENCE ON THE DIVINE WILL[168]

¶ 33

It is not an uncommon opinion that the time devoted to sleep is wasted. Renewed bodily strength, and a consequent freshness of the spirits, are at farthest all the uses which are supposed to result from it. It seems to be regarded as a necessary imperfection in creation. But it is not thus considered by the members of the New Church. To them it is revealed that the Lord, in the whole order of his creation, has respect

---

[165] Cf. *Nature*, 95.10-12.

[166] "Growth of the Mind," *E T E*, II, 17.

[167] "External Restraint," *N J M*, VI (1832-1833), 30-32. See pp. 31-32. Emerson refers to this article in *Journals*, II, 517. See chap. X, note 124.

[168] "Sleep," *N J M*, VI (1832-1833), 88-89. See p. 88. Cf. ¶ 70. See *Nature*, 7.7; 92.17; 93.4.

primarily to regeneration and salvation; and that the condition of the body and what is often called the animal spirits, is regarded only in relation to those ends. Sleep was not ordained because there must be nights, and this is the way in which they may be spent with the least inconvenience and anxiety. It necessarily belongs to all created beings, whether angels, men, or the inferior animals; and we see its image distinctly impressed on the vegetable world.

¶ 34

The use and necessity of sleep in accomplishing the work of regeneration can be understood only by means of the doctrines of the New Church. Were not the will alternately active and quiescent, it could never be brought to a sense and acknowledgement of its dependence on the Divine will.[169] Where human agency begins, there will be weariness and must be rest; and the law which imposes this necessity reveals also our total and constant dependence on the Lord; and makes this revelation where it needs to be felt and acknowledged, to the will itself.

DOCTRINE OF USE——EACH MAN AND EACH NATION MUST MAKE A DISTINCTIVE CONTRIBUTION TO THE WHOLE——————EDUCATION DISCUSSED[170]

¶ 35

Every individual . . . possesses peculiar powers, which should be brought to bear on society in the duties best fitted to receive them. The highest degree of cultivation of which the mind of any one is capable, consists in the most perfect development of that peculiar organization, which as really exists in infancy, as in maturer years. The seed which is planted, is said to possess in miniature the trunk, branches, leaves and fruit of the future tree. So it is with the mind; and the most that can possibly be done, is to afford facilities by which its development may be effected with the same order. In the process of the formation of our minds, there exists the spirit of prophecy; and no advancement can create surprise, because we have always been conscious of that from which it is produced. We must not seek to make one hair white·or black. . . . We should seek an employment for the mind, in which all its energies may be warmed into existence.[171]

¶ 36

Most sensibly do we feel that, as the true end of instruction is to prepare a man for some particular sphere of usefulness; that when he has found this sphere, his education has then truly commenced, and the finger of God is pointing to the very page of the book of his oracles, from which he may draw the profoundest wisdom. It was the design of Providence that there should be enough of science connected with the calling of each, for the highest and holiest purposes of heaven. . . . Truth is the way in which we should act; and then only is a man truly wise, when the body performs what the mind. perceives.[172]

¶ 37

[T]he several nations of the earth also, will at a future period, stand forth with a distinctness of character which cannot now be conceived of. The part which each is to perform in the regeneration of the world, will become more and more distinctly marked and universally acknowledged; and every nation will be found to possess resources in its own moral and intellectual character, and its own natural productions, which will render it essential to the well-being and happiness of the whole. Every government must find that the real good of its own people precisely harmonizes with that of others; and standing armies must be converted into willing labourers for the promotion of the same object.[173]

OPTIMISM——PROSPECTS——THE FUTURE——REVELATION——JOHN LOCKE'S INFLUENCE ALMOST ENDED[174]

¶ 38

The world is deriving vigour, not from that which is gone by, but from that which is coming; not from the unhealthy moisture of the evening, but from the nameless influences of the morning. The loud call on the past to instruct us, as it falls on the rock

---

[169] Emerson quotes this sentence in *Y E S*, 203.26 (Sept. 7, 1834).
[170] See also ¶ 61.
[171] "Growth of the Mind," *E T E*, II, 30.
[172] "Growth of the Mind," *E T E*, II, 31.
[173] "Growth of the Mind," *E T E*, II, 30.
[174] The spirit of these paragraphs appears in *Nature*, 94.1ff.

of ages, comes back in echo from the future. Both mankind, and the laws and principles by which they are governed, seem about to be redeemed from slavery. The moral and intellectual character of man has undergone, and is undergoing a change; and as this is effected it must change the aspect of all things, as when the position-point is altered from which a landscape is viewed. We appear to be approaching an age which will be the silent pause of merely physical force before the powers of the mind; the timid, subdued, awed condition of the brute, gazing on the erect and godlike form of man.[175]

¶ 39

All minds, whatever may be their condition, are not unconnected with God; and consequently not unconnected with each other. All nations, under whatever system of government, and in whatever state of civilization, are under the Divine Providence, surely but almost imperceptibly advancing to a moral and political order, such as the world has not yet seen. They are guided by the same hand, and with a view to the same destiny. Much remains to be done, and more to be suffered; but the end is certain. The humblest individual may, nay *must* aid in the accomplishment of this consummation. It is not for time or space to set limits to the effects of the life of a single man.[176]

¶ 40

[T]here is a society yet in its coming, unseen though not unseeing, shrouded from the rest of the world by the very brilliancy of its own light, which would resist the impulse of every evil affection, and look for heaven simply in the delight of that which is chaste, pure and holy; which by removing that which renders duty undelightful, would draw nigh to the only source of real enjoyment; which would find its happiness and its God, in the very commandments which have been the terrour of the world.[177]

¶ 41

[T]he human mind when revelation shall have accomplished its work, shall no longer regard the scene of sin and misery behind, but having completed the circle, shall rest as next to the present moment on the golden age, the infancy of the world.[178]

¶ 42

The light of this philosophy has begun to beam faintly on the world, and mankind will yet see their own moral and intellectual nature by the light of revelation, as it shines through the moral and intellectual character it shall have itself created. . . . It is the tendency of revelation to give a right direction to every power of every mind; and when this is effected, inventions and discoveries will follow of course, all things assume a different aspect, and the world itself again become a paradise.[179]

¶ 43

Science will be full of life, as nature is full of God. She will wring from her locks the dew which was gathered in the wilderness. By science, I mean natural science. The science of the human mind must change with its subject. Locke's mind will not always be the standard of metaphysics. Had we a description of it in its present state, it would make a very different book from "Locke on the Human Understanding." The time is not far distant. The cock has crowed. I hear the distant lowing of the cattle which are grazing on the mountains. "Watchman, what of the night? Watchman, what of the night? The watchman saith, The morning cometh."[180]

ALL TRUTH IS PRACTICAL——IT HAS REFERENCE TO OBJECTS[181]

¶ 44

Truth, all truth is practical. It is impossible from its nature and origin, that it should be otherwise. Whether its effect be directly to change the conduct, or it simply leave an impression on the heart, it is in the strictest sense practical. It should rather be our desire to use what we learn, than to remember it. If we desire to use it, we shall remember it of course; if we wish merely to remember, it is possible we may never use it. It is the tendency of all truth to effect some object. If we look at this

---

[175] "Growth of the Mind," *E T E*, II, 12.
[176] "Growth of the Mind," *E T E*, II, 24. See *Nature*, 80.3-4.
[177] "Growth of the Mind," *E T E*, II, 24.
[178] "Growth of the Mind," *E T E*, II, 14.
[179] "Growth of the Mind," *E T E*, II, 13-14. Cf. *Nature*, 88.9-10.
[180] "Oration on Genius," *E T E*, II, 11.
[181] "Growth of the Mind," *E T E*, II, 16. Cf. *Nature*, 7.2.

object, it will form a distinct and permanent image on the mind; if we look merely at the truth it will vanish away, like rays of light falling into vacancy.

SPIRITUAL LIGHT AND HEAT[182]

¶ 45

Spiritual heat warms the things of the spiritual world and causes them to live and grow, as natural heat does the things of the natural world; and spiritual light illuminates them and renders them visible, and thus determines their form and appearance, as natural light does the things of this world. . . . Nor are these things so strange to us, as we might perhaps be at first disposed to regard them. Our acquaintance with them is continually implied in our commonest forms of speech. We speak of the warmth of love as familiarly as of the warmth of fire; and of the light of wisdom as well as of the light of the natural sun. The affections are said to be warm or cold; the understanding, enlightened or dark. To excite the passions of men is to enflame their hearts: to render new truths intelligible is to communicate light to their understandings. So when one person entertains different views from another, he is said to see the subject in a different light.

TRUE GENIUS IS RECEPTION——FALSE GENIUS AND SELF-LOVE HAVE THEIR OWN CANKER——REJOICE IN THE TRUTH, NOT IN YOUR DISCOVERY OF IT——TRUTH COMES FROM GOD——IMPORTANCE OF HUMILITY[183]

¶ 46

The intellectual eye of man is formed to see the light, not to make it; and it is time that, when the causes that cloud the spiritual world are removed, man should rejoice in the truth itself, and not that *he* has found it.[184] More than once, when nothing was required but for a person to stand on this world with his eyes open, has the truth been seized upon as a thing of his own making. When the power of divine truth begins to dispel the darkness, the objects that are first disclosed to our view——whether men of strong understanding, or of exquisite taste, or of deep learning——are called geniuses. Luther, Shakspeare, Milton, Newton, stand with the bright side towards us.

¶ 47

There is something which is called genius, that carries in itself the seeds of its own destruction. There is an ambition which hurries a man after truth, and takes away the power of attaining it. There is a desire which is null, a lust which is impotence. There is no understanding so powerful, that ambition may not in time bereave it of its last truth, even that two and two are four. Know, then, that genius is divine, not when the man thinks that he is God, but when he acknowledges that his powers are from God. Here is the link of the finite with the infinite, of the divine with the human: this is the humility which exalts.[185]

POETRY——HOW EVALUATED——DEPENDS ON THE CREATIVE SPIRIT OF GOD——DRAWS ILLUSTRATIONS FROM NATURAL WORLD——FREE VERSE BEST——THE POET MUST BE FREE AND UNSHACKLED[186]

¶ 48

By poetry is meant all those illustrations of truth by natural imagery, which spring from the fact that this world is the mirror of him who made it. . . . The day will come, and it may not be far distant, when this art will have another test of merit than mere versification, or the invention of strange stories; when the laws by which poetry is

---

[182] "Remarks on the Nature of Spiritual Heat and Light," *N J M*, V (1831-1832), 94-100. See pp. 94-95. Cf. *Nature*, 34.5-7.

[183] "Oration on Genius," *E T E*, II, 9-10. (Cf. also top of page 13). See *Journals*, II, 363-364. See below ¶s. 61-62.

[184] Emerson quotes this line and applies it to himself in *Journals*, IV, 74 (June 22, 1836). He there calls Reed "my early oracle." See "Growth of the Mind," *E T E*, II, 13: ". . . to be proud of the truth is to cease to possess it."

[185] Emerson was probably thinking of this passage in *Journals*, III, 496 (June 26, 1835). Cf. *Nature*, 82.19-20.

[186] I believe that Reed had a definite influence upon Emerson's theory of poetry. See esp. "Poetry and the Imagination," *Letters and Social Aims* (*Works*, VIII), 64-66. See also Reed's review of William Gardiner's *The Music of Nature* in *N J M*, XI, 211ff.,

tested, will be as fixed and immutable as the laws of science. . . . It would seem that genius would be cramped; that the powers of invention would be destroyed; by confining the human mind, as it were, at home, within the bounds which nature has assigned. But what wider scope need it have? It reaches the throne of God; it rests on his footstool. All things spiritual and natural are before it. . . . [T]ruth presented in natural imagery, is only dressed in the garments[187] which God has given it.[188]

¶ 49

It belongs to the true poet to feel [the creative spirit of God], and to be governed by it; to be raised above the senses; to live and breathe in the inward efforts of things; to feel the power of creation, even before he sees the effect; to witness the innocence and smiles of nature's infancy, not by extending the imagination back to chaos, but by raising the soul to nature's origin. The true poetic spirit . . . is the soul of science. Without it, the latter is a cheerless, heartless study, distrusting even the presence and power of Him to whom it owes its existence. Of all the poetry which exists, that only possesses the seal of immortality, which presents the image of God which is stamped on nature.[189]

¶ 50

When there shall be a religion which shall see God in everything, and at all times; and the natural sciences not less than nature itself, shall be regarded in connexion with Him——the fire of poetry will begin to be kindled in its immortal part, and will burn without consuming. The inspiration so often feigned, will become real; and the mind of the poet will feel the spark which passes from God to nature.[190]

¶ 51

[T]o my ear, rhymes add nothing to poetry, but rather detract from its beauty. They possess too strongly the marks of art, and produce a sameness which tires, and sometimes disgusts. We seek for them in vain in nature, and may therefore reasonably presume that they spring out of the peculiar state of the public taste, without possessing any real foundation in the mind itself; that they are rather the fashion of the dress, than any essential part. In the natural world we find nothing which answers to them, or feels like them——but a happy assemblage of living objects springing up, not in straight lines and at a fixed distance, but in God's own order, which by its apparent want of design, conveys the impression of perfect innocence and humility. . . . The poet should be free and unshackled as the eagle; whose wings, as he soars in the air, seem merely to serve the office of a helm, while he moves on simply by the agency of the will.[191]

¶ 52

Had we a history of poetry, from the first rude effusions to where words make one with things,[192] and language is lost in nature, we should see the state of man in the language of licentious passion, in the songs of chivalry, in the descriptions of heroic valor, in the mysterious wildness of Ossian; till the beauties of nature fall on the heart, as softly as the clouds on the summer's water. The mind, as it wanders from heaven, moulds the arts into its own form, and covers its nakedness. Feelings of all kinds will discover themselves in music, in painting, in poetry; but it is only when the heart is purified from every selfish and worldly passion, that they are created in real beauty; for in their origin they are divine.[193]

THE GREAT LAW OF CRITICISM——ITS APPLICATION TO POETRY, SCIENCE AND THE BIBLE

¶ 53

There is one law of criticism, the most important to the thorough understanding of any work, which seems not to have been brought sufficiently into view in the study of the Bible. It is that by which we should be led by a continued exercise of those powers which are most clearly demonstrated in an authour;[194] by continued habits of

---

283ff., 354ff.

[187] See *Nature*, 44.15.
[188] "Growth of the Mind," *E T E*, II, 21.
[189] "Growth of the Mind," *E T E*, II, 21.
[190] "Growth of the Mind," *E T E*, II, 22.
[191] "Growth of the Mind," *E T E*, II, 22. Cf. *Nature*, 92.10-11.
[192] Emerson quotes this in *Journals*, III, 492 (June 20, 1835).
[193] "Oration on Genius," *E T E*, II, 10.
[194] See chap. VII, footnote 134. See *Nature*, 44.18-19.

mind and action; to approximate to that intellectual and moral condition, in which the work originated. If it were desired to make a child thoroughly acquainted with the work of a genuine poet, I would not put the poem and lexicon in his hand. . . . I would cultivate a sense of the constant presence and agency of God, and direct him inward to the presence chamber of the Most High, that his mind might become imbued with His spirit. I would endeavour by the whole course of his education to make him a living poem, that when he read the poetry of others, it might be effulgent with the light of his own mind. The poet stands on the mountain with the face of nature before him, calm and placid. If we would enter into his views, we must go where he is. We must catch the direction of his eye, and yield ourselves up to the instinctive guidance of his will. . . . The true poet, when his mind is full, fills his language to overflowing; and it is left to the reader to preserve what the words cannot contain. It is that part which cannot be defined; that which is too delicate to endure the unrestrained gaze; that which shrinks instinctively from the approach of any thing less chaste than itself.[195]

¶ 54

As it is requisite to a full sense of the beauties of poetry, that the individual should be himself a poet, and to a thorough knowledge of a work of science that he should not merely have scientific information, but a scientific mind; so it is necessary to a knowledge of the Bible, that the mind should be formed in the image and likeness of God. An understanding of the Word is the effect of a life according to its precepts.[196]

THE EVIL OF SELF-LOVE CHARACTERIZES THE NATURAL MAN——HE CONSIDERS HIS QUALITIES HIS OWN——FAILS TO DISTINGUISH BETWEEN GOOD AND EVIL IMPULSES WITHIN——IS IGNORANT OF THE ULTIMATE SPIRITUAL SOURCES OF BOTH[197]

¶ 55

The world knows still less in regard to what is good, than in regard to what is true. The distinction between truth and falsehood has never been entirely lost. . . . But with goodness it is otherwise.[198] The feelings obviously have an internal, not an external origin; and as the natural man, as he turns inward, does not look beyond himself, they seem to be wholly self-originated. The dispositions of individuals are subjects of praise or dispraise, without a thought that the good is from the Lord or the evil from the hells. Thus good and evil being ascribed to the same source, are necessarily confounded. True goodness is not known. . . . Thus has the natural man become as God, knowing good and evil. In the ascription of goodness to himself is latently involved the belief that he is himself divine.

MATERIALISTIC MEN THINK A SPIRITUAL WORLD UNREAL——THE CONCEPT, THEY SAY, IS MERELY POETIC——THE NEW CHURCH INSISTS UPON ITS REALITY——PURE LOVE DERIVES FROM THE SPIRITUAL SUN AND NOT FROM MAN HIMSELF——LOVE AND WISDOM[199]

¶ 56

The quality of self-love cannot be discerned without first understanding what love is. And here it must be remarked that although the word is and has been in the mouths of all men, the disclosure of its source and true quality is one of the distinguishing characteristics of the New Jerusalem. There is, ordinarily, in the minds of men, the moment they ascend above material things, a total want of reality. As the soul itself is not regarded as an organised substance, so neither does it seem to require to be acted upon by aught that is substantial. But there is a sun in the spiritual world, as there is in the natural; and as from the latter there is an emanation of heat and light which is essential to animal and vegetable life, so from the former there is an emanation of spiritual heat and light, the first of which is called love, and the last wisdom.

---

[195] "Growth of the Mind," *E T E*, II, 26.

[196] "Growth of the Mind," *E T E*, II, 27.

[197] "Self-Love Essential Evil," *N J M*, IV (1830-1831), 338-339. This thought was developed at length in the "Oration on Genius," *E T E*, II, 9-11. See also Swedenborg ¶ 30.   [198] See *Nature*, 93.15-19.

[199] "Self-Love Essential Evil," *N J M*, IV (1830-1831), 342. Emerson saw in New-Church terminology Coleridge's distinction between men dominated by the Understanding and those under sway of the Reason.

WHAT UNENLIGHTENED CHRISTIANS OF THE OLD CHURCH CONSIDERED MERE POETRY, THE NEW CHURCH CONSIDERS REAL AND THE SOURCE OF ALL REALITIES——ATTITUDES TOWARD THE ASCENSION ILLUSTRATE THE TWO POINTS OF VIEW[200]

¶ 57

The sober realities of the New Church are often the poetry of the Old.[201] That which seems real to the latter only on condition of their transferring to it somewhat of themselves, interweaving it with their own imaginations, giving it the indirect support of their own arm, and tracing its connexion with their own earth; with the former is not only real, but the source of all realities. That the Lord should be asked in prayer to warm the heart and enlighten the understanding, or when represented in a picture, that his head should be radiant with light, is considered as in good taste; but the simple truth that his face actually shines as the sun, and that he is really the source of heat and light to all the angels in heaven, is startling and visionary. Had it been possible for him, as he ascended up into heaven, to have been visible to those in opposite states of mind, the one would have been lost in wonder at the apparently miraculous suspension of the law of gravitation, the other in adoration of him from whose constant energy all worlds are held in their places.

THE SPIRITUAL SUN OR DIVINE LOVE SHINES INTO THE HEARTS OF GOOD AND EVIL MEN ALIKE——THE LATTER PERVERT IT——WITNESS THE EXTERNAL FORMS INTO WHICH OUR AFFECTIONS PROJECT THEMSELVES[202]

¶ 58

The Lord causes the sun of the spiritual world to rise on the evil and the good. But with the former it is turned into darkness, and they do not even know that it exists. To such its influence would even seem to be the source of darkness, because it would be inconsistent with all which they call light. Owls and bats are created through those who thus turn day into night and night into day, and exactly correspond to and represent their state. But with the good the Lord is a sun and a shield, and there shall be no night with them.

THE WORK OF CREATION——THE ACTIVITY OF THE SPIRITUAL SUN FINDS CORRESPONDENCE IN THE ACTIVITY OF THE NATURAL SUN——HOW MEN MAY BE SAID TO BUILD A NEW WORLD THROUGH SUBMISSION TO THE SPIRIT——THE DOCTRINE OF USE IS THE BEST ANTIDOTE TO SELF-LOVE[203]

¶ 59

[I]t is now revealed that the work of creation commences in the souls of angels and men, and that the spiritual heat and light which there impart warmth and intelligence, as they pass outward, actually create and sustain all things in the natural world. Something may be seen in regard to what love is, from the nature and effects of that which corresponds to it, the heat of the natural sun. In the winter, all vegetable and a considerable proportion of animal life is suspended. But in the spring the fields are clothed with verdure; the trees put forth their leaves and blossoms; those animals which have been in a state of torpor, revive; the birds choose their mates, build their nests, and fill the air with their music, and all things are filled with the effort of reproduction and preservation which is pressing into them from the Lord the Creator. The heat of spring as it descends on the vegetable world, does not change the qualities of any——it does not destroy the bad and preserve the good; it causes all to grow and bring forth fruit. But some bring forth fruit which is delightful to the taste and useful for the sustenance of man, and others that which is poisonous, or merely thorns and thistles. So also does this heat call forth the latent energies of all animals without changing the quality of any. Those which are torpid, it revives; and to those which are alive, it gives more life.

---

[200] "Self-Love Essential Evil," *N J M*, IV (1830-1831), 342-343. Cf. ¶ 15 above.

[201] See *Carlyle-Emerson Corr.*, I, 32-33, for a paraphrasing of this line. Emerson apparently enclosed a copy of the entire article in his letter to Carlyle.

[202] "Self-Love Essential Evil," *N J M*, IV (1830-1831), 343. Cf. ¶s. 18-22. See *Nature*, 81.2-11; 94.13-22.

[203] "Self-Love Essential Evil," *N J M*, IV (1830-1831), 343; 343-344; 344-345; 345. Cf. ¶s. 35-37. Cf. *Nature*, 94.22——95.7. See Swedenborg ¶ 29.

¶ 60

So is it with spiritual heat and light as it falls on the heavens and the hells. It causes both the one and the other to bring forth fruit; but the fruit of the one is good, and that of the other is evil. Those who are branches of the true vine, perceive and acknowledge the source of their life; and this life is the simple undivided effort to bring forth good fruit. But the evil are apparently men, and seem to themselves and to others to bear fruit. But this fruit, in consequence of not only the absence of all desire to be useful to others, but from the inward endeavor to do them injury, becomes in some cases like that of a poisonous tree; and in others results in the abortive and sterile effort of the thorn and the thistle. It should be remarked, however, that whereas the nature of beasts and vegetables is fixed,[204] and the heat simply causes the manifestation of their peculiar life; the quality of men in this world is not thus fixed, and it is the constant effort of the Divine Love and Wisdom to subdue our evil affections.

¶ 61

It is the simple undivided effort of spiritual heat and light to cause men to bring forth good fruit, without taking any thought for themselves. . . . It is an inverted effort for a man to think of himself. The creative endeavor is always that of developement; that by which the internal passes outward into the external——good affections into corresponding acts of usefulness. . . . There is no image of self-love in the uses of any of the organs of the human body; for these organs perform their functions from that life which is above the control of ourselves. The first traces of selfishness are discovered not in the healthy activity of the parts, but in their diseases; and that organ which refuses to perform its duty to the rest is the first occasion and seat of the disease. As all the organs of the body are instruments of usefulness, so is the human form which they go to compose, a perfect image, and when governed by life from the Lord, a perfect endeavor of use to the neighbor.

¶ 62

Thus it is that those who act from that life which is constantly flowing into them from the Lord, without perverting it, fill their own uses from the simple love of those uses. In doing this, they are indeed happy; and they are not permitted to be destitute of any means of use which would be made subservient to a true love of duty. But when does this love from the Lord, which is thus essentially expansive and communicative, become self-love? How totally is its quality changed, when, instead of passing forth in gladness into its own works, it becomes confined and self-directed? What would have been a creating and invigorating heat, now becomes a burning and consuming fire. . . . love deprived of every distinguishing property by which it is constituted.

TRUE DIGNITY——HOW TO PROTECT IT[205]
¶ 63

We want no education which shall raise a man out of the reach of the understanding or the sympathies of any of his species. We are disgusted with that kind of dignity which the possessor is himself obliged to guard; but venerate that which, having its origin in the actual character of the man, can receive no increase from the countenance of power, and suffer no diminution from the approach of weakness——that dignity in which the individual appears to live rather in the consciousness of the light which shines from above, than in that of his own shadow beneath. There is a spiritual atmosphere about such an one, which is at once its own protection, and the protection of him with whom it is connected——which while it is free as air alike to the most powerful and the most humble, conveys a tacit warning that too near an approach is not permitted.

DOCTRINE OF IMMORTALITY——MAN'S ASSURANCE SPRINGS FROM THE UNION OF THE DIVINE AND THE HUMAN WITHIN HIM——FEAR OF DEATH ABOLISHED[206]
¶ 64

All growth or development is effected from within, outward. It is so with animals; it is so with vegetables; it is so with the body; it is so with the mind. Were it not for

---

[204] Cf. *Nature*, 80.19-22.
[205] See "Growth of the Mind," *E T E*, II, 31. Emerson apparently echoes this passage in *Journals*, IV, 16 (Feb. 28, 1836).
[206] "Growth of the Mind," *E T E*, II, 25; 29. See also ¶ 4.

a power within the soul, as the soul is within the body, it could have no possibility of subsistence. That the growth of the material part depends on the presence of that which is spiritual, is obvious from the fact, that at death the former falls to decay. If it were possible for God to be detached from our spiritual part, this would decay likewise. The doctrine then of the immortality of the soul is simply, "I in my Father, and ye in me and I in you." It is the union of the Divine, with the human——of that from which all things are, and on which they depend the Divine Will, with man through the connecting medium of Divine Truth. It is the tendency of the Bible to effect this union, and of course to restore a consciousness of it. It is a union which God desires with all, therefore even the wicked who reject it, partake of his immortality, though not of his happiness. When in the process of regeneration, this union is accomplished, the fear of dissolution will be as impossible in this world as in the other. . . . It is not the place where a person is, but the condition of mind which is to be regarded; and there is no antidote against the fear of death, but the consciousness of being united with the fountain of life. . . . "He that believeth on the Son *hath* everlasting life;" and he will become conscious of living and growing from God.

¶ 65

Man alone of all created things, appears on his own account to want the full measure of his happiness; because he alone has left the order of his creation. He stands even at the present period half-convinced of the reality of the future state. It is the design of revelation to restore to him that moral condition, in which he will possess as necessarily the consciousness of immortality, as the brute does that of existence—— for a consciousness of existence united with that of union with God, is a consciousness of eternal life.

THE SPIRITUAL POWER ABOVE THE HUMAN WILL MAY BE CALLED *SUPERVOLUNTARY*[207]

¶ 66

We wish to use the word supervoluntary to express not only that which is above the will, but that which is *directly* above it——the inmost of the soul, which is operated upon by the Divine Love, which operation is there above the control of the individual, but becomes subject to his control as it descends and becomes voluntary. We mean, then, by supervoluntary, that which is voluntary in the highest sense of the word—— the very source and fountain of the will. Its freedom consists not in receiving or rejecting, for it cannot but will to receive; but in receiving only in accordance with its peculiar form, and of thus modifying the spiritual influence, and becoming a medium to the will, without which, this could not in freedom receive or reject either good or evil. The will does not act without the intervention of thought; but the supervoluntary is above the region of thought, is suggesting the thoughts themselves, and prompting the will to action.

OPERATION OF INFLUX BEFORE AND AFTER MAN'S FALL——–—MAN'S DISUNITED STATE[208]

¶ 67

With the most ancient church, the supervoluntary flowed directly into the will and thus into the understanding, whence resulted action; and here was a union of instinct and reason. But as the will, by aversion from God, became destroyed, had not this course of influx been changed, man could not but have willed what was evil and thence have thought what was false, and his reformation would have been impossible. Hence it was permitted the supervoluntary to act on the intellectual, and man, by doing what he saw to be true, was enabled to form a new will in his understanding. Hence resulted reason not in correspondence with, but in contradistinction to instinct. There is this essential difference between them. All which is in unbroken correspondence with the Divine Will is produced by developement; that which is without being formed directly from that which is within; but it is not thus with natural reason. It takes its survey

---

[207] "Review of Kirby and Spence," *N J M*, III (1829-1830), 138. Cf. *Nature*, 89.6-10: ". . . superior to his will. It is Instinct." See *Journals*, III, 337-338 (Sept. 14, 1834): "What is the doctrine of *infallible guidance if one will abdicate choice*, but striving to act unconsciously, to resume the simplicity of childhood?"
[208] "Review of Kirby and Spence," *N J M*, III (1829-1830), 138-139. Cf. *Nature*, 89.6-10.

and thence determines upon action; instead of both seeing and acting from a life within. There is thus miraculously given a return-power, by which internal evils may be resisted and removed.

DIGNITY OF INSTINCT IN THE REDEEMED MAN[209]

¶ 68

But when, by obedience to the commandments, the human will shall be brought into coincidence[210] with the Divine Will, then also will reason live from instinct and look towards it. The branch which is thus united to the vine, will, from the life it receives from within, put itself forth to meet the light. 'If therefore thine eye be single, thy whole body shall be full of light.'[211] Our instincts will no longer pass under the name of animal propensities by way of expressing their degraded inferiority to reason; as if we had only the heads of men, but the bodies of beasts. But what now appears to be the lowest, will, as it is purified and regenerated, become the most exalted part of our nature; and reason, like the preceptor of a prince, will delight to obey, where it had been accustomed to teach. We would remark, in passing, that many expressions applied to the Lord, such as 'plans,' 'schemes,' 'contrivance,' &c. are the effect of ascribing to him also reason like that of the natural man, in contradistinction to instinct.

THE SUPERVOLUNTARY POWER IS BEST VISIBLE IN INFANCY[212]

¶ 69

The supervoluntary power is particularly visible in infancy; for it is then presented to us in its native, unclothed state. The infant neither wills nor thinks according to our understanding of the words. There is indeed a continual but gentle effort of the supervoluntary, to press outward into that region of the mind where it becomes fully a subject of consciousness, and is under the voluntary control of the child; and this effort makes one with that by which he is becoming clothed with muscles suitable for the performance of the commands of the will..... The infant is an unresisting medium of the Divine influence, and there is in this influence a constant effort to make him a voluntary, rational medium, that 'his will may be done on earth as it is in heaven.' The very gradual process of growth is because the tendency of the supervoluntary to descend is so exceedingly gentle, that the formation of the will is under Providence effected in perfect freedom. In later periods of life, his hereditary evils discover themselves, and in the present state of society rarely fail to gain the ascendancy, though the Lord always provides strength for their resistance, if it be rightly used.

THE SUPERVOLUNTARY POWER IS ALSO EVIDENT IN SLEEP[213]

¶ 70

Next to the period of infancy, we witness the operation of the supervoluntary power most remarkably in sleep. The will is suspended, but this power continues its operation. . . . Sleep is the grand means, by which the states of infancy and childhood are preserved and revived. Indeed it approaches nearer the state of infancy than any other we experience, for in infancy the will has not come into action, and in sleep its operation is suspended. Such are the provisions of Him,

> 'Who did wrap the cloud
> Of infancy around us, that Himself
> Therein, with our simplicity awhile
> Might hold, on earth, communion undisturbed;
> Who from the anarchy of dreaming sleep,
> Or from its death-like void, with punctual care,
> And touch as gentle as the morning light,
> Restores us, daily, to the powers of sense,
> And reason's stedfast rule.' [214]

---

[209] "Review of Kirby and Spence," *N J M*, III (1829-1830), 140. Cf. *Nature*, 89.10.
[210] See *Nature*, 91.9-13.   [211] Matthew 6:12 and Luke 11:34.
[212] "Review of Kirby and Spence," *N J M*, III (1829-1830), 140-141. See ¶ 27 and also note on Swedenborg ¶s. 45-46. See *Nature*, 88.1-10.
[213] "Review of Kirby and Spence," *N J M*, III (1829-1830), 141-142. See ¶s. 33-34. Cf. *Nature*, 7.6; 11.18-19; 88.4-10.
[214] Wordsworth, "The Excursion," Bk. IV, lines 83-91, with slight variations.

THE NEW-CHURCH THEORY OF NATURE CONTAINS A "SOMEWHAT PROGRESSIVE"[213a]

¶ 71

To the New Church it is known that the natural world corresponds to the spiritual world; that the former is created from and through the latter——and that under Divine Providence it is not only adapted to subserve the wants of the body, and be a source of scientific truth to the mind; but to yield spiritual instruction, to develop the affections and to prepare men for that world of which this is only the outward effect. Now the development of higher and higher uses in the natural world, by which the wilderness is transformed into a paradise, is progressive. In this respect it resembles the successive revelations of different orders of truth in the Sacred Scripture, and is indeed the effect of these revelations. The language of nature is the same, whether it be understood or not. The Creator is always present doing His work, whether His presence be seen or unseen. The natural world is not the less useful to the savage, because it is so formed as to be the abode of civilized men. The scientific truths which are developed are not the less valuable, because there is still within them spiritual instruction, which the world has hitherto been unprepared to see and acknowledge.

THE *ANCIENT* CHURCH CONTRASTED WITH THE *NEW* CHURCH——WHY GOD NOW LIMITS HIS REVELATION TO THE BIBLE[213b]

¶ 72

[I]n the most ancient church, represented by Adam, when mankind were in a state of innocence and simplicity, their spiritual senses were opened and they saw and conversed with angels as with each other. But after they had fallen from that state of innocence and simplicity, this intercourse could no longer be permitted without great danger. Their internal senses were accordingly closed and they became ignorant of their connexion with the spiritual world and even of its existence. The Lord however did not leave himself entirely without witness, and this communication was permitted occasionally as the purposes of divine Providence required. Without it, the Sacred Scripture could not have been written. That the spiritual eyes of the prophets were opened, is evident from their being called seers. There could be no propriety in the use of this word, unless they saw in some peculiar sense.

HOW AFFECTIONS CLOTHE THEMSELVES——CONTRAST BETWEEN THE SPIRITUAL AND NATURAL WORLDS IN THE OPERATION OF THIS PROCESS[213c]

¶ 73

In the spiritual world, internals come directly forth, and form the externals in correspondence with themselves. Thus the spiritual body is formed from, and in correspondence with the internal, spiritual man. Its form is therefore beautiful, or truly human, in proportion as the internal, which is the man himself, is a true recipient and medium of love and wisdom from the Lord. So of the garments with which angels and spirits are clothed. These are not designed by their own understandings, and made with their own hands, nor even selected by their own taste and judgment. But every one's garments are provided by him who sees the internals; and they are provided in correspondence with the internals. They are in fact produced by an influx through the internals, and make, as it were, a part of the external man. So also with the habitations in which angels and spirits live, and with the animals, trees, fruits, and all things by which they are surrounded. All these things are formed through the spirits themselves, and change as they change. . . . When the affections and thoughts, or the state of mind which produced them passes away, they also pass away.

¶ 74

But in the natural world, it is well known that this is not the case. Material things possess a fixedness and maintain a kind of permanent existence. This, however, is not

---

[213a] See Sampson Reed, "Inspiration of the Sacred Scripture," *N J M*, VIII (1834-1835), 260-271; 331-343. Excerpt is on p. 266. Cf. *Nature*, 76.4-5, and *E T E*, chap. VIII.

[213b] "Inspiration of the Sacred Scripture," *N J M*, VIII (1834-1835), 260-271; 331-343. Excerpt is on pp. 334-335.

[213c] Sampson Reed, "Distinction Between the Laws of the Spiritual World and Those of the Natural, Arising from the Fixedness of Material Things," *N J M*, VIII (1834-

because they are independent of spiritual things. For on the contrary they are entirely dependent upon them; the natural world being a world of effects, while the spiritual world is the world of the causes of those effects. But then the natural world, which is the ultimate or lowest, is the general ultimate of all things in the spiritual world. And the things of the natural world by being permanent do not become independent of the spiritual world; but only independent of those particular individuals in whose natural vicinity they are situated. For instance, nothing can be produced in the natural world, except from a spiritual cause. But when it is once formed, it becomes an ultimate receptive of influx from the spiritual world, and from any and every part of the spiritual world, where there are qualities corresponding with it. And so long as these qualities any where remain in the spiritual world, they may continue to give it a life and soul.

A LIST OF SAMPSON REED'S ARTICLES IN THE *NEW JERUSALEM MAGAZINE* (1827-1872) [215]

1835), 95-101. Excerpts are from pp. 95-96.

[215] See the *New Jerusalem Magazine: Index to Vols. I-XLIV*, N.Y., 1882, pp. 196-198. Reed's articles published after 1872 are not given here. Articles about Reed, in addition to those cited in footnote 1, include: "Note of Carlyle Complimentary to the *Growth of the Mind*," *N J M*, XIII, 476ff.; "Reed Appointed Editor of the *N J M* by General Convention, 1854," *N J M*, XXVII, 2ff.; "Misrepresentation Concerning Reed Corrected," *N J M*, XXXI, 326ff.

Emerson heard Sampson Reed's "Oration on Genius"[216] at the Harvard Commencement on August 21, 1821. He secured a copy, which he considered "a treasure," and praised the work throughout his life as the creation of an original mind.[217] The preceding analysis makes quite clear the fact that many of Emerson's significant doctrines were announced or confirmed in Reed's remarks: self-reliance, or dependence on God within;

[216] Reprinted in *E T E*, II, 9-12.
[217] See *Letters*, III, 74; also I, 306. See *E T E*, II, 9, for evidence that Charles also received a copy—one from Joseph Lyman in Oct., 1830.

the reality of the world of spirit as opposed to the phenomenal order; the feebleness of the arts and sciences when separated from the Source of all being; the importance of the genuine man[218] rather than the successful or so-called "great" man; the necessary harmony of philosophy and religion; and the optimistic announcement of a better world to come. This early address, together with Reed's famous little book and the strong influence of Coleridge, had an important influence on Emerson's "Statement of the First Philosophy" and thereafter on all his speculations.[219] On September 10, 1826, Emerson hailed the appearance of the *Growth of the Mind* as a "revelation" the like of which had seldom been issued by the American press.[220] Three days later he wrote William that he had discovered one of the best books he had ever seen.[221] He undoubtedly had the same work in mind when he wrote to his Aunt Mary on September 23:[222]

> [I]t is one of the feelings of modern philosophy that it is wrong to regard ourselves so much in an historical light as we do,——putting Time between God and us,——and that it were fitter to regard every moment of the existence of the universe as a new creation, and all as a revelation proceeding each moment from the Divinity to the mind of the observer. . . . We ought not, therefore, to have this mighty regard to the long antiquity of its growth, and to the genuineness or fallacy of pretensions on which the dust of sixteen or eighteen centuries has gathered, but consider its present condition as a thing entirely independent of the ways and means whereby it came into that condition, and, neither seeing what it was nor hearing what it said to past generations, examine what it is, and hear what it saith to us.

On September 29, he again wrote to William about Reed's book, declaring it to be the richest work of its sort since Plato and asserting that its author merited the chair of philosophy at Harvard, recently vacated by Levi Frisbie. He was slightly amused, however, that such a profound essay could have been written entirely in a drug store.[223] Sometime in October he received an unenthusiastic letter from Aunt Mary and hastened to reply with questions:[224]

> Can anything be more greatly, more wisely writ? Has any modern hand touched the harp of great nature so rarely? Has any looked so shrewdly into the subtile and concealed connexion of man and nature, of earth and heaven? Has any, in short, produced such curiosity to see the farther progress, the remoter results, of the caste of intellect to which he belongs? I speak for myself, and not for another. I believe he must have admirers, but I have not seen any. The Sabbath after it came out, Dr. Channing delivered a discourse obviously founded upon it. And, as to his sect, you know they exult in the independent testimony of poor Wordsworth,[225] to the same truths which they get from Swedenborg.

On October 23, he promised to send the volume to William.[226] His first sermon (October 15) mentioned the preëxistent harmony between thoughts and things——a favorite theme with Reed and the Sweden-

---

[218] See Emerson's eloquent sermon on "The Genuine Man," delivered on the eve of his leaving the active ministry, *Y E S*, 180-190.   [220] *Journals*, II, 116-117 (Sept. 10, 1826).
[219] See chap. VII under June 10, 1835.   [221] *Letters*, I, 173 (Sept. 13, 1826).
[223] See Cabot, *Memoir*, I, 159-160. Cf. *Letters*, I, 174-175. See ¶s. 1-3.
[224] *Letters*, I, 176.
[224] *Journals*, II, 124.
[225] See *Letters*, I, 173. Aunt Mary had expressed her opinion in a letter dated Sept. 25, 1826. She thought it trite, obscure and Swedenish, and believed its best passages showed the influence of Wordsworth. (Reed had chosen lines from Wordsworth for his title page. See *supra*.)
[226] *Letters*, I, 178.

borgians. During November he seems to have applied Reed's theory of poetic form to the composition of "The spirits of the wise sit on the clouds."[227] The freedom and metrical irregularity seen in many of the philosophical or meditative poems still excluded from the canon are probably the result of Emerson's deliberate effort to follow that theory, and not evidence of incomplete or unpolished experiments.

In 1827,[228] Emerson described the age as one of Transcendentalism, with metaphysics and ethics looking *within*, and he selected Sampson Reed as the American representative of this philosophy. Having begun to write occasional sermons about this time, he found Reed's book and published articles both inspirational and suggestive. The fact, moreover, that contemporaries beheld much New-Church truth in his pulpit exercises leads me to believe that Reed and the *N J M* may have had a strong influence on at least the following compositions, still unpublished:[229]

"Change and Permanence"	"Acquiring True Knowledge"
"What is Man?"	"Reason and Revelation"
"Pride and Humility"[230]	"The Fear of Death"
"Progress of Religious Opinion"	"Doing the Will of God"
"Affections for God Can Be Cultivated"	"Spiritual Influence Reciprocal"[237]
"Religion is Doing One's Duty"[231]	"Spiritual Discernment"[238]
"Christianity the Medicine of Immortality"[232]	"We Are Not Our Own"[239]
"Cultivating the Mind"	"Freedom"
"A True Account of the Soul"	"No Harm Can Befall a Good Man"
"The Childlike Character"[233]	"All Truth is Related"
"Salvation, Now"[234]	"The Objects of Education"[240]
"The Virtue of Humility"[235]	"Words are Things"[241]
"Spiritual Improvement Unlimitable"[236]	"The Record of Time"

On February 10, 1830, Emerson quoted Reed on the miraculous.[242] On May 12, he wrote that there were a few men in every age who, like Jesus, taught as "having authority," and that Sampson Reed would be one if he were only a talker.[242a] On July 30 (?), he was reading Reed's articles along with Wordsworth and Montaigne.[243] On September 24, Charles sought to borrow William's copy of the "Oration on Genius." [244] On October 27, Emerson spoke of the generalization which gave elevation to all Reed's

---

[227] See *Journals*, II, 130-132. Cf. ¶s. 48-52.
[228] *Journals*, II, 164.
[229] See the remark of Dr. Artemas Stebbins, pastor at Bridgewater and vicinity, in *Journals*, III, 266 (Mar. 21, 1834). The following sermon titles are taken from *Y E S*, 263-271. The influence of Sampson Reed and the Swedenborgians in the published sermons, "Religion and Society" (Oct. 27, 1833), "The Miracle of Our Being" (Sept. 7, 1834) and others is unmistakable.
[230] See ¶ 47. See *Journals*, III, 496 (June 26, 1835).
[231] He may apply herein some aspects of the Swedenborgian Doctrine of Uses. Cf. also ¶ 62.
[232] Cf. ¶ 64.
[233] See ¶s. 27-28.
[234] See ¶s. 1-3.
[235] See note 230 above.
[241] See ¶s. 6 and 52.
[242a] See *Journals*, II, 296.
[243] *Letters*, I, 306.
[236] See ¶s. 38-43, 59-62. Cf. *Nature*, 80.3-4.
[237] Cf. *Journals*, II, 455-456 (Jan. 27, 1832).
[238] Cf. ¶ 8.
[239] Cf. ¶s. 46-47 and *Journals*, II, 363-364.
[240] See *Journals*, III, 416-417, and ¶s. 23-26; 35-37.
[242] See *Journals*, II, 289. Cf. ¶ 12.
[244] *Letters*, I, 306 fn. Cf. also p. 173 fn.

writing[245] and wrote to Edward on December 24 (?) that Reed had had no fear of death since college days ten years before.[246]

On January 10, 1831, Emerson echoed the "Oration on Genius" while discussing the subject of great men.[247] On March 4, he declared genius to be reception from God and in no sense an increase of a man's own individuality.[248] On July 8, he said that in good writing, *words were one with things*.[249]

On January 27, 1832, he wrote of his conversation with Reed and Thomas Worcester on the communication between men and spirits, on unconscious reciprocal influences and on the fact that God *dissolves*[250] men.[251] On September 14, he suggested that the cure for the fear of death was to animate the soul with *love* and *uses*——to give life worthy ends,[252] and two days later he preached on "Indifference to Death."[253] On October 2, he saw wisdom in Reed's article on "External Restraint" and soliloquized about our terrible inner freedom.[254] Almost a year later, on Sunday, August 25, 1833, he visited Thomas Carlyle and mentioned with enthusiasm his Swedenborgian druggist.[255]

1 8 3 4

On May 14, he sent Carlyle a copy of the *Growth of the Mind*.[256] Reed had earlier said in "Miracles" that the miraculous was the "measure of our alienation from God;"[257] on June 5, Emerson slightly modified the expression and added a figure which was later to appear in the Orphic Poet's lines: Christ's precepts, he said, flowed from periods of illumination like our own. Their value lies in the fact that they show *how high the waters flowed* when spiritual reception was at its best and also indicate a *measure of our deficiency*. "The wonder that is felt at these precepts is a measure of our unreason."[258] On September 7, he quoted Reed's "Sleep" in a sermon, "The Miracle of our Being."[259] On November 20, he sent Carlyle several of Reed's papers, including "Self-Love Essential Evil."[260]

[245] *Journals*, II, 331.
[246] See *Letters*, I, 315. Cf. ¶s. 4 and 64.
[247] See *Journals*, II, 354. Cf. *E T E*, II, 9-10.
[248] *Journals*, II, 363-364. Cf. ¶s. 46-47.
[249] See *Journals*, II, 401. Cf. ¶s. 5 and 52.
[250] See *Nature*, 88.12, and section XII of "A Statement of the First Philosophy," chap. VII under June 10, 1835.
[251] *Journals*, II, 455-456. The theme of reciprocal spiritual influence is developed in Emerson's "The Right Hand of Fellowship to the Rev. Hersey Bradford Goodwin" (Feb. 17, 1830), in *Uncollected Writings*, N.Y., [1912], pp. 11-14. In it Emerson mentions the beautiful sentiment of ancient philosophy that "God had so intimately linked all wise men to each other that, if one should only lift his finger in Rome, all the rest were benefited by it, through Egypt or Asia."
[252] See *Journals*, II, 511. Cf. ¶s. 4, 35-37, 59-62, 64.
[253] *Y E S*, 270.35 (Sept. 16, 1832). This sermon he preached ten times.
[254] See *Journals*, II, 517. Cf. ¶s. 29-32.
[255] This fact may be inferred from *Carlyle-Emerson Corr.*, I, 17.
[256] *Ibid.*, I, 17.
[257] See ¶ 12.
[258] See *Journals*, III, 303-304. Cf. *Nature*, 81.1 and 88.19-23.
[259] See *Y E S*, 203.26. Cf. ¶ 34. Sleep, says Emerson, prevents atheism. In *Journals* II, 64 (Mar., 1825) he said that the *eye* was proverbially called the cure for atheism.
[260] See *Carlyle-Emerson Corr.*, I, 32, and ¶ 57. The evidence lies in the paraphrase: "The poetry of the Old Church is the reality of the New."

On November 25, he wrote to James Freeman Clarke:[261] "Have you read Sampson Reed's *Growth of the Mind?* I rejoice to be contemporary with that man, and cannot wholly despair of the society in which he lives; there must be some oxygen yet, and La Fayette is only just dead." On November 26, he again reflected on the best means of overcoming the fear of death and stressed doing one's duty.[262] On December 27, the "Oration on Genius" once more suggested his blotting-book exercise:[263]

There is in every man a determination of character to a peculiar end, counteracted often by unfavorable fortune, but more apparent, the more he is left at liberty. This is called his genius, or his nature, or his turn of mind. The object of Education should be to remove all obstructions, and let this natural force have free play and exhibit its peculiar product. It seems to be true that no man in this is deluded. This determination of his character is to something in his nature; something real. This object is called his Idea.[264] It is that which rules his most advised actions, those especially that are most his, and is most distinctly discerned by him in those days or moments when he derives the sincerest satisfaction from his life. It can only be indicated by any action, not defined by anything less than the aggregate of all his genuine actions; perhaps then only approximated.

1835

On January 6, Emerson for the first time visited the Swedenborgian Chapel in Boston and after the service told Reed that the sermon, except at one point, would not have disturbed congregations of any other church.[265] On January 23, he complimented Benjamin Peter Hunt on having the discrimination to appreciate the writings of Sampson Reed.[266] On June 20, he again quoted Reed on language, remarking that in heaven it would be *one with things.*[267] On June 26, he listed Reed with Dante, Milton, Jesus and Chaucer as having discussed the mystery of humility.[268] In the rough draft of his "Historical Address" (June 29), he mentioned Reed's observation that the ant had no provision in its daily program for sleep.[269] On July 4, he seems to have recalled Reed's discussion of the character of genuine poetry and the fine arts.[270] On July 15, he called Webster, Wordsworth and Reed divine savages and natural thinkers.[271] Writing to Elizabeth P. Peabody on August 3, he indicated his belief in unconscious spiritual influences and his acceptance of the Swedenborgian position on the gradual improvement of the world through the righting of man's moral nature. A brighter future would dawn, he believed with Sampson Reed, when man occupied his *correct place* in the universal order. Part of the letter is redolent of Reed's remarks on the sciences in the *Growth of the Mind:*[272]

[261] See Oliver Wendell Holmes, *Ralph Waldo Emerson*, Boston, 1885, p. 80.
[262] See *Journals*, III, 373-374. See under Sept. 14, 1832, in the present chapter.
[263] See *Journals*, III, 416-417. See ¶s. 46-47. Cf. ¶s. 23-26; 35-37. See also Emerson's unpub. sermon, "The Objects of Education."
[264] Cf. *Nature*, 94.13-15.
[265] See *Journals*, III, 430; 432.
[266] *Letters*, I, 433.
[267] *Journals*, III, 492. See ¶s. 6 and 52.
[268] *Journals*, III, 496. See ¶ 47.
[269] *Journals*, III, 498. See ¶ 59 and *Nature*, 36.13-20.
[270] *Journals*, III, 501. See *E T E*, II, 10-11; 21-25.
[271] *Journals*, III, 505.
[272] See *Letters*, I, 450. See *Journals*, III, 530-532. Cf. *Journals*, III, 518.

The two attributes of wisdom & goodness[273] always face & always approach each
other. Each when perfect becomes the other. Yet to the moral nature belongs sovereignty, & so we have an instinctive faith that to it all things shall be added, that the moral
nature being righted, the circulations[274] of the Universe take effect thro' the man as a
member in its place, & so he learns sciences after a natural or divine way.[275] A good
deed conspires with all nature . . . but there's a kind of falsehood in the enunciation
of a chemical or astronomical law by an unprincipled savant.[276]

On August 5, he spoke of writers who wisely trusted the reception of their
first thoughts——who merely held the pen while the Spirit acted upon
and through them.[277] On November 5, in his "Introductory Lecture on
English Literature," he discoursed at length on the Doctrine of Correspondences and drew upon Reed and the Swedenborgians for much of the
substance and phraseology.[278]

1 8 3 6

On February 28, Emerson recalled Reed's views on dignity.[279] On June
22, while engaged in planning the last two chapters of *Nature*, he quoted
from the "Oration on Genius" and called Reed his "early oracle:"[280]

How hard to write the truth. "Let a man rejoice in the truth, and not that he has
found it," said my early oracle. Well, so soon as I have seen the truth I clap my hands
and rejoice, and go back to see it and forward to tell men. I am so pleased therewith
that presently it vanishes. Then am I submiss, and it appears "without observation."[281]
I write it down, and it is gone. . . . The Reason refuses to play at couples with Understanding; to subserve the private ends of the understanding.

On June 28, he wrote that *Nature* was almost completed and that it would
be approximately the size of Reed's *Growth of the Mind*.[282] On October 29,
he confessed that he had always considered Reed's "Oration on Genius"
together with William Collins' "Ode on the Passions" and each of Shakespeare's plays as a work of genius. The writers themselves, like all geniuses,
had become transparent to him, being only the manifestations of the love
of truth in God.[283]

It is difficult to summarize Reed's influence on *Nature*, but a few suggestions can be made. The prose form of the Orphic Poet's lines may be
indebted to Reed's theory of poetry.[284] Reed's views of time and eternity—
—of God acting in the eternal present as constant influx——undoubtedly
influenced the introductory and concluding chapters.[285] His defense of the
uniqueness of every individual mind[286] and his interpretation of the Doc-

---

[273] See ¶s. 55, 58-62.
[274] See *Nature*, 16.21. Cf. ¶ 19.
[275] See "Growth of the Mind," *E T E*, II, 20-21.
[276] Cf. *Nature*, 82.12.
[277] See *Journals*, III, 533. Cf. ¶ 46, 61-62.
[278] See my abstract of this lecture in a later section of the present volume.
[279] *Journals*, IV, 16. Cf. ¶ 46.
[280] See *Journals*, IV, 74-75. Cf. ¶s. 46 and 44.
[281] See *Nature*, 95.8, and Luke 17:20.
[282] See *Letters*, II, 26, and Cabot, *Memoir*, I, 259.
[283] See *Journals*, IV, 131-132. See *E T E*, II, 9-12.
[284] See ¶s. 48-52, esp. 51. See also Emerson's "The Poet," *Works*, III, 3-42. Walt Whitman's verse seems to be the best example of Reed's theory.
[285] See ¶s. 1-3, 17. The influence reappears in the essay on "Self-Reliance."
[286] See ¶s. 23-26.

trine of Uses, namely, that every man has a distinctive part to play in the whole,[287] strengthened Emerson's belief in self-reliance as well as his concept of Universal Man, who in time and space was obliged to appear divided into specialized functions of poet, mystic, scholar etc.[288] Reed encouraged Emerson by announcing a bright future, a universal religion and the end of the reign of John Locke.[289] He stressed the moral influence of nature and the relevance of the Ten Commandments to science and to all departments of life.[290] He discussed the great virtue of humility or dependence on the Source of spiritual influx, and asserted that the highest *use* of nature was to draw forth the latent energies of the soul, leading man away from his self-love.[291] He illustrated picturesquely that men are now strangers to both the worlds of spirit and of matter[292]——that they yet know the uses of only a few natural objects.[293] He offered explanations for pain and for the unpleasant appearances in nature by pointing to man's evil affections.[294] He provided Emerson with many useful illustrations: that man's departure from the divine order is attended by loss of knowledge and ignorance about his true condition;[295] that the Lord is ever trying to make men innocent, unconscious receivers of divine energy or grace; that the period of infancy seems best to illustrate the activity of unobstructed influx;[296] that man never entirely forgets his divine vocation;[297] that surprise at spiritual phenomena, like wonder in the presence of Biblical miracles, is an indication that men have departed from their original high plane of spiritual reception, have lost a view of the whole, and have forgotten to live like children, fully aware that they are never absent from their Father's house.[298]

But like other members of the "Old Church,"[299] Emerson considered Reed's concepts to be poetry——certainly poetry of a high order, but poetry nonetheless——and the quotation marks appearing in the orphic sections——to be discussed in a later chapter——are meant to indicate that some of the ideas so enclosed should not be interpreted literally. When, therefore, it became apparent that Emerson's view of Christianity was still a variety of Unitarianism so decorated with New-Church "poetry" that even New-Church readers were confused, it was inevitable that the Swedenborgians, whom he had earlier called the *transcendentalists* of the age,[300] should evaluate and openly repudiate the Concord transcendental school. Reed made the position of his church quite clear on February 28, 1838, as we have seen above. In the quiet of his study, on June 22 of that

---

[287] See ¶s. 35-37.
[288] See the introduction to *The American Scholar* as well as the general framework of *Representative Men*. See *Nature*, 87.13.
[289] See ¶s. 24, 38-43.
[290] See *Nature*, 51.12—52.10; 53.1-23. Cf. ¶s. 9-10.
[291] See *Nature*, 34.1-7; 76.1—77.2; 82.20; cf. ¶. 8-9, 45.
[292] See *Nature*, 81.4, and ¶ 11.
[293] See *Nature*, 81.7ff. and ¶ 22.
[294] See *Nature*, 34.1-3; 81.2ff.; 94.13-22. See ¶s. 18-21.
[295] See *Nature*, 88.11—89.11; cf. ¶ 21.
[296] See *Nature*, 88.6-10. Cf. ¶s. 27-28.
[297] See *Nature*, 89.3ff. and ¶ 11.
[298] See *Nature*, 95.10-12. Cf. ¶s. 11-16.
[299] See ¶ 57 and *Carlyle-Emerson Corr.*, I, 32-33.
[300] See *Journals*, II, 164.

year, Emerson retaliated by writing in his journals that it was now impossible to know "S. R.," entrenched as he was in the mind of Swedenborg and protected by the immense arrogance and sly bigotry of his organization.[301] Though the breach was irreparable, Reed's influence continued strong and significant. Emerson seems to have lent his own manuscript copy of the "Oration on Genius" for anonymous publication[302] in the *Æsthetic Papers*, edited by Miss Peabody in 1849,[303] and throughout the remainder of his life found in Reed's works many favorite ideas for both his public lectures and literary essays.[304]

---

[301] See *Letters*, I, 173 fn. See Reed's review of Emerson's *An Oration Delivered before the Phi Beta Kappa Society* (August 31, 1837) in *N J M*, XI (1837-1838), 67-72 (Oct., 1837), for further evidence of the growing rift. Reed began (p. 67): "Mr. Emerson has as yet published but little; at least under his own name. But he is a writer of very considerable power, and is favorably known as a popular lecturer on various subjects. We cannot at present pretend to enter into any analysis of his mind and character, even as exhibited in this oration; but shall confine ourselves to a few brief extracts and cursory remarks." He concluded (p. 72) as follows: "It is most true, that Swedenborg's 'literary value has never yet been rightly estimated;' and indeed it may well be doubted whether it ever will be, by those who look upon him, merely as a literary man. They may extol his imagination, and his precision and accuracy. But those can have but a poor idea, even of his literary character, who have not studied his writings too well to speak of his having attempted to engraft any thing 'on the popular Christianity of his time.' We have no doubt but Mr. Emerson intended to speak respectfully and truly of Swedenborg. But his remarks show that he has read him little;——or rather, to little purpose. We intended to have reserved more room for this part of the subject; and may perhaps recur to it again hereafter. It derives some importance from the fact, that many seem to suppose, that Mr. Emerson's general views are nearly allied to those of the New Church."

[302] It would be interesting to know why it was issued anonymously. Did Reed request it in view of the auspices of the new publication, or did Miss Peabody publish the work without seeking Reed's permission?

[303] I have noted in *E T E*, II, 11-12, the variants between the MS. used by Miss Peabody and that owned by Charles Emerson, the gift of Joseph Lyman in Oct., 1830.

[304] See, for example, the quotation in "Memory," *Natural History of the Intellect* (*Works*, XII), 104: "Sampson Reed says, 'The true way to store the memory is to develop the affections.'" Cf. ¶ 25.

G. OEGGER AND THE LANGUAGE OF NATURE

The subject of this sketch was born probably during the last decade of the eighteenth century at Bitche,[1] not far from Metz, in the Department of Moselle (northeastern France) in what came to be the Lorraine portion of Alsace-Lorraine. He seems to have been carefully trained in the language and literature of both Germany and France, for in later years he published his works in both languages, translated the writings of others and, it seems, exercised his ministry on both sides of the Franco-German border. These facts seem to account for the wide variety of forms which his name assumes on the title pages of his works and in the histories of the New Church:

Guillaume Caspar Lencroy Oegger[2]
Wilhelm Gaspar Lineweg Oegger[3]
Wilhelm Caspar Lineweg Oegger[4]
J. G. E. Oegger (or O'Egger)[5]
Gustave Oegger[6]
G. Oegger[7]
W. Oegger[8]

By 1822, it seems that he had entered the priesthood of the Church of Rome and had become "premier vicaire demissionnaire de la cathédrale [*i.e.*, Notre Dame] de Paris."[9] In that year he published a large volume called the *Manuel de Religion et de Morale*[10] and in the year following the *Traité Philosophique sur la Nature de L'âme*, a work that indicated his interest in psychic phenomena and hypnotism.[11] Just when he became confessor to the Queen of France or when his various speculations led him to become dissatisfied with the Church of Rome is uncertain. I cannot discover when he became "Professor of Philosophy at the French University."[12] It appears, however, that he received the doctrines of the New Church at Paris in 1826 through the zeal of Captain Jean Jacques Bernard (1791-1828), a French soldier who spread Swedenborgian tenets through-

[1] Joseph Marie Quérard, *La France Littéraire*, (10 vols.) Paris, 1827-1839, VI, 473.
[2] See *Journals*, III, 505 fn.
[3] C. G. Kayser, *Vollständiges Bücher-Lexikon*, Leipzig, vols. covering 1835-1840 and 1840-1846, *s.v.*
[4] Félix Bourguelot and Alfred Maury, *La Littérature Française Contemporaine, 1827-1849*, Paris, 1854, V, 546.
[5] See the catalogue of the Bibliothèque Nationale.
[6] See Carl Theophilus Odhner, *Annals of the New Church* [Vol. I, 1688-1850], Phila., 1898, index *et passim*.
[7] On title pages in the catalogue of the Bibliothèque Nationale.
[8] See C. G. Kayser, *op. cit.*, *s.v.*
[9] Joseph M. Quérard, *op. cit.*, VI, 473.
[10] *Manuel de religion et de morale, en forme de Livre de Prières, ou Réflexions et sentiments rédigés selon le véritable esprit de la religion de Jésus-Christ*, Paris, 1822.
[11] *Traité philosophique sur la nature de l'âme et ses facultés, où l'on examine le rapport qu'ont avec la morale le magnétisme de M. Mesmer et le système de Dr. Gall*, Paris, 1823.
[12] See *Intellectual Repository of the New Church* for 1846, p. 109, and Odhner, *op. cit.*, 328.

out France and Spain during the last eight years of his life.[13]

Bernard was about thirty-two when I first knew him. He was Captain of the Grenadiers of the 23d of the Line, and decorated with the ribbon of the Legion of Honor, from 1813. He had been Captain of the Young Guard under the empire. During all his life, he was studious; and carried, even into the camp, his taste for study. His leisure being great after the restoration, he delivered himself still more to it. He studied the various systems of philosophy; and was vividly impressed by the writings of St. Martin, of Jacob Boehm, and of Law. Some volume of Swedenborg's fell into his hands in 1820; and he had the presentiment, that there was the absolute truth for which he had been searching so long. In the same year (1820), he became acquainted at Paris with Madame de St. Amour, Mons. and Madame Gobert, and some other persons. Mr. Gobert had for some time adopted the truths of the New Church. Bernard was on terms of intimacy with him, and soon partook of all his convictions.[14]

In 1826, he went to Paris; and the house of Mr. Gobert was the usual place of meeting for the disciples of the New Church, the number of which increased. There lived the pious Oegger, who was yet ignorant of the existence of the New Dispensation; but, yielding to the cries of an honest conscience, he voluntarily resigned the place of First Vicar to the Cathedral of Paris. Bernard and Gobert, having encountered him, presented to him the truths of the New Church, which he adopted; and to them he devoted the remainder of his life.[15]

In 1827, he issued an enlarged edition of the *Manuel de Religion et de Morale*[16] with an introduction explaining his renunciation of the Roman Catholic priesthood and setting forth the ideas of the new faith. That same year he translated into French, apparently from the English, a small work entitled *Allocution Pastorale*[17] by Bishop Luscombe,[18] chaplain of the British Embassy in Paris and Anglican bishop for part of the continent. He also issued a pamphlet, *Éloge de Monsieur de Thou*.[19] In 1829, *Le Vrai Messie*,[20] his largest and, perhaps, most significant work came from the press. It appears to have been his first distinctly Swedenborgian treatise and was an elaborate exposition of the doctrine of correspondences as applied to the Bible. It must have occasioned some discussion, for the following year he issued a pamphlet *Lettre à Messieurs de Rothschild et à leurs coreligionnaires sur le Vrai Messie et la Langue de la Nature*.[21] It was followed, in 1831, by a book, *Essai d'un Dictionnaire de la Langue de la Nature*.[22] Another pamphlet appeared in 1832 in the form

---

[13] See S. A. Blanchet, "Letter from France," *N J M*, XXXI (1858-1859), 460-466. The letter is dated Jan. 3, 1859. See also Odhner, *op. cit.*, 328.

[14] Blanchet, *loc. cit.*, 460-461. [15] Blanchet, *loc. cit.*, 463.

[16] *Manuel de religion et de morale, ou Livre de Prières universel pour les chrétiens éclairés de toutes les communions*, Paris, 1827. The cover bears this additional note: "Précédé de quelques explications sur sa renonciation aux fonctions ecclésiastiques, et de quelques idées sur la Réforme."

[17] M. H. Thornhill Luscombe, *Allocution Pastorale Adressée aux Anglais qui sont en France*, Paris, 1827.

[18] Michael Henry Thornhill Luscombe (1776-1846) received the M.A. in 1805 and the D.C.L. in 1810. He was consecrated to a continental bishopric by the bishops of the Scottish Episcopal Church and appointed embassy chaplain at Paris in 1825. He helped found the *Christian Remembrancer* in 1841. Besides sermons his publications include *The Church of Rome Compared with the Bible, the Fathers of the Church and the Church of England* (1839). He died at Lausanne.

[19] *Éloge de Monsieur de Thou proposé par l'Académie Française pour le Prix d'Éloquence en 1824*, Paris, 1827.

[20] *Le Vrai Messie, ou l'Ancien et le Nouveau Testaments examinés d'après les principes de la langue de la nature*, Paris, 1829.

[21] Paris, 1830.

[22] *Essai d'un Dictionnaire de la Langue de la Nature, ou Explication de huit cents images hiéroglyphiques, sources de toutes les anciennes mythologies et clef de l'Ecriture*

of an open letter to the Minister of Public Instruction.[23] Two years later, he published *Rapports Inattendus établis entre le Monde Matériel et le Monde Spirituel*,[24] a work which had grown out of his own mystical experiences and which, therefore, seemed to his fellow churchmen to do harm to the cause. (Swedenborg had written that God no longer sent spirits to men, but confined revelation to the spiritual sense of the Bible!) In 1835, Oegger issued *Nouvelles Questions Philosophiques*,[25] a discussion of the principal New-Church doctrines. Meanwhile, the storm of criticism resulting from the appearance of *Rapports Inattendus* had been growing. The work had been widely circulated, both in the French original and in a German translation, *Stille Wege*, and appeared in a collection of books which Swedenborgians in America had commissioned Dr. J. F. Immanuel Tafel to distribute as a missionary enterprise. Tafel entered into an agreement with the university library at Tübingen,[26] but withheld Oegger's work, rebuking its author by letter and letting it be known that such "refractory opposition of presumptuous individuals against their mother, the New Church, constitutes a transgression of the fourth commandment, and, as it contains a menace at the same time, cannot remain unpunished."[27] The "worthy Oegger," however, wrote Tafel on December 15, 1836, authorizing him to publish correspondence in which he made "use of expressions amounting to a recantation" and said, in answer to the violent attacks made against the New Church by many journals because of his book, "that the New Church rests on its own foundation, and not upon a wretched pamphlet; that he had recovered his modesty, and would solemnly declare that he looked upon one half of his communications as spurious, and could not blame any of his brethren, who, being acquainted with the mode of revelation now existing, would look upon the remainder as false and imaginary."[28]

In 1840, Oegger translated from German into French Hofaker's *Elilytha*[29] and issued book one of a new work.[30] Two years later, Elizabeth Palmer Peabody of Boston published the first sixty pages[31] of his *Le Vrai Messie*, apparently from her own translation into English, made about seven years earlier and circulated in manuscript.[32] In 1845, Oegger published two letters, originally in French, but translated under the title, *Die Kirchenreformation*,[33] addressed to Roman Catholics in Germany. It

Sainte, Paris, 1831.

[23] *Lettre à Monsieur le Ministre de l'Instruction Publique et des Cultes sur quelques nouvelles questions de philosophie*, Paris, 1832.

[24] *Rapports Inattendus établis entre le monde matériel et le monde spirituel par la découverte de la langue de la Nature, ou ma Transition à la Nouvelle Église du Seigneur, dite la Nouvelle Jérusalem, et les circonstances surnaturelles qui ont accompagné cette démarche*, Paris, 1834. Odhner, *op. cit.*, 384, dates the work (I think, wrongly) 1832.

[25] *Nouvelles Questions Philosophiques*, Tubingue, Paris et Berne, 1835. Odhner dates it (I think, wrongly) 1833.

[26] See "Letter of Dr. J. F. Immanuel Tafel," *N J M*, XI (1837-1838), 17-22.

[27] *N J M*, XI, 19.   [28] *N J M*, XI, 19-20.

[29] Ludwig Wilhelm Hofaker, *Elilytha, ou le Portique des Amis de Dieu*, Paris, 1840.

[30] *Rapport entre la Nouvelle Jérusalem céleste et la Nouvelle Jérusalem terrestre, ou le Seigneur est avec nous*, Tubingue, 1840.

[31] Reprinted in *E T E*, II, 83-98.

[32] See *Journals*, III, 505.

[33] *Die Kirchenreformation: Zwei Briefe an die Neu-katholiken und eine Anrede an die Elberfelder Gemeinde*, von W. Oegger, Elberfeld, 1845.

contained also an address to a congregation of New Churchmen in Elberfeld, Germany, which he seems to have visited. Oegger had become interested in a movement within Roman Catholicism across the border, which seemed to indicate that a new spiritual era was about to dawn upon the world.[34] In the following year he published some of his correspondence in *Lettres sur la Nécessité de Rétablir l'Harmonie etc.*[35] Writing in November, 1848, after completing a tour of the continent, T. O. Prescott communicated the following information:[36] "I learned that at Versailles, in the neighborhood of Paris, there are a few Receivers of the Doctrines; and at their head, M. Oegger, who was formerly a clergyman of distinction in the Catholic Church, and held, as I understood, the post of Confessor to the Queen. . . . There are genuine and disinterested lovers of the truth, it thus appears, in all ranks and professions, and in all countries . . . ." In the same year, Oegger issued a pamphlet, *Nos Idées*,[37] consisting of two letters of a controversial nature addressed to the editor of *La Presse*. Probably in 1849, he translated into French from the German a pamphlet by P. E. Mullensiefen, *Révélation Progressive*.[38] He was present on August 19, 1851, at the great meeting of representatives of the New Church in Freemason's Hall, London,[39] and delivered one of the principal addresses.[40] The following year he issued a small book, *Philosophie du Christianisme*[41] and, in 1853, *Cinq Lettres sur Réforme Générale*.[42] He probably died soon afterwards, for I have been able to find no further evidence of activity or of publication.

The following excerpts from Miss Peabody's edition of the introductory pages of *Le Vrai Messie*, translated into English, will serve to round out my treatment of the New-Church influence upon Emerson before the year 1837 and give a rapid view of Oegger's presentation of the Doctrine of Correspondences.

MEN ARE ABOUT TO DISCOVER THE ORIGINAL LANGUAGE OF NATURE, WHICH EXISTED BEFORE MAN'S FALL[43]

¶ 1

What has most emboldened us in this great enterprise, is the entire certainty that we have acquired, of being definitely on the road to that language of Nature, which, as every one will easily conceive, must have preceded all languages of convention; in which, indeed, we have found the greater part of our holy books to be written, and which sheds over them collectively a light too strong and unexpected for deism to resist.

---

[34] See *Intellectual Repository of the New Church* for 1846, p. 109.

[35] *Lettres sur la nécessité de rétablir l'harmonie entre les principes religieux et les principes du gouvernement, adressées a MM^rs les archevêques de Reims et de Paris, etc. Réflexions sur les réponses reçues et appel au public*, Paris, 1846. Some of these letters were sent to *L'Ami de la Religion* and to the *Journal des Débats*.

[36] T. O. Prescott, "Intelligence and Miscellany," *N J M*, XXII (1848-1849), 29.

[37] *Nos Idées sur la Nature de l'Etre divin au XIXe Siècle*, Paris, 1848.

[38] P. E. Mullensiefen, *Révélation Progressive touchant la Nature de la très Sainte Trinité*, Paris, [1849?].

[39] See *N J M*, XXIV (1851), 431-498 (Nov.) for a full account of the convention.

[40] Summarized in *N J M*, XXIV, 486-487.

[41] *Philosophie du Christianisme, ou Précis de la Vraie Religion Chrétienne, d'après les doctrines de la Nouvelle Jérusalem . . . avec une courte notice sur la vie et les ouvrages d'Emmanuel Swedenborg*, Paris, 1852.

[42] *Cinq Lettres sur une Réforme Générale*, Paris, 1853.   [43] *E T E*, II, 84; 84.

¶ 2

The thinking moralist will easily believe that, even on our terrestrial globe, however material it may now be with its degraded inhabitants, there must have existed, in times of greater perfection, means of communication different from those which are of mere convention; for, to establish conventions, it is absolutely necessary to be able previously to explain one's self. Rousseau advanced the greatest of paradoxes, when he said that the savage state was the primitive state of man: on the contrary, the savage state is nothing but the state of our greatest degradation, when, as we have become incapable of raising ourselves, God is obliged to come to our relief. All knowledge, says Plato, is remembrance, and all ignorance is forgetting. Primitively man must have been perfect, at least, in his kind; and consequently he must have had a perfect language, a language which cannot have been lost but in the lapse of ages, and of which the traces may be found, when Philosophy will direct her researches to that point.

THE VISIBLE UNIVERSE WAS FRAMED TO REPRESENT BY CORRESPOND-ENCES THE SUBSTANTIAL THOUGHTS OF THE CREATOR——THE FATHER SYMBOL EXPLAINED[44]

¶ 3

People generally have an idea, before they have reflected more profoundly, that when God produced our visible universe, the choice that he made of forms and colors for animals, plants, and minerals, was entirely arbitrary on his part. But this idea is entirely false. Man may sometimes act from whim; God never can. The visible creation, then, can not, must not (if we may use such expression) be anything but the exterior circumference of the invisible and metaphysical world; and material objects are necessarily *scoriæ* of the substantial thoughts of the Creator; *scoriæ* which must always preserve an exact relation to their first origin; in other words, visible nature must have a spiritual and moral side.[45] For God every thing is, every thing exists: "create" conveys not the same idea to him as to us. For God, to create is only to manifest. The universe, even in its minutest details, existed for God as really before the creation as after it, because it existed in him substantially, as the statue exists in the block of marble from which the sculptor extracts it.

¶ 4

Every thing we see, touch, smell; every thing, from the sun to a grain of sand, from our own body with its admirable organs, to that of the worm; every thing has flowed forth, by a supreme reason, from that world where all is spirit and life. No fibre in the animal, no blade of grass in the vegetable kingdom, no form of crystalization in inanimate matter, is without its clear and well-determined correspondence in the moral and metaphysical world. And if this is true of colors and forms, it must, by a still stronger reason, be said of the instincts of animals, and the far more astonishing faculties of man.

¶ 5

We are created men, and God is uncreated man. It was at the immediate point between the infinite which is all, and the finite which is nothing, that God and man met. And this point is life, life manifested, life revealed by emblems. Before all languages of convention and of articulated sounds, when the Creator wished to manifest or reveal himself for the first time to man, how could he have done it but by showing himself to that man under the substantial form of a father,[46] the natural emblem of God Creator?

NATURE ADMITS NEW EMBLEMS AS A RESULT OF MAN'S GROWTH OR DEGRADATION[47]

¶ 6

An infinitely little degree of consent to receive, which forms our moral liberty, is the only thing that we have for our own. And merely by an inspection of the objects by which a man is surrounded, or of some of the customs which he has adopted, a superior intelligence can undoubtedly determine the moral worth of his being; for according as moral beings (for whom alone inferior nature exists) modify themselves, that nature must admit emblems analogous to the new perfections or degradations.[48]

---

[44] *E T E*, II, 84-85; 85; 86.
[45] Quoted in *Nature*, 44.8-13.
[46] See *Nature*, 35.1-4.

[47] *E T E*, II, 85.
[48] Cf. Sampson Reed ¶s. 18a-22.

THE FUTURE WORLD EXACTLY PARALLELS THE PRESENT ONE EXCEPT THAT IT IS SUBSTANTIAL AND NOT PHENOMENAL[49]

¶ 7

All these ideas, though new, will not surprise those philosophers who know that nature is always conformable to herself, or, as Leibnitz expresses it, she never does anything by leaps and bounds. According to this philosophic apothegm, our future existence will, in reality, differ from the present only by a slight variation; and this variation is that from a material to a substantial world. We shall pass to the future existence, as we enter into an agreeable dream; all nature will accompany us there.[50]

IN PROVIDING THE LANGUAGE FOR OUR MORAL AND INTELLECTUAL LIFE NATURE ENABLES MAN TO BECOME CONSCIOUS OF THE MORAL AND METAPHYSICAL WORLD[51]

¶ 8

Any one may learn these truths from daily experience, without any great reasoning. Do but take a dictionary of morals, and examine the terms in it. You will see that all of them, from the first to the last, are derived from corporeal and animal life. The birth, growth, decay and death of the body, its state of health or of sickness, of strength or of weakness, have alone furnished correspondent ideas in the moral man. Each member of that body, considered in relation to its terrestrial use and employment, offers the same results. All the emblems that can be supplied by agriculture, the arts and trades, the different manners among men of feeding and clothing themselves, have been laid under contribution to furnish the means for characterizing the different varieties of moral and intellectual life, in individuals as in societies; and, but for all those emblems furnished by nature herself, the moral and metaphysical world would have remained entirely buried in the eternal abyss.[52]

HOW ONE PROCEEDS TO DISCOVER THE LANGUAGE OF NATURE[53]

¶ 9

Finding ourselves thus placed on the road to the language of nature, by the inspired books, we may now, without fear of being misled, cite some of the emblems of nature, which men themselves have preserved in their speech without knowing that they really belonged to a distinct language. Thus the general instinct of mankind has long since determined the moral signification of the sun, as well as that of his heat and light. The sun has always been the principal emblem of the Divinity upon earth; his heat that of love, and his light that of truth: thence, in times of superstition and barbarity, the adoration of the sun, and the worship of fire, was found with almost all people. Gold also signifies, generally among all nations, what is precious; stone, what is solid; fat, what is rich; and a hundred other emblems, which it would be tedious to repeat. In general, the fewer conventional words people had, the more they needed natural emblems; and when they had no conventional terms at all, which is quite conceivable, at least of moral terms, then they had absolutely nothing but emblems in their language.[54]

THE SPIRIT LOVES THE HUMAN FORM——MAN, THE MICROCOSM, IS THE MOST PERFECT EMBLEM——HE ALONE IS PERPENDICULAR[55]

¶ 10

In all times, some profound minds have perceived that man was the most perfect possible emblem; consequently, the natural and true emblem of all that can be called intelligence and life. The name microcosm, or world in little, given to man by the ancient sages, would be enough to prove it. The human form is, in truth, a real form of love and wisdom; capable, in itself alone, of characterizing all the possible varieties of the moral being, taken in its complex state. Living, intelligent existence could not have any other form than the human. The angel is nothing but the man spirit, or the substantial man.

---

[49] *E T E*, II, 86.
[50] Adapted in *Nature*, 88.2-4.
[53] *E T E*, II, 91. See pp. 95-98 for the key vocabulary which he used in interpreting the spiritual sense of Holy Scripture.
[54] See *Nature*, 36.21—37.6.
[55] *E T E*, II, 91. Cf. *ibid.*, II, 69-75, and *Nature*, 57.4-23.

[51] *E T E*, II, 87.
[52] Cf. *Nature*, 45.9-12.

¶ 11

After this king of nature, all other animals, always less perfect forms of life, always inclining the head more and more towards the ground, are emblems of the different varieties of degraded life or intelligence. When man is what he ought to be, he differs from the angel only by the weight of matter; when man degrades himself, he runs through all the degrees of inferior life, figured by animals; each animal, by its forms and instincts, offering a particular variation of that life. The whole quadrant, from the zenith to the horizon, or from the perpendicular to the horizontal line, is thus filled up. Man and the serpent form the right angle; other animals fill the whole quadrant; and any other kind of beings is geometrically impossible.

THE LANGUAGE OF NATURE WAS SLOWLY LOST———RISE OF THE LANGUAGE OF CONVENTION[56]

¶ 12

The passage from the language of nature to languages of convention, was made by such insensible degrees that they who made it never thought of tracing the latter back to their source. They knew not the road they had traveled; but the distance appeared striking when they became attentive to it. Primitively, men could not name objects, they must show them; not corporeally, it is true, but substantially and by the force of thought; as those objects exist in God, and as we still perceive them in dreams, in which there is evidently something more than imagination.

¶ 13

When that primitive faculty of seeing and showing the immediate object of thought, and the natural emblem of sentiment was weakened, then, only, exterior signs came to join it. Thence the language of gestures, spoken at first more particularly by the eyes, the mouth, and the particular composition of the face, which at length introduced conventional sounds, and all exterior signs, such as are still found among the deaf and dumb; and, finally, those offered by hieroglyphics and writing the Scripture. At the epoch when the two manners of speaking (that by natural emblems and that by articulate sounds) were mixed, then resulted the language which is now called prophetic or extatic, in which conventional words are used only to recall the more significant emblems of nature.

HARMONY AND DISCORD IN NATURE———HOW EXPLAINED[57]

¶ 14

In the simultaneous order, the infinite is said to create, or produce the finite; the whole is said to create, or produce the part. All that produces, is Creator, or Father; all that is produced, is Son, or Truth. Substance produces form; form produces color, &c. Production refers to good, to affirmation, to reality, to order, to harmony; destruction, to evil, to negation, to falsity, to disorder, to discord. Nature, in her beauty, is the emblem of the first; terrible phenomena, elements in convulsion, the emblem of the second.

I have not been able to discover from whom Emerson secured the manuscript translation of *The True Messiah* in the summer of 1835.[58] The only available facts are these: (1) Miss Peabody published the manuscript in 1842;[59] (2) Emerson began his correspondence with her on June 12, 1835,[60] about one month before he began finding "good things" in Oegger;[61] (3) on August 3, he wrote Miss Peabody, sharing her aversion for Swedenborg's "associations" and the restrictions which they imposed.[62] It is possible and even probable that he was indebted to her

---

[56] *E T E*, II, 92. Cf. *Nature*, 37.17—38.22.

[57] *E T E*, II, 97. Cf. Sampson Reed ¶s. 18a-22, and *Nature*, 81.2-9; 94.13-22.

[58] See *Journals*, III, 505 fn.

[59] See *E T E*, II, 83-98. Emerson copied into his journals at least two passages that do not appear in the printed version. See *Journals*, III, 506 and 515 bottom.

[60] Evidence is given in *Letters*, I, 445, but the letter itself has not survived.

[61] *Journals*, III, 505.　　　　　　　　　[62] *Letters*, I, 449-451.

for the opportunity of becoming acquainted with the French Sweden-borgian. At all events, Oegger revealed to Emerson the richness of the Doctrine of Correspondences, though Emerson from the first refused to limit Nature's language to the symbolism of the family bible.[63] Oegger was welcomed, however, because he showed how God could speak to man through the phenomenal world and how the inner thoughts of man require an outer or material symbol for their complete expression.[64] Emerson copied unusually long passages from the manuscript into his blotting books[65] and later purchased a copy of the printed pamphlet for his library. Though he seems never to have mentioned Oegger by name in any of his published works, he quoted from this "French philosopher" in *Nature* and drew upon his ideas for the chapter on "Language."[66] It appears, also, that the essay on "Swedenborg" in *Representative Men* was meant to evaluate not only the Swedish mystic but also the work of his French, German and American disciples, of whom Oegger was not the least.

CONCORD RIVER — unchanged in its placid beauty
from Indian days to the present

---

[63] See *Works*, IV, 121, 134-135, and *Journals*, III, 505.
[64] *Journals*, III, 525 and 527.
[65] Not all of them appear in the printed record. See, however, *Journals*, III, 506, 512-515.
[66] See *Nature*, 35.1ff.; 39.10-20; 44.8-15.

ORATION ON GENIUS*

By SAMPSON REED

The world was always busy; the human heart has always had love of some kind; there has always been fire on the earth.[1] There is something in the inmost principles of an individual, when he begins to exist, which urges him onward; there is something in the centre of the character of a nation, to which the people aspire; there is something which gives activity to the mind in all ages, countries, and worlds. This principle of activity is love: it may be the love of good or of evil; it may manifest itself in saving life or in killing; but it is love.

The difference in the strength and direction of the affections creates the distinctions in society. Every man has a form of mind peculiar to himself. The mind of the infant contains within[2] itself the first[3] rudiments of all that will be hereafter, [59] and needs nothing but expansion; as the leaves and[4] branches and fruit of a tree are said to exist in the seed from which it springs. He[5] is bent in a particular direction; and, as some objects are of more value than others, distinctions must exist. What it is that makes a man great depends upon the state of society: with the savage, it is physical strength; with the civilized, the arts and sciences; in heaven, the[6] perception that love and wisdom are from the Divine.

There prevails an idea in the world,[7] that its[8] great men are more like God than others. This sentiment carries in its bosom sufficient evil to bar the gates of heaven. So far as a person possesses it, either with respect to himself or others, he has no connection with his Maker, no love for his neighbor, no truth in his understanding. This was at the root of heathen idolatry: it was this that[9] made men worship saints and images. It contains within[10] itself the seeds of atheism, and will ultimately make every man insane by whom it is cherished. The life which circulates in the body is found to commence in the head; but, unless it be traced through the soul up to God, it is merely corporeal, like that of the brutes.[11]

Man has often ascribed to his own power the effects of the secret operations[12] of divine truth. When the world is immersed in darkness, this is a judgment of the Most High; but the light is the effect of the innate strength of the[13] human intellect.

When the powers[14] of man begin[15] to decay, and approach an apparent dissolution,[16] who cannot see the Divinity? But what foreign aid[17] wants the man who is full of his own strength? God sends the lightning that[18] blasts the tree; but what credulity would ascribe to him the sap that[19] feeds its branches? The sight of idiotism leads to a train of religious reflections; but the face that is marked with lines of intelligence is admired for its own inherent beauty.[20] The hand of the Almighty is visible to all[21] in the stroke of death; but few see his face in the smiles of the new-born babe.

The intellectual eye of man is[22] formed to see the light, not to make it; and it is time that,[23] when the causes that[24] cloud the spiritual world are removed, man should rejoice in the [60] truth itself, and not that *he* has found it. More than once, when nothing was required but for a person to stand on this[25] world with his eyes open, has the truth been seized upon as a thing of his own making. When the power of divine truth begins to dispel the darkness, the objects that[26] are first disclosed to our view—whether men of strong understanding, or[27] of exquisite taste, or of deep learning—are called geniuses. Luther, Shakspeare, Milton, Newton, stand with the bright side towards us.

There is something which is called genius, that[28] carries in itself the seeds of its own destruction. There is an ambition which hurries a[29] man after truth, and takes away the power of attaining it. There is a desire which is null,[30] a lust which is impotence.[31] There is no understanding so powerful, that ambition may not in time bereave it of its

---

* This oration was delivered at Harvard on August 21, 1821, when Reed was candidate for the degree of Master of Arts. The text reproduced here is that found in *Æsthetic Papers*, ed. Elizabeth P. Peabody, Boston and N. Y., 1849, pp. 58-64. Verbal variations listed in the notes (to be found at the end of the oration) are those in a manuscript owned by the Ralph Waldo Emerson Memorial Association and formerly in the possession of Emerson himself. It bears the inscription: "Chas. C. Emerson from his friend, Joseph Lyman. Oct. 1830." See *Letters*, I, 306; III, 74. (Variants in capitalization, spelling and punctuation are ignored.)

last truth, even that two and two are[32] four. Know, then, that genius is divine, not when the[33] man thinks that[34] he is God, but when he acknowledges that his powers are from God. Here is the link of the finite with the infinite, of the divine with the human:[35] this is the humility which[36] exalts.

The arts have been taken from nature by human invention; and, as the mind returns to its God, they are in a measure swallowed up in the source from which[37] they came. We see, as they vanish, the standard to which we should refer them. They are not arbitrary, having no foundation[38] except in taste: they are only modified by taste, which varies according to the state of the human mind. Had we a history of music, from the war-song of the savage to the song of[39] angels, it would be a history of the affections that[40] have held dominion over the human heart. Had we a history of architecture, from the first building erected by man to the house not made with hands, we might trace the variations of the beautiful and the grand, alloyed[41] by human contrivance, to where they are lost in[42] beauty and grandeur. Had we a history of poetry, from the first rude effusions[43] to where words make one with things, and language is lost in nature, we should see the state of man in the language of licentious passion, in the songs[44] of chivalry, in the descriptions[45] of heroic valor, in the mysterious wildness of Ossian; till the [61] beauties of nature fall on the heart, as softly as the clouds on the summer's water. The mind, as it wanders from heaven, moulds the arts into its own form, and covers its nakedness. Feelings of all kinds will discover themselves in music, in painting, in poetry; but it is only when the heart is purified from every selfish and worldly passion, that they are created in real beauty; for in their origin they are divine.

Science is more fixed. It consists of the laws according to which natural things exist; and these must be either true or false. It is the natural world in the abstract, not in the concrete. But the laws according to which things exist, are from the things themselves, not the opposite. Matter has solidity: solidity makes no part of matter. If, then, the natural world is from God, the abstract properties, as dissected and combined, are from him also. If, then, science be from Him who gave the ten commandments, must not a life according to the latter facilitate[46] the acquirement of the former?[47] Can *he* love the works of God who does not love his commandments?[48] It is only necessary that the heart be purified, to have science like poetry its spontaneous growth. Self-love has given rise to many false theories, because a selfish man is disposed to make things differently from what God has made them. Because[49] God is love, nature exists; because God is love, the Bible is poetry. If, then, the love of God creates the scenery of nature, must not he whose mind is most open to this love be most sensible of natural beauties? But in nature both the sciences and the arts[50] exist embodied.

Science may be learned from ambition; but it must be by[51] the sweat of the brow. The filthy and polluted mind *may* carve beauties from nature, with which it has no allegiance:[52] the rose is blasted in the gathering. The olive and the vine had rather live with God, than crown the head of him whose love for them is a lust for glory. The man is cursed who would rob nature of her graces, that he may use them to allure the innocent virgin to[53] destruction.

Men say there is an inspiration in genius. The genius of the ancients was the good or evil spirit that attended the man. The moderns speak of the magic touch of the pencil, [62] and of the inspiration of poetry. But this[54] inspiration has been esteemed so unlike religion, that the existence of the one almost[55] supposes the absence of the other. The spirit of God is thought to be a very different thing when poetry is written, from what it is when the heart is sanctified.[56] What has the inspiration of genius in common with that of the cloister? The one courts the[57] zephyrs; the other flies them. The one is cheerful; the other, sad. The one dies; the other writes the epitaph. Would the Muses take the veil? Would they exchange Parnassus for a nunnery? Yet there has been learning, and even poetry, under ground. The yew loves the graveyard; but other trees have grown there.

It needs no uncommon eye[58] to see, that the finger of death has rested on the church. Religion and death have in the human mind been[59] connected with the same train[60] of associations. The churchyard is the graveyard. The bell which calls men to worship is to toll at their funerals, and the garments of the priests are of the color of the hearse and the coffin. Whether we view her in the strange melancholy that sits on her face, in her mad reasonings[61] about truth, or in the occasional convulsions that agitate her limbs, there are symptoms, not of life, but of disease and death. It is not strange, then, that genius, such as could exist on the[62] earth, should take its flight to the mountains. It[63] may be said, that great men are good men. But what I mean is, that, in the human mind, greatness is one thing, and goodness another; that philosophy is divorced from religion; that truth is separated from its source; that that which is called goodness is sad, and that which is called genius is proud.

Since things are so, let men take care[64] that the life which[65] is received be[66] genuine. Let the glow on the cheek spring from the warmth of the heart, and the brightness of the eyes beam[67] from the light of heaven. Let ambition and the love of the world be plucked up by their[68] roots. How can he love his neighbor, who desires to be above him? He may love him for a slave; but that is all. Let not the shrouds[69] of death be removed, till the living principle has entered. It was not till Lazarus was raised from the dead, and had received the breath of life, that the Lord said, "Loose him, and let him go."

[63] When the heart is purified from all selfish and worldly affections, then may genius find its seat in the church. As the human mind is cleansed of its lusts, truth will permit and invoke[70] its approach, as the coyness of the virgin subsides into the tender love of the wife. The arts will spring in full-grown[71] beauty from Him who is the source of beauty. The harps which have hung on the willows[72] will sound as sweetly as the first breath of heaven that moved the leaves in the garden of Eden. Cannot a man paint better when he knows that the picture ought not to be worshipped?

Here is no sickly aspiring after fame,—no filthy lust after philosophy, whose very origin is an eternal barrier to the[73] truth. But sentiments will flow from the heart warm as its blood, and speak eloquently; for eloquence is the language of love. There is a unison[74] of spirit and nature. The genius of the mind will descend, and unite with the genius of the rivers, the lakes, and the woods. Thoughts[75] fall to the earth with power, and make a language out of nature.

Adam and Eve knew[76] no language but their garden. They had nothing to communicate by words; for they had not the power of concealment. The sun of the spiritual world shone bright on their hearts, and their senses were open with delight to natural objects. In the eye were the beauties of paradise; in the ear was the music of birds; in the nose was the fragrance of the freshness of nature; in the taste was the fruit of the garden; in the touch, the seal of their eternal union.[77] What had they to *say?*

The people of the golden age have left us no monuments of genius, no splendid columns, no paintings, no poetry. They possessed nothing which evil passions might not obliterate; and, when their[78] "heavens were rolled together as a scroll," the curtain dropped between the world and their existence.

Science will be full of life, as nature is full of God.[79] She will wring from her locks the dew[80] which was gathered in the wilderness. By science, I mean natural science. The science of the human mind must change with its subject. Locke's mind will not always be the standard of metaphysics. Had we a description of it in its present state, it would make [64] a very different book from "Locke on the Human Understanding."

The time is not far distant. The cock has crowed. I hear the distant lowing of the[81] cattle which are grazing on the mountains. "Watchman, what of the night? Watchman, what of the night? The watchman saith, The morning cometh."[82]

TABLE OF VARIANTS

[1]*on earth*
[2]*in*
[3]Omitted.
[4]Ms. omits *leaves and*
[5]*Every one*
[6]Omitted.
[7]*in the world an idea*
[8]Omitted.
[9]*wh[ich].*
[10]*in*
[11]*corporeal life like the brute's.*
[12]*operation*
[13]Omitted.
[14]*power*
[15]*begins*
[16]*decay in apparent dissolution*
[17]Ms. reads *foresight* instead of *foreign aid.*

[18]*which*
[19]*which*
[20]Ms. omits entire sentence.
[21]Ms. omits *to all*
[22]*was*
[23]Ms. omits *that* and inserts it before the following *man.*
[24]*which*
[25]*the*
[26]*which*
[27]Omitted.
[28]*which*
[29]Omitted.
[30]*small*
[31]*importance*
[32]*make*
[33]*a*
[34]Omitted.

[35]*There is a kind of divine with human —of finite with infinite.*
[36]*that*
[37]*whence*
[38]*formation*
[39]*of the*
[40]*which*
[41]*(alloyed)?*
[42]*in the source of*
[43]*effusion*
[44]*song*
[45]*description*
[46]*participate*
[47]*this power.*
[48]Ms. omits entire sentence at this point, but records it at the bottom of the page without indicating its proper position.
[49]*Oh! because*
[50]*both science and the arts*
[51]*from*
[52]*alliance.*
[53]*to her*
[54]*the*
[55]Omitted.
[56]Entire sentence omitted.
[57]Omitted.
[58]*light*

[59]*been ever*
[60]*strain*
[61]*reasoning*
[62]Omitted.
[63]*It . . . proud.* appears in a footnote in the Ms.
[64]*beware*
[65]*that*
[66]*is*
[67]Omitted.
[68]*the*
[69]*shroud*
[70]*invite*
[71]*growth*
[72]*willow*
[73]Omitted.
[74]*union*
[75]*Thus it will*
[76]*had*
[77]Ms. omits *in the touch, the seal of their eternal union.*
[78]*the*
[79]*good*
[80]*the dew from her locks*
[81]Omitted.
[82]*the morning cometh and also the night.*

OBSERVATIONS ON THE GROWTH OF THE MIND*

By SAMPSON REED

Nothing is a more common subject of remark than the changed condition of the world. There is a more extensive intercourse of thought, and a more powerful action of mind upon mind than formerly. The good and the wise of all nations are brought nearer together, and begin to exert a power, which though yet feeble as infancy, is felt throughout the globe. Public opinion, that helm which directs the progress of events by which the world is guided to its ultimate destination, has received a new direction. The mind has attained an upward and onward look, and is shaking off the errours and prejudices of the past. The gothic structure of the feudal ages, the ornament of the desert, has been exposed to the light of heaven; and continues to be gazed at for its ugliness, as it ceases to be admired for its antiquity. The world is deriving vigour, not from that which is gone by, but from that which is coming; not from the unhealthy moisture of the evening, but from the nameless influences of the morning. The loud call on the past to instruct us, as it falls on the rock of ages, comes back in echo from the future. Both mankind, and the laws and principles by which they are governed, seem about to be redeemed from slavery. The moral and intellectual character of man has undergone, and is undergoing a change; and as this is effected it must change the aspect of all things, as when the position-point is altered from which a landscape is viewed. We appear [4] to be approaching an age which will be the silent pause of merely physical force before the powers of the mind; the timid, subdued, awed condition of the brute, gazing on the erect and godlike form of man.

---

* This is a reprint of the first edition, Boston, 1826, p. 3ff. (Copy in New York Public Library).

These remarks with respect to the present era are believed to be just, when it is viewed on the bright side. They are not made by one who is insensible to its evils. Least of all are they intended to countenance that feeling of self-admiration, which carries with it the seeds of premature disease and deformity; for to be proud of the truth is to cease to possess it. Since the fall of man, nothing has been more difficult for him than to know his real condition, since every departure from divine order is attended with a loss of the knowledge of what it is. When our first parents left the garden of Eden, they took with them no means by which they might measure the depths of degradation to which they fell; no chart by which they might determine their moral longitude. Most of our knowledge implies relation and comparison. It is not difficult for one age, or one individual, to be compared with another; but this determines only their relative condition. The actual condition of man, can be seen only from the relation in which he stands to his immutable creator; and this relation is discovered from the light of revelation, so far as by conforming to the precepts of revelation, it is permitted to exist according to the laws of divine order. It is not sufficient that the letter of the Bible is in the world. This may be, and still mankind continue in ignorance of themselves. It must be obeyed from the heart to the hand. The book must be eat, and constitute the living flesh. When only the relative condition of the world is regarded, we are apt to exult over other ages and other men, as if we ourselves were a different order of beings, till at length we are enveloped in the very mists from which we are proud of being cleared. But when the relative state of the world is justly viewed from the real state of the individual, the scene is lighted from the point of the beholder with the chaste light of humility which never deceives; it is not forgotten that the way lies forward; the cries of exultation cease to be heard in the march of progression, and the mind, in whatever it learns of the past and the present, finds food for improvement, and not for vain-glory.

[5] As all the changes which are taking place in the world originate in the mind, it might be naturally expected that nothing would change more than the mind itself, and whatever is connected with a description of it. While men have been speculating concerning their own powers, the sure but secret influence of revelation has been gradually changing the moral and intellectual character of the world, and the ground on which they were standing has passed from under them, almost while their words were in their mouths. The powers of the mind are most intimately connected with the subjects by which they are occupied. We cannot think of the will without feeling, of the understanding without thought, or of the imagination without something like poetry. The mind is visible when it is active; and as the subjects on which it is engaged are changed, the powers themselves present a different aspect. New classifications arise, and new names are given. What was considered simple is thought to consist of distinct parts, till at length the philosopher hardly knows whether the African be of the same or a different species; and though the soul is thought to continue after death, angels are universally considered a distinct class of intellectual beings. Thus it is that there is nothing fixed in the philosophy of the mind; it is said to be a science which is not demonstrative; and though now thought to be brought to a state of great perfection, another century under the providence of God, and nothing will be found in the structure which has cost so much labour, but the voice "he is not here, but is risen."

Is then every thing that relates to the immortal part of man fleeting and evanescent, while the laws of physical nature remain unaltered? Do things become changeable as we approach the immutable and the eternal? Far otherwise. The laws of the mind are in themselves as fixed and perfect as the laws of matter; but they are laws from which we have wandered. There is a philosophy of the mind, founded not on the aspect it presents in any part or in any period of the world, but on its immutable relations to its first cause; a philosophy equally applicable to man, before or after he has passed the valley of the shadow of death; not dependent on time or place, but immortal as its subject. The light of this philosophy has begun to beam faintly on the world, and mankind will yet see their own moral and in- [6] tellectual nature by the light of revelation, as it shines through the moral and intellectual character it shall have itself created. It may be remarked also that the changes in the sciences and the arts are entirely the effect of revelation. To revelation it is to be ascribed, that the genius which has taught the laws of the heavenly bodies and analyzed the material world, did not spend itself in drawing the bow or in throwing the lance, in the chase or in war; and that the vast powers of Handel did not burst forth in the wild notes of the war-song. It is the tendency of revelation to give a right direction to every power of every mind; and when this is effected, inventions and discoveries will follow of course, all things assume a different aspect, and the world itself again become a paradise.

It is the object of the following pages not to be influenced by views of a temporal or local nature, but to look at the mind as far as possible in its essential revealed character, and beginning with its powers of acquiring and retaining truth, to trace summarily that development which is required, in order to render it truly useful and happy. It is believed that they will not be found at variance with the state of the public mind on the subject of education, whether of the child or the man.

It was said, *the powers of acquiring and retaining truth,* because truth is not retained without some continued exertion of the same powers by which it is acquired. There is the most intimate connexion of the memory with the affections. This connexion is obvious from many familiar expressions; such as remember me to any one, by which is signified a desire to be borne in his or her affections—do not forget me, by which is meant do not cease to love me—get by heart, which means commit to memory. It is also obvious from observation of our own minds; from the constant recurrence of those subjects which we most love, and the extreme difficulty of detaching our own minds or the minds of others from a favourite pursuit. It is obvious from the power of attention on which the memory principally depends, which if the subject have a place in our affections requires no effort; if it have not, the effort consists principally in giving it a real or an artificial hold of our feelings, as it is possible if we do not love a subject, to attend to it because it may add to our fame or our wealth. It is obvious from the [7] never fading freshness retained by the scenes of childhood, when the feelings are strong and vivid, through the later periods of life. As the old man looks back on the road of his pilgrimage, many years of active life lie unseen in the valley, as his eye rests on the rising ground of his younger days; presenting a beautiful illustration of the manner in which the human mind when revelation shall have accomplished its work, shall no longer regard the scene of sin and misery behind, but having completed the circle, shall rest as next to the present moment on the golden age, the infancy of the world. The connexion of the memory with the affections is also obvious from the association of ideas; since the train of thoughts suggested by any scene or event in any individual, depends on his own peculiar and prevailing feelings; as whatever enters into the animal system whenever it may arise, seems first to be recognized as a part of the man, when it has found its way to the heart, and received from that its impulse. It is but a few years, (how strange to tell,) since man discovered that the blood circulated through the human body. We have perhaps, hardly learned the true nature of that intellectual circulation, which gives life and health to the human mind. The affections are to the soul, what the heart is to the body. They send forth their treasures with a vigour not less powerful, though not material, throughout the intellectual man, strengthening and nourishing; and again receive those treasures to themselves, enlarged by the effect of their own operation.

Memory is the *effect* of learning, through whatever avenue it may have entered the mind. It is said the *effect;* because the man who has read a volume and can perhaps tell you nothing of its contents, but simply express his own views on the same subject with more clearness and precision, may as truly be said to have remembered, as he that can repeat the very words. In the one case, the powers of the mind have received a new tone; in the other, they are encumbered with a useless burthen—in the one, they are made stronger; in the other they are more oppressed with weight—in the one, the food is absorbed and becomes a part of the man; in the other it lies on the stomach in a state of crude indigestion.

There is no power more various in different individuals, than the memory. This may be ascribed to two reasons. [8] First, this partakes of every power of the mind, since every mental exertion is a subject of memory, and may therefore be said to indicate all the difference that actually exists. Secondly, this power varies in its character as it has more or less to do with time. Simple divine truth has nothing to do with time. It is the same yesterday, to-day and tomorrow. The memory of this is simply the development of the mind. But we are so surrounded by facts of a local and temporal nature; the place where, and the time when, make so great a part of what is presented to our consideration; that the attribute is mistaken for the subject, and this power sometimes appears to have exclusive reference to time, though strictly speaking it has no relation to it. There is a power of growth in the spiritual man, and if in his progress we be able to mark as in the grain of the oak the number of the years, this is only a circumstance; and all that is gained would be as real if no such lines existed. The mind ought not to be limited by the short period of its own duration in the body, with a beginning and end comprising a few years; it should be poised on its own immortality, and what is learned, should be learned with a view to that real adaptation of knowledge to the mind which results from the harmony of creation, and whenever or wherever we exist, it will be useful to us. The memory has in reality, nothing to do with time, any more than the eye has with space. As the latter learns by experience to measure the distance of objects, so the consciousness of the present existence of states of mind, is referred to particular periods of the past. But when the soul has entered on its *eternal* state, there is reason to believe that the past and the future will be swallowed up in the present; that memory and anticipation will be lost in consciousness; that every thing of the past will be comprehended in the present, without any reference to time, and every thing of the future will exist in the divine effort of progression.

What is time? There is perhaps no question that would suggest such a variety of answers. It is represented to us from our infancy as producing such important changes, both in destroying some, and in healing the wounds it has inflicted on others, that people generally imagine, if not an actual person, it is at least a real existence. We begin with time in the primer, and end with reasoning about the [9] foreknowledge of God. What is time? The difficulty of answering the question, (and there are few questions more difficult,) arises principally from our having ascribed so many important effects to that which has no real existence. It is true that all things in the natural world are subject to change. But however these changes may be connected in our minds with time, it requires but a moment's reflection to see that time has no agency in them. They are the effects of chemical, or more properly perhaps, of natural decompositions and reorganizations. Time, or rather our idea of it, so far from having produced any thing, is itself the effect of changes. There are certain operations in nature, which depending on fixed laws, are in themselves perfectly regular; if all things were equally so, the question how long? might never be asked. We should never speak of a late season, or of premature old age; but every thing passing on in an invariable order, all the idea of time that would remain with respect to any object, would be a sort of instinctive sense of its condition, its progress or decay. But most of the phenomena in the natural world are exceedingly irregular; for though the same combination of causes would invariably produce the same effect, the same combination very rarely occurs. Hence in almost every change, and we are conversant with nothing but changes, we are assisted in ascertaining its nature and extent, by referring it to something in itself perfectly regular. We find this regularity in the apparent motions of the sun and moon. It is difficult to tell how much our idea of time is the effect of artificial means of keeping it, and what would be our feelings on the subject, if left to the simple operations of nature—but they would probably be little else than a reference of all natural phenomena to that on which they principally depend, the relative situation of the sun and earth; and the idea of an actual succession of moments, would be in a measure resolved into that of cause and effect.

Eternity is to the mind what time is to nature. We attain a perception of it, by regarding all the operations in the world within us, as they exist in relation to their first cause; for in doing this, they are seen to partake somewhat of the nature of that Being on whom they depend. We make no approaches to a conception of it, by heaping day upon day or year upon year. This is merely an accumu- [10] lation of time; and we might as well attempt to convey an idea of mental greatness by that of actual space, as to communicate a conception of eternity by years or thousands of years. Mind and matter are not more distinct from each other than their properties; and by an attempt to embrace all time we are actually farther from an approach to eternity than when we confine ourselves to a single instant—because we merely collect the largest possible amount of natural changes, whereas that which is eternal approaches that which is immutable. This resembles the attempt to ascend to heaven by means of the tower of Babel, in which they were removed by their pride from that which they would have approached, precisely in proportion to their apparent progress. It is impossible to conceive of either time or space without matter. The reason is, they are the effect of matter; and as it is by creating matter that they are produced, so it is by thinking of it that they are conceived of. It need not be said how exceedingly improper it is to apply the usual ideas of time and space to the Divine Being; making him subject to that which he creates.

Still our conceptions of time, of hours, days or years, are among the most vivid we possess, and we neither wish nor find it easy to call them in question. We are satisfied with the fact, that time is indicated on the face of the watch; without seeking for it among the wheels and machinery. But what is the idea of a year? Every natural change that comes under our observation, leaves a corresponding impression on the mind; and the sum of the changes which come under a single revolution of the earth around the sun, conveys the impression of a year. Accordingly, we find that our idea of a year is continually changing, as the mind becomes conversant with different objects, and is susceptible of different impressions; and the days of the old man as they draw near their close, seem to gather rapidity from their approach to the other world. We have all experienced the effect of pleasure and pain in accelerating and retarding the passing moments; and since our feelings are constantly changing, we have no reason to doubt, that they constantly produce a similar effect, though it may not be often noticed. The divisions of time then, however real they may seem to be, and however well they may serve the common purposes of conversation, cannot be supposed to convey the same im- [11] pression to any two minds, nor to any one mind in different periods of its existence. Indeed, unless this were the fact, all artificial modes of keeping it, would be unnecessary. Time then, is nothing real so far as it exists in our own minds.

Nor do we find a nearer approach to reality, by any analysis of nature. Every thing as was said, is subject to change, and one change prepares the way for another; by which there is growth and decay. There are also motions of bodies both in nature and art, which in their operation observe fixed laws; and here we end. The more we enter into an analysis of things, the farther are we from finding any thing that answers to the distinctness and reality which are usually attached to a conception of time; and there is reason to believe that when this distinctness and reality are most deeply rooted, (whatever may be the theory) they are uniformly attended with a practical belief of the actual motion of the sun, and are indeed the effect of it. Let us then continue to talk of time, as we talk of the rising and setting of the sun; but let us think rather of those changes in their origin and effect, from which a sense of time is produced. This will carry us one degree nearer the actual condition of things; it will admit us one step further into the temple of creation—no longer a temple created six thousand years ago, and deserted by him who formed it; but a temple with the hand of the builder resting upon it, perpetually renewing, perpetually creating—and as we bow ourselves to worship the "I am," "Him who liveth forever and ever, who created heaven and the things that are therein, and the earth and the things that are therein, and the sea and the things that are therein," we may hear in accents of divine love the voice that proclaims "that there shall be time no longer."

It is not the living productions of nature, by which the strongest impression of time is produced. The oak over which may have passed a hundred years, seems to drive from our minds the impression of time, by the same power by which it supports its own life, and resists every tendency to decay. It is that which is decayed, though it may have been the offspring of an hour—it is the ruined castle mouldering into dust, still more, if the contrast be strengthened by its being covered with the living productions of nature—it is [12] the half consumed remains of some animal, once strong and vigorous, the discoveries of the undertaker, or the filthy relics of the catacomb, by which the strongest impression of time is conveyed. So it is with the possessions of the mind. It is that which is not used, which seems farthest in the memory, and which is held by the most doubtful tenure; that which is suffered to waste and decay because it wants the life of our own affections; that which we are about to lose because it does not properly belong to us—whereas that truth, which is applied to the use and service of mankind, acquires a higher polish the more it is thus employed, like the angels of heaven, who forever approximate to a state of perfect youth, beauty and innocence. It is not a useless task then, to remove from our minds the usual ideas of time, and cultivate a memory of things. It is to leave the mind in the healthy, vigorous and active possession of all its attainments, and exercise of all its powers—it is to remove from it, that only which contains the seeds of decay and putrefaction; to separate the living from the dead; to take from it the veil by which it would avoid the direct presence of Jehovah, and preserve its own possessions without using them.

Truth, all truth is practical. It is impossible from its nature and origin, that it should be otherwise. Whether its effect be directly to change the conduct, or it simply leave an impression on the heart, it is in the strictest sense practical. It should rather be our desire to use what we learn, than to remember it. If we desire to use it, we shall remember it of course; if we wish merely to remember, it is possible we may never use it. It is the tendency of all truth to effect some object. If we look at this object, it will form a distinct and permanent image on the mind; if we look merely at the truth it will vanish away, like rays of light falling into vacancy.

Keeping in view what has been said on the subject of time then, the mind is presented to us, as not merely active in the acquirement of truth, but active in its possession. The memory is the fire of the vestal virgins, sending forth perpetual light; not the grave, which preserves simply because annihilation is impossible. The reservoir of knowledge should be seated in the affections, sending forth its influence throughout the mind and terminating in word and deed, if I [13] may be allowed the expression, merely because its channels and outlets are situated below the watermark. There prevails a most erroneous sentiment, that the mind is originally vacant, and requires only to be filled up; and there is reason to believe, that this opinion is most intimately connected with false conceptions of time. The mind is originally a most delicate germ, whose husk is the body; planted in this world, that the light and heat of heaven may fall upon it with a gentle radiance, and call forth its energies. The process of learning is not by synthesis, or analysis. It is the most perfect illustration of both. As subjects are presented to the operation of the mind, they are decomposed and reorganized in a manner peculiar to itself, and not easily explained.

Another object of the preceding remarks upon time, is that we may be impressed with the immediate presence and agency of God, without which a correct understanding of mind or matter can never be attained; that we may be able to read on every power of the mind, and on every particle of matter the language of our Lord, "My Father worketh hitherto, and I work." We usually put the Divine Being to an immense distance, by supposing that the world was created many years ago, and subjected to certain laws, by which it has since been governed. We find ourselves capable of constructing machines, which move on without our assistance, and imagine that the world was constructed in the same way. We forget that the motions of our machines depend on the uniform operation of what we call the laws of nature; and that there can be nothing beyond, on which these depend, unless it be the agency of that Being from whom they exist. The pendulum of the clock continues to move from the uniform operation of gravitation. It is no explanation, to say that it is a law of our machinery that the pendulum should move. We simply place things in a situation to be acted upon by an all-pervading power—but what all-pervading power is there by which gravitation is itself produced, unless it be the power of God?

The tendency of bodies to the earth, is something with which from our childhood we have been so familiar; something which we have regarded so much as a cause, since in a certain sense it is the cause of all the motions with which we are acquainted; that it is not agreeable to our habits of thinking, to look at it as an effect. Even the motions of [14] the heavenly bodies seem completely accounted for, by simply extending to these phenomena the feelings with which we have been accustomed to regard the tendency of bodies to the earth; whereas if the two things were communicated at the same period of life, they would appear equally wonderful. An event appears to be explained, when it is brought within the pale of those youthful feelings and associations, which in their simplicity do not ask the reason of things. There is formed in the mind of the child, from his most familiar observations, however imperfect they may be, as it were a little nucleus, which serves as the basis of his future progress. This usually comprises a large proportion of those natural appearances, which the philosopher in later periods of life, finds it most difficult to explain. The child grows up in his Father's house, and collects and arranges the most familiar operations and events. Into this collection, he afterwards receives whatever history or science may communicate, and still feels at home; a feeling with which wonder is never associated.

This is not altogether as it should be. It is natural for the mature mind to ask the cause of things. It is unsatisfied when it does not find one, and can hardly exclude the thought of that Being, from whom all things exist. When therefore we have gone beyond the circle of youthful knowledge, and found a phenomenon in nature, which in its insulated state fills us with the admiration of God; let us beware how we quench this feeling. Let us rather transfer something of this admiration to those phenomena of the same class, which have not hitherto directed our minds beyond the fact of their actual existence. As the mind extends the boundaries of its knowledge, let a holy reference to God descend into its youthful treasures. That light which in the distance seemed to be a miraculous blaze, as it falls on our own native hills may still seem divine, but will not surprise us; and a sense of the constant presence of God will be happily blended with the most perfect freedom.

Till the time of Newton, the motion of the heavenly bodies was in the strictest sense a miracle. It was an event which stood alone, and was probably regarded with peculiar reference to the Divine Being. The feeling of worship with which they had previously been regarded, had subsided into a feeling of wonder; till at length they were [15] received into the family of our most familiar associations. There is one step further. It is to regard gravitation wherever it may be found, as an effect of the constant agency of the Divine Being, and from a consciousness of his presence and co-operation in every step we take, literally "to walk humbly with our God." It is agreeable to the laws of moral and intellectual progression, that all phenomena, whether of matter or mind, should become gradually classified; till at length all things, wherever they are found; all events, whether of history or experience, of mind or matter; shall at once conspire to form one stupendous miracle, and cease to be such. They will form a miracle, in that they are seen to depend constantly and equally on the power of the Lord; and they will cease to be a miracle, in that the power which pervades them, is so constant, so uniform and so mild in its operation, that it produces nothing of fear, nothing of surprise. From whatever point we contemplate the scene, we feel that we are still in our Father's house; go where we will, the paternal roof, the broad canopy of heaven is extended over us.

It is agreeable to our nature, that the mind should be particularly determined to one object. The eye appears to be the point, at which the united rays of the sun within and the sun without, converge to an expression of unity; and accordingly the understanding can be conscious of but one idea or image at a time. Still there is another and a different kind of consciousness which pervades the mind, which is coextensive with every thing it actually possesses. There is but one object in nature on which the *eye* looks directly, but the whole body is pervaded with nerves which convey perpetual information of the existence and condition of every part. So it is with the possessions of the mind; and when an object ceases to be the subject of this kind of consciousness, it ceases to be remembered. The memory therefore, as was said, is not a dormant, but an active power. It is rather the possession than the retention of truth. It is a consciousness of the will; a consciousness of character; a consciousness which is produced by the mind's preserving in effort, whatever it actually possesses. It is the power which the mind has of preserving truth, without actually making it the subject of thought; bearing a relation to thought, anal[o]gous to what this bears to the actual [16] perception of the senses, or to language. Thus we remember a distant object without actually thinking of it, in the same way that we think of it, without actually seeing it.

The memory is not limited, because to the affections viewed simply as such, number is not applicable. They become distinct and are classified, when connected with truths, or from being developed are applied to their proper objects. Love may be increased, but not multiplied. A man may feel intensely, and the quantity and quality of his feeling may affect the character of his thought, but still it preserves its unity. The most ardent love is not attended with more than one idea, but on the contrary has a tendency to confine the mind to a single object. Every one must have remarked, that a peculiar state of feeling belongs to every exercise of the understanding; unless somewhat of this feeling remained after the thought had passed away, there would be nothing whereby the latter could be recalled. The impression thus left exists continually in the mind; though as different objects engage the attention, it may become less vivid. These impressions go to comprise the character of an individual; especially when they have acquired a reality and fixedness, in consequence of the feelings in which they originated, having resulted in the actions to which they tend. They enter into every subject about which we are thinking, and the particular modification they receive from that subject gives them the appearance of individuality; while they leave on the subject itself, the image of that character which they constitute. When a man has become acquainted with any science, that state of the affections which properly belongs to this science, (whatever direction his mind may take afterwards) still maintains a certain influence; and this influence is the creative power by which his knowledge on the subject is reproduced. Such impressions are to the mind, what logarithms are in numbers; preserving our knowledge in its fulness indeed, but before it has expanded into an infinite variety of thoughts. Brown remarks, "we will the existence of certain ideas, it is said, and they arise in consequence of our volition; though assuredly to will any idea is to know that we will, and therefore to be conscious of that very idea, which we surely need not desire to know, when we already know it so well as to will its actual existence." The author does not discriminate between look- [17] ing at an object and thence desiring it, and simply that condition of feeling between which and certain thoughts there is an established relation, so that the former cannot exist to any considerable degree without producing the latter. Of this exertion of the will, every one must have been conscious in his efforts of recollection. Of this exertion of the will the priest must be conscious, when (if he be sincere) by the simple prostration of his heart before his maker, his mind is crowded with the thoughts and language of prayer. Of this exertion of the will, the poet must be conscious, when he makes bare his bosom for the reception of nature, and presents her breathing with his own life and soul. But it is needless to illustrate that of which every one must be sensible.

It follows from these views of the subject, that the true way to store the memory is to develop the affections. The mind must grow, not from external accretion, but from an internal principle. Much may be done by others in aid of its development; but in all that is done, it should not be forgotten, that even from its earliest infancy, it possesses a character and a principle of freedom, which *should be* respected, and *cannot* be destroyed. Its peculiar propensities may be discerned, and proper nutriment and culture supplied—but the infant plant, not less than the aged tree, must be permitted, with its own organs of absorption, to separate that which is peculiarly adapted to itself; otherwise it will be cast off as a foreign substance, or produce nothing but rottenness and deformity.

The science of the mind itself will be the effect of its own development. This is merely an attendant consciousness, which the mind possesses of the growth of its own powers; and therefore it would seem, need not be made a distinct object of study. Thus the power of reason may be imperceptibly developed by the study of the demonstrative sciences. As it is developed, the pupil becomes conscious of its existence and its use. This is enough. He can in fact learn nothing more on the subject. If he learns to use his reason what more is desired? Surely it were useless, and worse than useless, to shut up the door of the senses, and live in indolent and laborious contemplation of one's own powers; when if any thing is learned truly, it must be what these powers are and therefore that they ought not to [18] be thus employed. The best affections we possess will find their home in the objects around us, and, as it were, enter into and animate the whole rational, animal and vegetable world. If the eye were turned inward to a direct contemplation of these affections, it would find them bereft of all their loveliness; for when they are active, it is not of them we are thinking, but of the objects on which they rest. The science of the mind then, will be the effect of all the other sciences. Can the child grow up in active usefulness, and not be conscious of the possession and use of his own limbs? The body and the mind should grow together, and form the sound and perfect man, whose understanding may be almost measured by his stature. The mind will see itself in what it loves and is able to accomplish. Its own works will be its mirror; and when it is present in the natural world, feeling the same spirit which gives life to every object by which it is surrounded, in its very union with nature it will catch a glimpse of itself, like that of pristine beauty united with innocence, at her own native fountain.

What then is that development which the nature of the human mind requires? What is that education which has heaven for its object, and such a heaven as will be the effect of the orderly growth of the spiritual man?

As all minds possess that in common which makes them human, they require to a certain extent the same general development, by which will be brought to view the same powers however distinct and varied they may be found in different individuals; and as every mind possesses something peculiar, to which it owes its character and its effect, it requires a particular development by which may be produced a full, sincere and humble expression of its natural features, and the most vigorous and efficient exertion of its natural powers. These make one, so far as regards the individual.

Those sciences which exist embodied in the natural world, appear to have been designed to occupy the first place in the development of all minds, or in that which might be called the general development of the mind. These comprise the laws of the animal, vegetable, and mineral kingdoms. The human mind, being as it were planted in nature by its heavenly Father, was designed to enter into matter, and detect knowledge for its own purposes of growth and nutrition. This gives us a true idea of memory, or rather of what memory [19] should be. We no longer think of a truth as being laid up in a mind for which it has no affinity, and by which it is perhaps never to be used; but the latent affections as they expand under proper culture, absolutely require the truth to receive them, and its first use is the very nutriment it affords. It is not more difficult for the tree to return to the seed from which it sprung, than for the man who has learned thus, to cease to remember. The natural sciences are the basis of all useful knowledge, alike important to man in whatever time, place or condition he is found. They are coeval with our race, and must continue so long as the sun, moon and stars endure. Before there were facts for the pen of history to record, or vices for the arm of law to restrain, or nations for the exhibition of institutions for the government of themselves, and intercourse with each other; at the very creation, these were pronounced good in the general benediction—and when history shall have finished her tale of sin and wo, and law shall have punished her millions of offenders, and civil society shall have assumed every possible form, they will remain the same as when presented in living characters to the first parents of the human race. Natural philosophy seems almost essential to an enlightened independence of thought and action. A man may lean upon others, and be so well supported by an equal pressure in all directions, as to be apparently dependent on no one; but his independence is apt to degenerate into obstinacy, or betray itself in weakness, unless his mind is fixed on this unchanging basis. A knowledge of the world may give currency to his sentiments and plausibility to his manners; but it is more frequently a knowledge of *the world* that gives light to the path and stability to the purposes. By the one he may learn what coin is current, by the other what possesses intrinsic value. The natural world was precisely and perfectly adapted to invigorate and strengthen the intellectual and moral man. Its first and highest use was not to support the vegetables which adorn, or the animals which cover its surface; nor yet to give sustenance to the human body—it has a higher and holier object, in the attainment of which these are only means. It was intended to draw forth and mature the latent energies of the soul; to impart to them its own verdure and freshness; to initiate them into its own mysteries; and by its silent and humble dependence on its creator, to leave on them [20] when it is withdrawn by death, the full impression of his likeness.

It was the design of Providence, that the infant mind should possess the germ of every science. If it were not so, they could hardly be learned. The care of God provides for the flower of the field, a place wherein it may grow, regale with its fragrance, and delight with its beauty. Is his providence less active over those, to whom this flower offers its incense? No. The soil which produces the vine in its most healthy luxuriance, is not better adapted to the end, than the world we inhabit to draw forth latent energies of the soul, and fill them with life and vigour. As well might the eye see without light, or the ear hear without sound; as the human mind be healthy and athletic, without descending into the natural world, and breathing the mountain air. Is there aught in eloquence, which warms the heart? She draws her fire from natural imagery. Is there aught in poetry to enliven the imagination? There is the secret of all her power. Is there aught in science to add strength and dignity to the human mind? The natural world is only the body, of which she is the soul. In books science is presented to the eye of the pupil, as it were in a dried and preserved state; the time may come when the instructer will take him by the hand, and lead him by the running streams, and teach him all the principles of science as she comes from her maker, as he would smell the fragrance of the rose without gathering it.

This love of nature, this adaptation of man to the place assigned him by his heavenly Father, this fulness of the mind as it descends into the works of God, is something which has been felt by every one, though to an imperfect degree; and therefore needs no explanation. It is the part of science, that this be no longer a blind affection, but that the mind be opened to a just perception of what it is, which it loves. The affection, which the lover first feels for his future wife, may be attended only by a general sense of her external beauty; but his mind gradually opens to a perception of the peculiar features of the soul, of which the external appearance is only an image. So it is with nature. Do we love to gaze on the sun, the moon, the stars and the planets? This affection contains in its bosom the whole science of astronomy, as the seed contains the future tree. It is the office of the instruct- [21] er, to give it an existence and a name, by making known the laws which govern the motions of the heavenly bodies, the relation of these bodies to each other, and their uses. Have we felt delight in beholding the animal creation, in watching their pastimes and their labours? It is the office of the instructer to give birth to this affection, by teaching the different classes of animals with their peculiar characteristics, which inhabit the earth, air, and sea. Have we known the inexpressible pleasure of beholding the beauties of the vegetable world? This affection can only expand in the science of botany. Thus it is that the love of nature in the mass, may become the love of all the sciences; and the mind will grow and bring forth fruit from its own inherent power of development. Thus it is that memory refers to the growth and expansion of the mind; and what is thus, as it were incorporated into its substance, can be forgotten only by a change in the direction of the affections, or the course of conduct of the individual analogous to that in his physical man, by which his very flesh and bones are exchanged for those of a different texture; nor does he then entirely cease to remember, inasmuch as he preserves a sense of his own identity.

It is in this way the continual endeavour of Providence, that the natural sciences should be the spontaneous production of the human mind. To these should certainly be added, poetry and music; for when we study the works of God as we should, we cannot disregard that inherent beauty and harmony in which these arts originate. These occasion in the mind its first glow of delight, like the taste of food as it is offered to the mouth; and the pleasure they afford, is a pledge of the strength and manhood afterwards imparted by the sciences.

By poetry is meant all those illustrations of truth by natural imagery, which spring from the fact that this world is the mirror of him who made it. Strictly speaking, nothing has less to do with fiction, than poetry. The day will come, and it may not be far distant, when this art will have another test of merit than mere versification, or the invention of strange stories; when the laws by which poetry is tested, will be as fixed and immutable as the laws of science; when a change will be introduced into taste corresponding to that which Bacon introduced into philosophy, by which both will [22] be confined within the limits of things as they actually exist. It would seem that genius would be cramped; that the powers of invention would be destroyed; by confining the human mind, as it were, at home, within the bounds which nature has assigned. But what wider scope need it have? It reaches the throne of God; it rests on his footstool. All things spiritual and natural are before it. There is as much that is true as false; and truth presented in natural imagery, is only dressed in the garments which God has given it.

The imagination was permitted for ages to involve the world in darkness, by putting theory in the place of fact; till at length the greatest man revealed the simplest truth, that our researches must be governed by actual observation. God is the source of all truth. Creation, (and what truth does not result from creation?) is the effect of the Divine Love and Wisdom. Simply to will and to think with the Divine Being, result in creating; in actually producing those realities, which form the ground-work of the thoughts and affections of man. But for the philosopher to desire a thing, and to think that it existed, produced nothing but his own theory. Hence it was necessary that he should bring his mind into coincidence with things as they exist, or in other words with the truth.

Fiction in poetry must fall with theory in science, for they depend equally on the works of creation. The word fiction however is not intended to be used in its most literal sense; but to embrace whatever is not in exact agreement with the creative spirit of God. It belongs to the true poet to feel this spirit, and to be governed by it; to be raised above the senses; to live and breathe in the inward efforts of things; to feel the power of creation, even before he sees the effect; to witness the innocence and smiles of nature's infancy, not by extending the imagination back to chaos, but by raising the soul to nature's origin. The true poetic spirit, so far from misleading any, is the strongest bulwark against deception. It is the soul of science. Without it, the latter is a cheerless, heartless study, distrusting even the presence and power of Him to whom it owes its existence. Of all the poetry which exists, that only possesses the seal of immortality, which presents the image of God which is stamped on nature. Could the poetry which now prevails, be viewed from the future, [23] when all partialities and antipathies shall have passed away, and things are left to rest on their own foundations; when good works shall have dwindled into insignificance from the mass of useless matter that may have fallen from them, and bad ones shall have ceased to allure with false beauty; we might catch a glimpse of the rudiments of this divine art, amid the weight of extraneous matter by which it is now protected, and which it is destined to throw off. The imagination will be refined into a chaste and sober view of unveiled nature. It will be confined within the bounds of reality. It will no longer lead the way to insanity and madness by transcending the works of creation, and as it were, wandering where God has no power to protect it; but finding a resting-place in every created object, it will enter into it and explore its hidden treasures, the relation in which it stands to mind, and reveal the love it bears to its Creator.

The state of poetry has always indicated the state of science and religion. The Gods are hardly missed more, when removed from the temples of the ancients, than they are when taken from their poetry; or than theory is when taken from their philosophy. Fiction ceases to be pleasing when it ceases to gain credence; and what they admired in itself, commands much of its admiration now, as a relic of antiquity. The painting which in a darkened room only impressed us with the reality, as the sun rises upon it discovers the marks of the pencil; and that shade of the mind can never again return, which gave to ancient poetry its vividness and its power. Of this we may be sensible, by only considering how entirely powerless it would be, if poetry in all respects similar were produced at the present day. A man's religious sentiments, and his knowledge of the sciences, are so entirely interwoven with all his associations; they shed such light throughout every region of the mind; that nothing can please which is directly opposed to them—and though the forms which poetry may offer, may sometimes be presented, where this light begins to sink into obscurity; they should serve, like the sky and the clouds, as a relief to the eye, and not like some unnatural body protruding on the horizon, disturb the quiet they are intended to produce. When there shall be a religion which shall see God in every thing, and at all times; and the natural [24] sciences not less than nature itself, shall be regarded in connexion with Him—the fire of poetry will begin to be kindled in its immortal part, and will burn without consuming. The inspiration so often feigned, will become real; and the mind of the poet will feel the spark which passes from God to nature. The veil will be withdrawn, and beauty and innocence displayed to the eye; for which the lasciviousness of the imagination and the wantonness of desire may seek in vain.

There is a language, not of words but of things. When this language shall have been made apparent, that which is human will have answered its end, and being as it were resolved into its original elements, will lose itself in nature. The use of language is the expression of our feelings and desires; the manifestation of the mind. But every thing which is, whether animal or vegetable, is full of the expression of that use for which it is designed, as of its own existence. If we did but understand its language, what could our words add to its meaning? It is because we are unwilling to hear, that we find it necessary to say so much; and we drown the voice of nature, with the discordant jargon of ten thousand dialects. Let a man's language be confined to the expression of that which actually belongs to his own mind; and let him respect the smallest blade which grows and permit it to speak for itself. Then may there be poetry which may not be written perhaps, but which may be felt as a part of our being. Every thing which surrounds us, is full of the utterance of one word, completely expressive of its nature. This word is its name; for God, even now could we but see it, is creating all things, and giving a name to every work of his love, in its perfect adaptation to that for which it is designed. But man has abused his power, and has become insensible to the real character of the brute creation, still more so, to that of inanimate nature, because in his selfishness, he is disposed to reduce them to slavery. Therefore he is deaf. We find the animal world, either in a state of savage wildness, or enslaved submission. It is possible that as the character of man is changed, they may attain a midway condition equally removed from both. As the mind of man acknowledges its dependance on the Divine Mind, brutes may add to their instinct submission to human reason; preserving an [25] unbroken chain from our Father in Heaven, to the most inanimate parts of creation. Such may be supposed to have been the condition of the animal, on which the King of Zion rode into Jerusalem; at once free and subject to the will of the rider. Every thing will seem to be conscious of its use; and man will become conscious of the use of every thing.

It may be peculiar, and is said with deference to the opinions of others, but to my ear, rhymes add nothing to poetry, but rather detract from its beauty. They possess too strongly the marks of art, and produce a sameness which tires, and sometimes disgusts. We seek for them in vain in nature, and may therefore reasonably presume that they spring out of the peculiar state of the public taste, without possessing any real foundation in the mind itself; that they are rather the fashion of the dress, than any essential part. In the natural world we find nothing which answers to them, or feels like them— but a happy assemblage of living objects springing up, not in straight lines and at a fixed distance, but in God's own order, which by its apparent want of design, conveys the impression of perfect innocence and humility. It is not for that which is human to be completely divested of the marks of art; but every approach towards this end, must be an approach towards perfection. The poet should be free and unshackled as the eagle; whose wings, as he soars in the air, seem merely to serve the office of a helm, while he moves on simply by the agency of the will.

By music is meant not merely that which exists in the rational world, whether in the song of angels or men; not merely the singing of birds and the lowing of cattle, by which the animal world express their affections and their wants—but that harmony which pervades also all orders of creation; the music of the harp of universal nature, which is touched by the rays of the sun, and whose song is the morning, the evening and the seasons. Music is the voice of God, and poetry his language, both in his word and works. The one is to the ear, what the other is to the eye. Every child of nature must feel their influence. There was a time, when the human mind was in more perfect harmony with the Divine Mind, than the lower orders of creation; and the tale of the harp of Orpheus, to which [26] the brutes, the vegetables and the rocks listened, is not altogether unfounded in reality—but when the selfish and worldly passions usurped the place of love to our God and our neighbour, the mind of man began to be mute in its praise. The original order was reversed. The very stones cry out, and we do well to listen to them.

There is a most intimate and almost inseparable connexion between poetry and music. This is indicated by the fact that they are always united. Nothing is sung which has not some pretensions to poetry; and nothing has any pretensions to poetry, in which there is not something of music. A good ear is essential to rhythm; and rhythm is essential to verse. It is the perfection of poetry, that it addresses two senses at once, the ear and the eye; that it prepares the affections for the object before it is presented; that it sends light through the understanding, by forming a communication between the heart of man, and the works of God. The character of music must have always harmonized with that of poetry. It is essential to the former that it should be in agreement with our feelings; for it is from this circumstance, that it derives its power. That music which is in unison with the Divine Mind, alone deserves the name. So various is it found in the different conditions of man, that it is hardly recognized as the same thing. There is music in the war-song of the savage, and in the sound for battle. Alas! how unlike that music which proclaimed peace on earth and good will towards men. Poetry and music like virtuous females in disguise, have followed our race into the darkest scenes to which the fall has brought them. We find them in the haunts of dissipation and vice; in the song of revelry and lewdness. We meet them again kindling the fire of devotion at the altar of God; and find them more and more perfect, as we approach their divine origin.

There prevail at present two kinds of music, as diverse as their origins; profane and religious. The one is the result of the free, unrestrained expression of natural feelings; the other, of a kind which indicates that these feelings are placed under restraint. In the one, there is often something of sensuality; in the other of sadness. There is a point in moral improvement, in which the sensual will be subdued, and the sorrowful disappear; which will combine the pleasure [27] of the one, with the sanctity of the other. When a sense of the presence of God shall be coextensive with the thoughts of the mind, and religion shall consecrate every word and action of our lives; the song of Zion will be no longer sung in a strange land. The Divine Love, the soul and essence of music, will descend, not in the thunders of Sinai, but will seem to acquire volume, as it tunes the heart in unison with itself, and the tongue in unison with the heart. The changes in the character of our music, which may be the effect of the gradual regeneration of the world, are hardly within the reach of conjecture.

Enough has been said to illustrate generally, the influence of the natural world in the development of the mind. The actual condition of society operates to produce the same effect, with hardly less power. In this, are comprised the religious and civil institutions of one's own country; that peculiar character in which they originate; and a knowledge of the past, as by disclosing the origin and progress of things, it throws light on the prospect actually before us. As the philosophy connected with the natural world, is that in which the mind may take root, by which it may possess an independence worthy a being whose eternal destiny is in his own hands—so the moral and civil institutions, the actual condition of society, is the atmosphere which surrounds and protects it; in which it sends forth its branches, and bears fruit. The spiritual part of man is as really a substance, as the material; and is as capable of acting upon spirit, as matter is upon matter. It is not from words of instruction and advice, that the mind of the infant derives its first impetus; it gathers strength from the warmth of those affections which overshadow it, and is nourished by a mother's love, even before it has attained the power of thought. It is the natural tendency of things, that an individual should be brought into a situation, in which the external condition of the place, and the circle of society in which he is, are particularly adapted to bring forth to view his hereditary character. The actual condition of the human mind, is as it were the solid substance, in which the laws of moral and intellectual philosophy and political economy, (whatever may be their quality) exist embodied, as the natural sciences do in the material world. A knowledge of those laws, such as they exist, is the natural consequence [28] of the development of the affections, by which a child is connected with those that surround him. The connexion of mind is not less powerful or universal than that of matter. All minds, whatever may be their condition, are not unconnected with God; and consequently not unconnected with each other. All nations, under whatever system of government, and in whatever state of civilization, are under the Divine Providence, surely but almost imperceptibly advancing to a moral and political order, such as the world has not yet seen. They are guided by the same hand, and with a view to the same destiny. Much remains to be done, and more to be suffered; but the end is certain. The humblest individual may, nay *must* aid in the accomplishment of this consummation. It is not for time or space to set limits to the effects of the life of a single man. Let then the child be so initiated into a knowledge of the condition of mankind, that the love at first indulged in the circle of his father's family, shall gradually subside into a chaste and sober love of his country; and of his country, not as opposed to other countries, but as aiding them in the same great object. Let the young mind be warmed and cherished by whatever is chaste and generous in the mind of the public; and be borne on to a knowledge of our institutions, by the rich current of the disposition to preserve them.

Thus it is that the child is no sooner brought into this world, than the actual condition both of the world itself, and of society, acts powerfully to draw forth the energies of his mind. If mankind had retained that order in which they were created, this influence in co-operation with the Divine, would have been sufficient, as it was designed to have been, for all the purposes of God. Nature, the very image of divine loveliness, and the purest affections of the heart, which approach still nearer the same origin, acting together on the infant mind; it would seem as if the effect would be almost as certain, as any process of growth which is witnessed among the productions of the natural world. But man is fallen—and the operation of this influence in different conditions of society, may produce different results; but in none is sufficient to capacitate him for that life of usefulness and happiness, for which he was designed. The influence of society cannot be sufficient, since this cannot raise a man above its own level; and the society of earth is no longer [29] the society of heaven. This influence may bring forward all the warlike energies of the young savage, and direct them in their utmost vigour to the destruction of his enemies and of the beasts of the forest; and he may look onward with rapture to the happy hunting grounds beyond the grave. What disappointment awaits him in the other world, all of us may easily imagine. This influence may bring forth and gratify the unchaste and beastly passions of the Turk; and he may look forward, with his Koran in his hand, to a heaven of sensuality and crime. It need not be said how widely different will be found the reality. Christians generally are standing in expectation of a happiness as boundless in extent, as it is undefined in its nature; and with an infinite variety of passions in whose gratification alone they have experienced delight, are expecting a heaven in which simple useless enjoyment will rise like a flood and immerse the mind. The result must of necessity be as various, as the condition of the individuals by whom it is anticipated. Still there is a society yet in its coming, unseen though not unseeing, shrouded from the rest of the world by the very brilliancy of its own light, which would resist the impulse of every evil affection, and look for heaven simply in the delight of that which is chaste, pure and holy; which by removing that which renders duty undelightful, would draw nigh to the only source of real enjoyment; which would find its happiness and its God, in the very commandments which have been the terrour of the world; to which the effect is no longer doubtful, since it is made acquainted with the cause, and which as it anticipates no reward, will meet with no disappointment. When this society shall be fully established on the earth, the voice of the Lord will be no longer obstructed as it descends from above the heavens;—"*Suffer little children to come unto me and forbid them not, for of such is the kingdom of God.*"

The influence of the natural world however beneficial it may prove, is not such as it **was** designed to have been. Man has ever sought a condition in nature, which should correspond with the state of his own mind. The savage would pine and droop, if too suddenly removed to scenes of civilization, like grass which had grown in rank luxuriance under the shade of the oak, if the branches were cleft and it was at once exposed to the power of the sun. The charac- [30] ter of all the lower orders of creation has suffered a change in consequence of that in the condition of man, the extent of which cannot be measured. That the sun was darkened at the crucifixion of our Lord, was no miracle. It was as much the natural consequence of that event, as its present lustre is of His glory. It is not then for these the objects of nature, to restore to us that moral order, the want of which has wrought such changes on themselves.

There is then another power which is necessary to the orderly development of the mind; the power of the Word of God. This indeed has been implied in all the preceding remarks. No possessions and no efforts of the mind are unconnected with it, whatever may be the appearance. Revelation so mingles with every thing which meets us, that it is not easy for us to measure the degree to which our condition is affected by it. Its effects appear miraculous at first, but after they have become established, the mind as in the ordinary operations of nature, is apt to become unconscious of the power by which they are produced. All growth or development is effected from within, outward. It is so with animals; it is so with vegetables; it is so with the body; it is so with the mind. Were it not for a power within the soul, as the soul is within the body, it could have no possibility of subsistence. That the growth of the material part depends on the presence of that which is spiritual, is obvious from the fact, that at death the former falls to decay. If it were possible for God to be detached from our spiritual part, this would decay likewise. The doctrine then of the immortality of the soul is simply, "I in my Father, and ye in me and I in you." It is the union of the Divine, with the human— of that from which all things are, and on which they depend the Divine Will, with man through the connecting medium of Divine Truth. It is the tendency of the Bible to effect this union, and of course to restore a consciousness of it. It is a union which God desires with all, therefore even the wicked who reject it, partake of his immortality, though not of his happiness. When in the process of regeneration, this union is accomplished, the fear of dissolution will be as impossible in this world as in the other; and before this is effected, the fear of dissolution may exist there, as well as here. It is not the place where a person is, but the condition of mind which is to be regarded; and [31] there is no antidote against the fear of death, but the consciousness of being united with the fountain of life. But it is asked, how can the fear of death exist after it has actually taken place? The separation of the spiritual and material part so far as the nature of their connexion is understood, can produce no fear. Were it not for evil in ourselves, it would rather wear the appearance of a state of uncommon quiet. There is upon no subject a more powerful tendency to instinctive knowledge, than upon that of death. The darkness with which it is veiled, presents but a lamentable picture of our present condition. It is its own dissolution of which the mind is afraid; and that want of conjunction with God which renders this fear possible here, may render it possible any where. It is the sole object of the Bible to conjoin the soul with God; and as this is effected it may be understood in what way the Holy Spirit operates interiously to produce its development. It is not a mere metaphor, it is a plain and simple fact, that the Spirit of God is as necessary to the development of the mind, as the power of the natural sun to the growth of vegetables and in the same way. But let us remember, that as in nature the heat and light may be converted into the most noxious poison; so the Spirit of God in itself perfectly pure and holy, may be converted into passions the most opposite to its nature. It is left to us to open our hearts to its influence, by obeying its commandments. "If ye love me, keep my commandments; and I will pray the Father, and he shall give you another comforter that he may abide with you forever." "He that believeth on the Son *hath* everlasting life;" and he will become conscious of living and growing from God.

It is not consistent with the nature of things, that the full practical effect of a subject should be at once revealed to the mind. The child is led on to a knowledge of his letters, by a thousand little enticements, and by the tender coercion of parental authority, while he is yet ignorant of the treasures mysteriously concealed in their combinations. The arts have been courted merely for the transient gratification they afford. Their connexion with religion and with the sciences is beginning to be discovered; and they are yet to yield a powerful influence in imparting to the mind, its moral harmony and proportions. The sciences themselves have been studied principally as subjects of speculation and [32] amusement. They have been sought for the gratification they afford, and for the artificial standing they give in society, by the line of distinction which is drawn between the learned and the vulgar. The discovery of their connexion with the actual condition of man, is of later origin; and though their application to use is yet in its infancy, they are beginning to throw a light on almost every department of labour, hitherto unexampled in the annals of the world. Religion too has been a subject of speculation, something evanescent, a theory, a prayer, a hope. It remains for this also to become practical, by the actual accomplishment of that which it promises. It remains for the promise of reward to be swallowed up in the work of salvation. It remains for the soul to be restored to its union with God—to heaven. Christianity is the tree of life again planted in the world; and by its own vital power it has been, year after year, casting off the opinions of men, like the external bark which partakes not of its life. It remains for the human mind to become conformed to its spirit, that its principles may possess the durability of their origin.

Such are the effects to be anticipated from the Bible in the development of the mind. It has begun the work, and will perfect it in each individual, so far as by a life according to the commandments he becomes willing that it should. There is within it a secret power, which exerts an influence on the moral and intellectual world, like that of the sun on the physical; and however long and successfully it may be resisted by some, not the less certain in its effect on the ultimate condition of society. I am aware that in these remarks, I am ascribing to the spirit of God, to the spirit of the Word, a power which some may be unwilling to allow to it. The Bible is thought to resemble other books, and to be subject to the same laws of criticism; and we may be sometimes in danger of becoming insensible to its internal power, from the very mass of human learning, with which it is encumbered. "Is not this the carpenter's son?"

There is one law of criticism, the most important to the thorough understanding of any work, which seems not to have been brought sufficiently into view in the study of the Bible. It is that by which we should be led by a continued exercise of those powers which are most clearly demonstrated in an authour; by continued habits of mind and action; to [33] approximate to that intellectual and moral condition, in which the work originated. If it were desired to make a child thoroughly acquainted with the work of a genuine poet, I would not put the poem and lexicon in his hand and bid him study and learn—I would rather make him familiar with whatever was calculated to call forth the power of poetry in himself, since it requires the exercise of the same powers to understand, that it does to produce. I would point him to that source from which the author himself had caught his inspiration, and as I led him to the baptismal fount of nature, I would consecrate his powers to that Being from whom nature exists. I would cultivate a sense of the constant presence and agency of God, and direct him inward to the presence chamber of the Most High, that his mind might become imbued with His spirit. I would endeavour by the whole course of his education to make him a living poem, that when he read the poetry of others, it might be effulgent with the light of his own mind. The poet stands on the mountain with the face of nature before him, calm and placid. If we would enter into his views, we must go where he is. We must catch the direction of his eye, and yield ourselves up to the instinctive guidance of his will, that we may have a secret foretaste of his meaning—that we may be conscious of the image in its first conception—that we may perceive its beginnings and gradual growth, till at length it becomes distinctly depicted on the retina of the mind. Without this, we may take the dictionary in our hands and settle the definition of every word, and still know as little of the lofty conceptions of the author, as the weary traveller who passes round in the farthest verge which is visible from the mountain, knows of the scenery which is seen from its summit. It has been truly said that Johnson was incapable of conceiving the beauties of Milton. Yet Johnson was himself a living dictionary of Milton's language. The true poet, when his mind is full, fills his language to overflowing; and it is left to the reader to preserve what the words cannot contain. It is that part which cannot be defined; that which is too delicate to endure the unrestrained gaze; that which shrinks instinctively from the approach of any thing less chaste than itself, and though present, like the inhabitants of the other world, is unperceived by flesh and blood, which is worth all the rest. This acknowledges no dwelling-place [34] but the mind. Stamp the living light on the extended face of nature, beyond the power of darkness at the setting of the sun, and you may preserve such light as this, when the mind rises not to meet it in its coming.

If it were desired to make an individual acquainted with a work in one of the abstract sciences, this might be best effected by leading him gradually to whatever conduced to the growth of those powers on which a knowledge of these sciences depend; by cultivating a principle of dependence on the Divine Being, a purity and chastity of the affections, which will produce a tranquil condition, of all things the most favourable to clear perceptions; by leading him to an habitual observation of the relations of things, and to such continued exertion of the understanding, as calling into use its full powers without inducing fatigue, may impart the strength of the labourer, without the degradation of the slave; in a word, by forming a penetrating, mathematical mind, rather than by communicating mathematical information. The whole character and complexion of the mind will be gradually changed; till at length it will become (chemically speaking) in its very nature an active solvent of these subjects. They fall to pieces as soon as they come in contact with it and assume an arrangement agreeable to that of the mind itself, with all the precision of crystallization. They are then understood—for the most perfect understanding of a subject is simply a perception of harmony existing between the subject and the mind itself. Indeed the understanding which any individual posseses of a subject might be mathematically defined $\frac{\text{the subject proposed,}}{\text{the actual character of his mind}}$; and there is a constant struggle for the numerator and denominator to become the same by a change in the one or the other, that the result may be unity, and the understanding perfect.

There is an analogy, (such as may exist between things human and things divine) between that discipline which is required in order to understand a production of taste or science, and that which is necessary to a clear perception of the truths of the Bible. As it is requisite to a full sense of the beauties of poetry, that the individual should be himself a poet, and to a thorough knowledge of a work of science that he should not merely have scientific information, but a scientific mind; so it is necessary to a knowledge of the Bible, [35] that the mind should be formed in the image and likeness of God. An understanding of the Word is the effect of a life according to its precepts. It requires, not the obedience of the rich man who went away sorrowful, but the obedience of him who holds every other possession, whether it consist in the acquirements of the mind or in earthly property, in subjection to the Holy Spirit within him. "If ye will do the will of God, ye shall know of the doctrines" is a law of exegesis, before which false sentiments will melt away like frost before the rising sun. There is within the mind the golden vein of duty, which if followed aright will lead to an increasing brightness, before which the proudest monuments of human criticism will present an appearance like that of the dark disk of this world, as the eye of the dying man opens on the scenes of the other.

The world is beginning to be changed from what it was. Physical power instead of boasting of its deeds of prowess, and pointing with the tomahawk or the lance to the bloody testimonies of its strength, is beginning to leave its image on the rugged face of nature, and to feel the living evidence of its achievements, in the happy circle of domestic life. It remains for intellectual strength to lose the consciousness of its existence in the passions subdued, and to reap the reward of its labours, not in the spoils of an enemy, but in the fruits of honest industry. It remains for us to become more thoroughly acquainted with the laws of moral mechanism. Instead of making unnecessary and ineffectual exertions in the direct attainment of truth, it remains for us to make equal efforts to cleanse our own minds and to do good to others; and what was before unattainable will become easy, as the rock which untutored strength cannot move, may be raised by a touch of the finger.

The Bible differs from other books as our Lord differed from men. He was born of a woman, but His Spirit was the everlasting Father. It is humble in its appearance, as nature is when compared to art; and some parts which Providence has permitted to remain within the same cover, have often attracted more attention than that which is really divine. From the very nature of perfect innocence its presence is unnoticed, save by him by whom it is loved. Divine Love, in its perfect thoughtlessness of itself, enters the atheistical [36] heart, unperceived. Such an one thinks meanly of those who think humbly of themselves, and with perfect humility the last vestige of reality disappears. To him, both nature and the Word are like a deserted building, through which as he passes, he is conscious of nothing but the sound of his own footsteps; but to him whose heart opens to the Divine Influence, this building appears to assume from the internal cause of its creation, the symmetry of perfect proportions, till at length as he becomes more and more conscious of the presence with which it is filled, he sees no temple, "for the Lord God Almighty, and the Lamb are the temple." The Word resembles the hebrew language in which much of it is written. To him who knows not its spirit, it is an empty form without sound or vowel; but to him who is alive to the Divine Influence it is filled with the living voice of God.

The Bible can never be fully understood, either by making it subservient to natural reason, or by blindly adopting what reason would reject; but by that illumination of the understanding and enlargement of the reason, which will result from a gradual conformity to its precepts. Reason now, is something very different from what it was a few centuries past. We are in the habit of thinking that the mode of reasoning has changed; but this appears to be merely an indication of a change which has taken place in the character of the mind itself. Syllogistic reasoning is passing away. It has left no permanent demonstration, but that of its own worthlessness. It amounts to nothing but the discernment and expression of the particulars which go to comprise something more general; and as the human mind permits things to assume a proper arrangement from their own inherent power of attraction, it is no longer necessary to bind them together with syllogisms. Few minds can now endure the tediousness of being led blindfold to a conclusion, and of being satisfied with the result merely from the recollection of having been satisfied on the way to it. The mind requires to view the parts of a subject, not only separately but together; and the understanding in the exercise of those powers of arrangement by which a subject is presented in its just relations to other things, takes the name of reason. We appear to be approaching that condition which requires the union of reason and eloquence, and will be satisfied with neither without the other. We neither wish to see an ana- [37] tomical plate of bare muscles, nor the gaudy daubings of finery; but a happy mixture of strength and beauty. We desire language neither extravagant nor cold; but bloodwarm. Reason is beginning to learn the necessity of simply tracing the relations which exist between created things, and of not even touching what it examines lest it disturb the arrangement in the cabinet of creation—and as in the progress of moral improvement, the imagination (which is called the creative power of man) shall coincide with the actively creative will of God, reason will be clothed with eloquence as nature is with verdure.

Reason is said to be a power given to man for his protection and safety. Let us not be deceived by words. If this were the particular design, it should be found in equal perfection in every condition of the mind; for all are in equal need of such a power. It is the office of the eye to discern the objects of nature, and it may protect the body from any impending injury; and the understanding may be useful in a similar way to the spiritual man. Reason is partly a natural and partly an acquired power. The understanding is the eye with simply the power of discerning the light; but reason in the eye whose powers have been enlarged by exercise and experience, which measures the distance of objects, compares their magnitudes, discerns their colours and selects and arranges them according to the relation they bear to each other. In the progress of moral improvement no power of the mind, or rather no mode of exercising the understanding, undergoes a more thorough and decisive change than this. It is like the change from chaos to creation; since it requires a similar exercise of the understanding in man to comprehend creation, to what it does in God to produce it; and every approach to Him by bringing us nearer the origin of things, enables us to discover analogies in what was before chaotic. This is a change which it is the grand design of revelation to accomplish; reason should therefore come to revelation in the spirit of prayer, and not in that of judgment. Nothing can be more intimately, and necessarily connected with the moral character of an individual, than his rational powers, since it is his moral character which is the grand cause of that peculiar classification and arrangement which characterizes his mind; hence revelation in changing the former, must change the latter also.

[38] The insufficiency of reason to judge of the Bible, is obvious on the very face of revelation from its miracles. The laws of Divine Operation are perfectly uniform and harmonious; and a miracle is a particular instance of Divine Power, which for a want of a more interiour and extended knowledge of the ways of God, appearing to stand alone, and to have been the result of an unusual exertion of the Divine Will, creates in the minds of men, what its name implies, a sensation of wonder. That there are miracles in the Bible, proves that there are laws of the Divine Operation and of the Divine Government, which are not embraced within the utmost limits of that classification and arrangement, which is the result of natural reason. While therefore human reason professes to be convinced of the reality of revelation from its miracles, let it humble

itself before them. Let it bow itself to the earth, that it may be exalted to a more intimate acquaintance with these heavenly strangers. Let it follow the Lord in the regeneration, till the wonderful disappear in the paternal. Miracles are like angels who have sometimes been visible to men—who would much more willingly have introduced them to an acquaintance with the laws and society of heaven, than have filled them with fear and consternation. They are insulated examples of laws as boundless as the universe, and by the manner in which we are affected by them, prove how much we have to learn, and how utterly incompetent we are to judge of the ways of God, from that reason, which is founded on our own limited and fallacious observation. The resurrection of our Lord must have been a very different miracle to the ang[el]s at the sepulchre, from what it was to Mary. They saw it from the other side of the grave, with a knowledge of the nature of that death which they had themselves experienced; she saw an insulated fact not at all coincident with her views on the subject of which it was an illustration. They saw the use and design of that which had been accomplished; she saw the sepulchre and the linen clothes lying. As they gazed intensely at the same subject, the veil of heaven was withdrawn, and they beheld each other, face to face. She was filled with fear; they with love and compassion. If Mary were to persist in judging of this subject from her own reason; from a knowledge of those laws with which she was previously acquainted; how could her views ever become an- [39] gelic? How could the dark cloud of admiration be ever filled with the rich light of the rising sun?

Man alone of all created things, appears on his own account to want the full measure of his happiness; because he alone has left the order of his creation. He stands even at the present period half-convinced of the reality of the future state. It is the design of revelation to restore to him that moral condition, in which he will possess as necessarily the consciousness of immortality, as the brute does that of existence—for a consciousness of existence united with that of union with God, is a consciousness of eternal life. Let us come to the Bible then, with no hopes of arbitrary reward, and no fears of arbitrary punishment; but let us come to it, as to that which if followed aright, will produce a condition of mind of which happiness will be the natural and necessary consequence.

It is often said that the Bible has nothing to do with metaphysics or the sciences. An individual, whatever be his condition, always retains to a certain extent, a consciousness of his moral and intellectual character, and the more this character is exalted, the more minute and discriminating will be this consciousness. Who is it that formed the human mind, and who is here endeavouring to restore it to its true order? The Bible has the mind for its subject, that condition of mind which is heaven for its object, and the Father of mind for its author. Has it nothing to do with metaphysics? It has indeed nothing to do with that metaphysics which we shall leave with our bodies in the graves; but of that, which will shine with more and more brilliancy, as the passage is opened, not through distant regions of space, but through the secret part of our own souls to the presence of God, it is the very life and being. Can omniscience contemplate the happiness of the mind, without regard to its nature? Were we disposed to improve the condition of the savage, what course should we pursue? Should we not endeavour to change his habits of mind and body, by teaching him the arts of civilization; instructing him in the sciences; and gradually introducing him to that portion of social order which is here attained? And are not all these most intimately connected with our own condition of mind? Are they not merely the expression of its countenance? In the same way is it the endeavour of the Divine Mind in the Bible, to restore all to his own image and likeness—and [40] to say that the Bible has nothing to do with metaphysics, is to say that the present condition of the mind has nothing to do with what it should be, and that present metaphysics have nothing to do with religion. It is said that the Bible has nothing to do with the sciences. It is true that it does not teach them directly, but it is gradually unfolding a condition of mind, out of which the sciences will spring as naturally, as the leaves and blossoms from the tree that bears them. It is the same power which acts simultaneously to develop the soul [it]self, and to develop nature—to form the mind and the mould which is destined to receive it. As we behold the external face of the world, our souls will hold communion with its spirit; and we shall seem to extend our consciousness beyond the narrow limits of our own bodies, to the living objects that surround us. The mind will enter into nature by the secret path of him who forms her; and can be no longer ignorant of her laws, when it is a witness of her creation.

I have endeavoured to illustrate generally, in what way the natural sciences, the actual condition of society, and the Word of God are necessary to the development of all minds, in a manner analogous to that in which the earth, the atmosphere and the sun combine to bring forth the productions of nature. I shall say but a few words with respect to that particular development, which is requisite to the full manifestation of the peculiar powers possessed by any individual.

It is well known that at a certain period of life, the character of a man begins to be more distinctly marked. He appears to become separated from that which surrounds him—to stand in a measure aloof from his associates—to raise his head above the shadow of any earthly object into the light of heaven, and to walk with a more determined step on the earth beneath. This is the manifestation of a character which has always existed, and which has, as it were been accumulating by little and little, till at length it has attained its full stature.

When a man has become his own master, it is left to himself to complete his own education. "He has one Father, God." For the formation of his character thus far, he is not in the strictest sense accountable; that is, his character is not as yet so fixed, but that it is yielding and pliable. It [41] is left to himself to decide, how far it shall remain in its present form. This is indeed a period of deep responsibility. He has taken the guidance of a human being, and is not the less accountable, that this being is himself. The ligament is now cut asunder by which his mind was bound to its earthly guardian, and he is placed on his own feet, exposed to the bleak winds and refreshing breezes, the clouds and the sunshine of this world, fully accountable to God and man for his conduct. Let him not be made dizzy from a sense of his own liberty, nor faint under his own weight; but let him remember that the eye of God is now fixed full, it might almost be said anxiously upon him.

It is with the human mind, as with the human body. All our race have those limbs and features, and that general aspect, from which they are denominated men. But on a nearer view we find them divided into nations possessed of peculiar appearance and habits, and these subdivided into families and individuals, in all of which there is something peculiarly their own. The human mind (speaking in the most general sense) requires to be instructed in the same sciences and needs the same general development, and is destined to make one common and universal effort for its own emancipation. But the several nations of the earth also, will at a future period, stand forth with a distinctness of character which cannot now be conceived of. The part which each is to perform in the regeneration of the world, will become more and more distinctly marked and universally acknowledged; and every nation will be found to possess resources in its own moral and intellectual character, and its own natural productions, which will render it essential to the well-being and happiness of the whole. Every government must find that the real good of its own people precisely harmonizes with that of others; and standing armies must be converted into willing labourers for the promotion of the same object. Then will the nations of the earth resemble the well organized parts of the same body, and no longer convert that light which is given them for the benefit of their brethren, into an instrument by which they are degraded and enslaved.

But we stop not here. Every individual also possesses peculiar powers, which should be brought to bear on society in the duties best fitted to receive them. The highest de-[42] gree of cultivation of which the mind of any one is capable, consists in the most perfect development of that peculiar organization, which as really exists in infancy, as in maturer years. The seed which is planted, is said to possess in miniature the trunk, branches, leaves and fruit of the future tree. So it is with the mind; and the most that can possibly be done, is to afford facilities by which its development may be effected with the same order. In the process of the formation of our minds, there exists the spirit of prophecy; and no advancement can create surprise, because we have always been conscious of that from which it is produced. We must not seek to make one hair white or black. It is in vain for us to attempt to add one cubit to our stature. All adventitious or assumed importance should be cast off, as a filthy garment. We should seek an employment for the mind, in which all its energies may be warmed into existence; which, (if I may be allowed the expression) may bring every muscle into action. There is something which every one can do better than any one else; and it is the tendency and must be the end of human events, to assign to each his true calling. Kings will be hurled from their thrones and peasants exalted to the highest stations, by this irresistible tendency of mind to its true level. These effects may not be fully disclosed in the short period of this life, but even the most incredulous must be ultimately convinced that the truth is no respecter of persons, by learning the simple fact that a man cannot be other than what he is. Not that endless progression in moral goodness and in wisdom are not within the reach of any one; but that the state will never arrive, when he may not look back to the first rudiments—the original stamina of his own mind; and be almost able to say, I possessed all at the time of my birth. The more a person lives in singleness of heart, in simplicity and sincerity, the more will this be apparent.

It becomes us then to seek and to cherish this *peculium* of our own minds, as the patrimony which is left us by our Father in heaven—as that by which the branch is united to the vine—as the forming power within us, which gives to our persons that by which they are distinguished from others—and by a life entirely governed by the commandments of God, to leave on the duties we are called to perform, the full impress of our real characters. Let a man's ambition to be great, [43] disappear in a willingness to be what he is; then may he fill a high place without pride, or a low one without dejection. As our desires become more and more concentrated to those objects which correspond to the peculiar organization of our minds, we shall have a foretaste of that which is coming, in those internal tendencies of which we are conscious. As we perform with alacrity whatever duty presents itself before us, we shall perceive in our own hearts, a kind of preparation for every external event or occurrence of our lives, even the most trivial, springing from the all-pervading tendency of the Providence of God to present the opportunity of being useful wherever there is the disposition.

Living in a country whose peculiar characteristick is said to be a love of equal liberty, let it be written on our hearts, that the end of all education is a life of active usefulness. We want no education which shall raise a man out of the reach of the understanding or the sympathies of any of his species. We are disgusted with that kind of dignity which the possessor is himself obliged to guard; but venerate that which, having its origin in the actual character of the man, can receive no increase from the countenance of power, and suffer no diminution from the approach of weakness—that dignity in which the individual appears to live rather in the consciousness of the light which shines from above, than in that of his own shadow beneath. There is a spiritual atmosphere about such an one, which is at once its own protection, and the protection of him with whom it is connected—which while it is free as air alike to the most powerful and the most humble, conveys a tacit warning that too near an approach is not permitted. We acknowledge the invisible chain which binds together all classes of society, and would apply to it the electric spark of knowledge with the hand of tenderness and caution. We acknowledge the healthy union of mental and bodily exercise, and would rather see all men industrious and enlightened, than to see one half of mankind slaves to the other, and these slaves to their passions. We acknowledge that the natural world is one vast mine of wisdom, and for this reason it is the scene of the labours of man; and that in seeing this wisdom, there is philosophy, and in loving it, there is religion. Most sensibly do we feel that, as the true end of instruction is to prepare a man for [44] some particular sphere of usefulness; that when he has found this sphere, his education has then truly commenced, and the finger of God is pointing to the very page of the book of his oracles, from which he may draw the profoundest wisdom. It was the design of Providence that there should be enough of science connected with the calling of each, for the highest and holiest purposes of heaven. It is the natural world from which the philosopher draws his knowledge; it is the natural world in which the slave toils for his bread. Alas! when will they be one? When we are willing to practise what we learn, and religion makes our duty our delight. The mass of mankind must always labour; hence it is supposed that they must be always ignorant. Thus has the pride of man converted that discipline into an occasion of darkness and misery, which was intended only to give reality to knowledge, and to make happiness eternal. Truth is the way in which we should act; and then only is a man truly wise, when the body performs what the mind perceives. In this way, flesh and blood are made to partake of the wisdom of the spiritual man; and the palms of our hands will become the book of our life, on which is inscribed all the love and all the wisdom we possess. It is the light which directs a man to his duty; it is by doing his duty that he is enlightened—thus does he become identified with his own acts of usefulness, and his own vocation is the silken chord which directs to his heart, the knowledge and the blessings of all mankind.

[A copy of Oegger's complete work of 503 pages,
published by F. Locquin in Paris in 1829 will
be found in the Yale University Library: Le
Vrai Messie, ou l'Ancien et le Nouveau Testaments examinés d'après les principes de la
langue de la Nature....]

THE TRUE MESSIAH*

By G. OEGGER

Introduction

There is but one way to form to ourselves a just and exact idea of the person of Jesus
Christ. This is, to bring ourselves into a state in which we shall not profane the holy
truth. If we succeed, (a condition without which God is forced to blind us,) we must
then look attentively and impartially at the Old and New Testaments. The first of these
conditions depends principally on individuals and on Him who holds in his hand the
heart of man; but history is within the domain of criticism, and reasoning may be submitted to analysis. It is then under this last interesting point of view that we intend to
perform a useful task. We hope to infuse into the spirits of our readers, some portion
of the salutary convictions which, for some years, have been our sweetest consolation.
We draw some hope of success from the career we have run; which has brought us to
those points of view, from which we could perceive the strong and the weak sides of
most of the philosophical and religious opinions in vogue in the nineteenth century. An
idea of the language of nature, must necessarily arouse the curiosity of even those who
are most indifferent on the subject of religion; and that idea is the predominent one in
our work. Yet, to shorten a work which may still be too serious for the frivolous tendency of the age, we shall confine ourselves principally to Saint John, the most sublime
of the evangelists, only tracing back, occasionally, to these two principal sources, the
most striking passages of the other extatic writers. Anticipating, on the other hand,
the impatience of those readers who, before engaging in our dissertations, inquire what
will be the result of the examination which we propose to make, we will here declare
directly, that this examination may result for him as it has resulted for us—in the
belief of the absolute divinity of Jesus Christ, and the thorough conviction that he who
believes this, believes the whole truth. Such a promise is well worth the trouble of
reading some pages with attention, even though it be previously known that the subject
is to be Christianity. The distinction of truth into Christian truth and philosophical
truth, is an absurdity which should never have entered any well organized mind. We will
inform the reader, then, that, when we began [4] our work, we were, what he perhaps
is, a deist, or something very near it, and that, when we finished it, we found ourself a
Christian, and a Christian more deeply convinced than any theologian, because our
conviction was the result of the free and lawful use of our individual reason. Indeed, the
evidence accumulated by this new method of studying the holy books, which consists in
reading them as written, from beginning to end, in the language of nature, are more
than sufficient to convince any man of good faith, or rather any man of good will, that
Jesus Christ was not merely an extraordinary man, or a Prophet, greater than the
others; that he was not merely an image of divinity, a spark of divinity, or an eternal
Son of God, distinct from him as to personality; but that he was Jehovah himself,
Jehovah in person; that, by making himself Jesus Christ, the hidden God, the metaphysical and incomprehensible God manifested himself; that it was by making himself Jesus
Christ, that the infinite Being entered into communication with finite beings engrossed
in matter; in a word, that, by appearing on the confines of his creation, to show his
erring children as much love as he had shown them power, the God became also
Redeemer.

---

* *The True Messiah; or The Old and New Testaments, examined according to the
Principles of the Language of Nature*, Boston (Pub. by E. P. Peabody), 1842, p. 3ff.
(Copy in Boston Public Library.) This work is a translation of the introductory por-
tions of Oegger's *Le Vrai Messie*, Paris, 1829, apparently made by Miss Peabody herself.
It was probably her uncorrected manuscript that Emerson used in July and August,
1835. See *Journals*, III, 505, 506, 512, 525, 527.

Our ideas will, without doubt, appear extraordinary to more than one class of readers; but who will dare to reproach us for them? When, in the nineteenth century, Christianity still appears in so precarious a state that philosophy dares to doubt its ultimate triumph, what danger can there be in trying some great means? Does not an impartial view of Christian society, for eighteen hundred years past, with its hateful and inconceivable divisions, authorize us in suspecting that, from the first, some great error has been committed which has obstructed the work of the regeneration of the universe? and that, in consequence, there is some great obstacle which must be removed before truth can make its way? Is it not more than probable that the Infidels, and all those Christians, who are Christians only in name, would long ago have embraced the true faith, if the true faith had been rightly presented to them? Is it not more than probable that the miserable descendants of Israel, as well as those of our philosophers, who seek truth sincerely, would long ago have acknowledged the God who has manifested himself upon our globe, if his majesty had not been degraded, as it were, before their eyes? If, in consequence, our deep conviction should be charged with temerity, if our courage should occasion scandal, we shall not retract, convinced as we are, with Saint Chrysostom, that, even if truth should cause scandal, it were better even to suffer this scandal than to let truth perish.

What has most emboldened us in this great enterprise, is the entire certainty that we have acquired, of being definitely on the road to that language of Nature, which, as every one will easily conceive, must have preceded all languages of convention; in which, indeed, we have found the greater part of our holy books to be written, and which sheds over them collectively a light too strong and unexpected for deism to resist.

Nothing is more comfortable to sound philosophy than the belief in the primitive existence of a language of nature. The greatest names in the learned world stand at the head of those philosophers who have occupied themselves with what they called a universal language, of which, accordingly, they experienced the advantages, and which they [5] did not believe it impossible to realize upon our globe among educated men. The only difference between the language of nature and that of which our philosophers had conceived the idea is, that the former would be of less service in our terrestrial relations than in those in which we are one day to stand, with the universality of beings, in that world in which all other worlds flow together, and in which we shall need means of communication much more extensive than those required by our material existence.

The philosophical moralist, who is fully convinced of the immortality of man, ought therefore to be convinced also of the actual existence of a language, quite distinct from that which consists in sounds which are articulated by means of the elasticity of the air, and which have merely a conventional meaning. The thinking moralist will easily believe that, even on our terrestrial globe, however material it may now be with its degraded inhabitants, there must have existed, in times of greater perfection, means of communication different from those which are of mere convention; for, to establish conventions, it is absolutely necessary to be able previously to explain one's self. Rousseau advanced the greatest of paradoxes, when he said that the savage state was the primitive state of man: on the contrary, the savage state is nothing but the state of our greatest degradation, when, as we have become incapable of raising ourselves, God is obliged to come to our relief. All knowledge, says Plato, is remembrance, and all ignorance is forgetting. Primitively man must have been perfect, at least, in his kind; and consequently he must have had a perfect language, a language which cannot have been lost but in the lapse of ages, and of which the traces may be found, when Philosophy will direct her researches to that point.

A general idea of the language of nature may be formed, from the application that we have made of its principles to a new explanation of several passages from the Holy Scriptures. We will here offer only a few preliminary reflections which may enable the reader to enter into our whole idea.

People generally have an idea, before they have reflected more profoundly, that when God produced our visible universe, the choice that he made of forms and colors for animals, plants, and minerals, was entirely arbitrary on his part. But this idea is entirely false. Man may sometimes act from whim; God never can. The visible creation, then, can not, must not (if we may use such expressions) be anything but the exterior circumference of the invisible and metaphysical world; and material objects are necessarily *scoriæ* of the substantial thoughts of the Creator; *scoriæ* which must always preserve an exact relation to their first origin; in other words, visible nature must have a spiritual and moral side. For God every thing is, every thing exists: "create" conveys not the same idea to him as to us. For God, to create is only to manifest. The universe, even in its minutest details, existed for God as really before the creation as after it, because it existed in him substantially, as the statue exists in the block of marble from which the sculptor extracts it. By the creation, we only have been enabled to perceive externally a portion of the infinite riches existing in the divine essence. The perfect, especially, must have always thus existed in God. The imperfect alone can have received a kind [6] of creation by means of man, a free agent, though under the influence of a Providence which never loses sight of him. Neither the form nor the color, then, of any object in nature, can have been chosen without a reason. Every thing we see, touch, smell; every thing, from the sun to a grain of sand, from our own body with its admirable organs, to that of the worm; every thing has flowed forth, by a supreme reason, from that world where all is spirit and life. No fibre in the animal, no blade of grass in the vegetable kingdom, no form of crystalization in inanimate matter, is without its clear and well-determined correspondence in the moral and metaphysical world. And if this is true of colors and forms, it must, by a still stronger reason, be said of the instincts of animals, and the far more astonishing faculties of man. Consequently the most imperceptible thoughts and affections which we imagine we have conceived by our own power; the compositions which we consider our own in the regions of philosophy and literature; the inventions which we believe we have made in the arts and sciences; the monuments that we think we are erecting; the customs that we fancy we establish in the things which men consider great, as in the most insignificant transactions of civil and animal life; all this existed before us; all this is simply given to us, and given with a supreme reason, according to our different immediate wants. An infinitely little degree of consent to receive, which forms our moral liberty, is the only thing that we have for our own. And merely by an inspection of the objects by which a man is surrounded, or of some of the customs which he has adopted, a superior intelligence can undoubtedly determine the moral worth of his being; for according as moral beings (for whom alone inferior nature exists) modify themselves, that nature must admit emblems analogous to the new perfections or degradations.

And, indeed, but for all these emblems of life which creation offers, there would be no appreciable moral idea or moral sentiment, no possible means, we fear not to say it, for God to communicate a thought, an affection, to his creature, any more than for one feeling creature to communicate it to another. Above all, there would be no possible communication between the present state of man and his state of transformation; all is annihilated, all is broken up in feeling or thinking nature; the most interior life of the intelligent being is effaced and returns to nothing.

This truth may be rendered palpable by examples. If there had never been a father according to nature, could you form any idea of that portion of the goodness of God which corresponds to the tenderness of a father for his children? Could you ever know anything of what paternal tenderness is? If there had never in nature existed a generous man, could you form any conception of what generosity is? If you had never loved anything upon earth, would it be possible for you to have the least idea of what love can be? Or, (to choose our own examples in the descending order,) could you, without the defects, the maladies, and the defilements of the human body, represent to yourself the shameful vices which are analogous to them in the moral man? If you had never seen animals tormented, killed, devoured, could the idea of cruelty and barbarity be communicated to your mind? In fine, if you had never heard anything of the persecutions, the treacheries [7] which sometimes reign upon earth, could your soul receive even the first germ of the ideas of hatred, perfidy, atrocity? The thing really appears impossible.

Besides, the consideration of the necessity of indicating, by visible and tangible emblems, moral distinctions which would be otherwise imperceptible, alone explains those terrible phenomena, those monstrosities and those disgusting images, evidently unworthy of the Creator, which nature offers to the eyes of degraded man. The abyss of our being cannot be revealed, but by the appreciable phenomena of life. It is with us, in this respect, as with the Creator himself, in whose image we were created, and to the knowledge of whom we cannot rise but by means of his visible wonders. Nature is like a book in which we may read the perfections of God, or as a mirror in which we may see them reflected. The same must be said of man, and of the different phenomena of his manner of living, of feeding and clothing himself. Matter furnishes us with steps by which to rise to pure substances; and we must have also emblematic substances and images, that we may dart into the moral and metaphysical world; for which reason the Creator has been obliged to come himself to meet us, crossing the abyss which separates us from his first essence. As Cre[a]tor, God must have means of communication analogous to those which he has imparted to us, that we might observe him. We are created men, and God is uncreated man. It was at the immediate point between the infinite which is all, and the finite which is nothing, that God and man met. And this point is life, life manifested, life revealed by emblems. Before all languages of convention and of articulated sounds, when the Creator wished to manifest or reveal himself for the first time to man, how could he have done it but by showing himself to that man under the substantial form of a father, the natural emblem of God Creator? In truth, the human mind could never find a different emblem, nor imagine any different means of communicating the first idea of the Creator to any secondary intelligence whatever. We shall learn, in another place, that, when men would not acknowledge for their Creator that ineffable Being who appeared to them as Father, that Being must employ, to defend his rights, the means which we call the Redemption of the human race, the divine means which he chose to show men that he was wiser, more powerful, and, above all, better than them all, that immense system, which, led down from the remotest times, to its entire execution, with an infinite knowledge, wisdom and goodness, at least overwhelms the mortal whose heart it cannot touch.

The indispensable necessity of what we call emblems of life, shows that our future existence itself cannot be so metaphysical as is sometimes imagined. There must still be, in our state of transformation, substantial images, appreciable forms, objects seen, felt, perceived, as in the material world. If not, any existence whatever, happy or unhappy, is but a real chimera. The future life is, evidently, Berkeley's world. That philosopher was wrong only in not making a clear distinction between the substance world and the matter world, or in not perceiving the shade which separates them; for if it is true that matter exists, it is also true that it has extension and impenetrability only as far as the Creator wills, and only for the beings whom he designs particularly for that purpose. If there were really the infinite [8] between matter and spirit, the impossibility of the creation might be reasonably maintained.*

---

* If we should here be asked, by a very natural curiosity, what we shall see in the other world, and what we shall do there, we would answer without hesitation, resting on the indispensable necessity of natural emblems, that we shall there see around us, as in the material world, a more or less extensive horizon, filled with a greater or less number of substantial images taken from known nature, and that we shall there be occupied nearly as we are occupied upon earth when we seek shelter, food and clothing: only these images will then be in exact correspondence with our moral being: the firmament representing our celestial relations; the different objects of nature, our social affections; and the soil which bears us, the nature of our confidence in Him who alone can make it firm under our feet. As to our different occupations, they will be those which Heaven shall judge most proper to characterize constantly the interior of our moral being, and the different ways in which we seek to appropriate to ourselves the spiritual nourishment of love and truth, in other words, to satisfy all our moral wants. All these ideas, though new, will not surprise those philosophers who know that nature is always conformable to herself, or, as Leibnitz expresses it, she never does anything by leaps and bounds. According to this philosophic apothegm, our future existence will, in reality, differ from the present only by a slight variation; and this variation is that from a material to a substantial world. We shall pass to the future existence, as we enter into an agreeable dream; all nature will accompany us there. This truth receives an increase of probability, or rather of proof, from the fact that, examined without those prejudices that rise from the vague idea of an infinite power, never checked by the bounds of the impossible, by simplicity or propriety, I might even say, geometrically examined, the chain of beings is nearly complete here below in the three kingdoms, and consequently that the nature which we know, itself contains all the elements necessary to the eternal happiness of sensitive creatures; which renders alike impossible and useless the destruction of the images of visible nature, for the future existence. It is sentiment which makes happiness, and not knowledge; and therefore the circle of possible things must be much more restricted than is commonly thought. Try to suppress the horizon of celest[i]al and terrest[r]ial images by which you are surrounded, the real Eden in which you are placed; what will remain to form the pretended heaven of a blessed spirit? There will remain nothing. And if those same images, clothed in an entirely spiritual and moral character, are sufficient for your happiness, why suppress them, or why even substitute others for them?

Then, in short, the moral and metaphysical universe, as rising successively to secondary degrees, (that is to say, to all which are not Jehovah,) cannot be conceived possible but by analogous emblems in the universe of phenomena; material phenomena for the physical world, substantial phenomena for that which is not physical. The moral and metaphysical world is, for us, as if anchored, as if rooted in the visible world, upon which it rests as upon an indispensable basis.

Any one may learn these truths from daily experience, without any great reasoning. Do but take a dictionary of morals, and examine the terms in it. You will see that all of them, from the first to the last, are derived from corporeal and animal life. The birth, growth, decay and death of the body, its state of health or of sickness, of strength or of weakness, have alone furnished correspondent ideas in the moral man. Each member of that body, considered in relation to its terrestrial use and employment, offers the same results. All the emblems that can be supplied by agriculture, the arts and trades, the different manners among men of feeding and clothing themselves, have been laid under contribution to furnish the means for characterizing the different varieties of moral and intellectual life, in individuals as in societies; and, but for all those emblems furnished by nature herself, the [9] moral and metaphysical world would have remained entirely buried in the eternal abyss.

Thence, then, the reality of a language of nature, which reality Philosophy should still admit, even if none of the letters of the immense alphabet which was made use of in speaking it, could be found; for that language is, after all, nothing but the perception of the emblems of life and intelligence, which nature contains in her bosom, and the faculty of transmitting that perception to other beings.

Still, we are very far from admitting that the dictionary of the language of nature is entirely lost; the traces of it might be found even in the languages of convention, necessarily derived from it, if the Bible were not alone sufficient to put us in possession of so precio[u]s a science. That book, so little known and so little appreciated by the self-styled enlightened universe, has not served to preserve for us the Hebrew language only, it has also furnished us with all the necessary materials for the understanding of the language of nature.

A certain number of our first ecclesiastical writers, such as the apostle Paul, Lactantius, Origen, Jerome and others, were evidently on the road to that language, as their particular manner of writing demonstrates; but by a secret judgment of Heaven, the precious traces were almost immediately abandoned by their successors. Men have treated these writers as mystics, as they now do all those who profess to see in the word of God something more than in an ordinary book. From the times of Theophilus, says Horsley, the great art of interpreting the Old Testament consisted in finding in everything types and emblems. If, instead of ridiculing this art, men had endeavored to learn how far it was well-founded, they would have better understood the mysteries of the love and wisdom of the Father, and they would not have wandered for eighteen centuries in the labyrinth of human thoughts. The word of God must necessarily be more rich and more fruitful in sense, than all the vain writings of the learned; its meaning must indeed be infinite.

Therefore, by abandoning the false method of the school, which consists in taking each text as if isolated, (by which the most contradictory things may be proved,) and studying the holy books as a whole, we may acquire an absolute certainty that all extatic men, from Abraham to the last of the prophets, and, after them all, the Redeemer himself, though expressing themselves by words of the conventional language in use at that time, yet always spoke the language of nature, and that the sense conveyed by it was the principal, if not the only one which they really meant to transmit to posterity. To speak only of Jesus Christ, it was to that language that he endeavored to accustom his apostles during the three years that he lived with them; it was that language that frequently perplexed them so much, which forced them to solicit explanations of their Master apart, and even to entreat him not [to] speak thus in parables. When a similitude, a comparison, is followed through all its branches, and sustained as long as those of Jesus Christ were, a real language results from it, which is inwoven with the ordinary discourse, and conveys a consistent sense, higher than the natural sense though parallel with it. Only recollect how far Jesus Christ carried the moral signification of the words eat and drink, and you will see that a new dictionary, a dictionary still to be made, is necessary to understand the Holy Scriptures; a book which not only is obscure, but which has been till now [10] closed and sealed in a thousand ways; and that, only by the aid of that dictionary, it will be possible to find the immense riches which the hand of the Eternal has concealed in it. He who has the least idea of the emblems of nature and their signification, reads the Bible as if with a microscope; he sees in it what he had never seen in it before; it seems to him like another book. It is like Egyptian hieroglyphics read by means of Champollion's system. Jesus Christ says, "Man lives by the word of God, as he lives by bread." The grain of which bread is made is that divine word. Bread is the substance of God, which man ought to appropriate to himself, because God is goodness and truth, and the moral man should be nothing else. Therefore the body and flesh of Jesus Christ are also that bread; because Jesus Christ is nothing but the Word or Divine Truth, incarnated through love for man. The daily bread recalls a daily appropriation of goodness and truth, which are God. The miraculous multiplications of bread, wrought by Jesus Christ, signify the abundance of the examples of virtue provided for men by infinite mercy. I have bread to eat that you know not of, said the Lord to the apostles; my food is to do the will of my Father. He who eats of the bread that I give him, shall not die, but he shall live forever. And this bread is my own flesh; you must eat me, or you can have no life in you. Inconceivable and repulsive expressions in the sense of the conventional language, but, in the language of nature, equally rich and true! I am, says Jesus Christ again, the bread of life come down from Heaven, grossly figured by the manna which your fathers ate in the desert: my flesh is consequently a true nourishment, as my blood is a true drink. And that, adds he, ought not to offend you; for these words are spirit and life; the flesh, inasmuch as it is flesh, profiteth nothing. Take and eat this bread in remembrance of me, says he, the evening before his death; it is the body which will be delivered for you to-morrow; and that means—Appropriate to yourself constantly more and more truth and love, which are God, by remembering unceasingly my examples. See, I stand at the door and knock; if any man will open to me, I will enter, and eat with him, and he with me.

Who does not see that the eating here spoken of, is entirely spiritual? and that these last words especially must be translated thus: If any man will open to me his heart, I will love him and he will love me. God cannot eat with us in any other way than by love, nor, consequently, we with him. That other passage of Saint John, where Jesus Christ says, Even as I live by the Father, so shall he who will eat with me live by me, makes this truth so clear, that the most marked folly alone could doubt it.

But this is not all. The comparison of material manducation, with the appropriation of love and truth which constitute the happiness of immortal man, is carried still farther in the Gospel. The sower, it is there said, is God; the field in which he sows, is the heart of man, in which that seed is to germinate; it is a whole church which is to bear fruit in the time of harvest. The wheat represents men loving God; the light straws, chaff,—souls without moral worth. The granary contains the riches of heaven; the fire of hell consumes the tares. The fan is the judgment upon the good and the bad. Three measures of flour or dough represents the kingdom of the heavens; the leaven of the Pharisees, false doctrines, hateful disputes. Even the mill pre- [11] serves an analogous signification; at the renewal of the Church two women shall be turning the mill-stone in a mill; the one shall be taken, the other left. Because of their different manner of announcing the word of God, such a particular church will be approved, such another disapproved, at the time of the arrival of the Son of Man. A mill-stone, hung to the neck of a scandalous man, and thrown with him into the sea, will be a blessing to him; for that mill-stone represents the means of appropriating to himself the word of God, and the sea is merely a collection of natural truths, by which man may be prepared for the reception of divine truths, as we shall soon see; water being everywhere in the discourses of Jesus Christ, the emblem of truth.

As to eat, is to appropriate to ourselves the love of God, or moral goodness, so to drink, is to appropriate to ourselves his truth. Truth dilutes goodness, which, otherwise, could not incorporate with our soul, as goodness without truth is not appreciable to creatures; or, in other words, as goodness manifested thereby becomes truth. If you had asked water of me, said Jesus Christ to the Samaritan woman, I would have given you water which springs up into everlasting life. He who will drink the water that I shall give him, shall never thirst again. He who receives my doctrine, rivers of water shall spring up from his heart. These words need no commentary; nor do these, which Jesus Christ pronounced aloud while teaching in the temple: Let him who thirsts, come and drink. Follow me, I will make you fishers of men, said he to the apostles when he associated them in the preaching of the Gospel; for, from natural truths, they were to raise men to spiritual knowledges. Thence the custom of baptism, which is evidently only the emblem of the acquisition of the true doctrine, leading man to repentance and reformation; for, we repeat it, water, as making the mirror and reflecting the images of objects, is the hieroglyphic of truth, even more than of purification. Wine and blood, in the mouth of Jesus Christ, considered as drinks, have analogous significations. Only, these emblems will be of a higher degree; blood being nearer life, and moistening the very flesh of men and animals, while water generally moistens only the objects on which they feed; and wine, on the other hand, having more affinity with the spirit of man whose heart it rejoices, according to the emblematic expression of David; the only reason why they play so great a part in the Holy Scriptures, in which mention is constantly made of the blood of victims and of the vine of the Lord; of the ancient law, and of the blood of the Lamb, of the wine that makes the virgins of the new law to germinate. The first miracle of Jesus Christ was changing of water into wine, because the principal object of his Advent was to change natural truths into divine truths, and to substitute his doctrine for that of human wisdom. New wine is put into new bottles, he says, speaking of that doctrine. Take and drink, cried he, at the Last Supper, after having long prepared the apostles for such a language, take and drink; this wine is the blood of the new covenant; this is my blood which is shed for the remission of sins; this is the New Testament in my blood. And the apostles so well understood the signification of all these discourses of their Master, that they afterwards generally gave the name of New Testament to the volume which contains his doctrine. The blood of Jesus Christ, then, wherever it is spoken of in the Gospel, recalls and represents the collection of the truths of salvation announced by him to the world; truths which the [12] world refused to receive, as it proved by the fact, and by a material emblem, by shedding, upon Calvary, the blood of the Redeemer. And the same is to be said of wine; for wine itself is only an emblem of blood. I will drink no more of this juice of the vine until I drink it new in my Father's kingdom, must signify, as will be fully proved in the body of our work, the complete union of divine truth and divine love in the person of Jesus Christ; in other words, the glorification of the Word in the heavens. When we know thus the real signification of the words eat and drink (inasmuch as these actions are moral emblems,) we can easily find the reason for the choice of those words, cup and platter, which Jesus Christ uses in this reproach to the Pharisees: Blind Pharisee, cleanse first the inside of the cup and platter, that the outside may be clean also. Man, as the receptacle of God's goodness, is represented by the platter; and, as the receptacle of His truth, by the cup. In a material vessel, the purity of the exterior, as is well known, does not necessarily follow from the purity of the interior. We perceive also that these words, happy are they who hunger and thirst after righteousness, are not chosen without reason, but that they are entirely in the genius of the language of nature. And, finally, we clearly understand that obscure text of Saint John: There are three in heaven who bear witness, the Father, the Word, and the Spirit; and these three are but one same thing: there are also three who bear witness upon earth; spirit, water, and blood, and these three relate to the same thing; in which water signifies the natural truths which announce God; blood, the evangelical truths which reveal him; and spirit, the invisible action of Him who alone can make us perceive any truth whatever, even if announced to us by a prophet. These three relate to the same thing, because reason and the Gospel, and extatic persons, speaking by the spirit, agree in declaring that the true God is no other than the Christ manifested in the flesh. We shall see, elsewhere, that Father is God in his essence, or as to his love and his power: Word, God in his form, or truth, divine wisdom, which has been called Speech or Son; and Spirit, God in his immediate action upon the soul, or the interior of all spiritual beings.

The knowledge of natural emblems, or of the universal language, has thrown, upon the whole word of God such a light, that even the mystery of the holy supper is fully revealed. Is it possible, indeed, after observing all the correspondences, which we have here pointed out to our readers, and after recollecting that Jesus Christ had said that his body was bread, before he said that bread was his body; and that before saying that wine was his blood, he had said that blood was truth—is it possible for any one to misunderstand it? Is it not clear as daylight that, in all this, he spoke only of the appropriation of the divine love and divine truth. And is not that dogma of the transubstantiation, which has had the effect of keeping men away from the holiest and most touching practice upon earth or in the heavens; is it not as absurd as it would be to attempt to maintain that the word of God is really corn, that Jesus Christ is a real vine, or that evangelical truths are indeed water and blood?*

[13] It would be easy for us to make the same remarks upon a number of other natural emblems, which were familiar to Jesus Christ in his instructions; such as stone, sand, house, door, shepherd, sheep, tree, sun, moon, stars; by which it may be seen, beyond a doubt, that, even in his apparently most simple discourses, he always spoke the language of nature. Stone, to select that example, is God, the eternal rock, and the eternal truth, general principles, mother truths, are particular stones detached from this rock; a house, a temple, built with these stones, is a religious system perfectly consistent in all its parts; built upon the rock, your house is eternal as God; built upon the incoherent sand of human thoughts, the torrent of tribulations overturns it; a whole city, founded upon the rock, is a collection of regular and unshakeable systems; built upon a mountain, such a city enlightens a whole country; finally, built entirely of precious stones, that same city is the general union of all the divine truths which can work the salvation of the human race; in other words, it is the New Jerusalem coming down out of heaven from God.

We must, in consequence, know something of the language of nature; we must have studied the genius of it a little, before we can understand what the extatic men intended to say; and, for want of this science, Rome, as well as the other Christian societies, successively detached from her, by the increase of light, have very naturally misinterpreted the Gospel upon different points. Indeed, it would be miraculous if this were not the case. For, how could men but be misled, when they took, grossly and literally, the words Father, Son, eat, drink, go up, come down, send, in discourses in which the divine essence only is spoken of? The truths of salvation were unavoidably enveloped in a human language by Him who came out from eternal splendors to visit our obscure retreat; and, to have the pure gold and silver of doctrine and truth, we must know how to separate his language from the dross and the scoriæ. The emblematic language is, as we have shown, founded upon the very nature of things; any other language would have been absurd in the mouth of God Redeemer. Discourses addressed to only a fraction of the creation of beings, would have been unworthy of Jesus Christ. The language of nature, or the universal language, has advantages which no conventional one can unite. That alone can be rendered as rich and concise as the Creator judges necessary on occasion; that alone can be understood in the eternal society of the univer- [14] sality of beings, in which the simple idea of a language, by articulate sounds, would appear an absurdity. Even while he made use of a conventional language as an instrument, the Being of beings still addressed himself to his whole creation, by weaving into that another language which was universal. In effect, the creation is to him but a unity; and it must always be comprehensible to all beings, from the highest angel to the most perverse of the demons; with only this difference, that the more intelligence a being has, the better he unravels the sense of these oracles; while he who is unworthy to receive them, seeing, seeth not, and hearing, understandeth not. This object, we repeat, is indispensable in the relations of the Creator with a society of degraded beings, and it can be attained only by natural emblems.

And if the contemporaries of Jesus Christ did not comprehend all the riches of his doctrine, it is because it could not and ought not to be: I should still have many things to say to you, but you are not now in a state to understand them, said the Lord to the

---

* I conjure those of my Roman Catholic brethren who still believe in a literal transmutation of substances, not to regard the word absurd as an insulting attack: nothing but the force of truth could wrest it from me. It will soon be seen that I also oppose, frequently and forcibly, not the Most Holy and Most Adorable Trinity, before which every created intelligence ought to be as nothing, but a Trinity of really distinct persons —and this without any hostile intention. I know that these two important points were so difficult to understand, without the knowledge of the language of nature, that all the errors into which they have led mankind, are excusable. As God was triple, it was easy to believe him three, and not to love him the less for it. Jesus Christ, in the idea of transcendental philosophy, might be supposed to be placed entirely out of time and space, even considered as man; and, therefore, some might easily persuade themselves of the possibility of eating, more or less really, the flesh of the Son of Man, and yet be very faithful and very loving Christians. In the eyes of the Lord, the zeal of the heart easily effaces the mistakes of the mind. And one proof that the errors we have mentioned, though serious in themselves, could be tolerated till now, is, that Eternal Wisdom has not seen fit to correct them sooner.

apostles. What would now be thought of Jesus Christ, if, to make his divine nature understood at his time, he had said, for example, suppressing the emblems of Father and Son: The first cause is the universal I; I who speak to you, I am that same universal I, particularly manifested! The world was really not then sufficiently advanced. It was necessary for the human race to be cultivated by degrees, under the influence of spirit and virtue from on high; it was requisite for it to learn to reflect profoundly; for it to rise, with Philosophy, entirely above the notions of time and space, that it might appreciate all the discourses and all the steps of its Eternal Benefactor. But that blessed epoch has arrived in its turn. Not only isolated individuals, but the whole mass of the human race is now ready to enter truly into the views of divine love. Eighteen hundred years have but just passed, and the eternal plan of God Redeemer may be developed! A third explosion of infinite mercy, to use the expression of a philosophical journal, may take place; and, at the moment when the universe believes itself nearest to deism, it may be on the point of becoming more truly Christian than it has ever been before.

Finding ourselves thus placed on the road to the language of nature, by the inspired books, we may now, without fear of being misled, cite some of the emblems of nature, which men themselves have preserved in their speech without knowing that they really belonged to a distinct language. Thus the general instinct of mankind has long since determined the moral signification of the sun, as well as that of his heat and light. The sun has always been the principal emblem of the Divinity upon earth; his heat that of love, and his light that of truth: thence, in times of superstition and barbarity, the adoration of the sun, and the worship of fire, was found with almost all people. Gold also signifies, generally among all nations, what is precious; stone, what is solid; fat, what is rich; and a hundred other emblems, which it would be tedious to repeat. In general, the fewer conventional words people had, the more they needed natural emblems; and when they had no conventional terms at all, which is quite conceivable, at least of moral terms, then they had absolutely nothing but emblems in their language.

There is one of these emblems at which we must stop, for a moment, because of its importance; it is that of man, which has not always [15] been remarked as much as those that are without us; because exterior objects generally strike us much more than our own being. In all times, some profound minds have perceived that man was the most perfect possible emblem; consequently, the natural and true emblem of all that can be called intelligence and life. The name microcosm, or world in little, given to man by the ancient sages, would be enough to prove it. The human form is, in truth, a real form of love and wisdom; capable, in itself alone, of characterizing all the possible varieties of the moral being, taken in its complex state. Living, intelligent existence could not have any other form than the human. The angel is nothing but the man spirit, or the substantial man. And God himself, when we would reflect on him, is really conceived by the human mind in no other way than as a divine man. The divine man is the only perceptible side of God; his infinite essence remaining eternally concealed in that man or in that form, which we conceive not as void and metaphysical, in the sense ordinarily attached to that word; but full and substantial; since God, to appear as man, need not create that man; he needs only show him. Another thing that renders man so interesting an emblem, is the relation in which he stands to all the other living beings that we perceive upon the earth. After this king of nature, all other animals, always less perfect forms of life, always inclining the head more and more towards the ground, are emblems of the different varieties of degraded life or intelligence. When man is what he ought to be, he differs from the angel only by the weight of matter; when man degrades himself, he runs through all the degrees of inferior life, figured by animals; each animal, by its forms and instincts, offering a particular variation of that life. The whole quadrant, from the zenith to the horizon, or from the perpendicular to the horizontal line, is thus filled up. Man and the serpent form the right angle; other animals fill the whole quadrant; and any other kind of beings is geometrically impossible.

We will not here cite a greater number of natural emblems to prove our theory; the body of our work will supply them in abundance; for, in looking, under this same point of view, upon all the objects of nature, both dead and living, and on the innumerable phenomena that they present in a whole globe as in every atom of that globe, it must be seen clearly that, always preserving a real, though distant relation with some variety of life or intelligence, they not only may serve to characterize them, but that they really do characterize them. Even the dust and the dirt have also their fixed significations. They represent all that is low and vile; for the low, the vile, the abject, and the disgusting, are found, in the moral world, by the side of the great, the noble, and the elevated. It is evidently from a dim remembrance of all those necessary relations between the moral and phenomenal worlds, that man derives his decided taste for comparisons, of which all the other figures of rhetoric are, in fact, only varieties. Thence comes man's irresistible taste for fables and parables; those sure means of making the multitude receive ideas of the just and the unjust, but by which people have been too often led to compose absurd mythologies. The passage from the language of nature to languages of convention, was made by such insensible degrees that they who made it never thought of tracing the latter back to their source. They knew [16] not the road they had traveled; but the distance appeared striking when they became attentive to it. Primitively, men could not name objects, they must show them; not corporeally, it is true, but substantially and by the force of thought; as those objects exist in God, and as we still perceive them in dreams, in which there is evidently something more than imagination.*

An immediate communication of thoughts and sentiments is quite as conceivable, and even more simple than all those which are made by means more or less distant; and such a communication is so rich that it suffers no comparison with the poverty of all the others. When that primitive faculty of seeing and showing the immediate object of thought, and the natural emblem of sentiment was weakened, then, only, exterior signs came to join it. Thence the language of gestures, spoken at first more particularly by the eyes, the mouth, and the particular composition of the face, which at length introduced conventional sounds, and all exterior signs, such as are still found among the deaf and dumb; and, finally, those offered by hieroglyphics and writing the Scripture. At the epoch when the two manners of speaking (that by natural emblems and that by articulate sounds) were mixed, then resulted the language which is now called prophetic or extatic, in which conventional words are used only to recall the more significant emblems of nature.

It is in this last language, evidently double, we repeat, that we have found to be written the greater number of the books which antiquity has transmitted to us as inspired. To understand the Bible, therefore, it is not enough to understand the Hebrew, the Greek, the Latin, or any other idiom into which it is translated; but it is necessary also to understand the language of nature; for the sacred writers, primitively, borrowed from the language used in their times, only the words necessary to retrace the natural images which speak of themselves. Hence those strange things found in the prophets, which have so much shocked superficial philosophers; those monstrous images, uniting the discordant members of many different animals; for, in speaking of collective societies, or of different traits of moral character in the same individual, the prophets were forced to amalgamate primitive emblems, and to form of them compounds, such as are remarked, principally, in Ezekiel, Daniel, and Saint John. All that was entirely in the genius of the language of nature, and, consequently in the essence of things; and to ridicule the animals, the horns, the wheels covered with eyes, of the prophets, the white horse of the Apocalypse, is like those ignorant beings who laugh when they see Chinese writing or Egyptian hieroglyphics.†

[17] Such are the considerations that have induced us to publish this essay. Studying the Holy Scriptures ourselves, with this new key, we have seen so clearly the real intentions of the Creator and Redeemer of the human race, that we should deem ourselves guilty, if we did not impart our ideas to a world, so bewildered in all its religious conceptions, that scarce anything is to be found in it but atheism or superstition.

Besides, the present is not an unfavorable moment to call on the world to examine anew, to examine seriously and reflectingly, those great events which have substituted Christianity for idolatry, upon our globe. The philosophy of the nineteenth century is really not that of the eighteenth. Since the last European revolutions, which were moral

---

* Unless it be admitted that by that imagination we can form Berkeley's whole world, and consequently all possible worlds.

† In speaking of religious matters, Voltaire most frequently joked; he did not reason. As to Dupuis, he had not made himself master of the subject he treated. An attentive perusal of Kreutzer's symbolics, (a very useful work to the philosopher who wishes to undertake the study of the language of Nature,) furnishes evidence excluding all doubt, that the ancient pagan religions, with their different mythologies and cosmogonies, generally arose from the language of Nature misunderstood; and that, consequently, the completion of the Christian religion, the only true one, will consist in that same language being regained and carried to a certain degree of perfection.

as well as physical, Philosophy, from being a materialist, as she was, has become, in a great measure, a spiritualist. Many of our modern thinkers have at length perceived the truth of that prediction of Plato, that "they who will deliver themselves to profound researches, (in all that belongs to morals and religion,) with a humble mind, and fly that irreligious and unphilosophic mania of deciding, of cutting short everything at the first sight of difficulties, will find that what seemed to them most incredible is often what was most certain and most evident. Some great names are already linked with those new and radiant doctrines, of a world of light, a world of substance, everywhere enclosed in a world of matter; the only true, the only life-giving doctrines; doctrines which must, sooner or later, triumph.*

We will not here speak of those phenomena which seem as if they must familiarize even the medical science with those ideas which extend our world through illimitable space. It is well known that some distinguished physicians in France, as well as in Germany, rising above the two opposite kinds of prejudice, have examined, with some attention, that particular state of organization produced by magnetic manipulations, or the laying on of hands, since called *provoked extasy*; and they have admitted the reality of surprising phenomena, evidently known to the ancients, which show that man, even while in the bonds of corporeal existence, may sometimes rise above organization, and thus be more or less free from time and space. The words seer, prophet, and inspired, thus begin to seem less strange to these philosophers; as the traces of the emblematic, or prophetic language, often reappear in the state of exaltation produced by magnetism. Some modern philosophers are even convinced by them, of the reality of certain communications between men, who, laying off their material envelope, have passed into that world of light, which plays in the midst of all the globes, as the rays of the sun play in a globe of crystal, and in which the emblematic language is spoken, and men still living upon earth who do not yet know any languages of convention and articulate sounds.†

---

* At the head of these names stands that of M. Royer Collard, and the school which he has formed.

† The proofs, by reasoning that we have offered, of the primitive existence of a natural language, among intelligent beings, appeared to us so clear and convincing, that we thought it unnecessary to crowd this introduction with citations from ancient authors who had the same opinion with ourselves, or related facts capable of supporting them. Yet the following remarks may find a place here, where we have touched on the delicate question of animal magnetism.

The Pythagorean Epicharmus already spoke as follows, of what I call substantial forms. "The art of playing on the flute, is undoubtedly separate from the man who plays on it. It is the same of what is well, or what is good; goodness is necessarily a thing separate from the man who possesses it." And Alcimus adds: "The soul learns certain things by means of the senses, and others without their aid, because it considers these things in themselves;" which very clearly proves that the ancients frequently attached the idea of reality to what, for the moderns, has been but an abstract quality. (See Diogenes Laertius, iii. 14, 12.) Philopones asserts that he has seen in one of the best books of Aristotle upon good, or philosophy, these expressions: "The ideas, or forms of things, contain their matter, as numbers contain the things numbered; for matter being in itself a thing undetermined, that is to say, without real attributes; it is only forms that make objects." (De An. page 17, Venice, 15, 35.) According to Pythagoras and his disciples, things alone were objects in themselves, that is to say, real and eternal, though immaterial objects: while material objects, as far as they were material, were in themselves nothing. Their ideas approached very near those brought forward among us by Berkeley, upon the non-existence of matter, as something in itself; and, consequently, when they spoke of the eternal world, they frequently meant only the substantial forms of this world; such as we see them, and feel them, in the state of dreaming. In this connection, the recent somnambulic phenomena, observed in Germany, seem to have enabled some of her philosophers to understand the ancients better than they have ever been understood before. "Timeus," says Tiedmann, in his Life of Pythagoras, page 545, "promises those who observe the prescribed rules, the sight of the gods, (that is, of their transformed ancestors); we cannot but conclude from this, that the Pythagoreans had found the means of being in a real state of extasy;" (that is, a state in which the interior and immortal man, being awake during a transient sleep of the body, can very naturally converse with those whose material organs sleep, definitely, the sleep of death.)

Stillingfleet, who is known to have studied antiquity most profoundly, was convinced, like ourselves, that, originally, the name of a thing signified its essence. Whoever will consult the "Origines Sacræ," will find there the confirmation of almost all our ideas.

[18] But, besides modern medicine being very far from consistent with itself, upon these various points; besides it being dangerous to seek to establish communications, of this kind, between the natural world and the universe of human spirits, on account of the degradation of our being, which necessarily prevents our entering into communication with any but the degraded beings who are found in unison with us; and as we are not in a state to understand them aright, even if they were disposed to be useful to us; we regard magnetic phenomena as of very little use to morals and religion, though we should be very far from discouraging any who wish to confirm their belief in immortality, by experiments in artificial somnambulism, by becoming eye-witnesses of the physical, or moral, penetration of certain extatic individuals, in whom the future state of man, disengaged from the dullness of matter, is seen as palpably as any other phenomenon in nature.

The enlightened Christian never needed those tardy experiments by which human sciences think, from time to time, to add to his faith. It was always enough, to make him perceive the finger of God, to observe with an impartial eye the admirable harmony of the old and new [19] Testaments, and the immense system evidently above the power of all created intelligences. But it is not thus with those merely nominal Christians, who, in reality, know not what they believe, and who, as they cannot disentangle the truth from the absurd pretensions, with which it has been mixed, envelope, in equal scorn, religious abuses and the most indispensable principles of morals and religion. It is not thus, above all, with those numerous miscreants of the day, who often have such terrible prejudices to surmount, who often have not the first idea, the first notion of an immortal life, disengaged from the clogs of matter. To all such, the most simple bridge becomes the most precious thing; and the idea of the language of Nature, found in the holy books, has appeared to us most proper to represent this bridge; and the eagerness with which we have seized on it, is proportioned to the number of those who are to pass over it.

We have divided our work into two parts; the first treats of the true nature of Jesus Christ; the second on the true sense of his doctrine.

Father Kircher was convinced that the first language could not be conventional. Clement, of Alexandria, said, in direct terms, that the ancients sometimes recounted their actions by a course of symbols. It was from Egypt that Greece received the use of symbols, her mythology, her temples for the cure of the sick, and the giving of oracles; and Egypt had found all those things only by means of her extatic men, her priests and priestesses. It is impossible to resist the evidence furnished by history, on this subject, and confirmed by new experience in these last times. Aristeus Proconensis, who lived at the time of Cyrus, is represented, by his contemporaries, as a man who could make his soul leave his body, and return to it, at will; he was, evidently, nothing else than a somnambulist. Socrates himself, as all know, entered, from time to time, into magnetic exaltation; this must be the origin of the demon, or familiar spirit, attributed to him. "These demons of the Pythagoreans, said Diogenes Laertius, (demons, who, as we have already said, were no other than the substantial men of their ancestors,) influence mortals by the presentiments and dreams which they give them; they send them health and sickness, and reveal to them hidden things and future events." Every one knows the cabalistic science of the Rabbins, which has been defended by more than one strong head, in past times, and which the progress of science has forced some modern philosophers to view with a little less disdain. Finally, all the passages of Saint Paul's epistles, in which he traces rules touching the order to be preserved among those who speak unknown tongues, those who have visions, revelations, and those who interpret dreams, prove that the laying on of hands, observed by him, resembled, entirely, our modern experiments on provoked extasy. It was necessary then, as now, to try the spirits if they be of God, and to set apart imaginary or simulated exaltation, imposture, and folly. And what the apostles themselves have taught us, on this subject, enables us to enter into details on what the Holy Fathers, and the first ecclesiastical writers, who, without a single exception, all admitted extasies, cures, and possessions, and spoke of them as phenomena known to all the world, the pagan as well as the Christian. Tertullian alone wrote seven books upon extasy; and he became a montanist only because he suffered himself to be deceived by the extatic Montan and his two companions, prophetesses or somnambulists, as they may be called. Really, he must be very ignorant of ancient authors, who can believe that the peculiar state of organization, which Dr. Bertrand calls the extatic crisis, has not been known to all ages; that it has not frequently constituted the principal object of the researches of nations, in relation to worship, as well as to the healing science, and that most of the religions in the world did not have those astonishing phenomena for a first principle.

Hieroglyphic Keys

[21] Before beginning our explanation of the principal pas[s]ages of the Holy Scriptures, according to the principles of the astonishing language, the existence of which we have just pointed at, we should most heartily wish to present, to our reader, the dictionary which has guided us. But, as the words of Rousseau will apply to this case, that our book would be as large as the world, and then we should not have exhausted our subject, we will limit ourselves to a few very general data; simple keys, by means of which the reader can, by himself, penetrate farther into the immense domains of nature. Meanwhile, our whole dictionary will be reduced to the following words:

    I.   GOD; LOVE, TRUTH.
    II.   SUN; HEAT, LIGHT.
    III.   MAN; GOODNESS, KNOWLEDGE.
    IV.   LIVE; EAT, DRINK.
    V.   ANIMAL KINGDOM; VEGETABLE KINGDOM, MINERAL KINGDOM.
    VI.   CREATION; PRODUCTION, DESTRUCTION.
    VII.   SUBSTANCE; FORM, COLOR.
    VIII.   TO WALK; TO ASCEND, TO DESCEND.
    XI.   MIDST; RIGHT, LEFT.
    X.   POINTS; NUMBERS, ELEMENTS.

I. GOD; LOVE, TRUTH. Because God, in his first essence, is the Great-Whole, the Infinite Being, he is nothing for us, unless he concentrate the rays of his eternal glory upon a determined point; in other words, unless he present himself to man, under man's image and likeness. Indeed, we cannot perceive, or grasp the idea of God, even when we consider him in the first great division of his being, as love, goodness, or power; and as truth, order, or wisdom. Not only does his being already escape us, when we turn our attention to those two great attributes, but those attributes themselves are not known to us, save by the natural emblems of which they are the abstractions. How, indeed, can we know love, if not by the heart? And how can we know truth, if not by the objects that reveal it to us? Thus arises an absolute im- [22] possibility for any created intelligence to reach God, except by means of the emblem of a man-God, or a God-man. Therefore, man is the true hieroglyphic of the Divinity; a hieroglyphic, infinite in its details, even when man is considered only as a material form, since his material form itself, is but the emblem of his moral being.

II. SUN; HEAT, LIGHT. The truth which we have just declared must be perceived by every impartial mind, which will give it the slightest attention; but men have not, generally, sought God in that most natural type, the perfection of human nature. Guided, probably, by the secret consciousness of the degradation of their own being, they have, almost invariably, begun by seeking God in an emblem of the second order, an inanimate emblem, and, on that account, less susceptible of degradation, but, also, less susceptible of a mere physical perfection; we speak of the star of day. Indeed, all the inconceivable qualities, remarked in the Divine Being, are found typified almost as inconceivably in the sun. The sun in the firmament, that star always the same, that star always new, appears as one only, dazzling the eyes of mortals, infinite by its light, present to the whole earth, and the principle of life to all nature. Its two essential qualities, heat and light, also correspond, the former to love, the latter to truth. Mysterious fire! in thy progress, as in the nature of thy rays, men know thee clearly, only by thy benefits. Everything in the world is nourished, formed, by thy substance, from the tenderest grass-blade to the hardest diamond. Hence the millions of hieroglyphics which any one may easily find. All the phenomena of reflected light, all the colors, preserve some distant relation with the moral world; from white, which represents complex truths, to black, which recalls the darkness of absolute ignorance; from scarlet, which casts the brilliancy of fire and flame, to the faintest violet, scarcely able to indicate the forms of objects. And this amazing comparison of dead light with spiritual light, may be carried into the mysteries of refraction and transmission. Light, in whatever way we view it, under whatever point of view we consider it, always answers to some variety of truth; and man's eye, the emblem of his soul, is really nourished by light, in the contemplation of the whole creation.

III. MAN; GOODNESS, SCIENCE. We have already, in our Introduction, said a word of man; and, in the body of our work, will be found quite a detailed sketch of the numerous hieroglyphics of his different organs. We will say, then, simply, that all that can be remarked in the vegetable, instinctive, and animal parts of his being, is likewise found in his moral being, and the former is but a detailed hieroglyphic of the latter. As the external man is constantly occupied in acquiring personal qualities, and in amassing possessions which will make him respected in the world, so the immortal man is every moment acquiring the celestial knowledges, and virtues, which render him worthy of the eternal society; and those different metaphysical qualities are made perceptible, even in their least varieties, by the infinite hieroglyphics of earthly acquisitions; hieroglyphics of which the substantial images will, necessarily, accompany man in his state of transformation; what do I say? which probably accompany him in his present state, though unknown to him. Man, like all animals, may be viewed [23] as a hollow cylinder, through which pass emblematic matters. Around this are ranged the different organs of the senses, more or less numerous, more or less developed, according to the subjects, and which, reviewed in the same way, give a mass of moral hieroglyphics, which it is not in human power to number. And here, also, may be remarked this characteristic difference, that goodness perfects, rather than science, because goodness relates to love, science to truth. Considered as a collection of levers, or of any powers whatever, man still offers an admirable subject of contemplation. The hand is, in itself, a whole apparatus; indeed, every finger is one. These apparatuses are always divided into three distinct levers, for reasons which we shall give when we speak of the hieroglyphic of numbers. The thumb, situated at the root of the hand, is the most considerable force of the same apparatus; and therein it corresponds to the shoulder and the hip, which are similarly situated. By an act of the will, of three levers man makes one. When a force is overcome, it is as if in three successive efforts; first, the hand is exerted, then the elbow, then the shoulder; and man is vanquished. Thus are distributed upon the human form, as upon a scale of proportion, the hieroglyphic points of all the possible varieties of moral powers. From the data that we already have on this subject, we may, one day, perhaps, give the particular correspondence of each finger and each joint.

IV. LIVE; EAT, DRINK. God is life; man lives: in other words, with man, life is progressive; with God, not. Everything in man is done by insensible degrees; the Creator himself cannot invert this order. For this reason, the human body increases, and decreases, equally, by accessions and losses, which are remarked only with time. Even love and truth, which are possessed exclusively by God, can be applied to man, only by imperceptible degrees. Hence that admirable economy of the restoration of the degraded human race, accomplished in a proportionate lapse of time; an essential truth, which we must never lose sight of, for an instant, when we wish to judge correctly of the course of God Redeemer. Eating, in the physical man, relates, also, to love, and drinking, to wisdom; and that, even in their minutest details. This is true of nourishment, in general, as of clothing, which also recalls love, or charity, by its warmth, and truth, by its colors and forms.

V. ANIMAL KINGDOM; VEGETABLE KINGDOM, MINERAL KINGDOM. All animals, by their corporeal forms, as well as by their instincts, are hieroglyphics of the different degradations of human nature, or of detached parts of the collection of organs of life, called man. Examine animal forms geometrically, from man, who represents the perpendicular, to the reptile which forms the horizontal line, and then applying to those forms the rules of the exact sciences, which God himself cannot change, we shall see that visible nature contains them all; that the combinations of the seven primitive forms, are entirely exhausted, and that, therefore, they can represent all possible varieties of morality. Hence the immense chain of moral types, offered by all animals, in their more and more imperfect manners of providing for their frail existence; types which appear, sometimes, arbitrary, and [24] even strange, to the eyes of the superficial philosopher, who is yet no more superficial than the philosophic naturalist, who has studied the delicate relation of forms, and instincts, in their endless details, and who knows that every fibre is placed, by a supreme reason, in the worm as in the elephant. As to the two other kingdoms, the vegetable kingdom is a degradation of the animal kingdom, by the suppression of all voluntary motion; and the mineral kingdom, a degradation of the vegetable kingdom by the suppression of all perceptible motion whatever. But the distant relation of the good and the true, is found to be always preserved. The young grass, for instance, is the symbol of a productive power in its germ; the tree, that of a faculty provided with all the means necessary for the production of fruits of all kinds. The same is true of minerals. The different manners of crystalization were certainly not abandoned to chance, nor chosen without some moral reason, by supreme Goodness and Wisdom. Only warmth, in the mineral kingdom, is generally less than in the preceding, as in that, it is less than in the first.

VI. CREATION; PRODUCTION, DESTRUCTION. If for God to create is not an act, properly speaking, that is to say, an effort, for man to do good is to create with God and by God. And to do evil is to create in a still more real sense; for, in evil, man acts alone; God does not create with him. The perfect emblems needed no Creation. They were all found in the Infinite Being, in the absolute Being, who can give everything because he has everything. But, as to the imperfect emblems, they were all necessarily created; from the emblem of fraternal hatred, pictured on the face of the first sinner, to that of a crucified, which is an outraged God. In the simultaneous order, the infinite is said to create, or produce the finite; the whole is said to create, or produce the part. All that produces, is Creator, or Father; all that is produced, is Son, or Truth. Substance produces form; form produces color, &c. Production refers to good, to affirmation, to reality, to order, to harmony; destruction, to evil, to negation, to falsity, to disorder, to discord. Nature, in her beauty, is the emblem of the first; terrible phenomena, elements in convulsion, the emblem of the second. The admirable economy of men and animals, reproducing themselves, offers the hieroglyphic of all moral bodies, which, also, have their birth, their time of growth, and of decay. When the moral body is considered as having life, it is represented by living being, more or less developed; when that body is without life, but regular, it is figured by a dead body, or a statue more or less perfect, more or less finished. All divine harmony is typified by different degrees of legitimate loves and unions; all discord, all sin, all error, by different degrees of illegitimate loves and unions. And this correspondence is sustained even in inorganic unions, the attractions or repulsions of matter. Otherwise, it would be metaphysically impossible that all those moral varieties should become appreciable to created intelligence.

VII. SUBSTANCE; FORM, COLOR. Substance is all that is real. The Creator is substance in the supreme degree. All that we see and touch, in nature, is emblematic of that substance. In this sense, the objects that we perceive in the state of dreaming, are as much sub- [25] tances as any others. In man, it is the flesh that represents the substance, or the foundation of his being; the various forms of this flesh represent his qualities. And, again, flesh, as substance, relates to love; forms and colors, to truth. Moreover, all possible geometrical forms are moral types; and, considered in their primitive developments, they cannot be more numerous than the primitive variety of colors. The three dimensions, length, breadth, and thickness, consequently, have their fixed significations; but thickness should be named first, as it relates to substance. These dimensions must make exactly the parallel of the centre, of the right and left, which will be spoken of soon. Just now, we considered men, and animals, as crooked cylinders, or as vases, containing such emblematic matters as may characterize their being. Let the reader now extend this idea to everything that is crooked; he will have, first, the horizon and the cope of the heavens surrounding him, like immense curves, figuring eternity; he will then have the edifices, made by the hand of man, of all forms and sizes, from the hieroglyphic temple, the abode of the divinity, or, rather, of Divine Truth, to the smallest vase, to the smallest box. And all the details, considered in their relation to the primitive form, with the universal form, which is man, supply the type of some moral variety, more or less distant from the first source.

VIII. WALK; GO UP, COME DOWN. The action of walking is the general emblem of life and social relations. In its origin, locomotion, with man, is of a very simple nature; but, afterwards, he varies it at will; the horse, the elephant, the carriage, the vessel, receive him by turns. He even makes to himself wings, and rises towards the heaven. Hence the innumerable hieroglyphics of life and social relations, all the different varieties of which may be found and appreciated. Human intelligence itself, as an abstract part, putting in motion all that apparatus, is figured by it in its different developments. And, in that, the degree of elevation of the soil has, also, its particular signification. To go up, is taken in a good sense, and recalls an approach to uncreated goodness; thence the custom of the ancients to worship upon mountains. To go down, is taken in the opposite sense. These two emblems are always the complete reverse of each other, when applied to the vice of pride and the virtue of humility, as, in general, all emblems may be. On the other side, to sit down is to cease to act, to be fixed, it is to rest, and even to rest upon ourselves. To be down, is to rest upon God, upon the eternal rock. The pagans called the earth the mother of all nature; the Christian knows that that mother is no other than He who would not forsake his children, even if a nursing mother could forget the child that she had borne beneath her bosom. Hence, then, the innumerable hieroglyphics of the sleep of night, of awakening, of the succession of days, and of labors, and even that of bed, which represents faith, and covering, which represents charity.

IX. MIDST; RIGHT, LEFT. The midst, in general, represents perfection, the centre of a whole; and thus, in the first place, the Being of beings, placed entirely out of time and space. The right recalls goodness, power; the left, truth, wisdom. The same may be said of that hieroglyphic, as of that of substance, form, and color. That of [26] points and directions, which follows, also relates to it, and will explain it entirely, so that we need say no more of it here.

X. POINTS; NUMBERS, ELEMENTS. Placing man at the zenith, he has behind him the east, before him the west, at his right the north, at his left the south. In this state of things, the east represents to him the invisible Creator, the hidden God, whom faith alone can reach. The east, characterized by the march of the sun, the material emblem of the Divinity, also designates an increase in goodness and truth; and, therefore, the west designates an analogous decrease; as the north recalls a loss in charity, and the south a progress in truth. Here, the order which we are about to remark, in relation to the good and the true, is found reversed,* since man has goodness, or love, at his left, and truth, or wisdom, at his right. But these things should always be judged, above all, with relation to that God in whose presence man stands. And, moreover, man himself, naturally placed by the Creator, at first, in a state of possible increase, consequently in a state of full and entire moral liberty, ought to make the first use of this noble faculty in seeking his Creator, in turning freely towards Him. Thence a moral signification of all the directions towards the different points of immensity, to which as many points in the human body correspond to characterize them. These points are still more real in the interior nature of our being, than they are in the physical universe. As we have already said, the human soul cannot be considered without that collection of organs called man; and, therefore, it cannot be conceived of without right, left, and all the other consequent directions. The points of height are already known to us, as recalling nobility, elevation of soul; those of depth, as recalling baseness and abjection. Considered in motion, the upward direction represents, also, celestial life; the opposite direction, infernal life. Beings of a superior perfection, when they appear, are seen descending from above; degraded beings arrive from below, though places, in themselves, are nothing determined, as forms offer only relative sizes. The whole front of man corresponds, also, to kindness, and the whole back, to aversion. The same instinct causes friendship to advance, and horror and disgust to recoil. Even the different forms of the body, among mankind, designate, as they create, the different affections.

The numbers which relate to points, have, also, their fixed significations. But they could not be understood without very extensive and metaphysical considerations. The analogy, which necessarily exists between this matter and all the rest, must supply the place of proof. Unity relates to God; duality to love and truth. Thus, duality relates to man, who, for this reason, was created male and female; the husband representing, rather, wisdom, the wife, rather, goodness. Trinity, or the number three, always designates the perfection of a being, or an object, probably, because of the three distinct relations that the human mind may discover therein. The astonishing properties of the number seven, and of the sabbath of human nature, will be amply discussed in [27] the body of our work. We will here add only a word, on the numbers ten and twelve, just to indicate to our readers that certain numbers cannot, in any case, be entirely arbitrary. The decimal which is taken from the number of our fingers, is, therefore, founded in the nature of things, since the Creator could not choose that number without reason. The same is true of the dozen. The different parts of the day and night, for example, could never have been divided in a different proportion. The four radical points, which serve as their base, two of which are in the horizon, the other two in the zenith and nadir, necessarily cause twelve or twenty-four numbers, which, likewise, have a proportionate importance in the Holy Scriptures, as we will show.

Finally, the four elements, in all their immense details, offer, to the reflecting mind, moral emblems so numerous, that no philosopher can count them. The earth, as a solid foundation, as a basis sustaining the king of nature, man with the upright brow, refers to God, the eternal support of his creatures. As productive of all sorts of fruits, agreeable to the taste and the sight, the earth may incessantly remind us of the human society, the church of God. The air, with its winged inhabitants, the atmosphere, with

---

* If the author here had turned man towards the east, as the angels always place themselves, in the heavens, he would not have found the order of right and left, with regard to good and truth, reversed.—TRANSLATOR.

its innumerable phenomena, everywhere announce the invisible action of a hidden God, his immensity, his inexhaustible goodness towards all that breathe, united to a majesty equally imposing and terrible. Water, as transparent element, reflecting with the exactness of a mirror, the images of objects, (when it is calm,) represents, with all the myriads that find life in it, the different kinds and degrees of truths; and that, in opposition to the habitable earth, which relates rather to goodness and substance. And as to fire, it refers us to the sun, from which it emanates; and, therefore, it represents charity, and knowledges among beings, weak images of their Author, who is uncreated Love and Truth.

We believe that this sketch, short and imperfect as it is, will be enough to awaken the attention of all classes of readers, and to prove to them that our explanations of the Holy Books will not be arbitrary, like those which have been hitherto given.

[This edition is in Emerson's library in Concord. Other copies survive at Boston Public, Rutgers University, the University of Virginia and at Union College at Schenectady.]

ON

THE INTERCOURSE

BETWEEN

THE SOUL AND THE BODY,

WHICH IS SUPPOSED TO TAKE PLACE

EITHER BY PHYSICAL INFLUX,

OR BY

SPIRITUAL INFLUX,

OR

BY PRE-ESTABLISHED HARMONY.

FROM THE LATIN OF

EMANUEL SWEDENBORG.

BOSTON:
ADONIS HOWARD, NO. 157, COURT STREET.
1828.

Press of the New Jerusalem Magazine.
Freeman & Bolles, Print.

CONTENTS.

ON

THE INTERCOURSE

BETWEEN

THE SOUL AND THE BODY, &c.

---

1. THERE are three opinions and traditions, which are hypothetical ones, concerning the intercourse between the soul and the body, or concerning the operation of one on the other, and of one in conjunction with the other; the first is that of physical influx, the second is that of spiritual influx, and the third is that of pre-established harmony, The FIRST hypothesis, which is that of PHYSICAL INFLUX, originates from the appearances of the senses, and the fallacies thence derived, because it appears as if the objects of sight, which affect the eyes, flowed-in into the thought, and produced it; in like manner speech, which affects the ears, appears to flow-in into the mind and produce ideas there; and the case appears to be similar with respect to the smell, taste, and touch: forasmuch as the organs of these senses first receive the impressions that flow from the world, and the mind appears to think, and also to will, according to the affections of those

1

organs, therefore the ancient philosophers and schoolmen supposed influx to be derived from them into the soul, and thus adopted the hypothesis of physical or natural influx. The SECOND hypothesis, which is that of SPIRITUAL INFLUX, called by some occasional influx, originates from order and its laws; for the soul is a spiritual substance, and is consequently purer, prior, and interior, but the body is material, and is consequently grosser, posterior, and exterior; and it is according to order for what is purer to flow-in into what is grosser, what is prior into what is posterior, and what is interior into what is exterior, thus what is spiritual into what is material, and not *vice versa*; consequently it is according to order for the thinking mind to flow-in into the sight according to the state induced on the eyes from the objects [before them], which state that mind also disposes at its pleasure; and likewise for the perceptive mind to flow-in into the hearing according to the state induced on the ears by speech. The THIRD hypothesis, which is that of PRE-ESTABLISHED HARMONY, originates from the appearances and fallacies of reason, since the mind, in every operation, acts in unity and simultaneously with the body; but nevertheless every operation is first successive and afterwards simultaneous, and successive operation is influx and simultaneous operation is harmony; as when the mind thinks and af-

terwards speaks, or when it wills and afterwards acts: wherefore it is a fallacy of reason to establish that which is simultaneous and exclude that which is successive. Besides these three opinions concerning the intercourse between the soul and the body, a fourth cannot be given, for either the soul must operate on the body, or the body on the soul, or both continually together.

2. Forasmuch as [the hypothesis of] spiritual influx originates from order and its laws, as was said above, therefore this opinion has been acknowledged and received by the wise in the learned world in preference to the other two: for every thing which originates from order, is truth, and truth manifests itself by virtue of its inherent light, even in the shade of reason in which hypothesis reside. There are three things which involve this hypothesis in shade, viz. ignorance of what the soul is, ignorance of what the spiritual [principle] is, and ignorance of the quality of influx; wherefore these three things must first be unfolded before reason can see the truth itself; for hypothetical truth is not truth itself, but a conjecture respecting it; it is like a picture seen at night on a wall by the light of the stars, to which the mind assigns various forms according to its fancy, which appears different when the sun illuminates it in the morning, and not only discovers and renders visible its gen-

eral form, but also its particular parts; in like manner, out of the shade of truth in which this hypothesis is involved, arises the open truth, when it is known what and of what quality the spiritual [principle] is respectively to the natural, what and of what quality the human soul is, and what is the quality of the influx that flows-in into the soul, and through that into the perceptive and thinking mind, and from this into the body. But these subjects can be explained by no man, unless it have been given him by the Lord to have consociation with angels in the spiritual world and with men in the natural world at the same time; and forasmuch as this has been given to me, I have been enabled to describe what and of what quality they are, which is done in the work on Conjugial Love, in the memorable relation concerning the SPIRITUAL [principle], n. 326 to 329; in that concerning the HUMAN SOUL, n. 315; in that concerning INFLUX, n. 380; and more fully in that at n. 415 to 422. Who does not know, or may not know, that the good of love and the truth of faith flow-in from God into man, and that they flow-in into his soul, and are felt in his mind, and flow-out from his thought into his speech, and from his will into his actions? That spiritual influx, and its origin and derivation are from thence, shall be manifested in the following order. I. That there are two worlds, the spiritual world, in

which are spirits and angels, and the natural world, in which are men. II. That the spiritual world [first] existed and [continually] subsists from its own sun, and that the natural world [first] existed and [continually] subsists from its own sun. III. That the sun of the spiritual world is pure love from Jehovah God, who is in the midst of it. IV. That from that sun proceeds* heat and light, and that the heat proceeding from it is in its essence love, and that the light thence is in its essence wisdom. V. That both that heat and that light flow-in into man, the heat into his will, where it produces the good of love, and the light into his understanding, where it produces the truth of wisdom. VI. That those two [principles], viz. heat and light, or love and wisdom, flow-in, conjointly from God into the soul of man, and through this into his mind, its affections and thoughts, and from these into the senses, speech and actions of the body. VII. That the sun of the natural world is pure fire, and that the world of nature [first] existed and [continually] subsists by means of this sun.

* This word is retained in the singular number in agreement with the Latin of the author; who frequently connects the terms heat and light, love and wisdom, good and truth, charity and faith, with a singular verb, to intimate that these principles are one in the Lord, and proceed as one from him, though they are variously received. The reader is requested to remember this explanation when he meets with this form of expression in the following pages.

VIII. That therefore every thing which proceeds from this sun, regarded in itself, is dead. IX. That what is spiritual [or the spiritual principle] clothes itself with what is natural [or the natural principle], as man clothes himself with a garment. X. That spiritual things thus clothed in man enable him to live a rational and moral man, thus a spiritually natural man. XI. That the reception of that influx is according to the state of love and wisdom with man. XII. That the understanding in man is capable of being elevated into the light, that is, into the wisdom, in which the angels of heaven are, according to the improvement of his reason, and that his will is capable of being elevated in like manner into heat, that is, into love, according to the deeds of his life; but that the love of the will is not elevated, except so far as man wills and does those things which the wisdom of the understanding teaches. XIII. That it is altogether otherwise with beasts. XIV. That there are three degrees in the spiritual world, and three degrees in the natural world, according to which all influx takes place. XV. That ends are in the first degree, causes in the second, and effects in the third. XVI. That hence may appear what is the quality of spiritual influx from its origin to its effects. Each of these propositions shall now be briefly illustrated.

I.—*That there are two worlds, the spiritual world in which are spirits and angels, and the natural world in which are men.*

3. THAT there is a spiritual world in which are spirits and angels, distinct from the natural world in which men are, is a truth which has been deeply hidden even in the christian world; the reason is, because no angel has descended and declared it, and no man has ascended and seen it; lest therefore from ignorance concerning that world, and the uncertain faith concerning heaven and hell that results from such ignorance, man should be infatuated to such a degree as to become an atheistic naturalist, it has pleased the Lord to open the sight of my spirit, and to elevate it into heaven, and also to let it down into hell, and to exhibit to its view the quality of each. It is thence manifest to me that there are two worlds which are distinct from each other; one in which all things are spiritual, which is thence called the spiritual world; and another in which all things are natural, which is thence called the natural world; and that spirits and angels live in their own world, and men in theirs; and also that every man passes by death from his own world into the other, and lives therein to eternity. A knowledge concerning each of these worlds should be premised, in order that [the doc-

trine of] influx, which is the subject here treated of, may be unfolded from its beginning; for the spiritual world flows-in into the natural world, and actuates it in all its particular parts as well with men as with beasts, and also constitutes the vegetative principle in trees and herbs.

II.—*That the spiritual world* [*first*] *existed and* [*continually*] *subsists from its own sun, and that the natural world* [*first*] *existed and* [*continually*] *subsists from its own sun.*

4. THE reason why there is one sun of the spiritual world and another sun of the natural world, is because those worlds are altogether distinct; and a world derives its origin from its sun; for a world in which all things are spiritual cannot originate from a sun from which all the things that proceed are natural, for thus influx would be physical, which, nevertheless, is contrary to order. That the world existed from the sun, and not *vice versa*, is manifest from an effect derived from this cause, viz. that the world in all and singular its parts subsists by means of the sun, and subsistence demonstrates existence, wherefore it is said that subsistence is perpetual existence; from whence it is evident, that if the sun were removed, its world would fall into chaos, and this chaos into no-

thing. That in the spiritual world there is a different sun from that in the natural world, I can testify, for I have seen it: it appears fiery like our sun, nearly of a similar magnitude, and is at a distance from the angels as our sun is from men: but it does not rise nor set, but stands immoveable in a middle altitude between the zenith and the horizon, whence the angels have perpetual light and perpetual spring. The man of [mere] reason, who knows nothing concerning the sun of the spiritual world, easily falls into absurdity *(delirat)* in his idea concerning the creation of the universe, which, when he deeply considers it, he apprehends no otherwise than as proceeding from nature; and as the origin of nature is the sun, he no otherwise apprehends the creation of the universe than as proceeding from its sun as a creator. Moreover no one can apprehend [the doctrine of] spiritual influx, unless he also knows the origin of it; for all influx proceeds from a sun, spiritual influx from its sun, and natural influx from its sun; the internal sight of man, which is that of his mind, receives influx from the spiritual sun, but his external sight, which is that of his body, receives influx from the natural sun; and both are conjoined in operation in like manner as the soul is conjoined with the body. Hence it is evident into what blindness, darkness, and fatuity they may fall, who know nothing concerning the spiritual world and its

sun: they may fall into *blindness*, because the mind which depends on the sight of the eye alone, becomes in its reasonings like a bat, which flies by night with a wandering course casually directed towards such linen cloths as may be hanging in its way; they may fall into *darkness*, because the sight of the mind, when the sight of the eye flows-in into it from within, is deprived of all spiritual light, and becomes like an owl; and they may fall into *fatuity*, because the man still continues to think, but he thinks from natural things concerning spiritual things, and not *vice versa*, thus he thinks madly, foolishly and fatuitously.

III.—*That the sun of the spiritual world is pure love, from Jehovah God, who is in the midst of it.*

5. SPIRITUAL things cannot proceed from any other source than from love, and love cannot proceed from any other source than from Jehovah God, who is love itself, wherefore the sun of the spiritual world, from which all spiritual things issue as from their fountain, is pure love proceeding from Jehovah God, who is in the midst of it: that sun itself is not God, but is from God, and is the proximate sphere about him from him. By means of this sun the universe was created by Jehovah God: by the universe all the worlds in one

complex are understood, which are as many as the stars in the expanse of our heaven. That creation was effected by means of that sun, which is pure love, thus by Jehovah God, is because love is the very *esse* of life, and wisdom is the *existere* of life thence derived, and all things were created from love by means of wisdom; this is understood by these words in John, "The Word was with God, and God was the Word, all things were made by him, and without him nothing was made which was made; and the world was made by [means of] him," i. 3, 10; the Word here is the divine truth, thus likewise the divine wisdom; wherefore also the Word is called the light which illuminates every man, ver. 9, in like manner as the divine wisdom illuminates by means of the divine truth. They who derive the origin of worlds from any other source than from the divine love [operating] by means of the divine wisdom, blunder like persons disordered in the brain *(cerebrosi)*, who see apparitions *(larvæ)* as men, phantoms as lights, and entities of the reason as real figures: for the created universe is a coherent work, originating from the divine love [operating] by means of the divine wisdom: you will see this if you are able to examine the connexions of things in their order from primaries to ultimates. As God is one, so also the spiritual sun is one; for the extension of space is not predicable of

spiritual things, which are the derivations of that sun; and essence and existence without space is every where in space without space; thus the divine love is from the beginning of the universe to all its boundaries: That the Divine fills all things, and by filling them preserves all things in the state in which they were created, reason has a distant view of, and also a near view, so far as it is acquainted with love as to its quality in itself; with its conjunction with wisdom for the perception of ends; with its influx into wisdom for the exhibition of causes; and with its operation by means of wisdom for the production of effects.

IV.—*That from that sun proceeds heat and light, and that the heat proceeding from it is in its essence love, and that the light thence is in its essence wisdom.*

6. It is known that in the Word, and thence in the common language of preachers, divine love is expressed by fire, as [when they pray] that heavenly fire may fill the heart and kindle holy desires to worship God: the reason is because fire corresponds to love, and thence signifies it; hence it is that Jehovah God was seen as a fire in a bush before Moses, and in like manner on mount Sinai before the sons of Israel; and that it was commanded that

fire should be perpetually kept upon the altar, and that the lights of the candlestick in the tabernacle should be kindled every evening; this was commanded because fire signified love. That there is heat proceeding from that fire appears manifestly from the effects of love; thus a man is incensed, grows warm, and is inflamed, as his love is exalted into zeal, or into the wrath of anger: the heat of the blood, or the vital heat of men, and of animals in general, is from no other source than from love, which constitutes their life: neither is the infernal fire any thing else than love opposite to heavenly love: this now is the reason that the divine love appears to the angels as the sun in their world, which is fiery like our sun, as was said above, and that the angels are in heat according to their reception of love from Jehovah God by means of that sun. It follows from hence that the light there is in its essence wisdom; for love and wisdom are indivisible, like esse and existere, as love exists by means of wisdom and according to it: this is similar to what takes place in our world, wherein, at the time of spring, heat unites itself with light, and produces germination and at length fructification: besides, every one knows that spiritual heat is love and spiritual light is wisdom: for a man grows warm in proportion as he loves, and his understanding is in light in proportion as he is wise. I have often seen

that spiritual light, which immensely exceeds natural light in whiteness *(candor)* and also in splendour, for it is as whiteness itself and splendour itself in themselves, and appears like resplendent and dazzling snow, such as the garments of the Lord appeared when he was transformed, Mark ix. 3, Luke ix. 28: as light is wisdom, therefore the Lord calls himself the light which illuminates every man, John i. 9, and says in other places that he is The Light, John iii. 19, chap. viii. 12, chap. xii. 35, 36, 47, that is, that he is divine truth itself, which is the Word, thus wisdom itself. It is believed that natural light *(lumen)*, which is also rational light, is derived from the light of our world: but it is derived from the light of the spiritual world; for the sight of the mind flows-in into the sight of the eye, thus also the light of the spiritual world flows-in into the light of the natural world, and not *vice versa;* if the contrary took place, there would be physical influx and not spiritual influx.

V.—*That both that heat and that light flow-in into man, the heat into his will, where it produces the good of love, and the light into his understanding, where it produces the truth of wisdom.*

7. It is known that all things universally have relation to good and truth, and that there

is not given a single entity which has not something relative to those two [principles]: hence it is that in man there are two receptacles of life, one which is the receptacle of good, called the will, and another which is the receptacle of truth, called the understanding; and as good is of love, and truth is of wisdom, the will is the receptacle of love, and the understanding is the receptacle of wisdom. The reason why good is of love, is because what a man loves, this he wills, and when he brings it into act he calls it good; and the reason why truth is of wisdom is, because all wisdom is derived from truths; even the good which a wise man thinks, is truth, and this becomes good when he wills it and does it. He who does not rightly distinguish between these two receptacles of life, which are the will and the understanding, and does not form to himself a clear notion concerning them, will in vain endeavour to comprehend [the nature of] spiritual influx: for there is influx into the will, and there is influx into the understanding; there is an influx of the good of love into the will of man, and there is an influx of the truth of wisdom into his understanding, each proceeding from Jehovah God immediately through the sun in the midst of which he is, and mediately through the angelic heaven. These two receptacles, the will and the understanding, are as distinct as heat and light are; for the will

receives the heat of heaven, which in its essence is love, and the understanding receives the light of heaven, which in its essence is wisdom, as was said above. There is given an influx from the human mind into the speech, and there is given an influx into the actions, the influx into the speech takes place from the will through the understanding, and the influx into the actions takes place from the understanding, through the will : they who are only acquainted with the influx into the understanding, and not at the same time with that into the will, are like one-eyed persons, who only see the objects on one side and not those on the other ; and they are like maimed persons, who do their work awkwardly with one hand only ; and they are like lame persons, who hop on one foot with a crutch. From these few considerations it is plain, that spiritual heat flows-in into the will of man, and produces the good of love, and that spiritual light flows-in into his understanding, and produces the truth of wisdom.

VI.—*That those two [principles], viz. heat and light, or love and wisdom, flow-in conjointly from God into the soul of man, and through this into the mind, its affections and thoughts, and from these into the senses, speech, and actions of the body.*

8. THE spiritual influx hitherto treated of by writers of acute genius, is the influx from the soul into the body, and not any influx into the soul, and through that into the body ; although it is known that all the good of love, and all the truth of faith flow-in from God into man, and that nothing thereof is from man ; and those things which flow-in from God, flow-in proximately into his soul, and through the soul into the rational mind, and through this into those things which constitute the body; if any person investigate spiritual influx in any other manner, he is like one who stops up the stream of a fountain and still looks for unfailing waters there ; or one who deduces the origin of a tree from the branch and not from the seed ; or one who examines principiates* without attending to the first principle. For the soul is not life in itself, but is a recipient of life from God, who is life in itself ; and all influx is of life, thus from God : this is under-

* Things derived from a first principle.

4

stood by this passage, "Jehovah God breathed into the nostrils of the man the soul of lives, and the man was made into a living soul," Gen. ii. 7 ; to breathe into the nostrils the soul of lives, signifies to implant the perception of good and truth ; and the Lord also says of himself, "As the Father hath life in himself, so hath he given also to the Son to have life in himself," John v. 26 ; [to have] life in himself is [to be] God ; and the life of the soul is life influent from God. Now forasmuch as all influx is of life, and life operates by means of its receptacles, and the inmost or first of the receptacles in man is his soul, therefore in order that influx may be rightly apprehended, it is necessary to begin from God, and not from an intermediate station ; if the beginning were taken from an intermediate station, the doctrine of influx would be like a chariot without wheels, or like a ship without sails : this being the case, therefore in the preceding articles we have treated of the sun of the spiritual world, in the midst of which is Jehovah God, n. 5 ; and of the influx of love and wisdom, thus of life, n. 6, 7. The reason that life from God flows-in into man through the soul, and through this into the mind, that is, into the affections and thoughts of the mind, and from these into the senses, speech, and actions of the body, is because these are [the derivatives] of life in successive order ; for the mind is

subordinate to the soul, and the body is subordinate to the mind : and the mind has two lives, one of the will and another of the understanding ; the life of its will is the good of love, the derivations of which are called affections, and the life of its understanding is the truth of wisdom, the derivations of which are called thoughts ; by means of these and the former the mind lives : but the life of the body are the senses, speech, and actions ; that these are derived from the soul through the mind, follows from the order in which they stand, and from which they manifest themselves to a wise man without scrutiny. The human soul, forasmuch as it is a superior spiritual substance, receives influx immediately from God ; but the human mind, forasmuch as it is an inferior spiritual substance, receives influx from God mediately through the spiritual world ; and the body, forasmuch as it originates from the substances of nature, which are called material, receives influx from God mediately through the natural world. That the good of love and the truth of wisdom flow-in from God into the soul of man conjointly, that is united into one, but that they are divided by man in their progress, and are conjoined only with those who suffer themselves to be led by God, will be seen in the following articles.

20

VII.—*That the sun of the natural world is pure fire, and that the world of nature [first] existed and [continually] subsists by means of this sun.*

9. THAT nature and its world, by which are understood the atmospheres, and the earths which are called planets, among which is the terraqueous globe on which we dwell, and also all and singular the things which annually adorn its surface, subsist solely from the sun, which constitutes their centre, and which, by the rays of its light, and the modifications *(temperies)* of its heat, is every where present, every one knows for certain from experience, from the testimony of the senses, and from the writings of those who have treated of such subjects; and as the perpetual subsistence of these things is from the sun, reason may with certainty conclude that their existence also is from thence; for perpetually to subsist is perpetually to exist as they first existed: hence it follows that the natural world was created by Jehovah God by means of this sun as a secondary cause *(secondario)*. That there are spiritual things and that there are natural things, which are entirely distinct from each other, and that the origin and support of spiritual things is derived from a sun which is pure love, in the midst of which is the Creator and Establisher of the

universe, Jehovah God, has been demonstrated before; but that the origin and support of natural things is derived from a sun which is pure fire, and that the latter is derived from the former, and both from God, follows of itself, as what is posterior follows from what is prior, and what is prior from the first. That the sun of nature and its worlds is pure fire, all its effects demonstrate; as the concentration of its rays into a focus by the art of optics, from which proceeds fire burning with vehemence, and also flame; the nature of its heat, which is similar to heat from elementary fire; the graduation of that heat according to its angle of incidence, whence proceed the varieties of climate, and also the four seasons of the year; besides other things, from which reason may be confirmed by means of the senses of its body, that the sun of the natural world is mere fire, and also, that it is fire in its purity itself. They who know nothing concerning the origin of spiritual things from their sun, but are only acquainted with the origin of natural things from theirs, can scarcely avoid confounding spiritual things and natural things, and concluding, through the fallacies of the senses and thence of the reason, that spiritual things are nothing but pure natural things, and that, from the activity of the latter excited by heat and light, arises wisdom and love: these persons, forasmuch as they see nothing else with their

eyes, and smell nothing else with their nostrils, and breathe nothing else in their breast, than nature, ascribe all rational things to it also, and thus imbibe naturalism, as a sponge sucks up water; such persons may be compared to charioteers who yoke the horses behind the chariot and not before it: the case is otherwise with those who distinguish between spiritual things and natural things, and deduce the latter from the former; these also perceive that the influx of the soul into the body is spiritual, and that natural things, which are those of the body, serve the soul for vehicles and means, that it may produce its effects in the natural world: if you conclude otherwise you may be compared to a crab, which assists its progress in walking by means of its tail, and draws its eyes backwards at every step; and your rational sight may be compared to the sight of the eyes of Argus in the back of his head, when those in his forehead were asleep; such persons also believe themselves to be Arguses when they reason, for they say, Who does not see that the origin of the universe is from nature? and what then is God but the inmost extension of nature? and the like irrational things; of which they boast more than wise men do of their rational sentiments.

VIII.—*That therefore every thing which proceeds from this sun, regarded in itself, is dead.*

10. WHO does not see from the reason of his understanding, if this is a little elevated above the sensual things of the body, that love regarded in itself is alive, and that its appearance of fire is life, and on the contrary that elementary fire regarded in itself is respectively dead; consequently, that the sun of the spiritual world, forasmuch as it is pure love, is alive, and that the sun of the natural world, forasmuch as it is pure fire, is dead; and that the case is the same with all the things which proceed and exist from them? There are two things which produce all the effects in the universe, LIFE AND NATURE, and they produce them according to order when life from the interior actuates nature: the case is otherwise when nature from the interior draws life to act, which takes place with those who place nature, which in itself is dead, above and within life, and thence only sacrifice to the pleasure of the senses and the concupiscences of the flesh, and esteem the spiritual things of the soul and the truly rational things of the mind as nothing: such persons, on account of that inversion, are they who are called THE DEAD; such are all atheistic naturalists in the world, and all satans in hell:

they are also called the dead in the Word, as in David, "They adhered to Baal-peor, and ate the sacrifices of THE DEAD," Ps. cvi. 28 ; "The enemy persecutes my soul, he makes me to sit in darkness as THE DEAD of the world," Ps. cxliii. 3 ; "To hear the groaning of the bound, and to open to THE SONS OF DEATH," Ps. cii. 21 ; and in the Revelation, "I know thy works that thou hast a name that thou livest, but thou art DEAD : be watchful and establish the things that remain which are ABOUT TO DIE," iii. 1, 2 : they are called the dead, because spiritual death is damnation, and damnation is the lot of those who believe life to be from nature, and thus believe the light of nature to be the light of life, and thereby hide, suffocate, and extinguish, every idea of God, of heaven, and of eternal life : such persons therefore are like owls, which see light in darkness and darkness in light, that is, such persons see falses as truths and evils as goods ; and forasmuch as the delights of evil are the delights of their hearts, they are not unlike those birds and beasts which feed on the bodies of the dead as dainties, and snuff up the fetid odours from sepulchres as balsams. Such persons do not see any other than physical or natural influx ; if notwithstanding they affirm influx to be spiritual, they do not do so from any idea of it, but from the dictate of a preceptor.

IX—*That what is spiritual [or the spiritual principle] clothes itself with what is natural, [or the natural principle] as a man clothes himself with a garment.*

11. IT is known that in every operation there is what is active and what is passive, and that from what is active alone nothing exists, and nothing from what is passive alone : the case is similar with what is spiritual and what is natural ; what is spiritual, forasmuch as it is a living power, being active, and what is natural, forasmuch as it is a dead power, being passive ; hence it follows that whatever has existed in this solar world from the beginning, and afterwards exists every moment, is from what is spiritual through what is natural, and this not only in the subjects of the animal kingdom, but also in the subjects of the vegetable kingdom. Another fact similar to this is also known, viz. that in every thing which is effected there is what is principal and what is instrumental, and that these two, when any thing is done, appear as one, though they are distinctly two ; wherefore it is one of the rules of wisdom that the principal cause and the instrumental cause make together one cause : so also do what is spiritual and what is natural : the reason that these two in producing effects appear as one, is because what is spiritual is

6

within what is natural as the fibre is within the muscle, and as the blood is within the arteries ; or as the thought is inwardly in the speech and the affection in the tones of the voice, causing themselves to be apprehended by means of what is natural ; from these considerations, but yet [obscurely] as [objects appear when seen] through a window, it appears, that what is spiritual clothes itself with what is natural as a man clothes himself with a garment. The organical body with which the soul clothes itself, is here compared to a garment, because a garment invests the body, and the soul also puts off the body, and casts it away as old clothes, *(exuviæ)* when it emigrates by means of death from the natural world into its own spiritual world : for the body grows old like a garment, but not the soul, because this is a spiritual substance, which has nothing in common with the changes of nature, which advance from their beginnings to their ends, and are periodically terminated. They who do not consider the body as the vesture or covering of the soul, and as being in itself dead, and only adapted to receive the living powers flowing in through the soul from God, cannot avoid concluding from fallacies, that the soul lives by itself, and the body by itself, and that there is a PRE-ESTABLISHED HARMONY between the life of each ; and likewise that the life of the soul flows-in into the life of the body, or

the life of the body into the life of the soul, [indifferently,] whence they conceive INFLUX to be both SPIRITUAL and NATURAL ; when nevertheless it is a truth which is testified by every thing that is created, that what is posterior does not act from itself, but from what is prior, from which it proceeded ; thus that neither does this act from itself, but from something still prior ; and thus that there is nothing which acts any otherwise than from that which is first, which acts from itself, which is God : besides, life is single *(unica)*, and this is not capable of being created, but is very capable of flowing-in into forms organically adapted to its reception ; such forms are all and singular the things in the created universe. It is believed by many that the soul is life, and thus that man, forasmuch as he lives from the soul, lives from his own life, thus from himself, consequently not by means of an influx of life from God : but such persons cannot avoid twisting a sort of Gordian knot of fallacies, and entangling in it all the judgments of their mind, whence follows mere insanity in spiritual things ; or they construct a labyrinth, from which the mind can never, by means of any clew of reason, retrace its way and extricate itself ; they also actually let themselves down into caverns under the earth, where they dwell in eternal darkness : for from such a belief proceed innumerable fallacies, each of which

7

is horrible ; as that God transferred and transcribed himself into men, and that thence every man is a sort of Deity, which lives from itself, and thus that he does good and is wise from himself ; likewise that he possesses faith and charity in himself, and thus displays them from himself, and not from God ; besides other enormous sentiments such as prevail with those in hell, who, when they were in the world, believed nature to live, or to produce life by its own activity ; when these look to heaven they see its light as mere darkness. I formerly heard a voice of one saying from heaven, that if a spark of life in man were his own, and not of God in him, there would be no heaven, nor any thing therein, and hence that there would not be any church on earth, and consequently no life eternal. Further particulars relating to this subject may be consulted in the memorable relation inserted in the work on CONJUGIAL LOVE, n. 132 to 136.

X.—*That spiritual things so clothed in man, cause him to be able to live a rational and moral man, thus a spiritually natural man.*

12. FROM the principle established above, viz. that the soul clothes itself with a body as a man clothes himself with a garment, this follows as a conclusion : for the soul flows-in into

the human mind, and through this into the body, and carries life with it, which it continually receives from the Lord, and thus transfers it mediately into the body, where by the closest union it makes the body appear to live ; whence, and from a thousand testimonies of experience, it is evident, that what is spiritual united to what is material, as a living power with a dead power, causes man to speak rationally and to act morally : it appears as if the tongue and lips spoke from a certain life in themselves, and that the arms and hands act in a like manner, but it is the thought, which in itself is spiritual, which speaks, and the will, which likewise is spiritual, which acts, both by means of their own organs, which in themselves are material, as being taken from the natural world : that this is the case appears in the light of day, provided this consideration is attended to ; remove thought from speech, is not the tongue dumb in a moment? and remove will from action, are not the hands in a moment quiescent? The unition of spiritual things with natural things and the consequent appearance of life in material things, may be compared to generous wine in a clean sponge, and to the saccharine juice in a grape, and to the savoury liquor in an apple, and also to the aromatic odour in cinnamon ; the fibres containing all these things are matters, which neither taste nor smell from themselves, but

from the fluids in and between them, wherefore if you squeeze out those juices, they are dead filaments ; so are the organs proper to the body, if life be taken away. That man is rational in consequence of the unition of spiritual things with natural things, is evident from the analytical [particulars] of his thought ; and that he is moral from the same cause, is evident from the propriety of his actions and the graces of his demeanour ; these he acquires from the faculty of being able to receive influx from the Lord through the angelic heaven, wherein is the very habitation of wisdom and love, thus of rationality and morality : hence it may be perceived, that what is spiritual and what is natural being united in man cause him to live a spiritually natural man. The reason that he lives in a similar and yet dissimilar manner after death, is because his soul is then clothed with a substantial body, as in the world it was clothed with a material body. It is believed by many that the perceptions and thoughts of the mind, forasmuch as they are spiritual, flow-in naked, and not by means of organized forms ; but let them dream thus who have not seen the interiors of the head, where perceptions and thoughts begin in their principles, and are ignorant that it contains the brains, interwoven and composed of the cineritious and medullary substances, together with glands, cavities, septa, and the meninges and matres

[*pia mater et dura mater*] which surround them all ; and who do not know that a man thinks and wills soundly or insanely according to the perfect or perverted state of all those things, consequently that he is rational and moral according to the organic formation of his mind : for nothing could be predicated of the rational sight of man, which is the understanding, without forms organized for the reception of spiritual light, as nothing could be predicated of the natural sight without the eyes ; and so in other instances.

XI.—*That the reception of that influx is according to the state of love and wisdom with man.*

13. THAT man is not life, but an organ recipient of life from God, and that love together with wisdom is life ; also, that God is love itself and wisdom itself, and thus life itself ; has been demonstrated above : hence it follows, that so far as a man loves wisdom, or so far as wisdom in the bosom of love is with him, so far he is an image of God, that is, a receptacle of life from God ; and on the contrary, so far as he is in opposite love, and thence in insanity, so far he does not receive life from God, but from hell, which life is called death. Love itself and wisdom itself are not life, but are the esse of life, but the delights of love and the pleas-

antnesses of wisdom, which are affections, constitute life, for the Esse of life Exists by means of these: the influx of life from God carries with it those delights and pleasantnesses, like the influx of light and heat at the time of spring into human minds, and also into birds and beasts of every kind, yea into vegetables, which then germinate and become prolific: for the delights of love and the pleasantnesses of wisdom expand men's minds (animi) and adapt them to reception, as joy and gladness expand the face, and adapt it to the influx of the hilarities of the soul. The man who is affected with the love of wisdom, is like a garden in Eden, in which are two trees, the one of life and the other of the science of good and evil; the tree of life is the reception of love and wisdom from God, and the tree of the science of good and evil is the reception of them from self; [the man who is] the latter is insane, but still believes himself to be wise like God, but [the man who is] the former is truly wise, and believes no one to be wise but God alone, and that man is wise so far as he believes this, and more so so far as he is sensible that he wills it; but more on this subject may be seen in the memorable relation inserted in the work on CONJUGIAL LOVE, n. 132 to 136. I will here add an arcanum confirming these things from heaven: all the angels of heaven turn their forehead to the Lord as a sun, and all the an-

gels of hell turn the back of the head to him, and the latter receive the influx into the affections of their will, which in themselves are concupiscences, and make the understanding favour them, but the former receive the influx into the affections of their understanding, and make the will favour them, whence these are in wisdom, but the others are in insanity; for the human understanding dwells in the cerebrum, which is under the forehead, and the will in the cerebellum, which is in the back of the head: who does not know that a man who is insane from falses, favours the cupidities of his own evil, and confirms them by means of reasons drawn from the understanding, and that a wise man sees from truths the quality of the cupidities of his own will and restrains them; a wise man does this because he turns his face to God, that is, he believes in God, and not in himself, but an insane man does the other because he averts his face from God, that is, he believes in himself and not in God; to believe in himself, is to believe that a man loves and is wise from himself and not from God, and this is signified by eating of the tree of the science of good and evil; but to believe in God, is to believe that a man loves and is wise from God and not from himself, and this is signified by eating of the tree of life, Rev. ii. 7. From these considerations, but still only as in the light of the moon by night, it may be perceiv-

ed that the reception of the influx of life from God is according to the state of love and wisdom with man. This influx may further be illustrated by the influx of light and heat into vegetables, which blossom and bear fruit according to the structure of the fibres which form them, thus according to reception; it may also be illustrated by the influx of the rays of light into precious stones, which modify them into colours according to the situation of the parts composing them, thus also according to reception; and likewise by optical glasses and the drops of rain, which exhibit rainbows according to the incidences, refractions, and thus the receptions, of light; the case is similar with human minds in respect to spiritual light, which proceeds from the Lord as a sun and perpetually flows-in, but is variously received.

35

XII—*That the understanding in man is capable of being elevated into the light, that is, into the wisdom, in which the angels of heaven are, according to the improvement of the reason; and that in like manner his will is capable of being elevated into the heat of heaven, that is, into the love of heaven, according to the deeds of the life; but that the love of the will is not elevated except so far as the man wills and does those things which the wisdom of the understanding teaches.*

14. By the human mind are understood its two faculties, which are called the understanding and the will; the understanding is the receptacle of the light of heaven, which in its essence is wisdom, and the will is the receptacle of the heat of heaven, which in its essence is love, as was shewn above: these two [principles], wisdom and love, proceed from the Lord as a sun, and flow-in into heaven universally and singularly [or individually], whence the angels have wisdom and love; and they also flow-in into this world universally and singularly [or individually], whence men have wisdom and love. But these two [principles] proceed unitedly from the Lord, and likewise flow-in unitedly into the souls of angels and men, but they are not received unitedly in their minds; light which constitutes the understanding being first received there, and love which

constitutes the will being received gradually : this also is of providence, as every man is to be created anew, that is, reformed, and this is effected by means of the understanding ; for he must imbibe from infancy the knowledges of truth and good, which are to teach him to live well, that is, to will and act rightly, thus the will is formed by means of the understanding. For the sake of this end, there is given to man the faculty of elevating his understanding almost into the light in which the angels of heaven are, that he may see what he ought to will and thence to do, in order that he may be prosperous in the world for a time, and blessed after death to eternity ; he becomes prosperous and blessed if he procures to himself wisdom, and keeps his will under its obedience ; but unprosperous and unhappy if he puts his understanding under the obedience of his will ; the reason is, because the will tends to evils from birth, even to those which are enormous ; wherefore unless it were restrained by means of the understanding, man would rush into acts of wickedness, yea, from his inrooted savage nature, he would destroy and slaughter for the sake of himself all those who do not favour and indulge him. Besides, unless the understanding could be separately perfected, and the will by means of it, man would not be man but a beast : for without that separation, and without the ascent of the understanding above the will,

he would not be able to think, and from thought to speak, but only to express his affection by sounds ; neither would he be able to act from reason, but only from instinct ; still less would he be able to know the things which are of God, and God by means of them, and thus to be conjoined to him, and to live to eternity : for man thinks and wills as from himself, and this *as from himself*, is the reciprocal [principle] of conjunction ; for conjunction cannot be given without reciprocality, as the conjunction of what is active with what is passive cannot be given without re-action ; God alone acts, and man suffers himself to be acted on, and re-acts in all appearance as from himself, though interiorly it is from God. From these considerations rightly apprehended, may be seen what is the quality of the will of man if it is elevated by means of the understanding, and what is its quality if it is not elevated, consequently, what is the quality of the man. But the latter subject, viz. what is the quality of man if the love of his will is not elevated by means of the understanding, shall be illustrated by comparisons : he is like an eagle flying on high, which, as soon as it sees the meats below which are the objects of its cupidity, as chickens, young swans, or even young lambs, casts itself down in a moment and devours them : he is also like an adulterer, who conceals a harlot in a cellar below, and

8

by turns goes up to the highest apartments of the house, and discourses wisely with those who dwell there concerning chastity, and alternately takes himself away from his companions, and indulges himself below with his harlot : he is also like a thief on a tower, who there pretends to act the part of a watchman, but who, as soon as he sees an object of plunder below, hastens down and seizes it : he may also be compared to marsh-flies, which fly in a column over the head of a horse that is running, but which fall down when the horse stops, and immerse themselves in the marsh : such is the man whose will or love is not elevated by means of the understanding, for he then stands still below at the threshold, immersed in the uncleannesses of nature and the lusts of the senses : the case is altogether otherwise with those who subdue the allurements of the cupidities of the will by means of the wisdom of the understanding ; with these the understanding afterwards enters into a conjugial covenant with the will ; thus wisdom with love, and they dwell together above with their delights.

39

XIII—*That it is altogether otherwise with beasts.*

15. THEY who judge of things only as they appear before the senses of the body, conclude that beasts have will and understanding as well as men, and hence that the only distinction consists in man's being able to speak, and thus to describe the things which he thinks and desires, while beasts can only express them by sounds : yet beasts, have not will and understanding, but only a resemblance of each, which the learned call something analogous. The reason that a man is a man, is because his understanding is capable of being elevated above the desires of his will, and thus can know and see them, and also govern them ; but a beast is a beast because its desires drive it to do whatever it does ; wherefore a man is a man in consequence of this, that his will is under the obedience of his understanding ; but a beast is a beast in consequence of this, that its understanding is under the obedience of its will : from these considerations this conclusion follows, viz. that the understanding of man, forasmuch as it receives the light influent from heaven, and apprehends and apperceives this as its own, and therefrom thinks analytically with all variety altogether as from itself, is alive, and is thence truly understand-

ing; and that the will of man, forasmuch as it receives the influent love of heaven, and therefrom acts as from itself, is alive, and is thence truly will; but that the contrary is the case with beasts. Wherefore they who think from the lusts of the will, are compared to beasts, and in the spiritual world they likewise at a distance appear as beasts; they also act like beasts, with this only difference, that they are able to act otherwise if they will: but they who restrain the lusts of their will by means of the understanding, appear in the spiritual world as men, and are angels of heaven. In a word, the will and the understanding in beasts always cohere, and forasmuch as the will is blind, being [the receptacle] of heat and not of light, it makes the understanding blind also; hence a beast does not know and understand its own actions, and yet it acts, for it acts by virtue of the influx from the spiritual world; and such action is instinct. It is believed that a beast thinks from understanding what to act, but this is by no means the case: it is led to act only from natural love, which is in it from creation, with the assistance of the senses of its body: the reason that man thinks and speaks is solely because his understanding is capable of being separated from his will, and of being elevated even into the light of heaven; for the understanding thinks, and thought speaks. The reason why beasts act according

to the laws of order inscribed on their nature, and some beasts in a moral and rational manner, differently from many men, is because their understanding is blind obedience to the desires of their will, and thence they are not able to pervert them by depraved reasonings, as men do. It is to be observed, that by the will and understanding of beasts here spoken of, is understood a resemblance of, and something analogous to, those faculties: things analogous are so named from appearance. The life of a beast may be compared with a sleep walker, who walks and acts by virtue of the will while the understanding sleeps: and also with a blind man, who walks through the streets with a dog leading him: and also with an idiot, who from custom and the habit thence acquired does his work in a regular manner: it it may likewise be compared with a person void of memory, and thence deprived of understanding, who still knows or learns how to clothe himself, to eat dainties, to love the sex, to walk the streets from house to house, and to do such things as sooth the senses and indulge the flesh, by the allurements and pleasures of which he is drawn along, though he does not think, and thence cannot speak. From these considerations it is evident, how much they are mistaken who believe beasts to be endowed with rationality, and only to be distinguished from men by the external figure and by their not being

9

able to speak of the rational things which they inwardly revolve: from which fallacies many even conclude, that if man lives after death, beasts will live after death likewise, and on the contrary, that if beasts do not live after death, neither will man; besides other dreams, arising from ignorance concerning the will and understanding, and also concerning degrees, by means of which, as by a ladder, the mind of man mounts up to heaven.

XIV.—*That there are three degrees in the spiritual world, and three degrees in the natural world, hitherto unknown, according to which all influx takes place.*

16. IT is discovered by means of the investigation of causes from effects, that degrees are of two kinds, one in which are things prior and posterior, and another in which are things greater and less: the degrees which distinguish things prior and posterior, are to be called DEGREES OF ALTITUDE, or DISCRETE DEGREES; but the degrees by which things greater and less are distinguished from each other, are to be called DEGREES OF LATITUDE, and also CONTINUOUS DEGREES: degrees of altitude, or discrete degrees, are like the generations and compositions of one thing from another; as for example, they are like the generation and com-

position of any nerve from its fibres, and of any fibre from its fibrillæ; or of any piece of wood, stone, or metal from its parts, and of any part from its particles: but degrees of latitude, or continuous degrees, are like the increments and decrements of the same degree of altitude with respect to breadth, length, height, and depth; as of greater and less bodies of water, or air, or ether; and as of large and small masses of wood, stone, or metal. All and singular the things in both worlds, both the spiritual world and the natural world, are, from creation, in degrees of both these kinds; the whole animal kingdom in this world is in those degrees both in general and in particular; so are the whole vegetable kingdom and the whole mineral kingdom likewise; and so is the expanse of atmospheres from the sun even to the earth. There are therefore three atmospheres discretely distinct according to the degrees of altitude both in the spiritual world and in the natural world, because each world has its sun: but the atmospheres of the spiritual world, by virtue of their origin, are substantial, and the atmospheres of the natural world, by virtue of their origin, are material: and forasmuch as the atmospheres descend from their origins according to those degrees, and are the continents of light and heat, and like vehicles to convey these principles to their destination, it follows that there are three degrees of light

10

and heat : and forasmuch as light in the spiritual world is in its essence wisdom, and heat there is in its essence love, as was demonstrated above in its proper article, it follows also that there are three degrees of wisdom and three degrees of love, consequently, three degrees of life ; for they are graduated by the atmospheres through which they pass. Hence it is that there are three angelic heavens ; a supreme, which is also called the third heaven, where are angels of the supreme degree ; a middle, which is also called the second heaven, where are angels of the middle degree ; and an ultimate, which is also called the first heaven, where are angels of the lowest degree : those heavens are also distinguished according to the degrees of wisdom and love ; they who are in the ultimate heaven are in the love of knowing truths and goods, they who are in the middle heaven are in the love of understanding them, and they who are in the supreme heaven are in the love of being wise, that is, of living according to those truths and goods which they know and understand. As the angelic heavens are distinguished into three degrees, so also is the human mind, because the human mind is an image of heaven, that is, it is a heaven in the least form : hence it is that man is capable of becoming an angel of one of those three heavens, and he becomes such according to his reception of wisdom and love from the

45

Lord ; an angel of the ultimate heaven if he only receives the love of knowing truths and goods ; an angel of the middle heaven if he receives the love of understanding them ; and an angel of the supreme heaven if he receives the love of being wise, that is, of living according to them : that the human mind is distinguished into three regions, according to the three heavens, may be seen in the memorable relation inserted in the work on CONJUGIAL LOVE, n. 270. Hence it is evident that all spiritual influx to man and into man descends from the Lord through these three degrees, and that it is received by man according to the degree of wisdom and love in which he is. The knowledge of these degrees is of the greatest utility at this day ; for many, in consequence of not knowing them, stand still and stick in the lowest degree, in which are the senses of their body, and on account of their ignorance, which is intellectual darkness, are incapable of being elevated into spiritual light, which is above them ; hence naturalism takes possession of them, as it were spontaneously, as soon as they enter on any investigation and scrutiny concerning the human soul and mind, and its rationality, and more so if they extend their inquiries to heaven and the life after death : whence they become like persons standing in the market places with telescopes in their hands, looking at the sky and uttering

vain predictions ; and also like those who prate and reason concerning every object they see, and every thing they hear, without any thing rational from an understanding [of the subject] being contained in their garrulity and reasonings ; but such persons are like butchers, who believe themselves to be skilful anatomists, because they have examined the viscera of oxen and sheep outwardly but not inwardly. But it is a truth, that to think from the influx of natural light (lumen) not enlightened by the influx of spiritual light, is nothing else but dreaming, and to speak from such thought is to utter idle ravings like soothsayers. But further particulars concerning degrees may be seen in the work on THE DIVINE LOVE AND THE DIVINE WISDOM, n. 173 to 281.

XV.—*That Ends are in the first degree, Causes in the second, and Effects in the third.*

17. WHO does not see that the end is not the cause, but that it produces the cause, and that the cause is not the effect, but that it produces the effect, consequently, that they are three distinct things which follow each other in order ? The end with man is the love of his will, for what a man loves, this he proposes to himself and intends ; the cause with him is the reason of his understanding, for the end,

by means of the reason, seeks for middle or efficient causes ; and the effect is the operation of the body from and according to those [prior principles] ; thus there are three things in man, which follow each other in order, as the degrees of altitude follow each other. When these three things are exhibited [in any act], then the end is inwardly in the cause, and the end through the cause is in the effect, wherefore these three things co-exist in the effect : on this account it is said in the Word, that every one shall be judged according to his works ; for the end, or the love of his will, and the cause, or the reason of his understanding, are contained together in the effects, which are the works of his body ; thus the quality of the whole man is contained therein. They who are unacquainted with these truths, and do not thus distinguish the objects of reason, cannot avoid terminating the ideas of their thought in the atoms of Epicurus, the monads of Leibnitz, or the simple substances of Wolff, whereby they shut up their understandings as with a bolt, so that they cannot even think from reason concerning spiritual influx, because they cannot think concerning any farther progression ; for the author of the doctrine of simple substances says, that if they are divided they fall into nothing : thus the understanding stands still in its first light (lumen), which is merely derived from the senses of the body,

and does not advance a step further : hence it is not known but that what is spiritual [or the spiritual principle] is something subtilely natural [or a subtile natural principle], and that beasts have a rational [principle] as well as men, and that the soul is a puff of wind which is breathed out of the breast when a person dies ; besides other notions, which do not partake of light but of darkness. As all things in the spiritual world and all things in the natural world proceed according to these degrees, as was shewn in the preceding article, it is evident that intelligence properly consists in knowing and distinguishing them, and seeing them in their order : by means of these degrees, also, every man is known as to his quality, when his love is known ; for as was said above, the end, which is of the will, and the causes, which are of the understanding, and the effects, which are of the body, follow from his love, as a tree from its seed, and as fruit from a tree. There are loves of three kinds, the love of heaven, the love of the world, and the love of self : the love of heaven is spiritual, the love of the world is material, and the love of self is corporeal : when the love is spiritual, all the things which follow from it, as forms from their essence, are spiritual likewise ; if the principal love is the love of the world or of wealth, and thus is material, all the things which follow from it, as principiates

from their principle, are material likewise ; and if the principal love is the love of self, or of eminence above all others, and thus is corporeal, all the things which follow from it are corporeal likewise, because the man who is in this love regards himself alone, and thus immerses the thoughts of his mind in his body : wherefore, as was just now said, he who knows the reigning love of any one, and is at the same time acquainted with the progression of ends to causes and of causes to effects, which three things follow each other in order according to the degrees of altitude, knows the [quality of the] whole man : thus the angels of heaven know [the quality of] every one with whom they speak ; they perceive his love from the sound of his voice, they see an image of it in his face, and the figure of it in the gestures of his body.

———

XVI.—*That hence it is evident what is the quality of Spiritual Influx from its origin to its effects.*

18. SPIRITUAL influx has hitherto been deduced [by those who have treated of it] from the soul into the body, but not from God into the soul and thus into the body : this has been done, because no one knew any thing concerning the spiritual world, and concerning the sun there, from whence all spiritual things issue as

from their fountain, and thus no one knew any thing concerning the influx of spiritual things into natural things. Now forasmuch as it has been given to me to be in the spiritual world and in the natural world at the same time, I am obliged by my conscience to declare these things : for what is the use of knowledge, unless what is known to one be also known to others? Without this, what is the acquisition of knowledge but like collecting and storing up riches in a casket, and only looking at them occasionally and counting them over, without any intention of applying them to use? spiritual avarice is nothing else. But in order that it may be fully known what and of what quality spiritual influx is, it is necessary to know what the SPIRITUAL [PRINCIPLE] is in its essence, and what the NATURAL [PRINCIPLE] is, and also what the HUMAN SOUL is : lest therefore this short lucubration should be defective through ignorance of these subjects, it will be useful to consult some memorable relations inserted in the work on CONJUGIAL LOVE ; viz. that concerning the SPIRITUAL [PRINCIPLE], n. 326 to 329 ; that concerning the HUMAN SOUL, n. 315 ; and that concerning THE INFLUX OF SPIRITUAL THINGS INTO NATURAL THINGS, n. 380 ; which latter subject is more fully treated of from n. 415 to 422.

———

19. I will here subjoin this MEMORABLE RE-

51

LATION. After these pages were written, I prayed to the Lord that I might be permitted to converse with some disciples of ARISTOTLE, and at the same time with some disciples of DES CARTES, and with some disciples of LEIBNITZ, in order that I might learn the opinions of their minds concerning the intercourse between the soul and the body. After my prayer [was ended] there were present nine men, three Aristotelians, three Cartesians, and three Leibnitzians ; and they stood round about me, the admirers of Aristotle being on the left side, the followers of Des Cartes on the right side, and the favourers of Leibnitz behind : at a distance off, and at intervals from each other, were seen three persons crowned with laurel, and I knew from an influent perception that they were those three great leaders or teachers themselves ; behind Leibnitz there stood a person holding the border of his garment, and I was told that it was Wolff. Those nine men, when they beheld one another, at first saluted and spake to each other in a gentle tone of voice. But presently there arose from below a spirit with a torch in his right hand, which he shook before their faces, whereupon they became enemies, three against three, and looked at each other with a fierce countenance : for they were seized with the lust of altercation and litigation. Then the Aristotelians, who were also schoolmen, began to speak, saying, Who does not see that objects flow in through the

senses into the soul, as a man enters through the doors into a chamber, and that the soul thinks according to such influx? When a lover sees a beautiful virgin or his bride, does not his eye sparkle and transmit the love of her into the soul? When a miser sees bags of money, do not all his senses burn towards them, and thence induce this ardour into the soul, and excite the cupidity of possessing them? When a proud man hears himself praised by another, does he not prick up his ears, and do not these transmit those praises to the soul? Are not the senses of the body like [outer] courts, through which alone entrance is obtained to the soul? From these considerations, and innumerable others of a similar kind, who can conclude otherwise than that influx takes place from nature, or is physical? While they were speaking thus the followers of Des Cartes held their fingers on their foreheads; and now withdrawing them they replied, saying, Alas, ye speak from appearances; do ye not know that the eye does not love a virgin or bride from itself, but from the soul? and likewise that the senses of the body do not covet the bags of money from themselves, but from the soul? and also that the ears do not devour the praises of flatterers in any other manner? Is not perception what causes sensation? and perception is of the soul and not of the organs of the body. Tell, if you can, what makes the tongue and lips to

speak but the thought? and what makes the hands to work but the will? and thought and will are of the soul and not of the body. Thus what makes the eye to see, and the ear to hear, and the other organs to feel, but the soul? From these considerations, and innumerable others of a similar kind, every one, whose wisdom is elevated above the sensual things of the body, must conclude, that influx does not take place from the body into the soul, but from the soul into the body, which influx we call occasional influx, and also spiritual influx. When these had finished, the three men who stood behind the former triads, who were the favourers of Leibnitz, began to speak, saying, We have heard the arguments on both sides, and have compared them, and we have perceived that in many particulars the latter are stronger than the former, and that in many others the former are stronger than the latter; wherefore, if it is permitted, we will compromise the dispute; and on being asked how? they replied, There is not any influx from the soul into the body, nor from the body into the soul, but there is a unanimous and instantaneous operation of both together, to which a celebrated author has assigned an elegant name, when he calls it pre-established harmony. After this the spirit with the torch appeared again, but the torch was now in his left hand, and he shook it behind the back of their heads, whence

their ideas of every thing became confused, and they cried out together, Neither our soul nor body knows what part to take, wherefore let us settle this dispute by lot, and we will abide by the lot which comes out first: and they took out three bits of paper, and wrote on one of them, PHYSICAL INFLUX, on another, SPIRITUAL INFLUX, and on the third, PRE-ESTABLISHED HARMONY; and they put them all into the crown of a hat. Then they chose one of their number to draw, and when he put in his hand he took hold of that on which was written SPIRITUAL INFLUX; which being seen and read, they all said, yet some with a clear and open, some with a faint and retracted voice, Let us abide by this because it came out first. But then an angel suddenly stood by, and said, Do not believe that the paper in favour of spiritual influx came out first by chance, for it was of providence; for you do not see the truth of that doctrine on account of the confusion of your ideas, but the truth itself offered itself to the hand of him that drew the lots, that you might assent to it.

———

20. I was formerly asked, How I, who was previously a philosopher, became a theologian? and I answered, In the same manner that fishers became the disciples and apostles of the Lord: and I added, that I also, from early

youth, had been a spiritual fisher. On this the inquirer asked, What a spiritual fisher was? To which I replied, That a fisher, in the spiritual sense of the Word, signifies a man who investigates and teaches natural truths, and afterwards spiritual truths, in a rational manner. On his inquiring, How this is demonstrated? I said, From these places in the Word, "Then the waters shall fail from the sea, and the rivers shall be dried up and burnt up, therefore the FISHERS shall mourn, and all that cast a hook into the sea shall be sad," Is. xix. 5, 8. In another place, "Upon the river whose waters were healed, the FISHERS stood from Engedi; they were there in the spreading forth of nets, according to its kind was their FISH, as the FISH of the great sea, exceedingly much," Ezekiel xlvii. 9, 10. And in another place, "The saying of Jehovah, Lo I will send to many FISHERS, who SHALL FISH THE SONS OF ISRAEL," Jerem. xvi. 16. Hence it is evident why the Lord chose fishers for his disciples, and said, "Come after me, and I will make you FISHERS of men," Matt. iv. 18, 19; Mark i. 16, 17: and why he said to Peter, after he had caught a multitude of fishes, "HENCEFORTH THOU SHALT CATCH MEN," Luke v. 9, 10. Afterwards I demonstrated the origin of this signification of fishers from THE APOCALYPSE REVEALED; viz. that forasmuch as water signifies natural truths, n. 50, 932; and likewise a river, n. 409, 932;

therefore a fish signifies those who are in natural truths, n. 405: whence fishers signify those who investigate and teach truth. On hearing this my interrogator raised his voice and said, Now I can understand why the Lord called and chose fishers to be his disciples, and therefore I do not wonder that he has also called and chosen you, since, as you have said, you were from early youth a fisher in a spiritual sense, that is an investigator of natural truths: the reason that you are now become an investigator of spiritual truths, is because these are founded on the former. To this he added, being a man of reason, that the Lord alone knows who is a proper person to apprehend and teach those things which should be revealed for his New Church, and whether such a person is to be found among the dignitaries of the Church or among their domestic servants. Besides, what theologian does not, amongst christians, first study philosophy at college, before he is ordained a divine; otherwise whence could he obtain [a sufficient degree of] intelligence? At last he said, Since you are become a theologian, explain what is your theology. I answered, These are the two principles of it, THAT GOD IS ONE, and THAT THERE IS A CONJUNCTION OF CHARITY AND FAITH. He replied, Who denies these principles? I rejoined, The theology of the present day, when interiorly examined.

[The End]

EXEGESIS
A - B
G - K

GENERAL
DOCTRINE
D - E - F
H - I - J

CHRISTOLOGY
D - I - J

ESCHATOLOGY
C - J - K

SWEDENBORG

1688 ~ 1772

PHILOSOPHY

PRINCIPAL ATTAINMENTS

1 - Systematic presentation of the Philosophy of Love
2 - Revived and expounded the knowledge of Correspondences
3 - First to formulate systematically the Doctrines of Influx, Degrees, Forms, Series and Order.

PRINCIPAL WRITINGS

Minor Principia [1720]
The Principia [1734]
Infinite and Final Cause of Creation [1734]
The Economy of the Animal Kingdom [1740] see note 4
The Animal Kingdom [1744] see note 3
Worship and Love of God [1745]
Divine Love and Wisdom [1763] see Theology
Intercourse Between the Soul and Body [1769] see Theology

THEOLOGICAL WORKS

A - ARCANA COELESTIA [1749 - 1756]
   Exposition of the spiritual sense of Genesis and Exodus.
B - APOCALYPSE EXPLAINED [1757 - 1759]
C - HEAVEN AND HELL
   From things heard and seen [1758]
D - FOUR DOCTRINES [1763]
   ① of the Lord   ② Sacred Scriptures
   ③ Life   ④ Faith
E - DIVINE LOVE AND WISDOM [1763]
F - DIVINE PROVIDENCE [1763]
G - APOCALYPSE REVEALED [1766]
   Exposition of the spiritual sense of Revelation.
H - CONJUGIAL LOVE [1767] On marriage.
   Translated "Marriage Love" [Rotch Edition]
I - TRUE CHRISTIAN RELIGION [1771]
J - MISCELLANEOUS THEOLOGICAL WORKS [1758 - 1769]
   Including "Earths in the Universe", "Last Judgement", "New Jerusalem and It's Heavenly Doctrine".
K - POSTHUMOUS THEOLOGICAL WORKS [1761 - 1772]
   Including "Prophets and Psalms", "The Coronis", and "The Canons."

NOTE:- A keyed identification is not to be taken as meaning that the given designation strictly limits the subject of the named work.

SCIENCE

PRINCIPAL ATTAINMENTS

1 - First to propound a "Nebular Hypothesis"
2 - Discoveries founded the Science of Chrystallography
3 - Anticipated the Doctrine of Energy
4 - Made first sketch of glider type airplane
5 - Constructed first mercurial air pump
6 - Discovered functions of corpora striata and motor areas of cerebral lobes
7 - Suggested particle construction of the magnet
8 - Discovered that the brain animates synchronously with the lungs
9 - Discovered function of the ductless glands
10 - Wrote and published first Swedish Algebra
11 - First with hypothesis of numerous galaxies of stars
12 - Researches founded science of Geology in Sweden
13 - First exhaustive works on Metallurgy
14 - Discovered circulation and uses of the cerebro - spinal fluid
15 - Invented the airtight, hot-air, stove once in common use

VALUES FOR EMERSON IN THE SWEDENBORGIAN SYSTEM

AN ABSTRACT OF EMERSON'S VIEW OF SWEDENBORGISM---THE PHILOSOPHIC
FRAMEWORK UPON WHICH ARE HUNG THE DOCTRINES OF THE SO-CALLED
"NEW CHURCH" OR "THE CHURCH OF THE NEW JERUSALEM"

[The student will find these titles Scriptural. See Revelation 3:12, 21:2, 2:17, 21:1 and 21:5. This small religious sect deserves great respect. It influenced Emerson, Alcott, Thoreau and Whitman.]

BIBLIOGRAPHY AND KEY TO ABBREVIATIONS

Soul and Body = Swedenborg, Intercourse Between the Soul and Body
Excerpts = Excerpts from Sampson Reed's early works
Genius = Sampson Reed's "Oration on Genius"
Genius-O = Outline of Sampson Reed's "Oration on Genius"
G O M = Synopsis of Reed's Observations on the Growth of the Mind
Rep. Men = "Swedenborg" in Emerson's Representative Men (Works, IV, 93ff.)

[This bibliography can be enriched by consulting Frederic Ives Carpenter, Emerson Handbook and the Instructor's Emerson the Essayist, both volumes. For a useful study of the history of Swedenborgism in America, see Marguerite Block's The New Church in the New World, New York, 1932.]

(A) THE SPIRITUAL UNIVERSE

1) GOD IS UNITY----THE COMPLETE OR GREATEST MAN----HE IS THE GOAL OF ALL SPIRITUAL BE-INGS----LIKE MERGES WITH LIKE IN CONSTITUTING THIS UNITY, WHICH REJECTS THE CHRIS-TIAN DOCTRINE OF THE TRINITY.

2) THE UNIVERSE IS COMPOSED OF LEVELS----SERIES AND DEGREES----A CONSTANT PROGRESS OR RETROGRESSION OPERATES THROUGHOUT THE NATURAL AND SPIRITUAL WORLDS. This and the preceding doctrine reflect the basic Platonic and Neo-Platonic patterns. See Soul and Body, chs. XIV-XV, and Rep. Men, 105, 106, 108-109.

3) INFLUX IS THE DYNAMIC FORCE ISSUING FROM THE SPIRITUAL CENTER----IT SWEEPS DOWN INTO EVEN THE LOWEST LEVELS OF CREATION----IT COMMUNICATES SPIRITUAL LIGHT AND HEAT (i.e., WISDOM AND LOVE)----IT CREATES IN THE NATURAL WORLD THE FORMS WHOSE PATTERNS OR PROTOTYPES FIRST EXIST IN THE SPIRITUAL WORLD----ALL NATURAL FORMS STRIVE UPWARD TOWARD MAN. See Soul and Body, chs. IX-XIV, esp. pp. 9-11; Rep. Men, 105, 115; cf. Nature (Boston, 1836), 57.1-23. Contrast Swedenborg's "love and wisdom" with Matthew Arnold's "sweetness and light." Compare the Neo-Platonic doctrine of EMANATION.

4) LIKE MOST RATIONALISTIC PHILOSOPHIES, SWEDENBORGISM IS DUALISTIC IN ONE OF THE MEAN-INGS OF THAT WORD----IT DIVIDES THE UNIVERSE INTO GOOD AND EVIL PRINCIPLES----ONLY THE SPIRITUAL WORLD IS GOOD----THE PHENOMENAL WORLD, APART FROM INFLUX, IS SPIRIT-UALLY DEAD AND EVIL----THIS DISTINCTION IS BROUGHT OUT IN THE NEW-CHURCH INTERPRE-TATION OF BIBLICAL MIRACLES. See Soul and Body, ch. VIII; Excerpts, ¶s. 11-12, 29-30, 32.

(B) MAN----THE CREATOR IN THE FINITE

1) MAN HOLDS THE CENTRAL POSITION IN THE UNIVERSE----HE STANDS BETWEEN THE REALMS OF SPIRIT AND NATURE----HE PARTICIPATES IN BOTH----HE IS THE MICROCOSM. See Rep. Men, 106; also 114-115: "Man is a kind of very minute heaven, corresponding to the world of spirits and to heaven. Every particular idea of man, and every affection, is an image and effigy of him. A spirit may be known from only a single thought."

2) DIVINE INFLUX CREATES THROUGH HIM ALL THE LOWER CREATION----ALL CREATION IS FROM
   WITHIN OUTWARDS----SPIRIT CREATES MEN'S BODIES----MAN'S AFFECTIONS OR SPIRITUAL
   STATES FLOW OUTWARD AND CLOTHE THEMSELVES IN THE WORLD OF NATURE. The good and
   bad "thoughts" or "affections" in man are projected respectively into good and ugly natural forms, thus
   accounting for useful and malevolent animals--edible and poisonous plants. Disorganizations of any
   kind in the natural world suggest men's evil condition. See Soul and Body, ch. IX. Emerson alludes to
   this chapter in Nature, 38.18-19, 79.18-23, 94.17. See G O M, ¶ 5; and Excerpts, ¶ 18d (cf. Nature,
   44.4); ¶ 18g (cf. Nature, 81.2ff., 88.11ff.); ¶s. 58, 73 (cf. Nature, 32ff., 81.2ff., 94.16ff.).

3) DAY BY DAY EACH MAN BUILDS HIS OWN ETERNAL CONDITION, POETICALLY CALLED HIS "SPIRIT-
   UAL HOUSE"----IT IS HIS INNER CONDITION, WHICH IS CONTINUALLY REFLECTED IN HIS OUTER
   WORLD----THE HEAVEN AND HELLS IN HIM CHANGE GRADUALLY AS HE OFFERS GREATER OR
   LESS RESISTANCE TO THE HEAVENLY INFLUX. See Rep. Men, 124: "All things in the universe arrange themselves to each person anew, according to his ruling love. Man is such as his affection and
   thought are. Man is man by virtue of willing.... As he is, so he sees. The [relationships and associ-
   ations] of the world are broken up. Interiors associate all in the spiritual world.... Nothing can resist states; every thing gravitates.... Every one makes his own house and state." Cf. Genius-O, ¶ 1.

4) THE FALL OF MAN IS NOT THAT OF TRADITIONAL CHRISTIANITY----IT IS MERELY A TEMPO-
   RARY BLINDNESS----IT RESULTS FROM MAN'S BECOMING INTERESTED IN THE MERE CREATURE
   INSTEAD OF THE SPIRITUAL MEANING BEHIND THINGS----THE RESULT IS A DEPARTURE FROM
   SPIRITUAL CONSCIOUSNESS OR "INNOCENCY"----SIGNIFICANCE OF THE LITTLE CHILD AND OF
   SLEEP----RESTORATION TO PARADISE IS ALWAYS POSSIBLE THROUGH AN AWAKENED MIND AND
   HEART. Swedenborg took over from Plato's Timaeus the myth of a "golden age" of superior men, add-
   ing it to the setting of the Biblical "Garden of Eden." (See D1 below.) According to his rationalistic
   system, earlier men knew the now-lost "language of Nature"---the key to natural symbolism---but when
   degeneration of spirituality set in, men began worshiping the symbol or thing rather than the truths
   which they represented. But blind eyes can always be opened in this or in any other mystical system.
   (See B5.) On the significance of the child and of sleep, see the following, and compare Wordsworth's
   "Ode on Intimations of Immortality": Soul and Body, ch. VIII; Genius-O, ¶ 2; G O M, ¶s. 1-2; Excerpts,
   ¶s. 27-28 (cf. Nature, 88.7, 95.10-12); ¶s. 29-30, 32 (cf. Emerson's poem, "Grace," Works, IX,
   359, and George Herbert's poem, "Sinne"); ¶s. 66, 69-70. The quotation in the last ¶ is from Wordsworth's Excursion, IV, 83-91. Cf. Nature, 89.6-11.

5) HOW SPIRITUAL PROGRESS IS ACHIEVED----THE PRINCIPLE OF PERSONAL ASSOCIATIONS----LIKE
   ONLY CAN KNOW LIKE----IMPERSONALITY OF THE SPIRITUAL WORLD----HEAVEN IS AN IM-
   MEDIATE SPIRITUAL STATE OR CONDITION----SOULS AND SPIRITS OF EQUAL ATTAINMENTS IN-
   FLUENCE EACH OTHER AT ALL TIMES----DEATH IS NO BARRIER TO RECIPROCAL INFLUENCES.
   As might be expected in such a rationalistic system, love, friendship and marriage (spiritually con-
   sidered) are transient, for two souls can never keep the same degree of Influx very long. (Spiritual
   fahrenheit varies from moment to moment!) New spiritual associations or alignments are inevitable.
   (Cf. the romantic view of secular marriage!) See Rep. Men, 128: "All loves and friendships are momentary. Do you love me? means, Do you see the same truth? If you do, we are happy with the same
   happiness; but presently one of us passes into the perception of new truth---we are [then automatically]
   divorced, and no tension in nature can hold us to each other." Though human love in human bodies is
   delicious, it is far too personal to be of spiritual value. In the highest spiritual levels of existence,
   there must be no personeity---only VALUES! Much of what we love in the personalities we see about
   us must perish. It is of the natural order and cannot endure. "I know how delicious is this cup of love,
   --I existing for you, you existing for me; but it is a child's clinging to his toy; an alphabet through
   which our first lessons are prettily conveyed." Obviously, such worldliness cannot endure the tests of
   eternity--at least in rationalistic or "spiritualistic" systems! See Rep. Men, 128-129: "Heaven is not
   the pairing of two, but the communion of all souls. We meet, and dwell an instant under the temple of
   one thought, and part, as though we parted not, to join another thought in other fellowships of joy."
   Hence in Swedenborg's (as in Emerson's) universe, the law of compensation and retribution worked instantaneously. See Nature, 58.1-20 and note. Swedenborg influenced Emerson's essay on "Friendship."

Summarizing the Swedenborgian position on human association: It is spiritual and impersonal at its best. To love a person merely because he returns the love or because his outer person is near by or attractive, is not to love interiorly. The spiritual world knows no time or space, and therefore ignores flesh, blood, muscle, coloring, pigmentation. The person is essentially evil and perishable; only the internal qualities (sustained by Influx) are good. When a person dies to the natural world, he continues the same close association with spirits sharing those qualities which he earlier shared internally and secretly. If we are internally and spiritually united to any person in the natural world, that union is not severed at death, for though we are then mutually invisible, we are always spiritually near each other. See G O M, ¶ 10; Soul and Body, chs. X-XII; Genius-O, ¶ 5; Genius, ¶s. 13-15.

6) DOCTRINE OF USES AND FUNCTIONS----MEN ARE ONLY PARTS OF THE "COMPLETE MAN"---- EACH HAS A SPECIALIZED GIFT TO BE DEVELOPED FOR THE GOOD OF THE WHOLE----HEAVEN IS COMPLETE UNITY----THE NATURAL WORLD, ON THE OTHER HAND, REQUIRES DIVERSITY. See Plato's discussion of "Universals" or "Ideas" in the Parmenides and the Sophista, as well as his view of justice or "rule of limitation." See Plotinus' "three kinds of souls" under "The Path of Enlightenment" on the Chart of Neo-Platonism in your Transcendental Workbook. Emerson develops the doctrine of USE and DIVISION OF GIFTS or APPORTIONING OF TALENTS in his famous essay, The American Scholar, q.v. See the commentary on "Universal Man" in the Transcendental Workbook chapter entitled, "Emerson's Daemon and the Orphic Poet." "Man in his perfect form is Heaven." See Rep. Men, 106, 126; Genius-O, ¶ 1; G O M, ¶s. 14-16; Excerpts, ¶s. 35-36.

(C) NATURE----AND ITS MINISTRY TO MAN

1) NATURE IS CREATED BY INFLUX AS THAT SPIRITUAL FORCE FLOWS THROUGH MANKIND----BUT IT IS PRODUCED AND SUSTAINED ALSO BY DIRECT DEPENDENCE UPON THE "FORMS" OF THE SPIRIT WORLD AND HENCE MAY ALWAYS SERVE IN A MEASURE TO INSTRUCT MAN, WHATEVER MAN'S FALLEN CONDITION, AND WARN MAN OF HIS CONDITION. Cf. Nature as "monitor" to man in Neo-Platonism and in Wordsworth's "Ode on Intimations." See G O M, ¶ 9; Excerpts, ¶ 74. Cf. Nature, 36.17 and 93.20ff.

2) THE OUTER WORLD SERVES MAN IN A VARIETY OF WAYS: FROM MINISTERING TO HIS PHYSICAL NEEDS UP TO TRAINING HIS SOUL FOR ETERNITY----NATURE'S CHIEF VALUE IS THE LAST: TO PROVIDE SYMBOLS OF SPIRITUAL AND MORAL TRUTHS----HER INSTRUCTION IS EXPLAINED IN THE "DOCTRINE OF CORRESPONDENCES" BY WHICH NATURAL OBJECTS OUTSIDE A MAN CORRE- SPOND TO IDEAS OR STATES OF MIND WITHIN HIM----ONE'S EDUCATION IS THE RESULT OF A PROCESS OF UNLOCKING OR "RECOLLECTION"----THE LANGUAGE OF NATURE, THEREFORE, IS ONE OF THINGS RATHER THAN WORDS.----THE SMALLEST BLADE OF GRASS MAY BE, NAY IS, A TEACHER----DOCTRINE OF THE ALL IN EACH. See Nature, 45.5-12. See Plato's Meno for a state- ment of the classical doctrine of education: "For all things in nature being linked and related, and the soul having heretofore known all, nothing hinders but that any man who has recalled to mind, or ac- cording to the common phrase has learned, one thing only, should of himself recover all his ancient [i.e., his prenatal] knowledge, and find out again all the rest, if he have but courage and faint not in the midst of his researches. For inquiry and learning is reminiscence all." See Wordsworth's "Ode on Intimations." See Rep. Men, 96, and Nature, 54.23--55.1 and 29.10-16----for the doctrine of the Microcosm. See Rep. Men, 101, 105, 115-117 on the Doctrine of Correspondences. More valuable are: Genius, ¶s. 15-16; G O M, ¶ 8 (cf. Nature, 32.8); Excerpts, ¶ 9 (cf. Nature, 76.10-12; 79.5ff.); ¶ 18f (cf. Nature, 32ff. and 36.19); ¶s. 22 and 71 (cf. Nature, 79.14-18; 76.3-17). On the range of Nature's service to man, see G O M, ¶ 6. Emerson makes use of these various levels and of the "pro- gressive principle" throughout Nature. Cf. esp. Nature, 76.3-17; 77.12-15. For the Microcosm, see Excerpts, ¶s. 6 et passim. This prophecy of a spiritual message in a single blade of grass lies behind Whitman's Leaves of Grass.

3) SINCE MAN HAS FALLEN, HE HAS LOST THE ABILITY TO SEE THROUGH MERE THINGS INTO THE DEEP TRUTHS BEHIND THEM----BUT GOD'S REVELATION TO SWEDENBORG COMES TO MEN AS A BOON----THOUGH THEY BE BLIND, THEY CAN THROUGH THE NEW-CHURCH USE SWEDENBORG'S KEY TO THESE MYSTERIES AND LOST CAPACITIES. See Genius, ¶ 17 and Excerpts, ¶ 74. Study Excerpts, ¶ 6 with Nature, 80-81.

4) THE EXTERNAL WORLD HAS SUFFERED SINCE MAN'S FALL----NATURE HERE AND THERE AP-
PEARS VICIOUS IN THE EYES OF DEGENERATE MANKIND BECAUSE MEN HAVE OBSTRUCTED THE
STREAM OF INFLUX WITH THEIR "HELLS". The view of Nature as modern science sees it (and as
Tennyson and Darwin saw it---as "red in tooth and claw"), evolving by cruelties and tremendous waste
of life---is largely unacceptable to "rationalistic" systems, which have a blind spot as regards matter.
Swedenborgism, like Neo-Platonism, places the chief emphasis upon the real world of MIND. (Matter is
not real.) In their theory of animals, Swedenborgians come as near a "naturalistic" view of the visible
world as they possibly can with their postulates. Study G O M, ¶s. 8 and 10 (cf. Nature, 81.2ff. and
94.13ff.); Excerpts, ¶ 18d (cf. Nature, 32ff., 81.2ff., 94.16ff.); ¶s. 18g and 22 (cf. Nature, 34.1-3;
81.2ff.); ¶s. 58, 69, 74.

(D) THE WORD OF GOD----HOLY SCRIPTURES

1) THE HEBREW-CHRISTIAN BIBLE IS CENTRAL IN REDEEMING A FALLEN WORLD BECAUSE IT CON-
TAINS IN ITS VOCABULARY A HIDDEN KEY TO THE SPIRITUAL MEANING OF NATURE----IT WAS
WRITTEN BY MEN WHO UNDERSTOOD THE LANGUAGE OF NATURE AND WHO LIVED IN A GOLDEN
AGE WHEN INFLUX OPERATED WITHOUT OPPOSITION TO ITS DOWNWARD SWEEP----BUT WHEN
MANKIND BECAME CORRUPT, THE LITERAL BIBLE REMAINED BUT ITS INNER MEANING VANISHED
----SWEDENBORGIANS (THROUGH THE REVELATIONS OF SWEDENBORG) CLAIM TO HAVE THE
KEY TO THE LOST LANGUAGE----THEY HAVE NO INTEREST IN LITERAL OR HISTORICAL IN-
TERPRETATION. (Cf. modern Christian Science or the recent cult of Unity.) New Churchmen, in
Emerson's day, like other types of Biblists or Biblical Fundamentalists, select rather carefully the
portions of the Bible which they find they can use in constructing their theological and ethical pattern.
They avoid coming to terms with the "higher" and "lower" criticism of Bible, i.e., Biblical scholarship
of the "form criticism" variety, now well established among objective critics. (Refer to B4 above.)
See Rep. Men, 120: "Having adopted the belief that certain books of the Old and New Testaments were
exact allegories, or written in angelic and ecstatic mode, [Swedenborg] employed his remaining years
in extricating from the literal, the universal sense.... He had borrowed from Plato the fine fable of
'a most ancient people, men better than we and dwelling nigher to the gods:' and Swedenborg added that
they used the earth symbolically; that these, when they saw terrestrial objects, did not think at all
about them, but only about those which they signified." The fable is recorded in Plato's Timaeus:
Egyptian priests told Solon of a race of great Athenians, who lived thousands of years before, but
whose civilization had been destroyed by an earthquake. See G O M, ¶s. 11-13; Excerpts, ¶ 18g.

2) BASED UPON SWEDENBORG'S COMMENTARIES ON HOLY WRIT, WILLIAM OEGGER AND OTHERS
HAVE WORKED OUT AN ELABORATE DICTIONARY OF THE LANGUAGE OF NATURE AS FOUND IN
THE BIBLE, AND CLAIM TO HAVE ARRIVED AT MUCH OF THE PRIMITIVE MEANING OF THE
NATURAL OBJECTS ROUND ABOUT US. Here is a typical passage from Oegger's The True Messiah:
The visible creation, he writes, is 'the exterior circumference of the invisible and metaphysical world;
and material objects are necessarily scoriae of the substantial thoughts of the Creator; scoriae [i.e.,
dross, slag, refuse, rubbish] which must always preserve an exact relation to their first origin; in
other words, visible nature must have a spiritual and moral side. For God everything is, every thing
exists.... For God, to create is only to manifest.... Every thing we see, touch, smell; every thing,
from the sun to a grain of sand, from our own body with its admirable organs, to that of a worm; every
thing has flowed forth, by a supreme reason, from the world where all is spirit and life." (A sentence
from this passage appears in Nature, 44.8-13.) For Oegger's "Hieroglyphic Keys" to the Scriptures,
see Emerson the Essayist, II, 95-98.

3) THE CANON OF THE BIBLE AND THE ROUTE TO FURTHER HEAVENLY REVELATIONS ARE DE-
CLARED "CLOSED"----SWEDENBORG'S VISIONS ARE DEFINITIVE----THE CHURCH WILL TOLER-
ATE NO FURTHER EXPLORATION----SWEDENBORG'S KEYS ARE THE ONLY ONES AUTHORIZED
(THE ONLY ONES THAT CAN BE AUTHORIZED) BY THE HIERARCHY OF THE NEW-CHURCH. (IN
OTHER WORDS, LIKE ALMOST EVERY RELIGIOUS BODY, THIS CHURCH HAS ITS DOCTRINE OF
INFALLIBILITY.)

(E) MISCELLANEOUS CONSIDERATIONS

1) SWEDENBORGIANS ARE A WARM AND BENEVOLENT LITTLE "CHRISTIAN" SECT ON THE BORDERS OF SECTARIAN PROTESTANTISM----IN APPEARANCE OR ATMOSPHERE THE CHURCH MIGHT BE SAID TO COMBINE THE QUIET GOODWILL OF QUAKERS WITH THE LITURGICAL AND CULTIC TRIMMINGS OF OLD LUTHERANISM----THE CHIEF EMPHASIS IS ON PRACTICAL LIVING--ON RECTITUDE----NEW-CHURCHMEN EXTOL THE MORAL SENTIMENT----CENTERED ON THE "TEN COMMANDMENTS," THEIR MORALITY SMACKS STRONGLY OF THE HEBRAIC QUALITY OF PURITANISM RATHER THAN OF THE HELENIC COLORING OF THE CATHOLIC CHURCHES. (In this connection, the student should remember that Swedenborg's father was a Lutheran bishop.) Emerson was strongly drawn to the New-Church because of its Neo-Platonic ("rationalistic") framework and especially because of its high ethical teaching. See Rep. Men, 94: "The atmosphere of moral sentiment is a region of grandeur which reduces all material magnificence to toys, yet opens to every wretch that has reason the doors of the universe." See ibid., 145: Swedenborg said: "'Nothing can keep you,--not fate, nor health, nor admirable intellect; none can keep you, but rectitude only, rectitude for ever and ever!' And with a tenacity that never swerved in all his studies, inventions, dreams, he adheres to this brave choice." See G O M, ¶ 1 etc.; Genius-O, ¶ 4; Excerpts, ¶ 9.

2) ESSENTIALLY ANTI-HISTORICAL, LIKE ALL RATIONALISTIC SYSTEMS, SWEDENBORGIANS EMPHASIZE A KIND OF EXISTENTIALISM---THE "ETERNAL PRESENT"----THEY ARE CONCERNED WITH THEIR "IMMEDIATE" SPIRITUAL CONDITION----FROM THE POINT OF VIEW OF MIND OR SOUL, TIME IS NOT REAL----THE BEST VIEW IS "SUB SPECIE AETERNITATIS"----WE HAVE ALREADY SEEN THAT NEW-CHURCH BIBLICAL ATTITUDES SHOW NO HISTORIC SENSE---NO CONCEPT OF A WRITING OF THE BIBLE IN HISTORY AS OTHER BOOKS ARE WRITTEN---TALMUD or ARABIAN NIGHTS, for example. NEW-CHURCHMEN DEPART FROM HISTORICAL PERSPECTIVE ON ANOTHER POINT: THEY SEE NOTHING BUT FUTILITY IN ORTHODOX CHRISTIANITY, IGNORING THE DOCTRINE OF "ORIGINAL SIN" WITH ITS CORRELATIVES, THE "INCARNATION" AND "ATONEMENT." ----IN ITS DUALISM, IT BREAKS WITH THE HEBREW-CHRISTIAN TRADITION, WHICH EVER ASSERTS THAT THE MATERIAL WORLD IS A DELIBERATE CREATION BY GOD WHO, FROM THE BEGINNING, HAS CALLED IT GOOD---- Cf. Genesis, 1 and the recurrence of the phrase, "it was good:" "‏כִּי טֹוב‎:"

3) EMERSON OBJECTED PRINCIPALLY TO THE LITERALISM OR FUNDAMENTALISM OF SWEDENBORG'S ALLEGORY----HE FELT THAT SWEDENBORG SAW INTO ONLY A HEBRAIC OR BIBLICAL HEAVEN----EMERSON DID NOT BELIEVE THAT THE HEBREW-CHRISTIAN SCRIPTURES WERE CAPABLE OF SUPPLYING A UNIVERSAL SYMBOLISM. See Rep. Men and Excerpts, ¶ 57.

4) THE FOLLOWING EXTRACT FROM A LETTER TO YOUR INSTRUCTOR FROM A FRIEND OF SWEDENBORGISM (BUT NOT AN ADHERENT) GIVES AN INTERESTING AND SOMEWHAT OBJECTIVE APPRAISAL OF THE FOUNDER OF THIS SECT: "Yes, you are right about the dearth of good concise pictures of Swedenborg's system, and I shall try my best to remedy that in my biography, because, really, his life is his thought, and his thought is his life. (He didn't have much real life outside his own brain.) I see him in the great stream of Platonic and Neo-Platonic thought, trying to do what Ficino and Pico had in mind, in reconciling the Platonic occult tradition with Christian dogma. I think he was trying to do for Plato what Thomas Aquinas did for (or to) Aristotle. I am sure that he got caught somewhere along the line in the 'occult tradition,' whether through the Rosicrucians, the Masons, the alchemists, the Hermetic writings, or whatever, but I don't think he was insane at all. I just think he got into some other realm of being, whether a 'world of spirits' as he thought, or Jung's 'collective unconscious,'---it doesn't matter much how we interpret it---it really does exist, whatever we call it. The mystics came into it through one door and the psychoanalysts through another. (I've peaked through both myself!) I don't think it is possible to understand fully a man like Swedenborg any more than Joan of Arc or Bernadette of Lourdes)--we can only make an attempt to clear up some of the debris of misunderstanding which has piled up around him, and let others make their own interpretations of the simple facts, according to their own temperamental predilections."

(F) SAMPSON REED'S DEVELOPMENTS OF SWEDENBORGIAN DOCTRINE IN THE
AREA OF BOSTON----HIS ROMANTICISM----HIS THEORY OF LITERATURE.
[Reed was a product of the Romantic Movement as well as of Swedenborgism.
A sketch of his life appears in Emerson the Essayist, volume I. He read Cole-
ridge eagerly and knew Wordsworth almost by heart. He claimed that the latter
was bearing an eloquent and independent witness to the truths which the New-
Church taught. A quotation from Wordsworth appeared on the title page of the
first edition of his Growth of the Mind (1826).]

1) TRUE OR "ORIGINAL GENIUS" IN MAN IS THAT SPECIAL GOD-GIVEN QUALITY OR USE IMPARTED
BY INFLUX----IT IS LENT TO MAN FROM HEAVEN----IT IS NOT HIS OWN POSSESSION----"IT IS
NOT OURS; WE ARE ITS."----IT IS GIVEN, NOT EARNED, AND MUST NOT BE USED SELFISHLY
----ALL GENIUS IS RECEPTION. See Genius, ¶ 2; Genius-O, ¶ 4; G O M, ¶s. 15-16.

2) TRULY GREAT MEN OR "REPRESENTATIVE MEN" ARE SUCH BECAUSE OF THEIR PARTAKING
LARGER DRAUGHTS OF DIVINE INFLUX THAN DO ORDINARY BEINGS----AT BEST, HOWEVER,
THEY ARE ONLY CREATURES----THEY ARE NOT TO BE WORSHIPED AS GODS----HUMILITY
CHARACTERIZES THE TRULY GREAT----GREATNESS AND GOODNESS ARE INSEPARABLE----
REED CONDEMNED THE BYRONIC OR NAPOLEONIC CONCEPT OF GREATNESS. Reed's doctrine
influenced Emerson's early poem, "Gnothi Seauton." Study Genius, ¶s. 3-7, 12; Excerpts, ¶s. 35-36;
Genius-O, ¶ 3. Neither Reed nor Emerson shared Carlyle's view of "great men."

3) MAN NEEDS TO RELY UPON GOD CONSTANTLY FOR EVERY QUALITY OF REAL LIFE----(COM-
PARE EMERSON'S SELF-RELIANCE)----THE FLESH FAILS----ONLY THE GODLIKE CHARACTER,
THE SOUL, OR THE REASON IN MAN IS ETERNAL----THAT PORTION OF US ILLUMINED BY THE
DIVINE INFLUX IS ALL THAT PERSISTS IN ETERNITY----SOCIETY AND THE WORLD'S NOTIONS
OF GREATNESS MUST BE RENOUNCED----THEY SMELL OF DEATH. See Genius-O, ¶ 5 and G O M,
¶s. 14-16. These thoughts lie behind Emerson's "Gnothi Seauton" and "Self-Reliance."

4) THE BASIC RULE OF LITERARY CRITICISM--ONE ESPECIALLY TRUE FOR INTERPRETING THE
BIBLE (OR ANY GREAT CLASSIC) IS THAT "A SCRIPTURE CAN BE INTERPRETED ONLY BY A SPIRIT
AKIN TO THAT WHICH GAVE IT FORTH."----LIKE ONLY CAN UNDERSTAND LIKE. ("QUANTUM
SUMUS, SCIMUS.") See G O M, ¶ 12. Cf. Nature, 44.18.

5) REED'S AESTHETIC THEORY----THE POET AS SEER----ALL TRUE ART ISSUES FROM THE
HEAVENLY INFLUX----THE NATURAL WORLD IS USEFUL ONLY INSOFAR AS IT SPEAKS OF
SPIRIT----FORM IS LESS IMPORTANT THAN INSPIRATION OR POWER OR CONTENT OR MESSAGE
----THE PRINCIPLE OF SPONTANEITY EMPHASIZED----RHYME IN POETRY IS NOT SANCTIONED
BY NATURE----SOME POETIC INSPIRATION IS TOO GREAT TO BE WRITTEN DOWN AND CAN ONLY
BE FELT AND NOT EXPRESSED----THE BEST PART OF MYSTICAL EXPERIENCE IS INEFFABLE
----THE WORK OF ART BUT HALF REVEALS----THE BEST PART OF AN EXPERIENCE CANNOT
BE COMMUNICATED!!!! See G O M, ¶s. 8-9; Genius, ¶ 8; Excerpts, ¶ 6; Genius-O, ¶ 3; Cf. Nature,
28.4--31.4; 32.10.

Reed's letter to Theophilus Parsons (edited in Emerson the Essayist) [May 31, 1823] is significant:
"If you keep the Word before you as essential poetry, I think you must know where to look for every
thing else, as instinctively as animals know the point of compass. The different kinds of poetry as
they have been classified by writers on the subject, are something, that I know very little about---but I
should think that the natural mind had made divisions here, as elsewhere, many of which would disappear before a single view of goodness and truth united. Whether Lyric, Pastoral, Heroic or what not
----poetry can have but one essence, love, but one form, nature. There may be infinite variety in
the time, but they all require articulation and sound. I can see no rhymes in nature, and hardly blank
verse, but a happy assemblage of living objects, not in straight lines and at fixed distances, but springing up in God's own order, which by its apparent want of design, leaves on the heart an image of its
essential innocence and humility."

He writes similarly in his Growth of the Mind (1826): "It is...the continual endeavour of Providence, that the natural sciences should be the spontaneous production of the human mind. To these should certainly be added, poetry and music.... By poetry is meant all those illustrations of truth by natural imagery, which spring from the fact that this world is the mirror of him who made it. Strictly speaking, nothing has less to do with fiction, than poetry.... The word fiction [means] whatever is not in exact agreement with the creative spirit of God. It belongs to the true poet to feel this spirit, and to be governed by it; to be raised above the senses; to live and breathe in the inward efforts of things; to feel the power of creation, even before he sees the effect.... Of all the poetry which exists, that only possesses the seal of immortality, which presents the image of God which is stamped on nature." [He is here condemning the works of that scoundrel, Byron!!]

"It may be peculiar, and is said with deference to the opinions of others, that to my ear, rhymes add nothing to poetry, but rather detract from its beauty. They possess too strongly the marks of art, and produce a sameness which tires, and sometimes disgusts. We seek for them in vain in nature, and may therefore reasonably presume that they spring out of the peculiar state of the public taste, without possessing any real foundation in the mind itself; that they are rather the fashion of the dress, than any essential part. In the natural world we find nothing which answers to them, or feels like them--but a happy assemblage of living objects springing up, not in straight lines and at a fixed distance, but in God's own order.... The poet should be free and unshackled as the eagle."

[Schyberg indicates that Whitman had contacts with the Swedenborgians in his early years. Whether he ever read Sampson Reed's Observations on the Growth of the Mind cannot be declared certainly, but as early as 1826, in Boston, Reed anticipated Emerson's "The Poet" and Whitman's Leaves of Grass.]

6) JOHN LOCKE'S MATERIALISM AND THE "NATURALISTIC SCHOOL" OF HOBBES MUST YIELD TO INTUITIONALISM----MIND (i.e., SPIRIT) IS PRIOR TO MATTER----OUR MOST IMPORTANT IDEAS ARE A PRIORI. See G O M, ¶s. 4, 7; Genius, ¶ 18; Genius-O, ¶ 5. Cf. Nature, 82.3--87.2; 89.12--90.4; 92.1-3.

7) THE SCIENTISTS CAN TRULY UNDERSTAND THE NATURAL WORLD ONLY BY ABANDONING THE INDUCTIVE METHOD AND LOOKING THROUGH SPIRITUAL OR RELIGIOUS EYES----SPIRITUAL STUDIES SHOULD HAVE PRIORITY OVER CHEMISTRY AND PHYSICS IN THE NATURALIST'S PREPARATION. See G O M, ¶ 7; Genius, ¶s. 9-10. Cf. Emerson on fact-grubbing scientists in Nature, 82.3--87.2; 89.12--90.4; 92.1-3.

8) THE NEW CHURCH BRINGS OPTIMISM FOR THE FUTURE----TRADITIONAL RELIGION IS DEAD---- THE NEW JERUSALEM WILL SOON DESCEND FROM HEAVEN. See G O M, ¶ 10; Genius, ¶s. 11-12, 19; Genius-O, ¶ 5. Emerson's optimism was greatly strengthened by the Swedenborgians while he was writing Nature. See G O M, ¶s. 1-2. Cf. Nature, "Introduction" and chapter VIII.

HILL BURYING GROUND — Its slate stones and brick tombs of the eighteenth century have elaborate inscriptions. John Jack's grave is down the path at the left.

THE INFLUENCE OF GERMAN, TRANSCENDENTAL KANT

Before 1837, at least, Emerson seems not to have read any of the works of Immanuel Kant, though they were available to him at Harvard, which, perhaps, by 1835 possessed the best collection in the United States.[1] His slow progress in the study of German partly accounts for this fact--his close friends were reading, discussing, and publishing about, Kant[2] and using the College holdings[3]--but, more significant, was his growing spiritual satisfaction with Swedenborgism and especially the philosophy of Coleridge, whose "system" drew less upon Kant than upon Kant's Neo-Platonic successors (notably Fichte and Schelling) and elevated (over an implied Kantian protest) spiritual enthusiasm and intuition. He appears to have been content to recognize in Kant the creator of the term "Transcendental," the establisher of the terms "Understanding" and "Reason," and the catalyst of German and British Romanticism, but he refused to go far outside the available works of Coleridge for interpretations.

Emerson's introduction to Kant at Harvard in or about November, 1820, moreover--Sir William Drummond's Academical Questions (London, 1805)[4]--did not encourage him to seek out the works of the German or his disciples. Drummond confused the founder of the Transcendental Philosophy with his successors, condemned a priori thinking (intuitionalism), and extolled the Scottish "Common Sense" school, especially the works of Thomas Reid, in which, at this early period, Emerson was much interested. The second book dealing with Kant--also discovered in the late Harvard years or soon thereafter--much recommended by Mary Moody Emerson but not immediately influential as it was to become in the early 1830's[5]--was Staël-Holstein's Germany (London, 1813), which appealed to him less for the exposition of Kant's principal works than for the general impressions it gave of Kant's successors--an appeal which did not become strong, however, until the crisis of 1831 and 1832, when, upon the death of his first wife, he was turning to the Quakers, Methodists, Swedenborgians, Wordsworth, Carlyle, but especially Coleridge for a world-view that might replace his outgrown Unitarianism. The third book on Kant on his reading list--F. A. Nitsch's A General and Introductory View of Professor Kant's Principles Concerning Man, the World and the Deity (London, 1796), which he withdrew from the Library of the Boston Athenaeum on March 21, 1832, and kept until April 3[6]--and which during that period and thereafter he never referred to in his Works, Journals or Letters--a dull, wordy, vague, pedantic, and poorly organized treatise--did Kant's system scant justice and offered little competition for The Friend or Aids to Reflection! The following November he apologetically grouped together some of those who had been influences: "We think so little that every new thought presented to us, even every old thought in a new dress of words takes us by surprize and we are thus at the mercy of Goethe, Kant, Cousin, Mackintosh, & even of Burton."[7] While completing Nature three and a half years later he developed this observation: "Each new mind we approach seems to require an abdication of all our past & present empire. A new doctrine seems at first a subversion of all our opinions, tastes, & manner of living. So did Jesus, so did Kant, so did Swedenborg, so did Cousin, so did Alcott seem. Take thankfully & heartily all they can give, exhaust them, leave father & mother & goods, wrestle with them, let them not go until their blessing be won, & after a short season the dismay will be overpast, the excess of influence will be withdrawn, & they will be no longer an alarming meteor but one more bright star shining serenely in your heaven & blending its light with all your day."[8] In neither reference, however, did he include the name of Coleridge, for whom, among the mottoes he assigned to great men of history in "A Laconic Biographical Dictionary," he quoted Plato (by way of Bacon): "He is a god to me who shall rightly define & divide."[9]

Indirectly, however, through his reading in periodicals[10] and especially through Wordsworth assisted by pre-Kantian Fénelon,[11] Kant's doctrines concerning morality expressed chiefly in the Metaphysic of Ethics (1785) and in the Critique of Practical Reason (1788) he permanently made his own. The period during which he wrote his sermons--still to be fully explored[12]--will provide evidence enough.

A glance at the hundreds of references to "Duty," "Voice Within," "Monitor," "Moral Sentiment," "Conscience," and synonyms of these in his more than one hundred and sixty homiletical manuscripts--most of them still unpublished--will convince one of the strong, indirect influence of Kant.[13] Let me, therefore, summarize--and badly, too--Kant's principal theories regarding morality.

Kant tried to discover a basis for ethics free from religious creeds and, at the same time, independent of sense experience--i.e., a priori: (1) The source of the moral law, he said, is not an external code like the Ten Commandments but man's own inner nature. (He might have said, quoting the New Testament, "The Kingdom of God is within you.")[14] (2) The fountainhead of right conduct is not the Intellect but the Will. Man's chief duty, then, is to endeavor to keep a "good will" functioning in himself at all times, since the moral law is derived from it. (3) An uncompromising, austere, but noble ethic results: "Respect the dignity of your own nature. Lean always toward your better self. You are not a mere animal!" Man, as Kant saw him, straddled two worlds--the phenomenal realm of space and time, on the one hand, and the spiritual or ideational order (whence right conduct springs), on the other. In the second, man can escape the limitations of the animal nature--especially domination by the passions--and be free. From it comes a voice of DUTY--an OUGHT--which he can hear, and hearing can perform. At the end of "Voluntaries" Emerson summarized Kant's speculations in four lines:[15]

> So nigh in grandeur to our dust,   When Duty whispers low, Thou must,
> So near is God to man,   The youth replies, I can.

Although, said Kant, the phenomenal world can cripple or limit one unless he makes a strong effort to counteract it, the spiritual world nonetheless shines into every man and tells him what he OUGHT to do and, at the same time, gives him power to execute the command. That will can become captive to the senses, of course, and then the Voice becomes less audible. This moral law or Conscience or Monitor, seated in man's moral nature, is universal and unconditional. One dares not deny it and expect to keep his integrity. Since it rules the universe and extends to everyone at all times and everywhere, said Kant, "Even the God of religion must yield to it."

He laid down three famous rules by way of interpretation: (1) So act that the principle of your action may be to your will a law universal. That is, when you act be sure your action can be safely and beneficially universalized--multiplied everywhere and by everybody without harmful consequences to the human race. (2) Treat humanity, whether in your own person, or in that of another, never as a means only, but always as an end. (This rule, often called a formal statement of Christ's "Golden Rule," applies to one's inferiors as well as superiors. All men resent being treated as mere conveniences. All have a sense of worth. All are human beings in whom GOOD WILL potentially resides.) (3) Act always as a member of the Kingdom of Ends. Continually ask yourself whether your proposed behavior is appropriate to such a membership, furthering the high ideals and good of all men.

Values in the foregoing ethical system are patent: (1) The first is discipline. Kant rightly urges men to beware of too much pleasure, since it frequently interferes with the stern commands of Duty. Only by keeping the beast within bounds through temperance can one become an apt instrument of the GOOD WILL. (2) The second value is universality of application. The Supreme Law, he maintains, is uniform semper, ubique, et ab omnibus. It does not vary for races, nations, times, or seasons. Great evil results from considering it "relatively binding." (3) A third value is the assurance that we have free will. When the OUGHT comes to a man, it brings CAN with it! Perhaps the best poetical paraphrase of the Kantian ethic is Wordsworth's "Ode to Duty," with which I conclude these incomplete (but, I hope, suggestive) remarks. Emerson carefully marked the second stanza in his edition of the Poetical Works (4 vols., Boston, 1824):

ODE TO DUTY

Stern Daughter of the Voice of God!
O Duty! if that name thou love
Who art a light to guide, a rod
To check the erring, and reprove;
Thou, who art victory and law
When empty terrors overawe;
From vain temptations dost set free;
And calm'st the weary strife of frail
    humanity!

There are who ask not if thine eye
Be on them; who, in love and truth,
Where no misgiving is, rely
Upon the genial sense of youth:
Glad Hearts! without reproach or blot
Who do thy work, and know it not:
Oh! if through confidence misplaced
They fail, thy saving arms, dread Power!
    around them cast.

Serene will be our days and bright,
And happy will our nature be,
When love is an unerring light,
And joy its own security.
And they a blissful course may hold
Even now, who, not unwisely bold,
Live in the spirit of this creed;
Yet seek thy firm support, according
    to their need.

I, loving freedom, and untried;
No sport of every random gust,
Yet being to myself a guide,
Too blindly have reposed my trust:

And oft, when in my heart was heard
Thy timely mandate, I deferred
The task, in smoother walks to stray;
But thee I now would serve more
    strictly, if I may.

Through no disturbance of my soul,
Or strong compunction in me wrought,
I supplicate for thy control;
But in the quietness of thought:
Me this unchartered freedom tires;
I feel the weight of chance-desires:
My hopes no more must change their name,
I long for a repose that ever is the
    same.

Stern Lawgiver! yet thou dost wear
The Godhead's most benignant grace;
Nor know we anything so fair
As is the smile upon thy face:
Flowers laugh before thee on their beds
And fragrance in thy footing treads;
Thou dost preserve the stars from wrong;
And the most ancient heavens, through
    Thee, are fresh and strong.

To humbler functions, awful Power!
I call thee: I myself commend
Unto thy guidance from this hour;
Oh, let my weakness have an end!
Give unto me, made lowly wise,
The spirit of self-sacrifice;
The confidence of reason give;
And in the light of truth thy Bondman
    let me live!

---

1 See A Catalogue of the Library of Harvard University in Cambridge, Massachusetts, (3 vols.) Cambridge, 1830, and the supplementary volume of 1834--especially the latter.
2 See Stanley M. Vogel, German Literary Influences on the American Transcendentalists, New Haven, 1955.
3 See my Transcendental Reading Patterns: Library Charging Lists for the Alcotts, James Freeman Clarke, Frederic Henry Hedge, Theodore Parker, George Ripley, Samuel Ripley of Waltham, Jones Very, and Charles Stearns Wheeler--New Areas for Fresh Explorations, Hartford, [1970], passim.
4 See my Emerson's Early Reading List, 1819-1824, N.Y., 1951, p. 6. Drummond discusses Kant (or, rather, his successors) in Bk. II, chap. IX, pp. 351-382.
5 See my book, A Commentary on Emerson's Early Lectures (1833-1836), with an Index-Concordance, Hartford, 1961, pp. 10-25.
6 See my Ralph Waldo Emerson's Reading, Raleigh, 1941, pp. 19 and 94.
7 See JMN, IV, p. 58 (Nov. 13, 1832).   8 Ibid., V, pp. 178-179 (June 22, 1836).
9 Ibid., VI, p. 209.
10 See my Emerson's Workshop: An Analysis of his Reading in Periodicals Through 1836 with the Principal Thematic Key to his Essays, Poems, and Lectures (2 vols.) Hartford, [1964], I, pp. 9-219.
11 For Fénelon's significance, see the following chapter.
12 I have indicated some of the rich possibilities for research with the unpublished sermons in my Index-Concordance to Emerson's Sermons with Homiletical Papers,

(2 vols.) Hartford, [1963].   Included in volume II (pages 654-661) is an article, "History and Biography in Emerson's Unpublished Sermons," originally published in the Proceedings of the American Antiquarian Society for October, 1956, pages 103-118.

13   In addition to the Index-Concordance to the unpublished sermons, cited above, one should consult the Index-Concordance to Young Emerson Speaks (the twenty-five manuscripts edited by A. C. McGiffert in 1938), published in my Emerson the Essayist, II, pp. 226-313.

14   See Luke 17:21.   New Testament scholars tell me that the Greek actually means: "The kingdom of God is in your midst"--a group rather than individualistic emphasis.

15   See Poems (volume in the Centenary edition of the Works, 1904), p. 207.

A

GENERAL AND INTRODUCTORY

V I E W

OF

PROFESSOR KANT's PRINCIPLES

CONCERNING

MAN, THE WORLD AND THE DEITY,

SUBMITTED TO

THE CONSIDERATION OF THE LEARNED.

BY

F. A. NITSCH,

LATE LECTURER OF THE LATIN LANGUAGE AND MA-
THEMATICS IN THE ROYAL FRIDERICIANUM COLLEGE
AT KÖNIGSBERG, AND PUPIL OF PROFESSOR KANT.

LONDON:

PRINTED, AND SOLD BY J. DOWNES, NO. 240, STRAND,
NEAR TEMPLE BAR.

1796.

[Entered at Stationers Hall.]

ELEMENTS

OF THE

CRITICAL PHILOSOPHY:

CONTAINING

A CONCISE ACCOUNT OF ITS ORIGIN AND TENDENCY;

A VIEW OF ALL THE WORKS PUBLISHED BY ITS FOUNDER,

PROFESSOR IMMANUEL KANT;

AND A GLOSSARY FOR THE EXPLANATION OF TERMS AND PHRASES.

TO WHICH ARE ADDED:

THREE PHILOLOGICAL ESSAYS;

Chiefly translated from the German of

JOHN CHRISTOPHER ADELUNG;

Aulic Counsellor and First Librarian to the Elector of Saxony.

BY

A. F. M. WILLICH, M. D.

LONDON:

PRINTED FOR T. N. LONGMAN,
No. 39. PATERNOSTER-ROW.

1798.

TWO BRITISH WORKS ABOUT KANT THAT CIRCULATED AMONG EMERSON'S FRIENDS

HOMILETICAL BACKGROUND OF

EMERSON'S POEM, "GNOTHI SEAUTON" (1831)[*]

While he was writing and preaching his sermons prior to 1832, and especially during the period of the meditations that led to the composition of "Gnothi Seauton" (ca. July, 1831), Emerson found confirmation for Kant's Metaphysic of Ethics--that is, reaffirmation of the "starry heavens above and the moral law within"--in the writings of Fénelon, Archbishop of Cambrai, who also extolled the Divinity that speaks through the conscience of man. In offering herein additional light on "Gnothi Seauton," therefore, I shall list selected passages from Fénelon and offer others from Emerson's unpublished sermons--these latter quoted through the kindness of the late Edward W. Forbes, Esq., Emerson's grandson. But first I reprint, because of its imagery, so like that of "Gnothi Seauton," a "Hymn on Deity" edited by Emerson's father in the Monthly Anthology and Boston Review, V (1808), pages 552-553. Whether Emerson himself ever saw it, I cannot be certain.

HYMN ON DEITY ASCRIBED TO ORPHEUS

I SPEAK to ears initiate. Far remov'd
Be every vulgar eye. Thou only, Moon,
Rolling full-orbed in silent majesty,
Witness my song. I utter truths sublime;
Truths, which the soul exalt. In mute attention
Listen; for I proclaim a DEITY!

The Almighty One, self-born, all glorious,
Exists; Creator blest, wide nature's sovereign,
Invisible to mortal eye; but he,
Watchful forever, guards his boundless works.
He, of his goodness, chastens man; he sends
War, famine, pestilence. He, he alone,
Uncounselled, governs and directs the whole.

O, come with me, my friend, adoring trace,
In all his works, the footsteps of a God.
His hand sustains, his powerful arm upholds
Creation; he himself invisible;

For clouds and darkness shroud him. He, remov'd
High in the heaven of heavens, dwells not with man;
No eye beholds him, save the Son belov'd,
Of wond'rous origin, Chaldea's hope.

God in the heavens resides. The rolling world,
The star-bespangled firmament, the sun,
Evening's mild lamp, creation's utmost bounds
Extended lie before him. He directs
The ceaseless flow of ocean. He, in storms,
Rides on the whirlwind, hurls the fire of heaven.

God in the heavens resides. He spreads his arms
To ocean's utmost bounds. At his approach
The mountains tremble; from their bases leap
The everlasting hills. To his high power
Earth bows submissive. He, the first and last.

No more. I tremble to proclaim his power;
God, from on high, the universe sustains.
My friend, restrain thy lips. In silent awe,
Bow, and adore the wonder-working God.

Note: ORPHEUS was one of the heroes who embarked in the Argonautick expedition, in the 79th year before the taking of Troy. The poems, which pass under his name, are, by Aristotle, attributed to a Pythagorean Philosopher, named Cecrops. Most of the moderns ascribe them to Onomacritus, who lived in the age of Pisistratus, Tyrant of Athens, B.C. 516. The author, whoever he was, had, undoubtedly, some acquaintance with the Jewish Scriptures.

---

[*] See above, pp. 175-179.

PASSAGES FROM FÉNELON QUOTED OR ALLUDED TO IN EMERSON'S SERMONS AND POEMS

[See François de Salignac de la Mothe Fénelon, Selections from the Writings of Fenelon. With a Memoir of his Life. By a Lady [Mrs. Eliza L. C. Follen]. (3rd ed., revised and enlarged) Boston, 1831. The "contents" are as follows:

¶ 1

A literary man, whose library was destroyed by fire, has been deservedly admired for saying, "I should have profited but little by my books, if they had not taught me how to bear the loss of them." The remark of Fenelon, who lost his in a similar way, is still more simple and touching. "I would much rather they were burnt than the cottage of a poor peasant." [Page 27]

¶ 2

One of the curates of his diocese complained to him that he was unable to put a stop to dances on the feast days. "Mr. Curate," said Fenelon to him, "let us abstain from amusement ourselves, but let us permit these poor people to dance. Why prevent them from forgetting for a moment their poverty and wretchedness?" [Page 27]

¶ 3

Although the spirit of love is manifest in all his writings, it is most deeply impressed on those that were composed for his pulpit. He seems, in writing them, to have ever repeated to himself, "What I am going to say to this child, will be the occasion of happiness or misery to twenty millions of people." [Page 31]

¶ 4

This interior guide is what I call my reason; but I speak of my reason, without comprehending the full import of the term, as I speak of nature and instinct, without comprehending what these things are. This law is perfect and immutable. I am changing and imperfect; I deceive myself, while this never loses its rectitude. When I am undeceived, it is not my reason that changes and returns to the right view, but it is this, which has never departed from it, recalling and forcing me to return to it. It is a controlling power within me, that silences or bids me speak; that makes me believe or makes me doubt; bids me confess my errors or confirms my decisions. In listening to it, I am instructed; in listening to myself, I go astray. This sovereign power is found everywhere; its voice is heard from one end of the universe to the other, by all mankind as it is by me. [Page 66]

¶ 5

There is a spiritual sun that enlightens the soul more fully than the material sun does the body. This sun of truth leaves no shadow, and it shines upon both hemispheres. It is as brilliant in the night as in the daytime; it is not without that it sheds its rays, it dwells within each one of us. One man cannot hide its rays from another: whatever corner of the earth we may go to, there it is.... This glorious sun never sets; no clouds intercept its rays, but those formed by our passions. It is one bright day. It sheds light upon the savage in the darkest caverns. [Pages 69-70]

¶ 6

Far from pronouncing judgment upon this [inward] teacher, we are in all cases judged by it. It is disinterested and superior to us. We may refuse to listen to it, and go astray from it; but if we do listen, we cannot contradict it. There seem to be two kinds of reason within me; one is self, the other superior to it.... Where is this all-perfect reason, so near me, yet so different from me? where is it? where dwells this supreme reason? Is it not God himself? [Page 70]

¶ 7

This [capacity to will] is the foundation of all merit or demerit; it is this that makes the justice of reward or punishment. Hence it is that we exhort, re-prove, menace, or promise. This is the foundation of all government, of all in-struction, and of all rules of conduct. Everything in human life brings us to this conclusion, that there is nothing over which we have such entire control, as our own wills; and that we have this free will, this power of election, between two things equally in our reach.... The internal evidence of this truth, is like that we have of those first principles, which have no need of demonstration, and by which we prove other truths less certain. [Pages 72-73]

¶ 8

There is nothing in the universe that does not equally bear these two opposite characters,--the stamp of the Creator, and the marks of nothingness from whence it is drawn, and into which it may at any moment be resolved. It is an incompre-hensible mixture of meanness and glory, of the frailty of the material, and of skill in its conformation. The hand of God is displayed everywhere, even in the worm; and weakness and nothingness are discoverable everywhere even in the most sublime geniuses. [Page 76]

¶ 9

Can we be astonished that poets have animated all nature; that they have given wings to the winds, and darts to the sun; that they have painted rivers hastening to precipitate themselves into the sea; and trees that reach the clouds, to over-come the rays of the sun by the thickness of their foliage? These figures have been adopted even in common conversation; so natural is it for man to feel the power and skill with which the universe is filled. [Page 77]

¶ 10

Poetry has only attributed to inanimate things, the design of the Creator. The language of the poets gave rise to the theology of the Pagans; their theolo-gians were poets.... The more enlarged our minds are when we contemplate nature, the more we discover of that inexhaustible wisdom which is the soul of the uni-verse. Then do we see the Infinite Creator represented in all his works, as in a mirror, to the contemplation of his intelligent offspring. [Page 77]

¶ 11

PRAYER TO GOD. Oh my God! while so many of thy children are unconscious of thy presence in this glorious scene of nature that thou presentest to them, still thou art not far from any one of them. Thou art near us, but we do not perceive thee; our passions blind us. Thus, Oh Lord, thy light shineth in the darkness, and the darkness comprehendeth it not. Thou discoverest thyself everywhere, but men do not see thee.... Thou art near them and within them, but they fly from themselves and from thee.... They live in thee without thinking of thee; or rather they die, for to be ignorant of thee is death.... It is because thou art within them, in the temple of the soul into which they never enter, that thou art hidden from them. [Pages 78-79]

¶ 12

The order and beauty of the creation, is like a veil that hides thee from their weak vision.... Frightful darkness that envelopes the children of men!... What do I see in all nature? God! God in everything, and God alone! Who does not see thee, has seen nothing. [Page 79]

¶ 13

How often do we hear those, who every day have to reproach themselves with un-faithfulness towards God, complain that he refuses to answer their prayers!

Ought they not to acknowledge, that it is their sins which have formed a thick cloud between Heaven and them, and that God has justly hidden himself from them?... If, then, the Almighty do not grant our petitions, let us adore his justice, let us be silent, let us humble ourselves, and let us pray without ceasing. This humble perseverance...will make us pass happily from darkness to light; for know, says St. Augustin, that God is near to us even when he appears far from us. [Page 106]

¶ 14

THE SPIRIT OF GOD TEACHES WITHIN. It is certain, that the scriptures declare that "the Spirit of God dwells within us," that it animates us, speaks to us in silence, suggests all truth to us, and that we are so united to it, that we are joined unto the Lord in one spirit.... [But certain learned men] do not attach sufficient importance to the teacher within us, which is the Spirit of God. This is the soul of our soul, and without it we could form no thought or desire. Alas! then, of what blindness we are guilty, if we suppose that we are alone in this interior sanctuary, while, on the contrary, God is there even more intimately than we are ourselves. [Page 111]

¶ 15

You will say, perhaps, Are we then inspired?... We are...always inspired; but we are ever stifling this inspiration. God never ceases to speak to us; but the noise of the world without, and the tumult of our passions within, bewilder us, and prevent us from listening to him.... It is a still small voice, and is only heard by those who listen to no other. [Pages 111-112]

¶ 16

What [God] demands of us is often what we most cherish; it is this Isaac of our hearts, this only son, this well beloved, that he commands us to resign; it is his will that we should yield up all that is most dear, and short of this obedience we have no repose.... Give up everything to him, and the God of peace will be with you. [Page 120]

¶ 17

My conclusion is, that we must listen to the voice of God in the silence of our souls, and pronounce for or against ourselves, whatever this pure light may reveal to us at the moment when we thus endeavor to know ourselves. We must often silently listen to this teacher within, who will make known all truth to us, and who, if we are faithful in attending to him, will often lead us to silence. When we hear this secret small voice within, which is the soul of our soul, it is a proof that self is silent, that it may listen to it. This voice is not a stranger there. God is in our souls, as our souls are in our bodies. It is something that we cannot distinguish exactly, but it is what upholds and guides us. This is not a miraculous inspiration, which exposes us to illusion and fanaticism. It is only a profound peace of the soul, that yields itself up to the spirit of God, believing his revealed word, and practising his commands as declared in the Gospel. [Pages 208-209. Quoted from Letter XXVII.]

¶ 18

I commit you to God, and I wish that you would commit yourself to him. You hope for repose elsewhere than in God. You shut your heart to him, and you try to repulse his merciful hand. "Who is it that has resisted God, and been at peace?" Return to him; give yourself up to him; hasten to him. Every moment of delay is a new infidelity. [Page 224]

¶ 19

You are willing to give yourself up to others, but this makes you an idol to yourself and to them. Here is the origin of this refined idolatry of self, that God would overthrow in your heart.... There is only one remedy for you, and it is the very one from which you fly.... You repulse the hand of God; you listen only to your self-love; you bear this venom in your heart; go where you will, you cannot escape God's displeasure. [¶] Yield yourself up to him, learn to see yourself as you are.... [Page 225]

¶ 20

I have given my attention to the difficulty you state, of discriminating between the operations of the spirit of God, and our own natural understanding. We
cannot have a precise and certain rule upon this subject within us. We only have
an exterior guide for our actions, which is conformity to the precepts, counsels,
and graces of Christianity. If we had, in addition to this, the means of distinguishing with certainty the Divine influence from the operation of our natural
powers, we should then be endowed with a sort of sanctity and infallibility, that
would amount to inspiration. This is exactly opposed to the uncertainty of faith
and to a state of pilgrimage.

¶ 21

We ought not to seek what our present condition does not permit us to obtain;
I mean a certain rule to decide when we are moved by a Divine influence, and when
it is our nature, which may imitate it.

¶ 22

On the other hand, it is of the utmost importance in our conduct, as a protection against illusion, to discern this difference, and to have a certain rule for
judging. We must, it is said, obey the Divine influence; not to do it, is to resist God, is to contrain the Holy Spirit, is to turn away from that perfection to
which we are called.

¶ 23

But how shall we follow this Divine guide, if we have no certain rule by which
to distinguish it from the operations of our own minds? A want of certainty upon
this subject, leaves us in continual danger of acting contrarily to what we really
desire; of being influenced by natural inclination, when we desire to be guided by
the spirit of God. This is the difficulty; let us seek the remedy.

¶ 24

These doubts can never relate, as I have before observed, to those things that
are forbidden by the precepts, the commands, the charities of our religion. This
holy influence not only can never lead us to violate the direct instructions, but
can never teach us to neglect any of the minor duties recommended in the Gospel.
Thus we see that there is no question about an entire purity and perfection of
manners in the case. The question must be, between two right actions, to know
which is the prompting of this inward teacher.

¶ 25

It is true, that in this choice, we have no certainty of internal evidence.
We have only external rules of christian prudence to enable us to judge by circumstances, and to decide which is the more expedient. And we have not within us
any certain rule to discern whether a decided preference for one right action,
over another, is from a Divine influence or from our own nature. And it would
not suit our condition here to have this certainty; it is the will of God that we
shall remain in this uncertainty, and that we shall not be able to distinguish between them. It is necessary, then, that this Divine influence be adapted to our
condition, and that it should operate always without our consciousness.

¶ 26

The danger of illusion as to venial acts, is not astonishing in a state in
which we are liable to far more perilous mistakes, which lead us to take the motions of self-love, that are the death of the soul, for its true life. What shall
we do in this state of darkness? All that depends upon us to do, and with this be
satisfied. Fidelity in duty, united to peaceful trust, in such a state of uncertainty, is the greatest self-sacrifice to those spirits that are eager to understand the ways of God.

¶ 27

It is true that notwithstanding the obscurity that rests upon this pilgrimage,
there are appearances, though without absolute certainty, that serve to cherish in
the heart an humble confidence, that the spirit of God guides it. There are gleams
of this light in the darkness of the most uncertain faith, making it visible occasionally, that we are led on to perfection by the Divine love: God mingles light

and darkness thus, that the soul may not be lost in uncertainty, yet not have a full assurance, and may not find here, in either state, a sufficient support.

¶ 28

The best proof that we are influenced by the spirit of God, is, first, when the action itself is pure and conformable to the perfection of his laws. Secondly, when we perform it simply, tranquilly, without eagerness to do it, contented if it is necessary to relinquish it. Thirdly, when, after the work is done, we do not seek by unquiet reflections to justify the action even to ourselves, but are willing it should be condemned, or to condemn it ourselves, if any superior light discovers it to be wrong; and when in fine, we do not appropriate the action to ourselves, but refer it to the will of God. Fourthly, when this work leaves the soul in its simplicity, in its peace, in its own uprightness, in humility, and in self-forgetfulness.

¶ 29

All these things, it is true, are very delicate in their operation upon the mind; and all we can say still gives little knowledge of them. But though there is so much obscurity in a state of faith, it is nevertheless true, that God, without teaching us by positive rules how to know his voice, accustoms the mind to understand it, to recognize it, and to obey it, although it cannot give an account, by any philosophical principle or precise rule, how it may be discerned. He gives to the soul, when it needs it, a momentary certainty; and then it is withdrawn, leaving no vestige behind. The greatest danger is from interrupting this influence by the inquietude with which we would escape from this state, and insist upon seeing clearly, when we are thus surrounded by darkness.

¶ 30

One thing that it appears to me desirable to observe is, that we can often more easily distinguish that which is nature, than that which is a Divine influence. Let us relinquish our own peculiar desires, whether they lead us to repose or to action; those that are induced by a refined intellectual taste, as entirely as those that grow out of the pleasures of sense; and in this peace of the soul, let us, in simplicity and truth, and in the presence of God, do all we can to die to ourselves and to please him.

¶ 31

But we must guard against useless scruples, against a mental constraint, and an anxiety to be assured that we perform all our actions under the influence of the spirit of God. We may extinguish this light in the endeavor to ascertain that we are following it. We may return, under a pretext of safety, into all the windings of that self-love that we pretend to avoid. We are in danger of losing the reality of this influence in our effort to obtain a certainty with regard to it, which it is not the will of God that we should possess. Thus we might pass our lives in reasoning upon the operation of the spirit of God, without daring to yield ourselves up to its influence.

¶ 32

Were I to propose anything personal and peculiar to yourself, my good Duke, it would be to remind you that the bent of your mind, and the temptation to illusion in you, arise, not from any gross disorders, but from the intemperance of wisdom and the excess of reasoning. Even wisdom ought to be sober and temperate. Sobriety and simplicity of mind are the same thing. The practice of true love to God dissipates doubts, and disgusts us with speculative reasonings.

¶ 33

You deserve that God should leave you to yourself, as a punishment for so long a resistance. But he loves you more than you know how to love yourself; he follows you with his mercy, he troubles your heart to subdue it: yield yourself to him, and finish this dangerous irresolution. This hesitation between two courses is in fact a choice; it is the secret, lurking desire of the heart in the illusion of self-love, fearing to yield itself up, and ready to fly from the restraints that religion imposes. [¶] Pardon the liberties I take; but I cannot moderate the zeal with which your confidence has inspired me. [¶s 20-33 come from pages 174-176.]

¶ 34

Nothing is easier than to confuse a man of good sense with regard to the reality of his own body, although it is still impossible for him to doubt of it seriously. Tell him that the time which he calls awaking, is only a time of more profound sleep than the sleep of the night; tell him that he will awake perhaps at death from the sleep of his whole life, which is only a dream, just as he thinks he awakes every morning from the dreams of the night; urge him to show you any difference that is precise and decisive between the illusion of a dream of the night, when a man is sure he is what he is not, and the illusion of the dream of a whole life;--you put it out of his power to answer you; but it is not less out of his power to believe you; he will smile at your ingenuity; he feels, though he is unable to demonstrate it, that your subtle reasons have only darkened a clear truth, instead of throwing light upon what was obscure. [Page 248]

¶ 35

Whosoever drinketh of this water shall thirst again. The more we drink of the corrupt waters of the world, the more shall we thirst. In proportion as we yield to evil, are our hearts dissatisfied.... [¶] Let us watch, then, over ourselves; let us beware of drinking of those waters that will only inflame our thirst. Let us keep our hearts with all diligence, lest the vain pleasures of the world should seduce them, and leave us at last in despair at finding ourselves deceived. [Page 272]

¶ 36

Humility is the source of all true greatness; pride is ever impatient, ready to be offended. He who thinks nothing is due to him, never thinks himself ill-treated; true meekness is not mere temperament, for this is only softness or weakness. To be meek to others, we must renounce self. The Saviour adds, lowly in heart; this is a humility to which the will entirely consents, because it is the will of God, and for his glory.

EXCERPTS FROM EMERSON'S UNPUBLISHED SERMONS

¶ 1

But let us be ashamed of an attempt to put a poor deception on others & feel that the best way to seem great & good is to be great & good; & that if we would accomplish the great objects for which God sent us into the world; if we would enter into the kingdom of heaven, we must be too great to be proud; we must forever abandon our arrogant pretensions.... [Sermon 16, Mar. 25, 1828]   [92]
[The bracketed numerals at the very end of this and the following quotations refer to page numbers in my typescripts of the unpublished Sermons.]

¶ 2

Life is a never ending succession of...alternatives; & the sentiment which approves one & condemns the other is the Conscience. It is not a simple perception that one action is good & another evil & ending there,--as the eye perceives that one leaf is green & another red, or that one is longer & another less & no more--but the distinction of the sentiment we call the Conscience, is, that it includes a command to adopt or to reject;--to perform one action, & to forbear another. [Sermon 21, July 30, 1828. This entire sermon is a background for the poem. It discusses the nature of the Conscience. Text: Romans 2:14-15.]   [118]

¶ 3

In this manner it would appear that Socrates designed to describe by a lively image that man within the breast which we call Conscience; & there is some reason for the distinction made, inasmuch as we can all feel we are rather commanded what not to do than urged to any performance. But in all our ordinary use of this word we understand something more; we speak of the whole power, of which this is a part; we imply its highest functions of reward to good & evil, as well as command to do & to forbear. I cite this instance only to show that the force of this principle was as familiar to the pagan & as fully understood by them as by us. [Ibid.]
                    [119]

¶ 4

[I]t is a matter of strange & terrible contemplation, the power of Conscience to punish human transgression, the manner in which God has secured the sanction of his laws. No precarious or tardy retribution--no imperfect judgment, as in human affairs, halts like a cripple after the daring offender, or wreaks its uncertain wrath upon the feeble accomplice, & lets the great criminal go; but a prompt, and unerring, & mighty power, which never falters, & never is deceived, treads on the steps of human offence. [Ibid.]   [119]

¶ 5

[W]hilst you defy blame from abroad, it is nearer than the nearest,--it is fastening its fangs on the memory, not of your patron, nor your neighbour, nor your brother, but on your own. By the force of an invisible & all uncontrollable event, that started out of darkness in the moment of your evil deed,--yourself are made the inflictor of vengeance, yourself is the victim. [Ibid.]   [120]

¶ 6

The peace of the creation is to be kept without making it needful that God should visit an offender with instant & signal misfortune or should strike the blasphemer with thunder. To do this he hath opened in every mind the Conscience;--this swift perception of approval or censure on all that is done or left undone. This law so sure so inevitable is the gravitation of the moral world. This Praise & this Blame are the two forces that keep mortal beings to their orbit. You will observe --it is not mere perception of right & wrong of accord & discord; it is more. it is a new element: After transgression, it is stern unrelenting envenomed pain, increasing with the crime & tending directly to the point at which moral government aims viz. an irresistible compunction which ends in Reformation. Thus Conscience is the police of the Universe; from which there is no escape, no hope of concealment, connecting every human soul with God its maker, & making it impossible to any to elude for a moment his irresistible dominion. [Ibid.]   [121]

¶ 7

It is a matter of lamentation & offence to many the fact that the more enlightened views of Christianity that prevail among us have thrown into the shade the strong oriental language in which in the scriptures the punishment of sin is described. But I apprehend that he who has once maturely considered the infinite force of Conscience to inflict pain & the invariable steadiness with which it follows up transgression can never bring himself to doubt the reality of future retribution. He needs not a revelation,--it is written in his nature y^t sin shall suffer--he will feel that the figurative language of darkness & fire & the undying worm are but faint representations of the real evils that wait on iniquity. [Ibid.]
[121]

¶ 8

I have read of those who doubted, I am told there are those who doubt the Being of God. But [t]here is no fable so extravagant that I cannot more easily admit than the possibility that this moral government is uncaused. I may believe that the stars have burned in their courses forever--that no hand hurled them into their eternal paths, but that they have walked in those circles from a frightful infinity without a Cause. I may believe when I daily see the ocean evaporate its clouds, that the precious burden is lifted by heat, & borne by the winds, & poured again over the land--by accident. I may believe that all the processes of vegetation originated without thought & go forward without being promoted by any regard to the wants of animal life;--Yes I may believe all this but I can never believe that the Conscience of man came to him without an author, a reason, or end. I hear the voice which it always utters, 'There is a God.' [Ibid.]   [121]

¶ 9

[T]his divine Director belongs to each of us. It will prove, as we use it, our good or our evil angel. It will scatter light or darkness in our path through this world. It will go with us when we go out of the world, & make for us the bliss of heaven or the pain of hell. [Ibid.]   [122]

¶ 10

It is because God is within us; it is because we are so formed that all things declare him to us, that we find it so hard to escape the conclusion. Day unto Day, night unto night bear witness to him; and every wise purpose, every happy thought, every beautiful feature, every good deed--is an argument to establish the being of God. These all plead more convincingly than the voice of thunder, the earthquake, the explosion of comets, for these last might chance in a chaos, but those can never <u>chance</u>. [Sermon 23, Sept. 24, 1828]   [131]

¶ 11

We see men daily who have no consciousness of their immortal gifts. They are full of superstitions about fortune, or the power of circumstances, or the laws of destiny, of which they think themselves the victims (& so they are, if so they think themselves,) & overlook the secret power of the human mind over circumstances, & its ability to make its own fate.... [W]e are masters of our own condition. [Sermon 27, Nov. 21, 1828]   [152]

¶ 12

"All things are yours." You are the Universe to yourself. We are not feeble, we are not pitiful, any more than we are vicious, except by our own fault. We are very powerful beings. We can, as we choose, be trained into angels or deformed into fiends. [<u>Ibid.</u>]   [154]

¶ 13

Be assured with a perfect assurance, that you shall be the better for all the knowledge & all the virtue that you add to yourself, exactly to the fulness of its amount & no more. that no particle of the spiritual <u>man</u> can ever be lost. As God has made you a law unto yourself, fulfil that law to <u>its</u> whole extent, & God shall be responsible for the event & the reward. [<u>Ibid.</u>]   [155]

¶ 14

[C]onsider that in the soul itself shall be the Paradise of God, or the abodes of the spirits of hell. So therefore let it be considered by you, how vain it is to utter a prayer of words, that is not the genuine breathing of your mind. [Sermon 32, Apr. 3, 1829]   [171]

¶ 15

My fate is in my own hands. Let me carry up my actions to the high level of my destiny. What can I not perform? What can I not know? no pitch of virtue is beyond my reach. Hasten, oh my soul, every event is an opportunity, a step to mount by; every moment contains a virtue. Awake, & live & ascend forever & ever. [Sermon 34, Apr. 26, 1829]   [182]

¶ 16

The experience of all good men conspires in one testimony that precisely in the same proportion as we advance in virtue...does the great Idea of God reveal itself & shine within the mind. Say not therefore 'I am good, but I do not love God.' You are not good think again; some deadly sin some fatal bar lies in your way, & keeps you out from heaven. [Sermon 35, May 3, 1829]   [185]

¶ 17

Thou art made sufficient to thyself. Thy joy, and thy glory, and thy punishment, thy heaven, and thy hell are within thee. There is the heavenly host; there is the eye of God. The heaven thou seekest thou shalt not find. Eternal mansions, streets of pearl, & streams of amber, & trees of life, & the music of innumerable harps praising God--these are but the types--the outward representations whereby to mortal ears the secrets of spiritual joy are faintly shadowed forth. Heaven is not a place, but a state of the mind. <u>Hell</u> is Vice, the rebellion of the passions, the army of cares, the night of self-made ignorance, the stings of self accusation. Heaven is the well ordered informed benevolent self-devoted mind when it adopts God's will for its own. [Sermon 37, May 23, 1829]   [198]

¶ 18

I would to God I might awaken the attention of every torpid hearer till he had measured with his eye the scope of his powers; till he saw how glorious this low life that we lead might be made; ...till he saw what degrees of self-command a human soul may attain; till he apprehended the death of the affections & the majesty of truth. till he apprehended the intimate connexion which can subsist between himself & God, when his own heart shall beat pulse for pulse in harmony with the universal whole, & by assimilating to the character begins to enjoy the beatitudes of the Divinity. [Ibid.]   [201]

¶ 19

We [Unitarians] have found out that God is merciful & we presume on his mercy. We have grown wiser than to fear the materialism of the Calvinists no longer interpret literally the figurative language of the Scriptures which surround God with clouds & darkness--& thunders. We have found out that fire & worm cannot touch the soul,--and so we brave the rest, we brave the terrors of the spiritual world,--& hug our vices under the name of liberal Christianity. My brethren, this is a dangerous mistake. [Sermon 43, July 11, 1829]   [224]

¶ 20

The main mischief...is, that Habit sears the conscience itself--the danger [is] that the conscience shd. cease to make a true report--so that our very compass is in a measure useless, & we do not know the way to right. But God has so far protected this, his minister in the soul, that though, as we sin, it points to lower & lower degrees of right, yet its divine instinct is never wholly subdued. It always points from hell. [Sermon 54, Nov. 6, 1829]   [271]

¶ 21

It [the soul] has this dangerous power of self-change, self-accommodation to whatsoever we do. As, in the heathen fable, the nymph who wept became a fountain, & the nymph who pined became an echo, so, in the stern law of moral nature, we are always changing from what we are to what we wish to be, from what we are to what we do. Be not deceived. We are not immoveably moored to any bottom--and if we do wrong & don't succeed we cannot come back to where we were. That where is gone. For as all our powers grow by their own exercise, so they die by disuse. As you follow new desires you are changed from what you were & those powers that once you had are dead. They do not exist. [Ibid.]   [271]

¶ 22

Our religion takes the individual out of the mass & reminds him of the burden he must bear alone. It recommends the duties of self-command, of the connexion of the soul with God;-- It teachers that to each soul is its own destiny which is stript of all connexions & friendships--the soul hath neither father nor mother nor wife nor sister. Its relation to God, itself alone knoweth & no stranger of all the vast family of intelligent being shall presume to intermeddle therein. All the day of its goodness it seeth him. All the night of its vice it mourneth & tosseth & lacketh his presence. [Sermon 55, Nov. 14, 1829]   [274]

¶ 23

Another of these facts--I call them revelations--...which perhaps [the soul] shall learn is that its own virtue is life, & so to teach it to expel the fear of death. If the soul can die, it is only by contracting deadly sin;--the seed of death is sin. Virtue is immortal unchangeable,--is of the very nature & substance of God Himself; & so that which is wholly virtuous lives as by God's life.... Without God we are nothing but with him we are all things. [Sermon 56, Nov. 21, 1829]
                                                                              [281]

¶ 24

[Emerson quotes 2 Peter 1:4--"Whereby are given unto us exceeding great and precious promises; that by these ye might be partakers of the divine nature, having escaped the corruption that is in the world through lust."] I feel that there is a glory in spiritual nature before which all other magnificence is straw....
[Sermon 67, Feb. 27, 1830]   [341]

¶ 25

It is the triumph of this part of our nature--its independance on circumstances.
The man of disciplined soul...is always in heaven. The city or the fields are
alike to him. In a shop, in a crowd, in a prison, he can separate himself from
impure contact, & embosom his soul in the sublime society of his recollections
his hopes & his affections. In every place there is a duty, in every event there
is occasion of prayer. It is a maxim of state, that an ambassador carries his
country with him. So do our minds. [Ibid.]   [346]

¶ 26

     If ever you have found in yourself any approbation of what is good, any love
of what is true, however mixed with imperfection or interrupted by vices, o honour
this spark this ray of God within you showing that its source is close at hand,
& hasten to break down every barrier, to open every door & chamber of your soul,
that this spirit of God from its hiding place in your inward parts may come forth
as a flood, may circulate through every part of you that the union may become perfect. [Sermon 88, Sept. 11, 1830]   [442]

¶ 27

[W]ill it not help us to keep unspotted to reflect that of all business our first
business is to build up such a character as shall be a fitting temple of God; that
everywhere, we are to carry ourselves worthily of this celestial inmate & that by
so doing there is no place or condition or occurrence from which something of
strength, some addition of truth or of virtue will not be gained. [Ibid.]   [443]

¶ 28

     My friends, I have no hope of giving any thing like accuracy or great distinct-
ness to this tho't. In our ignorance & sin we must dimly see it. I cannot find
out the Almighty unto perfection. I cannot tell how he is present to me, & yet I
can feel that he is present--that in him I live & move, & have my being. The best
& greatest men have in every age labored to give utterance to the same conviction
as this of Paul. Fenelon saith God is in our soul as our soul is in our body not
to be defined, but every where present. [See Fénelon ¶17.] We feel that tho' he
is present it is very darkly present. And that our ignorance & sins are clouds &
obstructions thro' which he speaks in a stifled voice but every effort to do his
will to obey this voice does something to remove these obstructions. It will
benefit us, if we seek good to meditate upon it until more of its meaning is apparent. [Ibid. Alternate conclusion and hence later than the original sermon.]
                                                                         [443]

¶ 29

I like very much the view of Lessing that revelation announces truths that are in
the natural path of the human mind but in its present state of sin & ignorance beyond its reach. that the same announcement of truth may be a revelation to one
mind & not to another which by its greater freedom from sin & its greater diligence in seeking truth has anticipated the progress of the general human mind.
[Sermon 91, Oct. 10, 1830]   [452]

¶ 30

A man contains all that is needful to his government within himself. He can only
do himself any good or any harm. Nothing can be given to him or taken from him
without an equivalent. The benevolence that bestows a cup of cold water is itself
enlarged enriched by the act; the malevolence that refuses the same is contracted
& impoverished thereby. Every act puts the agent in a new condition. The purpose
of life seems to be to acquaint a man with himself & whatever science or art or
course of action he engages in reacts upon & illuminates the recesses of his own
mind. Thus friends seem to be only mirrors to draw out & explain to us ourselves;
& that which draws us nearest to our fellow man, is, that the deep Heart in one,
answers to the deep Heart in another,--that we find we have a Common Nature--one
life which runs through all the individuals; & which is indeed Divine. [Sermon
93, Oct. 31, 1830. A fragment laid in.]   [463]

¶ 31

I know not--no man knoweth the nature of those changes that death shall bring
to pass in us. But there is not a syllable in all the word of God, there is not
the least breathing in all the voice of reason, that intimates any mitigation to
come from that change, to the evils that are suffered in this world for sin. The
consequences of sin in this world are painful thoughts, fear, further desire to
sin, and a blindness which hides our interest & happiness from us, &, beyond this,
the disapprobation & united opposition of all the rest of mankind. All these consequences may yet cleave to us, when the body is gone, & be far more intense
causes of pain when the relief of bodily pleasure, & the shield of bodily insens-
ibility is withdrawn. And the satisfactions of virtue may by the same change be
exalted. The connexions of friendship shall be more intimate, the pursuit of
knowledge far more rapid & extensive, the joys of meditation, of devotion, shall
be purified. [Sermon 95, Nov. 13, 1830]   [480]

¶ 32

Let a principle come from heaven to man such as Jesus presented, that he should
love & serve God. If I receive it into my soul forthwith, from a poor necessitous
sickly creature, occupying a spot of the earth, I become associated with God, I
prosper in the prosperity of the Universe. Wherever truth & virtue thrive, there
my interests are promoted; there is no star, or soul, or plant, or atom, but I
have my part & use of it, by my love of its Maker, & my part in Him. I am raised
by the reception of a great principle to its height and have by it a being greater
than my own. [Sermon 100, Dec. 26, 1830]   [511-512]

¶ 33

Is it a trial of poverty?... In the multitude of your thots By the help of Gods
spirit you may make the discovery that there is no low place; that where our duty
calls us there is dignity, as much in a menial as in a commanding office. And
when you have made this discovery, a light not of this world shall shine into the
closets & corners of your dwelling. [Sermon 102, Jan. 1, 1831]   [515]

¶ 34

Wisdom & goodness are the great means of power the communicable attributes of God,
& as men more fully apply themselves to God they receive larger measures of these.
He that wholly gives himself up to God, reaches the highest elevation the most
knowledge. And such men have grown wiser than the men who sought wisdom for bye
ends have outlearned the schools & have become conscious of the future as of the
present & wrought miracles. Probably all men have the same capacity of prophecy
& miracle. What is prophecy but more knowledge? What is miracle but more dominion of the soul over matter than is now evinced? [Sermon 110, Mar. 20, 1831]
                                                                          [545]

¶ 35

I believe one law prevails throughout the moral universe. There is not an economy
of spiritual influences different from the whole economy of the Creator. God does
to be sure differently endow different souls. That is his prerogative by which
one being is made a plant, & one a dog, & one a man. But having made us what we
are, we are all subjected to one law of improvement, which is shortly this, Draw
nigh to God & he will draw nigh to you. Every promise in the Scripture is conditional on our effort.... What is goodness but laboring to become good? [Ibid.]
                                                                          [546]

¶ 36

Was there ever a good man who did not ascribe every good thing to God? Then all
is spiritual influence, & its omnipresence excludes every superstitious distinction. O yes, I believe in spiritual influences. I believe the reason why we are
so weak & so ignorant is because we are so sinful. [Ibid.]   [547]

¶ 37

You may hold what views of ordinances you will; you may hold what views of the of-
fices of Christ, it will never add nor diminish one jot in the obligation of these
duties, nor, if you love truth, in the pressure of the obligation.... These are
written in lines that cannot be effaced. This [See Psalm 19:7] is
not a temporary law nor a covenant to a chosen nation. These are

the laws that exist yesterday today & forever. They are not to be abolished, nor
changed, nor shielded from. They make the substance of the soul. Heaven consists
in keeping them. Hell consists in violating them; simply because they are the
nature of God and mould according to which he hath formed man, coupling praise to
every right step & blame & pain to every wrong one. [Sermon 111, Mar. 27, 1831]

[551]

¶ 38

It is always the effect of the practice of Right to increase the love of the
Right--to quicken the Conscience. Men see by the light of their own virtue.
"True wisdom" said Lord Shaftesbury, "comes more from the heart than the head,"
and those ancients who loved what was true & did what was right were led to very
clear religious views, & learned to trust in God & pray to him & to speak humbly
of themselves, & kindly to others long before Jesus had bro't immortality to
light. [Ibid.]

[552]

¶ 39

I say to you you have much to learn of yourself. You do not yet know that this principle deciding on right & wrong within you is the parent of all good that the Universe contains for you; is your league with God himself, & shall minister to your
happiness & glory to the bounds of your being. This wonderful tho't is that which
makes all distinctions even. We cannot all be rich but we have this without which
riches are curses. We cannot all be popular or healthy or well-favoured or learned
but all, from the angel down to the poorest wretch that wears the form of man have
this transcendant thot which is the badge of immortal beings which is the stamp
of God on his own work. O my brother congratulate yourself on this. Humble yourself before God in devout gratitude for it. O cherish it as your dearest guest.
Honour it it shall honour you. Trust to that prompting. No man ever got above
it. Men have transgressed & hated & gainsaid it but no man ever sinned but he felt
this inward angel towering above him & threatening his well-being. Go sit alone &
think much of this feeling of right & wrong you will soon perceive that the principles by which you measure actions are true & unfailing though all your acquaintance tho you had never known a man who kept the law--oh yes you feel that the
nations are a handful before that multitude of beings for whom this law was made &
whose destinies shall be administered upon it   for wherever rational nature exists
there does this Law rule. He who thinks on this law of Right & Wrong thinks on
truth compared with which History in its highest antiquity is young & recent. He
thinks on that which ever was, which is, & which shall be & so is the measure of
all other things. [Sermon 112, Apr. 3, 1831]

[558]

¶ 40

But it [religion] cannot console a bad man, for he cannot receive the thoughts
that should soothe him. He cannot rightly believe that Gods will is done, for he
has incapacitated himself by his vices from seeing the evidence of Gods being. He
cannot have the joys of faith for he has no faith. Its realities are foolishness
to him, for they are spiritually discerned & he has no spiritual eye. [Sermon 117,
May 29, 1831]

[594]

¶ 41

[R]emember that it is a rule in morals that the merit of a good action is
greatest, when the motive to do it is most feeble in the presence of the most commanding motives to the contrary. The merit is measured by the difficulty encountered. Furthermore it is to my mind one of the most noble & one of the most
thrilling truths in moral science, that we gain the strength of the temptation we
resist. The savage in the Sandwich Islands believes that when he overcomes &
slays an enemy the strength & courage of that enemy passes into him. The soul
instructed by God knows that whenever it resists & overcomes a temptation, it becomes stronger by the strength of that temptation. Not in a remote heaven not
in a future hour but in the hour & moment of the contest the compensation the
power the peace of God enter into & possess him. [Ibid. On detached slip of
paper.]

[598]

¶ 42

I have no expectation of any happiness that is in store for me, in receiving which I am to be wholly passive. If I will not stretch out my hand, I do not believe it will be filled. If I will not work for the good, I must want it. It is always those who love men, that are loved again. It is always those who study that learn. It is always those who are meek, & upright, & diligent, who are at peace with themselves, & not the proud & dishonest & intemperate & lazy. And not only in thus taking advantage of moral laws, but in what is strictly Religion namely the directing of the tho'ts to God, the doing of what we suppose well pleasing in his sight, the abstaining from what we suppose moves his disapprobation and the addresses of the soul to him whether in silent contemplation or in uttered prayer we always know or always may know exactly how near is God to us & how acceptable is the tribute we pay him. And He is always in the language of Scripture 'waiting to be gracious.' He is always to be found of them that seek him & never of those who seek him not. [Sermon 118, June 18, 1831]   [599]

¶ 43

The whole secret is in one word, <u>Likeness</u>. The way to see a body is to draw near it with the eye. The way to perceive a spirit is to <u>become like it</u>. What is unlike us, we cannot perceive. We cannot perceive the spirit of purity without being pure; of justice, without being just; of wisdom, without being wise. The only way to understand what love means is to love; & what envy & hatred mean, is to covet & to hate. [Sermon 121, July 17, 1831]   [616]

¶ 44

He falls into temptation. Then he summons about him the invincible strength of his good tho'ts. his dependance upon God, the intimate sight which God hath of every action, nay more the stirring faith that every good man hath at the bottom of his soul, that he is not mortal, that he is not earthly, but draws his life from God; lives because God is within him & tho' now darkly & interruptedly seen, yet every good thot & good work goes to dispel the clouds & darkness of his outer nature, & fill him with divine light. These tho'ts are armies of angels which fight for him & resist temptation & then he rejoices in the beauty of right & the temptation which has once been resisted continually loses its force. [Sermon 125, Aug. 28, 1831]   [645]

¶ 45

Few men consider how sacred a possession is locked up within the narrow boundary of a human frame. If that which we must do & what we do every day, & that which we might be be considered, it will be seen that Heaven Hell Judgment the knowledge of all truth, the possession of indefinite power, & the love of innumerable beings, the choice of blessed or of accursed society are therein contained. And by reason of the retributions which in the nature of things are affixed to every act, a man is in some sort the Providence to himself which dispenses the events of his life. [Sermon 141, Jan. 15, 1832]   [729]

¶ 46

In the enlarged view of self which we have taken it is plain that the cause of a mans self is one with the Cause of God. I have spoken of self as it is presented to us by that inward monitor which seems to be the voice of our maker speaking to us from within in stifled tones often and very faint when we neglect them but always becoming more distinct as they are more obeyed. From the first dawn of reason to the day of death, it uses one voice that always is prophetic of a future state for which this being is to be thus carefully guarded & kept. If thou wouldst live forever do thyself no harm. [<u>Ibid</u>.]   [733]

¶ 47

The manner in which religion is presented to men in the infancy & ruder state of society is by <u>authority</u>.... Now this happens not I suppose because God speaks thus to man, but because man thus represents God as speaking. The voice of God does not go out of his prophet as it came in to him, but takes a new character from the prophets mind, just as the suns rays in passing through a glass do not come out pure but blue or red or green according to the colour of the medium.

[¶] If you give the same instruction to many men they will communicate it to others in a very different manner...tinged with the peculiar qualities of his own mind. And so in the night of the early ages men had imperfect views of Gods providence.... This I suppose is the defect not of the Revelation...but the unavoidable effect of the rude mind that received it. [Sermon 142, Jan. 29, 1832]   [741]

COMMENTARY ON "GNOTHI SEAUTON"   **[See pages 175-179.]**

Lines: 1-2 If thou canst bear / Strong meat of simple truth] See Hebrews 5:11-14--"...we have many things to say, and hard to be uttered, seeing ye are dull of hearing. For when for the time ye ought to be teachers, ye have need that one teach you again which be the first principles of the oracles of God; and are become such as have need of milk, and not of strong meat.... But strong meat belongeth to them that are of full age, even those who by reason of use have their senses exercised to discern both good and evil." Cf. 1 Cor. 3:1-3.

6 God dwells in thee] See Sermons par. 8 and 10. On the religion of Self-Reliance or God-Reliance and the "burden" involved in the relationship of the soul to God ("the alone to the Alone") see Sermons par. 22. (Cf. the isolating experience of the mystical state in Nature (1836), 13.5-12.) See Ovid's Ars Amatoria, III, 549: "Est deus in nobis; et sunt commercia coeli." (There is a god within us and intercourse with heaven.) Also Ovid's Fasti, VI, 5: "Est deus in nobis: agitante calescimus illo." (There is a god within us, and we glow when he stirs us.)

8 It is unknown to thousands, and to thee] See Sermons par. 11. On man's unconsciousness of the Deity he bears in his breast, see Fénelon par. 11.

9 Yet there is God] On Conscience's proclamation that "There is a God," see Sermons par 8. See also Fénelon par. 13: St. Augustine says "that God is near to us even when he appears far from us."

10 He is in thy world] On this "controlling power" within man, see Fénelon par. 4-5.

12 He is the mighty Heart] This imagery reappears in Nature (1836), 36.16ff. The ant is "seen to be a monitor, a little body with a mighty heart" and "all its habits...become sublime."

15-16 The Infinite / Embosomed in a man] The imagery may owe something to the description of the Father in Paradise Lost, III, 372-390. See Fénelon par. 5.

17 And thou art stranger to thy guest] Fénelon (par. 17) says that the voice of God is not a stranger to the soul.

19 The clouds that veil his light within] See Sermons par. 28, 40 and 44. The imagery suggests several famous Miltonic passages: Paradise Lost, II, 262-265; Paradise Regained, I, 41; etc. On the "veil" imagery, see the note on line 39. On "cloud" imagery, see Deut. 4:11, Job 22:14, and Psalm 97:2. On man's passions described as clouds, see Fénelon par. 5. On man's passions blinding him to the "God within," see Fénelon par. 11. On the veil that hides God from men, see Fénelon par. 12.

20 Clouds... / thy thick woven webs of sin] See Sermons par. 36. For this imagery, see also Fénelon par. 13.

21 his glory struggling through] For Emerson's discussion of how the Voice of God is tinged or modified by passing through the medium of an earthly spokesman, see Sermons par. 47. For Milton's frequent employment of this "glory" imagery, see Paradise Lost, I, 369-370, 594, 612; III, 63; IV, 32. Emerson copied into one of his blotting books the following fragment on Reason, which has pertinence here. See The Poetical Works of Samuel Taylor Coleridge, ed. James Dykes Campbell, London,

1925, p. 466:   "Finally, what is Reason?   You have often asked me; and this is my answer:--

> Whene'er the mist, that stands 'twixt God and thee,
> Defecates to a pure transparency,
> That intercepts no light and adds no stain--
> There Reason is, and then begins her reign!"

Emerson once spoke of his life as being optical, not practical.

22   Darkens to thine evil hue]   My original notes refer to the Swedenborgian Doctrine of Reception, here illustrated in the following quotation from Sampson Reed's "On Animals" (Emerson the Essayist, II, 34):   "The divine influx of love and wisdom is forever the same; but it is changed according to the state of the recipients.   The existing evils in the human race are thus satisfactorily accounted for, by the nature of free agency."   See also an anonymous Swedenborgian article, "On the Human Form," loc. cit., II, 69-75.   Cf. the transformation of Satan in Paradise Lost, I, 599.

27-28   The ambassador who bears / The royal presence where he goes]   Since our spiritual attainments or spiritual state or virtue may be achieved regardless of outward circumstances, we are like ambassadors who carry their true country with them even if they appear to live abroad.   Outward circumstances are indifferent matters as regards spiritual growth.   See Emerson's important commentary in Sermons par. 25 and 33.   As for the ambassador himself, Emerson remembered one of the textbooks in the Harvard Curriculum of 1817-1818:   Jean Jacques Burlamaqui, The Principles of Natural and Politic Law, tr. Thomas Nugent, (5th ed., 2 vols.) Cambridge, Mass., 1807, II, 251-252:   "When we say that the person of an ambassador is sacred, this signifies no more, than that we inflict a severer punishment on those, who offer violence to an ambassador, than on such, as commit an injury or insult to private persons; and the character of ambassadors is the reason of our inflicting so different a punishment for the same kind of offence.   [¶] Lastly, the reason, why we call the persons of ambassadors sacred, is because they are not subject to the jurisdiction of the sovereign, to whom they are deputed, either in their persons, their retinue, or effects; so that we cannot proceed against them, according to the ordinary course of justice; and it is in this that their privileges chiefly consist.   [¶] The foundation of these privileges, which the law of nations grants to ambassadors, is, that, as an ambassador represents the person of his master, he ought of course to enjoy all the privileges and rights, which his master himself, as a sovereign, would have, were he to come into the states of another prince, in order to transact his own affairs, to negociate, for instance, or conclude a treaty, or an alliance; to regulate some branch of commerce, and other things of a similar nature, &c.   Now when a sovereign goes into a foreign country, we cannot imagine, that he loses his character and independence, and that he becomes subject to the prince, whose territories he visits.   On the contrary, he ought to continue as he was before, equal and independent of the jurisdiction of the prince, whose territories he enters; and the latter receives him on the same footing, as he would choose to be received himself, if he went into the other's dominions.   Now we must grant the ambassador the same prerogative and immunities, in consequence of his representative character."

29   Give up to thy soul]   On "giving up" or yielding oneself to the "God within," see Fénelon par. 16, 18-19.   Emerson discusses ways of "giving up" in Sermons par. 42 and 44.   The Kantian ethic implies that man has the power to obey the voice of Duty.   On freedom of the will, see Sermons par. 32 and 41, Fénelon par. 7, and Emerson's "Voluntaries," section III:

| So nigh is grandeur to our dust | When Duty whispers low, Thou must, |
| So near is God to man, | The youth replies, I can. |

31   It is, I tell thee, God himself]   Fénelon uses almost the identical words in par. 6.

33   Tho' he speaks thro' thee with a stifled voice]   On "stifling" the still small voice within, see Fénelon par. 15.   Emerson uses Fénelon's imagery in Sermons par. 28:   "...our ignorance & sins are clouds & obstructions thro' which he speaks

in a stifled voice...." See God's "speaking to us from within in stifled tones
often and very faint when we neglect them" in Sermons par. 46.

34 shorn of his beams] A rich allusion to Satan, the fallen archangel, whose
glory was "obscured." See Paradise Lost, I, 594-596:

                        As when the Sun new ris'n
            Looks through the Horizontal misty Air
            Shorn of his Beams....

In Book IX, 1061-1062, Herculean Samson is described as rising "from the Harlot-
lap / of Philistean Dalilah...Shorn of his strength...." On the clouding of the
"inner sun" or Kantian Voice of Duty by man's passions, see Fénelon par. 5.

35 But if thou listen to his voice] For a definition of "voice" see Sermons
par. 2. On listening to Kant's Categorical Imperative, see Fénelon par. 4, 6 and
15.

36-37 If thou obey the royal thought, / It will grow clearer to thine ear] See
Emerson's illuminating commentary in Sermons par. 26, 28 and 46. Cf. Milton,
Comus, lines 169, 457, 569, and 783.

39 The clouds will burst that veil him now] For traditional elements in the
"cloud" imagery, see Sermons par. 19. The "veil" imagery is common in Coleridge's
poetry. See "The Destiny of Nations," lines 12ff. and 19ff.:

For what is freedom, but the un-   ...and we in this low world
    fettered use   Placed with our backs to bright Real-
Of all the powers which God for use   ity,
    had given?   That we may learn with young unwounded
But chiefly this, him first, him   ken
    last to view   The substance from its shadow. In-
Through meaner powers and secondary   finite Love,
    things   Whose latence is the plenitude of All,
Effulgent, as through clouds that   Thou with retracted beams, and self-
    veil his blaze.   eclipse
                                           Veiling, revealest thine eternal Sun.

See "Religious Musings" lines 395ff.:
                Believe thou, O my soul,   And lo! the Throne of the redeeming
Life is a vision shadowy of Truth;   God
And vice, and anguish, and the   Forth flashing unimaginable day
    wormy grave,   Wraps in one blaze earth, heaven, and
Shapes of a dream! The veiling   deepest hell.
    clouds retire.

40 And thou shalt see the Lord] As we advance in virtue, "the great Idea of
God" reveals itself and shines "within the mind." See Sermons par. 16. "Seeing
the Lord," therefore, means enjoying "the beatitudes of the Divinity" by living
spiritually here and now--and, of course, forever--a "glorious life." For details,
see Sermons par. 18.

41-42 Therefore be great, / Not Proud,--too great to be proud] See Sermons par.
1. Also Fénelon par. 36. Emerson here seems to reflect a principal theme of Sampson Reed's "Oration on Genius" (Emerson the Essayist, II, 9-11).

44-46 Peep not in corners; let thine eyes / Look straight before thee, as befits / The simplicity of Power.] See Journals, III, 343-344 (Sept. 16, 1834):
"Go forward and look straight ahead, though you die for it. Abernethy says in his
Hunter book, that the eyesockets are so formed in the gods and heroes of Greek
Sculpture that it would be impossible for such eyes to squint and take furtive
glances on this side and that...." See John Abernethy, Physiological Lectures,
exhibiting a general view of Mr. Hunter's Physiology, and his Researches in comparative anatomy delivered before the Royal College in...1817, London, 1817, pp.
86-87: "The intellect of the Greeks seems superior to that of most other nations;
their philosophers, poets, orators, and designers, have all left us models difficult to imitate, almost impossible to surpass. With a kind of intuitive perception

of the *Το Καλον* of whatever is excellent or beautiful, they formed an ideal perfect head, and have exaggerated those circumstances in which the human head differs from that of a brute; yet with a delicacy that leaves the excess beyond what is natural to man, not readily distinguishable. The head of a brute has its forehead oblique, or declining towards a horizontal line, drawn from the top of the face; and the sides of the forehead converge from the orbits, so as to make it narrower at the top than at the bottom. The Greeks made the human forehead advance a little before a perpendicular line, and they raised it to an uncommon height. They made it also diverge from the orbits, so as to be broader above than below. The eyes of animals are placed at the sides of the head, so that they see laterally, and some even behind them. The human eyes are made to look forwards; whenever they glance to a side, they indicate either fear or distrust. The Greeks seem to have paid attention to this point; the eyes are made to look strait forwards, and the outer edge of the orbit is so wrought up, as seemingly to preclude a contrary vision."

51 So do not thou to thine] The theme of "doing oneself no harm" Emerson found in a volume in his own library: The Meditations of St. Augustine, His Treatise of the Love of God, Soliloquies and Manual. To which are added Select Contemplations from St. Anselm and St. Bernard, tr. George Stanhope, London, 1818, p. 401 (a passage from "Devout Meditations of St. Bernard: with regard to the State of Human Nature, otherwise called his Book of the Soul"): "When any thing created me uneasiness, my impatience hath tempted me to wish that it might cease to be, or that it never had been at all; and yet upon recollection, I could not but acknowledge, that he who made every thing is good, and that every thing he made is very good in its own nature; and consequently, if it proved evil to me in the event, or the effects of it, the only reason must be, that I myself was evil, and wanted the grace and prudence to make a right use of it: for, after all, nothing can work me mischief except myself. The harm that I sustain, I carry about with me, and never am a real sufferer but by my own fault."

52 This is the reason why thou dost recognize] On the principle of "likeness," see Sermons par. 43. For the spiritual rule, "Quantum sumus, scimus" and "Like only can know like," see the index of Emerson the Essayist.

55 The Spirit that lives in all] This thought is repeated in line 116 of the poem, and is explained in Sermons par. 30. The expression is, probably, no more pantheistic than Wordsworth's "Lines Composed a Few Miles Above Tintern Abbey," 101-102:

> All thinking things, all objects of all thought,
> And rolls through all things.

60 Thou art unto thyself a law] Cf. also line 69. On being sufficient unto oneself and on the consequences of self-reliance, see Sermons par. 17 and 30. Cf. Paradise Lost, IX, 651ff.:

> But of this Tree we may not taste nor touch;
> God so commanded, and left that Command
> Sole Daughter of his voice; the rest, we live
> Law to ourselves, our Reason is our Law.

61 And since the soul of things is in thee] See Sermons par. 14 for the concept that heaven or hell is being formed inside us even now.

64 Heaven, Hell, the Judgment] This vocabulary appears in Sermons par. 45.

66-68 All these thou must find / Within thy single mind, / Or never find.] Emerson carefully explains that Heaven, Hell, harps, wings, rivers of milk and honey, and other symbols relate not to external states but to spiritual, internal conditions. See Sermons par. 17 and 45.

69 Thou art the law] I.e., the Moral Law. On being the "Universe to yourself" or a "law unto yourself" see Sermons par. 11-13. On the tremendous stakes involved in the choices made possible by man's self-reliance, see Sermons par. 39. See also

the note on line 60 of the poem. On the "temple of the soul" in which these momentous decisions are made, see Fénelon par. 11 and Sermons par. 27.

70-72 The gospel has no revelation / Of peace or hope until there is response / From the deep chambers of thy mind thereto] For Lessing's view of revelation, see Sermons par. 29. On the Doctrine of the necessary coincidence of Subject and Object in Coleridge's system, see Emerson the Essayist, I, 93, 112, 207 et passim. On the "response" see especially I, 147--a passage drawn from Coleridge's The Statesman's Manual. Cf. Coleridge's "Dejection: An Ode," lines 53ff. and 71ff.

> Ah! from the soul itself must issue forth
> A light, a glory, a fair luminous cloud
> Enveloping the Earth--
>
>   . . .
>
> Joy is the sweet voice, Joy the luminous cloud--
>   We in ourselves rejoice!
> And thence flows all that charms or ear or sight,
>   All melodies the echoes of that voice,
> All colours a suffusion from that light.

73 The rest is straw] Glory resides in "spiritual nature" or in living a divine life; "all other magnificence is straw." See Sermons par. 24. Cf. Milton's Comus, lines 596-598:

>   ...if this fail,
> The pillar'd firmament is rott'nness,
> And earths base built on stubble.

Luther called the Epistle of James an "Epistle of Straw, Epistola straminea." See Early Lectures, I, 121.11.

75 [Thou art] The Providence] On the human mind's ability to make its own fate, see Sermons par. 11 and 15. On man's being "in some sort the Providence to himself which dispenses the events of his life," see Sermons par. 45.

76-77 Thou art thyself that doth dispense / Wealth to thy work, want to thy sloth] On the working of the spiritual law of Compensation through the action of the Conscience, see Sermons par. 5 and 7. On the Conscience as rewarder, see Sermons par. 3 and 4. On men's being masters of their own condition, see Sermons par. 11. On our "dangerous power of self-change," see Sermons par. 21. On St. Bernard's theme that we only can do ourselves good or harm, see Sermons par. 30 and the note on line 51, supra. On the power that comes with wisdom and goodness, see Sermons par. 34. See also one of Emerson's journal notes, made while he was studying at Divinity Hall in November, 1828 (Works, VI, 407): "Don't you see you are the Universe to yourself? You carry your fortunes in your own hand. Change of place won't mend the matter. You will weave the same web at Pernambuco as at Boston, if you have only learned to make one texture."

84-85 Virtue sees by its own light; / Stumbleth sin in self-made night.] For an interesting variant, see Sermons par. 38. See Milton's Comus, lines 372-385:

> Vertue could see to do what vertue would
> By her own radiant light, though Sun and Moon
> Were in the flat Sea sunk....
>
> He that has light within his own cleer brest
> May sit i'th center, and enjoy bright day,
> But he that hides a dark soul, and foul thoughts
> Benighted walks under the mid-day Sun;
> Himself is his own dungeon.

On virtue's being God and immortality, see Sermons par. 23. By following virtue we enjoy "a being greater than our own" and may be said to "become God." See Sermons par. 32.

86 Who approves thee doing right?] For the activity of this "sovereign power" (called "God," "Reason," or "Conscience") see Fénelon par. 4. For Emerson on the Conscience as a rewarder, see Sermons par. 3 and 4.

87 God in thee] For an identification of God with the Conscience, see Sermons par. 8.

88 Who condemns thee doing wrong?] On the inward teacher that pronounces judgment on us, see Fénelon par. 6.

90 Who punishes thine evil deed?] See Sermons par. 9.

92 What is thine evil meed?] Emerson, in his moral order, presupposes "compensation" or immediate judgment through the activity of the Conscience. See Sermons par. 4-6.

93 Thy worse mind, with error blind] For Emerson's commentary on this line and for the significance of habit in our spiritual decline, see Sermons par. 20. He describes the progressive disintegration of the moral life in Sermons par. 31. Cf. Coleridge's "The Piccolomini," 4.7.251ff.:

> Every crime
> Has, in the moment of its perpetration,
> Its own avenging angel--dark Misgiving,
> An ominous Sinking at the inmost heart.

96 The loss of peace] See Sermons par. 6 and 41-42. See also Fénelon par. 16-18, 29, and 33.

97 this inmate] On our first business in life--the building up of one's character so that it may become a temple worthy of "this celestial inmate," see Sermons par. 27.

102 With Virtue rise.] Virtue in the soul is "life" and immortality. See Sermons par. 23. See the echo of Comus in Nature
admonishes me where the sources of wisdom and power lie, and points to virtue as to 'The golden key / Which opes the palace of eternity,' carries upon its face the highest certificate of truth, because it animates me to create my own world through the purification of my soul."

104 By the same law] Emerson discusses this law of improvement in Sermons par. 35, 37, and 39. "Draw nigh to God & he will draw nigh to you"--a variant of Quantum sumus, scimus. See note on line 52 above.

105-106 angels...devils] See Sermons par. 12 and 14.

108 There is nothing else but God] See Fénelon par. 12.

111 Light is but his shadow dim.] See Plato's remark: "God is truth, and light his shadow."

113 An image of himself to be my soul?] On this "interior sanctuary" or "soul of our soul," see Fénelon par. 14 and 17: "God is in our souls, as our souls are in our bodies."

116 For that which is in me lives in the whole] This thought is repeated in line 55 and explicated in Sermons par. 30. "Reason" in the thought-patterns of Fénelon and Coleridge is a synonym for God. See Fénelon par. 4.

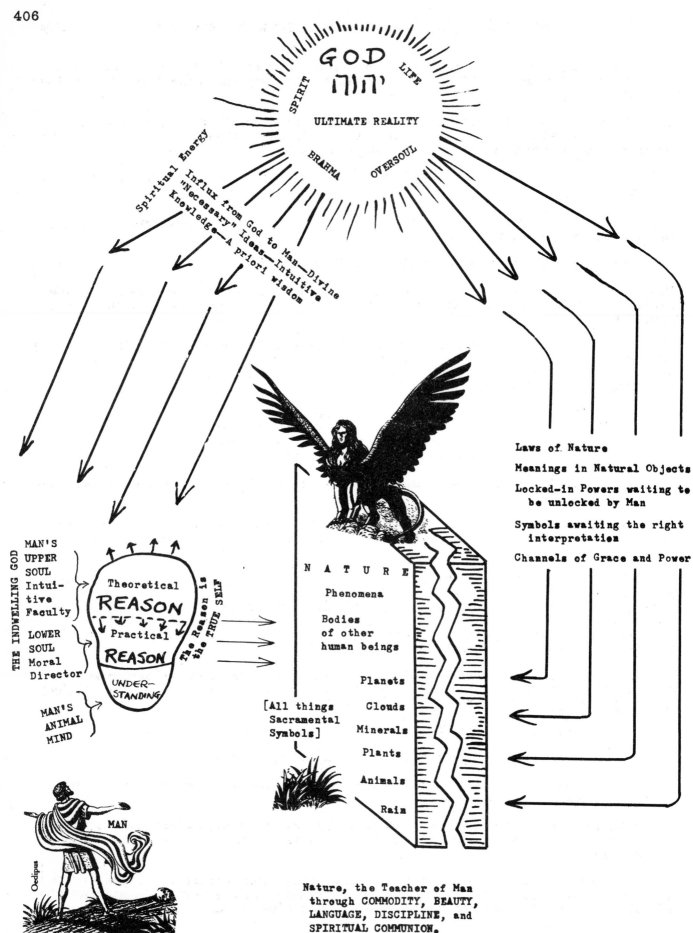

GOD
יהוה
SPIRIT
LIFE
ULTIMATE REALITY
BRAHMA
OVERSOUL

Spiritual Energy
Influx from God to Man—Divine
"Necessary" Ideas—Intuitive
Knowledge—A priori wisdom

Laws of Nature

Meanings in Natural Objects

Locked-in Powers waiting to
be unlocked by Man

Symbols awaiting the right
interpretation

Channels of Grace and Power

THE INDWELLING GOD

MAN'S
UPPER
SOUL
Intui-
tive
Faculty

LOWER
SOUL
Moral
Director

MAN'S
ANIMAL
MIND

Theoretical
REASON
Practical
REASON
UNDER-
STANDING

The Reason is the TRUE SELF

N A T U R E

Phenomena

Bodies
of other
human beings

Planets

Clouds

Minerals

Plants

Animals

Rain

[All things
Sacramental
Symbols]

MAN

Oedipus

Nature, the Teacher of Man
through COMMODITY, BEAUTY,
LANGUAGE, DISCIPLINE, and
SPIRITUAL COMMUNION.

Miss Margaret Fuller

With the respects of

R. W. Emerson.

Dieses Buch war ein Besitz Bettina's von Arnim, aus dem es in den meinigen überging.

Herman Grimm.

VERITAS

RADCLIFFE COLLEGE LIBRARY

THE GIFT OF
Miss Agnes Irwin

NATURE.

"Nature is but an image or imitation of wisdom, the last thing of the soul; nature being a thing which doth only do, but not know."

PLOTINUS.

BOSTON:
JAMES MUNROE AND COMPANY.

M DCCC XXXVI.

Cambridge Press:
Metcalf, Torry, & Ballou.

CONTENTS.

INTRODUCTION.

OUR age is retrospective. It builds the sepulchres of the fathers. It writes biographies, histories, and criticism. The foregoing gene-
5 rations beheld God and nature face to face; we, through their eyes. Why should not we also enjoy an original relation to the universe? Why should not we have a poetry and philosophy of insight and not of tradition, and a relig-
10 ion by revelation to us, and not the history of theirs? Embosomed for a season in nature, whose floods of life stream around and through us, and invite us by the powers they supply, to action proportioned to nature, why should we
15 grope among the dry bones of the past, or put the living generation into masquerade out of its faded wardrobe? The sun shines to-day also. There is more wool and flax in the fields.

1 There are new lands, new men, new thoughts. Let us demand our own works and laws and worship.

Undoubtedly we have no questions to ask
5 which are unanswerable. We must trust the perfection of the creation so far, as to believe that whatever curiosity the order of things has awakened in our minds, the order of things can satisfy. Every man's condition is a solution in
10 hieroglyphic to those inquiries he would put. He acts it as life, before he apprehends it as truth. In like manner, nature is already, in its forms and tendencies, describing its own design. Let us interrogate the great apparition, that
15 shines so peacefully around us. Let us inquire, to what end is nature?

All science has one aim, namely, to find a theory of nature. We have theories of races and of functions, but scarcely yet a remote
20 approximation to an idea of creation. We are now so far from the road to truth, that religious teachers dispute and hate each other, and speculative men are esteemed unsound and

1 frivolous. But to a sound judgment, the most abstract truth is the most practical. Whenever a true theory appears, it will be its own evidence. Its test is, that it will explain all phe-
5 nomena. Now many are thought not only unexplained but inexplicable; as language, sleep, dreams, beasts, sex.

Philosophically considered, the universe is composed of Nature and the Soul. Strictly
10 speaking, therefore, all that is separate from us, all which Philosophy distinguishes as the NOT ME, that is, both nature and art, all other men and my own body, must be ranked under this name, NATURE. In enumerating the values of
15 nature and casting up their sum, I shall use the word in both senses; — in its common and in its philosophical import. In inquiries so general as our present one, the inaccuracy is not material; no confusion of thought will occur.
20 *Nature*, in the common sense, refers to essences unchanged by man; space, the air, the river, the leaf. *Art* is applied to the mixture of his will with the same things, as in a house, a

canal, a statue, a picture. But his operations taken together are so insignificant, a little chipping, baking, patching, and washing, that in an impression so grand as that of the world on the human mind, they do not vary the result.

NATURE.

CHAPTER I.

To go into solitude, a man needs to retire as much from his chamber as from society. I am not solitary whilst I read and write, though nobody is with me. But if a man would be alone, let him look at the stars. The rays that come from those heavenly worlds, will separate between him and vulgar things. One might think the atmosphere was made transparent with this design, to give man, in the heavenly bodies, the perpetual presence of the sublime. Seen in the streets of cities, how great they are! If the stars should appear one night in a thousand years, how would men

1

believe and adore; and preserve for many generations the remembrance of the city of God which had been shown! But every night come out these preachers of beauty, and light the universe with their admonishing smile.

The stars awaken a certain reverence, because though always present, they are always inaccessible; but all natural objects make a kindred impression, when the mind is open to their influence. Nature never wears a mean appearance. Neither does the wisest man extort all her secret, and lose his curiosity by finding out all her perfection. Nature never became a toy to a wise spirit. The flowers, the animals, the mountains, reflected all the wisdom of his best hour, as much as they had delighted the simplicity of his childhood.

When we speak of nature in this manner, we have a distinct but most poetical sense in the mind. We mean the integrity of impression made by manifold natural objects. It is this which distinguishes the stick of timber of the wood-cutter, from the tree of the poet,

The charming landscape which I saw this morning, is indubitably made up of some twenty or thirty farms. Miller owns this field, Locke that, and Manning the woodland beyond. But none of them owns the landscape. There is a property in the horizon which no man has but he whose eye can integrate all the parts, that is, the poet. This is the best part of these men's farms, yet to this their land-deeds give them no title.

To speak truly, few adult persons can see nature. Most persons do not see the sun. At least they have a very superficial seeing. The sun illuminates only the eye of the man, but shines into the eye and the heart of the child. The lover of nature is he whose inward and outward senses are still truly adjusted to each other; who has retained the spirit of infancy even into the era of manhood. His intercourse with heaven and earth, becomes part of his daily food. In the presence of nature, a wild delight runs through the man, in spite of real sorrows. Nature says,— he is my creature,

1 and maugre all his impertinent griefs, he shall
be glad with me. Not the sun or the summer
alone, but every hour and season yields its
tribute of delight; for every hour and change
5 corresponds to and authorizes a different state
of the mind, from breathless noon to grimmest
midnight. Nature is a setting that fits equally
well a comic or a mourning piece. In good
health, the air is a cordial of incredible virtue.
10 Crossing a bare common, in snow puddles, at
twilight, under a clouded sky, without having
in my thoughts any occurrence of special good
fortune, I have enjoyed a perfect exhilaration.
Almost I fear to think how glad I am. In the
15 woods too, a man casts off his years, as the
snake his slough, and at what period soever of
life, is always a child. In the woods, is perpetual youth. Within these plantations of God,
a decorum and sanctity reign, a perennial
20 festival is dressed, and the guest sees not how
he should tire of them in a thousand years.
In the woods, we return to reason and faith.
There I feel that nothing can befal me in

1 life, — no disgrace, no calamity, (leaving me my
eyes,) which nature cannot repair. Standing
on the bare ground, — my head bathed by the
blithe air, and uplifted into infinite space, — all
5 mean egotism vanishes. I become a transparent eye-ball. I am nothing. I see all. The
currents of the Universal Being circulate
through me; I am part or particle of God.
The name of the nearest friend sounds then
10 foreign and accidental. To be brothers, to be
acquaintances, — master or servant, is then
a trifle and a disturbance. I am the lover
of uncontained and immortal beauty. In
the wilderness, I find something more dear
15 and connate than in streets or villages. In the
tranquil landscape, and especially in the distant
line of the horizon, man beholds somewhat as
beautiful as his own nature.

The greatest delight which the fields and
20 woods minister, is the suggestion of an occult
relation between man and the vegetable. I am
not alone and unacknowledged. They nod to
me and I to them. The waving of the boughs

1*

1 in the storm, is new to me and old. It takes
me by surprise, and yet is not unknown. Its
effect is like that of a higher thought or a
better emotion coming over me, when I deemed
5 I was thinking justly or doing right.

Yet it is certain that the power to produce
this delight, does not reside in nature, but in
man, or in a harmony of both. It is necessary
to use these pleasures with great temperance.
10 For, nature is not always tricked in holiday
attire, but the same scene which yesterday
breathed perfume and glittered as for the frolic
of the nymphs, is overspread with melancholy
today. Nature always wears the colors of the
15 spirit. To a man laboring under calamity, the
heat of his own fire hath sadness in it. Then,
there is a kind of contempt of the landscape
felt by him who has just lost by death a dear
friend. The sky is less grand as it shuts down
20 over less worth in the population.

CHAPTER II.

COMMODITY.

WHOEVER considers the final cause of the
world, will discern a multitude of uses that
5 enter as parts into that result. They all admit
of being thrown into one of the following
classes; Commodity; Beauty; Language; and
Discipline.

Under the general name of Commodity,
10 I rank all those advantages which our senses
owe to nature. This, of course, is a benefit
which is temporary and mediate, not ultimate,
like its service to the soul. Yet although low,
it is perfect in its kind, and is the only use of
15 nature which all men apprehend. The misery
of man appears like childish petulance, when
we explore the steady and prodigal provision
that has been made for his support and delight
on this green ball which floats him through the

1 heavens. What angels invented these splendid
ornaments, these rich conveniences, this ocean
of air above, this ocean of water beneath, this
firmament of earth between? this zodiac of
5 lights, this tent of dropping clouds, this
striped coat of climates, this fourfold year?
Beasts, fire, water, stones, and corn serve
him. The field is at once his floor, his
work-yard, his play-ground, his garden, and his
10 bed.

> " More servants wait on man
> Than he 'll take notice of." ——

Nature, in its ministry to man, is not only the
material, but is also the process and the result.
15 All the parts incessantly work into each other's
hands for the profit of man. The wind sows
the seed; the sun evaporates the sea; the
wind blows the vapor to the field; the ice, on
the other side of the planet, condenses rain on
20 this; the rain feeds the plant; the plant feeds
the animal; and thus the endless circulations
of the divine charity nourish man.

1 The useful arts are but reproductions or new
combinations by the wit of man, of the same
natural benefactors. He no longer waits for
favoring gales, but by means of steam, he
5 realizes the fable of Æolus's bag, and carries
the two and thirty winds in the boiler of his
boat. To diminish friction, he paves the road
with iron bars, and, mounting a coach with a
ship-load of men, animals, and merchandise
10 behind him, he darts through the country, from
town to town, like an eagle or a swallow
through the air. By the aggregate of these
aids, how is the face of the world changed,
from the era of Noah to that of Napoleon!
15 The private poor man hath cities, ships, canals,
bridges, built for him. He goes to the post-
office, and the human race run on his errands;
to the book-shop, and the human race read
and write of all that happens, for him; to the
20 court-house, and nations repair his wrongs.
He sets his house upon the road, and the
human race go forth every morning, and shovel
out the snow, and cut a path for him.

1 But there is no need of specifying particulars in this class of uses. The catalogue is endless, and the examples so obvious, that I shall
leave them to the reader's reflection, with the
5 general remark, that this mercenary benefit is
one which has respect to a farther good. A
man is fed, not that he may be fed, but that he
may work.

CHAPTER III.

BEAUTY.

A NOBLER want of man is served by nature,
namely, the love of Beauty.
5 The ancient Greeks called the world κοσμος,
beauty. Such is the constitution of all things,
or such the plastic power of the human eye,
that the primary forms, as the sky, the mountain, the tree, the animal, give us a delight *in
and for themselves*; a pleasure arising from
10 outline, color, motion, and grouping. This
seems partly owing to the eye itself. The eye
is the best of artists. By the mutual action of
its structure and of the laws of light, perspective is produced, which integrates every mass
15 of objects, of what character soever, into a
well colored and shaded globe, so that where
the particular objects are mean and unaffecting,
the landscape which they compose, is round and

symmetrical. And as the eye is the best composer, so light is the first of painters. There
is no object so foul that intense light will not
make beautiful. And the stimulus it affords to
the sense, and a sort of infinitude which it hath,
like space and time, make all matter gay.
Even the corpse hath its own beauty. But
beside this general grace diffused over nature,
almost all the individual forms are agreeable
to the eye, as is proved by our endless imitations of some of them, as the acorn, the grape,
the pine-cone, the wheat-ear, the egg, the
wings and forms of most birds, the lion's claw,
the serpent, the butterfly, sea-shells, flames,
clouds, buds, leaves, and the forms of many
trees, as the palm.

For better consideration, we may distribute
the aspects of Beauty in a threefold manner.

1. First, the simple perception of natural forms
is a delight. The influence of the forms and actions in nature, is so needful to man, that, in its
lowest functions, it seems to lie on the confines
of commodity and beauty. To the body and mind

which have been cramped by noxious work or
company, nature is medicinal and restores their
tone. The tradesman, the attorney comes out
of the din and craft of the street, and sees the
sky and the woods, and is a man again. In
their eternal calm, he finds himself. The
health of the eye seems to demand a horizon.
We are never tired, so long as we can see far
enough.

But in other hours, Nature satisfies the soul
purely by its loveliness, and without any mixture of corporeal benefit. I have seen the
spectacle of morning from the hill-top over
against my house, from day-break to sun-rise,
with emotions which an angel might share.
The long slender bars of cloud float like fishes
in the sea of crimson light. From the earth,
as a shore, I look out into that silent sea. I
seem to partake its rapid transformations : the
active enchantment reaches my dust, and I
dilate and conspire with the morning wind.
How does Nature deify us with a few and
cheap elements ! Give me health and a day,

2

and I will make the pomp of emperors ridiculous. The dawn is my Assyria; the sun-set
and moon-rise my Paphos, and unimaginable
realms of faerie ; broad noon shall be my England of the senses and the understanding; the
night shall be my Germany of mystic philosophy and dreams.

Not less excellent, except for our less sus-
ceptibility in the afternoon, was the charm, last
evening, of a January sunset. The western
clouds divided and subdivided themselves into
pink flakes modulated with tints of unspeakable
softness; and the air had so much life and
sweetness, that it was a pain to come within
doors. What was it that nature would say ?
Was there no meaning in the live repose of the
valley behind the mill, and which Homer or
Shakspeare could not re-form for me in words ?
The leafless trees become spires of flame in
the sunset, with the blue east for their background, and the stars of the dead calices of
flowers, and every withered stem and stubble
rimed with frost, contribute something to the
mute music.

The inhabitants of cities suppose that the
country landscape is pleasant only half the year.
I please myself with observing the graces of
the winter scenery, and believe that we are as
much touched by it as by the genial influences
of summer. To the attentive eye, each moment
of the year has its own beauty, and in the
same field, it beholds, every hour, a picture
which was never seen before, and which shall
never be seen again. The heavens change
every moment, and reflect their glory or gloom
on the plains beneath. The state of the crop
in the surrounding farms alters the expression
of the earth from week to week. The succession of native plants in the pastures and road-
sides, which make the silent clock by which
time tells the summer hours, will make even
the divisions of the day sensible to a keen
observer. The tribes of birds and insects, like
the plants punctual to their time, follow each
other, and the year has room for all. By water-
courses, the variety is greater. In July, the
blue pontederia or pickerel-weed blooms in

1 large beds in the shallow parts of our pleasant
river, and swarms with yellow butterflies in continual motion. Art cannot rival this pomp of
purple and gold. Indeed the river is a per-
5 petual gala, and boasts each month a new
ornament.

But this beauty of Nature which is seen and
felt as beauty, is the least part. The shows of
day, the dewy morning, the rainbow, moun-
10 tains, orchards in blossom, stars, moonlight,
shadows in still water, and the like, if too
eagerly hunted, become shows merely, and
mock us with their unreality. Go out of the
house to see the moon, and 't is mere tinsel ; it
15 will not please as when its light shines upon
your necessary journey. The beauty that
shimmers in the yellow afternoons of October,
who ever could clutch it ? Go forth to find it,
and it is gone : 't is only a mirage as you look
20 from the windows of diligence.

2. The presence of a higher, namely, of the
spiritual element is essential to its perfection.
The high and divine beauty which can be loved

1 without effeminacy, is that which is found in
combination with the human will, and never
separate. Beauty is the mark God sets upon
virtue. Every natural action is graceful. Every
5 heroic act is also decent, and causes the place
and the bystanders to shine. We are taught by
great actions that the universe is the property
of every individual in it. Every rational creature has all nature for his dowry and estate. It
10 is his, if he will. He may divest himself of it ;
he may creep into a corner, and abdicate his
kingdom, as most men do, but he is entitled to
the world by his constitution. In proportion to
the energy of his thought and will, he takes up
15 the world into himself. " All those things for
which men plough, build, or sail, obey virtue ; "
said an ancient historian. " The winds and
waves," said Gibbon, " are always on the side
of the ablest navigators." So are the sun and
20 moon and all the stars of heaven. When a
noble act is done, — perchance in a scene of
great natural beauty ; when Leonidas and his
three hundred martyrs consume one day in

2*

1 dying, and the sun and moon come each and
look at them once in the steep defile of Ther-
mopylæ ; when Arnold Winkelried, in the high
Alps, under the shadow of the avalanche, gath-
5 ers in his side a sheaf of Austrian spears to
break the line for his comrades ; are not these
heroes entitled to add the beauty of the scene to
the beauty of the deed ? When the bark of
Columbus nears the shore of America ; — before
10 it, the beach lined with savages, fleeing out of
all their huts of cane ; the sea behind ; and the
purple mountains of the Indian Archipelago
around, can we separate the man from the living picture ? Does not the New World clothe
15 his form with her palm-groves and savannahs as
fit drapery ? Ever does natural beauty steal in
like air, and envelope great actions. When Sir
Harry Vane was dragged up the Tower-hill,
sitting on a sled, to suffer death, as the cham-
20 pion of the English laws, one of the multitude
cried out to him, " You never sate on so glorious a seat." Charles II., to intimidate the citizens of London, caused the patriot Lord Rus-

1 sel to be drawn in an open coach, through the
principal streets of the city, on his way to the
scaffold. " But," to use the simple narrative of
his biographer, " the multitude imagined they
5 saw liberty and virtue sitting by his side." In
private places, among sordid objects, an act of
truth or heroism seems at once to draw to itself
the sky as its temple, the sun as its candle.
Nature stretcheth out her arms to embrace man,
10 only let his thoughts be of equal greatness.
Willingly does she follow his steps with the rose
and the violet, and bend her lines of grandeur
and grace to the decoration of her darling child.
Only let his thoughts be of equal scope, and the
15 frame will suit the picture. A virtuous man, is
in unison with her works, and makes the central figure of the visible sphere. Homer, Pindar, Socrates, Phocion, associate themselves
fitly in our memory with the whole geography
20 and climate of Greece. The visible heavens
and earth sympathize with Jesus. And in common life, whosoever has seen a person of powerful character and happy genius, will have re-

1 marked how easily he took all things along with him, — the persons, the opinions, and the day, and nature became ancillary to a man.

3. There is still another aspect under which
5 the beauty of the world may be viewed, namely, as it becomes an object of the intellect. Beside the relation of things to virtue, they have a relation to thought. The intellect searches out the absolute order of things as they stand in the
10 mind of God, and without the colors of affection. The intellectual and the active powers seem to succeed each other in man, and the exclusive activity of the one, generates the exclusive activity of the other. There is something
15 unfriendly in each to the other, but they are like the alternate periods of feeding and working in animals; each prepares and certainly will be followed by the other. Therefore does beauty, which, in relation to actions, as we have
20 seen comes unsought, and comes because it is unsought, remain for the apprehension and pursuit of the intellect; and then again, in its turn, of the active power. Nothing divine dies. All

1 good is eternally reproductive. The beauty of nature reforms itself in the mind, and not for barren contemplation, but for new creation.

All men are in some degree impressed by the
5 face of the world. Some men even to delight. This love of beauty is Taste. Others have the same love in such excess, that, not content with admiring, they seek to embody it in new forms. The creation of beauty is Art.
10 The production of a work of art throws a light upon the mystery of humanity. A work of art is an abstract or epitome of the world. It is the result or expression of nature, in miniature. For although the works of nature are
15 innumerable and all different, the result or the expression of them all is similar and single. Nature is a sea of forms radically alike and even unique. A leaf, a sun-beam, a landscape, the ocean, make an analogous impression on
20 the mind. What is common to them all,—that perfectness and harmony, is beauty. Therefore the standard of beauty, is the entire circuit of natural forms,—the totality of nature;

1 which the Italians expressed by defining beauty " il piu nell' uno." Nothing is quite beautiful alone: nothing but is beautiful in the whole. A single object is only so far beautiful as it sug-
5 gests this universal grace. The poet, the painter, the sculptor, the musician, the architect seek each to concentrate this radiance of the world on one point, and each in his several work to satisfy the love of beauty which stimu-
10 lates him to produce. Thus is Art, a nature passed through the alembic of man. Thus in art, does nature work through the will of a man filled with the beauty of her first works.

The world thus exists to the soul to satisfy the
15 desire of beauty. Extend this element to the uttermost, and I call it an ultimate end. No reason can be asked or given why the soul seeks beauty. Beauty, in its largest and profoundest sense, is one expression for the universe. God
20 is the all-fair. Truth, and goodness, and beauty, are but different faces of the same All. But beauty in nature is not ultimate. It is the herald of inward and eternal beauty, and is

1 not alone a solid and satisfactory good. It must therefore stand as a part and not as yet the last or highest expression of the final cause of Nature.

CHAPTER IV.

LANGUAGE.

A THIRD use which Nature subserves to man is that of Language. Nature is the vehicle of thought, and in a simple, double, and threefold degree.

1. Words are signs of natural facts.

2. Particular natural facts are symbols of particular facts. *spiritual*

3. Nature is the symbol of spirits.

1. Words are signs of natural facts. The use of natural history is to give us aid in supernatural history. The use of the outer creation is to give us language for the beings and changes of the inward creation. Every word which is used to express a moral or intellectual fact, if traced to its root, is found to be borrowed from some material appearance. *Right* originally means *straight*; *wrong* means *twisted*. *Spirit* primarily means *wind*; trans-

gression, the crossing of a *line*; *supercilious*, the *raising of the eye-brow*. We say the *heart* to express emotion, the *head* to denote thought; and *thought* and *emotion* are, in their turn, words borrowed from sensible things, and now appropriated to spiritual nature. Most of the process by which this transformation is made, is hidden from us in the remote time when language was framed; but the same tendency may be daily observed in children. Children and savages use only nouns or names of things, which they continually convert into verbs, and apply to analogous mental acts.

2. But this origin of all words that convey a spiritual import, — so conspicuous a fact in the history of language, — is our least debt to nature. It is not words only that are emblematic; it is things which are emblematic. Every natural fact is a symbol of some spiritual fact. Every appearance in nature corresponds to some state of the mind, and that state of the mind can only be described by presenting that natural appearance as its picture. An enraged

3

man is a lion, a cunning man is a fox, a firm man is a rock, a learned man is a torch. A lamb is innocence; a snake is subtle spite; flowers express to us the delicate affections. Light and darkness are our familiar expression for knowledge and ignorance; and heat for love. Visible distance behind and before us, is respectively our image of memory and hope.

Who looks upon a river in a meditative hour, and is not reminded of the flux of all things? Throw a stone into the stream, and the circles that propagate themselves are the beautiful type of all influence. Man is conscious of a universal soul within or behind his individual life, wherein, as in a firmament, the natures of Justice, Truth, Love, Freedom, arise and shine. This universal soul, he calls Reason: it is not mine or thine or his, but we are its; we are its property and men. And the blue sky in which the private earth is buried, the sky with its eternal calm, and full of everlasting orbs, is the type of Reason. That which, intellectually considered, we call Reason, considered in rela-

tion to nature, we call Spirit. Spirit is the Creator. Spirit hath life in itself. And man in all ages and countries, embodies it in his language, as the FATHER.

It is easily seen that there is nothing lucky or capricious in these analogies, but that they are constant, and pervade nature. These are not the dreams of a few poets, here and there, but man is an analogist, and studies relations in all objects. He is placed in the centre of beings, and a ray of relation passes from every other being to him. And neither can man be understood without these objects, nor these objects without man. All the facts in natural history taken by themselves, have no value, but are barren like a single sex. But marry it to human history, and it is full of life. Whole Floras, all Linnæus' and Buffon's volumes, are but dry catalogues of facts; but the most trivial of these facts, the habit of a plant, the organs, or work, or noise of an insect, applied to the illustration of a fact in intellectual philosophy, or, in any way associated to human nature, affects

us in the most lively and agreeable manner. The seed of a plant, — to what affecting analogies in the nature of man, is that little fruit made use of, in all discourse, up to the voice of Paul, who calls the human corpse a seed, — "It is sown a natural body; it is raised a spiritual body." The motion of the earth round its axis, and round the sun, makes the day, and the year. These are certain amounts of brute light and heat. But is there no intent of an analogy between man's life and the seasons? And do the seasons gain no grandeur or pathos from that analogy? The instincts of the ant are very unimportant considered as the ant's; but the moment a ray of relation is seen to extend from it to man, and the little drudge is seen to be a monitor, a little body with a mighty heart, then all its habits, even that said to be recently observed, that it never sleeps, become sublime.

Because of this radical correspondence between visible things and human thoughts, savages, who have only what is necessary, converse

in figures. As we go back in history, language becomes more picturesque, until its infancy, when it is all poetry; or, all spiritual facts are represented by natural symbols. The same symbols are found to make the original elements of all languages. It has moreover been observed, that the idioms of all languages approach each other in passages of the greatest eloquence and power. And as this is the first language, so is it the last. This immediate dependence of language upon nature, this conversion of an outward phenomenon into a type of somewhat in human life, never loses its power to affect us. It is this which gives that piquancy to the conversation of a strong-natured farmer or back-woodsman, which all men relish.

Thus is nature an interpreter, by whose means man converses with his fellow men. A man's power to connect his thought with its proper symbol, and so utter it, depends on the simplicity of his character, that is, upon his love of truth and his desire to communicate it without loss. The corruption of man is follow-

3*

ed by the corruption of language. When simplicity of character and the sovereignty of ideas is broken up by the prevalence of secondary desires, the desire of riches, the desire of pleasure, the desire of power, the desire of praise, — and duplicity and falsehood take place of simplicity and truth, the power over nature as an interpreter of the will, is in a degree lost; new imagery ceases to be created, and old words are perverted to stand for things which are not; a paper currency is employed when there is no bullion in the vaults. In due time, the fraud is manifest, and words lose all power to stimulate the understanding or the affections. Hundreds of writers may be found in every long-civilized nation, who for a short time believe, and make others believe, that they see and utter truths, who do not of themselves clothe one thought in its natural garment, but who feed unconsciously upon the language created by the primary writers of the country, those, namely, who hold primarily on nature.

But wise men pierce this rotten diction and fasten words again to visible things; so that picturesque language is at once a commanding certificate that he who employs it, is a man in alliance with truth and God. The moment our discourse rises above the ground line of familiar facts, and is inflamed with passion or exalted by thought, it clothes itself in images. A man conversing in earnest, if he watch his intellectual processes, will find that always a material image, more. or less luminous, arises in his mind, cotemporaneous with every thought, which furnishes the vestment of the thought. Hence, good writing and brilliant discourse are perpetual allegories. This imagery is spontaneous. It is the blending of experience with the present action of the mind. It is proper creation. It is the working of the Original Cause through the instruments he has already made.

These facts may suggest the advantage which the country-life possesses for a powerful mind, over the artificial and curtailed life of cities. We

know more from nature than we can at will communicate. Its light flows into the mind evermore, and we forget its presence. The poet, the orator, bred in the woods, whose senses have been nourished by their fair and appeasing changes, year after year, without design and without heed, — shall not lose their lesson altogether, in the roar of cities or the broil of politics. Long hereafter, amidst agitation and terror in national councils, — in the hour of revolution, — these solemn images shall reappear in their morning lustre, as fit symbols and words of the thoughts which the passing events shall awaken. At the call of a noble sentiment, again the woods wave, the pines murmur, the river rolls and shines, and the cattle low upon the mountains, as he saw and heard them in his infancy. And with these forms, the spells of persuasion, the keys of power are put into his hands.

3. We are thus assisted by natural objects in the expression of particular meanings. But how great a language to convey such peppercorn informations! Did it need such noble

races of creatures, this profusion of forms, this host of orbs in heaven, to furnish man with the dictionary and grammar of his municipal speech? Whilst we use this grand cipher to expedite the affairs of our pot and kettle, we feel that we have not yet put it to its use, neither are able. We are like travellers using the cinders of a volcano to roast their eggs. Whilst we see that it always stands ready to clothe what we would say, we cannot avoid the question, whether the characters are not significant of themselves. Have mountains, and waves, and skies, no significance but what we consciously give them, when we employ them as emblems of our thoughts? The world is emblematic. Parts of speech are metaphors because the whole of nature is a metaphor of the human mind. The laws of moral nature answer to those of matter as face to face in a glass. " The visible world and the relation of its parts, is the dial plate of the invisible." The axioms of physics translate the laws of ethics. Thus, " the whole is greater than its part;" " reaction is equal to

action;" " the smallest weight may be made to lift the greatest, the difference of weight being compensated by time;" and many the like propositions, which have an ethical as well as physical sense. These propositions have a much more extensive and universal sense when applied to human life, than when confined to technical use.

In like manner, the memorable words of history, and the proverbs of nations, consist usually of a natural fact, selected as a picture or parable of a moral truth. Thus; A rolling stone gathers no moss; A bird in the hand is worth two in the bush; A cripple in the right way, will beat a racer in the wrong; Make hay whilst the sun shines; 'T is hard to carry a full cup even; Vinegar is the son of wine; The last ounce broke the camel's back; Long-lived trees make roots first; — and the like. In their primary sense these are trivial facts, but we repeat them for the value of their analogical import. What is true of proverbs, is true of all fables, parables, and allegories.

This relation between the mind and matter is not fancied by some poet, but stands in the will of God, and so is free to be known by all men. It appears to men, or it does not appear. When in fortunate hours we ponder this miracle, the wise man doubts, if, at all other times, he is not blind and deaf;

> ——— " Can these things be,
> And overcome us like a summer's cloud,
> Without our special wonder?"

for the universe becomes transparent, and the light of higher laws than its own, shines through it. It is the standing problem which has exercised the wonder and the study of every fine genius since the world began; from the era of the Egyptians and the Brahmins, to that of Pythagoras, of Plato, of Bacon, of Leibnitz, of Swedenborg. There sits the Sphinx at the road-side, and from age to age, as each prophet comes by, he tries his fortune at reading her riddle. There seems to be a necessity in spirit to manifest itself in material

1 forms; and day and night, river and storm, beast and bird, acid and alkali, preexist in necessary Ideas in the mind of God, and are what they are by virtue of preceding affections,
5 in the world of spirit. A Fact is the end or last issue of spirit. The visible creation is the terminus or the circumference of the invisible world. "Material objects," said a French philosopher, "are necessarily kinds of *scoriæ* of
10 the substantial thoughts of the Creator, which must always preserve an exact relation to their first origin; in other words, visible nature must have a spiritual and moral side."

This doctrine is abstruse, and though the
15 images of "garment," "scoriæ," "mirror," &c., may stimulate the fancy, we must summon the aid of subtler and more vital expositors to make it plain. "Every scripture is to be interpreted by the same spirit which gave it forth,"
20 — is the fundamental law of criticism. A life in harmony with nature, the love of truth and of virtue, will purge the eyes to understand her text. By degrees we may come to know the

1 primitive sense of the permanent objects of nature, so that the world shall be to us an open book, and every form significant of its hidden life and final cause.

5 A new interest surprises us, whilst, under the view now suggested, we contemplate the fearful extent and multitude of objects; since "every object rightly seen, unlocks a new faculty of the soul." That which was unconscious truth, be-
10 comes, when interpreted and defined in an object, a part of the domain of knowledge, — a new amount to the magazine of power.

[46]

CHAPTER V.

DISCIPLINE.

In view of this significance of nature, we arrive at once at a new fact, that nature is a dis-
5 cipline. This use of the world includes the preceding uses, as parts of itself.

Space, time, society, labor, climate, food, locomotion, the animals, the mechanical forces, give us sincerest lessons, day by day, whose meaning
10 is unlimited. They educate both the Understanding and the Reason. Every property of matter is a school for the understanding, — its solidity or resistance, its inertia, its extension, its figure, its divisibility. The understanding adds,
15 divides, combines, measures, and finds everlasting nutriment and room for its activity in this worthy scene. Meantime, Reason transfers all these lessons into its own world of thought, by perceiving the analogy that marries Matter and
20 Mind.

1 1. Nature is a discipline of the understanding in intellectual truths. Our dealing with sensible objects is a constant exercise in the necessary lessons of difference, of likeness, of order,
5 of being and seeming, of progressive arrangement; of ascent from particular to general; of combination to one end of manifold forces. Proportioned to the importance of the organ to be formed, is the extreme care with which its
10 tuition is provided, — a care pretermitted in no single case. What tedious training, day after day, year after year, never ending, to form the common sense; what continual reproduction of annoyances, inconveniences, dilemmas; what
15 rejoicing over us of little men; what disputing of prices, what reckonings of interest, — and all to form the Hand of the mind; — to instruct us that "good thoughts are no better than good dreams, unless they be executed!"
20 The same good office is performed by Property and its filial systems of debt and credit. Debt, grinding debt, whose iron face the widow, the orphan, and the sons of genius fear and

1   hate ; — debt, which consumes so much time, which so cripples and disheartens a great spirit with cares that seem so base, is a preceptor whose lessons cannot be forgone, and is needed
5   most by those who suffer from it most. Moreover, property, which has been well compared to snow, — " if it fall level to-day, it will be blown into drifts to-morrow," — is merely the surface action of internal machinery, like the
10   index on the face of a clock. Whilst now it is the gymnastics of the understanding, it is hiving in the foresight of the spirit, experience in profounder laws.

      The whole character and fortune of the individual is affected by the least inequalities in the
15   culture of the understanding ; for example, in the perception of differences. Therefore is Space, and therefore Time, that man may know that things are not huddled and lumped, but sundered and individual. A bell and a plough
20   have each their use, and neither can do the office of the other. Water is good to drink, coal to burn, wool to wear ; but wool cannot be

1   drunk, nor water spun, nor coal eaten. The wise man shows his wisdom in separation, in gradation, and his scale of creatures and of merits, is as wide as nature. The foolish have
5   no range in their scale, but suppose every man is as every other man. What is not good they call the worst, and what is not hateful, they call the best.

      In like manner, what good heed, nature forms
10   in us ! She pardons no mistakes. Her yea is yea, and her nay, nay.

      The first steps in Agriculture, Astronomy, Zoölogy, (those first steps which the farmer, the hunter, and the sailor take,) teach that nature's
15   dice are always loaded ; that in her heaps and rubbish are concealed sure and useful results.

      How calmly and genially the mind apprehends one after another the laws of physics ! What noble emotions dilate the mortal as he enters
20   into the counsels of the creation, and feels by knowledge the privilege to BE ! His insight refines him. The beauty of nature shines in his own breast. Man is greater that he can see

4*

1   this, and the universe less, because Time and Space relations vanish as laws are known.

      Here again we are impressed and even daunted by the immense Universe to be explored.
5   ' What we know, is a point to what we do not know.' Open any recent journal of science, and weigh the problems suggested concerning Light, Heat, Electricity, Magnetism, Physiology, Geology, and judge whether the interest of
10   natural science is likely to be soon exhausted.

      Passing by many particulars of the discipline of nature we must not omit to specify two.

      The exercise of the Will or the lesson of power is taught in every event. From the child's
15   successive possession of his several senses up to the hour when he saith, " thy will be done ! " he is learning the secret, that he can reduce under his will, not only particular events, but great classes, nay the whole series of events, and
20   so conform all facts to his character. Nature is thoroughly mediate. It is made to serve. It receives the dominion of man as meekly as the ass on which the Saviour rode. It offers all its

1   kingdoms to man as the raw material which he may mould into what is useful. Man is never weary of working it up. He forges the subtile and delicate air into wise and melodious words,
5   and gives them wing as angels of persuasion and command. More and more, with every thought, does his kingdom stretch over things, until the world becomes, at last, only a realized will, — the double of the man.

10   2. Sensible objects conform to the premonitions of Reason and reflect the conscience. All things are moral ; and in their boundless changes have an unceasing reference to spiritual nature. Therefore is nature glorious with
15   form, color, and motion, that every globe in the remotest heaven ; every chemical change from the rudest crystal up to the laws of life ; every change of vegetation from the first principle of growth in the eye of a leaf, to the tropical forest
20   and antediluvian coal-mine ; every animal function from the sponge up to Hercules, shall hint or thunder to man the laws of right and wrong, and echo the Ten Commandments. Therefore

1   is nature always the ally of Religion : lends all
her pomp and riches to the religious sentiment.
Prophet and priest, David, Isaiah, Jesus, have
drawn deeply from this source.

5   This ethical character so penetrates the bone
and marrow of nature, as to seem the end for
which it was made. Whatever private purpose
is answered by any member or part, this is its
public and universal function, and is never omit-
10 ted. Nothing in nature is exhausted in its first
use. When a thing has served an end to the
uttermost, it is wholly new for an ulterior service. In God, every end is converted into a new
means. Thus the use of Commodity, regarded
15 by itself, is mean and squalid. But it is to the
mind an education in the great doctrine of Use,
namely, that a thing is good only so far as it
serves ; that a conspiring of parts and efforts to
the production of an end, is essential to any
20 being. The first and gross manifestation of this
truth, is our inevitable and hated training in
values and wants, in corn and meat.

1   It has already been illustrated, in treating of
the significance of material things, that every
natural process is but a version of a moral sentence. The moral law lies at the centre of na-
5   ture and radiates to the circumference. It is the
pith and marrow of every substance, every relation, and every process. All things with which
we deal, preach to us. What is a farm but a
mute gospel ! The chaff and the wheat, weeds
10 and plants, blight, rain, insects, sun, — it is a
sacred emblem from the first furrow of spring to
the last stack which the snow of winter overtakes in the fields. But the sailor, the shepherd,
the miner, the merchant, in their several resorts,
15 have each an experience precisely parallel and
leading to the same conclusions. Because all
organizations are radically alike. Nor can it be
doubted that this moral sentiment which thus
scents the air, and grows in the grain, and im-
20 pregnates the waters of the world, is caught by
man and sinks into his soul. The moral influence of nature upon every individual is that
amount of truth which it illustrates to him.

1   Who can estimate this ? Who can guess how
much firmness the sea-beaten rock has taught
the fisherman ? how much tranquillity has been
reflected to man from the azure sky, over whose
5   unspotted deeps the winds forevermore drive
flocks of stormy clouds, and leave no wrinkle or stain ? how much industry and providence and affection we have caught from the
pantomime of brutes ? What a searching preach-
10 er of self-command is the varying phenomenon
of Health !

        Herein is especially apprehended the Unity of
Nature, — the Unity in Variety, — which meets
us everywhere. All the endless variety of things
15 make a unique, an identical impression. Xenophanes complained in his old age, that, look
where he would, all things hastened back to
Unity. He was weary of seeing the same entity
in the tedious variety of forms. The fable of
20 Proteus has a cordial truth. Every particular
in nature, a leaf, a drop, a crystal, a moment of
time is related to the whole, and partakes of the
perfection of the whole. Each particle is a mi-

1   crocosm, and faithfully renders the likeness of
the world.

        Not only resemblances exist in things whose
analogy is obvious, as when we detect the type
5   of the human hand in the flipper of the fossil
saurus, but also in objects wherein there is great
superficial unlikeness. Thus architecture is
called ' frozen music,' by De Stael and Goethe.
' A Gothic church,' said Coleridge, ' is a petrified
10 religion.' Michael Angelo maintained, that, to
an architect, a knowledge of anatomy is essential. In Haydn's oratorios, the notes present to
the imagination not only motions, as, of the
snake, the stag, and the elephant, but colors also ;
15 as the green grass. The granite is differenced
in its laws only by the more or less of heat, from
the river that wears it away. The river, as it
flows, resembles the air that flows over it ; the
air resembles the light which traverses it with
20 more subtile currents ; the light resembles the
heat which rides with it through Space. Each
creature is only a modification of the other ; the
likeness in them is more than the difference, and

1   their radical law is one and the same. Hence it
is, that a rule of one art, or a law of one organization, holds true throughout nature. So intimate is this Unity, that, it is easily seen, it lies
5   under the undermost garment of nature, and betrays its source in universal Spirit. For, it pervades Thought also. Every universal truth
which we express in words, implies or supposes
every other truth. *Omne verum vero consonat*.
10   It is like a great circle on a sphere, comprising
all possible circles ; which, however, may be
drawn, and comprise it, in like manner. Every
such truth is the absolute Ens seen from one
side. But it has innumerable sides.

15   The same central Unity is still more conspicuous in actions. Words are finite organs of the
infinite mind. They cannot cover the dimensions of what is in truth. They break, chop,
and impoverish it. An action is the perfection
20   and publication of thought. A right action seems
to fill the eye, and to be related to all nature.
" The wise man, in doing one thing, does all ;
or, in the one thing he does rightly, he sees the
likeness of all which is done rightly."

1   Words and actions are not the attributes of
mute and brute nature. They introduce us to
that singular form which predominates over all
other forms. This is the human. All other or-
5   ganizations appear to be degradations of the
human form. When this organization appears
among so many that surround it, the spirit prefers it to all others. It says, ' From such as
this, have I drawn joy and knowledge. In such
10   as this, have I found and beheld myself. I will
speak to it. It can speak again. It can yield
me thought already formed and alive.' In fact,
the eye, — the mind, — is always accompanied
by these forms, male and female ; and these are
15   incomparably the richest informations of the
power and order that lie at the heart of things.
Unfortunately, every one of them bears the marks
as of some injury ; is marred and superficially
defective. Nevertheless, far different from the
20   deaf and dumb nature around them, these all
rest like fountain-pipes on the unfathomed sea of
thought and virtue whereto they alone, of all organizations, are the entrances.

5

1   It were a pleasant inquiry to follow into detail their ministry to our education, but where
would it stop ? We are associated in adolescent
and adult life with some friends, who, like skies
5   and waters, are coextensive with our idea ; who,
answering each to a certain affection of the soul,
satisfy our desire on that side ; whom we lack
power to put at such focal distance from us, that
we can mend or even analyze them. We can-
10   not chuse but love them. When much intercourse with a friend has supplied us with a
standard of excellence, and has increased our
respect for the resources of God who thus sends
a real person to outgo our ideal ; when he has,
15   moreover, become an object of thought, and,
whilst his character retains all its unconscious
effect, is converted in the mind into solid and
sweet wisdom, — it is a sign to us that his office
is closing, and he is commonly withdrawn from
20   our sight in a short time.

CHAPTER VI.

IDEALISM.

Thus is the unspeakable but intelligible and
practicable meaning of the world conveyed to
5   man, the immortal pupil, in every object of sense.
To this one end of Discipline, all parts of nature conspire.

       A noble doubt perpetually suggests itself,
whether this end be not the Final Cause of the
10   Universe ; and whether nature outwardly exists.
It is a sufficient account of that Appearance we
call the World, that God will teach a human
mind, and so makes it the receiver of a certain
number of congruent sensations, which we call
15   sun and moon, man and woman, house and trade.
In my utter impotence to test the authenticity of
the report of my senses, to know whether the
impressions they make on me correspond with
outlying objects, what difference does it make,
20   whether Orion is up there in heaven, or some

1 god paints the image in the firmament of the
soul ? The relations of parts and the end of
the whole remaining the same, what is the difference, whether land and ˉsea interact, and
5 worlds revolve and intermingle without number
or end, — deep yawning under deep, and galaxy
balancing galaxy, throughout absolute space, or,
whether, without relations of time and space,
the same appearances are inscribed in the con-
10 stant faith of man. Whether nature enjoy a
substantial existence without, or is only in the
apocalypse of the mind, it is alike useful and
alike venerable to me. Be it what it may, it is
ideal to me, so long as I cannot try the accuracy
15 of my senses.

The frivolous make themselves merry with the
Ideal theory, as if its consequences were bur-
lesque ; as if it affected the stability of nature.
It surely does not. God never jests with us, and
20 will not compromise the end of nature, by per-
mitting any inconsequence in its procession.
Any distrust of the permanence of laws, would
paralyze the faculties of man. Their perma-

1 nence is sacredly respected, and his faith therein
is perfect. The wheels and springs of man are
all set to the hypothesis of the permanence of
nature. We are not built like a ship to be toss-
5 ed, but like a house to stand. It is a natural
consequence of this structure, that, so long as
the active powers predominate over the reflective,
we resist with indignation any hint that nature
is more short-lived or mutable than spirit. The
10 broker, the wheelwright, the carpenter, the toll-
man, are much displeased at the intimation.

But whilst we acquiesce entirely in the permanence of natural laws, the question of the
absolute existence of nature, still remains open.
15 It is the uniform effect of culture on the human
mind, not to shake our faith in the stability of
particular phenomena, as of heat, water, azote ;
but to lead us to regard nature as a phenomenon, not a substance ; to attribute necessary
20 existence to spirit ; to esteem nature as an accident and an effect.

To the senses and the unrenewed understanding, belongs a sort of instinctive belief in the
5*

1 absolute existence of nature. In their view,
man and nature are indissolubly joined. Things
are ultimates, and they never look beyond their
sphere. The presence of Reason mars this
5 faith. The first effort of thought tends to relax
this despotism of the senses, which binds us to
nature as if we were a part of it, and shows us
nature aloof, and, as it were, afloat. Until this
higher agency intervened, the animal eye sees,
10 with wonderful accuracy, sharp outlines and colored surfaces. When the eye of Reason opens,
to outline and surface are at once added, grace
and expression. These proceed from imagination and affection, and abate somewhat of the
15 angular distinctness of objects. If the Reason
be stimulated to more earnest vision, outlines
and surfaces become transparent, and are no
longer seen ; causes and spirits are seen through
them. The best, the happiest moments of life,
20 are these delicious awakenings of the higher
powers, and the reverential withdrawing of nature before its God.

1 Let us proceed to indicate the effects of culture. 1. Our first institution in the Ideal philosophy is a hint from nature herself.

Nature is made to conspire with spirit to eman-
5 cipate us. Certain mechanical changes, a small
alteration in our local position apprizes us of a
dualism. We are strangely affected by seeing
the shore from a moving ship, from a balloon, or
through the tints of an unusual sky. The least
10 change in our point of view, gives the whole
world a pictorial air. A man who seldom rides,
needs only to get into a coach and traverse his
own town, to turn the street into a puppet-show.
The men, the women, — talking, running, bar-
15 tering, fighting, — the earnest mechanic, the
lounger, the beggar, the boys, the dogs, are un-
realized at once, or, at least, wholly detached
from all relation to the observer, and seen as apparent, not substantial beings. What new
20 thoughts are suggested by seeing a face of country quite familiar, in the rapid movement of the
rail-road car ! Nay, the most wonted objects,
(make a very slight change in the point of vis-

sion,) please us most. In a camera obscura, the butcher's cart, and the figure of one of our own family amuse us. So a protrait of a well-known face gratifies us. Turn the eyes upside down, by looking at the landscape through your legs, and how agreeable is the picture, though you have seen it any time these twenty years!

In these cases, by mechanical means, is suggested the difference between the observer and the spectacle, — between man and nature. Hence arises a pleasure mixed with awe; I may say, a low degree of the sublime is felt from the fact, probably, that man is hereby apprized, that, whilst the world is a spectacle, something in himself is stable.

2. In a higher manner, the poet communicates the same pleasure. By a few strokes he delineates, as on air, the sun, the mountain, the camp, the city, the hero, the maiden, not different from what we know them, but only lifted from the ground and afloat before the eye. He unfixes the land and the sea, makes them revolve around the axis of his primary thought, and dis-

poses them anew. Possessed himself by a heroic passion, he uses matter as symbols of it. The sensual man conforms thoughts to things; the poet conforms things to his thoughts. The one esteems nature as rooted and fast; the other, as fluid, and impresses his being thereon. To him, the refractory world is ductile and flexible; he invests dust and stones with humanity, and makes them the words of the Reason. The imagination may be defined to be, the use which the Reason makes of the material world. Shakspeare possesses the power of subordinating nature for the purposes of expression, beyond all poets. His imperial muse tosses the creation like a bauble from hand to hand, to embody any capricious shade of thought that is uppermost in his mind. The remotest spaces of nature are visited, and the farthest sundered things are brought together, by a subtile spiritual connexion. We are made aware that magnitude of material things is merely relative, and all objects shrink and expand to serve the passion of the poet. Thus, in his

sonnets, the lays of birds, the scents and dyes of flowers, he finds to be the *shadow* of his beloved; time, which keeps her from him, is his *chest*; the suspicion she has awakened, is her *ornament*;

> The ornament of beauty is Suspect,
> A crow which flies in heaven's sweetest air.

His passion is not the fruit of chance; it swells, as he speaks, to a city, or a state.

> No, it was builded far from accident;
> It suffers not in smiling pomp, nor falls
> Under the brow of thralling discontent;
> It fears not policy, that heretic,
> That works on leases of short numbered hours,
> But all alone stands hugely politic.

In the strength of his constancy, the Pyramids seem to him recent and transitory. And the freshness of youth and love dazzles him with its resemblance to morning.

> Take those lips away
> Which so sweetly were forsworn;
> And those eyes, — the break of day,
> Lights that do mislead the morn.

The wild beauty of this hyperbole, I may say, in passing, it would not be easy to match in literature.

This transfiguration which all material objects undergo through the passion of the poet, — this power which he exerts, at any moment, to magnify the small, to micrify the great, — might be illustrated by a thousand examples from his Plays. I have before me the Tempest, and will cite only these few lines.

> ARIEL. The strong based promontory
> Have I made shake, and by the spurs plucked up
> The pine and cedar.

Prospero calls for music to sooth the frantic Alonzo, and his companions;

> A solemn air, and the best comforter
> To an unsettled fancy, cure thy brains
> Now useless, boiled within thy skull.

Again;

> The charm dissolves apace
> And, as the morning steals upon the night,
> Melting the darkness, so their rising senses
> Begin to chase the ignorant fumes that mantle
> Their clearer reason.

Their understanding
Begins to swell : and the approaching tide
Will shortly fill the reasonable shores
That now lie foul and muddy.

The perception of real affinities between events, (that is to say, of *ideal* affinities, for those only are real,) enables the poet thus to make free with the most imposing forms and phenomena of the world, and to assert the predominance of the soul.

3. Whilst thus the poet delights us by animating nature like a creator, with his own thoughts, he differs from the philosopher only herein, that the one proposes Beauty as his main end ; the other Truth. But, the philosopher, not less than the poet, postpones the apparent order and relations of things to the empire of thought. "The problem of philosophy," according to Plato, " is, for all that exists conditionally, to find a ground unconditioned and absolute." It proceeds on the faith that a law determines all phenomena, which being known, the phenomena can be predicted. That law, when in the

mind, is an idea. Its beauty is infinite. The true philosopher and the true poet are one, and a beauty, which is truth, and a truth, which is beauty, is the aim of both. Is not the charm of one of Plato's or Aristotle's definitions, strictly like that of the Antigone of Sophocles? It is, in both cases, that a spiritual life has been imparted to nature ; that the solid seeming block of matter has been pervaded and dissolved by a thought ; that this feeble human being has penetrated the vast masses of nature with an informing soul, and recognised itself in their harmony, that is, seized their law. In physics, when this is attained, the memory disburthens itself of its cumbrous catalogues of particulars, and carries centuries of observation in a single formula.

Thus even in physics, the material is ever degraded before the spiritual. The astronomer, the geometer, rely on their irrefragable analysis, and disdain the results of observation. The sublime remark of Euler on his law of arches, " This will be found contrary to all experience,

6

yet is true ;" had already transferred nature into the mind, and left matter like an outcast corpse.

4. Intellectual science has been observed to beget invariably a doubt of the existence of matter. Turgot said, "He that has never doubted the existence of matter, may be assured he has no aptitude for metaphysical inquiries." It fastens the attention upon immortal necessary uncreated natures, that is, upon Ideas ; and in their beautiful and majestic presence, we feel that our outward being is a dream and a shade. Whilst we wait in this Olympus of gods, we think of nature as an appendix to the soul. We ascend into their region, and know that these are the thoughts of the Supreme Being. " These are they who were set up from everlasting, from the beginning, or ever the earth was. When he prepared the heavens, they were there ; when he established the clouds above, when he strengthened the fountains of the deep. Then they were by him, as one brought up with him. Of them took he counsel."

Their influence is proportionate. As objects of science, they are accessible to few men. Yet all men are capable of being raised by piety or by passion, into their region. And no man touches these divine natures, without becoming, in some degree, himself divine. Like a new soul, they renew the body. We become physically nimble and lightsome ; we tread on air ; life is no longer irksome, and we think it will never be so. No man fears age or misfortune or death, in their serene company, for he is transported out of the district of change. Whilst we behold unveiled the nature of Justice and Truth, we learn the difference between the absolute and the conditional or relative. We apprehend the absolute. As it were, for the first time, *we exist.* We become immortal, for we learn that time and space are relations of matter ; that, with a perception of truth, or a virtuous will, they have no affinity.

5. Finally, religion and ethics, which may be fitly called, — the practice of ideas, or the introduction of ideas into life, — have an analo-

gous effect with all lower culture, in degrading nature and suggesting its dependence on spirit. Ethics and religion differ herein; that the one is the system of human duties commencing from man; the other, from God. Religion includes the personality of God; Ethics does not. They are one to our present design. They both put nature under foot. The first and last lesson of religion is, "The things that are seen, are temporal; the things that are unseen are eternal." It puts an affront upon nature. It does that for the unschooled, which philosophy does for Berkeley and Viasa. The uniform language that may be heard in the churches of the most ignorant sects, is, — 'Contemn the unsubstantial shows of the world; they are vanities, dreams, shadows, unrealities; seek the realities of religion.' The devotee flouts nature. Some theosophists have arrived at a certain hostility and indignation towards matter, as the Manichean and Plotinus. They distrusted in themselves any looking back to these flesh-pots of Egypt. Plotinus was ashamed of his body. In

short, they might all better say of matter, what Michael Angelo said of external beauty, "it is the frail and weary weed, in which God dresses the soul, which he has called into time."

It appears that motion, poetry, physical and intellectual science, and religion, all tend to affect our convictions of the reality of the external world. But I own there is something ungrateful in expanding too curiously the particulars of the general proposition, that all culture tends to imbue us with idealism. I have no hostility to nature, but a child's love to it. I expand and live in the warm day like corn and melons. Let us speak her fair. I do not wish to fling stones at my beautiful mother, nor soil my gentle nest. I only wish to indicate the true position of nature in regard to man, wherein to establish man, all right education tends; as the ground which to attain is the object of human life, that is, of man's connexion with nature. Culture inverts the vulgar views of nature, and brings the mind to call that apparent, which it uses to call real, and that real, which

6*

it uses to call visionary. Children, it is true, believe in the external world. The belief that it appears only, is an afterthought, but with culture, this faith will as surely arise on the mind as did the first.

The advantage of the ideal theory over the popular faith, is this, that it presents the world in precisely that view which is most desirable to the mind. It is, in fact, the view which Reason, both speculative and practical, that is, philosophy and virtue, take. For, seen in the light of thought, the world always is phenomenal; and virtue subordinates it to the mind. Idealism sees the world in God. It beholds the whole circle of persons and things, of actions and events, of country and religion, not as painfully accumulated, atom after atom, act after act, in an aged creeping Past, but as one vast picture, which God paints on the instant eternity, for the contemplation of the soul. Therefore the soul holds itself off from a too trivial and microscopic study of the universal tablet. It respects the end too much, to immerse itself in

the means. It sees something more important in Christianity, than the scandals of ecclesiastical history or the niceties of criticism; and, very incurious concerning persons or miracles, and not at all disturbed by chasms of historical evidence, it accepts from God the phenomenon, as it finds it, as the pure and awful form of religion in the world. It is not hot and passionate at the appearance of what it calls its own good or bad fortune, at the union or opposition of other persons. No man is its enemy. It accepts whatsoever befals, as part of its lesson. It is a watcher more than a doer, and it is a doer, only that it may the better watch.

CHAPTER VII.

SPIRIT.

I⊤ is essential to a true theory of nature and of man, that it should contain somewhat progressive. Uses that are exhausted or that may be, and facts that end in the statement, cannot be all that is true of this brave lodging wherein man is harbored, and wherein all his faculties find appropriate and endless exercise. And all the uses of nature admit of being summed in one, which yields the activity of man an infinite scope. Through all its kingdoms, to the suburbs and outskirts of things, it is faithful to the cause whence it had its origin. It always speaks of Spirit. It suggests the absolute. It is a perpetual effect. It is a great shadow pointing always to the sun behind us.

The aspect of nature is devout. Like the figure of Jesus, she stands with bended head, and hands folded upon the breast. The happiest

man is he who learns from nature the lesson of worship.

Of that ineffable essence which we call Spirit, he that thinks most, will say least. We can foresee God in the coarse and, as it were, distant phenomena of matter; but when we try to define and describe himself, both language and thought desert us, and we are as helpless as fools and savages. That essence refuses to be recorded in propositions, but when man has worshipped him intellectually, the noblest ministry of nature is to stand as the apparition of God. It is the great organ through which the universal spirit speaks to the individual, and strives to lead back the individual to it.

When we consider Spirit, we see that the views already presented do not include the whole circumference of man. We must add some related thoughts.

Three problems are put by nature to the mind; What is matter? Whence is it? and Whereto? The first of these questions only, the ideal theory answers. Idealism saith: mat-

ter is a phenomenon, not a substance. Idealism acquaints us with the total disparity between the evidence of our own being, and the evidence of the world's being. The one is perfect; the other, incapable of any assurance; the mind is a part of the nature of things; the world is a divine dream, from which we may presently awake to the glories and certainties of day. Idealism is a hypothesis to account for nature by other principles than those of carpentry and chemistry. Yet, if it only deny the existence of matter, it does not satisfy the demands of the spirit. It leaves God out of me. It leaves me in the splendid labyrinth of my perceptions, to wander without end. Then the heart resists it, because it baulks the affections in denying substantive being to men and women. Nature is so pervaded with human life, that there is something of humanity in all, and in every particular. But this theory makes nature foreign to me, and does not account for that consanguinity which we acknowledge to it.

Let it stand then, in the present state of our knowledge, merely as a useful introductory hypothesis, serving to apprize us of the eternal distinction between the soul and the world.

But when, following the invisible steps of thought, we come to inquire, Whence is matter? and Whereto? many truths arise to us out of the recesses of consciousness. We learn that the highest is present to the soul of man, that the dread universal essence, which is not wisdom, or love, or beauty, or power, but all in one, and each entirely, is that for which all things exist, and that by which they are; that spirit creates; that behind nature, throughout nature, spirit is present; that spirit is one and not compound; that spirit does not act upon us from without, that is, in space and time, but spiritually, or through ourselves. Therefore, that spirit, that is, the Supreme Being, does not build up nature around us, but puts it forth through us, as the life of the tree puts forth new branches and leaves through the pores of the old. As a plant upon the earth, so a man rests

upon the bosom of God; he is nourished by unfailing fountains, and draws, at his need, inexhaustible power. Who can set bounds to the possibilities of man? Once inspire the infinite, by being admitted to behold the absolute natures of justice and truth, and we learn that man has access to the entire mind of the Creator, is himself the creator in the finite. This view, which admonishes me where the sources of wisdom and power lie, and points to virtue as to

> " The golden key
> Which opes the palace of eternity,"

carries upon its face the highest certificate of truth, because it animates me to create my own world through the purification of my soul.

The world proceeds from the same spirit as the body of man. It is a remoter and inferior incarnation of God, a projection of God in the unconscious. But it differs from the body in one important respect. It is not, like that, now subjected to the human will. Its serene order is inviolable by us. It is therefore, to us, the present expositor of the divine mind. It is a

fixed point whereby we may measure our departure. As we degenerate, the contrast between us and our house is more evident. We are as much strangers in nature, as we are aliens from God. We do not understand the notes of birds. The fox and the deer run away from us; the bear and tiger rend us. We do not know the uses of more than a few plants, as corn and the apple, the potato and the vine. Is not the landscape, every glimpse of which hath a grandeur, a face of him? Yet this may show us what discord is between man and nature, for you cannot freely admire a noble landscape, if laborers are digging in the field hard by. The poet finds something ridiculous in his delight, until he is out of the sight of men.

7

CHAPTER VIII.

PROSPECTS.

IN inquiries respecting the laws of the world and the frame of things, the highest reason is always the truest. That which seems faintly possible — it is so refined, is often faint and dim because it is deepest seated in the mind among the eternal verities. Empirical science is apt to cloud the sight, and, by the very knowledge of functions and processes, to bereave the student of the manly contemplation of the whole. The savant becomes unpoetic. But the best read naturalist who lends an entire and devout attention to truth, will see that there remains much to learn of his relation to the world, and that it is not to be learned by any addition or subtraction or other comparison of known quantities, but is arrived at by untaught sallies of the spirit, by a continual self-recovery, and by entire humility. He will perceive that there are far

more excellent qualities in the student than preciseness and infallibility; that a guess is often more fruitful than an indisputable affirmation, and that a dream may let us deeper into the secret of nature than a hundred concerted experiments.

For, the problems to be solved are precisely those which the physiologist and the naturalist omit to state. It is not so pertinent to man to know all the individuals of the animal kingdom, as it is to know whence and whereto is this tyrannizing unity in his constitution, which evermore separates and classifies things, endeavouring to reduce the most diverse to one form. When I behold a rich landscape, it is less to my purpose to recite correctly the order and superposition of the strata, than to know why all thought of multitude is lost in a tranquil sense of unity. I cannot greatly honor minuteness in details, so long as there is no hint to explain the relation between things and thoughts; no ray upon the *metaphysics* of conchology, of botany, of the arts, to show the relation of the forms of

flowers, shells, animals, architecture, to the mind, and build science upon ideas. In a cabinet of natural history, we become sensible of a certain occult recognition and sympathy in regard to the most bizarre forms of beast, fish, and insect. The American who has been confined, in his own country, to the sight of buildings designed after foreign models, is surprised on entering York Minster or St. Peter's at Rome, by the feeling that these structures are imitations also, — faint copies of an invisible archetype. Nor has science sufficient humanity, so long as the naturalist overlooks that wonderful congruity which subsists between man and the world ; of which he is lord, not because he is the most subtile inhabitant, but because he is its head and heart, and finds something of himself in every great and small thing, in every mountain stratum, in every new law of color, fact of astronomy, or atmospheric influence which observation or analysis lay open. A perception of this mystery inspires the muse of George Herbert, the beautiful psalmist of the

seventeenth century. The following lines are part of his little poem on Man.

"Man is all symmetry,
Full of proportions, one limb to another,
  And to all the world besides.
  Each part may call the farthest, brother ;
For head with foot hath private amity,
  And both with moons and tides.

"Nothing hath got so far
But man hath caught and kept it as his prey ;
  His eyes dismount the highest star ;
  He is in little all the sphere.
Herbs gladly cure our flesh, because that they
  Find their acquaintance there.

"For us, the winds do blow,
The earth doth rest, heaven move, and fountains flow ;
  Nothing we see, but means our good,
  As our delight, or as our treasure ;
The whole is either our cupboard of food,
  Or cabinet of pleasure.

"The stars have us to bed :
Night draws the curtain ; which the sun withdraws.
  Music and light attend our head.

7*

All things unto our flesh are kind,
  In their descent and being ; to our mind,
    In their ascent and cause.

"More servants wait on man
Than he 'll take notice of. In every path,
  He treads down that which doth befriend him
  When sickness makes him pale and wan.
Oh mighty love ! Man is one world, and hath
  Another to attend him."

The perception of this class of truths makes the eternal attraction which draws men to science, but the end is lost sight of in attention to the means. In view of this half-sight of science, we accept the sentence of Plato, that, " poetry comes nearer to vital truth than history." Every surmise and vaticination of the mind is entitled to a certain respect, and we learn to prefer imperfect theories, and sentences, which contain glimpses of truth, to digested systems which have no one valuable suggestion. A wise writer will feel that the ends of study and composition are best answered by announcing undiscovered regions of thought, and so

communicating, through hope, new activity to the torpid spirit.

I shall therefore conclude this essay with some traditions of man and nature, which a certain poet sang to me ; and which, as they have always been in the world, and perhaps reappear to every bard, may be both history and prophecy.

'The foundations of man are not in matter, but in spirit. But the element of spirit is eternity. To it, therefore, the longest series of events, the oldest chronologies are young and recent. In the cycle of the universal man, from whom the known individuals proceed, centuries are points, and all history is but the epoch of one degradation.

'We distrust and deny inwardly our sympathy with nature. We own and disown our relation to it, by turns. We are, like Nebuchadnezzar, dethroned, bereft of reason, and eating grass like an ox. But who can set limits to the remedial force of spirit ?

'A man is a god in ruins. When men are innocent, life shall be longer, and shall pass into the immortal, as gently as we awake from dreams. Now, the world would be insane and rabid, if these disorganizations should last for hundreds of years. It is kept in check by death and infancy. Infancy is the perpetual Messiah, which comes into the arms of fallen men, and pleads with them to return to paradise.

'Man is the dwarf of himself. Once he was permeated and dissolved by spirit. He filled nature with his overflowing currents. Out from him sprang the sun and moon; from man, the sun; from woman, the moon. The laws of his mind, the periods of his actions externized themselves into day and night, into the year and the seasons. But, having made for himself this huge shell, his waters retired; he no longer fills the veins and veinlets; he is shrunk to a drop. He sees, that the structure still fits him, but fits him colossally. Say, rather, once it fitted him, now it corresponds to him from far and on high.

He adores timidly his own work. Now is man the follower of the sun, and woman the follower of the'moon. Yet sometimes he starts in his slumber, and wonders at himself and his house, and muses strangely at the resemblance betwixt him and it. He perceives that if his law is still paramount, if still he have elemental power, "if his word is sterling yet in nature," it is not conscious power, it is not inferior but superior to his will. It is Instinct.' Thus my Orphic poet sang.

At present, man applies to nature but half his force. He works on the world with his understanding alone. He lives in it, and masters it by a penny-wisdom; and he that works most in it, is but a half-man, and whilst his arms are strong and his digestion good, his mind is imbruted and he is a selfish savage. His relation to nature, his power over it, is through the understanding; as by manure; the economic use of fire, wind, water, and the mariner's needle; steam, coal, chemical agriculture; the repairs of the human body by the dentist and the sur-

geon. This is such a resumption of power, as if a banished king should buy his territories inch by inch, instead of vaulting at once into his throne. Meantime, in the thick darkness, there are not wanting gleams of a better light, — occasional examples of the action of man upon nature with his entire force, — with reason as well as understanding. Such examples are; the traditions of miracles in the earliest antiquity of all nations; the history of Jesus Christ; the achievements of a principle, as in religious and political revolutions, and in the abolition of the Slave-trade; the miracles of enthusiasm, as those reported of Swedenborg, Hohenlohe, and the Shakers; many obscure and yet contested facts, now arranged under the name of Animal Magnetism; prayer; eloquence; self-healing; and the wisdom of children. These are examples of Reason's momentary grasp of the sceptre; the exertions of a power which exists not in time or space, but an instantaneous in-streaming causing power. The difference between the actual and the ideal force of man is happi-

ly figured by the schoolmen, in saying, that the knowledge of man is an evening knowledge, *vespertina cognitio*, but that of God is a morning knowledge, *matutina cognitio*.

The problem of restoring to the world original and eternal beauty, is solved by the redemption of the soul. The ruin or the blank, that we see when we look at nature, is in our own eye. The axis of vision is not coincident with the axis of things, and so they appear not transparent but opake. The reason why the world lacks unity, and lies broken and in heaps, is, because man is disunited with himself. He cannot be a naturalist, until he satisfies all the demands of the spirit. Love is as much its demand, as perception. Indeed, neither can be perfect without the other. In the uttermost meaning of the words, thought is devout, and devotion is thought. Deep calls unto deep. But in actual life, the marriage is not celebrated. There are innocent men who worship God after the tradition of their fathers, but their sense of duty has not yet extended to the use of all their

1   faculties.   And there are patient naturalists,
but they freeze their subject under the wintry
light of the understanding.   Is not prayer also
a study of truth, — a sally of the soul into the
5   unfound infinite ? No man ever prayed heartily,
without learning something.   But when a faithful thinker, resolute to detach every object from
personal relations, and see it in the light of
thought, shall, at the same time, kindle science
10 with the fire of the holiest affections, then will
God go forth anew into the creation.

   It will not need, when the mind is prepared
for study, to search for objects.   The invariable
mark of wisdom is to see the miraculous in the
15 common.   What is a day ?   What is a year ?
What is summer ? What is woman ? What is a
child ? What is sleep ? To our blindness, these
things seem unaffecting.   We make fables to
hide the baldness of the fact and conform it, as
20 we say, to the higher law of the mind.   But
when the fact is seen under the light of an idea,
the gaudy fable fades and shrivels.   We behold
the real higher law.   To the wise, therefore, a

1   fact is true poetry, and the most beautiful of fables.
These wonders are brought to our own door.
You also are a man.   Man and woman, and their
social life, poverty, labor, sleep, fear, fortune,
5   are known to you.   Learn that none of these
things is superficial, but that each phenomenon
hath its roots in the faculties and affections of
the mind.   Whilst the abstract question occupies your intellect, nature brings it in the con-
10 crete to be solved by your hands.   It were a
wise inquiry for the closet, to compare, point by
point, especially at remarkable crises in life,
our daily history, with the rise and progress of
ideas in the mind.

15   So shall we come to look at the world with
new eyes.   It shall answer the endless inquiry
of the intellect, — What is truth ? and of the
affections, — What is good ? by yielding itself
passive to the educated Will.   Then shall come
20 to pass what my poet said ; ' Nature is not fixed
but fluid.   Spirit alters, moulds, makes it.   The
immobility or bruteness of nature, is the absence
of spirit ; to pure spirit, it is fluid, it is volatile,
8

1   it is obedient.   Every spirit builds itself a house ;
and beyond its house, a world ; and beyond its
world, a heaven.   Know then, that the world
exists for you.   For you is the phenomenon per-
5   fect.   What we are, that only can we see.   All
that Adam had, all that Cæsar could, you have
and can do.   Adam called his house, heaven and
earth ; Cæsar called his house, Rome ; you perhaps call yours, a cobler's trade ; a hundred
10 acres of ploughed land ; or a scholar's garret.
Yet line for line and point for point, your dominion is as great as theirs, though without fine
names.   Build ; therefore, your own world.   As
fast as you conform your life to the pure idea in
15 your mind, that will unfold its great proportions.
A correspondent revolution in things will attend
the influx of the spirit.   So fast will disagreeable appearances, swine, spiders, snakes, pests,
mad-houses, prisons, enemies, vanish ; they are
20 temporary and shall be no more seen.   The
sordor and filths of nature, the sun shall dry up,
and the wind exhale.   As when the summer
comes from the south, the snow-banks melt, and

1   the face of the earth becomes green before it,
so shall the advancing spirit create its ornaments along its path, and carry with it the
beauty it visits, and the song which enchants it ;
5   it shall draw beautiful faces, and warm hearts,
and wise discourse, and heroic acts, around its
way, until evil is no more seen.   The kingdom of
man over nature, which cometh not with observation, — a dominion such as now is beyond his
10 dream of God, — he shall enter without more
wonder than the blind man feels who is gradually restored to perfect sight.'

AN INDEX—CONCORDANCE.*

---

* All lines on the printed page, except the running title, are counted in the numbering system used herein. The page number appears to the left of the decimal point; the line number is on the right. "V" before a page number refers the reader to the "Table of Verbal Variants" in the *Introduction*. "TP" stands for the title page. "Nature" throughout is indicated by "N." Other abbreviations will explain themselves.

EVERY scripture to be interpreted, 44.18

EVIDENCE: of our own being and of the world's, 78.3; a true theory is its own e., 7.3; soul not disturbed by historical e., 75.6

EVIL no more seen, 95.7

EXAMPLES: of Reason's grasp, 90.18; of man's full force, 90.6

EXCELLENCE, standard of, 58.12

EXCESS: creation is e. of love, 29.7

EXERCISE OF WILL in each act, 50.13

EXHILARATION enjoyed, 12.13

EXISTENCE: of matter doubted, 70.7; of world has no assurance, 78.5; absolute e. of N., 61.14

EXPERIENCE: blended with action, 39.16; parallel in all trades, 53.15

EXPERIMENTS, concerted, 83.6

EXPOSITOR of divine mind, 80.23

EXPOSITORS: vital e. needed, 44.17

EXPRESSION: of earth altered by crops, 23.13; e. of N. is single, 29.16; N. subordinated for e., 65.14

EYE: agent in beauty appreciation, 19.12; illuminated by sun, 11.14; integrates objects, 19.15; is best composer, 20.1; is best of artists, 19.13; pleased with N's forms, 20.10; reads omens, VTP; structure and perspective, 19.14; transforms ugly particulars into symmetrical landscape, 19.18; yields to male and female forms, 57.14; right action fills e., 56.20; poet's figures float before e., 64.21; plastic power of human e., 19.7; blank is in our own e., 91.7; animal e. sees outlines, 62.9; to the attentive e., 23.6; growth in e. of leaf, 51.19; e. (the mind) accompanied by forms, 57.13; e. of Reason beholds more, 62.11

EYE-BALL becomes transparent, 13.6

EYEBROW, raising of the, 33.2

EYE-HEALTH demands horizon, 21.7

EYES: upside down, 64.4; an exception, 13.2; will purge e., 44.22; new e. shall see world, 93.16; leaving me my e., 13.2; see SIGHT

F

FABLE: fades and shrivels, 92.22; of Proteus true, 54.19

FABLES: to hide baldness of fact, 92.18 similar to proverbs, 42.10; fact is most beautiful of f., 93.1

FACE: of earth becomes green, 95.1; of world impresses, 29.5; f. to f. in a glass, 41.19; iron f. of Debt, 47.22; well-known f. in portrait, 64.4

FACES: of the same All, 30.21; beautiful f. attend spirit, 95.5

FACT: baldness of, 92.19; conformed to law of mind, 92.19; in intellectual philosophy, 35.22; is last issue of spirit, 44.6; is true poetry, 93.1; linked with human N., 35.16; moral or intellectual, 32.17; most beautiful of fables, 93.1; of astronomy, 84.20; under light of idea, 92.21; natural f. selected as picture, 42.11

FACTS: have analogical value, 42.21; isolated and without value, 35.15; most trivial, 35.19; obscure and con-

tested, 90.16; shaped to character, 50.20; single and barren, 35.15; ending in statement, 76.6; trivial in primary sense, 42.20; natural f. are symbols, 32.8; 33.19; signs of natural f., 32.7; 32.11; spiritual f. symbolized, 32.8; 33.19; spiritual f. and natural symbols, 37.3

FACULTIES: find endless exercise, 76.8; man's f. in danger, 60.23; f. of mind, 93.7; all f. not used, 92.1

FACULTY: new f. of Soul, 45.8

FAERIE, realms of, 22.4

FAITH: of man constant, 60.10; that a law governs all, 68.21; culture gives a new f., 74.4; popular f. vs. Ideal theory, 74.7

FALSEHOOD ruins language, 38.6

FAMILY, member of our own, 64.3

FARM: is mute gospel, 53.8; is sacred emblem, 53.11

FARMER: conversation of, 37.16; first steps of, 49.13

FARMS: crop in surrounding, 23.12; Horizon is best part of, 11.9; twenty or thirty, 11.2

FATHER is term for Spirit, 35.4

FATHERS, sepulchres of the, 5.3

FEAR: glad to the brink of, V12.14; known to you, 93.4; almost I f. to think how glad I am, 12.14

FEEDING and working in animals, 28.16

FEMALE and male forms, 57.14

FEW: sun seen by f., 11.12; f. adults see N., 11.11

FIELD, hours in, 23.8; is floor, workyard, play-ground etc., 16.8; laborers digging in, 81.14; wind blows vapor to, 16.18; Miller owns this f., 11.3; see WOODS

FIELDS: last stack in the, 53.13; more wool and flax in, 5.18

FIGURE: N. like f. of Jesus, 76.19; f. of one of family, 64.2

FIGURES: poet's f. afloat, 64.21; used by savages, 36.23

FINAL CAUSE: of Universe, 59.9; of world considered, 15.3; parts of f.c. enumerated, 15.5; see CAUSE

FIRE: economic use of, 89.21; serves man, 16.7; f. of holiest affections, 92.10

FIRMAMENT, virtues shine in, 34.15

FIRMNESS taught by rock, 54.2

FIRST STEPS teach, 49.13

FISH: forms of, 84.5

FISHERMAN learns firmness, 54.3

FISHES, cloud floats like, 21.16

FLAKES: pink f. of clouds, 22.12

FLAME, trees become, 22.19

FLAMES imitated, 20.14

FLESHPOTS of Egypt, 72.22

FLIPPER of fossil saurus, 55.5

FLOODS of life stream around us, 5.12

FLORAS are dry catalogues, 35.17

FLOWERS: and affections, 34.4; dead calices of f., 22.22; forms of, 84.1; reflect wisdom, 10.14; scents and dyes, 66.1

FLUX of things, river symbolizes, 34.10

FOOD teaches lesson, 46.7

FOOLISH: have no range, 49.4; think men alike, 49.6

FOOLS and savages helpless, 77.8

FOOT, N. puts under f., 72.8

FORCE: actual and ideal in man, 90.23; man exerts but half, 89.13; remedial f. of Spirit, 87.22; entire f. of man on N., 90.7

FORCES: mechanical f. teach, 46.8

FOREST, tropical, 51.19

FORM: reducing many to one, 83.14; spires of VTP; N. glorious with f., 51.15; Spirit prefers human f., 57.6; every f. reveals its hidden life, 45.3; words and actions introduce us to human f., 57.3

FORMS: ascending order of, 57.5; bear marks of injury, 57.17; bizarre f., 84.5; male and female, 57.14; marred and defective, 57.18; of birds, 20.13; of flowers, shells, etc., 84.1; related to mind, 83.23; tedious variety of, 54.19; unwieldy and eccentric, 84.5; primary f. give delight in and for themselves, 19.8; individual f. please eye, 20.9; new f. of beauty, 29.8; poet's freedom with f., 68.8; material f. manifest Spirit, 43.22; sex f. are entrances, 57.23

FORMULA: centuries in single, 69.16

FORTUNE affected by Understanding, 48.14; is known to you, 93.4

FOSSIL SAURUS, flipper of, 55.5

FOUNDATIONS of man in Spirit, 87.9

FOUNTAIN-PIPES: forms rest like, 57.21

FOUNTAINS nourish man, 80.2

FOX, cunning man called, 34.1; f. and deer run away, 81.6

FRAME of things, 82.4; will suit the picture, 27.15

FREE WILL in our dealings with N., 25.10

FREEDOM arises and shines, 34.16

FRENCH PHILOSOPHER, 44.8

FRESHNESS of youth and Shak., 66.18

FRICTION diminished by rails, 17.7

FRIEND: answers to affection of soul, 58.6; character retains effect, 58.16; character converted, 58.16; lost by death, 14.19; name sounds foreign, 13.9; withdrawn from sight, 58.19

FRIENDS: coextensive with our idea, 58.4; hard to analyze, 58.9; in youth and adult life, 58.3; increase respect for God's resources, 58.13; like skies and waters, 58.4; satisfy a desire, 58.7; supply standard of excellence, 58.12; we cannot choose but love, 58.10; new f. supplant old, 58.14

FRIVOLOUS flout Ideal theory, 60.16

FROM such as this have I etc., 57.8

FROST, stem and stubble rimed with, 22.23

FROZEN MUSIC, architecture is, 55.8

FUNCTION, animal, 51.20

FUNCTIONS, knowledge of, 82.10

FURROW, first of spring, 53.11

G

GALA, river is perpetual, 24.5

N

NAMES, not fine, 94.13

NAPOLEON, era of, 17.14

NARRATIVE, simple, 27.3

NATION, long-civilized, 38.16

NATIONAL COUNCILS, agitation in, 40.10

NATIONS: repair wrongs, 17.20; proverbs of, 42.10

NATURAL ACTION is graceful, 25.4

NATURAL FACT selected as picture, 42.11

NATURAL HISTORY: and human hist., 35.16; cabinet of, 84.3; facts barren, 35.14; lively when married, 35.17; use of, 32.12

NATURAL LAWS permanent, 61.13

NATURAL OBJECTS: help us express ideas, 40.20; impress the mind, 10.8; manifold, 10.21

NATURAL PROCESS: version of moral sentence, 53.3

NATURALIST: best read, 82.13; has much to learn, 82.14; omits real problems, 83.7; overlooks congruity, 84.13; man cannot be a n., 91.14

NATURALISTS: patient n. freeze the subject with the Understanding, 92.1

NATURE: as beautiful as one's own n., 13.18; mind is part of n. of things, 78.6; n. of justice and truth shown, 71.13

NATURE (special sense): a discipline, 46.4; a perpetual effect, 76.15; a setting that fits a comic or mourning piece, 12.8; a show, if hunted, 24.12; a thing which doth only do, but not know, TP; absolute existence of, 61.14; 62.1; affronted by religion, 72.11; ally of religion, 52.1; aloof and afloat, 62.8; altered and moulded by spirit, 93.21; always speaks of spirit, 76.14; an accident and effect, 61.20; an apparent ruin or blank, 91.7; an interpreter, 37.17; N. and art are the NOT ME, 7.11; N. and God perceived directly, 5.5; N. and man joined, 62.2; N. and Soul compose universe, 7.9; N. and a wise man, 10.11; answers private purpose, 52.7; appendix to soul, 70.14; as interpreter of the will, 38.8; aspect is devout, 76.18; assistance given to genius, 27.28; beauty shines in man's breast, 49.22; becomes ancillary to man, 28.3; bows to man's dominion, 50.22; brings in concrete forms for man's exercise, 93.9; changes correspond to states of mind, 12.4; (chap. heading), 9.1; a chronometer, 23.6; clock of N. and states of mind, 12.5; colossal to 41.6; a common denominator, 29.20; common definition of, 7.20; conspires with Spirit to free us, 63.4; conveys world's meaning, 59.4; deaf and dumb, 57.20; decorates man, 27.13; degraded by religion and ethics, 72.1; deifies us, 21.22; delights childhood, delights young and old, 10.17; dependent on Spirit, 72.2; describing its own design, 6.13; dice ever loaded, 49.15; dictionary for man, 41.3; discipline—two particulars of, 50.11; discord with man, 81.12; distrust of N. and its results, 60.22; doctrine is abstruse,

44.14; dowery of each rational creature, 25.9; end is not compromise, 60.20; every particular in N., 54.20; faithful to originating cause, 76.13; filled with man's overflowing currents, 88.12; final cause of, 31.3; fits man colossally, 88.21; flouted by devotee, 72.18; fluid and volatile to pure Spirit, 93.23; follows man's steps, 27.11; forms good heed in us, 49.9; forms please eye, 20.9; forms radically alike, 29.17; garment reflects Unity, 56.5; given a spiritual life, 69.7; gives tedious training, 47.11; gives rose and violet, 27.11; glorious with form etc., 51.14; grammar of man, 41.3; grandeur and grace of N., 27.12; great shadow pointing to sun behind us, 76.16; hands folded upon breast, 76.20; has one expression, 29.16; her heaps and rubbish, 49.15; hints of Idealism, 63.3; hours sensible to keen observer, 23.17; hypothesis of permanence, 61.3; immobility and bruteness is absence of Spirit, 93.22; impression on the human mind, 8.4; in apocalypse of mind? 60.12; N. in miniature is art, 29.13; in presence of N., 11.21; inexhaustibility of, 52.10; integrity of impression, 10.20; is but an image of wisdom, TP; is discipline of Understanding, 47.1; is grand cipher, 41.4; is ideal to Emerson, 60.14; is last thing of soul, TP; is man's kingdom, 25.12; is material, process and result, 16.14; is medicinal, 21.2; is metaphor of mind, 41.17; is sea of forms, 29.17; kindles wild delight, 11.22; kingdoms of, 76.12; laws permanent, 61.12; lends pomp and riches, 52.2; light flows into mind, 40.2; made foreign by Idealism, 78.20; made to serve, 50.21; man's brave lodging, 76.7; man's house, 89.4; man's huge shell, 88.19; may be owned or disowned, 25.11; meanings of word, 7.8; meek as Savior's ass, 50.22; ministry to man, 16.13; moral influence on each one, 53.21; moral side of, 44.13; mouthpiece of universal Spirit, 77.13; my beautiful mother, 73.15; my gentle nest, 73.16; never a toy, 10.13; never omits moral, 52.9; never wears mean appearance, 10.10; noblest ministry as apparition of God, 77.11; not always tricked in holiday attire, 14.10; not built up around us, 79.20; not explicable by carpentry, etc., 78.10; not fixed but fluid, 93.20; not rivaled by art, 24.3; not shorter-lived than Spirit, 61.9; not yet put to use, 41.6; offers man raw materials, 51.1; once fitted man, 88.22; our house, 81.3; pardons no mistakes, 49.10; parts conspire to Discipline, 59.6; penetrated to bone by ethical, 52.5; perfection of, 10.3; permanence maintained, 60.23; permanent objects of, 45.1; permeated by spirit, 79.14; pervaded by correspondences, 35.6; pervaded with human life, 78.18; phenomenon, not substance, 61.18; pierced with informing soul, 69.12; poetical sense of, 10.19; procession of, 60.21; prodigality outweighs misery, 15.17; proportioned care, 47.8; public and universal function, 52.9; put forth thru us, 79.20; put under foot, 72.8; **puts three problems to mind, 77.20; refers to essences unchanged by man,**

7.20; regarded by senses and Understanding, 61.22; remotest spaces visited, 65.17; requires temperate use of pleasures, 14.9; revealed better by dream, 83.4; satisfies by loveliness, 21.11; says he is my creature, 11.23; secret impenetrable, 10.12; secret of, 83.5; seen as fluid by poet, 65.6; seen by few adults, 11.11; serves many ends, 52.11; shouts moral laws, 51.22; sordor and filths of, 94.21; source for Jesus, David etc., 52.3; stable despite Idealism, 60.18; stands like figure of Jesus, 76.19; stands with bended head, 76.19; stoned, 73.15; stretches arms, 27.9; strives to lead individual back to Spirit, 77.14; subordinated by Shak., 65.13; substantial existence? 60.11; suggests absolute, 76.15; symbol of spirit, 32.10; teaches lesson of worship, 77.1; test of a true theory of N., 7.4; the great apparition, 6.14; third use is language, 32.3; thoroughly mediate, 50.21; thru alembic of man, 30.11; tossed like bauble, 65.15; totality of, 29.23; traditions of man and N., 87.4; trains Understanding and Reason, 46.10; transferred into the mind, 70.1; true position in regard to man, 73.17; undermost garment of, 56.5; used in both senses, 7.16; useful and venerable, 60.12; unity apprehended, 54.12; values of, 7.14; vehicle of thought, 32.4; wears colors of the spirit, 14.14; what would it say? 22.15; floods of life, 5.12; wisdom of N. is ineffable, 40.1; works innumerable, 29.15; works thru will of man, 30.12; withdraws before God, 62.21; yea is yea, 49.10;—action proportioned to N., 5.14; action related to N., 56.21; all N's uses can be summed in one, 76.10; appearances in N. correspond to mental states, 33.20; beauty in N. not ultimate, 30.22; beauty of N's first works, 30.13; brute N. knows no words, 57.1; child's love of N., 73.12; deny our sympathy with N., 87.17; diff. between man and N., 64.10; doubt regarding N's existence, 59.8; embosomed for a season in N., 5.11; Emerson has no hostility to N., 73.12; essential to a true theory of N., 76.3; ethical penetrates bone of N., 52.5; Idealism is hypothesis to account for N., 78.9; kingdom of man over N., 95.8; life in harmony with N., 44.21; lover of N. described, 11.16; man acts with all his force on N., 90.7; man applies but half his force to N., 89.12; in harmony with law of N., 69.13; man's adjustment to N., 27.14; man's connection with N., 73.20; man's word sterling yet in N., 89.8; moral law at centre of N., 53.4; moral N. and laws of matter, 41.18; our least debt to N., 33.16; our relation to N. owned and disowned, 87.18; poet impresses self on N., 65.6; primary writers hold to N., 38.21; Reason in relation to N., 34.23; Reason mars faith in N. 62.4; rule of one art holds in all N., 56.2; scales as wide as N., 49.3; science aims to find theory of N., 6.17; senses bind us to N., 62.6; sensualist sees N. as rooted, 65.5; spirit behind and thru N., 79.14; strangers in N., 81.4; things refer to

love of, 44.21; nature unveiled, 71.13; never complete in words, 56.17; perception of, 71.19; philosopher seeks, 68.15; studied in prayer, 92.4; what is t.? 93.17; action precedes apprehension of, 6.11; language and love of t., 37.22; moral t. in picture or parable, 42.12; prayer a study of t., 92.3; such t is absolute Ens, 56.13; unconscious t. defined, 45.9; far from road to t., 6.21

TRUTHS: arise out of consciousness, 79.7; writers pretend to see t., 38.17; discipline of the Understanding in intellectual t., 47.1; this class of t., 86.10

TUITION: careful t. of N., 47.10

TURGOT quoted, 70.6

TWENTY YEARS, these, 64.7

TYPE of human hand detected, 55.4

U

UGLY is temporary, 94.18

ULTIMATES: things regarded as, 62.3

UNCONSCIOUS, world is projection of God in, 80.18

UNDERSTANDING: acts in separation and gradation, 49.2; affects character, 48.14; U. alone is used, 89.14; discipline of U. intellectually, 47.1; freezes subjects, 92.2; gymnastics of, 48.11; how it functions, 46.14; inequality in education of, 48.15; is noon, England of senses, 22.4; man lives in, 89.14; mastered by penny-wisdom, 89.14; relates man to N., 89.18; wintry light of, 92.3; words affect, 38.13; from U. to Spirit, 48.12; U. and Reason both used, 90.7; U. and Reason educated, 46.10; unrenewed U. trusts N., 61.22

UNISON with N's works, 27.16

UNITY: is central in actions, 56.15; in man's constitution, 83.12; in variety, 29.16; 54.13; intimate, 56.3; lies under garment of N., 56.5; of N. apprehended, 54.12; pervades thought, 56.6; separates and classifies things, 83.13; source and purpose, 83.11; source in Universal Spirit, 56.6; tranquil sense of, 83.18; tries to reduce to one form, 83.14; things ran back to, 54.17

UNIVERSE: becomes transparent, 43.11; composed of N. and Soul, 7.9; described, 16.2; expressed in beauty, 30.18; Final Cause of, 59.9; less, man greater, 49.23; lighted by stars, 10.4; original relation to, 5.7; property of all, 25.7; unexplored, 50.4; what angels invented? 16.1; see WORLD, NATURE

UNIVERSAL: essence defined, 79.10; U. Spirit is source of Unity, 56.6

UNKNOWN challenges us, 50.4

UNLIKENESS in things superficial, 55.7

UNREALITIES of world, 72.17

UNREALITY: of N. if hunted, 24.13; mocks us with u., 24.13

USE: of all faculties, 91.23; u. of commodity for itself is mean, 52.14; of fire, wind etc., 89.20; N. never is exhausted by u., 52.10; human life preferred to technical u., 42.7

USES: multitude classified, 15.4; of a few plants, 81.8; of N. can be summed in one, 76.10; u. that are exhausted, 76.5; other u. included in discipline, 46.5

UTTERMOST: extend to u., 30.15

V

VALLEY, live repose of, 22.17

VALUES, casting the sum of N's, 7.14

VALUES AND WANTS, training in, 52.22

VANE, death of Sir Harry, 26.18

VANITIES of world, 72.16

VARIETY: about water-courses, 23.22; of N's works, 29.15; unity of, 54.13; endless v. of things, 54.14; same entity in v., 54.18 v. provides identical impression, 54.15

VATICINATION of mind, 86.16

VEGETABLE and man, occult relationship, 13.21

VEGETATION, change of, 51.18

VEHICLE of thought, N. is, 32.4

VEINS and veinlets, and man, 88.20

VERITIES, eternal, 82.8

VERSION of a moral sentence, 53.3

VESPERTINA cognitio, 91.3

VESTMENT OF THOUGHT, an image is, 39.13

VIASA, philosophy aids, 72.13

VIEW: admonishes and animates me, 80.9ff.; points to virtue, 80.10

VIEWS: culture inverts vulgar v., 73.21

VINE and potato, 81.9

VINEGAR is the son of wine, 42.17

VIOLET and rose as adornment, 27.12

VIRTUE: all things obey, 25.15; is practical Reason, 74.11; love of, 44.22; relation of things to, 28.7; sea of, 57.22; sits with Russell, 27.5; subjects world to mind, 74.13; this view points to v., 80.10; beauty is God's mark on v., 25.3

VIRTUOUS MAN is in unison with N., 27.15

VISIBLE WORLD is dial plate, 41.19

VISION: axis of, 91.9; change in point of v., 63.23

VISIONARY becomes real, 74.1

VITRUVIUS: said architect should be musician, V55.8½

VOLCANO, cinders used to cook eggs, 41.8

W

WANTS, training in values and, 52.22

WARDROBE of past, faded, 5.17

WARRANTY-DEEDS for the horizon, V11.9

WASHING, see OPERATIONS OF MAN

WATER: cannot be spun, 49.1; economic use of, 89.21; good to drink, 48.22; ocean of w. beneath, 16.3; serves man, 16.7; stability of, 61.16

WATER-COURSES: variety about, 23.21

WATERS: friends like, 58.5; moral sentiment in, 53.20; man's w. retired, 88.19

WAVES: significant? 41.12; w. and winds, 25.17

WE EXIST for the first time, 71.17

WE SEE only what we are, 94.5

WEAPON of power, new, V45.12

WEED, beauty is frail and weary, 73.3

WEEDS and plants preach, 53.9

WEIGHT, smallest lifts greatest, 42.1

WHEAT AND CHAFF preach, 53.9

WHEAT-EAR imitated, 20.12

WHEELS and springs of man, 61.2

WHEELWRIGHT defends N., 61.10

WHENCE, WHERETO, matter? 77.21; 79.6

WHOLE: contemplation of, 82.11; each related to, 54.21; is greater than its part, 41.22; w. only is beautiful, 30.3

WHOLE OF NATURE is metaphor of mind, 41.16

WIDOW fears debt, 47.22

WILDERNESS, something dearer in, 13.14

WILL: acts in each event, 50.13; beauty combined with human w., 25.2; educated, 93.19; events reduced under w., 50.17; man's w. mixed with N., 7.23; power superior to his w., 89.9; stands in God's w., 43.2; a virtuous will in space and time, 71.20; N. uses w., of man, 30.12; Thy w. be done, 50.16; energy of w. and thought, 25.14; world becomes w., 51.8

WIND: blows vapor to field, 16.18; economic use of, 89.21; means spirit, 32.20; sows seed, 16.16; w. will exhale sordor and filths, 94.22; I dilate and conspire with w., 21.21

WINDS: drive stormy clouds, 54.5; w. and waves, 25.17

WINE: vinegar is son of, 42.17

WING: given to words, 51.5; imitated 20.13

WINKELRIED, Arnold, 26.3

WINTER: pleasant as summer, graces of w. scenery, 23.4

WISDOM: alone not universal essence, 79.10; imparted by N., 40.1; in separation and gradation, 49.2; of children, 90.18; of one's best hour, 10.16; to see miraculous in common, 92.14; where sources lie, 80.9; friends character becomes w., 58.18

WISE see fact as true poetry, 92.23

WIT OF MAN combines phenomena into useful arts, 17.2

WOMAN: a congruent sensation, 59.14; follower of moon, 89.2; is known to you, 93.3; source of moon, 88.15; is what? 92.16

WOMEN seen from coach, 63.14

WONDER of blind man, 95.11

WONDERS brought to our door, 93.2

WOODS: affirm N's power to repair our ills, 12.22; decorum and sanctity in, 12.19; liberate man, 12.15; make man a child, 12.17; no fatigue in, 12.21; offer perpetual youth, 12.17; plantations of God, 12.18; poet and orator in, 40.3; restore self-confidence, 12.23; return us to reason and faith, 12.22; suggest man's occult relation to vegetable, 13.20; wave again, 40.15; fear of calamity lost in w., 13.1; see WILDERNESS

WOOL: good to wear; cannot be drunk, 48.23; w. and flax in fields, 5.18

WORD: man's w. still sterling, 89.8

WORD-BUILDING process, 33.7

WORDS: angels of persuasion, 51.5; break and chop the truth, 56.18; em-

blematic, 33.17; introduce the human
form, 57.4; lose all power, 38.13;
made of air by man, 51.4; never
cover all truth, 56.17; of history and
natural facts, 42.10; of spiritual import, 33.15; old and perverted, 38.9;
origin of, 32.16; signs of facts, 32.7;
32.11; tied to visible things, 39.2; finite
organs of mind, 56.16; w. and actions
not of brutes, 57.1; w. and material
appearances, 32.18

WORK: aim of N's gifts that man
should w., 18.8; man adores his own
w., 89.1; w. of insects, 35.21; see
DILIGENCE, LABOR, ACTIVITY

WORK OF ART, produced, 29.10

WORKS, demand our own, 6.2

WORKS OF NATURE: all different,
29.14; first 30.13; unison with, 27.16

WORLD: a divine dream, 78.7; a fixed
point for measurement, 81.1; achieved
by thought and will, 25.14; always
phenomenal, 74.12; an appearance,
afterthought, 74.3; an open book,
45.2; becomes realized will, 51.8; believed in by children, 74.1; beyond
it is heaven, 94.2; brave lodging of
man, 76.7; build your own w., 94.13;
built beyond house, 94.2; called
Kosmos, 19.5; checked by death and
infancy, 88.6; create my own, 80.15;
different from body, 80.19; epitome
seen in work of art, 29.12; existence
without proof, 78.5; exists for you,
94.4; exists to satisfy, 30.14; expositor of divine mind, 80.23; face
changed, 17.13; face impresses, 29.4;
has pictorial air, 63.11; head and

heart is man, 84.17; is emblematic,
41.15; is flexible to poet, 65.7; is our
house, 81.3; is ours by constitution,
25.13; is remoter incarnation of God,
80.17; is spectacle, 64.14; is the double
of man, 51.9; justified as appearance
only, 59.11; lacks unity; lies broken
and in heaps, 91.12; likeness appears
in particle, 55.1; meaning given to
man, 59.4; most subtle inhabitant is
man, 84.16; original beauty of, 91.6;
passive to educated will, 93.19; presented best to the mind, 74.7; problem
of restoring w., 91.5; w. proceeds
from same spirit as body of man,
80.16; a projection of God in the unconscious, 80.18; reality of external
w., 73.7; relation to man, 82.15; seen
with new eyes, 93.15; shows of w.,
72.16; subordinated to mind, 74.13;
taken into self, 25.15; unlike body,
not subjected to human will, 80.19;
w. vs. soul, 79.4; will answer endless
inquiry of intellect, 93.16; would be
insane, 88.4; congruity between w.
and man, 84.14; Idealism sees w. in
God, 74.14; dial plate of invisible w.,
41.20; man is lord of w., 84.15; man
uses Understanding on w., 89.13; new
w. clothes his form, 26.14; problem
since beginning of w., 43.13; Reason's
use of the material w., 65.11; terminus
of unseen w., 44.7; visible w. is dial
plate of invisible, 41.19; see
NATURE

WORLD OF THOUGHT, Reason's,
46.18

WORLD ORDER inviolable by us,
80.22

WORLDS revolve and mingle, 60.5

WORM strives to be man, VTP

WORSHIP: demand our own, 6.3;
happiest man learns, 77.2

WORST, the "not good," 49.7

WRINKLE, winds leave no, 54.6

WRITER: wise w. seeks the undiscovered, 86.21

WRITERS: false to natural language,
38.15; primary w. of a nation, 38.21

WRITING: good w. is an allegory,
39.14

WRONG means *twisted*, 32.19

X

XENOPHANES: complained, 54.15;
weary of unity, 54.18

Y

YEA IS YEA, N's, 49.10

YEAR: created by man, 88.17; each
moment has beauty, 23.6; fourfold,
16.6; has room for all, 23.21; what
is a y.? 92.15; y. and earth's motion,
36.9; pleasant only half the y., 23.2

YEARS, hundreds of, 88.6

YORK MINSTER, an imitation, 84.9

YOU ALSO are a man, 93.3

YOU NEVER sate on so glorious a
seat, 26.21

YOUTH: freshness and love of, 66.18;
y. and the morning, 66.19; perpetual
y. in the woods, 12.18

Z

ZODIAC of lights, 16.4

ZOOLOGY, first steps in, 49.13

NECESSARY TRUTHS, 34.16; 44.18
NOTHING: I am n., 13.6
OEGGER, GUILLAUME, quoted, 44.8
ONE and the many, 29.16; 54.13
ORDER: world's serene o. is inviolable
  by us, 80.21
PAIN is unimportant, 12.1; 12.23ff.;
  15.15ff.; 71.9-20; 75.8-11; see
  MISERY.
PALACE of eternity, 80.12
PETULANCE, childish, 15.16
PIPES: these rest like fountain p. on
  the unfathomed sea of thought and
  virtue, 57.21
PLOTINUS, quoted, 43.4
POINT to what we do not know, 50.5
POLARITY: see SUBJECT, OBJECT, LAW,
  IDEA.
POLICY: it fears not p., that heretic,
  66.13
POLITIC: all alone stands hugely p.,
  66.15
POMP: it suffers not in smiling p.,
  66.11
POSITION: true p. of N. in re. to man,
  73.17
PROMONTORY, strong-based, 67.11
RELATION: an original r. to the uni-
  verse, 5.7
RIGHT: the laws of r. and wrong,
  51.22
ROOTS: long-lived trees make r. first,
  42.19
RUINS: man is a god in r., 88.1

SCENE: add beauty of the s. to the
  beauty of the deed, 26.7
SELF-RELIANCE: 5.7; 6.2; 6.9; 94.3ff.
SETTING: N. as a s., 12.7
SHAKSPEARE, WILLIAM: see TEMPEST etc.
SIDE: truth seen from one s., 56.14
SIDES: truth has many s., 56.14
SOMEWHAT progressive, 76.4
SPACE AND TIME: see TIME AND SPACE.
SPIRIT means wind, 32.20; see REASON.
SPURS: by the s. plucked up the pine
  and cedar, 67.13
STEWART, DUGALD: quotation from his
  Life and Writings of Thomas Reid,
  70.6-8
SWEDENBORG, EMANUEL: references to
  his Influx, 38.18-19; 79.18-23; 94.17
SYMPATHY: see LIKE ONLY CAN KNOW LIKE.
TIME AND SPACE: See SPACE AND TIME.
TIRED: never t. while you can see far
  enough, 21.8
TORPID: activity communicated to the
  t. spirit, 87.2
TRANSCENDENTALISM: 71ff.
TRUTH: he acts it as life before he
  apprehends it as t., 6.11
UNIVERSAL man, 87.13
WE ARE ITS, 34.18
WHAT WE ARE that only can we see, 94.5;
  see LIKE ONLY CAN KNOW LIKE.
WILL: world is not subjected to man's
  w., 80.21
WRONG: thunder the laws of right and
  w., 51.22

SURVEY OF EMERSON'S *NATURE* (1836) INTRODUCTION

"INTRODUCTION"

I) The theme of the "Introduction" is revolutionary (5.2-17). It sets aside the accepted views of the Industrial Revolution, machinery, churches, schools and books, concentrating on the development of individual human beings, each of whom contains the whole of creation within himself, i.e., the OVER-SOUL or DIVINE REASON or THE IMMEDIATE. He is to approach his new task through INTUITION or SELF-RELIANCE, which is GOD-RELIANCE. Emerson here declares his spiritual independence from New-England Calvinism, Unitarianism, Catholicism or any other ism.

II) What is the new task (5.17ff.)? It is to discover for our own day the voice of God (OVER-SOUL)--to confront Eternal Truth directly and not through secondary channels. "The sun shines today also." Why then conservatism and traditionalism? Though the Verities are always the same, the statement of them in any particular age will be unique. Hence, the task is to discover and report the eternal truths for our own day, i.e., write our own history, encourage our own poet, and establish our own literary tradition. As Thomas Mann says, "...For the mystery is timeless, but the form of timelessness is the now and here.... For the essence of life is presentness." [This anti-historical note is common to all intuitional systems and to the Perennial Philosophy. Cf. the Bhagavadgita.]

III) To achieve this confrontation with Deity and release the springs of intuition, Subject (the soul of man) and Object (the Natural world) must be brought together. Mind must spiritually align itself with Nature, which is a Mediatrix between God and man. Knowledge springs into life when these two electric poles are connected. Every man's condition or make-up is conducive to this happy union of poles, he having within him a spark of the Divine Mind and his body being under the dominion of Nature (6.9). [See Herbert's poem on "Man" in Nature, 85.3ff., esp. line 12. For the uniqueness of man, see 57.1ff. On his standing at the crossroads of time and eternity, see 79.18--80.15. Man is able to learn all spiritual truths today because the world (Nature) is the present or immediate revealer of the Divine Mind to the spiritually awakened (80.16--81.2).]

IV) The reason for this little book is suggested in the title (6.14): to find what Nature really is--not what her appearances suggest. A true theory of Nature will reveal her to have a "somewhat progressive" (76.4) whereby she can lead us into the mystery of things and allow floods of life to stream around and through us, for she is passive to the Great Spirit behind and operative in all things (79.5--80.15).

V) Emerson extols the value of Nature as representative of Deity (7.22ff.) Her art is infinitely superior to puny human art, which is derivative. [Cudworth, in his True Intellectual System, wrote of the "pre-eminences which [Nature] hath above human art; the first whereof is this, that whereas human art cannot act upon the matter otherwise than from without and at a distance, nor communicate itself to it, but with a great deal of tumult and hurliburly, noise and clatter, it using hands and axes, saws and hammers, and after this manner, with much ado, by knockings and thrustings, slowly introducing its form or idea into the materials; nature, in the mean time, is another kind of art, which, insinuating itself immediately into things themselves, and there acting more commandingly upon the matter as an inward principle, does its work easily, cleverly and silently. Nature is art as it were incorporated and embodied in matter, which doth not act upon it from without mechanically, but from within vitally and magically.... Another pre-eminence of nature above human art is this, that whereas human artists are often to seek and at a loss, and therefore consult and deliberate, as also upon second thoughts mend their former work; nature, on the contrary, is never to seek what to do, nor at a stand; and for that reason also...it doth never consult nor deliberate."]

VI) The implied optimistic conclusion is based on the fact that God is all in all. He speaks today. Man and Nature today are capable of sharing the divine life.

NATURE — ANALYSIS OF CHAPTER ONE

"NATURE"

[This chapter is an appetizer, calling the reader to a new awareness of the world about him and inviting him to read the following rich discussions of Nature's ministry to man. (1) Since Emerson's was an ocular age, the eye will be emphasized in the subject-object relationship. See 11.7ff., 13.1ff., 13.6 and compare Wordsworth's 'Daffodils.' (2) The occult relationship between man and nature operates on all levels of living, as Emerson noted in the Coleridgean system, which stressed in man a higher Reason and a lower Understanding (85.12-14, 86.1-3, 8-9). (3) The mystical experience or ecstasy in Nature arises from one's yielding oneself to the totality of experience and to the Oversoul behind and through it. This joyous intuition is genius and creates the orator, the artist, or the poet. Life at its best is ecstasy and miracle. (4) Nature, therefore, is to be approached more profoundly than men are wont to do. Cf. the poems, "The Apology" and "Earth Song."]

I) Emerson focuses the lens of his reading glass upon a Nature seldom seen by materialistic men. He writes in the spirit of Psalm 8:3ff. and Psalm 121:1ff. He urges an emancipation from the routine view of things, indicating that a change of position in Nature is not so important as a change of values regarding her. Then he skilfully turns the reader's attention to the stars before bringing it back to earth and its beauties.

II) But all natural objects can serve us as the stars have done if we will let them. All are filled with hidden meanings. The least important natural phenomenon is never exhausted in its meanings or potentials (10.8).

III) Emerson contrasts his religious view of Nature with the common view of the man in the street: The tree of Joyce Kilmer is infinitely more meaningful than the log of the woodcutter. Farms are less significant for their crops than for their horizons (10.22 and 11.6ff.).

IV) Why do so few people really see Nature in this higher perspective? The reason is that their inner or outer senses (or wave-lengths) are not adjusted, as they were in childhood. Subject and Object are not aligned--do not confront each other creatively. The Soul or Divine Reason within us are, therefore, not awakened. Wires from the two poles do not come together and spark. Hence, quantum sumus, scimus. Since we are spiritually lethargic within, we cannot rightly see what is outside of us. We can only know in accordance with the spiritual state in which we find ourselves.

V) Yet, if man only were spiritually awakened, Nature would be for him the most Admirable Companion (11.21ff.). She is capable of bereaving him of temporary sorrow, of reacting to all his moods and states of mind, of restoring him to health and sanity (as in the woods), and of indicating the spiritual basis of eternal youth. Cf. Bryant's "Thanatopsis."

VI) Emerson then indicates what possibilities there are in Nature for the religious or mystical experience, describing the glory and ecstasy of one of them (13.2ff.).

VII) He then discusses the mystical, occult relationship between man and Nature, wherein we are "at home." We are related to her on many levels. A moral quality pervades Nature (13.19ff.).

VIII) Nature, however, is not to be loved merely for herself but rather for that which is behind her (God) (14.6). The delight we experience in Nature--the mystical experience--comes not from Nature per se but from a harmony of Subject and Object. Without a spiritual outgoing from man, nature will reveal nothing. Our moods give evidence of this fact. Nature always wears the colors of the spirit (14.14). Again, quantum sumus, scimus.

NATURE — ANALYSIS OF CHAPTER TWO

"COMMODITY"

I) In the first paragraph, Emerson outlines the chapers that are to follow, inadvertently omitting Nature's fifth use ['Spirit'], which he was to develop in Chapter VII after a transitional Chapter VI ['Idealism']. (15.3-8)

II) Nature as Commodity offers advantages to our senses (15.9-11), which are usually under the dominion of the "Understanding"--Coleridge's term for the animal mind. [Emerson herein imitates the language of the conceit-writers of the Seventeenth Century.]

III) "Nature, in its ministry to man, is not only the material, but it is also the process and the result." Emerson seems to be saying that Nature in helping man is helping herself in him. The activity of the Spirit behind and in both man and Nature accounts for the unusual variety of Nature's ministrations 'the endless circulations of the divine charity' which nourish man.

IV) The useful or practical arts or crafts illustrate how Nature combines with man's ingenuity.

V) The utilitarian practical benefits do not stand alone in the pattern of Nature's beneficence. She intends that man, once his animal wants are satisfied, should look to higher uses and become creative. (Cf. the same idea expressed in Thoreau's <u>Walden</u>, Chapter I, "Economy.")

NATURE — ANALYSIS OF CHAPTER THREE

"BEAUTY"

I) Simple beauty which the <u>Understanding</u> can comprehend. This kind of beauty lies on the border between Commodity (treated in the preceding chapter) and Pleasure. (20.22) On the one hand, it is often useful, restoring us to health. On the other, it goes beyond utility. But it must not be too eagerly hunted for itself alone. (At its best it is FUNCTIONAL and must be related to the WHOLE) (24.7-20).

II) Beauty which the <u>Practical Reason</u>---the Conscience---The Will---can understand. It is beauty on a spiritual level---beauty of virtuous action---"Beauty of Holiness." (This is both a Hebraic <u>and</u> Platonic touch---and also quite characteristic of New England.) Beauty is, in this degree, the mark God sets upon virtue (25.3). Nature reveals this kind of beauty to the man whose THOUGHTS are great (27.9ff.). Cf. "Quantum sumus, scimus." Nature works with the virtuous man (27.15). Cf. Plato:

"But of beauty, I repeat again that we saw her there shining in company with the celestial forms; and coming to earth we find her here too, shining in clearness through the clearest aperture of sense. FOR SIGHT IS THE MOST PIERCING OF OUR BODILY SENSES; though not by that is Wisdom seen; her loveliness would have been transporting if there had been a visible image of her, and the other Ideas, if they had visible counterparts, would be equally lovely. But this is the privilege of beauty, that being the loveliest she is also the most palpable to SIGHT. Now he who is not newly initiated or who has become corrupted, does not easily rise out of this world to the sight of true Beauty in the other; he looks only at her earthly namesake, and instead of being awed at the sight of her, he is given over to pleasure, and like a brutish beast he rushes on to enjoy and beget. But he whose initiation is recent, and who has been the spectator of many glories in the other world, is amazed when he sees any one having a godlike face or form, which is the expression of divine beauty; and at first a shudder runs through him, and again the old awe steals over him; then looking upon the face of his beloved as of a god he reverences him, and if he were not afraid of being thought a downright madman, he would sacrifice to his beloved as to the image of a god."

---Phaedrus, 246ff.

"He who has been instructed so far in the mystery of love, and who has learned to see the beautiful correctly and in due order, when he comes toward the end will suddenly perceive a wondrous beauty (and this, Socrates, is the final cause of all our former toils). It is eternal, uncreated, indestructible, subject neither to increase or decay; not like other things partly beautiful, partly ugly; not beautiful at one time or in one relation or in one place, and deformed at other times.... It is Beauty absolute, separate, simple and everlasting, which without diminution, and without increase, or any change, is imparted to the ever-growing and perishing beauties of all other things. If a man ascends from these under the influence of the right love of a friend, and begins to perceive that beauty, he may reach his goal. And the true order of approaching the mystery of love is to begin from the beauties of earth and mount upwards for the sake of that other beauty, using these as steps only, and from one going on to two, and from two to all beautiful forms, and from beauty of conduct to beauty of knowledge, until from this we arrive at the knowledge of absolute beauty, and at last know what the essence of beauty is."

---Symposium, 202ff.

(Cf. chapter on Platonism and Neo-Platonism--under "Aesthetics.")

III) Beauty which only the <u>Theoretical Reason</u>---the highest level---the "God within"---can comprehend. This is the level of Abstract Thought or Spiritual Activity above the level of personality, individual behavior, active human life. This stage of beauty alternates with the preceding one, since both the Practical and Theoretical Reason are ONE REASON, divided only as regards its functions (28.19ff.). On this highest level, beauty passes from contemplation into CREATION OF NEW BEAUTY. This is the level of artistic conception and production (29.6-9). See the following paragraphs from Emerson's "The Poet":

"By virtue of this science the poet is the Namer, or Language-maker, naming things sometimes after their appearance, sometimes after their essence, and giving to every one its own name and not another's, thereby rejoicing the intellect, which delights in detachment or boundary. The poets made all the words, and therefore language is the archives of history, and, if we must say it, a sort of tomb of the muses. For, though the origin of most of our words is forgotten, each word was at first a stroke of genius, and obtained currency, because for the moment it symbolized the world to the first speaker and to the hearer. The etymologist finds the deadest word to have been once a brilliant picture. Language is fossil poetry. As the limestone of the continent consists of infinite masses of the shells of animalcules, so language is made up of images, or tropes, which now, in their secondary use, have long ceased to remind us of their poetic origin. But the poet names the thing because he sees it, or comes one step nearer to it than any other. This expression, or naming, is not art, but a second nature, grown out of the first, as a leaf out of a tree.... So when the soul of the poet has come to ripeness of thought, she detaches and sends away from it its poems or songs,---a fearless, sleepless, deathless progeny, which is not exposed to the accidents of the weary kingdom of time: a fearless, vivacious offspring clad with wings (such was the virtue of the soul out of which they came), which carry them fast and far, and infix them irrecoverably into the hearts of men. These wings are the beauty of the poet's soul."

"[Nature has a higher end than to provide a language for the Poet,] namely, ascension, or, the passage of the soul into higher forms. I knew, in my younger days, the sculptor who made the statue of the youth which now stands in the public garden. He was, as I remember, unable to tell directly, what made him happy, or unhappy, but by wonderful indirections he could tell. He rose one day, according to his habit, before the dawn, and saw the morning break, grand as the eternity out of which it came, and, for many days after, he strove to express this tranquillity, and, lo! his chisel had fashioned out of marble the form of a beautiful youth, Phosphorus, whose aspect is such that, it is said, all persons who look on it become silent. The poet also resigns himself to his mood, and that thought which agitated him is expressed, but alter idem, in a manner totally new. The expression is organic, or, the new type which things themselves take when liberated. As, in the sun, objects paint their images on the retina of the eye, so they, sharing the aspiration of the whole universe, tend to paint a far more delicate copy of their essence in his mind. Like the metamorphosis of things into higher organic forms, is their change into melodies. Over everything stands its daemon, or soul, and, as the form of the thing is reflected by the eye, so the soul of the thing is reflected by a melody.... The pairing of the birds is an idyl, not tedious as our idyls are; a tempest is a rough ode, without falsehood or rant; a summer, with its harvest sown, reaped, and stored, is an epic song, subordinating how many admirably executed parts. Why should not the symmetry and truth that modulate these, glide into our spirits, and we participate the invention of nature?"

"This insight, which expresses itself by what is called Imagination, is a very high sort of seeing, which does not come by study, but by the intellect being where and what it sees, by sharing the path or circuit of things through forms, and so making them translucid to others. The path of things is silent. Will they suffer a speaker to go with them? A spy they will not suffer; a lover, a poet, is the transcendency of their own nature,---him they will suffer. The condition of true naming, on the poet's part, is his resigning himself to the divine aura which breathes through forms, and accompanying that."

"It is a secret which every intellectual man quickly learns, that, beyond the energy of his possessed and conscious intellect, he is capable of a new energy (as of an intellect doubled on itself), by abandonment to the nature of things; that, beside his privacy of power as an individual man, there is a great public power, on which he can draw, by unlocking, at all risks, his human doors, and suffering the ethereal tides to roll and circulate through him: then he is caught up into the life of the Universe, his speech is thunder, his thought is law, and his words are universally intelligible as the plants and animals. The poet knows that he speaks adequately, then, only when he speaks somewhat wildly, or, 'with the flower of the mind'; not with the intellect, used as an organ, but with the intellect released from all service, and suffered to take its direction from its celestial life; or, as the ancients were wont to express themselves, not with intellect alone, but with the intellect inebriated by nectar. As the traveller who has lost his way, throws his reins on his horse's neck, and trusts to the instinct of the animal to find his road, so must we do with the divine animal who carries us through this world. For if in any manner we can stimulate this instinct, new passages are opened for us into nature, the mind flows into and through things hardest and highest, and the metamorphosis is possible."

[Note the interesting parallels in the Swedenborgian notion of "creation through Influx." The outer world of Nature and Art is created THROUGH MAN. See Swedenborg's System, ¶s. B1, C2, F5. Compare what is said on the Poet and the Imagination in Nature, 64.16ff.]

SIGNIFICANT POINTS IN THE CHAPTER

1) THE EYE THE BEST OF ARTISTS. See Plato above. Cf. Nature, 11.14, 19.7ff., 20.1ff., 57.14, 56.20, 64.21, 91.7, 23.6, 62.11, 11.7, 64.4, 13.2ff., 95.12. ("The light of the body is the eye.") Cf. Matthiessen, 44-55.

2) DESCRIPTIONS OF CONCORD, Massachusetts: 21.10-23, 22.8-24, 23.6--24.6, 12.8-22.

3) MAN'S KINGDOM----HIS POWER LIES IN THE SPIRITUAL AND MORAL, not in the mechanical or materialistic gadget (25.8-15). Cf. 45.5-12, 90.2, 94.3ff., 95.7ff. For the unprofitable realm of the UNDERSTANDING, see 89.12ff.

4) POSITION OF BEAUTY IN THE NEO-PLATONIC TRIAD (TRUTH, BEAUTY and GOODNESS): All three are different faces of the SAME ALL, as in Neo-Platonism and as the Grecian Urn of Keats would have us believe. And Emerson, following Plato and Plotinus, would lead us through simple beauty up to the realm where the three IDEAS are ONE. (Aesthetics is therefore related to Truth and Goodness----ultimately. Emerson has little in common with the modern Hedonistic school of "art for art's sake.")

"According to the [Hedonistic] school, it is profanation of literary criticism so much as to hint the question of morals. This view, which, in modern times at least, rose as a reaction from strongly moralistic criticism, errs as much on one side as moralistic criticism does on the other. Hedonistic criticism is quite right in maintaining that the criticism of literature, as an activity distinct from other activities of the mind, concerns itself with aesthetic value and not with moral utility.... But the hedonist errs in forgetting that, as literature is speech, it is the whole of speech, and that as speech has been evolved to express and communicate the whole nature of man, including his moral nature, it is impossible to use speech in such a way that it will have practical meaning without either stating or implying moral concepts. The concept of pure poetry (art whose significance could be exhausted by a strictly aesthetic judgment) is useful and necessary in theory, but no pure poetry exists in practice.... The dilemma is easily solved if we will agree to maintain both points of view and protect our judgment on the one side from being encroached upon by our judgment on the other...."

Pottle, Idiom of Poetry (2nd ed.), 196-197.

THE CREATIVE PROCESS (28.4ff.)

1) Wherein the average man differs from the poet: Both are impressed by the beauty of the face of the world, but the artist makes a better response. The beauty of external objects mounts to his highest Reason and their reforms for new creation (29.4-9, 29.1-3). Compare the following from Emerson's "The Poet":

"If the imagination intoxicates the poet, it is not inactive in other men. The metamorphosis excites in the beholder an emotion of joy. The use of symbols has a certain power of emancipation and exhilaration for all men. We seem to be touched by a wand, which makes us dance and run about happily, like children. We are like persons who come out of a cave or cellar into the open air. This is the effect on us of tropes, fables, oracles, and all poetic forms. Poets are thus liberating gods. Men have really got a new sense, and found within their world, another world, or nest of worlds.... The ancient British bards had for the title of their order, "Those who are free throughout the world." They are free, and they make free. An imaginative book renders us much more service at first, by stimulating us through its tropes, than afterward, when we arrive at the precise sense of the author. I think nothing is of any value in books, excepting the transcendental and extraordinary.... That also is the best success in conversation, the magic of liberty, which puts the world, like a ball, in our hands. How cheap even the liberty then seems; how mean to study, when an emotion communicates to the intellect the power to sap and upheave nature: how great the perspective! nations, times, systems, enter and disappear, like threads in tapestry of large figure and many colors; dream delivers us to dream, and, while the drunkenness lasts, we will sell our bed, our philosophy, our religion, in our opulence."

"There is good reason why we should prize this liberation. The fate of the poor shepherd, who, blinded and lost in the snow-storm, perishes in a drift within a few feet of his cottage door, is an emblem of the state of man. On the brink of the waters of life and truth, we are miserably dying. The inaccessibleness of every thought but that we are in, is wonderful. What if you come near to it, ---you are as remote, when you are nearest, as when you are farthest. Every thought is also a prison; every heaven is also a prison. Therefore we love the poet, the inventor, who in any form, whether in an ode, or in an action, or in looks and behavior, has yielded us a new thought. He unlocks our chains and admits us to a new scene.... Therefore all books of the imagination endure, all which ascend to that truth, that the writer sees nature beneath him, and uses it as his exponent. Every verse or sentence, possessing this virtue, will take care of its own immortality. The religions of the world are the ejaculations of a few imaginative men."

2) Emerson shares the concept of the "Organic Principle" with Coleridge. He has no interest in a mechanical or arbitrary construction of a work of art. Rhyme or meter are usually too consciously adopted to suit him. Form, he believes, is innate. It is shaped by the thought, or not at all. It comes from within out. Ultimately, it comes, through the Poet's high intuition, from the Creative Mind behind the Universe. (Cf. Sampson Reed and the Swedenborgians on poetry.) [The danger to look for in the application of this view is FORMLESSNESS and a scattering of artistic power.]

3) Emerson subscribed to the theory (if not always to the practice) that the duty of the artist was continually to renew his elemental experiences (29.1-3). Cf. "The Poet." One sees a possible denial to this view in his tendency to "spiritualize experience" and thereby deny its ugliness or its reality (20.2-7). (This "doctoring" is a facet of Emerson's optimism.) Cf. "The Poet."

4) The Work of Art must demonstrate its relationship to the WHOLE----its universality----its being "in composition." Since each work of art is the product of the impact of the entire external world upon the Reason of man, and since it is therefore a "microcosm," it is to be tested for validity by being considered against the "totality of nature" (29.10ff., 19.6--20.1). This relatedness is manifested by its FUNCTIONAL VALUE (24.7-20). Study the poem, "Each and All."

5) Human Art receives greater appreciation in this chapter (30.10-13) than it seemed to merit at the end of the Introduction (7.20--8.5). The fact is that he drew both positive and negative aspects of human art as compared with Nature's art, from Ralph Cudworth's True Intellectual System. Compare the excerpt from Cudworth cited in connection with 7.20ff. with the following:

HOW NATURE FALLS SHORT OF HUMAN ART

"...we must here take notice also of the imperfections and defects of it, in which respect it falls short of human art, which are likewise two: and the first of them is this, that though it act artificially for the sake of ends, yet itself doth neither intend those ends, nor understand the reason of that it doth. Nature is not master of that consummate art and wisdom, according to which it acts, but only a servant to it, and a drudging executioner of the dictates of it. This difference betwixt nature and abstract art or wisdom is expressed by Plotinus in these words: How doth wisdom differ from that which is called nature? verily in this manner, that wisdom is the first thing, but nature the last and lowest; for nature is but an image or imitation of wisdom, the last thing of the soul,** which hath the lowest impress of reason shining upon it; as when a thick piece of wax is thoroughly impressed upon a seal, that impress, which is clean and distinct in the superior superficies of it, will in the lower side be weak and obscure; and such is the stamp and signature of nature, compared with that of wisdom and understanding, nature being a thing, which doth only do, but not know....**

"There is, in the next place, another imperfection to be observed in the plastic nature, that as it doth not comprehend the reason of its own action, so neither is it clearly and expressly conscious of what it doth; in which respect, it doth not only fall short of human art, but even of that very manner of acting, which is in brutes themselves.... In a word, nature is a thing that hath no such self-perception or self-enjoyment in it, as animals have."

————————

**Compare title page of Nature.

[For an illustration of Emerson's theory, see the discussion of his composition of "The Rhodora" in Matthiessen, American Renaissance, pp. 49-50.]

NATURE — ANALYSIS OF CHAPTER FOUR

"LANGUAGE"

[Note to the Student: For a general background, study Matthiessen, American Renaissance, pp. 30-44; 92-99; 100-119. Note especially the following strong influences on Emerson at this point.]

COLERIDGE'S INFLUENCE: See the chart of his system for identity of Subject and Object---for necessity of coincidence for awakening or unlocking truth. (Compare also Plato's doctrine of reminiscence or recollection in Workbook, I, "Miscellaneous Observations," #6.) See especially section VIII on "Language" and the Doctrine of Correspondences in "Coleridge as Key to Nature" (Workbook, XI). See also sections VI and VII of "Coleridge as Key to Nature" for Coleridge's views on polarity and education through the unlocking process. See Nature, 45.5-12---MAN'S SOURCE OF POWER. Cf. Excerpts from "The Poet," ¶s. 14-15.

SWEDENBORG'S INFLUENCE: Pervades the entire chapter. See sheets on Philosophic System of Emanuel Swedenborg, ¶s. B2, C2, C4. His "Doctrine of Correspondences" is basic for understanding Emerson's lustres. The terminology of the Swedenborgians appears especially at:

32.10	Nature is symbol of Spirit. Cf. System, F5.
34.1-3	Enraged man is a lion...fox...rock...torch. Cf. System, C4.
36.17	Ray of relation from man to all created things. Cf. System, C1-2.
38.18-19	Clothing thought in its natural garment. Cf. System, B2.
44.4	Influx from preceding affections in world of spirit. Cf. System, B2.
44.8-13	French philosopher is Guillaume Oegger, for an account of whom see Emerson the Essayist, I, pp. 295-302; II, pp. 83-99. Cf. System, D3.
44.18	Every scripture to be interpreted by same spirit which gave it forth. Cf. System, F4.
45.5-12	Unconscious truth when interpreted becomes power. Cf. System, C2.

BACON'S INFLUENCE: "Knowledge is power." "Man is the priest and interpreter of Nature." See Emerson the Essayist, I, p. 333. See Emerson's essay on "Power" in The Conduct of Life (Works, VI, esp. pp. 53-54). Cf. Nature, 18.19, 45.5-12, 50.13--51.9, 80.1-10, 89.12ff., 95.7-12.

OUTLINE AND ANALYSIS

I) WORDS ARE SIGNS OF NATURAL FACTS. Every word that is used to express a moral or intellectual fact was borrowed from some material appearance. Nature has furnished us our everyday language. "Language is fossil poetry." Cf. Emerson's "The Poet."

II) PARTICULAR NATURAL FACTS ARE SYMBOLS OF PARTICULAR SPIRITUAL FACTS. Every appearance in Nature corresponds to some state of the mind. Natural objects become symbols. When a man wishes to refer to the spiritual world or to spiritual experiences, the best he can do is to choose the appropriate natural object to represent or "half reveal" his thought. Only such a symbol can bridge the gap between the phenomenal world and the spiritual state. The power of the symbol lies in its indirection.

When a man is spiritually inspired---utterly truthful---under the dominion of the Reason---he is able to connect his thought with the proper outward symbol, and thus he can become communicative to others of like spirituality. (See Emerson's Journals, II, 402.) For Emerson's own use of analogy, see Matthiessen, p. 65 top. For the inspired poet's use of nature for a language, see "The Poet." When the poet is receptive to the divine influx, his mind is endowed directly with the word that embodies the THING.

"There is every degree of remoteness from the line of things in the line of words. By and by comes a word true and closely embracing the thing. That is not Latin, nor English, nor any language but thought. The aim of the author is not to <u>tell</u> the truth---that he cannot do, but to <u>suggest</u> it. He has only approximated it himself and hence his cumbrous, embarrassed speech: he uses many words, hoping that one, if not another, will bring you as near to the fact as he is. For language itself is young and unformed. In heaven it will be, as Sampson Reed said, 'one with things.' Now, there are many things that refuse to be recorded,---perhaps the larger half. The unsaid part is the best of every discourse." <u>Journals</u>, III, 491-92.

See Sampson Reed on the "language, not of words but of things" in his <u>Oration on Genius</u>, ¶ 8.

"In good writing, every word means something. In good writing, words become one with things. I take up a poem; if I find that there is not a single line there nor word but expresses something that is true for me as well as for him...it is adamant.... No critic can hurt it; he will only hurt himself by tilting against it." ---Emerson in his <u>Journals</u>, II, 401.

Emerson illustrates how the particular natural fact becomes a symbol of a spiritual fact---and his power to connect his thought with its proper symbol (37.19)---in the poem, "The Two Rivers." Cf. Thoreau's line in <u>Walden</u>: "Time is but the stream I go a-fishing in. I drink at it; but while I drink, I see the sandy bottom and detect how shallow it is. Its thin current slides away, but eternity remains. I would drink deeper; fish in the sky, whose bottom is pebbly with stars."

III) NATURE----THE LANGUAGE OF MYSTICAL COMMUNION. THE WHOLE OF NATURE ANSWERS TO THE WHOLE OF MIND----THE VISIBLE WORLD IS A CLOCK'S FACE, STANDING FOR THE HIDDEN OR INVISIBLE WORLD.

All visible nature, therefore, has a spiritual or moral side, if our Reasons were only awakened to understand and profit. But just as one can understand a scripture only if he is of the same spiritual quality as the author (44.18), so a person can understand nature ONLY IF LOVE AND VIRTUE have purged his eyes---his inward sight (44.22). Only when he is spiritually awakened will the natural world really reveal its secrets---the primitive sense of the permanent objects of nature (45.1)---and through them the SPIRIT---their "hidden life" and FINAL CAUSE. In this connection, study Whitman's "Crossing Brooklyn Ferry," section 9.

The miracle of the "mystical trance" is discussed (43.4). It arises from the coincidence of subject and object. It is God-given---coming upon us when we least expect it (43.4). All men are eligible because of possessing the Reason, but all men do not experience it because of lethargy or apathy (43.3). Cf. 13.2ff. for excellent example of Nature furnishing the means of mystical or spiritual communion. See "Statement of the First Philosophy," sections XIII--XIV.

Emerson calls attention to some of the great men of the world who have tried to learn Nature's great spiritual meaning. Nature is, and has always been, a kind of Sphinx by the roadside, offering rich rewards to anyone who, like Oedipus of old, will read her riddle. For such a person, she becomes transparent (43.11). Then only does a man seem to live (43.7, 71.17). He apprehends the Absolute (71.16). He becomes immortal, and time-and-space relations vanish (71.17).

And when the faculties of his soul are unlocked, and what was once unconscious truth becomes alive, he is conscious of increased power over Nature, the mirage, the vicegerent of God (45.5-12, 94.13--95.12, 40.18-19, 51.6-9, 26.6-15, 71.17-20, 93.15-19).

For a fuller statement of Nature's use as a language of the Spirit, see 77.9-15, 76.12-17, 79.8--80.15.

But if we remain degenerate and asleep, how little Nature reveals to us! (81.2-16, 89.12--90.4) Study Emerson's "Days."

NATURE — ANALYSIS OF CHAPTER FIVE

"DISCIPLINE"

INTRODUCTION: Nature, as a DISCIPLINE, educates both the Understanding <u>and</u> the Reason (46.10). Every property of matter trains the former (46.11); the latter is benefited also because of the occult relationship between SUBJECT and OBJECT, <u>i.e.</u>, between mind and matter (46.19). Through the affinity between the OUTER and INNER worlds, Emerson approaches his subject, in this chapter, from two points of view: (I) by starting from the outer world of Nature and proceeding into man's Understanding, thence up to the Reason; (II) by starting with the Reason, proceeding to the outer world and observing how spiritual and ethical the DISCIPLINE from Nature becomes when the SUBJECT (the inner man) is spiritually awake. Cf. the discipline imposed by Nature in this chapter with Emerson's earlier, Unitarian view of the subject, expressed in his poem, "Grace," an obvious imitation of George Herbert's poem, "Sinne":

> Lord, with what care hast thou begirt us round!
>   Parents first season us: then schoolmasters
>   Deliver us to laws; they send us bound
> To rules of reason, holy messengers,
>
> Pulpits and sundayes, sorrow dogging sinne,
>   Afflictions sorted, anguish of all sizes,
>   Fine nets and stratagems to catch us in,
> Bibles laid open, millions of surprises,
>
> Blessings beforehand, tyes of gratefulnesse,
>   The sound of glorie ringing in our eares;
>   Without, our shame; within, our consciences;
> Angels and grace, eternall hopes and fears.
>
>   Yet all these fences and their whole aray
>   One cunning bosome-sinne blows quite away.

I) HOW THE OUTER WORLD TRAINS THE UNDERSTANDING, NOT ONLY MAKING IT EFFICIENT AND DISCRIMINATING, BUT ALSO AROUSING IT TO AN AWARENESS OF SOMETHING ABOVE ITSELF. THIS DISCIPLINE ULTIMATELY CAUSES THE EYE OF REASON TO OPEN and IDEAS BEGIN TO FLOW, HAVING BEEN UNLOCKED BY THE CORRESPONDENT LAWS IN THE NATURAL WORLD. Occasionally a man may pass from mere intellectual awakening into the mystical experience---into a state of BEING---into the joys of the Eternal "Now" (49.21). This bringing of the outer and inner worlds together tends to strengthen the WILL, which is the key to man's increasing dominion over Nature (51.6-9).

A) The training of man's common sense:

1) By sensible objects etc. (47.2-19).

2) By property, debt and credit, in particular (47.20ff.).

B) The character and fortune of a person depend upon a well-trained Understanding. Example: importance of the ability to perceive differences---to make distinctions (48.14--49.8).

C) Nature does not spoil us or pamper us. She means what she says. She is an exacting preceptress. Nothing she does is useless. (49.9-16)

D) The Mystical Moment described (49.17--50.2). Compare Emerson's other references to "mystical union" and note his fondness for the word "transparent" (13.2-18, 43.1-13, 62.11-22, 71.2-20).

E) As man's will becomes strengthened by an awakened Reason, he extends his power or kingdom over Nature (50.13--51.9). (Cf. 25.6-15, 40.18-19, 45.5-12, 71.17-20, 93.15-19, 94.13--95.12.)

II) HOW THE INNER WORLD (i.e., THE PRACTICAL OR MORAL REASON) ASSISTS THE OUTER WORLD IN ITS WORK OF MORAL DISCIPLINE----BY MAKING IT SPEAK TO MAN'S CONSCIENCE ----BY MAKING IT SHOUT THE TEN COMMANDMENTS THROUGH EVERY OBJECT (51.10--54.11). (Cf. 41.18-21.)

A) All things are moral (51.12).

B) Nature is never exhausted in its first use (as commodity), but is always ready for new uses---such as that of moral discipline (52.10-18). (Cf. 50.3-10.)

C) Therefore all things preach the SAME lesson or make the same impact on the mind, no matter what a person's specialized work may be or what natural phenomena he may encounter (53.7-23).

"The moral influence of nature upon every individual is that amount of truth which it illustrates to him"--that is to say, "the amount of truth he will allow it to illustrate to him" (53.21-33).

III) MISCELLANEOUS CONSIDERATIONS BEARING ON NATURE'S FUNCTION AS DISCIPLINER:

A) Why all things teach the same moral lesson: UNITY OF NATURE----UNITY IN VARIETY (54.12--56.24). (On the subject of the Microcosm or the "All in Each," see Swedenborg System, C2, and the chapter on Neo-Platonism.)

1) All things resemble each other in making the same impression upon us (54.15).

2) This unity or resemblance which all things share extends to those which are superficially unlike. So every universal truth, in whatever field, implies or supposes every other truth, just as a great circle on a sphere includes all other circles (55.3--56.14). Cf. sections I-II of "A Statement of the First Philosophy."

3) The same unity applies to ACTIONS, which are ultimately superior to words. "The wise man in doing one thing does all" (56.15-24). Cf. Thoreau's parable of the Artist from the City of Kouroo in the final chapter of Walden.

B) Whom does Nature discipline? The answer is: "MAN, THE HIGHEST OF ALL FORMS." The Spirit prefers the HUMAN FORM because man can exercise the Reason. Each man or woman, however, is defective. Still, man is unique among all animals because he rests upon the "sea of thought and virtue" (57.1-24).

Thought = function of the Theoretical Reason
Virtue = function of the Practical Reason

On man, see Swedenborg System, A3, B1. Compare the following passage in one of Emerson's journals:

"Every animal in our scale of creatures leans upward on man, and man leans downward on it; lynx, dog, tapir, lion, lizard, camel, & crocodile, ---all find their perfection in him; all add a support, & some essential contribution to him. He is the grand lion, he the grand lynx, the grand worm, the fish of fishes, and bird of birds; so that, if one of these tribes were struck out of being, he would lose some one property of his nature, and no doubt, to each of these creatures man appears as of its own kind, to a lion, the arch-lion; to a stork, the arch-stork. He is the master key for which you must go back, to open each door in this thousand-gated Thebes."

C) Nature's discipline through the INFLUENCE OF MAN UPON MAN----Chief value of human friendship is ultimately IMPERSONAL. How a friend serves his purpose and is withdrawn from us, leaving an unconscious effect or "solid and sweet wisdom" in our minds (58.1-20).

See "Notes on the Text of Nature" covering lines 58.4-15.

For similar views on Friendship, see Emerson's poem on the subject. See the passages from Plato's Symposium and Phaedrus, cited above in the outline for Chapter III of Nature.

See "Art" and "Aesthetics" in the systems of Plato and Neo-Platonism. See Swedenborg System, B5.

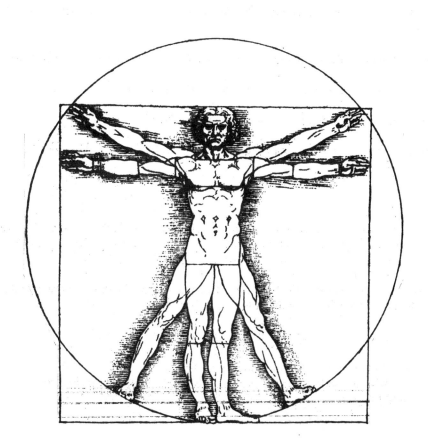

NATURE — ANALYSIS OF CHAPTER SIX

"IDEALISM"

[Note to the Student: Review Bishop George Berkeley's system of "idealism," which is the one being considered here. In his earlier years, and before he had discovered Coleridge and Swedenborg, he had been much impressed by it. Chapter VI is an "interim" chapter, a foil for Chapter VII, which essentially repudiates Berkeley and affirms Coleridge and Swedenborg. He includes it partly out of gratitude and partly because Berkeley's system served as "a useful introductory hypothesis" (79.2-3) to the better ones summarized in Chapter VII.]

OUTLINE

I) We have been considering Nature as it affects us in a practical way---through the senses. We have called it a disciplining agent, BUT whether it actually exists or not is uncertain. (The "noble" doubt. 59.8) As Berkeley suggests, Nature may be only an appearance which God uses to achieve his purpose.

II) Even so, there is no need to distrust the permanence of natural laws. For all practical purposes, the "appearance" is dependable (60.22ff.).

III) The practical and sense-loving Understanding, of course, takes Nature's existence (its absolute existence) for granted, but Reason sees beyond the animal eye (61.22--62.22). The mystical trance casts doubts on the absolute existence of Nature (62.19-22).

IV) Evidence supporting Berkeleian Idealism: (The following cast doubt upon belief in the real existence of the outer world:)

    A) Motion---changing the position (This is a hint from nature herself) (63.2--64.15).

    B) Poetry and the Poet---The Poet's use of the Imagination (64.16--68.10).

    C) General Philosophy and Physical Science (Euler) (68.11--70.3).

    D) Metaphysics---Ontology (Science of Being)---Pure Philosophy (called "intellectual science") (70.4--71.20).

    E) Religion and Ethics (71.21--73.4).

V) Though the evidence is rather conclusive against the reality of the natural world, Emerson does not wish to underestimate the value of Nature even as a mirage. He merely wishes to classify or characterize her adequately. She is still his "beautiful mother" (73.5--74.5).

VI) The Advantage of the Ideal Theory of Berkeley---It supports the Reason's view of things; i.e., it supports Coleridge's view of mind and matter (74.6--75.14).

SOME POINTS TO NOTICE

1) This natural world which we perceive is essentially illusion and must not be valued too much for itself but rather for what it represents (62.4-22, 77.12). Compare the following from "Illusions" in Emerson's Conduct of Life [Works, VI, 319ff.]:

"There are deceptions of the senses, deceptions of the passions, and the structural, beneficent illusions of sentiment and of the intellect. There is the illusion of love, which attributes to the beloved person all which that person shares with his or her family, sex, age or condition, nay, with the human mind itself.... There is the illusion of time, which is very deep; who has disposed of it?---or come to the conviction that what seems the succession of thought is only the distribution of wholes into causal series? [Compare Nature, 74.13-20.] The intellect sees that every atom carries the whole of nature; that the mind opens to omnipotence; that, in the endless striving and ascents, the metamorphosis is entire, so that the soul doth not know itself in its own act when that act is perfected. There is illusion that shall deceive even the elect...

"From day to day the capital facts of human life are hidden from our eyes. Suddenly the mist rolls up and reveals them, and we think how much good time is gone that might have been saved had any hint of these things been shown. A sudden rise in the road shows us the system of mountains, and all the summits, which have been just as near us all the year, but quite out of mind....

"In this kingdom of illusions we grope eagerly for stays and foundations. There is none but a strict and faithful dealing at home and a severe barring out of all duplicity or illusion there. Whatever games are played with us, we must play no games with ourselves, but deal in our privacy with the last honesty and truth. [Self-Reliance]

"The Hindoos...express the liveliest feeling, both of the essential identity and of that illusion which they conceive variety to be. 'The notions, I am, and This is mine, which influence mankind, are but delusions of the mother of the world. Dispel, O Lord of all creatures, the conceit of knowledge which proceeds from ignorance.' And the beatitude of man they hold to lie in being freed from fascination. [Cf. "Hamatreya."]

"There is no chance and no anarchy in the universe. All is system and gradation. Every god is there sitting in his sphere. The young mortal enters the hall of the firmament; there is he alone with them alone, they pouring on him benedictions and gifts, and beckoning him up to their thrones. On the instant, and incessantly, fall snow-storms of illusions. He fancies himself in a vast crowd which sways this way and that and whose movement and doings he must obey: he fancies himself poor, orphaned, insignificant. The mad crowd drives hither and thither, now furiously commanding this thing to be done, now that. What is he that he should resist their will, and think or act for himself? Every moment new changes and new showers of deceptions to baffle and distract him. And when, by and by, for an instant, the air clears and the cloud lifts a little, there are the gods still sitting around him on their thrones---they alone with him alone."

2) The FLOWING or FLUX of the Phenomenal world about us---River Imagery. On Heraclitus and the doctrine of flux, see Emerson the Essayist, I, 33-36. On Xenophanes, see Nature, 54.15-19; Nature is fluid, 65.6; River symbolizes the flux, 34.10; Nature is not fixed but fluid, 93.20-24; This green ball which floats us through the heavens, 15.19ff.; see also 5.11-12. The following passage comes from Emerson's "Lecture on the Times" (1841), in Works, I, 287:

"The main interest which any aspects of the Times can have for us, is the great spirit which gazes through them, the light which they can shed on the wonderful questions, What we are? and Whither we tend? We do not wish to be deceived. Here we drift, like white sail across the wild ocean, now bright on the wave, now darkling in the trough of the sea;---but from what port did we sail? Who knows? Or to what port are we bound? Who knows? There is no one to tell us but such poor weather-tossed mariners as ourselves, whom we speak as we pass, or who have hoisted some signal, or floated to us some letter in a bottle from far. But what know they more than we? They also found themselves on this wondrous sea and the loud winds answer, Not in us; not in Time. Where then but in Ourselves, where but in that Thought through which we communicate with absolute nature [i.e., God], and are made aware that whilst we shed the dust of which we are built, grain by grain, till it is all gone, the law which clothes us with humanity remains anew? where but in the intuitions which are vouchsafed us from within, shall we learn the Truth.... Underneath all these appearances lies that which is, that which lives, that which causes. This ever renewing generation of appearances rests on a reality, and a reality that is alive." [Cf. Nature, 5.6-17.]

3) THE POET AND THE IMAGINATION (64.16--68.10). See Emerson's "The Poet." See Coleridge's distinction between the <u>Imagination</u> and the <u>Fancy</u> in <u>Biographia Literaria</u> and in <u>Emerson the Essayist</u>, I, 91-93. The imagination is defined in 65.10.

4) THE DEFINITION OF POETRY (65.4, 64.20-21). In this connection, one ought to study the penetrating observations of Matthiessen, <u>American Renaissance</u>, pp. 52-53 and 55.

5) EMERSON'S DEEPENING INTEREST IN IDEALISM----HIS ULTIMATE TURNING TO THE ORIENT AND ITS WRITINGS----to the Hindus. See Emerson's Poem, "Brahma."

Note the following summary of the <u>Bhagavadgita</u> by Victor Cousin, reprinted from <u>Emerson the Essayist</u>, I, 310-311.

THE *BHAGAVAD-GITA*——WHAT IT REVEALS OF INDIAN CIVILIZATION

Open, for instance, the Bhagavad-Gita; it is a short episode in an immense poem. Two great armies, the Pandoos and the Kouroos, are in the presence of each other, and are ready to engage in battle. A boundless carnage is at hand. In one of the two armies there is a young warrior, individually very brave, but who, upon the eve of shedding the blood of his relations and friends, for the two armies are composed of friends and relations, finds his courage failing. He requests another personage to advance his chariot into the middle of the plain, for the purpose of ascertaining the situation of affairs, and having cast a brief glance upon the two hosts, the good Ardschunas vows to Crishna, his uncertainty. What is the reply? "Truly, Ardschunas, your pity is exceedingly ridiculous. Why do you speak of friends and of relations? Why of men? Relations, friends, men, beasts, or stones, all are one. A perpetual and eternal energy has created all which you see and renews it without cessation. What is today a man, was yesterday a plant, and tomorrow may become a plant once more. The principle of every thing is eternal; what value has aught else? You are, as a Schatrias, a man of the caste of warriors, doomed to the combat. Therefore, do battle; a fearful carnage will be the result. Be it so; tomorrow the sun will shine upon the world, and will illuminate new scenes, and the eternal principle will continue to subsist. Beyond this principle, every thing is illusion. The fundamental error is, to consider as true that which is only apparent. If you attach any value to appearances, you deceive yourself; if you attach it to your actions, you deceive yourself again; for as all is illusion, action itself, when it is regarded as real, is illusion also; the beauty and the merit of an action consist in performing it with profound indifference as to the results which it may produce. It is necessary to act, undoubtedly, but to act as if one acted not. Nothing exists but the eternal principle; being, in itself. It follows that it is the supreme of wisdom to let things pass, to do what we are compelled to do, but as if we did it not, and without concerning ourselves about the result, interiorly motionless, with our eyes fixed unceasingly upon the absolute principle which alone exists with a true existence."

Such, under a somewhat occidental form, is the philosophy of this sublime episode. ... You will comprehend how human nature must tremble and shrink into nothingness, before a theism so terrible and filled with chimeras, and represented by symbols that are extravagant and gigantic; how art, in its powerless endeavor to represent being in itself, must fall, without reserve, into colossal and irregular creations; how God being all and man nothing, a formidable theocracy must press upon humanity, take away all liberty, all movement, all practical interest, and consequently all true morality; and how man, despising himself, was unable to recall the memory of actions in which he supposed himself not the real agent; and therefore, why there is no history of man in India, and no chronology.

NATURE — ANALYSIS OF CHAPTER SEVEN

"SPIRIT"

[Note to the Student: This chapter fulfils the promise of the "Introduction"---to find an adequate theory of Nature (6.17-18)---and is, essentially, the conclusion to Emerson's little book. The last chapter ("Prospects") is an afterword, speculating about the future of the age based on the optimistic dogmas expressed in Chapter VII. The Orphic Poet's lines are an illustration or recapitulation of the high points of Chapter VII.]

I) A true theory of Nature and of man must provide sufficient scope and purpose. Nature is not a mere spectacle or maze of mirages (as implied in Bishop Berkeley's epistemology) but an active revealer of the Absolute, an agent of the Absolute, and an arena providing man a maximum opportunity for infinite moral and spiritual development. It is not static (as in Berkeley's system) but dynamic (as in Swedenborg's, Coleridge's and Schelling's systems).

II) According to this high view of the subject, Nature qualifies as the Divine Mediatrix between God and Man or as a Divine Redemptress, having somewhat the role of Jesus in the historic Christian religions. She creates an atmosphere of worship and must be approached worshipfully.

III) Though the Deity or Spirit behind man and Nature is ineffable and beyond man's comprehension or any credal statement, when the fragment of the Divine Mind in every man (Coleridge calls it the "Theoretical Reason" or "Divine Intellect") becomes active or inspired, then external Nature appears godlike, assumes a sacerdotal or sacramental character, and through moments of man's ecstasy beckons him to his spiritual home. (For a good illustration, see Wordsworth's "Tintern Abbey.")

IV) We know all this from our experience of the Indwelling Spirit. Berkeley's view of Nature, expressed in the preceding chapter, therefore, is inadequate. It does not deal with Ultimates, it does not account for intuition or the mystic experience, and it does not fully account for matter (Nature) and its manifold ministries. Berkeley's system may tell us what matter is; Coleridge and Swedenborg go further and explain its origin and sublime purposes.

V) Of course, Berkeley's system is useful in distinguishing between, on the one hand, the mind's awareness of itself and, on the other, its inability to test the validity of what comes in through the senses. To Berkeley, the mind is real. As for the outer world, for him it is or may be just a dream. He tends to deny its actual existence.

VI) Berkeley's system, therefore, fails to satisfy the requirements of our spiritual experience. Its epistemology leaves God out of a man. Because it ignores Nature's true ministry, the human heart resists it. In fact, since the human body is a part of Nature, Berkeley essentially denies substantive being even to men and women! He also denies what appear at every turn in Nature those rays of relation between it and man---its kinship, consanguinity, identity, warmth and communion. (Cf. Emerson's experience in the Jardin des Plantes in Paris.) In view of our experience in the Romantic Period, therefore, Berkeley's post-Lockian theory says too little about Nature and, in fact, makes it foreign to us. Let it stand, however, as a useful "introductory hypothesis" (79.3).

VII) For the deeper explanations we turn to Coleridge and Swedenborg. They show us that when we lift ourselves into the highest level of our being (into the God-given Intellect or Reason), then God speaks by flowing (Influx) or intuitional Truth, convincing us that (1) the Dread Universal Spirit is present within each of us; (2) it is also behind and throughout Nature; (3) it is the same Spirit in both. Truth is a priori, not a posteriori. Berkeley's epistemology, based upon John Locke's tabula rasa theory or "sensualism," asserted that Nature or Deity acted upon us only from without. (Nihil in intellectu sine in sensu.) On the contrary, as we know from our experience (and as

Coleridge and Swedenborg state), the Spirit acts <u>intuitionally from within us</u> and works its way out through ourselves into Nature. A man, like a tree, is a part of a vast organicism. And because man and Nature both rest upon Deity, and because Nature is God's agent to help man, who dares set bounds to man's possibilities for growth and spiritual expansion? Once he allows his mind to mount into the Theoretical Reason within him, through intuition he can have access to the entire mind of God. In fact, like the Godhead, he, too, through Influx, becomes a creator---though only in the finite world. As Deity creates all below it through Influx, so man creates his external universe by allowing Influx to pass through him and out into Nature. He can create the world he dreams about if only he will not put obstructions (sins, materialism, etc.) in the way of God's lethean stream. (These views are further elucidated in Emerson's "Statement of the First Philosophy" and in the lines of the Orphic Poet in Chapter VIII.)

VIII) We have, then, answers to the questions which Berkeley's system could not deal with (77.21-22): The world, like man's body, proceeds from God. "It is a remoter and inferior incarnation," but an incarnation nonetheless. The differences are these: the human body is a <u>conscious</u> incarnation; Nature is <u>unconscious</u>. The human body is dominated by a human will, which (as Coleridge shows us) may be good or bad, free or bound. Nothing of this sort troubles Nature. Because its serene order is inviolable by man, it can be man's teacher---even his model---certainly the "present expositor of the divine mind" (80.23).

IX) Nature's ministry or purpose, in part, then, is to make man aware of his "fallen will" or "fallen nature." (See the Orphic Poet's lines.) Man can recognize his fallen condition in any estrangement he experiences between himself and Nature---in any failure to understand Nature or to receive from her spiritual exaltation or solace. In other words, evidence of a temporary "fall" lies in man's failure to establish the Subject-Object relationship. (For classic examples of this estrangement, see Wordsworth's "Ode on Intimations of Immortality" and Coleridge's "Dejection--An Ode.")

NATURE — ANALYSIS OF CHAPTER EIGHT

"PROSPECTS"

I) A description of our present world, which lives largely under the dominion of the Understanding. (Scientists, technicians, gatherers of facts, classifiers, research scholars, catalogers, sensualists, empiricists---these characterize our age, and Emerson reproaches them.) They work without "SELF-recovery"---i.e., dependence upon the true SELF---the Reason (82.3--84.15, 89.12--90.4, 92.1-3). Cf. "Statement of the First Philosophy," sections VI, VIII, XI. Cf. Swedenborg System, F6, F7.

II) The "Practical Men" do not account for the tyrannizing unity which wise men see existing between THINGS and THOUGHTS (SUBJECT vs. OBJECT) (83.21) or the congruity subsisting between man and the world, because man is its head and heart (Microcosm) (84.14-17, 85.3--86.9). See "Statement of the First Philosophy," sections XII--XIII.

III) A GUESS or intuition from the Reason should be ranked above dead, scientific classifications or systems (83.2, 86.13-20). We have evidence that the Reason or Divine Influx isn't yet dead. It lights our present darkness---here and there (90.4--91.4). Cf. "Coleridge as Key to Nature," section XII.

IV) The chief Problem of our Age is essentially religious. We can usher in the Utopia by redeeming the soul or mind or Reason of man so that the axis of vision WITHIN will coincide with the axis of things WITHOUT (Subject and Object becoming coincident). Quantum sumus, scimus. Old traditional religions will not help because they are content with second-hand religious experience (91.5--92.11). Cf. "Coleridge as Key to Nature," sections VI, VII, IX, X, XI.

V) When the Reason is awakened, the entire world and all its component parts will take on spiritual meaning. One will see the miraculous in the commonest objects. Natural symbols will reveal the "higher law" or the mystical truth behind them. We shall look upon the world with new eyes, and the outer world will answer our every question (6.9-10, 92.12--93.20). "Coleridge as Key to Nature," section XIII.

VI) The above points are compressed into mythological form in the Orphic Poet's paragraphs. (For general commentary see "Coleridge as Key to Nature," section XIII.)

POINTS FOR THE STUDENT ESPECIALLY TO NOTICE

1) OPTIMISM----INFINITUDE OF THE INDEPENDENT MAN----THE INDIVIDUAL IS HIS OWN MESSIAH. Cf. Swedenborg System, F8 and "Coleridge as Key to Nature," section XIII. For the optimism of all Rationalistic systems see Reinhold Niebuhr, The Nature and Destiny of Man, early chapters.

2) HINT OF THE ROMANTIC CULT OF THE FUTURE----CULT OF PROGRESS----"UP AND ONWARD" Against this cult, Hawthorne and Melville were to rebel. See Matthiessen, American Renaissance, 652-654.

3) EVIDENCE OF THE MYTH-MAKING FACULTY OF THE AGE (Melville shared it in creating Moby-Dick; Whitman created his "representative American" in Song of Myself; the ballad singers in West Virginia created versions of the ballad of "John Henry." Myths emerged from the Great Plains. The "Orphic Poet" in Nature is a mythological statement. See Matthiessen, American Renaissance, 57, 65, 73, 626ff., 631. For the related forms of "fable" and "proverb" see Nature, 92.18-23,

54.19-23, 42.1ff. The Apostles Creed (<u>Symbolum Apostolorum</u>) is a mythological statement of Christian experience. Every profound or meaningful philosophy of life of necessity has its myth. For an application of the myth-making faculty in Emerson's day, see Coleridge's <u>On the Constitution of Church and State</u>. Witness what I. A. Richards says in his <u>Coleridge on Imagination</u>:

"The saner and greater mythologies are not fancies; they are the utterance of the whole soul of man and, as such, inexhaustible to meditation. They are no amusement or diversion to be sought as a relaxation and an escape from the hard realities of life. They <u>are</u> those hard realities <u>in projection</u>, their symbolic recognition, co-ordination and acceptance. Through such mythologies our will is collected, our powers unified, our growth controlled. Through them the infinitely divergent strayings of our being are brought into 'balance or reconciliation.' The 'opposite and discordant qualities' of things in them acquire a form; and such integrity as we possess as 'civilized' men is our inheritance through them. Without his mythologies man is only a cruel animal without a soul--- for a soul is a central part of his governing mythology---he is a congeries of possibilities without order and without aim."

EMERSON'S DAEMON AND THE ORPHIC POET[1]

It would require too much space to list the scholarly works which have assigned the lines of the Orphic Poet either to Bronson Alcott or to some unknown ancient Neo-Platonic sage, but for nearly fifty years the weight of authority has certainly been against Emerson's authorship of what constitutes a very considerable portion of the crowning chapter of his first significant prose work. The implication has been that Emerson was indifferent to sources, careless about making acknowledgments, and, perhaps, a trifle unfair in borrowing from an unmentioned poet lines that could command the prominent position which they now occupy in the Orphic paragraphs. He is made to appear somewhat unworthy of his well-known reputation for generosity by seeming to deny to a friend during the first stage of a long friendship, an appropriate word of thanks. On the other hand, all fair critics will confess that both in his journals and letters Emerson consistently defended Alcott and praised him highly. They will also see in the anonymity of the first edition of *Nature* some palliation of the supposed offense, but the implication still remains unpleasant, even though every scholar who has attributed the lines or the ideas to Alcott―― or to any other "poet"――has *never* proved his case by any conclusive evidence, or, for that matter, by any evidence at all. Yet the myth has been exceedingly tenacious. The available facts――and there have been many since the publication of Emerson's journals――make it clear that the Orphic Poet could have been no one but the daemon of Emerson himself ――the daemon whose law was self-reliance. In fact, the whole argument of *Nature* is summed up in the Orphic lines, ten years of philosophic development (1825-1835) are symbolized in them, and through them Emerson uttered his most earnest challenge and prophecy to the nineteenth century. To miss their significance is to ignore the first trumpet blast of New England Transcendentalism.

What caused the legend of Alcott's authorship to spring up half a century after the publication of *Nature?* I suspect that Alcott's Orphic *Sayings,* published in the *Dial* a few years after the appearance of Emerson's first book, seemed to legitimize the assignment to Alcott of *all* Orphic utterances in the Concord School. Then, too, it was inevitable that some of the thoughts――especially the commonplaces which Emerson confessed had appeared "to every bard"[2]――in some form or other should have found their way into the writings of his fellow-Transcendentalist, fellow-Platonist and fellow-admirer of Coleridge, yet even these few parallel ideas have never been collected or their relationship and common sources demonstrated. The greatest mistake of early scholarship was that it ignored all chronological perspective. The traditional view, therefore, was

---

[1] I have divided the Orphic Poet's lines into six sections: (a) 87.9-16; (b) 87.17-22; (c) 88.1-10; (d) 88.11―89.11; (e) 93.20―94.12; (f) 94.13―95.12. On the concept of every man's *daemon* or ruling idea, see chap. III and *Journals,* III, 416-417 (Dec. 27, 1834). Emerson was fond of relating his doctrine of Self-Reliance with Socrates' dependence on his daemon. See *Journals,* III, 260 (Feb. 12, 1834), as well as the sermon of Sept. 12, 1830: "The Oracle Within." See *Nature,* 94.14.   [2] See *Nature,* 87.7.

based *only on opinion,* at least until the publication of Emerson's journals in 1909-1914, when it was revealed that the composition of many of the Orphic Poet's lines almost coincided with one of Alcott's visits to Concord. Here was a bit of *circumstantial evidence.* In 1938, an additional straw—— the only one furnished by Alcott himself——was added to the scaffolding. Alcott's journals, published in that year,[3] revealed that after reading *Nature* in September, 1836, Alcott had written: "Mr. E. adverts, *indirectly,* to my 'Psyche,' now in his hands, in the work." He was thinking, quite understandably, of only one non-Orphic or possibly four Orphic lines,[4] for the inspiration of which, as we shall see, Sampson Reed and the Swedenborgians were chiefly responsible. At all events, the first draft of *Psyche,* which, in 1938, was believed lost and which many thought might contain conclusive evidence, has since come to light. I have carefully read it, have partly edited it in the present work,[5] and have found nothing that could have justified Alcott's comment, apart from the four or five lines mentioned above. On the basis of his own words, therefore, and other evidence to be submitted, I believe that Emerson once for all can be exonerated from the charge of ingratitude, without injury to his good friend Alcott and without any diminution of that friend's literary reputation by more than the four or five lines which he believed he had only *indirectly* suggested.

On the basis of the preceding chapters, it is now possible to select the two chief influences on Emerson's speculation during the period before the publication of *Nature* in September, 1836——Coleridge and the Swedenborgians. Those influences appear together in the published and unpublished sermons and can be seen clearly in "Religion and Society" (Oct. 27, 1833),[6] an essay which might better have been called "Prospects," for it points in the same direction as the last chapter of *Nature.* The same two influences are seen in "The Miracle of Our Being" (Sept. 7, 1834),[7] which provides an excellent commentary on the Orphic Poet's concluding lines. The same influences reappear in the "Statement of the First Philosophy" (*ca.* June 10, 1835),[8] with Coleridge's contribution dominant and the Swedenborgian, as usual, largely supplementary and decorative. The same prevail in the "Introductory Lecture on English Literature" (Nov. 5, 1835),[9] which may be considered as a kind of "rough draft" of *Nature.* It is hardly surprising, then, that the Orphic lines in *Nature,* which is the product of all the earlier compositions and their final development, should manifest the same traditions, the one predominantly philosophic and the other essentially religious. The fusion of the two was to become Emerson's distinctive Transcendentalism, for, since there is nothing new under the sun, originality must be defined in terms of a God-given power of selection and combination.

In chapter VIII, I pointed out in some detail that the content and method of Emerson's first great literary work were indebted chiefly to the poet of Highgate. That analysis should be kept in mind during the following dis-

---

[3] *The Journals of Bronson Alcott,* ed. Odell Shepard, Boston, 1938, 78 (italics mine).
[4] *Nature,* 88.6-10 and 90.18.   [6] See *Y E S,* 191-202.
[5] See *E T E,* II, 101-125.   [7] See *Y E S,* 203-212.
[8] This "Statement" appears edited in chap. VII *supra.*
[9] My abstract of this lecture appears elsewhere in this volume.

cussion. In chapters X-XII, I indicated how the Swedenborgians contributed a rich religious spirit together with lustres and illustrations which, considered *poetically* rather than literally,[10] Emerson did not hesitate to join to Coleridge's philosophy as a substitute for the latter's Anglican theology. For example, the activity of Coleridge's Divine Reason was made synonymous with Swedenborg's Influx of the Spirit. Emerson wrote in the "Language" chapter of *Nature*:[11] "That which, intellectually considered, we call Reason, considered in relation to nature, we call Spirit. Spirit is the Creator. Spirit hath life in itself." In the chapter on "Spirit" he said:[12] "Therefore, that spirit, that is, the Supreme Being, does not build up nature around us, but puts it forth through us, as the life of the tree puts forth new branches and leaves through the pores of the old." In his final chapter, "Prospects," he portrayed the "revolution in things" which would attend "the influx of the spirit."[13] The chapter on "Language," moreover, is an example of his use of Swedenborgian lustres to illustrate the progressive quality of Coleridge's *true method*.[14]

The outlines and rough drafts appearing in the journals for the first six months of 1836 indicate that the early chapters of *Nature* were in rather definite form before Alcott's visit in June. The final chapter or chapters still remained to be completed. Emerson wished to conclude his work on a prophetic note, following the example of Coleridge's *The Friend*, the *Statesman's Manual*, and Sampson Reed's "Oration on Genius." "The highest science is prophecy," he wrote on June 22, 1836,[15] and in "Prospects" he attempted to portray a brave new world which, he believed, was one day to dawn——a world externally beautiful because it was to be dependent upon a rich spiritual universe *within* men. He sought for some way of setting forth the rich themes of the preceding seven years——self-reliance, know thyself, trust thyself, man the microcosm, God within, the eternal in the present, like only can know like, what we are within that only can we see without, follow your instincts, build your own world, be genuine, the world exists for you——to name only the chief——but he quite rightly wished to avoid the homiletic form. How was he to announce the truths of the Reason and the moral laws underlying all religions in such a manner as to command attention? Coleridge had shown him that, according to man's relative position in this life, "Sacred History becomes prophetic" and the "Sacred Prophecies historical" and suggested the Biblical style of writing for its twofold significance——because it had "a past and a future, a temporary and a perpetual, a particular and a universal application."[16] Its narrative was fabulous, speaking to the Understanding as well as to the Reason. On April 16, 1835, Emerson himself wrote:[17] "Fable avoids the difficulty, is at once exoteric and esoteric, and is clapped by both sides. Plato and Jesus used it. And History is such a

[10] See *Carlyle-Emerson Corr.*, I, 32-33; *Journals*, IV, 70-71.
[11] *Nature*, 34.22—35.2. See also Coleridge ¶ 28.
[12] *Nature*, 79.18-23.
[13] *Nature*, 94.16-17.   [15] See *Journals*, IV, 73. Cf. *Nature*, 87.8.
[14] See Coleridge ¶s. 127ff.   [16] See Coleridge ¶ 248.
[17] *Journals*, III, 468. See also the long extract on "Mythology" taken from Coleridge's tr. of Schiller's *Wallenstein* and published in *Parnassus*, Boston, 1875, 120. See sections III and VII of Emerson's "Statement of the First Philosophy" for an excellent commentary on the use of orphic or fabulous elements.

fable." But what fable should he use, and how might he disown responsibility for its literal meaning when it should fall into the hands of men under the dominion of the Understanding? He decided, finally, to construct a composite oracle, drawing upon Plato and others, but especially upon the Swedenborgians, putting the whole into the mouth of an anonymous "poet." He had observed earlier that one's words always gained force when quoted by another.[18] Had not Coleridge employed a "voice" in the first essay of *The Friend?* Had not Carlyle prophesied in the person of Diogenes Teufelsdröckh, whose remarks Emerson had recently edited?[19] Ever since college days, moreover, Emerson had liked to assume pseudonyms in his journals and letters,[20] and he frequently addressed himself as if writing to a stranger or described himself in the third person.[21] Since the word *Orphic* was exceedingly common in his period and bore no greater significance than "oracular" or "proverbial,"[22] it was easily appropriated for his *alter ego.* Later on, in his second series of *Essays,* he repeated the little trick by putting his remarks on genius into the mouth of "a bard."[23]

Emerson always made an effort to collect for his journals all "necessary truths"[24] and examples of the *moral sublime*[25] that he could discover. These, for him, were Orphic, as he confessed in the first of two passages that must be considered in any discussion of the Orphic Poet:[26]

In what I call the *cyclus* of orphic words, which I find in Bacon, in Cudworth, in Plutarch, in Plato, in that which the new Church[27] would indicate when it speaks of the truths possessed by the primeval church broken up into fragments and floating hither and thither in the corrupt church,[28] I perceive myself addressed thoroughly. They do

---

[18] See *Journals,* III, 466. " 'Already my opinion has gained infinitely in force when another has adopted it.' This is the reason why a writer appears ever to so much more advantage in the pages of another man's book than in his own. Coleridge, Wordsworth, Schelling are conclusive, when Channing or Carlyle or Everett quotes them, but if you take up their own books, then instantly they become, not lawgivers, but modest, peccable candidates for your approbation."

[19] Emerson's preface to the first American ed. of *Sartor Resartus* was dated March, 1836.

[20] See "Junio" in *Journals,* I, 11, 23, 32; cf. *Letters,* I, 33, 34. See also his treatment of Aunt Mary's name in *Journals,* I, 97. See George E. Woodberry, *Ralph Waldo Emerson,* N.Y., 1914: "He was intimately aware of the poetic part of his nature, and early idealized it and set it apart as a higher self. 'A certain poet told me,' he was afterward accustomed to write, and later he named him Osman; it was this poet known within."

[21] He addresses himself as "Son of man" in *Letters,* I, 376 (Apr. 18, 1833); he describes himself objectively in *Journals,* III, 470 (Apr. 19, 1835). Cf. also *Journals,* III, 260.

[22] See *Works of Plato* (tr. Taylor), I, xxxvii: "And he who desires to signify divine concerns through symbols is Orphic." See "Orphic Sayings from Goethe," *The Western Messenger,* II, 59-62 (August, 1836); Cudworth's *Intellectual System* (1820), II, 69ff. and 78ff. discussed Orphism at length. Coleridge's poem "To a Gentleman" [*i.e.,* Wordsworth] dealt with ·

An orphic song indeed
A song divine of high and passionate thoughts
To their own music chaunted!

and quoted the lines in *The Friend* [*Complete Works* (Shedd), II], 338. See Sampson Reed ¶ 20 on Orpheus.   [24] *Journals,* II, 357-358 (Feb. 23, 1831).
[23] See "The Poet," *Works,* III, 22-24.   [25] *Journals,* II, 404-405.
[26] *Journals,* IV, 154-155 (Nov. 28, 1836) and IV, 168 (Dec. 10, 1836).
[27] *I.e.,* the Swedenborgians.
[28] Consult John F. Potts, *The Swedenborg Concordance,* London (5 vols.), 1888. See Swedenborg ¶ 51, and Sampson Reed, "Inspiration of the Sacred Scripture," *N J M,* VIII (1834-1835), 122-128, esp. p. 127. Cf. also Samuel Worcester *et al.* in *N J M,* IX (1835-1836), 342-350.

touch the intellect and cause a gush of emotion which we call the moral sublime; they pervade also the moral nature. Now the universal man,[29] when he comes, must so speak. He must not be one-toned.[30] He must recognize by addressing the whole nature. Of these truths Jesus uttered many, such as: God is no respecter of persons:[31] His kingdom cometh without observation.[32] His kingdom is a little child.[33]

Believe Christianity. What else can you do? It is not matter of doubt. What is good about it is self-affirming. When Jesus says the kingdom of God comes without observation; comes as a little child; is within you,[34] etc., these are not propositions upon which you can exercise any election, but are philosophical verities quite independent of any asseveration, or testimony, or abnegation.

It is clear from the earlier paragraph, therefore, that the New Church provided Emerson with Orphic words and examples of the moral sublime. He had written Carlyle on November 20, 1834, that the Swedenborgians were a sect which he thought "must contribute more than all other sects to the new faith which must arise out of all,"[35] and they were again in his mind on June 16, 1836, when he wrote[36] that Swedenborg would soon become popular. One merely had to forget his religious dogmatism, regard him as a poet, and admire him "for his verities." On June 22, after Alcott had returned to Boston, Emerson appears to have sought inspiration in the works of a certain "early oracle"——especially in an unpublished essay by the same, from which he copied a specimen of the moral sublime. It was Sampson Reed's "Oration on Genius."[37] We shall do well to remember, therefore, thàt Reed and Swedenborg were among the influences which nourished Emerson's daemon while it dictated the following journal,[38] elements from which found their way into the last two chapters of *Nature*. The reader will note that Emerson carefully put quotation marks around two of Alcott's utterances.[39] He needed none, of course, around the Orphic lines inspired by his own poetic muse.

WEDNESDAY, JUNE 22, 1836.

Mr Alcott has been here with his Olympian dreams. He is a world-builder.[40] Evermore he toils to solve the problem, Whence is the World? The point at which he prefers to begin is the Mystery of the Birth of a child. I tell him it is idle for him to affect to feel an interest in the compositions[41] of any one else.[42]
5 Particulars,——particular tho'ts, sentences, facts even, cannot interest him except

[29] See *Nature*, 87.13 (Orphic Poet I).
[30] Alcott is, therefore, eliminated. For his monomania and "single tone" see *Journals*, IV, 71-72; IV, 403 etc.
[31] St. Paul in Romans 2:11 said: "For there is no respect of persons with God." St. Peter in Acts 10:34 said: "Of a truth I perceive that God is no respecter of persons." See *Journals*, II, 409-410: "God does not use personal authority. It is the direct effect of all spiritual truth to abrogate, nullify, personal authority,—to make us love the virtue and the person exactly by the measure of his virtues, but not to honour the inherent evils for the sake of any person. He is no respecter of *persons*."
[32] Luke 17:20——"The kingdom of God cometh not with observation." The following verse contains Emerson's favorite line: ". . . the kingdom of God is within you." See *Nature*, 95.7-9 (Orphic Poet VI) for a modification of the first.
[33] Emerson somewhat modifies Mark 10:15 and Luke 18:17.
[34] See notes 32 and 33 above.   [36] *Journals*, IV, 70-71.
[35] *Carlyle-Emerson Corr.*, I, 33.   [37] *Journals*, IV, 74. See Sampson Reed ¶ 46.
[38] The following extract is taken from the *Typescript Journals*, "B," Part II, pp. 250-257.   [39] See lines 17 and 99.
[40] See the significance of this expression in *Nature*, 94.13ff. (Orphic Poet VI).
[41] MS. originally had "thoughts."   [42] See note 30 above.

as for a moment they take their place as a ray from his orb. The Whole,——
Nature proceeding from himself, is what he studies. But he loses like other
sovereigns great pleasures by reason of his grandeur   I go to Shakspear Goethe
Swift even to Tennyson submit myself to them become merely an organ of
10 hearing & yield to the law of their being   I am paid for thus being nothing
by an entire new mind & thus a Proteus[43] I enjoy the Universe through the
powers & organs of a hundred different men. But Alcott cannot delight in Shakspear cannot get near him. And so with all things. What is characteristic also, he
cannot recal one word or part of his own conversation or of any one's let the
15 expression be never so happy. He made here some majestic utterances but so
inspired me that even I forgot the words often. The grass the earth[44] seemed to
him "the refuse of spirit."

Jesus says, Leave father & mother, house & lands & follow me.[45] And there is
no man who hath left all but he receives more. This is as true intellectually
20 as morally. Each new mind we approach seems to require an abdication of all
our past & present empire. A new doctrine seems at first a subversion of all our
opinions, tastes, & manner of living   So did Jesus, so did Kant, so did
Swedenborg, so did Cousin, so did Alcott seem. Take thankfully & heartily all
they can give, exhaust them, leave father & mother & goods, wrestle with them
25 let them not go until their blessing be won[46] & after a short season the dismay
will be overpast, the excess of influence will be withdrawn & they will be no
longer an alarming meteor but one more bright star shining[47] serenely in your
heaven & blending its light with all your day.[48]

I love the wood god. I love the mighty PAN.

30   Yesterday I walked in the storm

And truly in the fields I am not alone or unacknowledged.[49] They nod to me
& I to them. The waving of the boughs of trees in a storm is new to me & old.
It takes me by surprize & yet is not unknown. Its effect is like that of a higher
thought or a better emotion coming over me when I deemed I was thinking
35 justly or doing right. We distrust & deny inwardly our own sympathy with
nature. We own & disown our relation to it. We are like Nebuchadnezzar cast
down from our throne bereft of our reason & eating grass like an ox.

Man is the dwarf of himself

Is it not true that spirit in us is dwarfed by clay?   that once Man was
40 permeated & dissolved by spirit. He filled Nature with his overflowing currents.
Out from him sprang the sun & moon   from man the sun from woman the
moon   The laws of his mind   the periods of his deeds   externized themselves into day & night into the year & seasons   But having made for himself
this vast shell the waters retired, he no longer fills its veins & veinlets he
45 is shrunk into a drop. He sees it still fits him but fits him colossally. He adores
timidly his own work. Say rather once it fitted him now it corresponds to him
from far &[50] on high. Yet now he starts occasionally in his slumber & wonders[51]
at himself & his house & muses strangely at the resemblance betwixt him & it.

---

[43] See Coleridge ¶ 65 for Emerson's source.
[44] Originally the MS. read "animals."
[45] See Matthew 19:29; Mark 10:29-30; Luke 18:29-30.
[46] An allusion to Genesis 32:26.
[47] Followed originally by the word "peace[fully?]."
[48] A possible allusion to Wordsworth's *Ode on Intimations of Immortality*, line 152.
[49] The first part of this paragraph appears in *Nature*, 13.21—14.5.
[50] Originally followed by "from."   [51] See below lines 62, 63, 127.

If now he have power "if that his word is sterling yet in England" he sees that
50 it is unconscious power; power superior to his will; or Instinct

Now all man's power over nature is by the understanding; as by manure,
steam, the economic use of the wind & water & needle, coal, filling teeth with
gold; making wooden legs; &c, &c. It is a[52] recovering his world an inch at a
time & not a[53] resumption of power by vaulting at once into his seat.[54]

55   But Animal Magnetism, the Miracles of enthusiasts as Hohenlohe & the
Shakers & the Swedenborgian prayer, eloquence, self healing as weak eyes,[55]
the achievements of a principle as in Revolutions & in the abolition of Slave
Trade——& the wisdom (often observed) of children[56]——these are the examples
of the Reason's momentary grasp of the sceptre. the exertions of a power not in
60 time or in space but an instantaneous causing in-streaming power.[57]
                                         2   1

The kingdom of man over nature shall not come with observation[58]   To all
these wonders,[59] to a dominion such as now is beyond his dream of God, he shall
return[60] without more wonder[61] than the blind man feels who is gradually restored
to perfect sight.

65   The sordor & filths of nature the sun shall exhale & the wind dry up.

It is the property of the divine[62] to be reproductive.[63] The harvest is seed.[64]
The good sermon becomes a text in the hearer's mind. That is the good book[65]
which sets us at work. The highest science is prophecy.[66] Jesus is but the
harbinger & announcer of the Comforter to come, & his continual office is to
70 make himself less to us by making us demand more.[67]

---

[52] Originally followed by "reascending his throne by."
[53] Originally followed by "vaulting into his seat by."
[54] This paragraph appears in *Nature*, 89.18—90.4. For a discussion of the Understanding, see Coleridge ¶s. 1-56 and chap. VII *passim*.
[55] The bracketed words were inserted between the lines, and it is not clear exactly
where in the sequence they were intended to go.
[56] At this point Emerson almost certainly was thinking of Wordsworth's *Ode*, the
experiments described in Elizabeth P. Peabody's *Record of a [Alcott's] School* (1835),
Alcott's earlier MS. of *Psyche*, and Alcott's manuscript of *Conversations with Children
on the Gospels*. For the last, see lines 92-98 below.   [58] See lines 87 and 125 below.
[57] This paragraph is expanded in *Nature*, 90.4—22.   [60] Originally followed by "&."
[59] Originally followed by "he returns."
[61] See lines 47, 62, 63, 127; Sampson Reed ¶s. 15, 17, 28; Swedenborg ¶ 47.
[62] Originally "true."   [63] See *Nature*, 28.23—29.1.
[64] See *Y E S*, 55.1ff. ("A Feast of Remembrance," Sept. 27, 1829): "Great truths
which ages toiled to prove they did prove and we begin where they ended. The results
of an old philosopher are the elements of his pupil. Their harvest is our seed." Emerson
liked to use *seed* illustrations. For other examples see *Letters*, I, 148, 181, 291, 412;
Journals, III, 351, 497. See *Nature*, 36.2-7 and Mark 4:3ff.
[65] In his sermon, "Charity," (June 14, 1829) he calls good books the "seeds of civilization," "silent benefactors," and "modest missionaries that carry light and truth and
virtue from one generation to another." See *Y E S*, 240.41ff.
[66] See *Nature*, 87.8.
[67] See *Y E S*, 195.6ff. ("Religion and Society," Oct. 27, 1833): "I cannot but think that
Jesus Christ will be better loved by not being adored. He has had, as we all know, an
unnatural, an artificial place for ages in human opinions—a place too high for love.
There is a recoil of the affections from all authority and force. To the barbarous state
of society it was thought to add to the dignity of Christ to make him king, to make him
demigod, to make him God." *Ibid.*, 196.33ff.: "He never said, All truth have I revealed
—but that which was committed to me. He plainly affirms the direct contrary. I will
send you another Teacher, another Comforter, even the spirit of Truth; he will guide
you into all truth. He promised that continual effort of the divine Providence which is
always instructing those who are in the attitude of scholars." See *Y E S*, 177.31ff.

The Understanding, the Usurping Understanding the lieutenant of Reason,[68] his[69] hired man,[70] the moment the Master is gone[71] steps into his place this usher commands sets himself to finish what He was doing, but instantly proceeds with his own dwarf[72] Architecture & thoroughly cheats us until presently for
75 a moment Reason returns & the slave obeys, & his work shrinks into tatters & cobwebs.

Not whilst the wise are one class & the good another,[73] not whilst the physiologist & the psychologist are twain, can a Man exist, & Messiah[74] come.

A man is a god in ruins. When men are child-like, life may[75] be longer. Now
80 the world would be more monstrous yet, if these disorganizations were more permanent. Infancy[76] is the perpetual messiah which comes into the arms of these lost beings, & pleads with them to return to paradise.

How hard to write the truth. "Let a man rejoice in the truth and not that he has found it," said my early oracle.[77] Well, so soon as I have seen the truth I
85 clap my hands & rejoice & go back to see it & forward to tell men. I am so pleased therewith that presently it vanishes. Then am I submiss & it appears "without observation."[78] I write it down, & it is gone.[79] Yet is[80] the benefit of others & their love of receiving truth from me the reason of my interest & effort to obtain it & thus do I double & treble with God.[81] The Reason refuses
90 to play at couples with Understanding; to subserve the private ends of the Understanding.[82]

FRIDAY, JUNE 24, 1836.

I have read with great pleasure sometimes with delight No. 5 of Mr Alcott's Record of Conversations in the Gospels.[83] The internal evidence of the

---

Emerson says Jesus saves us only "by inducing us to save ourselves." See *Journals*, III, 324 (Aug. 10, 1834).
[68] See Coleridge ¶s. 1-56.   [70] Originally followed by "&."
[69] Originally "the."   [71] Originally followed by "he."
                                                         [72] See lines 38-39 above.
[73] Emerson here reflects his meditation on Sampson Reed's "Oration on Genius," *E T E*, II, 10-11. Reed therein laments that what is called *genius* is nothing but a partial ability. Men are extolled as *great* who are not *good*, and true genius requires *both* qualities, especially a dependence upon God, who is the source of all our Being. He blames the "Old Church" in large measure for the unhappy separation of greatness and goodness—of religion and philosophy: "It needs no uncommon eye to see, that the finger of death has rested on the church. Religion and death have in the human mind been connected with the same train of associations. . . . It is not strange, then, that genius, such as could exist on the earth, should take its flight to the mountains . . . that, in the human mind, greatness is one thing, and goodness another; that philosophy is divorced from religion; that truth is separated from its source; that that which is called goodness is sad, and that which is called genius is proud. . . . When the heart is purified from all selfish and worldly affections, then may genius find its seat in the church. . . . The arts will spring in full-grown beauty from Him who is the source of beauty. . . . Science will be full of life, as nature is full of God. . . . The time is not far distant." See also Sampson Reed ¶s. 46ff.
[74] By the coming of the Messiah Emerson is probably referring figuratively to Reed's optimistic picture of the new era set forth in the "Oration on Genius" and later in his own *Nature*, 94-95.   [75] Originally "will."   [76] Originally "Childhood."
[77] The oracle is Sampson Reed, and the line appears in his ¶ 46. See also "Growth of the Mind," *E T E*, II, 13.4: ". . . . to be proud of the truth is to cease to possess it."
[78] See lines 61 and 125 above.
[79] This thought he expressed in his "Statement of the First Philosophy," sections XII-XIV, edited in chap. VII above.   [80] Originally "for."
[81] Emerson is here paraphrasing Sampson Reed ¶ 44.   [82] See Coleridge ¶s. 1-56.
[83] Apparently the first draft of Alcott's MS. The first volume was not published until

genuineness of the thinking on the part of the children is often very strong.[84]
95   Their wisdom is something the less surprizing because of the simplicity of the
instrument on which they play these fine airs. It is a harp of two strings, Matter
& Spirit, & in whatever combination or contrast or harmony you strike them,
always the effect is sublime.

"And no man gave him. He was alone with the swine; himself a swine."[85]
100   Alcott.

Is it not plain that prayer is a true study of truth. No man ever prayed heartily
without learning something.[86]

Every one has a trust of power.[87]   every man——every boy——a jurisdiction, if it be only over a cow, or a rood of a potato field, or a fleet of ships, or
105   the laws of a state.

Magnitude is nothing to Science. The ocean is a large drop; the drop, a small
ocean.[88]

It is essential to a true theory of Nature & Man, that it should contain
somewhat progressive,[89] should ascribe freedom to the will, or benevolent de-
110   signs to the Deity   And the effect of the ideal theory truly seen is this;[90]
Nature is not stable but fluid. Spirit alters, moulds, makes it. The immobility or
bruteness of nature is the absence of spirit; to pure spirit it is fluid, it is
volatile, it is obedient. Believe that the[91] world exists for you.   for you
is the phenomenon perfect & what we are, that only we see. All that Adam
115   had,[92] all that Caesar could, you have & can do   Adam called it the earth,
Caesar called life Rome; you perhaps call it a cobbler's trade, yet line for
line & point for point, you have the whole circle   As fast as your spirit
quits its earth, disagreeable appearances, prisons, spiders, snakes, pests, mad-
houses, vanish.   they are temporary & shall be no more seen   the sordor
120   & filths of nature, the sun shall dry up & the wind exhale.[93] As before the
Summer, the snowbanks melt and the face of the earth becomes green so[94]
the spirit shall create its ornaments along its path & carry with it the beauty
it visits & the song which enchants it.——creates intelligent faces & warm
hearts and sweet discourse heroic acts around its way until evil is no more
125   seen   This kingdom of man over nature which shall not come with observation.[95]   a dominion such as now is beyond his dream of God he shall enter
without more wonder[96] than the blind man feels who is gradually restored to
perfect sight.

Insist upon seeing Nature as a problem to be solved. It is a question addressed
130   to you   What is a child? What is a woman? What is a year or a season?

---

late December, 1836.
[84] See line 58 above.
[85] He refers apparently to the "Parable of the Prodigal Son" in Luke 15:11-24.
[86] See *Nature*, 92.3-6.
[87] Preceding this sentence in the typescript is the following cancellation: "Every one
has a charge trust of power, one talent, if it be only a jurisdiction." Above the line is
written "men & boys." See below lines 114-117.
[88] This thought was expressed earlier on June 4, 1836. See *Journals*, IV, 60. Cf. Coleridge ¶ 253 and lines 136-137 *infra*.   [89] See *Nature*, 76.3-5.
[91] The *Typescript Journals* repeat "the."   [90] See *Nature*, 74.6-7.
[92] Originally followed by "saw."   [93] Originally "dissipate."
[94] Originally followed by "shall the path of P." The "shall" of this phrase is still
uncancelled in the typescript.
[95] See lines 61 and 87 above.   [96] See note 61 above.

What do they signify & say to ME?[97]

Then it occurs as a question whether the Ideal Theory is not merely introductory[98] to Spiritual views   It diminishes & degrades matter in order to
receive a new view of it, namely this, that the world is the new fruit of Spirit
135 evermore.

There is one drop in the number of its drops which makes the ocean greater
than any sea.[99]

WEDNESDAY, JUNE 29, 1836.

In this pleasing contrite wood life which God allows me, let me record day
by day my honest thoughts, & the record ought to have the interest to a
140 philosopher which the life of a gymnosophist or stylit had.[100]

The last two chapters of *Nature* were composed at one time, and it is
not surprising, therefore, to find that the Orphic paragraphs in "Prospects" should have interesting parallels at the close of the preceding chapter on "Spirit" or that one should provide illustrations and commentary
for the other. I here list the analogues, assigning to them the numbers
corresponding to those of the complete Orphic passages, which will be
discussed exhaustively later in the present chapter:

I

As a plant upon the earth, so a man rests upon the bosom of God; he is nourished by unfailing fountains, and draws, at his need, inexhaustible power. Who can set bounds to the possibilities of man? (79.23—80.4).

The foundations of man are not in matter, but in spirit. But the element of spirit is eternity. (87.9-11).

II

We are as much strangers in nature, as we are aliens from God. . . . Yet this may show us what discord is be-tween man and nature, for you cannot freely admire a noble landscape, if

We distrust and deny inwardly our sympathy with nature. We own and dis-own our relation to it, by turns. . . . But who can set limits to the remedial force of spirit? (87.17-22).

---

[97] See *Y E S*, 204.16-25. The Swedenborgians stimulated Emerson to ask these questions. They more than others were able to give him spiritual answers. See *Nature*,
92.12-18.   [98] See *Nature*, 79.1-4.

[99] This sentence appears in *Letters*, I, 200 (May 19? 1827). Emerson wrote to Charles
as follows (italics mine): "Give yourself to study with boundless ambition. despising as
much as you please the primary & vulgar landmarks of success in the consciousness y^t
you aim to raise your rank not among your compeers alone but in that great scale of
moral beings which embraces the invisible & the visible. *There is one drop in the
number of its drops wh makes the ocean greater than any sea.* & by every discovery of
a thot or a relation wh. your diligence accumulates perchance you overtop another &
another individual in those enormous congregations of aspirants which in the body &
out of the body environ you."

[100] Continued in "Self-Reliance," *Works*, II, 58. Emerson earlier referred to Simeon
Stylites in *Journals*, III, 369 and 439. See S. Cheetham, *A History of the Christian
Church During the First Six Centuries*, London, 1894, 353: "Simeon, the most noted of
these pillar-saints, who lived in the early part of the fifth century, established himself
on a column which was finally raised to the height of sixty feet from the ground. There
he remained some thirty years, exhorting to repentance those who flocked to him,
settling disputes, making enemies to be at one, converting pagans. Men otherwise careless were arrested by so extraordinary a spectacle."

laborers are digging in the field hard by. (81.3-14). Who can set bounds to the possibilities of man? (80.3-4).

IV

As we degenerate, the contrast between us and our house is more evident. (81.2-3). The world proceeds from the same spirit as the body of man. It is a remoter and inferior incarnation of God, a projection of God in the unconscious. . . . Its serene order is inviolable by us. It is therefore, to us, the present expositor of the divine mind. It is a fixed point whereby we may measure our departure. (80.16—81.2).

Man is the dwarf of himself. Once he was permeated and dissolved by spirit. He filled nature with his overflowing currents. . . ; he is shrunk to a drop. He sees, that the structure still fits him, but fits him colossally. (88.11-22).

V

We learn . . . that spirit creates; that behind nature, throughout nature, spirit is present; that spirit is one and not compound; that spirit does not act upon us from without, that is, in space and time, but spiritually, or through ourselves. Therefore, that spirit, that is, the Supreme Being, does not build up nature around us, but puts it forth through us, as the life of the tree puts forth new branches and leaves through the pores of the old. (79.8-23).

Nature is not fixed but fluid. Spirit alters, moulds, makes it. The immobility or bruteness of nature, is the absence of spirit; to pure spirit, it is fluid, it is volatile, it is obedient. Every spirit builds itself a house; and beyond its house, a world; and beyond its world, a heaven. (93.20——94.3).

VI

This view . . . animates me to create my own world through the purification of my soul. (80.8-15). Once inspire the infinite, by being admitted to behold the absolute natures of justice and truth, and we learn that man has access to the entire mind of the Creator, is himself the creator in the finite. (80.4-8). We do not understand the notes of birds. The fox and the deer run away from us; the bear and tiger rend us. We do not know the uses of more than a few plants . . . . (81.5-9).

Build, therefore, your own world. As fast as you conform your life to the pure idea in your mind, that will unfold its great proportions. A correspondent revolution in things will attend the influx of the spirit. So fast will disagreeable appearances, swine, spiders, snakes, pests . . . vanish; they are temporary and shall be no more seen. (94.13-20).

Anyone who has studied carefully chapters X-XII will have no difficulty in identifying the ideas expressed in the above parallels.[101] They are echoes of the Swedenborgian doctrine that creation is accomplished by spiritual influx from the Heavens through the sun of the natural world and also through man; that the soul makes the body and proceeds to make the world of appearances; that good and bad affections are clothed in pleasant and unpleasant external objects; that evil animals are the notable results of man's unregenerate state; that disorganizations of any kind in

---

[101] Study the ¶s. in chaps. X and XI.

the external world are proof of man's fallen condition; that nature, though
in one sense disorganized by man's fall, in another sense, because of certain fixed patterns, does not vary with man's changing states in certain
basic functions and, therefore, is a monitor to him of spiritual and moral
truth; that man through degeneration becomes blind to the spiritual sun
and moon and begins to worship the luminaries of the world of nature;
that even though degraded man still experiences enough of the Divine
Influx to remember something of his original state; that his improvement
comes only through submission to the spiritual stream that tries to pass
through him unhindered by his inner hell; that the unspiritual man loses
a knowledge of the language of nature, especially the true use of animals
and plants and their spiritual significance; that man builds his eternal
condition (his eternal heaven and hell) while still in this life and gradually
passes into the next as in a dream and without surprise; that infancy
illustrates the ideal of spiritual consciousness, for at the early stage of
life in man the Divine Influx flows unimpeded; that in the mature individual the condition of childlikeness is called "innocency;" that the Divine
Influx, when unhindered, purifies man's instincts, and his whole life becomes "instinctive"——guided by the "supervoluntary" or that which is
above his own will. More of these Swedenborgian ideas will appear in the
complete Orphic paragraphs to follow.[102] I shall discuss each section
separately, placing on the right the form in which it appears in the
Typescript Journals for June 22 and 24, which I have reproduced completely in the foregoing.

In chapter VII of *Nature*, Emerson essentially concluded the philosophical development of his book, and the work might well have ended on
the lofty ethical and spiritual note observable in its final pages. He felt
obliged, however, to prolong the conclusion by discussing the contemporary
scene and by giving an account of the results to be anticipated from a
transcendental or spiritual outlook on life. The chapter on "Prospects,"
therefore, threatened to become a prosy anticlimax, but in the Orphic
Poet's lines, Emerson found the means of reascending to the eloquent level
of the chapter on "Spirit" and of maintaining it to the very end. The first
Orphic paragraph,[103] as might be expected, contains an allusion to the
parallels in the earlier chapter, set forth above.[104]

COMMENTARY ON EMERSON'S ORPHIC POETRY

I

'The foundations of man are not in
matter, but in spirit. But the element
of spirit is eternity. To it, therefore,
the longest series of events, the oldest
chronologies are young and recent. In
the cycle of the universal man, from
whom the known individuals proceed,
centuries are points, and all history is
but the epoch of one degradation.
(87.9-16).

---

[102] See chap. VIII for the plan followed by Emerson in combining Coleridge and
Swedenborg.
[103] Note that this has no parallel in the journals.   [104] See *Nature*, 79.5—81.16.

Emerson's sermons are an excellent commentary on the fact that man's foundation is in Spirit rather than matter,[105] and they are conveniently summarized in "Gnothi Seauton:"[106]

> He is in thy world,
> But thy world knows him not.
> He is the mighty Heart
> From which life's varied pulses part.
> Clouded and shrouded there doth sit
> The Infinite
> Embosomed in a man;
> And thou art stranger to thy guest,
> And know'st not what thou dost invest.
> The clouds that veil his life within
> Are thy thick woven webs of sin,
> Which his glory struggling through
> Darkens to thine evil hue.

The later sermons show a developed and more impersonal transcendentalism, especially "The Genuine Man" (Oct. 21, 1832), "Religion and Society" (Oct. 27, 1833)——which might better have been called "Prospects"——and "The Miracle of Our Being" (Sept. 7, 1834).[107] In his "Statement of the First Philosophy" (June 10, 1835),[108] moreover, he followed Coleridge in indicating that *Spirit* and the *Reason* are synonymous terms for the Reality behind men and phenomena,[109] *i.e.*, for that Transcendental Force whose *element is eternity*. This eternal Spirit "does not act upon us from without, that is, in space and time, but spiritually, or through ourselves."[110] The Sun behind all suns, therefore, shines every day,[111] making religion an immediate experience rather than a venerable tradition. Emerson had expressed this view as early as September 23, 1826, in his letter to Aunt Mary,[112] twenty-five days after the publication[113] of the *Growth of the Mind*. He had apparently been influenced by Reed's discussion of time and eternity in that work,[114] but he did not then, or ever, agree with Reed's Christology. To Emerson, the religion of the future was to be a lofty transcendentalism based on the eternal principles of a moral and spiritual universe without the limitations of conventional religious channels and the unjustified veneration of prophets and martyrs:[115]

The Revival that comes next must be preached to man's moral nature, and from a height of principle that subordinates all persons. It must forget historical Christianity

---

[105] *E.g.*, "Salvation, Now" (June 13, 1830); "Self-Culture" (Sept. 5, 1830); "The Oracle Within" (Sept. 12, 1830); "Trust Yourself" (Dec. 3, 1830); "Reason and Revelation" (Oct. 24, 1830); "The Kingdom of Heaven Is Within" (Oct. 31, 1830); "God in the Soul" (Mar. 6, 1831); "We Are Not Our Own" (July 24, 1831). See esp. *Y E S*, 132.14-21.

[106] It is edited in chap. VII above, under the date indicated. I quote here lines 10-22.

[107] These appear in *Y E S*, 180-212.

[108] Edited in chap. VII under the date indicated.

[109] See *Nature*, 34.22ff.: "That which, intellectually considered, we call Reason, considered in relation to nature, we call Spirit. Spirit is the Creator." Cf. Coleridge ¶ 28.

[110] *Nature*, 79.16-18.

[111] Cf. *Nature*, 5.17. See also *Journals*, III, 399: "Within and Above are synonyms."

[112] See *Letters*, I, 174-175.

[113] *The Boston Daily Advertiser* gave the date of publication as Aug. 29, 1826.

[114] See *E T E*, II, 15-17. See also Sampson Reed ¶s. 1-5.

[115] See *Journals*, IV, 15-16 (Feb. 28, 1836). See also note 67 above.

and preach God who is, not God who was. *Eripitur persona, manet res.*[115a] It must preach the Eternity of God as a practical doctrine.

Christianity he definitely regarded as a time-and-space tradition. The Spirit or the sublime Reason, therefore, transcended it——functioned in all ages, both universally and immediately. Why follow the dogmas of a sect when one might go to the immediate source of all sects?[116]

> Time & Space are below [Reason's] sphere. It considers things according to more intimate properties. It beholds their essence wherein is seen what they can produce. It is in all men, even in the worst, & constitutes them men. In bad men it is dormant; in the good, efficient. But it is perfect & identical in all, underneath the peculiarities, the vices, & the errors of the individual. A man feels that his fortune, friendships, opinions, yea, all the parts of his individual existence, are merely superficial to the principle of Right. Compared with the self-existence of the laws of Truth & Right whereof he is conscious, his personality is a parasitic deciduous atom. Hence the doctrine of Cosmism,[117] that the Soul which was, shall be, but that our private life which was created, may be dissipated.

Thus man rests upon an eternal world which is immediately accessible. When he is aware of its presence, he is "in Heaven," for

> Heaven is the name we give to the True State, the world of Reason, not of the Understanding; of the Real, not the Apparent. It exists always, whether it is ever to be separated from the Hell[118] or not. It is, as Coleridge said, another world, but not to come.[119] The world I describe is that, where only the laws of mind are known; the only economy of time is saying and doing nothing untrue to self.[120]

The chronological systems of the Greeks and Romans, of the early Hebrews, and of Christian civilization must fade, he believed, when compared with an eternal moral order.[121]

Emerson's concept of Universal Man seems to have come from Plato's discussion of "Universals" or "Ideas" in the *Parmenides* and in the *Sophista.*[122] It was corroborated by Victor Cousin[123] and by Swedenborg's

---

[115a] See note 117 *infra* and context. See *Journals*, II, 324-325 (Dec. 10, 1830).

[116] Section V of the "Statement of the First Philosophy" (June 10, 1835). See the complete "Statement" in chap. VII.

[117] See note 115a above. In 1826, Emerson had rebelled against the thought of an impersonal spiritual existence. By 1831, in "Γνωθι Σεαυτον," he had come to favor it. Compare *Journals*, II, 101 (June 15, 1826): " 'T is not in man to thank the philosopher that merges his selfish in the social nature. 'T was a foolish vanity in the Stoic to talk in this wise. It suggested or else grew out of that primeval dogma of the Mundane Soul. No man loves it; the meanest loses more than he gains by parting with his identity to make an integral atom of the Whole." See also *Journals*, II, 109 (June 30, 1826): ". . . but let the glory and virtue of other worlds be as they may, in parting with our identity we part with happiness." See also *Y E S*, 245.10-16 (May 3, 1829). See his reference to Mary Rotch in *Journals*, III, 399. For his riper view with its emphasis on the *impersonal* see *Journals*, II, 363 on the subject of genius, based upon Sampson Reed's "Oration." Genius is *not* a characteristic of individuality; it doesn't increase individuality; it is the impersonal or Divine element, available to all men but too often thwarted or denied. It is *reception* from the Reason or from the Spiritual Center of the universe. It is not ours, but we are ITS.

[118] See Swedenborg ¶s. 8-9.   [119] See Coleridge ¶ 275.

[120] See *Journals*, III, 488 (June 4, 1835). See also stanza VIII of the "Statement of the First Philosophy" (June 10, 1835): "Heaven is the projection of the Ideas of Reason on the plane of the understanding." See notes 209 and 276 and context.

[121] He was probably thinking of the background presupposed by Plato in the legend of the reign of Cronos in *The Statesman* and of the ancient chronology discussed in the "Tale of Solon" (*Timaeus*); also of *Critias, or the Island of Atlantis.*

[122] See *The Works of Plato* (tr. Thomas Taylor), III, 1-200 *et passim.*

[123] See the chapter on Cousin.

portrayal of heaven as the "Greatest Man" or the "Divine Man."[124] As early as November 15, 1834,[125] Emerson tried to clarify his thinking on the individual *versus* the universal and to prepare a statement that might be both "history and prophecy."[126] It will be well, therefore, to trace the development of his thought on a doctrine extremely important in all his later works:

Shakspeare immortalizes his characters. They live to every age and, as we say of Christianity, have a prospective adaptation. Ben Jonson's are all dead. . . . But universal man appreciates Shakspeare,——boys, rabble, every man of strong sense though uncultivated as——.[127]

[W]e find there is a certain *standard idea of man* which we all have in our thoughts, in our conversation. In every dispute, we have tacit reference to it all along. If we talk on any question of speculation with a man who seems to us to be in great error, we always believe that at last, perhaps not in this life, but somewhere, sometime, he will come to the truth; he will see as we see; will come nearer to this standard-man, which we believe exists for both. This feeling amounts to so strong a confidence, when a man is very wrongheaded, that we do not feel it to be of great importance to set him right, sure that he will come right hereafter if left to himself.[128]

Every man has an idea of a greatness that was never realized. Take the history of a great and good man, of Newton, or Franklin, or Washington, and explain all its details to the most obscure and ignorant wretch that wears the human form, you shall find that whilst he understands its elevation he will be able to put his finger upon imperfections in that life. Which shows that in his heart there is a greater man than any that has lived in the world.[129]

Every man is one-half of a man, either benevolent and weak, or firm and unbenevolent; either a speaker and no doer, or a doer and no speaker, either contemplative or practical, and excellence in any one kind seems to speak defect in the others. This wisely ordered for the *social* state; and the individual expectation and effort seems to promise completeness of character in the whole future.[130]

When we look at the world of past men, we say, what a host of heroes; but when we come to particularize, it is like counting the stars which we thought innumerable, but which prove few and rare. Bacon, Shakspeare, Cæsar, Scipio, Cicero, Burke, Chatham, Franklin,——none of them will bear examination, or furnish the type of a *Man*.[131]

Reverence man, and not Plato and Cæsar. Wherever there is sense, reflexion, courage, admit it to the same honour,——embrace it, quote it from a truckman as quick as from Webster.[132]

There is a man in us, we have not seen executed out of us. Survey the whole circle of your acquaintance, of your neighborhood, of your town and if you can[,] fix upon one complete man, a man independent of his circumstances, a mind which fills and satisfies your idea of the perfection of human nature——one whom you venerate *as a man*; whose value to your eye consists entirely in the richness of his own nature.[133]

---

[124] See Swedenborg ¶ 14.

[125] See *Journals*, III, 362: "I suppose the materials may now exist for a Portraiture of Man which should be at once history and prophecy. Does it not seem as if a perfect parallelism existed between every great and fully developed man and every other?"

[126] He significantly enough uses the phrase in *Nature*, 87.7-8, in introducing the Orphic Poet's lines.　　　　　　　　　　　[128] See *Y E S*, 64-65 (Oct. 18, 1829).

[127] See *Journals*, II, 234 (1828?).　　　　[129] See *Y E S*, 110 (Oct. 3, 1830).

[130] See *Journals*, II, 435 (Dec. 10, 1831). See also note 264 and context.

[131] See *Journals*, II, 505 (Aug. 12, 1832).

[132] *Journals*, II, 507 (Aug. 19, 1832).　　　[133] *Y E S*, 181 (Oct. 21, 1832).

The wise man, the true friend, the finished character, we seek everywhere, and only find in fragments. Yet I cannot persuade myself that all the beautiful souls are fled out of the planet, or that always I shall be excluded from good company and yoked with green, dull, pitiful persons. . . . God's greatest gift is a Teacher, and when will he send me one full of truth and of boundless benevolence and of heroic sentiments? I can describe the man. I know the idea well, but where is its real blood-warm counterpart?[134]

The reason why the Luther, the Newton, the Bonaparte, concerning whom we read, was made the subject of panegyric, is, that in the writer's opinion, in some one respect this particular man represented the idea of Man. And so far as we accord with his judgment, we take the picture for a Standard Man, and so let every line accuse or approve our own ways of thinking and living by comparison.[135]

[Shakspeare's] best works are of doubted authenticity, and what was his, and what his novelist's, and what the players', seems yet disputed: a sharp illustration of that relentless disregard of the individual in regard for the race which runs through history. It is not an individual, but the general mind of man[136] that speaks from time to time, quite careless and quite forgetful of what mouth or mouths it makes use of.[137]

The world looks poor and mean so long as I think only of its great men; most of them of spotted reputation. But when I remember how many obscure persons I myself have seen possessing gifts that excited wonder, speculation and delight in me; when I remember that the very greatness of Homer, of Shakspeare, of Webster and Channing, is the truth with which they reflect the mind of all mankind; when I consider that each fine genius that appears is already predicted in our constitution, inasmuch as he only makes apparent shades of thought in us of which we hitherto knew not (or actualizes an idea) . . . I feel the riches of my inheritance in being set down in this world, gifted with organs of communication with this accomplished company.[138]

Out of these fragmentary, lob-sided mortals shall the heaven unite Phidias, Demosthenes, Shakspear, Newton, Napoleon, Bacon and Saint John in one person.[139]

You affirm that the moral development contains all the intellectual, and that Jesus was the perfect man. I bow in reverence unfeigned before that benign man. I know more, hope more, am more, because he has lived. But, if you tell me that in your opinion he has fulfilled all the conditions of man's existence, carried out to the utmost, at least by implication, all man's powers, I suspend my assent. I do not see in him cheerfulness: I do not see in him the love of natural science: I see in him no kindness for art; I see in him nothing of Socrates, of Laplace, of Shakspear. The perfect man should remind us of all great men. Do you ask me if I would rather resemble Jesus than any other man? If I should say Yes, I should suspect myself of superstition.[140]

[P]erfect in the sense of complete man [Jesus] seems not to me to be, but a very exclusive & partial development of the moral element such as the great Compensation that balances the universe provides to repair accumulated depravity. The weight of his ethical sentences deserves more than all the consideration they have, & his life is one original pure beam of truth but a perfect man should exhibit all the traits of humanity & should expressly recognize the intellectual nature. Socrates I call a complete universal man fulfilling all the conditions of man's existence. Sublime as he is I compare him not as an ethical teacher to Christ, but his life is more humane.[141]

He, the preacher, let him then acquiesce in being nothing that he may move mountains: let him be the mere tongue of us all; no individual, but a universal man, let him leave his nation, his party, his sect, his town-connexion, even his vanity and self-love at home, and come hither to say what were equally fit at Paris, at Canton, and at

[134] See *Journals*, III, 100-101 (Apr. 22, 1833).
[135] *Journals*, III, 249 (Jan. 19, 1834). See the chapter on Cousin.
[136] See Coleridge ¶ 90.
[137] *Journals*, III, 329 (Aug. 17, 1834).
[138] *Journals*, III, 383-384 (Dec. 8, 1834).
[139] *Journals*, III, 409 (Dec. 23, 1834).
[140] See *Journals*, III, 518 (July 30, 1835).
[141] *Letters*, I, 451 (Aug. 3, 1835).

Thebes.[142]

> It is in the nature not of any particular man but of universal man *to think;* though the act of reflexion is very rare.[143]

But Emerson encountered difficulty in his speculation regarding the identification of the individual man with his prototype——that is, with the Reason or Spirit. One's personality kept asserting itself, kept denying the universality of the mind, and continued to stand in the way of mystical experiences.[144]

> The mind is very wise, could it be roused into action. But the life of most men is aptly signified by the poet's personification, "Death in Life." We walk about in a sleep. A few moments in the year, or in our lifetime, we truly live; we are at the top of our being; we are pervaded, yea, dissolved by the Mind; but we fall back again presently. . . . Such is the inaction of men. We have an obscure consciousness of our attributes. We stand on the edge of all that is great, yet are restrained in inactivity and unconscious of our powers, like neuters of the hive, every one of which is capable of transformation into the Queen Bee. We are always on the brink, etc. . . . What a benefit if a rule could be given whereby the mind, dreaming amid the gross fogs of matter, could at any moment EAST ITSELF and FIND THE SUN!

Writing to Miss Peabody on August 3, 1835, Emerson indicated his general acceptance of the Swedenborgian opinion that when man's moral nature has been improved[145] and he has returned to his proper place at the head of the natural order,[146] then the circulations[147] of spiritual influx through him[148] will find no opposition, and his moral and intellectual natures will tend to become *one nature.*[149] Though most considerate persons would accept this "general confession," however, he was frank in facing a few uncontested facts, namely:[150]

> that in our experience is almost no proportioned cultivation; the blacksmith has a strong arm, the dancer a strong foot; great proficiency in the mathematics may coexist with extreme moral insensibility, & the splendours of holiness with a contempt for learning, Such lobsided one eyed half men are we now, & such a yawning difference between our *esse* & our *posse.*

He wrote that he was content to face these refractory details even if they did not permit him to see anything more than a "great tendency" in the direction of Universal Man. That *tendency,* however, meant more to him than any narrow sectarian revelation that claimed *certainty.* Writing on October 15, 1835, he maintained the same view:[151]

> Far off, no doubt, is the perfectibility; so far off as to be ridiculous to all but a few. Yet wrote I once that, God keeping a private door to each soul, nothing transcends the

---

[142] See *Journals,* III, 565 (Oct. 25, 1835).

[143] From the unpublished "Introductory Lecture on English Literature" (Nov. 5, 1835). See my abstract elsewhere in this volume. Cf. *Journals,* III, 406 (Dec. 22, 1834). See *Y E S,* 181.6 and 110.19.

[144] See sections XII-XIV of "A Statement of the First Philosophy" (June 10, 1835), above in chap. VII. See also section IV: "Reason is the superior principle. Its attributes are Eternity & Intuition. We belong to it, not it to us. Human individuality is an upstart just now added to this Eternal Beatitude."

[145] See the commentary on section VI of the Orphic Poet, *infra.*

[146] See the commentary on Orphic Poet IV, *infra.*

[147] See Swedenborg ¶s. 24ff.

[148] See Sampson Reed ¶s. 18d and 66-70.   [150] *Letters,* I, 450. Italics are mine.

[149] See Swedenborg ¶s. 24 and 29.   [151] *Journals,* III, 557.

bounds of reasonable expectation from a man. Now what imperfect tadpoles we are! an arm or a leg, an eye or an antenna, is unfolded,——all the rest is yet in the chrysalis.

On December 26, 1835, he again acknowledged the fact that he had not chosen an easy solution to the great problems of life, but indicated his willingness to endure the inconvenience and the suspense which are corollaries of an open mind:[151a]

There are two objects between which the mind vibrates like a pendulum; One, the desire of truth; the other, the desire of Repose. He in whom the love of Repose predominates, will accept the first creed he meets, Arianism, Calvinism, Socinianism; he gets rest & reputation; but he shuts the door of Truth. He in whom the love of Truth predominates will keep himself aloof from all moorings & afloat. He will abstain from dogmatism & recognize all the opposite negations between which as walls his being is swung. On one side he will feel that God is impersonal. One [sic] the other, that the Universe is his work. He submits to the inconvenience of suspense & imperfect opinion but he is a candidate for truth & respects the highest law of his being.

He seems never to have wavered in his belief that the progress of the human race could be achieved only by individual effort[152]——an idea which found vigorous expression in paragraphs V and VI of the Orphic Poet. Shortly after the publication of *Nature* his speculations continued in the same vein:

Whilst thus I use the Universal Humanity, I see plainly the fact that there is no progress to the race, that the progress is of individuals. One element is predominant in one; another is carried to perfection in the next; Art in the Greek; power in the Roman; piety in the Hebrew; letters in the Old English; commerce in the late English; Empire in Austria; erudition in Germany; free institutions in America. But in turn the whole man is brought to the light. It is like the revolution of the globe in the ecliptic: each part is brought in turn under the more direct beams of the sun to be illuminated and warmed.[153]

Fear God, and where you go men shall feel as if they walked in hallowed cathedrals. Make your perceptions accurate, and the sound of your voice, or sight of your name, shall be useful to men as Institutes and Scientific societies are, suggesting the just use of the faculties to great ends. This is the way to be a Universal man, or take the ages up into an hour and one person.[154]

The Individual. Who shall define to me an Individual? I behold with awe and delight many illustrations of the One Universal Mind. I see my being imbedded in it; as a plant in the earth so I grow in God.[155] I am only a form of him. He is the soul of me. I can even with a mountainous aspiring say, *I am God*,[156] by transferring my *me* out of the flimsy and unclean precinct of my body, my fortunes, my private will, and meekly

[151a] *Typescript Journals*, "B," Part I, p. 158. The passage appears revised in *Works*, II, 341-342. Cf. *Nature*, 6.20—7.5.
[152] See the poem, "Γνωθι Σεαυτον," in chap. VII. See his sermons: "Self-Direction and Self-Command," "The Heaven of a Common Life," "The Christian is Free and Solitary," "Self-Command," "Man is Improvable," "Solitude and Society," "Non-Conformity," "Improvement by Small Degrees," "The Individual and the State," "Salvation, Now," "Self-Culture," "The Oracle Within," "Trust Yourself," "The Kingdom of Heaven is Within," "Why Christianity Advances," "God in the Soul," "Find Your Calling," "Self-Improvement," "Judging Right for Ourselves," "The Education of the Soul," and "The Genuine Man." See esp. *Y E S*, 80 (Apr. 8, 1830).
[153] See *Journals*, IV, 158-159 (Nov. 28, 1836). See the chapter on Cousin.
[154] See *Journals*, IV, 182 (Jan. 7, 1837).
[155] See *Nature*, 79.23—80.3.
[156] See *Y E S*, 4.11-15 (Oct. 15, 1826); *Y E S*, 133 (Jan. 12, 1831); *Journals*, II, 173-174 (Feb., 1827); III, 267 (Mar. 22, 1834); Psalm 82:6 and John 10:34.

retiring upon the holy austerities of the Just and the Loving, upon the secret fountains of nature. That thin and difficult ether, I also can breathe. The mortal lungs and nostrils burst and shrivel, but the soul itself needeth no organs; it is all element and all organ. Yet why not always so? How came the Individual, thus armed and impassioned, to parricide thus murderously inclined, ever to traverse and kill the Divine Life? Ah, wicked Manichee! Into that dim problem I cannot enter. A believer in Unity, a seer of Unity, I yet behold two. Whilst I feel myself in sympathy with nature, and rejoice with greatly beating heart in the course of Justice and Benevolence overpowering me, I yet find little access to this me of me. I fear what shall befal: I am not enough a party to the great order to be tranquil. I hope and I fear. I do not see. At one time, I am a Doer.[157] A divine life, I create scenes and persons around and for me, and unfold my thought by a perpetual, successive projection.[158] At least I so say, I so feel,——but presently I return to the habitual attitude of suffering. . . . Cannot I conceive the Universe without a contradiction?[159]

Still later, Emerson called the poet alone the "complete man" or "universal man."[160] For the fable of the degradation and fall of humanity, the reader is referred to sections III and IV below.[161]

II

'We distrust and deny inwardly our sympathy with nature. We own and disown our relation to it, by turns. We are, like Nebuchadnezzar, dethroned, bereft of reason, and eating grass like an ox. But who can set limits to the remedial force of spirit? (87.17-22).

We distrust & deny inwardly our own sympathy with nature. We own & disown our relation to it. We are like Nebuchadnezzar cast down from our throne bereft of our reason & eating grass like an ox.

The key word in the second section is *inwardly*. Man's relation to nature is too often merely *outward* and utilitarian, that is, through the Understanding alone.[162] His inner world of the Reason remains sleepy and unawakened. The concurrence of subject and object——the liaison between mind and matter,[163] which either "appears to men, or it does not"[164]——is not established. Man, therefore, fails to see the correspondence between his inner thoughts and external phenomena, and understands few of the uses of plants and animals. He is unaware that nature's highest function is to teach and discipline him, unlocking the powers of his soul. The price one pays for living outwardly is the loss of self-knowledge, which is the only certain answer to the Sphinx.[165] Emerson was thinking of two types of people who failed to discover their own spiritual significance and to venerate the God within them: (1) the practical man or the business man, who denies his "sympathy with nature" by living to no sufficient end.[166]

[157] See *Nature*, 75.13.
[158] See *Nature*, 94.1ff. (Orphic Poet V).
[159] For these paragraphs, see *Journals*, IV, 247-249 (May 26, 1837). In section IV of "A Statement of the First Philosophy" (see chap. VII) he accounted for the contradiction as follows: "Man is conscious of a twofold nature which manifests itself in perpetual self-contradiction. Our English philosophers to denote this quality, distinguish the Reason and the Understanding."
[160] See *Works*, II, 30; III, 5. For further views on "Universal Man" see Coleridge ¶s. 142 and 224.
[161] See Plato's legend of the reign of Cronos in *The Statesman*.
[162] See Orphic Poet IV.
[163] See chap. VIII above.
[164] *Nature*, 43.4.
[165] See *Nature*, 43.19-21.
[166] He is described in the sermons, esp. in *Y E S*, 206.17—207.14; in section XII of "A Statement of the First Philosophy" (June 10, 1835); in Coleridge ¶s. 149-152; in *Nature*, 89.12—90.1.

He merely accumulates property and rejoices in the world of appearances, whereas it is only "in the closing the senses to the exclusive commerce with outward things and in the opening of the interior senses to the acknowledgment of [a] better kingdom does true life consist. In the spiritual world only can we live."[167] (2) The scientists deny their "sympathy with nature" by being content to gather particulars without seizing the fundamental natural Laws which correspond to Ideas within themselves.[168] They see in nature only commodity and not the words of a spiritual language. Nature is a book in which are recorded spiritual meanings, which only those who know themselves can understand. "What we are [within], that only can we see [without]."[169]

A life in harmony with nature, the love of truth and of virtue, will purge the eyes to understand her text. By degrees we may come to know the primitive sense of the permanent objects of nature, so that the world shall be to us an open book, and every form significant of its hidden life and final cause.[170]

In owning and disowning our relation to nature *by turns*, Emerson probably meant the alternation of our loyalties discussed above. At one moment we are aware of the rich spiritual universe of the Reason and find our thoughts clothing themselves in natural garments.[171] Then the Understanding mounts the throne after overthrowing the Reason and leaves us like Nebuchadnezzar,[172] our higher faculties useless,[173] eating grass[174] and content to satisfy merely our animal wants. The world, then, lacks a meaning, and our lives lack purpose:

I take it to be a main object of that education which this world administers to each soul to touch the springs of wonder in us, and make us alive to the marvel of our condition. That done, all is done. Before, he was so wrongheaded, so at discord with things around him, that he was ridiculous: now, he is at one with all. He accepts his lot: he perceives the great astonishment. He adores. Awaked to truth and virtue——which is the two fold office of Reason, he passes out of the local and finite, he inspires and expires immortal breath.[175]

The problem of restoring to the world original and eternal beauty, is solved by the redemption of the soul. The ruin or the blank, that we see when we look at nature, is in our own eye. The axis of vision is not coincident with the axis of things, and so they

---

[167] See "How Old Art Thou," *Y E S*, 114.10-14. The whole sermon provides an excellent gloss on the present section.

[168] See *Nature*, 83.7—84.2; 84.12-21. See Emerson's early lecture on "The Naturalist" (May 7, 1834) in Cabot, *Memoir*, II, 712; I, 224-227. See Coleridge on method, ¶s. 127-147. See chap. VIII.

[169] See *Nature*, 94.5 (Orphic Poet V). See footnote 43 of chap. VII.

[170] *Nature*, 44.20ff. Cf. *Nature*, 25.8-15.

[171] Cf. *Nature*, 38.14-22. See sections XIII-XIV of "A Statement of the First Philosophy" (chap. VII).

[172] See Daniel 4:25, 32-33. Emerson might have got the idea of "un roi depossédé" from Blaise Pascal's *Pensées*, sections 397-399. Nebuchadnezzar is mentioned in section 721. It is more likely, however, that it was suggested by Swedenborgian literature, in which Nebuchadnezzar is an excellent subject for correspondences of all kinds. Cf. *Nature*, 25.8-15.

[173] Probably intentional *double-entendre*. Nebuchadnezzar temporarily demented (*i.e.*, in Coleridge's language, without his *Understanding*). Emerson is toying with the idea that our own loss is that of the *Reason*—that our contentment to live in the Understanding alone is shameful.

[174] The Swedenborgian dictionaries of correspondences assign to "eating grass" the meaning of "to become sensuous."

[175] "The Miracle of Our Being" (Sept. 7, 1834), *Y E S*, 207.6ff. Cf. Sampson Reed ¶s. 9-10.

appear not transparent but opake. The reason why the world lacks unity, and lies broken and in heaps, is, because man is disunited with himself. He cannot be a naturalist, until he satisfies all the demands of the spirit. Love is as much its demand, as perception. Indeed, neither can be perfect without the other. In the uttermost meaning of the words, thought is devout, and devotion is thought. Deep calls unto deep.[176]

But the Reason can always be awakened from its sleep by the influx of Spirit, which is able to change the entire scene.[177] The affections can be purged so that they will clothe themselves only in appropriate objects. Unimpeded by man's frailties the Supervoluntary may yet find its way through human beings out into nature.[178] Being confident, then, that this divine force can offer great remedy, who dares

set bounds to the possibilities of man? Once inspire the infinite, by being admitted to behold the absolute natures of justice and truth, and we learn that man has access to the entire mind of the Creator, is himself the creator in the finite.[179]

III

'A man is a god in ruins. When men are innocent, life shall be longer, and shall pass into the immortal, as gently as we awake from dreams. Now, the world would be insane and rabid, if these disorganizations should last for hundreds of years. It is kept in check by death and infancy. Infancy is the perpetual Messiah, which comes into the arms of fallen men, and pleads with them to return to paradise. (88.1-10).

A man is a god in ruins. When men are child-like, life may be longer. Now the world would be more monstrous yet, if these disorganizations were more permanent. Infancy is the perpetual messiah which comes into the arms of these lost beings, & pleads with them to return to paradise.

Emerson liked to emphasize the spiritual wealth which the Universal Reason[180] brings to a man by calling those in whom the Spirit is most active—GODS. To many who cannot appreciate Emerson's terminology, the assertion seems blasphemous, yet there are scriptural parallels for the words quoted in the following:[181]

I feel that close by meanness is grandeur. In a beggar's weeds, in a servile office, the imagination starts out with a noble recoil, and in that moment whispers "Ye are gods." Never so lowly but we remember that we are tenants of infinite spaces and survivors of the sun and the stars.

In his sermons, Emerson was careful to justify his use of the phrase by listing several eminent authorities, as may be seen in the following:[182]

[176] *Nature*, 91.5-19 (chiefly Coleridgean with Swedenborgian touches).
[177] See Orphic Poet VI.
[178] See Coleridge ¶s. 152, 245-246, 254, 263; Swedenborg ¶s. 24-34, 47; Sampson Reed ¶s. 5, 18a—18g, 38-43, 56, 59-62, 66-70.
[179] See *Nature*, 80.3-8. See also Sampson Reed ¶ 39: "Much remains to be done . . . but the end is certain. The humblest individual may, nay *must* aid in the accomplishment of this consummation. It is not for time or space to set limits to the effects of the life of a single man."
[180] See Coleridge ¶s. 1-54. See *Journals*, III, 267.
[181] *Journals*, II, 173-174 (Feb., 1827). For scriptural references, see note 156 above. The last line reflects classical thought. See note 218.
[182] *Y E S*, 132; 133 (Jan. 12, 1831). See also *Journals*, III, 324 (Aug. 10, 1834): "See two sincere men conversing together. They deport themselves as if self-existent. Are they not for the time two gods? . . . Is not man in our day described by the very attributes which once he gave his God?"

We are sad aliens from the heavenly life, we grievously break the commandments, if we are thus strangers to Him. The Scriptures teach us that nothing is more intimate than our relation to Him. They teach that we are God's children, not by any metaphor but in a far stricter sense than we are the children of men. We are made of him. We live but in him, as the leaf lives in the tree. 'Know ye not that the spirit of God dwelleth in you. God worketh in us, both to will and to do, of his own good pleasure.' We are his children . . . . We shall be parts of God, as the hand is part of the body . . . . It is I that do wrong; it is God in me who does right.

Be ye merciful as your Father is merciful, Be ye perfect as your father in Heaven is perfect,——commandments which would be wholly incomprehensible but for the great truth that men, in the words of Saint Peter, are partakers of the divine nature. . . . The pious men of the Stoic sect received this faith, saying that the wise man differed from God in nothing but duration. It was also a maxim of their school that mind was God in man. The devout Fénelon, a bishop of the church of Rome, declares that God is in our souls as our soul is in our bodies. Archbishop Leighton, one of the most esteemed and one of the best divines of the Church of England, writes that 'by the love of God the soul is made divine and one with him;' and quotes with approbation the language of Saint Austin, 'If you love the earth, you become earth; if you love God——shall I not say?——you become God.'

Emerson's poem, "Gnothi Seauton"[183] (July 6, 1831), is an eloquent statement of this belief and can be said to summarize the thought of most of his early sermons. His very first composition for the pulpit contained the following:[184]

[God] is not so much the observer of your actions, as he is the potent principle by which they are bound together; not so much the reader of your thoughts, as the active Creator by whom they are aided into being; and, casting away the deceptive subterfuges of language, and speaking with strict philosophical truth, that every faculty is but a mode of his action; that your reason is God, your virtue is God, and nothing but your liberty, can you call securely and absolutely your own.

Lamartine had written: "Limited in his nature, infinite in his desires, man is a fallen god who remembers the heavens,"[185] and the phrase was not uncommon, but I believe Emerson's daemon created the expression, "a god in ruins," quite spontaneously. Equivalent phrases appear in the journals:[185a]

I never read Wordsworth without chagrin; a man of such great powers and ambition, so near to the Dii majores, to fail so meanly in every attempt! A genius that hath epilepsy, a deranged archangel.[186]

Every man is an angel in disguise, a god playing the fool. It seems as if Heaven had sent its insane angels into our world as an asylum, and here they will break out into rare music and utter at intervals the words they have heard in Heaven, and then the mad fit returns and they mope and wallow like dogs. When the gods come among men they are not known. Jesus was not. Socrates and Shakspear were not.[187]

---

[183] It appears edited in chap. VII above.

[184] See his first sermon, "Pray Without Ceasing," *Y E S*, 4.7ff. (Oct. 15, 1826).

[185] Alphonse de Lamartine, *Méditations*, ser. II (1823), quoted in Burton Stevenson's *Home Book of Quotations* (3d. ed.).

[185a] See *Journals*, III, 467-468: "Empedocles said bravely, 'I am God; I am immortal; I contemn human affairs;' and all men hated him. Yet every one of the same men had had his religious hour when he said the same thing."

[186] *Journals*, II, 534 (Dec. 1, 1832).

[187] *Journals*, III, 443 (Jan. 14, 1835). See also IV, 16 (Feb. 28, 1836): "I must treat my fellow as Empire treats Empire, and God, God." See also III, 318: "How much is an assembly of men restrained! It seems often like a collection of angels, and a collection of demons in disguise." See III, 353: "Whilst [a man] sits alone in his studies and

By *innocence* or *childlikeness* Emerson meant submission of the individual will to the Reason or the Divine Spirit——a constant awareness of the God within and a readiness at all times to listen to his voice. It was synonymous with the Swedenborgian concept of "unconscious reception" of the Divine Influx——the rule of the "supervoluntary." Emerson combined the thought of Coleridge[188] and Sampson Reed[189] in the following:[190]

How precisely parallel are the biographies of religious enthusiasts——Swedenborg, Guyon, Fox, Luther, and perhaps Boehmen. Each owes all to the discovery that God must be sought within, not without. That is the discovery of Jesus. Each perceives the worthlessness of all instruction, and the infinity of wisdom that issues from meditation. Each perceives *the nullity of all conditions but one, innocence;* the absolute submission which attends it. All becomes simple, plain in word and act.[191]

What is the doctrine of *infallible guidance if one will abdicate choice,* but striving to act unconsciously, to resume the simplicity of childhood? It is to act on the last impression derived from a knowledge of all the facts, and not wilfully to secure a particular advantage. The single-minded actor insists on the tranquillity of his own mind.[192]

The age of puberty is a crisis in the life of the man worth studying. It is the passage from the Unconscious to the Conscious; from the sleep of the Passions to their rage; from careless receiving to cunning providing; from beauty to use; from omnivorous curiosity to anxious stewardship; from faith to doubt; from maternal Reason to hard, short-sighted Understanding; from unity to disunion.[193]

Sampson Reed[194] explained how the Lord helps preserve innocency in men by strengthening their resistance to the hereditary evils of the flesh, that is——to use Coleridge's terminology——by helping them overcome the blindness of the Understanding:

The infant is an unresisting medium of the Divine influence, and there is in this influence a constant effort to make him a voluntary, rational medium, that 'his will may be done on earth as it is in heaven.' The very gradual process of growth is because the tendency of the supervoluntary to descend is so exceedingly gentle, that the formation of the will is under Providence effected in perfect freedom. In later periods of life, his hereditary evils discover themselves, and in the present state of society rarely fail to gain the ascendancy, though the Lord always provides strength for their resistance, if it be rightly used.

Earthly life can be lengthened as evil, sickness, calamities and the other evidences of our spiritual maladjustment are eliminated. Emerson again was thinking of the Swedenborgian idea of "affections clothed," which explains terrible appearances and ferocious animals as the projection of man's internal condition.[195] For the thought that transition from this

---

opens not his mouth, he is God manifest, in flesh. Put him in a parlor with unfit company, and he shall talk like a fool." See III, 362: "Respect a man! assuredly, but in general only as the potential God . . . . Now he is only a scrap, an ort, an end, and in his actual being no more worthy of your veneration than the poor lunatic. But the simplest person who, in his integrity, worships God, becomes God: at least no optics of human mind can detect the line where man, the effect, ceases, and God; the Cause, begins." See also *Journals*, III, 278: ". . . your prosy, selfish sensualist awakes, a god. . . ."

[188] Cf. Coleridge ¶s. 1-54, 75, 122a, 126, 174, 226, 262.
[189] See Sampson Reed ¶s. 18a *et seq.*, 27, 46, 66-70.
[190] Cf. also his "The Childlike Character," delivered Apr. 25, 1830. Cf. *Nature*, 11.18-19. See *Journals*, III, 275 top.
[191] *Journals*, III, 432-433 (Jan. 7, 1835). Italics are mine.
[192] *Journals*, III, 337-338 (Sept. 14, 1834).
[193] *Journals*, III, 376-377 (Dec. 2, 1834). Cf. the similar thought in Wordsworth's *Ode.*
[194] See Sampson Reed ¶ 69.
[195] See Nature, 81.3-9 and 94.16-22 (Orphic Poet VI). See Sampson Reed ¶s. 18a-22.

present life to the next will be *gradual*, Emerson was indebted principally to Oegger's lines on the exact correspondence of the natural and spiritual worlds:[196]

> All these ideas, though new, will not surprise those philosophers who know that nature is always conformable to herself, or . . . never does anything by leaps and bounds. According to this philosophic apothegm, *our future existence will, in reality, differ from the present only by a slight variation;* and this variation is that from a material to a substantial world. *We shall pass to the future existence, as we enter into an agreeable dream; all nature will accompany us there.*

The disorganizations to which Emerson referred are the result of man's evil affections, which inevitably clothe themselves externally in all manner of unpleasantness, as mentioned above. The key is man's inner life, and when that is not changed, death is the only corrective. At least, it eliminates the cause even if it does not provide a remedy. Infancy, on the other hand, by providing a new generation under the sway of the "supervoluntary," gives us hope that the future may witness further progress in the solution of great human problems.[197]

> The problem of restoring to the world original and eternal beauty, is solved by the redemption of the soul. The ruin or the blank, that we see when we look at nature, is in our own eye. The axis of vision is not coincident with the axis of things, and so they appear not transparent but opake. The reason why the world lacks unity, and lies broken and in heaps, is, because man is disunited with himself.[198]

> Should the Whig party fail, which God avert! the patriot will still have some confidence in the . . . regenerative Nature of Man, which ever reproduces a healthful moral sense even out of stupidity and corruption. Thus the children of the convicts at Botany Bay are found to have sound moral sentiments.[199]

The word *Messiah* appeared in the title of Oegger's manuscript,[200] which Emerson was reading in 1835. In the same year, A. P. Peabody issued *An Essay on the Prophecies Relating to the Messiah.*[201] Emerson, of course, never accepted the traditional Christian view of Jesus, and by 1836 had an interest only in what he considered elemental or universal facts. He scarcely, therefore, needed suggestions from Wordsworth's *Ode on Intimations of Immortality*,[202] Alcott's *Psyche*, Henry More's *Psychozoia* or the body of Romantic poetry to find a perpetual messiah in childhood. The Bible alone would have been sufficient.[203] In 1834, he wrote:

> Blessed is the child; the unconscious is ever the act of God himself. Nobody can reflect upon his *unconscious* period, or any particular word or act in it, with regret or

---

See Swedenborg ¶s. 25-27.

[196] See "The True Messiah," *E T E*, II, 86. Italics are mine. Emerson enthusiastically quotes the significant lines in *Journals*, III, 506 (July 15, 1835). The same idea is expressed in Swedenborg ¶s. 11-13, and 47. See *Y E S*, 244.

[197] See note 195 above.

[198] See *Nature*, 91.5-13.

[199] See *Journals*, III, 357 (Nov. 5, 1834). Botany Bay, an inlet on the west of the County of Cumberland, New South Wales, Australia, was discovered by Capt. [James] Cook in 1770. It became a penal colony, but the transportation of criminals ceased in 1840.

[200] "The True Messiah," *E T E*, II, 83-98.

[201] Boston, 1835.

[202] For his great admiration of the *Ode*, even in his early years, see *Journals*, II, 53-54, 108, 109, 147, 217, 230, 436; IV, 246. See *Works*, V, 298.

[203] See esp. Isaiah 11:6; Matt. 18:2-6; Mark 10:13-16; Luke 9:47-48 and 18:15-17. The Emersons were expecting young Waldo at the time *Nature* was being composed.

contempt. Bard or Hero cannot look down upon the word or gesture of a child; it is as great as they.[204]

I am inclined to believe that Sampson Reed suggested the perpetual messiahship of the child at the end of one of his eloquent discourses on that theme, not only because of the verbal similarity therein evident but also because Emerson's idea of innocency and childlikeness, as we have seen above, was definitely Swedenborgian:[205]

The infant is nearly passive, and his motions are mostly involuntary. He does not will or think, according to the usual understanding of volition and thought; but possesses that kind of consciousness which we should have, if we ascended, within ourselves, above those principles which appear to be at all the work of our own hands. Thus to ascend into the elements and beginning of our own creation, where the Lord *stretcheth forth the heavens*; and thence, by our cooperation, to permit the lower principles of the mind to be formed after the same pattern, is *to be born again, to become as little children*, to ascend to where the good and the true are perpetually born within us from the Lord, to return, as it were, to our own infancy, save that the innocence of infancy, as it now descends, becomes clothed with the wisdom and strength of manhood. . . . [T]he term of infancy is of considerable duration, in order that the highest principles of the mind may acquire strength to overcome the resistance to divine order, which hereditary evil will perpetually offer beneath; or if, in later periods, he be borne away by his own will, he may yet not be entirely insensible to the presence of the Lord within him, by which his evils may still possibly be curbed and subdued. . . . Each succeeding period of life presents an image of what is seen in infancy. *It is the perpetual endeavour of the Lord, as the interior principles are formed, thence to descend into those which are beneath*, that all may be made in his image and likeness; and this is effected so far as it can be done consistently with the freedom of the individual.

By "fallen men" Emerson intended to convey the thought, expressed above, that men drift gradually from the dominion of the Reason into the baser rule of the Understanding.[206] The word *Paradise* meant a world of men living by the Reason or the Supervoluntary. The *Garden of Eden* or *Primitive Church* was an approximate equivalent.[207] The Swedenborgian thought is well expressed in the following:[208]

It is the tendency of revelation [said Sampson Reed] to give a right direction to every power of every mind; and when this is effected, inventions and discoveries will follow of course, all things assume a different aspect, and the world itself again become a paradise.

Emerson made his meaning quite clear in the following:

Heaven is the name we give to the True State, the world of Reason, not of the Understanding; of the Real, not the Apparent. It exists always, whether it is ever to be separated from the Hell or not. It is, as Coleridge said, another world, but not to come.[209]

He was born on Oct. 30, 1836. See *Journals*, IV, 134.

[204] *Journals*, III, 325 (Aug. 13, 1834).

[205] See Sampson Reed ¶ 27. Italics at the end are mine. See also "On Simplicity of Character," *N J M*, II (1828-1829), 145-151.

[206] See Coleridge ¶ 221: "Man was and is a *fallen* Creature, not by accidents of bodily constitution, or any other cause, which *human* Wisdom in a course of ages might be supposed capable of removing; but diseased in his *Will*, in that Will which is the true and only strict synonime of the Word, I, or the intelligent Self." Cf. the thought of Wordsworth's *Ode*.

[207] See Coleridge ¶s. 148 and 224; Sampson Reed ¶s. 4-5; and Swedenborg's *Works, passim*. [208] See Sampson Reed ¶ 42.

[209] See *Journals*, III, 488 (June 4, 1835). See notes 120 and 276 and context.

Heaven is the projection of the Ideas of Reason on the plane of the understanding.[210]

IV

'Man is the dwarf of himself. Once he was permeated and dissolved by spirit. He filled nature with his overflowing currents. Out from him sprang the sun and moon; from man, the sun; from woman, the moon. The laws of his mind, the periods of his actions externized themselves into day and night, into the year and the seasons. But, having made for himself this huge shell, his waters retired; he no longer fills the veins and veinlets; he is shrunk to a drop. He sees, that the structure still fits him, but fits him colossally. Say, rather, once it fitted him, now it corresponds to him from far and on high. He adores timidly his own work. Now is man the follower of the sun, and woman the follower of the moon. Yet sometimes he starts in his slumber, and wonders at himself and his house, and muses strangely at the resemblance betwixt him and it. He perceives that if his law is still paramount, if still he have elemental power, "if his word is sterling yet in nature," it is not conscious power, it is not inferior but superior to his will. It is Instinct.' (88.11——89.11).

Man is the dwarf of himself   Is it not true that spirit in us is dwarfed by clay?[210a] that once Man was permeated & dissolved by spirit. He filled Nature with his overflowing currents. Out from him sprang the sun & moon   from man the sun   from woman the moon
The laws of his mind   the periods of his deeds externized themselves into day & night into the year & seasons   But having made for himself this vast shell the waters retired, he no longer fills its veins & veinlets   he is shrunk into a drop. He sees it still fits him but fits him colossally. He adores timidly his own work. Say rather once it fitted him   now it corresponds to him from far & on high. Yet now he starts occasionally in his slumber & wonders at himself & his house & muses strangely at the resemblance betwixt him & it. If now he have power "if that his word is sterling yet in England" he sees that it is unconscious power; power superior to his will; or Instinct

"Man is great, not in his goals, but in his transition from state to state. Great in act, but instantly *dwarfed* by self-indulgence," wrote Emerson in 1834.[211] He gave another clue to his meaning when he declared that the Understanding usurps the place of the Reason, "proceeds with his own *dwarf Architecture* & thoroughly cheats us until presently for a moment Reason returns & the slave obeys, & his work shrinks into tatters & cobwebs."[212]

This little creature . . . capable by intellect and affection, of acting upon remote men as upon himself . . . and from his little hour, extending the arms of his influence through thousands of years and to millions of millions of rational men: Nay, by means of Virtue, of entering instantly upon a life that makes the whole grandeur of the Creation pale and visionary. Yet this little creature quite unmindful of these vast prerogatives, struts about with immense activity to procure various meats to eat and stuffs to wear, and most of all, salutations and marks of respect from his fellows.[213]

---

[210] From section VIII of "A Statement of the First Philosophy."

[210a] See *Journals*, III, 394 (Dec. 17, 1834): "If it has so pleased God, it is very easy for you to surpass your fellows in genius; but surpass them in generosity of sentiment; see not their meanness, whilst your eyes are fixed on everlasting virtues; being royal, being divine, in your sentiment . . . . This shall be your own,—O no; God forbid! not your own, but a vast accession of the Divinity *into your trembling clay*." (Italics mine.) See also *Journals*, III, 401 bottom.

[211] *Journals*, III, 349 (Oct. 27, 1834). Italics are mine. Cf. also III, 477 and 337.7-12.

[212] See above under June 22, 1836. Italics are mine. Emerson calls those under the dominion of the Understanding, "half-men" (*Nature*, 89.16ff.).

[213] "The Miracle of Our Being," *Y E S*, 205 (Sept. 7, 1834). In this paragraph Emerson is thinking both of the instantaneous or immediate spiritual power which one

Only occasionally in life are men *"pervaded, yea dissolved* by the Mind,"* wrote Emerson, adopting the imagery of Thomas Worcester and the Swedenborgians.[214] Originally the Divine Influx[215] from the spiritual world poured into them unceasingly, directed their affections and, finally, overflowed into the world of appearances.[216] Their affections projected themselves into nature.[217] The outer world sprang into being from the inner world of man: planets, days, seasons and phenonema in general. In this connection, one should reread Sampson Reed's discussion of the *laws of the mind* and of time and eternity.[218] Man's *waters retired,* however, and he found himself in

> An Edifice too large for him to fill,
> Lodg'd in a small partition . . . .[219]

Emerson once before had used the metaphor of a retreating flood in discussing the example of Jesus Christ:[220]

Fatal tendency to hang on to the letter and let the spirit go. We will debate the precept about "turning the cheek to the smiter," the "coat and cloke," the "not taking thought what ye shall speak," etc., and question whether it is now practicable, and is now obligatory. Yet every one of us has had his hours of illumination by the same spirit, when he fully understood those commands and saw that he did not need them. He had the Commander, giving fresh precepts fit for the moment and the act. Yet it is well that Christ's are recorded. *They show how high the waters flowed when the spirit brooded upon them, and are a measure of our deficiency. The wonder that is felt at these precepts is a measure of our unreason.*

As men shrank to a drop[221] or degenerated, the contrast between them and their house became more evident, and they discovered themselves "as

---

unconsciously shares with one's fellows (Law of Compensation) as well as the influence one casts into the stream of history. See his unpub. sermon, "Spiritual Influences Reciprocal" (June 19, 1831), written with a strong Swedenborgian emphasis, and *Journals*, II, 296 (probably Apr. 21, 1830): "The power that we originate outlives us, takes imposing and stable forms, and Cæsar becomes a dynasty; and Luther and Calvin each a Church; and Mohomet represents himself in a third of the human race."

[214] From section XII of "A Statement of the First Philosophy." The word *dissolved* as used to describe the influx of the Spirit seems to have entered Emerson's vocabulary when he was talking with the Rev. Thos. Worcester and Sampson Reed in January, 1832. See *Journals*, II, 455-456.

[215] See Swedenborg ¶s. 21ff.

[216] Cf. Coleridge ¶ 263.

[217] See Sampson Reed ¶s. 18a-22.

[218] See Sampson Reed on "Time and Eternity:" ¶s. 2-3; also *E T E*, II, 13; 15-17. Emerson is Swedenborgian rather than classical. For the latter view of creation see Cudworth, *Intellectual System* (1845), I, 392 fn.: "Plato maintains in the Timæus the same opinion concerning the origin of the human race, which is well known to have been entertained by the Egyptian and many other philosophers, that men were procreated and produced from the elements according to a certain law by the sun and other heavenly bodies. But this he remodels agreeably to his own system of philosophy, and presents to us in a kind of rhetorical dress; nor does he exclude the Deity from so important an office, as most others did both before and after him. God, he tells us, first ordered and disposed rude matter, agitated by disorderly motion; he then made the sun, moon and stars, endowed with mind and intelligence, which the philosopher calls the visible and junior gods; to these again he assigned the task of forming men and of uniting in them body and soul: the heavenly bodies in obedience to the commands of God gave to men a body from the four elements, and then a soul from themselves." See note 181 above, and observe its context.

[219] Milton, *Paradise Lost*, Bk. VIII, 104-105.

[220] *Journals*, III, 303-304 (June 5, 1834). Italics are mine. The word "brooded" is possibly an echo of Milton's *Paradise Lost*, Bk. I, line 21.

[221] The hyperbole is justified in Sampson Reed ¶s. 21, 66-70. See also *Letters*, I, 235-236: ". . . the doctor's dominion will shrink back into an advisory council." Cf. Coleridge ¶s. 257 and 277. Emerson, in his "Introductory Lecture on English Literature" (Nov.

much strangers in nature" as they were "aliens from God" within them.[222] The Swedenborgians showed how man gradually became blind to the Sun and Moon of the Spiritual World, turned his back on them, and began to worship the sun and moon in nature——mere creatures.[223] Coleridge emphasized the same truth:[224]

> They built cities, invented musical instruments, were artificers in brass and in iron, and refined on the means of sensual gratification, and the conveniencies of courtly intercourse. They became the great masters of the agreeable, which fraternized readily with cruelty and rapacity; these being, indeed, but alternate moods of the same sensual selfishness. . . . [They] determined to receive nothing as true, but what they derived, or believed themselves to derive from their senses . . . *à posteriori*; they became idolaters of the heavens and the material elements.

The sex of Emerson's planets reverses most oriental folklore,[225] and I suggest that Milton was his authority for a *male* sun and a *female* moon:[226]

> . . . and other Suns perhaps
> With thir attendant Moons thou wilt descry
> Communicating Male and Female Light,
> Which two great Sexes animate the World,
> Stor'd in each Orb perhaps with some that live.

Though man be a drowsy dwarf, still he starts in his slumber. He recalls his better or higher self and is conscious of the present discrepancy. There is still hope for him:

> The generic soul in each individual is a giant overcome with sleep which locks up almost all his senses, and only leaves him a little superficial animation. Once in an age at hearing some deeper voice, he lifts his iron lids, and his eyes straight pierce through all appearances, and his tongue tells what shall be in the latest times: then is he obeyed like a God, but quickly the lids fall, and sleep returns.[227]

> The whole secret of the teacher's force lies in the conviction that men are convertible. And they are. They want awakening. Get the soul out of bed, out of her deep habitual sleep, out into God's universe, to a perception of its beauty, and hearing of its call, and your vulgar man, your prosy, selfish sensualist awakes, a god, and is conscious of force to shake the world.[228]

> The slowness with which the *stirps generosa, seu historica* in Europe opened their eyes to the monstrous lie of Popery, might startle us as to the possible depth of our own degradation through the sleep of Reason, and prompt a hope of what height we may yet attain.[229]

5, 1835), remarked that the tyranny of divine Ideas crushes man's skepticism and that man shrivels into an insignificant onlooker in the midst of magnificent Laws. See the abstract of this lecture in the chapter on the Early Lectures.

[222] *Nature*, 81.2-5.

[223] See Swedenborg ¶s. 40-41.

[224] See Coleridge ¶ 149. Cf. also ¶ 160. Cf. Deut. 4:19; 17.3; Ezekiel 8:16.

[225] See the usual tradition, expressed by John Donne in Epithalamion VII (italics mine):

> Here lies a *she Sun*, and a *he Moon* here,
> She gives the best light to his Sphere,
> Or each is both, and all, and so
> They unto one another nothing owe . . . .

Emerson quoted these lines in *Letters*, I, 10 (June 2-3, 1815).

[226] *Paradise Lost*, Bk. VIII, 148ff.   [228] See *Journals*, III, 278 (Apr. 20, 1834).

[227] *Journals*, IV, 53 (May 19, 1836).   [229] See *Journals*, III, 365 (Nov. 19, 1834).

We are always on the brink of an ocean of thought into which we do not yet swim. We are poor lords,——have immense powers which we are hindered from using. I am kept out of my heritage. . . .[230]

The mind is very wise, could it be roused into action. But the life of most men is aptly signified by the poet's personification, "Death in Life." We walk about in a sleep. A few moments in the year, or in our lifetime, we truly live; we are at the top of our being; we are pervaded, yea dissolved by the Mind; but we fall back again presently. Those who are styled Practical Men are not awake, for they do not exercise the Reason; yet their sleep is restless. The most active lives have so much routine as to preclude progress almost equally with the most inactive. We bow low to the noted merchants whose influence is felt, not only in their native cities, but in most parts of the globe; but our respect does them and ourselves great injustice, for their trade is without system, their affairs unfold themselves after no law of the mind, but are bubble built on bubble without end; a work of arithmetic, not of commerce, much less of humanity. . . .

Such is the inaction of men. We have an obscure consciousness of our attributes. We stand on the edge of all that is great, yet are restrained in inactivity and unconscious of our powers, like neuters of the hive, every one of which is capable of transformation into the Queen Bee. We are always on the brink, etc. Much preparation, little fruit. But suddenly in any place, in the street, in the chamber, will the heavens open and the regions of wisdom be uncovered, as if to show how thin the veil, how null the circumstances. As quickly, a Lethean stream washes through us and bereaves us of ourselves.[231]

Both Coleridge and Swedenborg also wrote on man's dim recollection of his higher self.[232]

Sampson Reed explained how, with the degeneration of man, love of self took the place of the love of the Lord and the neighbor, and how a *practical* or utilitarian knowledge was substituted for a knowledge of the laws of the divine order, so that when God communicated with men in His usual manner, they could no longer understand the means and declared all such manifestations "miracles." The fact that man is *astonished and filled with wonder* at the normal operation of spiritual laws indicates his departure and alienation from God.[233]

As divine things became less and less familiar to the human mind, there was more and more a feeling of something strange and incongruous when they were presented. Mankind were as one who has been stolen in his childhood by a band of robbers, and made familiar to all their scenes of violence: to whom the recollections of his infancy appear like a strange dream, by which he is terrified far more than by crimes.[234]

The *elemental power* of man comes, of course, from self-knowledge—— that is, knowledge of the God within, of the indwelling Reason, of Universal Spirit or Soul. Man finds himself able to use this force only insofar as he yields to it:

We are taught by great actions that the universe is the property of every individual in it. Every rational creature has all nature for his dowry and estate. It is his, if he

---

[230] See *Journals*, III, 272 (Apr. 12, 1834). See also *Carlyle-Emerson Corr.*, I, 51 (Mar. 12, 1835): "Men live on the brink of mysteries and harmonies into which yet they never enter, and with their hand on the door-latch they die outside."
[231] See sections XII-XIII of "A Statement of the First Philosophy."
[232] See Coleridge ¶s. 44, 203, 246; also *Aids* (1829), notes, 258-259; Swedenborg ¶ 44. See Wordsworth's *Ode*.
[233] Sampson Reed ¶s. 11, 12, 15. See the frequent repetition of the word *wonder* in the journals for June 22-24, 1836, printed above.
[234] Sampson Reed ¶ 11. Cf. the last lines of Orphic Poet VI.

will. He may divest himself of it; he may creep into a corner, and abdicate his kingdom, as most men do, but he is entitled to the world by his constitution. In proportion
to the energy of his thought and will, he takes up the world into himself.[235]

What learned I this morning in the woods, the oracular woods? Wise are they, the
ancient nymphs . . . . But thus they said:——Power is one great lesson which Nature
teaches man. The secret that he can, not only reduce under his will, that is, conform to
his character particular events, but classes of events, and so harmonize all the outward
occurrences with the states of mind,——that must he learn.[236]

Very appropriate for a discussion of gods in ruin and kings deposed was
Emerson's allusion to King Richard II. in a line which he adapted from
Shakespeare's play. (The typescript parallel offers the better evidence.)

> An if my word be sterling yet in England,
> Let it command a mirror hither straight,
> That it may show me what a face I have.[237]

The best interpretation of Emerson's words, *instinct, involuntary* and
unconscious power superior to the will, will be found in the writings of
Sampson Reed.[238] The general meaning is preserved in the following excerpts from Emerson himself:

> Give up to thy soul——
> Let it have its way——
> It is, I tell thee, God himself,
> The selfsame One that rules the Whole,
> Tho' he speaks thro' thee with a stifled voice,
> And looks through thee, shorn of his beams.
> But if thou listen to his voice,
> If thou obey the royal thought,
> It will grow clearer to thine ear,
> More glorious to thine eye.
> The clouds will burst that veil him now
> And thou shalt see the Lord.[239]

I will trust my instincts. For always a reason halts after an instinct, and when I
have deviated from the instinct, comes somebody with a profound theory teaching that
I ought to have followed it: some Goethe, Swedenborg, or Carlyle.[240]

The exercise of reason, the act of reflexion redeems a man at once out of this
brutishness. The man who reflects, is a man, and not an animal. By the act of reflexion
man perceives 'that he is wonderfully made.' . . . He accepts his lot: he perceives the
great astonishment. He adores. Awaked to truth and virtue——which is the two fold
office of Reason, he passes out of the local and finite, he inspires and expires immortal
breath.[241]

---

[235] *Nature*, 25.6-15. Part also appears in *Journals*, III, 570 (Nov. 14, 1835) and part
in *Typescript Journals*, "B," Part I, p. 118.

[236] *Journals*, IV, 66-67 (June 14, 1836). Cf. *Nature*, 50.13-20. Cf. Coleridge, *Church
and State* [*Complete Works* (Shedd), VI], 137. On man's power over nature, see also
Journals, III, 360, 488; Cousin ¶ 1; Miscellaneous Selections ¶s. 14-20.

[237] See Shakespeare's *Richard II.*, IV, i, 265-267. Note in the journal for June 22
(ptd. above) that Alcott could not "delight in Shakspear cannot get near him."

[238] See Sampson Reed ¶s. 66-70, 33-34, 27; Swedenborg ¶s. 29ff. and 48. See *Y E S*,
234.35ff. (Nov. 28, 1830): Emerson says Jesus is distinguished from other men by the
"presence of a Superior Will to his own or to that of any created being in every one
of his actions." For the "infallible guidance" one receives by abdicating choice, see
Journals, III, 337-338 (Sept. 14, 1834). See also III, 344 top, 345, and 471 bottom. See
index for "First and third thoughts coincide."

[239] See lines 29-40 of "Γνωθι Σεαυτον" in chap. VII.

[240] See *Journals*, III, 299 (May 21, 1834).   [241] See *Y E S*, 206-207 (Sept. 7, 1834).

To him who, by God's grace, has seen that by being a mere tunnel or pipe through which the divine Will flows, he becomes great, and becomes a Man,——the future wears an eternal smile, and the flight of time is no longer dreadful. I assure myself always of needed help, and go to the grave undaunted because I go not to the grave. I am willing also to be as passive to the great forces I acknowledge as is the thermometer or the clock, and quite part with all will as superfluous.[241a]

V

'Nature is not fixed but fluid. Spirit alters, moulds, makes it. The immobility or bruteness of nature, is the absence of spirit; to pure spirit, it is fluid, it is volatile, it is obedient. Every spirit builds itself a house; and beyond its house, a world; and beyond its world, a heaven. Know then, that the world exists for you. For you is the phenomenon perfect. What we are, that only can we see. All that Adam had, all that Cæsar could, you have and can do. Adam called his house, heaven and earth; Cæsar called his house, Rome; you perhaps call yours, a cobbler's trade; a hundred acres of ploughed land; or a scholar's garret. Yet line for line and point for point, your dominion is as great as theirs, though without fine names. (93.20——94.13).

Nature is not stable but fluid. Spirit alters, moulds, makes it. The immobility or bruteness of nature is the absence of spirit; to pure spirit it is fluid, it is volatile, it is obedient.

Believe that the world exists for you. for you is the phenomenon perfect & what we are, that only we see. All that Adam had, all that Cæsar could, you have & can do   Adam called it the earth, Cæsar called life Rome; you perhaps call it a cobbler's trade, yet line for line & point for point, you have the whole circle

Every one has a trust of power. every man——every boy——a jurisdiction, if it be only over a cow, or a rood of a potato field, or a fleet of ships, or the laws of a state.

This section was intended originally to complete the chapter on "Spirit," as may be seen from the sentence introducing it in the typescripts,[242] but Emerson enlarged his original plan, keeping the paragraph for the conclusion of "Prospects." It contains his favorite themes of "self-reliance" and "compensation." That nature was plastic in the presence of Spirit he found especially in Cudworth,[242a] though also in Coleridge and the Swedenborgians. Nearly a year before the publication of *Nature* he had discussed the Ideal Theory and indicated the power of "thought" in making the natural world "fluid," as may be seen in his "Introductory Lecture on English Literature" (Nov. 5, 1835).[243] Bruteness in man he had recognized earlier as evidence of the absence of Reason.[244] He took his imagery of a Spirit's building its house (the body) and through the affections of the body an external world, and finally a spiritual home in eternity——from the Swedenborgians.[245]

How does every institution, every man, every thought embody, clothe itself externally with dress, houses, newspapers, societies. . . . Why then should the Swedenborgian doctrine be obnoxious, that in the spiritual world the affections clothe themselves with appropriate garments, dwellings, and other circumstances?[246]

[241a] See *Journals*, III, 555 (Oct. 15, 1835). Cf. *Nature*, 57.19-23.
[242] See line 110 in the *Typescript Journals*, edited above.
[242a] See the chapter on Cudworth and also the motto on the title page of *Nature* (1836).
[243] See my abstract elsewhere in this volume.
[244] See *Y E S*, 206.33ff. (Sept. 7, 1834).
[245] See Swedenborg ¶s. 21-27; 34-37; 39; 6-13; Sampson Reed ¶s. 18a *et seq.*
[246] *Journals*, III, 370 (Nov. 23, 1834).

Let a man under the influence of strong passion go into the fields, and see how readily every thought clothes itself with a material garment. (Is it not illustration to us of the manner in which every spirit clothes itself with body?) Now I say, is it not time that something was done to explain this attractiveness which the face of Nature has for us?[247]

This Spirit is the "immediate" within man, and it is not circumscribed by temporal institutions or considerations. On it Emerson built his doctrine of self- (that is, God-) reliance:

[The] soul converses with the past and the distant, and the future, and is conscious that its thoughts have no relation to time or to corruption. A stronger and stronger word of assurance comes from the undeceiving inward Monitor, who speaks as with the voice of the whole creation. I perceive no terrors, no shrinking in that inmost shrine at the approach of death . . . all is calm within.[248]

It is the perception of this depth in human nature——this infinitude belonging to every man that has been born——which has given new value to the habits of reflexion and solitude. This has caused the virtue of independent judgment to be so much praised. This has given its odour to spiritual interpretations. Many old and almost forgotten maxims have been remembered up from where they lay in the dust of centuries and are seen to beam new light . . . . 'Know Thyself' . . . 'Revere Thyself.'[249]

The whole universe exists, indeed, for the development of each man's soul ——for the exercise of the God within him. Rank, occupation or external condition means nothing. All men have a priceless stake in the Godhead or Universal Reason. None can afford to ignore the divine voice or deny its oracles:

Wherever is life, wherever is God, there the Universe evolves itself as from a centre to its boundless irradiation. Whosoever therefore apprehends the infinite,—— and every man can,——brings all worth and significance into that spot of space where he stands, though it be a ditch, a potato-field, a work-bench; or, more properly, into that state of thought in which he is, whether it be the making a statue or designing a church like Michel Angelo, or holding silent meetings like George Fox, and Job Scott, or fighting battles like Leonidas, Washington, Lafayette; exploring the law of laws like Plotinus . . . . Therefore is it in the option of every generous spirit to denominate that place in which he now is, his Rome, his world; his sunshine shall be Susa;[249a] his shade, Ecbatana; and let him rest assured, if he invite them, not one deity will stay away from his feast.[250]

A day is a rich abyss of means, yet mute and void. It demands something godlike in him who has cast off the common yokes and motives of humanity, and has ventured to trust himself for a taskmaster. High be his heart, faithful his will, vast his contemplations, that he may truly be a world, society, law to himself; that a simple purpose may be to him as strong as iron necessity is to others. It is a faithful saying worthy of all acceptation, that a reasoning Man, conscious of his powers and duties, annihilates all distinction of circumstances. What is Rome? what is royalty? what is wealth? His place is the true place, and superior therefore in dignity to all other places. Linnæus at Copenhagen, Oberlin on the high Alps, White at Selborne, Roger Bacon at Oxford, Rammohun Roy in India, and Heber at Bombay, Washington in the Jerseys——these are the Romes, the Empires, the Wealth of these men. The place which I have not sought, but in which my duty places me, is a sort of royal palace. If I am faithful in it, I move in it with a pleasing awe at the immensity of the chain

---

[247] *Journals*, III, 227 (Nov. 2, 1833). Cf. *Nature*, 84.12-21.
[248] See "Religion and Society," *Y E S*, 202 (Oct. 27, 1833). Cf. *Journals*, I, 253 (Apr. 8, 1823) and *Letters*, I, 409.
[249] *Y E S*, 200.
[249a] For commentary on Susa and Ecbatana, see *Journals*, II, 450 (Jan. 12, 1832).
[250] *Journals*, III, 402 (Dec. 22, 1834). Cf. *Y E S*, 54.5.

of which I hold the last link in my hand and am led by it. I perceive my commission to be coeval with the antiquity of the eldest causes.[251]

The perfect world exists to every man,——to the poorest drover in the mountains, the poorest laborer in his ditch. Quite independent of his work are his endowments. There is enough in him (grant him capable of thought and virtue) to puzzle and outwit all our philosophy. The history of one man, inasmuch as it is searching and profound, is as valuable as the history of a nation. Thoroughly acquaint me with the heart of one living man,——though the humblest, and what can Italy or England teach me more with all their wars and all their laws? Sharpen these obtuse perceptions of ours and show us the motives, the fancy, the affection, the distorting and colouring lenses that pauper makes use of, and the redeeming power that still sets him right after countless errors, and that promises him a kingdom of heaven whilst he shuffles about in his barnyard, and we shall be able to do without Tacitus and Clarendon.[252]

Reverence man, and not Plato and Cæsar. Wherever there is sense, reflexion, courage, admit it to the same honour,——embrace it, quote it from a truckman as quick as from Webster.[253]

Then what Boswellism it is to travel! Illustrate, eternize your own woodhouse. It is much cheaper, and quite possible to any resolute thinker.[254]

Who can resist this influence [of wealth, social position etc.] and feel that the reason of Caesar is really no more weighty than our own?[255]

[T]he Spirit of truth . . . speaks by a thousand thousand lips, in all countries, in public and in private places, to mankind. He is never silent. There is no one so remote but he is addressed by him. To drop all personification——the progress of society, the simple occurrences of every day, are always instructing men, undeceiving them.[256]

Him I call rich, that soul I call endowed, whether in man or woman, who by poverty or affliction or love has been driven home so far as to make acquaintance with the spiritual dominion of every human mind. Henceforward he is introduced into sublime society, henceforward he can wave the hand of adieu to all the things he coveted most . . . . him I leave in his heaven, and all others I call miserably poor.[257]

There is a revolution of religious opinion taking effect around us as it seems to me the greatest of all revolutions which have ever occurred that, namely, which has separated the individual from the whole world and made him demand a faith satisfactory to his own proper nature, whose full extent he now for the first time contemplates. A little while ago men were supposed to be saved or lost as one race; Adam was the federal head and, in books of theology, his sin was a federal sin which cut off the hopes of all his posterity. . . . But now, men have begun to feel and to inquire for their *several stake* in the joy and the suffering of the whole. What is *my* relation to Almighty God? What is *my* relation to my fellow man? What am I designed for? What are my duties? What is my destiny?[258]

> Therefore, O happy youth,
> Happy if thou dost know and love this truth,
> Thou art unto thyself a law,
> And since the soul of things is in thee,
> Thou needest nothing out of thee.
> The law, the gospel, and the Providence,
> Heaven, Hell, the Judgment, and the stores
> Immeasureable of Truth and Good,

[251] *Journals*, III, 285-286 (Apr. 28, 1834). The last lines express Emerson's thought about chronologies in Orphic Poet I.
[252] "The Miracle of Our Being," *Y E S*, 209 (Sept. 7, 1834).
[253] *Journals*, II, 507 (Aug. 19, 1832).   [254] *Journals*, III, 340 (Sept. 15, 1834).
[255] "The Genuine Man," *Y E S*, 182.2-3 (Oct. 21, 1832).
[256] "Religion and Society," *Y E S*, 194 (Oct. 27, 1833).
[257] *Journals*, III, 410 (Dec. 24, 1834).
[258] "Religion and Society," *Y E S*, 199 (Oct. 27, 1833).

> All these thou must find
> Within thy single mind,
> Or never find.[259]

One should consult the chapters on Coleridge for an extensive commentary on the line, "What we are, that only can we see."[260] The inner dominion of each man, Emerson believed, should seem so rich to those who discovered it that they would thereafter be quite contented with their lot in life. Your dominion is as great as that enjoyed by any hero or conqueror. It needs only to be recognized and developed:

Know thyself. To him who has reached this wisdom how ridiculous is Caesar and Bonaparte wandering from one extreme of civilization to the other to conquer men,——himself, the while, unconquered, unexplored, almost wholly unsuspected to himself. Yet Europe and Asia are not so broad and deep, have nothing so splendid, so durable as the possessions of this empire. What shall it profit a man though he gain the whole world and lose his own soul?[261]

You seem to be a point or focus upon which all objects, all ages concentrate their influence.[262] Nothing past but affects *you*. Nothing remote but through some means reaches *you*. Every superficial grain of sand may be considered as the fixed point round which all things revolve, so intimately is it allied to all and so truly do all turn as if for it alone. . . . All that [man] sees and hears gives him a lesson. Do not the ages that are past report their experience for his tuition and millions of millions of rational spirits epitomize their fate for his behoof? Is he not continually moved to joy or grief by things said a thousand years ago? He understands them. His soul embraces the act or the sentiment as if it were done or said for him only. Is not his condition different for every one of the men that has acted upon the world? . . . Does not Socrates, and Solomon, and Bacon, and Shakespear counsel him alone? Jesus lives as for him only? God exists for him only? And Right and Wrong, and Wisdom and Folly? the whole of Pleasure; and of Pain; and all the heaven of thought? Are they not all poured into his bosom as if the world had no other child?[263]

When I read a problem, I would be a geometer; poetry, a poet; history, a historian; sermons, a preacher; when I see paintings, I would paint; sculpture, carve; and so with all things, the manifold soul in me vindicates its acquaintance with all these things. Similar delight we have in the admirable artist's, soldier's, or sailor's life. We individuate ourselves with him, and judge of his work. What is this but our first ride round our estate to take possession, promising ourselves withal, after a few visits more, to have an insight and give a personal direction to all the affairs that go on within our domain, which is the All?[264]

Let it be remembered that it is not ourselves so much as Providence that appoints our situation in life, that appoints us to great or to humble occasions of usefulness. But our virtue is in all cases determined by ourselves. It is ours to say whether we will rise in our daily life to the dignity of angels or whether we will creep nameless and worthless through infamous years of selfishness and sin to a dishonourable old age of shame and sorrow. One who contemplates the beauty of a life that is nobly led under the unerring guidance of religious principle is sometimes astonished how there

---

[259] See lines 58-68 of "Γνωθι Σεαυτον," in chap. VII. Cf. the theme of George Herbert's poem, "Man," in *Nature*, 85.3——86.9. See *Journals*, II, 348 (1830) for Emerson's quoting St. Paul (I Cor. 3:21): "All things are yours."

[260] See esp. chap. VII, note 43. See *Journals*, II, 357-358. See also Gérando, *Histoire* (1822), I, 485-486: "Le même ne peut être conçu que par le même."

[261] "Trust Yourself," *Y E S*, 111 (Dec. 3, 1830).

[262] Cf. the Doctrine of the Microcosm. See the index.

[263] "The Miracle of Our Being," *Y E S*, 207-208 (Sept. 7, 1834). Cf. *Journals*, III, 570: "[E]ach rational creature is dowried with all the gifts of God. The universe—nothing less—is totally given to each new being."

[264] *Journals*, III, 438 (Jan. 12, 1835).

should be hesitation upon its advantage; that all men do not run to render the homage of their obedience to the law of God.[265]

Our time is yet present. That span out of his measureless eternity which the Almighty Father allows to each, to be tried and instructed, to hear his name and to read his commandments, to make friends, to deal with men, to choose our part and make our character, that time which is nearly equal in all, (a few years making little difference when compared with the boundless duration out of which it rose and into which it recedes,)——is now ours. It is all that the great and the wise have had. It is all that saints and heroes had. It is all that Paul or Luther or Newton or Washington had, to lift themselves by humility and the love of truth and sublime energy into the spiritual world and help the human race. It is now our turn of life. It is a singular proof of the independence of spiritual nature on space and time that this life is long enough for the vast purposes to be answered by it. It is long enough for useful men to work their ends. It is long enough to the wise to instruct men. It has been long enough for tyrants to enslave men. It has been long enough for the patriots to free nations.[266]

Make much of your own place. The stars and celestial awning that overhang our simple Concord walks and discourses are as brave as those that were visible to Coleridge as he talked, or Dryden, or Ben Jonson and Shakspear, or Chaucer and Petrarch and Boccaccio when they met.[267]

Why are you dazzled with the name of Caesar? A part as important, a soul as great, a name as dear to God as his or any other's is your own.[268]

The mind reveals that Virtue is happiness; that good spirits associate; that the only Rank is Character; that Virtue is the key to the secrets of the world.[269]

VI

'Build, therefore, your own world. As fast as you conform your life to the pure idea in your mind, that will unfold its great proportions. A correspondent revolution in things will attend the influx of the spirit. So fast will disagreeable appearances, swine, spiders, snakes, pests, mad-houses, prisons, enemies, vanish; they are temporary and shall be no more seen. The sordor and filths of nature, the sun shall dry up, and the wind exhale. As when the summer comes from the south, the snow-banks melt, and the face of the earth becomes green before it, so shall the advancing spirit create its ornaments along its path, and carry with it the beauty it visits, and the song which enchants it; it shall draw beautiful faces, and warm hearts, and wise discourse, and heroic acts, around its way, until evil is no more seen. The

As fast as your spirit quits its earth, disagreeable appearances, prisons, spiders, snakes, pests, madhouses, vanish.
    they are temporary & shall be no more seen   The sordor & filths[270] of nature, the sun shall dry up & the wind exhale. As before the Summer, the snowbanks melt and the face of the earth becomes green so the spirit shall create its ornaments along its path & carry with it the beauty it visits & the song which enchants it.——creates intelligent faces & warm hearts and sweet discourse
    heroic acts   around its way until evil is no more seen   This kingdom[271] of man over nature which shall not come with observation.   a dominion such as now is beyond his dream of God he shall enter without more wonder than the blind man feels who is gradually restored to perfect sight

---

[265] "On Showing Piety at Home," *Y E S*, 16 (Aug. 12, 1827).
[266] "How Old Art Thou," *Y E S*, 117 (Dec. 31, 1830).
[267] *Journals*, III, 536 (Aug. 5, 1835).
[268] *Journals*, III, 103 (Apr. 22, 1833). Cf. Coleridge ¶s. 177 and 261.
[269] From sect. IX of "A Statement of the First Philosophy."
[270] [Variant:] The sordor & filths of nature the sun shall exhale & the wind dry up.
[271] [Variant:] The kingdom of man over nature shall not come with observation To all these wonders, to a dominion such as now is beyond his dream of God he shall return

kingdom of man over nature, which
cometh not with observation,——a dominion such as now is beyond his dream
of God,——he shall enter without more
wonder than the blind man feels who is
gradually restored to perfect sight.'
(94.13——95.12).

Build your own world! "Every man makes his own religion, his own God, his own charity; takes none of these from the Bible or his neighbour entire."[272] "Every man has a form of mind peculiar to himself," wrote Sampson Reed in the "Oration on Genius,"[273] and "it becomes us then to seek and to cherish this *peculium* of our own minds, as the patrimony which is left us by our Father in heaven. . . . Let a man's ambition to be great disappear in a willingness to be what he is." Agreeing with Reed, Emerson emphasized the doctrine of self-reliance (*i.e.*, God-reliance) as the only true means of improving the world and redeeming one's own soul:[274]

There is in every man a determination of character to a peculiar end, counteracted often by unfavorable fortune, but more apparent, the more he is left at liberty. This is called his genius, or his nature, or his turn of mind. The object of Education should be to remove all obstructions, and let this natural force have free play and exhibit its peculiar product. It seems to be true that no man in this is deluded. This determination of his character is to something in his nature; something real. This object is called his Idea. It is that which rules his most advised actions, those especially that are most his, and is most distinctly discerned by him in those days or moments when he derives the sincerest satisfaction from his life.

It is loyalty or disloyalty to this Idea that can make a heaven of hell, a hell of heaven. This Idea is the element of the timeless within us, our special *use*, our God-given vocation. It is not limited by the fleeting present, but is superior to it as, indeed, Sampson Reed demonstrated in his treatment of time and eternity.[275] The general Swedenborgian view can be summed up as follows:[276]

[H]eaven is not a place, nor is hell. They are states,——conditions of the will and the understanding. He is in heaven, in whom the love of the Lord and of the neighbor are not only predominant, but absolute; holding all things within the man in due subservience to them. He is in hell, in whom the love of self and the love of the world have the mastery, and exercise entire dominion.

From such thoughts Emerson developed his sermon on "Salvation, Now."[277] "That life alone is beautiful," he wrote, "which is conformed to an Idea. Let us not live from hand to mouth *now*, that we may not *ever*."[278] But Coleridge's concept of the Divine Reason and its necessary Ideas[279] are also implied in the final paragraph of the Orphic Poet:

---

without more wonder than the blind man feels who is gradually restored to perfect sight.

[272] See *Journals*, II, 290 (Feb. 11, 1830).

[273] See Sampson Reed ¶s. 23 and 26. See also ¶ 28.

[274] *Journals*, III, 416-417 (Dec. 27, 1834). For the same theme see *Journals*, III, 511 and *Y E S*, 165.19; 210.34. See also note 151a *supra* and its context.

[275] See *E T E*, II, 15-18; see ¶s. 1-3.

[276] Swedenborg ¶ 8. See notes 120 and 209 and their context.

[277] Sermon no. 78, delivered June 13, 1830.

[278] *Journals*, IV, 16 (Feb. 28, 1836).   [279] See Coleridge ¶s. 1-56.

[T]he moment Reason assumes its empire over a man, he finds that he has nothing low and injurious in him but it is, under this dominion, the root of power and beauty. His animal nature is ennobled by serving the soul: that which was debasing him will now prove the sinews of his character . . . the worst calamities, the sorest sorrow, are changed, are glorified. He owns his deep debt to them, and acknowledges in them the omnipresent energy of the God who transforms all things into the divine. . . . Let him consider that all riches, though convenient to the senses, cannot profit *himself*, but that a true thought, a worthy deed, puts him at once in harmony with the real and eternal. . . . What does the world suggest but a lofty faith that all will be, that all is well: that the Father who thus vouchsafes to reveal himself in all that is. great, and all that is lovely, will not forsake the child for whom he provideth such costly instruction——whom every hour and every event of memory and hope educate. What does it intimate but presages of an infinite and perfect life?[280]

By listening to this inward voice, by following this invisible Leader, it is in the power of a man to cast off from himself the responsibility of his words and actions and to make God responsible for him. It is beautiful, it is venerable to see the majesty which belongs to the man who leans directly upon a principle. . . . [T]he conviction must be produced in our minds that *this truth of character is identical with a religious life;* that they are one and the same thing; that this voice of your own mind is the voice of God; that the reason why you are bound to reverence it, is because it is the direct revelation of your Maker's Will, not written in books many ages since nor attested by distant miracles but in the flesh and blood, in the faculties and emotions of your constitution.[281]

A human mind once persuaded of a simple abstract proposition becomes the servant of that thought and puts the whole material creation as far as its power reaches into subjection to it. And a few men persuaded of the same thing will cooperate and by cooperation make more intense each other's conviction and soon exert a power that multiplies itself in a compound ratio. . . . For there is in all moral truth that fruitfulness, that inborn creative force, that ever unfolding power that promises to act upon human society with an energy which nothing can adequately represent.[282]

Sampson Reed promised the "correspondent revolution" in external things which would follow upon the *influx of the Spirit.*[283] "It is the tendency of revelation," he wrote, "to give a right direction to every power of every mind; and when this is effected, inventions and discoveries will follow of course, all things assume a different aspect, and the world itself again become a paradise." These views strengthened Emerson's belief in universal compensation:

There is nothing in material nature . . . so splendid and perfect as the law of compensations—the law according to which an act done by any moral being draws after it its inevitable fruit which no chance and no art can elude. The nature of these laws, their extent, their omnipotence he can learn only by *acting*, and observing how they determine and reward every action. The Creation is so magically woven that nothing can do him any mischief but himself. An invisible immortal fence surrounds his being which defends him from all harm he wills to resist; the whole creation cannot bend him whilst he stands upright; but, on the other hand, every act of his, is instantaneously judged and rewarded.[284]

Such is the force of spiritual nature that every thing takes the hue of our thought. The peevish man finds his way full of crosses; the benevolent man full of charities. The world is but a mirror in which every mind sees its own image reflected. Everything speaks wisdom to the wise, and sensuality to the sensual, and worldly hope to

[280] See "The Miracle of Our Being," *Y E S*, 210-212 (Sept. 7, 1834).
[281] "The Genuine Man," *Y E S*, 188-189 (Oct. 21, 1832).
[282] "Religion and Society," *Y E S*, 198 (Oct. 27, 1833).
[283] "Growth of the Mind," *E T E*, II, 13-14. On the influx of the Spirit, see Swedenborg ¶ 21. For an optimistic picture of the future and for signs of a change, see Sampson Reed ¶s. 38-43.   [284] See *Y E S*, 209-210 (Sept. 7, 1834).

the ambitious, folly to the frivolous, and God to the good. As a man thinketh so he is
and so he receives. . . . So is this the law of all action. All things are double, one
against another. Love and you shall be loved. Hate and you shall be hated. Judge not
and ye shall not be judged, saith our Saviour, for whatsoever measure ye mete, it shall
be measured to you again.[285]

"More and more, with every thought," he wrote early in *Nature*,[286] "does
his kingdom stretch over things, until the world becomes, at last, only a
realized will,——the double of the man." In his concluding lines, he was
probably also thinking of the Psalmist: "Thou sendest forth thy spirit,
they are created; and thou renewest the face of the earth."[287]

We have seen above that the "disagreeable appearances" in nature——
the result of the clothing of man's evil affections——must be explained by
familiar Swedenborgian doctrines, set forth most clearly in the articles
of Sampson Reed.[288] Reed also seems to have suggested the beautiful
imagery of the summer coming from the South and, doubtless, contributed
something to the optimism with which *Nature* closes.[289] As the Spirit
advances its influence multiplies:[290]

[Jesus] has always in his mouth expressions of his sense of the littleness of the
present and strong assurance of the greatness of the future. His word is a mustard
seed——it is a little leaven,——it is a single pearl——but with a prophet's eye he sees
that the omnipotence of truth is in it, and beholds already its prolific effects——he
sees it quicken in the minds of good men and run like something endued with life from
soul to soul . . . preparing hearts to conceive and tongues to utter yet more lofty and
significant revelations.

At last, evil will be no longer seen. As we noted in the comment on section
one, Emerson did not anticipate an early state of perfection for all, but
rather one that crowned a long and difficult development of individuals.[291]
His optimism, nevertheless, was strong because his source of encouragement was the great, unfailing, omnipresent Spirit. With the Reason in his
breast, man's worst troubles might be converted into benefits; his aches
and pains should become mere trifles:

Misery is superficial, and the remedy, when it can be attained, of presenting to the
mind Universal Truths, is a perfect one. The wise may, that is, the healthy mind learns
. . . that every event, every pain, every misfortune, seen in the perspective of the
past, is beautiful; that we are embosomed[292] in beauty; and if, in long retrospect,
things are yet ugly, it is because the mind is diseased, and the rays are dislocated and
not suffered to fall in a focus and so present a just perspective to the Reason. Of
course the aim of the wise physician will then be to repair the general health.[293]

To you and to me does this sublime doctrine come home . . . with such power of
consolation and of command as to make adversity no longer adverse, the fears and

[285] See "Self-Culture," *Y E S*, 101-102 (Sept. 5, 1830). Cf. *Nature*, 14.14-15.
[286] See *Nature*, 51.6-9. For the world as man's *double*, see Cousin ¶ 1.
[287] Psalm 104:30.
[288] See Sampson Reed ¶s. 18a-22, 58; Swedenborg ¶s. 30, 35-39. See also *Nature*, 80.16
—81.16. See *Journals*, III, 533-534 (Aug. 5, 1835).
[289] See Sampson Reed ¶s. 59-60; 38-43.
[290] "Religion and Society," *Y E S*, 197 (Oct. 27, 1833).
[291] See the summary of Emerson's attitude toward the problem of evil by Arthur C.
McGiffert, Jr., in *Y E S*, 258-259. See *Nature*, 12.1, 12.23ff., 15.15ff., 71.9-20, 75.8-11.
[292] See *Nature*, 5.11.
[293] *Journals*, IV, 23 (Mar. 14, 1836).

vexations of time no disturbance of our peace, and human life a part of the Eternity of God.[294]

We are wonderfully protected. We have scarce a misfortune, a hindrance, an infirmity, an enemy, but it is somehow productive of singular advantage to us. After groaning through years of poverty and hard labor, the mind perceives that really it has come the shortest road to a valuable position, that, though the rough climate was not good for leaves and flowers, it was good for timber. . . . God brings us by ways we know not and like not into Paradise.[295]

The "kingdom of man over nature," which will be accomplished by man's yielding to the spiritual universe within himself, will require the ownership of no tangible property, will necessitate no travel or change of scene, and will involve no particular occupation. It will come to pass——first in the individual and ultimately in society——very slowly and almost imperceptibly, for it will be, indeed, the "kingdom of God:"[296]

And when he was demanded of the Pharisees when the kingdom of God should come, he answered them and said, The kingdom of God cometh not with observation: Neither shall they say, Lo here! or, lo there! for, behold, the kingdom of God is within you.[297]

It will excite no surprise or wonder, because those who welcome it will perceive and understand the spiritual forces which attend it.[298] So gradually[299] will men awaken that the human race will resemble a blind man,[300] the recovery of whose sight is so slow as to seem in no sense miraculous or extraordinary.

---

[294] "Self and Others," *Y E S*, 136.3ff. (Jan. 12, 1831).

[295] *Journals*, III, 315-316 (July? 1834). Cf. III, 555. On the unimportance of poverty or riches see III, 341-342. Cf. *Y E S*, 21.2; 160.3.

[296] "The Miracle of Our Being," *Y E S*, 205.31ff. (Sept. 7, 1834). Cf. also section XII of the "Statement of the First Philosophy." See *Nature*, 44.20—45.4, and *Journals*, III, 227 (Nov. 2, 1833).

[297] See Luke 17:20. See Emerson's sermon, "The Kingdom of Heaven Is Within," delivered on Oct. 31, 1830. See also footnote 26 above as well as its context and the *Typescript Journals*, line 87 above.

[298] See Sampson Reed ¶s. 11-16, 28, 15, 17. See above footnotes 96 and 233, with their context.

[299] See Swedenborg ¶s. 47, 11-13. See note 196 above and its context.

[300] Cf. Swedenborg ¶ 33.

NOTES ON THE TEXT OF *NATURE*

5.3 It writes biographies, histories and criticism.] See *Journals*, II, 349 (Oct., 1830), for condensed quotation from Goethe's *Wilhelm Meister* (tr. Carlyle).

5.9 not of tradition] See *Nature*, 91.21-23; Early Lectures ¶ 12 (May 7, 1834); and *Journals*, III, 420 (Dec. 28, 1834).

5.10 a religion of revelation to us] See comment on Dr. Channing's sermons, *Letters*, I, 138 (Oct. 16, 1823); see Coleridge ¶s. 1-56, 157, 273-277 and references to "know thyself" and "self-knowledge;" see Sampson Reed ¶s. 1-3, 17, 27-28, 38-43, 50, 62, 66, 69 and "Growth of the Mind" *passim*; see Swedenborg ¶s. 21, 24, 48; and *Y E S*, 189.2, 193.25, 196.26, 199-200, 245.18, 267.28. Cf. "The Oversoul," *Works*, II, 280-281: "We distinguish the announcements of the soul, its manifestations of its own nature, by the term *Revelation*. These are always attended by the emotion of the sublime. For this communication is an influx of the Divine mind into our mind. It is the ebb of the in-dividual rivulet before the flowing surges of the sea of life." Cf. "Revelation," *N J M*, II (1828-1829), pp. 56-58.

5.17 The sun shines to-day also.] Cf. the phrase in *Letters*, I, 123 (Nov. 12, 1822).

6.1 new lands, new men, new thoughts] See *Journals*, II, 195 middle (Apr. 17, 1827). Cf. the corollary in Early Lectures ¶ 12 (May 7, 1834).

6.4 no questions unanswerable] Because of the correlation of mind and matter (Coleridge ¶s. 67-68, 96, 131, 138, 200, 247, 256, 260, 287, 289) and the consequent language of nature by the law of correspondence (Swedenborg ¶s. 1-4, 22-23; Sampson Reed ¶s. 6, 9, 18f, 59; Oegger *passim*), "the external world is an answer in hiero-glyphics to the questions the mind would put concerning itself." See Early Lectures ¶ 3 (Nov. 5, 1833).

6.9 Every man's condition is a solution in hieroglyphic] The basis of all wisdom or the solution to all problems in the outer world is self-knowledge, dependence on the Reason, or regard for the spiritual world within oneself. See Coleridge ¶s. 1-56, 67, 69-70, 152, 155, 216, 226-228, 258, 260, 264. Nature reveals answers (see 6.4 above) only when the spirit within man speaks *first*. *Quantum sumus scimus*. This is the meta-physical basis of Emerson's doctrine of self-reliance (*i.e.*, God-reliance). For the term *hieroglyphic*, see Coleridge ¶ 258 end, and Oegger, "The True Messiah," *E T E*, II, 95ff.

6.11 He acts it as life, before he apprehends it as truth.] See Coleridge ¶s. 67, 200, 174 fn. On this concurrence of mind and matter or the relationship between subject and object, Emerson builds his doctrine of compensation. For an excellent commentary, see *Y E S*, 209.24——210.13.

6.16 to what end is nature?] Emerson says it is progressively to serve as com-modity, beauty, language, discipline and, finally, the revelation of Spirit (*Nature*, 76.14-15). For its use as language, see the chapters on Coleridge, Swedenborg, Sampson Reed and Oegger; for its value as discipline of the moral being, see Sampson Reed ¶s. 9-10.

6.17 to find a theory of nature] For the requirements of a *true* theory, see Cole-ridge ¶s. 127-146. On the problem in general, see Coleridge ¶ 253 and Sampson Reed, "On Animals," *E T E*, II, 34 top.

7.2 abstract truth is the most practical] Cf. Coleridge ¶s. 282, 76, 250, and Plato, *Works* (Taylor), I, lxxxi: "*That* demonstration likewise is the best which furnishes the mind with the most ample knowledge; and this is alone the province of universals. We may also add, that he who knows universals knows particulars likewise in capacity; but we cannot infer that he who has the best knowledge of particulars knows any thing of universals. And lastly, that which is universal is the object of intellect and reason; but particulars are coordinated to the perceptions of sense."

8.1 Man's operations are insignificant compared with Nature's] See *Typescript Journals*, "B," Pt. II, p. 186 (May 28, 1836): "You cannot build your house or pagoda as you will but as you must. Gravity, Wind, sun, rain, the size of men & animals, & such other aliens have more to say than the architect. Beneath the almighty necessity therefore I regard what is artificial in man's life & works as petty & insignificant by the side of what is natural." Cf. *Works*, XI, 29-30 (Sept. 12, 1835).

9.3 go into solitude] For a standard treatment of this theme in Emerson's period, see Johann Georg Zimmerman, *Solitude, or the Effect of Occasional Retirement*, (2 vols.) London, 1779. It appeared as *Solitude considered with respect to its influence*, tr. from the French by J. B. Mercier, London, 1795; as *The Advantages and Disadvantages of Solitude Considered*, London, 1808; and as *Solitude*, (2 vols.) Exeter, 1836. The book was much read at Harvard.

9.7 look at the stars] See *Journals*, II, 491 (May 26, 1832); III, 197 (Sept. 8, 1833); and III, 464 (Apr. 10, 1835). See "Astronomy," Y E S, 170-179 (May 27, 1832), and *Works*, I, 405 (notes). Emerson owned John Hubbard Wilkins, *Elements of Astronomy*, Boston, 1825, and Mrs. Mary Fairfax Somerville, *A Preliminary Dissertation on the Mechanism of the Heavens*, Phila., 1832. The latter is inscribed: "R. W. Emerson 1832." See Cabot, *Memoir*, I, 44, for an account of Emerson's Latin-school theme on astronomy, still extant among his papers.

9.14 If the stars should appear one night in a thousand years] Cf. Lucretius, *On the Nature of Things*, tr. H. A. J. Munro, London, 1932, pp. 76-77 [Bk. II]: "Look up at the bright and unsullied hue of heaven and the stars which it holds within it, wandering all about, and the moon and the sun's light of dazzling brilliancy: if all these things were now for the first time, if I say they were now suddenly presented to mortals beyond all expectation, what could have been named that would be more marvellous than these things, or that nations beforehand would less venture to believe could be? nothing, methinks: so wondrous strange had been this sight. Yet how little, you know, wearied as all are to satiety with seeing, any one now cares to look up into heaven's glittering quarters!"

11.3 Miller owns this field, Locke that] For the original form, see *Typescript Journals*, "B," Pt. I, p. 123 (Jan. 16, 1836): "Mr Meriam owns this field, Mr Bacon that, & Mr Butterfield the next, but the poet owns the whole . . . . And the best part of all these men's farms the . . . face which they show to the poet's eye, they do not possess but he. The view of the field & wood at the distance of a quarter of a mile has no property in it." Cf. *Journals*, IV, 64. Mr. Meriam's name appears also in the "Historical Discourse at Concord" (Sept. 12, 1835) [*Works*, XI, 30] and at the beginning of the poem "Hamatreya" [*Works*, IX, 35].

12.1 maugre all his impertinent griefs he shall be glad] Cf. lines 1-8 of William Cullen Bryant's "Thanatopsis." Emerson owned the *Poems*, N.Y., 1832. For Emerson's view of the problem of evil—for his belief that griefs were impertinent to the religious man——see the commentary on Orphic Poet VI. See also *Journals*, II, 120 (Sept. 23, 1826) and his sermon, "Calamities" (May 29, 1831). See also *Nature*, 12.23ff., 15.15ff., 71.9-20, 75.8-11.

12.3 every hour and season yields its tribute] In *Journals*, III, 460-461 (Mar. 28, 1835) Emerson said that he would like to prepare a better book than William Howitt's *The Book of the Seasons, or The Calendar of Nature*, London, 1831; Phila., 1831. Howitt attempted to lay before his readers in prospect "all the objects and appearances which the month would present." Emerson may also have known a similar work by Henry Duncan, *Sacred Philosophy of the Seasons*, (4 vols.) Edinburgh, 1836-1837, and Leigh Hunt, *The Months, descriptive of the Successive Beauties of the Year*, London, 1821. The interest in making natural chronologies for each region was common in the period. See "The Arts——Hints to Amateurs," *Blackwood's Edinburgh Magazine*, XL (1836), 134 (July): "A rood of green earth, the veriest nook of landscape, is, to my inglorious taste, worth Babylon and Ninevah, real or imaginary; and so will I venture to mark down an item for the Amateur's Almanac, who should keep one for himself, in which he should note the peculiarities of every division and subdivision of the year, and catalogue trees and plants by the months.' Cf. *Nature*, 23.6—24.20. See note on *Nature*, 23.6 below.

12.4   every change corresponds to a different state of mind]   See the index for the Swedenborgian Doctrine of Correspondences. See also *Journals*, III, 226 bottom (Nov. 2, 1833) and *Nature*, 33.20 and 35.5ff.

12.14-23 , in the woods]   See *Journals*, I, 354; III, 222, 392, 453.

13.1   leaving me my eyes]   See *Letters*, I, 134 (July 2, 1823): "In short, particoloured Nature makes a man love his eyes. I thought tonight when I watched in the West 'Parting day die like a dolphin' what a mutilated mind & existence belongs to the blind." Cf. the "Rhodora."

13.5ff.   mean egotism vanishes. I become a transparent eyeball . . . part or particle of God.]   The highest part of man (*i.e.*, the Reason) is impersonal. Whatsoever is good in a man springs from the Universal Mind or the Soul. His personality is a mere time-and-space limitation. When the Reason functions, a man easily forgets his petty human achievements. Self-reliance (*i.e.*, reliance on the Reason or on the God within) has nothing selfish or egotistical in it. See the commentary on Orphic Poet I as well as sections III and V of "A Statement of the First Philosophy" (chap. VII *supra*) and *Journals*, II, 310-311 (Sept. 27, 1830). On the *transparent-eyeball* passage, see *Y E S*, 207.11: "He accepts his lot: he perceives the great astonishment. He adores. Awaked to truth and virtue——which is the two fold office of Reason, he passes out of the local and finite, he inspires and expires immortal breath." See also *Y E S*, 100.4-25. See also Coleridge ¶s. 298-299 and *Journals*, III, 425 (Dec. 29, 1834). Cf. the "inward eye" of Reason in Wordsworth's "Daffodils" and in *Journals*, II, 283 (Jan. 4, 1830). The best glosses on the Divine in man are sections III-V, XII-XIV of "A Statement of the First Philosophy" and the poem "Γνωθι Σεαυτον"——both edited in chap. VII. See also *Journals*, II, 354 (Jan. 10, 1831) and III, 452 (Mar. 19, 1835).

13.7   currents of the Universal Being circulate through me]   See section XIII of "A Statement of the First Philosophy" and Sarah Austin, *Characteristics of Goethe*, (3 vols.) London, 1833, II, 313: "Think only that with every breath we draw, an etherial lethean stream flows through our whole being, so that we remember our joys but imperfectly, our cares and sorrows scarcely at all. This high gift of God I have long known how to value, to use, and to enhance; and in this I was strengthened by that saying of the antient which comes renewed to me, 'I cease not to learn;——thence only do I mark that I grow older.'" Similar thoughts appear in *Journals*, III, 454 and 425.

13.10   To be brothers . . . is then a trifle]   When the impersonal Reason or God in a man functions, personal relations have little or no importance. One is raised above human associations to Ideas. For the original passage, see *Journals*, III, 452 (Mar. 19, 1835): "And if then I walk with a companion, he should speak from his Reason to my Reason; that is, both from God. To be brothers, to be acquaintances, master or servant, is then a trifle too insignificant for remembrance." On the impersonality of the Spirit in man, see the commentary on Orphic Poet I.

13.13   uncontained and immortal beauty]   Since Truth, Beauty and Goodness are different faces of the same All (*Nature*, 30.20-21), Emerson found himself communing with beauty in his mystical experiences. Cf. *Nature*, 79.8-13. See *Journals*, III, 254 (Feb. 1, 1834): "Some thoughts always find us young, and keep us so. Such a thought is the love of the universal and eternal beauty. Every man leaves that contemplation with the feeling that it rather belongs to ages than to mortal life."

13.20   an occult relation]   See *Nature*, 84.4; *Journals*, III, 163 (July 13, 1833) and IV, 41 (May 16, 1836); Early Lectures ¶s. 1-2.

14.14   Nature wears the colors of the spirit.]   See *Y E S*, 101.25——102.22 (Sept. 5, 1830) and xxiv.11. Emerson quoted the following from Hermann, Prince Pückler-Muskau's *Tour of England, Ireland and France*, Phila., 1833, in *Typescript Journals*, "B," Pt. I, p. 131 (Feb. 8, 1836): "Great poets work like Nature herself. To every man they assume the garb & color of his own mind and thence admit of various interpretations They are so rich that they distribute their gifts among a thousand poor & yet have abundance in reserve." See Charles Bucke, *The Philosophy of Nature*, (2 vols.) London, 1813, II, 170: "By the charm of combination, scenery, in a variety of ways, appears to partake of our delights, or to sympathize in our misfortunes.——As are our feelings, so does all nature seem to accord.——Are we cheerful and gay?——every bird, every field, every flower are objects of delight.——Are our spirits worn down with sorrow?——Melancholy 'round us throws a death-like silence and a dread repose.' "

16.11   More servants wait on man]   From George Herbert's poem, "Man," quoted at greater length in *Nature*, 85.3——86.9. See *Journals*, II, 348 (1830).

16.13   Nature in its ministry is material, process and result]   Emerson seems to mean that Nature in helping man is helping herself in him. The activity of the Spirit behind and in both man and Nature accounts for the unusual variety of Nature's ministrations. See Cudworth ¶ 11, which Emerson marked in his copy, for further elucidation.

16.17ff.   the sun evaporates the sea . . . endless circulations nourish man]   See Early Lectures ¶ 8 and *Y E S*, 208.1-2. There is possibly a hint here of the doctrine of the conservation of energy or of convertibility. See *Works*, I, 85.

17.5   fable of Æolus's bag]   See Thomas Bulfinch, *The Age of Fable*, (Everyman's ed.), 245.

17.7   paves the road with iron bars]   The Boston-Worcester railroad was opened in the spring of 1834. Cf. *Journals*, III, 305 (June 10, 1834); III, 482 (May 14, 1835); the *Christian Examiner*, XIV (Boston, Sept. 27, 1834), p. 27.

17.17   the human race run on his errands]   The original passage in *Typescript Journals*, "B," Pt. II, p. 163 (Mar. 22, 1836) reads: "I admire specially three advantages of civilization: the post office, the newspaper, and the road. Hereby the human race run on my errands, the human race read & write of all that happens for me; the human race turn out, every morning, and shovel away the snow and cut a path for me." Cf. Goethe's remark in *Journals*, II, 349 (1830).

18.7   man is fed that he may work]   Cf. Carlyle, *Sartor Resartus*, 198: "Produce! Produce! Were it but the pitifullest, infinitesimal fraction of a product, produce it, in God's name! 'T is the utmost thou hast in thee; out with it, then. Up, up! Whatsoever thy hand findeth to do, do it with thy whole might. Work while it is called to-day, for the night cometh wherein no man can work." See also p. 166: "A certain inarticulate self-consciousness dwells dimly in us; which only our works can render articulate and decisively discernible. Our works are the mirror wherein the spirit first sees its natural lineaments. Hence, too, the folly of that impossible precept, *Know thyself;* till it be translated into this partially possible one, *Know what thou canst work at.*" Cf. *Nature*, 93.8-10 and Coleridge ¶s. 67-68, 174 fn., 200, 289.

19.18   particular objects are mean and unaffecting]   See *Journals*, III, 247, 293, 298.

20.7   the corpse hath its own beauty]   See *Journals*, III, 563 (Oct. 25, 1835).

21.2   nature is medicinal]   See *Journals*, IV, 14-15.

22.4ff.   England of the senses and the understanding and Germany of mystic philosophy]   Cf. *The Friend*, section II, essay I, for Coleridge's table of characteristics of England, Germany and France. Emerson was, doubtless, influenced especially by Madame de Staël-Holstein's *The Influence of Literature Upon Society*, (2 vols.) Boston, 1813, chap. XVII, "Of German Literature," and chap. XVI, "Of the Philosophy and Eloquence of the English."

22.17   valley behind the mill]   See *Journals*, III, 418, for the original form: "the live repose which the amphitheatre of a valley behind Ball's Hill reflects to my eye." See Cabot, *Memoir*, I, 229-230, for a description of the hillside opposite the Manse. See

Franklin B. Sanborn and Wm. T. Harris, *A. Bronson Alcott: His Life and Philosophy*, (2 vols.) Boston, 1893, II, 457: "This was a favorite walk of Emerson's, from the Old Manse down the river to Peter's Field and Cæsar's Woods, then across the meadows and hills to the Virginia Road, near Bedford, where Thoreau was born, and thence back to Emerson's house."

23.6   each moment of the year has its own beauty]   See note on *Nature*, 12.3. Emerson borrowed, from the Athenæum, James L. Drummond, *Letters to a Young Naturalist*, London, 1831. See p. 74: "That broad and smiling sea, which now lies beneath us in such stillness and beauty, would in time lose its interest did it never alter; but one great characteristic of the works of the Deity is, that with endless beauty there is endless variety and change. The ocean is scarcely ever, even for one hour, the same; the morning breeze may sink into a mid-day calm, and that again may, before another day, be exchanged for the careering blast that is maddening the billows into foam, and dashing them in thunder on the leeward shore."

24.14   the moon is mere tinsel]   See *Journals*, I, 394; II, 232-233, 454; III, 293.

25.3   Beauty is the mark God sets upon virtue]   Cf. *Journals*, III, 342, and *Y E S*, 93.35; 127.11-14. The doctrine was common. See George Berkeley, *Alciphron, or The Minute Philosopher*, New Haven, 1803, p. 121: "And as . . . beauty is found in the shape and form of corporeal things; so also is there analogous to it, a beauty of another kind, an order, a symmetry, and comeliness, in the moral world. And, as the eye perceiveth the one, so the mind doth, by a certain interior sense, perceive the other; which sense, talent, or faculty, is ever quickest and purest in the noblest minds." See Charles Bucke, *The Philosophy of Nature* (ed. cit.), II, 27: "Hence arises the connection between beauty and virtue; and as nothing produces so many agreeable emotions, as the practice of virtue, (for virtue is a medal, whose reverse is happiness,) whatever is virtuous, or conducive thereto, is really and essentially beautiful."

25.15   "All those things obey virtue," said an ancient historian]   The 1849 edition of *Nature* reads "Sallust." Emerson's quotation is probably only a summary. See "Catiline's Conspiracy" in *The Works of Sallust*, tr. Arthur Murphy, London, 1807, p. 2: "It is virtue, and virtue only, that ennobles the human character, and lives in the memory of after-times." See p. 3: "The labours of man, whether he choose to cultivate the land, to explore the ocean, or to raise the lofty dome, agriculture, navigation, architecture, and all the arts of life, owe their success to the faculties of the mind." See p. 4: "He only . . . can be said to live, and to answer the ends of his being, who devotes his time to some worthy employment."

25.17   "The winds and the waves etc."]   Quoted from Edward Gibbon, *Decline and Fall of the Roman Empire*, chap. 68.

25.22   Leonidas and his three hundred]   Leonidas (*fl.* 489-480 B.C.) was king of Sparta. In 480, he attempted to hold the pass of Thermopylae against the army of Xerxes. Through the treachery of Ephialtes, he was surprised from the rear and forced to divide his army. He and three hundred Spartans chose to remain in the pass, and there they were slowly annihilated. See Herodotus, *History*, V, VII, IX; Plutarch's *Morals*, I, IV and V; Montaigne's *Essays*, (tr. Charles Cotton), (3 vols.) London, 1711, I, 297-299.

26.3   Arnold Winkelried in the high Alps]   Arnold von Winkelried, a Swiss patriot whom tradition associates with the victory of Sempach against the Austrians in 1386. The ranks of the enemy were too dense to penetrate until Winkelried rushed forward, seized a number of the Austrian pikes which were immediately directed against his breast, and fell, pulling the weapons to the ground as he died. His companions broke through the gap thus created and carried the day.

26.9   Columbus nears the shore of America]   Emerson may have drawn his details from the early pages of Thomas Southey, *Chronological History of the West Indies*, (3 vols.) London, 1827. See *Emerson's Reading*, 20, 106.

26.18   Sir Harry Vane dragged up Tower-hill]   Emerson probably secured his information from a work by his classmate, Charles Wentworth Upham, "Life of Sir Henry Vane, Fourth Governor of Massachusetts" in *The Library of American Biography*, ed. Jared Sparks, vol. IV (Boston & London, 1835), pp. 85-403. See pp. 357-358: "One of the sheriff's men came and told him, there must be a sled; to which Sir Henry replied, 'Any way, how they please, for I long to be at home, to be dissolved and to be with Christ. . . .' " See p. 359: "Being passed within the rails on Tower Hill, there were many loud exclamations of the people, crying out, 'The Lord Jesus go with your dear soul,' &c. One told him, that was the most glorious seat he ever sate on; he answered, 'It is so indeed,' and he rejoiced exceedingly." Vane was executed on June 14, 1662.

26.23   the patriot Lord Russell]   The account of Lord William Russell (1639-1683) appears in *The General Biographical Dictionary*, ed. Alexander Chalmers, new ed., London, 1812-1817, XXVI, 493: "The execution was performed July 21, not on Tower-hill, the common place of execution for men of high rank, but in Lincoln's-inn-fields; and as he passed on in his coach, the multitude imagined they beheld virtue and liberty sitting by his side." See also David Hume, *The History of England*, (8 vols.) Oxford, 1826, VIII, 172: ". . . it was probably intended, by conducting Russell through so many streets, to show the mutinous city their beloved leader, once the object of all their confidence, now exposed to the utmost rigours of the law." Emerson refers to the account in *Journals*, III, 525-526 (Aug. 1, 1835) in connection with observations on the fancy and the imagination.

27.17   Homer, Pindar, Socrates, Phocion]   For Emerson's interest in these men, see *Journals*, III, 426-427; 439. See his Bowdoin Prize essay on "The Character of Socrates."

27.19   geography and climate of Greece]   Emerson had read Johann Gottfried von Herder, *Outlines of a Philosophy of the History of Man*, London, 1800; (2 vols.) London, 1803. Herder had been among the first to show the relationship between climate and character. See Cousin, *Introduction* (1832), 227ff., on the part played by geography in the history of man.

27.20   heavens and earth sympathize with Jesus]   Emerson intended something more than pathetic fallacy. The Swedenborgian doctrine of "affections clothed" accounted for the agreement of external nature with man's mental states. See Sampson Reed ¶s. 18a—20 and "Growth of the Mind," *E T E*, II, 25 top: "That the sun was darkened at the crucifixion of our Lord, was no miracle. It was as much the natural consequence of that event, as its present lustre is of His glory."

28.23   Nothing divine dies.]   Cf. Carlyle, "Boswell's Life of Johnson," *Essays*, (Everyman ed.) II, 21: "Nothing dies, nothing can die. No idlest word thou speakest but is a seed cast into Time, and grows through all Eternity!"

35.5   nothing lucky or capricious in these analogies]   See *Journals*, III, 226-227 (Nov. 2, 1833); *Nature*, 12.4 and note.

35.9   man is an analogist]   See *Journals*, IV, 28 and 70.

35.18   Linnæus' and Buffon's volumes]   Emerson probably had in mind especially George Louis Leclerc, comte de Buffon, *Histoire Naturelle*, ed. Charles S. Sonnini de Manoncourt, (127 vols.) Paris, 1800-1808. A set of Buffon——a new edition——in 20 vols. was advertised for $50.00 in the *U. S. Literary Gazette*, I (Boston, 1824), p. 160.

36.2   seed of a plant]   See *Journals*, III, 497 (June 29, 1835) and index to *E T E*.

36.6   "It is sown a natural body."]   See I Cor. 15:44.

36.11   analogy between man's life and the seasons]   See *Y E S*, 44.18ff.

36.13   The instincts of the ant]   See *Journals*, IV, 70 (June 16, 1836) on the ant's significance; also Sampson Reed ¶ 18f. Emerson had examined Jean Pierre Huber, *The Natural History of Ants*, tr. J. R. Johnson, London, 1820, at the Athenæum in July, 1832.

37.15   conversation of a farmer or back-woodsman]   See *Journals*, II, 449; III, 306, 482, 509-510, 529, 567. Cf. Madame de Staël-Holstein, *The Influence of Literature upon Society*, (2 vols.) Boston, 1813, II, 92: "I think it always interesting to examine what would be the prevailing character of the literature of a great and enlightened people, in whose country should be established liberty, political equality, and manners in unison with its institutions: there is but one nation in the world to whom some of these reflections may be applied in the present day;——America. The American literature, indeed, is not yet formed; but when their magistrates are called upon to address themselves on any subject to the public opinion, they are eminently gifted with the power of touching all the affections of the heart, by expressing simple truth and pure sentiments; and to do this, is already to be acquainted with the most useful secret of elegant style."

38.20   the primary writers of the country]   Cf. Samuel Johnson, *Rasselas*, chap. X: "And yet it fills me with wonder, that, in almost all countries, the most ancient poets are considered as the best: whether it be that every other kind of knowledge is an acquisition gradually attained, and poetry is a gift conferred at once; or that the first poetry of every nation surprised them as a novelty, and retained the credit by consent, which it received by accident at first; or whether, as the province of poetry is to describe Nature and Passion, which are always the same, the first writers took possession of the most striking objects for description, and the most probable occurrences for fiction, and left nothing to those that followed them, but transcription of the same events, and new combinations of the same images. Whatever be the reason, it is commonly observed that the early writers are in possession of nature, and their followers of art; that the first excel in strength and invention, and the latter in elegance and refinement." For other possible influence by Johnson, see T. Percy Armstrong, "Emerson and Dr. Johnson," 12 *N & Q*, X, 167 (March 4, 1922).

39.2   fasten words again to visible things]   See Emerson's sermon, "Words are Things" (Nov. 6, 1831) and Sampson Reed ¶ 6 and the Doctrine of Correspondences.

39.21   advantage which country-life possesses]   See the journal of the literary society (in *E T E*, part IV) under Mar. 21, 1821: "Br. Emerson next advanced, with a neat, concise and pithy comparison of country and city life, much to the edification of the Brotherhood." See *Journals*, I, 347-351, 354-356, 368; II, 307, 367.

40.11   These solemn images shall reappear]   Cf. Wordsworth, *Tintern Abbey*, lines 22ff. See Early Lectures ¶ 30   and *Journals*, III, 567 (Nov. 6, 1835).

41.7   cinders of a volcano to roast their eggs]   Possibly an echo of Bacon, *Works*, (10 vols.) London, 1824, II, 469: "Extreme self-lovers will set a man's house on fire, though it were but to roast their eggs." The same appears in Bacon's *Essays*, no. xxiii.

41.12   Have waves no significance?]   See *Journals*, III, 291 (Apr. 30, 1834): "The philosophy of the Wave. The wave moves onward, but the water of which it is composed does not. The same particle does not rise from the valley to the ridge. Its unity is only phenomenal. So it is with men." Cf. *Works*, II, 87.

41.18   laws of moral nature answer those of matter as face to face in a glass]   See Swedenborg ¶s. 1-5, 25-28; Sampson Reed ¶s. 6, 9-10; Coleridge ¶s. 67, 96, 131, 138, 260, 287-288. Emerson has marked his Cudworth, *Intellectual System* (1820), I, 371: "For the plastic life of nature is but the mere umbrage of intellectuality, a faint and shadowy imitation of mind and understanding; upon which it doth as essentially depend, as the shadow doth upon the body, the image in the glass upon the face, or the echo upon the original voice." The metaphor of the "glass" is common. Cf. Young, *Night Thoughts*, Night IX, line 1004: "Nature is the glass reflecting God." Cf. I Cor. 13:12.

41.21   axioms of physics translate the laws of ethics etc.]   Cf. Coleridge ¶s. 72, 112, 115. See Emerson's letter in *Carlyle-Emerson Corr.*, I, 50 (Mar. 12, 1835): "There is a part of ethics, or in Schleiermacher's distribution it might be physics, which possesses all attraction for me; to wit, the compensations of the Universe, the equality and the coexistence of action and reaction, that all prayers are granted, that every debt is paid.

And the skill with which the great All maketh clean work as it goes along, leaves no rag, consumes its smoke,——will I hope make a chapter in your thesis." See also *Journals*, III, 247 (Jan. 2, 1834).

42.10   the proverbs of nations]   A large collection of proverbs and epigrams appears in *Typescript Journals*, Cabot's "T," "U" and "V" Blotting Books (*ca.* 1826-1827). See *Y E S*, 62.33—63.13; 93.10-15; 225.24-27; and Early Lectures ¶ 30.

43.8   Can these things be etc.]   See *Macbeth*, III,iv,110ff. For *these* Shakespeare wrote *such.*

43.17   era of Pythagoras]   See Gérando, *Histoire* (1822), I, 396-432.

43.18   era of Leibnitz]   Emerson's introduction to Leibnitz probably came by way of Dugald Stewart's "Second Dissertation," which strongly emphasized Leibnitz's lofty conceptions, his optimism, his revolt against the prevailing materialism and the fatalism of his contemporaries, etc. See *The Collected Works of Dugald Stewart,* (11 vols.) Edinburgh, 1854-1860, I, 265: "The scheme of necessity was still farther adorned and sublimed in the *Theodicæa* of Leibnitz, by an imagination nurtured and trained in the school of Plato. 'May there not exist,' he asks on one occasion, 'an immense space beyond the region of the stars? and may not this *empyreal* heaven be filled with happiness and glory? It may be conceived to resemble an ocean, where the rivers of all those created beings that are destined for bliss shall finish their course, when arrived in the starry system, at the perfection of their respective natures.' " Stewart writes in conclusion (I, 286): "I am almost tempted to retract part of what I have written, when I reflect on the benefits which the world has derived even from the *errors* of Leibnitz. It has been well and justly said, that 'every *desideratum* is an imperfect discovery;' to which it may be added, that every new problem which is started, and still more every attempt, however abortive, towards its solution, strikes out a new path, which must sooner or later lead to the truth. If the problem be solv[a]ble, a solution will in due time be obtained; if insolv[a]ble, it will soon be abandoned as hopeless by general consent; and the legitimate field of scientific research will become fertile . . . . In this point of view, what individual in modern times can be compared to Leibnitz! To how many of those researches, which still usefully employ the talents and industry of the learned, did he not point out and open the way! From how many more did he not warn the wise to withhold their curiosity, by his bold and fruitless attempts to burst the barriers of the invisible world!"

43.19   There sits the Sphinx]   See *Journals*, II, 121 (Sept. 23, 1826); III, 525 (Aug. 1, 1835); *Works*, II, 32-33; IX, 20-25. See Carlyle, *Sartor Resartus*, 53: "The secret of man's being is still like the Sphinx's secret: a riddle that he cannot rede; and for ignorance of which he suffers death, the worse death, a spiritual." See p. 128: "The universe . . . was as a mighty Sphinx-riddle, which I knew so little of, yet must rede, or be devoured." See Bacon, "Sphinx, sive Scientia," in his "De Sapientia Veterum," *Works,* (10 vols.) London, 1824, X, 214-217. Emerson had a small sphinx in his study; the Manse had a sphinx-head door knocker.

44.4   preceding affections in the world of spirit]   For the Swedenborgian doctrine of "affections clothed" see the index. See *Journals*, III, 370.

44.5   A Fact is the last issue of spirit]   This may be an echo of a similar utterance by Alcott in *Psyche*. See *Journals*, IV, 11. See *Nature*, 56.19.

44.18   "Every scripture is to be interpreted by the same spirit which gave it forth."]   Taught by George Fox. See *Journals*, II, 497-499 (July 15, 1832). Emerson had been reading Wm. Sewell's *The History of . . . the . . . Quakers*, Phila., 1823. (See *Letters,* I, 438.) For the wide use of this remark and its variations, see index to *E T E*.

45.7   extent and multitude of objects]   The original passage in *Typescript Journals*, "B," Pt. II, 222 (Aug. 12, 1836) reads: "The reason of the variety & infinity of objects is given in the doctrine that external objects are mere signs of internal essences. Therefore 'every object rightly seen unlocks a new faculty of the Soul.' that is to say, it becomes a part of the domain of Consciousness; before it was unconscious truth, now is available Knowledge." See Coleridge ¶s. 261, 67-68, 174 fn., 200. See *Nature*, 50.13.

46.2   Discipline]   See *Journals*, II, 9 (Oct. 8, 1824); II, 241 middle (1828); III, 289 (Apr. 30, 1834); *Y E S*, 160.3-5 (Dec. 4, 1831); 258.29-37.

47.18   "good thoughts . . . executed!"]   A slightly modified quotation from Francis Bacon's "Of Great Place" in *Essays* (Everyman ed.), 31-32: "But power to do good is the true and lawful end of aspiring. For good thoughts (though God accept them) yet towards men are little better than good dreams, except they be put in act. . . ."

47.20   same good office performed by Property]   See *Journals*, III, 256-257 (Feb. 10, 1834). Cf., however, *Y E S*, 205-206.

48.16   culture of the understanding]   See Early Lectures ¶ 11 (May 7, 1834); the quotation from Plato in *Journals*, III, 529; and the same in *Works*, IV, 47.

48.20   a bell and a plough]   See *Typescript Journals*, "B," Pt. I, p. 149: "a pump & a plough. . . ."

49.1   nor coal eaten]   This phrase is followed, in *Typescript Journals*, "B," Pt. I, p. 149 (Mar. 5, 1836), by: "We never snatch a corkscrew to cut down an oak nor a shoe to sew up a rent in a garment. Yet among men we make analogous blunders without shame. We expect of one, anothers talent. We do not separate them & apprehend that each is a system & has ends of his own. The wise man . . . ." On making distinctions, see *Y E S*, 86, and Early Lectures ¶ 12.

49.10   Her yea is yea, and her nay, nay.]   See Matt. 5:37 (*Sermon on the Mount*); James 5:12; 2 Cor. 1:17.

49.14   nature's dice are always loaded]   See variations of fragment no. 763 of Sophocles in Burton Stevenson, *Home Book of Quotations*, (3rd ed.) 229. Emerson used the phrase again in *Works*, II, 102; VI, 221-222. See *Typescript Journals*, "B," Pt. I, p. 137 (Feb. 24, 1836): "It takes the first steps by geology, astronomy, zoology, to learn that nature's dice are always loaded; that in the most promiscuous heaps & rubbish, an informed eye can find harmonious, inevitable, & beneficial results, and these are premises to the later conclusion that matter flows out from spirit, & does not find its cause in itself." See also Sarah Austin, *Characteristics of Goethe*, (3 vols.) London, 1833, I, 59: "Figure to yourself Nature, how she sits, as it were at a card-table, incessantly calling '*au double!*' *i.e.* exulting in what she has already won, through every region of her operations; and thus plays on into infinitude. Animal, vegetable, mineral, are continually set up anew after some such fortunate throws; and who knows, whether the whole race of man is any thing more than a throw for some higher stake."

50.13   The exercise of the will or the lesson of power]   See *Journals*, III, 249. See note on *Nature*, 45.7.

50.16   "thy will be done!"]   See Matt. 26:42 rather than Matt. 6:10 and Luke 11:2. Cf. *Journals*, IV, 43-44. See the theme in Emerson's poem, "Γνωθι Σεαυτον" and in "A Statement of the First Philosophy," edited in chap. VII. See the sermon, "Doing the Will of God," *Y E S*, 259.22-23. The phrase is especially emphasized by the Swedenborgians. See "Thy Will Be Done," *N J M*, I, 145-148; "Thy Will Be Done etc.," *N J M*, IV, 178-185; and Theophilus Parsons, "On the Doctrine of Progressive Order," *N J M*, IX, 194.

51.12   All things are moral]   See *Y E S*, 122.33——123.15.

51.19   growth in the eye of a leaf]   A reference to Goethe's idea in botany. See *Journals*, IV, 22; *Works*, IV, 275. Cabot, *Memoir*, II, 725.

51.23   echo the Ten Commandments]   The Swedenborgians put a strong emphasis on the Commandments. See Sampson Reed ¶ 10; see, for example, the following articles in the *N J M:* V, 9-14, 50-54, 251-253, 363-368.

53.8 What is a farm?] The original form as it appears in *Typescript Journals*, "B," Pt. II, p. 208 (June 17, 1836) reads: "What is a farm but a chapter in the bible almost? Pull out the weeds, water the plants; blight, rain, insects, sun,——it is a mere holy emblem from its first process to the last."

53.15 an experience precisely parallel] See *Journals*, IV, 28 and 70; also the commentary on Orphic Poet V.

54.15 Xenophanes complained] See *Journals*, II, 342, 389 and 398-399; III, 310; IV, 21. Cf. Emerson's poem, "Xenophanes."

54.19 fable of Proteus] See Homer, *Odyssey*, IV, 354-569, or Thomas Bulfinch, *Age of Fable* (Everyman ed.), 194-195. See index of *E T E* under "Proteus" and under "each in all."

54.21 a leaf, a drop, a crystal, a moment of time is related to the whole] See *Journals*, IV, 22, 28 etc.; Cabot, *Memoir*, II, 725 (Dec. 8, 1836). See index of *E T E* under "microcosm" and "all in each."

55.7 architecture called "frozen music"] See *Journals*, III, 147 (June 10, 1833); III, 363 (Nov. 15, 1834); III, 403 (Dec. 22, 1834). See under Mar. 23, 1829, in Johann Peter Eckermann, *Words of Goethe, Being the Conversations*, N.Y., 1933, p. 300: "I have found a paper of mine among some others . . . in which I call architecture 'petrified music.' Really there is something in this; the tone of mind produced by architecture approaches the effect of music." See Burton Stevenson, *Home Book of Quotations* (3rd ed.), 95, for a quotation from Schelling's *Philosophie der Kunst*, p. 576: "Architecture is music in space, as it were a frozen music." See Cotton Mather, *The Christian Philosopher*, Charlestown, [Mass.], 1815, 235: "Vitruvius instructs us that the most exquisite and accurate figure for a temple will be found in a conformity to a human body; indeed a human body ought for ever to be beheld and employed, as designed for a holy temple."

55.10 Michael Angelo maintained a knowledge of anatomy is essential] Emerson here recalled his lecture of Feb. 5, 1835. See *Journals*, III, 403 (Dec. 22, 1834) and Richard Duppa, *The Life of Michel Angelo Buonarroti*, London, 1807, 224: "It is also certain, that the members of architecture have a reference to those of the human body, and he who does not understand the human figure, and particularly anatomy, can know nothing of the subject."

56.7 Every universal truth implies every other] See Emerson's sermon, "All Truth is Related" (Sept. 18, 1831), listed in *Y E S*, 269.10.

56.16 Words cannot cover the dimensions of truth] This thought or an analogous one appears in *Journals*, III, 280, 492. See Francis Bacon, *Works*, (10 vols.) London, 1824, II, 471: "The best part of beauty is that which a picture cannot express." See Coleridge ¶s. 77-83.

56.19 An action is the perfection and publication of thought] See *Journals*, IV, 32. See *Nature*, 44.5.

56.22 "The wise man in doing one thing does all."] Emerson's translation from Goethe. See *Journals*, IV, 17 (Feb. 28, 1836).

57.3-21 the form which predominates over all others] See "On the Human Form," *E T E*, II, 69-75. See also the chapter on Goethe and Moritz.

58.4-15 friends coextensive with our idea . . . object of thought] On a man's ruling "idea" see the commentary on Orphic Poet VI. Emerson believed that what we call "personality" in a man was a mere product of time and space, and that his better part (his Reason or Spirit) was impersonal and divine. It followed, therefore, that people who have merited great love or veneration have necessarily had a large share of the

divine, impersonal Reason in them and therefore have existed independent of temporal
or external characteristics (*Journals*, III, 506-507). The relationship between high-
minded men is, therefore, from "Reason to Reason"———that is, from the God in one
to the God in the other (*Journals*, III, 452). The highest value in anyone, according to
Emerson, is his Godlikeness or his essential character. There can, therefore, be no
"personeity" in true and deep spiritual friendship, and the presence or absence of a
friend is not of any real importance. The God within does not require clutching and
clawing; He is no respecter of persons. See *Journals*, IV, 62, and "A Statement of the
First Philosophy," section IV. As friends ceased to exist for Emerson in time and space,
he found that he held them still—but by *real* ties, for they ceased to be phenomenal and
assumed the quality of Ideas (*Journals*, IV, 12 and 25). After Edward's death he wrote,
accordingly, that Edward had served his family best, not by length of days or by
material goods, but by the "healthful influence of his perfect moral health" and believed
that Edward's great value continued present in the family because spiritual influences
are *reciprocal* in the universe. See *Journals*, III, 404 and *Y E S*, 268.36; this last belief
he found corroborated by the teaching of the Swedenborgians (*Journals*, II, 455-456).
The foregoing provides the background for the passage under consideration, which
reflects the death of Charles Chauncy Emerson on May 9, 1836. The original lines
(*Journals*, IV, 67-68) were written down on June 14 and have more beauty than the
revised form in *Nature*. Emerson's later essay on "Friendship" is based upon the ideas
which he here expresses. Below I reproduce (1) Charles' letter to Dr. Henry Ingersoll
Bowditch of Boston, written less than three months before his death; and (2) Charles'
autobiographical sketch for his Harvard Class Book. They both appear in the records
of the Class of 1828 (H.U. 338.28.5.F) on folios 348 and 303 respectively.

Concord   Feby. 16. 1836

Dear Bowditch.

I suppose to answer a letter the same day in which it is received is very business like
& inelegant; but as I happen to find myself sitting with my Portfolio on my knees in the
very attitude of preparation, having already despatched sundry letters, I am moved to
reply to yours likewise.

I do not think, indeed I am sure, I have not a letter of James Jackson's which it
would do any good to print. Those I got from him were hastily written, for friendship's
sake, that we might shake hands now & then, rather than for the expression of his
opinions, or the describing of what he saw. To what class of persons do you expect the
memoir & letters you propose to reprint, will address itself? To 'whose condition is it
to speak'?

Of Mr   Withington I know nothing, not even that he is my Successor, as you
intimate.

I am heartily glad at the prospect of escaping a war, & especially by the humane &
rational expedient of mediation. A year or two ago I considered at some length & as
well as I was able the question of a "Congress of Nations for the settling of interna-
tional disputes," & it seemed to me then as if war must be pretty near its end amongst
civilized nations. It is such an expensive, disagreeable, & inappropriate method of
determining the right between country & country, & so disturbs the commercial relations all round the globe, that I am satisfied it is coming to be looked upon with as evil
an eye by the statesman as the Christian. By & by God will be praised not only out of
the mouths of babes, but of the very devils———& the law will be kept if not from love
from self interest.

Do you study the newspapers, & calculate out of these leaves the future fortunes of
your own & other countries? I am on the whole pleased with the present face of things
at Washington. The Congress contains in itself hostile & bitter elements, but I think I
see principles as well as passions, & if I see aright, the corrupt Party Influence has well
nigh spent its force. We shall never be at our ease in this country. Every man has got
to bestir himself in politics, & every man must make up his mind to see things always

going awry——You cannot keep power from being shared amongst both bad & good, & the result must be not white but grey. The projectile force of our Republican Institutions continually modified by the gravitation towards Democracy will hold us in our orbit, even as the moon is held in hers, while each instant she falls towards the Earth. If I had time I could show you how just & admirable the illustration is, but no matter.

You are a disciple, I learn, of Miss Martineau. Tell me what truth you learn of her.

You must come to Concord some pleasant day & see us—— I will introduce you to all my friends whom you are curious to see.

Give my love to Weston, & tell him the Philosopher said "The wise man differeth from the fool in————a good hope."

I am

                                                            Yours,
                                                            C. C. EMERSON

———

[Autobiography]

I was born in Chauncey Place, Boston, in that blessed year of our Lord 1808 (towards the close, however,) & after a puny & unhappy childhood, was sent to be beatten with many stripes by the gentleman who now conducts the Massachusetts Journal, then sub-master of the Public Latin School. I deem it my duty to mention him by name—— David L. Child——the fag end of the old Disciplinarian school. I then migrated by a sort of retrograde Metempsychosis, to the English High school. Here I endured more pangs & woes than war or women have or give. For they abused me (as the hens in the fable abused the partridge) as being 'αλλοτριος.' But I contemned them; & after a year's sojourning in this Sodom, some good angels guided me back to my ancient seat under the eye of B. A. Gould esq. This worthy man (Heaven reward him with long life & numerous issue!) gave me that recommendation for moral & literary merits, which secured the approbation of my deluded friends & an entrance into the University at Cambridge—— Of the four years here spent, I would speak more seriously—— They have been happy, God knows how happy. My studies I liked well & my friends more. To my Class I owe a great deal, for their confidence & kindness. May they be worthily rewarded!

Graduated 1828 aged 19————intending (I know not when) to study Law.————Per se Scrip.————

———

59.2   Idealism]   An interesting comment of Carlyle on this subject is found in his review of "Novalis" (1829) in *Critical and Miscellaneous Essays*, (2 vols.) London, 1899, II, 24-25: "The Idealist . . . boasts that his Philosophy is Transcendental, that is, 'ascending *beyond* the senses;' which, he asserts, *all* Philosophy, properly so called, by its nature is and must be: and in this way he is led to various unexpected conclusions. To a Transcendentalist, Matter has an existence, but only as a Phenomenon: were *we* not there, neither would it be there; it is a mere Relation, or rather the result of a Relation between our living Souls and the great First Cause; and depends for its apparent qualities on *our* bodily and mental organs; having itself *no* intrinsic qualities; being, in the common sense of that word, Nothing. The tree is green and hard, not of its own natural virtue, but simply because my eye and my hand are fashioned so as to discern such and such appearances under such and such conditions. . . . There is, in fact, says Fichte, no Tree there; but only a Manifestation of Power from something which is *not I*."

61.22   the unrenewed understanding]   *I.e.*, the understanding without guidance or help from an awakened Reason. See *Nature*, 89.12————91.4.

62.9   the animal eye sees sharp outlines and colored surfaces]   See note on *Nature*, 62.11, below, and *Michael Angelo*, 3: "The common eye is satisfied with the surface on which it rests. The wise eye knows that it is surface, and, if beautiful, only the result of interior harmonies, which, to him who knows them, compose the image of higher beauty. . . . The walls of houses are transparent to the architect. The symptoms disclose the constitution to the physician; and to the artist it belongs by a better knowledge of anatomy, and, within anatomy, of life and thought, to acquire the power of true drawing."

62.11 When the eye of Reason opens] For the original passage, see *Typescript Journals*, "B," Pt. I, p. 136 (Feb. 24, 1836): "When the eye of Reason is closed the animal eye is very clear & sees outlines & surfaces with preternatural distinctness; when the eye of Reason opens,——to the clear outline & surface is added color & grace not natural but supernatural, the gift of fancy, imagination, affection; as the eye of Reason grows more clear & strong, the outlines & surfaces become so transparent as to be no longer seen & causes & spirits are seen through them." Cf. sections III-VIII and XIII-XIV of "A Statement of the First Philosophy" in chap. VII.

63.3 a hint from nature herself] See *Journals*, IV, 25 and 32.

63.6 alteration of our local position] This illustration was possibly suggested by Sampson Reed ¶ 38.

65.4-17 The poet conforms things to his thoughts and tosses creation like a bauble. Imagination is the use his Reason makes of the material world.] See *Journals*, IV, 25: "Virtue is, subordinating things to thoughts." See Coleridge ¶s. 62-63, 238, 292-295 and *Biographia Literaria* (Everyman ed.), p. 169: "[I]mages, however beautiful, though faithfully copied from nature, and as accurately represented in words, do not of themselves characterize the poet. They become proofs of original genius only as far as they are modified by a predominant passion; or by associated thoughts or images awakened by that passion; or when they have the effect of reducing multitude to unity, or succession to an instant; or lastly when a human and intellectual life is transferred to them from the poet's own spirit." See also p. 170: "As of higher worth, so doubtless still more characteristic of poetic genius does the imagery become, when it moulds and colours itself to the circumstances, passion, or character, present and foremost in the mind." See p. 171: "Scarcely less sure, or if a less valuable, not less indispensable mark . . . will the imagery supply, when, with more than power of the painter, the poet gives us the liveliest image of succession with the feeling of simultaneousness." See *A Midsummer Night's Dream*, V,i,7-17 and the relevant description of the poet's passion in *Journals*, II, 380. *Nature* may be slightly indebted to William Hazlitt's *Lectures on the English Poets*. See items 161, 262 and 768 in the B.L.S. reading record in *E T E*, II.

65.8. he invests dust and stones with humanity] Possibly an echo of *As You Like It*, II,i,15ff.

66.6 "The ornament of beauty is Suspect"] See Shakespeare, *Sonnets*, LXX, 3-4.

66.10 "No, it was builded far from accident"] See Shakespeare, *Sonnets*, CXXIV, 5ff.

66.17 Pyramids seem recent and transitory] See Shakespeare, *Sonnets*, CXXIII, 2.

66.20 "Take those lips away"] Slightly misquoted from *Measure for Measure*, IV, i,1-4. Cf. Beaumont and Fletcher, *The Tragedy of Rollo, Duke of Normandy*, V,ii,21ff.

67.11 Ariel etc.] The speaker should be "Prospero." See *The Tempest*, V,i,46ff.

67.16 "A solemn air etc."] See *The Tempest*, V,i,58ff.

67.20 "The charm dissolves etc."] See *The Tempest*, V,i,64ff.

68.1 "Their understanding etc."] See *The Tempest*, V,i,79ff.

68.21 a law determines all phenomena] See Coleridge ¶s. 131, 134, 100, 127-128, 155.

See index of *E T E* for the Swedenborgian doctrine of Influx.

69.2   The true philosopher and the true poet are one.]   See Early Lectures ¶ 28 and a quotation from Novalis in Carlyle's "Novalis" (1829), *ed. cit.*, II, 41: "The division of Philosopher and Poet is only apparent, and to the disadvantage of both. It is a sign of disease, and of a sickly constitution."

69.11   penetrated nature with an informing soul]   See Coleridge ¶s. 170-171.

69.14   the memory disburthens itself of particulars]   See *Journals*, III, 291 (Apr. 30, 1834) middle.

70.13   we wait in this Olympus of gods]   The allusion becomes clear from Early Lectures, ¶s. 27-28 and section VII of "A Statement of the First Philosophy" in chap. VII. Cf. Bacon's sentence: "Not only virtues but also divinities surround a soul which shall strive for magnanimous ends." See *Journals*, II, 405 and *Nature*, 71.5.

70.17   "These are they etc."]   A modification of Proverbs 8:23ff., esp. verses 23, 27a, 28, 30a.

71.3   all men are capable of being raised by piety or by passion into their region]   See Coleridge ¶s. 237-238 and the excerpts on idealism at the end of chap. V. By *piety* Emerson meant *virtue* (*Nature* 74.13). See the index-concordance to the sermons, *s.v.* The drudging scientist is not included among those raised to the region of great "necessary ideas."

71.5   becoming, in some degree, himself divine]   For a discussion of Emerson's view of the God within and of the divinity of man, see the commentary on Orphic Poet III.

72.9   "The things that are seen are temporal."]   See 2 Cor. 4:18b.

72.12   philosophy for Berkeley and Viasa]   See *Typescript Journals*, "B," Pt. I, p. 172: "Religion does that for the uncultivated which philosophy does for Berkeley & Viasa; makes the mountains dance & smoke & disappear before the steadfast gaze of the Reason." See chap. V *supra* for a survey of Berkeley's Idealism. Abraham Rees, *The Cyclopædia or Universal Dictionary*, Phila., [1810-1842], XXXIX, describes Vyasa as "a personage of great celebrity and sanctity in the history of the Hindoos, as arranger or compiler of their sacred books called the Veda. His real name is supposed to have been Dwapayana, or Krishna Dwapayana; and his surname of Vyasa, or *Divider*, to have been given him from his great work . . . . To Vyasa is likewise ascribed a celebrated and popular system of philosophy, grounded wholly on the doctrines of the Veda, and thence named *Vedanta*." See lectures V-VI of Friedrich von Schlegel, *The Philosophy of History*, (2 vols.) London, 1835, which Emerson owned.

72.22   flesh-pots of Egypt]   See Exodus 16:3.

72.23   Plotinus was ashamed of his body.]   See *Journals*, II, 377 (Apr. 25, 1831); Coleridge, *Aids* (1829), 54: "Plotinus thanked God, that his Soul was not tied to an immortal body."

73.3   frail and weary weed]   See *Michael Angelo*, pp. 10-11: "He spoke of external grace as 'the frail and weary weed, in which God dresses the soul which he has called into Time.' . . . He sought, through the eye, to reach the soul . . . and to seek Beauty in its highest form, that of Goodness."

73.12   no hostility to nature]   See *Journals*, IV, 12 and 32.

73.17   true position of nature]   For the "true position of man," see *Y E S*, 211.16ff.

74.9   Reason both speculative and practical]   See Coleridge ¶ 2.

74.21   the soul holds itself off from a trivial study of the universal tablet]   See *Nature*, 13.2-13 (and notes); *Journals*, III, 433-434 (Jan. 8, 1835); *Y E S*, 201.24ff.

75.4 incurious concerning persons or miracles] On the "impersonal" in the highest levels of spiritual experience, see note on *Nature*, 58.4-15 and its references. For Emerson's early attitude toward miracles (reflecting Coleridge) see *Y E S*, 120-126; for the influence on his later attitude, see Sampson Reed ¶s. 11-17.

75.11-12 The soul accepts whatsoever befals it] See "The Miracle of Our Being" (Sept. 7, 1834), *Y E S*, 206.33—207.14, esp. line 11.

76.15 It suggests the absolute] See *Typescript Journals*, "B," Pt. II, p. 201 (June 7, 1836): "The Use of Nature is to awaken the feeling of the Absolute. Nature is a perpetual effect. It is the great shadow pointing to an unseen Sun."

76.17 pointing always to the sun behind us] Add "both" to this line for the intended meaning. A good commentary is *Nature*, 80.16ff.

76.18 nature, like Jesus, hands folded upon the breast] The hint for this figure of speech probably came from Charles Chauncy Emerson. See *Journals*, IV, 43-44.

79.9 the highest is present to the soul of man] The best commentary is the poem "Γνωθι Σεαυτον" and the "Statement of the First Philosophy," both edited in chap. VII. See *Journals*, III, 432 and the commentary on Orphic Poet V-VI.

80.3 Who can set bounds to man's possibilities] See the sermon, "Spiritual Improvement Unlimitable" (July 25, 1830) and the commentary on Orphic Poet I and VI. Cf. *Nature*, 87.21 and Sampson Reed ¶s. 38-39, 41-42.

80.8 man is the creator in the finite] See Sampson Reed ¶ 18d and in *E T E*, II, 21: "Simply to will and to think with the Divine Being, result in creating; in actually producing those realities, which form the ground-work of the thoughts and affections of man."

80.11 "The golden key etc."] A slight variation of Milton's *Comus*, lines 13-14.

81.5 We do not understand the notes of birds.] For the Swedenborgian doctrine of "affections clothed" see the index and Sampson Reed ¶s. 18a-22. Cf. *Works*, I, 112-113 and *Journals*, III, 533-534 (Aug. 5, 1835): "The birds fly from us, and we do not understand their music. The squirrel, the musquash, the insect have no significance to our blind eyes; such is now the discord betwixt man and nature. Yet it is strange that all our life is accompanied by Dreams on one side, and by the Animals on the other, as monuments of our ignorance, or Hints to set us on the right road of inquiry."

81.13 laborers digging in the field] In *Journals*, IV, 76, he gives them names—Wyman and Tuttle.

82.19 by a continual self-recovery] The true "self" according to Emerson is the Reason or Soul or the God within. Compare the meaning of "self-reliance" or God-reliance. The scientist in working with particulars must continue cultivating his highest nature or his facts will lose all significance.

85.3ff. George Herbert's poem, "Man"] An excellent prose commentary will be found in *Y E S*, 207.17—209.15.

91.10 not transparent but opake] Coleridge ¶s. 167 and 254. Misc. Selections ¶ 4.

91.19 Deep calls unto deep.] See Psalm 42:7.

91.21 worship God after tradition] See *Journals*, III, 369, 420, and Carlyle's *Sartor Resartus*, p. 70: "Thou . . . who too probably art no psalmist, but a prosaist, knowing God only by tradition, knowest thou any corner of the world where at least FORCE is not?"

92.7 detach every object from personal relations] See note on *Nature*, 13.10 and 58.4-15 and Early Lectures ¶ 31 (Nov. 5, 1835).

92.14   see the miraculous in the common]   See *Y E S*, 122.6-21 and Coleridge ¶s. 63, 75, 174. See the "Preface" to the *Lyrical Ballads* for further discussion. Cf. *Nature*, 93.1.

92.22   the gaudy fable fades and shrivels]   On the use of fable, see the index of *E T E*; *Journals*, III, 468; the chapter on the Orphic Poet; sections III and VII of "A Statement of the First Philosophy" (chap. VII); and ¶ J of the excerpts from Schiller's *Wallenstein* (chap. VII).

SUPPLEMENT—MISCELLANEOUS NOTES ON *NATURE*

7.5 unexplained...inexplicable; as language, sleep, dreams, beasts, sex.] These subjects were much discussed on a spiritual level in contemporary articles in the N J M, q.v. See also Staël-Holstein's Germany, (3 vols.) London, 1813, III, 378-379: "How can we consider animals without being plunged into the astonishment which their mysterious existence causes? A poet has called them the dreams of Nature, and man her waking. For what end were they created? what mean those looks which seem covered with an obscure cloud, behind which an idea strives to show itself? what connexion have they with us? what part of life is it they enjoy? A bird survives a man of genius, and I know not what strange sort of despair seizes the heart when we have lost what we love, and when we see the breath of existence still animate an insect which moves upon the earth, from which the most noble object has disappeared. The contemplation of Nature overwhelms our thoughts. We feel ourselves in a state of relation with her, which does not depend upon the good or evil which she can do; but her visible soul endeavours to find ours in her bosom, and holds converse with us."

9-14 Chapter I. Nature.] This chapter, I believe, shows stylistic indebtedness to Selections from the Writings of Fenelon, Boston, 1831, chap. I: "Upon the Proofs of the Existence of God, Drawn from a View of Nature, and of the Mind of Man."

10.2 the remembrance of the city of God which had been shown!] Emerson might have recalled Immanuel Kant's remark about man's two great awarenesses--of the starry heavens above and the moral law within. See also his quotation from St. Augustine by way of John Norris, An Essay Towards the Theory of an Ideal or Intelligible World, in Early Lectures, I, 383. Also A Commentary on Emerson's Early Lectures (1833-1836), p. 122.

12.14-15 In the woods too, a man casts off his years....] Cf. a passage quoted in Edward Waldo Emerson, Emerson in Concord, Boston & N.Y., [1888], p. 192, headed "To the Woods": "Whoso goeth in your paths readeth the same cheerful lesson, whether he be a young child or a hundred years old. Comes he in good fortune or in bad, ye say the same things, and from age to age. Ever the needles of the pine grow and fall, the acorns on the oak; the maples redden in autumn, and at all times of the year the ground-pine and the pyrola bud and root under foot. What is called fortune and what is called time by men, ye know them not. Men have not language to describe one moment of your life. When you shall give me somewhat to say, give me also the tune wherein to say it. Give me a tune like your winds or brooks or birds, for the songs of men grow old, when they are repeated; but yours, though a man have heard them for seventy years, are never the same, but always new, like Time itself, or like love."

12.19-20 a perennial festival is dressed] The phrase is apparently derived from Plutarch's Morals, tr. from the Greek by Several Hands [Matthew Morgan et al.], (5 vols.) London, 1718 [Copy in Emerson's library], "Of the Tranquillity of the Mind," I, 159: "That Saying of Diogenes extreamly pleaseth me, who seeing one sprucing himself up very neatly to go to a great Entertainment, asked him, Whether every Day was not a Festival to a good Man?"

13.1-2 no disgrace, no calamity, (leaving me my eyes,)....] Cf. the eloquent passage in Emerson's letter to Mary Moody Emerson on the importance of eyes in Journals, II, 99-100 (June 15, 1826).

13.5 I become a transparent eye-ball.] Cf. Journals, IX, 285 (Oct., 1860): "Plotinus says of the heavens, 'There, however, everybody is pure (transparent), and each inhabitant is as it were an eye.'"

13.20-21 an occult relation between man and the vegetable] For Swedenborgian commentary on the doctrine of correspondence and "affections clothed," see Thomas H. Perry, "The Physical Condition of the World Dependent upon the Moral Character of Man," N J M, IX (Oct., 1835), pp. 58-62, reprinted in E T E, II, pp. 99-101.

19-31 Chapter III. Beauty.] This chapter, I believe, shows stylistic indebtedness to Selections from the Writings of Fenelon, ed. cit., chap. I.

22.6-7 Germany of mystic philosophy and dreams] See "Menzel on German Literature," Foreign Quarterly Review, XVI, no. 31 (Oct., 1835), pp. 1-26, esp. p. 7: "Madame de Staël long ago drew the proper line of designation, when she said that 'Germany is the native country of thought.' The Germans are a sort of 'intellectual miners,' and spiritual moles--and this is one among the many reasons why their merits are so often concealed from superficial eyes. As the Hindoo philosophers convert every thing into religion, and every thing in nature is with them a mere modification of Brahma, Vishnu, and Siva, these sacred three themselves being mere modifications of the one eternal Brahm--so the Germans can do nothing without metaphysics. They must have a principle and a soul in every thing, and the whole of external nature and life is valuable to them only in so far as it is a revelation of the internal Divinity, in whom we live and move and have our being."

24.13-20 when its light shines upon your necessary journey...the windows of diligence.] Emerson had carefully read Abraham Tucker, The Light of Nature Pursued, (8 vols.) London, 1768-1777. See chap. XXII ("Pleasure") in II, 95-121, esp. 117: "Yet pleasures of the tempting kind if properly chosen have their value, not so much for their intrinsic worth as for the fruits they produce: for pleasing sensations or reflections rarely come upon us of their own accord, much the greater part of our enjoyment lies in the exercise of our activity when engaged in some pursuit or employment...." See also II, 111-112: "...we have found that objects however qualified please us or not according to the disposition of our organs, translation or resemblance casting a lustre upon what had it not before; and that the same thing appears agreable [sic] or indifferent or loathsome in the eyes of different beholders: which if it depended solely upon the qualities of the object, then the opposite qualities of beauty and deformity must reside at once in the same subject." See also II, 102: "Beauty is a species of taste: it may be defined an aptness of things to please immediately upon sight.... But this aptness to please is a relative term, not solely a quality residing in objects but depending equally upon the cast of our imagination.... We find the taste of beauty infinitely various and variable, the same thing appearing charming to one person, indifferent to another and disgustfull to a third...according to the disposition of body or humour of mind we happen to be in. Therefore nothing is beautifull in itself...."

25.15-17 All those things...obey virtue;" said an ancient historian.] Emerson's source was Milton's "An Apology for Smectymnuus," The Prose Works, ed. Charles Symmons, (7 vols.), I, pp. 207-272. See page 234: "That ye may know, not only as the historian speaks, 'that all those things for which men plough, build, or sail, obey virtue,' but that all words, and whatsoever may be spoken, shall at some time in an unwonted manner wait upon her purposes."

25.22 Leonidas and his three hundred martyrs] Emerson here recalled his early reading about the hero in Jean Jacques Barthélemy, Travels of Anacharsis the Younger in Greece, (5 vols.) London, 1796, I, 124-132.

26.3-6 Arnold Winkelried...sheaf of Austrian spears] Cf. Wordsworth's poem, "The Church of San Salvador, seen from the Lake of Lugano" in Poetical Works, (4 vols.) Boston, 1824, III, 338-340. See Wordsworth's note and compare the similarity of language in the following lines:

> He, too, of battle-martyrs chief!   By gathering with a wide embrace,
> Who, to recall his daunted peers,   Into his single heart, a sheaf
> For victory shaped an open space,   Of fatal Austrian spears.

27.19 geography and climate of Greece] Emerson might have known a book by William Falconer in the Harvard College Library: Remarks on the Influence of Climate, Situation, Nature of Country, Population, Nature of Food, and Way of Life, on the Disposition and Temper, Manners and Behavior, Intellects, Laws and Customs, Form of Government, and Religion, of Mankind, London, 1781.

35.7ff. These are not the dreams of a few poets] See Francis Jeffrey's review of Felicia Hemans in <u>Edinburgh Review</u>, L, no. 99 (1829-1830), pp. 32-47, esp. page 35: It has always been our opinion, that the very essence of poetry, apart from the pathos, the wit, or the brilliant description which may be embodied in it, but may exist equally in prose, consists in the fine perception and vivid expression of that subtle and mysterious analogy which exists between the physical and the moral world--which makes outward things and qualities the natural types and emblems of inward gifts and emotions, and leads us to ascribe life and sentiment to every thing that interests us in the aspects of external nature. The feeling of this analogy, obscure and inexplicable as the theory of it may be, is so deep and universal in our nature, that it has stamped itself on the ordinary language of men of every kindred and speech: and that to such an extent, that one half of the epithets by which we familiarly designate moral and physical qualities, are in reality so many metaphors, borrowed reciprocally, upon this analogy, from those opposite forms of existence. The very familiarity, however, of the expression, in these instances, takes away its poetical effect--and indeed, in substance, its metaphorical character. The original sense of the word is entirely forgotten in the derivative one to which it has succeeded; and it requires some etymological recollection to convince us that it was originally nothing else than a typical or analogical illustration. Thus we talk of a penetrating understanding, and a furious blast--a weighty argument, and a gentle stream--without being aware that we are speaking in the language of poetry, and transferring qualities from one extremity of the sphere of being to another.... It has substantially two functions, and operates in two directions. In the <u>first</u> place, it strikes vividly out, and flashes at once on our minds, the conception of an inward feeling or emotion, which it might otherwise have been difficult to convey, by the presentment of some bodily form or quality, which is instantly felt to be its true representative, and enables us to fix and comprehend it with a force and clearness not otherwise attainable; and, in the <u>second</u> place, it vivifies dead and inanimate matter with the attributes of living and sentient mind, and fills the whole visible universe around us with objects of interest and sympathy, by tinging them with the hues of life, and associating them with our own passions and affections. This magical operation the poet too performs, for the most part, in one of two ways--either by the direct agency of similes and metaphors, more or less condensed or developed, or by the mere graceful presentment of such visible objects on the scene of his passionate dialogues or adventures, as partake of the character of the emotion he wishes to excite, and thus form an appropriate accompaniment or preparation for its direct indulgence or display. The former of those methods has perhaps been most frequently employed, and certainly has most attracted attention. But the latter, though less obtrusive, and perhaps less frequently resorted to of set purpose, is, we are inclined to think, the most natural and efficacious of the two; and is often adopted, we believe, unconsciously by poets of the highest order;--the predominant emotion of their minds overflowing spontaneously on all the objects which present themselves to their fancy, and calling out from them, and colouring with its own hues, those that are naturally emblematic of its character, and in accordance with its general expression. It would be easy to show how habitually this is done by Shakspeare, and Milton especially, and how many of their finest passages are indebted both for force and richness of effect to this general and diffusive harmony of the external character of their scenes with the passions of their living agents....

37.1-3 As we go back in history, language becomes more picturesque, until its infancy, when it is all poetry.] See R. T. Clark, Jr., "Herder, Percy, and the Song of Songs," <u>P M L A</u>, LXI (1946), pp. 1087ff., on the theory that the perfection of poetry had been attained in primitive times.

40.19 keys of power] See <u>Nature</u>, 45.7ff. and 51.6-9; also 25.13-15.

41.8 volcano to roast their eggs] See Francis Bacon, "Ornamenta Rationalia: or Elegant Sentences," <u>The Miscellaneous Writings...in Philosophy</u>, <u>Morality and Religion</u> (London, 1802), p. 83: "Extreme self-lovers will set a man's house on fire, tho' it were but to roast their eggs." (This is a volume in <u>The Works</u>, ed. Peter Shaw (12 vols.) London, 1802-1803.)

41.21-22 axioms of physics translate the laws of ethics] For variants, see <u>A</u> <u>Commentary on Emerson's Early Lectures (1833-1836)</u>, Hartford, 1961, p. 131. See especially the famous passage in Staël-Holstein's <u>Germany</u>, (3 vols.) London, 1813, III, pp. 150-152: "It is a fine conception, that has a tendency to discover the resemblance between the laws of the human understanding and those of nature, and that considers the physical world as the basso-relievo of the moral. If the same genius was capable of composing the Iliad, and of carving like Phidias, the Jupiter of the sculptor would resemble the Jupiter of the poet. Why then should not the supreme Intelligence, which formed nature and the soul, have made one the emblem of the other? There is no vain play of fancy in those continual metaphors which aid us in comparing our sentiments with external phaenomena; sadness, with the clouded heaven; composure, with the silver moonlight; anger, with the stormy sea:--it is the same thought of our Creator, transfused into two different languages, and capable of reciprocal interpretation. Almost all the axioms of physics correspond with the maxims of morals. This species of parallel progress, which may be perceived between the world and the mind, is the indication of a great mystery; and every understanding would be struck with it, if any positive discoveries had yet been drawn from this source;--but still, the uncertain lustre that already streams from it carries our views to a great distance. The analogies between the different elements of external nature together constitute the chief law of the creation--variety in unity, and unity in variety. For example, What is there more astonishing than the connexion between sounds and forms, and between sounds and colours? A German (Chladni) lately proved by experiment, that the vibrations of sound put grains of sand upon a glass plate in motion after such a manner, that when the tones are pure, the sand arranges itself into regular forms, and when the tones are discordant, there is no symmetry in the figures traced upon the glass. Sanderson, who was blind from his birth, said, that the colour of scarlet, in his idea, was like the sound of a trumpet; and a mathematician wished to make a harpsichord for the eyes, which might imitate, by the harmony of colours, the pleasure excited by music. We incessantly compare painting to music; because the emotions we feel discover analogies where cold observation would only have seen differences."

42.14 A cripple in the right way....] See Francis Bacon, <u>Novum Organum Scientiarum</u>, tr. from the Latin by Peter Shaw (2 vols.) London, 1802, I, pp. 28-29: "But for the Idols of the Theatre, they are neither innate, nor secretly insinuated into the understanding, but plainly palmed upon it, and received from fabulous theories, and the perverted laws of demonstration. To undertake a confutation of these, is by no means congruous with what we have already advanced, for where neither principles nor demonstrations are agreed upon, there can be no arguing. And this happens fortunately, to leave the ancients possessed of their glory; we can detract nothing from them, whilst the question is only concerning the way. And a cripple in the right way may beat a racer in the wrong one. Nay, the fleeter and better the racer is, who has once missed his way, the farther he leaves it behind. Our method, however, of discovering the sciences, does not much depend upon subtilty, and strength of genius, but lies level to almost every capacity and understanding."

42.16 'T is hard to carry a full cup even] Emerson attributed this line to Robert Leighton. See <u>The Select Works of Archbishop Leighton</u>, ed. George B. Cheever, Boston, 1832, and <u>JMN</u>, VI, p. 140.

43.4 It appears to men, or it does not appear.] See Plotinus on intuitive knowledge in <u>JMN</u>, V, 103 (Oct. 28, 1835): "it is not lawful to inquire whence it sprang as if it were a thing subject to place & motion for it neither approached hither nor again departs from hence, to some other place, but it either appears to us, or it does not appear." Emerson found it quoted in Coleridge, <u>Biographia Literaria</u>, N.Y. & Boston, 1834, pp. 144-145, where one finds the additional line (developed in the "Statement of the First Philosophy"): "So that we ought not to pursue it with a view of detecting its secret source, but to watch in quiet till it suddenly shines upon us; preparing ourselves for the blessed spectacle, as the eye waits patiently for the rising sun."

43.18 era of Leibnitz] Emerson drew his knowledge of Leibnitz principally from Staël-Holstein's <u>Germany</u>, tr. from the French, (3 vols.) London, 1813, III, 53-69.

43.19 the Sphinx....] See Julius Charles Hare and Augustus William Hare, <u>Guesses at Truth</u>, various editions after the first: "It is a subtle and profound remark of Hegel's (Vol. X, p. 465), that the riddle which the Sphinx, the Egyptian symbol for the mysteriousness of Nature, propounds to Œdipus, is only another way of expressing the command of the Delphic Oracle, γνῶθι σεαυτόν. And when the answer is given, the Sphinx casts herself down from her rock: when man does know himself, the mysteriousness of Nature, and her terrours, vanish also; and she too walks in the light of knowledge, of law, and of love."

45.7-8 "every object rightly seen, unlocks a new faculty of the soul."] Possibly a rewriting of Goethe's maxim: "Der Mensch kennt nur sich selbst, insofern er die Welt kennt, die er in sich und sich in ihr gewahr wird. Jeder neue Gegenstand wohl beschaut, schliesst ein neues Organ in uns auf." (One understands himself only to the extent that he knows the world.... Every new object well regarded reveals a new faculty in us.)

45.11-12 a part of the domain of knowledge,--a new amount to the magazine of power.] Cf. 95.7-8: "The kingdom of man over nature...." Note the concluding paragraph of Francis Bacon's <u>Novum Organum Scientiarum</u>, tr. Peter Shaw, (2 vols.) London, 1802, II, 196-197: "And now we should proceed to the helps and rectification of induction, then to concretes, latent processes, concealed structures, &c. as mentioned in order, under the twenty-first aphorism; that at len[g]th, like faithful guardians, we might possess mankind of their fortunes, and release and free the understanding from its minority, upon which an amendment of the state and condition of mankind, and an enlargement of their power over nature, must necessarily ensue. For by the fall man at once forfeited his innocency, and his dominion over the creatures, though both of them are, in some measure, recoverable, even in this life: the former by religion and faith; and the latter by arts and sciences. For the world was not made absolutely rebellious by the curse, but in virtue of that denunciation. "In the sweat of thy brow thou shalt eat thy bread," it is at length, not by disputes, or indolent magical ceremonies, but by various real labours, subdued, and brought in some degree to afford the necessaries of life." Cf. also I, 1-2: "Man, who is the servant and interpreter of nature, can act and understand no farther than he has, either in operation, or in contemplation, observed of the method and order of nature.... The knowledge and power of man are coincident; for whilst ignorant of causes, he can produce no effects: Nor is nature to be conquered but by submission. And that which in speculation stands for the cause, is what in practice stands for the rule."

50.5 'What we know, is a point to what we do not know.'] Quoted with variations and assigned to Bishop Joseph Butler in <u>JMN</u>, VI, p. 64. I have been unable to locate it where it would seem to belong--in <u>The Analogy of Religion</u> or in such sermons as "Upon the Ignorance of Man" and assume that Emerson came upon it in one of the many contemporary discussions of Butler in the <u>Quarterly Review</u> or <u>Edinburgh Review</u>--that is, outside the canonical works.

51.6-9 More and more...does his kingdom stretch over things] See <u>Nature</u>, 45.7-12; 40.19; 25.13-15.

54.19 The fable of Proteus has a cordial truth.] See "The Mythology of the Ancients," <u>The Works of Francis Bacon</u>, (12 vols.) London, 1802-1803, V, pp. 47-50: "Proteus, according to the poets, was Neptune's herdsman; an old man, and a most extraordinary prophet; who understood things past and present as well as future; so that besides the business of divination, he was the revealer and interpreter of all antiquity, and secrets of every kind. He lived in a vast cave; where his custom was to tell over his herd of sea-calves at noon, and then to sleep. Whoever consulted him, had no other way of obtaining an answer, but by binding him with manacles and fetters; when he, endeavouring to free himself, would change into all kinds of shapes and miraculous forms; as of fire, water, wild beasts, &c. till at length he resumed his own shape again. / This fable seems to point at the secrets of nature, and the states of matter. For the person of Proteus denotes matter, the oldest of all things, after God himself; that resides, as in a cave, under the vast concavity of the heavens. He is represented as the servant of Neptune; because the various operations and modifications of matter, are principally wrought

in a fluid state. The herd, or flock of Proteus, seems to be no other than the
several kinds of animals, plants, and minerals, in which matter appears to dif-
fuse and spend itself; so that after having formed these several species, and as
it were finished its task, it seems to sleep and repose, without otherwise attempting to produce any new ones. And this is the moral of Proteus's counting
his herd, then going to sleep. / This is said to be done at noon, not in the morning or evening; by which is meant the time best fitted and disposed for the production of species; from a matter duly prepared, and made ready before-hand, and
now lying in a middle state, between its first rudiments and decline: which, we
learn from sacred history, was the case at the time of the creation; when, by the
efficacy of the divine command, matter directly came together, without any transformation or intermediate changes, which it affects; instantly obeyed the order,
and appeared in the form of creatures. / And thus far the fable teaches of Proteus
and his flock, at liberty and unrestrained. For the universe, with the common
structures and fabrics of the creatures, is the face of matter, not under constraint, or as the flock wrought upon, and tortured, by human means. But if any
skilful minister of nature shall apply force to matter, and by design tortune and
vex it, in order to its annihilation, it, on the contrary, being brought under
this necessity, changes and transforms itself into a strange variety of shapes and
appearances; for nothing but the power of the Creator can annihilate, or truly destroy it: so that at length, running through the whole circle of transformations,
and compleating its period, it in some degree restores itself, if the force be
continued. And that method of binding, torturing, or detaining, will prove the
most effectual and expeditious, which makes use of manacles and fetters; that is,
lays hold and works upon matter in the extremest degrees. / The addition in the
fable that makes Proteus a prophet, who had the knowledge of things past, present,
and future, excellently agrees with the nature of matter; as he who knows the properties, the changes, and the processes of matter, must, of necessity, understand
the effects and sum of what it does, has done, or can do; though his knowledge extends not to all the parts and particulars thereof."

55.7 architecture is called 'frozen music,' by De Stael] See the biography of
Madam de Staël (Staël-Holstein) in Lydia Maria Child, <u>The Biographies of Madame
de Staël and Madame Roland</u>, Boston, 1832--a quotation from Lord Byron's journal--
on p. 89: "At Lord Holland's I was trying to recollect a <u>quotation</u> (as I think)
of Staël's, from some Teutonic sophist about architecture. 'Architecture reminds
me of frozen music,' says this Macaronico Tedescho. It is somewhere--but where?
The demon of perplexity must know, and won't tell. I asked M----- and he said it
was not hers; but P-----r said it must be <u>hers</u>, it was so <u>like</u>."

56.22 "The wise man in doing one thing does all."] See <u>Journals</u>, III, 147.
Iarno says approximately these words in <u>Wilhelm Meister</u>, tr. Thomas Carlyle.

58.3ff. We are associated in adolescent and adult life with some friends....]
Reminiscent of a tribute paid to his lately deceased brother, Charles Chauncy
Emerson. See his revision of Sermon 114, read in Concord before his mother and
family on June 5, 1836. (I quote from my "History and Biography in Emerson's
Unpublished Sermons," <u>Proceedings of the American Antiquarian Society</u>, Oct., 1956,
pp. 103-118, esp. p. 109: "It may be you have been called to mourn the loss of a
dear friend connected with yourself by all those bonds that make friendship dearest & its loss sorest. And what is it that such events say? Why this, certainly.
The chasm of the loss, these bursting tears, this broken voice, this wearisome
sense of privation,--what is it but so much eulogy of the departed? what is it but,
under another form, a thanksgiving to God that he had so highly blessed us? It
is an acknowledgement (how unsuspicious) of the privilege of being associated with
a noble character. Indeed, brethren, I prize above all prosperity that which is
sometimes called the joy of grief. I value every tear that is shed for departed
men, because it is a certificate of the excellent endowments, the graces, the
character which have dwelt with us. What good shall we compare with this good?
with the reverence & love which human character has inspired in closest intimacy,
where all hypocrisy & veil were impossible,--seen in the practice of common duties,
& in the gaiety & vexations, the plans & failures, the opinions & actions of daily
life, passing from duty to duty, at home, & abroad. When we have been made acquainted in our own familiar circle with one who was so severe an adorer of truth

that it would have been as easy for him to steal as to dissemble; with one who so reverenced the oracle in his own mind that he held all men's opinion light in the balance with its softest whisper; with one who had such a value for time that he thought men's frugality of it the measure of their worth; with one who adding to his virtues the finest accomplishments, had no vanity, and never added to his necessary discourse one word for the sake of display; with one who amidst all the attractions which the world offered had so high a standard of action & character that more life had nothing to charm him & in his most ambitious hour held the world very cheap, with one who prized the religious sentiment as God's greatest gift to man, & was impatient of any discourse or speculations in the Church which led the mind away from this, because it was the basis of human strength, the succor in trouble, & especially the right of the great number who have almost no education but that which the Sabbath supplies them...."

59.2 Idealism.] See Journals, VI, 26 (Aug., 1841): "I remember, when a child, in the pew on Sundays amusing myself with saying over common words as 'black,' 'white,' 'board,' etc., twenty or thirty times, until the word lost all meaning and fixedness, and I began to doubt which was the right name for the thing, when I saw that neither had any natural relation, but all were arbitrary. It was a child's first lesson in Idealism."

65.1 Possessed himself by a heroic passion, he uses matter as symbols of it.] See Francis Jeffrey's views of poetry in the note on 35.7ff.

65.12ff. Shakspeare possesses the power of subordinating nature....] Emerson was probably indebted to William Hazlitt, Lectures on the English Poets, (1st Am. ed.) Philadelphia, 1818 [or London, 1818], Lecture III ("On Shakspeare and Milton"), esp. pp. 105-106, beginning: "Shakspeare's imagination is of the same plastic kind as his conception of character or passion. 'It glances from heaven to earth, from earth to heaven.' Its movement is rapid and devious. It unites the most opposite extremes...." (See the Boston Library Society reading list, items 161, 262, 768.) See also Thomas Carlyle, "Goethe's Works," Foreign Quarterly Review, X, no. 19 (Aug., 1832), pp. 1-44, esp. 40: "A nobler power of insight than this of Goethe you in vain look for, since Shakspeare passed away.... Shakspeare too does not look at a thing, but into it, through it; so that he constructively comprehends it, can take it asunder, and put it together again; the thing melts, as it were, into light under his eye, and anew creates itself before him. That is to say, he is a Thinker in the highest of all senses: he is a Poet. For Goethe, as for Shakspeare, the world lies all translucent, all fusible (we might call it), encircled with WONDER; the Natural in reality the Supernatural, for to the seer's eyes both become one. What are the Hamlets and Tempests, the Fausts and Mignons, but glimpses accorded us into this translucent, wonder-encircled world; revelations of the mystery of all mysteries, Man's Life as it actually is?"

70.6-8 Turgot said, "He that has never doubted the existence of matter...."] See Dugald Stewart, Account of the Life and Writings of Thomas Reid, Edinburgh & London, 1803, p. 271: "It is recorded as a saying of M. Turgot, (whose philosophical opinions in some important points approached very nearly to those of Dr Reid), That 'he who had never doubted of the existence of matter, might be assured he had no turn for metaphysical disquisitions.'" See also p. 271 of the review of Stewart's book in the Edinburgh Review, III (1803-1804), pp. 269-287.

71.2-4 Yet all men are capable of being raised by piety...into their region.] See Letters, II, 7. Writing to Frederic Henry Hedge from Concord, Mar. 14, 1836: "A man feels like one who has lost his way in the Universe when he discovers that he has aims which he has no faculties to satisfy. Yet in better hours we own that there is medicine for this disease. The sentiment of piety restores us our property in the Universe...."

72.13 Berkeley and Viasa.] See Emerson's Indian Superstition, ed. Cameron, pp. 28-30 et passim.

73.14-16 I do not wish to...soil my gentle nest.] Emerson here alludes to the English proverb, "It's an ill bird that fouls its own nest," appearing as early as

John Skelton's <u>Poems Against Garneshe</u>: "Old proverbe says, / That byrd ys not honest / That fyleth his owne nest." See William S. Walsh, <u>Handy-book of Literary Curiosities</u>, London, 1898, p. 239.

74.16-17 not as painfully accumulated...but...on the instant eternity] Cf. <u>Journals</u>, III, 425: "For to the soul in her pure action all the virtues are natural, and not painfully acquired. Excite the soul, and it becomes suddenly virtuous."

76.17 a great shadow pointing always to the sun behind us.] This figure may have been suggested by lines 17ff. in Coleridge's "The Destiny of Nations." See E T E, II, 113 bottom. Cf. also Plato's famous myth of the cave in his <u>Republic</u>.

82.4-18 the highest reason is always the truest.... Empirical science is apt to cloud the sight.... But the best read naturalist...much to learn...by untaught sallies of the spirit] See Staël-Holstein's <u>Germany</u>, (3 vols.) London, 1813, III, 159-163, from the chapter entitled: "Influence of the New Philosophy on the Sciences":

Pascal says, "that astrologers and alchemists have some principles, but that they abuse them." There were, perhaps, of old, more intimate relations between man and nature than now exist. The mysteries of Eleusis; the religion of the Egyptians; the system of emanations among the Indians; the Persian adoration of the elements and the sun; the harmony of numbers, which was the basis of the Pythagorean doctrine--are vestiges of some curious attraction which united man with the universe.... The Germans promote the true perfection of the human mind, when they endeavour to awaken the inspirations of nature by the light of thought.

Experience every day leads the learned to recognise phaenomena, which men had ceased to believe, because they were mingled with superstitions, and had been the subjects of presages. The ancients have related that stones fell from heaven; and in our days the accuracy of this fact, the existence of which had been denied, is established. The ancients have spoken of showers red as blood, and of <u>earth-lightnings</u>--we have lately been convinced of the truth of their assertions in these respects.

Astronomy and music are the science and art which men have known from all antiquity: why should not sounds and the stars be connected by relations which the ancients perceived, and which we may find out again? Pythagoras maintained that the planets were proportionably at the same distance as the seven chords of the lyre; and it is affirmed, that he predicted the new planet which has been discovered between Mars and Jupiter. It appears that he was not ignorant of the true system of the heavens, the fixedness of the sun; since Copernicus supports himself in this instance upon the opinion of Pythagoras, as recorded by Cicero. From whence then arose these astonishing discoveries, without the aid of experience, and of the new machines of which the moderns are in possession? The reason is this--the ancients advanced boldly, lit by the sun of genius. They made use of reason, the resting-place of human intellect; but they also consulted imagination, the priestess of nature.

Those which we call errors and superstitions may, perhaps, depend upon laws of the universe, yet unknown to man. The relations between the planets and metals, the influence of these relations, even oracles and presages--may they not be caused by occult powers, of which we have no idea? And who knows whether there is not a germ of truth hidden under every apologue, under every mode of belief, which has been stigmatized with the name of madness? It assuredly does not follow that we should renounce the experimental method, so necessary in the sciences. But why not furnish a supreme director for this method in a philosophy more comprehensive, which would embrace the universe in its <u>collective character</u>, and which would not despise <u>the nocturnal side of nature</u>, in the expectation of being able to throw light upon it?...

Doubtless, the French are right in recommending the Germans to have a respect for experience; but they are wrong in turning into ridicule the presages of reflection, which perhaps will hereafter be confirmed by the knowledge of facts. The greater part of grand discoveries have at first appeared absurd; and the man of genius will never do any thing if he dreads being exposed to ridicule.--Ridicule is nerveless when despised, and ascends in influence just as it is feared. We see in fairy tales phantoms that oppose the enterprises of knights, and harrass them until they have passed beyond the weird dominion. Then all the witchcraft vanishes, and the fruitful open country is spread before their sight. Envy and mediocrity have also their sorceries; but we ought to march on towards the truth, without caring for the seeming obstacles that impede our progress.

87.19-21   like Nebuchadnezzar...eating grass like an ox.] Cf. Edinburgh Review, XI (1807-1808), p. 206, a review of John Sinclair's The Code of Health and Longevity: "In treating of salads, however, he informs us, that 'there are instances of persons living only upon grass and hay;' and quotes, in confirmation of this assertion, the 4th chapter and 32d verse of the prophet Daniel! We really did not expect to find the diet of poor Nebuchadnezzar commemorated in a modern treatise on vegetable food; but we cannot help admiring the accuracy with which the learned President of the Board of Agriculture speaks upon this interesting subject. The prophet says only, that the humbled monarch ate grass like an ox; but Sir John is too learned in the feeding of cattle, to let this pass uncorrected; he therefore makes the addition of hay also; taking it for granted, no doubt, that his Babylonish majesty grazed only during the summer season, but was stalled and fed with good dry hay in the winter." See also The Works of Plato Abridg'd: With an Account of his Life...by M. Dacier, (3d ed., 2 vols.) London, 1772, I, 124: "And perhaps it would be no ill-founded Opinion, that this Idea came into the Head of Pythagoras, upon what happened in the Time of King Nebuchadnezzar, who for his Sins, was turned out among the Beasts, and for seven Years grazed like an Ox."

94.5-7 All that Adam had, all that Caesar could, you have and can do.] Cf. Jeremy Taylor, Discourses on Various Subjects, (3 vols.) Boston, 1816. From Sermon XVIII ("The Foolish Exchange"), II, 347-348: "Can the greatest prince enclose the sun, and set one little star in his cabinet for his own use? or secure to himself the gentle and benign influences of any one constellation? are not his subjects' fields bedewed with the same showers that water his gardens of pleasure? Nay those things which he esteems his ornament and the singularity of his possessions, are they not of more use to others than to himself?... The poorest artizan of Rome walking in Caesar's gardens, had the same pleasures which they ministered to their lord: and although it may be he was put to gather fruits to eat from another place, yet his other senses were delighted equally with Caesar's: ...save only that Caesar paid for all that pleasure vast sums of money, the blood and treasure of a province, which the poor man had for nothing."

SOURCES FOR EMERSON'S EARLY ORIENTALISM

The student interested in the impact of India on young Emerson might do well to begin his explorations with a perusal of "A Dissertation on Emerson's Orientalism at Harvard," "Notes on Massachusetts Orientalism," "Oriental Themes and Climate in Harvard Commencement and Exhibition Parts (1800-1834)," and "Emerson's Reading for his Poem ['Indian Superstition']"[1]--supplemented by some of my more recent studies on this subject.[2] This body of evidence along with records of his reading[3] indicates that Emerson was aware of the attractiveness of Hindoo philosophy from college days even if, like Southey, he found the terrifying cult life of Hindoo castes a more congenial subject for his early verse. Although he did not come upon a translation of the Bhagavadgita until 1845,[4] he read a challenging summary in Victor Cousin's Introduction to the History of Philosophy (1832),[5] which he acquired soon after publication[6] and was reading in January of that year:[7]

THE *BHAGAVAD-GITA*——WHAT IT REVEALS OF INDIAN CIVILIZATION

Open, for instance, the Bhagavad-Gita; it is a short episode in an immense poem. Two great armies, the Pandoos and the Kouroos, are in the presence of each other, and are ready to engage in battle. A boundless carnage is at hand. In one of the two armies there is a young warrior, individually very brave, but who, upon the eve of shedding the blood of his relations and friends, for the two armies are composed of friends and relations, finds his courage failing. He requests another personage to advance his chariot into the middle of the plain, for the purpose of ascertaining the situation of affairs, and having cast a brief glance upon the two hosts, the good Ardschunas vows to Crishna, his uncertainty. What is the reply? "Truly, Ardschunas, your pity is exceedingly ridiculous. Why do you speak of friends and relations? Why of men? Relations, friends, men, beasts, or stones, all are one. A perpetual and eternal energy has created all which you see and renews it without cessation. What is today a man, was yesterday a plant, and tomorrow may become a plant once more. The principle of every thing is eternal; what value has aught else? You are, as a Schatrias, a man of the caste of warriors, doomed to the combat. Therefore, do battle; a fearful carnage will be the result. Be it so; tomorrow the sun will shine upon the world, and will illuminate new scenes, and the eternal principle will continue to subsist. Beyond this principle, every

thing is illusion. The fundamental error is, to consider as true that which is only apparent. If you attach any value to appearances, you deceive yourself; if you attach it to your actions, you deceive yourself again; for as all is illusion, action itself, when it is regarded as real, is illusion also; the beauty and the merit of an action consist in performing it with profound indifference as to the results which it may produce. It is necessary to act, undoubtedly, but to act as if one acted not. Nothing exists but the eternal principle; being, in itself. It follows that it is the supreme of wisdom to let things pass, to do what we are compelled to do, but as if we did it not, and without concerning ourselves about the result, interiorly motionless, with our eyes fixed unceasingly upon the absolute principle which alone exists with a true existence."

Such, under a somewhat occidental form, is the philosophy of this sublime episode. . . . You will comprehend how human nature must tremble and shrink into nothingness, before a theism so terrible and filled with chimeras, and represented by symbols that are extravagant and gigantic; how art, in its powerless endeavor to represent being in itself, must fall, without reserve, into colossal and irregular creations; how God being all and man nothing, a formidable theocracy must press upon humanity, take away all liberty, all movement, all practical interest, and consequently all true morality; and how man, despising himself, was unable to recall the memory of actions in which he supposed himself not the real agent; and therefore, why there is no history of man in India, and no chronology.

As early as 1820,[8] moreover, he had access to Sir William Jones's translations of Hindoo poems--especially "Narayena," to which his Aunt Mary Moody Emerson called his special attention in 1822.[9] This he laid in his journals[10] and years later included among religious classics in Parnassus.[11] Since it belongs in the tradition of his own exalted "Gnothi Seauton," it, doubtless, served as an early pointer in his lifelong quest for a sustaining Transcendental religious faith:[12]

---

1 See Indian Superstition by Ralph Waldo Emerson, ed. with a Dissertation on Emerson's Orientalism at Harvard by Kenneth Walter Cameron, Hanover, N.H., 1954; reprinted in the Emerson Society Quarterly, no. 32 (III Quarter 1963), Part 1.

A HYMN

TO

NÁRÁYENA.

THE ARGUMENT.

A COMPLETE introduction to the following Ode would be no lefs than a full comment on the VAYDS and PURA'NS of the HINDUS, the remains of *Egyptian* and *Perfian* Theology, and the tenets of the *Ionick* and *Italick* Schools ; but this is not the place for fo vaft a difquifition. It will be fufficient here to premife, that the inextricable difficulties attending the *vulgar notion* of *material fubftances*, concerning which

" We know this only, that we nothing know,"

induced many of the wifeft among the Ancients, and fome of the moft enlightened among the Moderns, to believe, that the whole Creation was rather an *energy* than a *work*, by which the Infinite Being, who is prefent at all times in all places, exhibits to the minds of his creatures a fet of perceptions, like a wonderful picture or piece of mufick, always varied, yet always uniform ; fo that all bodies and their qualities exift, indeed, to every wife and ufeful purpofe, but exift only as far as they are *perceived ;* a theory no lefs pious than fublime, and as different from any principle of Atheifm, as the brighteft funfhine differs from the blackeft midnight. This *illufive operation* of the Deity the *Hindu* philofophers call MA'YA', or *Deception ;* and the word occurs in this fenfe more than once in the commentary on the *Rig Vayd*, by the great VASISHTHA, of which Mr. HALHED has given us an admirable fpecimen.

---

2 See "More Remarks on 'Indian Superstition' and Emerson's Oriental Resources while at Harvard" in my Transcendentalists and Minerva, (3 vols.) Hartford, 1958, III, 829-854. Also "Emerson and Southey's Oriental Books," Ibid., II, 433-437. Also "Indian Superstition and Orientalism in Emerson's Harvard," E S Q, no. 33 (IV Quarter 1963), pp. 7-16, and "More Notes on Orientalism in Emerson's Harvard," E S Q, no. 22 (I Quarter 1961), pp. 81-90. See also "More Background for Emerson's Indian Superstition--Parish Circulating Libraries," E S Q, no 47 (II Quarter 1967), pp. 130-138.

3 Notably "Emerson's Reading in Periodicals Through 1836" and the chapters immediately following in my Emerson's Workshop, (2 vols.) Hartford, [1964], I, pp. 8-219.
4 The Bhagvat-Geeta, or Dialogues of Kreeshna and Arjoon; in Eighteen Lectures with Notes, tr. Charles Wilkins, London, 1785--recently reprinted in facsimile with an "Introduction" by George Hendrick by Scholars' Facsimiles & Reprints (Gainesville, Florida, 1959).
5 Tr. Henning Gotfried Linberg, Boston, 1832, pp. 71-73. See also my Emerson the Essayist, I, 310-311.
6 See Walter Harding, Emerson's Library, [Charlottesville, 1967], p. 71.
7 See J M N, III, 320-323.
8 These poems appeared in The Asiatick Miscellany; consisting of Original Productions, Translations, Fugitive Pieces etc., [ed. F. Gladwin?], (2 vols.) Calcutta, 1785-1786, only vol. I of which Emerson was reading in 1820. See my Emerson's Early Reading List (1819-1824), N.Y., 1951, p. 4.
9 See Letters, I, p. lx.   10 See Journals, I, 157.
11 See Parnassus, ed. R. W. Emerson, Boston, 1875, p. 180.
12 See The Works of Sir William Jones, (6 vols.) London, 1799, VI, pp. 367-373.

The *firſt* ſtanza of the Hymn repreſents the ſublimeſt attributes of the Supreme Being, and the three forms, in which they moſt clearly appear to us,
Power, Wiſdom, and *Goodneſs,* or, in the language of ORPHEUS and his diſciples,
Love: the *ſecond* compriſes the *Indian* and *Egyptian* doctrine of the Divine Eſſence
and Archetypal *Ideas;* for a diſtinct account of which the reader muſt be referred to a noble deſcription in the ſixth book of PLATO'S *Republick;* and
the fine explanation of that paſſage in an elegant diſcourſe by the author of
CYRUS, from whoſe learned work a hint has been borrowed for the conclu-
ſion of this piece. The *third* and *fourth* are taken from the Inſtitutes of
MENU, and the eighteenth *Puran* of VYA'SA', entitled *Srey Bhagawat,* part of
which has been tranſlated into *Perſian,* not without elegance, but rather too
paraphraſtically. From BREHME, or the *Great Being,* in the *neuter* gender, is
formed BREHMA', in the *maſculine;* and the ſecond word is appropriated to
the *creative power* of the Divinity.

The ſpirit of GOD, called NA'RA'YENA, or *moving on the water,* has a multiplicity of other epithets in *Sanſcrit,* the principal of which are introduced,
expreſsly or by alluſion, in the *fifth* ſtanza; and two of them contain the
names of the *evil beings,* who are feigned to have ſprung from the ears of
VISHNU; for thus the divine ſpirit is entitled, when conſidered as the *pre-
ſerving power:* the *ſixth* aſcribes the perception of *ſecondary* qualities by our
ſenſes to the immediate influence of MA'YA'; and the *ſeventh* imputes to her
operation the *primary* qualities of *extenſion* and *ſolidity.*

THE HYMN.

SPIRIT of Spirits, who, through ev'ry part
    Of ſpace expanded and of endleſs time,
    Beyond the ſtretch of lab'ring thought ſublime,
    Badſt uproar into beauteous order ſtart,
        Before Heav'n was, Thou art:
Ere ſpheres beneath us roll'd or ſpheres above,
    Ere earth in firmamental ether hung,
    Thou ſatſt alone; till, through thy myſtick **Love,**
    Things unexiſting to exiſtence ſprung,
        And grateful deſcant ſung.
What firſt impell'd thee to exert thy might?
    Goodneſs unlimited. What glorious light
    Thy pow'r directed? Wiſdom without bound.
    What prov'd it firſt? Oh! guide my fancy right;
        Oh! raiſe from cumbrous ground
        My ſoul in rapture drown'd,
    That fearleſs it may ſoar on wings of fire;
For Thou, who only knowſt, Thou only canſt inſpire.

Wrapt in eternal folitary fhade,
 Th' impenetrable gloom of light intenfe,
 Impervious, inacceffible, immenfe,
 Ere fpirits were infus'd or forms difplay'd,
  BREHM his own Mind furvey'd,
As mortal eyes (thus finite we compare
 With infinite) in fmootheft mirrors gaze:
 Swift, at his look, a fhape fupremely fair
 Leap'd into being with a boundlefs blaze,
  That fifty funs might daze.
Primeval MAYA was the Goddefs nam'd,
 Who to her fire, with Love divine inflam'd,
 A cafket gave with rich *Ideas* fill'd,
 From which this gorgeous Univerfe he fram'd;
  For, when th' Almighty will'd
  Unnumber'd worlds to build,
 From Unity diverfified he fprang,
While gay Creation laugh'd, and procreant Nature rang.

Firft an all-potent all-pervading found
 Bade flow the waters——and the waters flow'd,
 Exulting in their meafurelefs abode,
 Diffufive, multitudinous, profound,
  Above, beneath, around;
Then o'er the vaft expanfe primordial wind
 Breath'd gently, till a lucid bubble rofe,
 Which grew in perfect fhape an Egg refin'd:
 Created fubftance no fuch luftre fhows,
  Earth no fuch beauty knows.
Above the warring waves it danc'd elate,
 Till from its burfting fhell with lovely ftate
 A form cerulean flutter'd o'er the deep,
 Brighteft of beings, greateft of the great:
  Who, not as mortals fteep,
  Their eyes in dewy fleep,
 But heav'nly-penfive on the Lotos lay,
That bloffom'd at his touch and fhed a golden ray.

Hail, primal bloffom! hail empyreal gem!
 KEMEL, or PEDMA, or whate'er high name
 Delight thee, fay, what four-form'd **Godhead came**,
 With graceful ftole and beamy diadem,

Forth from thy verdant ftem ?
Full-gifted BREHMA ! Rapt in folemn thought
  He ftood, and round his eyes fire-darting threw ;
  But, whilft his viewlefs origin he fought,
  One plain he faw of living waters blue,
    Their fpring nor faw nor knew.
Then, in his parent ftalk again retir'd,
  With reftlefs pain for ages he inquir'd
  What were his pow'rs, by whom, and why conferr'd :
  With doubts perplex'd, with keen impatience fir'd
    He rofe, and rifing heard
    Th' unknown all-knowing Word,
  " BREHMA ! no more in vain refearch perfift :
My veil thou canft not move—Go ; bid all worlds exift."

Hail, felf-exiftent, in celeftial fpeech
  NARAYEN, from thy watry cradle, nam'd ;
  Or VENAMALY may I fing unblam'd,
  With flow'ry braids, that to thy fandals reach,
    Whofe beauties, who can teach ?
Or high PEITAMBER clad in yellow robes
  Than funbeams brighter in meridian glow,
  That weave their heav'n-fpun light o'er circling globes ?
  Unwearied, lotos-eyed, with dreadful bow,
    Dire Evil's conftant foe !
Great PEDMANABHA, o'er thy cherifh'd world
  The pointed *Checra*, by thy fingers whirl'd,
  Fierce KYTABH fhall deftroy and MEDHU grim
  To black defpair and deep deftruction hurl'd.
    Such views my fenfes dim,
    My eyes in darknefs fwim :
  What eye can bear thy blaze, what utt'rance tell
Thy deeds with filver trump or many-wreathed fhell ?

Omnifcient Spirit, whofe all-ruling pow'r
  Bids from each fenfe bright emanations beam ;
  Glows in the rainbow, fparkles in the ftream,
  Smiles in the bud, and gliftens in the flow'r
    That crowns each vernal bow'r ;
Sighs in the gale, and warbles in the throat
  Of ev'ry bird, that hails the bloomy fpring,
  Or tells his love in many a liquid note,
  Whilft envious artifts touch the rival ftring,

Till rocks and forefts ring;
Breathes in rich fragrance from the fandal grove,
  Or where the precious mufk-deer playful rove;
  In dulcet juice from cluft'ring fruit diftills,
  And burns falubrious in the tafteful clove:
    Soft banks and verd'rous hills
    Thy prefent influence fills;
In air, in floods, in caverns, woods, and plains;
Thy will infpirits all, thy fov'reign MAYA reigns.

Blue cryftal vault, and elemental fires,
  That in th' ethereal fluid blaze and breathe;
  Thou, toffing main, whofe fnaky branches wreathe
  This penfile orb with intertwifted gyres;
    Mountains, whofe radiant fpires
Prefumptuous rear their fummits to the fkies,
  And blend their em'rald hue with fapphire light;
  Smooth meads and lawns, that glow with varying dyes
  Of dew-befpangled leaves and bloffoms bright,
    Hence! vanifh from my fight:
Delufive Pictures! unfubftantial fhows!
  My foul abforb'd One only Being knows,
  Of all perceptions One abundant fource,
  Whence ev'ry object ev'ry moment flows:
    Suns hence derive their force,
    Hence planets learn their courfe;
But funs and fading worlds I view no more:
GOD only I perceive; GOD only I adore.

EMBODIMENT of rhythmic cosmic energy is Hindu god Shiva as religion's King of Dance.